Financial Accounting Principles

Kermit D. Larson
The University of Texas at Austin

Michael Zin
University of Windsor
Windsor, Ontario

Morton Nelson
Wilfrid Laurier University
Waterloo, Ontario

First Canadian Edition

Homewood, IL 60430
Boston, MA 02116

Cover photo: Eric Meola—*The Image Bank/Chicago*.

Sponsoring editor: *Roderick T. Banister*
Project editor: *Gladys True*
Production manager: *Irene H. Sotiroff*
Designer: *Michael Warrell*
Artist: *Precision Graphics*
Compositor: *York Graphic Services, Inc.*
Typeface: *10/12 Times Roman*
Printer: *Von Hoffmann Press, Inc.*

ISBN 0-256-09386-5
Library of Congress Catalog Card No. 90–85614
Printed in the United States of America
1 2 3 4 5 6 7 8 9 0 VH 7 6 5 4 3 2 1 0

Preface

Financial Accounting Principles and its supplements provide a complete, fully integrated teaching and learning system for colleges and universities that wish to concentrate solely on Financial Accounting. Based on the highly successful *Fundamental Accounting Principles*, Sixth Canadian Edition, this text has been updated to reflect current accounting practices through 1990. The objectives of this course generally include: (1) developing a general understanding of financial reports and analyses that students will use in their personal affairs regardless of their fields of specialization, (2) providing a strong foundation for future courses in business and finance, and (3) initiating the course work that leads to a career in accounting. *Financial Accounting Principles* serves all of these objectives.

The central focus of *Financial Accounting Principles* is to explain the development of accounting information for the use of business managers and other parties who are interested in the financial affairs of a business. Underlying this focus is a primary goal of helping students interpret and use accounting information intelligently and effectively. The concepts and principles that govern accounting processes are explained and persistently emphasized so that students will be able to generalize and apply their knowledge to a variety of new situations.

The early chapters of *Financial Accounting Principles* use the single proprietorship to illustrate the accounting cycle. However, corporations are gradually introduced through the first four chapters in a manner that does not interrupt or confuse the discussion of the cycle. As a result, students gain a clear understanding of unincorporated entities and are also prepared for the corporate illustrations of Chapter 5. The assignment material for Chapter 5 is divided equally between corporate and proprietorship businesses so instructors can easily move to full reliance on corporate illustrations or defer an emphasis on corporations until the later chapters in the book.

Learning through More Student Involvement

The educational philosophy behind the development of *Financial Accounting Principles* is that learning occurs most effectively when students are actively involved. Our objective is to have students use as much of their study time as possible in active behaviour such as answering questions and solving problems. This means that the use of student time in passive, low-retention behaviour such as reading must be held to a minimum. To accomplish this objective, *Financial Accounting Principles* uses a concise yet conceptually thorough writing style and provides a rich source of assignment material that includes a wide range of questions, multiple-choice questions, mini discussion cases, exercises, problems, provocative problems, and analytical and review problems. In addition, to encourage students to hold a more active, participative mindset, the text is written in an active voice.

Specific features in the text that contribute to this process of learning through active student involvement include the following:

Introductions. Each part of the book and each chapter opens with an introduction that invites personal involvement and generally describes the personal benefit that will result from studying the part or chapter.

Careful Integration of Concepts and Applications. Throughout the book, the definitions and explanations of important concepts and principles are presented in close proximity to illustrations and practical applications of those concepts and principles. As a result, students need not hold abstract concepts in limbo before they see how the concepts are applied.

Diagrams. A variety of illustrative diagrams are intended to maintain interest and to clarify or summarize the relationships between the items under discussion.

Chapter Summaries. To help students review their understanding of the topical coverage, each chapter contains a summary whose structure is parallel to the learning objectives.

Demonstration Problems in Each Chapter. Although the authors present illustrative problems in close proximity to typical explanations, each chapter also concludes with a demonstration problem and solution. These present integrated examples of how the concepts in the chapters are applied in solving problems.

Assignment Material. There are nearly 600 exercise and problem assignments in this edition. Several problems are based on facts drawn from real-world companies. A large number have relatively short solution times that give students the positive incentive of quick feedback and frequent encouragement that results from successful completion.

Annotation of Selected Assignments. Brief annotations are provided for the exercises and problems so that students can move quickly to the active process of preparing their solutions.

Unannotated Provocative and Analytical and Review Problems. The role of the provocative and analytical and review problems is to challenge students with somewhat more complex situations in which they must take greater responsibility for analyzing the problems and structuring their solutions. To facilitate this, annotations are not provided and working papers are not specifically designed for these problems. Nevertheless, the working papers booklets include a variety of extra forms that students can adapt to these problems. Provocative and analytical and review problems can help instructors challenge their best students and demonstrate to the entire class the contemporary relevance of the course.

Comprehensive Review Problems. To support the integration of topics across several chapters and to provide structured review on a periodic basis, the text includes three comprehensive assignment problems. They appear after Chapters 4, 6, and 12.

Appendixes

The book contains ten appendixes. Some of the topics in these appendixes represent expanded coverage. Each of the topical appendixes is supported by separate learning objectives, assignment material, coverage in the Study Guides, and the examination bank.

a. Appendix A (after Chapter 3) expands the discussion of adjusting entries to include a clearer treatment of items that are originally recorded in expense and revenue accounts.

b. Appendix B (after Chapter 4) contains a discussion of reversing entries. The placement of this material in an appendix permits optional coverage of these procedures.

c. Appendix C (after Chapter 5) gives a thorough explanation of the adjusting entry approach to accounting for merchandise inventories.

d. Appendix D (also after Chapter 5) contains a review of accounting principles and concise coverage of CICA's financial statement concepts and of the FASB's conceptual framework.

e. Appendix E (after Chapter 6) focuses on the application of microcomputers to accounting.

f. Appendix F (after Chapter 7) explains the use of vouchers in a manual accounting system.

g. Appendix G (at the end of the book) supplements the present value discussion in Chapter 10 with an expanded analysis of present and future values.

h. Given that the *CICA Handbook* recommends disclosure on the effect of price changes as supplementary information, this topic is covered in Appendix H.

i. Appendix I includes a discussion of accounting for corporate income taxes.

j. Appendix J contains all of the financial disclosures that appear in the 1989 annual report of Abitibi-Price Inc.

Other Important Features that Affect Several Chapters

In addition to the above features, there are several highlights found throughout the text. Some of these are itemized below:

An Emphasis on Ethics in Accounting. The text begins with a new prologue on the importance of ethics in accounting. Thereafter, many chapters include brief cases under the common title ''As a Matter of Ethics.'' These cases are intended to encourage student reflection on the ethical issues confronted by accountants and others who use accounting information. The *Instructor's Resource Manual* includes helpful points for discussion related to each ethical case and copies of the ethical codes adopted by the CICA, CGAAC, and SMAC. Some instructors may use these materials in support of class discussions; others may simply post the notes or distribute them for student use.

Questions. Approximately 425 questions for class discussion address the conceptual issues explained in the text.

Glossaries. The glossaries include well over 400 important terms with concise definitions that focus on the conceptual essence of the terms. The glossaries are located at the end of each chapter so they can be used effectively when students are reviewing the chapter. However, each glossary term is also highlighted in colour in the index to the book.

Integrated Learning Objectives. Learning objectives are clearly stated at the beginning of each chapter. To support instructional approaches that focus on learning objectives, *Financial Accounting Principles* integrates these objectives throughout the text and supporting materials. In the text, they are presented in the margins next to relevant topical coverage and next to related problem assignments.

Comprehensive Accounting Cycle Illustration. A comprehensive illustration, Jerry Dow, Lawyer, is used throughout Chapters 1–4. This illustration contains several highlights that make the book more teachable and easier to understand. For example, all of the financial statements introduced in Chapter 1 (including the statement of changes in financial position) are drawn from this illustration. Also, Chapter 3 presents the unadjusted trial balance, the adjustments, and the adjusted trial balance in a manner that better prepares students for the Chapter 4 discussion of the work sheet. And in Chapter 4, a series of overlay transparencies are used to show much more clearly the process of developing a work sheet. Throughout these chapters, special care has been taken to ensure that problem requirements never precede a thorough explanation of the issues.

Descriptive Titles of Illustrations. Descriptive titles have been given to the illustrations whenever this adds clarity.

Treatment of Dividends. Dividends are recorded in a Dividends Declared account to make the corporate procedures parallel to the withdrawals accounts used in unincorporated businesses.

Real-World Examples. The real-world examples and problems were selected especially for the first edition. These have been drawn primarily from the published financial reports of corporations.

Problem Assignments Solvable with Computer Package. Many exercises, problems, and provocative problems can be solved using Spreadsheet Applications Template Software (SPATS) developed by Will Garland of Coastal Carolina College and Raymond F. Carroll of Dalhousie University. SPATS contains innovatively designed templates based on Lotus® 1-2-3® and also includes a very effective tutorial for Lotus® 1-2-3®. The exercises and problems that are solvable with SPATS are identified in the *Instructor's Resource Manual*.

Use of Colour to Enhance Learning. The use of colour in *Financial Accounting Principles* has been carefully designed to support and encourage student learning. Financial reports that are the output of the accounting process are identified by their blue background. A bold blue is used to emphasize key terms, titles of statements, and items of special importance in illustrations. Textual headings require a "hot," bold colour to draw attention. These are printed in red, which also is used to emphasize alternative points of special importance in illustrations. A noninterruptive, cream colour softly highlights the end-of-chapter material where student involvement in the learning process is greatest. Cream also serves as a background for illustrations.

Highlights in Specific Chapters

Most of the chapters in this text reflect specific highlights in addition to those described above. These include the following:

- Chapter 1 contains coverage of the institutional environment of financial reporting and its relationship to standards setting.
- Chapter 3 reflects a conceptual discussion of the realization and matching principles and of accrual versus cash basis accounting.
- Overlay transparencies are used in the work sheet illustrations of Chapter 4 to present more effectively the sequence of steps in the preparation of a work sheet.
- Illustrations in Chapter 7 highlight the principles of internal control and diagram the flow of business papers related to purchases when a voucher system is used. The concept of asset liquidity is also explained in this chapter.
- A discussion of temporary investments and lower of cost or market is provided in Chapter 8.
- The discussion in Chapter 10 has been organized to emphasize the concept of cost recovery through depreciation and to place less emphasis on accelerated depreciation methods.
- In Chapter 12, the criteria for classifying leases as capital or operating leases are clearly explained.
- Chapter 15 includes a discussion and illustration of corporate management structures.
- The material on reporting income and retained earnings items is presented in Chapter 16, as is the explanation of earnings per share. This organization provides a connected set of topics and makes room for the separate chapter on stock investments, consolidations, and international operations (Chapter 19).
- Also found in Chapter 16 is a discussion of extraordinary items as covered by the *CICA Handbook,* section 3480.
- The statement of changes in financial position is explained in Chapter 18. Both the direct and working paper approaches to preparing the statement are explained.
- The discussion of financial statement ratios in Chapter 20 includes coverage of profit margin, total asset turnover, and their relationship to return on total assets. The calculations of all ratios are reviewed at the end of the chapter.

- Diagrams are used in Chapter 21 to support explanations of product costs versus period costs, the flow of product costs in manufacturing companies, and the relationship between overhead items, the manufacturing statement, and the income statement.

For the Instructor

The support package for *Financial Accounting Principles* includes many of the items published for *Fundamental Accounting Principles,* Sixth Canadian Edition. They include the following:

- Two *Solutions Manuals* that have extensive supporting calculations in this edition.
- Solution transparencies that include selected exercises and problems. These transparencies are printed in boldface in an exceptionally large typeface so that visibility from a distance is strikingly improved.
- A set of Teaching Transparencies, many of which are in colour.
- Computerized Teaching Transparencies that are designed to support teaching the course using a computer, data display, and an overhead projector.
- Video tapes that are available upon adoption. The tapes reinforce important topics and procedures. They may be used in the classroom or media lab.
- *Spreadsheet Applications Template Software (SPATS),* a software package developed for use with the text by Will Garland of Coastal Carolina College and Raymond F. Carroll of Dalhousie University. SPATS includes a Lotus® 1-2-3® tutorial and innovatively designed templates that may be used with Lotus® 1-2-3® to solve many of the exercises and problems in the text. Upon adoption, this package is available to instructors for classroom or laboratory use.
- *Computerized Tutorials* by Leland Mansuetti and J. Russell Curtis. These software packages include glossary reviews, journalizing problems, multiple-choice exercises, and analyses of financial statements. Upon adoption, these computerized tutorials are available to instructors for classroom or laboratory use.
- A comprehensive test bank to accompany this text. The bank includes a variety of multiple-choice and true/false questions.
- *Computest III,* an improved test generator program that allows editing of questions, provides up to 99 different versions of each test, and allows question selection based on type of question, level of difficulty, or learning objectives.
- *Teletest,* which is a system for obtaining laser-printed tests by telephoning the publisher and specifying the questions to be drawn from the test bank.
- The *Instructor's Resource Manual* includes sample course syllabi, suggested homework assignments, a series of lecture outlines, demon-

stration problems, suggested points for emphasis, and background materials for discussions of ethics in accounting.

For the Student

In addition to the text, the package of support items for the student includes the following:

- *Working Papers,* which includes working papers for the Problems, Alternate Problems, and Comprehensive Problems, with additional forms that may be adapted for the Exercises and Provocative Problems.
- The *Study Guide,* which provides a basis for independent study and review, has been expanded to include multiple-choice and true/false questions as well as several additional problems with solutions for each chapter and appendix.
- *Class Notes,* for use with the Computerized Teaching Transparencies. These are designed to help students be actively involved and take effective notes when the computerized transparencies are used to teach the course.
- Check Figures for the Problems and Alternate Problems.
- *World of Sports,* a manual, single proprietorship practice set with business papers that may be assigned after Chapter 6.
- Student's Name Book Centre, a manual, single proprietorship practice set covering a one-month accounting cycle. Authored by Harvey C. Freedman of Humber College, this practice set may be assigned after Chapter 6.
- *New Tech Incorporated,* a manual practice set with a narrative of transactions for a manufacturing corporation. This may be assigned after Chapter 21.
- *Kellogg Business Systems, Inc.,* an extended corporate practice set that may be assigned after Chapter 20. Like the other computerized items for students, it can be ordered on either $5\frac{1}{4}$- or $3\frac{1}{2}$-inch disks.
- *ESP—Electronic Spreadsheet Program,* a computerized spreadsheet package by John Wanlass and Kermit Larson that can be used to solve many of the problems in the text and is also broad enough to be used in a separate computer accounting course.
- *DeeJay Sound and Vision,* an accounting practice set using ACCPAC® plus General Ledger and Bedford Integrated Accounting. Authored by John W. Yu and David Harrison.
- *DeeJay Sound and Vision,* an accounting practice set using New Views®.

Acknowledgments

We are indebted to those individuals who have been the source of many improvements in the book through their thoughtful and insightful reviews. They include:

Robert C. Bell, British Columbia Institute of Technology.

Bob Duff, New Brunswick Community College.

Harvey C. Freedman, Humber College of Applied Arts and Technology.

Henry Funk, Red River Community College.

Bob Gordon, New Brunswick Community College.

Roger Melanson, New Brunswick Community College.

Paul Poirier, New Brunswick Community College.

Ralph Sweet, Durham College of Applied Arts and Technology.

During the development of this text, a focus group was held to solicit feed-back, ideas, and suggestions for the revision of *Fundamental Accounting Principles*. We are indebted to the instructors that attended this informative session. They include:

Richard Farrar, Conestoga College.

Jeremy Frape, Humber College of Applied Arts and Technology.

John Glendenning, Centennial College.

Tom McMillan, George Brown College.

Doug Mann, Georgian College.

Michael Perretta, Sheridan College

We especially want to recognize the contribution of Ray Carroll, Dalhousie University. Professor Carroll prepared the *Instructor's Resource Manual* that accompanies this text and checked every problem and solution for accuracy. We would also like to thank Sharon Roth, University of Windsor, and public accountants Danny Guida and Tony Ianni for their work on the *Solutions Manual*. Along with the authors, they conducted a very thorough four-stage check of illustrations, problems, and solutions for accuracy. We are indebted to Frank Reichardt, Red River Community College, for his preparation of the computerized test bank that accompanies this text.

Last but not least, we gratefully acknowledge the contribution from the faculty members and secretarial staff at the University of Windsor and Wilfrid Laurier University, especially Sandra J. Berlasty, Susanne Burns, and Kim Susanna.

Michael Zin
Morton Nelson

Contents

Disbursements Journal or Cheque Register Testing the Accuracy
of the Ledgers Sales Taxes Using Sales Invoices as a Sales
Journal Sales Returns General Journal Entries Computerized
Data Processing Recording Actual Transactions Appendix E:
Application Programs for Business

Part Three
Accounting for Assets   331

7 Internal Control and Accounting for Cash   332

Internal Control Computers and Internal Control Internal Control
for Cash The Voucher System and Control The Voucher System
and Expenses Recording Vouchers The Petty Cash Fund Petty
Cash Fund Illustrated Cash Over and Short Reconciling the Bank
Balance Illustration of a Bank Reconciliation Other Internal
Control Procedures Appendix F: Recording Vouchers, Manual
System

8 Temporary Investments and Receivables   385

Temporary Investments Credit Card Sales Maintaining a Separate
Account for Each Customer Bad Debts Matching Bad Debt
Losses with Sales Allowance Method of Accounting for Bad Debts
Bad Debt Recoveries Estimating the Amount of Bad Debts
Expense Direct Write-Off Method of Accounting for Bad Debts
Installment Accounts and Notes Receivable Promissory Notes
Calculating Interest Recording the Receipt of a Note
Dishonoured Notes Receivable Discounting Notes Receivable
Dishonour of a Discounted Note End-of-Period Adjustments
Alternative Method of Interest Calculation

9 Inventories and Cost of Goods Sold   436

Matching Merchandise Costs with Revenues Items to Include in
Merchandise Inventory Elements of Inventory Cost Taking an
Ending Inventory Assigning Costs to Inventory Items Changing
Accounting Procedures Lower of Cost or Market Principle of
Conservatism Perpetual Inventory Systems Comparing Journal
Entries under Periodic and Perpetual Inventory Systems
Subsidiary Inventory Records—Perpetual System First-In, First-
Out—Perpetual Inventory System Weighted Average—Perpetual
Inventory System The Difference between Weighted Average
(Perpetual) and Weighted Average (Periodic) The Retail Method of
Estimating Inventories Gross Profit Method of Estimating
Inventories

Nature of Partnership Earnings Division of Earnings Earnings
Allocated on a Stated Fractional Basis Division of Earnings Based
on the Ratio of Capital Investments Salaries and Interest
Allowances Partnership Financial Statements Withdrawal or
Addition of a Partner Death of a Partner Liquidations

of a Manufacturing Company   Manufacturing Statement   Work
Sheet for a Manufacturing Company   Preparing the Financial
Statements   Adjusting Entries   Closing Entries   Inventory
Valuation Problems of a Manufacturer

Introduction

Accounting in one form or another touches the lives of everyone: young people add and subtract figures to decide how to spend their weekly allowances; newspaper carriers keep payment records of their customers; students determine where the money for their education is coming from and how to spend it; taxpayers account for their taxable deductions; and businesses account for the profits from their operations. All of us use accounting to make economic decisions of one kind or another.

As you study this accounting text, a new world of understanding and knowledge will unfold. You will be better prepared to earn a living and to live on what you earn; newspaper stories of record sales, bankruptcies, and government regulations will have more meaning; and gradually you will come to understand the important role accounting plays in our economic society.

Part One of *Financial Accounting Principles* consists of:

To the Student Reader

Prologue: Ethics: The Most Fundamental Accounting Principle

1. Accounting: An Introduction to Its Concepts

To the Student Reader

Financial Accounting Principles is designed to get you actively involved in the learning process so that you will learn quickly and more thoroughly. The more time you spend expressing what you are learning, the more effectively you will learn. In accounting, you do this primarily by answering questions and solving problems. However, you can also express your ideas by using the wide margins for taking notes, summarizing a phrase, or writing down a question that remains unanswered in your mind. These notes will assist in your later review of the material, and the simple process of writing them will help you learn.

As you read the text, you will be exposed to many important new terms. The first time a key term is used, it is printed in blue. In addition to being defined and discussed in the chapter, these terms are listed with concise definitions in a glossary at the end of each chapter. The glossary is a good place to begin your review of important concepts. You can also find the key terms in the Index at the back of the book.

As a guide to your study, specific learning objectives are listed at the beginning of each chapter, repeated in the margins next to the related topics throughout the chapter, and used as a basis for summary at the end of the chapter. The exercises and problems are also coded in terms of these objectives.

The use of colour in the book has been carefully planned to facilitate your learning. Financial reports, which are the output of the accounting process, are printed on a blue background. Blue is also used to emphasize key terms, titles of statements, and items of special importance in illustrations. Red is used for headings and for emphasizing alternative points of special importance in illustrations. A soft, noninterruptive cream colour is used as a background in the illustrations and the end-of-chapter material.

In addition to a summary and glossary, each chapter contains a Demonstration Problem and related solution that illustrate many of the issues discussed in the chapter. The exercises and problems in each chapter have brief annotations. However, to challenge you to identify the topical issues involved, the provocative problems are not annotated.

Ethics: The Most Fundamental Accounting Principle

"Each person capable of making moral decisions is responsible for making his own decisions. The ultimate locus of moral responsibility is in the individual."[1]

As college students, you no doubt realize that ethics and ethical behaviour are important features of civilized society. Ethical considerations abound in daily life, both privately and professionally. The media often remind us of the importance of ethics to society. These reminders come in the form of news stories about such things as civil rights violations, fraudulent attempts to "rip off" the elderly, credit card scams, parents who failed to make child support payments, children who ignored or abused their elderly parents, politicians who failed to disclose past instances of misconduct, the alleged bribery of government officials, and Wall Street moguls who used inside information for personal gain.

The Meaning of Ethics

As a discipline of study, ethics deals "with what is good and bad or right and wrong or with moral duty and obligation." In practice, ethics are "principles of conduct that govern an individual or a profession."[2] Some unethical actions are unlawful. Other actions may be within the law but, nevertheless, are widely recognized as being ethically wrong. In addition, some actions are not clearly right or wrong but are ethically questionable.

Many of the issues we face in school, in the workplace, and beyond have ethical dimensions; they are unavoidable aspects of life. How well we deal with ethical matters influences how we feel about ourselves, how we are perceived by others, and in the aggregate, the quality of our society. But why begin an accounting text with a prologue on ethics? How do ethics relate to business, and more specifically, to the discipline of accounting?

---

[1] Harold H. Titus and Morris Keeton, *Ethics for Today,* 4th ed. (New York: American Book–Stratford Press, 1966), p. 131.

[2] *Webster's Third New International Dictionary of the English Language, Unabridged* (Springfield, Mass.: G & C Merriam Co., 1971), p. 780.

Ethics in Business

To answer the question of why we begin this text with a prologue on ethics, we must recognize that ethical standards in business and accounting are a matter of public concern. In recent years, many people have expressed concern about deteriorating ethical standards in business. Touche Ross, an international public accounting firm, recently conducted an opinion survey on business ethics. The survey included over 1,100 business executives, deans of business schools, and members of Congress. Of those in the survey, 94% agree that "the business community is troubled by ethical problems today."[3] Ironically, those surveyed also believe that companies that are successful over the long run seem to have high ethical standards. You may infer from this that "ethics is good business." Ethical business practices can help create loyal customers and suppliers, trustworthy and productive employees, and a solid reputation.

Because of the widespread public interest in business ethics, many banks, insurance companies, and other businesses have recently revised or written new codes of ethics. Others are currently in the process of developing new codes of ethics. Companies generally use these codes as public statements of their commitment to ethical business practices and also as guides for employees to follow.

Ethics in Accounting

In accounting, many professional organizations such as the American Institute of Certified Public Accountants have had codes of ethics for years. Most of these codes have been reevaluated and revised in recent years. Ethics is important in accounting because accountants often are required to make decisions that have ethical implications. The activities performed by accountants have a profound impact on many individuals, businesses, and other institutions. An accountant's decisions can affect such things as the amount of money a corporation distributes to its shareholders, the price a buyer pays for a business enterprise, the compensation levels of managers and executives, the success or failure of specific products and divisions, and the amount of provincial and federal taxes paid by an individual or a business.

To see how an accountant's decisions can have an ethical dimension, consider the following example. Assume that Smith and Jones agreed to be partners in a business venture that would last two years. Because the original idea for the business venture was Smith's, they agreed that Smith would receive 75% of the first year's profits and Jones would receive 25%. However, their agreement was that Smith and Jones would split the profits evenly in years after the first year. At the end of the first year, their accountant discovers that there are two alternative methods for recording a recent transaction. If method A is used, a profit of $100,000 will be recognized in year 1. If method B is used, the profit of $100,000 will not be recognized until year 2. Clearly, the accountant's decision about which method should be used will affect each partner's compensation. If method A is used, Smith will receive $75,000 of the profit and

---

[3] Touche Ross & Co., *Ethics in American Business* (New York, 1988), pp. 1–2.

Jones will receive $25,000. But if method B is used, each partner will receive $50,000.

In the above example, more information is needed to help the accountant choose between methods A and B. As an ethical matter, however, the accountant's decision should not be influenced by the fact that method A is more favourable to Smith and method B is more favourable to Jones.

The above example is not unusual. Accountants are frequently called on to choose between alternative methods for recognizing profits. These decisions cannot be made lightly because, as the example shows, the decisions may shift wealth from one party to another.

Another aspect of accounting that illustrates the importance of ethical behaviour involves the issue of confidentiality. Accountants, by the very nature of their duties, frequently work with private, confidential information. For example, accountants have access to individual salary records, future business plans and budgets, and a variety of information about the financial status of their clients or employers. As an ethical matter, accountants must respect and maintain the confidentiality of this type of information.

The Ethical Challenge

As you proceed in your study of accounting, you will encounter many other situations in which ethical considerations are important. We encourage you to seek out and explore any ethical issues that may arise. Accounting must be done ethically if it is to be an effective tool in the service of society. This is, perhaps, the most fundamental principle of accounting.

Ethical decisions and the development of ethical standards are areas in your life where you are in control. Each one of us as individuals is free to shape our own moral positions. Adapting a phrase originally spoken by Supreme Court Justice Earl Warren in reference to the law: "In civilized life, [accounting] floats on a sea of ethics." It is your choice how you elect to navigate this sea.

1 Accounting: An Introduction to Its Concepts

Your study begins in this chapter with the questions: What is accounting? and, Why study accounting? Many students will follow careers in accounting, and many others will work closely with accountants. As a result, this chapter discusses the accounting profession, the work accountants do, the periodic financial statements that accountants prepare, the general principles that accountants follow in preparing financial statements, and some of the organizations that govern or influence accounting practices. The chapter also describes the different ways a business might be organized and takes an introductory look at how accountants analyze the effects of business transactions.

Learning Objectives

After studying Chapter 1, you should be able to:

1. Describe the function of accounting and the nature and purpose of the information it provides.
2. List the main fields of accounting employment and the kinds of work carried on in each field.
3. Describe the information contained in the financial statements of a business and be able to prepare simple financial statements.
4. Briefly explain the accounting concepts and principles introduced in the chapter and describe the process by which generally accepted accounting principles are established.
5. Briefly explain the differences between a single proprietorship, a partnership, and a corporation, comparing the differing responsibilities of their owners for the debts of the business.
6. Recognize and be able to indicate the effects of transactions on the elements of an accounting equation.
7. Define or explain the words and phrases listed in the chapter Glossary.

What Is Accounting?

Describe the function of accounting and the nature and purpose of the information it provides. (L. O. 1)

Accounting is a service activity. Its function is to provide quantitative information about economic entities. The information, essentially financial in nature, is primarily provided by reports referred to as financial statements and is intended to be useful in making economic decisions. These reports are used in describing the activities and financial status of many different kinds of economic entities. They include hospitals, schools, cities, governmental agencies, and profit-oriented businesses. The "Financial Statement Concepts" (*CICA Handbook,* par. 1000.12) state:

> The objective of financial statements is to communicate information that is useful to investors, creditors and other users in making resource allocation decisions and/or assessing management stewardship. Consequently, financial statements provide information about:
>
> (a) an entity's economic resources, obligations and equity;
> (b) changes in an entity's economic resources, obligations and equity; and
> (c) the economic performance of the entity.

In making decisions about an economic entity, individuals generally must begin by asking questions about the entity. The answers to many such questions are found in accounting reports. If, for example, the entity is a business, the managers of the business would look to accounting for answers to questions such as:

What are the resources of the business?

What debts does it owe?

Does it have earnings?

Are expenses too large in relation to sales?

Is too little or too much merchandise being kept?

Are amounts owed by customers being collected rapidly?

Will the business be able to pay its debts as they mature?

Should the plant be expanded?

Should a new product be introduced?

Should selling prices be increased?

In addition, grantors of credit such as banks, wholesale houses, and manufacturers use accounting information in answering such questions as:

Are the customer's earning prospects good?

What is its debt-paying ability?

Has it paid its debts promptly in the past?

Should it be granted additional credit?

Likewise, governmental units use accounting information in regulating businesses and collecting taxes. Labour unions use it in negotiating working conditions and wage agreements. And last but certainly not least among the users of accounting information are individual investors, who make wide use of accounting data in their investment decisions.

Accounting and Bookkeeping

Many people confuse **accounting** and **bookkeeping** and look on them as one and the same. In effect, they identify the whole with one of its parts. Actually, bookkeeping is only part of accounting, the record-making part. To keep books is to record transactions, and a bookkeeper is one who records transactions either on a computer or manually or with a bookkeeping machine. Accounting includes much more than this. The accountant should have the ability to design the accounting system; to analyze and record complex, nonroutine transactions; and to analyze and interpret accounting information.

Accounting and Computers

Computers are used for many tasks in our modern society, including the processing of accounting data. A computer can accept and store accounting data, sort and rearrange it, perform arithmetic calculations on it, and prepare reports from the data. Furthermore, a computer can perform these functions very rapidly and with little or no human intervention. However, before a computer can do this, a set of detailed instructions must be prepared and entered into the computer to tell it how to process the data. The person who prepares these instructions must have a thorough understanding of accounting procedures and accounting principles. Thus, while computers have had a tremendous impact on accounting, they are not substitutes for understanding the fundamental concepts and principles of accounting.

Why Study Accounting?

Considering the wide range of questions that are answered by referring to accounting information, perhaps every educated person in our society should be regarded as a user of accounting information. If you are to use accounting information effectively, you must have some understanding of how the data are gathered and the figures are put together. You must appreciate the limitations of the data and the extent to which portions are based on estimates rather than on precise measurements. And, you must understand accounting terms and concepts. Needless to say, this knowledge is gained in a study of accounting. With regard to understandability, the *CICA Handbook* (par. 1000.16) states:

> For the information provided in financial statements to be useful,
> it must be capable of being understood by investors, creditors and
> other users. Investors, creditors and other users are assumed to
> have a reasonable understanding of business and economic activi-
> ties and accounting, together with a willingness to study the infor-
> mation with reasonable diligence.

Another reason to study accounting is to make it one's lifework. A career in accounting can be very interesting and highly rewarding.

Accountancy as a Profession

Over the past half century, accountancy as a profession has attained a stature comparable with that of law or medicine. Most provinces license *public accountants* just as they license doctors and lawyers. The licensing helps ensure a high standard of professional service. Only individuals who have passed a rigorous examination of their accounting and related knowledge, met other education and experience requirements, and have received a license may designate themselves as public accountants.

In Canada, there are a number of accounting organizations providing education and professional training. These include the provincial Institutes of Chartered Accountants, the Certified General Accountants' Association of Canada, and the Society of Management Accountants **(SMA).** Successful completion of the prescribed courses of instruction and practical experience lead to the following appellations:

Chartered Accountant (CA)

Certified General Accountant **(CGA)**

Certified Management Accountant (CMA)

An activity of the three accounting organizations that has shaped accounting thought has been the education and the publication program. Each has an extensive educational program and has maintained the publication of journals which enjoy wide readership.

In the past decade reliance on post-secondary accounting education has become a significant part of the educational process and complements the extensive correspondence and lecture programs of both the Certified General Accountants' Association of Canada and the Society of Management Accountants—The Canadian Institute of Chartered Accountants **(CICA)** requires a university degree with specified course content.

Accountancy is the fastest growing of the professions. This growth is in response to the expansion and complexity of the economy, the increasing involvement of the accountant in the process of management decision making, and a growing number of financial reporting activities.

The Work of an Accountant

Accountants are employed in three broad fields: (1) in public accounting, (2) in private accounting, or (3) in government.

List the main fields of accounting employment and the kinds of work carried on in each field. (L. O. 2)

Public Accounting

Auditing. The principal service offered by public accountants is auditing. Banks commonly require an **audit** of the financial statements of companies that apply for a sizable loan. Such audits are performed by public accountants who are not employees of the audited concern but are independent professional persons working for a fee. Also, companies whose securities are offered for sale to the public generally must be audited before their securities may be sold. Thereafter, additional audits must be made periodically if the securities are to continue being traded.

The purpose of an audit is to lend credibility to a company's financial statements. In making the audit, the auditors carefully examine the company's statements and the accounting records from which they were prepared. In the examination, the *auditors seek to determine whether the statements fairly reflect the company's financial position and operating results, in accordance with generally accepted accounting principles.* Based on their examination, the auditors prepare a report that expresses their opinion about the financial statements. The auditors' report is published together with the audited financial statements.

Banks, investors, and other users of financial statements rely on independent auditors to determine that a company's financial statements are fairly presented. The audit gives these financial statement users the confidence to use financial statement information in making loans, in granting credit, and in buying and selling securities.

Management Advisory Services. In addition to auditing, public accountants commonly offer **management advisory services.** An accountant gains from an audit an intimate knowledge of the audited company's accounting and operating procedures. Thus, the accountant is in an excellent position to offer constructive suggestions for improving the company's methods of operation. Clients expect these suggestions as a useful audit by-product. They also commonly engage public accountants to conduct additional investigations for the purpose of determining ways in which their operations may be improved. Such investigations and the suggestions growing from them are known as management advisory services.

Management advisory services include the design, installation, and improvement of a client's general accounting system and any related information systems it may have for managing the company. This may involve selecting appropriate computers, developing software, and installing the procedures necessary to bring an information system into effective operating use. Management advisory services may also include financial planning, budgeting, forecasting, and inventory control.

Tax Services. In this day of highly complex tax laws and high tax rates, few important business decisions are made without consideration being given to their tax effect. A professional accountant, through training and experience, is well qualified to render important service in this area. **Tax services** include not only the preparation and filing of tax returns but also advice as to how transactions may be completed so as to incur the smallest tax.

Private Accounting

Accountants employed by a single enterprise are said to be in private accounting. A small business may employ only one accountant or it may depend on the services of a public accountant and employ none. A large business, on the other hand, may have more than 100 employees in its accounting department. They commonly work under the supervision of a chief accounting officer called the **controller.** The title *controller* stems from the fact that one of the chief uses of accounting data is to control the operations of a business.

The one accountant of the small business and the accounting department of a large business do a variety of work, including general accounting, cost accounting, budgeting, and internal auditing.

General Accounting. The task of recording transactions, processing the recorded data, and preparing financial reports for the use of management, owners, creditors, and governmental agencies is called **general accounting.**

Private accountant employees may design a company's accounting information system, perhaps with the help of the company's auditors. The private accountant employees also supervise the clerical or data processing staff in recording transactions, maintaining financial records, and preparing the company's financial reports.

Cost Accounting. The phase of accounting that has to do with determining and controlling costs and assessing the performance of managers who are responsible for costs is called cost accounting. This may involve accounting for the costs of producing a given product or service, or the costs of performing some other specific function. A knowledge of costs and controlling costs is vital to good management. Therefore, a large company may have a number of accountants engaged in this activity.

Budgeting. The process of developing formal plans for future business activities is called budgeting. The objective of budgeting is to provide management with a clear understanding of all the activities that must be undertaken and completed in order to accomplish their objectives for the company. Then, after the budget plan has been put into effect, it provides a basis for evaluating actual accomplishments. Many large companies have a number of people who devote all their time to this phase of accounting.

Internal Auditing. In addition to an annual audit by an independent firm of public accountants, many companies maintain a staff of internal auditors. These employees move from one department of the company to another, checking the records and operating procedures of each department. It is the responsibility of internal auditing to make sure that established accounting procedures and management directives are being followed throughout the company. Also, internal auditors are often asked to evaluate the operating efficiency of each department.

Governmental Accounting

Furnishing governmental services is a vast and complicated operation in which accounting is just as indispensable as in business. Elected and appointed officials must rely on data accumulated by means of accounting if they are to complete their administrative duties effectively. Accountants are responsible for the accumulation of this data. Accountants also review and audit the millions of income, payroll, and sales tax returns that accompany the tax payments on which governmental units depend. Criminal investigation agencies employ accountants to assist in the process of detecting crimes such as fraud. And finally, federal and provincial agencies, such as the Board of Transport Commissioners, Restrictive Trade Practices Commission, and Security Commissions, use accountants in many capacities in their regulation of business.

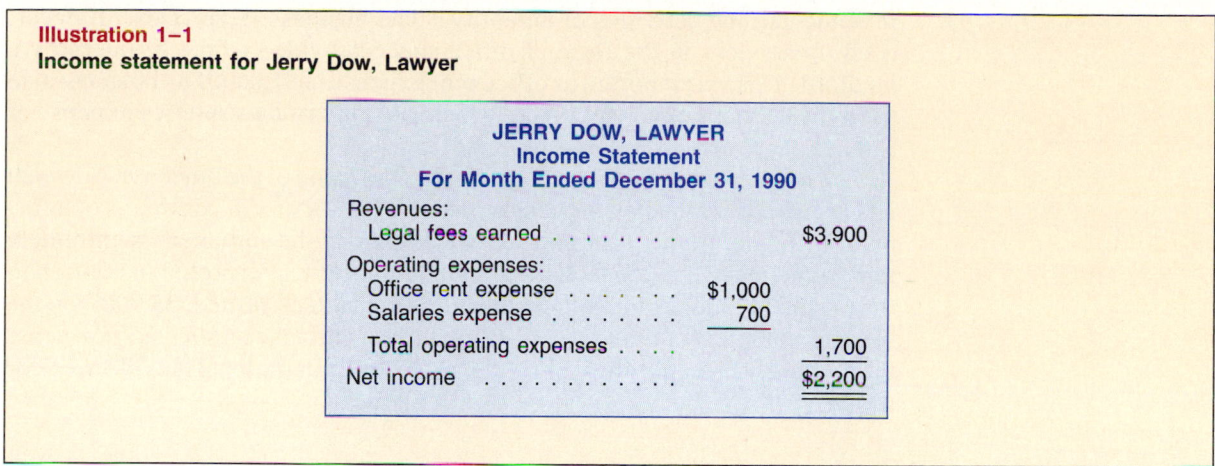

Illustration 1–1
Income statement for Jerry Dow, Lawyer

JERRY DOW, LAWYER
Income Statement
For Month Ended December 31, 1990

Revenues:		
Legal fees earned		$3,900
Operating expenses:		
Office rent expense	$1,000	
Salaries expense	700	
Total operating expenses		1,700
Net income		$2,200

Financial Statements

Describe the information contained in the financial statements of a business and be able to prepare simple financial statements.
(L. O. 3)

Financial statements are used to communicate accounting information. They are a primary product of the accounting process. As such, they are a good place to begin the study of accounting. Financial statements are used to convey a concise picture of the results of operations and the financial position of a business. We begin by considering two widely used financial statements: the income statement and the balance sheet.

The Income Statement

Many people would argue that a company's **income statement** (see Illustration 1–1) is the most important financial statement. The income statement shows whether or not the business achieved or failed to achieve one of its primary objectives—earning a profit, or net income. A **net income** is earned when revenues exceed expenses, but a **net loss** is incurred if the expenses exceed the revenues. An income statement is prepared by listing the revenues earned by the business, then listing the expenses incurred in earning the revenues, and finally subtracting the expenses from the revenues to determine if a net income or a net loss was incurred.

Revenues are increases in economic resources, either by way of inflows or enhancements of assets or reductions of liabilities, resulting from the ordinary activities of an entity, normally from the sale of goods, the rendering of services, or the use by others of entity resources yielding rent, interest, royalties, or dividends.[1] As shown in Illustration 1–1, the business of Jerry Dow, Lawyer, had $3,900 of revenues resulting from legal services provided to clients (customers). Other examples of revenues would be product sales, rent earned, dividends earned, and interest earned.

Expenses are decreases in economic resources, either by way of outflows or reductions of assets or incurrences of liabilities, resulting from the ordinary

---

[1] *CICA Handbook*, ''Financial Statement Concepts,'' par. 1000.32.

revenue-earning activities of an entity.[2] The business, Jerry Dow, Lawyer, used up services in the form of office space provided to the business by a landlord. This was reported as office rent expense of $1,000. The business also used the services of an employee, which was reported as salaries expense of $700.

The heading of an income statement tells the name of the business for which it is prepared and the time period covered by the statement. Both bits of information are important. The time period covered by the statement is extremely important, since the items on the statement must be interpreted in relation to the period of time. For example, the item ''Legal fees earned, $3,900'' on the income statement of Illustration 1–1 has little significance until it is known that the amount represents one month's legal fees and not the legal fees of a week or a year.

The Balance Sheet

The purpose of a **balance sheet** is to show the financial position of a business on a specific date. As a matter of fact, the statement is often called a **statement of financial position**. This statement reports the financial position of a business by showing the business's assets, liabilities, and equity. To begin with, you may think of an asset as a property or property right. Liabilities are debts, and equity is the residual claim of the business's owner or owners. The name of the business and the date are given in the balance sheet heading. It is understood that the amounts shown are as of the close of business on that date.

A balance sheet for Jerry Dow, Lawyer, appears in Illustration 1–2. Note that it is dated December 31, 1990. This balance sheet shows that as of the close of business on December 31, the business of Jerry Dow, Lawyer, had three different types of assets: cash, law library, and office equipment. The total dollar amount of these assets was $10,860. The statement also shows that the business had one liability, amounting to $760, and the owner's equity in the business amounted to $10,100.

Observe that the two sides of the financial statement are equal. This is where it gets the name *balance sheet*. Its two sides must always be equal because one side shows the resources of the business and the other shows who supplied the resources. For example, the business of Jerry Dow, Lawyer, had $10,860 of resources (assets) of which $760 were supplied by its creditors and $10,100 were supplied by its owner. **Creditors** are the individuals or organizations to whom debts are owed. The individuals or organizations who are obligated to pay are called **debtors**.

Assets, Liabilities, and Owner's Equity

The **assets** of a business are, in general, the properties or economic resources owned by the business. More precisely, assets are ''economic resources controlled by an entity as a result of past transactions or events and from which future economic benefits may be obtained.''[3] Assets include such things as cash, amounts owed to the business by its customers for goods and services

---

[2] Ibid., par. 1000.33.

[3] *CICA Handbook*, par. 1000.25.

Illustration 1–2
Balance sheet for Jerry Dow, Lawyer

JERRY DOW, LAWYER
Balance Sheet
December 31, 1990

Assets		Liabilities	
Cash	$ 1,100	Accounts payable	$ 760
Law library	2,880	**Owner's Equity**	
Office equipment	6,880	Jerry Dow, capital	10,100
Total assets	$10,860	Total liabilities and owner's equity	$10,860

sold to them on credit (called **accounts receivable**), merchandise held for sale by the business, supplies, equipment, buildings, and land. Assets may also include such intangible rights as those granted by a patent or copyright.

The **liabilities** of a business are its debts. They are defined more precisely as "obligations of an entity arising from past transactions or events, the settlement of which may result in the transfer or use of assets, provision of services or other yielding of economic benefits in the future."[4] Liabilities include obligations such as amounts owed to creditors for goods and services bought on credit (called **accounts payable**), salaries and wages owed employees, taxes payable, notes payable, and interest payable.

The **equity,** or **net assets,** of a business is "the residual interest in the assets of an entity that remains after deducting its liabilities."[5] When a business is owned by one person, the owner's interest or equity is shown on a balance sheet by listing the person's name, followed by the word *capital,* and then the amount of the equity. The use of the word capital comes from the idea that the owner has furnished the business with resources, or capital, equal to the amount of the equity.

A liability represents a claim, or right, to be paid. The law recognizes this right. If a business fails to pay its creditors, the law gives the creditors the right to force the sale of the assets of the business to secure money to meet creditor claims. Furthermore, if the assets are sold, the creditors are paid first, with any remainder going to the business owner.

Since creditor claims take precedence over those of an owner, an owner's equity in a business is always a residual amount. Creditors recognize this. When they examine the balance sheet of a business, they are always interested in the share of its assets furnished by creditors and the share furnished by its owner or owners. The creditors recognize that if the business must be liquidated and its assets sold, the shrinkage in converting assets into cash must exceed the equity of the owner or owners before the creditors will lose.

---

[4] Ibid., par. 1000.28.

[5] Ibid., par. 1000.31.

Generally Accepted Accounting Principles (GAAP)

Briefly explain the accounting concepts and principles introduced in the chapter and describe the process by which generally accepted accounting principles are established.
(L. O. 4)

An understanding of financial statement information requires a knowledge of the generally accepted accounting principles that govern the accumulation and presentation of the data appearing on such statements. A common definition of the word *principle* is: ''A broad general law or rule adopted or professed as a guide to action; a settled ground or basis of conduct or practice. . . .'' Consequently, **generally accepted accounting principles (GAAP)** may be described as broad rules adopted by the accounting profession as guides in measuring, recording, and reporting the financial affairs and activities of a business. They consist of a number of concepts, principles, and procedures that are summarized in Chapter 5, Appendix D. They also are referred to again and again throughout this text in order to increase your understanding of the information conveyed by accounting data.

Sources of Accounting Principles

Generally accepted accounting principles are not natural laws in the sense of the laws of physics and chemistry but man-made rules that depend for their authority upon their general acceptance by the accounting profession. They have evolved from the experience and thinking of the accounting profession, influenced by the financial community and governmental regulations. Primary among the organizations that fostered and continue to foster development of accounting principles are the Canadian Institute of Chartered Accountants (CICA), the American Institute of Certified Public Accounts **(AICPA)**, the Securities and Exchange Commission, and the American Accounting Association.

Over the years the accounting profession has devoted much time and attention to the problem of generally accepted accounting principles. For three decades prior to 1968, the Accounting and Auditing Committee of the CICA issued bulletins on financial disclosure, accounting principles, terminology, reporting, and auditing procedures. In 1968 these bulletins were consolidated to form a major part of the *CICA Handbook*. Since 1968 the *Handbook* has been constantly updated by the **Accounting Standards Committee** (formerly the Accounting Research Committee) through the issuance of recommendations on various current topics. These recommendations are issued only after due consideration of comments by interested parties on the exposure drafts. Added importance was given these recommendations when the regulations of the Canada Business Corporations Act, 1975, required that financial statements and the auditor's report be prepared in accordance with the recommendations of the CICA set out in the *Handbook*. The *Handbook* and the regulations permit departure from the recommendations in circumstances where departure would achieve a fairer disclosure. The fact of a departure from the recommendations of the *Handbook* and an explanation of the effect of the accounting method or statement presentation used must, however, be clearly set out in the financial statements, in a note thereto, or in a summary of accounting policies. This requirement parallels that of the AICPA's 1964 rule that its members must disclose in footnotes to published financial statements any departure from generally accepted accounting principles as set forth in the *Opinions of the Accounting Principles Board*. *Opinions* of the **APB** have the same status in the United States as the recommendations in the *CICA Hand-*

book in Canada. In 1959 the AICPA established the APB and gave it the authority to issue authoritative expressions of generally accepted accounting principles. In 1973 the APB was replaced by a seven-member Financial Accounting Standards Board *(FASB)*, independent of the AICPA, with authority to formulate rules governing the practice of accounting. In Canada, the Accounting Standards Authority of Canada (ASAC), an independent rules-setting body, has, to date, met with limited success.

The American Accounting Association, an organization with strong academic ties, has also been influential in describing and defining generally accepted accounting principles. It has sponsored a number of research studies and has published many articles dealing with accounting principles.

On the international scene, Canadian accounting bodies were in 1973 signatories of an Agreement establishing the International Accounting Standards Committee (IASC). This Agreement (revised in 1977) gave the IASC, now comprising 60 accounting bodies in 48 countries, the authority to ''formulate and publish in the public interest, standards to be observed in the preparation of audited financial statements and to promote their world wide acceptance and observance.'' Canadian agreement to require disclosure of compliance and any material departure from the international standards gave added weight to IASC recommendations. All organizations are continuing active research in accounting theory and the updating of accounting standards. Numerous references to these statements will be made throughout the discussion in this book.

Understanding Generally Accepted Accounting Principles (GAAP)

We believe that an understanding of GAAP is best conveyed with examples illustrating the application of each concept or principle. Consequently, we introduce only three **accounting concepts** and two *accounting principles* at this point. Discussions of the others are delayed until later in the text when meaningful examples of their application can be developed.

Business Entity Concept

For accounting purposes, every business is perceived and treated as if it is a separate entity that is distinct from its owner or owners and from every other business. This point of view in accounting is called the **business entity concept**. Businesses are perceived and treated as separate entities because, insofar as a specific business is concerned, the purpose of accounting is to record its transactions and periodically report its financial position and profitability. Consequently, the records and reports of a business should not include either the transactions or assets of another business or the personal assets and transactions of its owner or owners. To include either would distort the financial position and profitability of the business.

Cost Principle

One of the most fundamental principles in accounting is called the **cost principle**. Under this principle, all goods and services purchased are recorded at cost. For example, if a business pays $50,000 for land to be used in carrying on its operations, the purchase should be recorded at $50,000. It makes no difference if the buyer and several competent outside appraisers think that the land is worth at least $60,000. If the price paid for the land is $50,000, it must be recorded at that amount.

In applying the *cost principle*, costs are measured on a cash or cash-equivalent basis. If the consideration given for an asset or service is cash, cost is measured as the entire cash outlay made to secure the asset or service. If the consideration is something other than cash, cost is measured as the cash-equivalent value of the consideration given or the cash-equivalent value of the asset received, whichever is more clearly evident.

Objectivity Principle

Why are assets and services recorded at cost rather than some other amount such as estimated market value? The answer is because of the **objectivity principle.** This principle requires that accounting records be based on verifiable events such as business transactions between independent parties. **Business transactions** involve completed exchanges of economic consideration, for example, goods, services, money, or the rights to collect money, between two or more parties. Whims and fancies—for example, management opinion that an asset is "worth more than it cost"—have no place in accounting. To be dependable, accounting information must be based on objective data. As a rule, costs are objective, since they normally are established by buyers and sellers, each striking the best possible bargain for themselves.

Continuing-Concern Concept

When a business purchases and holds assets for use in its operations, the market values of those assets may change over time. Nevertheless, the accounting records for those assets are not adjusted to reflect market value changes. This is because of the **continuing-concern** or **going-concern concept.** Unless there is strong evidence to the contrary, a balance sheet is prepared under the assumption that the business for which it is prepared will continue in operation. As a continuing or going concern, the assets used in carrying on the operations of the business are not for sale. In fact, they cannot be sold without disrupting the business. Therefore, since the assets are held for use in the business and are not for sale, their current market values are not particularly relevant and need not be shown. Also, without a sale, their current market values usually cannot be objectively established, as is required by the *objectivity principle*.

The *continuing-concern* or *going-concern concept* applies in most situations. However, if a business is about to be sold or liquidated, the *continuing-concern concept* and the *cost principle* do not apply in the preparation of its statements. In such cases, amounts other than costs, such as estimated market values, become more useful and informative.

The Stable-Dollar Concept

In Canada, accounting transactions are measured, recorded, and reported in terms of dollars. In the measuring, recording, and reporting process, the dollar is treated as a stable unit of measure, like a litre, a metre, or a kilometre. However, the dollar, like other currencies, is not a stable unit of measure.

When the general price level (the average of all prices) changes, the value of money (its purchasing power) also changes.

Nevertheless, although the instability of the dollar is understood, accountants in their reports continue to add and subtract items acquired in different years with dollars of different sizes. In effect, they ignore changes in the size of the measuring unit. For example, assume a company purchased land some years ago for $10,000 and sold it today for $20,000. If during this period the purchasing power of the dollar declined from 100 cents to 50 cents, it can be said that the company is no better off for having purchased the land for $10,000 and sold it for $20,000 because the $20,000 will buy no more goods and services today than did the $10,000 at the time of the purchase. Yet, using the dollar to measure both transactions, the accountant reports a $10,000 gain from the purchase and sale.

The instability of the dollar as a unit of measure is recognized. However, at the present time, many people do not believe that accounting reports would be more informative if adjustments were made for changes in price levels. Consequently, instead of making such adjustments, accountants rely on the **stable-dollar concept,** which states that accounting reports should be based on the assumption that the value of the dollar does not change.

From the discussions of the *cost principle,* the *continuing-concern concept,* and the *stable-dollar concept,* it should be recognized that in most instances a balance sheet does not show the amounts at which the listed assets can be sold or replaced. Nor does it show the ''worth'' of the business for which it was prepared, since some of the listed assets may be salable for much more or much less than the dollar amounts at which they are shown.

Business Organizations

Briefly explain the differences between a single proprietorship, a partnership, and a corporation, comparing the differing responsibilities of their owners for the debts of the business.
(L. O. 5)

Accounting is applicable to all economic entities such as business concerns, schools, churches, fraternities, and so on. However, this text is focused on accounting for business concerns organized as **single** or **sole proprietorships, partnerships,** and **corporations.**

Single Proprietorships

If a business is owned by one person and the business is not organized under provincial or federal laws as a separate legal entity, the business is called a *single proprietorship,* or *sole proprietorship.* Small retail stores and service enterprises are commonly operated as single proprietorships. There are no legal requirements to be met in starting a single proprietorship business. Furthermore, single proprietorships are the most numerous of all business concerns.

In accounting for a single proprietorship, the *business entity concept* is applied and the business is treated as a separate entity that is distinct from its owner. However, insofar as the debts of the business are concerned, no such legal distinction is made. The owner of a single proprietorship business is personally responsible for its debts. As a result, if the assets of such a business are not sufficient to pay its debts, the personal assets of the proprietor may be taken to satisfy the claims of the business creditors.

Partnerships

When a business is owned by two or more people (partners) and is not organized as a separate legal entity, it is called a *partnership*. Like a single proprietorship, there are no special legal requirements to be met in starting a partnership business. All that is required is for two or more people to enter into an agreement to operate a business as partners. The agreement becomes a contract and may be either oral or written. However, to avoid disagreements, a written contract is preferred.

For accounting purposes, a partnership business is treated as a separate entity that is distinct from its owners. However, just as with a single proprietorship, no such legal distinction is made insofar as the debts of the business are concerned. A partner is personally responsible for all the debts of the partnership, both his or her own share and the shares of any partners who are unable to pay. Furthermore, the personal assets of a partner may be taken to satisfy all the debts of a partnership if other partners cannot pay.

Corporations

A *corporation* is formed, or *incorporated,* under the laws of a province or the federal government as a separate legal entity. Unlike a single proprietorship or partnership, a corporation is a separate entity under the law; it is separate and distinct from its owners. The owners of a corporation are called **shareholders** or **stockholders** because their ownership of the corporation's equity is divided into units that are called shares of **stock.** For example, a corporation that has issued 1,000 shares of stock has divided its equity into 1,000 units. A shareholder that owns 500 of these shares would own 50% of the corporation's equity. Such shares of stock may be sold and transferred from one shareholder to another without affecting the operation of the corporation.

Perhaps the most important characteristic of a corporation is its status as a separate legal entity. This characteristic makes a corporation responsible for its own acts and its own debts and relieves its shareholders of liability for either. It enables a corporation to buy, own, and sell property in its own name, to sue and be sued in its own name, and to enter into contracts for which it is solely responsible. In short, the separate legal entity status enables a corporation to conduct its business affairs as a legal person with all the rights, duties, and responsibilities of a person. However, unlike a person, a corporation must act through agents.

A corporation is created by securing approval of articles of incorporation from one of the provinces or the federal government. The requirements for incorporation vary, but in general, they call for filing an application with the proper governmental official and paying certain fees and taxes. If the application complies with the law and all fees and taxes have been paid, the articles of incorporation are approved and the corporation comes into existence. At that point, the corporation's organizers and perhaps others buy the corporation's stock and become shareholders. Then, the shareholders meet and elect a board of directors. The board then meets, appoints the corporation's president and other officers, and makes them responsible for managing the corporation's business affairs.

Corporations have multiplied, grown, and become the dominant form of business organization in our country. The primary reasons for this have been the lack of shareholder liability and the ease with which stock may be sold and transferred. Nevertheless, the single proprietorship is a simpler form of business. As a result, we begin the study of accounting in the early chapters of this book by focusing primarily on single proprietorships.

The Balance Sheet Equation

As previously stated, a balance sheet is so called because its two sides must always balance. The sum of the assets shown on the balance sheet must equal the liabilities plus the equity of the owner or owners of the business. This equality may be expressed in equation form as follows:

$$\text{Assets} = \text{Liabilities} + \text{Owner's Equity}$$

When balance sheet equality is expressed in equation form, the resulting equation is called the **balance sheet equation.** It is also known as the **accounting equation,** since all double-entry accounting is based on it. Like any mathematical equation, its elements may be transposed and the equation expressed:

$$\text{Assets} - \text{Liabilities} = \text{Owner's Equity}$$

The equation in this form illustrates the residual nature of the owner's equity. An owner's claims are secondary to the creditors' claims.

Effects of Transactions on the Accounting Equation

Recognize and be able to indicate the effects of transactions on the elements of an accounting equation.
(L. O. 6)

As mentioned earlier, a *business transaction* is a completed exchange of economic consideration such as goods or services; business transactions affect the elements of the accounting equation. However, regardless of what transactions a business completes, its accounting equation always remains in balance. In other words, the total assets of a business always equal the combined claims of its creditors and the equity of its owner or owners. This may be demonstrated with the following transactions of Jerry Dow's law practice, a single proprietorship business.

On December 1, Jerry Dow began a new law practice by investing $9,000 of his personal cash, which he deposited in a bank account opened in the name of the business, Jerry Dow, Lawyer. After the investment, the one asset of the new business and the equity of Dow in the business are shown in the following equation:

$$\text{Assets} = \text{Owner's Equity}$$

Cash, $9,000   Jerry Dow, capital, $9,000

Observe that after its first transaction, the new business has one asset, cash, $9,000. It has no liabilities, and the equity of Dow in the business is $9,000.

To continue the illustration, after the investment, Dow used $2,500 of the business cash to purchase books for a law library (transaction 2). Next, he used $5,600 of the business cash to buy office equipment (transaction 3). These transactions were exchanges of cash for other assets. Their effects on the accounting equation are shown in colour in Illustration 1–3. Observe that the equation remains in balance after each transaction.

Illustration 1–3
The effect on the balance sheet equation of asset purchases for cash

	Assets					=	Owner's Equity	
	Cash	+	Law Library	+	Office Equipment	=	Jerry Dow, Capital	Explanation of Change
(1)	$9,000						$9,000	Investment
(2)	−2,500		+$2,500					
Bal.	$6,500		$2,500				$9,000	
(3)	−5,600				+$5,600			
Bal.	$ 900	+	$2,500	+	$5,600	−	$9,000	

Illustration 1–4
The effect on the balance sheet equation of asset purchases on credit

	Assets					=	Liabilities	+	Owner's Equity	
	Cash	+	Law Library	+	Office Equipment	=	Accounts Payable	+	Jerry Dow, Capital	Explanation of Change
Bal.	$900		$2,500		$5,600				$9,000	
(4)			+ 380		+1,280		+$1,660			
Bal.	$900	+	$2,880	+	$6,880	=	$1,660	+	$9,000	

Continuing the illustration, assume that Dow needed additional equipment and more library items in the law office. However, the cash balance of the business was not adequate to make these purchases. Consequently, he purchased on credit from Equip-it Company law library items that cost $380 and office equipment that cost $1,280. The effects of this purchase (transaction 4) are shown in Illustration 1–4. Note that the assets were increased by the purchase. However, Dow's equity did not change because Equip-it Company acquired a claim against the assets equal to the increase in the assets. The claim or amount owed Equip-it Company is called an *account payable*.

A primary objective of a business is to increase the equity of its owner or owners by earning a profit or a net income. Dow's law practice will accomplish this objective by providing legal services to its clients on a fee basis. Of course, the practice will earn a net income only if legal fees earned are greater than the expenses incurred in earning the fees. Legal fees earned and expenses incurred affect the elements of an accounting equation. To illustrate their effects, assume that on December 10, Jerry Dow completed legal work for a client and immediately collected $2,200 in cash for the services rendered (transaction 5). On the same day, he paid $1,000 for the expense of renting office space during December (transaction 6). On December 12, Dow paid the $700 salary of the office secretary (transaction 7). The effects of these transactions are shown in Illustration 1–5.

Observe the effects of the legal fee. The $2,200 fee is a revenue, an inflow of assets from the sale of services. Note that the revenue not only increased assets (cash) but also caused a $2,200 increase in Dow's equity. Dow's equity increased because total assets increased without an increase in liabilities.

Illustration 1–5
The effect on the balance sheet equation of revenues received in cash and expenses paid in cash

	Assets			=	Liabilities +		Owner's Equity	
	Cash +	Law Library +	Office Equipment	=	Accounts Payable +		Jerry Dow, Capital	Explanation of Change
Bal.	$ 900	$2,880	$6,880		$1,660		$ 9,000	
(5)	+2,200						+ 2,200	Revenue
Bal.	$3,100	$2,880	$6,880		$1,660		$11,200	
(6)	−1,000						− 1,000	Expense
Bal.	$2,100	$2,880	$6,880		$1,660		$10,200	
(7)	− 700						− 700	Expense
Bal.	$1,400 +	$2,880 +	$6,880	=	$1,660 +		$ 9,500	

Next, observe the effects of paying the $1,000 office rent and the secretary's $700 salary. Both transactions were expenses of the business. Note that the effects are opposite those of a revenue. Simply stated, expenses are outflows or the using up of goods and services in the operation of a business. In the present instance, the business's use of both the office space and the secretary's time may be understood as the using up of services. When the services were paid for, both the assets and Dow's equity in the business decreased. Dow's equity decreased because cash decreased without an increase in other assets or a decrease in liabilities.

Remember that a business earns a net income when its revenues exceed its expenses; and the effect of a net income is to increase the net assets or equity of the owner or owners. (Recall that net assets are the excess of assets over liabilities.) Net assets increase because more assets flow into the business from revenues than are used up or flow out for expenses. The equity of the owner or owners increases as net assets increase. A net loss has the opposite effect.

In this first chapter, to simplify the material and emphasize the effects of revenues and expenses to owner's equity, revenues are added directly to and expenses are deducted from the owner's capital. However, this is not done in actual practice. In actual practice, revenues and expenses are first accumulated in separate categories. They are then combined; and their combined effect, the net income or loss, is added to or deducted from owner's capital. Further discussion of this is deferred to later chapters.

Realization Principle

In transaction 5, the revenue inflow was in the form of cash. However, revenue inflows are not always in the form of cash. This is because of the **realization principle**, which governs the recognition of revenue. This principle, also called the **recognition principle**, (1) states that the inflow of assets associated with a revenue does not have to be in the form of cash. (2) It requires that the revenue be recognized (entered in the accounting records as revenue) at the time, but not before, it is earned. (Generally, revenue is considered to be earned at the time services are rendered or at the time title to goods sold is transferred.) (3) The principle also requires that the amount of revenue recognized be mea-

Illustration 1–6
The effect on the balance sheet equation of noncash revenues and the later receipt of cash

		Assets				=	Liabilities	+	Owner's Equity	
	Cash	+	Accounts Receivable	+	Law Library	+	Office Equipment	=	Accounts Payable	+	Jerry Dow, Capital	Explanation of Change
Bal.	$1,400				$2,880		$6,880		$1,660		$ 9,500	
(8)			+$1,700								+ 1,700	Revenue
Bal.	$1,400		$1,700		$2,880		$6,880		$1,660		$11,200	
(9)	+1,700		−1,700									
Bal.	$3,100	+	$ –0–	+	$2,880	+	$6,880	=	$1,660	+	$11,200	

sured by the cash received plus the cash equivalent (fair value) of any other asset or assets received.

For most businesses, the realization principle is satisfied and revenue is recognized in the accounting records at the time goods are sold to a customer or when services have been performed and are billable. This is known as the *sales basis of revenue recognition*. In many cases, cash is received from the customer at the time the sale is completed. Even if cash is not received, the sale gives the seller the legal right to collect cash in the future. Theoretically, revenue is earned throughout the entire performance of a service or throughout the whole process of securing goods for sale, taking a customer's order, and delivering the goods. Yet, until all steps are completed and there is a right to collect the sales price, the requirements of the *objectivity principle* are not fulfilled and revenue is not recognized.

To demonstrate the recognition of a revenue inflow in a form other than cash, assume that Jerry Dow completed legal work for a client and billed the client $1,700 for the services rendered (transaction 8). Also assume that 10 days later, the client paid in full for the services rendered (transaction 9). The effects of the two transactions are shown in Illustration 1–6.

Observe in transaction 8 that the asset flowing into the business was the right to collect $1,700 from the client, an account receivable. Next observe that the receipt of cash (10 days after the services were rendered) is nothing more than an exchange of assets, cash for the right to collect from the client. Also note that the receipt of cash did not affect Dow's equity because the revenue was recognized in accordance with the *realization principle* and Dow's equity was increased upon completion of the services rendered.

Illustration 1–7 shows all of the previously discussed transactions. It also discloses two additional transactions. The first (transaction 10) occurred on December 24, when Jerry Dow paid Equip-it Company $900. This was in partial settlement of the $1,660 owed for the library and equipment items that had been purchased on credit (transaction 4). The effects of the payment transaction are to reduce in equal amounts both assets and liabilities. As a final transaction, assume that on December 24, Jerry Dow took $1,100 out of the business chequing account for his personal use. The effect of this withdrawal by the owner (transaction 11) is to reduce both the assets and the owner's equity in the business.

Illustration 1–7
The effect on the balance sheet equation of debt repayments and withdrawals by owner

	Cash	+	Accounts Receivable	+	Law Library	+	Office Equipment	=	Accounts Payable	+	Jerry Dow, Capital	Explanation of Change
				Assets				**=**	**Liabilities**	**+**	**Owner's Equity**	
(1)	$9,000										$ 9,000	Investment
(2)	−2,500					+$2,500						
Bal.	$6,500					$2,500					$ 9,000	
(3)	−5,600							+$5,600				
Bal.	$ 900					$2,500		$5,600			$ 9,000	
(4)						+ 380		+1,280		+$1,660		
Bal.	$ 900					$2,880		$6,880		$1,660		$ 9,000	
(5)	+2,200										+ 2,200	Revenue
Bal.	$3,100					$2,880		$6,880		$1,660		$11,200	
(6)	−1,000										− 1,000	Expense
Bal.	$2,100					$2,880		$6,880		$1,660		$10,200	
(7)	− 700										− 700	Expense
Bal.	$1,400					$2,880		$6,880		$1,660		$ 9,500	
(8)			+$1,700								+ 1,700	Revenue
Bal.	$1,400		$1,700			$2,880		$6,880		$1,660		$11,200	
(9)	+1,700		−1,700									
Bal.	$3,100		$ –0–			$2,880		$6,880		$1,660		$11,200	
(10)	**− 900**									**− 900**		
Bal.	$2,200		$ –0–			$2,880		$6,880		$ 760		$11,200	
(11)	**−1,100**										**− 1,100**	**Withdrawal**
Bal.	$1,100	+	$ –0–	+	$2,880	+	$6,880	=	$ 760	+	$10,100	

Important Transaction Effects

Look at Illustration 1–7 and observe that every transaction affected at least two items in the equation. In each case, after the effects were entered in the columns the equation remained in balance. The accounting system you are beginning to study is called a *double-entry system*. It is based on the fact that every transaction affects two or more items in an accounting equation and requires a "double entry" or, in other words, entries in two or more places. Also, the fact that the equation remains in balance after each transaction is important in that it helps you discover errors. If the equation does not balance, you know an error has been made.

Also note in Illustration 1–7 the types of transactions that had an effect on the owner's equity. They include investments by the owner, revenues, expenses, and withdrawals by the owner. In Illustration 1–8, you may observe that owner's equity is increased as a result of the owner's investments in the business and also by revenues. Owner's equity is decreased as a result of withdrawals by the owner and by expenses.

When financial statements are prepared, these changes in the owner's equity are summarized as shown in Illustration 1–9. Note that the income statement reports the revenues and expenses that were presented in Illustration 1–7. The resulting net income is reported, along with owner's investments and owner's withdrawals, in the **statement of changes in owner's equity.** And the resulting balance in Jerry Dow, Capital is reported in the balance sheet. For

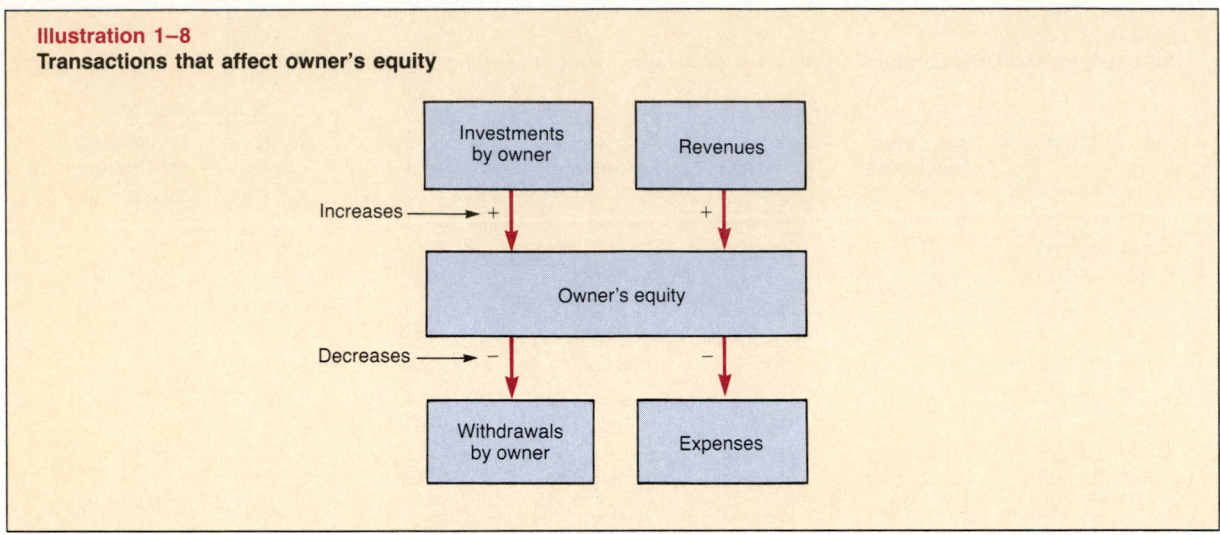

Illustration 1–8
Transactions that affect owner's equity

purposes of comparison, note that the income statement and balance sheet shown in Illustration 1–9 are the same as those first shown in Illustrations 1–1 and 1–2.

Statement of Changes in Financial Position

The financial statements of a business that are presented to its owners and other outside parties include four primary statements. Three of these have already been illustrated. They are the income statement, the balance sheet, and the statement of changes in owner's equity. The fourth financial statement is called the **statement of changes in financial position.** This statement shows the cash inflows and cash outflows of the business, summarized in three categories. They are cash flows from operations, cash flows from investing activities, and cash flows from financing activities. Observe in Illustration 1–10 the statement of cash flows for Jerry Dow, Lawyer. A detailed explanation of the statement of changes in financial positions is presented in Chapter 18.

Summary of the Chapter in Terms of Learning Objectives

1. Accounting provides quantitative information about economic entities that is intended to be useful in making economic decisions. Accounting reports are used to describe the activities and financial status of many different types of economic entities.

2. Accountants work in public accounting, private accounting, and government. In public accounting, their work includes auditing, management advisory services, and tax services. In private accounting, their work includes general accounting, cost accounting, budgeting, and internal auditing. Accountants in government work in the same areas as private accounting plus in the areas of crime detection and business regulation.

Illustration 1–9
Financial statements for Jerry Dow, Lawyer

JERRY DOW, LAWYER
Income Statement
For Month Ended December 31, 1990

Revenues:		
Legal fees earned		$ 3,900
Operating expenses:		
Office rent expense	$1,000	
Salaries expense	700	
Total operating expenses		1,700
Net income		$ 2,200

JERRY DOW, LAWYER
Statement of Changes in Owner's Equity
For Month Ended December 31, 1990

Jerry Dow, capital, November 30, 1990 . .		$ –0–
Plus: Investments by owner	$9,000	
Net income	2,200	11,200
Total		$11,200
Less withdrawals by owner		1,100
Jerry Dow, capital, December 31, 1990 . .		$10,100

JERRY DOW, LAWYER
Balance Sheet
December 31, 1990

Assets		Liabilities	
Cash	$ 1,100	Accounts payable . .	$ 760
Law library	2,880	**Owner's Equity**	
Office equipment . .	6,880		
		Jerry Dow, capital . .	10,100
Total assets	$10,860	Total liabilities and owner's equity . . .	$10,860

3. The income statement shows revenues, expenses, and net income or net loss. The balance sheet shows assets, liabilities, and owner's equity. The statement of changes in owner's equity shows the increase in owner's equity from investments by the owner, the decrease from owner withdrawals, and the increase or decrease from net income or net loss. The statement of changes in financial position shows the cash inflows and outflows from operations, from investing activities, and from financing activities.

4. Accounting concepts introduced in this chapter include the business entity concept, the continuing-concern concept, and the stable-dollar concept. The accounting principles introduced in the chapter include the cost principle, the objectivity principle, and the realization principle. Accounting principles in Canada are established primarily by the Accounting Standards Committee, and the recommendations are published in the *CICA Handbook*.

Illustration 1–10
A statement of changes in financial position for Jerry Dow, Lawyer

JERRY DOW, LAWYER
Statement of Changes in Financial Position
For Month Ended December 31, 1990

Cash flows from operations:		
Cash received from customers	+$3,900	
Cash paid for rent	−1,000	
Cash paid to employee	− 700	
Net cash provided by operating activities . .		+$2,200
Cash flows from investing activities:		
Purchase of office equipment.	−$5,600	
Purchase of law library	−2,500	
Net cash used by investing activities		−8,100
Cash flows from financing activities:		
Investments by owner	+$9,000	
Withdrawals by owner	−1,100	
Repayment of debt	− 900	
Net cash provided by financing activities . .		+7,000
Net increase in cash		$1,100
Cash balance, November 30, 1990.		−0−
Cash balance, December 31, 1990.		$1,100

5. A single or sole proprietorship is a business that is owned by one individual and that is not established as a separate entity under the law. A partnership differs from a single proprietorship only in that it has more than one owner. The owner or owners of proprietorships and partnerships are personally liable for the debts of the business. A corporation is established under the law as a separate entity; hence, its owners (shareholders) are not liable for the debts of the corporation.

6. Business transactions always affect at least two elements in the accounting equation. After a transaction is recorded, the accounting equation must be in balance.

Demonstration Problem

After planning for several months, Barbara Schmidt decided to start her own haircutting business called The Cutlery. During its first month of operation, The Cutlery completed the following transactions:

a. On August 1, 1990, Schmidt put $2,000 of her savings into a chequing account in the name of The Cutlery.

b. On August 2, she bought $600 of supplies for the shop.

c. On August 3, she paid $500 rent for the month of August for a small store.

d. On August 5, she furnished the store, installing new fixtures that the supplier sold to her for $1,200. This amount is to be repaid in three equal payments at the end of August, September, and October.

e. The Cutlery opened August 12; and in the first week of business ended August 16, receipts from cash sales amounted to $825.

f. On August 17, Schmidt paid $125 to an assistant for working during the business's grand opening.

g. Receipts from cash sales during the two-week period ended August 30 amounted to $1,930.

h. On August 31, Schmidt paid the first installment on the fixtures.

i. On August 31, she withdrew $1,100 cash for her personal expenses.

Required

1. Arrange the following asset, liability, and owner's equity titles in an equation like the one in Illustration 1–7: Cash, Store Supplies, Store Equipment (fixtures), Accounts Payable, and Barbara Schmidt, Capital. Show by additions and subtractions the effects of each of the above transactions on the equation.

2. Prepare an August income statement for The Cutlery.

3. Prepare a statement of changes in owner's equity for August 1990.

4. Prepare a statement of changes in financial position for August 1990.

5. Prepare an August 31, 1990, balance sheet for the business.

Solution to Demonstration Problem

1.

	Cash +	Store Supplies +	Store Equipment =	Accounts Payable +	Barbara Schmidt, Capital	Explanation of Change
	Assets			**= Liabilities +**	**Owner's Equity**	
(a)	$2,000				$2,000	Investment
	$2,000				$2,000	
(b)	− 600	+$600				
	$1,400	$600			$2,000	
(c)	− 500				− 500	Expense
	$ 900	$600			$1,500	
(d)			+$1,200	+$1,200		
	$ 900	$600	$1,200	$1,200	$1,500	
(e)	+ 825				+ 825	Revenue
	$1,725	$600	$1,200	$1,200	$2,325	
(f)	− 125				− 125	Expense
	$1,600	$600	$1,200	$1,200	$2,200	
(g)	+1,930				+1,930	Revenue
	$3,530	$600	$1,200	$1,200	$4,130	
(h)	− 400			− 400		
	$3,130	$600	$1,200	$ 800	$4,130	
(i)	−1,100				−1,100	Withdrawal
	$2,030 +	$600 +	$1,200 =	$ 800 +	$3,030	

2.

THE CUTLERY
Income Statement
For Month Ended August 31, 1990

Sales		$2,755
Expenses:		
Rent	$(500)	
Wages	(125)	
Total expenses		(625)
Net income		$2,130

3.

THE CUTLERY
Statement of Changes in Owner's Equity
For Month Ended August 31, 1990

Barbara Schmidt, capital, August 1, 1990 . .		$ –0–
Plus: Investment by owner	$2,000	
Net income	2,130	4,130
Total		$ 4,130
Less withdrawal by owner		(1,100)
Barbara Schmidt, capital, August 31, 1990 . .		$ 3,030

4.

THE CUTLERY
Statement of Changes in Financial Position
For Month Ended August 31, 1990

Cash flows from operations:		
Cash received from customers (e) and (g) . .	$ 2,755	
Cash paid for rent (c)	(500)	
Cash paid for wages (f)	(125)	
Net cash provided by operations		$2,130
Cash flows from investing activities:		
Purchase of store supplies (b)		(600)
Cash flows from financing activities:		
Investment by owner (a)	$ 2,000	
Withdrawal by owner (i)	(1,100)	
Repayment of debt (h)	(400)	
Net cash from financing activities		500
Net increase in cash		$2,030
Cash balance, August 1, 1990		–0–
Cash balance, August 31, 1990		$2,030

5.

THE CUTLERY
Balance Sheet
August 31, 1990

Assets		Liabilities	
Cash	$2,030	Accounts payable	$ 800
Store supplies	600	**Owner's Equity**	
Store equipment	1,200	Barbara Schmidt, capital	3,030
		Total liabilities and	
Total assets	$3,830	owner's equity	$3,830

Glossary

Define or explain the words and phrases listed in the chapter Glossary. (L. O. 7)

AAA the American Accounting Association, an organization of persons interested in accounting; generally identified as the professional association of academic accountants. p. 16

Accounting a service activity that provides quantitative information about economic entities; the information is primarily financial in nature and is intended to be useful in making economic decisions. p. 8

Accounting concept an abstract idea that serves as an important assumption underlying generally accepted accounting principles and procedures. p. 17

Accounting equation another name for the *balance sheet equation*. p. 21

Accounting Standards Committee the committee of CICA charged with developing recommendations for inclusion in the *CICA Handbook*. p. 16

Accounts payable liabilities resulting from the credit purchase of goods or services. p. 15

Accounts receivable amounts owed to a business by its customers for goods or services sold to them on credit. p. 15

AICPA American Institute of Certified Public Accountants, the professional association of certified public accountants in the United States. p. 16

APB Accounting Principles Board, a committee of the AICPA that was responsible for formulating generally accepted accounting principles prior to the FASB. p. 16

Assets probable future economic benefits obtained or controlled by a particular entity as a result of past transactions or events. p. 14

Audit a critical examination of an entity's accounting records and statements that is made for the purpose of determining whether the statements fairly reflect the entity's financial position and operating results, in accordance with generally accepted accounting principles. p. 10

Balance sheet a financial report showing the assets, liabilities, and equity of an enterprise on a specific date. Also called a *statement of financial position*. p. 14

Balance sheet equation an expression in dollar amounts of the equivalency of the assets, liabilities, and equity of an enterprise, usually stated as Assets = Liabilities + Owner's Equity. p. 21

Bookkeeping the record-making phase of accounting. p. 9

Budgeting the process of developing formal plans for future business activities, which then serve as bases for evaluating actual accomplishments. p. 12

Business entity concept the idea that a business is a separate entity that is distinct from its owner or owners and from every other business. p. 17

Business transaction a completed exchange of economic consideration, for example, goods, services, money, or the right to collect money, between two or more parties. p. 18

CGA—Canada Certified General Accountants' Association of Canada. p. 10.

CICA Canadian Institute of Chartered Accountants. p. 10

Continuing-concern concept the assumption that a business will continue to operate and that the assets held for use in the business will not be sold. p. 18

Controller the chief accounting officer of a large business. p. 11

Corporation a business that is established under the laws of a state or the federal government as a separate entity. p. 20

Cost accounting the phase of accounting that has to do with determining and controlling costs, and assessing the performance of managers who are responsible for costs. p. 12

Cost principle the accounting rule that requires assets and services plus any resulting liabilities to be recorded in the accounting records at cost, which is the cash or cash-equivalent amount of the consideration given in exchange for the purchased assets and services. p. 17

Creditor an individual or organization to whom a debt is owed. p. 15

Debtor a person or organization that is obligated to pay a liability. p. 15

Equity the residual interest in the assets of an entity that remains after deducting its liabilities. Also called *net assets*. p. 15

Expense outflows or the using up of assets as a result of the major or central operations of a business; also, the incurrence of liabilities may result as an alternative to outflows of assets. p. 13

FASB Financial Accounting Standards Board, the seven-member board that currently has the authority to issue pronouncements of generally accepted accounting principles. p. 17

GAAP generally accepted accounting principles. p. 16

General accounting that phase of accounting dealing primarily with recording transactions, processing the recorded data, and preparing financial statements. p. 11

Generally accepted accounting principles broad rules adopted by the accounting profession as guides in measuring, recording, and reporting the financial affairs and activities of a business. p. 16

Going-concern concept another name for the *continuing-concern concept*. p. 18

Income statement a financial statement showing revenues earned by a business, the expenses incurred in earning the revenues, and the resulting net income or net loss. p. 13

Internal auditing the use of a business's own accounting employees to check records and operating procedures for the purpose of making sure that established accounting procedures and management directives are being followed. Also includes evaluations of operating efficiency. p. 12

Liabilities probable future sacrifices of economic benefits arising from present obligations of a particular entity to transfer assets or provide services to other entities in the future as a result of past transactions or events. p. 15

Management advisory services the phase of public accounting dealing with the design, installation, and improvement of a client's accounting system, plus advice on financial planning, budgeting, forecasting, and inventory control. p. 11

Net assets another name for *equity,* or the residual interest in the assets of an entity that remains after deducting its liabilities. p. 15

Net income the excess of revenues over expenses. p. 13

Net loss the excess of expenses over revenues. p. 13

Objectivity principle the accounting rule that wherever possible the amounts used in recording transactions be based on verifiable evidence such as business transactions between independent parties. p. 18

Partnership a business that is owned by two or more people and that is not organized as a separate legal entity. p. 20

Realization principle the accounting rule which states that: (1) the inflow of assets associated with a revenue does not have to be in the form of cash, (2) a revenue should be recorded as a revenue at the time, but not before, it is earned, and (3) the amount of a revenue should be measured in terms of the cash plus cash equivalent amount of other assets received. p. 23

Recognition principle another name for the *realization principle.* p. 23

Revenue an inflow of assets received in exchange for goods or services provided to customers as part of the major or central operations of the business; may take the form of a decrease in liabilities as well as an inflow of assets. p. 13

Shareholder another name for *stockholder.* p. 20

Single proprietorship a business owned by one individual. p. 19

SMA Society of Management Accountants. p. 10

Stable-dollar concept the idea that accounting reports should be based on the assumption that the purchasing power of the unit of measure used in accounting, the dollar, does not change. p. 18

Statement of changes in financial position a financial statement that discloses the inflows and outflows of cash during the period, classified in terms of cash flows from operations, cash flows from investing activities, and cash flows from financing activities. p. 26

Statement of changes in owner's equity a financial statement that discloses all changes in owner's equity during the period, including investments by the owner, withdrawals by the owner, and net income or net loss. p. 25

Statement of financial position another name for the *balance sheet.* p. 14

Stock equity of a corporation that is divided into units or shares. p. 20

Stockholders the owners of a corporation; also called *shareholders.* p. 20

Tax services the phase of public accounting dealing with the preparation of tax returns and with advice as to how transactions may be completed in a way as to incur the smallest tax liability. p. 11

1. What is the nature of accounting and what is its function?
2. What are three or four examples of questions that a business manager might try to answer by looking to accounting information?
3. What is the difference between accounting and bookkeeping?
4. Why is the study of accounting necessary for a person who is responsible for using a computer to process accounting data?
5. What are three broad fields of employment for accountants?
6. What are three types of services typically offered to the public by public accountants?
7. What is the purpose of an audit? What do public accountants do when they make an audit?
8. What are some examples of the management advisory services typically provided by public accountants?
9. What do the tax services of a public accountant include beyond preparing tax returns?
10. Why is the chief accounting officer of a large company called a controller?
11. What are four broad areas of work performed in private accounting?
12. Government accounting may involve some unique types of work. Give some examples.
13. What does an income statement show?
14. As the words are used in accounting, what is a revenue? An expense?
15. Why is the period of time covered by an income statement of extreme importance?
16. What does a balance sheet show?
17. Does a balance sheet relate to a period of time? Explain.
18. Define (*a*) assets, (*b*) liabilities, (*c*) equity, and (*d*) net assets.
19. Are generally accepted accounting principles natural laws or laws of nature?
20. What are generally accepted accounting principles?
21. Why are the recommendations of the *CICA Handbook* of importance to accounting students?
22. Why is a business treated as a separate entity for accounting purposes?
23. What is required by the cost principle? Why is such a principle necessary?
24. Why are the balance sheet amounts for assets held for use in a business not changed from time to time to reflect changes in market values?
25. A business shows office stationery on its balance sheet at its $350 cost, although the stationery can be sold for not more than $5 as scrap paper. What accounting principles and concept justify this treatment?
26. In accounting, transactions are measured, recorded, and reported in terms of dollars, and the dollar is assumed to be a stable unit of measure. Is the dollar a stable unit of measure?

27. How does a corporation's status as a separate legal entity affect the responsibility of its shareholders for the debts of the corporation? Does this responsibility or lack of responsibility for the debts of the business apply to the owner or owners of a single proprietorship or partnership business?

28. What is the balance sheet equation? What is its importance to accounting students?

29. Is it possible for a transaction to increase or decrease a single liability without affecting any other asset, liability, or owner's equity item?

30. In accounting, what does the realization principle require?

31. Name four financial statements that businesses present to their owners and other outside parties.

Multiple Choice

1. Accountants who are employed in public accounting generally work in one or more of the following fields:
   a. Internal auditing, tax services, and management advisory services.
   b. General accounting, auditing, and budgeting.
   c. Governmental accounting, private accounting, and auditing.
   d. Tax services, cost accounting, and budgeting.
   e. Tax services, management advisory services, and auditing.

2. The financial statements usually presented to the owner of a business and to other outside parties are the:
   a. Income statement and balance sheet.
   b. Income statement, statement of changes in owner's equity, and balance sheet.
   c. Revenues, expenses, assets, liabilities, and owner's equity.
   d. Balance sheet, statement of changes in financial position, income statement, and statement of changes in owner's equity.
   e. Income statement, balance sheet, and statement of changes in financial position.

3. The realization principle states that:
   a. Revenues must be in the form of cash.
   b. Revenues should be recognized at the time they are earned but not before.
   c. The inflow of assets associated with a revenue does not have to be in the form of cash.
   d. Revenues should be measured by the cash received plus the cash equivalent of any other asset or assets received.
   e. (b), (c), and (d) are all correct.

4. A new business has the following transactions: (1) the owner invested $2,500; (2) $1,500 of supplies were purchased for cash; (3) $1,200 was received in payment for services rendered by the business; (4) a salary of $900 was paid to an employee; and (5) $2,000 was borrowed from the

bank. After these transactions were completed, the total assets, total liabilities, and total owner's equity of the business are:
  a. $4,800; $2,000; $2,800.
  b. $6,300; $3,500; $2,800.
  c. $4,800; $3,200; $1,600.
  d. $4,800; $2,300; $2,500.
  e. $4,800; $–0–; $4,800.

5. Compared to a partnership or corporation, the nature of a single proprietorship is that:
  a. It is a separate legal entity.
  b. Its owner holds all of the shares of stock issued by the business.
  c. It is not a separate legal entity but is owned by more than one person.
  d. It is not a separate legal entity and its owner is personally responsible for its debts.
  e. The debts of the business are the responsibility of the business but not of the owner.

6. If the assets of a business increased $15,000 during a period of time and its liabilities increased $6,000 during the same period, owner's equity in the business must have:
  a. Increased $9,000.
  b. Decreased $9,000.
  c. Increased $21,000.
  d. Decreased $21,000.
  e. Changed by some other amount.

Mini Discussion Cases

Case 1–1

In order to realize a lifelong dream, Catherine Swazzee decides to open a video and audio rental and sales business. Catherine worked for such a business on a part-time basis while attending school and learned much about the operation of such a business. However, she needs help setting up the business—especially with determining available sources of financing because her own resources are insufficient to provide for all the necessary assets.

Required
Prepare for Catherine a possible balance sheet that will show the necessary assets to start the business and the proposed sources of these assets. Support your proposal.

Case 1–2

Studies indicate that 50% of small business fail within the first two years of their life. These studies also indicate that the failure rate would be substantially reduced if serious planning preceded the starting of a business.

Required
Discuss the type of preplanning indicated by the balance sheet, income statement, and a statement of changes in financial position.

Case 1–3

James Haddad located a business he was interested in and started negotiations with the owner, Caspar Fitz, for its purchase. Fitz supplied Haddad with a balance sheet. The balance sheet, which Fitz had prepared personally, listed four assets, two liabilities, and the owner's capital account. The listed assets were cash, accounts receivable, merchandise, and building and equipment.

The purchase was completed, and James Haddad took over with satisfaction and enthusiasm. Sales the first month of operations were up to Haddad's expectation. But prior to the end of the month, Haddad received a disturbing letter from Millie Fitz, which he turned over to a lawyer. A couple of days later he learned from the lawyer that Millie Fitz was indeed the sole owner of the building. Haddad was certain he had purchased the building since it was listed on the balance sheet Caspar Fitz had given him.

Required

Discuss the GAAP applicable to the situation and what Haddad should have done prior to concluding the purchase.

Exercises

Exercise 1–1
Balance sheet for a single proprietorship
(L. O. 3, 5, 6)

On March 31, 1990, the accounting equation for Rae's Antiques, a single proprietorship, showed the following:

Cash	$ 3,000
Other assets	80,000
Accounts payable	30,000
Rae Wong, capital	53,000

On that date, Rae Wong sold the "Other assets" for $40,000 in preparation for ending and liquidating the business of Rae's Antiques.

Required

1. Prepare a balance sheet for the shop as it would appear immediately after the sale of the assets.
2. Tell how the shop's cash should be distributed in ending the business and why.

Exercise 1–2
The accounting equation
(L. O. 6)

Determine the missing amount on each of the following lines:

	Assets	= Liabilities	+ Owner's Equity
a.	$46,500	$9,400	?
b.	35,600	?	$18,600
c.	?	8,700	25,800

Exercise 1–3
Effects of transactions on the accounting equation
(L. O. 6)

The effects of five transactions on the assets, liabilities, and owner's equity of Lee Fox in his dental practice are shown in the following equation with each transaction identified by a letter. Write a short sentence or phrase telling the probable nature of each transaction.

		Assets			= Liabilities +	Owner's Equity
	Cash +	Accounts + Receivable	Office + Supplies	Land	= Accounts + Payable	Lee Fox, Capital
	$11,200		$5,250	$ 2,900		$19,350
a.	−10,000			+10,000		
	$ 1,200		$5,250	$12,900		$19,350
b.			+ 450		+$450	
	$ 1,200		$5,700	$12,900	$450	$19,350
c.		+$750				+ 750
	$ 1,200	$750	$5,700	$12,900	$450	$20,100
d.	− 450				−450	
	$ 750	$750	$5,700	$12,900	$−0−	$20,100
e.	+ 750	−750				
	$ 1,500 +	$−0−	+ $5,700 +	$12,900 =	$−0− +	$20,100

Exercise 1–4
Use of the accounting equation
(L. O. 6)

Determine:

a. The equity of the owner in a business having $145,200 of assets and owing $22,800 of liabilities.

b. The liabilities of a business having $109,200 of assets and in which the owner has a $77,100 equity.

c. The assets of a business with $9,400 of liabilities and in which the owner has a $47,500 equity.

Exercise 1–5
Analyzing the accounting equation
(L. O. 6)

On September 1, Bob Crane began operating a new real estate agency. After each of the agency's first five transactions, the accounting equation for the agency showed the following balances. Analyze the equations and describe each of the five transactions with their amounts.

Balances after Transaction	Cash +	Accounts Receivable +	Office Supplies +	Office Furniture =	Accounts Payable +	Bob Crane, Capital
1	$15,000	$ −0−	$ −0−	$ −0−	$−0−	$15,000
2	14,600	−0−	1,000	−0−	600	15,000
3	5,600	−0−	1,000	9,000	600	15,000
4	5,600	1,200	1,000	9,000	600	16,200
5	4,100	1,200	1,700	9,800	600	16,200

Exercise 1–6
Determination of net income
(L. O. 3, 6)

A business had the following assets and liabilities at the beginning and at the end of a year:

	Assets	Liabilities
Beginning of the year	$78,000	$24,000
End of the year	90,000	12,000

Determine the net income or net loss of the business during the year under each of the following unrelated assumptions:

a. The owner of the business made no additional investments in the business and no withdrawals of assets from the business during the year.

b. The owner made no additional investments in the business during the year but had withdrawn $1,800 per month to pay personal living expenses.

c. During the year, the owner had made no withdrawals but had made a $30,000 additional investment in the business.

d. The owner had withdrawn $2,400 from the business each month to pay personal living expenses and near the year-end had invested an additional $12,000 in the business.

Exercise 1–7
Effects of transactions on the accounting equation
(L. O. 6)

Hannah Neal began the practice of dentistry on December 1, and will prepare financial statements at the end of each month. During December, Ms. Neal completed these transactions:

a. Invested $9,600 in cash and dental equipment having a $2,400 fair market (cash equivalent) value.

b. Paid the rent on the office space for December, $1,800.

c. Purchased additional dental equipment on credit, $6,600.

d. Completed dental work for a patient and immediately collected $150 cash for the week.

e. Completed dental work for a patient on credit, $1,700.

f. Purchased additional dental equipment for cash, $480.

g. Paid the dental assistant's wages for December, $1,200.

h. Collected $1,000 of the amount owed by the patient of transaction (*e*).

i. Paid for the equipment purchased in transaction (*c*).

Required

Arrange the following asset, liability, and equity titles in an equation form like Illustration 1–7: Cash; Accounts Receivable; Dental Equipment; Accounts Payable; and Hannah Neal, Capital. Then, show by additions and subtractions the effects of the transactions on the elements of the equation. Show new totals after each transaction.

Exercise 1–8
Analysis of transaction effects on the accounting equation
(L. O. 3)

List a transaction for each of the following that will:

a. Increase an asset and decrease an asset.

b. Increase an asset and increase a liability.

c. Decrease an asset and decrease a liability.

d. Decrease a liability and increase a liability.

e. Increase an asset and increase equity.

f. Decrease an asset and decrease equity.

Exercise 1–9
An income statement for a single proprietorship
(L. O. 3)

On February 1, 1990, Deborah Norris began the practice of law under the name of Deborah Norris, Lawyer. On February 28, her records showed the following assets, liabilities, owner's investments, owner's withdrawals, revenues, and expenses.

Cash	$ 500	Owner's withdrawals	$2,000
Accounts receivable	300	Legal fees earned	3,800
Office supplies	700	Miscellaneous expense	50
Law library	3,000	Rent expense	600
Office equipment	1,500	Salaries expense	900
Accounts payable	1,150	Telephone expense.	400
Owner's investments	5,000		

From the information above, prepare a February income statement for the business.

Exercise 1–10
A statement of changes in owner's equity for a single proprietorship
(L. O. 3)

Based on the facts provided in Exercise 1–9, prepare a February statement of changes in owner's equity for the business of Deborah Norris, Lawyer.

Exercise 1–11
A balance sheet for a single proprietorship
(L. O. 3)

Based on the facts provided in Exercise 1–9, prepare a February 28 balance sheet for the business of Deborah Norris, Lawyer.

Exercise 1–12
Identifying the information in each financial statement
(L. O. 3)

Karen Smith is in the business of managing apartment houses. Examine each of the following items related to the business and state with the appropriate letter (*a, b, c,* or *d*) whether the item should appear on (*a*) an income statement, (*b*) a statement of changes in owner's equity, (*c*) a balance sheet, or (*d*) a statement of changes in financial position. If an item should appear on two statements, state both letters.

1. Management fees earned.
2. Accounts receivable.
3. Investments of cash by owner.
4. Cash received from customers.
5. Rent expense paid in cash.
6. Cash withdrawals by owner.
7. Office supplies.
8. Accounts payable.

Problems

Problem 1–1
Effects of transactions on the accounting equation
(L. O. 6)

Carol Olds, began a public accounting practice and during a short period completed these transactions:

a. Sold for $43,750 a personal investment in General Motors stock and deposited $40,000 of the proceeds in a bank account opened in the name of the practice.

b. Purchased for $100,000 a small building to be used as an office. She paid $35,000 in cash and signed a note payable promising to pay the balance over a period of years.

c. Took office equipment from home for use in the practice. The equipment had a $500 fair value.

d. Purchased office supplies for cash, $350.

e. Purchased office equipment on credit, $6,000.

f. Completed accounting work for a client and immediately collected $530 for the work done.

g. Paid a local newspaper $160 for a notice of the opening of the practice.

h. Completed $900 of accounting work for a client on credit.

i. Made a $600 installment payment on the equipment purchased in transaction (e).

j. The client of transaction (h) paid $600 of the amount he owed.

k. Paid the office secretary's wages, $550.

l. Carol Olds withdrew $300 from the bank account of the practice to pay personal living expenses.

Required

1. Arrange the following asset, liability, and owner's equity titles in an equation like Illustration 1–7: Cash; Accounts Receivable; Office Supplies; Office Equipment; Building; Accounts Payable; Notes Payable; and Carol Olds, Capital. Leave space for an Explanation column to the right of Carol Olds, Capital.

2. Show by additions and subtractions the effects of each transaction on the elements of the equation. Show new totals after each addition or subtraction. Next to each change in Carol Olds, Capital, state whether the change was caused by an investment, a revenue, an expense, or a withdrawal.

Problem 1–2
Analyzing transactions and preparing financial statements
(L. O. 3, 6)

Gary Meyer began a new law practice and completed these transactions during May 1990:

May   1   Transferred $6,000 from his personal savings account to a chequing account opened in the name of the law practice, Gary Meyer, Lawyer.

1   Rented the furnished office of a lawyer who was retiring and paid cash for May's rent, $1,000.

1   Purchased the law library of the retiring lawyer for $4,000, paying $2,000 in cash and agreeing to pay the balance in six months.

2   Purchased office supplies for cash, $200.

7   Completed legal work for a client and immediately collected $680 in cash for the work done.

10   Purchased office equipment on credit, $400.

13   Completed legal work for National Bank on credit, $1,875.

17   Purchased office supplies on credit, $35.

20   Paid for the office equipment purchased on May 10.

23   Completed legal work for Nash Realty on credit, $1,200.

25   Received $1,875 from National Bank for the work completed on May 13.

31   Paid the office secretary's salary, $1,300.

May 31   Paid the monthly utility bills, $125.
     31   Gary Meyer took $1,500 out of the business for his personal use.

Required

1. Arrange the following asset, liability, and owner's equity titles in an equation like Illustration 1–7: Cash; Accounts Receivable; Office Supplies; Law Library; Office Equipment; Accounts Payable; and Gary Meyer, Capital. Leave space for an Explanation column to the right of Gary Meyer, Capital.

2. Show by additions and subtractions the effects of each transaction on the items of the equation. Show new totals after each transaction. Next to each change in Gary Meyer, Capital, state whether the change was caused by an investment, a revenue, an expense, or a withdrawal.

3. Analyze the increases and decreases in the last column of the equation and prepare a May income statement for the practice.

4. Prepare a May statement of changes in owner's equity.

5. Prepare a May 31 balance sheet.

Problem 1–3
Preparation of balance sheet; calculation of net income
(L. O. 3, 6)

The records of Bart James, Realtor, show the following assets and liabilities as of the end of 1989 and 1990:

	December 31	
	1989	1990
Cash	$2,300	$ 500
Accounts receivable	1,200	600
Office supplies	300	150
Automobile	6,200	6,200
For Sale signs	400	400
Office equipment	2,800	6,250
Land.		37,500
Building		127,500
Accounts payable	750	1,050
Notes payable		112,500

Late in December 1990 (just before the amounts above were calculated), Mr. James purchased in the name of the business, Bart James, Realtor, a small office building and moved the business from rented quarters to the new building. The building and the land cost $165,000. The business paid $52,500 in cash, and a note payable was signed for the balance. Mr. James had to invest an additional $45,000 in the business to enable it to pay the $52,500. The business earned a satisfactory net income during 1990, which enabled Mr. James to withdraw $3,000 per month from the business to pay personal living expenses.

Required

1. Prepare two balance sheets for the business, as of the end of 1989 and the end of 1990. (Remember that the owner's equity equals assets less liabilities.)

2. By comparing the owner's equity amounts in the balance sheets and using the additional information presented above, prepare a calculation to show the net income earned by the business during 1990.

Problem 1–4
Preparation of balance sheet and income statement
(L. O. 3)

Hank Seta graduated from university in May 1990 with a degree in architecture. On June 1, he invested $4,500 in a new business under the name Hank Seta, Architect. Financial statements for the business will be prepared at the end of each month. The following transactions occurred during June:

June 1 Rented the furnished office and equipment of an architect who was retiring, paying $900 cash for June's rent.

1 Purchased drafting supplies for cash, $115.

3 Paid $150 for June's janitorial expense.

6 Completed architectural work for a client and immediately collected $375 cash for the work done.

9 Completed architectural work for Hills Realty on credit, $1,150.

16 Paid the draftsman's salary for the first half of June, $750.

19 Received payment in full for the work completed for Hills Realty on June 9.

21 Completed architectural work for Northern Contractors on credit, $1,200.

22 Purchased additional drafting supplies on credit, $100.

24 Completed architectural work for Ann Trent on credit, $900.

28 Purchased on credit the service of having blueprint copies made; the copies (of architectural plans) were delivered to customers. Cost was $140.

29 Received payment in full from Northern Contractors for the work completed on June 21.

30 Paid for the drafting supplies purchased on June 22.

30 Paid the June telephone bill, $135.

30 Paid the June utilities expense, $95.

30 Paid the draftsman's salary for the second half of June, $750.

30 Purchased insurance protection for the next 12 months (beginning July 1) by paying an $1,800 premium. Since none of this insurance protection had been used up on June 30, it was at that time an asset called Prepaid Insurance.

30 Mr. Seta withdrew $1,000 from the business for his personal use.

Required

1. Arrange the following asset, liability, and owner's equity titles in an equation like Illustration 1–7: Cash; Accounts Receivable; Prepaid Insurance; Drafting Supplies; Accounts Payable; and Hank Seta, Capital. Include an Explanation column for changes in owner's equity.

2. Show the effects of the transactions on the elements of the equation by recording increases and decreases in the appropriate columns. Indicate an increase with a + and a decrease with a − before the amount. *Do not determine new totals for the items of the equation after each transaction.*

3. After recording the last transaction, determine and insert on the next line the final total for each item of the equation and determine if the equation is in balance.

4. Analyze the items in the last column of the equation and prepare a June income statement for the practice.

5. Prepare a June statement of changes in owner's equity.

6. Prepare a June 30 balance sheet.

Problem 1–5
Calculating financial
statement amounts
(L. O. 3)

Financial statement information about five unrelated companies is as follows:

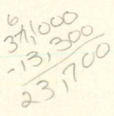

	Company 1	Company 2	Company 3	Company 4	Company 5
December 31, 1989:					
Assets	$24,000	$28,000	$35,000	$18,000	$52,000
Liabilities	15,000	20,000	20,000	11,000	?
December 31, 1990:					
Assets	26,000	37,000	64,000	?	77,000
Liabilities	12,700	?	27,000	16,000	30,000
During 1990:					
Net income	?	5,000	10,000	9,000	12,000
Owner investments .	3,500	6,000	?	12,000	–0–
Owner withdrawals .	1,000	1,500	3,000	4,000	6,000

Required

1. Answer the following questions about Company 1:
   a. What was the owner's equity on December 31, 1989?
   b. What was the owner's equity on December 31, 1990?
   c. What was the net income for 1990?

2. Answer the following questions about Company 2:
   a. What was the owner's equity on December 31, 1989?
   b. What was the owner's equity on December 31, 1990?
   c. What was the amount of liabilities owed on December 31, 1990?

3. For Company 3, calculate the amount of owner investments during 1990.

4. For Company 4, calculate the amount of assets on December 31, 1990.

5. For Company 5, calculate the amount of liabilities owed on December 31, 1989.

Alternate Problems

Problem 1–1A
Effects of transactions on
the accounting equation
(L. O. 6)

Carol Olds secured her broker's license and opened a real estate office. During a short period, she completed these transactions:

a. Sold for $62,500 a personal investment in General Electric stock, which she had inherited, and deposited $60,000 of the proceeds in a bank account opened in the name of the business, Carol Olds, Realtor.

b. Purchased for $150,000 a small building to be used as an office. She paid $45,000 in cash and signed a note payable promising to pay the balance over a period of years.

c. Purchased office equipment for cash, $11,600.

d. Took from home for use in the business office equipment having a $700 fair value.

e. Purchased on credit office supplies, $100, and office equipment, $5,000.

f. Paid the local paper $165 for advertising.

g. Completed a real estate appraisal for a client on credit and billed the client $250 for the work done.

h. Sold a house and collected a $10,000 cash commission on completion of the sale.

i. Carol Olds withdrew $2,000 from the business to pay personal expenses.

j. The client paid for the appraisal of transaction (g).

k. Made a $2,500 installment payment on the amount owed from transaction (e).

l. Paid the office secretary's wages, $950.

Required

1. Arrange the following asset, liability, and owner's equity titles in an equation like Illustration 1–7: Cash; Accounts Receivable; Office Supplies; Office Equipment; Building; Accounts Payable; Notes Payable; and Carol Olds, Capital. Leave space for an Explanation column to the right of Carol Olds, Capital.

2. Show by additions and subtractions the effects of each transaction on the elements of the equation. Show new totals after each transaction. Next to each change in Carol Olds, Capital, state whether the change was caused by an investment, a revenue, an expense, or a withdrawal.

Problem 1–2A
Analyzing transactions and preparing financial statements
(L. O. 3, 6)

Gary Meyer graduated from law school in May 1990, and on June 1 began a law practice by investing $5,000 in cash in the practice. He also transferred to the business office equipment having a cash value of $8,500. Then, he completed these additional transactions during June:

June 1 Rented the office of a lawyer who was retiring and paid the rent for June, $800.

1 Moved from home to the law office law books acquired at university. (In other words, invested the books in the practice.) The books had a $600 fair value.

2 Purchased office supplies for cash, $120.

4 Purchased additional law books costing $1,500. Paid $500 in cash and promised to pay the balance within 90 days.

5 Completed legal work for a client and immediately collected $500 for the work done.

10 Completed legal work for Village Bank on credit, $1,500.

15 Purchased additional office supplies on credit, $50.

20 Received $1,500 from Village Bank for the work completed on June 10.

25 Completed legal work for Astor Realty on credit, $1,300.

30 Made a $300 installment payment on the law books purchased on June 4.

30 Paid the June telephone bill, $70.

30 Paid the office secretary's wages, $1,200.

30 Gary Meyer took $1,400 out of the business for his personal use.

Required

1. Arrange the following asset, liability, and owner's equity titles in an equation like Illustration 1–7: Cash; Accounts Receivable; Office Supplies; Law Library; Office Equipment; Accounts Payable; and Gary Meyer, Capital. Leave space for an Explanation column to the right of Gary Meyer, Capital.

2. Show by additions and subtractions the effects of each transaction on the elements of the equation. Show new totals after each transaction. Next to each change in Gary Meyer, Capital, state whether the change was caused by an investment, a revenue, an expense, or a withdrawal.

3. Analyze the items in the last column of the equation and prepare a June income statement for the practice.

4. Prepare a June statement of changes in owner's equity.

5. Prepare a June 30 balance sheet.

Problem 1–3A
Preparation of balance sheet; calculation of net income
(L. O. 3, 6)

The accounting records of Viola Nunez's medical practice show the following assets and liabilities as of the end of 1989 and 1990:

	December 31	
	1989	**1990**
Cash	$ 9,600	$ 1,600
Accounts receivable	5,700	7,000
Office supplies	1,000	800
Automobile	4,800	4,800
Office equipment	18,500	23,200
Land		70,000
Building		125,000
Accounts payable	1,400	1,600
Notes payable		145,000

During the last week of December 1990 (just before the amounts above were calculated), Dr. Nunez purchased a small office building in the name of the medical practice, Viola Nunez, M.D., and moved her practice from rented quarters to the new building. The building and the land it occupies cost $195,000; the practice paid $50,000 in cash and signed a note payable for the balance. Dr. Nunez had to invest an additional $40,000 in the practice to enable it to pay the $50,000. The practice earned a satisfactory net income during 1989, which enabled Dr. Nunez to withdraw $3,200 per month from the practice to pay her personal living expenses.

Required

1. Prepare two balance sheets for the business, as of the end of 1989 and the end of 1990. (Remember that the owner's equity equals assets less liabilities.)

2. Using the information presented above and by comparing the owner's equity amount in the balance sheets, prepare a calculation to show the net income earned by the business during 1990.

Problem 1–4A
Preparation of balance sheet and income statement
(L. O. 3)

Hank Seta graduated from university, completed his internship, and on May 1 of the current year began an architectural practice by investing $6,000 in the practice. Financial statements for the business will be prepared at the end of each month. The following transactions occurred during May:

May 1 Rented the office and equipment of an architect who was retiring, paying $1,500 cash for May's rent.

1 Paid $180 for janitorial expense during May.

2 Purchased drafting supplies for cash, $50.

4 Completed an architectural assignment for a client and immediately collected $2,600 cash for the work done.

7 Purchased additional drafting supplies on credit, $160.

9 Completed architectural work for Apex Contractors on credit, $1,500.

15 Paid the draftsman's salary for May 1–15, $800.

16 Paid for the drafting supplies purchased on May 7.

19 Received payment in full from Apex Contractors for the work completed on May 9.

21 Completed architectural work for Wright Realtors on credit, $1,100.

25 Purchased additional drafting supplies on credit, $150.

30 Completed additional architectural work for Apex Contractors on credit, $1,050.

31 Paid the draftsman's salary for May 16–31, $800.

31 Paid the May telephone bill, $50.

31 Paid the May hydro bill, $185.

31 Purchased liability insurance protection for the next year (beginning June 1) by paying a premium of $2,000. Since none of this insurance protection had been used up on May 31, it was at that time an asset called Prepaid Insurance.

31 Mr. Seta withdrew $1,700 from the business's account to pay for some personal items.

Required

1. Arrange the following asset, liability, and owner's equity titles in an equation like Illustration 1–7: Cash; Accounts Receivable; Prepaid Insurance; Drafting Supplies; Accounts Payable; and Hank Seta, Capital. Include an Explanation column for changes in owner's equity.

2. Show the effects of the transactions on the elements of the equation by recording increases and decreases in the appropriate columns. Indicate an increase with a + and a decrease with a − before the amount. *Do not determine new totals for the items of the equation after each transaction.*

3. After recording the last transaction, determine and enter on the next line the final total for each item and determine if the equation is in balance.

4. Analyze the items in the last column of the equation and prepare a May income statement for the practice.

5. Prepare a May statement of changes in owner's equity.

6. Prepare a May 31 balance sheet.

Financial statement information about five unrelated companies is as follows:

	Company A	Company B	Company C	Company D	Company E
December 31, 1989:					
Assets	$62,000	$57,000	$29,000	$55,000	$72,000
Liabilities	46,000	41,000	14,000	38,000	?
December 31, 1990:					
Assets	79,000	86,000	?	70,000	94,000
Liabilities	?	59,000	18,000	32,000	49,000
During 1990:					
Net income	13,000	?	7,500	15,000	18,000
Owner investments .	7,000	10,000	10,000	?	12,000
Owner withdrawals .	2,000	4,000	2,500	–0–	5,000

Required

1. Answer the following questions about Company A:
   a. What was the owner's equity on December 31, 1989?
   b. What was the owner's equity on December 31, 1990?
   c. What was the amount of liabilities owed on December 31, 1990?

2. Answer the following questions about Company B:
   a. What was the owner's equity on December 31, 1989?
   b. What was the owner's equity on December 31, 1990?
   c. What was the net income for 1990?

3. For Company C, calculate the amount of assets on December 31, 1990.

4. For Company D, calculate the amount of owner investments during 1990.

5. For Company E, calculate the amount of liabilities owed on December 31, 1989.

Provocative Problems

Devon Bailey invested $750 in a short-term enterprise, the sale of soft drinks during the annual July First Weekend Fair in his small rural town. He paid $150 for the right to sell soft drinks in the fairgrounds. He constructed a stand from which to make the sales at a cost of $50 for lumber and crepe paper, none of which had any value at the end of the fair. He bought ice for which he paid $40 and purchased soft drinks costing $750. At this point, he had only $510 in cash and could not pay in full for the drinks. However, since his credit rating was good, the soft drink company accepted $500 in cash and the promise that he would pay the balance the day after the fair ended. During the fair, he collected $1,540 in cash from sales; at the end of the fair, he paid a young man $90 for helping with the sales. He had soft drinks left over that cost $35 and could be returned to the soft drink company. At this point, Devon stopped to decide whether he should cease operations or look for similar opportunities and continue the business.

Assemble the information in such a way that will enable you to prepare an income statement for the three-day period of the fair, which ended on July 2. Also prepare a statement of changes in owner's equity for the three-day period and a balance sheet dated July 3, 1990.

Provocative Problem 1–2
Megan's Delivery Service
(L. O. 3)

Megan Brinks ran out of money at the end of the first semester of her sophomore year in college. She had to go to work, but she could not find a satisfactory job. However, since she had an automobile, she decided to go into business for herself. Consequently, she began Megan's Delivery Service with no assets other than the automobile, which had a fair market value of $2,400. She kept no accounting records; and now, at the year-end, she has engaged you to determine the net income earned by the service during its first year. You find that the service has a $700 year-end bank balance plus $50 of undeposited cash. Local stores owe the service $125 for delivering packages during the past month. In the last week of the year, Megan sold the automobile for $1,350, and used the cash proceeds to help buy a new delivery truck that cost $6,800. The service still owes a finance company $4,000 as a result of the truck's purchase. Also, when the truck was purchased, Megan borrowed $1,500 from her father to help make the down payment. The loan was made to the delivery service, was interest free, and has not been repaid. Finally, since the service has been profitable from the beginning, Megan has withdrawn $200 of its earnings each week for the 52 weeks of its existence to pay personal living expenses.

Determine and present a calculation to prove the net income earned by the business during the first year of its operations.

Provocative Problem 1–3
WICAT Systems, Inc.
(L. O. 4)

WICAT Systems manufactures, markets, and services a complete line of computer systems, software, and courseware for training, education, and general-purpose markets. In the company's 1986 annual report, revenues for the year were reported as $39,405,000. Net income was $389,000. The notes to the 1986 financial statements included the following comments:

Related-Party Transactions

The Company is affiliated with The WICAT Education Institute, a shareholder, and is the general partner in WISTRAN Partners and BASICS Partnership. The Company has billed The WICAT Education Institute for system sales and services amounting to $291,000, $580,000, and $136,000 for the years ended 1984, 1985, and 1986, respectively. The WICAT Education Institute has billed the Company for services and rent amounting to $75,000, $199,000, and $4,000 for the years ended 1984, 1985, and 1986, respectively.

Why do you think WICAT Systems included the above comments in its annual report? What accounting principle might be compromised by related-party transactions?

Analytical and Review Problems

A&R Problem 1–1

John Hope began his Auto Repair Shop the first part of this month. The balance sheet, prepared by an inexperienced part-time bookkeeper is shown below:

HOPE AUTO REPAIR SHOP
Balance Sheet
November 30, 1990

Assets		Liabilities and Owner's Equity	
Cash	$ 2,000	Parts and supplies	$ 3,500
Accounts payable	11,000	Accounts receivable	15,000
Equipment	7,000	Prepaid rent	1,000
John Hope, capital	8,500		
		Mortgage payable	9,000
Total assets	$28,500	Total equities	$28,500

Required

1. Prepare a correct balance sheet.
2. Explain why the incorrect balance sheet can also be in balance.

A&R Problem 1–2

An analysis of cash and accounts receivable transactions of Townsend Office Services for the month of October 199A indicates the following:

Cash account:

Beginning balance	$ 900
Sandy Townsend, additional investment	9,000
Collection of accounts receivable	4,500
Payment of office rent for 3 months (Oct.–Dec.)	1,800
Rental payment for office equipment (for October)	450
Payment of wages including Townsend of $2,250	5,250
Payment of utilities, telephone, and advertising	900
Partial payment for office supplies (cost $1,500)	750

Accounts receivable:

Beginning balance	1,800
Billings during the month	6,750
Collection of accounts receivable	4,500

Additional information

$1,400 of office supplies were on hand on October 31.

Required

1. Prepare the October income statement.
2. Prepare the October 31 balance sheet.
3. Determine the October 1, 199A, balance in Sandra Townsend's capital account.

A&R Problem 1–3

Joan Blake began the practice of law the first day of October with an initial investment of $3,000 in cash and a law library valued at $3,600. After completing the first month of practice, the financial statements were being prepared by John Gilbert, the secretary/bookkeeper Ms. Blake had hired. The statements were completed, and Ms. Blake almost burst out laughing when she saw them. She had completed a course in legal accounting in law school and knew the statements prepared by Mr. Gilbert left much to be desired. Consequently, she asks you to revise the statements. The Gilbert version is presented below:

JOAN BLAKE, LAWYER
Balance Sheet
October 31, 199A

Assets		**Owner's Equity**	
Cash	$1,305	Joan Blake, capital	$2,340
Prepaid rent	900		
Supplies expense	60		
Accounts payable	75		
	$2,340		$2,340

JOAN BLAKE, LAWYER
Income Statement
For the Month Ended October 31, 199A

Revenues:		
Legal fees	$3,950	
Accounts receivable	1,500	$5,450
Expenses:		
Salaries expense	$1,500	
Telephone expense	45	
Rent expense	900	
Supplies	165	
Law library	4,050*	6,860
Loss		$1,410

*Purchase of law books in October, $450.

Required

Prepare the corrected financial statements for Joan Blake.

A&R Problem 1–4

The following notes are exerpted from the financial statements of two companies headquartered in Canada:

> The consolidated financial statements have been prepared by management following accounting policies generally accepted in Canada. Except as indicated in Note 19(a), they are also in conformity, in all material respects, with accounting policies generally accepted in the United States. The consolidated financial statements are presented in U.S. dollars. This currency best reflects the economic environment in which the Company operates and provides for a more meaningful measurement of operating results in consideration of the international scope of its operations. Such presentation also affords a better basis of comparison with major companies in the industry, the larger of which are U.S. based and report their results in U.S. dollars.

and

> The consolidated financial statements have been prepared by management on a historical cost basis in accordance with Canadian generally accepted accounting principles consistently applied and conform in all material respects with International Accounting Standards.

Required

1. Are there differences between the generally accepted accounting principles or accounting policies in Canada and the United States? May there be differences with the International Accounting Standards? If yes, what in your opinion may account for differences?
2. Do you believe disclosure of any differences is desirable? Why?

Processing Accounting Data

The next five chapters are perhaps more important than any others you will study in your accounting education. In these chapters, we describe the accounting process that starts with an analysis of a business's transactions and ends with the periodic preparation of financial statements. Your careful study of these chapters will pay great dividends. It will make the later parts of the book easier to understand.

Part Two consists of the following chapters:

2 Recording Transactions

In Chapter 1, you were introduced to the accounting equation (Assets = Liabilities + Owner's Equity) and the effect of business transactions on the accounting equation. In this chapter, you will learn how the effects of business transactions are recorded and stored in the accounting records. We begin the chapter with a discussion of business papers that provide evidence of transactions and a description of several commonly used accounts in which the effects of the transactions are recorded. Then, we explain the process of recording the effects of transactions. The procedures that you learn in the chapter can be used to record the effects of any type of business transactions you may encounter.

Learning Objectives

After studying Chapter 2, you should be able to:

1. State the names of several commonly used accounts and the nature of the items recorded in those accounts.
2. Explain the mechanics of double-entry accounting and tell why transactions are recorded with equal debits and credits.
3. Apply the rules of debit and credit in recording transactions.
4. Tell the normal balance of any asset, liability, or owner's equity account.
5. Record transactions in a General Journal, post to the ledger accounts, and prepare a trial balance to test the accuracy of the recording and posting.
6. Define or explain the words and phrases listed in the chapter Glossary.

The Accounting Process Starts by Analyzing Economic Events

In Chapter 1, we said that accounting provides quantitative (primarily financial) information about economic entities. This information is intended to be useful in economic decision making. The accounting process involves (1) analyzing the economic events of an entity and recording the effects of those events, and (2) classifying and summarizing the recorded effects in reports or financial statements that individuals find useful in making economic decisions about the entity. This process is presented graphically in Illustration 2–1.

Business Transactions

In Illustration 2–1, note that economic events consist of business transactions and other (internal) events. Remember from Chapter 1 that business transactions are completed exchanges of economic consideration between two or more parties. Whenever an entity engages in a business transaction, the transaction will have an effect on the entity's accounting equation. The accounting process begins by analyzing such transactions to determine their effects on the accounting equation. Then, those effects are recorded in the accounting records (the books). Because business transactions are between the entity and some other (outside) party, they are sometimes called *external transactions*.

Other (Internal) Events

Some economic events have an effect on an entity's accounting equation even though they are not transactions with outside parties. For example, a business uses a machine in its operations. As a result, the remaining usefulness of the machine is decreased. In other words, the economic benefit of the machine is partially used up. The using up of the machine's economic benefit is an economic event that decreases the assets and decreases the owner's equity in the business. Internal economic events of this sort are not transactions between two or more parties. Nevertheless, because they have an effect on the accounting equation, they are sometimes called **internal transactions.** The analysis and recording of internal economic events is the central topic of Chapter 3.

Many years ago, most companies used pen and ink to manually record and process the data resulting from transactions. Today, only a few, very small companies use this method. Now, large and small companies use computers in recording transactions and in processing the recorded data. A few companies use electric bookkeeping machines, which were developed as an intermediate step in the path of progress from manual to computerized systems.

Nevertheless, you will begin your study of accounting by learning to process accounting data manually. By manually processing the data, you will more readily understand the importance of each step in the accounting process. Also, the general concepts you learn through manual methods will apply equally well to computerized accounting systems.

Business Papers

The printed documents that businesses use in the process of completing transactions are called **business papers.** They include such things as sales slips or invoices, cheques, purchase orders, customer billings, employee earnings records, and bank statements. Because they provide evidence of business transactions and are the basis for accounting entries, business papers are also called **source documents**

Illustration 2–1
The accounting process

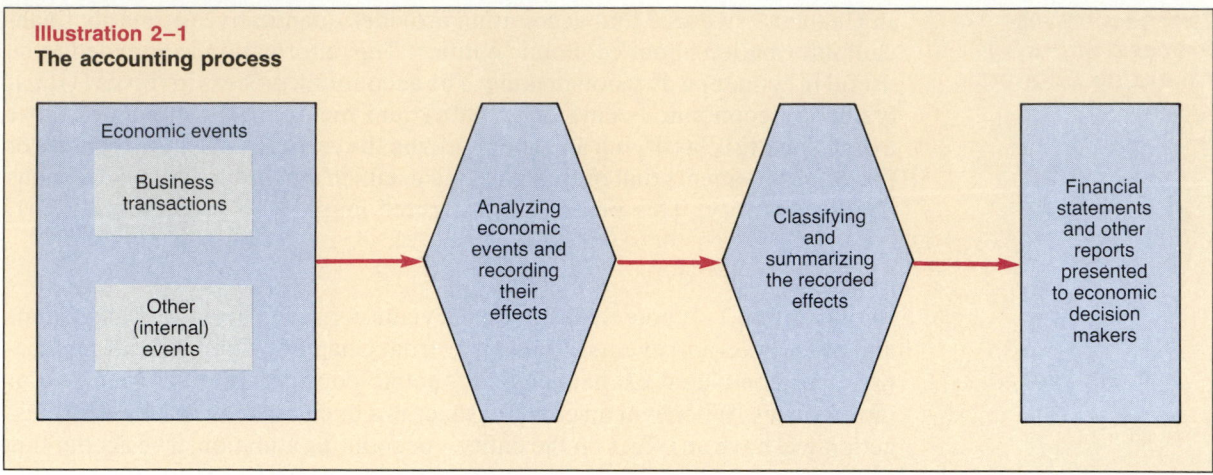

For example, if you buy a tennis racket on credit, two or more copies of an invoice or sales ticket are prepared. One copy is given to you. The other is sent to the store's accounting department and becomes the basis for an entry to record the sale. On the other hand, if you paid cash for the tennis racket and did not buy it on credit, the sale typically would have been "rung up" on a cash register that prints the amount of each sale on a paper tape locked inside the register. At the end of the day, when the proper key is depressed, the register prints on the tape the total cash sales for the day. The tape is then removed and becomes the basis for an entry to record the sales.

Business papers such as a sales invoice often are used by both the seller and the buyer as a basis for recording the transaction in their accounting records. For example, if you bought the tennis racket for use in your business, your copy of the invoice or sales ticket would provide the information you would need to record the transaction in the accounting records of your business.

To summarize, business papers are the starting point in the accounting process. Furthermore, verifiable business papers, particularly those originating outside the business, are also objective evidence of transactions completed and the amounts at which they should be recorded. As you learned in Chapter 1, this type of evidence is important because of the *objectivity principle*.

Accounts

In accounting for an entity, the different effects of its business transactions must be recorded and stored in separate "locations" so that they can be sorted and combined when financial reports are prepared. These locations in the accounting system are called **accounts.** A number of accounts are normally required. A separate account is used for summarizing the increases and decreases in each asset, liability, and owner's equity item appearing on the balance sheet and each revenue and expense item appearing on the income statement.

In its simplest form, an account looks like the letter **T**, is called a **T-account**, and appears as follows:

(Place for the Name of the Item Recorded in this Account)

(Left side)	(Right side)

Note that the **T** format gives the account a left side, a right side, and a place for the name of the account. The name indicates the type of items or effects to be stored in this particular account. For example, the *Cash* account is the location where all cash increases and decreases are recorded and stored.

When a T-account is used to record increases and decreases in an item, the increases are placed on one side of the account and the decreases on the other. For example, recall the transactions of Jerry Dow's law practice that were discussed in Chapter 1. Many of those transactions affected cash. If the increases and decreases in the cash of Jerry Dow's law practice are recorded in a T-account, they appear as follows:

Cash

Investment	9,000	Purchase of law books	2,500
Legal fee earned	2,200	Purchase of office equipment	5,600
Collection of account receivable	1,700	Rent payment	1,000
		Payment of salary	700
		Payment of account payable	900
		Withdrawal by owner	1,100

Balance of an Account

The reason for putting the increases on one side and the decreases on the other is that it is easy to add the increases and then add the decreases. The sum of the decreases may then be subtracted from the sum of the increases to determine the remaining balance of the account. Regardless of the type of account, the **account balance** is the difference between its increases and decreases. Also, the balance of an asset account is the amount of that asset owned by the entity on the date the balance is calculated. The balance of a liability account is the amount owed by the entity on the date of the balance.

In the case of the Cash account for Jerry Dow's law practice, the total increases were $12,900, the total decreases were $11,800, and the account balance is $1,100, as shown below.

Cash			
Investment	9,000	Purchase of law books	2,500
Legal fee earned	2,200	Purchase of office equipment	5,600
Collection of account receivable	1,700	Rent payment	1,000
		Payment of salary	700
		Payment of account payable	900
		Withdrawal by owner	1,100
Total increases	12,900	Total decreases	11,800
Less decreases	−11,800		
Balance	1,100		

Accounts Commonly Used

State the names of several commonly used accounts and the nature of the items recorded in those accounts.
(L. O. 1)

A business uses a number of accounts to record and store the effects of its transactions. However, the specific accounts a business uses depend on the assets owned, the debts owed, and the information the business needs to obtain from the accounting records. Nevertheless, although there are variations in the accounts different businesses use, the following accounts are common:

Asset Accounts

If the accounting system is to provide useful information about the different assets of a company, you must keep a separate account for each kind of asset owned. Generally, accounts are maintained for the following common assets.

Cash. Increases and decreases in cash are recorded in an account called Cash. The cash of a business consists of money or any medium of exchange that a bank will accept at face value for deposit. It includes coins, currency, cheques, and postal and bank money orders. The balance of the Cash account shows both the cash on hand in the store or office and that on deposit in the bank.

Notes Receivable. A **promissory note** is an unconditional written promise to pay a definite sum of money on demand or at a fixed or determinable future date. When amounts due from others are evidenced by promissory notes, the notes are known as notes receivable and are recorded in a Notes Receivable account.

Accounts Receivable. Goods and services are commonly sold to customers on the basis of oral or implied promises of future payment. Such sales are called credit sales or sales on account; and the oral or implied promises to pay are called accounts receivable. Accounts receivable are increased by credit sales and are decreased by customer payments. Since a company must know the amount currently owed by each customer, a separate record must be kept of each customer's purchases and payments. However, we will discuss this separate record in a later chapter. For the present, all increases and decreases in accounts receivable are recorded in a single account called Accounts Receivable.

Prepaid Insurance. Fire, liability, and other types of insurance protection are normally paid for in advance. The amount paid is called a premium, which expires as time passes. Many times, an insurance premium gives protection for a long time, perhaps as much as three years. As a result, a large portion of the premium is an asset for a considerable time after payment. When an insurance premium is paid in advance, assets are increased by the amount paid. The increase is normally recorded in an account called Prepaid Insurance. Therefore, whenever financial statements are prepared, the insurance that has expired is calculated and recorded as an expense, and the balance of the Prepaid Insurance account is reduced accordingly.

Office Supplies. Stamps, stationery, paper, pencils, and similar items are called office supplies. They are assets when purchased and continue to be assets until used up. As they are used up, the cost of the supplies becomes an expense. Increases and decreases in the asset are commonly recorded in an account called Office Supplies.

Store Supplies. Wrapping paper, cartons, bags, string, and similar items used by a store are called store supplies. Increases and decreases in store supplies are recorded in an account of that name.

Other Prepaid Expenses. When payments are made for economic benefits that do not expire until some later time, the payments create assets called **prepaid expenses.** Then, as the economic benefits are used up or expire, the assets become expenses. As a practical matter, if a purchased benefit will fully expire before the next income statement is prepared, the payment is generally recorded as an expense. But, when purchased benefits will not be used up or will not fully expire in the current time period, the payments are recorded as prepaid expenses (assets). Examples of prepaid expenses include prepaid insurance, office supplies, and store supplies. Rent that is paid for more than one period in advance is another example. Others include legal fees and management fees when they are paid in advance of receiving the legal or management services. Each type of prepaid expense is accounted for in a separate asset account.

Equipment. Increases and decreases in physical assets such as typewriters, desks, chairs, and office machines are commonly recorded in an account called Office Equipment. In a similar manner, physical assets that are used in the selling operations of a store—for example, counters, showcases, and cash registers—are recorded in an account called Store Equipment.

Buildings. A building used by a business in carrying on its operations may be a store, garage, warehouse, or factory. Such assets are commonly recorded and accounted for in an account called Buildings. If several buildings are owned, a separate account may be kept for each building.

Land. An account called Land is commonly used in recording increases and decreases in the land owned by a business. Land and the buildings placed on it are physically inseparable. Nevertheless, the land and the buildings must be recorded in separate accounts because buildings wear out or depreciate while the land on which they are placed does not.

Liability Accounts

Recall from Chapter 1 that liabilities are present obligations to transfer assets or provide services to other entities in the future. A business may have several different types of liabilities, each of which requires a separate account. The following are common:

Notes Payable. When an entity makes a formal written promise to pay a definite sum of money at a fixed future date, the liability is called a note payable. Increases and decreases in such promissory notes given to creditors are accounted for in an account called Notes Payable.

Accounts Payable. When purchases are made on the basis of oral or implied promises to pay, the amounts owed are called accounts payable. The items purchased on credit may be merchandise, supplies, equipment, or services. Since a business must know the amount owed each creditor, an individual record must be kept of the purchases from and the payments to each. However, we will discuss this individual record in a later chapter. For the present, all increases and decreases in accounts payable are recorded in a single Accounts Payable account.

Unearned Revenue. As you learned in Chapter 1, the *realization principle* requires that revenue not be recognized until it is earned. Therefore, when a company collects for its products or services before delivery, the amounts collected are received in advance of being earned and are called **unearned revenues.** An unearned revenue is a liability that will be satisfied by delivering the product or service paid for in advance. Examples are subscriptions collected in advance by a magazine publisher, rent collected in advance by a landlord, and legal fees collected in advance by a lawyer. On receipt, the amounts collected are recorded in liability accounts such as Unearned Subscriptions, Unearned Rent, and Unearned Legal Fees. When earned by delivery, the amounts earned are transferred to the revenue accounts: Subscriptions Earned, Rent Earned, and Legal Fees Earned.

Other Short-Term Payables. Wages payable, taxes payable, and interest payable are other short-term liabilities, each of which requires a separate account.

Owner's Equity Accounts

In Chapter 1, we illustrated four different types of transactions that affected the owner's equity in a proprietorship. They are: (1) investments by the owner, (2) withdrawals of cash or other assets by the owner, (3) revenues, and (4) expenses. Recall that in the previous chapter, all such transactions were entered in a column under the name of the owner. This procedure was used to show the effect of transactions on the accounting equation. However, the procedure made it necessary to analyze the items entered in the column in order to prepare an income statement and a statement of changes in owner's equity. Fortunately, such an analysis is not necessary. All that you need is a number of accounts, a separate one for each owner's equity item that appears on the balance sheet and a separate one for each revenue and expense item on the income statement. Then, as each transaction affecting owner's equity is completed, it is recorded in the proper account. The required accounts are as follows:

Capital Account. When a person invests in his or her own business, the investment is recorded in an account carrying the owner's name and the word *Capital*. For example, an account called Jerry Dow, Capital is used to record the investment of Jerry Dow in his law practice. In addition to the original investment, the **capital account** is used for any permanent additional increases or decreases in owner's equity.

Withdrawals Account. Usually a person invests in a business to earn income. Then, as the business earns income, the net assets of the business increase. From time to time, the owner may withdraw some of the business's assets to pay living expenses or for other personal uses. These withdrawals reduce both assets and owner's equity. To record them, you use an account that has the name of the business owner and the word *Withdrawals*. For example, an account called Jerry Dow, Withdrawals is used to record the withdrawals of cash by Jerry Dow from his law practice. The **withdrawals account** is also known as the **personal account** or **drawing account.**

An owner of an unincorporated business often withdraws a fixed amount each week or month to pay personal living expenses, and often thinks of these withdrawals as a salary. However, in a legal sense they are not a salary because the owner of an unincorporated business cannot enter into a legally binding contract with himself to hire himself and pay himself a salary. Consequently, by law and by custom, such withdrawals are neither a salary nor an expense of the business. They are simply the opposite of investments by the owner.

Revenue and Expense Accounts. When you prepare an income statement for an entity, you need to know the amount of each kind of revenue earned and each kind of expense incurred during the period covered by the statement. To accumulate this information, you need a number of revenue and expense accounts. However, all concerns do not have the same revenues and expenses. Therefore, it is impossible to list all revenue and expense accounts that you might encounter. Nevertheless, common examples of revenue accounts are Revenue from Repairs, Commissions Earned, Legal Fees Earned, Rent Earned, and Interest Earned. Common examples of expense accounts are Advertising Expense, Store Supplies Expense, Office Salaries Expense, Office Supplies Expense, Rent Expense, Utilities Expense, and Insurance Expense. Note that the kind of revenue or expense recorded in each above-mentioned account is evident from its title. This is generally true of such accounts.

The Ledger

A business may use from two dozen to several thousand accounts to record its transactions. In a computerized system, each account is stored on a disk or on a tape. In a manual system, each account is placed on a separate page in a bound or loose-leaf book, or on a separate card in a tray of cards. If the accounts are kept in a book, the book is called a **ledger.** If they are kept on cards in a file tray, the tray of cards is a ledger. Actually, as used in accounting, the word *ledger* means a group of accounts.

Debit and Credit

Recall that a T-account has a left side and a right side. However, in accounting, the left side is called the **debit** side, abbreviated ''Dr.''; and the right side is called the **credit** side, abbreviated ''Cr.'' Also, when amounts are entered on the left side of an account, they are called *debits,* and the account is said to be *debited.* When amounts are entered on the right side, they are called *credits,* and the account is said to be *credited.* The difference between the total debits and the total credits recorded in an account is the *account balance.* The balance may be either a *debit balance* or a *credit balance.* It is a debit balance when the sum of the debits exceeds the sum of the credits. It is a credit balance when the sum of the credits exceeds the sum of the debits.

The words *to debit* and *to credit* should not be confused with *to increase* and *to decrease.* To debit means to enter an amount on the left side of an account. To credit means to enter an amount on the right side. Either may be an increase or a decrease. For example, notice the way in which the investment of Jerry Dow is recorded in the Cash and capital accounts that follow:

Cash		Jerry Dow, Capital	
Investment 9,000			Investment 9,000

When Dow invested $9,000 in his law practice, both the cash of the business and Dow's equity increased. Observe in the accounts that the increase in cash is recorded on the left or debit side of the Cash account, while the increase in owner's equity is recorded on the right or credit side. The transaction is recorded in this manner because of the mechanics of **double-entry accounting**

Mechanics of Double-Entry Accounting

Explain the mechanics of double-entry accounting and tell why transactions are recorded with equal debits and credits.
(L. O. 2)

The mechanics of double-entry accounting are such that every transaction affects and is recorded in two or more accounts with equal debits and credits. One by-product of having equal debits and credits is that many errors are easy to discover. If every transaction is recorded with equal debits and credits, then the debits in the ledger must equal the credits. If you find that the sum of the debits in the ledger does not equal the sum of the credits, you know that an error has been made.

In double-entry accounting, increases in assets are recorded on the debit side of asset accounts. Why do assets have debit balances? There is no good reason; it is simply a matter of convention. However, since assets have debit balances, we can reason that increases in liabilities and owner's equity must be recorded as credits. This results from the accounting equation, $A = L + OE$, and from the requirement that debits equal credits. In other words, if assets have debit balances, equal debits and credits are possible only if increases in liabilities and owner's equity are recorded on the opposite or credit side. Therefore, increases and decreases in all balance sheet accounts have to be recorded as follows:

Assets		=	Liabilities		+	Owner's Equity	
Debit for increases	**Credit for** decreases		**Debit for** decreases	**Credit for** increases		**Debit for** decreases	**Credit for** increases

As pictured in these T-accounts, the rules for recording transactions under a double-entry system may be expressed as follows:

1. Increases in assets are debited to asset accounts; therefore, decreases must be credited.
2. Increases in liability and owner's equity items are credited to liability and owner's equity accounts; therefore, decreases must be debited.

Recall from Chapter 1 that owner's equity is increased by the owner's investments and by revenues. Owner's equity is decreased by expenses and by withdrawals. With this recollection, we offer these additional rules:

3. Investments by the owner of a business are credited to the owner's capital account.
4. Since the owner's withdrawals of assets decrease owner's equity, they are debited to the owner's withdrawals account.
5. Since revenues increase owner's equity, they are credited in each case to a revenue account that shows the kind of revenue earned.
6. Since expenses decrease owner's equity, they are debited in each case to an expense account that shows the kind of expense incurred.

At this stage, you will find it helpful to memorize these rules. You will apply them over and over in the course of your study. Eventually, the rules will become second nature to you.

Transactions Illustrating the Rules of Debit and Credit

Apply the rules of debit and credit in recording transactions.
(L. O. 3)

The following transactions for Jerry Dow's law practice illustrate how you should apply the rules of debit and credit while recording transactions in the accounts. The number before each transaction is used throughout the illustration so that you can identify the transaction in the accounts. Note that the first 11 transactions are the same ones used in Chapter 1 to illustrate the effects of transactions on the accounting equation. Five additional transactions (12 through 16) are presented in this chapter.

To record a transaction, you must first analyze it to determine what items were increased or decreased. The rules of debit and credit are then applied to determine the debit and credit effects of the increases or decreases. An analysis of each of the following transactions is given in order to demonstrate the process.

1. On December 1, Jerry Dow invested $9,000 in a new law practice.

Cash

(1) 9,000	

Jerry Dow, Capital

	(1) 9,000

Analysis of the transaction: The transaction increased the cash of the practice and at the same time it increased Dow's equity in the business. Increases in assets are debited, and increases in owner's equity are credited. Therefore, to record the transaction, Cash should be debited and Jerry Dow, Capital should be credited for $9,000.

2. Purchased books for a law library, paying cash of $2,500.

Cash

(1) 9,000	(2) 2,500

Law Library

(2) 2,500	

Analysis of the transaction: The law library is an asset that is increased by the purchase of books; and cash is an asset that is decreased. Increases in assets are debited, and decreases are credited. Therefore, to record the transaction, debit Law Library and credit Cash for $2,500.

3. Purchased office equipment for cash, $5,600.

Cash

(1) 9,000	(2) 2,500
	(3) 5,600

Office Equipment

(3) 5,600	

Analysis of the transaction: The asset office equipment is increased, and the asset cash is decreased. Debit Office Equipment and credit Cash for $5,600.

4. Purchased on credit from Equip-it Company law library items, $380, and office equipment, $1,280.

Law Library

(2) 2,500	
(4) 380	

Office Equipment

(3) 5,600	
(4) 1,280	

Accounts Payable

	(4) 1,660

Analysis of the transaction: This transaction increased the assets, law library and office equipment, but it also created a liability. Increases in assets are debits, and increases in liabilities are credits; therefore, debit Law Library for $380 and Office Equipment for $1,280, and credit Accounts Payable for $1,660.

5. Completed legal work for a client and immediately collected a $2,200 fee.

Cash

(1)	9,000	(2)	2,500
(5)	**2,200**	(3)	5,600

Legal Fees Earned

		(5)	**2,200**

Analysis of the transaction: This revenue transaction increased both assets and owner's equity. Increases in assets are debits, and increases in owner's equity are credits. Since revenues increase owner's equity, revenue accounts are increased with credits. Therefore, debit Cash to record the increase in assets. Credit Legal Fees Earned to increase owner's equity and accumulate information for the income statement.

6. Paid the office rent for December, $1,000.

Cash

(1)	9,000	(2)	2,500
(5)	2,200	(3)	5,600
		(6)	**1,000**

Rent Expense

(6)	**1,000**		

Analysis of the transaction: The cost of renting the office during December is an expense, the effect of which is to decrease owner's equity. Since decreases in owner's equity are debits, expenses are recorded as debits. Therefore, debit Rent Expense to decrease owner's equity and to accumulate information for the income statement. Also, credit Cash to record the decrease in assets.

7. Paid the secretary's salary for the two weeks ended December 12, $700.

Cash

(1)	9,000	(2)	2,500
(5)	2,200	(3)	5,600
		(6)	1,000
		(7)	**700**

Salaries Expense

(7)	**700**		

Analysis of the transaction: The secretary's salary is an expense that decreased owner's equity. Debit Salaries Expense to have the effect of decreasing owner's equity and to accumulate information for the income statement. Also, credit Cash to record the decrease in assets.

8. Completed legal work for a client on credit and billed the client $1,700 for the services rendered.

Accounts Receivable

(8)	**1,700**		

Legal Fees Earned

		(5)	2,200
		(8)	**1,700**

Analysis of the transaction: This revenue transaction gave the law practice the right to collect $1,700 from the client, and thus increased assets and owner's equity. Therefore, debit Accounts Receivable for the increase in assets and credit Legal Fees Earned to increase owner's equity and at the same time accumulate information for the income statement.

9. The client paid the $1,700 legal fee billed in transaction 8.

	Cash		
(1)	9,000	(2)	2,500
(5)	2,200	(3)	5,600
(9)	**1,700**	(6)	1,000
		(7)	700

Analysis of the transaction: One asset was increased, and the other decreased. Debit Cash to record the increase in cash, and credit Accounts Receivable to record the decrease in the account receivable, or the decrease in the right to collect from the client.

	Accounts Receivable		
(8)	1,700	**(9)**	**1,700**

10. Paid Equip-it Company $900 of the $1,660 owed for the items purchased on credit in transaction 4.

	Cash		
(1)	9,000	(2)	2,500
(5)	2,200	(3)	5,600
(9)	1,700	(6)	1,000
		(7)	700
		(10)	**900**

Analysis of the transaction: Payments to creditors decrease in equal amounts both assets and liabilities. Decreases in liabilities are debited, and decreases in assets are credited. Debit Accounts Payable and credit Cash.

	Accounts Payable		
(10)	**900**	(4)	1,660

11. Jerry Dow withdrew $1,100 from the law practice for personal use.

	Cash		
(1)	9,000	(2)	2,500
(5)	2,200	(3)	5,600
(9)	1,700	(6)	1,000
		(7)	700
		(10)	900
		(11)	**1,100**

Analysis of the transaction: This transaction reduced in equal amounts both assets and owner's equity. Cash is credited to record the asset reduction; and the Jerry Dow, Withdrawals account is debited to decrease owner's equity and to accumulate information for the statement of changes in owner's equity.

	Jerry Dow, Withdrawals		
(11)	**1,100**		

12. Signed a contract with Chemical Supply to do its legal work on a fixed-fee basis for $500 per month. Received the fee for the first six months in advance, $3,000.

	Cash		
(1)	9,000	(2)	2,500
(5)	2,200	(3)	5,600
(9)	1,700	(6)	1,000
(12)	**3,000**	(7)	700
		(10)	900
		(11)	1,100

Analysis of the transaction: The $3,000 receipt of cash increased assets but is not a revenue until earned. Receipt of cash before it is earned creates a liability, which will be satisfied by doing the client's legal work for the next six months. Record the asset increase by debiting Cash. Record the liability increase by crediting Unearned Legal Fees.

Unearned Legal Fees

	(12)	3,000

13. Paid a $2,400 premium for liability insurance protection that lasts two years.

Cash

(1)	9,000	(2)	2,500
(5)	2,200	(3)	5,600
(9)	1,700	(6)	1,000
(12)	3,000	(7)	700
		(10)	900
		(11)	1,100
		(13)	2,400

Analysis of the transaction: The advance payment of an insurance premium creates an asset by decreasing another asset. The new asset is recorded with a debit to Prepaid Insurance, and the payment is recorded with a credit to Cash.

Prepaid Insurance

(13)	2,400	

14. Purchased office supplies for cash, $120.
15. Paid the December utilities bill for hydro and water, $230.
16. Paid the secretary's salary for the two weeks ended December 26, $700.

Cash

(1)	9,000	(2)	2,500
(5)	2,200	(3)	5,600
(9)	1,700	(6)	1,000
(12)	3,000	(7)	700
		(10)	900
		(11)	1,100
		(13)	2,400
		(14)	120
		(15)	230
		(16)	700

Analysis of the transaction: These transactions are alike because each decreased cash; but they differ in that office supplies are assets while the utilities and secretary's services have been used up and are expenses. The cost of the supplies should be debited to an asset account, while the utilities and the salary should be debited to separate expense accounts. Each transaction involves a credit to Cash.

Office Supplies

(14)	120	

Utilities Expense

(15)	230	

Salaries Expense

(16)	700	

The Accounts and the Equation

Illustration 2–2 shows the accounts of the Dow law practice after the transactions have been recorded in them. The accounts are classified according to the elements of the accounting equation.

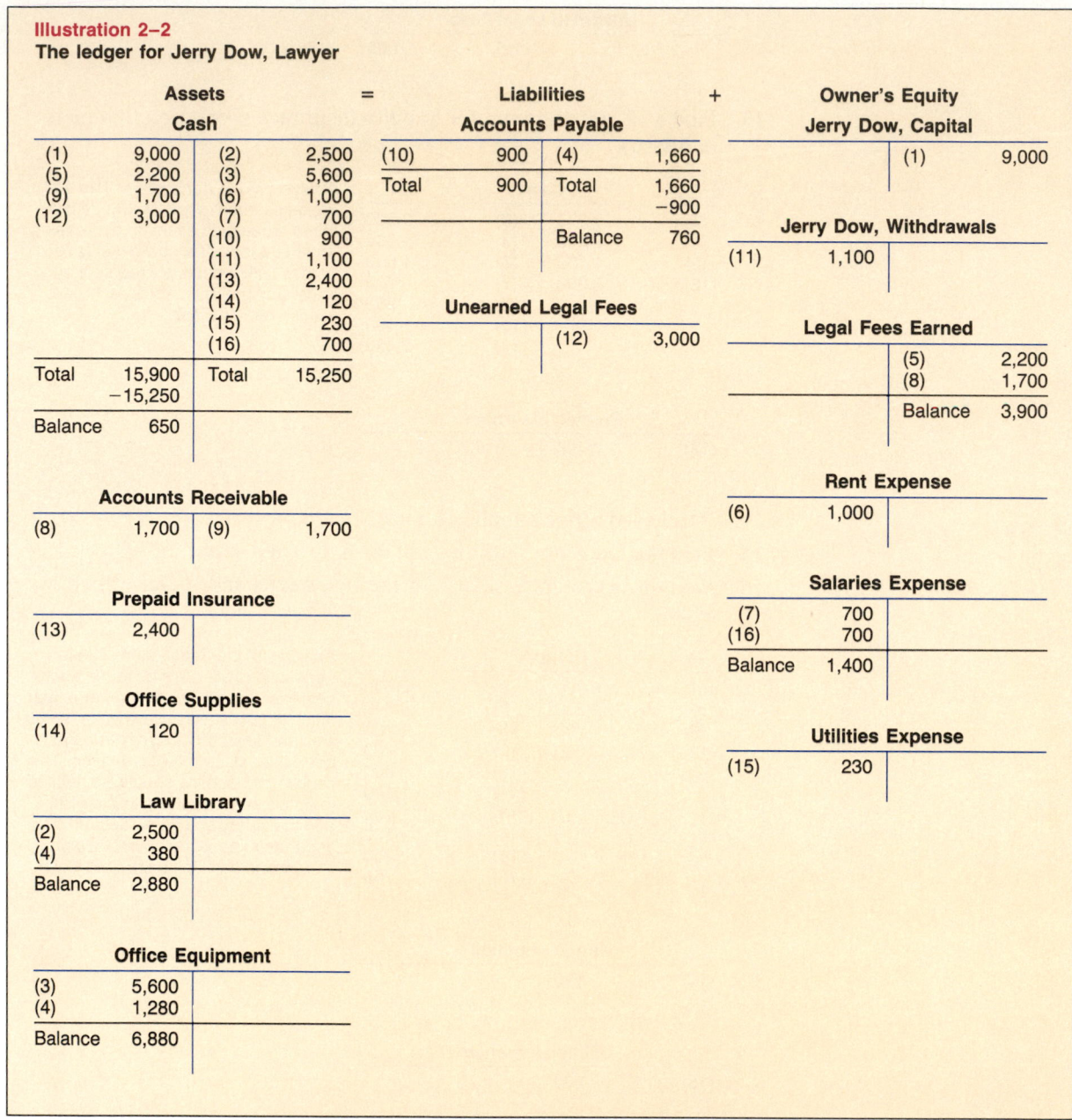

Illustration 2–2
The ledger for Jerry Dow, Lawyer

| Assets | = | Liabilities | + | Owner's Equity |

Cash

(1)	9,000	(2)	2,500
(5)	2,200	(3)	5,600
(9)	1,700	(6)	1,000
(12)	3,000	(7)	700
		(10)	900
		(11)	1,100
		(13)	2,400
		(14)	120
		(15)	230
		(16)	700
Total	15,900	Total	15,250
	−15,250		
Balance	650		

Accounts Receivable

| (8) | 1,700 | (9) | 1,700 |

Prepaid Insurance

| (13) | 2,400 | | |

Office Supplies

| (14) | 120 | | |

Law Library

(2)	2,500		
(4)	380		
Balance	2,880		

Office Equipment

(3)	5,600		
(4)	1,280		
Balance	6,880		

Accounts Payable

(10)	900	(4)	1,660
Total	900	Total	1,660
			−900
		Balance	760

Unearned Legal Fees

| | | (12) | 3,000 |

Jerry Dow, Capital

| | | (1) | 9,000 |

Jerry Dow, Withdrawals

| (11) | 1,100 | | |

Legal Fees Earned

		(5)	2,200
		(8)	1,700
		Balance	3,900

Rent Expense

| (6) | 1,000 | | |

Salaries Expense

(7)	700		
(16)	700		
Balance	1,400		

Utilities Expense

| (15) | 230 | | |

Preparing a Trial Balance

Recall that in a double-entry accounting system, every transaction is recorded with equal debits and credits. As a result, you know that an error has been made if the total of the debits in the ledger does not equal the total of the credits. Also, when the balances of the accounts are determined, the sum of the debit balances must equal the sum of the credit balances; otherwise, you know an error has been made. This equality is tested by preparing a **trial balance**. Preparing a trial balance requires five steps:

Illustration 2–3
Trial balance drawn from the ledger of Jerry Dow, Lawyer

JERRY DOW, LAWYER
Trial Balance
December 31, 1990

Cash	$ 650	
Prepaid insurance	2,400	
Office supplies	120	
Law library	2,880	
Office equipment	6,880	
Accounts payable		$ 760
Unearned legal fees		3,000
Jerry Dow, capital		9,000
Jerry Dow, withdrawals	1,100	
Legal fees earned		3,900
Rent expense	1,000	
Salaries expense	1,400	
Utilities expense	230	
Totals	$16,660	$16,660

1. Determine the balance of each account in the ledger.
2. List the accounts with balances other than zero, with the debit balances in one column and the credit balances in another (see Illustration 2–3).
3. Add the debit balances.
4. Add the credit balances.
5. Compare the sum of the debit balances with the sum of the credit balances.

The trial balance in Illustration 2–3 was prepared from the accounts in Illustration 2–2. Note that its column totals are equal; in other words, the trial balance is in balance. Therefore, debits equal credits in the ledger.

The Evidence of Accuracy Offered by a Trial Balance

If you prepare a trial balance that does not balance, one or more errors have been made. The error(s) may have been in recording transactions, in determining the account balances, in copying the balances on the trial balance, or in adding the columns of the trial balance. On the other hand, if your trial balance balances, you may assume that the accounts are free of those errors that would cause an inequality in debits and credits.

However, a trial balance that balances is not absolute proof of accuracy. Some errors do not affect the equality of the trial balance columns. For example, you may record a correct debit amount to the wrong account. This error will not cause a trial balance to be out of balance. Another example would be to record, with an equal debit and credit, a wrong amount. Because errors of this sort do not affect the equality of debits and credits, a trial balance that balances does not prove recording accuracy. It does, however, provide evidence that several types of errors have not been made.

Balance Column Accounts

T-accounts like the ones shown so far are commonly used in textbook illustrations and also in accounting classes for demonstrations. In both cases, their use eliminates details and lets you concentrate on ideas. However, although widely used in textbooks and in teaching, T-accounts are not used in real-world accounting systems. Instead, accounts like the one in Illustration 2–4 are generally used.

The account of Illustration 2–4 is called a **balance column account.** It differs from a T-account in that it has columns for specific information about each debit and credit entered in the account. Also, its Debit and Credit columns are placed side by side, and it has a third, "Balance," column. In this Balance column, the account's new balance is entered each time the account is debited or credited. As a result, the last amount in the column is the account's current balance. For example, on December 1, the illustrated account was debited for the $9,000 investment of Jerry Dow, which caused it to have a $9,000 debit balance. It was then credited for $2,500, and its new $6,500 balance was entered. On December 3, it was credited again for $5,600, which reduced its balance to $900. Then, on December 10, it was debited for $2,200, and its balance was increased to $3,100.

When a balance column account like that of Illustration 2–4 is used, the heading of the Balance column does not tell whether the balance is a debit balance or a credit balance. However, this should not create a problem. You should be able to determine the normal balance of any account by reading the account title and recognizing what type of account it is. These normal balances result from the rules of debit and credit, and are as follows:

Tell the normal balance of any asset, liability, or owner's account.
(L. O. 4)

Account Classification	Since Increases Are Recorded as—	The Normal Balance Is—
Asset	Debits	Debit
Liability	Credits	Credit
Owner's equity: . . .		
Capital	Credits	Credit
Withdrawals	Debits	Debit
Revenue	Credits	Credit
Expense	Debits	Debit

When an unusual transaction causes an account to have a balance opposite from its normal kind of balance, this opposite-from-normal kind of balance is indicated in the account by circling the amount or by entering it in red. Also, when a debit or credit entered in an account causes the account to have no balance, some bookkeepers place a –0– in the Balance column on the line of the entered amount. Others write 0.00 in the column to indicate the account does not have a balance.

Transactions Should First Be Recorded in a Journal

It is possible to record transactions by entering debits and credits directly in the accounts, as was done earlier in this chapter. However, if you do this and you make an error, the error will be difficult to locate. Even with a transaction that has only one debit and one credit, the debit is entered on one ledger page or card and the credit on another, and there is nothing to link the two together.

Therefore, to link together the debits and credits of each transaction and to

Illustration 2–4
A Cash account formatted as a balance column account

Cash				Account No. 111

Date		Explanation	PR	Debit		Credit		Balance	
1990 Dec.	1		G1	9,000	00			9,000	00
	2		G1			2,500	00	6,500	00
	3		G1			5,600	00	900	00
	10		G1	2,200	00			3,100	00

Illustration 2–5
The sequence of steps in recording transactions

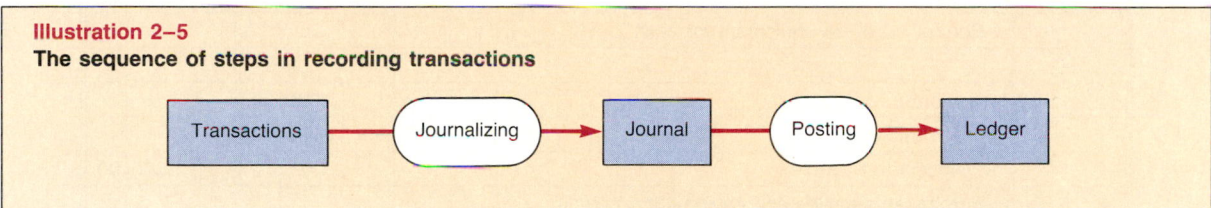

provide in one place a complete record of each transaction, it is the universal practice in manual accounting systems to record all transactions first in a **journal.** Then, the debit and credit information about each transaction is copied from the journal to the ledger accounts. These procedures reduce the tendency to make errors in posting. And if errors are made, the journal record makes it possible to trace the debits and credits into the accounts for the purpose of locating the errors.

The process of recording transactions in a journal is called *journalizing transactions*. The process of copying journal entry information from a journal to a ledger is called **posting.** Remember the sequence of these steps, as shown in Illustration 2–5. Since transactions are first journalized and then posted to the ledger, a journal is called a **book of original entry** and a ledger a **book of final entry**

The General Journal

The simplest and most flexible type of journal is a **General Journal.** The General Journal is designed so flexibly that it can be used to record any kind of transaction. For each transaction, it provides places for recording (1) the transaction date, (2) the names of the accounts involved, (3) the amount of each debit and credit, and (4) an explanation of the transaction. And when the amounts are copied from the journal to the accounts in the ledger, the General Journal provides (5) a column in which to mark the identifying number of the

Illustration 2–6
A General Journal showing four transactions of Jerry Dow, Lawyer

General Journal				Page 1

Date	Account Titles and Explanation	PR	Debit	Credit
1990 Dec. 1	Cash		9,000 00	
	Jerry Dow, Capital			9,000 00
	Investment by owner.			
2	Law Library		2,500 00	
	Cash			2,500 00
	Purchased law books for cash.			
3	Office Equipment		5,600 00	
	Cash			5,600 00
	Purchased office equipment for cash.			
6	Law Library		380 00	
	Office Equipment		1,280 00	
	Accounts Payable			1,660 00
	Purchased supplies and equipment on credit.			

account to which each debit or credit was copied. Illustration 2–6 shows a typical general journal page on which the first four transactions of the Dow law practice have been recorded.

In Illustration 2–6, the last entry records the credit purchase of law books and office equipment. Note that three accounts are involved. When a transaction involves three or more accounts and is recorded with a general journal entry, a **compound journal entry** is required. A compound journal entry is one that involves three or more accounts.

Recording Transactions in a General Journal

Record transactions in a General Journal, post to the ledger accounts, and prepare a trial balance to test the accuracy of the recording and posting. (L. O. 5)

Use the following procedures to record transactions in a General Journal:

1. Write the year in small figures at the top of the first column.
2. Write the month on the first line in the first column. The year and the month are not repeated except at the top of a new page or at the beginning of a new month or year.
3. Write the day of each transaction in the second column on the first line of the transaction.
4. Write the names of the accounts to be debited and credited and an explanation of the transaction in the Account Titles and Explanation

column. *The name of the account debited is written first, beginning at the left margin of the column. The name of the account credited is written on the following line, indented about one inch.* The explanation is placed on the next line, indented about a half inch from the left margin. The explanation should be short but sufficient to explain the transaction and set it apart from other transactions.

5. Write the debit amount in the Debit column opposite the name of the account to be debited. Write the credit amount in the Credit column opposite the account to be credited.

6. Skip a single line between each journal entry to set the entries apart.

At the time transactions are recorded in the General Journal, nothing is entered in the **Posting Reference (PR) column.** However, when the debits and credits are copied from the journal to the ledger, the account numbers of the ledger accounts to which the debits and credits are copied are entered in this column. The Posting Reference column is sometimes called the **Folio column.**

Posting Transaction Information

The process of posting journal entry information from the journal to the ledger is usually done near the end of a day. All transactions recorded in the journal that day are posted. In the posting procedure, journal debits are copied and become ledger account debits and journal credits are copied and become ledger account credits.

Illustration 2–7 shows the posting procedures for a journal entry. As shown in the illustration, the procedures you should use to post a journal entry are as follows:

For the debit:

1. Find in the ledger the account named in the debit of the entry.
2. Enter in the account the date of the entry as shown in the journal.
3. In the Debit column of the account, write the debit amount shown in the journal.
4. Enter the letter G and the **journal page number** from which the entry is being posted in the posting Reference column of the account. The letter G indicates that the amount was posted from the General Journal. We will discuss other journals later in the text, and each is identified by a letter.
5. Determine the effect of the debit on the account balance and enter the new balance.
6. Enter in the Posting Reference column of the journal the account number of the account to which the amount was posted.

For the credit:

Repeat the above steps. However, the credit amount is entered in the Credit column and has a credit effect on the account balance.

Illustration 2–7
Procedures to follow in posting a general journal entry

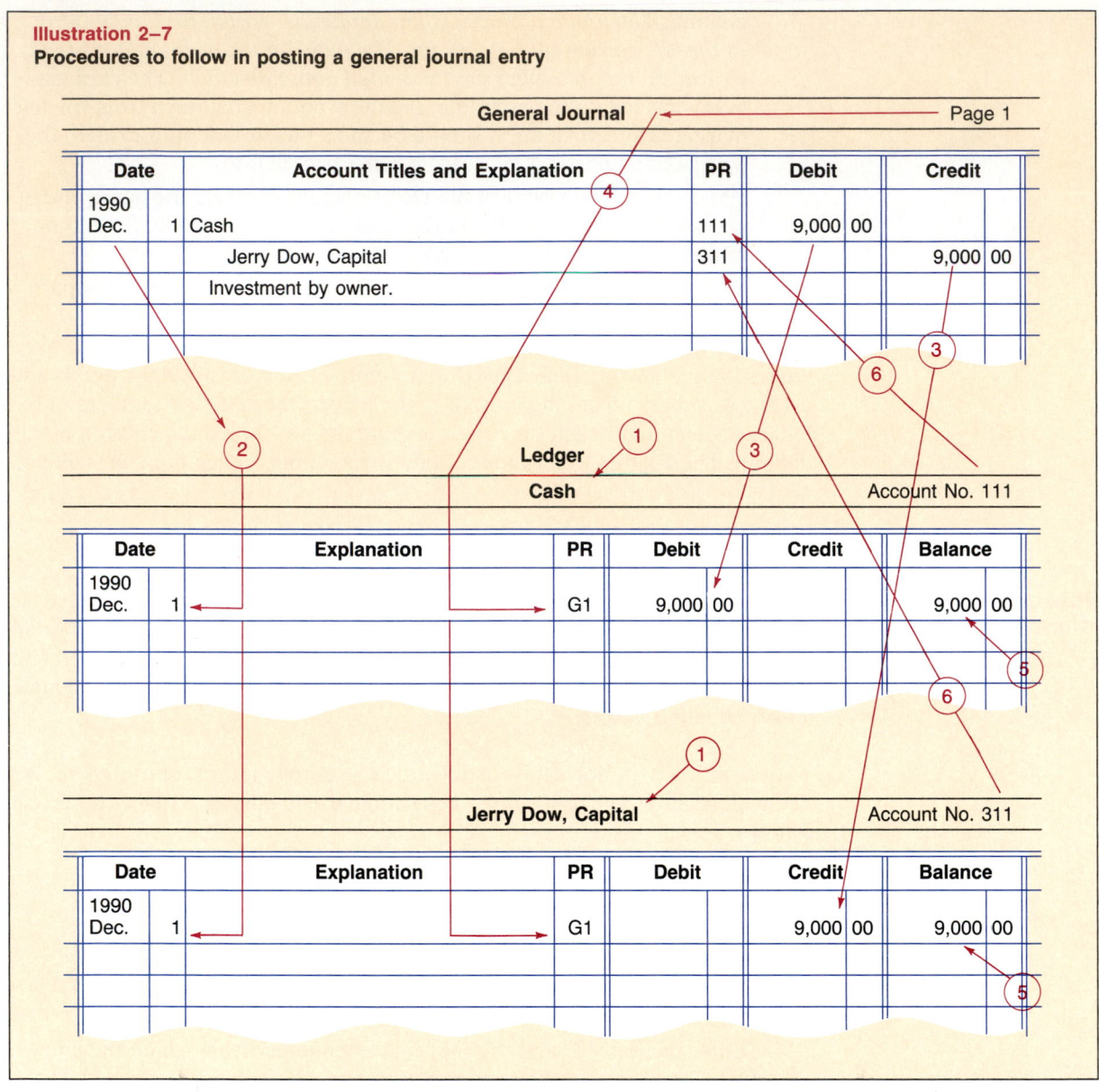

Observe that the last step (step 6) in the posting procedure for either the debit or the credit of an entry is to insert the **account number** in the Posting Reference column of the journal. Inserting the account number in this column serves two purposes: (1) The account number in the journal and the journal page number in the account act as a cross-reference when you want to trace an amount from one record to the other. (2) Writing the account number in the journal as a last step in posting indicates that posting is completed. If posting is interrupted, the bookkeeper, by examining the journal's Posting Reference column, can easily see where posting stopped.

Account Numbers

All companies should follow a systematic method of assigning identifying numbers to their accounts. A list of all the accounts used by a company, showing the identifying number assigned to each account, is called a **chart of accounts.** One example of a system that service businesses might use in developing a chart of accounts is to assign numbers as follows:

Asset accounts, 111 through 199.

Liability accounts, 211 through 299.

Owner's equity accounts, 311 through 399.

Revenue accounts, 411 through 499.

Operating expense accounts, 511 through 699.

Observe that asset accounts are assigned numbers with first digits of 1, liability accounts are assigned numbers with first digits of 2, and so on. In each case, the first digit of an account's number tells its balance sheet or income statement classification. The second and third digits further identify the account. However, we will describe this type of account numbering system more completely in the next chapter.

Locating Errors

When a trial balance does not balance, one or more errors have been made. To locate the error or errors, you should check the journalizing, posting, and trial balance preparation steps in their reverse order. First check the addition of the columns in the trial balance to see that no addition errors were made. Then check to see that the account balances were correctly copied from the ledger. Then recalculate the account balances. If at this stage the error or errors are not found, check the posting and then the original journalizing of the transactions.

Correcting Errors

When an error is discovered in either the journal or the ledger, it must be corrected. Such an error is never erased, for this may indicate an effort to conceal something. However, the method of correction will vary with the nature of the error and the stage in the accounting procedures at which it is discovered.

If an error is discovered in a journal entry before the error is posted, it may be corrected by ruling a single line through the incorrect amount or account name and writing the correct amount or account name above. Likewise, if an incorrect amount was posted to an account, you may correct it in the same manner. However, if an amount was posted to the wrong account, it is best to correct the error with a correcting journal entry. For example, the following journal entry to record the purchase of office supplies was made and posted:

Oct.	14	Office Furniture and Fixtures	160.00	
		Cash		160.00
		To record the purchase of office supplies.		

Obviously, the debit of the entry is to the wrong account; therefore, the following entry is needed to correct the error:

Oct.	17	Office Supplies	160.00	
		Office Furniture and Fixtures		160.00
		To correct the entry of October 14 in which the Office Furniture and Fixtures account was debited in error for the purchase of office supplies.		

The debit of the second entry correctly records the purchase of supplies, and the credit cancels the error of the first entry. Note the full explanation of the correcting entry. Such an explanation should always be full and complete so that anyone can see exactly what occurred.

Bookkeeping Techniques

When amounts are entered in a journal or a ledger, it is not necessary to use commas indicating thousands of dollars or decimal points to separate dollars and cents. The ruled lines accomplish this. However, when statements are prepared on unruled paper, the decimal points and commas should be used.

Dollar signs are not used in journals or ledgers. However, you should use them on financial reports prepared on unruled paper. On such reports, a dollar sign is placed (1) before the first amount in each column of figures and (2) before the first amount appearing after a ruled line to indicate an addition or a subtraction. Examine Illustration 3–5 for examples of the use of dollar signs on a financial report.

When an amount to be entered in a ledger or a journal is an amount of dollars and no cents, some bookkeepers save time by using a dash in the cents column in the place of two zeros to indicate that there are no cents. However, on financial reports, two zeros are preferred because they are neater in appearance.

In this text, exact dollar amounts are used in order to save space. In such cases, neither zeros nor dashes are used to show that there are no cents involved.

Summary of the Chapter in Terms of Learning Objectives

1. Commonly used asset accounts include Cash, Notes Receivable, Accounts Receivable, Prepaid Insurance, Office Supplies, Store Supplies, Equipment, Buildings, and Land. Commonly used liability accounts include Notes Payable and Accounts Payable, as well as other unearned revenue accounts. The owner's investments in a proprietorship and other relatively permanent changes in the owner's equity are recorded in the owner's capital account. Revenue, expense, and withdrawals accounts are used to accumulate changes in owner's equity.

2. In double-entry accounting, every transaction is recorded in two or more accounts with equal debits and credits. Although this procedure does not guarantee accuracy, it provides evidence that several possible errors have not been made.

3. Double-entry accounting is based on the accounting equation, A = L + OE. Debits are used to record increases in assets, withdrawals, and expenses. Decreases in liabilities, the owner's capital account, and revenues are also recorded with debits. Credits are used to record increases in liabilities, the owner's capital account, and revenues. Credits are also used to record decreases in assets, withdrawals, and expenses.

4. Asset and expense accounts normally have debit balances. Liability, owner's equity, and revenue accounts normally have credit balances.

5. The effects of the economic events on an entity's accounting equation are recorded first in a journal such as the General Journal. After they have been journalized, the amounts are copied from the journal to the accounts in the ledger. After the amounts have been posted to the ledger accounts, a trial balance may be prepared to prove that the equality of debits and credits has been maintained.

Demonstration Problem

This demonstration problem is based on the same facts as the demonstration problem presented at the end of Chapter 1. During its first month of operation, Barbara Schmidt's haircutting business (The Cutlery) completed the following transactions:

a. On August 1, 1990, Schmidt put $2,000 of her savings into a chequing account in the name of The Cutlery.
b. On August 2, she bought $600 of supplies for the shop.
c. On August 3, she paid $500 rent for the month of August for a small store.
d. On August 5, she furnished the store, installing new fixtures which the supplier sold to her for $1,200. This amount was to be repaid in three equal payments at the end of August, September, and October.
e. The Cutlery opened August 12, and in the first week of business ended August 16, receipts from cash sales amounted to $825.
f. On August 17, Schmidt paid $125 to an assistant for working during the business's grand opening.
g. Receipts from cash sales during the two-week period ended August 30 amounted to $1,930.
h. On August 31, Schmidt paid the first installment on the fixtures.
i. On August 31, she withdrew $1,100 cash for her personal expenses.

Required

1. Prepare general journal entries to record the above transactions.
2. Open the following accounts: Cash, 111; Store Supplies, 112; Store Equipment, 131; Accounts Payable, 211; Barbara Schmidt, Capital, 311; Barbara Schmidt, Withdrawals, 312; Sales, 411; Rent Expense, 611; and Wages Expense, 612.
3. Post the journal entries to the proper ledger accounts.
4. Prepare a trial balance for The Cutlery.

Solution to Demonstration Problem

1.

Page 1

	Date		Account Titles and Explanations	PR	Debit	Credit
	1990					
a.	Aug.	1	Cash.	111	2,000.00	
			Barbara Schmidt, Capital	311		2,000.00
			Invested $2,000 in business.			
b.		2	Store Supplies	112	600.00	
			Cash	111		600.00
			Purchased store supplies.			
c.		3	Rent Expense.	611	500.00	
			Cash	111		500.00
			Paid rent for August.			
d.		5	Store Equipment	131	1,200.00	
			Accounts Payable	211		1,200.00
			Purchased fixtures on credit.			
e.		16	Cash.	111	825.00	
			Sales.	411		825.00
			Cash sales to customers.			
f.		17	Wages Expense	612	125.00	
			Cash	111		125.00
			Paid wages to assistant.			
g.		30	Cash.	111	1,930.00	
			Sales.	411		1,930.00
			Two weeks' sales to customers.			
h.		31	Accounts Payable.	211	400.00	
			Cash	111		400.00
			Paid first payment on store equipment purchased on August 5.			
i.		31	Barbara Schmidt, Withdrawals.	312	1,100.00	
			Cash	111		1,100.00
			Withdrew cash for personal use.			

2., 3.

Cash Account No. 111

Date		Explanation	PR	Debit	Credit	Balance
1990						
Aug.	1		1	2,000		2,000
	2		1		600	1,400
	3		1		500	900
	16		1	825		1,725
	17		1		125	1,600
	30		1	1,930		3,530
	31		1		400	3,130
	31		1		1,100	2,030

Store Supplies — Account No. 112

Date	Explanation	PR	Debit	Credit	Balance
1990 Aug. 2		1	600		600

Store Equipment — Account No. 131

Date	Explanation	PR	Debit	Credit	Balance
1990 Aug. 5		1	1,200		1,200

Accounts Payable — Account No. 211

Date	Explanation	PR	Debit	Credit	Balance
1990 Aug. 5		1		1,200	1,200
31		1	400		800

Barbara Schmidt, Capital — Account No. 312

Date	Explanation	PR	Debit	Credit	Balance
1990 Aug. 1		1		2,000	2,000

Barbara Schmidt, Withdrawals — Account No. 312

Date	Explanation	PR	Debit	Credit	Balance
1990 Aug. 31		1	1,100		1,100

Sales — Account No. 411

Date	Explanation	PR	Debit	Credit	Balance
1990 Aug. 16		1		825	825
30		1		1,930	2,755

Rent Expense — Account No. 611

Date	Explanation	PR	Debit	Credit	Balance
1990 Aug. 3		1	500		500

Wages Expense — Account No. 612

Date	Explanation	PR	Debit	Credit	Balance
1990 Aug. 17		1	125		125

4.

THE CUTLERY
Trial Balance
August 31, 1990

Cash	$2,030	
Store supplies	600	
Store equipment	1,200	
Accounts payable		$ 800
Barbara Schmidt, capital		2,000
Barbara Schmidt, withdrawals	1,100	
Sales		2,755
Rent expense	500	
Wages expense	125	
Totals	$5,555	$5,555

Glossary

Define or explain the words and phrases listed in the chapter Glossary. (L. O. 6)

Account balance the difference between the increases and decreases recorded in an account. p. 57

Account number a unique number that is assigned to an account as a means of identifying that account. p. 74

Accounts separate locations in an accounting system, one of which is used in recording and summarizing the increases and decreases in each type of revenue, expense, asset, liability, or owner's equity item. p. 56

Balance column account an account that has Debit and Credit columns for entering changes in the account and a column for entering the new account balance after each debit or credit is posted to the account. p. 70

Book of final entry a ledger to which amounts are posted. p. 71

Book of original entry a journal in which transactions are first recorded. p. 71

Business papers printed documents that businesses use in the process of completing business transactions and that provide evidence of the transactions; sometimes called *source documents*. p. 55

Capital account an account used to record the owner's investments in the business plus any more or less permanent changes in the owner's equity. p. 61

Chart of accounts a list of all the accounts used by a company, showing the identifying number assigned to each account. p. 75

Compound journal entry a journal entry that has more than one debit or more than one credit. p. 72

Credit the right-hand side of a T-account, or entries that decrease assets, or increase liabilities, or increase owner's equity. p. 62

Debit the left-hand side of a T-account, or entries that increase assets, or decrease liabilities, or decrease owner's equity. p. 62

Double-entry accounting a system of accounting in which each transaction affects and is recorded in two or more accounts with equal debits and credits. p. 62

Drawing account another name for the *withdrawals account*. p. 61

Folio column another name for the *Posting Reference column*. p. 73

General Journal a book of original entry that is designed so flexibly that it can be used to record any type of transaction. p. 71

Internal transactions a name sometimes given to economic events that have an effect on an entity's accounting equation but that do not involve transactions with outside parties. p. 55

Journal a book of original entry in which a complete record of transactions is first recorded and from which transaction amounts are posted to the ledger accounts. p. 71

Journal page number a posting reference number entered in the Posting Reference column of each account to which an amount is posted and which shows the page of the journal from which the amount was posted. p. 73

Ledger a group of accounts used by a business in recording its transactions. p. 62

Personal account another name for the *withdrawals account*. p. 61

Posting transcribing the debit and credit amounts from a journal to the ledger accounts. p. 73

Posting Reference (PR) column a column in a journal and in each account that is used for cross-referencing amounts that have been posted from a journal to the account. Also called a *Folio column*. p. 73

Prepaid expenses assets created by payments for economic benefits that do not expire until some later time; then, as the benefits expire or are used up, the assets become expenses. p. 59.

Promissory note a formal written promise to pay a definite sum of money on demand or at a fixed or determinable future date. p. 58

Source documents another name for *business papers*. p. 55

T-account a simple form of account that is widely used in accounting education to illustrate the debits and credits required in recording a transaction. p. 56

Trial balance a list of the accounts that have balances in the ledger, the debit or credit balance of each account, the total of the debit balances, and the total of the credit balances. p. 68

Unearned revenues liabilities created by the receipt of cash from customers in payment for products or services that have not yet been delivered to the customers; the liabilities will be satisfied by delivering the product or service. p. 60

Withdrawals account the account used to record the transfers of assets from a business to its owner; also known as *personal account* or *drawing account*. p. 61

Questions for Class Discussion

1. What are two types of occurrences that affect an entity's accounting equation?
2. What are the two fundamental steps in the accounting process?
3. Why are business papers called source documents?
4. Why is the evidence provided by business papers important to accounting?
5. What is an account? What is a ledger?
6. What determines the number and type of accounts a business will use?
7. What is the difference between a note receivable and an account receivable?
8. What types of transactions increase the owner's equity in a business? What types decrease owner's equity?
9. What are the meanings of the following words and terms: (*a*) debit, (*b*) to debit, (*c*) credit, and (*d*) to credit?

10. Does debit always mean increase and credit always mean decrease?

11. If a transaction has the effect of decreasing an asset, is the decrease recorded as a debit or as a credit? If the transaction has the effect of decreasing a liability, is the decrease recorded as a debit or as a credit?

12. Why are some accounting systems called *double-entry* accounting systems?

13. Given that assets have economic value and that they have debit balances, why do expenses also have debit balances?

14. What entry (debit or credit) would you make to (*a*) increase a revenue, (*b*) decrease an expense, (*c*) record an owner's withdrawals, and (*d*) record an owner's investment?

15. Why are the rules of debit and credit the same for both liability and owner's equity accounts?

16. List the steps in the preparation of a trial balance.

17. Why is a trial balance prepared?

18. What kinds of errors would cause the column totals of a trial balance to be unequal? What are some examples of errors that would not be revealed by a trial balance?

19. Should transactions be recorded first in a journal or first in the ledger? Why?

20. In recording transactions in a General Journal, which is written first, the debit or the credit? Which is indented?

21. What is a compound entry?

22. What kind of transactions can be recorded in a General Journal?

23. What is the purpose of posting reference numbers that are entered in the journal at the time entries are posted to the accounts?

24. What is a chart of accounts?

25. If a wrong amount was journalized and posted to the accounts, how should it be corrected?

26. When are dollar signs used in accounting?

27. Define or describe each of the following:
    a. Journal.
    b. Ledger.
    c. Folio column.
    d. Posting.
    e. Posting Reference column.

Multiple Choice

1. The requirements of double-entry accounting are such that:
    a. All transactions that involve debits to asset accounts must also involve credits to liability or owner's equity accounts.
    b. All transactions are recorded with equal debits and credits.

c. The total debits of all recorded transactions will equal the total credits of all recorded transactions.

d. The effects on the balance sheet equation of external transactions can be recorded but the effects of other economic events, sometimes called internal transactions, cannot be recorded.

e. Both (b) and (c) are correct.

2. The following types of accounts normally have credit balances:

a. Revenue, asset, and owner's equity accounts.

b. Revenue, expense, and owner's equity accounts.

c. Revenue, liability, and owner's equity accounts.

d. Liability and expense accounts.

e. Asset and expense accounts.

3. The trial balance of a company shows a Wages Expense account with a balance of $700, which resulted from a single transaction. This account:

a. Was recorded in the General Journal in the process of journalizing.

b. Was journalized when the $700 amount was copied from the General Journal to the ledger account.

c. Was posted when the ledger account was listed in the trial balance.

d. Represents an increase in owner's equity that resulted from the use of labor.

e. Would normally be listed in the trial balance as a credit balance.

4. In a trial balance, if the sum of the debit balances equals the sum of the credit balances:

a. You know that all transactions were journalized correctly.

b. You know that all entries were posted correctly.

c. You know that every transaction involving the business has been recorded.

d. The trial balance has failed to disclose any errors involving journalizing and posting and therefore provides some evidence that these steps were done correctly.

e. All of the above are correct.

5. The following are commonly used accounts: (1) Equipment; (2) Unearned Rent; (3) Store Supplies; (4) Owner, Capital; (5) Accounts Payable; (6) Owner, Withdrawals; and (7) Land. These accounts should be classified as assets, liabilities, or owner's equity as follows:

	Assets	Liabilities	Owner's Equity
a.	1, 3, 7	2, 5	4, 6
b.	1, 3, 7	2, 5, 6	4
c.	1, 3, 7	5, 6	2, 4
d.	1, 7	5, 6	2, 3, 4
e.	1, 7	2, 5	3, 4, 6

6. Of the following errors, the one that by itself will cause the trial balance to be out of balance is:

a. A $200 salary payment posted as a $200 debit to cash and a $200 credit to salaries expense.

b. A $100 receipt from a customer in payment of his account posted as a $100 debit to cash and a $10 credit to accounts receivable.

   c. A $75 receipt from a customer in payment of his account posted as a $75 debit to cash and a $75 credit to cash.

   d. A $50 payment for office supplies purchased for cash posted as a $50 debit to office equipment and a $50 credit to cash.

   e. Any one and all of the foregoing errors.

Mini Discussion Case

Case 2–1

Archibald and Amanda, students in accounting class, were overheard discussing problems they encountered in the first test after Chapter 2. Their problem centered around their inability to understand the rules of debit and credit. They just could not understand why, when they deposit their allowances at the Campus Bank, their accounts are credited, reflecting an increase in the amount of money they have on deposit. When they withdraw money from the bank their accounts are debited, reflecting a decrease in the amount of money they have left on deposit. Yet in their class and in their textbook they are told just the opposite.

The two students decided to go to their instructor for a resolution of their dilemma. The instructor welcomed them and began to explain their apparent problem.

Required

Put yourself in the position of the instructor and explain to Archibald and Amanda the source of their problem and why the rules of debit and credit are correct as stated in the textbook.

Exercises

Exercise 2–1
Increases, decreases, and normal balances of accounts
(L. O. 3, 4)

Prepare the following columnar form. Then enter the word *debit* or *credit* in each of the last three columns to indicate the action necessary to increase the account, the action to decrease the account, and to show the normal balance of the account.

Kind of Account	Increases	Decreases	Normal Balance
Revenue			
Asset			
Owner's withdrawals			
Liability			
Expense			
Owner's capital			

Exercise 2–2
Entering transactions in T-accounts
(L. O. 3)

Place the following T-accounts on a sheet of notebook paper: Cash; Accounts Receivable; Office Supplies; Office Equipment; Accounts Payable; Gae Neff, Capital; Revenue from Services; and Utilities Expense. Then record these transactions by entering debits and credits directly in the accounts. Use the transaction letters to identify amounts entered in the accounts.

a. Gae Neff began a service business, called N-E Errands, by investing $5,000 in the business.
b. Purchased office supplies for cash, $60.
c. Purchased office equipment on credit, $3,000.
d. Received $300 cash for services provided to a customer.
e. Paid for the office equipment purchased in transaction (c).
f. Billed a customer $875 for services provided to the customer.
g. Paid the monthly utility bills, $45.
h. Collected $350 of the amount owed by the customer of transaction (f).

Exercise 2–3
Preparing a trial balance
(L. O. 5)

After recording the transactions of Exercise 2–2, prepare a trial balance for N-E Errands. Use the current date.

Exercise 2–4
Analyzing a trial balance
(L. O. 1, 3, 4)

James Nelson began a real estate agency and completed seven transactions. The transactions included a cash investment by Nelson, a purchase on credit, and other cash transactions. After completing these transactions, he prepared the trial balance that follows. Analyze the trial balance and prepare a list describing each transaction and its amount. (Hint: T-accounts may help.)

JAMES NELSON, REALTOR
Trial Balance
November 7, 1990

Cash	$ 5,925	
Office supplies	225	
Prepaid insurance	2,700	
Office equipment	6,000	
Accounts payable		$ 6,000
James Nelson, capital		7,500
James Nelson, withdrawals	3,000	
Commissions earned		4,500
Advertising expense	150	
Totals	$18,000	$18,000

Exercise 2–5
Trial balance errors
(L. O. 5)

Prepare a form with the following three column headings: (1) Error, (2) Amount Out of Balance, and (3) Column Having Larger Total. Then for each of the following errors: (1) in the first column list the error by letter, (2) in the second column show the difference in the trial balance column totals that will result from the error, and (3) in the third column indicate which trial balance column (Debit or Credit) will have the larger total as a result of the error. If the error does not affect the trial balance, write ''none'' in each of the last two columns.

a. A $100 debit to Office Supplies was debited to Office Equipment.
b. A $135 credit to Office Equipment was credited to Sales.
c. A $90 credit to Sales was credited to the Sales account twice.
d. A $60 debit to Office Supplies was posted as a $65 debit.
e. A $55 debit to Office Supplies was not posted.
f. A $22 credit to Sales was posted as a $220 credit.

Exercise 2–6
Analyzing a trial balance error
(L. O. 5)

A trial balance does not balance. In looking for the error, you notice that Accounts Payable has a credit balance of $6,000. However, you discover that a transaction for the credit purchase of a computer for $525 had been recorded with a $525 debit to Office Equipment and a $525 debit to Accounts Payable. Answer each of the following questions, giving the dollar amount of the misstatement, if any.

a. Was the balance of the Office Equipment account overstated, understated, or correctly stated in the trial balance?

b. Was the balance of the Accounts Payable account overstated, understated, or correctly stated in the trial balance?

c. Was the Debit column total of the trial balance overstated, understated, or correctly stated?

d. Was the Credit column total of the trial balance overstated, understated, or correctly stated?

e. If the Credit column total of the trial balance was $144,000 before the error was corrected, what was the total of the Debit column?

Exercise 2–7
Preparing a corrected trial balance
(L. O. 5)

A careless bookkeeper prepared the following trial balance which does not balance, and you have been asked to prepare a corrected trial balance. In examining the records of the concern, you discover the following: (1) The debits to the Cash account total $49,850, and the credits total $45,125. (2) A $115 receipt of cash from a customer in payment of the customer's account was not posted to Accounts Receivable. (3) A $35 purchase of shop supplies on credit was entered in the journal but was not posted to any account. (4) The bookkeeper made a transposition error in copying the balance of the Revenue from Services account in the trial balance. The correct amount was $52,350.

FRED'S REPAIR SHOP
Trial Balance
December 31, 1990

Cash	$ 4,825	
Accounts receivable		$ 5,765
Shop supplies	5,950	
Shop equipment	10,750	
Accounts payable	900	
Fred Mason, capital	12,265	
Fred Mason, withdrawals . . .	27,000	
Revenue from services		53,250
Rent expense		10,800
Advertising expense	640	
Totals	$62,330	$69,815

Exercise 2–8
Analyzing account entries and balances
(L. O. 1, 2)

a. During the month of July, Ray Company had cash receipts of $12,000 and cash disbursements of $13,500. The July 31 cash balance was $4,200. Calculate the beginning (June 30) cash balance.

b. On June 30, Ray Company had an Accounts Receivable balance of $26,000. During the month of July, total credits to Accounts Receivable were $24,000, which resulted from customer payments. The July 31

Accounts Receivable balance was $32,000. Calculate the amount of credit sales during July.

c. Earl Ray, the owner of Ray Company, had a capital account balance of $57,500 on June 30 and $74,000 on July 31. Net income for the month of July was $18,000. Calculate the owner's withdrawals during July.

Exercise 2–9
Analyzing transactions from T-accounts
(L. O. 2, 3)

The following accounts contain seven transactions keyed together with letters. Write a short explanation of each transaction with the amount or amounts involved.

Cash					Office Equipment				Bill Edwards, Capital	
(a)	7,500	(b)	2,475	(d)	11,250				(a)	12,000
(e)	450	(c)	75							
		(f)	3,750							
		(g)	90							

Office Supplies			Law Library			Legal Fees Earned		
(c)	75		(a)	4,500			(e)	450
(d)	50							

Prepaid Rent			Accounts Payable				Utilities Expense	
(b)	2,475		(f)	3,750	(d)	11,300	(g)	90

Exercise 2–10
General journal entries
(L. O. 1, 3, 5)

Prepare a form like Illustration 2–6 and then prepare general journal entries to record the following transactions. Omit the year in the journal date column.

May 1 Jeff Sims invested $3,000 in cash and an automobile having a $15,000 fair value in a real estate agency he called Sims Realty.

 1 Rented furnished office space and paid two months' rent in advance, $1,500.

 2 Purchased office supplies for cash, $90.

 15 Sold a building lot for a client and collected a $3,750 commission on the sale.

 31 Paid for gas and oil used in the agency car during May, $60.

Exercise 2–11
T-accounts and the trial balance
(L. O. 1, 3, 5)

1. Open T-accounts for each of the following items: Cash; Prepaid Rent; Office Supplies; Automobile; Jeff Sims, Capital; Commissions Earned; and Gas and Oil Expense.

2. Post the transactions of Exercise 2–10 to the T-accounts. Omit posting reference numbers.

3. Prepare a trial balance of the T-accounts.

Exercise 2–12
Analyzing and journalizing revenue transactions
(L. O. 1, 5)

Examine each of the following transactions and prepare general journal entries to record only the revenue transactions. Explain why the remaining transactions are not revenue transactions.

a. Received $800 cash for consulting services provided to customer.

b. Received $2,000 cash from Karen Smith, the owner of the business.

c. Received $500 from a customer in partial payment of his account receivable.

d. Rendered consulting services to a customer on credit, $700.

e. Borrowed $4,000 from the bank by signing a promissory note.

f. Received $1,000 from a customer in payment for services to be rendered next year.

Exercise 2–13
Analyzing and journalizing expense transactions
(L. O. 1, 5)

Examine each of the following transactions and prepare general journal entries to record only the expense transactions. Explain why the remaining transactions are not expense transactions.

a. Paid $1,000 cash for store equipment.

b. Paid $1,400 in partial payment for supplies purchased 30 days previously.

c. Paid utility bill of $640.

d. Paid $1,200 to owner of the business for his personal use.

e. Paid $1,600 salary of office employee.

Problems

Problem 2–1
Recording transactions in T-accounts; preparing a trial balance
(L. O. 3, 4, 5)

Carol Blake opened a real estate business and during a short period as an agent completed these business transactions:

a. Invested $42,000 in cash and office equipment with a $6,000 fair value in a real estate agency she called Blake Realty.

b. Purchased land valued at $30,000 and a small office building valued at $105,000, paying $35,000 cash and signing a note payable to pay the balance over a period of years.

c. Purchased office supplies on credit, $60.

d. Carol Blake contributed her personal automobile, which had a $7,200 fair value, for exclusive use in the business.

e. Purchased additional office equipment on credit, $720.

f. Paid the office secretary's salary, $600.

g. Sold a house and collected an $8,500 cash commission on the sale.

h. Paid $150 for newspaper advertising that had appeared.

i. Paid for the supplies purchased on credit in transaction (c).

j. Purchased a new typewriter for the business, paying $840 cash plus an old typewriter carried in the accounting records at $140.

k. Completed a real estate appraisal on credit and billed the client $210 for the appraisal.

l. Paid the secretary's salary, $600.

m. Received payment in full for the appraisal of transaction (k).

n. Carol Blake withdrew $1,500 from the business to pay personal expenses.

Required

1. Open the following T-accounts: Cash; Accounts Receivable; Office Supplies; Office Equipment; Automobile; Land; Building; Accounts Payable; Notes Payable; Carol Blake, Capital; Carol Blake, Withdrawals; Commissions Earned; Appraisal Fees Earned; Office Salaries Expense; and Advertising Expense.

2. Record the transactions by entering debits and credits directly in the accounts. Use the transaction letters to identify each debit and credit amount.

3. Determine the balance of each account in the ledger and prepare a trial balance using the current date and the title Blake, Realty.

Problem 2–2
Posting from general journal entries; preparing a trial balance
(L. O. 5)

Jack Fish, Public Accountant, completed these transactions during September of the current year:

Sept. 1   Began a public accounting practice by investing $4,200 in cash and office equipment having a $4,800 fair value.
       1   Prepaid two months' rent in advance on suitable office space, $1,800.
       2   Purchased on credit office equipment, $420, and office supplies, $75.
       4   Completed accounting work for a client and immediately received payment of $180 cash.
       8   Completed accounting work on credit for Frontier Bank, $700.
       10 Paid for the items purchased on credit on September 2.
       14 Paid the annual $750 premium on an insurance policy.
       18 Received payment in full from Frontier Bank for the work completed on September 8.
       24 Completed accounting work on credit for Travis Realty, $500.
       28 Jack Fish withdrew $300 cash from the practice to pay personal expenses.
       29 Purchased additional office supplies on credit, $45.
       30 Paid the September utility bills, $165.

Required

1. Open the following accounts: Cash; Accounts Receivable; Office Supplies; Prepaid Insurance; Prepaid Rent; Office Equipment; Accounts Payable; Jack Fish, Capital; Jack Fish, Withdrawals; Accounting Fees Earned; and Utilities Expense.

2. Prepare general journal entries to record the transactions.

3. Post to the accounts.

4. Prepare a trial balance. Title the trial balance Jack Fish, Public Accountant.

Problem 2–3
Recording transactions in T-accounts; preparing a trial balance
(L. O. 3, 5)

Wayne Seale began business as an excavating contractor and during a short period completed these transactions:

a. Began business by investing cash, $18,000; office equipment, $1,500; and machinery, $51,000.

b. Purchased land for an office site and for parking machinery, $21,000. Paid $6,500 in cash and signed a promissory note payable for the balance.

c. Purchased for cash a used prefabricated building and moved it onto the land for use as an office, $6,000.

d. Prepaid the annual premium on two insurance policies, $875.

e. Completed an excavating job and collected $1,050 cash in full payment.

f. Purchased additional machinery costing $8,150. Gave $2,150 in cash and signed a note payable for the balance.

g. Completed an excavating job on credit for Northern Contractors, $1,500.

h. Purchased additional office equipment on credit, $450.

i. Completed an excavating job for Valley Contractors on credit, $1,150.

j. Received and recorded as an account payable a bill for rent on a special machine used on the Valley Contractors job, $200.

k. Received $1,500 from Northern Contractors for the work of transaction (g).

l. Paid the wages of the machinery operator, $1,050.

m. Paid for the office equipment purchased in transaction (h).

n. Paid $150 cash for repairs to a machine.

o. Wayne Seale wrote a $75 cheque on the bank account of the business to pay for repairs to his personal automobile. (The car is not used for business purposes.)

p. Paid the wages of the machinery operator, $1,100.

q. Paid for gas and oil that had been used by the excavating machinery, $250.

Required

1. Open the following T-accounts: Cash; Accounts Receivable; Prepaid Insurance; Office Equipment; Machinery; Building; Land; Accounts Payable; Notes Payable; Wayne Seale, Capital; Wayne Seale, Withdrawals; Excavating Revenue; Machinery Repairs Expense; Wages Expense; Machinery Rentals Expense; and Gas and Oil Expense.

2. Record the transactions by entering debits and credits directly in the accounts. Use the transaction letters to identify each debit and credit. Prepare a trial balance using the current date and the title Wayne Seale, Contractor.

Problem 2–4
Journalizing, posting, and preparing a trial balance
(L. O. 5)

Paula Hill completed these transactions during June of the current year:

June 1 Began an architectural practice by investing cash, $5,500; drafting supplies, $200; and office and drafting equipment, $4,500.

      1 Prepaid two months' rent in advance on suitable office space, $1,500.

      3 Paid the annual premium on an insurance policy taken out in the name of the practice, $675.

June 4 Purchased drafting equipment, $575, and drafting supplies, $45, on credit.
      9 Delivered a set of plans to a contractor and collected $600 cash in full payment.
     15 Paid the draftsman's salary, $780.
     16 Completed and delivered a set of plans to Carver Contractors on credit, $850.
     18 Purchased drafting supplies on credit, $50.
     19 Paid for the equipment and supplies purchased on June 4.
     26 Received $850 from Carver Contractors for the plans delivered on June 16.
     27 Paula Hill withdrew $250 from the practice for personal use.
     28 Paid for the supplies purchased on June 18.
     29 Completed architectural work for Blake Realty on credit, $600.
     30 Paid the draftsman's salary, $780.
     30 Paid the June utility bill, $140.
     30 Paid the blueprinting expenses incurred in June, $105.

Required

1. Open the following accounts: Cash; Accounts Receivable; Prepaid Rent; Prepaid Insurance; Drafting Supplies; Office and Drafting Equipment; Accounts Payable; Paula Hill, Capital; Paula Hill, Withdrawals; Architectural Fees Earned; Salaries Expense; Blueprinting Expense; and Utilities Expense.

2. Prepare and post general journal entries to record the transactions. Prepare a trial balance, titling it Paula Hill, Architect.

Problem 2–5
Journalizing, posting, and preparing financial statements
(L. O. 5)

Amy Tuck completed these transactions during April of the current year:

Apr. 1 Began a new law practice by investing $3,000 in cash and law books having a $1,500 fair value.
      1 Rented the furnished office of a lawyer who was retiring because of illness, and paid the rent (expense) for April, $600.
      1 Took out a liability insurance policy giving one year's protection and paid the premium (expense) for the month of April, $45.
      3 Purchased office supplies on credit, $50.
      9 Completed legal work for a client and immediately collected $300 cash for the work.
     13 Paid for the office supplies purchased on April 3.
     16 Completed legal work for Knox Realty on credit, $1,000.
     23 Completed legal work for National Bank on credit, $900.
     26 Received $1,000 from Knox Realty for the work completed on April 16.
     28 Amy Tuck wrote a $20 cheque on the bank account of the legal practice to pay her home telephone bill.
     29 Purchased additional office supplies on credit, $54.
     30 Paid the April telephone bill of the office, $30.
     30 Paid the salary of the office secretary, $1,150.

Apr. 30   Prepaid the rent on the office for May and June, $1,200.

    30   Prepaid the liability insurance premium for the next 11 months, $495.

Required

1. Open the following accounts: Cash; Accounts Receivable; Prepaid Rent; Prepaid Insurance; Office Supplies; Law Library; Accounts Payable; Amy Tuck, Capital; Amy Tuck, Withdrawals; Legal Fees Earned; Rent Expense; Salaries Expense; Telephone Expense; and Insurance Expense.

2. Prepare general journal entries to record the transactions, post to the accounts, and prepare a trial balance titled Amy Tuck, Lawyer.

3. Prepare an income statement for the month ended April 30.

4. Prepare a statement of changes in owner's equity for the month ended April 30.

5. Prepare a balance sheet dated April 30.

Alternate Problems

Problem 2–1A
Recording transactions in T-accounts; preparing a trial balance
(L. O. 3, 4, 5)

Carol Blake completed these transactions during a short period:

a. Opened a real estate agency by investing the following assets at their fair values: cash, $4,000; office equipment, $4,500; automobile, $8,000; land, $37,500; and building, $112,500. The business should also assume responsibility for a $90,000 promissory note that was given to the bank to finance the purchase of the land and building.

b. Purchased office supplies, $90, and additional office equipment, $525, on credit.

c. Collected a $9,500 commission from the sale of property for a client.

d. Purchased additional office equipment on credit, $630.

e. Paid for advertising that had appeared in the local paper, $190.

f. Traded the agency's automobile and $7,000 in cash for a new automobile.

g. Paid the office secretary's salary, $785.

h. Paid for the supplies and equipment purchased in transaction (b).

i. Completed a real estate appraisal for a client on credit, $265.

j. Collected a $3,750 commission from the sale of a building lot for a client.

k. The client of transaction (i) paid $115 of the amount owed.

l. Paid the secretary's salary, $785.

m. Paid $175 for newspaper advertising that had appeared.

n. Carol Blake withdrew $2,500 from the business for personal use.

Required

1. Open the following T-accounts: Cash; Accounts Receivable; Office Supplies; Office Equipment; Automobile; Land; Building; Accounts Paya-

ble; Notes Payable; Carol Blake, Capital; Carol Blake, Withdrawals; Commissions Earned; Appraisal Fees Earned; Office Salaries Expense; and Advertising Expense.

2. Record the transactions by entering debits and credits directly in the accounts. Use the transaction letters to identify the amounts in the accounts.

3. Determine the balance of each account in the ledger and prepare a trial balance using the current date and the title Blake Realty.

Problem 2–2A
Posting from general journal entries; preparing a trial balance
(L. O. 5)

Jack Fish began a public accounting practice and completed these transactions during April of the current year:

Apr. 1   Invested $7,000 in a public accounting practice begun this day.
      1   Rented suitable office space and prepaid two months' rent in advance, $2,400.
      2   Purchased office supplies, $95, and office equipment, $5,650, on credit.
      4   Paid the annual premium on a liability insurance policy, $650.
      6   Completed accounting work for a client and immediately collected $265 in cash for the work done.
     12   Completed accounting work for Heritage Bank on credit, $675.
     16   Purchased additional office supplies on credit, $55.
     22   Received $675 from Heritage Bank for the work completed on April 12.
     25   Jack Fish withdrew $375 from the accounting practice to pay personal expenses.
     29   Completed accounting work for Blake Realty on credit, $525.
     30   Made an installment payment of $1,245 on the equipment and supplies purchased on April 2.
     30   Paid the April utility bills of the accounting practice, $150.

Required

1. Open the following accounts: Cash; Accounts Receivable; Office Supplies; Prepaid Insurance; Prepaid Rent; Office Equipment; Accounts Payable; Jack Fish, Capital; Jack Fish, Withdrawals; Accounting Fees Earned; and Utilities Expense.

2. Prepare general journal entries to record the transactions.

3. Post to the accounts.

4. Prepare a trial balance titled Jack Fish, Public Accountant.

Problem 2–3A
Recording transactions in T-accounts; preparing a trial balance
(L. O. 3, 5)

Wayne Seale completed these transactions during a short period:

a. Began business as an excavating contractor by investing cash, $37,500; office equipment, $2,200; and excavating machinery, $67,500.

b. Purchased for $37,500 land to be used as an office site and for parking equipment. Paid $15,000 in cash and signed a promissory note payable for the balance.

c. Purchased additional excavating machinery costing $32,650. Paid $10,150 in cash and signed a promissory note payable for the balance.

d. Paid $6,700 cash for a used prefabricated building and moved it on the land for use as an office.

e. Completed an excavating job and immediately collected $1,275 in cash for the work.

f. Prepaid the premium on an insurance policy giving one year's protection, $960.

g. Completed an $1,875 excavating job for City-Wide Contractors on credit.

h. Paid the wages of the equipment operator, $1,200.

i. Paid $250 cash for repairs to excavating machinery.

j. Received $1,875 from City-Wide Contractors for the work of transaction (g).

k. Completed a $1,200 excavating job for SMK Contractors on credit.

l. Received and recorded as an account payable a $165 bill for the rent of a special machine used on the SMK Contractors job.

m. Purchased additional office equipment on credit, $790.

n. Wayne Seale withdrew $750 from the business for personal use.

o. Paid the wages of the equipment operator, $1,350.

p. Paid the $165 account payable resulting from renting the machine of transaction (l).

q. Paid for gas and oil consumed by the excavating machinery, $335.

Required

1. Open the following T-accounts: Cash; Accounts Receivable; Prepaid Insurance; Office Equipment; Machinery; Building; Land; Accounts Payable; Notes Payable; Wayne Seale, Capital; Wayne Seale, Withdrawals; Excavating Revenue; Machinery Repairs Expense; Wages Expense; Machinery Rentals Expense; and Gas and Oil Expense.

2. Record the transactions by entering debits and credits directly in the accounts. Use the transaction letters to identify each debit and credit. Prepare a trial balance using the current date and headed Wayne Seale, Contractor.

Problem 2–4A
Journalizing, posting, and preparing a trial balance
(L. O. 5)

Paula Hill completed these transactions during May of the current year:

May 1   Began an architectural practice by opening a bank account in the name of the practice, Paula Hill, Architect, and deposited $7,500 therein.

1   Rented suitable office space and prepaid two months' rent in advance, $1,500.

2   Purchased for $7,125 office and drafting equipment under an agreement calling for a $1,125 down payment and the balance in monthly installments. Paid the down payment and recorded the account payable.

May   4   Purchased drafting supplies for cash, $265.
       8   Completed and delivered a set of plans to a contractor and immediately received $785 cash in full payment.
      12   Paid the annual premium on a liability insurance policy, $720.
      14   Purchased on credit additional drafting supplies, $55, and drafting equipment, $175.
      15   Paid the salary of the draftsman, $825.
      17   Completed and delivered a set of plans to Valley Developers on credit, $1,800.
      21   Paid in full for the supplies and equipment purchased on May 14.
      25   Completed additional architectural work for Valley Developers on credit, $1,800.
      27   Received $1,800 from Valley Developers for the plans delivered on May 17.
      28   Paula Hill withdrew $300 cash from the practice to pay personal expenses.
      31   Paid the salary of the draftsman, $825.
      31   Paid the May utility bills, $120.
      31   Paid $200 cash for blueprinting expense.

Required

1. Open the following accounts: Cash; Accounts Receivable; Prepaid Rent; Prepaid Insurance; Drafting Supplies; Office and Drafting Equipment; Accounts Payable; Paula Hill, Capital; Paula Hill, Withdrawals; Architectural Fees Earned; Salaries Expense; Blueprinting Expense; and Utilities Expense.
2. Prepare general journal entries to record the transactions, post to the accounts, and prepare a trial balance.

Problem 2–5A
Journalizing, posting, and preparing financial statements
(L. O. 5)

Amy Tuck graduated from law school with a law degree in June of the current year, and during July, she completed these transactions:

July 1   Began the practice of law by investing $3,000 in cash and law books acquired in school and having a $1,200 fair value.
      1   Rented the furnished office of a lawyer who was retiring and paid the rent (expense) for July, $725.
      2   Purchased law books costing $1,125 under an agreement calling for a $150 down payment and the balance in monthly installments. Paid the down payment and recorded the remaining $975 as an account payable.
      5   Purchased office supplies on credit, $70.
      6   Took out a liability insurance policy giving one year's protection and paid the premium (expense) for the month of July, $50.
      8   Completed legal work for a client and immediately collected $450 for the work done.
      12   Paid for the office supplies purchased on credit on July 5.
      16   Completed legal work for York Bank on credit, $1,275.
      22   Amy Tuck wrote a $30 cheque on the bank account of the legal practice to pay her home telephone bill.

July 24 Received $1,275 from York Bank for the work completed July 16.
    26 Completed legal work for Royal Realty on credit, $900.
    30 Paid the telephone bill of the legal practice, $40.
    31 Paid the salary of the office secretary, $1,350.
    31 Prepaid the rent on the office for August and September, $1,450.
    31 Prepaid the liability insurance premium for the next 11 months, $550.

Required

1. Open the following accounts: Cash; Accounts Receivable; Prepaid Rent; Prepaid Insurance; Office Supplies; Law Library; Accounts Payable; Amy Tuck, Capital; Amy Tuck, Withdrawals; Legal Fees Earned; Rent Expense; Salaries Expense; Telephone Expense; and Insurance Expense.

2. Prepare general journal entries to record the transactions, post to the accounts, and prepare a trial balance titled Amy Tuck, Lawyer.

3. Prepare an income statement for the month ended July 31.

4. Prepare a statement of changes in owner's equity for the month ended July 31.

5. Prepare a balance sheet dated July 31.

Provocative Problems

Provocative Problem 2–1
Barry Holk, Consultant
(L. O. 1)

Barry Holk operates an engineering consulting business. Through the month of February, the accounting records for the business had been maintained by a public accountant. Those records showed that Holk's February 28 capital balance was $44,600. However, Holk believed that the public accountant had overcharged for his work in the past. As a result, Holk decided to keep his own records. At the end of March, he prepared the statements shown below. He was shocked to discover how unprofitable his business had become, and asked you to review the statements. You should prepare new financial statements including a statement of changes in owner's equity.

BARRY HOLK, CONSULTANT
Income Statement
For Month Ended March 31, 19—

Revenues:		
Unearned consulting fees		$12,000
Investments by owner		1,000
Total revenues		$13,000
Operating expenses:		
Rent expense.	$1,000	
Telephone expense	800	
Technical library	3,500	
Utilities expense	700	
Withdrawals by owner	5,000	
Travel and customer entertainment	4,400	
Insurance expense	200	
Total operating expenses		15,600
Net income (loss)		$(2,600)

BARRY HOLK, CONSULTANT
Balance Sheet
March 31, 19—

Assets		Liabilities	
Cash	$ 5,600	Accounts payable	$ 1,400
Accounts receivable	8,800	Consulting fees earned	21,700
Prepaid rent	3,000	Notes payable	25,000
Prepaid insurance	1,200	Total liabilities	$48,100
Office supplies	500		
Land	18,000	**Owner's Equity**	
Buildings	47,000	Barry Holk, capital	42,000
Salary payments	6,000	Total liabilities and	
Total assets	$90,100	owner's equity	$90,100

Provocative Problem 2–2
DeShazo's Tennis Camp
(L. O. 1, 3, 5)

Scott DeShazo opened a new business as a tennis instructor and completed a number of transactions during May, the first month of operation. He recorded all transactions with double entries in just two accounts, Cash and "Income." At the end of the first month, he asks you to review his records and improve his ledger. Based on the following information, you should present a compound general journal entry dated May 31 to show your corrections and improvements.

Cash   Account No. 111

Date		Explanation	PR	Debit		Credit		Balance	
May	1	Investment by owner	G1	3,000	00			3,000	00
	1	Purchased tennis supplies	G1			400	00	2,600	00
	1	Purchased ball machine	G1			2,400	00	200	00
	5	Signed note payable to bank	G1	2,500	00			2,700	00
	11	Paid for May rental of courts	G1			800	00	1,900	00
	14	Received cash for lessons given	G1	1,600	00			3,500	00
	14	Paid wages of assistants	G1			700	00	2,800	00
	27	Received cash for June lessons	G1	1,000	00			3,800	00
	28	Purchased tennis supplies	G1			200	00	3,600	00
	29	Received cash for lessons given	G1	2,300	00			5,900	00
	29	Paid wages of assistants	G1			750	00	5,150	00
	30	Withdrew cash for personal use	G1			900	00	4,250	00

Date		Explanation	PR	Debit		Credit		Balance	
May	1		G1			3,000	00	3,000	00
	1		G1	400	00			2,600	00
	1		G1	2,400	00			200	00
	5		G1			2,500	00	2,700	00
	11		G1	800	00			1,900	00
	14		G1			1,600	00	3,500	00
	14		G1	700	00			2,800	00
	27		G1			1,000	00	3,800	00
	28		G1	200	00			3,600	00
	29		G1			2,300	00	5,900	00
	29		G1	750	00			5,150	00
	30		G1	900	00			4,250	00

Income — Account No. 411

Provocative Problem 2–3
Boats and Grub
(L. O. 3, 5)

Karen Harris, a graduate student, has just completed the first summer's operation of a concession on Green Lake, at which she rents boats and sells sandwiches, soft drinks, and candy. She began the summer's operation with $7,000 in cash and a five-year lease on a boat dock and a small concession building on the lake. The lease requires a $1,200 annual rental, although the concession is open only from June 1 through August 31. On opening day, Karen paid the first year's rent and purchased three boats at $1,250 each, paying cash.

During the summer, she purchased food, soft drinks, and candy costing $6,400, all of which was paid for by summer's end, excepting food costing $340 that was purchased during the last week's operation. By summer's end, she had paid electric bills, $430, and wages of a part-time helper, $1,200. She had also withdrawn $125 of earnings of the concession each week for 12 weeks for personal expenses.

She took in $3,100 in boat rentals during the summer and sold $13,600 of food and drinks, all of which was collected in cash, except $235 owed by Lax Company for food and drinks for an employees' picnic.

On August 31, when she closed for the summer, Karen was able to return to the soft drink company several cases of soft drinks for which she received a $75 cash refund. However, she had to take home for personal consumption a number of candy bars and soft drinks that cost $50 and could have been sold for $100. She then sold the three boats to a used boat dealer for $500 each.

Prepare an income statement showing the results of the summer's operations, a statement of changes in owner's equity, and an August 31 balance sheet. Head the statements Boats and Grub. (T-accounts may be helpful in organizing the data.)

Provocative Problem 2–4
Clay's Lawn Service
(L. O. 3, 5)

Upon graduation from high school last summer, Clay Stocks needed a job to earn a portion of his first-year college expenses. He was unable to find anything satisfactory and decided to go into the lawn-care business. He had $1,450 in a savings account that he used to buy a lawn mower and other lawn-care tools. However, to haul the tools from job to job, he needed a truck. Consequently, he borrowed $2,800 from a bank by signing a promissory note that had an interest rate of 1% per month in exchange for a secondhand truck.

From the beginning, he had as much work as he could do, and after two months, he repaid the bank loan plus two months' interest. On August 28, he ended the business after exactly three months' operations. Throughout the summer, he followed the practice of depositing in the bank all cash received from customers. An examination of his chequebook record showed he had deposited $4,350. He had written cheques to pay $180 for gas, oil, and lubricants used in the truck and mower and a $65 cheque for mower repairs. A notebook in the truck contained copies of credit card tickets that showed the business owed $90 for additional gas and oil used in the truck and mower. The notebook also showed that customers owed Clay $260 for lawn-care services. He decided to give his lawn-care equipment to his parents, and estimated it had a fair value of $500. He received a good offer on the truck and sold it for $3,100. Under the assumption that Clay had withdrawn $600 from the business during the summer for spending money and to buy clothes, prepare an income statement showing the results of the summer's operations. Also prepare a statement of changes in owner's equity and an August 28 balance sheet. Head the statements Clay's Lawn Service. (T-accounts should be helpful in organizing the data.)

Analytical and Review Problems

A&R Problem 2–1

Mary Senn just dismissed her inexperienced bookkeeper and asked you to help out until she finds a replacement. Since you had a few days before your Florida winter break, you agreed to see Senn through a proper trial balance. Senn was grateful for your offer and turned over all the accounting records. You found that the trial balance prepared by the bookkeeper (shown below) was nothing more than a listing of account balances.

SENN COMPANY
Trial Balance
December 31, 199A

Cash	$ 2,960
Accounts receivable.	2,040
Equipment	6,000
Prepaid rent	2,400
Accounts payable	1,120
M. Senn, capital	12,000
M. Senn, withdrawals	1,440
Service revenue	18,000
Salaries expense	14,000
Insurance expense	2,000
Miscellaneous expenses	360
Total	$62,320

After classifying the accounts into debit and credit balances, you found that the trial balance did not balance. Consequently, you proceeded to examine the accounting records. In searching back through the accounting records, you discovered that the accounts as listed had normal balances and that the following errors were made by the bookkeeper.

a. An entire entry was not posted. It included a debit to Cash and a credit to Accounts Receivable for $220.

b. In computing the balance of Accounts Payable, a credit of $100 was omitted from the computation.

c. In copying Senn's Capital account, the bookkeeper entered $12,000 instead of $12,100, the correct amount in the ledger.

d. A withdrawal of $60 by Senn was posted as a credit to Senn's withdrawal account.

e. Equipment of $200 was debited to Prepaid Rent when purchased.

Required

Prepare a corrected trial balance for the Senn Company as of December 31, 199A.

A&R Problem 2–2

The following T-accounts show the October transactions of Cindy Etsell's service business which was organized on the first day of October this year. Since the bookkeeper is very inexperienced, some dates and amounts are missing.

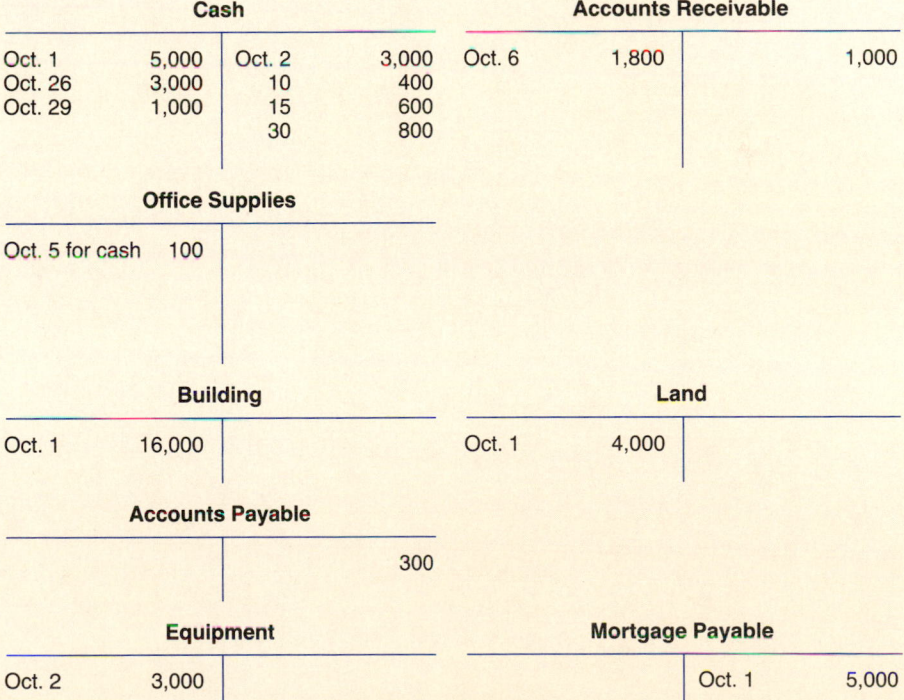

	Cash				Accounts Receivable	
Oct. 1	5,000	Oct. 2	3,000	Oct. 6	1,800	1,000
Oct. 26	3,000	10	400			
Oct. 29	1,000	15	600			
		30	800			

Office Supplies	
Oct. 5 for cash 100	

	Building			Land	
Oct. 1	16,000		Oct. 1	4,000	

Accounts Payable	
	300

Equipment			Mortgage Payable	
Oct. 2	3,000		Oct. 1	5,000

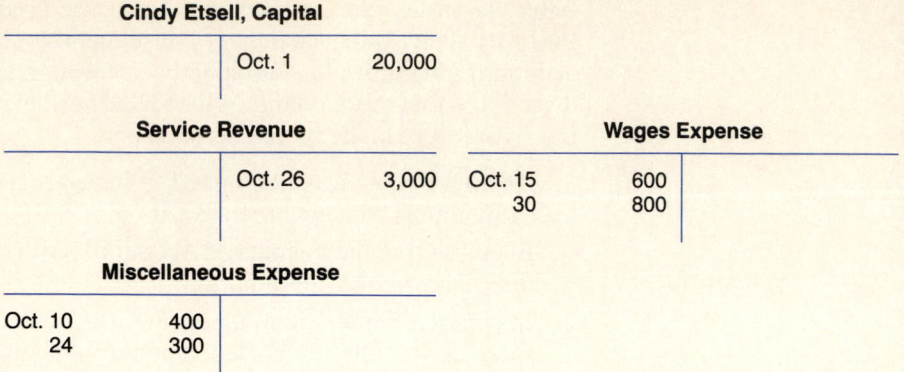

Cindy Etsell, Capital

| | | Oct. 1 | 20,000 |

Service Revenue

| | | Oct. 26 | 3,000 |

Wages Expense

| Oct. 15 | 600 | | |
| 30 | 800 | | |

Miscellaneous Expense

| Oct. 10 | 400 | | |
| 24 | 300 | | |

Required

1. Prepare journal entries (omit narratives) to reconstruct all transactions for the month of October.
2. Identify the missing data.

3 Adjusting the Accounts and Preparing the Statements

At the beginning of Chapter 2, we recognized that an entity's accounting equation is affected by business transactions and by other (internal) economic events. The primary focus of Chapter 2 was to teach you the double-entry process of recording the effects of business transactions. This process involves journalizing the transactions in a book of original entry and then posting to the accounts. In studying Chapter 3, you will learn that some of the account balances which result from recording business transactions must be adjusted. These adjustments are recorded so that the entity's internal economic events will be reflected in the account balances.

Learning Objectives

After studying Chapter 3, you should be able to:

1. Explain why the life of a business is divided into accounting periods of equal length and why the accounts of a business must be adjusted at the end of each accounting period.

2. Prepare adjusting entries for prepaid expenses, accrued expenses, unearned revenues, accrued revenues, and depreciation.

3. Explain the difference between the cash and accrual bases of accounting.

4. Prepare entries to record cash receipts and cash disbursements of items that were recorded at the end of the previous period as accrued revenues and accrued expenses.

5. Define each asset and liability classification appearing on a balance sheet, classify balance sheet items, and prepare a classified balance sheet.

6. Define or explain the words and phrases listed in the chapter Glossary.

After studying the appendix to Chapter 3 (Appendix A), you should be able to:

7. Explain why some companies record prepaid and unearned items in income statement accounts and prepare adjusting entries when this procedure is used.

Explain why the life of a
business is divided into
accounting periods of
equal length and why the
accounts of a business
must be adjusted at the
end of each accounting
period.
(L. O. 1)

The life of a business often spans many years, during which its activities go on without interruption. However, decision makers such as managers and investors cannot wait for the business to conclude its operations before they evaluate its financial progress. Instead, they expect a business to provide financial reports periodically. To accomplish this, the accounting process is based on a **time-period concept**. In other words, the activities of a business are identified as occurring during specific time periods such as months, or three-month periods, or years. Then, financial reports that show the results of operations are prepared for each period. Since this division of the life of a business into time periods is done for accounting purposes, the time periods are called **accounting periods**. The primary accounting period used by most businesses is one year, for which they prepare annual financial statements. However, businesses also prepare **interim financial reports** based on one-month or three-month accounting periods.

Businesses do not always adopt the calendar year ending December 31 as the annual accounting period. They may adopt a period of any 12 consecutive months. The specific 12-month period that a business adopts as its annual accounting period is called the **fiscal year** of the business. In choosing a fiscal year, businesses that do not have much seasonal fluctuation in their sales volume often choose the calendar year. Those that have wide fluctuations in volume tend to choose their **natural business year**, which ends when inventories are at their lowest point and business activities are at their lowest ebb. For example, in department stores, the natural business year begins on February 1, after the Christmas and January sales, and ends the following January 31. Therefore, the annual accounting periods of department stores commonly begin on February 1 and end the following January 31.

Need for Adjustments at the End of an Accounting Period

At the end of an accounting period, after all transactions are recorded, several of the accounts in a company's ledger typically do not show proper end-of-period balances for presentation in the financial statements. This occurs even though all transactions were recorded correctly. The balances are incorrect for statement purposes, not through error, but because internal economic events have occurred and have not yet been recorded. One event of this type involves costs that expire with the passage of time. For example, the second item on the trial balance of Dow's law practice, as prepared in Chapter 2 and reproduced again as Illustration 3–1, is "Prepaid insurance, $2,400." This $2,400 represents the insurance premium for two years. The insurance protection began on December 1. However, by December 31, $2,400 is not the correct balance sheet account for this asset. During December, one month's insurance ($2,400 ÷ 24 = $100) expired and became an expense. Only $2,300, or ($2,400 − $100), remains as an asset. Likewise, the $120 balance in Office Supplies includes the cost of some supplies that have been used up and become an expense during December. Also, the items in the law library have a limited useful life and part of their usefulness expired during December. Therefore, part of the $2,880 cost of the law library should be reported as expense during December. Furthermore, the office equipment has begun to wear out. Because of these events, the balances of the Prepaid Insurance, Office Supplies, Law Library, and Office Equipment accounts are not the proper amounts to

JERRY DOW, LAWYER
Trial Balance
December 31, 1990

Cash	$ 650	
Prepaid insurance	2,400	
Office supplies	120	
Law library	2,880	
Office equipment	6,880	
Accounts payable		$ 760
Unearned legal fees		3,000
Jerry Dow, capital		9,000
Jerry Dow, withdrawals	1,100	
Legal fees earned		3,900
Rent expense	1,000	
Salaries expense	1,400	
Utilities expense	230	
Totals	$16,660	$16,660

appear on the December 31 balance sheet. These items must be *adjusted* before financial statements are prepared.

Some of the other accounts in the trial balance of Dow's law practice also must be adjusted before financial statements are prepared. They include Office Salaries Expense, Unearned Legal Fees, and Legal Fees Earned.

Adjusting the Accounts

Prepare adjusting entries for prepaid expenses, accrued expenses, unearned revenues, accrued revenues, and depreciation.
(L. O. 2)

The process of adjusting the accounts is essentially the same as the process of analyzing and recording business transactions. Each account balance and the economic events that affect that account are analyzed to determine whether an adjustment is needed. If an adjustment is required, an **adjusting entry** is prepared to correct the asset or liability account and to correct the related expense or revenue account. After the adjusting entries are journalized, they are posted to the accounts. In the following paragraphs, we will explain why adjusting entries are needed to account for prepaid expenses, **depreciation**, **accrued expenses**, unearned revenues, and **accrued revenues**

Prepaid Expenses

As the name implies, a prepaid expense is an economic benefit that has been paid for in advance of its use. At the time of payment, an asset is acquired that will expire or be used up, and as it is used up, it becomes an expense.

For example, during December, the Dow law practice paid a $2,400 premium for liability insurance protection that would last for two years. Although the payment was made on December 26, the policy went into effect on December 1. As each day of December went by, the benefit of insurance protection expired, and a portion of the prepaid insurance became an expense. On December 31, one month's insurance, valued at 1/24 of $2,400, or $100, had expired. Therefore, the following adjusting entry is required so that the accounts will reflect proper asset and expense amounts on December 31:

		Adjustment (a)		
Dec.	31	Insurance Expense.	100.00	
		Prepaid Insurance		100.00
		To record the expired insurance.		

Posting the adjusting entry has the following effect on the accounts:

Prepaid Insurance				Insurance Expense		
Dec. 26	2,400	Dec. 31	100	Dec. 31	100	

After the entry is posted, the Prepaid Insurance account with a $2,300 balance and the Insurance Expense account with a $100 balance show proper statement amounts.

The allocation of the insurance premium cost to December 1990, to 1991, and to 1992 is shown graphically in Illustration 3–2. In looking at this illustration, you should recognize the adjusting entries will be required to allocate $1,200, or ($2,400 ÷ 24) × 12, to 1991, and to allocate $1,100, or ($2,400 ÷ 24) × 11, to 1992.

To continue, during December, the Dow law practice purchased some office supplies and placed them in the office for use. In the following days, the secretary used some of the supplies. The amount used up was an expense that reduced the supplies on hand. However, the daily reductions were not recognized in the accounts because day-by-day information about amounts used and remaining was not needed. Also, labor is saved by recording only a single amount, the total of all supplies used during the month.

Therefore, for the accounts to reflect proper statement amounts on December 31, the dollar amount of office supplies used during the month must be determined and recorded. To learn the amount used, you must count, or "take an inventory of," the unused supplies remaining. Then, the cost of the remaining supplies is deducted from the cost of the supplies purchased. If, for example, $75 of unused supplies remain, then $45 ($120 − $75 = $45) of supplies were used and became an expense. The following adjusting entry is required to record the using up of the supplies:

		Adjustment (b)		
Dec.	31	Office Supplies Expense	45.00	
		Office Supplies		45.00
		To record the supplies used.		

The effect of the adjusting entry on the accounts is:

Office Supplies				Office Supplies Expense		
Dec. 26	120	Dec. 31	45	Dec. 31	45	

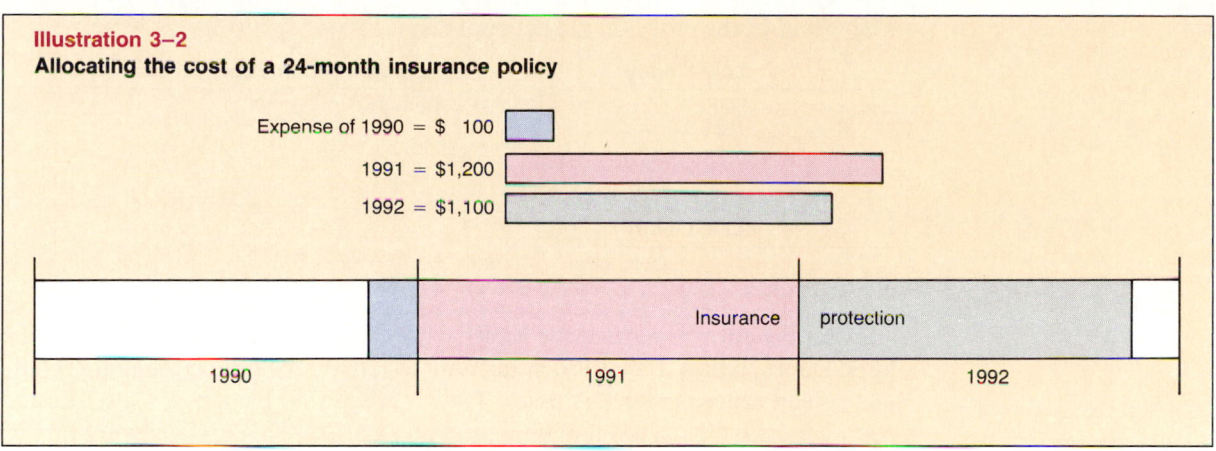

Illustration 3–2
Allocating the cost of a 24-month insurance policy

Expense of 1990 = $ 100
1991 = $1,200
1992 = $1,100

Insurance   protection

1990   1991   1992

Unlike the two previous examples, some items that are prepaid expenses at the time of purchase are both bought and fully used up within a single accounting period. For example, a company might pay its rent in advance on the first day of each month. Each month, the amount paid results in a prepaid expense that fully expires before the month's end and before the end of the accounting period. In such cases, you should ignore the fact that an asset results from each prepayment because an adjustment can be avoided if each prepayment is originally recorded as an expense.

Depreciation

Tangible, long-lived assets that are held for use in the production or sale of other assets or services are called **plant and equipment.** They include assets such as land, buildings, machines, professional libraries, and automobiles. All items of plant and equipment, except for land, will eventually wear out or lose their usefulness. Therefore, the cost of these assets must be charged off to expense over their useful lives. This process of allocating the cost of these items to expense is called *depreciation*. Depreciation is recorded with adjusting entries similar to those used for prepaid expenses.

For example, the Dow law practice owns a law library that cost $2,880. Dow estimates that the items in this library will be useful for three years, beginning December 1, 1990, after which they will have to be discarded and replaced. Based on this estimate, the depreciation expense for December is calculated as $2,880 ÷ 36 months = $80. You record this expense with the following adjusting entry:

		Adjustment (c)		
Dec.	31	Depreciation Expense, Law Library	80.00	
		Accumulated Depreciation, Law Library.		80.00
		To record depreciation for December.		

The effect of the entry on the accounts is:

Law Library		Depreciation Expense, Law Library	
Dec. 2	2,500	Dec. 31	80
6	380		

Accumulated Depreciation, Law Library	
Dec. 31	80

After the entry is posted, the Law Library account and its related Accumulated Depreciation, Law Library account together show the December 31 balance sheet amounts for this asset. The Depreciation Expense, Law Library account shows the amount of depreciation expense that should appear on the December income statement.

In most cases, a decrease in an asset is recorded with a credit to the account in which the asset is recorded. However, note in the illustrated accounts that this procedure is not followed in recording depreciation. Rather, depreciation is recorded in a **contra account**, in this case the Accumulated Depreciation, Law Library account. (A contra account is an account the balance of which is subtracted from the balance of an associated account to show a more proper amount for the item recorded in the associated account.)

Why are contra accounts used to record depreciation? The reason is that depreciation entries are not supported by as much objective evidence as are most other entries. Depreciation is only an estimate. You cannot determine the amount of depreciation without estimating how long the asset will last. Contra accounts are used so that readers of a balance sheet can observe both the original cost of the asset and the estimated amount of depreciation that has been charged to expense. For example, the original cost of the law library is shown in the Law Library account to be $2,880. The $80 depreciation that has been charged to expense as of December 31, 1990, is shown in the Accumulated Depreciation, Law Library account.

Note the word *accumulated* in the title of the contra account. This emphasizes the fact that depreciation taken in all prior periods is recorded in this account. For example, if monthly financial statements are prepared for Dow's law practice, the Law Library account and its related accumulated depreciation account at the end of February 1991 will appear as follows:

Law Library		Accumulated Depreciation, Law Library	
Dec. 2	2,500	Dec. 31	80
6	380	Jan. 31	80
		Feb. 28	80

And the law library's cost and three months' **accumulated depreciation** will be shown on its February 28 balance sheet thus:

Law library	$2,880	
Less accumulated depreciation	240	$2,640

The office equipment of Dow's law practice is another type of plant and equipment that must be depreciated. Early in December, Dow made two purchases of office equipment for $5,600 and $1,280. For convenience, we will assume that all of the items purchased are estimated to have a four-year useful life. Also, Dow estimates that at the end of the four-year useful life, the business will receive $880 for the equipment as a trade-in allowance on new equipment. Therefore, the cost that will expire over the 48-month life is $6,880 − $880, or $6,000. Depreciation expense for each month may be calculated as $6,000 ÷ 48 = $125, and the entry to record depreciation for December is:

		Adjustment (d)		
Dec.	31	Depreciation Expense, Office Equipment	125.00	
		Accumulated Depreciation, Office Equipment		125.00
		To record depreciation for December.		

The effects of posting this entry to the accounts appear as follows:

Office Equipment			Depreciation Expense, Office Equipment		
Dec. 3	5,600		Dec. 31	125	
6	1,280				

Accumulated Depreciation, Office Equipment		
	Dec. 31	125

Accumulated depreciation accounts are sometimes titled *Allowance* for Depreciation. However, the word *Accumulated* is more descriptive of the depreciation procedure.

Accrued Expenses

Most expenses are recorded at the time they are paid. That is because when the cash payment is recorded, the credit to Cash is balanced by a debit to the expense account. However, at the end of an accounting period, some expenses that were incurred during the period may remain unrecorded because payment is not due. Incurred expenses that are unpaid and therefore unrecorded are called *accrued expenses*. One common example is earned but unpaid wages.

For example, the Dow law practice has a secretary who earns $70 per day or $350 per week for a week that begins on Monday and ends on Friday. The secretary's wages are due and payable every two weeks on Friday. During December, these wages were paid on the 12th and 26th and were recorded as follows:

Cash			Salaries Expense		
	Dec. 12	700	Dec. 12	700	
	26	700	26	700	

DECEMBER
S M T W T F S
1 2 3 4 5 6
7 8 9 10 11 12 13
14 15 16 17 18 19 20
21 22 23 24 25 26 27
28 29 30 31

If the calendar for December is as shown at the left and the secretary worked on December 29, 30, and 31, then at the close of business on Wednesday, December 31, the secretary has earned three days' wages that are not paid and recorded because payment is not due. However, this $210 of earned but unpaid wages is as much a part of the December expenses as the $1,400 of wages that have been paid. Also, on December 31, the unpaid wages are a liability. Therefore, for the accounts to show the correct salary expense for December and all liabilities owed on December 31, you must make an adjusting entry like the following:

		Adjustment (e)		
Dec.	31	Salaries Expense	210.00	
		Salaries Payable		210.00
		To record the accrued wages.		

The effect of the entry on the account is:

Salaries Expense			**Salaries Payable**	
Dec. 12	700		**Dec. 31**	**210**
26	700			
31	**210**			

Unearned Revenues

An unearned revenue results when payment is received for goods or services in advance of their delivery. For instance, Jerry Dow entered into an agreement with Chemical Supply to do its legal work on a fixed-fee basis of $500 per month, beginning December 15. On December 26, Dow received $3,000 in payment for providing legal services for the six-month period beginning December 15. The fee was recorded with this entry:

Dec.	26	Cash	3,000.00	
		Unearned Legal Fees		3,000.00
		Received a legal fee in advance.		

Receiving the fee in advance increased the cash of the law practice and created a liability, the obligation to do Chemical Supply's legal work for the next six months. However, by December 31, the law practice has discharged $250 of the liability and earned that much revenue, which according to the *realization principle* should appear on the December income statement. Therefore, on December 31, the following adjusting entry is required:

		Adjustment (f)		
Dec.	31	Unearned Legal Fees	250.00	
		Legal Fees Earned		250.00
		Earned legal fees that had been received in advance.		

Posting the entry has this effect on the accounts:

Unearned Legal Fees				Legal Fees Earned		
Dec. 31	250	Dec. 26	3,000		Dec. 10	2,200
					12	1,700
					31	250

The effect of the entry is to transfer the $250 earned portion of the fee from the liability account to the revenue account. It reduces the liability and records as a revenue the $250 that has been earned.

Accrued Revenues

Many revenues are recorded when cash is received. Others are recorded at the time the goods or services are sold on credit and a bill is given to the customer. However, at the end of an accounting period, some revenues may remain unrecorded even though they have been earned. Earned revenues that are unrecorded because payment has not been received are called *accrued revenues*. For example, assume that on December 20, Jerry Dow agreed with Guaranty Bank to do its legal work on a fixed-fee basis of $600 per month to be paid at the end of each month's work on the 20th of the month. Under this assumption, by December 31, the law practice has earned one third of a month's fee, or $200. According to the *realization principle,* this revenue should be reported on the December income statement. Therefore, you should make the following adjusting entry:

		Adjustment (g)		
Dec.	31	Accounts Receivable	200.00	
		Legal Fees Earned		200.00
		To record accrued legal fees.		

Posting the entry has this effect on the accounts:

Accounts Receivable				Legal Fees Earned		
Dec. 12	1,700	Dec. 22	1,700		Dec. 10	2,200
31	200				12	1,700
					31	250
					31	200

The Adjusted Trial Balance

A trial balance that is prepared before adjustments have been recorded is called an **unadjusted trial balance.** By comparison, an **adjusted trial balance** reflects the effects of the adjustments. Illustration 3–3 shows the December 31, 1990, unadjusted trial balance, the adjustments, and the adjusted trial balance for the law practice of Jerry Dow. Note that in the Adjustments columns a letter is used to identify each debit and credit with the adjusting entries explained earlier in the chapter.

Illustration 3–3
The December 31, 1990, unadjusted and adjusted trial balances for Jerry Dow, Lawyer

	Unadjusted Trial Balance		Adjustments		Adjusted Trial Balance	
	Dr.	Cr.	Dr.	Cr.	Dr.	Cr.
Cash	650				650	
Prepaid insurance	2,400			(a) 100	2,300	
Office supplies	120			(b) 45	75	
Law library	2,880				2,880	
Office equipment	6,880				6,880	
Accounts payable		760				760
Unearned legal fees		3,000	(f) 250			2,750
Jerry Dow, capital		9,000				9,000
Jerry Dow, withdrawals	1,100				1,100	
Legal fees earned		3,900		(f) 250		4,350
				(g) 200		
Rent expense	1,000				1,000	
Salaries expense	1,400		(e) 210		1,610	
Utilities expense	230				230	
Totals	16,660	16,660				
Insurance expense			(a) 100		100	
Office supplies expense			(b) 45		45	
Depreciation expense, law library			(c) 80		80	
Accumulated depreciation, law library				(c) 80		80
Depreciation expense, office equipment			(d) 125		125	
Accumulated depreciation, office equipment				(d) 125		125
Salaries payable				(e) 210		210
Accounts receivable			(g) 200		200	
Totals			1,010	1,010	17,275	17,275

Preparing Statements from the Adjusted Trial Balance

An adjusted trial balance shows proper balance sheet and income statement amounts. Therefore, you can use it to prepare the financial statements. When this is done, the income statement is prepared first because the net income, as calculated on the income statement, is needed to complete the statement of changes in owner's equity.

Illustration 3–4 shows how the revenues and expenses of Dow's law practice are arranged into an income statement and a statement of changes in owner's equity. In preparing the statement of changes in owner's equity, you may have to refer back to the ledger to determine how much of the owner's capital account balance existed at the beginning of the period and how much resulted from the owner's investments during the current period.

Illustration 3–5 shows how the asset, liability, and owner's equity items are drawn from the adjusted trial balance and arranged into a balance sheet. The balance sheet is prepared last, since the owner's equity is calculated in the statement of changes in owner's equity.

Illustration 3–4
Preparing the income statement and statement of changes in owner's equity from the adjusted trial balance

JERRY DOW, LAWYER
Adjusted Trial Balance
December 31, 1990

Cash	$ 650	
Prepaid insurance	2,300	
Office supplies	75	
Law library	2,880	
Office equipment	6,880	
Accounts payable		$ 760
Unearned legal fees		2,750
Jerry Dow, capital		9,000
Jerry Dow, withdrawals	1,100	
Legal fees earned		4,350
Rent expense	1,000	
Salaries expense	1,610	
Utilities expense	230	
Insurance expense	100	
Office supplies expense	45	
Depreciation expense, law library	80	
Accumulated depreciation, law library		80
Depreciation expense, office equipment	125	
Accumulated depreciation, office equipment		125
Salaries payable		210
Accounts receivable	200	
Totals	$17,275	$17,275

JERRY DOW, LAWYER
Income Statement
For the Month Ended December 31, 1990

Revenues:		
Legal fees earned		$ 4,350
Operating expenses:		
Rent expense	$1,000	
Salaries expense	1,610	
Utilities expense	230	
Insurance expense	100	
Office supplies expense	45	
Depreciation expense, law library	80	
Depreciation expense, office equipment	125	
Total operating expenses		3,190
Net income		$ 1,160

JERRY DOW, LAWYER
Statement of Changes in Owner's Equity
For the Month Ended December 31, 1990

Jerry Dow, capital, November 30, 1990		$ –0–
Plus:		
Investments by owner	$9,000	
Net income	1,160	
Total		$10,160
Less:		
Withdrawals by owner		1,100
Jerry Dow, capital, December 31, 1990		$ 9,060

Illustration 3–5
Preparing the balance sheet from the adjusted trial balance

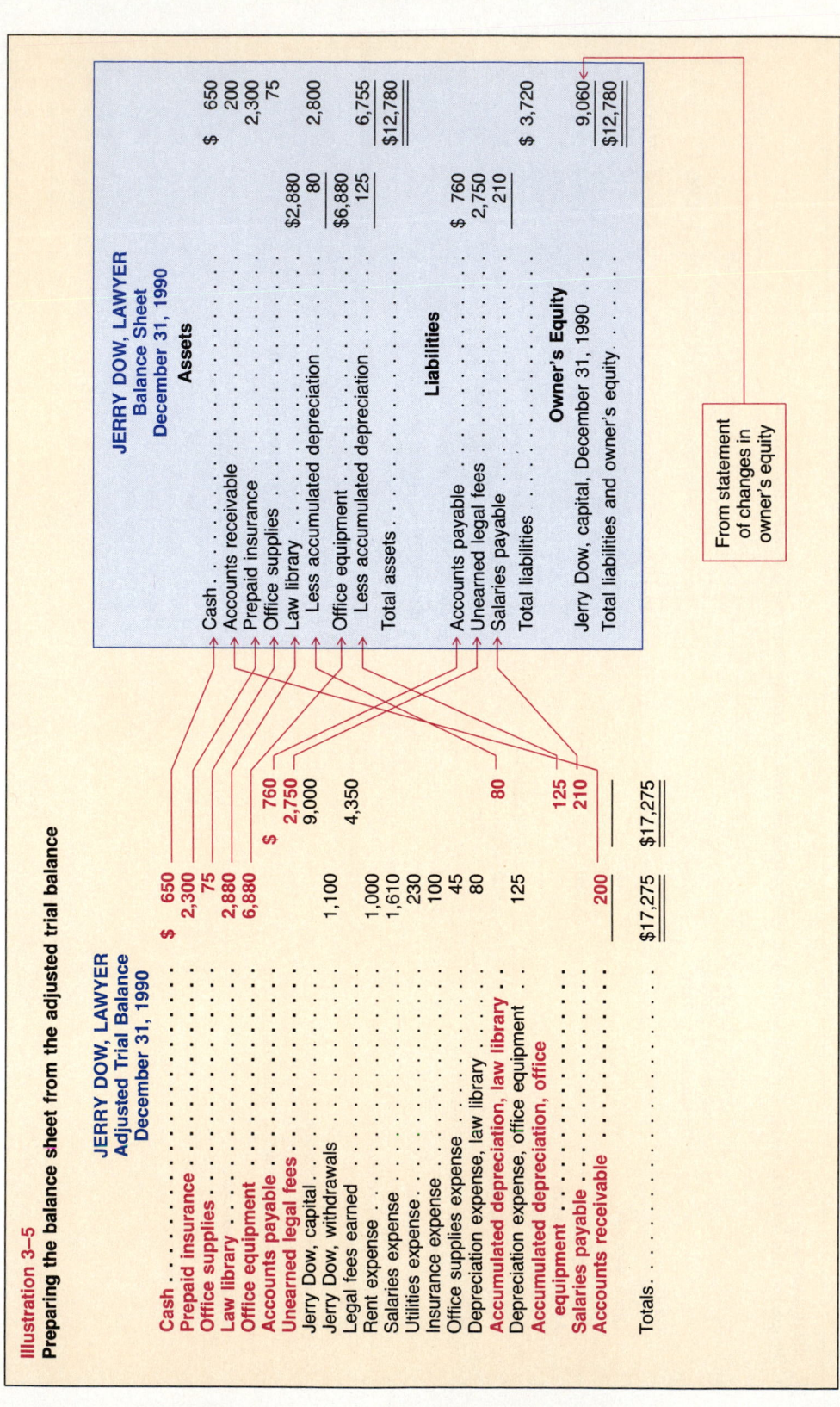

JERRY DOW, LAWYER
Adjusted Trial Balance
December 31, 1990

Cash	$ 650	
Prepaid insurance	2,300	
Office supplies	75	
Law library	2,880	
Office equipment	6,880	
Accounts payable		$ 760
Unearned legal fees		2,750
Jerry Dow, capital		9,000
Jerry Dow, withdrawals	1,100	
Legal fees earned		4,350
Rent expense	1,000	
Salaries expense	1,610	
Utilities expense	230	
Insurance expense	100	
Office supplies expense	45	
Depreciation expense, law library	80	
Accumulated depreciation, law library		80
Depreciation expense, office equipment	125	
Accumulated depreciation, office equipment		125
Salaries payable		210
Accounts receivable	200	
Totals	$17,275	$17,275

JERRY DOW, LAWYER
Balance Sheet
December 31, 1990

Assets

Cash		$ 650
Accounts receivable		200
Prepaid insurance		2,300
Office supplies		75
Law library	$2,880	
Less accumulated depreciation	80	2,800
Office equipment	$6,880	
Less accumulated depreciation	125	6,755
Total assets		$12,780

Liabilities

Accounts payable	$ 760	
Unearned legal fees	2,750	
Salaries payable	210	
Total liabilities		$ 3,720

Owner's Equity

Jerry Dow, capital, December 31, 1990		9,060
Total liabilities and owner's equity		$12,780

From statement of changes in owner's equity

The Adjustment Process

The adjustment process is based on two accounting principles, the *realization principle* and the **matching principle**. As explained in Chapter 1, the *realization principle* requires that revenue be reported in the income statement when it is earned, not before and not after. For most firms, revenue is earned at the time a service is rendered or a product is sold to the customer. For example, if a lawyer renders legal services to a client during December, the legal fees are earned during December and must be reported in the December income statement, even though the cash receipt from the client may take place in November or January. In cases such as this, the adjustment process is used to assign the revenue to December, when it was earned.

The *matching principle* requires that expenses be reported on the income statement in the same accounting period as are the revenues that were earned as a result of the expenses. For example, assume that a business uses an office to earn revenues during December. According to the *realization principle,* the revenues must be reported on the December income statement. One expense the business incurred in the pursuit of those December revenues was the December office rent. Therefore, the *matching principle* requires that the rent for December be reported on the December income statement; this must be accomplished even if the December rent was paid in November (or in January). In such cases, the adjustment process is used to match the cost of December's rent with the revenues earned during December.

Accrual Basis Accounting versus Cash Basis Accounting

Explain the difference between the cash and accrual bases of accounting.
(L. O. 3)

When the adjustment process is used to assign revenues to the periods in which they are earned and to match expenses with revenues, the accounting system is described as **accrual basis accounting.** Accrual basis accounting attempts to report revenues and expenses when the economic or financial effects of the transactions impact on the entity. It is based on the understanding that the economic effect of a revenue generally occurs when it is earned, not when cash is received. And the economic effect of an expense is incurred when the benefit expires or is used up, not when cash is paid.

An alternative to accrual basis accounting is the **cash basis of accounting.** Under the cash basis, revenues are reported when cash is received and expenses are reported when cash is paid. No adjustments are made for prepaid, unearned, and accrued items. Since revenues are reported when cash is received and expenses are deducted when cash is paid, net income is calculated as the difference between revenue receipts and expense disbursements.

The conclusion of "Financial Statement Concepts" is: "Items recognized in financial statements are accounted for in accordance with the accrual basis of accounting. The accrual basis of accounting recognizes the effect of transactions and events in the period in which the transactions and events occur, regardless of whether there has been a receipt or payment of cash or its equivalent."[1] Some concerns use a cash basis, but it is acceptable only if the amount of prepaid, unearned, and accrued items is unimportant.

One important benefit of accrual accounting is that it makes the information on accounting statements comparable from period to period. For example, in

---

[1] *CICA Handbook,* par. 1000.41.

AS A MATTER OF ETHICS

At the end of Mystic Company's first business year, its accountant is about to prepare the adjusting entries to record accrued expenses. After discussing these items with the accountant, the company's president instructed the accountant not to make the accruals because the bills will not be received until January or later and thus should not be included in this year's expenses.

In addition, the president asked how much this year's revenues will be increased by the sales to Brown Company under a contract that was just signed. The accountant explained that there will be no effect on sales until January because Brown Company will not take delivery until after the first of the year.

The president was exasperated and told the accountant to record the sales in December because the contract was already signed, and the company is ready to make the deliveries even though the customer does not want to have the items delivered until later.

The combination of not accruing the expenses and recording the sales to Brown Company will substantially increase the company's net income for this year. What should the accountant do? Would your answer be different if the company's statements are or are not to be audited? What if the accountant knows that the president's bonus depends on the amount of income reported in the first year? What if the accountant's job depends on complying with the president's wishes?

December 1990, the Dow law practice paid $2,400 for two years of insurance coverage. Under accrual accounting, insurance expense of $100 is reported in the December 1990 income statement, and $100 will be reported as expense each month for the next 23 months. In contrast, a cash basis income statement for December 1990 would show insurance expense of $2,400; and the monthly income statements for the next 23 months would show $–0– expense. When the monthly income statements are compared, the accrual basis correctly shows that all 24 months incurred the expense of insurance coverage. The cash basis would suggest that December 1990 was much less profitable than the following 23 months.

Disposing of Accrued Items

Prepare entries to record cash receipts and cash disbursements of items that were recorded at the end of the previous period as accrued revenues and accrued expenses. (L. O. 4)

Accrued Expenses

Earlier in this chapter, the December 29, 30, and 31 accrued wages of the secretary were recorded as follows:

Dec.	31	Salaries Expense	210.00	
		Salaries Payable		210.00
		To record the accrued wages.		

When these wages are paid on Friday, January 9, you must make the following entry:

Jan.	9	Salaries Payable	210.00	
		Salaries Expense	490.00	
		Cash		700.00
		Paid two weeks' wages.		

The first debit in the January 9 entry cancels the liability for the three days' wages accrued on December 31. The second debit records the wages of January's first seven working days as an expense of the January accounting period. The credit records the amount paid to the secretary.

Accrued Revenues

On December 20, Jerry Dow agreed to do the legal work of Guaranty Bank on a fixed-fee basis for $600 per month. On December 31, the following adjusting entry was made to record one third of a month's revenue earned under this contract.

Dec.	31	Accounts Receivable	200.00	
		Legal Fees Earned		200.00
		To record the legal fees.		

And when payment of the first month's fee is received on January 20, you should make the following entry:

Jan.	20	Cash	600.00	
		Accounts Receivable		200.00
		Legal Fees Earned		400.00
		Received cash for accrued and earned legal fees.		

The first credit in the January 20 entry records the collection of the fee accrued at the end of December. The second credit records as revenue the fee earned during the first 20 days of January.

Classification of Balance Sheet Items

Define each asset and liability classification appearing on a balance sheet, classify balance sheet items, and prepare a classified balance sheet. (L. O. 5)

The balance sheets that we have presented up to this point (for example, see Illustration 3–5) may be described as **unclassified balance sheets.** This means that no attempt was made to divide the assets or liabilities into classes. However, a balance sheet becomes more useful when you classify its assets and liabilities into meaningful groups. Readers of such **classified balance sheets** can better judge the adequacy of the different kinds of assets used in the business. Also, they can better estimate the probable availability of funds to meet the various liabilities as they become due.

Businesses do not all use the same system of classifying assets and liabilities on their balance sheets. However, most businesses classify them as shown in Illustration 3–6. Assets are classified as (1) current assets, (2) investments, (3) plant and equipment, and (4) intangible assets. Liabilities are classified as (1) current liabilities and (2) long-term liabilities. We explain the nature of these classes in the following paragraphs.

Illustration 3–6
A classified balance sheet

NATIONAL ELECTRICAL SUPPLY
Balance Sheet
December 31, 1990
Assets

Current assets:

Cash	$ 1,050	
Temporary investments	2,145	
Accounts receivable	3,961	
Notes receivable	600	
Merchandise inventory	10,248	
Prepaid expenses	405	
Total current assets		$ 18,409

Investments:

Chrysler Corporation common stock	$ 2,400	
Land held for future expansion	8,000	
Total investments		10,400

Plant and equipment:

Store equipment	$ 3,200		
Less accumulated depreciation	800	$ 2,400	
Buildings	$70,000		
Less accumulated depreciation	18,400	51,600	
Land		24,200	
Total plant and equipment			78,200

Intangible assets:

Franchise	10,000
Total assets	117,009

Liabilities

Current liabilities:

Accounts payable	$ 2,715	
Wages payable	480	
Notes payable	3,000	
Current portion of long-term liabilities . . .	1,200	
Total current liabilities		$ 7,395

Long-Term liabilities:

Notes payable	48,800	
Total liabilities		$56,195

Owner's Equity

Bruce Brown, capital	60,814
Total liabilities and owner's equity	$117,009

Current Assets

Current assets are defined as cash and other assets that are reasonably expected to be realized in cash or to be sold or consumed within one year or within the normal **operating cycle of the business,** whichever is longer. In addition to cash, current assets typically include temporary investments in marketable securities, accounts receivable, notes receivable, products held for resale (merchandise inventory), and prepaid expenses.

Illustration 3–7
The operating cycle of a manufacturing business

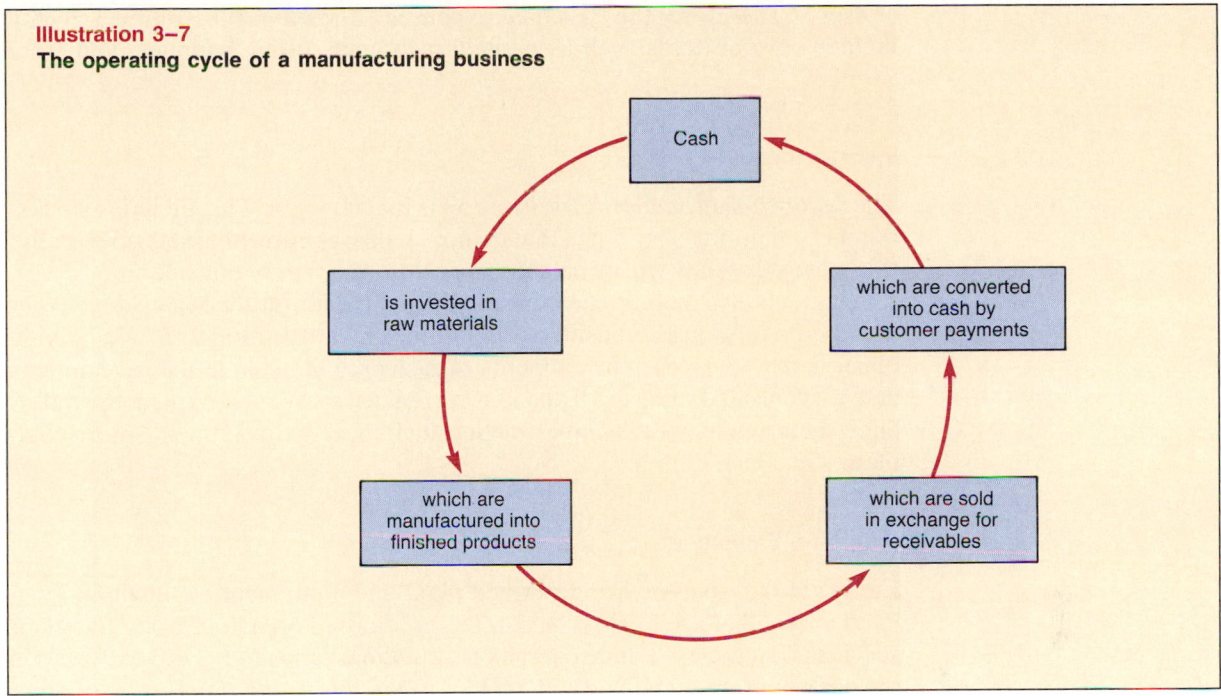

The operating cycle of a business is the average period of time between its acquisition of merchandise or raw materials and the realization of cash from the sale of the merchandise or the sale of the products manufactured from the raw materials. Illustration 3–7 shows a typical operating cycle for a manufacturer. In many companies, this interval is less than one year; as a result, these companies use a one-year period in classifying current assets. However, some companies have an operating cycle longer than one year. For example, distilleries must age some products for several years before the products are ready for sale. Consequently, in such companies, inventories or raw materials, manufacturing supplies, and products made from the inventories will not be ready for sale for more than a year.

Return to Illustration 3–6 and note that current assets are listed first. This is because they are more easily converted into cash than are other types of assets. In other words, current assets are said to be more *liquid* than other assets. Also, within the current asset category, the items are listed in the order of their liquidity, the most liquid first and the least liquid last. Note that prepaid expenses are listed last among the current assets. Unlike other current assets, prepaid expenses will not be converted into cash. Nevertheless, prepaid expenses substitute for future cash payments that would be required if the expenses had not been prepaid. Therefore, prepaid expenses are listed as current assets until their benefits expire or they are used up.

The prepaid expenses of a business, as a total, are seldom a major item on its balance sheet. As a result, instead of listing them individually, they are commonly totaled and only the total is shown under the caption ''Prepaid expenses.'' Therefore, the ''Prepaid expenses'' shown in Illustration 3–6 may include several items such as prepaid insurance, office supplies, and store supplies.

Investments

The second balance sheet classification is investments. This includes stocks, bonds, and promissory notes that do not qualify as current assets. Generally, this means that they will be held for more than one year or one operating cycle. Investments also include such things as land held for future expansion but not now being used in the business operations. In Illustration 3–6, you should observe that temporary investments of cash are not listed in the Investments category; instead, they are listed as a current asset. We will explain the differences between temporary investments and long-term investments more completely in a later chapter.

Plant and Equipment

Earlier in this chapter, we described plant and equipment as tangible, long-lived assets that are held for use in the production or sale of other assets or services. Examples include equipment, buildings, and land. The key words in the definition are *long lived* and *held for use in the production or sale of other assets or services*. Land held for future expansion is not a plant asset because it is not being used to produce or sell other assets, goods, or services.

The words *Plant and equipment* are commonly used as a balance sheet caption. Alternative captions are *Property, plant, and equipment* or *Land, buildings, and equipment* or simply *Plant assets*. The order in which plant assets are listed within the balance sheet classification is not uniform.

Intangible Assets

Economic benefits or resources that do not have a physical substance are called **intangible assets.** Their value stems from the privileges or rights that accrue to their owner. Examples of intangible assets are goodwill, patents, trademarks, copyrights, and franchises.

Current Liabilities

Obligations that are due to be paid or liquidated within one year or one operating cycle of the business, whichever is longer, are classified as **current liabilities.** Current liabilities usually are satisfied by paying current assets or by incurring new current liabilities. Common current liabilities are accounts payable, notes payable, wages payable, taxes payable, interest payable, and unearned revenues. Also, since long-term liabilities often require periodic payments, the portion of long-term liabilities that comes due within one year or one operating cycle must be classified as a current liability. Illustration 3–6 shows how this item usually is described. The order in which current liability items are listed is not uniform.

Unearned revenues are classified as current liabilities because current assets will normally be required in their liquidation. For example, advance receipts for future delivery of merchandise will be earned and the liability liquidated by delivering merchandise, which is a current asset.

Long-Term Liabilities

The second liability classification is **long-term liabilities**. Liabilities that are not due and payable within one year or the current operating cycle are listed under this classification. Common long-term liability items are notes payable and bonds payable. Because businesses may owe both long-term notes payable and notes payable that are current liabilities, they sometimes use two different accounts, one called Short-Term Notes Payable and the other Long-Term Notes Payable.

Owner's Equity on the Balance Sheet

The equity section of a balance sheet differs depending on whether the business is organized as a single proprietorship, a partnership, or a corporation.

Single Proprietorships and Partnerships

When a business is organized as a single proprietorship, the equity section of the balance sheet is presented as a single line that reports the owner's equity as of the date of the balance sheet. Thus, Illustration 3–5 shows "Jerry Dow, capital, December 31, 1990 . . . . 9,060." In the unusual case where total liabilities exceed total assets, the negative (or debit) equity amount is shown in parentheses and subtracted from total liabilities.

When a business is organized as a partnership, separate capital accounts and withdrawals accounts are maintained for each partner. Changes in the partners' equities are reported in a statement of changes in partners' equities similar to the statement of changes in owner's equity. In the equity section of the balance sheet, the equity of each partner is listed as follows:

Partner's Equities		
Rebecca Matthews, capital	$17,300	
Amy Searcy, capital	24,800	
Total equities of the partners		$42,100

Corporations

Corporations are established under the laws of a province or under federal laws. These laws generally distinguish between amounts a corporation receives from its shareholders through investments, and the increase or decrease in shareholders' equity due to net incomes, net losses, and **dividends**. The amounts shareholders have invested are classified as **contributed capital**, or **paid-in capital**. The equity that represents the corporation's cumulative net incomes less net losses and dividends is called **retained earnings.** Therefore, shareholders' equity is shown on a corporation balance sheet as follows:

Shareholders' Equity		
Contributed capital:		
Common stock	$400,000	
Retained earnings	124,400	
Total shareholders' equity		$524,400

If a corporation issues only one kind of stock (others are discussed later), it is called **common stock.** The $400,000 amount shown here for this item is the amount originally contributed to the corporation by its shareholders through the purchase of the corporation's stock. The $124,400 of retained earnings represents the increase in the shareholders' equity resulting from cumulative net incomes that exceeded any net losses and any dividends paid to the shareholders. (A dividend is a distribution, generally of assets, made by a corporation to its shareholders. Such a dividend reduces the assets and the equity of a corporation in the same way a withdrawal reduces the assets and equity of a proprietorship.)

Alternative Balance Sheet Arrangements

The balance sheet in Illustration 1–2, with the liabilities and owner's equity placed to the right of the assets, is called an **account form balance sheet.** Such an arrangement emphasizes that assets equal liabilities plus owner's equity. Alternatively, when balance sheet items are arranged vertically, such as in Illustration 3–5, the format is called a **report form balance sheet.** Both forms are commonly used, and neither is preferred.

Identifying Accounts by Number

A typical three-digit account numbering system was introduced in Chapter 2. In such a system, the number assigned to an account usually identifies the account and also identifies the balance sheet or income statement classification of the account. For example, in the following system, the first digit in an account's number tells its primary balance sheet or income statement classification. Account numbers with first digits of 1 are assigned to asset accounts. Liability accounts are assigned numbers with first digits of 2, and the accounts in each balance sheet and income statement classification of a concern selling merchandise are assigned numbers as follows:

111 to 199 are assigned to asset accounts.

211 to 299 are assigned to liability accounts.

311 to 399 are assigned to owner's equity accounts.

411 to 499 are assigned to sales or revenue accounts.

511 to 599 are assigned to cost of goods sold accounts.

611 to 699 are assigned to operating expense accounts.

711 to 799 are assigned to other revenue and expense accounts.

In this system, the second digit of each account number identifies the sub-classification of the account, as follows:

111 to 199. Asset accounts.
    111 to 119. Current asset accounts (second digits of 1).
    121 to 129. Long-term investment accounts (second digits of 2).
    131 to 139. Plant asset accounts (second digits of 3).
    141 to 149. Intangible asset accounts (second digits of 4).
211 to 299. Liability accounts.
    211 to 219. Current liability accounts (second digits of 1).
    221 to 229. Long-term liability accounts (second digits of 2).
611 to 699. Operating expense accounts.
    611 to 629. Selling expense accounts (second digits of 1 and 2).
    631 to 649. General and administrative expense accounts (second digits of 3 and 4).

Finally, each account is assigned a third digit that, within the subclass, is unique to that account. For example, specific current asset accounts might be assigned numbers as follows:

111 to 199. Asset accounts.
    111 to 119. Current asset accounts.
        111. Cash.
        112. Temporary Investments.
        113. Accounts Receivable.
        114. Short-Term Notes Receivable.

The sales and cost of goods sold accounts listed in this account numbering system are discussed in Chapter 5. The division of the operating expense accounts into selling expense accounts and general and administrative expense accounts is also discussed in that chapter. In businesses that sell services rather than tangible products, all expense accounts usually are classified as operating expenses without subdividing them.

Summary of the Chapter in Terms of Learning Objectives

1. The life of a business is divided into accounting periods so that periodic financial reports can be prepared and used to evaluate the financial progress of the business. Adjustments at the end of each period are necessary to correct some of the asset, liability, expense, and revenue accounts and to show the effects of previously unrecorded internal economic events of the business.

2. Adjusting entries are used: (*a*) to charge the expired portion of prepaid expenses to expense, (*b*) to charge the expired portion of plant and equipment cost to depreciation expense, (*c*) to accrue expenses and record the related liabilities, (*d*) to recognize as revenues the earned portion of unearned revenue liabilities, and (*e*) to accrue revenues and record the related assets.

3. Cash basis accounting does not make adjustments for prepaid expenses, accrued expenses, unearned revenues, and accrued revenues. Revenues are recorded when cash is received, and expenses are recorded when cash is paid. Accrual accounting adjusts for prepaid, unearned, and accrued items; therefore, it reports revenues when earned and expenses when the expiration of benefits is incurred.

4. When accrued expenses are paid early in a new accounting period, the entry to record the payment includes a debit to the previously recorded liability and a debit to expense for the portion that expired during the new period. When payment of accrued revenues is received, the entry includes a credit to the previously recorded asset and a credit to revenue for the portion earned during the new period.

5. Classified balance sheets usually report four classes of assets: current assets, investments, plant and equipment, and intangible assets. Liabilities are classified as current liabilities and long-term liabilities. The equity of a single proprietorship is reported on one line, while a separate capital account is reported for each partner in a partnership. Corporations report the investments of its shareholders as contributed capital; the equity from net incomes less net losses and dividends is reported as retained earnings.

Demonstration Problem

The following information relates to Bidder Company on December 31, 1991. The company prepares financial statements annually on a calendar-year basis.

a. Bidder Company's weekly payroll is $2,800, paid every Friday for a five-day workweek. At the 1991 year-end, the employees have worked Monday through Wednesday.

b. On December 1, 1991, the company borrowed $45,000 from a local bank for 90 days at 12% interest.

c. During December, the company advertised in the local paper at a cost of $600, which amount is unpaid and unrecorded.

d. Equipment that cost $10,000 and has no salvage value was purchased on July 1, 1990. It has a five-year useful life.

e. At the beginning of the year, office supplies amounted to $210. During the year, $650 of supplies were purchased and charged to the asset account. At year-end, there were $280 of supplies on hand.

f. On October 1, 1991, Bidder Company contracted to install plumbing for a new housing project. The contract was for $144,000 to install plumbing in 24 new houses. The $144,000 was received on October 1, 1991, and credited to Unearned Plumbing Revenue. As of December 31, 1991, 18 houses have been completed.

g. On September 1, 1991, a one-year insurance policy was purchased for $1,200 and was debited to Prepaid Insurance.

h. The previous year, on December 1, 1990, the company had purchased a one-year policy for $900. The portion of the cost that relates to 1991 exists in the Prepaid Insurance account.

Required

1. Prepare the necessary adjusting journal entries on December 31, 1991.
2. Complete the following schedule:

Entry	Account	Amount of Adjustment	Amount that Will Appear on Balance Sheet	Classification of Account on Balance Sheet*
a	Wages payable	$	$	
b	Interest payable			
c	Advertising payable			
d	Accumulated depreciation			
e	Office supplies			
f	Unearned revenues			
g and h	Prepaid insurance			

*Indicate whether the account is a current asset, plant and equipment, current liability, or long-term liability.

3. State whether the effect of each adjustment was to increase or decrease or leave unchanged each of the following: net income, total assets, total liabilities.

Solution to Demonstration Problem

1. Adjusting journal entries.

a.	Dec.	31	Wages Expense	1,680.00	
			Wages Payable		1,680.00
			To accrue wages for the last three days of the year (3/5 × $2,800).		
b.		31	Interest Expense.	450.00	
			Interest Payable		450.00
			To accrue interest for one month ($45,000 × .12 × 1/12).		
c.		31	Advertising Expense.	600.00	
			Advertising Payable		600.00
			To record advertising expense.		
d.		31	Depreciation Expense, Equipment	2,000.00	
			Accumulated Depreciation, Equipment		2,000.00
			To record depreciation expense for the year ($10,000 ÷ 5 = $2,000).		
e.		31	Office Supplies Expense	580.00	
			Office Supplies		580.00
			To record office supplies used ($210 + $650 − $280).		
f.		31	Unearned Plumbing Revenues	108,000.00	
			Plumbing Revenues		108,000.00
			To recognize plumbing revenues earned ($144,000 × 18/24).		

g.	Dec.	31	Insurance Expense . . . .
			    Prepaid Insurance . . . .
			    To adjust for the expired portion of
			    insurance ($1,200 × ⁴⁄₁₂).
				400.00	400.00

h.		31	Insurance Expense . . . .
			    Prepaid Insurance . . . .
			    To record the expiration of insurance
			    ($900 × ¹¹⁄₁₂).
				825.00	825.00

2.

Entry	Account	Amount of Adjustment	Amount that Will Appear on Balance Sheet	Classification of Account on Balance Sheet
a	Wages payable	$ 1,680	$ 1,680	Current liability
b	Interest payable	450	450	Current liability
c	Advertising payable	600	600	Current liability
d	Accumulated depreciation	2,000	3,000	Plant and equipment
e	Office supplies	(580)	280	Current asset
f	Unearned revenues	(108,000)	36,000	Current liability
g and h	Prepaid insurance	(1,225)	800*	Current asset

*$825 + $1,200 − $825 − $400 = $800.

3.

Entry	Net Income Increase (Decrease)	Total Assets Increase (Decrease)	Total Liabilities Increase (Decrease)
a	$ (1,680)	$ –0–	$ 1,680
b	(450)	–0–	450
c	(600)	–0–	600
d	(2,000)	(2,000)	–0–
e	(580)	(580)	–0–
f	108,000	–0–	(108,000)
g	(400)	(400)	–0–
h	(825)	(825)	–0–

Appendix A

RECORDING PREPAID AND UNEARNED ITEMS IN INCOME STATEMENT ACCOUNTS

Prepaid Expenses

Explain why some companies record prepaid and unearned items in income statement accounts and prepare adjusting entries when this procedure is used.
(L. O. 7)

The discussion in Chapter 3 emphasized the fact that prepaid expenses are assets at the time they are purchased. Therefore, at the time of purchase, we recorded prepaid expenses with debits to asset accounts. Then, at the end of the accounting period, adjusting entries were made to transfer the cost that had expired to expense accounts. In the chapter, we also recognized that some prepaid expenses are purchased and will fully expire before the end of the accounting period. When this is expected, it is easier to charge prepaid expenses to expense accounts at the time of purchase. Then, no adjusting entry is necessary.

Some companies follow a practice of recording *all* prepaid expenses with debits to expense accounts. Then, at the end of the accounting period, if any amounts remain unused or unexpired, adjusting entries are made to transfer the cost of the unused portions from the expense accounts to prepaid expense (asset) accounts. This practice is perfectly acceptable. The reported financial statements will be exactly the same under either procedure.

To illustrate the difference between the two procedures, recall that on December 26, the Dow law practice purchased office supplies for $120. That purchase was recorded with a debit to an asset account, but could have been recorded with a debit to an expense account. Both alternatives are shown below:

		Purchase Recorded as Asset		Purchase Recorded as Expense	
Dec. 26	Office Supplies	120.00			
	Cash		120.00		
26	Office Supplies Expense			120.00	
	Cash				120.00

At the end of the accounting period (December 31), an inventory of the unused office supplies was taken and $75 of supplies were found to be unused. That means $120 − $75 = $45 of office supplies were used and became an expense of December. The required adjusting entry depends on how the original purchase was recorded. The alternative adjusting entries are as follows:

		Purchase Recorded as Asset		Purchase Recorded as Expense	
Adjusting entries:					
Dec. 31	Office Supplies Expense	45.00			
	Office Supplies		45.00		
31	Office Supplies			75.00	
	Office Supplies Expense				75.00

When these entries are posted to the accounts, you can see that the two alternative procedures give the same results. Regardless of which procedure is followed, the December 31 adjusted account balances show office supplies of $75 and office supplies expense of $45.

Purchase Recorded as Asset				Purchase Recorded as Expense			
Office Supplies				**Office Supplies**			
Dec. 26	120	Dec. 31	45	Dec. 31	75		
	−45						
Balance	75						
				Office Supplies Expense			
				Dec. 26	120	Dec. 31	75
Office Supplies Expense					−75		
Dec. 31	45			Balance	45		

To continue the example for another month, assume that during January, Dow's law practice purchased $150 of supplies; on January 31, an inventory of unused supplies showed $100 of supplies on hand. As you can see in the above accounts, the December 31 balance in the Office Supplies account was $75, regardless of which procedure is used. Therefore, the total supplies available for use during January was $75 + $150 = $225. Since $100 of supplies remain unused on January 31, the adjusting entry on January 31 must be designed to report a supplies asset of $100 and a supplies expense of $225 − $100 = $125. Depending on how the purchases were recorded, the alternative adjusting entries are:

		Purchase Recorded as Asset		Purchase Recorded as Expense	
Adjusting entries:					
Jan. 31	Office Supplies Expense	125.00			
	Office Supplies		125.00		
31	Office Supplies.			25.00	
	Office Supplies Expense . . .				25.00

Note that if purchases are debited to expense accounts, the required adjusting entry increases the Office Supplies account balance $25, from $75 to $100. The credit in the entry reduces the Office Supplies Expense account debit balance from $150 to $125.

Unearned Revenues

The procedures used to record unearned revenues are similar to those used to record prepaid expenses. Receipts of unearned revenues may be recorded with credits to liability accounts (as described in Chapter 3) or they may be recorded with credits to revenue accounts. The adjusting entries at the end of the period will be different, depending on which procedure is followed. Nevertheless, either procedure is acceptable. The amounts reported in the financial statements will be exactly the same, regardless of which procedure is used.

To illustrate the alternative procedures of recording unearned revenues, recall that on December 26, the Dow law practice received $3,000 in payment for legal services to be provided over the six-month period beginning December 15. In Chapter 3, that receipt was recorded with a credit to a liability account. The alternative would be to record it with a credit to a revenue account. Both alternatives are shown below:

		Receipt Recorded as a Liability		Receipt Recorded as a Revenue	
Dec. 26	Cash	3,000.00			
	Unearned Legal Fees		3,000.00		
26	Cash			3,000.00	
	Legal Fees Earned				3,000.00

By the end of the accounting period (December 31), the Dow law practice had earned $250 of these legal fees. That means $250 of the liability had been satisfied. Depending on how the original receipt was recorded, the required adjusting entry is as follows:

	Receipt Recorded as a Liability	Receipt Recorded as a Revenue
Adjusting entries:		
Dec. 31 Unearned Legal Fees	250.00	
Legal Fees Earned	250.00	
31 Legal Fees Earned		2,750.00
Unearned Legal Fees		2,750.00

Posting these entries shows that the two alternative procedures give the same results. Regardless of which procedure is followed, the December 31 adjusted account balances show unearned legal fees of $2,750 and legal fees earned of $250.

Receipt Recorded as a Liability

Unearned Legal Fees

Dec. 31	250	Dec. 31	3,000
			−250
		Balance	2,750

Legal Fees Earned

		Dec. 31	250

Receipt Recorded as a Revenue

Unearned Legal Fees

		Dec. 31	2,750

Legal Fees Earned

Dec. 31	2,750	Dec. 26	3,000
			−2,750
		Balance	250

Summary of the Appendix in Terms of the Learning Objective

7. Because many prepaid expenses expire during the same period they are purchased, some companies choose to charge all prepaid expenses to expense accounts at the time they are purchased. When this is done, end-of-period adjusting entries are required to transfer any unexpired amounts from the expense accounts to appropriate asset accounts. Also, unearned revenues may be credited to revenue accounts at the time cash is received. If so, end-of-period adjusting entries are required to transfer any unearned amounts from the revenue accounts to appropriate unearned revenue accounts.

Glossary

Define or explain the words and phrases listed in the chapter Glossary. (L. O. 6)

Account form balance sheet a balance sheet that is arranged so that the assets are listed on the left and the liability and owner's equity items are listed on the right. p. 122

Accounting period the length of time into which the life of a business is divided for the purpose of preparing periodic financial statements. p. 104

Accrual basis of accounting a system of accounting in which the adjustment process is used to assign revenues to the periods in which they are earned and to match expenses with revenues. p. 115

Accrued expenses expenses that are incurred during an accounting period but that, prior to end-of-period adjustments, remain unrecorded because payment is not due. p. 109

Accrued revenues revenues that are earned during an accounting period but that, prior to end-of-period adjustments, remain unrecorded because payment has not been received. p. 111

Accumulated depreciation the total amount of depreciation recorded against an asset or group of assets during the entire period of time the asset or assets have been owned. p. 108

Adjusted trial balance a trial balance that shows the account balances after they have been revised to reflect the effects of end-of-period adjustments. p. 111

Adjusting entry a journal entry made at the end of an accounting period for the purpose of assigning revenues to the period in which they are earned, assigning expenses to the period in which the expiration of benefit is incurred, and to correct related liability and asset accounts. p. 105

Cash basis of accounting an accounting system in which revenues are reported in the income statement when cash is received and expenses are reported when cash is paid; no adjustments are made for prepaid, unearned, and accrued items. p. 115

Classified balance sheet a balance sheet that shows assets and liabilities grouped in meaningful subclasses. p. 117

Common stock the name given to a corporation's stock when it issues only one kind or class of stock. p. 122

Contra account an account the balance of which is subtracted from the balance of an associated account to show a more proper amount for the item recorded in the associated account. p. 108

Contributed capital the portion of a corporation's equity that represents investments in the corporation by its shareholders. p. 121

Current assets cash or other assets that are reasonably expected to be realized in cash or to be sold or consumed within one year or one operating cycle of the business, whichever is longer. p. 118

Current liabilities obligations that are due to be paid or liquidated within one year or one operating cycle of the business, whichever is longer. p. 120

Depreciation the expiration of the usefulness of plant and equipment, and the related process of allocating the cost of such assets to expense of the periods during which the assets are used. p. 107

Dividends a distribution, generally of assets, made by a corporation to its shareholders. p. 121

Fiscal year a period of any 12 consecutive months used by a business as its annual accounting period. p. 104

Intangible assets economic benefits or resources without physical substance, the value of which stems from the privileges or rights that accrue to their owner. p. 120

Interim financial reports financial reports of a business that are based on one-month or three-month accounting periods. p. 104

Long-term liabilities obligations that are not due to be paid within one year or the current operating cycle of the business. p. 121

Matching principle the accounting requirement that expenses be reported in the same accounting period as are the revenues that were earned as a result of the expenses. p. 115

Natural business year the 12-month period that ends when the activities of a business are at their lowest point. p. 104

Operating cycle of a business the average time a business takes to invest cash in merchandise or raw materials that are manufactured into finished products, sell the products, and convert the receivables (if sales are on credit) back into cash. p. 118

Paid-in capital another name for *contributed capital*. p. 121

Plant and equipment tangible, long-lived assets that are held for use in the production or sale of other assets or services. p. 107

Report form balance sheet a balance sheet with a vertical format that shows the assets above the liabilities and the liabilities above the owner's equity. p. 122

Retained earnings the portion of a corporation's equity that represents its cumulative net incomes, less net losses and dividends. p. 122

Time-period concept the idea that the life of a business is divisible into time periods of equal length for the purpose of preparing periodic financial reports of the business. p. 104

Unadjusted trial balance a trial balance that is prepared before any adjustments have been recorded. p. 111

Unclassified balance sheet a balance sheet that presents a single list of assets and a single list of liabilities with no attempt to divide them into classes. p. 117

An asterisk (*) identifies the questions, exercises, and problems that are based on Appendix A at the end of the chapter.

Questions for Class Discussion

1. Why is the life of a business divided into time periods of equal length?
2. If a business adopts the calendar year as its annual accounting period, how would you describe financial reports of the business that are based on one-month or three-month accounting periods?

3. Which month would most likely end the natural business year of a business that operates outdoor tennis camps in Manitoba: August or April?

4. In selecting a fiscal year, what type of businesses are most apt to select their natural business year intead of the calendar year?

5. Why would you expect some account balances of a concern to be incorrect for statement purposes at the end of an accounting period even though all transactions were correctly recorded?

6. What purposes are served by making end-of-period adjustments?

7. A prepaid expense is an asset at the time of its purchase or prepayment. When is it best to ignore this and record the prepayment as an expense? Why?

8. What kind of assets require adjusting entries for depreciation?

9. What is a contra account? Give an example.

10. What contra account is used to record depreciation? Why is such an account used?

11. If a building is purchased for $100,000 and depreciation of $2,500 is taken each year, what amount of accumulated depreciation will appear in the balance sheet at the end of five years?

12. What is an accrued expense? Give an example.

13. How does an unearned revenue arise? Give an example of an unearned revenue.

14. What is the balance sheet classification of an unearned revenue?

15. What is an accrued revenue? Give an example.

16. When financial statements are prepared from an adjusted trial balance, why should the income statement be prepared first? What statement is prepared next?

17. Which accounting principles provide the basis for the adjustment process?

18. What is required by the matching principle?

19. Is the cash basis of accounting consistent with the matching principle?

20. What is the difference between the cash and accrual bases of accounting?

21. What are the typical classes of assets and liabilities shown on a classified balance sheet?

22. What are characteristics of a current asset?

23. What is meant by the operating cycle of a business?

24. What are some examples of assets that are shown in the investments category of the balance sheet?

25. What are the characteristics of assets classified as plant and equipment?

26. A local fast-food restaurant paid $20,000 for a franchise that identifies the restaurant as belonging to a nationally recognized chain of restaurants. How should this asset be classified on the local restaurant's balance sheet?

27. What are current liabilities? Long-term liabilities?

28. What are the two classes of equity on the balance sheet of a corporation?

*29. If a company records its prepaid expenses with debits to expense accounts, what type of account does it debit in making end-of-period adjustments for prepaid expenses?

*30. Bee Company records revenues received in advance with credits to liability accounts, while Cee Company records revenues received in advance with credits to revenues accounts. Will these companies have differences in their financial statements as a result of this difference in their procedures? Why or why not?

Multiple Choice

1. For purposes of preparing financial statements, the act of dividing the life of a business into equal time periods:
   a. Always is done so that the annual accounting period ends at the close of the natural business year.
   b. Always is done so that the annual accounting period ends at the close of the calendar year.
   c. Results in an annual accounting period that is called the fiscal year.
   d. Results in annual financial reports called interim financial reports.
   e. None of the above are correct.

2. On December 31, 1990, Craft Company failed to make an adjustment for $300 of accrued service revenues earned and also failed to record the expiration of $500 of insurance premiums that had been debited to Prepaid Insurance. As a result of these errors, on the 1990 income statement:
   a. Revenues will be overstated $300 and expenses will be understated $500.
   b. Revenues will be understated $300 and expenses will be overstated $500.
   c. Revenues will be overstated $300 and expenses will be overstated $500.
   d. Revenues will be understated $300 and expenses will be understated $500.
   e. Net income will be understated by $200.

3. On December 31, 1990, Watt Company made an entry to record $400 of accrued salaries. On January 5, the next payment of salaries was $2,000. Related to these transactions only:
   a. The entry on January 5 will include a $1,600 credit to Cash.
   b. You can be sure that Watt Company is using the cash basis of accounting.
   c. The salaries expense charged to 1991 will be $1,600.
   d. The salaries expense charged to 1991 will be $2,000.
   e. The salaries expense charged to 1990 will be $1,600.

4. On April 1, 1990, Flay Company paid $3,000 for two years' insurance coverage. In accounting for this item:

a. Under the cash basis of accounting, 1991 insurance expense will be $–0–.
b. Under the cash basis of accounting, 1992 insurance expense will be $375.
c. Under the accrual basis of accounting, 1991 insurance expense will be $1,500.
d. Under the accrual basis of accounting, an adjusting entry for insurance will not be required at the end of 1990.
e. Both (a) and (c) are correct.

5. A company owns the following items: (1) land used in the operations of the business, (2) office supplies, (3) receivables from customers due in 10 months, (4) a three-year note receivable from the purchaser of land previously owned by the company, (5) the right to receive insurance protection for the next 9 months, (6) land held in case expanded operations require it, (7) trucks used in servicing customers, and (8) trademarks used in selling the company's services. These items should be classified as follows:

	Current Assets	Investments	Plant and Equipment	Intangible Assets
a.	2, 3, 5	4	1, 6, 7	8
b.	2, 3, 5	4, 6	1, 7	8
c.	2, 3	4, 6	1, 7	5, 8
d.	2, 3, 4	6	1, 7	5, 8
e.	2	4, 6	1, 7	3, 5, 8

6. If throughout an accounting period the fees for legal services paid in advance by clients are recorded in an account called Unearned Legal Fees, the end-of-the-period adjusting entry to record the portion of these fees that has been earned is:
a. Debit Cash and credit Legal Fees Earned.
b. Debit Cash and credit Unearned Legal Fees.
c. Debit Unearned Legal Fees and credit Legal Fees Earned.
d. Debit Legal Fees Earned and credit Unearned Legal Fees.
e. Some other entry.

Mini Discussion Cases

Case 3–1

The president of Seneca Company called in the controller to personally express his displeasure with the length of time the accounting department took to produce the monthly financial statements. The controller replied that he appreciated the president's frustration; however, the month-end adjustments did require time, which was reduced to the absolute minimum. The president responded that he did not know why these adjustments were necessary. In fact, in his opinion, the time spent on adjustments was nothing more than a "make-work" procedure. It was unnecessary since these adjustments were repetitions of the same items which, if left alone, would cancel out the effects and result in financial statements that were just as accurate. For example, the president continued, with accrued wages payable at the end of each month, why then waste time on adjustments?

Required

Discuss whether the president's underlying assumptions are realistic and apply equally to all types of adjustments normally encountered at the end of each period.

Case 3–2

Durham Company's president believed that the monthly executive meetings, which considered the results of previous month's activity, could be "pushed up" a couple of days if the financial statements were available. After a discussion with the controller, the president found out that the month-end adjustments were the cause of delays. Consequently, he is contemplating asking the controller to speed up month-end statement preparation without the benefit of month-end adjustments. However, before taking such a step, he asks you to evaluate such an alternative.

Required

Discuss the short-comings of "unadjusted" financial statements. Focus your discussion on (*a*) compliance with GAAP, (*b*) treatment of such items as supplies and insurance, and (*c*) manipulation of results.

Exercises

Exercise 3–1
Adjusting entries for accrued expenses
(L. O. 2)

A company's two employees earn a total of $225 per day for a five-day week that begins on Monday and ends on Friday. They were paid for the week ended Friday, December 28, and both worked a full day on Monday, December 31. January 1 of the next year was an unpaid holiday, but the employees all worked on Wednesday, Thursday, and Friday, January 2, 3, and 4. Journalize the year-end adjusting entry to record the accrued wages and the entry to pay the employees on January 4.

Exercise 3–2
Adjusting entries for expenses
(L. O. 2)

Prepare adjusting journal entries on December 31, 1990, prior to the preparation of annual financial statements, for the following independent situations:

a. The Shop Supplies account had a $350 debit balance on January 1, 1990; $625 of supplies were purchased during the year; and a year-end inventory showed $180 of supplies on hand.

b. The Prepaid Insurance account had a $950 debit balance at the end of the accounting period before adjustment for expired insurance. An examination of insurance policies showed $560 of insurance expired.

c. The Prepaid Insurance account had a $780 debit balance at the end of the accounting period before adjustment for expired insurance. An examination of insurance policies showed $375 of unexpired insurance.

d. Depreciation on shop equipment was estimated at $1,350 for the accounting period.

e. Four months' property taxes, estimated at $848, have accrued but are unrecorded and unpaid at the accounting period end.

Exercise 3–3
Omission of adjusting entries
(L. O. 1, 2)

Assume that the required adjustments of Exercise 3–2 were not made at the end of the accounting period. For each adjustment, tell the effect of its omission on the income statement and balance sheet prepared at that time.

Exercise 3–4
Missing data in calculations of supplies
(L. O. 2)

Determine the amounts indicated by the question marks in the columns below. The amounts in each column constitute a separate problem.

	(a)	(b)	(c)	(d)
Supplies on hand on January 1	$350	$210	$560	$?
Supplies purchased during the year	675	795	?	945
Supplies remaining at the year-end	250	?	325	360
Supplies expense for the year	?	720	905	840

Exercise 3–5
Adjustments and payments of accrued items
(L. O. 2, 4)

Prepare adjusting journal entries dated April 30 for the following items. Then prepare journal entries to record the May payments.

a. Employees are paid total salaries of $2,400 each Friday after they complete a five-day workweek. As of April 30, the employees had worked four days since the last payment. The next payment date is May 1.

b. On April 1 the company retained a lawyer at a monthly fee of $250 payable on the 12th of the following month.

c. The company owes a $15,000 note payable, which requires that 1% interest be paid each month on the 20th of the month. The interest was paid April 20 and the next payment is due May 20.

Exercise 3–6
Cash basis versus accrual basis expense amounts
(L. O. 3)

A company paid the $1,080 premium on a three-year insurance policy on October 1, 1990. The policy gave protection beginning on that date.

a. Assuming the accrual basis of accounting, how many dollars of the premium will appear as an expense on the annual income statement for 1990? for 1991? for 1992? for 1993?

b. Assuming the accrual basis, how many dollars of the premium will appear as an asset on each December 31 balance sheet for 1990? for 1991? for 1992? for 1993?

c. Assuming the cash basis of accounting, how many dollars of the premium will appear as an expense on the annual income statement for 1990? for 1991? for 1992? for 1993?

d. Assuming the cash basis, how many dollars of the premium will appear as an asset on each December 31 balance sheet for 1990? for 1991? for 1992? for 1993?

Exercise 3–7
Unearned and accrued revenues
(L. O. 2, 4)

The owner of a building prepares annual financial statements based on a calendar-year accounting period.

a. A tenant rented space in the building on November 1 at $450 per month, paying six months' rent in advance. The receipt was credited to Unearned Rent. Give the December 31 adjusting entry of the building owner, prior to the preparation of annual financial statements.

b. Another tenant rented space in the building at $525 per month on November 1. The tenant paid the November rent on the first day of November, but by December 31 the December rent had not yet been paid. Give the December 31 adjusting entry of the building owner.

c. Assume the tenant in (b) paid the rent for December and January on January 3 of the new year. Give the entry to record the receipt of the $1,050.

Exercise 3–8
Classified balance sheet
(L. O. 5)

The adjusted trial balance that follows was taken from the ledger of Laura Shipley, Lawyer. Calculate the amount of owner's equity on December 31, 1990, and prepare a classified year-end balance sheet for the practice.

LAURA SHIPLEY, LAWYER
Adjusted Trial Balance
December 31, 1990

Cash	$ 2,250	
Accounts receivable	4,800	
Prepaid insurance	1,050	
Office supplies	150	
Investment in X-Ray Corporation common stock . .	20,000	
Office equipment	15,750	
Accumulated depreciation, office equipment		$ 4,500
Building	145,000	
Accumulated depreciation, building		15,000
Land	60,000	
Salaries payable		300
Unearned legal fees		1,200
Long-term notes payable	142,500	
Laura Shipley, capital		72,000
Laura Shipley, withdrawals	54,000	
Legal fees earned		127,500
Operating expenses (combined)	60,000	
Totals	$363,000	$363,000

Exercise 3–9
Analyzing statements for adjusting entries
(L. O. 2)

An inexperienced bookkeeper prepared the income statement shown below in columns 1 and 2, but he forgot to adjust the accounts before its preparation. However, the oversight was discovered, and the statement in columns 3 and 4 was prepared. Analyze the statements and prepare the adjusting journal entries that were made between the preparation of the two statements. Assume that one third of the additional property management fees resulted from recognizing accrued fees and two thirds resulted from previously recorded unearned fees that were earned by the date of the statements.

MASON REALTY
Income Statement
For Year Ended December 31, 1990

	Prepared without Adjustments	Prepared after Adjustments
Revenues:		
Commissions earned	$82,125	$82,125
Property management fees	4,500	5,625
Total revenues	$86,625	$87,750
Operating expenses:		
Salaries expense	$17,250	$18,000
Rent expense	13,500	13,500
Advertising expense	3,750	3,750
Gas, oil, and repairs expense	750	750
Office supplies expense		150
Insurance expense.		1,350
Depreciation expense, office equipment . .		1,500
Depreciation expense, automobile		3,000
Total operating expenses	35,250	42,000
Net income	$51,373	$45,750

Exercise 3–10
Balance sheet equity section for a corporation
(L. O. 5)

A corporation had $375,000 of common stock issued and outstanding during all of 1990. It began the year with $95,000 of retained earnings, and it declared and paid $30,000 of cash dividends to its shareholders. It also earned a $75,000 1990 net income. Prepare the equity section of the corporation's year-end balance sheet.

Exercise 3–11
Calculating elements of change in owner's equity
(Review exercise)

Calculate the missing item in each of the following cases:

	Case 1	Case 2	Case 3	Case 4	Case 5
The Owner, capital, January 1, 1990	$95,900	$76,000	$ (c)	$55,500	$38,000
Total revenues during 1990	84,000	(b)	65,200	67,600	46,600
Total expenses during 1990	56,500	37,200	72,000	(d)	37,500
Withdrawals during the year	45,000	21,000	12,800	18,000	(e)
The Owner, capital, December 31, 1990 . .	(a)	84,400	49,300	52,100	32,000

*Exercise 3–12
Adjustments for prepaid items recorded in expense and revenue accounts
(L. O. 7)

Ace Consulting was organized on December 1 and follows the procedure of debiting expense accounts when it records prepayments of expenses; also, revenue accounts are credited when unearned revenues are received. Prepare adjusting journal entries on December 31 for the following items:

a. Shop Supplies were purchased during December for $975. A December 31 inventory showed that $180 of supplies were on hand.

b. The company paid insurance premiums of $1,260 during December. On December 31, an examination of the insurance policies showed that $210 of insurance had expired.

c. During December, the business received $1,900 from one client for two consulting projects. As of December 31, only one project, for which the client was charged $1,100, had been completed.

d. Late in December, the business received $1,500 from a second client for consulting services to be performed in January.

*Exercise 3–13
Adjustments for supplies when purchases were recorded as expenses
(L. O. 7)

Ideas Company prepares monthly financial statements. On June 30, the balance in the Office Supplies account was $400. During July, $740 of supplies were purchased and debited to Office Supplies Expense.

a. Prepare an adjusting journal entry on July 31 to account for the supplies, assuming a July 31 inventory of supplies showed that $325 of supplies were on hand.

b. Prepare an adjusting journal entry on July 31 to account for the supplies, assuming a July 31 inventory of supplies showed that $500 of supplies were on hand.

Problems

Problem 3–1
Adjusting journal entries
(L. O. 2, 4)

The following information for adjustments was available on December 31, 1990, the end of Tuft Company's annual accounting period:

a. The Store Supplies account had a $150 debit balance at the beginning of the year, $675 of supplies were purchased during the year, and an inventory of unused supplies at year-end totaled $180.

b. An examination of insurance policies showed three policies, as follows:

Policy	Date of Purchase	Life of Policy	Cost
1	September 1, 1989	3 years	$2,100
2	March 1, 1990	2 years	840
3	July 1, 1990	1 year	576

Prepaid Insurance was debited for the cost of each policy at the time of its purchase. Expired insurance was correctly recorded at the end of 1989.

c. The company's two employees earn $60 per day and $70 per day, respectively. They are paid each Friday for a five-day workweek that begins on Monday. This year, December 31 fell on Wednesday, and the employees both worked on Monday, Tuesday, and Wednesday. The next payment for five days' work will be on January 2.

d. The company purchased a building on April 1, 1990. The building cost $435,000, has an estimated 25-year life, and is not expected to have any salvage value at the end of that time.

e. The company occupies most of the space in its building but it also rents space. One tenant rented a small amount of space on October 1 at $500 per month. The tenant paid the rent on the first day of October and November, and the amounts paid were credited to Rent Earned. However, the tenant did not pay the December rent until January 10, 1991, at which time he also paid the rent for January.

f. Another tenant agreed on November 1 to rent a small amount of space at $540 per month, and on that date paid three months' rent in advance. The receipt was credited to Unearned Rent.

Required

1. Given the above information, journalize adjusting entries dated December 31, 1990, prior to the preparation of annual financial statements.

2. Prepare journal entries to record the January payments and receipts that involve amounts which were accrued on December 31.

Problem 3–2
Adjusting entries and the adjusted trial balance
(L. O. 2, 5)

Century Realty's unadjusted trial balance on December 31, 1990, the end of its annual accounting period, is as follows:

CENTURY REALTY
Trial Balance
December 31, 1990

Cash	$ 2,500	
Prepaid insurance	2,100	
Office supplies	555	
Office equipment	7,500	
Accumulated depreciation, office equipment . .		$ 2,500
Automobile	15,350	
Accumulated depreciation, automobile		3,000
Accounts payable		275
Unearned management fees.		540
Don Miller, capital.		15,000
Don Miller, withdrawals.	22,500	
Sales commissions earned		49,400
Office salaries expense	12,360	
Advertising expense	1,200	
Rent expense	6,000	
Telephone expense.	650	
Totals	$70,715	$70,715

Required

1. Set up accounts for the items in the trial balance plus these additional accounts: Accounts Receivable; Office Salaries Payable; Management Fees Earned; Insurance Expense; Office Supplies Expense; Depreciation Expense, Office Equipment; and Depreciation Expense, Automobile. Enter the trial balance amounts in the accounts.

2. Use the following information to prepare and post adjusting entries:
   a. An examination of insurance policies shows $775 of expired insurance.
   b. An inventory shows $75 of unused office supplies on hand.
   c. Estimated annual depreciation on the office equipment is $935.
   d. Estimated annual depreciation on the automobile is $2,100.
   e. Century Realty offers property management services. On November 1, the company agreed to manage an office building for a client. The contract calls for a $180 monthly fee, and the client paid the first three months' fees in advance at the time the contract was signed. The amount paid was credited to the Unearned Management Fees account.
   f. On October 15, the company agreed to manage an apartment building for $120 per month payable at the end of each three-month period. Fees for two and one-half months have accrued.

g. The one office employee is paid weekly; and on December 31, three days' wages at $55 per day have accrued.

3. After posting the adjusting entries, prepare an adjusted trial balance, an income statement, a statement of changes in owner's equity, and a classified balance sheet. Miller did not make additional investments in the business during the year.

Problem 3–3
Adjusting entries and the adjusted trial balance
(L. O. 2, 5)

The unadjusted trial balance of Countrywide Moving and Storage follows:

COUNTRYWIDE MOVING AND STORAGE
Trial Balance
December 31, 1990

Cash	$ 2,990	
Accounts receivable	775	
Prepaid insurance	4,500	
Office supplies	485	
Investment in Trail, Inc., common stock	10,000	
Office equipment	4,500	
Accumulated depreciation, office equipment		$ 2,000
Trucks	54,000	
Accumulated depreciation, trucks		14,000
Building	160,000	
Accumulated depreciation, building		35,000
Land	21,000	
Franchise	30,000	
Unearned storage fees		2,075
Long-term notes payable		144,000
Dennis Meade, capital		65,000
Dennis Meade, withdrawals	29,000	
Revenue from moving services		110,000
Storage fees earned		8,325
Office salaries expense	13,745	
Drivers' and helpers' wages expense	32,950	
Gas, oil, and repairs expense	3,525	
Interest expense	12,930	
Totals	$380,400	$380,400

Required

1. Set up accounts for the items in the trial balance plus these additional accounts: Salaries and Wages Payable; Insurance Expense; Office Supplies Expense; Depreciation Expense, Office Equipment; Depreciation Expense, Trucks; and Depreciation Expense, Building. Enter the trial balance amounts in the accounts.

2. Journalize and post adjusting entries given the following information:
    a. Insurance premiums of $2,820 expired during the year.
    b. An inventory showed $165 of unused office supplies on hand.
    c. Estimated depreciation on the office equipment, $545; (d) on the trucks, $5,300; and (e) on the building, $6,700.
    f. Of the $2,075 credit balance in Unearned Storage Fees, $1,700 was earned by the year-end.
    g. Accrued storage fees earned but unrecorded at year-end totaled $315.
    h. There were $730 of earned but unrecorded drivers' and helpers' wages at the year-end.

3. Prepare an adjusted trial balance, an income statement for the year, a statement of changes in owner's equity, and a classified year-end balance sheet. Meade's capital account balance reflects the December 31, 1989, balance plus a January 1, 1990, investment of $50,000. A $4,800 installment on the note payable is due within one year.

Problem 3–4
Adjusting entries and the adjusted trial balance
(L. O. 2, 5)

Crestview Trailer Park's unadjusted trial balance is as follows:

CRESTVIEW TRAILER PARK
Trial Balance
December 31, 1990

Cash	$ 3,350	
Prepaid insurance	1,830	
Office supplies	415	
Office equipment	2,940	
Accumulated depreciation, office equipment		$ 975
Buildings and improvements	110,000	
Accumulated depreciation, buildings and improvements		25,620
Land	114,000	
Unearned rent		935
Long-term notes payable		142,000
Ida Henry, capital		50,100
Ida Henry, withdrawals	22,000	
Rent earned		62,235
Wages expense	12,200	
Utilities expense	995	
Property taxes expense	2,455	
Interest expense	11,680	
Totals	$281,865	$281,865

Required

1. Set up accounts for the items in the trial balance plus these additional accounts: Accounts Receivable; Wages Payable; Property Taxes Payable; Interest Payable; Insurance Expense; Office Supplies Expense; Depreciation Expense, Office Equipment; and Depreciation Expense, Buildings and Improvements. Enter the trial balance amounts in the accounts.

2. Use the following information to prepare and post adjusting journal entries:
   a. An insurance policy examination showed $1,400 of expired insurance.
   b. An inventory showed $140 of unused office supplies on hand.
   c. Estimated depreciation expense on office equipment, $350; and (d) on buildings and improvements, $5,500.
   e. By year-end, $690 of the Unearned Rent account balance was earned.
   f. A tenant is in arrears on rent payments, and this $100 of accrued revenue was unrecorded at the time the trial balance was prepared.
   g. The one employee of the trailer park works a five-day workweek at $50 per day. The employee was paid last week but has worked three days this week for which he has not been paid.
   h. Three months' property taxes, totaling $789, have accrued. This additional amount of property taxes expense has not been recorded.

    i. One month's interest on the note payable, $1,000, has accrued but is unrecorded.

3. Post the adjusting entries and prepare an adjusted trial balance, an income statement for the year, a statement of changes in owner's equity, and a classified balance sheet. Ms. Henry's capital account balance has not been increased by investments during 1990. A $7,200 installment on the note payable is due within one year.

Problem 3–5
Accrual basis income statement
(L. O. 3, 5)

Lily Kent purchased Pecan Grove, a mobile home park, last September 1, and she has operated it four months without keeping formal accounting records. However, she has deposited all receipts in the bank and has kept an accurate chequebook record of payments. An analysis of the cash receipts and payments follows:

	Receipts	Payments
Investment	$52,000	
Purchased Pecan Grove:		
Office equipment	$ 1,500	
Buildings and improvements	90,000	
Land	105,000	
Total	$196,500	
Less long-term note payable signed . .	145,000	
Cash paid.		$51,500
Insurance premium paid		1,140
Office supplies purchased		144
Wages paid		4,000
Utilities paid		450
Property taxes paid		1,500
Owner's withdrawals of cash.		4,800
Mobile home space rentals collected	19,380	
Totals	$71,380	$63,534
Cash balance, December 31.		7,846
Totals	$71,380	$71,380

Ms. Kent wants you to prepare an accrual basis income statement for the village for the four-month period she has operated the business, a statement of changes in owner's equity, and a December 31 balance sheet. You ascertain the following (T-accounts may be helpful in organizing the data):

The buildings and improvements were estimated to have a 25-year remaining life when purchased and at the end of that time will be wrecked. It is estimated that the sale of salvaged materials will just pay the wrecking costs and the cost of clearing the site. The office equipment is in good condition. At the time of purchase, Ms. Kent estimated she would use the equipment for three years and would then trade it in on new equipment of like kind. She thought $150 a fair estimate of what she would receive for the old equipment when she traded it in at the end of three years.

The $1,140 payment for insurance was for a policy taken out on September 1. The policy's protection was for one year beginning on that date. Ms. Kent estimates that one third of the office supplies purchased have been used. She also says that the one employee of the park earns $50 per day for a five-day week that ends on Friday. The employee was paid last week but has worked four days, December 28 through 31, for which he has not been paid.

Included in the $19,380 of mobile home rentals collected is $360 received from a tenant for three months' rent beginning on December 1. Also, a tenant has not paid his $120 rent for the month of December.

The long-term note payable requires an annual payment of 12% interest on the beginning principal balance plus a $6,000 annual payment on the principal. The first payment is due next September 1. The property tax payment was for one year's taxes that were paid on October 1 for the tax year beginning on September 1, the day Ms. Kent purchased the business.

*Problem 3–6
Recording prepayments and unearned items in income statement accounts
(L. O. 2, 7)

Setter Company debits expense accounts when recording prepaid expenses; it credits revenue accounts when recording unearned receipts. The following information was available on December 31, 1990, the end of the company's annual accounting period.

a. The Store Supplies account had a $340 debit balance at the beginning of the year, $1,250 of supplies were purchased during the year, and an inventory of unused supplies at the year-end totaled $620.

b. An examination of insurance policies showed two policies, as follows:

Policy	Date of Purchase	Life of Policy	Cost
1	May 1, 1988	3 years	$2,340
2	October 1, 1990	2 years	2,280

Insurance Expense was debited for the cost of each policy at the time of its purchase. However, the correct amount of Prepaid Insurance was recorded during the adjustment processes at the end of 1988 and 1989.

c. On October 15, 1990, Setter Company agreed to provide consulting services to a client and received advance payment of $8,500. At year-end, the client agreed that three fourths of the services had been provided.

d. The company occupies most of the space in its building but it also rents space to one tenant. The tenant agreed on November 1 to rent a small amount of space at $750 per month, and on that date paid three months' rent in advance.

e. The Office Supplies account had a $550 debit balance at the beginning of the year and $750 of supplies were purchased during the year. A year-end inventory of office supplies indicated that supplies amounting to $990 had been used during the year.

Required

Prepare adjusting journal entries dated December 31, 1990, prior to the preparation of annual financial statements. For item (b), prepare a separate adjusting entry for each insurance policy.

Alternate Problems

Problem 3–1A
Adjusting journal entries
(L. O. 2, 4)

The following information for preparing adjusting entries was available on December 31, 1990, the end of Shiff Company's annual accounting period.

a. The Store Supplies account had a $175 debit balance at the beginning of the year, $845 of supplies were purchased during the year, and an inventory of unused supplies at year-end totaled $185.

b. An examination of insurance policies showed three policies, as follows:

Policy	Protection Began on	Life of Policy	Cost
1	March 12, 1989	3 years	$1,260
2	May 1, 1990	2 years	810
3	April 1, 1990	1 year	600

Prepaid Insurance was debited for the cost of each policy at the time of purchase. Expired insurance was correctly recorded at the end of 1989.

c. The company's two employees earn $60 per day and $75 per day, respectively. They are paid each Friday for a five-day workweek that begins on Monday. December 31 fell on Tuesday, and the employees both worked on Monday and Tuesday but have not been paid. The next payment for five days' work will be on January 3.

d. The company purchased a building on July 1, 1990. The building cost $675,000, has an estimated 25-year life, and is not expected to have any salvage value at the end of its life.

e. The company occupies most of the space in its building, but it also rents space. One tenant rented a small amount of space on September 1 at $300 per month. The tenant paid the rent on the first day of each month, September through November, and the amounts paid were credited to Rent Earned. However, the tenant did not pay the December rent until January 12, at which time he also paid the rent for January.

f. Another tenant agreed on November 1 to rent a small amount of space at $335 per month and on that date paid three months' rent in advance. The amount paid was credited to Unearned Rent.

Required

1. Given the above information, journalize adjusting entries dated December 31, 1990, prior to the preparation of annual financial statements.

2. Prepare journal entries to record the January payments and receipts that involve amounts which were accrued on December 31.

Problem 3–2A
Adjusting entries and the
adjusted trial balance
(L. O. 2, 5)

Miller Realty's unadjusted trial balance on December 31, 1990, the end of its annual accounting period, is as follows:

MILLER REALTY
Trial Balance
December 31, 1990

Cash	$ 2,910	
Prepaid insurance	1,375	
Office supplies	435	
Office equipment	9,375	
Accumulated depreciation, office equipment . .		$ 2,880
Automobile	19,150	
Accumulated depreciation, automobile		3,225
Accounts payable		335
Unearned management fees		675
Don Miller, capital		16,700
Don Miller, withdrawals	27,900	
Sales commissions earned		61,920
Office salaries expense	15,450	
Advertising expense	1,245	
Rent expense	7,200	
Telephone expense	695	
Totals	$85,735	$85,735

Required

1. Set up accounts for the items in the trial balance plus these additional accounts: Accounts Receivable; Office Salaries Payable; Management Fees Earned; Insurance Expense; Office Supplies Expense; Depreciation Expense, Office Equipment; and Depreciation Expense, Automobile. Enter the trial balance amounts in the accounts.

2. Use the information that follows to prepare and post adjusting entries:

    a. An examination of insurance policies shows $1,085 of expired insurance.

    b. An inventory shows $120 of unused office supplies on hand.

    c. Estimated annual depreciation on the office equipment is $1,225.

    d. Estimated annual depreciation on the automobile is $2,665.

    e. The December telephone bill arrived after the trial balance was prepared, and its $60 amount was not included in the trial balance amounts. Also, a $165 bill for newspaper advertising that had appeared in December was not included in the trial balance amounts.

    f. A client who was taking a tour around the world signed a contract with Miller Realty for the management of his apartment building. The contract calls for a $225 monthly fee, and management began on December 1. The client paid three months' fees in advance, and the amount paid was credited to the Unearned Management Fees account.

    g. Miller Realty agreed to manage the small office building of a second client for $250 per month payable at the end of each three months. The contract was signed on November 15, and one and one-half months' fees have accrued.

    h. The one office employee is paid weekly; and on December 31, four days' wages at $60 per day have accrued.

3. After posting the adjusting entries, prepare an adjusted trial balance, an income statement, a statement of changes in owner's equity, and a classified balance sheet. Miller's capital account balance of $16,700 consists of a $6,700 balance on December 31, 1989, plus a $10,000 investment during 1990.

Problem 3–3A
Adjusting entries and the adjusted trial balance
(L. O. 2, 5)

The unadjusted trial balance of United Moving and Storage follows:

UNITED MOVING AND STORAGE
Trial Balance
December 31, 1990

Cash	$ 3,360	
Accounts receivable	815	
Prepaid insurance	5,370	
Office supplies	480	
Investment in Trail, Inc., common stock	25,000	
Office equipment	5,475	
Accumulated depreciation, office equipment . .		$ 2,520
Trucks	66,300	
Accumulated depreciation, trucks		17,300
Building	207,000	
Accumulated depreciation, building		42,900
Land.	26,250	
Franchise	20,000	
Unearned storage fees		2,595
Long-term notes payable		180,000
Dennis Mead, capital		81,170
Dennis Meade, withdrawals	36,000	
Revenue from moving services		135,170
Storage fees earned		11,660
Office salaries expense	17,100	
Drivers' and helpers' wages expense	39,945	
Gas, oil, and repairs expense	4,020	
Interest expense	16,200	
Totals	$473,315	$473,315

Required

1. Set up accounts for the items in the trial balance plus these additional accounts: Salaries and Wages Payable; Insurance Expense; Office Supplies Expense; Depreciation Expense, Office Equipment; Depreciation Expense, Trucks; and Depreciation Expense, Building. Enter the trial balance amounts in the accounts.

2. Use the information that follows to prepare and post adjusting entries:
    a. Insurance premiums of $4,225 expired during the year.
    b. An inventory shows $165 of unused office supplies on hand.
    c. Estimated depreciation on the office equipment, $775; (d) on the trucks, $8,000; and (e) on the building, $9,300.
    f. Of the $2,595 balance in the Unearned Storage Fees account, $1,985 was earned by the year-end.
    g. Accrued storage fees earned but unrecorded at year-end totaled $515.
    h. There were $200 of earned but unrecorded office salaries and $1,135 of earned but unrecorded drivers' and helpers' wages at the year-end.

3. Prepare an adjusted trial balance, an income statement for the year, a statement of changes in owner's equity, and a classified year-end balance sheet. Meade's $81,170 capital balance reflects the December 31, 1989, balance plus a January 15, 1990, investment of $30,000. A $9,000 installment on the long-term note payable is due within one year.

Problem 3–4A
Adjusting entries and the adjusted trial balance
(L. O. 2, 5)

Bel-Aire Trailer Park's unadjusted trial balance, at the end of its annual accounting period, follows:

BEL-AIRE TRAILER PARK
Trial Balance
December 31, 1990

Cash	$ 3,810	
Prepaid insurance	2,285	
Office supplies	390	
Office equipment	3,675	
Accumulated depreciation, office equipment		$ 1,225
Buildings and improvements	138,000	
Accumulated depreciation, buildings and improvements		32,025
Land	142,500	
Unearned rent		1,170
Long-term notes payable		177,000
Ida Henry, capital		62,710
Ida Henry, withdrawals	27,300	
Rent earned		77,800
Wages expense	15,180	
Utilities expense	1,240	
Property taxes expense	2,950	
Interest expense	14,600	
Totals	$351,930	$351,930

Required

1. Set up accounts for the items in the trial balance plus these additional accounts: Accounts Receivable; Wages Payable; Property Taxes Payable; Interest Payable; Insurance Expense; Office Supplies Expense; Depreciation Expense, Office Equipment; and Depreciation Expense, Buildings and Improvements. Enter the trial balance amounts in the accounts.

2. Use the information that follows to prepare and post adjusting journal entries:
    a. An insurance policy examination shows $1,850 of expired insurance.
    b. An inventory shows $125 of unused office supplies on hand.
    c. Estimated depreciation of office equipment, $465; and (d) of buildings and improvements, $7,875.
    e. An examination reveals that $665 of the Unearned Rent balance was earned by the year-end.
    f. One tenant is in arrears on rent payments, and this $150 of accrued revenue was unrecorded at the time the trial balance was prepared.
    g. Four months' property taxes expense, estimated at $1,500, has accrued but was not recorded at the time the trial balance was prepared.

> *h.* The one employee of the trailer park works a five-day week at $60 per day. He was paid last week but has worked four days this week for which he has not been paid.
>
> *i.* Three months' interest on the note payable, $4,866, has accrued but is unpaid on the trial balance date.
>
> 3. Post the adjusting entries and prepare an adjusted trial balance, an income statement for the year, a statement of changes in owner's equity, and a classified balance sheet. Ms. Henry's capital account balance has not been increased by investments during 1990. An $8,250 payment on the long-term note payable is due within one year.

Problem 3–5A
Accrual basis income statement
(L. O. 3, 5)

James Piper, a lawyer, has always kept his records on a cash basis; at the end of 1990, he prepared the following cash basis income statement:

JAMES PIPER, LAWYER
Income Statement
For Year Ended December 31, 1990

Revenues	$95,500
Expenses	40,450
Net income	$55,050

In preparing the statement, the following amounts of prepaid, unearned, and accrued items were ignored at the end of 1989 and 1990:

	End of 1989	End of 1990
Prepaid expenses	$2,310	$1,800
Accrued expenses	2,595	3,270
Unearned revenues	3,300	5,430
Accrued revenues	4,550	3,660

Required

Under the assumptions that the 1989 prepaid expenses were consumed or expired in 1990, the 1989 unearned revenues were earned in 1990, and the 1989 accrued items were either paid or received in cash in 1990, prepare a 1990 accrual basis income statement for James Piper's law practice. Attach to your statement calculations showing how you arrived at each 1990 income statement amount.

*Problem 3–6A
Recording prepayments and unearned items in income statement accounts
(L. O. 2, 7)

In recording prepaid expenses and unearned revenues, Nickle Company debits the disbursements to expense accounts and credits the receipts to revenue accounts. The following information was available on December 31, 1990, the end of the Nickle Company's annual accounting period:

a. The Store Supplies account had an $880 debit balance at the beginning of the year, $1,790 of supplies were purchased during the year, and an inventory of unused supplies at the year-end totaled $1,320.

b. An examination of insurance policies showed two policies, as follows:

Policy	Date of Purchase	Life of Policy	Cost
1	April 1, 1988	3 years	$3,528
2	August 1, 1990	2 years	3,408

Insurance Expense was debited for the cost of each policy at the time of its purchase. However, the correct amount of Prepaid Insurance was recorded during the adjustment processes at the end of 1988 and 1989.

c. On July 20, 1990, Nickle Company agreed to provide consulting services to a client and received advance payment of $12,900. At year-end, the client agreed that two thirds of the services had been provided.

d. The company occupies most of the space in its building but it also rents space to one tenant. The tenant agreed on October 1 to rent a small amount of space at $900 per month, and on that date paid four months' rent in advance.

e. The Office Supplies account had a $620 debit balance at the beginning of the year and $1,350 of supplies were purchased during the year. A year-end inventory of office supplies indicated that supplies amounting to $1,050 had been used during the year.

Required

Prepare adjusting journal entries dated December 31, 1990, prior to the preparation of annual financial statements. For item (b), prepare a separate adjusting entry for each insurance policy.

Provocative Problems

Provocative Problem 3–1
Kidd Management Services
(L. O. 3)

The 1989 and 1990 balance sheets of Kidd Management Services show the following assets and liabilities at the end of each of the years:

	December 31	
	1989	1990
Prepaid insurance	$1,580	$1,140
Property management fees receivable	900	1,675
Interest payable	375	310
Unearned property management fees	890	1,220

The concern's records show the following amounts of cash disbursed and received for these items during 1990:

Cash disbursed to pay insurance premiums . .	$2,470
Cash disbursed to pay interest	1,750
Cash received for managing property	9,720

Present calculations to show the amounts to be reported on Kidd Management Services' 1990 income statement for (a) insurance expense, (b) interest expense, and (c) property management fees earned.

Provocative Problem 3–2
Field Electrical Service
(L. O. 3, 5)

Jay Field began Field Electrical Service, a new business, on January 2, 1990. After one year's operations, Jay feels the business has done a lot of work during its first year. However, the bank has begun to dishonour its cheques. The company's creditors are dunning it for bills it is unable to pay, and Jay just cannot understand why. Consequently, he has asked your help in determining the results of the first year's operations.

You find that the service's accounting records, such as they are, have been kept by Jay's son, who has no formal training in record-keeping. However, he has prepared for your inspection the following statement of cash receipts and disbursements:

FIELD ELECTRICAL SERVICE
Cash Receipts and Disbursements
For Year Ended December 31, 1990

Receipts:		
Owner's investment	$18,000	
Received from customers for services	53,300	$71,300
Disbursements:		
Rent expense	$ 4,875	
Repair equipment purchased	8,100	
Service truck expense	15,470	
Wages expense	28,080	
Insurance expense	1,905	
Repair parts and supplies	12,975	71,405
Bank overdraft		$ (105)

There were no errors in the statement, and you learn these additional facts:

1. The lease contract for the shop space runs for five years and requires rent payments of $375 per month, with the first and last month's rent to be paid in advance. All required payments were made on time.

2. The repair equipment has an estimated six-year life, after which it will be valueless. It has been used a full year.

3. The service truck expense consists of $13,800 paid for the truck on January 2, plus $1,670 paid for gas and oil. Mr. Field expects to use the truck four years, after which he thinks he will get $1,800 for it as a trade-in on a new truck.

4. The wages expense consists of $4,680 paid the service's one employee who was hired on September 1, plus $23,400 of personal withdrawals by Mr. Field. Also, the one employee is owed $150 of earned but unpaid wages.

5. The $1,905 of insurance expense resulted from paying premiums on two insurance policies on January 2. One policy cost $825 and gave protection for one year. The other policy cost $1,080 for two years' protection.

6. In addition to the $12,975 of repair parts and supplies paid for during the year, creditors have billed the business $800 for parts and supplies purchased and delivered but not paid for. Also, an inventory shows $1,430 of unused parts and supplies on hand.

7. Mr. Field reports that the business does most of its work for cash, but customers owe $400 for repair work done on credit.

Prepare an accrual basis income statement for the year, a statement of changes in owner's equity, and a classified balance sheet showing its year-end financial position.

Provocative Problem 3–3
Repairs Fast
(L. O. 3, 5)

During the first week of January 1990, Ray Slovak began a repair business he calls Repairs Fast. He has kept no accounting records, but he does keep any unpaid invoices in a box near his workbench. He has kept a good record of the year's receipts and payments, which follows:

	Receipts	Payments
Investment	$ 7,500	
Shop equipment		$ 6,000
Repair parts and supplies		6,315
Rent payments		3,900
Insurance premiums paid		1,176
Newspaper advertising paid		375
Utility bills paid		970
Part-time helper's wages paid		9,345
Ray Slovak for personal use		22,500
Revenue from repairs	44,930	
Subtotals	$52,430	$50,581
Cash balance, December 31, 1990		1,849
Totals	$52,430	$52,430

Ray would like to know how much the business actually earned during its first year. Therefore, he would like for you to prepare an accrual basis income statement, a statement of changes in owner's equity, and a year-end classified balance sheet for the shop.

You learn that the shop equipment has an estimated eight-year life, after which it will be worthless. There is a $475 unpaid invoice in the box near Ray's workbench for supplies received, and an inventory shows $495 of unused supplies on hand. The shop space rents for $300 per month on a five-year lease. The lease contract requires payment of the first and last months' rents in advance, which were paid. The insurance premiums were for two policies taken out on January 2. The first is a one-year policy that cost $360. The second is a two-year policy that cost $816. There are $90 of earned but unpaid wages owed the helper, and customers owe the shop $580 for repair services they have received.

Analytical and Review Problems

A&R Problem 3–1

The Salaries Payable account of James Bay Company Limited appears below:

Salaries Payable

Entries during 19A5	94,560	Bal. Jan. 1, 19A5	1,260
		Entries during 19A5	94,420

The company records the salary expense and related liability at the end of each week and pays the employees on the last Friday of the month.

Required

Calculate:

1. Salary expense for 19A5.
2. How much was paid to employees in 19A5 for work done in 19A4?
3. How much was paid to employees in 19A5 for work done in 19A5?
4. How much will be paid to employees in 19A6 for work done in 19A5?

A&R Problem 3–2

The Prepaid Insurance account of Hobby Shops is reproduced below:

Prepaid Insurance

Bal. Jan. 1, 19A5	580	Entry Dec. 31, 19A5	2,100
Entries during 19A5	1,800		

Required

Reconstruct the journal entries made by Hobby Shops in 19A5.

A&R Problem 3–3

Ida M. Smart, the accountant for Longview Company, believes that the need for adjusting entries at the end of the accounting period is caused by the lack of anticipation on the part of the accountant. She holds that if all transactions are recorded properly, with the year-end adjustments fully anticipated at the time the transactions occur, the need for year-end adjustments will be completely eliminated. To prove her point, she cites the following journal entries recorded in the books for the current year.

Jan.	1	Insurance expense	300	
		Prepaid insurance.	600	
		Cash		900
		To record the payment of a three-year insurance.		
	1	Rent expense	1,800	
		Cash		1,800
		One year's rent paid.		
	1	Depreciation expense.	900	
		Accumulated depreciation		900
		One-year depreciation for office equipment costing $9,000 with an estimated useful life of 10 years and no salvage value.		
July	1	Cash	1,200	
		Commission earned		600
		Commission received in advance.		600
		Receipt of 12 months' commissions.		
	1	Office supplies used	300	
		Office supplies	200	
		Accounts payable		500
		Purchase of office supplies, half of which will probably be used during the year.		

Required

1. By anticipating year-end adjustments at the time the transactions are recorded, what problems or difficulties do you think Ms. Smart will most likely encounter at the year-end date?

2. Is it usually true that some adjustments are not susceptible to accurate anticipation? Explain and give examples to support your answer.

3. If you follow Ms. Smart's approach of anticipating adjustments at the time the transactions occur, what entries should you make at the beginning of year two, based on the entries recorded in year one?

4. What is to be gained by Ms. Smart's approach of anticipating adjustments? Explain.

A&R Problem 3–4

Robert Butler, a local dentist, asked you to help him prepare an income statement that would be acceptable by Revenue Canada. Butler's secretary/nurse maintained all the records and had developed the following statement for the year ended December 31, 1990.

DR. ROBERT BUTLER
Income and Expense Statement
1990

Dental fees collected		125,800
Expenses paid:		
Rent for office	$ 7,200	
Rent for dental equipment	18,000	
Utilities	600	
Telephone	360	
Supplies	1,500	
Wages of secretary/nurse	26,000	53,660
Profit for the year		$72,140

Since the statement was prepared on a 100% cash basis you realized that it would not be acceptable by Revenue Canada. Consequently, you conducted an investigation of records of the current year as well as of the previous year. You discovered the following:

a. Of the $125,800 of fees collected in 1990, $1,800 was for work performed in 1989.

b. On December 31, 1990, uncollected fees for work performed during 1990 were $4,700.

c. When Butler started his dental practice in 1989 he entered into a 10-year agreement with Universal Dental Supply, Inc. Under the agreement Butler obtained all the necessary equipment for a monthly rental of $1,500. The payments are made on the 15th of each month.

d. Office rent is paid at the rate of $600 on the 1st of each month.

e. On December 31, 1990, a count of supplies indicated $300 were on hand. It was estimated that on January 1, 1990, supplies of $100 were on hand.

f. The secretary/nurse started working in February 1990 and on December 31, 1990, wages amounting to $400 remained unpaid.

g. Unpaid utilities and telephone for December 1990 were expected to be greater by $40 and $30 respectively than for December 1989.

Required

Prepare an income statement for 1990 on an accrual basis. Support all changes in amounts from the statement prepared by the secretary/nurse.

A&R Problem 3–5

The following situations relate to McLean Company. The books are adjusted on December 31 in order to prepare year-end statements. The current year is 1990.

Required

For each case below, you are to give the December 31, 1990, adjusting entry or entries (omit narratives).

Case A. On January 2, 1990, the company purchased equipment to be used in the business at a cost of $30,800. The equipment is expected to be used for 10 years at which time it would be sold for an estimated $3,800.

Case B. At the beginning of 1990, office supplies amounted to $300. During 1990, office supplies in the amount of $1,400 were purchased and debited to Office Supplies Expense. A count on December 31, 1990, showed supplies on hand amounted to $500.

Case C. On July 2, 1990, the company paid a three-year insurance premium amounting to $1,800. This amount was debited to Prepaid Insurance.

Case D. On October 1, 1990, the compay paid rent on a leased office space. The payment of $6,000 was for a 12-month period. At the time of payment, Rent Expense was debited for the $6,000.

Case E. On April 1, 1990, the company leased to Vachon Company its un-used land for a 12-month period for $4,800. On April 1, the entire amount was credited to Unearned Rent Revenue.

A&R Problem 3–6

An income statement prepared on an accrual basis reflects the application, primarily, of two of the generally accepted accounting principles.

Required

1. Identify the two principles.
2. Discuss their application.
3. Do these principles apply equally to the balance sheet? If yes, explain how.

4

The Work Sheet and Closing the Accounts of Proprietorships, Partnerships, and Corporations

Your study of Chapter 4 will focus on some of the procedures that are performed at the end of each accounting period. You will learn to use a work sheet to show the effects of the adjustments and to organize the data prior to preparing financial statements. Also, you will learn the necessary steps to get the accounts ready for use in the following accounting period.

Learning Objectives

After studying Chapter 4, you should be able to:

1. Explain why a work sheet is prepared and be able to prepare a work sheet for a service-type business.
2. Prepare closing entries for a service business and explain why it is necessary to close the temporary accounts at the end of each accounting period.
3. Prepare a post-closing trial balance and explain its purpose.
4. Explain the nature of a corporation's retained earnings and its relationship to the declaration of dividends.
5. Prepare entries to record the declaration and payment of a dividend and to close the temporary accounts of a corporation.
6. List the steps in the accounting cycle in the order in which they are completed and perform each step.
7. Define or explain the words and phrases listed in the chapter Glossary.

After studying the appendix to Chapter 4 (Appendix B), you should be able to:

8. Prepare reversing entries and explain when and why they are used.

Using a Work Sheet at the End of Each Accounting Period

Explain why a work sheet is prepared and be able to prepare a work sheet for a service-type business. (L. O. 1)

In the process of organizing the data that go into the formal financial reports given to managers and other interested parties, accountants prepare numerous memoranda, analyses, and informal papers. These analyses and memoranda, called **working papers,** are invaluable tools of the accountant. One important example of such working papers is the **work sheet** described in this chapter. The work sheet for a business is not given to the owner or manager. It is prepared solely for the accountant's use and is kept by the accountant.

Recall the end-of-period procedures that we discussed in Chapter 3. After all transactions were recorded, an unadjusted trial balance was prepared and adjusting entries were entered in the journal and posted to the accounts. Then, an adjusted trial balance was prepared and used as a basis for preparing the financial statements.

For a very small business, these procedures are satisfactory. However, if a company has more than a few accounts and adjustments, you will make fewer errors if you insert an additional step in the procedures. The additional step is to prepare a work sheet. A work sheet is prepared before the adjusting entries are journalized or posted to the accounts.

On the work sheet, the accountant (1) shows the unadjusted trial balance, (2) shows the effects of the adjustments on the account balances, (3) shows the adjusted trial balance, and (4) sorts the adjusted amounts into columns according to whether the accounts are used in preparing the income statement or the statement of changes in owner's equity or balance sheet. Also, the amount of net income is calculated on the work sheet. After the work sheet is completed, the work sheet information is used to prepare the financial statements and to journalize the adjusting entries and the closing entries. (Closing entries are discussed later in this chapter.)

Preparing a Work Sheet

Illustration 4–1 shows the multicolumn form that is used to prepare a work sheet. Note that two columns each are provided for the unadjusted trial balance, the adjustments, the adjusted trial balance, the income statement, and the statement of changes in owner's equity or balance sheet. A work sheet could be prepared with two separate columns for the statement of changes in owner's equity and two separate columns for the balance sheet. However, since the statement of changes in owner's equity includes only a few items, this usually is not done. Instead, most work sheets provide only two columns for both statements, as Illustration 4–1 shows.

When a work sheet is used, the unadjusted trial balance is not prepared on a separate form. Instead, the first step in preparing the work sheet is to prepare the unadjusted trial balance in the first two money columns of the work sheet. Turn the first transparency overlay to see Illustration 4–2, which shows this first step in preparing the work sheet for Jerry Dow, Lawyer. This is the same example that we used in Chapters 1 through 3.

Remember that Dow's law practice completed a number of transactions during December 1990. The unadjusted trial balance in Illustration 4–2 reflects the account balances after these December transactions were recorded but *before any adjusting entries were journalized or posted.*

In Illustration 4–2, a blank line was left after the Legal Fees Earned account. Based on past experience, the accountant may realize that more than one line will be needed to show the adjustments to a particular account. When you turn the second transparency overlay, you will see in Illustration 4–3 that Legal Fees Earned is an example. Another alternative is to "squeeze" two adjustments on one line or to combine the effects of two or more adjustments in one amount.

The next step in preparing a work sheet is to enter the adjustments in the columns labeled "Adjustments," as in Illustration 4–3. The adjustments in Illustration 4–3 are the same ones that we discussed in Chapter 3. Notice that an identifying letter is used to relate the debit and credit of each adjustment. After you prepare a work sheet, you still have to enter the adjusting entries in the journal and post them to the ledger. At that time, the identifying letters help you to match correctly the debit and credit of each adjusting entry.

Explanations of the adjustments on the illustrated work sheet are as follows:

Adjustment (*a*): To adjust for expired insurance.
Adjustment (*b*): To adjust for the office supplies used.
Adjustment (*c*): To adjust for depreciation of the law library.
Adjustment (*d*): To adjust for depreciation of the office equipment.
Adjustment (*e*): To adjust for accrued salaries.
Adjustment (*f*): To adjust for unearned revenue.
Adjustment (*g*): To adjust for accrued revenue.

Most of the adjustments on the illustrated work sheet required one or two additional accounts to be written in below the original trial balance. These accounts did not have balances when the trial balance was prepared. Therefore, they were not listed in the trial balance. However, if you anticipate that additional accounts will be required, you may list them in the process of preparing the unadjusted trial balance.

After the adjustments are entered in the Adjustments columns, the columns are totaled to prove the equality of the debit and credit adjustments. Then you proceed to prepare the adjusted trial balance. To do so, each amount in the Unadjusted Trial Balance columns is combined with its adjustments in the Adjustments columns, if any, and is entered in the Adjusted Trial Balance columns.

For example, in Illustration 4–3, the Prepaid Insurance account has a $2,400 debit balance in the Unadjusted Trial Balance columns. This $2,400 debit is combined with the $100 credit in the Adjustments columns to give Prepaid Insurance a $2,300 debit in the Adjusted Trial Balance columns. Insurance Expense has no balance in the Unadjusted Trial Balance columns, but it has a $100 debit in the Adjustments columns. Therefore, no balance combined with a $100 debit gives Insurance Expense a $100 debit in the Adjusted Trial Balance columns. Cash, Office Equipment, and several other accounts have trial balance amounts but not adjustments, As a result, their unadjusted trial balance amounts are carried unchanged into the Adjusted Trial Balance columns.

After the combined amounts are carried to the Adjusted Trial Balance columns, the Adjusted Trial Balance columns are added to prove their equality. Then, the amounts in these columns are sorted to the financial statement columns, as shown in Illustration 4–4. (Turn the next transparency overlay.) Expenses are sorted to the Income Statement Debit column. Revenues are sorted to the Income Statement Credit column. Assets and the owner's withdrawals are sorted to the Statement of Changes in Owner's Equity or Balance Sheet Debit column. Liability items and the owner's capital account are sorted to the Statement of Changes in Owner's Equity or Balance Sheet Credit column. This task requires answers to only two questions: (1) Is the item to be sorted a debit or a credit? and (2) On which statement does it appear?

After the amounts are sorted to the proper columns, the columns are totaled as shown in Illustration 4–5. (Turn the last transparency overlay.) At this point, the difference between the totals of the Income Statement columns is the net income or loss. The difference is the net income or loss because revenues are entered in the Credit column and expenses in the Debit column. If the Credit column total exceeds the Debit column total, the difference is a net income. If the Debit column total exceeds the Credit column total, the difference is a net loss. In the illustrated work sheet, the Credit column total exceeds the Debit column total, and the result is a $1,160 net income.

After the net income is calculated in the Income Statement columns, it is added to the Statement of Changes in Owner's Equity or Balance Sheet Credit column. In that final column, the balance of the capital account does not yet reflect the increase in capital that resulted from net income. Therefore, adding the net income to this column has the effect of adding it to the capital account.

Had there been a loss, it would have been necessary to add the loss to the Debit column. This is because losses decrease owner's equity, and adding the loss to the Debit column has the effect of subtracting it from the capital account.

When the net income or net loss is added to the appropriate Statement of Changes in Owner's Equity or Balance Sheet column, the totals of the last two columns should balance. If they do not balance, you know that one or more errors were made in constructing the work sheet. Either the error or errors may have been mathematical or an amount may have been sorted to a wrong column.

Although balancing the last two columns is done in an effort to discover errors, the fact that they balance is not proof that the work sheet is free from error. These columns will balance even when certain types of errors have been made. For example, if you incorrectly carry an asset amount into the Income Statement Debit column, the columns will still balance. Or, if you carry a liability amount into the Income Statement Credit column, the columns will still balance. Either error will cause the net income amount to be incorrect. But, the columns will be in balance. Therefore, you must exercise care in sorting the adjusted trial balance amounts into the correct financial statement columns.

Preparing Financial Statements from the Work Sheet

We should emphasize that a work sheet is not a substitute for the financial statements. The work sheet is nothing more than a supporting tool that the accountant uses at the end of an accounting period to help organize the data. However, as soon as it is completed, the accountant uses the work sheet to prepare the financial statements. The items in the Income Statement columns provide the information necessary to prepare the formal income statement.

Illustration 4–1

Preparing a worksheet at the end of the accounting period

The heading should identify the entity, the nature of the document, and the time period

JERRY DOW, LAWYER
Work Sheet for Month Ended December 31, 1990

Account Titles	Unadjusted Trial Balance		Adjustments		Adjusted Trial Balance		Income Statement		Statement of Changes in Owner's Equity or Balance Sheet	
	Dr.	Cr.	Dr.	Cr.	Dr.	Cr.	Dr.	Cr.	Dr.	Cr.

The multicolumn work sheet can be prepared manually or with a computer spreadsheet program

The work sheet collects and summarizes the information used to prepare financial statements and to journalize adjusting and closing entries

Illustration 4-6
Financial statements prepared from the worksheet

JERRY DOW, LAWYER
Income Statement
For the Month Ended December 31, 1990

Revenues:		
Legal fees earned		$ 4,350
Operating expenses:		
Rent expense	$1,000	
Salaries expense	1,610	
Utilities expense	230	
Insurance expense	100	
Office supplies expense	45	
Depreciation expense, law library	80	
Depreciation expense, office equipment	125	
Total operating expenses		3,190
Net income		$ 1,160

JERRY DOW, LAWYER
Statement of Changes in Owner's Equity
For the Month Ended December 31, 1990

Jerry Dow, capital, November 30, 1990		$ –0–
Plus:		
Investments by owner	$9,000	
Net income	1,160	10,160
Total		$10,160
Less withdrawals by owner		1,100
Jerry Dow, capital, December 31, 1990		$ 9,060

JERRY DOW, LAWYER
Balance Sheet
December 31, 1990

Assets			Liabilities		
Cash		$ 650	Accounts payable		$ 760
Accounts receivable		200	Unearned legal fees		2,750
Prepaid insurance		2,300	Salaries payable		210
Office supplies		75	Total liabilities		$ 3,720
Law library	$2,880				
Less accumulated depreciation	80	2,800			
Office equipment	$6,880		**Owner's Equity**		
Less accumulated depreciation	125	6,755	Jerry Dow, capital		9,060
			Total liabilities and		
Total assets		$12,780	owner's equity		$12,780

Next, information is taken from the last two columns to prepare the statement of changes in owner's equity and the balance sheet. The financial statements prepared from the information in Illustration 4–5 are shown in Illustration 4–6.

Preparing Adjusting Entries from the Work Sheet

Entering the adjustments in the Adjustments columns of a work sheet does not get these adjustments into the ledger accounts. Therefore, after the work sheet is completed, you must prepare adjusting journal entries like the ones described in Chapter 3. The adjusting entries must be entered in the General Journal and posted to the accounts in the ledger. The work sheet makes this easy, because its Adjustments columns provide the information for these entries. All that is needed is an entry for each adjustment. If you prepare adjusting entries from the information in Illustration 4–5, you will see that they are the same adjusting entries we discussed in the last chapter.

Closing Entries

Prepare closing entries for a service business and explain why it is necessary to close the temporary accounts at the end of each accounting period. (L. O. 2)

After the work sheet and statements are completed and the adjusting entries are recorded, you also must journalize and post **closing entries.** Closing entries are designed to transfer the balances in the revenue accounts, the expense accounts, and the withdrawals account to a balance sheet equity account. In a single proprietorship, they are transferred to the owner's capital account. After the closing entries are posted, the revenue, expense, and withdrawals accounts have zero balances. Thus, these accounts are said to be closed, or cleared.

Why Closing Entries Are Made

When closing entries are prepared at the end of each accounting period, the revenue and expense accounts are closed by transferring their balances first to a summary account called **Income Summary.** Then, the Income Summary account balance, which is the net income or loss, is transferred in a single proprietorship to the owner's capital account. Finally, the owner's withdrawals account is transferred to the owner's capital account. These transfers, as shown in Illustration 4–7, are necessary because—

a. Revenues increase owner's equity, while expenses and withdrawals decrease owner's equity.
b. During an accounting period these increases and decreases are temporarily accumulated in revenue, expense, and withdrawals accounts rather than in the owner's capital account.
c. Closing entries are needed at the end of each accounting period to transfer the net effect of these increases and decreases out of the revenue, expense, and withdrawals accounts and on to the owner's capital account.

Also, closing entries cause the revenue and expense accounts to begin each new accounting period with zero balances. This is necessary because—

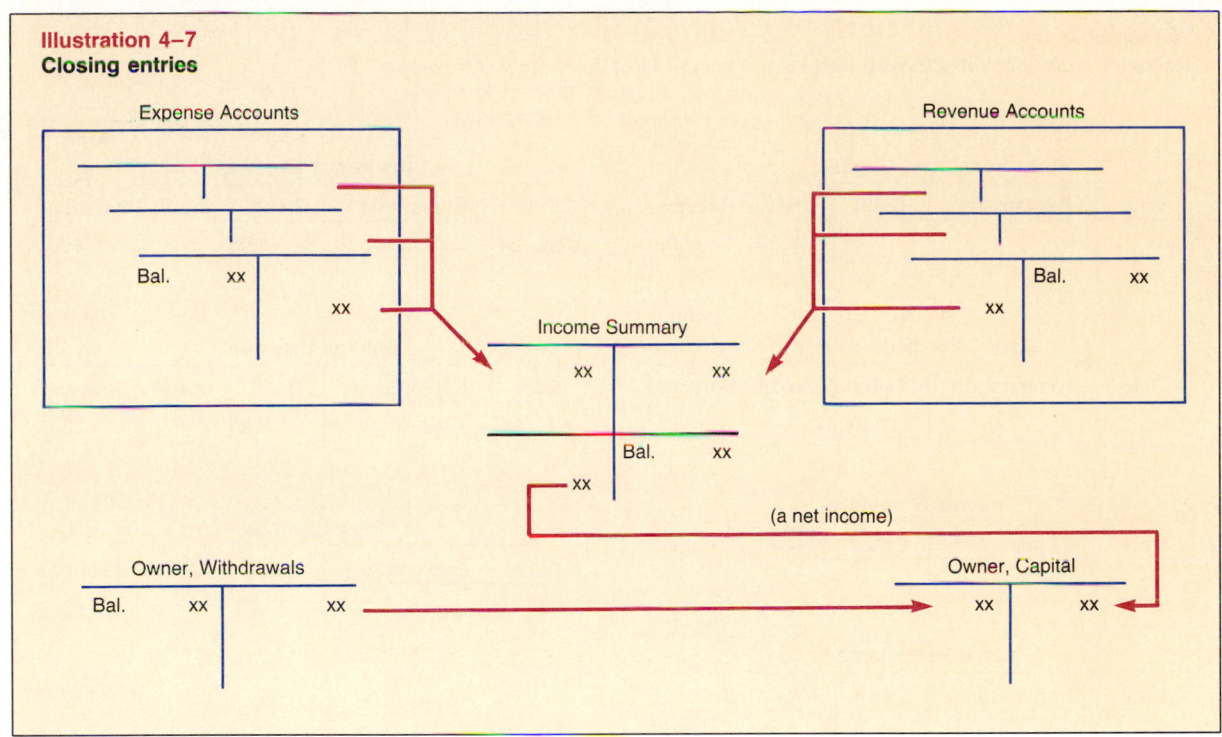

Illustration 4–7
Closing entries

a. An income statement reports the revenues earned and expenses incurred during *one accounting period* and is prepared from information recorded in the revenue and expense accounts.

b. The revenue and expense accounts are not discarded at the end of each accounting period but are used to record the revenues and expenses of succeeding periods.

c. If the balances of these accounts are to reflect only one period's revenues and expenses, the accounts must begin each period with zero balances.

d. Since the statement of changes in owner's equity reports the owner's withdrawals during only one period, the withdrawals account must begin each period with a zero balance.

Closing Entries
Illustrated

At the end of December, after its adjusting entries were posted but before its accounts were closed, the revenue, expense, withdrawals, and capital accounts of Dow's law practice had the balances shown in Illustration 4–8. (As a rule, an account's Balance column heading does not tell whether the balance is debit or credit. However, in Illustration 4–8 and in the illustrations that immediately follow, the nature of each account's balance is shown as a study aid.)

In Illustration 4–8, notice that Dow's capital account shows only the $9,000 investment by Dow made on December 1. This is not the amount of Dow's equity on December 31. Closing entries are required to make this account show the December 31 equity.

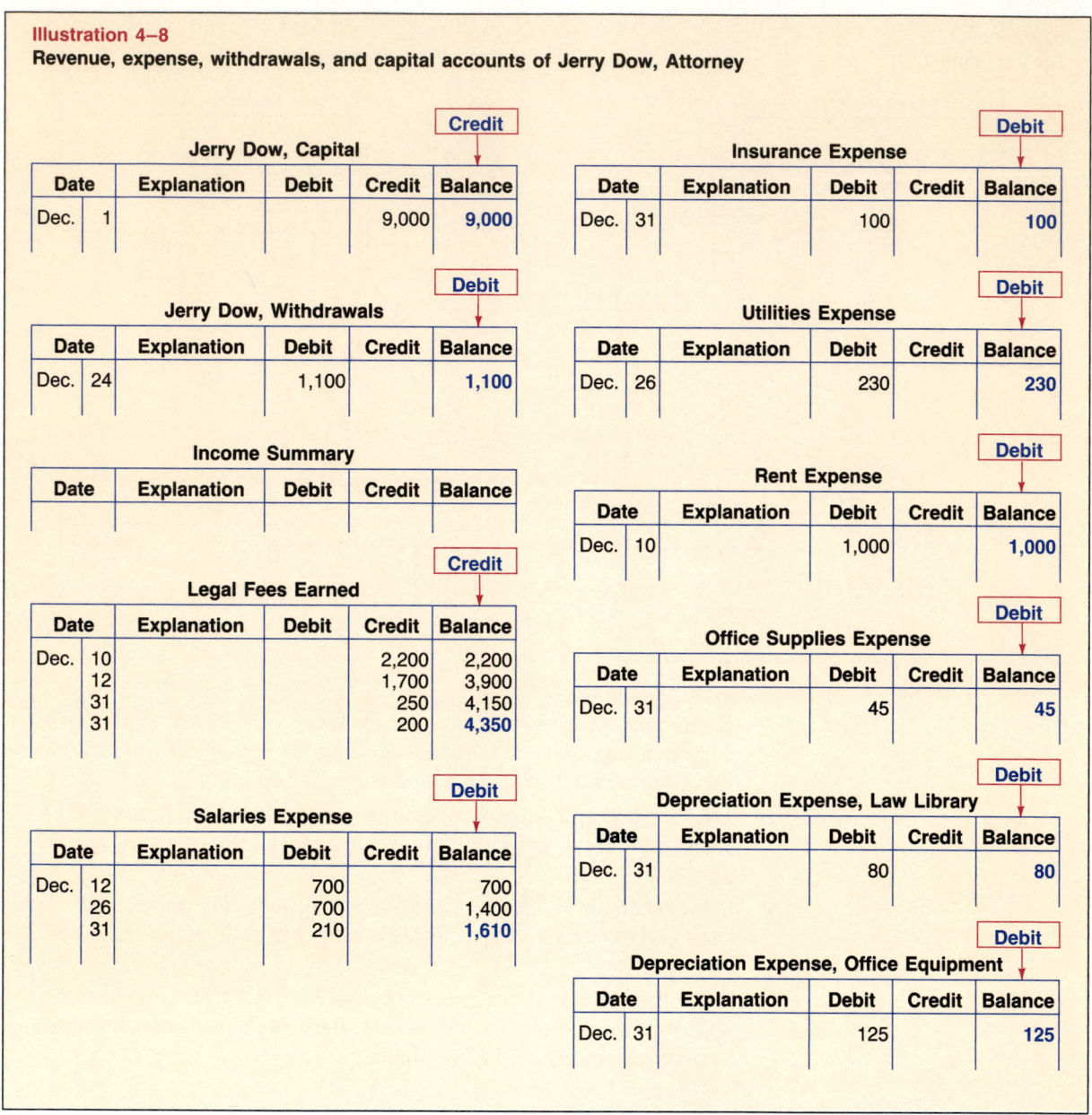

Illustration 4–8
Revenue, expense, withdrawals, and capital accounts of Jerry Dow, Attorney

Jerry Dow, Capital   *(Credit)*

Date	Explanation	Debit	Credit	Balance
Dec. 1			9,000	9,000

Jerry Dow, Withdrawals   *(Debit)*

Date	Explanation	Debit	Credit	Balance
Dec. 24		1,100		1,100

Income Summary

Date	Explanation	Debit	Credit	Balance

Legal Fees Earned   *(Credit)*

Date	Explanation	Debit	Credit	Balance
Dec. 10			2,200	2,200
12			1,700	3,900
31			250	4,150
31			200	4,350

Salaries Expense   *(Debit)*

Date	Explanation	Debit	Credit	Balance
Dec. 12		700		700
26		700		1,400
31		210		1,610

Insurance Expense   *(Debit)*

Date	Explanation	Debit	Credit	Balance
Dec. 31		100		100

Utilities Expense   *(Debit)*

Date	Explanation	Debit	Credit	Balance
Dec. 26		230		230

Rent Expense   *(Debit)*

Date	Explanation	Debit	Credit	Balance
Dec. 10		1,000		1,000

Office Supplies Expense   *(Debit)*

Date	Explanation	Debit	Credit	Balance
Dec. 31		45		45

Depreciation Expense, Law Library   *(Debit)*

Date	Explanation	Debit	Credit	Balance
Dec. 31		80		80

Depreciation Expense, Office Equipment   *(Debit)*

Date	Explanation	Debit	Credit	Balance
Dec. 31		125		125

Notice also the third account in Illustration 4–8, the Income Summary account. This account is used only at the end of the accounting period to summarize and clear the revenue and expense accounts.

Closing Revenue Accounts

Before closing entries are posted, revenue accounts have credit balances. Therefore, to close revenue accounts, you must debit each revenue account and credit Income Summary.

The Dow law practice has only one revenue account, and the entry to close it is:

Dec.	31	Legal Fees Earned	4,350.00	
		Income Summary		4,350.00
		To close the revenue account.		

Posting this entry has the following effect on the accounts:

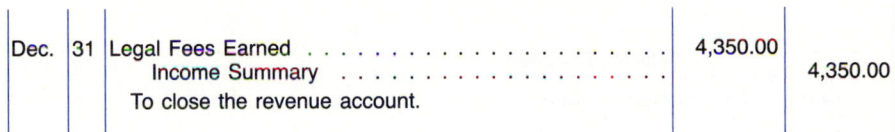

Legal Fees Earned

Date		Explanation	Debit	Credit	Balance
Dec.	10			2,200	2,200
	19			1,700	3,900
	31			250	4,150
	31			200	4,350
	31		4,350		–0–

Income Summary

Date		Explanation	Debit	Credit	Balance
Dec.	31			4,350	4,350

Note that the entry clears the revenue account by transferring its balance as a credit to the Income Summary account. It also causes the revenue account to begin the new accounting period with a zero balance.

Closing Expense Accounts

Before closing entries are posted, expense accounts have debit balances. Therefore, to close a concern's expense accounts, you debit the Income Summary account and credit each individual expense account. The Dow law practice has seven expense accounts, and the compound entry to close them is:

Dec.	31	Income Summary	3,190.00	
		Salaries Expense		1,610.00
		Insurance Expense		100.00
		Utilities Expense		230.00
		Rent Expense		1,000.00
		Office Supplies Expense		45.00
		Depreciation Expense, Law Library		80.00
		Depreciation Expense, Office Equipment		125.00
		To close the expense accounts.		

Posting the entry has the effect shown in Illustration 4–9. In that illustration, notice that the entry clears the expense accounts of their balances by transferring the balances in a total as a debit to the Income Summary account. Also, the entry causes the expense accounts to begin the new period with zero balances.

Illustration 4–9
The entry to close the expense accounts

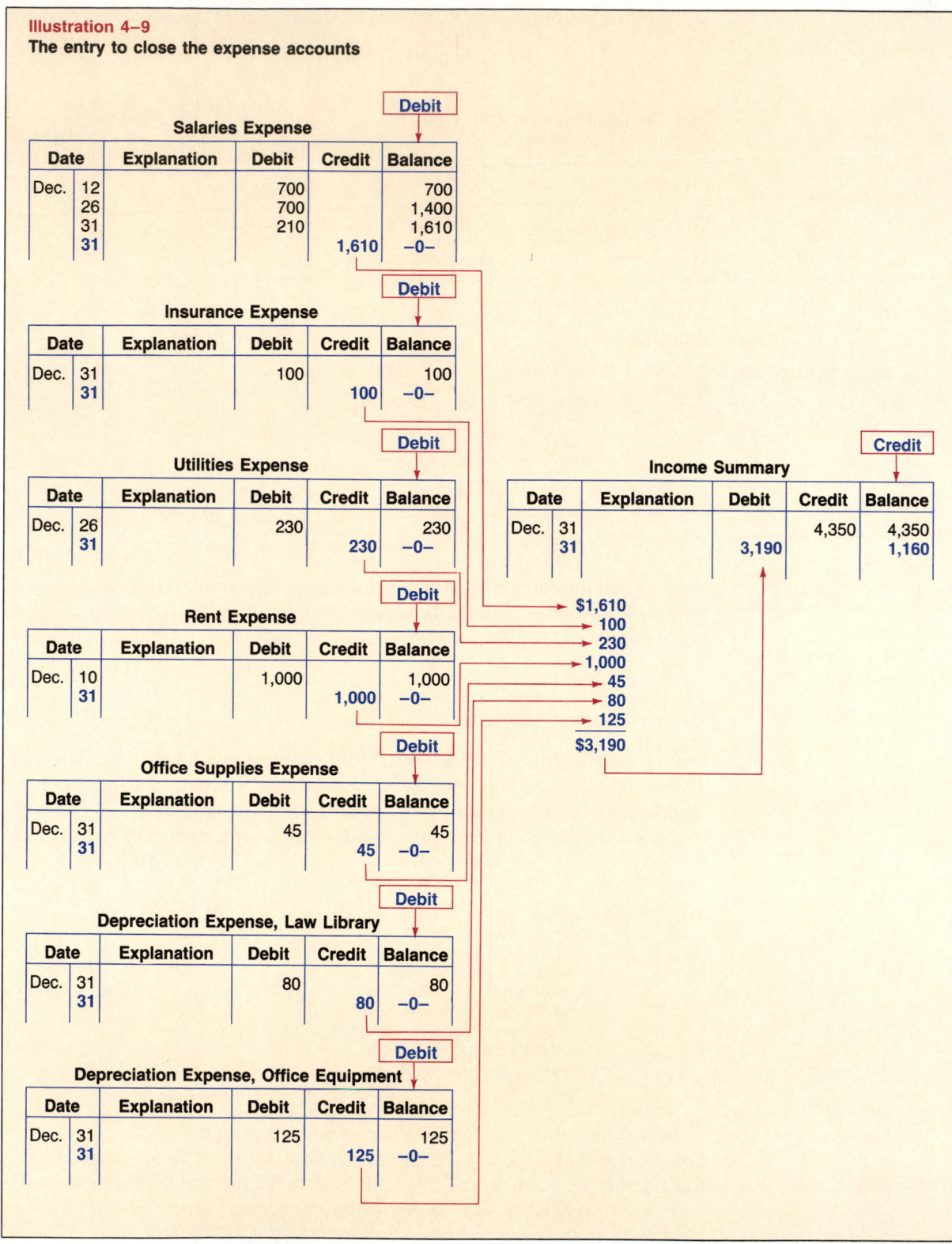

Closing the Income Summary Account

After a business's revenue and expense accounts are closed to Income Summary, the balance of the Income Summary account is equal to the net income or loss. When revenues exceed expenses, there is a net income, and the Income Summary account has a credit balance. On the other hand, when expenses exceed revenues, there is a loss and the account has a debit balance. But, regardless of the nature of its balance, the Income Summary account must be closed by transferring its balance to the capital account.

The Dow law practice earned $1,160 during December. Therefore, after its revenue and expense accounts are closed, its Income Summary account has a $1,160 credit balance. This balance is transferred to the Jerry Dow, Capital account with an entry like this:

Dec.	31	Income Summary	1,160.00	
		Jerry Dow, Capital		1,160.00
		To close the Income Summary account.		

Posting this entry has the following effect on the accounts:

Income Summary

| | | | Credit | |
Date	Explanation	Debit	Credit	Balance
Dec. 31			4,350	4,350
31		3,190		1,160
31		1,160		–0–

Jerry Dow, Capital

| | | | Credit | |
Date	Explanation	Debit	Credit	Balance
Dec. 1			9,000	9,000
31			1,160	10,160

Notice that the entry clears the Income Summary account, transferring its balance, the amount of the net income in this case, to the capital account.

Closing the Withdrawals Account

At the end of an accounting period, the withdrawals account shows the decrease in the owner's equity due to the owner's withdrawals. The account is closed, and its debit balance is transferred to the capital account with an entry like this:

Dec.	31	Jerry Dow, Capital	1,100.00	
		Jerry Dow, Withdrawals		1,100.00
		To close the withdrawals account.		

Posting the entry has this effect on the accounts:

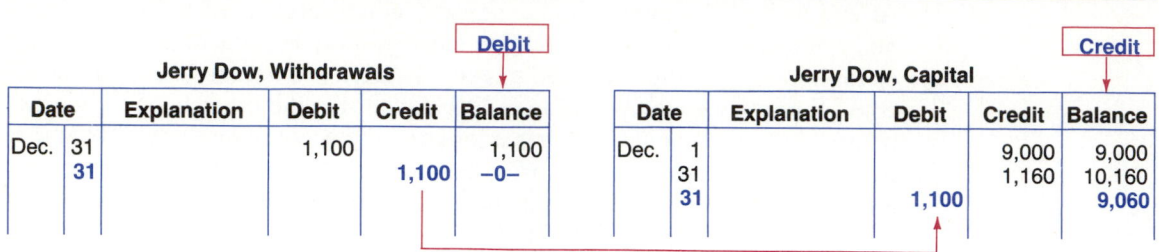

After you post the entry to close the withdrawals account, notice that the two reasons for making closing entries are accomplished: (1) All revenue, expense, and withdrawal accounts have zero balances. (2) The net effect of the period's revenue, expense, and withdrawal transactions on the owner's equity is shown in the capital account.

Temporary (Nominal) Accounts and Permanent (Real) Accounts

Revenue accounts, expense accounts, withdrawals accounts, and the Income Summary account are often called **temporary accounts** or **nominal accounts**. These terms are used because amounts are stored in these accounts only temporarily. Such accounts are closed at the end of each accounting period. By contrast, accounts that appear in the balance sheet are often called **permanent accounts** or **real accounts**, because they remain open as long as the asset, liability, or owner's equity items recorded in the accounts continue in existence.

Sources of Closing Entry Information

Information for closing entries may be taken from the individual revenue and expense accounts. However, the work sheet provides this information in a more convenient form. Look at the work sheet in Illustration 4–5. Every account that has a balance in the Income Statement columns must be closed. In addition, the withdrawals account must be closed.

The Accounts after Closing

After both adjusting and closing entries are posted, the Dow law practice accounts appear as in Illustration 4–10. Observe that the asset, liability, and owner's capital accounts show their end-of-period balances. Also, note that the revenue and expense accounts have zero balances and are ready to be used when revenues and expenses are recorded in the next accounting period.

The Post-Closing Trial Balance

Prepare a post-closing trial balance and explain its purpose.
(L. O. 3)

Because errors may have been introduced in the process of adjusting and closing the accounts, a new trial balance is prepared after all adjusting and closing entries have been posted. This **post-closing trial balance** is prepared to retest the equality of the accounts. The post-closing trial balance for Dow's law practice appears in Illustration 4–11.

Illustration 4–10
The general ledger for Jerry Dow, Lawyer

Cash   Account No. 111

Date		Explanation	PR	Debit		Credit		Balance	
1990 Dec.	1		G1	9,000	00			9,000	00
	2		G1			2,500	00	6,500	00
	3		G1			5,600	00	900	00
	10		G1	2,200	00			3,100	00
	10		G1			1,000	00	2,100	00
	12		G1			700	00	1,400	00
	22		G1	1,700	00			3,100	00
	24		G2			900	00	2,200	00
	24		G2			1,100	00	1,100	00
	26		G2	3,000	00			4,100	00
	26		G2			2,400	00	1,700	00
	26		G2			120	00	1,580	00
	26		G2			230	00	1,350	00
	26		G2			700	00	650	00

Accounts Receivable   Account No. 114

Date		Explanation	PR	Debit		Credit		Balance	
1990 Dec.	12		G1	1,700	00			1,700	00
	22		G2			1,700	00	–0–	
	31		G3	200	00			200	00

Prepaid Insurance   Account No. 115

Date		Explanation	PR	Debit		Credit		Balance	
1990 Dec.	26		G2	2,400	00			2,400	00
	31		G3			100	00	2,300	00

Illustration 4–10 *(continued)*

Office Supplies   Account No. 116

Date		Explanation	PR	Debit		Credit		Balance	
1990 Dec.	26		G2	120	00			120	00
	31		G3			45	00	75	00

Law Library   Account No. 131

Date		Explanation	PR	Debit		Credit		Balance	
1990 Dec.	2		G1	2,500	00			2,500	00
	6		G1	380	00			2,880	00

Office Equipment   Account No. 132

Date		Explanation	PR	Debit		Credit		Balance	
1990 Dec.	3		G1	5,600	00			5,600	00
	6		G1	1,280	00			6,880	00

Accumulated Depreciation, Law Library   Account No. 133

Date		Explanation	PR	Debit		Credit		Balance	
1990 Dec.	31		G3			80	00	80	00

Accumulated Depreciation, Office Equipment   Account No. 134

Date		Explanation	PR	Debit		Credit		Balance	
1990 Dec.	31		G3			125	00	125	00

Illustration 4–10 *(continued)*

Accounts Payable   Account No. 212

Date		Explanation	PR	Debit	Credit	Balance
1990 Dec.	6		G1		1,660 00	1,660 00
	24		G2	900 00		760 00

Salaries Payable   Account No. 213

Date		Explanation	PR	Debit	Credit	Balance
1990 Dec.	31		G3		210 00	210 00

Unearned Legal Fees   Account No. 214

Date		Explanation	PR	Debit	Credit	Balance
1990 Dec.	26		G2		3,000 00	3,000 00
	31		G3	250 00		2,750 00

Jerry Dow, Capital   Account No. 311

Date		Explanation	PR	Debit	Credit	Balance
1990 Dec.	1		G1		9,000 00	9,000 00
	24		G2	1,100 00		7,900 00
	31		G3		1,160 00	9,060 00

Jerry Dow, Withdrawals   Account No. 312

Date		Explanation	PR	Debit	Credit	Balance
1990 Dec.	24		G2	1,100 00		1,100 00
	31		G3		1,100 00	–0–

Illustration 4–10 *(continued)*

Income Summary   Account No. 313

Date		Explanation	PR	Debit		Credit		Balance	
1990 Dec.	31		G3			4,350	00	4,350	00
	31		G3	3,190	00			1,160	00
	31		G3	1,160	00			—0—	

Legal Fees Earned   Account No. 411

Date		Explanation	PR	Debit		Credit		Balance	
1990 Dec.	10		G1			2,200	00	2,200	00
	12		G1			1,700	00	3,900	00
	31		G3			250	00	4,150	00
	31		G3			200	00	4,350	00
	31		G3	4,350	00			—0—	

Salaries Expense   Account No. 511

Date		Explanation	PR	Debit		Credit		Balance	
1990 Dec.	12		G1	700	00			700	00
	26		G2	700	00			1,400	00
	31		G3	210	00			1,610	00
	31		G3			1,610	00	—0—	

Insurance Expense   Account No. 512

Date		Explanation	PR	Debit		Credit		Balance	
1990 Dec.	31		G3	100	00			100	00
	31		G3			100	00	—0—	

Illustration 4–10 *(concluded)*

Utilities Expense   Account No. 513

Date		Explanation	PR	Debit		Credit		Balance	
1990 Dec.	26		G2	230	00			230	00
	31		G3			230	00	–0–	

Rent Expense   Account No. 514

Date		Explanation	PR	Debit		Credit		Balance	
1990 Dec.	10		G1	1,000	00			1,000	00
	31		G3			1,000	00	–0–	

Office Supplies Expense   Account No. 516

Date		Explanation	PR	Debit		Credit		Balance	
1990 Dec.	31		G3	45	00			45	00
	31		G3			45	00	–0–	

Depreciation Expense, Law Library   Account No. 517

Date		Explanation	PR	Debit		Credit		Balance	
1990 Dec.	31		G3	80	00			80	00
	31		G3			80	00	–0–	

Depreciation Expense, Office Equipment   Account No. 518

Date		Explanation	PR	Debit		Credit		Balance	
1990 Dec.	31		G3	125	00			125	00
	31		G3			125	00	–0–	

Illustration 4–11
The post-closing trial balance

JERRY DOW, LAWYER
Post-Closing Trial Balance
December 31, 1990

Cash	$ 650	
Accounts receivable	200	
Prepaid insurance	2,300	
Office supplies	75	
Law library	2,880	
Office equipment	6,880	
Accumulated depreciation, law library		$ 80
Accumulated depreciation, office equipment		125
Accounts payable		760
Salaries payable		210
Unearned legal fees		2,750
Jerry Dow, capital		9,060
Totals	$12,985	$12,985

Compare Illustration 4–11 with the accounts that have balances in Illustration 4–10. Note that only asset, liability, and the owner's capital accounts have balances in Illustration 4–10. Note also that these are the only accounts that appear on the post-closing trial balance. The revenue and expense accounts have been cleared and have zero balances at this stage.

Accounting for Partnerships and Corporations

Partnership Accounting

Accounting for a partnership is like accounting for a single proprietorship except for transactions that directly affect the partners' capital and withdrawal accounts. For these transactions, you need a capital account and a withdrawals account for each partner. Also, you close the Income Summary account with a compound entry that allocates to each partner his or her share of the net income or loss.

Corporate Accounting

Accounting for a corporation also differs from that of a single proprietorship for transactions that affect the equity accounts of the corporation. The differences occur because accounting principles require a corporation to distinguish between shareholders' equity resulting from amounts invested in the corporation by its shareholders and shareholders' equity resulting from earnings. This distinction is also important because in most jurisdictions a corporation cannot pay a legal dividend unless it has shareholders' equity resulting from earnings. In making the distinction, two kinds of shareholders' equity accounts are kept: (1) *contributed capital accounts* and (2) *retained earnings accounts.* Amounts invested in a corporation (contributed) by its shareholders are shown in a contributed capital account such as the Common Stock account.

Shareholders' equity resulting from earnings is shown in a retained earnings account.

To demonstrate corporate accounting, assume that five persons secured a charter for a new corporation. Each invested $10,000 in the corporation by buying 1,000 shares, at $10 per share, of its common stock. The corporation's entry to record their investments is:

Jan.	5	Cash	50,000.00	
		Common Stock		50,000.00
		Issued 5,000 shares of common stock for cash.		

If during its first year the corporation earned $20,000, the entry to close its Income Summary account is:

Dec.	31	Income Summary	20,000.00	
		Retained Earnings		20,000.00
		To close the Income Summary account.		

If these are the only entries that affected the Common Stock and Retained Earnings accounts during the first year, the corporation's year-end balance sheet will show the shareholders' equity as follows:

<table>
<tr><td colspan="3" align="center">Shareholders' Equity</td></tr>
<tr><td>Common stock, 5,000 shares . . . .</td><td></td><td></td></tr>
<tr><td>outstanding . . . .</td><td>$50,000</td><td></td></tr>
<tr><td>Retained earnings . . . .</td><td>20,000</td><td></td></tr>
<tr><td>Total shareholder's equity . . . . . .</td><td></td><td>$70,000</td></tr>
</table>

Explain the nature of a corporation's retained earnings and its relationship to the declaration of dividends. (L. O. 4)

Since a corporation is a separate legal entity, the names of its shareholders usually are of little interest to a balance sheet reader and are not shown in the equity section. However, in this case, the section does show that the net assets or equity of the corporation's shareolders is $70,000. Of this amount, $50,000 resulted from their purchase of the corporation's stock, and $20,000 was the result of net income that has not been paid out as dividends.

Perhaps the concept of retained earnings would be clearer if the balance sheet item were labeled "Shareholders' equity resulting from earnings." However, the retained earnings caption is commonly used. You should understand that it does not represent a specific amount of cash or any other asset. These are shown in the asset section of the balance sheet. Retained earnings represents nothing more than shareholders' equity resulting from earnings.

To continue, assume that on January 10 of the corporation's second year, its board of directors met and by vote declared a $1 per share dividend payable on February 1 to the January 25 **shareholders of record** (shareholders according to the corporation's records). The entry to record the declaration of the dividend is as follows:

Jan.	10	Dividends Declared	5,000.00	
		Common Dividend Payable		5,000.00
		Declared a $1 per share dividend.		

The **Dividends Declared** account is a temporary account that serves the same function for a corporation as does a withdrawals account for a proprietorship. At the end of each period, the Dividends Declared account is closed to Retained Earnings.

The entry to record the payment of the dividend is as follows:

Feb.	1	Common Dividend Payable	5,000.00	
		Cash		5,000.00
		Paid the dividend declared on January 10.		

Note from the two entries that a dividend declaration and payment reduce the corporation's assets and shareholders' equity just as a withdrawal of cash by the owner of a single proprietorship reduces assets and the owner's equity.

A cash dividend is normally paid by mailing cheques to the shareholders. Also, as in this case, three dates are normally involved in a dividend declaration and payment: (1) the **date of declaration**, (2) the **date of record**, and (3) the **date of payment**. Since shareholders may sell their stock to new investors, the three dates give new shareholders an opportunity to have their ownership entered in the corporation's records in time to receive the dividend. Otherwise, the dividend would go to the old shareholders.

A dividend must be formally voted by a corporation's board of directors. Also, courts have generally held that the board is the final judge of when a dividend should be paid. Therefore, shareholders have no right to a dividend until declared. However, as soon as a cash dividend is declared, it becomes a liability of the corporation (normally a current liability) and must be paid. Furthermore, shareholders have the right to sue and force payment of a cash dividend once it is declared.

If during its second year (1991) the corporation suffered a $7,000 net loss, the entries to close its Income Summary and Dividends Declared accounts are:

1991				
Dec.	31	Retained Earnings	7,000.00	
		Income Summary		7,000.00
		To close the Income Summary account.		
	31	Retained Earnings	5,000.00	
		Dividends Declared		5,000.00
		To close the Dividends Declared account.		

Now assume that during 1992, the corporation paid no dividends but suffered a net loss of $14,000. The entry to close the Income Summary account at the end of 1992 is:

1992				
Dec.	31	Retained Earnings	14,000.00	
		Income Summary		14,000.00
		To close the Income Summary account.		

Posting these entries has the following effects on the Retained Earnings account:

Retained Earnings

Date	Explanation	PR	Debit	Credit	Balance
1990					
Dec. 31	Net income	G4		20,000.00	20,000.00
1991					
Dec. 31	Net loss	G5	7,000.00		13,000.00
31	Dividends declared	G7	5,000.00		8,000.00
1992					
Dec. 31	Net loss	G9	14,000.00		(6,000.00)

Due to the dividend and the net losses, the Retained Earnings account has a $6,000 debit balance. A debit balance in a Retained Earnings account indicates a negative amount of retained earnings. A corporation with a negative amount of retained earnings is said to have a **deficit**. A deficit may be shown on a corporation's balance sheet as follows:

Shareholders' Equity

Common stock, 5,000 shares		
outstanding	$50,000	
Deduct retained earnings deficit . .	(6,000)	
Total shareholder's equity		$44,000

In most jurisdictions, it is illegal for a corporation with a deficit to pay a cash dividend. Such dividends are illegal because as a separate legal entity a corporation is responsible for its own debts. If its creditors are to be paid, they must be paid from the corporation's assets. Therefore, making a dividend illegal when there is a deficit helps prevent a corporation in financial difficulties from paying all of its assets in dividends and leaving nothing for payment of its creditors.

The Accounting Cycle

List the steps in the accounting cycle in the order in which they are completed and perform each step.
(L. O. 6)

In Chapters 2, 3, and 4, we have discussed all of the accounting procedures that must be completed each accounting period, beginning with the recording of transactions in a journal and ending with a post-closing trial balance. Since these steps are repeated each period, they are called the **accounting cycle.** A knowledge of accounting requires that you understand each step and its relation to the others. The steps in the order of their occurrence are as follows:

1. **Journalizing** . . . . . . Analyzing and recording transactions in a journal.

2. **Posting** . . . . Copying the debits and credits of the journal entries into the ledger accounts.

3. **Preparing an unadjusted trial balance** . Summarizing the ledger accounts and testing the recording accuracy.

4. **Completing the work sheet** . . . . Gaining the effects of the adjustments before entering the adjustments in the accounts. Then sorting the account balances into the proper financial statement columns and calculating the net income or net loss.

5. **Preparing the statements** . . . . . . Rearranging the work sheet information onto an income statement, a statement of changes in owner's equity, and a balance sheet.

6. **Adjusting the ledger accounts** . . . . . . Preparing adjusting journal entries from information in the Adjustments columns of the work sheet and posting the entries in order to bring the account balances up to date.

7. **Closing the temporary accounts** . . . . . . Preparing and posting entries to close the temporary accounts and to transfer the net income or loss to the capital account or accounts in a single proprietorship or partnership and to the Retained Earnings account in a corporation.

8. **Preparing a post-closing trial balance** . . Proving the accuracy of the adjusting and closing procedures.

Summary of the Chapter in Terms of Learning Objectives

1. A work sheet is a tool the accountant uses at the end of an accounting period to show the effects of the adjustments and to organize the data for use in preparing financial statements and recording the adjusting and closing entries.

2. Closing the temporary accounts at the end of each accounting period serves to transfer the effects of these accounts to the proper owner's equity account that appears on the balance sheet. It also gives the revenue, expense, and withdrawals or Dividend Declared accounts zero balances, preparing them for use in the following period.

3. A post-closing trial balance tests the equality of debits and credits in the ledger after the adjusting and closing entries have been posted. It also confirms the fact that all temporary accounts have been closed.

4. Retained earnings is the total amount of net incomes a corporation has earned since it was organized, less the total amount of net losses it has incurred and the total amount of dividends it has declared.

5. Dividend declarations are recorded with a debit to a temporary account called Dividends Declared and a credit to a liability account. When paid in cash, the liability account is debited and Cash is credited.

6. The steps in the accounting cycle are to journalize and post transactions, prepare a trial balance and complete the work sheet, prepare the financial statements, record the adjustments, close the temporary accounts, and prepare a post-closing trial balance.

Demonstration Problem

The December 31, 1990, adjusted trial balance of The Shoemaker, Inc., is as follows:

Cash	$ 83,300	
Prepaid insurance	19,000	
Prepaid rent	5,000	
Accounts receivable	45,000	
Equipment	165,000	
Accumulated depreciation, equipment		$ 52,000
Notes receivable	60,000	
Accounts payable		37,000
Notes payable		58,000
Income taxes payable		21,500
Common stock		55,000
Retained earnings		99,000
Dividends declared	75,000	
Sales		420,000
Interest earned		6,500
Wages expense	179,000	
Rent expense	47,000	
Insurance expense	7,000	
Depreciation expense	26,000	
Interest expense	4,700	
Income taxes expense	33,000	
Totals	$749,000	$749,000

Required

1. Prepare closing entries for The Shoemaker, Inc.

2. Prepare a post-closing trial balance for the business.

3. Set up a Retained Earnings account, and post all necessary amounts to the account.

Solution to Demonstration Problem

1.

Closing Entries

1990				
Dec.	31	Sales	420,000.00	
		Interest Earned	6,500.00	
		Income Summary		426,500.00
	31	Income Summary	296,700.00	
		Wages Expense		179,000.00
		Rent Expense		47,000.00
		Insurance Expense		7,000.00
		Depreciation Expense		26,000.00
		Interest Expense		4,700.00
		Income Taxes Expense		33,000.00
	31	Income Summary	129,800.00	
		Retained Earnings		129,800.00
	31	Retained Earnings	75,000.00	
		Dividends Declared		75,000.00

2.

THE SHOEMAKER, INC.
Post-Closing Trial Balance
December 31, 1990

Cash	$ 83,300	
Prepaid insurance	19,000	
Prepaid rent	5,000	
Accounts receivable	45,000	
Equipment	165,000	
Accumulated depreciation, equipment		$ 52,000
Notes receivable	60,000	
Accounts payable		37,000
Notes payable		58,000
Income taxes payable		21,500
Common stock		55,000
Retained earnings		153,800
Totals	$377,300	$377,300

3.

Retained Earnings

Date		Explanation	PR	Debit	Credit	Balance
1990						
Jan.	1	Beginning balance			99,000	99,000
Dec.	31	Close Income Summary			129,800	228,800
	31	Close Dividends Declared		75,000		153,800

Appendix B

REVERSING ENTRIES

Prepare reversing entries
and explain when and why
they are used.
(L. O. 8)

In this appendix, we explain some optional entries accountants may use in accounting for accrued items. These optional entries, called *reversing entries,* are used to make the bookkeeping process easier.

In accounting for Jerry Dow's law practice, the December 31, 1990, adjusting entries included an accrual of the secretary's salary. This entry was as follows:

1990 Dec.	31	Salaries Expense	210.00	
		Salaries Payable		210.00
		To record accrued wages.		

Then on December 31, the Salaries Expense account was closed to Income Summary.

Since the secretary is paid every two weeks, the next payment is on January 9, and is recorded as follows:

Jan.	9	Salaries Payable.	210.00	
		Salaries Expense	490.00	
		Cash		700.00
		Paid wages for two weeks.		

To correctly record a transaction like that of the January 9 entry, a bookkeeper must remember that part of the cash payment is accrued salaries and part is expense of the current period. Since the accrual is easy to forget, you can avoid "the need to remember" by preparing and posting entries to reverse any end-of-period adjustments of accrued items. These reversing entries are made after the adjusting and closing entries are posted and are normally dated the first day of the new accounting period.

Also, when prepaid and unearned items are initially recorded in income statement accounts, the end-of-period adjusting entries transfer the unused or unearned portions to asset and liability accounts. Thereafter, reversing entries may be used to transfer the prepaid asset and unearned liability account balances back into the expense and revenue accounts.

To reverse the accrual of wages, you would make the following entry:

Jan.	1	Salaries Payable.	210.00	
		Salaries Expense		210.00
		To reverse the accrual of salaries.		

Observe that the reversing entry is the exact opposite of the original adjusting entry. After the adjusting, closing, and reversing entries are posted, the Salaries Expense and Salaries Payable accounts appear as follows:

Salaries Expense						Salaries Payable				
Date	**Explanation**	**Dr.**	**Cr.**	**Bal.**		**Date**	**Explanation**	**Dr.**	**Cr.**	**Bal.**
Dec. 12	Paid wages	700		700		Dec. 31	Accrued wages		210	210
26	Paid wages	700		1,400		1991				
31	Accrued wages	210		1,610		Jan. 1	Reversal	210		–0–
31	Closing		1,610	–0–						
1991										
Jan. 1	Reversal		210	(210)						

Notice that the reversing entry cancels the $210 of salaries that appeared in the Salaries Payable account. It also causes the accrued salaries to appear in the Salaries Expense account as a $210 credit. (Remember that a circled balance means a balance opposite from normal.) Therefore, due to the reversing entry, when the salaries are paid on January 9, you can record the transaction with this entry:

Jan.	9	Salaries Expense	700.00	
		Cash		700.00
		Paid wages for two weeks.		

The entry's $210 debit to Salaries Expense includes both the $210 salary incurred during 1990 and the $490 salary expense incurred during 1991. However, when the entry is posted, because of the previously posted reversing entry, the balance of the Salaries Expense account shows only the $490 expense of the current period, as follows:

Salaries Expense				
Date	**Explanation**	**Dr.**	**Cr.**	**Bal.**
Dec. 12	Paid wages	700		700
26	Paid wages	700		1,400
31	Accrued wages	210		1,600
31	Closing		1,610	–0–
1991				
Jan. 1	Reversal		210	(210)
9	Paid wages	700		490

Summary of the Appendix in Terms of the Learning Objective

8. Reversing entries are applicable to all accrued items, such as accrued interest earned, accrued interest expense, accrued taxes, and accrued salaries and wages. Reversing entries are also used for prepaid and unearned items if (and only if) the business records prepaid expenses with debits to expense accounts, and records unearned revenues with credits to revenues accounts. (This practice was explained in Appendix A at the end of Chapter 3.) In any case, however, reversing entries are not required. The financial statements appear exactly the same whether or not reversing entries are used. Reversing entries are used as a convenience in bookkeeping.

Glossary

Define or explain the words and phrases listed in the chapter Glossary. (L. O. 7)

Accounting cycle the recurring accounting steps that are performed each accounting period and that begin with the recording of transactions and proceed through posting the recorded amounts, preparing a trial balance and completing a work sheet, preparing the financial statements, preparing and posting adjusting and closing entries, and preparing a post-closing trial balance. p. 176

Closing entries entries made at the end of each accounting period to establish zero balances in the temporary accounts and to transfer the temporary account balances to a capital account or accounts or to the Retained Earnings account. p. 160

Date of declaration the date on which a dividend is declared by a corporation's board of directors. p. 174

Date of payment the date on which a dividend liability of a corporation is satisfied by mailing checks to the shareholders. p. 174

Date of record the date on which the shareholders who are listed in a corporation's records are determined to be those who will receive a dividend. p. 174

Deficit a negative amount (debit balance) of retained earnings. p. 175

Dividends Declared a temporary account that serves the same function for a corporation as does a withdrawals account for a proprietorship, and which is closed to Retained Earnings at the end of each accounting period. p. 174

Income Summary the account used in the closing process to summarize the amounts of revenues and expenses, and from which the amount of the net income or loss is transferred to the owner's capital account in a single proprietorship, the partners' capital accounts in a partnership, or the Retained Earnings account in a corporation. p. 160

Nominal accounts another name for *temporary accounts*. p. 166

Permanent accounts accounts that remain open as long as the asset, liability, or owner's equity items recorded in the accounts continue in existence; therefore, accounts that appear in the balance sheet. p. 166

Post-closing trial balance a trial balance prepared after all adjusting and closing entries have been posted. p. 166

Real accounts another name for *permanent accounts*. p. 166

Reversing entries optional entries that transfer the balances in balance sheet accounts which arose as a result of certain adjusting entries (usually accruals) to income statement accounts. p. 179

Shareholders of record the shareholders of a corporation as reflected in the records of the corporation. p. 173

Temporary accounts accounts that are closed at the end of each accounting period; therefore, the revenue, expense, Income Summary, and withdrawals accounts. p. 166

Working papers the memoranda, analyses, and other informal papers prepared by accountants in the process of organizing the data that goes into the formal financial reports given to managers and other interested parties. p. 157

Work sheet a working paper on which the accountant shows the unadjusted trial balance, shows the effects of the adjustments on the account balances, calculates the net income or loss, and sorts the adjusted amounts according to the financial statements on which the amounts will appear. p. 157

An asterisk (*) identifies the questions, exercises, and problems that are based on Appendix B at the end of the chapter.

Questions for Class Discussion

1. What is the difference between working papers and a work sheet?
2. What tasks are performed on a work sheet?
3. Is it possible to complete the statements and adjust and close the accounts without preparing a work sheet? What is gained by preparing a work sheet?
4. At what stage in the accounting process is a work sheet prepared?
5. Where do you obtain the amounts that are entered in the Unadjusted Trial Balance columns of a work sheet?
6. Why are the adjustments in the Adjustments columns of a work sheet keyed together with letters?
7. What is the result of combining the amounts in the Unadjusted Trial Balance columns with the amounts in the Adjustments columns of a work sheet?
8. Why must you exercise care in sorting the items in the Adjusted Trial Balance columns to the proper Income Statement or Balance Sheet columns?
9. In extending the items in the Adjusted Trial Balance columns of a work sheet, what would be the effect on the net income of extending (*a*) an expense into the Statement of Changes in Owner's Equity or Balance Sheet Debit column, (*b*) a liability into the Income Statement Credit column, and (*c*) a revenue into the Statement of Changes in Owner's Equity or Balance Sheet Debit column? Would each of these errors be detected automatically on the work sheet? Which would be detected automatically? Why?
10. Why are revenue and expense accounts called temporary accounts? Are there any other temporary accounts?
11. What two purposes are accomplished by recording closing entries?
12. What accounts are affected by closing entries? What accounts are not affected?
13. Explain the difference between adjusting and closing entries.
14. What is the purpose of the Income Summary account?
15. Why is a post-closing trial balance prepared?
16. An accounting student listed the item, ''Depreciation expense, building, $1,800,'' on a post-closing trial balance. What did this indicate?
17. What two kinds of accounts are shown in the shareholders' equity section of a corporation's balance sheet?

18. Explain how the retained earnings item found on corporate balance sheets arises.

19. What three dates are normally involved in the declaration and payment of a cash dividend?

20. What is the purpose of using a Dividends Declared account?

21. One corporation uses a Dividends Declared account and another corporation does not. What effect does this difference have on the entries to be made by the corporations?

22. Explain why the payment of a cash dividend by a corporation with a deficit generally is illegal.

*23. If one company uses reversing entries and another does not, what differences between the two companies will show up on the financial statements?

*24. Why do reversing entries make the bookkeeping process easier?

*25. If a company made an adjusting entry to accrue salaries expense of $500 at the end of an accounting period, what reversing entry would be made for this accrual?

*26. At what stage in the accounting cycle are reversing entries recorded? When are they dated?

Multiple Choice

1. In preparing a work sheet at the end of the annual accounting period, Fritz Company's accountant incorrectly extended a $6,000 salaries expense amount from the adjusted trial balance to the Statement of Changes in Owner's Equity or Balance Sheet Debit column. As a result of this error:
   a. The net income calculated on the work sheet will be understated.
   b. On the bottom row of the work sheet, the totals of the last two columns will not be equal.
   c. The Adjusted Trial Balance columns will not balance.
   d. The net income calculated on the work sheet will be overstated.
   e. Both (a) and (b) are correct.

2. Related to the process of preparing closing entries:
   a. All expense accounts are first closed to the revenue accounts, which are then closed to Income Summary.
   b. After the process is completed, all temporary accounts will have zero balances.
   c. Expenses, revenues, and the withdrawals account are closed to Income Summary.
   d. After the process is completed, the Income Summary account balance will equal net income or net loss for the period.
   e. None of the above is correct.

3. A post-closing trial balance:
   a. Must be prepared as the first step in the end-of-period procedures that lead to the preparation of financial statements.
   b. Is one of the important financial statements presented to the owner of a business and other outside parties.

  c. Should include only balances of accounts that appear on the balance sheet.

  d. Includes the balances of all accounts that appear on the financial statements.

  e. Should include only balances of accounts that appear on the statement of changes in owner's equity or on the balance sheet.

4. The retained earnings of a corporation:

  a. Include the sum of all past net incomes (less net losses) of the corporation plus any dividends that have been declared but not paid.

  b. Represent cash balances the corporation has available to pay dividends.

  c. Less any contributed capital amounts equal the total stockholders' equity of the corporation.

  d. Will be reported as a deficit if the sum of all prior net losses plus all dividend declarations exceed the sum of all prior net incomes.

  e. Will be reported as a positive amount if net income for the current period exceeds dividend declarations during the period.

5. In accounting for dividends that a corporation declares and pays:

  a. The Dividends Declared account is closed to Income Summary.

  b. A dividend declaration is debited to Retained Earnings and credited to Dividends Declared.

  c. A payment of a previously recorded dividend declaration is debited to Dividends Declared and credited to Cash.

  d. No entry is required on the date of record.

  e. The Dividends Declared account is reported on the balance sheet as a liability.

6. The steps in the accounting cycle:

  a. Begin with the preparation of an unadjusted trial balance.

  b. Are completed once during the life of each business.

  c. Are concluded with the preparation of a post-closing trial balance.

  d. Are the eight procedures that are followed in preparing a work sheet.

  e. All of the above are correct.

Mini Discussion Case

Case 4–1

In the "heyday" of exploration and the quest for finding alternate routes to sources of spices, group-financed individual ventures were the order of the day. A venture lasted for two, three, or more years and once completed involved a windup. Financial statements were prepared with precision without the need for adjusting entries. Closing entries were, however, required to close out the profit on the venture and the capital accounts to complete the windup.

Required

Discuss the similarities and differences between venture accounting of yesteryear and present-day accounting for similar ventures that would be required under GAAP.

Exercises

The balances of the following accounts appeared in the Adjusted Trial Balance columns of a work sheet. Copy the account numbers in a column on a sheet of note paper, and beside each number indicate by letter the Income Statement or Balance Sheet column to which the account's balance would be sorted in completing the work sheet. Use the letter *a* to indicate the Income Statement Debit column, *b* to indicate the Income Statement Credit column, *c* to indicate the Statement of Changes in Owner's Equity or Balance Sheet Debit column, and *d* to indicate the Statement of Changes in Owner's Equity or Balance Sheet Credit column.

1. Cash.
2. Accounts Payable.
3. Accumulated Depreciation, Repair Equipment.
4. Advertising Expense.
5. Leo Walken, Capital.
6. Accounts Receivable.
7. Revenue from Repairs.
8. Leo Walken, Withdrawals.
9. Rent Expense.
10. Repair Equipment.
11. Repair Supplies.
12. Wages Expense.
13. Prepaid Insurance.

The following item amounts are from the Adjustments columns of a work sheet. Use this information to prepare adjusting journal entries dated December 31.

	Adjustments	
	Debit	Credit
Prepaid insurance		(*a*) 1,020
Office supplies		(*b*) 235
Accumulated depreciation, office equipment . .		(*c*) 650
Accumulated depreciation, shop equipment. . .		(*d*) 4,015
Office salaries expense.	(*e*) 65	
Shop wages expense.	(*e*) 335	
Insurance expense, office equipment	(*a*) 100	
Insurance expense, shop equipment	(*a*) 920	
Office supplies expense	(*b*) 235	
Depreciation expense, office equipment.	(*c*) 650	
Depreciation expense, shop equipment.	(*d*) 4,015	
Salaries and wages payable		(*e*) 400
Totals	6,320	6,320

On a sheet of paper, copy the following T-accounts and their end-of-period balances. Below the accounts, prepare entries to close the accounts. Post to the T-accounts.

Mac Boss, Capital		Rent Expense	
	Dec. 31 15,000	Dec. 31 2,800	

Mac Boss, Withdrawals		Salaries Expense	
Dec. 31 18,500		Dec. 31 12,250	

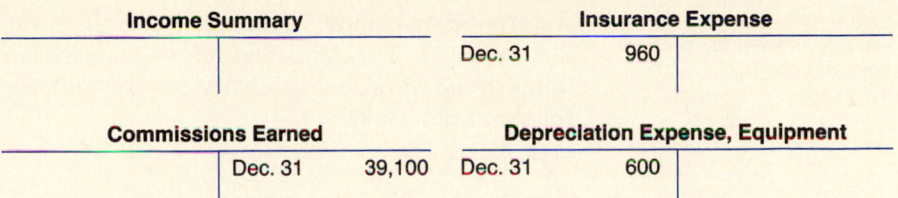

Income Summary		Insurance Expense	
		Dec. 31 960	

Commissions Earned		Depreciation Expense, Equipment	
	Dec. 31 39,100	Dec. 31 600	

Exercise 4–4

Using work sheet information to prepare closing entries

(L. O. 2)

The following items appeared in the Income Statement columns of a December 31 work sheet prepared for Donald Cole, a lawyer. Assume that Mr. Cole withdrew $28,000 from his law practice during the year and prepare entries to close the accounts.

	Income Statement	
	Debit	**Credit**
Legal fees earned		64,000
Office salaries expense	15,000	
Rent expense	7,200	
Insurance expense	1,500	
Office supplies expense	350	
Depreciation expense, office equipment . .	2,800	
	26,850	64,000
Net income	37,150	
	64,000	64,000

Exercise 4–5

Preparing and posting closing entries for a corporation

(L. O. 2, 5)

Open the following T-accounts on note paper for a corporation that does repair work for other companies. Below the T-accounts, prepare entries to close the accounts. Post to the T-accounts.

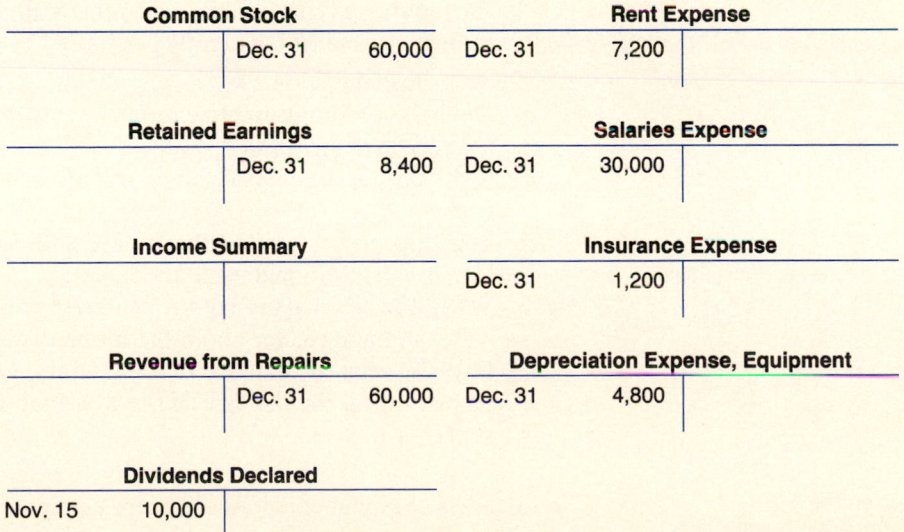

Common Stock		Rent Expense	
	Dec. 31 60,000	Dec. 31 7,200	

Retained Earnings		Salaries Expense	
	Dec. 31 8,400	Dec. 31 30,000	

Income Summary		Insurance Expense	
		Dec. 31 1,200	

Revenue from Repairs		Depreciation Expense, Equipment	
	Dec. 31 60,000	Dec. 31 4,800	

Dividends Declared	
Nov. 15 10,000	

Exercise 4–6
Closing entries for a corporation
(L. O. 3)

A corporation debited Dividends Declared for $18,000 during the year ended December 31. The items that follow appeared in the Income Statement columns of the work sheet prepared at year-end. Prepare closing journal entries for the corporation.

	Income Statement	
	Debit	Credit
Revenue from services		106,300
Office salaries expense	32,000	
Rent expense	15,000	
Insurance expense	2,100	
Office supplies expense	500	
Depreciation expense, office equipment . .	6,200	
	55,800	106,300
Net income	50,500	
	106,300	106,300

Exercise 4–7
Recording corporate transactions in T-accounts
(L. O. 4, 5)

1. On a sheet of note paper, open the following T-accounts: Cash, Accounts Receivable, Equipment, Notes Payable, Common Dividend Payable, Common Stock, Retained Earnings, Income Summary, Dividends Declared, Revenue from Services, and Operating Expenses.

2. Record directly in the T-accounts these transactions of a new corporation:
   a. Issued common stock for $12,000 cash.
   b. Purchased equipment for $10,000 cash.
   c. Sold and delivered $30,000 of services on credit.
   d. Collected $26,000 of accounts receivable.
   e. Paid $20,000 of operating expenses.
   f. Declared cash dividends of $4,000.
   g. Paid the dividends declared in (f).
   h. Purchased $6,000 of additional equipment, giving $4,000 in cash and a $2,000 promissory note.
   i. Closed the revenue accounts, (j) the expense accounts, (k) Income Summary, and (l) Dividends Declared.

3. Answer these questions:
   a. Does the corporation have retained earnings?
   b. Does it have any cash?
   c. If the corporation has retained earnings, why does it not also have cash?
   d. Can the corporation legally declare additional cash dividends?
   e. Can it pay additional cash dividends?
   f. What does the balance of the Notes Payable account tell the financial statement reader about the makeup of the corporation's assets?
   g. Explain what the balance of the Common Stock account represents.
   h. Explain what the balance of the Retained Earnings account represents.

Exercise 4–8
Preparing a work sheet
(L. O. 1)

Following is an alphabetical list of Seeger Company's accounts and their unadjusted balances. All are normal balances. To save you time, the balances are in one- and two-digit numbers.

Trial Balance Accounts and Balances

Accounts payable	$3	Rent expense	$ 3
Accounts receivable	4	Revenue from repairs	22
Accumulated depreciation,		Rick Seeger, capital	13
shop equipment	3	Rick Seeger, withdrawals	3
Cash	6	Shop equipment	8
Notes payable	2	Shop supplies	5
Prepaid insurance	4	Wages expense	10

Required

1. Prepare a work sheet form and enter the trial balance accounts and amounts on the work sheet in their alphabetical order.

2. Complete the work sheet using the following information:
   a. Estimated depreciation of shop equipment, $2.
   b. Expired insurance, $2.
   c. Unused shop supplies per inventory, $2.
   d. Earned but unpaid wages, $3.

Exercise 4–9
Preparing a work sheet
(L. O. 1)

The unadjusted trial balance of Medium Company, Inc., as of December 31, 1990, the end of its annual accounting period, follows:

Cash	$ 4,500	
Prepaid insurance	1,500	
Repair supplies	2,400	
Repair equipment	18,000	
Accumulated depreciation, repair equipment		$ 1,200
Common stock		17,000
Retained earnings		1,800
Dividends declared	5,000	
Revenue from repairs		48,000
Salaries expense	25,800	
Rent expense	10,800	
Totals	$68,000	$68,000

Required

1. Prepare a work sheet form on note paper and enter the trial balance.

2. Complete the work sheet using the information that follows:
   a. Expired insurance, $900.
   b. Unused repair supplies per inventory, $400.
   c. Estimated depreciation of repair equipment, $2,500.
   d. Earned but unpaid salaries, $600.

Exercise 4–10
Adjusting and closing entries
(L. O. 5)

Prepare adjusting and closing journal entries for the corporation of Exercise 4–9.

Exercise 4–11
The steps in the accounting cycle
(L. O. 6)

List the letters identifying the following steps in the accounting cycle in the order in which the steps are performed.

a. Preparing an unadjusted trial balance.
b. Journalizing and posting closing entries.

   c. Journalizing transactions.

   d. Preparing a post-closing trial balance.

   e. Completing the work sheet.

   f. Posting the entries to record transactions.

   g. Preparing the financial statements.

   h. Journalizing and posting adjusting entries.

*Exercise 4–12
Reversing entries
(L. O. 8)

On December 31, adjusting entry information for Janes Company is as follows:

   a. Depreciation on office equipment, $3,000.

   b. Four hundred dollars of the Prepaid Insurance balance has expired.

   c. Employees have earned salaries of $800 that have not been paid.

   d. The Unearned Service Fees account balance includes $1,000 that has been earned.

   e. The company has earned $2,400 of service fees that have not been collected or recorded.

Required

List the letters that identify adjustments for which reversing entries should be made. Assuming the appropriate adjusting entries have been recorded, prepare the reversing entries.

*Exercise 4–13
Reversing entries
(L. O. 8)

The following information relates to Dawson Company on December 31, 1990, the end of its annual accounting period.

   a. Dawson rents office space for $2,000 per month. The company failed to pay the rent for December until January 6, at which time it paid the rent for December and January.

   b. Because Dawson does not use all of its office space, it subleases space to a tenant for $400 per month. The tenant failed to pay the December rent until January 8, at which time it paid the rent for December and January.

Required

1. Assuming that Dawson does not use reversing entries, prepare adjusting journal entries dated December 31. Also prepare entries to record Dawson's payment of rent in January and the receipt of rent in January from Dawson's tenant.

2. Assuming that Dawson uses reversing entries, prepare adjusting journal entries dated December 31 and reversing entries dated January 1. Also prepare entries to record Dawson's payment of rent in January and the receipt of rent in January from Dawson's tenant.

Problems

Problem 4–1
Closing entries for partnerships and corporations
(L. O. 2, 3, 4, 5)

Roy Red, Ben Blue, and George Green started a business on January 7, 1989, and each invested $45,000 in the business. During 1989, the business lost $11,250; and during 1990, it earned $49,500. On January 5, 1991, the three owners agreed to pay out to themselves $27,000 of the accumulated earnings of the business. On January 9, the $27,000 was paid out.

Required

1. Assume that the business is a partnership and the partners share net incomes and net losses equally. Give the entries to record the investments and to close the Income Summary account at the end of 1989 and again at the end of 1990. Also assume that the partners shared equally in the $27,000 of earnings paid out. Give the entry to record the withdrawals.

2. Assume that the business is organized as a corporation and that each owner invested $45,000 in it by buying 4,500 shares of its common stock at $10 per share. Give the entry to record the investments. Also, give the entries to close the Income Summary account at the end of 1989 and again at the end of 1990 and to record the declaration and payment of the $2 per share dividend. (Ignore corporate income taxes and assume that the three owners are the corporation's board of directors.)

Problem 4–2
The work sheet; financial statements and closing entries
(L. O. 1, 2)

At the end of its annual accounting period, a trial balance from the ledger of Rip's Repair Service appeared as follows:

RIP'S REPAIR SERVICE
Unadjusted Trial Balance
December 31, 1990

Cash	$ 1,825	
Prepaid insurance	1,300	
Repair supplies	4,375	
Repair equipment	7,860	
Accumulated depreciation, repair equipment		$ 1,920
Accounts payable		295
Rip Horn, capital		6,185
Rip Horn, withdrawals	28,200	
Revenue from repairs		55,845
Wages expense	15,210	
Rent expense	4,500	
Utilities expense	975	
Totals	$64,245	$64,245

Required

1. Enter the trial balance on a work sheet form and complete the work sheet using the information that follows:
    a. Expired insurance, $800.
    b. A repair supplies inventory showed $1,160 of unused supplies on hand.
    c. Estimated depreciation on repair equipment, $990.
    d. Wages earned by the one employee but unpaid and unrecorded, $120.

2. From the work sheet prepare an income statement, a statement of changes in owner's equity, and a classified balance sheet. Mr. Horn did not make additional investments in the business during 1990.

3. Prepare adjusting journal entries and compound closing entries.

Problem 4–3
All steps in the accounting cycle (covers two accounting cycles)
(L. O. 1, 2, 3, 4, 6)

Tami Martin opened a real estate office she called Martin Realty. During May, she completed these transactions:

May 3   Invested in the real estate agency $3,000 in cash and an automobile having a $15,000 fair value.
     3   Rented furnished office space and paid one month's rent, $750.
     4   Purchased office supplies for cash, $225.
     8   Paid the premium on a one-year insurance policy, $1,080.
    14   Paid the salary of the office secretary for two weeks, $600.
    16   Sold a house and collected an $8,010 commission.
    28   Paid the salary of the office secretary for two weeks, $600.
    31   Paid the May telephone bill, $75.
    31   Paid for gas and oil used in the agency car during May, $90.

Required Work for May

1. Open these accounts: Cash; Prepaid Insurance; Office Supplies; Automobile; Accumulated Depreciation, Automobile; Salaries Payable; Tami Martin, Capital; Tami Martin, Withdrawals; Income Summary; Commissions Earned; Rent Expense; Salaries Expense; Gas, Oil, and Repairs Expense; Telephone Expense; Insurance Expense; Office Supplies Expense; and Depreciation Expense, Automobile.

2. Prepare and post journal entries to record the transactions.

3. Prepare an unadjusted trial balance on a work sheet form and complete the work sheet using the following information:
   a. Two thirds of a month's insurance has expired.
   b. An inventory shows $185 of unused office supplies remaining.
   c. Estimated depreciation on the automobile, $250.
   d. Earned but unpaid salary of the office secretary, $60.

4. Prepare an income statement and a statement of changes in owner's equity for May, and prepare a May 31 classified balance sheet.

5. Journalize and post adjusting and closing entries.

6. Prepare a post-closing trial balance.

During June, Tami Martin completed these transactions:

June 1   Paid the June rent on the office space, $750.
      4   Purchased additional office supplies for cash, $45.
     11   Paid the salary of the office secretary for two weeks, $600.
     15   Tami Martin withdrew $3,000 cash from the business for personal use.
     18   Sold a building lot and collected a $2,200 commission.
     25   Paid the salary of the office secretary for two weeks, $600.
     30   Paid for gas and oil used in the agency car during June, $80.
     30   Paid the June telephone bill, $65.

Required Work for June

1. Prepare and post journal entries to record the transactions.
2. Prepare an unadjusted trial balance on a work sheet form and complete the work sheet using the following information:
    a. One month's insurance has expired.
    b. An office supplies inventory shows $185 of unused supplies.
    c. Estimated depreciation on the automobile, $250.
    d. Earned but unpaid secretary's salary, $180.
3. Prepare an income statement and a statement of changes in owner's equity for June and prepare a June 30 classified balance sheet.
4. Journalize and post adjusting and closing entries.
5. Prepare a post-closing trial balance.

Problem 4–4
End-of-period accounting procedures
(L. O. 1, 2, 3)

The accounts of Strait Alleys, showing balances as of the end of its annual accounting period, appear in the booklet of working papers that accompanies this text, and a trial balance of its ledger is reproduced on a work sheet form provided there. The trial balance has the items that follow:

STRAIT ALLEYS
Unadjusted Trial Balance
December 31, 1990

Cash	$ 1,250	
Bowling supplies	2,150	
Prepaid insurance	2,000	
Bowling equipment	74,325	
Accumulated depreciation, bowling equipment . .		$ 11,460
Accounts payable		205
Long-term notes payable		15,000
Paul Strait, capital		31,800
Paul Strait, withdrawals	23,500	
Bowling revenue		81,750
Wages expense	24,300	
Equipment repairs expense	630	
Rent expense	7,200	
Utilities expense	3,200	
Business tax expense	760	
Interest expense	900	
Totals	$140,215	$140,215

Required

1. Enter the unadjusted trial balance on a work sheet form and complete the work sheet using the information that follows:
    a. Bowling supplies inventory, $315.
    b. Expired insurance, $1,680.
    c. Estimated depreciation on bowling equipment, $7,125.
    d. The December hydro bill for the bowling alley arrived in the mail after the trial balance was prepared. Its $330 amount was unrecorded.
    e. Wages earned but unpaid and unrecorded, $420.
    f. The lease contract on the building calls for an annual rent equal to 10% of the annual bowling revenue, with $600 payable each month

on the first day of the month. The $600 was paid each month and debited to the Rent Expense account.

g. Business tax amounting to $285 has accrued but is unrecorded and unpaid.

h. The long-term note payable was signed on September 1, and interest on the debt is at a 12% annual rate or $150 per month. The note calls for payment in advance of $450 interest every three months. Interest payments were made on September 1 and December 1. A $1,500 payment on the note principal is due next September 1.

2. Prepare an income statement, a statement of changes in owner's equity, and a classified balance sheet. Mr. Strait did not make additional investments in the business during 1990.

3. Journalize adjusting and closing entries.

4. Post the adjusting and closing entries and prepare a post-closing trial balance. (Omit this requirement if you are not using the working papers.)

Problem 4–5
End-of-period accounting procedures
(L. O. 1, 2, 3)

The unadjusted trial balance of Doc's Delivery Service is as follows:

DOC'S DELIVERY SERVICE
Unadjusted Trial Balance
December 31, 1990

Cash	$ 785	
Accounts receivable	1,000	
Prepaid insurance	3,400	
Office supplies	365	
Prepaid rent	375	
Office equipment	3,690	
Accumulated depreciation, office equipment		$ 855
Delivery equipment	22,185	
Accumulated depreciation, delivery equipment		4,725
Accounts payable		1,335
Unearned delivery service revenue		825
Mark Welby, capital		34,355
Mark Welby, withdrawals	18,000	
Delivery service revenue		63,085
Rent expense	4,500	
Telephone expense	540	
Office salaries expense	15,090	
Delivery wages expense	30,480	
Gas, oil, and repairs expense	4,770	
Totals	$105,180	$105,180

Required

1. Enter the unadjusted trial balance on a work sheet form and complete the work sheet using the information that follows:

a. Insurance expired on the office equipment, $150, and on the delivery equipment, $2,835.

b. An inventory showed $165 of unused office supplies on hand.

c. Estimated depreciation on the office equipment, $450.

d. Estimated depreciation on the delivery equipment, $3,625.

e. In December 1989, the company had prepaid the January 1990 rent for garage and office space occupied by the delivery service. This amount appears as the balance of the Prepaid Rent account. Rents for February through November were paid each month and debited to the Rent Expense account. Also, $750 was paid for extra space used during the summer. As of the trial balance date, the December rent had not been paid.

f. Three stores signed contracts with the delivery service in which they agreed to pay a fixed fee for the delivery of packages. Two of the stores made advance payments on their contracts, and the amounts paid were credited to the Unearned Delivery Service Revenue account. An examination of their contracts shows $420 of the $825 paid was earned by the end of the accounting period. The third store's contract provides for a $300 monthly fee to be paid at the end of each month's service. It was signed on December 15, and one half of a month's revenue has accrued but is unrecorded.

g. A $55 December telephone bill and a $90 bill for repairs to a motorcycle used in the business arrived in the mail on December 31. Neither bill was paid or recorded before the trial balance was prepared.

h. Office salaries, $120, and delivery wages, $265, have accrued but are unpaid and unrecorded.

2. Prepare an income statement, a statement of changes in owner's equity, and a classified balance sheet. Mr. Welby did not make additional investments in the business during 1990.

3. Journalize adjusting and closing entries.

4. Post the adjusting and closing entries to the accounts and prepare a post-closing trial balance. (If you are not using the working papers, omit this requirement.)

*Problem 4–6
Reversing entries
(L. O. 2, 8)

Windward Service Company's unadjusted trial balance on December 31, 1990, the end of its annual accounting period, is as follows:

WINDWARD SERVICE COMPANY
Unadjusted Trial Balance
December 31, 1990

Cash.	$ 49,150	
Notes receivable	25,000	
Office supplies	2,800	
Land	30,000	
Unearned service fees		$ 12,000
Notes payable.		60,000
J. Cass, capital		25,000
J. Cass, withdrawals	40,000	
Service fees earned		178,000
Interest earned		1,700
Rent earned		8,250
Salaries expense	129,000	
Insurance expense	3,300	
Interest expense	5,700	
Totals	$284,950	$284,950

Information necessary to prepare adjusting entries is as follows:

a. Employees, who are paid $5,000 every two weeks, have earned $3,500 since the last payment. The next payment of $5,000 will be on January 4.

b. Windward rents office space to a tenant who has paid only $300 of the $750 rent for December. On January 10, the tenant will pay the remainder along with the rent for January.

c. An inventory of office supplies discloses $450 of unused supplies.

d. Premiums for insurance against injuries to employees are paid monthly. The $300 premium for December will be paid January 12.

e. Windward owes $60,000 on a note payable that requires quarterly payments of accrued interest. The quarterly payments of $1,800 each are made on the 15th of January, April, July, and October.

f. An analysis of Windward's service contracts with customers shows that $4,200 of the amount customers have prepaid remains unearned.

g. Windward has a $25,000 note receivable on which interest of $125 has accrued. On January 20, the note and the total accrued interest of $375 will be repaid to Windward.

h. Windward has earned but unrecorded revenue of $5,500 for services provided to a customer that will pay for the work on January 23. At that time, the customer will also pay $2,100 for services Windward will perform in early January.

Required

1. Prepare adjusting journal entries.
2. Prepare closing journal entries.
3. Prepare reversing entries.
4. Prepare journal entries to record the January 1991 cash receipts and cash payments identified in the above information.

Alternate Problems

Problem 4–1A
Closing entries for partnerships and corporations
(L. O. 2, 3, 4, 5)

On January 5, 1989, Bob Long, Kim Wong, and Phil Song started a business in which Bob Long invested $15,000, Kim Wong invested $30,000, and Phil Song invested $45,000. During 1989, the business lost $4,500; and during 1990, it earned $27,000. On January 5, 1991, the three business owners agreed to pay out to themselves $18,000 of the accumulated earnings of the business; and on January 10, the $18,000 was paid out.

Required

1. Assume that the business is a partnership and that the partners share net incomes and net losses in proportion to their investments. Give the entries to record the investments and to close the Income Summary account at the end of 1989 and again at the end of 1990. Also assume that the partners paid out the accumulated earnings in proportion to their investments. Give the entry to record the withdrawals.

2. Assume that the business is organized as a corporation and that the owners invested in the corporation by buying its common stock at $10 per share, with Bob Long buying 1,500 shares, Kim Wong buying 3,000 shares, and Phil Song buying 4,500 shares. Give the entry to record the investments. Also give the entries to close the Income Summary ac-

count at the end of 1989 and again at the end of 1990. Then give the entries to record the declaration and payment of the $2 per share dividend. (Ignore corporation income taxes and assume the investors are the corporation's board of directors.)

Problem 4–2A
The work sheet; financial statements and closing entries
(L. O. 1, 2)

A trial balance of the ledger of Ms. Shine Janitorial Service at the end of its annual accounting period appeared as follows:

MS. SHINE JANITORIAL SERVICE
Unadjusted Trial Balance
December 31, 1990

Cash	$ 1,600	
Accounts receivable	320	
Prepaid insurance	1,980	
Cleaning supplies	1,225	
Prepaid rent	450	
Cleaning equipment	3,915	
Accumulated depreciation, cleaning equipment		$ 1,710
Trucks	24,840	
Accumulated depreciation, trucks		5,720
Accounts payable		965
Unearned janitorial revenue		600
Jane Adams, capital		17,615
Jane Adams, withdrawals	23,175	
Janitorial revenue earned		51,915
Wages expense	18,660	
Rent expense	1,200	
Gas, oil, and repairs expense	1,160	
Totals	$78,525	$78,525

Required

1. Enter the trial balance on a work sheet form and complete the work sheet using the information that follows:

   a. Expired insurance, $1,425.

   b. An inventory of cleaning supplies showed $185 of unused supplies on hand.

   c. The cleaning service rents garage and equipment storage space. At the beginning of the year, three months' rent was prepaid as shown by the debit balance of the Prepaid Rent account. Rents for April through November were paid on the first day of each month and debited to the Rent Expense account. The December rent was unpaid on the trial balance date.

   d. Estimated depreciation on the cleaning equipment, $545, and (e) on the trucks, $3,255.

   f. On November 15, the janitorial service contracted and began cleaning the office of Troy Realty for $300 per month. The realty company paid for two months' service in advance, and the amount paid was credited to the Unearned Janitorial Revenue account. The janitorial service also entered into a contract and began cleaning the office of Knox Insurance Agency on December 15. By the month's end, a half month's revenue, $180, had been earned on this contract but was unrecorded.

   g. Employee's wages amounting to $270 had accrued but were unrecorded on the trial balance date.

2. Prepare an income statement, a statement of changes in owner's equity, and a classified balance sheet for the business. Ms. Adams did not make additional investments in the business during 1990.

3. Prepare adjusting journal entries and compound closing entries.

Problem 4–3A
All steps in the accounting cycle (covers two accounting cycles)
(L. O. 1, 2, 3, 4, 6)

Tami Martin started a business she called Martin Realty. During May, she completed the transactions that follow:

May 2 Invested in the real estate agency $3,500 in cash and an automobile having a $12,000 fair value.

2 Rented furnished office space and paid one month's rent, $600.

2 Paid the premium on an insurance policy giving one year's protection, $996.

3 Purchased office supplies for cash, $210.

13 Paid the salary of the office secretary for two weeks, $670.

19 Sold a building lot and collected a $2,400 commission on the sale.

27 Paid the salary of the office secretary for two weeks, $670.

31 Paid the May telephone bill, $65.

31 Paid for gas and oil used in the agency car during May, $70.

Required Work for May

1. Open these accounts: Cash; Prepaid Insurance; Office Supplies; Automobile; Accumulated Depreciation, Automobile; Salaries Payable; Tami Martin, Capital; Tami Martin, Withdrawals; Income Summary; Commissions Earned; Rent Expense; Salaries Expense; Gas, Oil, and Repairs Expense; Telephone Expense; Insurance Expense; Office Supplies Expense; and Depreciation Expense, Automobile.

2. Prepare and post journal entries to record the transactions.

3. Prepare an unadjusted trial balance on a work sheet form and complete the work sheet using the information that follows:
   a. One month's insurance has expired.
   b. An inventory shows $165 of unused office supplies remaining.
   c. Estimated depreciation on the automobile, $240.
   d. Earned but unpaid wages of the secretary, $134.

4. Prepare an income statement and a statement of changes in owner's equity for May, and prepare a May 31 classified balance sheet.

5. Journalize and post adjusting and closing entries.

6. Prepare a post-closing trial balance.

These transactions were completed by Tami Martin during June:

June 1 Paid the June rent on the office space, $600.

5 Sold a house and collected a $7,275 commission.

7 Tami Martin withdrew $2,250 from the business to pay personal expenses.

10 Paid the salary of the office secretary for two weeks, $670.

21 Purchased additional office supplies for cash, $55.

24 Paid the salary of the office secretary for two weeks, $670.

June 30   Paid the June telephone bill, $60.
    30   Paid for gas and oil used in the agency car, $75.

Required Work for June

1. Prepare and post journal entries to record the transactions.
2. Prepare an unadjusted trial balance on a work sheet form and complete the work sheet using the information that follows:
   a. One month's insurance has expired.
   b. An office supplies inventory shows $180 of unused office supplies.
   c. Estimated depreciation on the automobile, $240.
   d. Earned but unrecorded salary of the secretary, $268.
3. Prepare an income statement and a statement of changes in owner's equity for June, and prepare a June 30 classified balance sheet.
4. Journalize and post adjusting and closing entries.
5. Prepare a post-closing trial balance.

Problem 4–4A
End of period accounting procedures
(L. O. 1, 2, 3)

The accounts of Strait Alleys, showing the end of its annual accounting period balances, appear in the booklet of working papers that accompanies this text, and a trial balance of the accounts is reproduced on a work sheet form provided there. The trial balance has the items that follow:

STRAIT ALLEYS
Unadjusted Trial Balance
December 31, 1990

Cash	$ 1,265	
Bowling supplies	2,230	
Prepaid insurance	2,000	
Bowling equipment	74,295	
Accumulated depreciation, bowling equipment		$ 11,460
Accounts payable		205
Long-term notes payable		15,000
Paul Strait, capital		32,250
Paul Strait, withdrawals	23,475	
Bowling revenue		81,700
Wages expense	24,580	
Equipment repairs expense	690	
Rent expense	7,200	
Utilities expense	3,200	
Business tax expense	780	
Interest expense	900	
Totals	$140,615	$140,615

Required

1. Enter the unadjusted trial balance on a work sheet form and complete the work sheet using the information that follows:
   a. Bowling supplies inventory, $270.
   b. Expired insurance, $1,795.
   c. Estimated depreciation on the bowling equipment, $7,075.
   d. A $245 bill for equipment repairs arrived in the mail after the trial balance was prepared. It is unrecorded and unpaid.
   e. Wages earned but unpaid and unrecorded, $335.
   f. The lease contract on the bowling alley space calls for an annual rental equal to 11% of the annual bowling revenue, with $600 paya-

   ble each month on the first day of the month. The $600 was paid each month and debited to the Rent Expense account.

   g. Business tax amounting to $325 has accrued but is unrecorded and unpaid.

   h. The long-term note payable was signed on August 1. The interest on the debt is at a 12% annual rate or $150 per month. The note requires the payment in advance of $450 interest each three months. Interest was paid on August 1 and November 1. A $3,000 payment on the note principal is due next August 1.

2. Prepare an income statement, a statement of changes in owner's equity, and a classified balance sheet. Mr. Strait did not make any additional investments in the business during 1990.

3. Journalize adjusting and closing entries.

4. Post the adjusting and closing entries and prepare a post-closing trial balance. (Omit this requirement if the working papers are not being used.)

Problem 4–5A
End-of-period accounting procedures
(L. O. 1, 2, 3)

The unadjusted trial balance of Doc's Delivery Service is as follows:

DOC'S DELIVERY SERVICE
Unadjusted Trial Balance
December 31, 1990

Cash	$ 785	
Accounts receivable	1,000	
Prepaid insurance	3,415	
Office supplies	365	
Prepaid rent	375	
Office equipment	3,690	
Accumulated depreciation, office equipment		$ 855
Delivery equipment	22,185	
Accumulated depreciation, delivery equipment		4,725
Accounts payable		1,335
Unearned delivery service revenue		825
Mark Welby, capital		34,355
Mark Welby, withdrawals	18,000	
Delivery service revenue		62,325
Rent expense	3,750	
Telephone expense	515	
Office salaries expense	15,090	
Delivery wages expense	30,480	
Gas, oil, and repairs expense	4,770	
Totals	$104,420	$104,420

Required

1. Enter the unadjusted trial balance on a work sheet form and complete the work sheet using the information that follows:

   a. Expired insurance on the office equipment, $165, and on the delivery equipment, $2,665.

   b. An inventory showed $180 of unused office supplies on hand.

   c. Estimated depreciation on the office equipment, $435, and (d) on the delivery equipment, $3,495.

   e. In December 1989, the company had prepaid the January 1990 rent for garage and office space occupied by the delivery service. This amount appears as the balance of the Prepaid Rent account. Rents for February through November were paid each month and debited to the Rent Expense account. As of December 31, 1990, the December rent had not been paid.

f. The delivery service has contracts with three stores for the delivery of packages on a fixed-fee basis. Two of the stores made advance payments on their contracts, and the amounts paid were credited to the Unearned Delivery Service Revenue account. An examination of the contracts shows that $480 of the $825 paid was earned by the end of the accounting period. The third store's contract provides for a $380 monthly fee to be paid at the end of each month's service. One half of a month's revenue has accrued on this contract but it is unrecorded.

g. A $125 bill for repairs to a delivery truck during December arrived in the mail after the trial balance was prepared. The bill is unpaid and unrecorded.

h. Office salaries, $60, and delivery wages, $145, have accrued but are unpaid and unrecorded.

2. Prepare an income statement, a statement of changes in owner's equity, and a classified balance sheet.

3. Journalize adjusting and closing entries.

4. Post the adjusting and closing entries to the accounts and prepare a post-closing trial balance. (If the working papers are not being used, omit this requirement.)

*Problem 4–6A
Reversing entries
(L. O. 2, 8)

Leeward Service Company's unadjusted trial balance on December 31, 1990, the end of its annual accounting period, is as follows:

LEEWARD SERVICE COMPANY
Unadjusted Trial Balance
December 31, 1990

Cash.	$ 73,725	
Notes receivable	37,500	
Office supplies	4,200	
Land	45,000	
Unearned service fees		$ 18,000
Notes payable.		90,000
J. Boat, capital		37,500
J. Boat, withdrawals	60,000	
Service fees earned		267,000
Interest earned		2,550
Rent earned		12,375
Salaries expense	193,500	
Insurance expense	4,950	
Interest expense	8,550	
Totals	$427,425	$427,425

Information necessary to prepare adjusting entries is as follows:

a. Employees, who are paid $7,500 every two weeks, have earned $5,250 since the last payment. The next payment of $7,500 will be on January 4.

b. Leeward rents office space to a tenant who has paid only $450 of the $1,125 rent for December. On January 12, the tenant will pay the remainder along with the rent for January.

c. An inventory of office supplies discloses $675 of unused supplies.

d. Premiums for insurance against injuries to employees are paid monthly. The $450 premium for December will be paid January 12.

e. Leeward owes $90,000 on a note payable that requires quarterly payments of accrued interest. The quarterly payments of $2,700 each are made on the 15th of January, April, July, and October.

f. An analysis of Leeward's service contracts with customers shows that $6,300 of the amount customers have prepaid remains unearned.

g. Leeward has a $37,500 note receivable on which interest of $175 has accrued. On January 22, the note and the total accrued interest of $575 will be repaid to Leeward.

h. Leeward has earned but unrecorded revenue of $8,250 for services provided to a customer who will pay for the work on January 24. At that time, the customer will also pay $3,100 for services Leeward will perform in early January.

Required
1. Prepare adjusting journal entries.
2. Prepare closing journal entries.
3. Prepare reversing entries.
4. Prepare journal entries to record the January 1991 cash receipts and cash payments identified in the above information.

Provocative Problems

Provocative Problem 4–1
Strongarm Moving Service
(Review problem)

During his second year in college, Wesley Smith inherited Strongarm Moving Service when his father died. He immediately dropped out of school and took over management of the business. At the time he took over, Wesley recognized he knew little about accounting. However, he reasoned that since the business performed its services strictly for cash, if the cash of the business increased, the business was doing OK. Therefore, he was pleased as he watched the cash balance grow from $2,100 when he took over to $20,950 at year-end. Furthermore, since he had withdrawn $30,000 from the business to buy a new car and to pay personal expenses, he reasoned that the business must have earned $48,850 during the year. He arrived at the $48,850 by adding the $18,850 increase in cash to the $30,000 he had withdrawn from the business. Wesley was shocked when he received the income statement that follows and learned that the business had earned less than the amounts withdrawn.

STRONGARM MOVING SERVICE
Income Statement
For Year Ended December 31, 1990

Revenue from moving services		$120,565
Operating expenses:		
Salaries and wages expense	$54,825	
Gas, oil, and repairs expense	4,835	
Telephone expense	525	
Taxes expense	3,710	
Insurance expense.	3,485	
Office supplies expense	375	
Depreciation expense, office equipment	600	
Depreciation expense, trucks	9,375	
Depreciation expense, building	7,500	
Total operating expenses		85,230
Net income		$ 35,335

After thinking about the statement for several days, Wesley asked you to explain how, in a year in which the cash increased $18,850 and he withdrew $30,000, the business earned only $35,335. In examining the accounts of the business, you note that accrued salaries and wages payable at the beginning of the year were $185 but increased to $575 at year's end. Also, the accrued taxes payable were $675 at the beginning of the year but had increased to $715 at year-end. Also, the balance of the Prepaid Insurance account was $300 less and the balance of the Office Supplies account was $75 less at the end of the year than at the beginning. However, except for the changes in these accounts, the change in cash, and the changes in the balances of the accumulated depreciation accounts, there were no other changes in the balances of the concern's asset and liability accounts between the beginning of the year and the end. Back your explanation with a calculation that accounts for the increase in the business's cash.

Provocative Problem 4–2
Victoria Shaw, Lawyer
(L. O. 2, 6)

During the first year-end closing of the accounts of Victoria Shaw's law practice, the office bookkeeper became seriously ill and entered the hospital, unable to have visitors. Ms. Shaw is certain the bookkeeper prepared a work sheet and complete financial statements, but she has only the income statement and cannot find the work sheet or remaining statements. She does have the unadjusted trial balance. She has asked you to take the information she has and prepare adjusting and closing entries. She also wants you to prepare a statement of changes in owner's equity and a classified balance sheet. She says the $1,800 of unearned legal fees on the trial balance represents a retainer fee paid by Guaranty Bank. The bank retained Victoria Shaw on November 1 to do its legal work, and agreed to pay her $600 per month for her services. She says she has also agreed with Eastside Realty to do its legal work on a fixed-fee basis. The agreement calls for a $450 monthly fee payable at the end of each three months. The agreement was signed on December 1, and one month's fee has accrued but has not been recorded. Ms. Shaw did not make any additional investments in the business during the year.

VICTORIA SHAW, LAWYER
Unadjusted Trial Balance
December 31, 1990

Cash	$ 1,835	
Legal fees receivable	2,250	
Office supplies	490	
Prepaid insurance	1,350	
Furniture and equipment	18,750	
Accounts payable		$ 525
Short-term notes payable		7,500
Unearned legal fees		1,800
Victoria Shaw, capital		11,250
Victoria Shaw, withdrawals	27,000	
Legal fees earned		55,985
Salaries expense	17,625	
Rent expense	7,200	
Telephone expense	560	
Totals	$77,060	$77,060

VICTORIA SHAW, LAWYER
Income Statement
For Year Ended December 31, 1990

Revenue:		
Legal fees earned		$57,635
Operating expenses:		
Salaries expense	$18,000	
Rent expense	7,200	
Telephone expense	560	
Office supplies expense	300	
Insurance expense	1,125	
Depreciation expense, furniture and equipment	1,800	
Interest expense	900	
Total operating expenses		29,885
Net income		$27,750

Provocative Problem 4–3
Valleyview Realty
(L. O. 1)

The balance sheet that follows was prepared for Valleyview Realty at the end of its annual accounting period.

VALLEYVIEW REALTY
Balance Sheet
December 31, 1990
Assets

Current assets:			
Cash		$ 2,285	
Prepaid insurance		750	
Office supplies		165	
Total current assets			$ 3,200
Plant and equipment:			
Office equipment	$ 7,860		
Less accumulated depreciation	1,515	$ 6,345	
Automobile	$18,600		
Less accumulated depreciation	4,050	14,550	
Total plant and equipment			20,895
Total assets			$24,095

Liabilities

Current liabilities:		
Accounts payable	$ 315	
Unearned property management fees	375	
Salaries payable	270	
Total liabilities		$ 960

Owner's Equity

Gail Banks, capital, December 31, 1990	23,135
Total liabilities and owner's equity	$24,095

After completing the balance sheet, Valleyview Realty's accountant prepared and posted the following adjusting and closing entries for the concern:

Dec.	31	Insurance Expense	1,725.00	
		Prepaid Insurance		1,725.00
	31	Office Supplies Expense	315.00	
		Office Supplies		315.00
	31	Depreciation Expense, Office Equipment	960.00	
		Accumulated Depreciation, Office Equipment		960.00
	31	Depreciation Expense, Automobile	3,150.00	
		Accumulated Depreciation, Automobile		3,150.00
	31	Unearned Property Management Fees	750.00	
		Property Management Fees Earned		750.00
	31	Salaries Expense	270.00	
		Salaries Payable		270.00
	31	Commissions Earned	74,400.00	
		Property Management Fees Earned	2,640.00	
		Income Summary		77,040.00
	31	Income Summary	33,750.00	
		Salaries Expense		16,500.00
		Rent Expense		9,000.00
		Telephone Expense		690.00
		Gas, Oil, and Repairs Expense		1,410.00
		Insurance Expense		1,725.00
		Office Supplies Expense		315.00
		Depreciation Expense, Office Equipment		960.00
		Depreciation Expense, Automobile		3,150.00
	31	Income Summary	43,290.00	
		Gail Banks, Capital		43,290.00
	31	Gail Banks, Capital	36,000.00	
		Gail Banks, Withdrawals		36,000.00

Enter the relevant information from the balance sheet and the adjusting and closing entries on a work sheet form and complete the work sheet by working backward to the items that appeared in its Unadjusted Trial Balance columns.

Analytical and Review Problems

A&R Problem 4–1

The owner of Dynasty Stores has come to you for assistance because his book-keeper has just moved to another city. The following is the only information his bookkeeper left him.

(1) Balance sheets as at December 31, 199A and 199B.

	199A	199B
Assets.	$150,000	$120,000
Liabilities	$ 45,000	$ 30,000
Capital.	105,000	90,000
	$150,000	$120,000

(2) The owner withdrew $75,000 in 199B for his personal use.

(3) The business incurred total expenses of $120,000 for 199B, of which $90,000 was for wages and $30,000 for advertising.

Required

1. Compute the total revenue and net income for 199B.

2. Prepare closing or clearing entries for 199B (omit narratives).

A&R Problem 4–2

The partially completed work sheet for the current fiscal year of Joan Turner Delivery Service appears below.

Required

Complete the work sheet on page 207.

A&R Problem 4–3

Required

Based on the data of the completed work sheet of A&R Problem 4–2:

1. Prepare for Joan Turner Delivery Service the income statement and balance sheet.

2. Journalize the adjusting and closing entries (omit narratives).

A&R Problem 4–4

Philip Kersh operates a management consulting firm and uses a cash basis for recording transactions. The trial balance presented below reflects the operations for the first year of business.

PHILIP KERSH, MANAGEMENT CONSULTANT
Trial Balance
December 31, 1990

Cash	$ 3,600	
Office equipment expense	28,000	
P. Kersh, capital		$ 1,000
Management consulting fees		98,000
Office salaries expense	31,000	
Telephone expense	1,000	
Insurance expense	3,000	
Office supplies expense	800	
P. Kersh, withdrawals	31,600	
Totals	$99,000	$99,000

JOAN TURNER DELIVERY SERVICE
Work Sheet
For the Year Ended December 31, 1990

Account Titles	Trial Balance Dr.	Trial Balance Cr.	Adjustments Dr.	Adjustments Cr.	Adjusted Trial Balance Dr.	Adjusted Trial Balance Cr.	Income Statement Dr.	Income Statement Cr.	Balance Sheet Dr.	Balance Sheet Cr.
Cash	10,650									
Accounts receivable	5,200				6,000					
Supplies on hand	1,400				900					
Prepaid insurance	2,400									
Prepaid rent	1,200									
Delivery trucks					40,000					
Accounts payable		3,130				3,130				
Unearned delivery fees		4,500				3,000				
Joan Turner, capital, Dec. 31, 1989		50,000								
Joan Turner, drawing	3,000									
Delivery service revenue		10,700								
Advertising expense	50									
Gas and oil expense	680									
Salaries expense	3,600									
Utilities expense	150									
	68,330	68,330								
Insurance expense					200					
Rent expense					400					
Supplies expense										
Depreciation expense—delivery trucks										
Accumulated depreciation—delivery trucks						750				
Accrued salaries payable						180				
Net income										

Additional information

a. Amount of office supplies still on hand at the end of the year was $200.

b. The office equipment was estimated to have a 10-year useful life with no salvage value.

c. Consulting services rendered for which no payment has been received amounted to $6,000.

d. Telephone bill for the month of December 1990 was paid in January 1991, $150.

e. Advertising expenses incurred but not yet paid, $1,200.

f. Golden, Ltd., paid $1,000 consulting fee for services to be performed in 1991.

Required

1. Prepare all necessary adjusting entries (omit narratives) to reflect Kersh's operation on an accrual basis of accounting.
2. Prepare a trial balance on the accrual basis of accounting.
3. What is the difference in net income between the cash and the accrual bases of accounting for Kersh's business?
4. Which basis, in your opinion, more realistically reflects the operations of Kersh? Why?
5. What are the similarities and dissimilarities between the adjusting entries to convert a cash basis to an accrual basis and the adjusting entries for an accrual basis?

A&R Problem 4–5

Your examination of the books of Dr. Milton Vacon, a local general practitioner, revealed that his nurse/secretary followed the cash basis of accounting in all matters with the exception of equipment. The equipment which cost $42,000 at the time Dr. Vacon started practice (January 2, 1988) was set up as an asset and to date not depreciated. The equipment had an estimated useful life of 10 years at which time it would be sold for an estimated $2,000. Upon further examination you were able to identify the relevant data as follows:

	1988	1989	1990
Reported income	$91,000	$96,000	$89,000
Supplies on hand at year-end	500	300	1,200
Wages not paid at year-end	1,600	1,800	1,500
Billings to the Provincial Hospital Insurance during December for which a cheque has not been received	10,000	8,000	12,000
Miscellaneous expenses owing at year-end	1,300	1,700	1,200

Required

Compute the correct net income for each year using the accrual basis of accounting (show all supporting calculations).

COMPREHENSIVE PROBLEM

Satellite Theatre
(Review of Chapters 1 through 4)

Presented below is the November 30, 1990, unadjusted trial balance of Satellite Theatre, which is owned by J. R. Thompson. The temporary account balances represent the results of entries recorded during the first 11 months of 1990, and the balance in J. R. Thompson's capital account has not changed since December 31, 1989.

SATELLITE THEATRE
Unadjusted Trial Balance
November 30, 1990

	Acct. No.	Debits	Credits
Cash	111	$ 4,000	
Concessions inventory	112	11,200	
Supplies inventory	113	750	
Prepaid movie rental	114	880	
Equipment	131	5,500	
Accumulated depreciation, equipment	132		$ 1,100
Building	135	75,000	
Accumulated depreciation, building	136		14,500
Accounts payable	211		1,550
Wages payable	212		–0–
Utilities payable	213		250
Interest payable	214		–0–
Long-term notes payable	231		42,000
J. R. Thompson, capital	311		14,970
J. R. Thompson, withdrawals	312	8,000	
Income summary	313		–0–
Admissions revenue	411		39,850
Concessions revenue	412		28,650
Wages expense	511	14,000	
Movie rental expense	512	16,500	
Concessions expense	513	–0–	
Supplies expense	514	–0–	
Utilities expense	515	2,800	
Advertising expense	516	3,200	
Maintenance expense	517	1,040	
Depreciation expense, equipment	518	–0–	
Depreciation expense, building	519	–0–	
Interest expense	520	–0–	
Totals		$142,870	$142,870

The following transactions occurred during the month of December 1990:

Dec. 2 Paid a $250 utility bill that was recorded as accrued on November 30.
5 Paid accounts payable of $950.
6 Paid movie rental of $1,500 in advance.
7 Deposited $1,000 of admissions receipts.
10 Purchased $350 of concessions items on credit.
12 Acquired additional equipment worth $4,000 by paying $500 cash and giving a long-term note payable for the balance.
14 Paid wages of $520 for the period December 1 through 14.
17 Purchased $100 of supplies on credit.

Dec. 21   Deposited $1,750 from concessions sales and $1,660 of admissions receipts.

24   Paid $500 for repairs to roof and marquee for weather damage.

28   Paid wages of $720 for the period December 15 through 28.

30   Paid $400 to newspaper for advertisements that appeared in December.

31   Deposited $2,000 from admissions receipts and $850 from concessions sales.

Required

1. Set up accounts for the items listed in the November 30 trial balance, and enter the November 30 balances in them.

2. Prepare and post journal entries to record the December transactions listed above.

3. Prepare a 10-column work sheet and enter the December 31 unadjusted balances from the accounts. Also enter adjusting entries for the following items, and complete the work sheet.
   a. Unpaid wages were $160 as of December 31.
   b. The December 31 concessions inventory was $960.
   c. The supplies inventory was $125 on December 31.
   d. The unexpired portion of the prepaid movie rental was $510 as of December 31.
   e. Depreciation for the year on the equipment was $1,900.
   f. Depreciation for the year on the building was $3,750.
   g. Unpaid utilities expense for December was $330.
   h. Thompson had withdrawn $1,000 cash on December 30, but he had not taken the time to record it.
   i. Interest expense on the note payable for 1990 was $4,300.

4. Prepare an income statement and a statement of changes in owner's equity for the year ended December 31, 1990, and a December 31, 1990, classified balance sheet.

5. Journalize and post the adjusting entries.

6. Journalize and post the closing entries.

7. Prepare a post-closing trial balance.

5

Accounting for a Merchandising Concern

The illustrations we have used in previous chapters were of businesses that provided services to their customers: businesses such as law firms, accounting firms, and real estate agencies. In this chapter, we shift our attention to merchandising businesses; they buy goods or products and resell them to their customers. Your study of this chapter will focus on the problem of accounting for the goods that merchandising companies purchase for resale. You will learn to identify the elements of cost of goods sold and to complete the end-of-period procedures that are used to account for merchandising companies, whether they are organized as corporations or as proprietorships.

Learning Objectives

After studying Chapter 5, you should be able to:

1. Analyze and record transactions that involve the purchase and resale of merchandise.
2. Explain the nature of each item entering into the calculation of cost of goods sold and gross profit from sales.
3. Prepare a work sheet and the financial statements for a merchandising business that uses a periodic inventory system and that is organized as a corporation or as a single proprietorship.
4. Prepare adjusting and closing entries for a merchandising business organized as either a corporation or a single proprietorship.
5. Define or explain the words and phrases listed in the chapter Glossary.

After studying the appendixes to Chapter 5 (Appendixes C and D), you should be able to:

6. Explain the adjusting entry approach to accounting for inventories and prepare a work sheet, adjusting entries, and closing entries according to the adjusting entry approach. (Appendix C)
7. Discuss financial statement concepts and the qualitative characteristics accounting information should possess. (Appendix D)

The accounting records and reports of the Dow law practice, as described in previous chapters, are those of a service enterprise. Other examples of service enterprises are laundries, taxicab companies, hairdressers, theatres, and golf courses. Each performs a service for a commission or fee, and the net income of each is the difference between fees or commissions earned and operating expenses.

A merchandising company, on the other hand, whether a wholesaler or retailer, earns revenue by selling goods or **merchandise.** In such a company, a net income results when revenue from sales exceeds the cost of the goods sold plus operating expenses, as illustrated below:

EASTSIDE HARDWARE STORE
Condensed Income Statement
For Month Ended July 31, 1990

Revenue from sales	$100,000
Less cost of goods sold	60,000
Gross profit from sales	$ 40,000
Less operating expenses . . .	25,000
Net income	$ 15,000

This income statement shows you that Eastside Hardware Store sold goods to customers for $100,000. The goods that were sold had cost Eastside $60,000. As a result, the company earned a $40,000 **gross profit.** Also, the company incurred operating expenses of $25,000, which resulted in a $15,000 net income for the month.

Gross profit, also called *gross margin,* is defined as the amount by which revenue from sales exceeds the cost of goods sold. The elements of this calculation are what make accounting for a merchandising company different from accounting for a service company. To account for a merchandising company, you must understand how to account for the elements of gross profit: for revenue from sales and for cost of goods sold.

Revenue from Sales

Analyze and record transactions that involve the purchase and resale of merchandise.
(L. O. 1)

Revenue from sales consists of gross proceeds from merchandise sales less returns, allowances, and discounts. It may be reported on an income statement as follows:

SOWA SALES, INCORPORATED
Income Statement
For Year Ended December 31, 1990

Revenue from sales:		
Gross sales.		$306,200
Less: Sales returns and allowances . .	1,900	
Sales discounts	4,300	6,200
Net sales		$300,000

Gross Sales

On the partial income statement, the gross sales item is the total cash and credit sales made by the company during the year. Cash sales were "rung up" on the cash register as each sale was completed. At the end of each day, the register total showed the amount of that day's cash sales, which was recorded with an entry like this:

Nov.	3	Cash	1,205.00	
		Sales		1,205.00
		To record the day's cash sales.		

Also, the following entry was used to record credit sales:

Nov.	3	Accounts Receivable	45.00	
		Sales		45.00
		Sold merchandise on credit.		

Sales Returns and Allowances

In most stores, customers are allowed to return any unsatisfactory merchandise they bought. Sometimes, customers are allowed to keep the unsatisfactory goods and are given an allowance or an amount off the sales price. Either way, returns and allowances result from dissatisfied customers. Therefore, it is important for management to know the amount of such returns and allowances and their relation to sales. The Sales Returns and Allowances account supplies this information because each return or allowance is recorded as follows:

Nov.	4	Sales Returns and Allowances	20.00	
		Accounts Receivable (or Cash)		20.00
		Customer returned unsatisfactory merchandise.		

Sales Discounts

When goods are sold on credit, the terms of payment must be stated clearly so there will be no misunderstanding as to the amount and time of payment. These **credit terms** normally appear on the invoice or sales ticket and are part of the sales agreement. Exact terms usually depend on the custom of the trade. In some areas of business, it is customary for invoices to become due and payable 10 days after the end of the month **(EOM)** in which the sale occurred. These credit terms are stated on the sales invoices as "n/10 EOM." In other trades, invoices become due and payable 30 days after the invoice date and carry terms of "n/30." This means that the net amount of the invoice is due 30 days after the invoice date.

When credit periods are long, creditors often grant discounts, called **cash discounts,** for early payments. This reduces the amount invested in accounts receivable, which means that less money is needed to carry on business operations. When discounts for early payment are granted, they are made part of the credit terms and appear on the invoice as, for example, "Terms: 2/10, n/60." Terms of 2/10, n/60 mean that the **credit period** is 60 days but that the debtor may deduct 2% from the invoice amount if payment is made within 10 days after the invoice date. The 10-day period is known as the **discount period.**

At the time of a sale, you do not know if the customer will pay within the discount period and take advantage of a cash discount. As a result, sales discounts usually are not recorded until the customer pays. For example, on November 12, Sowa Sales, Incorporated, sold $100 of merchandise to a customer on credit, terms 2/10, n/60, and recorded the sale as follows:

Nov.	12	Accounts Receivable	100.00	
		Sales		100.00
		Sold merchandise, terms 2/10, n/60.		

The customer has two alternative ways to satisfy this $100 obligation. One option is to pay $98 any time on or before November 22. Or, the customer could wait 60 days, until January 11, and pay the full $100. If the customer elects to pay by November 22 and take advantage of the cash discount, Sowa Sales, Incorporated, will record the receipt of the $98 as follows:

Nov.	22	Cash	98.00	
		Sales Discounts	2.00	
		Accounts Receivable		100.00
		Received payment for the November 12 sale less the discount.		

Cash discounts granted to customers are called **sales discounts,** and are accumulated in the Sales Discounts account until the end of an accounting period. Their total is then deducted from gross sales in calculating net revenue from sales. This is logical. A sales discount is an "amount off" the regular price of goods that is granted for early payment. As a result, it reduces revenue from sales.

Periodic and Perpetual Inventory Systems

Businesses such as automobile dealers or major appliance stores make a limited number of sales each day. Therefore, they can easily refer to their records at the time of each sale and record the cost of the car or appliance sold. On the other hand, a drugstore or a hardware store may find this difficult. For instance, if a drugstore sells a customer a tube of toothpaste, a box of aspirin, and a magazine, it can easily record with a cash register the sale of these items at marked selling prices. However, with large-volume, low-priced items, it may be quite difficult to determine quickly the cost of each item so that the "cost of goods sold" can be recorded at the time of sale. Some computerized systems allow this to be done. But many stores that sell a large volume of low-priced items often make no effort to record the cost of goods sold at the time of each sale. Rather, they wait until the end of an accounting period, take a physical inventory, and from the inventory and their accounting records determine at that time the cost of all goods sold during the period.

The end-of-period inventories that drug, hardware, grocery, or similar stores take to learn the cost of the goods they have sold are called periodic inventories. Also, the systems such stores use to account for inventories and the cost of goods sold are called **periodic inventory systems.** These systems are described and explained in this chapter. An alternative system of accounting for inventories and cost of goods sold, which involves recording the cost of goods sold each time a sale is made and keeping an up-to-date record of the goods on hand, is called a **perpetual inventory system.** These systems are discussed in Chapter 9.

Cost of Goods Sold, Periodic Inventory System

Explain the nature of each item entering into the calculation of cost of goods sold and gross profit from sales.
(L. O. 2)

As we mentioned before, a store that uses a periodic inventory system does not record the cost of items sold at the time they are sold. Rather, it waits until the end of an accounting period and determines the cost of all the goods sold during the period. To do this, it must have information about (1) the cost of the merchandise on hand at the beginning of the period, (2) the cost of merchandise purchased during the period, and (3) the cost of unsold goods that remain at the period end. With this information, a store can calculate the cost of goods sold during a period, as follows:

Cost of goods on hand at beginning of period . .	$ 19,000
Cost of goods purchased during the period . . .	232,000
Goods available for sale during the period	$251,000
Less unsold goods on hand at the period end . .	21,000
Cost of goods sold during the period	$230,000

In the above calculation, the company had $19,000 of merchandise at the beginning of the accounting period. During the period, it purchased additional merchandise that cost $232,000. Therefore, it had merchandise that cost $251,000 available for sale during the period. However, $21,000 of this merchandise remained on hand (unsold) at the period end. Therefore, the cost of the goods it sold during the period was $230,000.

The following paragraphs explain how you accumulate the information needed to calculate cost of goods sold.

Merchandise Inventories

The merchandise on hand at the beginning of an accounting period is called the beginning inventory; the merchandise on hand at the end is the ending inventory. Also, since accounting periods follow one after another, the ending inventory of one period is the beginning inventory of the next.

When a periodic inventory system is in use, the dollar amount of the ending inventory is determined by (1) counting the unsold items on the shelves in the store and in the stockroom, (2) multiplying the count for each type of goods by its cost, and (3) adding the costs of the different types of goods.

After the dollar cost of the ending inventory is determined in this manner, it is subtracted from the cost of the goods available for sale to determine cost of goods sold. Also, a journal entry is prepared and posted to record the ending inventory amount in an account called Merchandise Inventory. This ending inventory amount remains as the balance in the Merchandise Inventory account throughout the next accounting period. Thus, throughout the new accounting period, the balance of the Merchandise Inventory account represents the cost of the inventory on hand at the end of the previous period, which also is the beginning inventory of the current period.

We should emphasize the fact that, other than to correct errors, entries are made in the Merchandise Inventory account *only* at the end of each accounting period. As time passes during an accounting period and merchandise is both purchased and sold, neither the purchases nor the cost of goods sold amounts are entered in the Merchandise Inventory account. Therefore, as soon as goods are purchased or sold, the account does not show the dollar amount of merchandise on hand. Rather, the account's balance reflects the beginning inventory of the period.

Cost of Merchandise Purchased

To determine the cost of merchandise purchased, you must note the invoice price of goods purchased and subtract any discounts, returns, and allowances. Then, you add any freight or other transportation costs incurred by the purchaser to ship the goods from the supplier to the purchaser's place of business. The following paragraphs explain how these amounts are accumulated in the accounts.

Under a periodic inventory system, when merchandise is bought for resale, its cost is debited to an account called Purchases, as follows:

Nov.	5	Purchases	1,000.00	
		Accounts Payable		1,000.00
		Purchased merchandise on credit, invoice dated November 2, terms 2/10, n/30.		

The sole purpose of the Purchases account is to accumulate the cost of all merchandise bought for resale during an accounting period. The account does not at any time show whether the merchandise is on hand or has been disposed of through sale or other means.

If a credit purchase is eligible for a cash discount, payment within the discount period results in a credit to **Purchases Discounts,** as in the following entry:

Nov.	12	Accounts Payable	1,000.00	
		Purchases Discounts		20.00
		Cash		980.00
		Paid for the purchase of November 5 less the discount.		

When a supplier offers cash discounts, the total amount to be saved by taking the discounts often is important. Therefore, whenever the invoices offer a discount, many companies take special care to pay within the discount period so that no discounts are lost. On the other hand, good cash management requires that no invoice be paid until the last day of its discount period. To accomplish these objectives, every invoice must be filed in such a way that it automatically comes to the attention of the person responsible for its payment on the last day of its discount period. A simple way to do this is to have a file with 31 folders, one for each day in a month. Then, after an invoice is recorded, it is placed in the file folder of the last day of its discount period. For example, if the last day of an invoice's discount period is November 12, it is filed in folder number 12. Then, on November 12, this invoice, together with any other invoices in the same folder, are removed and paid or refiled for payment without a discount on a later date.

Sometimes, merchandise received from suppliers is not acceptable and must be returned. Or, defective merchandise may be kept by the purchaser because the supplier grants an allowance or reduction in its price. When merchandise is returned, the purchaser "gets its money back." Nevertheless, the process of receiving, inspecting, evaluating, and perhaps returning defective merchandise is costly and should be held to a minimum. As a result, the amount of purchase returns or allowances must be controlled and a purchaser may look for another supplier if purchased merchandise is frequently defective.

An important element in controlling the problem of defective merchandise purchases is to obtain information about the amount of returns and allowances. To gain this information, returns and allowances on purchases are commonly recorded in an account called Purchases Returns and Allowances, as follows:

Nov.	14	Accounts Payable	65.00	
		Purchases Returns and Allowances		65.00
		Returned defective merchandise.		

When an invoice for purchased goods is subject to a cash discount and a portion of the goods is returned before the invoice is paid, the discount only applies to the goods kept. For example, assume that you buy merchandise for $500, subject to a 2% cash discount. Then, you return $100 of the goods before the invoice is paid. When you pay the amount due before the discount period expires, the discount of 2% applies only to the remaining $400. In other words, the amount you will pay is $400 - (.02 \times \$400) = \$392$.

AS A MATTER OF ETHICS

Marti Roberts was recently hired to be the accountant for a medium-sized company, and was given responsibility for managing accounts payable. Specifically, she is to assure that the accounts are paid promptly in order to maintain the company's credit standing with its suppliers and to take advantage of all cash discounts. Marti overlapped for several days on the job with Peter Bailey, the outgoing accountant, so that they could spend time together to help her learn the ropes.

Peter told Marti that the system in place has accomplished both goals easily but has also made another contribution to the company's profits. Because the accounts are always paid, there has been no difficulty with the creditors. However, with respect to the discounts, the system has always been to prepare cheques for the "net of discount" amounts and then wait until *after* the end of the discount period before mailing the cheques. The cheques are dated the last day of the discount period but are not mailed until five days later. "It's simple," Peter said, "we get the free use of the cash for an extra five days, and who's going to complain? Even if someone gripes, we can always blame the computer or the mail room."

Only a few days later, on March 17, Peter has departed and Marti recognizes that the discount period on a $10,000 payable is about to lapse. The purchase was made on March 8 subject to terms of 2/10, n/30. Marti is trying to decide whether she should pay the bill on March 18 or wait until March 23.

Sometimes a supplier assumes responsibility for the costs of transporting the sold goods to the customer. When this is the case, the total cost of the goods to the purchaser is the amount the purchaser must pay to the supplier. Other times the purchaser must pay transportation costs. When this occurs, such charges are a proper addition to the cost of the goods purchased and may be recorded with a debit to the Purchases account. However, more complete information is obtained if such costs are debited to an account called **Transportation-In**, as follows:

Nov.	24	Transportation-In	22.00	
		Cash		22.00
		Paid express charges on merchandise purchased.		

When there are transportation charges, the buyer and seller must understand which party is responsible for the charges. Normally, in quoting a price, the seller makes this clear by quoting a price of, say $300, **FOB** factory. FOB factory means free on board or loaded on board the means of transportation at the factory, free of loading charges. The buyer then is responsible for transportation costs from there. Likewise, FOB destination means the seller is responsible for transportation costs to the destination of the goods.

Sometimes, even though the terms are FOB factory, the seller will prepay the transportation costs as a service to the buyer, and add the amount to the invoice. In this case, if the credit terms include a cash discount, the discount does not apply to the transportation charges. In other words, the purchaser must reimburse the seller for 100% of the transportation charges, even if the invoice is paid within the discount period.

At the end of the period, the balances of the Purchases, Purchases Returns and Allowances, Purchases Discounts, and Transportation-In accounts must be combined to determine the cost of the merchandise purchased during the period. This calculation may be shown on the income statement of a merchandising company, as follows:

Purchases			$235,800
Less: Purchases returns and allowances . .	$1,200		
Purchases discounts	4,100	5,300	
Net purchases			$230,500
Add transportation-in			1,500
Cost of goods purchased			$232,000

Cost of Goods Sold

In the above calculation, the last item is the cost of the merchandise purchased during the accounting period. To calculate cost of goods sold, you must combine this amount with the beginning and ending inventories, as follows:

Cost of goods sold:			
Merchandise inventory, December 31, 1989 . .			$ 19,000
Purchases		$235,800	
Less: Purchases returns and allowances . .	$1,200		
Purchases discounts	4,100	5,300	
Net purchases		$230,500	
Add transportation-in		1,500	
Cost of goods purchased			232,000
Goods available for sale			$251,000
Merchandise inventory, December 31, 1990 . .			21,000
Cost of goods sold			$230,000

Inventory Losses

Merchandising companies lose merchandise in a variety of ways such as from shrinkage, spoilage, or shoplifting. When merchandise is lost and a periodic inventory system is used, the cost of lost merchandise is automatically included in cost of goods sold. For example, assume a store lost $500 of merchandise to shoplifters during a year. This caused its year-end inventory to be $500 less than it otherwise would have been, since these goods were not available for inclusion in the year-end count. Therefore, since the year-end inventory was $500 smaller because of the loss, the cost of the goods the store sold was $500 greater.

Many merchandisers are troubled with shoplifting or other types of inventory losses. A disadvantage of the periodic inventory system is that it fails to provide clear information about the amount of such losses. Instead, the amount of such losses is "hidden" in the cost of goods sold figure. The perpetual inventory systems described in Chapter 9 provide more complete information about merchandise losses. Chapter 9 also discusses a method of estimating inventory losses when a periodic inventory system is being used.

Income Statement of a Merchandising Company

A classified income statement for a merchandising company has (1) a revenue section, (2) a cost of goods sold section, and (3) an operating expenses section. Note in Illustration 5–1 how the first two sections are brought together to show gross profit from sales.

Also notice in Illustration 5–1 how operating expenses are classified as either ''Selling expenses'' or ''General and administrative expenses.'' **Selling expenses** include expenses of storing and preparing goods for sale, promoting sales, actually making sales, and delivering goods to customers. **General and administrative expenses** support the overall management and operations of a business. Examples are the central office, accounting, personnel, and credit and collection expenses.

Sometimes an expenditure should be divided or prorated between selling expenses and general and administrative expenses. Sowa Sales, Incorporated, divided the rent on its store building in this manner, as you can see in Illustration 5–1. However, it did not prorate its insurance expense because the amount involved was so small the company felt the extra exactness did not warrant the extra work.

In Illustration 5–1, the last item subtracted is income taxes expense. This income statement was prepared for Sowa Sales, Incorporated, a corporation. Of the three kinds of business organizations, only corporations are subject to the payment of provincial and federal income taxes. Notice in Illustration 5–1 that the result of subtracting operating expenses from gross profit is called ''Income from operations.'' Income taxes expense is then subtracted to obtain the final net income.

Work Sheet of a Merchandising Company

Prepare a work sheet and the financial statements for a merchandising business that uses a periodic inventory system and that is organized as a corporation or as a single proprietorship.
(L. O. 3)

In organizing the end-of-period procedures, the work sheet that you use for a merchandising company is just like the work sheet for a service-type company. In both cases, the work sheet serves as a tool to help bring together the end-of-period information needed to prepare the financial statements and prepare the adjusting and closing entries. Illustration 5–2 shows the work sheet for Sowa Sales, Incorporated.

Illustration 5–2 differs from the Chapter 4 work sheet in several ways, the first of which is that it was prepared for a corporation. This is indicated by the word *Incorporated* in the company name. Also, the heading of the last two columns is Retained Earnings Statement or Balance Sheet. Later in this chapter, we will explain how the changes in retained earnings are reported in the retained earnings statement.

In Illustration 5–2, notice the appearance of the Common Stock and Retained Earnings accounts on lines 13 and 14. The balances of these two accounts are carried unchanged from the Unadjusted Trial Balance Credit column into the Retained Earnings Statement or Balance Sheet Credit column.

Illustration 5–2 also differs from the work sheet presented in Chapter 4 in that it does not have any Adjusted Trial Balance columns. Experienced accountants commonly omit these columns from a work sheet in order to reduce the time and effort required in its preparation. They enter the adjustments in

Illustration 5–1
A classified income statement for a merchandising company

SOWA SALES, INCORPORATED
Income Statement
For Year Ended December 31, 1990

Revenue from sales:			
Gross sales..............................			$306,200
Less: Sales returns and allowances		$ 1,900	
Sales discounts...............		4,300	6,200
Net sales			$300,000
Cost of goods sold:			
Merchandise inventory, December 31, 1989 ..		$ 19,000	
Purchases	$235,800		
Less: Purchases returns and allowances ...	$1,200		
Purchases discounts	4,100	5,300	
Net purchases		$230,500	
Add transportation-in		1,500	
Cost of goods purchased		232,000	
Goods available for sale		$251,000	
Merchandise inventory, December 31, 1990 ..		21,000	
Cost of goods sold.................			230,000
Gross profit from sales..............			$ 70,000
Operating expenses:			
Selling expenses:			
Sales salaries expense	$ 18,500		
Rent expense, selling space	8,100		
Advertising expense.............	700		
Store supplies expense...........	400		
Depreciation expense, store equipment ...	3,000		
Total selling expenses		$ 30,700	
General and administrative expenses:			
Office salaries expense.............	$ 25,800		
Rent expense, office space...........	900		
Insurance expense	600		
Office supplies expense	200		
Depreciation expense, office equipment....	700		
Total general and administrative expenses ..		28,200	
Total operating expenses			58,900
Income from operations			$ 11,100
Less income taxes expense			1,700
Net income			$ 9,400

the Adjustments columns, combine the adjustments with the unadjusted trial balance amounts, and sort the combined amounts directly to the proper financial statement columns in a single operation. In other words, the adjusted trial balance columns may be omitted in preparing a work sheet.

The remaining similarities and differences of Illustration 5–2 are best described column by column.

Illustration 5–2
A work sheet for a merchandising company

SOWA SALES, INCORPORATED
Work Sheet
For Year Ended December 31, 1990

	Unadjusted Trial Balance		Adjustments		Income Statement		Retained Earnings Statement or Balance Sheet	
Account Titles	Dr.	Cr.	Dr.	Cr.	Dr.	Cr.	Dr.	Cr.
1 Cash	8,200						8,200	
2 Accounts receivable	11,200						11,200	
3 Merchandise inventory	19,000				19,000	21,000	21,000	
4 Prepaid insurance	900			(a) 600			300	
5 Store supplies	600			(b) 400			200	
6 Office supplies	300			(c) 200			100	
7 Store equipment	29,100						29,100	
8 Accum. depr., store equipment		2,500		(d) 3,000				5,500
9 Office equipment	4,400						4,400	
10 Accum. depr., office equipment		600		(e) 700				1,300
11 Accounts payable		3,600						3,600
12 Income taxes payable				(f) 100				100
13 Common stock		50,000						50,000
14 Retained earnings		8,600						8,600
15 Dividends declared	4,000						4,000	
16 Sales		306,200				306,200		
17 Sales returns and allowances	1,900				1,900			
18 Sales discounts	4,300				4,300			
19 Purchases	235,800				235,800			
20 Pur. returns and allowances		1,200				1,200		
21 Purchases discounts		4,100				4,100		
22 Transportation-in	1,500				1,500			
23 Sales salaries expense	18,500				18,500			
24 Rent expense, selling space	8,100				8,100			
25 Advertising expense	700				700			
26 Store supplies expense			(b) 400		400			
27 Depr. expense, store equipment			(d) 3,000		3,000			
28 Office salaries expense	25,800				25,800			
29 Rent expense, office space	900				900			
30 Insurance expense			(a) 600		600			
31 Office supplies expense			(c) 200		200			
32 Depr. expense, office equipment			(e) 700		700			
33 Income taxes expense	1,600		(f) 100		1,700			
34	376,800	376,800	5,000	5,000	323,100	332,500	78,500	69,100
35 Net income					9,400			9,400
36					332,500	332,500	78,500	78,500

Account Titles Column

In the Account Titles column of the work sheet, several accounts that do not
have unadjusted trial balance amounts are listed in the order of their appearance on the financial statements. These accounts are debited and credited in
making the adjustments. Entering their names on the work sheet in statement

order at the time the work sheet is begun makes later preparation of the statements somewhat easier. If you find that you need accounts that were not listed, they may be entered below the trial balance totals as was done in Chapter 4.

Unadjusted Trial Balance Columns

In Illustration 5–2, the amounts in the Unadjusted Trial Balance columns are the account balances of Sowa Sales, Incorporated, as of December 31, 1990, the end of its annual accounting period. They were taken from the company's ledger after all transactions were recorded but before any end-of-period adjustments were made.

Note the $19,000 inventory amount that appears in the Unadjusted Trial Balance Debit column on line 3. This is the amount of inventory the company had on December 31, 1989. As the ending inventory for 1989, this amount is also the beginning inventory for 1990. The $19,000 was debited to the Merchandise Inventory account at the end of the previous period and remained in the account as its balance throughout the current accounting period.

Adjustments Columns

Of the adjustments that appear on the illustrated work sheet, only the adjustment for income taxes is new. A business organized as a corporation is subject to the payment of income taxes. As to the income tax, near the beginning of each year a corporation must estimate the amount of income it expects to earn during the year. Then, it must pay, in advance installments, an estimated tax on this income. The advance payments are debited to the Income Taxes Expense account as each installment is paid. Therefore, a corporation that expects to earn a profit normally reaches the end of the year with a debit balance in its Income Taxes Expense account. However, since the balance is an estimate and usually less than the full amount of the tax, an adjustment like that on lines 12 and 33 normally must be made to reflect the additional tax owed.

Combining and Sorting the Items

After all adjustments are entered and totaled on the work sheet, the amounts in the Unadjusted Trial Balance and Adjustments columns are combined and sorted to the proper financial statement columns. Revenue, cost of goods sold, and expense items go on the income statement and are sorted to the Income Statement columns. Asset, liability, and shareholders' equity items plus Dividends Declared are sorted to the Retained Earnings Statement or Balance Sheet columns.

Income Statement Columns

Observe in Illustration 5–2 that revenue, cost of goods sold, and expense items maintain their debit and credit positions when sorted to the Income Statement columns. Since sales returns and sales discounts are entered in the Debit column, the effect is to subtract them from sales when the columns are totaled and the net income is determined.

The Beginning Inventory Amount. Look at the beginning inventory amount on line 3. Note that the $19,000 unadjusted trial balance amount is sorted to the Income Statement Debit column. It is put in the Income Statement Debit column because, as a debit account balance, it is a positive element in the calculation of cost of goods sold. Recall that on the income statement, the calculation of cost of goods sold begins by adding the beginning inventory plus the net cost of purchases to determine the cost of goods available for sale.

The Ending Inventory Amount. Recall that when the periodic inventory system is used, you must take a physical inventory of merchandise on hand at the end of each accounting period. The December 31, 1990, physical inventory of Sowa Sales, Incorporated, showed that it had a $21,000 ending inventory. This amount was determined by counting the items of unsold merchandise and multiplying by the cost of each item.

In preparing a work sheet, after all items are sorted to the proper columns, the ending inventory amount is simply inserted in the Income Statement Credit column and in the Retained Earnings Statement or Balance Sheet Debit column. In Illustration 5–2, note that the $21,000 ending inventory was inserted in these columns on line 3 of the work sheet. The ending inventory amount is placed in the Income Statement Credit column because when cost of goods sold is calculated on the income statement, the ending inventory must be subtracted from cost of goods available for sale.

The ending inventory amount is put in the Retained Earnings Statement or Balance Sheet Debit column because it is an asset that will appear on the balance sheet. (Later in this chapter, we will discuss the journal entry to record the ending inventory in the accounts.)

Cost of Goods Sold on the Work Sheet

The amounts that enter into the calculation of cost of goods sold are shown in colour in the Income Statement columns of Illustration 5–2. The beginning inventory, purchases, and transportation-in amounts appear in the Debit column. The amounts of the ending inventory, purchases returns and allowances, and purchases discounts appear in the Credit column. Note in the following calculations that the sum of the three debit items minus the sum of the three credit items equals the $230,000 cost of goods sold shown in the income statement of Illustration 5–1.

Beginning inventory	$ 19,000	Ending inventory	$21,000
Purchases	235,800	Purchases returns.	1,200
Transportation-in	1,500	Purchases discounts	4,100
Total debits	$256,300	Total credits	$26,300
Less total credits	(26,300)		
Cost of goods sold	$230,000		

Therefore, the net effect of putting the six cost of goods sold amounts in the Income Statement columns is to put the $230,000 cost of the goods sold into the columns.

Completing the Work Sheet and Preparing Financial Statements

After all items are sorted to the proper columns and the ending inventory amount is entered, you complete a work sheet like Illustration 5–2 by adding the columns and determining and adding in the net income or loss, as we explained in the last chapter. When the work sheet for a corporation is completed, it is used to prepare an income statement, a retained earnings statement, and a balance sheet.

Preparing the Income Statement

After the work sheet is completed, the items in the Income Statement columns are used to prepare a formal income statement. A classified income statement prepared from information in the Income Statement columns of Illustration 5–2 is shown in Illustration 5–1.

Preparing the Retained Earnings Statement

The **retained earnings statement** reports the changes that have occurred in the corporation's retained earnings during the period. Therefore, the statement accounts for the difference between the retained earnings reported on successive, end-of-period balance sheets.

The information you need to prepare the retained earnings statement is found in the last two columns of the work sheet. The beginning retained earnings balance appears on the line showing the Retained Earnings account. The net income (or net loss) appears on a line near the bottom of the work sheet and the amount of dividends declared also appears on a separate line.

Illustration 5–3 shows the retained earnings statement of Sowa Sales, Incorporated. The statement shows that the company began the year with $8,600 of retained earnings, which is also the amount of retained earnings it reported on its previous year-end balance sheet. Its retained earnings balance was reduced by the declaration of $4,000 of dividends and increased by the $9,400 net income. The result is the final balance of $14,000, which is reported on the December 31, 1990, balance sheet.

Preparing the Balance Sheet

The classified balance sheet for Sowa Sales, Incorporated, appears in Illustration 5–4. Since none of the company's prepaid items are material in amount, you will observe that they have been totaled and are shown as a single item on the balance sheet. Also, the $14,000 retained earnings amount on the balance sheet is the final amount that was calculated on the retained earnings statement, as shown in Illustration 5–3.

Adjusting and Closing Entries

Prepare adjusting and closing entries for a merchandising business organized as either a corporation or a single proprietorship. (L. O. 4)

After the work sheet and statements are completed, you must prepare and post adjusting and closing entries. Illustration 5–5 shows the entries for Sowa Sales, Incorporated. They differ from previously illustrated adjusting and closing entries because an explanation for each entry is not given. Individual explanations may be given but are unnecessary. The words *Adjusting Entries* before the first adjusting entry and *Closing Entries* before the first closing entry are sufficient to explain the entries.

As we previously explained, the Adjustments columns of its work sheet provide the information you need to prepare a concern's adjusting entries.

Illustration 5–3
A corporation's retained earnings statement

SOWA SALES, INCORPORATED
Retained Earnings Statement
For Year Ended December 31, 1990

Retained earnings, December 31, 1989 . .	$ 8,600
Add 1990 net income	9,400
Total	$18,000
Deduct dividends declared	4,000
Retained earnings, December 31, 1990 . .	$14,000

Illustration 5–4
A corporation's classified balance sheet

SOWA SALES, INCORPORATED
Balance Sheet
December 31, 1990
Assets

Current assets:		
Cash	$ 8,200	
Accounts receivable	11,200	
Merchandise inventory	21,000	
Prepaid expenses	600	
Total current assets		$41,000
Plant and equipment:		
Store equipment	$29,100	
Less accumulated depreciation	5,500	$23,600
Office equipment.	$ 4,400	
Less accumulated depreciation	1,300	3,100
Total plant and equipment		26,700
Total assets.		$67,700

Liabilities

Current liabilities:		
Accounts payable	$ 3,600	
Income taxes payable	100	
Total liabilities.		$ 3,700

Shareholders' Equity

Common stock, 10,000 shares		
outstanding	$50,000	
Retained earnings	14,000	
Total shareholders' equity		64,000
Total liabilities and shareholders' equity . .		$67,700

Illustration 5–5

Adjusting and closing entries for a merchandising corporation

Date		Account Titles and Explanation	PR	Debit	Credit
1990 Dec.		Adjusting Entries			
	31	Insurance Expense		600.00	
		Prepaid Insurance			600.00
	31	Store Supplies Expense		400.00	
		Store Supplies			400.00
	31	Office Supplies Expense		200.00	
		Office Supplies			200.00
	31	Depreciation Expense, Store Equipment		3,000.00	
		Accumulated Depreciation, Store Equipment			3,000.00
	31	Depreciation Expense, Office Equipment		700.00	
		Accumulated Depreciation, Office Equipment . . .			700.00
	31	Income Taxes Expense		100.00	
		Income Taxes Payable			100.00
		Closing Entries			
	31	Income Summary		323,100.00	
		Merchandise Inventory			19,000.00
		Sales Returns and Allowances			1,900.00
		Sales Discounts			4,300.00
		Purchases			235,800.00
		Transportation-In			1,500.00
		Sales Salaries Expense			18,500.00
		Rent Expense, Selling Space			8,100.00
		Advertising Expense			700.00
		Store Supplies Expense			400.00
		Depreciation Expense, Store Equipment			3,000.00
		Office Salaries Expense			25,800.00
		Rent Expense, Office Space			900.00
		Insurance Expense			600.00
		Office Supplies Expense			200.00
		Depreciation Expense, Office Equipment			700.00
		Income Taxes Expense			1,700.00
	31	Merchandise Inventory		21,000.00	
		Sales		306,200.00	
		Purchases Returns and Allowances		1,200.00	
		Purchases Discounts		4,100.00	
		Income Summary			332,500.00
	31	Income Summary		9,400.00	
		Retained Earnings			9,400.00
	31	Retained Earnings		4,000.00	
		Dividends Declared			4,000.00

Each adjustment in the Adjustments columns requires an adjusting entry that is journalized and posted. Compare the adjusting entries in Illustration 5–5 with the adjustments on the work sheet of Illustration 5–2.

A work sheet like Illustration 5–2 also contains the information you need to prepare closing entries. Look at the first closing entry of Illustration 5–5 and the items in the Income Statement Debit column of Illustration 5–2. Note that Income Summary is debited for the column total and each account that has an amount in the column is credited. This entry removes the $19,000 beginning inventory amount from the Merchandise Inventory account. It also closes all the revenue, cost of goods sold, and expense accounts that have debit balances.

Now compare the second closing entry with the items in the Income Statement Credit column of Illustration 5–2. Note that each account which has an amount in the column is debited and the Income Summary account is credited for the column total. This entry closes the revenue and cost of goods sold accounts that have credit balances. It also enters the $21,000 ending inventory amount in the Merchandise Inventory account.

The third closing entry transfers the net income from Income Summary to Retained Earnings, and the fourth closing entry closes the Dividends Declared account by transferring its balance to Retained Earnings.

Closing Entries and the Inventories

There is nothing especially new about the closing entries of a merchandising company except for the beginning and ending inventory amounts. You need to understand clearly the effect of the closing entries on the Merchandise Inventory account.

Before closing entries were posted, the Merchandise Inventory account of Sowa Sales, Incorporated, showed the $19,000 beginning-of-period inventory as follows:

Merchandise Inventory						Account No. 113
Date		Explanation	PR	Debit	Credit	Balance
1989 Dec.	31		G10	19,000		19,000

Then, when the first closing entry is posted, its $19,000 credit to Merchandise Inventory clears the beginning inventory amount from the inventory account as follows:

Merchandise Inventory						Account No. 113
Date		Explanation	PR	Debit	Credit	Balance
1989 Dec.	31		G10	19,000		19,000
1990 Dec.	31		G20		19,000	–0–

When the second closing entry is posted, its $21,000 debit to Merchandise Inventory puts the amount of the ending inventory into the inventory account, as follows:

	Merchandise Inventory					Account No. 113
Date	Explanation	PR	Debit	Credit	Balance
1989 Dec. 31		G10	19,000		19,000
1990 Dec. 31		G20		19,000	–0–
31		G23	21,000		21,000

The $21,000 remains throughout the succeeding year as the debit balance of the inventory account and as a historical record of the amount of inventory at the end of 1990 and the beginning of 1991.

Other Inventory Methods

There are several ways to handle the inventories in the end-of-period procedures. However, all have the same objectives. These are (1) to remove the beginning inventory amount from the inventory account and to charge (debit) it to Income Summary, and (2) to enter the ending inventory amount in the inventory account and credit it to Income Summary. These objectives may be achieved with closing entries as explained in this chapter. Or, for example, adjusting entries to accomplish the same objectives may be used. Either method is satisfactory. The adjusting entry method is explained in Appendix C at the end of this chapter.

Multiple-Step and Single-Step Income Statements

The income statement shown in Illustration 5–1 is called a classified income statement because its items are classified in significant groups. It is also a **multiple-step income statement** because cost of goods sold and the expenses are subtracted in steps to get net income. Illustration 5–6 shows another statement format, the **single-step income statement**. Note how cost of goods sold and the expenses are added together in the illustration and are subtracted in "one step" from net sales to get net income. This format is commonly used for published statements. Also, note that the information in the income statement is condensed. This is frequently done in published statements.

Combined Income and Retained Earnings Statement

Many companies combine their income and retained earnings statements into a single statement. Such a statement may be prepared in either single-step or multiple-step form. Illustration 5–7 shows a single-step statement.

Debit and Credit Memoranda

Merchandise purchased that does not meet specifications, goods received that were not ordered, goods received short of the amount ordered and billed, and invoice errors are matters for adjustment between the buyer and seller. In some cases, the buying company can make the adjustment, for example, when there is an invoice error. If the buying company makes the adjustment, it must

Illustration 5–6
A single-step income statement

SOWA SALES, INCORPORATED
Income Statement
For Year Ended December 31, 1990

Revenue from sales		$300,000
Expenses:		
Cost of goods sold	$230,000	
Selling expenses	30,700	
General and administrative expenses . .	28,200	
Income taxes expense	1,700	
Total expenses.		290,600
Net income		$ 9,400

Illustration 5–7
Combining the income statement and the retained earnings statement

SOWA SALES, INCORPORATED
Statement of Income and Retained Earnings
For Year Ended December 31, 1990

Revenue from sales		$300,000
Expenses:		
Cost of goods sold	$230,000	
Selling expenses	30,700	
General and administrative expenses	28,200	
Income taxes expense	1,700	
Total expenses		290,600
Net income		$ 9,400
Add retained earnings, December 31, 1989 . .		8,600
Total		$ 18,000
Deduct dividends declared		4,000
Retained earnings, December 31, 1990		$ 14,000

notify the seller of its action. It commonly does this by sending a **debit memorandum** or a **credit memorandum.**

A debit memorandum is a business form that has spaces for the name and address of the concern to which it is directed and the printed words, ''WE DEBIT YOUR ACCOUNT,'' followed by space for typing in the reason for the debit. A credit memorandum has the words, ''WE CREDIT YOUR ACCOUNT.''

To illustrate the use of a debit memorandum, assume that a buyer discovers an invoice error that reduces the invoice total by $10. For such an error, the buyer notifies the seller with a debit memorandum reading: ''WE DEBIT YOUR ACCOUNT to correct a $10 error on your November 17 invoice.'' A debit memorandum is sent because the correction reduces an account payable of the buyer, and a debit is required to reduce an account payable. To record the purchase, the buyer normally marks the correction on the invoice and attaches a copy of the debit memorandum to show that the seller was notified. The buyer then debits Purchases and credits Accounts Payable for the corrected amount.

An adjustment, such as merchandise that does not meet specifications, normally requires negotiations between the buyer and the seller. In such a case, the buyer may debit Purchases for the full invoice amount and then negotiate with the seller for a return or a price adjustment. If the seller agrees to the return or adjustment, the seller notifies the buyer with a credit memorandum. A credit memorandum is used because the return or adjustment reduces an account receivable on the books of the seller, and a credit is required to reduce an account receivable. When the credit memorandum is received, the buyer records it by debiting Accounts Payable and crediting Purchases Returns and Allowances, if the purchase was originally recorded at the full invoice price.

From this discussion you can see that a debit or a credit memorandum may originate with either party to a transaction. The memorandum gets its name from the action of the originator. If the originator debits, the originator sends a debit memorandum. If the originator credits, a credit memorandum is sent.

Trade Discounts

When a manufacturer or wholesaler prepares a catalogue of the items it offers for sale, each item typically is given a **list** or catalogue price. A **trade discount** is a deduction (often as much as 40% or more) from a list (or catalogue) price that is used to determine the invoice or sales price of the goods to which it applies. Trade discounts are commonly used by manufacturers and wholesalers to avoid republication of catalogues when selling prices change. If selling prices change, catalogue prices can be adjusted simply by issuing a new list of discounts to be applied to the catalogue prices.

Understand that trade discounts are quite different from the cash discounts we discussed earlier in this chapter. *Trade discounts are not entered in the accounts by either party to a sale*. Instead, they are used to calculate the sales price. For example, if a manufacturer sells on credit an item listed in its catalogue at $100, less a 40% trade discount, it will record the sale as follows:

Dec.	10	Accounts Receivable [$100 − (.40 × $100)]	60.00	
		Sales		60.00
		Sold merchandise on credit.		

The buyer will also enter the purchase in its records at $60. Also, if a cash discount is involved, it applies only to the amount of the purchase, $60.

Summary of the Chapter in Terms of Learning Objectives

1. In determining the amount to record as a purchase (or sale), trade discounts are subtracted from list prices to calculate the invoice price, which is debited to Purchases (or credited to Sales). Purchases discounts, purchases returns and allowances, transportation-in, sales discounts, and sales returns and allowances are recorded in separate accounts.

2. Sales discounts and sales returns and allowances are subtracted from sales to get net sales. The ending inventory is subtracted from the cost of goods available for sale to get cost of goods sold, which is subtracted from net sales to get gross profit. The beginning inventory plus net purchases equals the cost of goods available for sale.

3. When the closing entry approach is used on the work sheet, the beginning inventory is extended to the Income Statement Debit column and the ending inventory is inserted in the Income Statement Credit column and the Statement of Retained Earnings or Balance Sheet Debit column. A corporation's retained earnings statement shows the changes in retained earnings during the period.

4. When the closing entry approach is used, the beginning inventory is transferred from Merchandise Inventory to Income Summary in the closing process. Also, the ending inventory is debited to Merchandise Inventory and credited to Income Summary as part of a closing entry.

Demonstration Problem

Below is a partially completed work sheet prepared for Continental Sales, Inc., as of December 31, 1990, the end of its annual accounting period.

CONTINENTAL SALES, INC.
Work Sheet
For Year Ended December 31, 1990

Account Titles	Unadjusted Trial Balance Dr.	Unadjusted Trial Balance Cr.	Adjustments Dr.	Adjustments Cr.
Cash	19,000			
Merchandise inventory	52,000			
Supplies	7,000			(a) 6,000
Equipment	40,000			
Accumulated depreciation, equipment		11,000		(b) 5,500
Accounts payable		3,000		
Income taxes payable		6,000		(c) 1,000
Common stock		50,000		
Retained earnings		19,000		
Dividends declared	8,000			
Sales		320,000		
Sales discounts	20,000			
Purchases	147,000			
Purchases discounts		12,000		
Transportation-in	11,000			
Salaries expense	43,000			
Rent expense	24,000			
Advertising expense	21,000			
Supplies expense			(a) 6,000	
Depreciation expense			(b) 5,500	
Insurance expense	12,000			
Income taxes expense	17,000		(c) 1,000	
	421,000	421,000	12,500	12,500

Required

1. Complete the work sheet. (Ending inventory is $50,000.)
2. Prepare the 1990 income statement.
3. Prepare the 1990 retained earnings statement.
4. Prepare a balance sheet as of December 31, 1990.
5. Prepare closing entries.

Solution to Demonstration Problem

1.

CONTINENTAL SALES, INC.
Work Sheet
For Year Ended December 31, 1990

Account Titles	Unadjusted Trial Balance Dr.	Cr.	Adjustments Dr.	Cr.	Income Statement Dr.	Cr.	Retained Earnings Statement or Balance Sheet Dr.	Cr.
Cash	19,000						19,000	
Merchandise inventory	52,000				52,000	50,000	50,000	
Supplies	7,000			(a) 6,000			1,000	
Equipment	40,000						40,000	
Accumulated depreciation, equipment		11,000		(b) 5,500				16,500
Accounts payable		3,000						3,000
Income taxes payable		6,000		(c) 1,000				7,000
Common stock		50,000						50,000
Retained earnings		19,000						19,000
Dividends declared	8,000						8,000	
Sales		320,000				320,000		
Sales discounts	20,000				20,000			
Purchases	147,000				147,000			
Purchases discounts		12,000				12,000		
Transportation-in	11,000				11,000			
Salaries expense	43,000				43,000			
Rent expense	24,000				24,000			
Advertising expense	21,000				21,000			
Supplies expense			(a) 6,000		6,000			
Depreciation expense			(b) 5,500		5,500			
Insurance expense	12,000				12,000			
Income taxes expense	17,000		(c) 1,000		18,000			
	421,000	421,000	12,500	12,500	359,500	382,000	118,000	95,500
Net income					22,500			22,500
					382,000	382,000	118,000	118,000

2.

CONTINENTAL SALES, INC.
Income Statement
For Year Ended December 31, 1990

Revenue from sales:			
Gross sales			$320,000
Less: Sales discounts			20,000
Net Sales			$300,000
Cost of goods sold:			
Merchandise inventory, December 31, 1989 . .		$ 52,000	
Purchases	$147,000		
Less: Purchases discounts	12,000		
Net purchases	$135,000		
Plus: Transportation-in	11,000		
Cost of goods purchased		146,000	
Cost of goods available for sale		$198,000	
Merchandise inventory, December 31, 1990 . .		50,000	
Cost of goods sold			148,000
Gross profit from sales			$152,000
Operating expenses:			
Salaries expense		$ 43,000	
Rent expense		24,000	
Advertising expense		21,000	
Supplies expense		6,000	
Depreciation expense		5,500	
Insurance expense		12,000	
Total operating expenses			111,500
Income from operations			40,500
Less income taxes expense			18,000
Net income			$ 22,500

3.

CONTINENTAL SALES, INC.
Retained Earnings Statement
For Year Ended December 31, 1990

Retained earnings, December 31, 1989 . .	$19,000
Add 1990 net income	22,500
Total	$41,500
Deduct dividends declared	8,000
Retained earnings, December 31, 1990 . .	$33,500

4.

CONTINENTAL SALES, INC.
Balance Sheet
December 31, 1990

Assets

Current assets:		
Cash		$19,000
Merchandise inventory		50,000
Supplies		1,000
Total current assets		$70,000
Equipment	$40,000	
Less accumulated depreciation	16,500	
Total equipment		23,500
Total assets		$93,500

Liabilities

Current liabilities:
Accounts payable	$ 3,000	
Income taxes payable	7,000	
Total liabilities		$10,000

Shareholders' Equity

Common stock	$50,000	
Retained earnings	33,500	
Total shareholders' equity		83,500
Total liabilities and shareholders' equity . .		$93,500

5.

1990					
Dec.	31	Merchandise Inventory	50,000.00	
		Sales	320,000.000	
		Purchases Discounts	12,000.00	
		Income Summary		382,000.00
	31	Income Summary	359,500.00	
		Merchandise Inventory		52,000.00
		Sales Discounts		20,000.00
		Purchases		147,000.00
		Transportation-In		11,000.00
		Salaries Expense		43,000.00
		Rent Expense		24,000.00
		Advertising Expense		21,000.00
		Supplies Expense		6,000.00
		Depreciation Expense		5,500.00
		Insurance Expense		12,000.00
		Income Taxes Expense		18,000.00
	31	Income Summary	22,500.00	
		Retained Earnings		22,500.00
	31	Retained Earnings	8,000.00	
		Dividends Declared		8,000.00

Appendix C

THE ADJUSTING ENTRY APPROACH TO ACCOUNTING FOR MERCHANDISE INVENTORIES

Explain the adjusting entry approach to accounting for inventories and prepare a work sheet, adjusting entries, and closing entries according to the adjusting entry approach.
(L. O. 6)

In Chapter 5, we transferred the beginning inventory to Income Summary in the process of making the closing entries. Also, the ending inventory was recorded in the Merchandise Inventory account as part of a closing entry. An alternative approach is to show these transfers as adjustments on the work sheet and to journalize the transfers as adjusting entries.

Some accountants prefer to use the closing entry approach and others prefer to use the adjusting entry approach. Also, some computerized accounting systems prepare the closing entries automatically. In other words, the person who uses such a system does not prepare closing entries. Instead, a single command ''to close'' is given, and the computer automatically closes all of the temporary accounts. When such a system is used, you do not have the opportunity to insert the beginning and ending inventory amounts in the closing entries. Instead, the adjusting entry approach must be used to bring the Merchandise Inventory account balance up-to-date.

To illustrate the differences between the closing entry approach and the adjusting entry approach, we return to the example of Sowa Sales, Incorporated. In Chapter 5, when the *closing entry approach* was used, the beginning inventory was transferred to Income Summary and the ending inventory was recorded in the Merchandise Inventory account as part of the closing entries. In the *adjusting entry approach,* an adjusting entry is prepared to transfer the beginning inventory from the Merchandise Inventory account to Income Summary. Another adjusting entry records the ending inventory as a debit balance in the Merchandise Inventory account and as a credit in Income Summary. The adjusting and closing entries under both approaches are presented in Illustration C–1.

In Illustration C–1, notice that both approaches accomplish exactly the same changes in the Merchandise Inventory account. The beginning inventory of $19,000 was removed from the account, and the $21,000 ending inventory was recorded in the account.

Also, both approaches result in exactly the same credit balance of $9,400 in the Income Summary account. Under the adjusting entry approach, the effects of the beginning and ending inventories on Income Summary are recorded with adjusting entries. And under the closing entry approach, these effects are recorded with closing entries.

The Work Sheet under the Adjusting Entry Approach

When the adjusting entry approach is used, the beginning inventory transfer from Merchandise Inventory to Income Summary is entered in the Adjustments columns of the work sheet. Also, the ending inventory amount is debited to Merchandise Inventory and credited to Income Summary in the Adjustments columns. This procedure is followed in Illustration C–2, which shows the work sheet for Sowa Sales, Incorporated.

On line 3 of Illustration C–2, note that the adjustment (*g*) eliminates the beginning inventory from the Merchandise Inventory account. Adjustment (*h*) establishes the ending inventory amount in the account. Because this is an asset on December 31, 1990, the ending amount is carried directly to the Statement of Retained Earnings or Balance Sheet Debit column.

Also in Illustration C–2, you can see that the Income Summary account (line 15) was listed at the time the Unadjusted Trial Balance was first prepared. Note that the debit and credit adjustments to this account are individually carried into the Income Statement columns. Both of these amounts, the beginning inventory and the ending inventory amounts, are used in preparing the income statement. Therefore, you should not subtract one from the other and carry over only the net amount. Rather, the $19,000 beginning inventory is extended to the Income Debit column and the $21,000 ending inventory is extended to the Income Statement Credit column.

The remaining steps to complete the work sheet are exactly the same, whether the adjusting entry approach or the closing entry approach is used. To see the work sheet differences between the two methods, compare Illustration C–2 (the adjusting entry approach) with Illustration 5–2 on page 222 (the closing entry approach).

Illustration C-1

Adjusting and closing entries for a merchandising corporation

		Closing Entry Approach		Adjusting Entry Approach	
	Adjusting Entries				
1990 Dec. 31	Insurance Expense	600.00		600.00	
	Prepaid Insurance		600.00		600.00
31	Store Supplies Expense	400.00		400.00	
	Store Supplies		400.00		400.00
31	Office Supplies Expense	200.00		200.00	
	Office Supplies		200.00		200.00
31	Depreciation Expense, Store Equipment .	3,000.00		3,000.00	
	Accumulated Depreciation, Store Equipment		3,000.00		3,000.00
31	Depreciation Expense, Office Equipment .	700.00		700.00	
	Accumulated Depreciation, Office Equipment		700.00		700.00
31	Income Taxes Expense	100.00		100.00	
	Income Taxes Payable		100.00		100.00
31	**Income Summary**	—		**19,000.00**	
	Merchandise Inventory		—		**19,000.00**
31	**Merchandise Inventory**	—		**21,000.00**	
	Income Summary		—		**21,000.00**
	Closing Entries				
31	Income Summary	323,100.00		304,100.00	
	Merchandise Inventory		**19,000.00**		—
	Sales Returns and Allowances		1,900.00		1,900.00
	Sales Discounts		4,300.00		4,300.00
	Purchases		235,800.00		235,800.00
	Transportation-In		1,500.00		1,500.00
	Sales Salaries Expense		18,500.00		18,500.00
	Rent Expense, Selling Space		8,100.00		8,100.00
	Advertising Expense		700.00		700.00
	Store Supplies Expense		400.00		400.00
	Depreciation Expense, Store Equipment		3,000.00		3,000.00
	Office Salaries Expense.		25,800.00		25,800.00
	Rent Expense, Office Space		900.00		900.00
	Insurance Expense		600.00		600.00
	Office Supplies Expense		200.00		200.00
	Depreciation Expense, Office Equipment		700.00		700.00
	Income Taxes Expense		1,700.00		1,700.00
31	**Merchandise Inventory**	**21,000.00**		—	
	Sales	306,200.00		306,200.00	
	Purchases Returns and Allowances	1,200.00		1,200.00	
	Purchases Discounts	4,100.00		4,100.00	
	Income Summary		332,500.00		311,500.00
31	Income Summary	9,400.00		9,400.00	
	Retained Earnings		9,400.00		9,400.00
31	Retained Earnings	4,000.00		4,000.00	
	Dividends Declared		4,000.00		4,000.00

Illustration C–2
The work sheet when the adjusting entry approach is used

SOWA SALES, INCORPORATED
Work Sheet
For Year Ended December 31, 1990

	Account Titles	Unadjusted Trial Balance		Adjustments		Income Statement		Retained Earnings Statement or Balance Sheet	
		Dr.	Cr.	Dr.	Cr.	Dr.	Cr.	Dr.	Cr.
1	Cash	8,200						8,200	
2	Accounts receivable	11,200						11,200	
3	Merchandise inventory	19,000		(h) 21,000	(g) 19,000			21,000	
4	Prepaid insurance	900			(a) 600			300	
5	Store supplies	600			(b) 400			200	
6	Office supplies	300			(c) 200			100	
7	Store equipment	29,100						29,100	
8	Accum. depr., store equipment		2,500		(d) 3,000				5,500
9	Office equipment	4,400						4,400	
10	Accum. depr., office equipment		600		(e) 700				1,300
11	Accounts payable		3,600						3,600
12	Income taxes payable				(f) 100				100
13	Common stock		50,000						50,000
14	Retained earnings		8,600						8,600
15	Income summary			(g) 19,000	(h) 21,000	19,000	21,000		
16	Dividends declared	4,000						4,000	
17	Sales		306,200				306,200		
18	Sales returns and allowances	1,900				1,900			
19	Sales discounts	4,300				4,300			
20	Purchases	235,800				235,800			
21	Purchases returns and allowances		1,200				1,200		
22	Purchases discounts		4,100				4,100		
23	Transportation-in	1,500				1,500			
24	Sales salaries expense	18,500				18,500			
25	Rent expense, selling space	8,100				8,100			
26	Advertising expense	700				700			
27	Store supplies expense			(b) 400		400			
28	Depr. expense, store equipment			(d) 3,000		3,000			
29	Office salaries expense	25,800				25,800			
30	Rent expense, office space	900				900			
31	Insurance expense			(a) 600		600			
32	Office supplies expense			(c) 200		200			
33	Depr. expense, office equipment			(e) 700		700			
34	Income taxes expense	1,600		(f) 100		1,700			
35		376,800	376,800	45,000	45,000	323,100	332,500	78,500	69,100
36	Net income					9,400			9,400
37						332,500	332,500	78,500	78,500

Summary of Appendix C in Terms of the Learning Objective

6. When the adjusting entry approach is used, adjusting entries are designed to update the Merchandise Inventory account and to record the beginning and ending inventory elements of cost of goods sold in the Income Summary account. On the work sheet, these adjustments are entered in the

Adjustments columns. Then, the ending inventory is extended to the Retained Earnings Statement or Balance Sheet Debit column. Both the debit and credit adjustments to Income Summary are individually extended to the Income Statement columns.

Appendix D:

ACCOUNTING PRINCIPLES AND FINANCIAL STATEMENT CONCEPTS

Discuss financial statement concepts and the qualitative characteristics accounting information should possess.
(L. O. 7)

Accounting concepts and principles are not laws of nature. They are broad ideas that are developed as a way of describing current accounting practices and prescribing new and improved practices. In studying this appendix, you will learn about some new accounting concepts that the Accounting Standards Committee has developed in an effort to guide future changes and improvements in accounting.

To fully understand the importance of financial accounting concepts and principles, you must realize that they serve two purposes. First, they provide general descriptions of existing accounting practices. In doing this, concepts and principles serve as guidelines that help you learn about accounting. Thus, after learning how the concepts and principles are applied in a few situations, you develop the ability to apply them in different situations. This is easier and more effective than memorizing a very long list of specific practices.

Second, accounting concepts and principles help accountants analyze unfamiliar situations and develop procedures to account for those situations. This purpose is especially important for developing uniform practices for financial reporting and for improving the quality of financial reporting.

In prior chapters we defined and illustrated several important accounting concepts and principles. These concepts and principles, which are listed below, describe in general terms the practices currently used by accountants.

Generally accepted concepts:
  Business entity concept   Stable-dollar concept
  Continuing-concern concept   Time-period concept

Generally accepted principles:
  Cost principle   Full-disclosure principle
  Realization principle   Consistency principle
  Matching principle   Conservatism principle
  Objectivity principle   Materiality principle

The concepts and principles listed above, and for learning convenience defined later in this supplement, are useful for teaching and learning about accounting practice and are helpful for dealing with some unfamiliar transactions. However, as business practices have evolved in recent years, these concepts have become less useful as guides for accountants to follow in dealing with new and different types of transactions. This problem has occurred because the concepts are intended to provide general descriptions of current accounting practices. In other words, they describe what accountants currently do; they do not necessarily describe what accountants should do. Also, since these concepts do not identify weaknesses in accounting practices, they do not lead to major changes or improvements in accounting practices. Thus, a need exists to expand upon the concepts and principles in order to promote what ought to be done to make things better.

During the 1970s the accounting profession in both Canada and the United States turned its attention to the apparent need for improvement in financial reporting. In 1980 *Corporate Reporting: Its Future Evolution,* a research study, was published by the Canadian Institute of Chartered Accountants, and in 1989 "Financial Statement Concepts," Section 1000 of the *CICA Handbook,* was approved. In the United States the Financial Accounting Standards Board (FASB) published, in the 1978–85 period, six statements regarded as the most comprehensive pronouncement of the conceptual framework of accounting. FASB (*SFAC 1*) and Accounting Standards Committee (*CICA Handbook,* Section 1000) identified the broad objectives of financial reporting.

The Objectives of Financial Reporting

"Financial Statement Concepts" identified the broad objectives of financial reporting. The most general objective stated in the *CICA Handbook,* par. 1000.12, is to:

> communicate information that is useful to investors, creditors and other users in making resource allocation decisions and/or assessing management stewardship.

From this beginning point the Accounting Standards Committee (AcSC) expressed other more specific objectives. These objectives recognize that (1) financial reporting should help users predict future cash flow and (2) in making such predictions, information about a company's resources and obligations is useful if it possesses certain qualities. All of the concepts in the "Financial Statement Concepts" are intended to be consistent with these general objectives. Of course, present accounting practice already provides information about a company's resources and obligations. Thus, although the conceptual framework is intended to be prescriptive of new and improved practices, the concepts in the framework are also descriptive of many current practices.

The Qualities of Useful Information

The AcSC discussed the fact that information can be useful only if it is understandable to users. However, the users are assumed to have the training, experience, and motivation to analyze financial reports. With this decision, the AcSC indicated that financial reporting should not try to meet the needs of unsophisticated or other casual report users.

The AcSC said that information is useful if it is (1) relevant, (2) reliable, and (3) comparable. Information is *relevant* if it can make a difference in a decision. Information has this quality when it helps users either predict the future or evaluate the past, as long as it is received in time to affect their decisions.

Information is *reliable* if users can depend on it to be free from bias and error. Reliable information is verifiable and faithfully represents what is supposed to be described. In addition, users can depend on information only if it is neutral. This means that the rules used to produce information should not be designed so that they lead users to accept or reject any specific decision alternative.

Information is *comparable* if users can use it to identify differences and similarities between companies. Comparability is possible only if companies follow uniform practices. However, even if all companies uniformly follow the same practices, comparable reports do not result if the practices are not appropriate. For example, comparable information would not be provided if all companies were to ignore the useful lives of their assets and depreciate all assets over two years.

Comparability also requires consistency, which means that a company should not change its accounting practices unless the change is justified as a reporting improvement. Another important principle discussed is materiality (see Chapter 8).

Elements of Financial Statements

Another important step was to determine the elements of financial statements. This involved defining the categories of information that should be contained in financial reports. The AcSC's discussion of financial statement elements includes definitions of important elements such as assets, liabilities, equity, revenues, expenses, gains, and losses. In earlier chapters we referred to many of these definitions when we explained various accounting procedures.

Recognition and Measurement

The AcSC, in paragraphs 36–47 of Section 1000, established concepts for deciding (1) when items should be presented (or ''recognized'') in the financial statements and (2) how to assign numbers (or ''measure'') those items. In general, items should be recognized in the financial statements if they meet the following criteria:

1. Definitions—The item meets the definition of an element of financial statements.
2. Measurability—It has a relevant attribute measurable with sufficient reliability.
3. Relevance—The information about it is capable of making a difference in user decisions.
4. Reliability—The information is representationally faithful, verifiable, and neutral.

The question of how items should be measured raises the fundamental question of whether financial statements should be based on cost or on value. Since this question is quite controversial, the AcSC's discussion of this issue is perhaps more descriptive of current practice than it is prescriptive of new measurement methods.

Accounting Concepts

An understanding of accounting principles begins with the recognition of four broad concepts as to the nature of the economic setting in which accounting operates.

The Business Entity Concept

Every business unit or enterprise is treated in accounting as a separate entity, with the affairs of the business and those of the owner or owners being kept entirely separate.

The Going-Concern Concept

Unless there is strong evidence to the contrary, it is assumed that a business will continue to operate as a going concern, earning a reasonable profit for a period longer than the life expectancy of any of its assets.

The Stable-Dollar Concept

Under this concept it is held that the function of accounting is not to account for value; rather, it is (1) to record ''dollars invested'' and ''dollars borrowed,'' (2) to trace the various commitments of these ''dollars of capital'' as they are invested and reinvested in the business activities, and finally, (3) to measure out of gross ''dollars of revenue'' the recapture of ''dollars of capital'' with any excess being designated as ''dollars of income.''

It is conceded that value can only subjectively be measured. It is also recognized that the ''value'' (purchasing power) of the accountant's unit of measure, the dollar, is itself constantly changing. Therefore, it is recognized that a balance sheet prepared under this concept simply shows the number of dollars received from all sources and shows where these dollars are committed. A reader cannot interpret the dollar amounts of the various assets as the values of these assets.

The Time-Period Concept

The environment in which accounting operates—the business community and the government—requires that the life of a business be divided into relatively short periods and that changes be measured over these short periods. Yet, it is generally agreed that earnings cannot be measured precisely over a short period and that it is impossible to learn the exact earnings of a business until it has completed its last transaction and converted all its assets to cash.

Accounting Principles

Cost Principle

The cost principle specifies that cash-equivalent cost is the most useful basis for the initial accounting of the elements that are recorded in the accounts and reported on the financial statements. It is important to note that the cost principle applies to the initial recording of transactions and events.

The cost principle is supported by the fact that at the time of a completed arm's-length business transaction, the market value of the resources given up in the transaction provides reliable evidence of the valuation of the item acquired in the transaction.

When a noncash consideration is involved, cost is measured as the market value of the resources given or the market value of the item received, whichever is more reliably determinable. For example, an asset may be acquired with a debt given as settlement. Cost in this instance is the present value of the amount of cash to be paid in the future, as specified by the terms of the debt. The cost principle applies to all of the elements of financial statements, including liabilities.

The cost principle provides guidance at the original recognition date. However, the original cost of some items acquired is subject to depreciation, depletion, amortization, and write-down in conformity with the matching principle and the conservatism constraint (discussed in the sections that follow).

Realization or Revenue Principle

The realization or revenue principle specifies when revenue should be recognized in the accounts and reported in the financial statements. Revenue is measured as the market value of the resources received or the product or service given, whichever is the more reliably determinable. The realization or revenue principle requires that all discounts be viewed as adjustments of the amount of revenue earned. For example, in determining the net cash exchange value of sales subject to a discount, sales discounts should be subtracted from gross sales revenue in measuring the net amount of sales revenue.

Under the realization or revenue principle, revenue from the sale of goods is recognized according to the sales method (i.e., at the time of sale) because the earning process usually is complete at the time of sale. At that time, the relevant information about the asset inflows to the seller would be known with reliability.

The conditions for completion of the earning process are (a) collection from the buyer is reasonably assured and (b) the expenses of making the sale can be determined reliably. Condition (a)—reasonable assurance of collection—provides the basis for the conclusion that the transaction provided a "probable future economic benefit" (i.e., an asset) to the seller. Without this condition, the principle of revenue realization would be altogether lacking in substantive economic content. Condition (b)—reliable determination of related expenses—provides the basis for measurement of the net economic benefit of the transaction. Without this condition, measurement of the effect of the revenue would ignore the related expenses. It would therefore be partial at best. Condition (b) is closely related to the matching principle, which is discussed below.

Under the realization or revenue principle, revenue from the sale of services is recognized on the basis of performance because performance determines the extent to which the earning process is complete.

The realization or revenue principle requires accrual basis accounting rather than cash basis accounting for revenues. For example, completed transactions for the sale of goods or services on credit usually are recognized as revenue in the period in which the sale or service occurred rather than in the period in which the cash is eventually collected.

Other types of revenue transactions posing problems of revenue recognition are installment sales, long-term construction contracts, sales of land with minimal down payments, and sales of franchises that require a certain level of performance on the part of the purchaser. In these and many other cases, both determination of when the earning process is complete and measurement of the amount of revenue are difficult tasks, and consideration of them is beyond the scope of this textbook.

Matching Principle

A major objective of accounting is the determination of periodic net income by matching appropriate costs against revenues. The principle recognizes that streams of revenues continually flow into a business, and it requires: (1) that there be a precise ''cutoff'' in these streams at the end of an accounting period, (2) that the inflows of the period be measured, (3) that the costs incurred in securing the inflows be determined, and (4) that the sum of the costs be deducted from the sum of the inflows to determine the period's net income.

The pattern of expense recognition varies. Some expenses reflect a direct cause-and-effect relationship with revenues. That is, the revenue and expense occur simultaneously. Examples are cost of goods sold, sales commission expense, and delivery expense. Other expenses are recognized on a time basis because the asset counterparts expire over time rather than reflect direct cause-and-effect relationships with revenues. Examples are depreciation expense of the home office, interest expense, and property tax expense. For other expenses, there is no direct relationship with either revenue or time. Therefore, these expenses must be allocated to reporting periods on some subjective basis. Examples are expenditures for advertising, research and development, and charitable contributions. A common system of allocation is to recognize such costs as expense in full in the period in which they are incurred.

The Objectivity Principle

The objectivity principle holds that changes in account balances should be supported to the fullest extent possible by objective evidence.

Bargained transactions supported by verifiable business documents originating outside the business are the best objective evidence obtainable; and whenever possible, accounting data should be supported by such documents.

Full-Disclosure Principle

The full-disclosure principle requires that the financial statements of a business clearly report all of the relevant information about the economic affairs of the enterprise. This principle rests upon the primary characteristic of relevance. Full disclosure requires (a) reporting of all information that can make a difference in a decision and (b) that the accounting information reported must be understandable (i.e., not susceptible to misleading inferences). Full disclosure also requires that the major accounting policies and any special accounting policies used by the company be explained in the notes to the financial statements.

The Consistency Principle

In many cases two or more methods or procedures have been derived in accounting practice to accomplish a particular accounting objective. While recognizing the validity of different methods under varying circumstances, it is still necessary in order to ensure a high degree of comparability in any concern's accounting data to insist on a consistent application in the company of any given accounting method, period after period. It is also necessary to insist that any departures from this doctrine of consistency be fully disclosed in the financial statements and the effects thereof on the statements be fully described.

The Principle of Conservatism

The principle of conservatism holds that the accountant should be conservative in his/her estimates and opinions and in the selection of procedures, choosing those that neither unduly understate nor overstate the situation.

Balance sheet conservatism was once considered the "first" principle of accounting, the objective being to place every item on the balance sheet at a conservative figure. This in itself was commendable; but it commonly resulted in overconservatism, which in turn resulted in (1) an understatement of asset and equity amounts, (2) an overstatement of costs in the year the assets were first understated, and (3) an understatement of costs on each income statement thereafter throughout the lives of the understated assets. Today, accountants recognize that balance sheet conservatism is not desirable when it misrepresents true situations; and they recognize that full, fair, and free-from-bias disclosure is a more important accounting objective.

The Principle of Materiality

A strict adherence to accounting principles is not required for items of little significance. Consequently, the accountant must always weigh the costs of complying with an accounting principle against the extra accuracy gained thereby; and in those situations where the cost is relatively great and the lack of compliance will have no material effect on the financial statements, compliance is not necessary.

There is no clear-cut distinction between material and immaterial items. Each situation must be individually judged, and an item is material or immaterial as it relates to other items. As a guide, the amount of an item is material if its omission, in the light of the surrounding circumstances, makes it probable that the judgment of a reasonable person would have been changed or influenced.

Implementation Constraints

Two of the principles listed, materiality and conservatism, are different from the other principles. In fact, some regard these as constraints which exert a modifying influence on financial accounting and reporting. The two other constraints are cost-benefit and industry peculiarities.

The cost of preparing and reporting accounting information should not exceed the value or usefulness of such information. Accounting focuses on usefulness and substance over form. Thus, peculiarities and practices of an industry may warrant selective exceptions to accounting principles and practices. These exceptions are permitted for specific items where there is a clear precedent in the industry based on uniqueness and usefulness.

Departure from the strict application of accounting principles and concepts must be fully disclosed whether it be on the basis of (*a*) materiality, (*b*) conservatism, (*c*) cost-benefit, or (*d*) industry peculiarity.

This review and summary of accounting concepts and principles and the constraints in their application provides an opportunity for reflection on the five chapters already covered and a frame of reference for study of subsequent chapters.

Summary of Appendix D in Terms of the Learning Objective

7. Some accounting concepts provide general descriptions of the accounting practices currently in use. These descriptive concepts are most useful in learning about accounting. Other accounting concepts prescribe the practices accountants should follow. These prescriptive concepts are most useful in developing accounting procedures for new types of transactions and making improvements in accounting practice.

"Financial Statement Concepts" (Section 1000, *CICA Handbook*) identifies the broad objectives of financial reporting. Then, the qualitative characteristics accounting information should possess are identified. Thereafter, the elements contained in the financial reports are defined and the recognition and measurement criteria to be used are identified. The accounting concepts and principles are defined and brought together in one place.

Glossary

Define or explain the words and phrases listed in the chapter Glossary. (L. O. 5)

Cash discount a deduction from the invoice price of goods that is granted if payment is made within a specified period of time. p. 214

Credit memorandum a memorandum sent to notify its recipient that the business sending the memorandum has in its records credited the account of the recipient. p. 230

Credit period the agreed period of time for which credit is granted and at the end of which payment is expected. p. 214

Credit terms the specified amounts and timing of payments that a buyer agrees to make in return for being granted credit to purchase goods or services. p. 213

Debit memorandum a memorandum sent to notify its recipient that the business sending the memorandum has in its records debited the account of the recipient. p. 230

Discount period the period of time during which, if payment is made, a cash discount may be deducted from the invoice price. p. 214

EOM an abbreviation for the words *end-of-month* that is sometimes used in expressing the credit terms of a sales agreement. p. 213

FOB the abbreviation for *free on board,* which is used to denote that goods purchased are placed on board the means of transportation at a specified geographic point with all loading and transportation charges to that point to be paid by the seller. p. 218

General and administrative expenses expenses to support the management and overall operations of a business, such as central office, accounting, personnel, and credit and collections expenses. p. 220

Gross margin another name for **gross profit.** p. 212

Gross profit net sales minus cost of goods sold; also called **gross margin** p. 212

List price the catalogue price of an item from which a trade discount, if offered, is deducted to determine the invoice or gross sales price of the item. p. 231

Merchandise assets purchased and held for resale. p. 212

Multiple-step income statement an income statement on which cost of goods sold and the expenses are subtracted in steps to get net income. p. 229

Periodic inventory system a method of accounting for inventories in which the inventory account is brought up to date once each period, at the end of the period, by counting the units of each product on hand, multiplying the count for each product by its cost, and adding the costs of the various products. p. 215

Perpetual inventory system a method of accounting for inventories in which cost of goods sold is recorded each time a sale is made and an up-to-date record of goods on hand is maintained. p. 215

Purchases discounts deductions from the invoice price of purchased items, which are granted by suppliers in return for early payment, i.e., cash discounts from suppliers. p. 216

Retained earnings statement a financial statement that reports the changes in a corporation's retained earnings that occurred during an accounting period. p. 225

Sales discounts deductions from the invoice price granted to customers in return for early payment, i.e., cash discounts to customers. p. 214

Selling expenses the expenses of preparing and storing merchandise for sale, promoting sales, making sales, and delivering goods to customers. p. 220

Single-step income statement an income statement on which cost of goods sold and operating expenses are added together and subtracted in one step from net sales to get net income. p. 229

Trade discount a deduction from a catalogue or list price that is used to determine the invoice price of goods. p. 231

Transportation-in costs incurred by a business for transporting merchandise purchases to the business. p. 218

An asterisk (*) identifies the questions, excercises, and problems that are based on Appendixes C and D at the end of the chapter.

Questions for Class Discussion

1. What is gross profit?
2. May a business earn a gross profit on its sales and still suffer a net loss? How?
3. Why should a business be interested in the amount of its sales returns and allowances?
4. Since sales returns and allowances are subtracted from sales on the income statement, why not save the effort of this subtraction by debiting all such returns and allowances directly to the Sales account?
5. What is a cash discount?
6. What is the difference between sales discounts, cash discounts, and purchases discounts?
7. If terms are 2/10, n/60, what is the length of the credit period? What is the length of the discount period?
8. How and when is cost of goods sold determined in a store that uses a periodic inventory system?
9. Which of the following are debited to the Purchases account of a grocery store: (*a*) the purchase of a cash register, (*b*) the purchase of a refrigerated display case, (*c*) the purchase of advertising space in a newspaper, and (*d*) the purchase of a case of tomato soup?
10. If a business is allowed to return all unsatisfactory merchandise purchased and receive full credit for the purchase price, why should it be interested in controlling the amount of its returns?
11. When applied to transportation terms, what do the letters FOB mean? What does FOB destination mean?

12. At the end of an accounting period, which inventory, the beginning inventory or the ending inventory, appears on the unadjusted trial balance of a company that uses a periodic inventory system?

13. What information appears on a retained earnings statement?

14. What relationship does a retained earnings statement have to the balance sheets at the end of the prior period and at the end of the current period?

15. How does a single-step income statement differ from a multiple-step income statement?

16. During the year, a company purchased merchandise that cost $150,000. What was the company's cost of goods sold if there were: (*a*) no beginning or ending inventories? (*b*) a beginning inventory of $26,000 and no ending inventory? (*c*) a $20,000 beginning inventory and a $32,000 ending inventory? and (*d*) no beginning inventory and an $11,000 ending inventory?

17. In counting the merchandise on hand at the end of an accounting period, a clerk failed to count and consequently omitted from the inventory all the merchandise on one shelf. If the cost of the merchandise on the shelf was $100, what was the effect of the omission on (*a*) the balance sheet and (*b*) the income statement?

18. Suppose that the omission of the $100 from the inventory (question 17) was not discovered. What would be the effect on the balance sheet and income statement prepared at the end of the next accounting period?

19. Distinguish between cash discounts and trade discounts. Is the amount of a trade discount on purchased merchandise credited to the Purchases Discounts account?

20. When a debit memorandum is issued, who debits, the originator of the memorandum or the company receiving it?

*21. Where is the ending inventory entered on the work sheet when the adjusting entry approach to accounting for inventories is used?

*22. What are the procedural differences between the adjusting entry and closing entry approaches to accounting for inventories?

*23. In comparing the adjusting entry and closing entry approaches to accounting for inventories, what effect does the adjusting entry approach have on the reported amount of the ending inventory? What effect does it have on the net income or net loss?

*24. What three qualitative characteristics of accounting information did "Financial Statement Concepts" identify as being necessary if the information is to be useful?

*25. What is implied by saying that financial information should have the qualitative characteristic of relevance?

*26. What are the characteristics of accounting information that makes it reliable?

*27. What is the meaning of the phrase "elements of financial statments"?

*28. What are the four criteria an item should satisfy to be recognized in the financial statements?

Multiple Choice

1. With a periodic inventory system, cost of goods sold:
    a. Is subtracted from the cost of goods available for sale to determine gross profit from sales.
    b. Plus the net cost of purchases equals the cost of goods available for sale.
    c. Is calculated as the cost of the beginning inventory plus the cost of purchases less the cost of the ending inventory.
    d. Is subtracted from gross sales to determine net sales.
    e. Includes all operating expenses related to merchandising operations.

2. In recording transactions that involve the purchase and resale of merchandise when a periodic inventory system is used:
    a. The sales price of merchandise returned by customers is credited to Sales Returns and Allowances.
    b. The purchase price of merchandise returned to a supplier is debited to Purchases Returns and Allowances.
    c. The Sales account is credited for the cost of merchandise sold to customers.
    d. The amount of any sales discounts taken by customers is debited to a Sales Discounts account.
    e. The amount of any purchases discounts is debited to a Purchases Discounts account.

3. If a concern's income statement showed cost of goods sold at $78,000, purchases of $80,000, freight-in at $300, purchases returns of $500, and end-of-the-period inventory at $11,900, its beginning-of-the-period inventory must have been:
    a. $10,400.
    b. $10,100.
    c. $9,900.
    d. $9,200.
    e. None of these amounts.

4. On the work sheet for a merchandising company that uses the closing entry approach to account for inventories:
    a. The beginning inventory is extended from the trial balance to the Income Statement Credit column.
    b. The ending inventory is inserted in the Income Statement Debit column and then extended to the Retained Earnings Statement or Balance Sheet Debit column.
    c. The amount of cost of goods sold is calculated in the Adjustments columns.
    d. The beginning inventory and ending inventory amounts appear in the Income Statement Debit and Income Statement Credit columns, respectively.
    e. The elements that make up the cost of purchases are extended to the Retained Earnings Statement or Balance Sheet Debit column.

5. When closing entries are used to account for merchandise inventories:
    a. The closing entries include a credit to Merchandise Inventory for the cost of the beginning inventory.

        b. The closing entries include a debit to Merchandise Inventory for the cost of the ending inventory.

        c. The cost of goods sold is recorded in a separate Cost of Goods Sold account which is closed to Income Summary.

        d. Cost of goods sold is calculated as the difference between the beginning and ending merchandise inventory amounts.

        e. Both (*a*) and (*b*) are correct.

6. If a bookkeeper recorded a cash sale with a debit to cash and a credit to purchases, the error would:

        a. Have no effect on reported net income.

        b. Cause an overstatement of net income.

        c. Cause an overstatement of cost of goods sold.

        d. Cause an understatement of gross profit.

        e. Cause an overstatement of net sales.

Mini Discussion Cases

Case 5–1
The case of unrecorded invoices

Part 1. One month after purchasing a profitable wholesale plumbing distribution company, Mr. Gerald Innocente realized he had a nightmare on his hands. The head accountant resigned after only two weeks with the new owner, and Gerald was getting calls from suppliers with regard to overdue accounts. He could not understand why because he had instructed the staff to pay all accounts as they became due.

Part 2. Gerald's wife, Jennifer, offered to help. She had been the accountant for a family owned firm, which had been sold about 15 years previously. With the aid of the assistant accountant, Jennifer found a folder of unpaid and unrecorded invoices all dated prior to the purchase date. Further investigation and discussion with the former head accountant's secretary revealed that Jennifer's discovery was nothing new. The secretary told the Innocentes that her former boss told her that he delayed the recordng of invoices in order to make the statements look good. He told her that no one was hurt, the goods went into inventory as they arrived, the invoices were eventually recorded, and the suppliers paid. She also informed them that the amount of $90,000 of the current unrecorded invoices was about $40,000 more than at the last year-end.

Required

If Mr. Innocente could turn the clock back one month, what do you believe he would have done with regard to accounts payable prior to finalizing the purchase of the business?

Case 5–2

Consider Part 2 of Case 5–1.

Required

Discuss which statements were affected and how they were affected.

Exercises

Exercise 5–1
Analyzing and recording purchases and purchases discounts
(L. O. 1)

Corner Store purchased merchandise having a $6,000 invoice price, terms 2/10, n/60, from a manufacturer and paid for the merchandise within the discount period. (*a*) Give without dates the journal entries made by the store to record the purchase and payment. (*b*) Give without dates the entries made by the manufacturer to record the sale and collection. (*c*) If the store borrowed sufficient money at a 13% annual rate of interest on the last day of the discount period to pay the invoice, how much did the store save by borrowing to take advantage of the discount?

Exercise 5–2
Journalizing merchandise transactions
(L. O. 1)

Prepare journal entries to record the following transactions of Baird Variety Store.

Jan. 3 Purchased merchandise from West Company subject to the following terms: $500 invoice price, 2/15, n/60, FOB factory.

5 Paid McLean Trucking $45 for shipping charges on purchase of January 3.

7 Returned to West Company unacceptable merchandise with list price of $100.

17 Sent West Company a cheque to pay for January 3 purchase net of discount and return.

18 Purchased merchandise from North Company subject to the following terms: $800 list price, 2/10, n/30, FOB North Company factory. The invoice showed that North Company had paid a trucking company $60 to ship the merchandise to Baird.

22 After advising North Company that some merchandise was damaged, received a credit memorandum granting Baird a $200 allowance on the January 18 purchase.

28 Paid North Company for the January 18 purchase, net of the allowance, and the shipping charges prepaid by North.

Exercise 5–3
Journal entries for purchases and sales and returns
(L. O. 1)

On January 5, 1990, Q Company received $6,000 of merchandise and an invoice dated January 4, terms of 2/10, n/30, FOB T Company's factory. On the day the goods were received, Q Company paid Quick Freight Company $180 of shipping charges on the merchandise purchased. The next day, Q Company returned to T Company $500 of the goods that were defective, and on January 14 it mailed T Company a cheque for the amount owed. Prepare general journal entries to record the foregoing transactions (*a*) on the books of Q Company and (*b*) on the books of T Company. Assume that T Company recorded the return and the cheque the next day after each was sent.

Exercise 5–4
Calculating expenses and income
(L. O. 2)

Copy the following tabulation and fill in the missing amounts. Indicate a loss by placing parentheses around the amount. Each horizontal row of figures is a separate problem situation.

Sales	Beginning Inventory	Purchases	Ending Inventory	Cost of Goods Sold	Gross Profit	Expenses	Net Income or Loss
$132,000	$ 96,000	$ 84,000	$?	$114,000	$?	$60,000	$?
222,000	78,000	?	90,000	96,000	?	66,000	60,000
180,000	60,000	?	36,000	?	102,000	54,000	48,000
?	90,000	132,000	72,000	?	120,000	48,000	?
192,000	72,000	114,000	?	126,000	?	84,000	?
60,000	18,000	?	30,000	36,000	?	?	6,000
?	138,000	264,000	156,000	?	168,000	?	60,000
96,000	?	60,000	42,000	?	36,000	?	12,000

Exercise 5–5
Multiple-step income statement for a proprietorship
(L. O. 3)

The Place is a single proprietorship business that ends its annual accounting period on December 31. The Income Statement columns of The Place's December 31, 1990, work sheet appeared as shown below. Use the information in these columns to prepare a 1990 multiple-step income statement for The Place.

	Income Statement	
	Debit	**Credit**
Merchandise inventory	43,000	48,000
Sales		240,000
Sales returns and allowances	1,500	
Sales discounts	1,800	
Purchases	144,000	
Purchases returns and allowances.		1,000
Purchases discounts		3,000
Transportation-in	700	
Selling expenses	36,000	
General and administrative expenses	25,000	
	252,000	292,000
Net income	40,000	
	292,000	292,000

Exercise 5–6
Preparing and posting proprietorship closing entries
(L. O. 4)

Part 1. Assume that The Place of Exercise 5–5 is owned by Rose Callen and prepare entries to close the temporary accounts of the business.

Part 2. Construct a balance column Merchandise Inventory account and enter the $43,000 beginning inventory of Exercise 5–5 as its balance on December 31, 1989. Then post to the account the portions of the closing entries that affect the account.

Exercise 5–7
Preparing an income statement from closing entries
(L. O. 3, 4)

The following two closing entries (with expenses combined to shorten the exercise) were made by Northwest Sales at the end of its 1990 annual accounting period.

Dec.	31	Income Summary	316,800.00	
		Merchandise Inventory		42,000.00
		Sales Returns and Allowances		2,400.00
		Sales Discounts		3,600.00
		Purchases		180,000.00
		Transportation-In		4,800.00
		Selling Expenses		48,000.00
		General and Administrative Expenses		36,000.00
	31	Merchandise Inventory	55,000.00	
		Sales	300,000.00	
		Purchases Returns and Allowances	1,200.00	
		Purchases Discounts	2,400.00	
		Income Summary		358,600.00

Required

Use the information in the closing entries to prepare an income statement for Northwest Sales.

Exercise 5–8

Multiple-step income statement and retained earnings statement
(L. O. 3)

The following items, with expenses condensed to conserve space, appeared in the last four columns of a work sheet prepared for Small Shop, Incorporated, as of December 31, 1990, the end of its annual accounting period. Use this information to prepare a 1990 multiple-step income statement and a retained earnings statement for the corporation.

	Income Statement		Retained Earnings Statement or Balance Sheet	
	Debit	Credit	Debit	Credit
Merchandise inventory	48,000	60,000	60,000	
Other assets			150,000	
Common stock				75,000
Retained earnings				107,000
Dividends declared			20,000	
Sales		360,000		
Sales returns and allowances	1,800			
Sales discounts	3,600			
Purchases	216,000			
Purchases returns and allowances		1,200		
Purchases discounts		3,000		
Transportation-in	600			
Selling expenses	54,000			
General and administrative expenses	42,600			
Income taxes expense	9,600			
	376,200	424,200	230,000	182,000
Net income	48,000			48,000
	424,200	424,200	230,000	230,000

Exercise 5–9

Preparing and posting closing entries
(L. O. 4)

Part 1.   Prepare entries to close the temporary accounts of Small Shop, Incorporated (Exercise 5–8).

Part 2.   Construct a Merchandise Inventory account in the form of a balance column account and enter the $48,000 beginning inventory of Exercise 5–8 as its December 31, 1989, balance. Then post to the account the portions of the store's closing entries that affect the account.

Exercise 5–10
Calculating operating expenses and cost of goods sold
(L. O. 2, 3)

The information that follows was taken from a single proprietorship's income statement.

Sales	$180,000	Purchases returns	$ 600
Sales returns	1,200	Purchases discounts	1,800
Sales discounts	2,400	Transportation-in	3,600
Beginning inventory	48,000	Gross profit from sales	56,400
Purchases	114,000	Net loss	4,800

Required

Prepare calculations to determine (*a*) total operating expenses, (*b*) cost of goods sold, and (*c*) ending inventory.

Exercise 5–11
Preparing a work sheet for a merchandising corporation
(L. O. 3)

The trial balance that follows was taken from the ledger of Bexar, Incorporated, at the end of its annual accounting period. (To simplify the problem and to save you time, the account balances are in one- and two-digit numbers.)

BEXAR, INCORPORATED
Unadjusted Trial Balance
December 31, 1990

Cash	$ 2	
Accounts receivable	7	
Merchandise inventory	6	
Store supplies	4	
Store equipment	10	
Accumulated depreciation, store equipment		$ 3
Accounts payable		4
Salaries payable	—	—
Common stock, 12 shares		12
Retained earnings		10
Dividends declared	1	
Sales		42
Sales returns and allowances	2	
Purchases	19	
Purchases discounts		3
Transportation-in	2	
Salaries expense	11	
Rent expense	7	
Advertising expense	3	
Depreciation expense, store equipment	—	—
Store supplies expense	—	—
Totals	$74	$74

Required

Prepare a work sheet form (do not include columns for an adjusted trial balance). Copy the unadjusted trial balance onto the work sheet and complete the work sheet using the following information:

a. Ending store supplies inventory, $2.

b. Estimated depreciation on the store equipment, $4.

c. Accrued salaries payable, $2.

d. Ending merchandise inventory, $7.

*Exercise 5–12
Work sheet for a merchandising corporation adjusting entry approach
(L. O. 6)

Use the information in Exercise 5–11 to prepare a work sheet according to the adjusting entry approach to accounting for merchandise inventories.

*Exercise 5–13
Updating the merchandise Inventory account; adjusting entry approach
(L. O. 6)

Use the adjusting entry approach to accounting for merchandise inventories and prepare adjusting journal entries and closing journal entries for Bexar, Incorporated, the company described in Exercise 5–11.

Exercise 5–14
Preparing a work sheet for a merchandising proprietorship
(L. O. 3)

The trial balance that follows was taken from the ledger of Linder Sales at the end of its annual accounting period. Bob Linder, the owner of Linder Sales, did not make additional investments in the business during 1990.

LINDER SALES
Unadjusted Trial Balance
December 31, 1990

Cash.	$ 8	
Accounts receivable	11	
Merchandise inventory	16	
Store supplies.	9	
Accounts payable.		$ 19
Salaries payable	—	—
Bob Linder, capital		26
Bob Linder, withdrawals	6	
Sales		62
Sales returns and allowances	5	
Purchases.	25	
Purchases discounts		4
Transportation-in	5	
Salaries expense	19	
Rent expense	7	
Store supplies expense	—	—
Totals	$111	$111

Required

Prepare a work sheet form (do not include columns for an adjusted trial balance). Copy the unadjusted trial balance onto the work sheet and complete the work sheet using the following information:

a. Ending store supplies inventory, $5.

b. Accrued salaries payable, $3.

c. Ending merchandise inventory, $21.

Exercise 5–15
Work sheet for a merchandising proprietorship; adjusting entry approach
(L. O. 6)

Use the information in Exercise 5–14 to prepare a work sheet according to the adjusting entry approach to accounting for merchandise inventories.

Exercise 5–16
Updating the Merchandise Inventory account; adjusting entry approach
(L. O. 6)

Use the adjusting entry approach to accounting for merchandise inventories and prepare adjusting journal entries and closing journal entries for Linder Sales, the company described in Exercise 5–14.

Problems

Problem 5–1
Journal entries for merchandising transactions
(L. O. 1)

Prepare general journal entries to record the following transactions of Hart Sales Company:

Dec. 1   Purchased merchandise priced at $3,600 on credit, terms 1/15, n/30, FOB the seller's factory.

2   A new computer for office use was purchased on credit for $9,000.

2   Sold merchandise on credit, terms 2/10, 1/30, n/60, $1,800.

3   Paid $115 cash for freight charges on the merchandise shipment of the December 1 transaction.

7   Sold merchandise for cash, $360.

9   Purchased merchandise on credit, terms 2/15, n/30, $1,500.

11   Received a $300 credit memorandum for merchandise purchased on December 9 and returned for credit.

18   Sold merchandise on credit, terms 2/10, n/30, $1,350.

21   Issued a $225 credit memorandum to the customer of December 18 who returned a portion of the merchandise purchased.

22   Purchased office supplies on credit, $185.

23   Received a credit memorandum for unsatisfactory office supplies purchased on December 22 and returned for credit, $60.

24   Paid for the merchandise purchased on December 9, less the return and the discount.

28   The customer who purchased merchandise on December 2 paid for the purchase of that date less the applicable discount.

28   Received payment for the merchandise sold on December 18, less the return and applicable discount.

31   Paid for the merchandise purchased on December 1.

Problem 5–2
Corporate income and retained earnings statements, and closing entries
(L. O. 2, 3, 4)

On December 31, 1990, the end of Griffin Sales, Inc.'s annual accounting period, the financial statement columns of the company's work sheet were as follows:

	Income Statement		Retained Earnings Statement or Balance Sheet	
	Debit	Credit	Debit	Credit
Merchandise inventory	33,765	35,790	35,790	
Other assets			260,000	
Common stock				100,000
Retained earnings				186,070
Dividends declared			25,000	
Sales		330,510		
Sales returns and allowances	1,970			
Purchases	216,765			
Purchases returns and allowances		780		
Purchases discounts		3,255		
Transportation-in	1,405			
Sales salaries expense	32,760			
Rent expense, selling space	16,200			
Advertising expense	1,185			
Store supplies expense	825			
Depreciation expense, store equipment	3,175			
Office salaries expense	15,975			
Rent expense, office space	1,800			
Telephone expense	855			
Office supplies expense	325			
Insurance expense	2,160			
Depreciation expense, office equipment	795			
Income taxes expense	5,655			
	335,615	370,335	320,790	286,070
Net income	34,720			34,720
	370,335	370,335	320,790	320,790

Required

1. Prepare a 1990 classified, multiple-step income statement for the corporation, showing in detail the expenses and the items that make up cost of goods sold.

2. Prepare a 1990 retained earnings statement.

3. Journalize compound closing entries for the corporation.

4. Open a Merchandise Inventory account and enter a December 31, 1989, balance of $33,765. Then post the portions of the closing entries that affect the account.

5. Prepare a combined, single-step income and retained earnings statement. Condense each revenue and expense category into a single item.

Problem 5–3
Proprietorship work sheet, income statement, and closing entries
(L. O. 2, 3, 4)

A December 31, 1990, year-end, unadjusted trial balance from the ledger of The Value Store, a single proprietorship, is as follows:

THE VALUE STORE
Unadjusted Trial Balance
December 31, 1990

Cash.	$ 2,000	
Merchandise inventory	50,960	
Store supplies.	1,175	
Office supplies	365	
Prepaid insurance	2,730	
Store equipment	31,815	
Accumulated depreciation, store equipment		$ 12,810
Office equipment	8,870	
Accumulated depreciation, office equipment		3,200
Accounts payable.		7,305
Don Boise, capital		60,450
Don Boise, withdrawals	27,000	
Sales		285,645
Sales returns and allowances	1,745	
Sales discounts	3,180	
Purchases.	171,375	
Purchases returns and allowances		1,110
Purchases discounts		4,410
Transportation-in	965	
Sales salaries expense.	31,920	
Rent expense, selling space	19,350	
Advertising expense	570	
Store supplies expense	–0–	
Depreciation expense, store equipment	–0–	
Office salaries expense	18,630	
Rent expense, office space	2,280	
Office supplies expense	–0–	
Insurance expense	–0–	
Depreciation expense, office equipment	–0–	
Totals	$374,930	$374,930

Required

1. Copy the unadjusted trial balance on a work sheet form and complete the work sheet using the following information:
   a. Store supplies inventory, $200.
   b. Office supplies inventory, $125.
   c. Expired insurance, $2,235.
   d. Estimated depreciation of store equipment, $3,180.
   e. Estimated depreciation of office equipment, $575.
   f. Ending merchandise inventory, $52,320.

2. Journalize closing entries for the store.

3. Open a balance column Merchandise Inventory account and enter a December 31, 1989, balance of $50,960. Then post the portions of the closing entries that affect the account.

*Problem 5–4
Adjusting entry approach to proprietorship work sheet, adjusting and closing entries
(L. O. 6)

Use the information presented in Problem 5–3 for The Value Store in solving this problem. However, in satisfying the following requirements, use the adjusting entry approach to accounting for merchandise inventories.

Required

1. Copy the unadjusted trial balance on a work sheet form and complete the work sheet. (Note the adjustments information presented in requirement 1 of Problem 5–3.)

2. Journalize adjusting and closing entries for the store.

3. Open a balance column Merchandise Inventory account and enter a December 31, 1989, balance of $50,960. Then post those portions of the closing entries that affect the account.

Problem 5–5
Corporate work sheet, income and retained earnings statements, and closing entries
(L. O. 3, 4)

The unadjusted trial balance of Gizmo Shop, Incorporated, on December 31, 1990, the end of the annual accounting period, is as follows:

GIZMO SHOP, INCORPORATED
Unadjusted Trial Balance
December 31, 1990

Cash.	$ 5,475	
Merchandise inventory	52,315	
Store supplies.	920	
Office supplies	475	
Prepaid insurance	3,165	
Store equipment	55,795	
Accumulated depreciation, store equipment		$ 5,310
Office equipment	12,660	
Accumulated depreciation, office equipment		1,385
Accounts payable.		1,195
Salaries payable		–0–
Income taxes payable		–0–
Common stock, 6,000 shares		60,000
Retained earnings		21,825
Dividends declared	15,000	
Sales		412,230
Sales returns and allowances	2,790	
Purchases.	251,715	
Purchases returns and allowances		1,120
Purchases discounts		4,385
Transportation-in.	3,275	
Sales salaries expense.	36,975	
Rent expense, selling space	15,750	
Advertising expense	5,150	
Store supplies expense	–0–	
Depreciation expense, store equipment	–0–	
Office salaries expense	37,740	
Rent expense, office space	2,250	
Insurance expense	–0–	
Office supplies expense	–0–	
Depreciation expense, office equipment	–0–	
Income taxes expense	6,000	
Totals	$507,450	$507,450

Required

1. Copy the unadjusted trial balance on a work sheet form and complete the work sheet using the information that follows:
   a. Ending store supplies inventory, $245.
   b. Ending office supplies inventory, $185.
   c. Expired insurance, $2,465.
   d. Depreciation on the store equipment, $5,415.
   e. Depreciation on the office equipment, $1,485.
   f. Accrued sales salaries payable, $335; and accrued office salaries payable, $240.
   g. Additional income taxes expense, $635.
   h. Ending merchandise inventory, $49,740.
2. Prepare a multiple-step classified income statement showing in detail the expenses and the items that make up cost of goods sold.
3. Prepare a retained earnings statement.
4. Prepare compound closing entries for the corporation.
5. In addition to the foregoing, prepare a single-step statement of income and retained earnings with the items condensed as is commonly done in published statements.

*Problem 5–6
Adjusting entry approach to corporate work sheet, income and retained earnings statements, adjusting and closing entries
(L. O. 6)

Use the information presented in Problem 5–5 for Gizmo Shop, Incorporated, in solving this problem. However, in satisfying the following requirements, use the adjusting entry approach to accounting for merchandise inventories.

Required

1. Copy the unadjusted trial balance on a work sheet form and complete the work sheet. (Note the adjustments information presented in Requirement 1 of Problem 5–5.)
2. Prepare a multiple-step classified income statement showing in detail the expenses and the items that make up cost of goods sold.
3. Prepare a retained earnings statement.
4. Prepare adjusting and closing entries for the corporation.
5. In addition to the foregoing, prepare a single-step statement of income and retained earnings with the items condensed as is commonly done in published statements.

Problem 5–7
Proprietorship work sheet, financial statements, and closing entries
(L. O. 2, 3, 4)

The unadjusted trial balance of Classic Threads on December 31, 1990, the end of the annual accounting period, is as follows:

CLASSIC THREADS
Unadjusted Trial Balance
December 31, 1990

Cash.	$ 10,275	
Accounts receivable	22,665	
Merchandise inventory	51,845	
Store supplies.	2,415	
Office supplies	775	
Prepaid insurance	3,255	
Store equipment	61,980	
Accumulated depreciation, store equipment		$ 10,830
Office equipment	12,510	
Accumulated depreciation, office equipment		2,825
Accounts payable.		8,310
Salaries payable		–0–
Sally Fowler, capital		106,015
Sally Fowler, withdrawals	15,000	
Sales		562,140
Sales returns and allowances	5,070	
Purchases.	385,085	
Purchases returns and allowances		1,820
Purchases discounts		4,710
Transportation-in	5,125	
Sales salaries expense.	43,220	
Rent expense, selling space	20,250	
Store supplies expense	–0–	
Depreciation expense, store equipment	–0–	
Office salaries expense	48,330	
Rent expense, office space	8,850	
Office supplies expense	–0–	
Insurance expense	–0–	
Depreciation expense, office equipment	–0–	
Totals	$696,650	$696,650

Required

1. Copy the unadjusted trial balance on a work sheet form and complete the work sheet using the information that follows:
    a. Ending store supplies inventory, $445.
    b. Ending office supplies inventory, $225.
    c. Expired insurance, $2,805.
    d. Depreciation on the store equipment, $5,415.
    e. Depreciation on the office equipment, $1,485.
    f. Accrued sales salaries payable, $445; and accrued office salaries payable, $210.
    g. Ending merchandise inventory, $54,365.
2. Prepare a multiple-step income statement showing in detail the expenses and the items that make up cost of goods sold.

3. Prepare a statement of changes in owner's equity. On December 31, 1989, the Sally Fowler, Capital account had a balance of $36,015. Early in 1990, Ms. Fowler invested an additional $70,000 in the business.

4. Prepare a year-end classified balance sheet with the prepaid expenses combined.

5. Prepare adjusting and closing entries.

Alternate Problems

Problem 5–1A
Journal entries for merchandising transactions
(L. O. 1)

Prepare general journal entries to record the following transactions of Schafer Merchandising:

Oct. 1   Purchased merchandise on credit, terms 2/10, n/30, $7,200.

    2   Sold merchandise for cash, $750.

    7   Purchased merchandise on credit, terms 2/10, n/30, $5,250, FOB the seller's factory.

    7   Paid $225 cash for freight charges on the merchandise shipment of the previous transaction.

    8   Purchased delivery equipment on credit, $12,000.

  12   Sold merchandise on credit, terms 2/15, 1/30, n/60, $3,000.

  13   Received a $750 credit memorandum for merchandise purchased on October 7 and returned for credit.

  13   Purchased office supplies on credit, $240, n/30.

  15   Sold merchandise on credit, terms 2/10, 1/30, n/60, $2,100.

  15   Paid for the merchandise purchased on October 7, less the return and the discount.

  16   Received a credit memorandum for unsatisfactory office supplies purchased on October 13 and returned, $60.

  19   Issued a $210 credit memorandum to the customer who purchased merchandise on October 15 and returned a portion for credit.

  25   Received payment for the merchandise sold on October 15, less the return and applicable discount.

  27   The customer of October 12 paid for the purchase of that date, less the applicable discount.

  31   Paid for the merchandise purchased on October 1.

Problem 5–2A
Corporate income and retained earnings statements, and closing entries
(L. O. 2, 3, 4)

On December 31, 1990, the end of Seaside Sales, Inc.'s, annual accounting period, the financial statement columns of its work sheet appeared as follows:

	Income Statement		Retained Earnings Statement or Balance Sheet	
	Debit	Credit	Debit	Credit
Merchandise inventory	69,330	66,545	66,545	
Other assets			487,785	
Common stock				200,000
Retained earnings				312,370
Dividends declared			50,000	
Sales		963,720		
Sales returns and allowances	5,715			
Sales discounts	14,580			
Purchases	651,735			
Purchases returns and allowances		2,730		
Purchases discounts		8,970		
Transportation-in	9,205			
Sales salaries expense	70,080			
Rent expense, selling space	33,000			
Store supplies expense	1,620			
Depreciation expense, store equipment	8,910			
Office salaries expense	56,820			
Rent expense, office space	3,000			
Office supplies expense	735			
Insurance expense	3,390			
Depreciation expense, office equipment	2,760			
Income taxes expense	19,125			
	950,005	1,041,965	604,330	512,370
Net income	91,960			91,960
	1,041,965	1,041,965	604,330	604,330

Required

1. Prepare a 1990 classified, multiple-step income statement for the corporation, showing in detail the expenses and the items that make up cost of goods sold.

2. Prepare a 1990 retained earnings statement.

3. Prepare compound closing entries for the corporation.

4. Open a Merchandise Inventory account and enter a December 31, 1989, balance of $69,330. Then post those portions of the closing entries that affect the account.

5. Prepare a combined, single-step income and retained earnings statement. Condense each revenue and expense category into a single item.

Problem 5–3A
Proprietorship work sheet, income statement, and closing entries
(L. O. 2, 3, 4)

The December 31, 1990, year-end, unadjusted trial balance of the ledger of Eastman Store, a single proprietorship business, is as follows:

EASTMAN STORE
Unadjusted Trial Balance
December 31, 1990

Cash.	$ 7,305	
Merchandise inventory	47,000	
Store supplies.	1,715	
Office supplies	645	
Prepaid insurance	3,840	
Store equipment	57,735	
Accumulated depreciation, store equipment		$ 9,575
Office equipment	14,130	
Accumulated depreciation, office equipment		3,670
Accounts payable.		4,680
Bob Eastman, capital.		93,585
Bob Eastman, withdrawals	31,500	
Sales		478,850
Sales returns and allowances	3,185	
Sales discounts	5,190	
Purchases.	331,315	
Purchases returns and allowances		1,845
Purchases discounts		4,725
Transportation-in	2,810	
Sales salaries expense.	34,710	
Rent expense, selling space	24,000	
Advertising expense	1,220	
Store supplies expense	–0–	
Depreciation expense, store equipment	–0–	
Office salaries expense	27,630	
Rent expense, office space	3,000	
Office supplies expense	–0–	
Insurance expense	–0–	
Depreciation expense, office equipment	–0–	
Totals	$596,930	$596,930

Required

1. Copy the unadjusted trial balance on a work sheet form and complete the work sheet using the following information:
   a. Store supplies inventory, $385.
   b. Office supplies inventory, $180.
   c. Expired insurance, $2,765.
   d. Depreciation on the store equipment, $5,865.
   e. Depreciation on the office equipment, $1,755.
   f. Ending merchandise inventory, $48,980.
2. Journalize closing entries for the store.
3. Open a balance column Merchandise Inventory account and enter a December 31, 1989, balance of $47,000. Then post those portions of the closing entries that affect the account.

*Problem 5–4A
Adjusting entry approach to proprietorship work sheet, adjusting and closing entries
(L. O. 6)

Use the information presented in Problem 5–3A for the Eastman Store in solving this problem. However, in satisfying the following requirements, use the adjusting entry approach to accounting for merchandise inventories.

Required

1. Copy the unadjusted trial balance on a work sheet form and complete the work sheet. (Note the adjustments information presented in requirement 1 of Problem 5–3A.)

2. Journalize adjusting and closing entries for the store.

3. Open a balance column merchandise Inventory account and enter a December 31, 1989, balance of $47,000. Then post those portions of the adjusting entries that affect the account.

Problem 5–5A
Corporate work sheet, income and retained earnings statements, and closing entries
(L. O. 3, 4)

The unadjusted trial balance of Ho Sales, Inc., on December 31, 1990, the end of the annual accounting period, is as follows:

HO SALES, INC.
Unadjusted Trial Balance
December 31, 1990

Cash.	$ 8,835	
Merchandise inventory	66,810	
Store supplies.	1,460	
Office supplies	660	
Prepaid insurance	4,340	
Store equipment	65,070	
Accumulated depreciation, store equipment		$ 9,350
Office equipment	14,505	
Accumulated depreciation, office equipment		2,285
Accounts payable.		3,375
Salaries payable		–0–
Income taxes payable		–0–
Common stock, 7,500 shares		75,000
Retained earnings		13,955
Dividends declared	7,500	
Sales		534,810
Sales returns and allowances	3,180	
Purchases.	352,345	
Purchases returns and allowances		2,165
Purchases discounts		4,930
Transportation-in	3,325	
Sales salaries expense.	42,145	
Rent expense, selling space	19,500	
Advertising expense	5,495	
Store supplies expense	–0–	
Depreciation expense, store equipment	–0–	
Office salaries expense	39,300	
Rent expense, office space	3,000	
Insurance expense	–0–	
Office supplies expense	–0–	
Depreciation expense, office equipment	–0–	
Income taxes expense	8,400	
Totals	$645,870	$645,870

Required

1. Copy the unadjusted trial balance on a work sheet form and complete the work sheet using the information that follows:
   a. Ending store supplies inventory, $395.
   b. Ending office supplies inventory, $185.
   c. Expired insurance, $3,715.
   d. Depreciation on the store equipment, $6,390.
   e. Depreciation on the office equipment, $1,715.
   f. Accrued sales salaries payable, $515; and accrued office salaries payable, $125.
   g. Additional income taxes expense, $785.
   h. Ending merchandise inventory, $64,305.

2. Prepare a multiple-step classified income statement showing in detail the expenses and the items that make up cost of goods sold.

3. Prepare a retained earnings statement.

4. Prepare compound closing entries for the corporation.

5. In addition to the foregoing, prepare a single-step statement of income and retained earnings with the items condensed as is commonly done in published statements.

---

*Problem 5–6A
Adjusting entry approach to corporate work sheet, income and retained earnings statements, adjusting and closing entries
(L. O. 6)

Use the information presented in Problem 5–5A for Ho Sales, Inc., in solving this problem. However, in satisfying the following requirements, use the adjusting entry approach to accounting for merchandise inventories.

Required

1. Copy the unadjusted trial balance on a work sheet form and complete the work sheet. (Note the adjustments information presented in Requirement 1 of Problem 5–5A.)

2. Prepare a multiple-step classified income statement showing in detail the expenses and the items that make up cost of goods sold.

3. Prepare a retained earnings statement.

4. Prepare adjusting and closing entries for the corporation.

5. In addition to the foregoing, prepare a single-step statement of income and retained earnings with the items condensed as is commonly done in published statements.

Problem 5–7A
Proprietorship work sheet, financial statements, and closing entries
(L. O. 2, 3, 4)

The unadjusted trial balance of Hanson's Rags on December 31, 1990, the end of the annual accounting period, is as follows:

HANSON'S RAGS
Unadjusted Trial Balance
December 31, 1990

Cash.	$ 10,170	
Accounts receivable	23,915	
Merchandise inventory	51,855	
Store supplies.	2,225	
Office supplies	840	
Prepaid insurance	3,570	
Store equipment	56,280	
Accumulated depreciation, store equipment		$ 9,170
Office equipment	11,885	
Accumulated depreciation, office equipment		2,750
Accounts payable.		3,840
Salaries payable		–0–
Bruce Hanson, capital		112,840
Bruce Hanson, withdrawals	25,000	
Sales		551,760
Sales returns and allowances	4,485	
Purchases.	382,020	
Purchases returns and allowances		1,920
Purchases discounts		4,315
Transportation-in	4,425	
Sales salaries expense.	39,525	
Rent expense, selling space	20,250	
Store supplies expense	–0–	
Depreciation expense, store equipment	–0–	
Office salaries expense	41,900	
Rent expense, office space	8,250	
Office supplies expense	–0–	
Insurance expense	–0–	
Depreciation expense, office equipment	–0–	
Totals	$686,595	$686,595

Required

1. Copy the unadjusted trial balance on a work sheet form and complete the work sheet using the following information:
   a. Ending store supplies inventory, $515.
   b. Ending office supplies inventory, $275.
   c. Expired insurance, $2,955.
   d. Depreciation on the store equipment, $4,965.
   e. Depreciation on the office equipment, $1,415.
   f. Accrued sales salaries payable, $485; and accrued office salaries payable, $275.
   g. Ending merchandise inventory, $53,835.

2. Prepare a multiple-step classified income statement showing in detail the items that make up cost of goods sold and the expense items.

3. Prepare a statement of changes in owner's equity. On December 31, 1989, the Bruce Hanson, Capital account had a balance of $37,840. Early in the year, Mr. Hanson invested an additional $75,000 in the business.

4. Prepare a year-end classified balance sheet with the prepaid expenses combined.

5. Prepare adjusting and closing entries.

Provocative Problems

Provocative Problem 5–1
Nan's Nursery
(L. O. 2, 3)

Nan Hall and Mike Linden were partners in a nursery. They disagreed, closed the business, and ended their partnership. In settlement for her partnershp interest, Nan Hall received an inventory of trees, plants, and garden supplies having a $22,500 cost. Since there was nothing practical she could do with the inventory, except to open a new nursery, she did so by investing the inventory and $18,000 in cash. She used $15,000 of the cash to buy equipment, and she opened for business on May 1. During the succeeding eight months, she paid out $63,750 to creditors for additional trees, plants, and garden supplies and $21,000 in operating expenses. She also withdrew $15,000 for personal expenses, and at the year-end, she prepared the balance sheet that follows:

NAN'S NURSERY
Balance Sheet
December 31, 1990

Cash		$ 8,550	Accounts payable (all for	
Merchandise inventory .		26,650	merchandise)	$ 3,300
Equipment	$15,000		Nan Hall, capital	45,700
Less depreciation . . .	1,200	13,800	Total liabilities and	
Total assets		$49,000	owner's equity	$49,000

Based on the information given, prepare calculations to determine the net income earned by the business, the cost of goods sold, and the amount of its sales. Then prepare an income statement showing the result of the nursery's operations during its first eight months.

Provocative Problem 5–2
Westwood Store
(L. O. 3)

Tony Falk, the owner of Westwood Store, has not maintained an adequate accounting system and has asked you to help him prepare an income statement for the business. Based on information he has provided, the following balance sheet information is now available:

	December 31	
	1989	**1990**
Cash	$ 3,750	$12,150
Accounts receivable	9,300	10,950
Merchandise inventory	45,600	42,750
Equipment (net after depreciation)	37,200	30,900
Total assets	$95,850	$96,750
Accounts payable	$13,950	$12,300
Accrued wages payable	450	750
Tony Falk, capital	81,450	83,700
Total liabilities and owner's equity	$95,850	$96,750

Also, the store's record of cash receipts and disbursements shows the following:

Collection of accounts receivable	$402,600
Payments for:	
Accounts payable	249,300
Employees' wages	72,150
Other operating expenses	27,750
Tony Falk, withdrawals	45,000

Under the assumption that the store makes all purchases and sales on credit, prepare calculations to determine the 1990 amounts of its accrual basis sales, purchases, and wages expense. Then prepare an accrual basis income statement for 1990.

Provocative Problem 5–3
Phil's Paints
(L. O. 3)

Phil Potter worked in the Western National Bank for 20 years, until his aunt died, leaving him a sizable estate. After sitting around long enough to get bored and see his bank balance dwindle, Phil decided to open a retail paint store. When he started the business on July 1, 1990, Valley Hills had no such store, and it appeared to Phil that the business would succeed.

On July 1, Phil deposited $53,500 in a bank account under the name Phil's Paints. He then paid $12,000 cash for store equipment, which he expected to last 10 years before it became valueless. He also bought merchandise for $37,500 cash, and paid $3,600 in advance for six months' store rent.

Phil estimated that most paint stores marked their goods for sale at prices averaging 35% above cost. In other words, an item that cost $10.00 was marked for sale at $13.50. But to entice customers, he decided to mark his merchandise for sale at 30% above cost. Since his overhead would be low, he thought this would still leave a net income equal to 10% of sales.

On December 31, 1990, six months after opening his store, Phil has come to you for advice. He thinks business has been good. However, he doesn't quite understand why his cash balance has fallen to $1,200.

In talking with Phil and examining his records, you determine that the inventory was replaced three times during the six months, each time at a cost of $37,500. All merchandise suppliers have been paid except for $10,850, which is not yet due. A full stock of merchandise (cost of $37,500) is on hand and customers owe Phil $29,100. In addition to the rent paid in advance, Phil paid $14,700 for other expenses.

Prepare an income statement for the business covering the six-month period ended December 31, a statement of changes in owner's equity, a December 31, 1990, balance sheet, and a statement that explains the $1,200 cash balance by showing the cash receipts and cash disbursements during the six months ended December 31.

Analytical and Review Problems

A&R Problem 5–1 The partially completed work sheet of Incomplete Data Company appears below:

INCOMPLETE DATA COMPANY
Work sheet for the Year Ended December 31, 199A

Account Titles	Trial Balance		Adjustments		Income Statement		Balance Sheet	
	Debit	Credit	Debit	Credit	Debit	Credit	Debit	Credit
Cash	34,780							
Accounts receivable							4,600	
Merchandise inventory					31,400	26,400		
Prepaid fire insurance	720						480	
Prepaid rent	4,800							
Office equipment							12,000	
Accumulated depreciation—office equipment		4,500						
Accounts payable		8,000						
Clay Camp, capital		22,000						
Clay Camp, drawing							20,000	
Sales		300,000						
Sales returns and allowances					1,000			
Purchases	199,200							
Purchases returns and allowances		1,000				1,400		
Advertising expense	1,000							
Supplies expense	1,800							
Salaries expense	23,200							
Utilities expense	1,400							
Fire insurance expense								
Rent expense					2,400			
Depreciation expense—office equipment					1,500			
Salaries payable								660

Required

Complete the work sheet for the year ended December 31, 199A.

A&R Problem 5–2

ET Company has prepared the following unadjusted trial balance at the end of its fiscal year ended December 31, 199A:

Cash.	$160	
Accounts receivable	290	
Merchandise inventory (periodic system) . .	180	
Prepaid insurance	40	
Equipment.	390	
Accumulated depreciation (equipment) . . .		$190
Note payable		280
Accounts payable.		100
ET, Capital		400
Sales revenue		890
Purchases.	510	
Rent expense	60	
Salary expense	190	
Other expenses.	50	
Sales returns	10	
Purchases returns and allowances.		20

At December 31, 199A, the company:

a. Owes interest of $20 on the note payable.

b. Has unpaid other expenses at year-end, $20.

c. Owes salaries of $40.

d. Should record depreciation expense of $40.

e. Has unexpired insurance of $20.

f. Discovered that sales revenue (as recorded in the ledger and listed on the unadjusted trial balance) is understated by $110 (a sale was not invoiced).

g. Has merchandise inventory on hand of $260.

Required

1. Determine the following for the year ended December 31, 199A:
   a. Revenue.
   b. Cost of goods sold.
   c. Gross margin.
   d. Total of expenses.
   e. Net income.

2. Determine the following as of December 31, 199A:
   a. Total of assets.
   b. Total of liabilities.
   c. ET, capital.

3. Prepare all the closing entries (omit narratives).

A&R Problem 5-3   The following are the selected data for the Allen Sales Company for the year 1991.

1. Selected closing entries:

Income Summary	273,000	
Purchases Returns and Allowances	2,500	
Purchases		180,000
Freight-In		4,000
Purchase Discounts Lost		200
Sales Salaries Expense		40,000
Advertising Expense		10,000
Rent Expense, Office Space		8,000
Delivery Expense		4,800
Office Salaries Expense		26,000
Depreciation, Office Equipment		2,000
Miscellaneous Expense		500
To close expense and other nominal accounts.		
G. Allen, Capital	28,000	
G. Allen, Withdrawals		28,000
To close the withdrawals account.		

2. G. Allen follows the practice of withdrawing half of the annual net income from the business.

3. There were no sales returns and allowances for the year. However, sales discounts amounted to $2,000.

4. Inventories:
   December 31, 1990—$25,000
   December 31, 1991—$20,000

Required

1. Compute the amount of net income for 1991.
2. Compute the amount of sales for 1991.
3. Prepare a classified income statement for 1991.

A&R Problem 5-4   Discuss the qualitative characteristics accounting information should possess.

*A&R Problem 5-5   Reconstruct your solution to A&R Problem 5-1 (show adjustments column only) to conform to Appendix C.

6 Accounting Systems

Even in small businesses, the quantity of data that is processed through the accounting system is large. As a result, the accounting system should be designed so that the data can be processed efficiently. This chapter explains some general procedures and techniques that you can use in designing an accounting system so that it will efficiently process data.

Learning Objectives

After studying Chapter 6, you should be able to:

1. Describe the type of transaction that is recorded in each journal when special journals are used and record all types of transactions in an accounting system that uses special journals.
2. Explain how a controlling account and its subsidiary ledger operate and, when special journals are used, post the amounts recorded in the journals to the General Ledger and any subsidiary ledgers.
3. Explain how to test the accuracy of the account balances in the Accounts Receivable and Accounts Payable Ledgers and prepare schedules of the accounts in each subsidiary ledger.
4. Describe how data are processed in computerized accounting systems.
5. Define or explain the words and phrases listed in the chapter Glossary.

After studying the appendix to Chapter 6 (Appendix E), you should be able to:

6. Explain how microcomputers can be used in the accounting process.

Accounting Systems

An **accounting system** consists of the business papers, records, reports, and procedures that a business uses to record transactions and report their effects. The operation of an accounting system includes three important steps. First, you must capture on business papers or source documents the quantities, dollar amounts, and other important data related to business transactions. Second, you must classify and record in the accounting records the data contained in the source documents. Third, you must summarize in timely reports to management and other interested parties the information contained in the accounting records.

Even in a small business, the quantity of data that is processed through the accounting system is large. As a result, the accounting system should be designed so that the data can be processed efficiently. To help you learn how to accomplish this goal, we begin Chapter 6 with a discussion of techniques that are used primarily in manual accounting systems. You should understand that the basic concepts introduced in this discussion are generally applicable to both manual and computerized accounting systems. Later in the chapter, we turn the discussion specifically to electronic and computerized accounting systems.

Using Special Journals to Save Labour

Describe the type of transaction that is recorded in each journal when special journals are used and record all types of transactions in an accounting system that uses special journals. (L. O. 1)

The General Journal is a flexible journal in which you can record any transaction. However, each debit and credit entered in a General Journal must be individually posted. As a result, if a General Journal is used to record all the transactions of a business, much time and labour are required to post the individual debits and credits.

One way to reduce the writing and the posting labour is to divide the transactions of a business into groups of similar transactions and to provide a separate **special journal** for recording the transactions in each group. For example, most of the transactions of a merchandising business fall into four groups. These are sales on credit, purchases on credit, cash receipts, and cash disbursements. If a special journal is provided for each group, the journals are:

1. A Sales Journal for recording credit sales.
2. A Purchases Journal for recording credit purchases.
3. A Cash Receipts Journal for recording cash receipts.
4. A Cash Disbursements Journal for recording cash payments.

Also, you must have a General Journal for the miscellaneous transactions that you cannot record in the special journals and also for adjusting, closing, and correcting entries.

The following illustrations show that special journals require less writing in recording transactions than does a General Journal. Also, special journals save posting labour by providing special columns for accumulating the debits and credits of similar transactions. The amounts entered in the special columns are then posted as column totals rather than as individual amounts. For example, if you record credit sales for a month in a Sales Journal like the one at the top of Illustration 6–1, you can save posting labour. To do so, you wait until the end of the month, total the sales recorded in the journal, and then debit Accounts Receivable and credit Sales for the total.

Illustration 6–1

Sales Journal

Page 3

Date	Account Debited	Invoice Number	PR	Amount
Feb. 2	James Henry	307	√	450.00
7	Albert Smith.	308	√	500.00
13	Sam Moore.	309	√	350.00
15	Paul Roth	310	√	200.00
22	James Henry	311	√	225.00
25	Frank Booth.	312	√	175.00
28	Albert Smith.	313	√	250.00
28	Total—Accounts Receivable, Dr.; Sales, Cr..			2,150.00
				(112/411)

Individual amounts are posted daily to the subsidiary ledger.

Total is posted at the end of the month to the general ledger accounts.

Accounts Receivable Ledger

Frank Booth

Date	PR	Debit	Credit	Balance
Feb. 25	S3	175.00		175.00

James Henry

Date	PR	Debit	Credit	Balance
Feb. 2	S3	450.00		450.00
22	S3	225.00		675.00

Sam Moore

Date	PR	Debit	Credit	Balance
Feb. 13	S3	350.00		350.00

Paul Roth

Date	PR	Debit	Credit	Balance
Feb. 15	S3	200.00		200.00

Albert Smith

Date	PR	Debit	Credit	Balance
Feb. 7	S3	500.00		500.00
28	S3	250.00		750.00

General Ledger

Accounts Receivable   No. 112

Date	PR	Debit	Credit	Balance
Feb. 28	S3	2,150.00		2,150.00

Sales   No. 411

Date	PR	Debit	Credit	Balance
Feb. 28	S3		2,150.00	2,150.00

The ruled lines around the accounts are meant to convey the idea that the customer accounts are in one ledger and the financial statement accounts are in a different ledger.

Explanation columns are omitted from the accounts due to a lack of space.

Only seven sales are recorded in the illustrated journal. However, if you assume the seven sales represent 700 sales, you can better appreciate the posting labour saved by the one debit to Accounts Receivable and the one credit to Sales, rather than 700 debits and 700 credits.

The special journal in Illustration 6–1 is also called a **columnar journal** because it has columns for recording the date, the customer's name, the invoice number, and the amount of each charge sale. Only charge sales are recorded in it, and they are recorded daily, with the information about each sale placed on a separate line. Normally, the information is taken from a copy of the sales ticket or invoice prepared at the time of the sale. However, before discussing the journal further, you need to understand the role played by **subsidiary ledgers**.

Maintaining a Separate Account for Each Customer

In previous chapters, when we recorded credit sales, we debited a single account called Accounts Receivable. However, when a business has more than one credit customer, the accounts must be designed so that they show how much each customer has purchased, how much each customer has paid, and how much remains to be collected from each customer. To provide this information, businesses with credit customers must maintain a separate account receivable for each customer.

One possible way of keeping a separate account for each customer would be to keep all of these accounts in the same ledger that contains the financial statement accounts. However, this usually is not done. Instead, the ledger that contains the financial statement accounts, now called the **General Ledger**, continues to hold a single Accounts Receivable account. Then, a supplementary record is established in which a separate account is maintained for each customer. This supplementary record is called the **Accounts Receivable Ledger**. This subsidiary ledger may exist on tape or disk storage in a computerized system. In a manual system, the Accounts Receivable Ledger may take the form of a book or tray that contains the customer accounts. In either case, the customer accounts in the subsidiary ledger are kept separate from the Accounts Receivable account in the General Ledger.

Posting the Sales Journal

When customer accounts are placed in a subsidiary ledger, a Sales Journal is posted as in Illustration 6–1. The individual sales recorded in the Sales Journal are posted each day to the proper customer accounts in the Accounts Receivable Ledger. These daily postings keep the customer accounts up-to-date. This is important in granting credit because the person responsible for granting credit should know the amount the credit-seeking customer currently owes. The source of this information is the customer's account, and if the account is not up-to-date, an incorrect decision may be made.

Note the check marks in the Sales Journal's Posting Reference column. They indicate that the sales recorded in the journal were individually posted to the customer accounts in the Accounts Receivable Ledger. Check marks rather than account numbers are used because customer accounts may not be numbered. If the accounts are not numbered, they are arranged alphabetically in the Accounts Receivable Ledger so they can be located easily.

In addition to the daily postings to customer accounts, at the end of the month, the Sales Journal's Amount column is totaled. Then, the total is debited to Accounts Receivable and credited to Sales. The credit records the month's revenue from charge sales. The debit records the resulting increase in accounts receivable.

In Illustration 6–1, pay attention to the fact that the individual customer accounts in the subsidiary Accounts Receivable Ledger do not replace the Accounts Receivable account in the General Ledger. The general ledger Accounts Receivable account is maintained because it serves three functions: (1) It shows the total amount owed by all customers. (2) It allows the General Ledger to be a balancing ledger in which debits equal credits. (3) It offers a way of testing the accuracy of the customer accounts in the subsidiary Accounts Receivable Ledger.

Identifying Posted Amounts

When several journals are posted to ledger accounts, you must indicate in the Posting Reference column before each posted amount the journal and the page number of the journal from which the amount was posted. The journal is indicated by using its initial. Thus, items posted from the Cash Disbursements Journal carry the initial "D" before their journal page numbers in the Posting Reference columns. Likewise, items from the Cash Receipts Journal carry the letter "R." Those from the Sales Journal carry the initial "S." Items from the Purchases Journal carry the initial "P," and from the General Journal, the letter "G."

Controlling Accounts

Explain how a controlling account and its subsidiary ledger operate and, when special journals are used, post the amounts recorded in the journals to the General Ledger and any subsidiary ledgers.
(L. O. 2)

You should understand that when debits (or credits) to Accounts Receivable are posted twice (once to Accounts Receivable and once to the customer's account), this does not violate the requirement that debits equal credits. The equality of debits and credits is maintained *in the General Ledger*. The Accounts Receivable Ledger is simply a supplementary record that provides detailed information concerning each customer.

After all items are posted, the balance in the Accounts Receivable account should be equal to the sum of the balances in the customers' accounts. As a result, the Accounts Receivable account is said to control the Accounts Receivable Ledger and is called a **controlling account**. And since the Accounts Receivable Ledger is a supplementary record that is controlled by an account in the General Ledger, it is called a *subsidiary ledger*. After posting is completed, if the Accounts Receivable balance does not equal the sum of the customer account balances, you know an error has been made.

The Accounts Receivable account and the Accounts Receivable Ledger are not the only examples of controlling accounts and subsidiary ledgers. Most companies buy on credit from several suppliers and must use a controlling account and subsidiary ledger for accounts payable. Another example might be an Office Equipment account, which would control a subsidiary ledger in which each item of equipment is recorded in a separate account.

Cash Receipts Journal

A Cash Receipts Journal designed to save labour through posting column totals must be a multicolumn journal. A multicolumn journal is necessary because when cash is received from different sources, different accounts are credited. For example, the cash receipts of a store normally fall into three groups: (1) cash from charge customers in payment of their accounts, (2) cash from cash sales, and (3) cash from miscellaneous sources. Note in Illustration 6–2 that a special column is provided for the credits that result when cash is received from each of these sources.

Cash from Charge Customers

When a Cash Receipts Journal like Illustration 6–2 is used to record cash received in payment of the customer's account, the customer's name is entered in the journal's Account Credited column. The amount credited to the customer's account is entered in the Accounts Receivable Credit column, and the debits to Sales Discounts and Cash are entered in the journal's last two columns.

Look at the Accounts Receivable Credit column. Observe that (1) only credits to customer accounts are entered in this column. (2) The individual credits are posted daily to the customer accounts in the subsidiary Accounts Receivable Ledger. (3) The column total is posted at the end of the month as a credit to the Accounts Receivable controlling account. This is the normal recording and posting procedure when you use special journals and controlling accounts with subsidiary ledgers. Transactions are normally entered in a special journal column. Then, the individual amounts are posted to the subsidiary ledger accounts and the column totals are posted to the general ledger accounts.

Cash Sales

After cash sales are entered on one or more cash registers and totaled at the end of each day, the daily total is recorded with a debit to Cash and a credit to Sales. When a Cash Receipts Journal like that of Illustration 6–2 is used, the debits to Cash are entered in the Cash Debit column, and the credits are entered in a special column headed Sales Credit. By using a separate Sales Credit column, you can post the total cash sales for a month as a single amount, the column total. (Although cash sales are normally recorded daily from the cash register reading, the cash sales of Illustration 6–2 are recorded only once each week in order to shorten the illustration.)

At the time daily cash sales are recorded in the Cash Receipts Journal, some bookkeepers, as in Illustration 6–2, place a check mark in the Posting Reference (PR) column to indicate that no amount is individually posted from that line of the journal. Other bookkeepers use a double check ($\sqrt{\sqrt{}}$) to distinguish amounts that are not posted from amounts that are posted to customer accounts.

Illustration 6–2

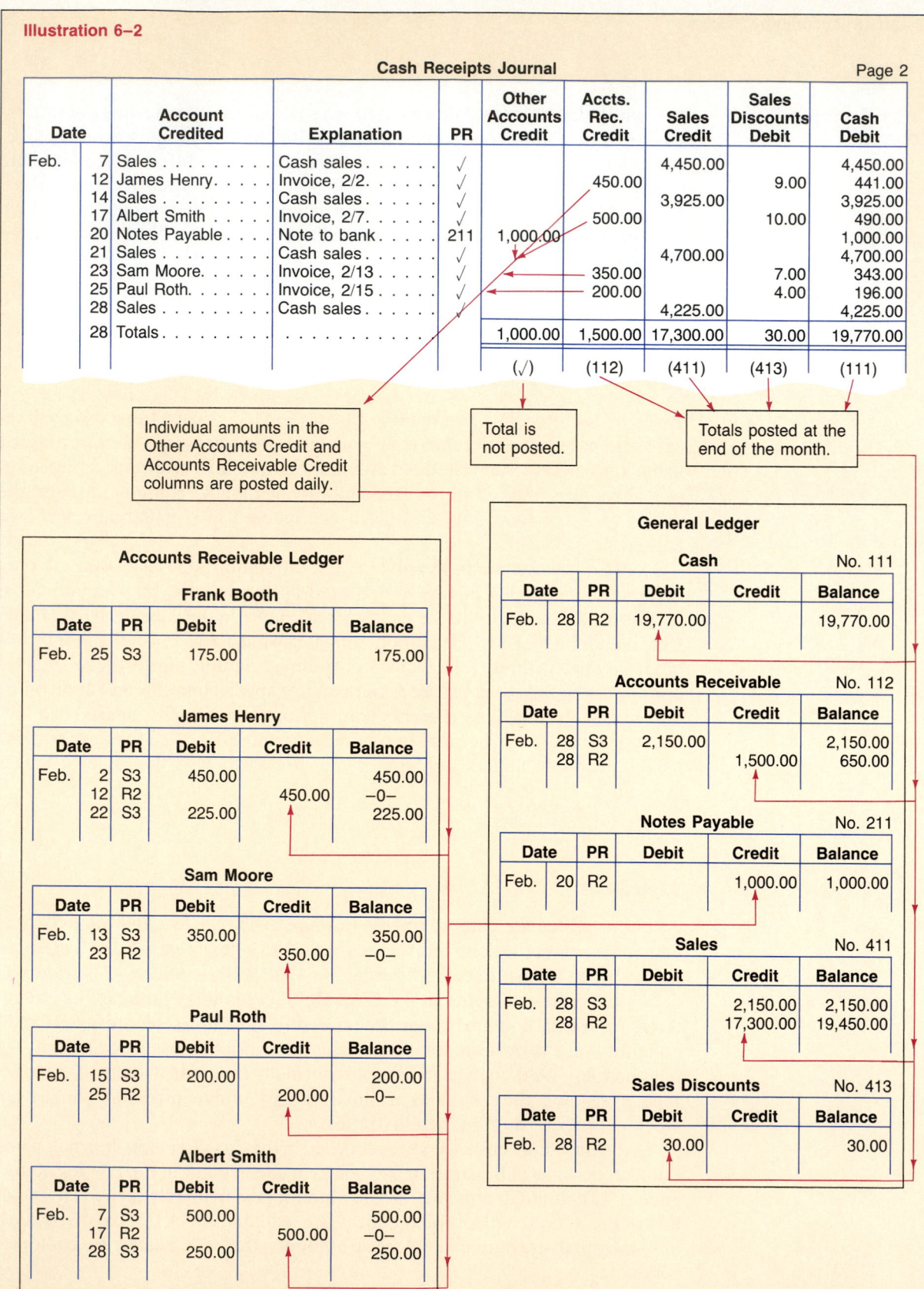

Miscellaneous Receipts of Cash

Most cash receipts are from collections of accounts receivable and from cash sales. However, other less frequent sources of cash include borrowing money from a bank or selling unneeded assets. The Other Accounts Credit column is provided for receipts that do not occur often enough to warrant a separate column. In an average company, the items entered in this column are few and are posted to a variety of general ledger accounts. As a result, postings are less apt to be omitted if these items are posted daily.

The Cash Receipts Journal's Posting Reference column is used only for daily postings from the Other Accounts and Accounts Receivable columns. The account numbers that appear in the Posting Reference column indicate items that were posted to general ledger accounts. The check marks indicate either that an item like a day's cash sales was not posted or that an item was posted to the subsidiary Accounts Receivable Ledger.

Month-End Postings

At the end of the month, the amounts in the Accounts Receivable, Sales, Sales Discounts, and Cash columns of the Cash Receipts Journal are posted as column totals. However, the transactions recorded in any journal must result in equal debits and credits to general ledger accounts. Therefore, to be sure that the total debits and credits in a columnar journal are equal, you must **crossfoot** or cross add the column totals before they are posted. To **foot** a column of numbers is to add it. To crossfoot, the Debit column totals are added, the Credit column totals are added, and the two sums are compared for equality. For Illustration 6–2, the two sums appear as follows:

Debit Columns		Credit Columns	
Sales discounts debit	$ 30	Other accounts credit	$ 1,000
Cash debit	19,770	Accounts receivable credit	1,500
		Sales credit	17,400
Total	$19,800	Total	$19,800

Since the sums are equal, you may assume the debits in the journal equal the credits.

After you crossfoot the journal to show that debits equal credits, the totals of the last four columns are posted as indicated in each column heading. As for the Other Accounts column, since the individual items in this column are posted daily, the column total is not posted. Note in Illustration 6–2 the check mark below the Other Accounts column. The check mark indicates that the column total was not posted. The account numbers of the accounts to which the remaining column totals were posted are shown in parentheses below each column.

Posting items daily from the Other Accounts column with a delayed posting of the offsetting items in the Cash column (total) causes the General Ledger to be out of balance throughout the month. However, this does not matter because before the trial balance is prepared, the offsetting amounts reach the General Ledger in posting the Cash column total.

Posting Rule

Now that we have illustrated the procedures for posting from two different journals to a subsidiary ledger and its controlling account, the rule that governs all such postings should be clear. The rule is: *In posting to a subsidiary ledger and its controlling account, the controlling account must be debited periodically for an amount or amounts equal to the sum of the debits to the subsidiary ledger, and it must be credited periodically for an amount or amounts equal to the sum of the credits to the subsidiary ledger.*

Maintaining a Separate Account for Each Creditor

As with accounts receivable, a company must keep a separate account for each creditor. To accomplish this, an Accounts Payable controlling account is maintained in the General Ledger and a separate account for each creditor is maintained in a subsidiary **Accounts Payable Ledger**. Also, the controlling account, subsidiary ledger, and columnar journal techniques demonstrated thus far with accounts receivable apply to the creditor accounts. The only difference is that a Purchases Journal and a Cash Disbursements Journal are used to record most of the transactions that affect these accounts.

Purchases Journal

A Purchases Journal that has one money column may be used to record purchases of merchandise on credit. However, a Purchases Journal usually is more useful if it is designed as a multicolumn journal in which purchases of both merchandise and supplies can be recorded. Such a journal may have columns like those shown in Illustration 6–3. In the illustrated journal, the invoice date and terms together indicate the date on which payment for each purchase is due. The Accounts Payable Credit column is used to record the amounts credited to each creditor's account. These amounts are posted daily to the individual creditor accounts in the subsidiary Accounts Payable Ledger. At the end of the month, the column total is posted to the Accounts Payable controlling account. The items purchased are recorded in the Debit columns and are posted in the column totals.

The Cash Disbursements Journal or Cheque Register

The Cash Disbursements Journal, like the Cash Receipts Journal, has columns so that you can post repetitive debits and credits in column totals. The repetitive cash payments involve debits to the Accounts Payable controlling account and credits to both Purchases Discounts and Cash. In most companies, merchandise is usually purchased on credit. Therefore, a Purchases column is not needed. Instead, the occasional cash purchase is recorded as on line 2 of Illustration 6–4.

Observe that the illustrated journal has a column headed Cheque Number (Ch. No.). In order to gain control over cash disbursements, all such disbursements, except petty cash disbursements, should be made by cheque. The cheques should be prenumbered by the printer and should be entered in the journal in numerical order with each cheque's number in the column headed Ch. No. This makes it possible to scan the numbers in the column for omitted cheques. When a Cash Disbursements Journal has a column for cheque numbers, it is often called a **Cheque Register.**

Illustration 6–3

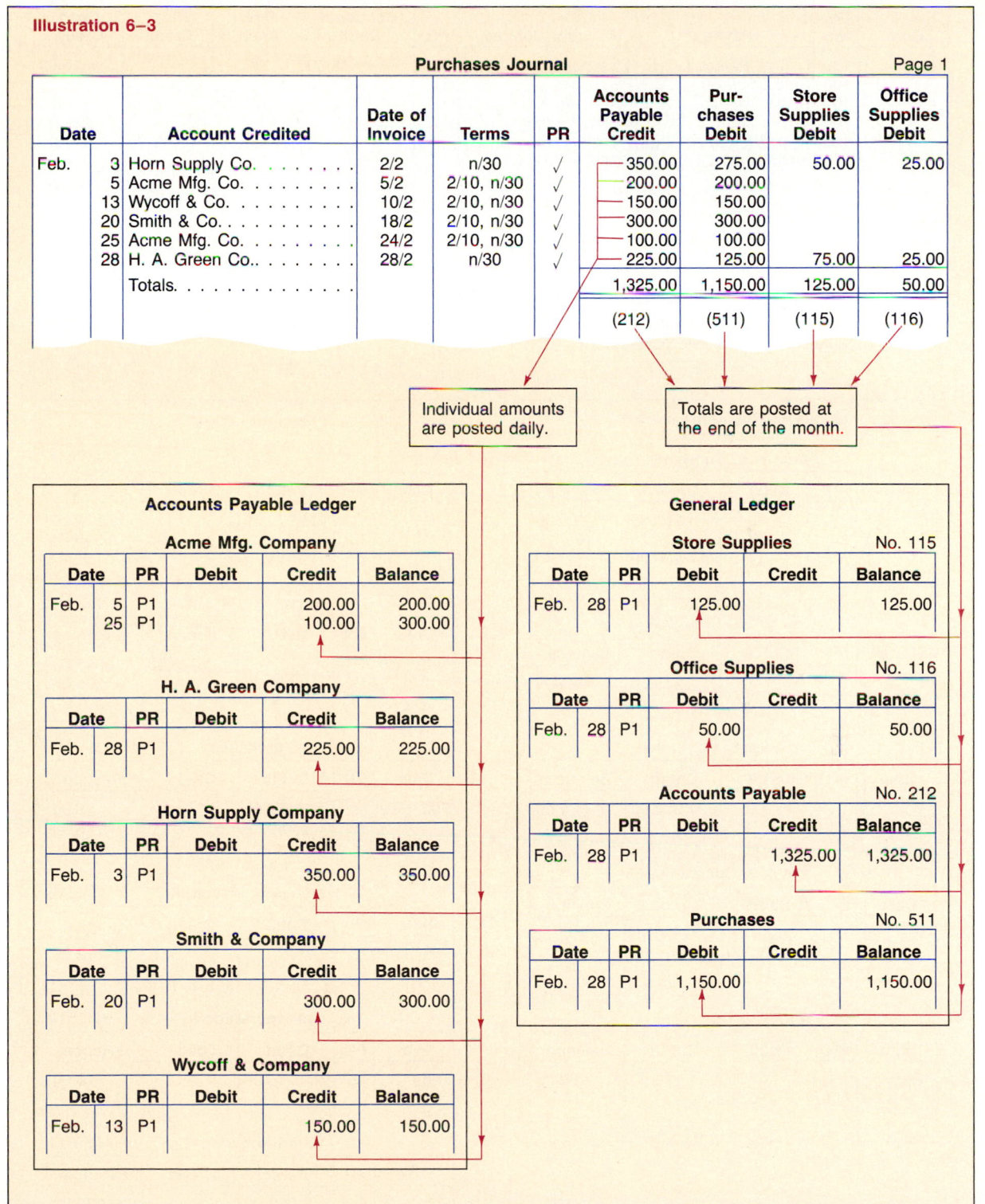

Illustration 6–4

Cash Disbursements Journal

Page 2

Date		Ch. No.	Payee	Account Debited	PR	Other Accounts Debit	Accts. Pay. Debit	Pur. Disc. Credit	Cash Credit
Feb.	3	105	L. & N. Railroad. . . .	Transportation-In . . .	514	15.00			15.00
	12	106	East Sales Co.	Purchases	511	25.00			25.00
	15	107	Acme Mfg. Co.	Acme Mfg. Co.	✓		200.00	4.00	196.00
	15	108	Jerry Hale	Salaries Expense . . .	611	250.00			250.00
	20	109	Wycoff & Co.	Wycoff & Co.	✓		150.00	3.00	147.00
	28	110	Smith & Co.	Smith & Co.	✓		300.00	6.00	294.00
	28		Totals			290.00	650.00	13.00	927.00
						(✓)	(212)	(513)	(111)

Individual amounts in the Other Accounts Debit column and Accounts Payable Debit column are posted daily.

Totals posted at the end of the month.

Accounts Payable Ledger

Acme Mfg. Company

Date		PR	Debit	Credit	Balance
Feb.	5	P1		200.00	200.00
	15	D2	200.00		–0–
	25	P1		100.00	100.00

H. A. Green Company

Date		PR	Debit	Credit	Balance
Feb.	28	P1		225.00	225.00

Horn Supply Company

Date		PR	Debit	Credit	Balance
Feb.	3	P1		350.00	350.00

Smith & Company

Date		PR	Debit	Credit	Balance
Feb.	20	P1		300.00	300.00
	28	D2	300.00		–0–

Wycoff & Company

Date		PR	Debit	Credit	Balance
Feb.	13	P1		150.00	150.00
	20	D2	150.00		–0–

General Ledger

Cash   No. 111

Date		PR	Debit	Credit	Balance
Feb.	28	R2	19,770.00		19,770.00
	28	D2		927.00	18,843.00

Accounts Payable   No. 212

Date		PR	Debit	Credit	Balance
Feb.	28	P1		1,325.00	1,325.00
	28	D2	650.00		675.00

Purchases   No. 511

Date		PR	Debit	Credit	Balance
Feb.	12	D2	25.00		25.00
	28	P1	1,150.00		1,175.00

Purchases Discounts   No. 513

Date		PR	Debit	Credit	Balance
Feb.	28	D2		13.00	13.00

Transportation-In   No. 514

Date		PR	Debit	Credit	Balance
Feb.	3	D2	15.00		15.00

Salaries Expense   No. 611

Date		PR	Debit	Credit	Balance
Feb.	15	D2	250.00		250.00

Illustration 6–5
Schedule of accounts payable, December 31, 19——

Acme Mfg. Company	100
H. A. Green Company	225
Horn Supply Company	350
Total accounts payable	$675

To post a Cash Disbursements Journal or Cheque Register like Illustration 6–4, you do the following. Each day, post the individual amounts in the Other Accounts column to the debit of the general ledger accounts named. Also on a daily basis, post the individual amounts in the Accounts Payable column to the subsidiary Accounts Payable Ledger as debits to the named creditors' accounts. At the end of the month, after you crossfoot the column totals, post the Accounts Payable column total to the debit of the Accounts Payable controlling account. Then, credit the Purchases Discounts column total to the Purchases Discounts account, and credit the Cash column total to the Cash account. Since the items in the Other Accounts column are posted individually, the column total is not posted.

Testing the Accuracy of the Ledgers

Explain how to test the accuracy of the account balances in the Accounts Receivable and Accounts Payable Ledgers and prepare schedules of the accounts in each subsidiary ledger. (L. O. 3)

Periodically, after all posting is completed, the account balances in the General Ledger and the subsidiary ledgers should be tested for accuracy. To do this, you first prepare a trial balance of the General Ledger to confirm that debits equal credits. If the trial balance balances, the accounts in the General Ledger, including the controlling accounts, are assumed to be correct. Then you test the subsidiary ledgers by preparing schedules of accounts receivable and accounts payable. To prepare a **schedule of accounts payable**, for example, you list the Accounts Payable Ledger accounts with balances and calculate the sum of the balances. If the total is equal to the balance of the Accounts Payable controlling account, the accounts in the Accounts Payable Ledger are assumed to be correct. Illustration 6–5 shows a schedule of accounts payable drawn from the Accounts Payable Ledger of Illustration 6–4. A **schedule of accounts receivable** is prepared in the same way as a schedule of accounts payable. Also, if its total equals the balance of the Accounts Receivable controlling account, the accounts in the Accounts Receivable Ledger are assumed to be correct.

Sales Taxes

Most provinces require retailers to collect sales taxes from their customers and periodically remit these taxes to the provincial treasurer. When a columnar Sales Journal is used, a record of taxes collected can be obtained by adding special columns in the journal as shown in Illustration 6–6.

Illustration 6–6

Sales Journal

Date	Account Debited	Invoice No.	PR	Accounts Receivable Debit	Sales Taxes Payable Credit	Sales Credit
Dec. 1	D. R. Horn	7-1698		103.00	3.00	100.00

In posting the journal, the individual amounts in the Accounts Receivable column are posted daily to customer accounts in the Accounts Receivable Ledger. Then, at the end of the month, you post the column total to the Accounts Receivable controlling account. The individual amounts in the Sales Taxes Payable and Sales columns are not posted. Instead, at the end of the month, you credit the total of the Sales Taxes Payable column to the Sales Taxes Payable account, and credit the total of the Sales column to Sales.

A business that collects sales taxes on its cash sales may add a special Sales Taxes Payable column in its Cash Receipts Journal.

Using Sales Invoices as a Sales Journal

To save labour, you may avoid using a Sales Journal for credit sales. Instead, you can post each sales invoice total directly to the customer's account in a subsidiary Accounts Receivable Ledger. Then, copies of the invoices are bound in numerical order in a binder. At the end of the month, all the invoices of that month are totaled, and you make a general journal entry to debit Accounts Receivable and credit Sales for the total. In effect, the bound invoice copies act as a Sales Journal. Such a procedure is known as direct posting of sales invoices.

Sales Returns

If a business has only a few sales returns, you may record them in a General Journal with an entry like the following:

Oct.	17	Sales Returns and Allowances	412	17.50	
		Accounts Receivable—George Ball	112/√		17.50
		Customer returned merchandise			

The debit of the entry is posted to the Sales Returns and Allowances account. The credit is posted both to the Accounts Receivable controlling account and to the customer's account. Note the account number and the check mark, 112/√, in the PR column on the credit line. This indicates that both the Accounts Receivable controlling account in the General Ledger and the George Ball account in the Accounts Receivable Ledger were credited for $17.50.

Illustration 6–7

Sales Returns and Allowances Journal

Date		Account Credited	Explanation	Credit Memo No.	PR	Amount
Oct.	7	Robert Moore	Defective merchandise . . .	203	√	10.00
	14	James Warren	Defective merchandise . . .	204	√	12.00
	18	T. M. Jones	Not ordered	205	√	6.00
	23	Sam Smith	Defective merchandise . . .	206	√	18.00
	31	Sales Returns and Allowances, Dr.; Accounts Receivable, Cr.				46.00
						(412/112)

Companies that have sufficient sales returns can save posting labor by recording them in a special Sales Returns and Allowances Journal like the one in Illustration 6–7. Note that this is in keeping with the idea that a company can design and use a special journal for any group of similar transactions if there are enough transactions to warrant the journal. When a Sales Returns and Allowances Journal is used to record returns, the amounts entered in the journal are posted daily to the customers' accounts. At the end of the month, the journal total is debited to Sales Returns and Allowances and credited to Accounts Receivable.

General Journal Entries

When special journals are used, a General Journal always is necessary for adjusting, closing, and correcting entries and for a few transactions that cannot be recorded in the special journals. Examples of such transactions would be purchases returns and purchases of plant assets, which would be recorded as follows:

Oct.	8	Accounts Payable—Medford Company	212/√	32.00	
		Purchases Returns and Allowances	512		32.00
		Returned defective merchandise.			
	11	Office Equipment	133	685.00	
		Accounts Payable—ABC Supply Co.	212/√		685.00
		Purchased a typewriter.			

Computerized Data Processing

Describe how data are processed in computerized accounting systems. (L. O. 4)

Manual accounting systems like the ones described thus far are used only by small businesses. In fact, even very small businesses now are able to use computers to process their accounting data. Computerized data processing allows data to be entered in the system, classified, stored, and summarized on printed reports with very little human intervention. A computer is capable of—

1. Inputing and storing data.
2. Performing arithmetic calculations on the data.

3. Comparing units of the data to find which are larger or smaller.
4. Sorting or rearranging data.
5. Printing reports from the data stored in the machine.

Computers vary in size and in the speed with which they process data. They range from small desktop microcomputers to machines that with their peripheral equipment occupy a large room. Peripheral equipment includes devices to input or output data and to store data on reels of magnetic tape or on magnetic disks.

Data may be entered into a computer by means of a computer terminal, with previously prepared punched cards, reels of magnetic tape, magnetic disks, and in other ways. For example, one means of entry is to use a laser beam that reads a bar code such as is found on many consumer products.

Inside the computer each alphabetical letter or numerical digit of data becomes a combination of electrical or magnetic states that the computer can manipulate at very high rates of speed. Computers can do thousands or even millions of additions, subtractions, multiplications, and divisions per second, all without error in a predetermined sequence according to instructions stored in the machine.

A computer can do nothing without a previously prepared set of instructions that is entered and stored in the computer. However, with a properly prepared program of instructions, a computer will accept data, store and process the data, and produce the processed results in the form of a report displayed on a monitor, or typed out on an electric typewriter at the rate of approximately 10 characters per second, or printed by a laser printer at up to 2,000 lines per minute.

The Program

A **computer program** is a set of instructions written in a language the computer "understands." Some of the widely used languages are COBOL, BASIC, RPG, and FORTRAN. The instructions specify each operation a computer is to perform and are entered into the computer before the data to be processed. The program may contain only a few or several thousand detailed instructions. For example, the following shows the steps that must be programmed to have a computer process customers' orders for merchandise.

Instructions to Be Programmed for Processing Customers' Orders

1. For the first item on the customer's order, compare the quantity ordered with the quantity on hand as shown by inventory data stored in the computer.
    a. If the quantity ordered is not on hand:
       (1) Prepare a back order notifying the customer that the goods are not available but will be shipped as soon as a new supply is received.
       (2) Go to the next item on the customer's order.
    b. If the quantity on hand is greater than the amount ordered:
       (1) Deduct the amount ordered from the amount on hand.
       (2) Prepare instructions to ship the goods.

(3) Compare the amount of the item remaining after filling the customer's order with the reorder point for the item.
   (a) If the amount remaining is greater than the reorder point:
      1. Go to the next item on the customer's order.
   (b) If the amount remaining is less than the reorder point:
      1. Compute the amount to be purchased and prepare documents for the purchase.
      2. Go to the next item on the customer's order.

In addition to these instructions, a program for processing customer orders would have instructions for preparing invoices, recording sales, and updating customer accounts.

Designing the Program

Computers have the ability to compare two numbers and decide which is larger. This ability makes it possible for the computer to process data one way or another, depending on the result of the comparison. Note that this ability to compare numbers is essential if the comptuer is to follow instructions such as those for processing customer orders.

If a computer is to process data correctly, a person (the programmer) must first design a program for the computer to follow. In designing the program, the programmer determines in advance the alternative sets of calculations or processing steps to be made. Then, the programmer must devise the appropriate comparisons that will identify the circumstances under which each particular set of processing steps should be performed. Finally, the programmer must write specific instructions telling the computer how to process the data. A computer can follow through the program's maze of decisions and alternate instructions rapidly and accurately. However, if it encounters an exception not anticipated in the program, it is helpless and can only process the exception incorrectly or stop.

Modes of Operation

Computers operate in one of two modes: either **batch processing** or **online processing.** In the batch mode, the program and data to be processed are inputed to the computer, processed, and then removed from the computer before another batch is begun. Then, the program for a new job and a new set of data are entered, and the new job is processed. Batch processing may result in customers' orders being processed daily, the payroll being run each week, financial statements being prepared monthly, and the processing of other jobs on a periodic basis. Because transactions are processed in groups or batches, this mode of operation may require less computer capacity, is usually less expensive than online operation, and is used when an immediate processing or an immediate computer response is not required.

In online processing, the program is kept in the computer along with any required data. As new data are entered, they are instantly processed by the computer. For example, in some department stores, the cash registers are connected directly into the store's computer. In addition to cash sales, the

Illustration 6–8
Machine-readable inventory tag

registers are used as follows in recording charge sales: After the customer selects merchandise for purchase, the salesperson uses the customer's plastic credit card to print the customer's name on a blank sales ticket. The sales ticket is then placed in the Forms Printer of the cash register, and the sale is recorded. The register prints all pertinent information on the sales ticket and totals it. In order to finalize the sale, controls within the register require that the salesperson depress the proper register keys to record the customer's account number. This, in effect, posts the sale to the customer's account. The salesperson does not actually post to the account. Rather, the data entered with the cash register's keys causes the store's computer to update the customer's account. The computer will also produce the customer's month-end statement, ready for mailing.

Another example of online operation is found in supermarkets, where each item of merchandise is imprinted with a machine-readable inventory tag similar to Illustration 6–8. At one of the store's checkout stands, each item of merchandise selected by a customer is passed over an optical scanner in the countertop, or an optical scanner in a wand is passed over each item's price tag. This actuates the cash register and eliminates the need for handkeying information into the register. It also transmits the sales information to a computer that updates the store's inventory records and prepares orders to a central warehouse to restock any item in low supply. At closing time, the computer prints out detailed summaries of the day's sales and item inventories. It thus provides management with up-to-the-minute information that could not otherwise be obtained.

Other examples of online operations are found in banks, airlines, and factories. However, all have the same results: they reduce human labor, create more accurate records, and provide management with both better and more up-to-date reports. Furthermore, when there are sufficient transactions, they do the work at less cost per transaction.

Time Sharing

Computer service companies provide computer service to many concerns on a time-sharing basis, using computers that are capable of working on many jobs simultaneously. In providing such service, the computer service company installs an input-output device on the premises of a subscriber to its service. The

AS A MATTER OF ETHICS

A public accountant has a client whose business has grown significantly over the last couple of years and has reached the point where its accounting system has become inadequate for handling both the volume of transactions and management's needs for financial information. The client asks the accountant for advice on which software system would work best for the company.

The accountant has been offered a 10% commission by a software company for each purchase of its system by one of the accountant's clients. The price of one of these systems falls within the range specified by the client. Do you think that the accountant's evaluation of the alternative systems could be affected by this commission arrangement? Should it be? Should the accountant feel compelled to tell the client about the commission arrangement before making a recommendation?

input-output device is connected to the service company's computer by means of a telephone line. The subscriber uses the input-output device to input data into the service company's computer. The data is held in storage there until processing time is available, usually within a few seconds. The computer then processes the data and transmits the results to the subscriber. For this service the subscriber pays a monthly fee plus a charge for the computer time used.

Through **time sharing**, a growing number of concerns are using computers, even very small businesses. For example, a dentist or a physician practicing alone is a small business. Yet a significant number of such dentists and physicians have their accounts receivable and customer billing done by computer service companies.

Microcomputers

Another important factor leading to the expanded use of computers is the development of microcomputers. These computers have become less expensive in recent years and are now affordable by very small businesses and individuals. As more and more people become proficient in using these machines, manual accounting systems are being replaced by computerized systems.

Recording Actual Transactions

Depending on the accounting system of a business, transactions may be recorded manually in a General Journal or in special journals. Also, if the accounting system is computerized, the recording of transactions must be done in a form that is acceptable to the company's computer. Nevertheless, in the remainder of this text, we use general journal entries to illustrate the recording of most transactions. The general journal entries are intended to show the items increased and decreased by the transactions.

Summary of the Chapter in Terms of Learning Objectives

1. Columnar journals are designed so that repetitive debits to a specific account are entered in a separate column. The same is done for repetitive credits. When special journals are used, all credit sales are entered in a Sales Journal. Credit purchases of merchandise and usually of supplies are entered in a Purchases Journal. All cash receipts are entered in the Cash Receipts Journal, and all cash payments, except for those from petty cash, are entered in the Cash Disbursements Journal (or Cheque Register). Any transactions that cannot be entered in the special journals are entered in the General Journal.

To enter a transaction when special journals are used, you first decide which journal must be used. Then, the transaction is recorded in accordance with the columns provided in the journal and the nature of the transaction.

2. When transactions are posted from special journals to the accounts, individual debits and credits to subsidiary Accounts Receivable and Accounts Payable Ledgers are posted daily. Other amounts that must be posted individually also may be posted daily. Normally, the columns of each special journal are totaled and crossfooted at the end of each month. Then, the column totals are posted to the appropriate general ledger accounts.

3. To test the accuracy of a subsidiary ledger after all posting is completed, you prepare a schedule of the accounts in the ledger and compare the total of the account balances with the balance in the related controlling account. If they are not equal, you know an error has been made. If they are equal, you assume the balances are correct.

4. In a computerized accounting system, data may be entered in the computer in a variety of ways, such as from a terminal, punched cards, magnetic tape, magnetic disk storage, or laser beam scanners. Following the instructions contained in the computer program, the computer accepts, classifies, and stores the data and prepares summarized reports that may be printed or displayed on a monitor.

Appendix E

APPLICATION PROGRAMS FOR BUSINESS

Explain how micro-
computers can be used in
the accounting process.
(L. O. 6)

Numerous application programs run on microcomputers. These application programs include accounting and business software, graphics software, statistical software, education software, and games. The concern in this appendix is the accounting software. Accounting programs are used to manage the accounting records of a business.

Features of Accounting Programs

Accounting programs can be used to computerize a company's accounting system. Automated transaction processing is faster and more accurate than manual methods. Accounting programs can be used to manage the major accounting applications of general ledger, accounts payable, accounts receivable, inventory, payroll, and job costing. The better built accounting systems integrate these major accounting applications.

The term *integrate* refers to an accounting system that links the general ledger, accounts payable, accounts receivable, inventory, payroll, and job costing programs. Information (usually in the form of transactions) can be posted from one program to another automatically (without rekeying). Almost all integrated accounting systems available on microcomputers permit individual programs to run independently as well as enable the user to add programs later. Accounting systems that are not integrated require information to be rekeyed from one program to another. Such systems are not as desirable as integrated ones.

Basic Features of Accounting Programs

An accounting system is usually made up of a collection of programs that accept and keep financial transactions. Most accounting systems provide menus that are displayed on the screen. By selecting one of the choices presented in a menu, users can direct the accounting system to take a specific action—for example, accept new transactions from the keyboard, post a batch of transactions into the general ledger, or print a set of financial statements. A computerized accounting system stores information in files. A file is a collection of related information saved on a disk. In general, three types of files are used:

1. *Profile file*. A file that keeps permanent information on the company, such as company name, address, and fiscal periods.
2. *Master file*. A file that keeps the information essential for the operation of the accounting program. The information stored in a master file is permanent, and it is usually organized into accounts. The following are examples of the various master files:
   a. The master file of a general ledger program keeps information on the *chart of accounts* and the account balances.
   b. The master file of an accounts payable keeps information on the *vendors* and account balances.
   c. The master file of an accounts receivable keeps information on the *customers* and account balances.
   d. The master file of an inventory system keeps information on the *inventory* items, cost, markup, and count.
3. *Transaction file*. A file that holds detailed information on transactions. The information stored in a transaction file is not permanent. A transaction file is purged after all the totals have been distributed to the master file and an audit trail has been printed. The transaction file of a general ledger holds records of invoices and payment receipts.

An integrated accounting system is generally designed so that a transaction only needs to be entered into the system once. A transaction is the entry of a single value (either debit or credit) into the computer files. Therefore, a journal entry is represented by two transactions; for example:

Journal Entry on Paper.

Interest Expense.	500.00	
Bond Interest Payable		500.00

Transactions. The following illustrates how to enter the above journal entry into a computerized accounting system. The text on the left would appear on the screen as ''prompts'' to the accountant. The actual keystrokes used to enter the figures as shown in boldface.

```
Transaction Number  [   1]
Account           [      750]
Amount    Dr.[    50000]     Cr.[              ]

Transaction Number  [   2]
Account           [      550]
Amount      Dr.[         ]     Cr.[    50000]
```

Most accounting systems have built-in facilities to control the posting of transaction entries so the general ledger is always in balance. For an integrated accounting system, transaction files (say, in the general ledger program and accounts receivable program) are cross-referenced by account numbers so account balances from one program can be posted to another automatically.

For some accounting systems (e.g., ACCPAC, a popular accounting system), transactions are entered into an accounting system via a *video form*, also known as a *video screen*, or *input screen*. A video form is functionally equivalent to a paper form. Some accounting systems use on-screen dialogues instead of video forms—instead of ''filling'' a video form, users type the answers to the questions presented on the screen.

General Ledger Programs

The general ledger (G/L) is the heart of an integrated accounting system. Like the manually kept general ledger, it keeps all the financial records of a business. The master file of a general ledger program is the chart of accounts. The major activities carried out by the general ledger program can be grouped into four types:

1. Transaction processing.
2. Account posting.
3. Working paper printing.
4. Financial statement preparation.

Illustration E–1 shows the flow of activities of a typical general ledger program.

Some general ledger programs provide flexible numbering for the chart of accounts, while some use account names rather than account numbers. Many programs can handle data identified by department. Department codes are usually coded into account numbers. Some general ledger programs use fixed account number ranges; for example, account numbers 100 to 199 are reserved for assets; 200 to 299, for liabilities; and so on. Although most businesses can work within this constraint, it is an undesirable feature of an accounting program. All except the very basic general ledger programs can handle a large number of accounts. A general ledger program that can handle only a small number of accounts is usually not worthwhile.

Illustration E–1
General ledger activity chart

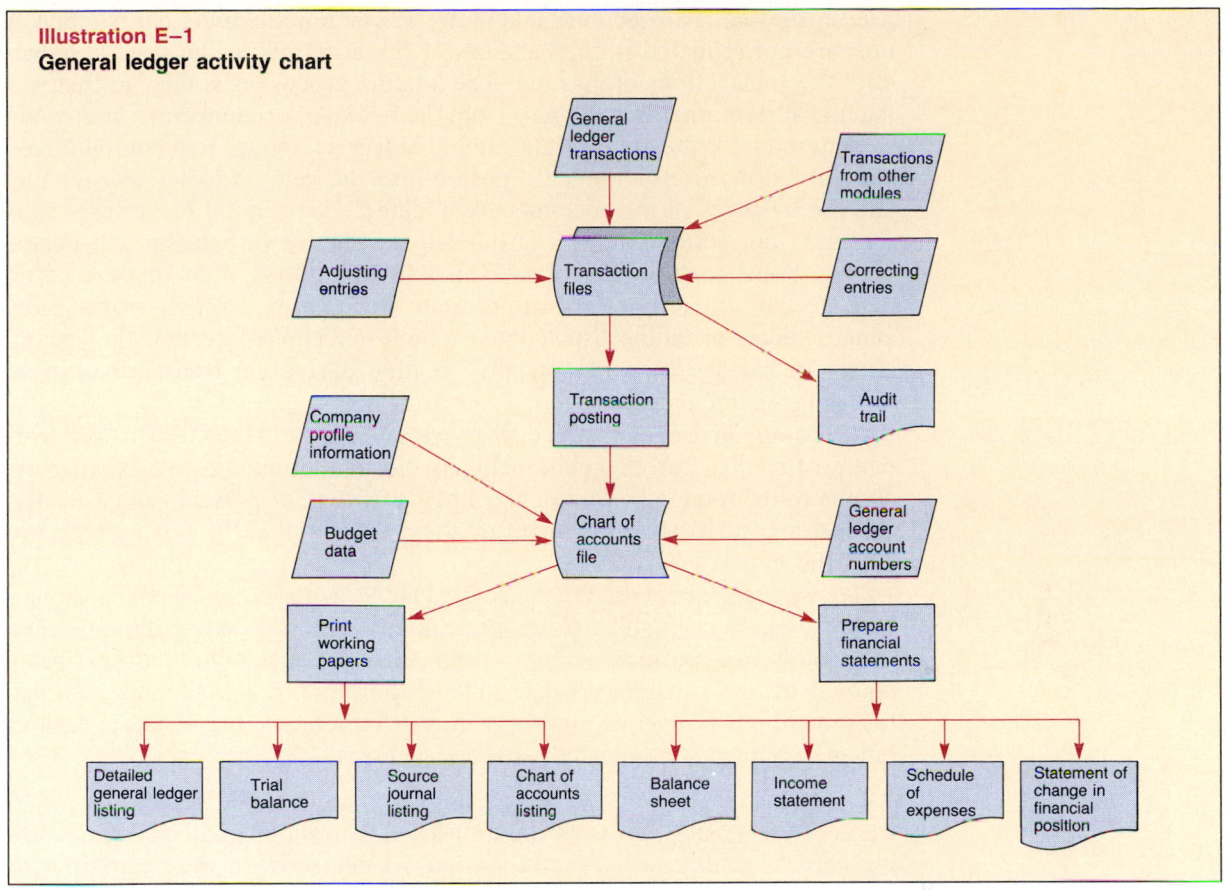

Transaction Processing. Many general ledger programs use transaction batches. A transaction *batch* is a group of transactions usually but not necessarily related by activity or by date. Transaction batches are held in the transaction file until posted to the general ledger. Transactions held in the transaction file can be edited anytime prior to posting to the master file of the general ledger. For an integrated accounting system, the general ledger program also accepts transaction batches from other programs such as accounts receivable or accounts payable. Some general ledger programs accept transactions directly into the transaction file without going through batches. Many general ledger programs can handle transactions that recur monthly. Many expenses that occur once a year but are distributed on a monthly basis can be structured as recurring transactions; for example, monthly distribution of insurance costs, fixed asset depreciation, and payable accruals.

For most general ledger programs running on a hard disk, the maximum number of transactions per fiscal period is only limited by the amount of hard disk space available. Because of the limited amount of storage space on floppy disks, there is usually some restriction on the number of transactions per fiscal period.

Account Posting. Transactions held in the transaction file (whether batched or not) are not reflected in the balances of the accounts in the general ledger until the transactions are posted. The posting process is similar to that in a manual system; that is, the totals from the books of original entry are posted to (entered into) the appropriate general ledger accounts. In a computerized general ledger, transactions are posted into the general ledger master file, and the balances of the accounts are updated. For general ledger programs that use transaction batches, any batch that is not in balance will not be posted. Some general ledger programs will post transactions that are not in balance but will provide the appropriate warning or error message. Such general ledger programs usually have a built-in means of keeping the general ledger in balance by automatically creating correcting transactions in an error-correcting account.

All computerized general ledger programs have a means to perform year-end posting. This process automatically closes the income and expense accounts to the retained earnings accounts at the end of a fiscal year. Usually, the income and expense accounts are then zeroed out in the general ledger to start the new fiscal year.

Transactions are posted to the general ledger without the use of subsidiary ledgers. Instead of subsidiary ledgers, many general ledger programs allow the grouping of transactions into *source journals,* each source journal being equivalent to a subsidiary ledger. These source journals, such as cash disbursement, cash receipts, and payroll distribution, are not separate entities but merely names associated with transactions.

Working Paper Printing. Most accounting systems print an audit trail and working papers on demand. Printed journal listings provide the audit trail for internal control purposes. To enforce an audit trail, many general ledger programs require that the posted transactions be printed before they can be purged (deleted) from the transaction file. The transaction listing forms part of the working file for the auditor.

Other working papers produced by most general ledger programs include:

1. Detailed general ledger listing.
2. Trial balance.
3. Listing of the source journals.
4. Chart of account listing.

As explained in this chapter, in a manual accounting system of any size, transaction details are usually kept in subsidiary ledgers. To review transactions, the subsidiary ledgers must be examined. In a computerized general ledger, transactions are reviewed by examining a printout called the *general ledger listing,* which provides a list of all transactions posted to the general ledger accounts. Most general ledger programs permit the user to select all accounts or ranges of accounts for the general ledger listing. Some programs permit the listing of transactions for specified fiscal periods.

With a manual system, a *trial balance* is prepared at the end of an accounting period after all of the regular entries have been entered into the general ledger. As described in Chapter 2, a trial balance is a work sheet used to verify that the debits equal the credits in the general ledger. A trial balance is used to review accounting balances and prepare adjusting entries before the financial statements are prepared. Doing a trial balance by hand can be time-consuming and frustrating, particularly if it does not balance. A computerized general ledger system can produce a trial balance by a few simple keystrokes. Because the general ledger is always in balance, the debits and credits in such a trial balance always match. The trial balance in a general ledger system is used to review account balances. Almost all general ledger systems permit the listing of the trial balance at any time.

Source journals are used in general ledger programs to group transactions of the same nature, much the same way subsidiary ledgers do. Most general ledger programs provide a facility to print a *source journal listing*, which shows all the transactions belonging to the same source journal.

The *chart of accounts listing* is a handy reference when entering transactions into the transaction file. All general ledger programs provide a means of listing the chart of accounts on the printer. The information printed usually includes all the general ledger accounts in numeric sequence (or alphabetical order if numbers are not used for accounts), account name, and type.

Financial Statement Preparation. One of the major differences between general ledger programs is in the preparation of financial statements. Many general ledger programs provide standard formats for financial statements as well as some means of customizing these statements. Some formats offer very limited capabilities in customizing financial statements; others offer powerful but complex commands. A kind of specification language for the user to indicate required statement format is often provided in the program. A specification language is similar to a programming langue—it is used to control how financial statements appear. Unfortunately, most specification languages require practice before they can be mastered. The ability to customize financial reports is one of the most important features to consider in selecting a computerized general ledger program. Such a function must be easy to use but powerful enough to meet all of a company's statement preparation needs. Financial statement formats available from most general ledger programs include:

1. Balance sheet.
2. Income statement.
3. Schedule of expenses.
4. Statement of changes in financial position.

All the popular general ledger programs provide a means of producing statements that compare the current period with prior periods. Some of the more sophisticated general ledger programs include the capability to produce financial statements for any prior period (within certain limits) as well as for the current period. Many programs provide a means to enter budget figures into the general ledger accounts and to produce statements comparing the actual figures with the budget.

The ability to group several accounts into one entry in the financial statements is an important feature. For example, in a balance sheet, it may be desirable to show the total for all current asset accounts in one line. Different general ledger programs offer various capabilities to show subtotals and totals. For the income statement, subtotals and totals should be provided for gross income, cost of goods sold, administrative and selling expenses, and net income. For the balance sheet, subtotals and totals should be provided for current assets, fixed assets, and total assets on the asset side; and current liabilities, long-term liabilities, equity, and retained earnings on the liabilities and equity side. In general, the more sophisticated the financial statement preparation capabilities of the general ledger program, the harder the program is to learn. Ideally, the general ledger program should combine sophisticated format control with ease of use.

Accounts Receivable Programs

Managing accounts receivable is a critical activity for many enterprises. In many integrated accounting systems, the accounts receivable program can be used separately. Later, when the general ledger program is added, the accounts receivable program can be integrated into the general ledger program with relative ease. Some businesses start computerizing their accounting systems by installing the accounts receivable program first. The following are activities carried out by the accounts receivable program:

1. Invoice processing.
2. Payment receipts.
3. Report printing.
4. Interface to the general ledger.

Illustration E–2 shows the flow of activities in a typical accounts receivable program. The customer file contains the key information for an accounts receivable program. This information usually includes customer number, customer name, address, telephone number, contact person, year-to-date sales, and credit limit. The customer file should be able to handle the company's total number of customers. However, the customer file in some accounts receivable programs has a very limited capacity. On a hard disk, the maximum number of vendors and invoices is only limited by the amount of space available. Many small businesses can work quite comfortably within this space. Floppy disks, however, place more restrictions on how many transactions can be stored. A good accounts receivable program should show the user how to determine the maximum number of transactions permissible for either a hard or floppy disk.

Invoice Processing. There are basically three types of accounts receivable transactions: (1) invoices, (2) cash receipts, and (3) adjustments. As with general ledger programs, some accounts receivable programs require that invoices and adjustments be entered in batches. Others allow direct entry into the transaction file. In either case, the entries in the transaction file can be modified before they are posted to the customer file. In order to provide an audit trail, transactions posted to the customer file are usually printed. Invoice information that needs to be entered includes customer number, invoice number, invoice date, and invoice amount.

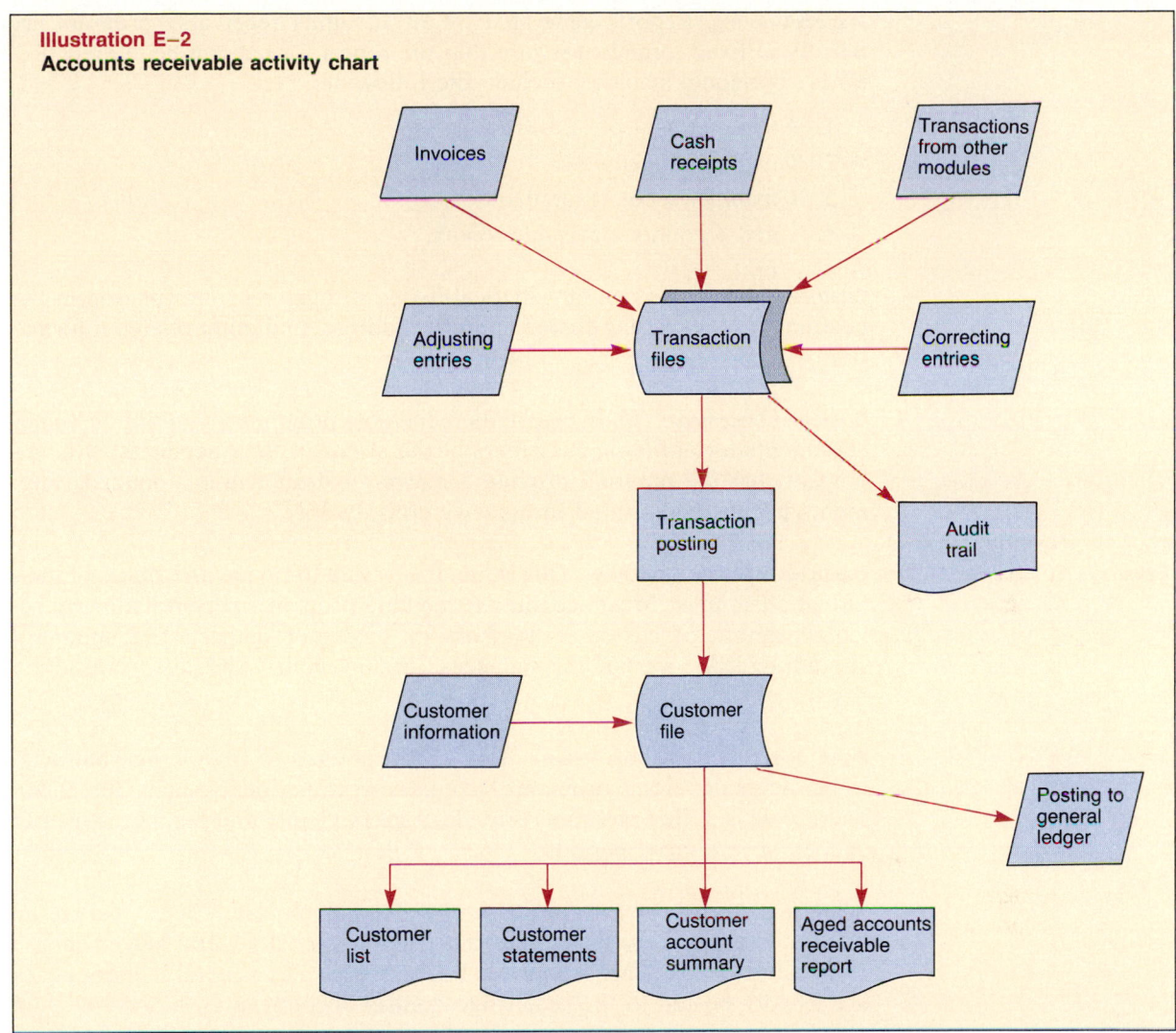

Illustration E–2
Accounts receivable activity chart

Payment Receipts. Two methods of accounting for payment receipts are normally used. One is the *open item* method, in which payment receipts are matched to open invoices. The other is the *balance forward* method, in which payment receipts are applied to customers' account balances. Many accounts receivable programs can handle either method. To record a payment for the open item method, the payment receipts must be credited against an open invoice. In this case, the customer number and invoice number must be specified. If the balance forward method is used, the customer number is the key for recording the payment. The accounts receivable program must also provide a means of recording miscellaneous cash transactions, including cash sales and interest.

Report Printing. Reports generated by an accounts receivable program are usually in fixed format; it is rare that the report format can be altered. Reports commonly available include the following:

1. Customer list.
2. Customer statements.
3. Customer account summary.
4. Aged accounts receivable report.

Customer List. This is an alphabetical listing of customer information in the customer file, including customer name, address, and other related information.

Customer Statements. Many accounts receivable programs can print customer statements for notifying customers of the status of their accounts. It is important that the program provide a means of designing customized statements because preprinted forms vary considerably.

Customer Account Summary. This summary is used to review the status of individual customers. Most accounts receivable programs permit listing by selected ranges of customer numbers or customer names. The summary should include outstanding balances, credit limits, and last transaction dates.

Aged Accounts Receivable Report. This report is used to review overdue customer accounts. Some programs have fixed aged periods, usually 30, 60, 90, and 120 days. Other programs provide more flexibility and permit the user to specify several aged periods.

Interface to General Ledger. An accounts receivable program that is part of an integrated accounting system can automatically post general ledger entries resulting from accounts receivable transactions. The general ledger entries are usually posted to the receivable control account, a cash account, and possibly an interest account and a discount account. Some integrated accounting systems have predetermined general ledger accounts for posting from the accounts receivable program; others allow these accounts to be specified at system setup time.

Accounts Payable Program

Any business that handles a large number of cheques and has a multitude of vendors should consider using a computerized accounts payable program. An accounts payable program can be used to optimize the timing of payments and to take maximum advantage of early payment discounts. It can also be used to plan cash requirements. Many accounts receivable programs also print cheques and cheque registers. In many integrated accounting systems, the accounts payable program can run separately or as one part of the integrated accounting system. In the latter case, the accounts payable program accumulates and summarizes general ledger entries that result from accounts payable

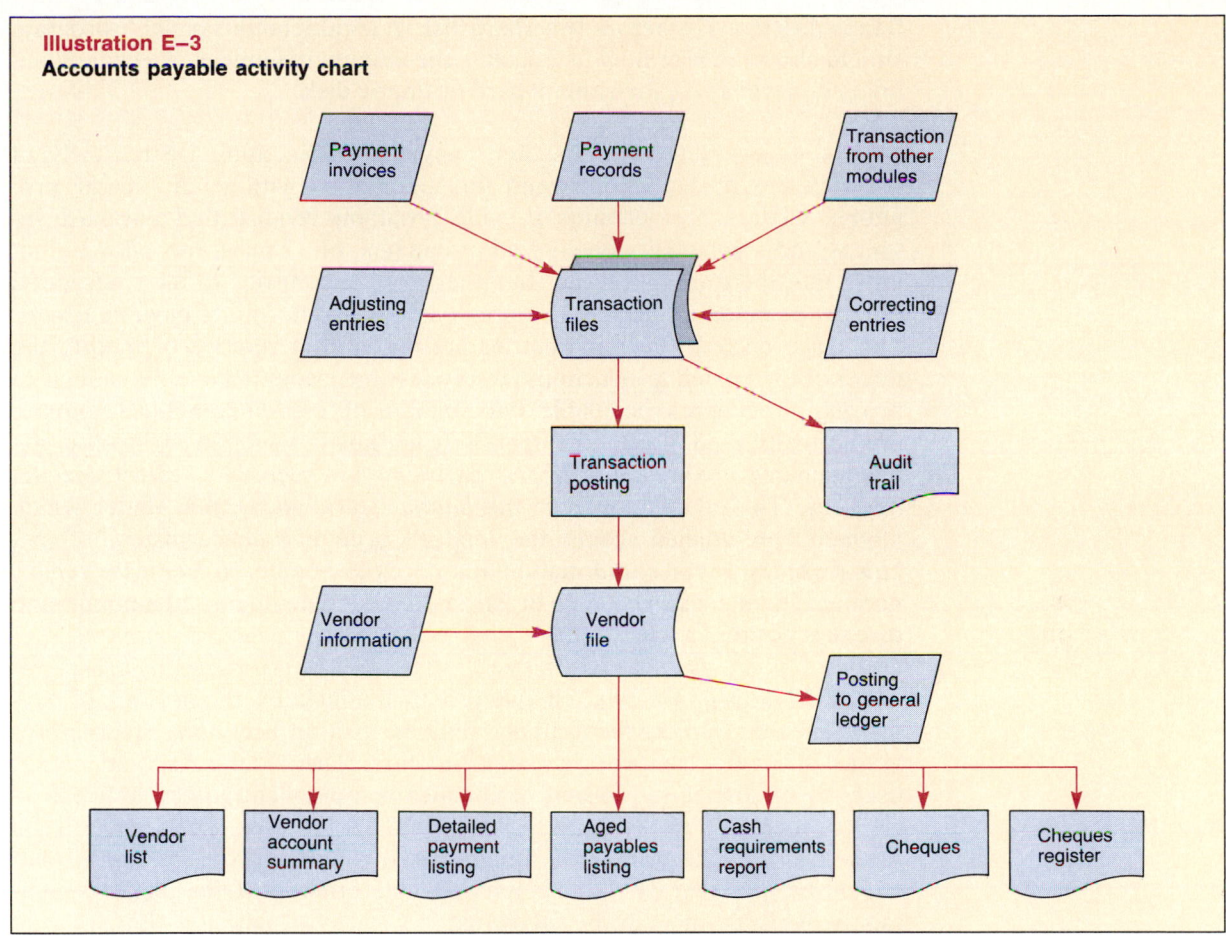

Illustration E–3
Accounts payable activity chart

transactions. Usually only the totals are posted to the general ledger control accounts. In this manner, the accounts payable program keeps the accounts payable subsidiary ledger used in manual accounting systems. The major activities carried out by the accounts payable program are:

1. Payment invoice processing.
2. Cheque processing.
3. Report printing.
4. Interface to the general ledger.

Illustration E–3 shows the flow of activities of a typical accounts payable program.

The vendor file contains the key information for an accounts payable program including vendor number, vendor name, address, telephone number, contact person, and terms of payment. It is important that the vendor file be able to handle the total number of vendors for the business. The vendor file in some accounts payable programs has a very limited capacity. The maximum number of vendors and invoices is more limited if the vendor file is stored on a floppy disk than if it is stored on a hard disk. A good accounts payable program should show the user how to calculate the maximum number of vendors and invoices permissible for either a hard or floppy disk.

Payment Invoice Processing. Accounts payable transactions are basically of two types: purchase invoices and adjustments. As with general ledger programs, while some accounts payable programs require that purchase invoices and adjustments be entered in batches, other programs allow direct entry into the transaction file. In either case, the entries in the transaction file can be modified before they are posted to the accounts payable master file. Once posted, reversing entries are required to remove or modify the effect of the posted transactions. In processing accounts payable, similar to processing accounts receivable, two methods of recording payment invoices are normally used. One is the *open item* method in which every transaction has a unique invoice number and payments are recorded against specific invoices. The other method is the *balance forward* method under which payments are applied against the vendor's account balance instead of specific invoices. Invoice information that needs to be entered includes: vendor number, invoice number, date invoice received, date due, total amount, and discount option.

Cheque Processing. Usually, cheque processing includes the printing of payment cheques and payment advice notices. Not all accounts payable programs include a cheque-processing function. The program should permit users to customize the format of cheques and payment advice notices.

Report Printing. The printing of an audit trail is an important safeguard that should be provided by the accounts payable program. Other reports commonly available include the following:

1. Vendor list.
2. Vendor account summary.
3. Detailed payment listing.
4. Aged payables listing.
5. Cash requirement report.

Vendor List. This is a listing of vendor information in alphabetical order from the vendor file. Vendor information printed includes vendor name, address, phone number, and contact person.

Vendor Account Summary. Usually, accounts payable programs provide a means to print a vendor account summary for selected vendors. Selection is either by vendor number or vendor name. The summary should at least include year-to-date purchases, total payment outstanding, and last payment date.

Detailed Payment. This listing is a printout of all outstanding payment invoices and associated transactions in the vendor accounts. Usually, only vendors with amounts owing are listed.

Aged Payable Listing. Most account payable programs provide some means to age outstanding payables. An aged payable listing is one such means. This report lists all outstanding payables, aged either by fixed time intervals (usually 30, 60, and 90 days) or by user specification.

Cash Requirement Report. One of the most useful reports from an accounts payable program is the cash requirement report. This report is used to plan cash requirements to pay the outstanding payables.

Interface to General Ledger. For an accounts payable program that is part of an integrated accounting system, this facility automatically summarizes and posts general ledger entries resulting from accounts payable transactions.

Summary of Appendix E in Terms of the Learning Objective

6. Microcomputers can be used to computerize a company's accounting system. Automated transaction processing is faster, more accurate, and labour-saving than manual methods. Accounting programs can be used to manage the major accounting applications of general ledger, accounts payable, accounts receivable, inventory, payroll, and job costing.

Glossary

Define or explain the words and phrases listed in the chapter Glossary. (L. O. 5)

Accounting system the business papers, records, reports, and procedures used by a business in recording transactions and reporting their effects. p. 275

Accounts Payable Ledger a subsidiary ledger having an account for each creditor. p. 282

Accounts Receivable Ledger a subsidiary ledger having an account for each customer. p. 277

Batch processing a mode of computer operation in which a program and data are entered in the computer, processed, and removed from the computer before the next program and data are entered. p. 289

Cheque Register a book of original entry for recording cash payments by cheque. p. 282

Columnar journal a book of original entry having columns, each of which is designated as the place for entering specific data about each transaction of a group of similar transactions. p. 277

Computer program a set of instructions that are entered into a computer and that specify the operations the computer is to perform. p. 288

Controlling account a general ledger account the balance of which (after posting) equals the sum of the balances of the accounts in a related subsidiary ledger, thereby proving the sum of those subsidiary account balances. p. 278

Crossfoot to add the Debit column totals of a journal, add the Credit column totals, and then compare the sums to prove that total debits equal total credits. p. 281

Foot to add a column of numbers. p. 281

General Ledger the ledger containing the financial statement accounts of a business. p. 277

Online processing a mode of computer operation in which the program and required data are maintained in the computer so that as new data are entered, they are processed instantly. p. 289

Schedule of accounts payable a list of the balances of all the accounts in the accounts payable ledger that is summed to show the total amount of accounts payable outstanding. p. 285

Schedule of accounts receivable a list of the balances of all the accounts in the accounts receivable ledger that is summed to show the total amount of accounts receivable outstanding. p. 285

Special journal a book of original entry that is designed and used for recording only a specified type of transaction. p. 275

Subsidiary ledger a group of accounts other than general ledger accounts which show the details underlying the balance of a controlling account in the General Ledger. p. 277

Time sharing a process by which several users of a computer, each having an input-output device, can input data into a single computer and, as processing time becomes available, have their data processed and transmitted back to their output device. p. 290

Questions for Class Discussion

1. What are three steps in the operation of an accounting system?
2. How does a columnar journal save posting labour?
3. Most transactions of a merchandising business fall into four groups. What are these four groups?
4. Why should sales to and receipts of cash from charge customers be recorded and posted daily?
5. What functions are served by the Accounts Receivable controlling account?
6. Both credits to customer accounts and credits to miscellaneous accounts are individually posted from a Cash Receipts Journal like that of Illustration 6–2. Why not put both kinds of credits in the same column and thus save journal space?
7. How is a multicolumn journal crossfooted? Why is such a journal crossfooted?
8. How is the equality of a controlling account and its subsidiary ledger accounts maintained?
9. Describe how copies of a company's sales invoices may be used as a Sales Journal.
10. When a general journal entry is used to record a returned charge sale, the credit of the entry must be posted twice. Does this cause the trial balance to be out of balance? Why or why not?
11. How does one tell from which journal a particular amount in a ledger account was posted?
12. How is a schedule of accounts payable prepared? How is it used to prove the balances of the creditor accounts in the Accounts Payable Ledger?
13. After all posting is completed, the balance of the Accounts Receivable controlling account does not agree with the sum of the balances in the Accounts Receivable Ledger. If the trial balance is in balance, where is the error apt to be?
14. Are computerized accounting systems used by small businesses?
15. What are some of the ways data can be entered into a computer?

Multiple Choice

1. When special journals are used:
   a. All sales transactions are recorded in the Sales Journal.
   b. All purchase transactions are recorded in the Purchases Journal.
   c. All cash payments by cheque are recorded in the Cash Disbursements Journal.
   d. All cash receipts except from cash sales of merchandise are recorded in the Cash Receipts Journal.
   e. A General Journal is not used.

2. If an accounting system includes an Accounts Receivable controlling account and an Accounts Receivable Ledger:
    a. Two accounts are debited when posting sales on credit.
    b. The rule that debits must equal credits is not maintained.
    c. Two accounts are debited when posting cash sales.
    d. Two accounts are credited when posting cash receipts from credit customers.
    e. Both (a) and (d) are correct.

3. When testing the accuracy of the balances in the Accounts Receivable Ledger:
    a. You know absolutely that an error has been made if the sum of the customer account balances does not equal the controlling account balance.
    b. You can be sure that transactions involving credit customers were correctly journalized if the sum of the customer account balances equals the balance in the controlling account.
    c. The sum of the balances in the customer accounts should equal the balance in the Sales account.
    d. You can be sure that transactions involving credit customers were correctly posted if the sum of the customer account balances equals the balance in the controlling account.
    e. You should foot and crossfoot each of the special journals.

4. In computerized accounting systems:
    a. At least five special journals are used.
    b. Errors are most often made in the process of posting transactions.
    c. A standard computer program is used by all businesses.
    d. Cash registers are used to enter all of a business's transactions in the accounting system.
    e. Errors in posting and in transferring account balances to financial reports are less apt to occur than they are in manual accounting systems.

5. A set of computer instructions for processing data is a:
    a. Working paper.
    b. Peripheral unit.
    c. Computer model.
    d. Computer program.
    e. None of the above.

6. The processing of data without human intervention is known as:
    a. General accounting processing.
    b. Objectivity processing.
    c. Automated data processing.
    d. Internal auditing.
    e. Intangible data processing.

Mini Discussion Case

Case 6–1

Two students were discussing the similarities and dissimillarities of manual and computerized accounting systems. Their discussion focused on the following:

a. Recording of data—use of specialized journals, etc.

b. Processing of data—posting, etc.

c. Necessity and function of trial balance.

d. Problems of tracing entries in connection with verification and tracing of errors.

Required

Present your comparison of the two systems focusing on the four areas given in the case.

Exercises

Exercise 6–1
Special journals
(L. O. 1)

A company that uses a Sales Journal, a Purchases Journal, a Cash Receipts Journal, a Cash Disbursements Journal, and a General Journal like the ones described in the chapter completed the following transactions. List the transactions by letter and opposite each letter give the name of the journal in which the transaction would be recorded.

a. Sold merchandise for cash.

b. Sold merchandise on credit.

c. Purchased merchandise on credit.

d. A customer returned merchandise sold for cash; a cheque was issued.

e. Paid a creditor.

f. Returned merchandise purchased on credit.

g. A customer paid for merchandise previously purchased on credit.

h. Purchased office supplies on credit.

i. Gave a customer credit for merchandise purchased on credit and returned.

j. Purchased office equipment on credit.

k. Recorded adjusting and closing entries.

Exercise 6–2
The Sales Journal
(L. O. 1)

A company uses a Sales Journal, a Purchases Journal, a Cash Receipts Journal, a Cash Disbursements Journal, and a General Journal. The following transactions occurred during the month of August:

Aug. 3 Purchased merchandise for $18 on credit from Z Company.
6 Sold merchandise to M. Isak for $35 cash, Invoice No. 15.
10 Sold merchandise to C. Judd for $135, terms 2/15, n/60, Invoice No. 16.
12 Borrowed $25 from the bank by giving a note to the bank.
14 Sold merchandise to S. Clark for $90, terms n/30, Invoice No. 17.

Aug. 20   Sold used store equipment to G Company for $150.
     25   Received $132.30 from C. Judd to pay for the purchase of August 10.
     31   Sold merchandise to B. Witten for $115, terms n/30, Invoice No. 18.

Required

On a sheet of notebook paper, draw a Sales Journal like the one that appears in Illustration 6–1. Journalize the transactions during August that should be recorded in the Sales Journal.

Exercise 6–3
The Cash Receipts Journal
(L. O. 1)

A company uses a Sales Journal, a Purchases Journal, a Cash Receipts Journal, a Cash Disbursements Journal, and a General Journal. The following transactions occurred during the month of August:

Aug. 3   L. Fox, the owner of the business, invested $30 in the business.
      6   Purchased merchandise for $18 on credit from J Company.
     10   Sold merchandise on credit to D. Roy for $12, subject to a $2 sales discount if paid by the end of the month.
     12   Borrowed $25 from the bank by giving a note to the bank.
     13   Sold merchandise to B. Maddox for $9 cash.
     27   Paid J Company $18 for the merchandise purchased on August 6.
     28   Received $10 from D. Roy to pay for the purchase of August 10.
     31   Paid salaries of $8.

Required

1. On a sheet of notebook paper, draw a multicolumn Cash Receipts Journal like the one that appears in Illustration 6–2. (Dollar amounts in this exercise are small so that you may use narrow columns.)

2. Journalize the transactions during August that should be recorded in the Cash Receipts Journal.

Exercise 6–4
The Purchases Journal
(L. O. 1)

A company uses a Sales Journal, a Purchases Journal, a Cash Receipts Journal, a Cash Disbursements Journal, and a General Journal. The following transactions occurred during the month of August:

Aug. 1   K. Neile, the owner of the business, invested $45 in the business.
      3   Purchased merchandise for $21 on credit from F Company, terms n/30.
      6   Purchased store supplies from P Company for $5 cash.
      8   Sold merchandise on credit to D. Saw for $15, subject to a $2 sales discount if paid by the end of the month.
     11   Purchased on credit from P Company office supplies for $6 and store supplies for $10, terms n/30.
     18   Sold merchandise to T. Rey for $24 cash.
     30   Paid F Company $21 for the merchandise purchased on August 3.

Required

1. On a sheet of notebook paper, draw a multicolumn Purchases Journal like the one that appears in Illustration 6–3. (Dollar amounts in this exercise are small so that you may use narrow columns.)

2. Journalize the transactions during August that should be recorded in the Purchases Journal.

Exercise 6–5
The Cash Disbursements
Journal
(L. O. 1)

A company uses a Sales Journal, a Purchases Journal, a Cash Receipts Journal, a Cash Disbursements Journal, and a General Journal. The following transactions occurred during the month of August:

Aug. 1 Purchased merchandise for $60 on credit from Z Company, terms 2/10, n/30.

      2 Purchased merchandise for $75 on credit from B Company, terms 2/15, n/60.

      5 Issued Cheque No. 5 to Q Company to buy store supplies for $15.

   15 Sold merchandise on credit to F. Hane for $120, terms n/30.

   16 Issued Cheque No. 6 for $55 to repay a note payable to Provincial Bank.

   17 Issued Cheque No. 7 to B Company to pay the amount due for the purchase of August 2, less the discount.

   31 Issued Cheque No. 8 to Z Company to pay the amount due for the purchase of August 1.

   31 Paid salary of $30 to D. Jones by issuing Cheque No. 9.

Required

1. On a sheet of notebook paper, draw a multicolumn Cash Disbursements Journal like the one that appears in Illustration 6–4. (Dollar amounts in this exercise are small so that you may use narrow columns.)

2. Journalize the transactions during August that should be recorded in the Cash Disbursements Journal.

Exercise 6–6
General Journal
transactions
(L. O. 1)

A company uses a Sales Journal, a Purchases Journal, a Cash Receipts Journal, a Cash Disbursements Journal, and a General Journal. The following transactions occurred during the month of August:

Aug. 1 N. Fount, the owner of the business, invested $150 in the business.

      5 Purchased merchandise for $125 on credit from B Company, terms 2/10, n/30.

   11 N. Fount, the owner of the business, contributed an automobile worth $750 to the business.

   13 Issued Cheque No. 5 to G Company to buy store supplies for $15.

   15 Sold merchandise on credit to J. Kirk for $120, terms n/30.

   16 Returned $35 of defective merchandise to B Company from the purchase on August 5.

Aug. 19 Issued Cheque No. 7 to M Company to pay the $225 due for a purchase of July 20.

26 J. Kirk returned $45 of merchandise originally purchased on August 15.

31 Accrued salaries payable were $30.

Required

Journalize the transactions during August that should be recorded in the General Journal.

Exercise 6–7
Special journal
transactions
(L. O. 1)

A company uses the following journals: Sales Journal, Purchases Journal, Cash Receipts Journal, Cash Disbursements Journal, and General Journal. On March 15, the company purchased merchandise priced at $15,000, subject to credit terms of 2/10, n/30. On March 25, the company paid the net amount due. However, in journalizing the payment, the bookkeeper debited Accounts Payable for $15,000 and failed to record the cash discount. Cash was credited for the actual amount paid. In what journals would the March 15 and the March 25 transactions have been recorded? What procedure is likely to disclose the error in journalizing the March 25 transaction?

Exercise 6–8
Subsidiary ledger accounts
(L. O. 2, 3)

At the end of March, the Sales Journal of Crockett Company appeared as follows:

Sales Journal

Date	Account Debited	Invoice No.	PR	Amount
Mar. 4	Wanda Slater	532	√	615.00
7	Ted Atkinson	533	√	1,020.00
13	Hana Moore	534	√	855.00
22	Wanda Slater	535	√	285.00
31	Total			2,775.00

The company had also recorded the return of merchandise with the following entry:

Mar. 21	Sales Returns and Allowances	150.00	
	Accounts Receivable—Hana Moore.		150.00
	Customer returned merchandise.		

Required

1. On a sheet of notebook paper, open a subsidiary Accounts Receivable Ledger having a T-account for each customer listed in the Sales Journal. Post to the customer accounts the entries of the Sales Journal and also the portion of the general journal entry that affects a customer's account.

2. Open a General Ledger having T-accounts for Accounts Receivable, Sales, and Sales Returns and Allowances. Post the Sales Journal and the portions of the general journal entry that affect these accounts.

3. Test the accuracy of the subsidiary ledger accounts with a schedule of accounts receivable.

Exercise 6–9
Accounts Receivable Ledger
(L. O. 2, 3)

Maxmann Company, a company that posts its sales invoices directly and then binds the invoices to make them into a Sales Journal, had the following sales during July:

July	3	Freida Jenz	.	.	.	.	$ 7,200
	6	Bob Gibson	.	.	.	.	9,900
	14	Earl Waites	.	.	.	.	14,400
	20	Bob Gibson	.	.	.	.	15,840
	22	Earl Waites	.	.	.	.	6,300
	30	Donald Betz	.	.	.	.	13,500
		Total	.	.	.	.	$67,140

Required

1. On a sheet of notebook paper, open a subsidiary Accounts Receivable Ledger having a T-account for each customer listed above. Post the invoices to the subsidiary ledger.

2. Give the general journal entry to record the end-of-month total of the Sales Journal.

3. Open an Accounts Receivable controlling account and a Sales account and post the general journal entry.

4. Prove the subsidiary Accounts Receivable Ledger with a schedule of accounts receivable.

Exercise 6–10
Errors related to the Sales Journal
(L. O. 1, 2, 3)

A company that records credit sales in a Sales Journal and records sales returns in its General Journal made the following errors. List each error by letter, and opposite each letter tell when the error should be discovered:

a. Posted a sales return recorded in the General Journal to the Sales Returns and Allowances account and to the Account Receivable account but did not post to the customer's account.

b. Made an addition error in determining the balance of a customer's account.

c. Made an addition error in totaling the Amount column of the Sales Journal.

d. Posted a sales return to the Accounts Receivable account and to the customer's account but did not post to the Sales Returns and Allowances account.

e. Correctly recorded a $300 sale in the Sales Journal but posted it to the customer's account as a $3,000 sale.

Exercise 6–11
Posting from special journals to T-accounts
(L. O. 2)

Following are the condensed journals of a merchandising concern. The journal column headings are incomplete in that they do not indicate whether the columns are Debit or Credit columns.

Required

1. Prepare T-accounts on a sheet of ordinary notebook paper for the following general ledger and subsidiary ledger accounts. Separate the accounts of each ledger group as follows:

General Ledger Accounts	**Accounts Receivable Ledger Accounts**
Cash	Customer One
Accounts Receivable	Customer Two
Prepaid Insurance	Customer Three
Store Equipment	
Notes Payable	**Accounts Payable Ledger Accounts**
Accounts Payable	Company X
Sales	Company Y
Sales Returns	Company Z
Sales Discounts	
Purchases	
Purchases Returns	
Purchases Discounts	

2. Without referring to any of the illustrations showing complete column headings for the journals, post the following journals to the proper T-accounts.

Sales Journal

Account	Amount
Customer One . . .	5,250
Customer Two	7,800
Customer Three . . .	10,500
Total	23,550

Purchases Journal

Account	Amount
Company X	6,300
Company Y	7,350
Company Z	8,400
Total	22,050

General Journal

. . . .	. .			
		Sales Returns.	1,050.00	
		Accounts Receivable—Customer Three.		1,050.00
	. .	Accounts Payable—Company Z	1,575.00	
		Purchases Returns		1,575.00

Cash Receipts Journal

Account	Other Accounts	Accounts Receivable	Sales	Sales Discounts	Cash
Customer One	. . .	5,250	. . .	105	5,145
Cash Sales	. . .	. . .	7,615	. . .	7,615
Notes Payable	10,000	. . .	. . .	. . .	10,000
Cash Sales	. . .	. . .	8,665	. . .	8,665
Customer Two	. . .	7,800	. . .	156	7,644
Store Equipment	785	. . .	. . .	. . .	785
Totals	10,785	13,050	16,280	261	39,854

Cash Disbursements Journal

Account	Other Accounts	Accounts Payable	Purchases Discounts	Cash
Prepaid Insurance	525	. . .	. . .	525
Company Y	. . .	7,350	147	7,203
Company Z	. . .	6,825	137	6,688
Store Equipment	2,625	. . .	. . .	2,625
Totals	3,150	14,175	284	17,041

Problems

Problem 6–1
Special journals and subsidiary ledgers
(L. O. 1, 2, 3)

Zenobia Company completed these transactions during April of the current year:

Apr. 2 Purchased merchandise on credit from Barclay Company, invoice dated March 31, terms 2/10, n/60, $5,400.

2 Issued Cheque No. 660 to *The City Times* for advertising expense, $575.

3 Sold merchandise on credit to Mark Loftis, Invoice No. 742, $9,650. (The terms of all credit sales are 2/10, n/60.)

4 Purchased on credit from Nixen Company merchandise, $7,125; store supplies, $375; and office supplies, $300. Invoice dated April 3, terms n/10 EOM.

6 Received a $75 credit memorandum from Nixen Company for unsatisfactory merchandise received on April 4 and returned for credit.

8 Sold merchandise on credit to Helen Stone, Invoice No. 743, $8,750.

9 Purchased store equipment on credit from Rexor Company, invoice dated April 9, terms n/10 EOM, $13,200.

10 Issued Cheque No. 661 to Barclay Company in payment of its March 31 invoice, less the discount.

12 Sold merchandise on credit to Regina Niser, Invoice No. 744, $3,450.

13 Received payment from Mark Loftis for the April 3 sale, less the discount.

14 Sold merchandise on credit to Mark Loftis, Invoice No. 745, $4,800.

15 Issued Cheque No. 662, payable to Payroll, in payment of the sales salaries for the first half of the month, $3,345. Cashed the cheque and paid the employees.

15 Cash sales for the first half of the month, $22,305. (Cash sales are usually recorded daily from the cash register readings. However, they are recorded only twice in this problem to reduce the repetitive transactions.)

18 Received payment from Helen Stone for the April 8 sale, less the discount.

19 Purchased merchandise on credit from Long Company, invoice dated April 18, terms 2/10, n/60, $5,150.

Apr. 20   Borrowed $18,000 from Eastern Bank by giving a note payable.

22   Received payment from Regina Niser for the April 12 sale, less the discount.

23   Purchased on credit from Rexor Company merchandise, $1,650; store supplies, $270; and office supplies, $180. Invoice dated April 22, terms n/10 EOM.

24   Received payment from Mark Loftis for the April 14 sale, less the discount.

24   Purchased merchandise on credit from Barclay Company, invoice dated April 23, terms 2/10, n/60, $3,150.

25   Received a $350 credit memorandum from Long Company for defective merchandise received on April 19 and returned.

28   Issued Cheque No. 663 to Long Company in payment of its April 18 invoice, less the return and the discount.

28   Sold merchandise on credit to Helen Stone, Invoice No. 746, $4,260.

29   Sold merchandise on credit to Regina Niser, Invoice No. 747, $2,475.

30   Issued Cheque No. 664, payable to Payroll, in payment of the sales salaries for the last half of the month, $3,345.

30   Cash sales for the last half of the month were $23,880.

Required

1. Open the following general ledger accounts: Cash, Accounts Receivable, Notes Payable, Sales, and Sales Discounts. Also open subsidiary accounts receivable ledger accounts for Mark Loftis, Regina Niser, and Helen Stone.

2. Prepare a Sales Journal and a Cash Receipts Journal like the ones illustrated in this chapter.

3. Review the transactions of Zenobia Company and enter those transactions that should be journalized in the Sales Journal and those that should be journalized in the Cash Receipts Journal. Ignore any transactions that should be posted in a Purchases Journal, a Cash Disbursements Journal, or a General Journal.

4. Post the items that should be posted as individual amounts from the journals. (Normally, such items are posted daily; but since they are few in number, in this problem you are asked to post them only once.)

5. Foot and crossfoot the journals and make the month-end postings.

6. Prepare a trial balance of the General Ledger and test the accuracy of the subsidiary ledger by preparing a schedule of accounts receivable.

Problem 6–2
Special journals, subsidiary ledgers, schedule of accounts payable
(L. O. 1, 2, 3)

On March 31, Zenobia Company had a cash balance of $75,000 and a Notes Payable balance of $75,000. The April transactions of Zenobia Company included those listed in Problem 6–1.

Required

1. Open the following general ledger accounts: Cash, Store Supplies, Office Supplies, Store Equipment, Notes Payable, Accounts Payable, Pur-

chases, Purchases Returns and Allowances, Purchases Discounts, Advertising Expense, and Sales Salaries Expense. Enter the March 31 balances of Cash and Notes Payable ($75,000 each).

2. Open subsidiary accounts payable ledger accounts for Barclay Company, Long Company, Nixen Company, and Rexor Company.

3. Prepare a General Journal, a Purchases Journal, and a Cash Disbursements Journal like the ones illustrated in this chapter.

4. Review the April transactions of Zenobia Company and enter those transactions that should be journalized in the General Journal, the Purchases Journal, or the Cash Disbursements Journal. Ignore any transactions that should be posted in a Sales Journal or Cash Receipts Journal.

5. Post the items that should be posted as individual amounts from the journals. (Normally, such items are posted daily; but since they are few in number, in this problem you are asked to post them only once.)

6. Foot and crossfoot the journals and make the month-end postings.

7. Prepare a trial balance and a schedule of accounts payable.

Problem 6–3
Special journals, subsidiary ledgers, and a trial balance
(L. O. 1, 2, 3)

(If the working papers that accompany this text are not being used, omit this problem.)

It is January 19, and you have just taken over the accounting work of Webster Company, a concern operating with annual accounting periods that end each January 31. The company's previous accountant journalized its transactions through January 18 and posted all items that required posting as individual amounts, as an examination of the journals and ledgers in the booklet of working papers will show.

The company completed these transactions beginning on January 19:

Jan. 19 Purchased on credit from Reed Suppliers merchandise, $2,450; store supplies, $360; and office supplies, $245. Invoice dated January 19, terms n/10 EOM.

20 Received a $385 credit memorandum from Younger Company for merchandise received on January 17 and returned for credit.

21 Received a $90 credit memorandum from Reed Suppliers for office supplies received on January 19 and returned for credit.

22 Sold merchandise on credit to Brenda Simms, Invoice No. 741, $2,765. (Terms of all credit sales are 2/10, n/60.)

23 Issued a credit memorandum to Sam Trent for defective merchandise sold on January 18 and returned for credit, $295.

24 Purchased store equipment on credit from Reed Suppliers, invoice dated January 24, terms n/10 EOM, $3,305.

25 Issued Cheque No. 450 to Younger Company in payment of its January 15 invoice less the return and the discount.

25 Received payment from Brenda Simms for the January 15 sale less the discount.

26 Issued Cheque No. 451 to Vax Company in payment of its January 16 invoice less a 2% discount.

Jan. 27   Sold merchandise on credit to Frank Urich, Invoice No. 742, $3,715.

27   Sold a neighboring merchant a roll of wrapping paper (store supplies) for cash at cost, $135.

28   Received payment from Sam Trent for the January 18 sale less the return and the discount.

29   Received merchandise and an invoice dated January 27, terms 2/10, n/60, from Vax Company, $4,250.

29   Susan Linder, the owner of Webster Company, used Cheque No. 452 to withdraw $4,500 cash from the business for personal use.

31   Issued Cheque No. 453 to Max Davis, the company's only sales employee, in payment of his salary for the last half of January, $1,440.

31   Issued Cheque No. 454 to Central Power Company in payment of the January hydro bill, $835.

31   Cash sales for the last half of the month, $44,975. (Cash sales are usually recorded daily but are recorded only twice in this problem in order to reduce the repetitive transactions.)

Required

1. Record the transactions in the journals provided.

2. Post to the customer and creditor accounts and also post any amounts that should be posted as individual amounts to the general ledger accounts. (Normally, these amounts are posted daily, but they are posted only once by you in this problem because they are few in number.)

3. Foot and crossfoot the journals and make the month-end postings.

4. Prepare a January 31 trial balance and test the accuracy of the subsidiary ledgers by preparing schedules of accounts receivable and payable.

Problem 6–4
Special journals, preparing and proving the trial balance
(L. O. 1, 2, 3)

Henderson Company completed these transactions during May of the current year:

May 2   Received merchandise and an invoice dated May 1, terms 2/10, n/60, from Bradley Company, $7,850.

3   Sold merchandise on credit to Omar Hanes, Invoice No. 632, $3,600. (Terms of all credit sales are 2/10, n/60.)

4   Purchased on credit from Abell Company merchandise, $8,345; store supplies, $335; and office supplies, $155. Invoice dated May 2, terms n/10 EOM.

4   Sold merchandise on credit to Leigh Rogers, Invoice No. 633, $5,650.

8   Borrowed $25,000 by giving Central National Bank a promissory note payable.

9   Purchased office equipment on credit from Telecore Company, invoice dated May 8, terms n/10 EOM, $2,815.

10   Sent Bradley Company Cheque No. 282 in payment of its May 1 invoice less the discount.

May 12 Sold merchandise on credit to Carl Chase, Invoice No. 634, $7,450.

13 Received payment from Omar Hanes for the May 3 sale less the discount.

14 Received payment from Leigh Rogers for the May 4 sale less the discount.

15 Received merchandise and an invoice dated May 14, terms 2/10, n/60, from Thomas Company, $8,935.

15 Issued Cheque No. 283, payable to Payroll, in payment of sales salaries for the first half of the month, $3,845. Cashed the cheque and paid the employees.

15 Cash sales for the first half of the month, $83,070. (Normally, cash sales are recorded daily; however, they are recorded only twice in this problem to reduce the number of repetitive entries.)

15 *Post to the customer and creditor accounts and also post any amounts that should be posted as individual amounts to the general ledger accounts. (Normally, such items are posted daily; but you are asked to post them on only two occasions in this problem because they are few in number.)*

18 Purchased on credit from Abell Company merchandise, $1,845; store supplies, $205; and office supplies, $135. Invoice dated May 17, terms n/10 EOM.

18 Received a credit memorandum from Thomas Company for unsatisfactory merchandise received on May 15 and returned for credit, $385.

19 Received a credit memorandum from Telecore Company for office equipment received on May 9 and returned for credit, $585.

22 Received payment from Carl Chase for the sale of May 12 less the discount.

24 Issued Cheque No. 284 to Thomas Company in payment of its invoice of May 14 less the return and the discount.

25 Sold merchandise on credit to Carl Chase, Invoice No. 635, $3,755.

28 Sold merchandise on credit to Leigh Rogers, Invoice No. 636, $3,485.

29 Issued Cheque No. 285, payable to Payroll, in payment of sales salaries for the last half of the month, $3,845. Cashed the cheque and paid the employees.

29 Cash sales for the last half of the month, $90,965.

31 *Post to the customer and creditor accounts and post any amounts that should be posted as individual amounts to general ledger accounts.*

31 Foot and crossfoot the journals and make the month-end postings.

Required

1. Open the following general ledger accounts: Cash, Accounts Receivable, Store Supplies, Office Supplies, Office Equipment, Notes Payable, Accounts Payable, Sales, Sales Discounts, Purchases, Purchases Returns and Allowances, Purchases Discounts, and Sales Salaries Expense.

2. Open the following accounts receivable ledger accounts: Carl Chase, Omar Hanes, and Leigh Rogers.

3. Open the following accounts payable ledger accounts: Abell Company, Bradley Company, Telecore Company, and Thomas Company.

4. Enter the transactions in a Sales Journal, a Purchases Journal, a Cash Receipts Journal, a Cash Disbursements Journal, and a General Journal similar to the ones illustrated in this chapter. Post when instructed to do so.

5. Prepare a trial balance and test the accuracy of the subsidiary ledgers by preparing schedules of accounts receivable and payable.

Problem 6–5
Special journals, subsidiary ledgers, and the trial balance
(L. O. 1, 2, 3)

Donnybrook Company completed these transactions during August of the current year:

Aug. 1 Received merchandise and an invoice dated July 31, terms 2/10, n/60, from Lakes Company, $18,900.

1 Purchased store equipment on credit from Barbour Company, invoice dated August 1, terms n/10 EOM, $7,050.

4 Sold merchandise on credit to Robert Sunbeck, Invoice No. 830, $8,250. (Terms of all credit sales are 2/10, n/60.)

6 Sold merchandise on credit to Sheila Jost, Invoice No. 831, $10,650.

8 Cash sales for the week ended August 8, $22,200.

8 *Post to the customer and creditor accounts and also post any amounts that should be posted as individual items to the general ledger accounts. (Normally, such items are posted daily; but to simplify the problem, you are asked to post them only once each week.)*

9 Issued Cheque No. 940 to The Blue Pages for advertising, $600.

10 Sold merchandise on credit to Kurt Han, Invoice No. 832, $4,800.

10 Issued Cheque No. 941 to Lakes Company in payment of its July 31 invoice less the discount.

11 Purchased on credit from Outlet Company merchandise, $5,850; store supplies, $555; and office supplies, $390. Invoice dated August 10, terms n/10 EOM.

12 Sold unneeded store equipment at cost for cash, $510.

15 Cash sales for the week ended August 15, $17,250.

15 Received payment from Robert Sunbeck for the sale of August 4 less the discount.

15 Issued Cheque No. 942, payable to Payroll, in payment of the sales salaries for the first half of the month, $3,900. Cashed the cheque and paid the employees.

15 *Post to the customer and creditor accounts and also post any amounts that should be posted as individual items to the general ledger accounts.*

16 Received payment from Sheila Jost for the sale of August 6 less the discount.

17 Sold merchandise on credit to Kurt Han, Invoice No. 833, $6,525.

Aug. 18   Sold merchandise on credit to Robert Sunbeck, Invoice No. 834, $3,750.

     20   Received merchandise and an invoice dated August 19, terms 2/10, n/60, from Elgin Company, $9,450.

     20   Received payment from Kurt Han for the sale of August 10 less the discount.

     21   Issued a credit memorandum to Kurt Han for defective merchandise sold on August 17 and returned for credit, $675.

     22   Cash sales for the week ended August 22, $20,700.

     22   *Post to the customer and creditor accounts and also post any amounts that should be posted as individual items to the general ledger accounts.*

     24   Received a $300 credit memorandum from Elgin Company for defective merchandise received on August 20 and returned for credit.

     25   Purchased on credit from Outlet Company merchandise, $4,050; store supplies, $450; and office supplies, $225. Invoice dated August 24, terms n/10 EOM.

     26   Received merchandise and an invoice dated August 25, terms 2/10, n/60, from Lakes Company, $8,550.

     27   Received payment from Kurt Han for the August 17 sale less the return and the discount.

     28   Sold merchandise on credit to Sheila Jost, Invoice No. 835, $2,775.

     29   Issued Cheque No. 943 to Elgin Company in payment of its August 19 invoice, less the return and the discount.

     29   Issued Cheque No. 944, payable to Payroll, in payment of the sales salaries for the last half of the month, $3,900.

     29   Cash sales for the week ended August 29 were $19,125.

     29   *Post to the customer and creditor accounts and also post any amounts that should be posted to the general ledger accounts as individual items.*

     31   *Foot and crossfoot the journals and make the month-end postings.*

Required

1. Open the following general ledger accounts: Cash, Accounts Receivable, Store Supplies, Office Supplies, Store Equipment, Accounts Payable, Sales, Sales Returns and Allowances, Sales Discounts, Purchases, Purchases Returns and Allowances, Purchases Discounts, Sales Salaries Expense, and Advertising Expense.

2. Open the subsidiary accounts receivable ledger accounts: Kurt Han, Sheila Jost, and Robert Sunbeck.

3. Open these subsidiary accounts payable ledger accounts: Barbour Company, Elgin Company, Lakes Company, and Outlet Company.

4. Prepare a Sales Journal, a Purchases Journal, a Cash Receipts Journal, a Cash Disbursements Journal, and a General Journal like the ones illustrated in this chapter. Enter the transactions in the journals and post when instructed to do so.

5. Prepare a trial balance and test the accuracy of the subsidiary ledgers with schedules of accounts receivable and payable.

Alternate Problems

Problem 6–1A
Special journals and
subsidiary ledgers
(L. O. 1, 2, 3)

Youngstown Company completed these transactions during May of the current year:

May 1   Issued Cheque No. 101 to *The Weekly Journal* for advertising expense, $1,080.

     2   Purchased merchandise on credit from Barclay Company, invoice dated May 1, terms 2/10, n/60, $6,500.

     4   Sold merchandise on credit to Mark Loftis, Invoice No. 203, $6,500. (The terms of all credit sales are 2/10, n/60.)

     4   Purchased on credit from Nixen Company merchandise, $7,050; store supplies, $495; and office supplies, $255. Invoice dated May 4, terms n/10 EOM.

     5   Sold merchandise on credit to Helen Stone, Invoice No. 204, $12,300.

     6   Received a $525 credit memorandum from Nixen Company for unsatisfactory merchandise received on May 4 and returned for credit.

     8   Purchased store equipment on credit from Rexor Company, invoice dated May 8, terms n/10 EOM, $17,400.

    10   Issued Cheque No. 102 to Barclay Company in payment of its May 1 invoice, less the discount.

    12   Sold merchandise on credit to Regina Niser, Invoice No. 205, $4,650.

    14   Received payment from Mark Loftis for the May 4 sale, less the discount.

    15   Issued Cheque No. 103, payable to Payroll, in payment of the sales salaries for the first half of the month, $4,875. Cashed the cheque and paid the employees.

    15   Sold merchandise on credit to Mark Loftis, Invoice No. 206, $7,350.

    15   Cash sales for the first half of the month, $14,835. (Cash sales are usually recorded daily from the cash register readings. However, they are recorded only twice in this problem to reduce the repetitive transactions.)

    15   Received payment from Helen Stone for the May 5 sale, less the discount.

    16   Purchased merchandise on credit from Long Company, invoice dated May 16, terms 2/10, n/60, $8,250.

    18   Borrowed $15,000 from Pioneer Trust Bank by giving a note payable.

    22   Received payment from Regina Niser for the May 12 sale, less the discount.

    23   Received a $300 credit memorandum from Long Company for defective merchandise received on May 16 and returned.

    24   Purchased on credit from Rexor Company merchandise, $4,410; store supplies, $345; and office supplies, $195. Invoice dated May 23, terms n/10 EOM.

    25   Received payment from Mark Loftis for the May 15 sale, less the discount.

May 26   Purchased merchandise on credit from Barclay Company, invoice dated May 25, terms 2/10, n/60, $3,900.

26   Issued Cheque No. 104 to Long Company in payment of its May 16 invoice, less the return and the discount.

27   Sold merchandise on credit to Helen Stone, Invoice No. 207, $5,085.

29   Sold merchandise on credit to Regina Niser, Invoice No. 208, $3,495.

31   Issued Cheque No. 105, payable to Payroll, in payment of the sales salaries for the last half of the month, $4,875.

31   Cash sales for the last half of the month were $20,820.

Required

1. Open the following general ledger accounts: Cash, Accounts Receivable, Notes Payable, Sales, and Sales Discounts. Also open subsidiary accounts receivable ledger accounts for Mark Loftis, Regina Niser, and Helen Stone.

2. Prepare a Sales Journal and a Cash Receipts Journal like the ones illustrated in this chapter.

3. Review the transactions of Youngstown Company and enter those transactions that should be journalized in the Sales Journal and those that should be journalized in the Cash Receipts Journal. Ignore any transactions that should be posted in a Purchases Journal, a Cash Disbursements Journal, or a General Journal.

4. Post the items that should be posted as individual amounts from the journals. (Normally, such items are posted daily; but since they are few in number, in this problem you are asked to post them only once.)

5. Foot and crossfoot the journals and make the month-end postings.

6. Prepare a trial balance of the General Ledger and test the accuracy of the subsidiary ledger by preparing a schedule of accounts receivable.

Problem 6–2A
Special journals, subsidiary ledgers, schedule of accounts payable
(L. O. 1, 2, 3)

On April 30, Youngstown Company had a cash balance of $30,000 and a Notes Payable balance of $30,000. The May transactions of Youngstown Company included those listed in Problem 6–1A.

Required

1. Open the following general ledger accounts: Cash, Store Supplies, Office Supplies, Store Equipment, Notes Payable, Accounts Payable, Purchases, Purchases Returns and Allowances, Purchases Discounts, Sales Salaries Expense, and Advertising Expense. Enter the April 30 balances of Cash and Notes Payable ($30,000 each).

2. Open subsidiary accounts payable ledger accounts for Barclay Company, Long Company, Nixen Company, and Rexor Company.

3. Prepare a General Journal, a Purchases Journal, and a Cash Disbursements Journal like the ones illustrated in this chapter.

4. Review the May transactions of Youngstown Company and enter those transactions that should be journalized in the General Journal, the Pur-

chases Journal, or the Cash Disbursements Journal. Ignore any transactions that should be posted in a Sales Journal or Cash Receipts Journal.

5. Post the items that should be posted as individual amounts from the journals. (Normally, such items are posted daily; but since they are few in number, in this problem you are asked to post them only once.)

6. Foot and crossfoot the journals and make the month-end postings.

7. Prepare a trial balance and a schedule of accounts payable.

Problem 6–3A
Special journals, subsidiary ledgers, and a trial balance
(L. O. 1, 2, 3)

(If the working papers that accompany this text are not being used, omit this problem.)

It is January 19, and you have just taken over the accounting work of Crowe Company, a concern operating with annual accounting periods that end each January 31. The company's previous accountant journalized its transactions through January 18 and posted all items that required posting as individual amounts, as an examination of the journals and ledgers in the booklet of working papers will show.

The company completed these transactions beginning on January 19:

Jan. 19 Sold merchandise on credit to Brenda Simms, Invoice No. 741, $8,300. (Terms of all credit sales are 2/10, n/60.)

20 Received a $685 credit memorandum from Younger Company for merchandise received on January 17 and returned for credit.

20 Purchased on credit from Reed Suppliers merchandise, $7,350; store supplies, $1,080; and office supplies, $745. Invoice dated January 19, terms n/10 EOM.

22 Issued a credit memorandum to Sam Trent for defective merchandise sold on January 18 and returned for credit, $445.

23 Received a $270 credit memorandum from Reed Suppliers for office supplies received on January 20 and returned for credit.

23 Purchased store equipment on credit from Reed Suppliers, invoice dated January 22, terms n/10 EOM, $9,925.

24 Sold merchandise on credit to Frank Urich, Invoice No. 742, $11,135.

25 Issued Cheque No. 450 to Younger Company in payment of its January 15 invoice less the return and the discount.

25 Received payment from Brenda Simms for the January 15 sale less the discount.

26 Issued Cheque No. 451 to Vax Company in payment of its January 16 invoice less a 2% discount.

28 Received merchandise and an invoice dated January 28, terms 2/10, n/60, from Vax Company, $12,750.

28 Received payment from Sam Trent for the January 18 sale less the return and the discount.

30 Sold a neighbouring merchant a carton of computer ribbons (store supplies) for cash at cost, $405.

31 Issued Cheque No. 452 to Valley Power Company in payment of the January hydro bill, $2,495.

31 Issued Cheque No. 453 to Max Davis, the company's only sales

employee, in payment of her salary for the last half of January, $1,440.

Jan. 31   Cash sales for the last half of the month, $54,510. (Cash sales are usually recorded daily but are recorded only twice in this problem in order to reduce the repetitive transactions.)

31   Susan Linder, the owner of Crowe Company, used Cheque No. 454 to withdraw $7,500 cash from the business for personal use.

Required

1. Record the transactions in the journals provided.

2. Post to the customer and creditor accounts and also post any amounts that should be posted as individual amounts to the general ledger accounts. (Normally, these amounts are posted daily, but they are posted only once by you in this problem because they are few in number.)

3. Foot and crossfoot the journals and make the month-end postings.

4. Prepare a January 31 trial balance and test the accuracy of the subsidiary ledgers by preparing schedules of accounts receivable and payable.

Problem 6–4A
Special journals, preparing and proving the trial balance
(L. O. 1, 2, 3)

Jarrett Company completed these transactions during October of the current year:

Oct. 2   Borrowed $36,000 by giving Regional Bank a promissory note payable.

3   Received merchandise and an invoice dated October 1, terms 2/10, n/60, from Bradley Company, $12,600.

4   Purchased on credit from Abell Company merchandise, $10,950; store supplies, $450; and office supplies, $225. Invoice dated October 3, terms n/10 EOM.

5   Sold merchandise on credit to Omar Hanes, Invoice No. 520, $9,300. (Terms of all credit sales are 2/10, n/60.)

6   Purchased office equipment on credit from Telecore Company, invoice dated October 5, terms n/10 EOM, $14,550.

9   Sold merchandise on credit to Leigh Rogers, Invoice No. 521, $8,850.

10   Sent Bradley Company Cheque No. 312 in payment of its October 1 invoice less the discount.

11   Received merchandise and an invoice dated October 10, terms 2/10, n/60, from Thomas Company, $12,900.

15   Received payment from Omar Hanes for the October 5 sale less the discount.

15   Issued Cheque No. 313, payable to Payroll, in payment of sales salaries for the first half of the month, $7,200. Cashed the cheque and paid the employees.

15   Cash sales for the first half of the month, $44,700. (Normally, cash sales are recorded daily; however, they are recorded only twice in this problem to reduce the number of repetitive entries.)

15   *Post to the customer and creditor accounts and also post any amounts that should be posted as individual amounts to the general*

ledger accounts. (Normally, such items are posted daily; but you are asked to post them on only two occasions in this problem because they are few in number.)

Oct. 16   Sold merchandise on credit to Carl Chase, Invoice No. 522, $10,850.

    18   Purchased on credit from Abell Company merchandise, $5,475; store supplies, $525; and office supplies, $420. Invoice dated October 17, terms n/10 EOM.

    19   Received payment from Leigh Rogers for the October 9 sale less the discount.

    20   Received a credit memorandum from Thomas Company for unsatisfactory merchandise received on October 10 and returned for credit, $1,200.

    20   Issued Cheque No. 314 to Thomas Company in payment of its invoice of October 10 less the return and the discount.

    23   Sold merchandise on credit to Carl Chase, Invoice No. 523, $7,050.

    26   Received payment from Carl Chase for the sale of October 16 less the discount.

    27   Received a credit memorandum from Telecore Company for office equipment received on December 6 and returned for credit, $750.

    28   Sold merchandise on credit to Leigh Rogers, Invoice No. 524, $6,150.

    31   Issued Cheque No. 315, payable to Payroll, in payment of sales salaries for the last half of the month, $7,200. Cashed the cheque and paid the employees.

    31   Cash sales for the last half of the month, $50,550.

    31   *Post to the customer and creditor accounts and post any amounts that should be posted as individual amounts to general ledger accounts.*

    31   Foot and crossfoot the journals and make the month-end postings.

Required

1. Open the following general ledger accounts: Cash, Accounts Receivable, Store Supplies, Office Supplies, Office Equipment, Notes Payable, Accounts Payable, Sales, Sales Discounts, Purchases, Purchases Returns and Allowances, Purchases Discounts, and Sales Salaries Expense.

2. Open the following accounts receivable ledger accounts: Carl Chase, Omar Hanes, Leigh Rogers.

3. Open the following accounts payable ledger accounts: Abell Company, Bradley Company, Telecore Company, and Thomas Company.

4. Enter the transactions in a Sales Journal, a Purchases Journal, a Cash Receipts Journal, a Cash Disbursements Journal, and a General Journal similar to the ones illustrated in this chapter. Post when instructed to do so.

5. Prepare a trial balance and test the accuracy of the subsidiary ledgers by preparing schedules of accounts receivable and payable.

Problem 6–5A
Special journals, subsidiary ledgers, and the trial balance
(L. O. 1, 2, 3)

Jocelyn Company completed these transactions during December of the current year:

Dec. 2 Received merchandise and an invoice dated December 1, terms 2/10, n/60, from Lakes Company, $26,850.

3 Sold merchandise on credit to Robert Sunbeck, Invoice No. 825, $12,150. (Terms of all credit sales are 2/10, n/60.)

4 Issued Cheque No. 240 to *The Weekly Times* for advertising, $2,340.

5 Purchased store equipment on credit from Barbour Company, invoice dated December 4, terms n/10 EOM, $36,300.

6 Sold merchandise on credit to Sheila Jost, Invoice No. 826, $13,950.

7 Cash sales for the week ended December 7, $24,600.

7 *Post to the customer and creditor accounts and also post any amounts that should be posted as individual items to the general ledger accounts. (Normally, such items are posted daily; but to simplify the problem, you are asked to post them only once each week.)*

9 Sold merchandise on credit to Kurt Han, Invoice No. 827, $8,950.

10 Received a credit memorandum from Barbour Company for the return of defective equipment originally purchased on December 5, $1,050.

11 Issued Cheque No. 241 to Lakes Company in payment of its December 1 invoice less the discount.

12 Sold unneeded store equipment at cost for cash, $720.

13 Received payment from Robert Sunbeck for the sale of December 3 less the discount.

14 Cash sales for the week ended August 14, $22,950.

14 Issued Cheque No. 242, payable to Payroll, in payment of the sales salaries for the first half of the month, $4,950. Cashed the cheque and paid the employees.

14 *Post to the customer and creditor accounts and also post any amounts that should be posted as individual items to the general ledger accounts.*

16 Purchased on credit from Outlet Company merchandise, $11,250; store supplies, $930; and office supplies, $570. Invoice dated December 16, terms n/10 EOM.

16 Received payment from Sheila Jost for the sale of December 6 less the discount.

17 Received merchandise and an invoice dated December 17, terms 2/10, n/60, from Elgin Company, $16,650.

17 Sold merchandise on credit to Kurt Han, Invoice No. 828, $13,350.

19 Sold merchandise on credit to Robert Sunbeck, Invoice No. 829, $11,800.

19 Received payment from Kurt Han for the sale of December 9 less the discount.

20 Issued a credit memorandum to Kurt Han for defective merchandise sold on December 17 and returned for credit, $150.

21 Cash sales for the week ended December 21, $27,450.

21 *Post to the customer and creditor accounts and also post any*

amounts that should be posted as individual items to the general ledger accounts.

Dec. 22 Received a $450 credit memorandum from Elgin Company for defective merchandise received on December 17 and returned for credit.

23 Purchased on credit from Outlet Company merchandise, $10,200; store supplies, $330; and office supplies, $420. Invoice dated December 22, terms n/10 EOM.

24 Received merchandise and an invoice dated December 23, terms 2/10, n/60, from Lakes Company, $15,300.

27 Received payment from Kurt Han for the December 17 sale less the return and the discount.

27 Issued Cheque No. 243 to Elgin Company in payment of its December 17 invoice, less the return and the discount.

28 Sold merchandise on credit to Sheila Jost, Invoice No. 830, $8,925.

28 Issued Cheque No. 244, payable to Payroll, in payment of the sales salaries for the last half of the month, $4,950.

28 Cash sales for the week ended December 28 were $14,625.

31 *Post to the customer and creditor accounts and also post any amounts that should be posted to the general ledger accounts as individual items.*

31 *Foot and crossfoot the journals and make the month-end postings.*

Required

1. Open the following general ledger accounts: Cash, Accounts Receivable, Store Supplies, Office Supplies, Store Equipment, Accounts Payable, Sales, Sales Returns and Allowances, Sales Discounts, Purchases, Purchases Returns and Allowances, Purchases Discounts, Sales Salaries Expense, and Advertising Expense.

2. Open the subsidiary accounts receivable ledger accounts: Kurt Han, Sheila Jost, and Robert Sunbeck.

3. Open these subsidiary accounts payable ledger accounts: Barbour Company, Elgin Company, Lakes Company, and Outlet Company.

4. Prepare a Sales Journal, a Purchases Journal, a Cash Receipts Journal, a Cash Disbursements Journal, and a General Journal like the ones illustrated in this chapter. Enter the transactions in the journals and post when instructed to do so.

5. Prepare a trial balance and test the accuracy of the subsidiary ledgers with schedules of accounts receivable and payable.

Analytical and Review Problems

A&R Problem 6–1

The following problem is designed to test your ability in the use of special journals and subsidiary ledgers. The special journals of E.T. Notea Department Store are reproduced below, followed by a number of representative transactions which occurred during the period. The money columns in the journals are numbered to minimize clerical work in recording each transaction.

Accounts Receivable Debit	Sales Credit						Sales Tax Credit
	Men's Clothing	Women's Clothing	Appliances	Furniture	Bargain Basement	Other Departments	
1	2	3	4	5	6	7	8

Cash Debit	Sales Discounts Debit	Sales Credit						Accounts Receivable Credit	Other Accounts Credit	Sales Tax Credit
		Men's Clothing	Women's Clothing	Appliances	Furniture	Bargain Basement	Other Departments			
9	10	11	12	13	14	15	16	17	18	19

Purchases Debit						Accounts Payable Credit
Men's Clothing	Women's Clothing	Appliances	Furniture	Bargain Basement	Other Departments	
20	21	22	23	24	25	26

Accounts Payable Debit	Supplies Expense Debit	Other Accounts Debit	Cash Credit
27	28	29	30

Debit	Credit
31	32

Transactions (*Note:* All sales are subject to sales tax of 8%):

		Debit	Credit
a.	Purchases of $8,200 on account of Appliances from E. G. Inc.		
b.	Sale on account $1,400 of Furniture to Gates Brown.		
c.	Sale for cash $1,000 less 5% discount—Appliances.		
d.	Collection of account receivable from Cec Oak, $600.		
e.	Payment of account payable to J. T. Inglis, $4,200.		
f.	Borrowed $25,000 from Great Northern Bank on note payable.		
g.	Sale on account $300 to J. C. Snead—Men's Clothing.		
h.	Sale for cash of baked goods—$10.		
i.	Purchases of $7,500 on account of goods—Bargain Basement from C. L. Co.		
j.	J. C. Snead returned for credit a shirt that had a flaw—$40.		

Required

1. Identify each of the journals.
2. Journalize by indicating the column number in the spaces provided after each transaction. For example: Purchase for cash of supplies (immediately expensed).

Debit	Credit
28	30

3. Indicate how the data in the special journals are posted to various accounts by filling in the spaces provided with the following posting possibilities.
    a. Posted as a *debit* to some general ledger account.
    b. Posted as a *debit* to some subsidiary ledger account.
    c. Posted as a *credit* to some general ledger account.
    d. Posted as a *credit* to some subsidiary ledger account.
    e. Not posted.

Note: The numbers in parentheses are the identification numbers for the money columns of the special journals. For example: (31) money column.

	Posted as
(00) Total of column (31)Example	e
a. Total of column (1).	
b. Detail items of column (3).	
c. Detail items of column (8).	
d. Total of column (9).	
e. Detail items of column (17).	
f. Total of column (20).	
g. Total of column (26).	
h. Detail items of column (27).	
i. Detail items of column (32).	
j. Detail items of column (1).	
k. Total of column (19).	
l. Detail items of column (18).	
m. Total of column (29).	
n. Total of column (5).	
o. Detail items of column (10).	

COMPREHENSIVE PROBLEM

Centaur Company
(Review of Chapters 1
through 6)

Assume it is Monday, March 2, the first business day of the month, and you have just been hired as an accountant by Centaur Company, a company that operates with monthly accounting periods. All of the company's accounting work has been completed through the end of February. Its ledgers show February 28 balances, and you are ready to begin work by recording the following transactions:

Mar. 2 Purchased on credit from Reston Suppliers merchandise, $5,505; store supplies, $480; and office supplies, $165. Invoice dated March 2, terms n/10 EOM.

3 Sold merchandise on credit to Anchor Company, Invoice No. 541, $5,550. (The terms of all credit sales are 2/10, n/60.)

3 Issued Cheque No. 320 to District Realty in payment of the March rent, $2,925. (Use two lines to record the transaction. Charge 80% of the rent to Rent Expense, Selling Space and the balance to Rent Expense, Office Space.)

4 Received a $390 credit memorandum from Hardman Products for merchandise received on February 27 and returned for credit.

4 Issued a $225 credit memorandum to Blutex Company for defective merchandise sold on February 28 and returned for credit.

5 Purchased office equipment on credit from Reston Suppliers, invoice dated March 4, terms n/10 EOM, $5,900.

6 Sold store supplies to the merchant next door at cost for cash, $35.

6 Issued Cheque No. 321 to Hardman Products to pay for the $3,540 of merchandise received on February 27 less the return and a 2% discount.

9 Received payment from Blutex Company for the sale of February 28 less the return and the discount.

11 Received merchandise and an invoice dated March 10, terms 2/10, n/60, from Thomas Brothers, $6,450.

12 Received a $260 credit memorandum from Reston Suppliers for defective office equipment received on March 5 and returned for credit.

13 Received payment from Anchor Company for the March 3 sale less the discount.

15 Issued Cheque No. 322, payable to Payroll, in payment of sales salaries, $1,315, and office salaries, $1,125. Cashed the cheque and paid the employees.

15 Cash sales for the first half of the month, $21,435. (Such sales are normally recorded daily. They are recorded only twice in this problem in order to reduce the number of repetitive transactions.)

15 *Post to the customer and creditor accounts and post any amounts that should be posted to the general ledger accounts as individual amounts. (Such items are normally posted daily, but you are asked*

to post them only twice each month because they are few in number.)

Mar. 16 Received merchandise and an invoice dated March 16, terms 2/10, n/60, from Worth Materials, $7,950.

16 Sold merchandise on credit to Pete's Repairs, Invoice No. 542, $4,150.

18 Issued Cheque No. 323 to Thomas Brothers in payment of its March 10 invoice less the discount.

18 Sold merchandise on credit to Blutex Company, Invoice No. 543, $3,300.

20 Purchased on credit from Reston Suppliers merchandise, $4,995; store supplies, $165; and office supplies, $240. Invoice dated March 19, terms n/10 EOM.

23 Sold merchandise on credit to Maxwell Constructors, Invoice No. 544, $6,245.

24 Issued Cheque No. 324 to Worth Materials in payment of its March 16 invoice less the discount.

25 Received merchandise and an invoice dated March 25, terms 2/10, n/60, from Thomas Brothers, $4,170.

26 Received payment from Pete's Repairs for the March 16 sale less the discount.

29 Henry Sutton, the owner of Centaur Company, used Cheque No. 325 to withdraw $2,700 from the business for personal use.

30 Issued Cheque No. 326, payable to Payroll, in payment of sales salaries, $1,315, and office salaries, $1,125. Cashed the cheque and paid the employees.

30 Issued Cheque No. 327 to City Utility in payment of the March hydro bill, $745.

30 Cash sales for the last half of the month were $23,415.

31 *Post to the customer and creditor accounts and post any amounts that are posted as individual amounts to the general ledger accounts.*

31 Foot and crossfoot the journals and make the month-end postings.

Required

1. Enter the transactions in the journals and post when instructed to do so.

2. Prepare a trial balance in the Trial Balance columns of the work sheet form provided and complete the work sheet using the following information:

    a. Ending merchandise inventory, $48,660.

    b. Expired insurance, $510.

    c. Ending store supplies inventory, $455; and office supplies inventory, $240.

    d. Estimated depreciation of store equipment, $450; and of office equipment, $300.

3. Prepare a multiple-step classified March income statement and a March 31 classified balance sheet.

4. Prepare and post adjusting and closing entries.

5. Prepare a post-closing trial balance and test the accuracy of the subsidiary ledgers with schedules of accounts payable and accounts receivable.

Accounting for Assets

Businesses use many different kinds of assets in carrying on their operations. These include items such as cash, receivables, merchandise inventories, land, buildings, equipment, natural resources, and intangible assets. As you study the next four chapters, you will learn the basic principles of accounting for all these different types of assets. You will see how transactions that involve assets are recorded and how the assets are reported in the financial statements. In addition, you will learn several accounting procedures that help management safeguard and control the assets of the business.

Part Three consists of the following chapters:

7 Internal Control and Accounting for Cash

Cash is an asset that every business owns and uses. Cash includes such specific items as currency, coin, demand deposits (or chequing accounts), and perhaps savings accounts. In studying this chapter, you will learn the principles of internal control that guide businesses in managing and accounting for cash. The chapter will show you how to establish and use a petty cash fund and how to reconcile a chequing account. Also, you will learn a method of accounting for purchases that helps management monitor the extent to which cash discounts are being lost.

Learning Objectives

After studying Chapter 7, you should be able to:

1. Explain why internal control procedures are needed in a large concern and state the broad principles of internal control.
2. Describe internal control procedures to protect cash received from cash sales, cash received through the mail, and cash disbursements.
3. Explain the operation of a petty cash fund and be able to journalize entries to record petty cash fund transactions.
4. Explain why the bank balance and the book balance of cash are reconciled and be able to prepare such a reconciliation.
5. Tell how recording invoices at net amounts helps gain control over cash discounts taken and be able to account for invoices recorded at net amounts.
6. Define or explain the words and phrases listed in the chapter Glossary.

After studying Appendix F at the end of Chapter 7, you should be able to.

7. Explain the use of a Voucher Register and Cheque Register and prepare entries to record and pay liabilities when these registers are used in a manual accounting system.

Cash can be converted into other types of assets or used to buy services or satisfy obligations more easily than any other type of asset. As such, cash is said to be the most **liquid asset.** Because cash has a high degree of **liquidity,** it also is most likely to be the object of fraud or theft. Therefore, in accounting for cash, the procedures for protecting it from theft or other misuse are very important. These *internal control procedures* apply to all assets owned by a business and to all phases of its operations; but they are particularly important with respect to cash.

Internal Control

Explain why internal control procedures are needed in a large concern and state the broad principles of internal control.
(L. O. 1)

In a small business, the owner-manager often controls the entire operation through personal supervision and direct participation in the activities of the business. For example, he or she commonly buys all the assets and services that are used in the business. Such a manager also hires and supervises all employees, negotiates all contracts, and signs all cheques. As a result, the manager knows from personal contact and observation that the business actually received the assets and services for which the cheques were written. However, as a business grows, it becomes increasingly difficult to maintain this personal contact. Therefore, at some point the manager must delegate responsibilities and rely on internal control procedures rather than personal contact in controlling the operations of the business.

A properly designed **internal control system** encourages adherence to prescribed managerial policies. It also promotes operational efficiencies; protects the business assets from waste, fraud, and theft; and ensures accurate and reliable accounting data.

Internal control procedures vary from company to company and depend on such factors as the nature of the business and its size. However, the same broad principles of internal control apply to all companies. These broad principles, itemized in Illustration 7–1, are discussed in the following paragraphs.

Clearly Establish Responsibilities

In order to have good internal control, responsibilities must be clearly established and one person made responsible for each task. When responsibility is shared and something goes wrong, it is difficult to determine who is at fault. For example, when two salesclerks share the same cash drawer and there is a shortage, it is usually impossible to tell which clerk is at fault. Each will tend to blame the other. Neither can prove that he or she is not responsible. To correct this problem, each clerk should have a separate cash drawer, or one of the clerks should be given responsibility for making all change.

Maintain Adequate Records

To protect assets and assure that employees follow prescribed procedures, good record-keeping is required. Reliable records are also a source of information that management uses to monitor the operations of the business. For example, if detailed records of manufacturing equipment and tools are not maintained, items may disappear without any discrepancy being noticed. And if a comprehensive chart of accounts is not documented carefully and followed

---

Illustration 7–1
Seven principles of good internal control

1. Clearly establish responsibilities.
2. Maintain adequate records.
3. Insure assets and bond employees.
4. Separate record-keeping and custody over assets.
5. Divide responsibilities for related transactions.
6. Use mechanical devices where practicable.
7. Perform regular and independent reviews.

---

precisely, some expenses may be debited to the wrong accounts. As a result, management may never discover that some expenses are excessive.

Numerous forms and internal business papers must be designed and properly used to maintain good internal control. For example, if sales slips are properly designed, sales personnel can record the proper information efficiently and without irritating delays to customers. And if all sales slips are prenumbered and controlled, each salesperson can be held responsible for the sales slips under his or her control. Thus, a salesperson is not apt to make a sale, destroy the sales slip, and pocket the cash.

Insure Assets and Bond Key Employees

Assets should be covered by adequate casualty insurance, and employees who handle cash and negotiable assets should be bonded. Bonding of employees involves the purchase of an insurance policy against losses from employee theft. Bonding also tends to prevent theft, since bonded employees are less apt to take assets if the employees know a bonding company must be dealt with when the shortage is revealed.

Separate Record-Keeping and Custody over Assets

A fundamental principle of internal control requires that the person who has access to or is responsible for an asset should not maintain the accounting record for that asset. When this principle is followed, the custodian of an asset, knowing that a record of the asset is being kept by another person, is not likely to misappropriate the asset or waste it; and the record-keeper, who does not have access to the asset, has no reason to falsify the record. Furthermore, if the asset is to be misappropriated and the theft concealed in the records, collusion is necessary.

Divide Responsibility for Related Transactions

Responsibility for a divisible transaction or a series of related transactions should be divided between individuals or departments so that the work of one acts as a check on that of another. This does not mean there should be duplication of work. Each employee or department should perform an unduplicated portion. For example, responsibility for placing orders, receiving the merchandise, and paying the vendors should not be given to one individual or department. To do so invites laxity in checking the quality and quantity of goods received, and carelessness in verifying the validity and accuracy of invoices. It also invites the purchase of goods for an employee's personal use and the payment of fictitious invoices.

Use Mechanical Devices Whenever Practicable

Cash registers, cheque protectors, time clocks, and mechanical counters are examples of control devices that should be used whenever practicable. A cash register with a locked-in tape makes a record of each cash sale. A cheque protector, by perforating the amount of a cheque into its face, makes it difficult to change the amount. A time clock registers the exact time an employee arrived on the job and when the employee departed.

Perform Regular and Independent Reviews

Even if an internal control system is well designed, there is a tendency for it to deteriorate over time. Changes in personnel and the stress of time pressures tend to bring about shortcuts and omissions. Regular reviews of internal control procedures are necessary to be sure that the procedures are being followed. These reviews should be performed by internal auditors who are not directly involved in operations. From this independent perspective, internal auditors can evaluate the overall efficiency of operations as well as the effectiveness of the internal control system.

Many companies also have audits by external public accountants. After testing the company's financial records, the public accountants give an opinion as to whether the company's financial statements are presented fairly in accordance with generally accepted accounting principles. However, before public accountants can decide on how much testing they must do, they first must evaluate the effectiveness of the internal control system.

Computers and Internal Control

The broad principles of internal control should be followed whether the accounting system is manual or computerized. However, computers have several important effects on internal control. Perhaps the most obvious is that computers provide more rapid access to large quantities of information. As a result, management's ability to monitor and control business operations is greatly improved.

Computers Reduce Processing Errors

Computers reduce the number of errors in processing information. After the data are entered correctly, the human tendency to make mechanical and mathematical errors is largely eliminated. On the other hand, data entry errors may occur because the process of entering data sometimes appears less logical in a computerized system. Also, the lack of human involvement in later processing may cause data entry errors to go undiscovered.

Computers Allow More Extensive Testing of Records

The regular review and audit of records can include more extensive testing if a computerized system is used. To reduce the cost of testing when manual methods are used, only small samples of data might be tested. But when computers are used to process data, large samples or even complete data files can be reviewed and analyzed.

Computerized Systems May Limit Hard Evidence of Processing Steps

Because many data processing steps are performed by the computer, less hard evidence in the form of written forms and analyses may be available for review. Therefore, internal control may depend more on reviews of the design and operation of the computerized processing system and less on reviews of the documents left behind by the system.

Separation of Duties Must Be Maintained

A common risk with computerized systems is that the separation of critical responsibilities is not maintained. Companies that use computers must have employees with special skills to program and operate the computers. The duties of these employees must be carefully controlled to avoid the risk of fraud. The person who designs and programs the system generally should not also serve as the operator. Control over cash receipts and disbursements should be separated. And cheque-writing should not be controlled by the computer operator. This problem is particularly difficult in small companies.

Internal Control for Cash

Describe internal control procedures to protect cash received from cash sales, cash received through the mail, and cash disbursements.
(L. O. 2)

A good system of internal control for cash should provide adequate procedures for protecting both cash receipts and cash disbursements. In the procedures, three basic principles should always be observed. First, there should be a separation of duties so that the people responsible for handling cash and for its custody are not the same people who keep the cash records. Second, all cash receipts should be deposited in the bank, intact, each day. Third, all payments should be made by cheque. The one exception to the last principle is that small disbursements may be made in cash from a petty cash fund. Petty cash funds are discussed later in this chapter.

The reason for the first principle is that a division of duties necessitates collusion between two or more people if cash is to be embezzled and the theft concealed in the accounting records. The second, requiring that all receipts be deposited intact each day, prevents an employee from making personal use of the money for a few days before depositing it. And if all receipts are deposited intact and all payments are made by cheque, the bank records provide a separate and external record of all cash transactions. These bank records are used to confirm the accuracy of the company's own records.

The exact procedures used to achieve control over cash vary from company to company. They depend on such things as company size, number of employees, cash sources, and so on. Therefore, you should understand that the procedures described in the following paragraphs are only illustrative of some that are used.

Cash from Cash Sales

Cash sales should be rung up on a cash register at the time of each sale. To help ensure that correct amounts are rung up, each register should be placed so that customers can see the amounts rung up. Also, the clerks should be required to ring up each sale before wrapping the merchandise. Finally, each cash register should be designed to provide a permanent, locked-in record of each transaction. In some cases, this is accomplished by a direct connection between the register and a computer. The computer is programmed to accept cash register transactions and enter them in the accounting records. In other cases, the register prints a record of each transaction on a paper tape that is locked inside the register.

As we previously stated, custody over cash should be separated from record-keeping for cash. For cash sales, this separation begins with the cash register. The salesclerk who has access to the cash in the register should not have access to its locked-in record. At the end of each day, the salesclerk is usually required to count the cash in the register and to turn the cash and its count over to an employee in the cashier's office. The employee in the cashier's office, like the salesclerk, has access to the cash and should not have access to the computerized accounting records (or the register tape if one is used). A third employee, commonly from the accounting department, examines the computerized record of register transactions (or the register tape) and compares its daily total with the total cash receipts reported by the cashier's office. If a register tape is used, it becomes the basis for the journal entry to record cash sales. The accounting department employee has access to the records for cash but does not have access to the actual cash. The salesclerk and the employee from the cashier's office do not have access to the accounting records and cannot take any cash without the shortage being revealed.

Cash Received through the Mail

Control of cash that comes in through the mail begins with the person who opens the mail. Preferably, two people should be present when the mail is opened. One of those should make a list in triplicate of the money received. The list should give each sender's name, the purpose for which the money was sent, and the amount. One copy of the list is sent to the cashier with the money. The second copy goes to the bookkeeper. The third copy is kept by the mail clerk. The cashier deposits the money in the bank, and the bookkeeper records the amounts received in the accounting records. Then, if the bank balance is reconciled (discussed later) by a fourth person, errors or fraud by the mail clerk, the cashier, or the bookkeeper will be detected. They will be detected because the cash deposited and the records of three people must agree. Furthermore, fraud is impossible, unless there is collusion. The mail clerk must report all receipts or customers will question their account balances. The cashier must deposit all receipts because the bank balance must agree with the bookkeeper's cash balance. The bookkeeper and the person who reconciles the bank balance do not have access to cash and, therefore, have no opportunity to withhold any.

Cash Disbursements

It is important to gain control over cash from sales and cash received through the mail. However, most large embezzlements do not involve cash receipts. More often, they are accomplished through the payment of fictitious invoices. Therefore, procedures for controlling cash disbursements are equally as important and sometimes more important than those for cash receipts.

To control cash disbursements, all disbursements should be made by cheque, except very small payments from petty cash. If authority to sign cheques is delegated to some person other than the business owner, that person should not have access to the accounting records. This helps prevent fraudulent disbursements that are concealed in the accounting records.

In a small business, the owner-manager usually signs cheques and normally knows from personal contact that the items to be paid for were actually received. However, this is impossible in a large business. In a large business, internal control procedures must be substituted for personal contact. The procedures are designed to tell the cheque-signer that the obligations for which the cheques were written are proper obligations, properly incurred, and should be paid. Often these procedures take the form of a **voucher system.**

The Voucher System and Control

A voucher system helps gain control over cash disbursements. Such a system: (1) permits only authorized individuals to incur obligations that will result in cash disbursements; (2) establishes procedures for incurring such obligations and for their verification, approval, and recording; (3) permits cheques to be issued only in payment of properly verified, approved, and recorded obligations; and (4) requires that every obligation be recorded at the time it is incurred and every purchase be treated as an independent transaction, complete in itself. This is required even though a number of purchases may be made from the same company during a month or other billing period.

When a voucher system is used, control over cash disbursements begins with the incurrence of obligations that will result in cash disbursements. Only specified departments and individuals are authorized to incur such obligations, and the kind each may incur is limited. For example, in a large store, only the purchasing department may incur obligations by purchasing merchandise. However, to gain control, the purchasing, receiving, and paying procedures are divided among several departments. These are the departments that request the purchases, the purchasing department, the receiving department, and the accounting department. To coordinate and control the responsibilities of these departments, several different business papers are used as shown in Illustration 7–2. An explanation of each paper will show you how large companies gain control over cash disbursements for merchandise purchases.

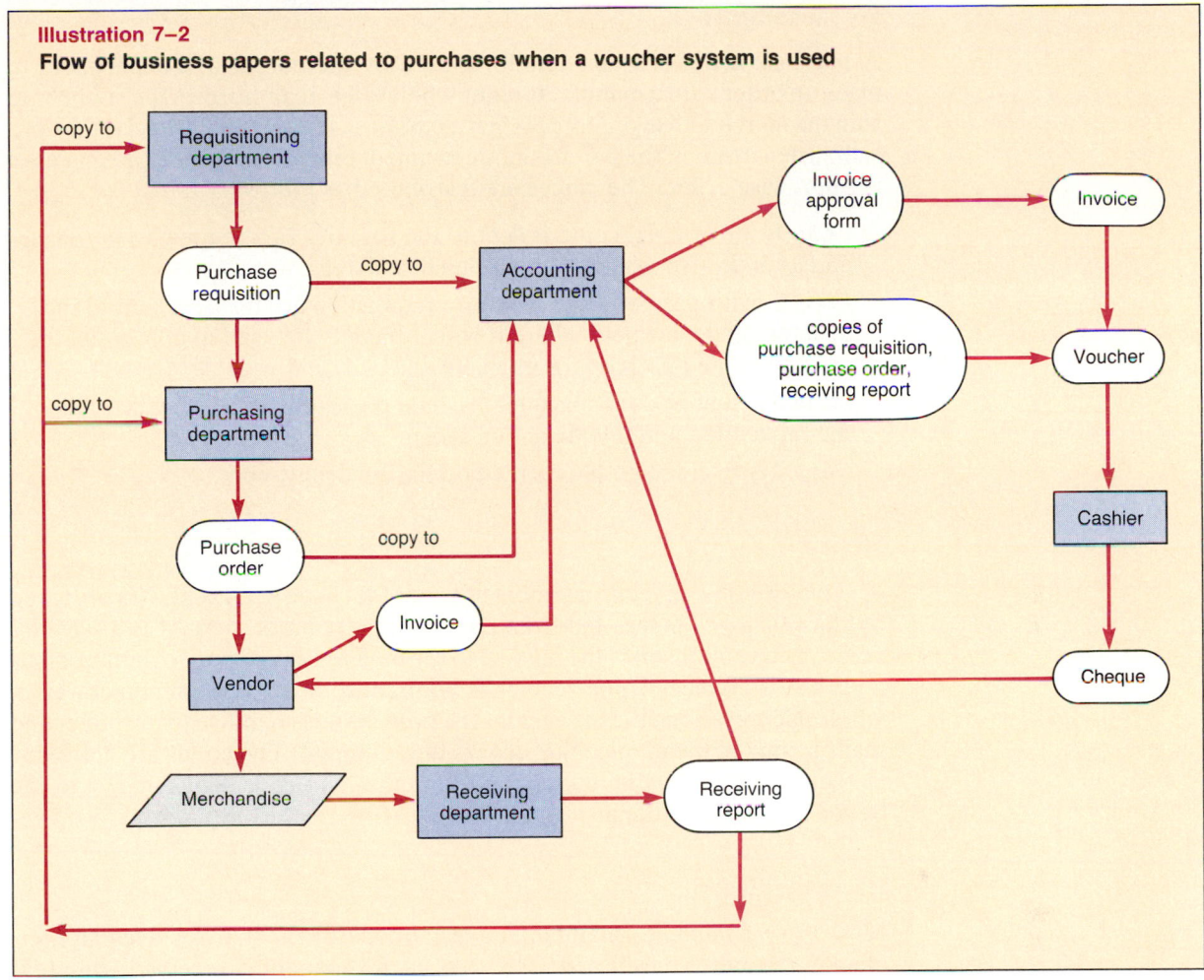

Illustration 7–2
Flow of business papers related to purchases when a voucher system is used

Purchase Requisition

In a large store, the department managers cannot be allowed to place orders directly with supply sources. If each manager could deal directly with suppliers, the amount of merchandise purchased and the resulting liabilities could not be controlled. Therefore, to gain control over purchases and resulting liabilities, department managers are commonly required to place all orders through the purchasing department. In such cases, the function of the selling department managers in the purchasing procedure is to inform the purchasing department of their needs. Each manager performs this function by preparing in triplicate and signing a business paper called a **purchase requisition.** On the requisition, the manager lists the merchandise needs of his or her department. The original and a duplicate copy of the purchase requisition are sent to the purchasing department. The requisitioning department keeps the third copy as a check on the purchasing department.

Purchase Order

A **purchase order** is a business form used by the purchasing department to place an order with a manufacturer or wholesaler. It authorizes the supplier to ship the merchandise ordered. When a purchase requisition is received from a selling department, the purchasing department prepares four or more copies of the purchase order. The copies are distributed as follows:

Copy 1, the original copy, is sent to the supplier as a request to purchase and as authority to ship the merchandise listed.

Copy 2, with a copy of the purchase requisition attached, is sent to the accounting department where it will ultimately be used in approving the invoice of the purchase for payment.

Copy 3 is sent to the department issuing the requisition to acknowledge the requisition and tell the action taken.

Copy 4 is retained on file by the purchasing department.

Invoice

An **invoice** is an itemized statement of goods that have been sold. It is prepared by the seller or **vendor**; and from the vendor's point of view, it is a sales invoice. The vendor sends the invoice to the buyer or **vendee,** who thinks of it as a purchase invoice. Upon receipt of a purchase order, the manufacturer or wholesaler receiving the order ships the ordered merchandise to the buyer and mails a copy of the invoice that covers the shipment. The goods are delivered to the buyer's receiving department, and the invoice is sent directly to the buyer's accounting department.

Receiving Report

Most large companies maintain a special department that receives all merchandise or other purchased assets. As each shipment is received, counted, and checked, the receiving department prepares four or more copies of a **receiving report.** This report lists the quantity, description, and condition of the items received. One copy is sent to the accounting department. To notify the requisitioning and purchasing departments that the goods have arrived, copies are sent to each of those departments. Finally, the receiving department retains a copy in its files.

Invoice Approval Form

When the receiving report arrives in the accounting department, it should have in its possession copies of the—

1. Requisition listing the items that were to be ordered.
2. Purchase order that lists the merchandise actually ordered.
3. Invoice showing quantity, description, unit price, and total of the goods shipped by the seller.
4. Receiving report that lists quantity and condition of the items received.

Illustration 7–3
An invoice approval form

```
Purchase order number _____
Requisition check _____
Purchase order check _____
Receiving report check _____
Invoice check:
  Price approval _____
  Calculations _____
  Terms _____
Approved for payment: _____
```

With the information on these papers, the accounting department is in a position to approve the invoice for entry on the books and to approve ultimate payment. In approving the invoice, the accounting department checks and compares the information on all the papers. To facilitate the checking procedure and to ensure that no step is omitted, an **invoice approval form** is commonly used. This form may be a separate business paper that is attached to the invoice, or the information shown in Illustration 7–3 may be stamped directly on the invoice with a rubber stamp.

As each step in the checking procedure is finished, the clerk making the check initials the invoice approval form. Initials in each space on the form indicate:

1. **Requisition check** . . . . . The items on the invoice agree with the requisition and were requisitioned.

2. **Purchase order check** . . . The items on the invoice agree with the purchase order and were ordered.

3. **Receiving report check** . . The items on the invoice agree with the receiving report and were received.

4. **Invoice check:**
   Price approval . . . . . The invoice prices are the agreed prices.
   Calculations . . . . . . The invoice has no mathematical errors.
   Terms . . . . The terms are the agreed terms.

The Voucher

When a voucher system is used, after an invoice is checked and approved, a **voucher** is prepared. A voucher is a business paper on which a transaction is summarized, its correctness certified, and its recording and payment approved. Vouchers vary somewhat from company to company. However, in general, they are designed so that the invoice, bill, or other documents from which they are prepared are attached to and folded inside the voucher. This makes for ease in filing. The inside of a voucher is shown in Illustration 7–4, and the outside in Illustration 7–5. The preparation of a voucher requires only that a clerk enter the required information in the proper blank spaces on a voucher form. The information is taken from the invoice, and its supporting documents are attached to and folded inside the voucher. The voucher is then sent to the desk of the chief clerk or auditor who makes an additional check, approves the accounting distribution (the accounts to be debited), and approves the voucher for recording.

After a voucher is approved and recorded, it is filed until its due date, when it is sent to the office of the company cashier or other disbursing office for payment. Here the person responsible for issuing cheques depends on the approved voucher and its signed supporting documents to verify that the obligation was properly incurred and should be paid. For example, the purchase requisition and purchase order attached to the voucher confirm that the purchase was authorized. The receiving report shows that the items were received, and the invoice approval form verifies that the invoice was checked for errors. As a result, there is little chance for fraud, unless all the documents were stolen and the signatures forged, or there was collusion.

The Voucher System and Expenses

Under a voucher system, obligations should be approved for payment and recorded as liabilities when they are incurred, or as soon as possible thereafter. This includes all expenses. For example, when a company receives the monthly telephone bill, the charges, including long-distance calls, should be examined for correctness. A voucher is then prepared, and the telephone bill is attached to and folded inside the voucher. The voucher is then recorded, and a cheque is issued in its payment, or the voucher is filed for payment at a later date.

The requirement that expenses be approved and recorded when incurred helps ensure that every expense payment is approved when information for its approval is available. However, invoices or statements (bills) for such things as equipment repairs sometimes are not received until weeks after the work is done. If no record of the repairs exists, it is difficult at the time to determine whether the invoice or bill is a correct statement of the amount owed. Also, if no records exist, it is possible for a dishonest employee to arrange with an outsider for more than one payment of an obligation, or for payment of excessive amounts, or for payment for goods and services not received, all with kickbacks to the dishonest employee.

Recording Vouchers

Normally, a company large enough to use a voucher system will use a computer in recording its transactions. For this reason and also because the primary purpose of this discussion is to describe the control techniques of a voucher system, a manual system of recording vouchers is not described here. However, such a system is described in Appendix F at the end of this chapter.

Illustration 7–4
Inside of a voucher

VALLEY SUPPLY COMPANY   Voucher No. __767__
Halifax, Nova Scotia

Date __Oct. 1, 19--__
Pay to __A. B. Seay Wholesale Company__
City __Digby__   Province __Nova Scotia__

For the following: (attach all invoices and supporting papers)

Date of invoice	Terms	Invoice Number and Other Details	Amount
Sept. 30, 19--	2 / 10, n / 60	Invoice No. C-11756 Less Discount Net Amount Payable	800.00 16.00 784.00

Payment approved

R. L. Tucker
Auditor

Illustration 7–5
Outside of a voucher

ACCOUNTING DISTRIBUTION   Voucher No. __767__

Account Debited	Amount
Purchases	800.00
Transportation-In	
Store Supplies	
Office Supplies	
Sales Salaries	
Total Vouch. Pay. Cr.	800.00

Due Date __October 6, 19--__

Pay to __A. B. Seay Wholesale Co.__
City __Digby__
Province __Nova Scotia__

Summary of Charges:
Total Charges __800.00__
Discount __16.00__
Net Payment __784.00__

Record of Payment:
Paid _____
Cheque No. _____

The Petty Cash Fund

Explain the operation of a
petty cash fund and be
able to journalize entries
to record petty cash fund
transactions.
(L. O. 3)

In controlling cash disbursements, a basic principle is to require that all disbursements be made by cheque. However, an exception to this rule is made for petty cash disbursements. Every business must make many small payments for items such as postage, express charges, telegrams, and small items of supplies. If such payments are made by cheque, many cheques for immaterial amounts are written. This is both time-consuming and expensive. Therefore, to avoid writing cheques for small amounts, you need to establish a petty cash fund and use the money in this fund to make small payments such as those listed above.

To establish a petty cash fund, you should estimate the total amount of small payments likely to be made during a short period, usually not more than a month. Then, a cheque is drawn for an amount slightly in excess of this estimate. You record the cheque with a debit to the Petty Cash account and a credit to Cash. The cheque is cashed, and the money is turned over to a member of the office staff who is called the *petty cashier*. This person is responsible for keeping the petty cash and for making payments from this fund.

The petty cashier usually keeps the petty cash in a locked box in the office safe. As each disbursement is made, a *petty cash receipt* (see Illustration 7–6) is signed by the person receiving payment and is placed with the remaining money in the petty cashbox. Under this system, the petty cashbox should always contain paid petty cash receipts and money equal to the amount of the fund.

Each disbursement reduces the money and increases the sum of the receipts in the petty cashbox. When the money is nearly gone, the fund is reimbursed. To reimburse the fund, the petty cashier presents the receipts for petty cash payments to the company cashier. The company cashier stamps each receipt "paid" so that it may not be reused, retains the receipts, and gives the petty cashier a cheque for their sum. When this cheque is cashed and the proceeds returned to the petty cashbox, the money in the box is restored to its original amount, and the fund is ready to begin a new cycle of operations.

At the time a cheque is written to reimburse the petty cash fund, you should sort the paid petty cash receipts into groups according to the expense or other accounts to be debited in recording payments from the fund. Each group is then totaled, and the totals are used in making the reimbursing entry.

Petty Cash Fund Illustrated

To avoid writing numerous cheques for small amounts, a company established a petty cash fund on November 1, designating one of its office clerks, Ned Fox, petty cashier. A $75 cheque was drawn, cashed, and the proceeds turned over to the clerk. The entry to record the cheque is shown in Illustration 7–7. The effect of the entry was to transfer $75 from the regular Cash account to the Petty Cash account.

Notice that the entry transfers $75 from the regular Cash account to the Petty Cash account. After the petty cash fund is established, the Petty Cash account is not debited or credited again unless the size of the fund is changed. If the fund is exhausted and reimbursements occur too often, the fund should be increased. To record an increase in the size of the fund, debit Petty Cash and credit Cash for the amount of the increase. If the fund is too large, some of the

Illustration 7–6
A petty cash receipt

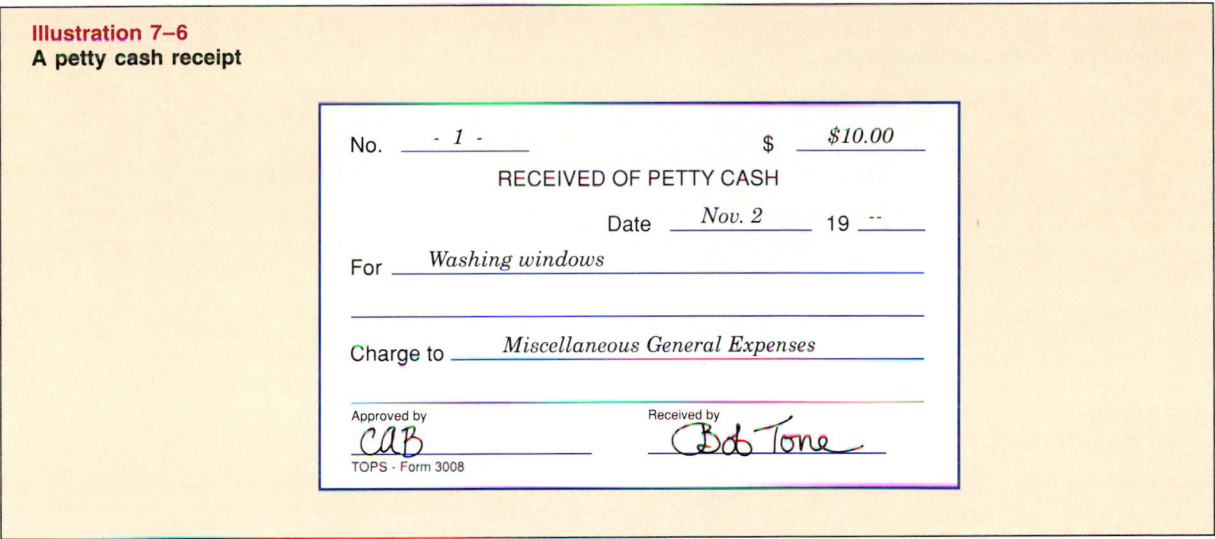

No. ___ - 1 - ___ $ ___$10.00___

RECEIVED OF PETTY CASH

Date ___Nov. 2___ 19 __

For ___Washing windows___

Charge to ___Miscellaneous General Expenses___

Approved by
CAB

Received by
Bob Tone

TOPS - Form 3008

Illustration 7–7
Entry to establish the petty cash fund

Cash Disbursements Journal

Date	Ch. No.	Payee	Account Debited	PR	Other Accts. Debit	Cash Credit
Nov. 1	58	Ned Fox, Petty Cashier	Petty Cash		75.00	75.00

money in the fund should be redeposited in the chequing account. Such a reduction in the fund is recorded with a debit to Cash and a credit to Petty Cash.

During November, Ned Fox, the petty cashier, made several payments from the petty cash fund. Each time he asked the person who received payment to sign a receipt. Then, on November 27, after making a $26.50 payment for repairs to an office typewriter, Mr. Fox realized there was not enough cash in the fund for another payment. Therefore, he summarized and totaled the petty cash receipts as shown in Illustration 7–8. The summary and the petty cash receipts were then given to the company cashier in exchange for a $71.30 cheque to reimburse the fund. Mr. Fox cashed the cheque, put the $71.30 proceeds in the petty cashbox, and was then ready to make additional payments from the fund.

The reimbursing cheque was recorded in the Cash Disbursements Journal with the second entry of Illustration 7–9. Information for this entry came from

Illustration 7–8
Summary of petty cash payments

Miscellaneous general expenses:
Nov. 2, washing windows $10.00
Nov. 17, washing windows 10.00
Nov. 27, typewriter repairs 26.50 $46.50

Transportation-in:
Nov. 5, delivery of merchandise purchased . . $ 6.75
Nov. 20, delivery of merchandise purchased . .   8.30   15.05

Delivery expense:
Nov. 18, customer's package delivered 5.00

Office supplies:
Nov. 15, purchased paper clips 4.75

Total $71.30

Illustration 7–9
Entry to reimburse the petty cash fund

Cash Disbursements Journal

Date	Ch. No.	Payee	Account Debited	PR	Other Accts. Debit	Cash Credit
Nov. 1	58	Ned Fox, Petty Cashier	Petty Cash		75.00	75.00
Nov. 27	106	Ned Fox, Petty Cashier	Transportation-In		15.05	
			Miscellaneous General Expenses.		46.50	
			Delivery Expense		5.00	
			Office Supplies.		4.75	71.30

the petty cashier's summary of payments. Note that the debits in the entry record the petty cash payments. Such an entry is necessary to get the debits into the accounts. Therefore, even if the petty cash fund is not low on funds, it should be reimbursed at the end of each accounting period. Otherwise, the financial statements will show an overstated petty cash asset and understated expenses and assets that were paid for out of petty cash.

Occasionally, a petty cashier will forget to get a receipt for a payment. Then, by the time the fund is reimbursed, the petty cashier will have forgotten the expenditure. This causes the fund to be short. If, for whatever reason, the petty cash fund is short at reimbursement time, the shortage is recorded as an expense in the reimbursing entry with a debit to the **Cash Over and Short account**.

AS A MATTER OF ETHICS

Nancy Tucker is an internal auditor for a large corporation and is in the process of making surprise counts of several $100 petty cash funds in various offices in the headquarters building. She arrived at the office of one of the fund custodians shortly before lunch while he was on the telephone. Nancy explained the purpose of her visit, and the custodian asked politely that she come back after lunch so that he could finish the business he was conducting by long distance. She agreed and returned about 1:30. The custodian opened the petty cash box and showed her five new $20 bills with consecutive serial numbers. Would you suggest that the auditor take any further action or comment on these events in her report to management?

Cash Over and Short

Even though a cashier is careful in making change, customers are sometimes given too much change or are shortchanged. As a result, at the end of a day, the actual cash from a cash register is commonly not equal to the cash sales "rung up" on the register. For example, assume that a cash register shows cash sales of $550 but the actual count of cash in the register is counted as $555. The entry in general journal form to record the cash sales and the overage is:

Nov.	23	Cash	555.00	
		Cash Over and Short		5.00
		Sales		550.00
		Day's cash sales and overage.		

On the other hand, if there is a shortage of cash in the register on the next day, the entry to record cash sales and the shortage would look like the following:

Nov.	24	Cash	621.00	
		Cash Over and Short	4.00	
		Sales		625.00
		Day's cash sales and shortage.		

Normally, customers are more likely to report being shortchanged than being given too much change. As a result, by the end of each accounting period, the Cash Over and Short account usually has a debit balance. If so, the balance represents an expense. You may show this expense on the income statement as a separate item in the general and administrative expense section. Or, if the amount is small, you may combine it with other small expenses and report them as a single item called miscellaneous expenses. If Cash Over and Short has a credit balance at the end of the period, it usually is shown on the income statement as part of the item, miscellaneous revenues.

Reconciling the Bank Balance

Explain why the bank balance and the book balance of cash are reconciled and be able to prepare such a reconciliation. (L. O. 4)

At least once every month, banks send each commercial depositor a bank statement that shows the activity in the depositor's account during the month. Different banks use a variety of formats for their bank statements. However, all of them include in one place or another: (1) the balance of the depositor's account at the beginning of the month, (2) deposits and any other amounts added to the account, (3) cheques and any other amounts deducted from the account, and (4) the account balance at the end of the month, according to the records of the bank. Illustration 7–10 shows a typical bank statement.

Note that the changes in the account are summarized in part A of Illustration 7–10. Specific debits and credits to the account (other than canceled cheques) are listed in part B. All canceled cheques are listed in numerical order in part C, and the daily account balances are shown in part D.

Banks usually mail the bank statement to the depositor each month. With the statement are the depositor's **canceled cheques** and any debit or credit memoranda that have affected the account. These cheques are the ones that the bank has paid during the month. They are called canceled cheques because they have been stamped or perforated to show that they were paid. Other deductions that may appear on the bank statement include withdrawals through automatic teller machines (ATM withdrawals) and periodic payments arranged in advance by the depositor. Also, the bank may deduct from the depositor's account amounts for service charges and fees, items deposited that are uncollectible, and amounts to correct previous errors. The bank notifies the depositor of each such deduction with a debit memorandum. A copy of each memorandum is sent with the monthly statement.

In addition to deposits made by the depositor, the bank may add amounts to the depositor's account. Examples of additions would be amounts the bank has collected for the depositor and corrections of previous errors. A credit memorandum is used to notify the depositor of any such additions.

Another addition might be for interest the depositor has earned. Some chequing accounts pay the depositor interest based on the daily cash balance maintained in the account. The bank calculates the amount of interest earned and credits it to the depositor's account each month. In Illustration 7–10, note that the bank credited $78.89 of interest to the account of Valley Company. The methods used to calculate interest are discussed in the next chapter.

When all receipts are deposited intact and all payments, other than petty cash payments, are drawn from the chequing account, the bank statement is a device for proving the accuracy of the depositor's cash records. The proof normally begins by preparing a **bank reconciliation.**

Need for Reconciling the Bank Balance

Normally, when the bank statement arrives, the balance of cash as shown by the statement does not agree with the balance in the depositor's accounting records. Therefore, in order to prove the accuracy of both the depositor's records and those of the bank, you should **reconcile** the two balances. To reconcile the balances, you must explain or account for the differences between the two balances.

Illustration 7–10
A typical bank statement

Canada Trust

```
VALLEY COMPANY                          CANADA TRUSTCO
39 MAPLE STREET                         NOV 30
LONDON, ONTARIO                         DAILY INTEREST
K2M 4K6                                 ACCOUNT
```

	BRANCH	ACCOUNT NUMBER	BALANCE FORWARD
	LONDON MAIN	007-500865	7,502.02

DATE	SYMBOL	WITHDRAWALS	DEPOSITS	BALANCE
OCT 31	756	1,102.31		6,399.71
OCT 31	757	179.00		6,220.71
NOV 02	NBD		20,000.00	26,220.71
NOV 02	755	835.17		25,385.54
NOV 03	NBW	250.00		25,135.54
NOV 04	759	1,116.00		24,019.54
NOV 08	749	32.00		23,987.54
NOV 08	747	4,212.00		19,775.54
NOV 09	751	50.00		19,725.54
NOV 10	762	1,906.81		17,818.73
NOV 14	NBW	250.00		17,568.73
NOV 14	764	940.43		16,628.30
NOV 14	750	113.78		16,514.52
NOV 15	CM		2,075.05	18,589.57
NOV 15	770	10,000.00		8,589.57
NOV 15	763	267.29		8,322.28
NOV 15	767	86.46		8,235.82
NOV 17	766	125.00		8,110.82
NOV 17	769	164.00		7,946.82
NOV 21	765	89.78		7,857.04
NOV 23	771	150.00		7,707.04
NOV 24	768	178.29		7,528.75
NOV 30	INT		78.89	7,607.64
NOV 30	S/C	1.00		7,606.64**

EXPLANATION OF SYMBOLS

Each transaction is identified by one of the following symbols.
Talk to your branch staff if you have any questions.

AID	Investment Certificate Interest	**INT**	Interest	**OBC**	Other Bank Service Charge
CHQ	Cheque	**JCW**	Johnny Cash Withdrawal	**PAY**	Payroll Deposit
CM	Miscellaneous Credit	**MCM**	Merchant MasterCard Credit	**PL**	Loan Payment
COR	Correction	**MDM**	Merchant MasterCard Debit	**PWR**	Powerline Payment
CSB	Canada Savings Bond Transaction	**MTC**	MasterTeller Service Charge	**RTD**	Returned Item
DEP	Deposit	**MTG**	Mortgage Payment	**SC**	Service Charge
DM	Miscellaneous Debit	**MTW**	MasterTeller Withdrawal	**SDB**	Safe Deposit Box Payment
ECM	Electronic Funds Credit	**NBD**	No Book Deposit	**WD**	Withdrawal
EDM	Electronic Funds Debit	**NBW**	No Book Withdrawal		
ICW	Interac Withdrawal	**NRT**	Non Resident Tax		

Numerous factors may cause the bank statement balance to differ from the depositor's book balance of cash. Some are:

1. **Outstanding cheques.** These are cheques that were drawn by the depositor, deducted on the depositor's records, sent to the payees, but have not reached the bank for payment and deduction.

2. **Unrecorded deposits.** Companies often make deposits at the end of each business day, after the bank is closed. These deposits are made in the bank's night depository and are not recorded by the bank until the next business day. Therefore, if a deposit is placed in the night depository the last day of the month, it does not appear on the bank statement for that month.

3. **Charges for uncollectible items and for service.** Sometimes, a company deposits a customer's cheque that is found to be uncollectible. Usually, the problem is nonsufficient funds in the customer's account to cover the cheque. Thus, the cheque is called a nonsufficient funds (NSF) cheque. The bank first credits the depositor's account for the full amount of the deposit. Then, when the bank learns that the cheque is uncollectible, it debits the depositor's account for the amount of the cheque. Also, the bank may charge the depositor a fee for processing the NSF cheque. The bank notifies the depositor of each such deduction with a debit memorandum. If the item is material in amount, the memorandum is mailed to the depositor on the day of the deduction. Although each deduction should be recorded on the day the memorandum is received, sometimes an entry is not made until the bank reconciliation is prepared. Also, memoranda for small amounts may not be sent to the depositor until the bank statement is mailed.

    Other charges to a depositor's account that a bank might report on the bank statement include the printing of new cheques. Also, a monthly service charge may be made for processing the cheques of the depositor.

4. **Credits for collections and for interest.** Banks often act as collection agents for their depositors, collecting promissory notes and other items. When the bank collects an item, the bank usually deducts a small fee and adds the net proceeds to the depositor's account. It then sends a credit memorandum as notification of the transaction. As soon as the memorandum is received, it should be recorded. However, these items may remain unrecorded until the time of the bank reconciliation.

    Many bank accounts earn interest on the average cash balance in the account during the month. If an account earns interest, the bank statement will include a credit for the amount earned during the past month.

5. **Errors.** Regardless of care and systems of internal control for automatic error detection, both the banks and depositors make errors. Errors by the bank may not be discovered until the depositor completes the bank reconciliation. Also, the depositor's errors often are not discovered until the balance is reconciled.

Steps in Reconciling the Bank Balance

The steps in reconciling the bank balance are the following:

1. Compare deposits listed on the bank statement with deposits shown in the accounting records. Note any discrepancies and discover which is correct. List any errors or unrecorded items.

2. Examine all other credits to the account shown on the bank statement and determine whether each one was recorded in the books. These items include collections by the bank, correction of previous bank statement errors, and interest earned by the depositor. List any unrecorded items.

3. Compare the list of canceled cheques on the bank statement with the actual cheques returned with the statement. For each cheque, make sure that the correct amount was deducted by the bank and that the returned cheque was properly charged to the company's account. Note any discrepancies or errors.

4. Compare the outstanding cheques listed on the previous month's bank reconciliation with the canceled cheques listed on the bank statement. Prepare a list of any cheques that remain outstanding at the end of the current month.

5. Compare the canceled cheques listed on the bank statement with the cheques recorded in the books since the last reconciliation. To make this process easier, the bank statement normally lists canceled cheques in the same numerical order as the cheques are numbered. List any outstanding cheques. Although companies with reasonable internal controls would rarely if ever write a cheque without recording it, an individual may occasionally write a cheque and fail to record it in the books. List any canceled cheques that are unrecorded in the books.

6. Examine all other debits to the account as shown on the bank statement and determine whether each one was recorded in the books. These include bank charges for newly printed cheques, NSF cheques, stop payment orders, and monthly service charges.

7. Prepare a reconciliation of the bank statement balance with the book balance of cash. Such a reconciliation is shown in Illustration 7–11.

8. Determine if any debits or credits appearing on the bank statement are unrecorded in the books. Make journal entries to record them.

Illustration of a Bank Reconciliation

To illustrate a bank reconciliation, assume that in preparing to reconcile its bank balance of October 31, Valley Company discovered the following items. The bank balance as shown by the bank statement was $2,050. However, the cash balance according to the accounting records was $1,404.58. A $145 deposit, placed in the bank's night depository on October 31, was unrecorded by the bank at the time the bank statement was mailed. With the bank statement was a credit memorandum showing that the bank had collected a note receivable for the company on October 23. The note's proceeds of $500 less a $15

Illustration 7–11
A typical bank reconciliation

VALLEY COMPANY
Bank Reconciliation
October 31, 1990

Book balance of cash		$1,404.58	Bank statement balance		$2,050.00
Add:			Add:		
Proceeds of note less			Deposit of 10/31		145.00
collection fee	$485.00				
Interest earned	8.42	493.42			
		$1,898.00			$2,195.00
Deduct:			Deduct:		
NSF cheque plus			Outstanding cheques:		
service charge	$ 30.00		No. 124	$150.00	
Cheque printing charge	23.00	53.00	No. 126	200.00	350.00
		$1,845.00			$1,845.00

collection fee were credited to the company's account. The bank statement also showed a credit of $8.42 for interest earned on the average cash balance in the account. Neither the collection of the note nor the interest had been recorded on the company's books.

A comparison of canceled cheques with the company's books showed that two cheques were outstanding. Cheque No. 124 for $150 and Cheque No. 126 for $200 were outstanding and unpaid by the bank. Other debits on the bank statement that had not been recorded on the books included: (1) a $23 debit memorandum for cheques printed by the bank; and (2) an NSF (nonsufficient funds) cheque for $20 plus related processing fee of $10. The NSF cheque had been received from a customer, Frank Jones, on October 16, and had been included in that day's deposit.

Illustration 7–11 shows the bank reconciliation that reflects the above items.

A bank reconciliation helps locate any errors made by either the bank or the depositor. It discloses any items that have been entered on the company's books but have not come to the bank's attention. Also, it discloses items that should be recorded on the company's books but are unrecorded on the date of the reconciliation. For example, in Valley Company's reconciliation, the reconciled cash balance, $1,845, is the true cash balance. However, at the time of the reconciliation, Valley Company's accounting records show a $1,404.58 book balance. Therefore, entries must be made to adjust the book balance, increasing it to the true cash balance. This requires four entries. The first is:

Nov.	2	Cash	485.00	
		Collection Expense	15.00	
		Notes Receivable		500.00
		To record the collection fee and proceeds of a note collected by the bank.		

This entry records the net proceeds of Valley Company's note receivable which had been collected by the bank, the expense of having the bank perform that service, and the reduction in the Notes Receivable account.

The second entry records the interest credited to Valley Company's account by the bank. Interest earned is a revenue, and the entry recognizes both the revenue and the related increase in Cash. As mentioned earlier, interest calculations are discussed in the next chapter. The entry is:

Nov.	2	Cash	8.42	
		Interest Earned		8.42
		To record interest earned on the average cash balance maintained in the chequing account.		

The third entry is:

Nov.	2	Accounts Receivable—Frank Jones	30.00	
		Cash		30.00
		To charge Frank Jones's account for his NSF cheque and for the bank's fee.		

This entry records the NSF cheque that was returned as uncollectible. The $20 cheque was received from Jones in payment of his account and was deposited as cash. The bank, unable to collect the cheque, charged $10 for handling the NSF cheque and deducted $30 from the Valley Company account. Therefore, the company must reverse the entry made when the cheque was received and also record the $10 processing fee. Valley Company charged the $10 fee to Jones's account and will try to collect the entire $30 from Jones.

The fourth entry debits Miscellaneous General Expenses for the cheque printing charge. The entry is:

Nov.	2	Miscellaneous General Expense	23.00	
		Cash		23.00
		Cheque printing charge.		

Other Internal Control Procedures

Tell how recording invoices at net amounts helps gain control over cash discounts taken and be able to account for invoices recorded at net amounts.
(L. O. 5)

Internal control procedures apply to every phase of a company's operations from purchases through sales, cash receipts, cash disbursements, and the control of plant assets. Many of these procedures are discussed in later chapters. However, a way that a company can gain control over purchases discounts is discussed here, and the technique is illustrated below.

Recall that entries like the following have been used to record the receipt and payment of an invoice for merchandise purchased.

Oct.	2	Purchases	1,000.00	
		Accounts Payable		1,000.00
		Purchased merchandise, terms 2/10, n/60.		
	12	Accounts Payable	1,000.00	
		Purchases Discounts		20.00
		Cash		980.00
		Paid the invoice of October 2.		

These entries reflect the **gross method of recording purchases.** Thus, the invoice was recorded at its gross amount of $1,000. This is the way invoices are recorded in many companies. However, a better method is to record invoices at their **net** (after discount) amounts. To illustrate, a company that records invoices at net amounts purchased merchandise that had a $1,000 invoice price, terms 2/10, n/60. On receipt of the goods, the purchasing company deducted the offered $20 discount from the gross invoice amount and recorded the purchase with this debit and credit:

Oct.	2	Purchases	980.00	
		Accounts Payable		980.00
		Purchased merchandise on credit.		

If the invoice for this purchase is paid within the discount period, the entry to record the payment has a debit to Accounts Payable and a credit to Cash for $980. However, if payment is not made within the discount period and the discount is *lost,* an entry like the following must be made either before or when the invoice is paid:

Dec.	1	Discounts Lost	20.00	
		Accounts Payable		20.00
		To record the discount lost.		

A cheque for the full $1,000 invoice amount is then drawn, recorded, and mailed to the creditor.

Advantage of the Net Method

When invoices are recorded at gross amounts, the amount of discounts taken is deducted from the balance of the Purchases account on the income statement to arrive at the cost of merchandise purchased. However, when invoices are recorded at gross amounts, the amount of any discounts that are lost does not appear in any account or on the income statement. Therefore, discounts lost may not come to the attention of management. On the other hand, when purchases are recorded at net amounts, the amount of discounts taken does not appear on the income statement. Instead, the amount of **discounts lost** is called to management's attention through the appearance on the income state-

---

Illustration 7–12
Reporting discounts lost when the net method of recording purchases is used

XYZ COMPANY
Income Statement
For Year Ended December 31, 1990

Sales	$100,000
Cost of goods sold	60,000
Gross profit from sales	$ 40,000
Operating expenses	28,000
Income from operations	$ 12,000
Other revenues and expenses:	
Discounts lost	(150)
Net income	$ 11,850

---

ment of an expense called discounts lost. This is shown in the condensed income statement of Illustration 7–12.

Of the two methods, recording invoices at their net amounts probably supplies management with the more valuable information, the amount of discounts lost through oversight, carelessness, or other cause. It also gives management better control over the work of the people responsible for taking cash discounts. If discounts are lost, someone must explain why. As a result, fewer discounts are lost through carelessness.

Summary of the Chapter in Terms of Learning Objectives

1. Internal control procedures are designed to protect assets against theft or misuse, to promote operational efficiencies, and to encourage adherence to prescribed managerial policies. Principles of good internal control include having clearly established responsibilities, maintaining adequate records, insuring assets and bonding employees, separating record-keeping and custody over assets, dividing responsibilities for related transactions, using mechanical devices where practicable, and regularly performing independent reviews of the internal control practices.

2. To maintain control over cash, custody over the assets must be separated from record-keeping for cash. Also, all cash receipts should be deposited in the bank on a daily basis, and all payments, except for minor petty cash payments, should be made by cheque. A voucher system helps maintain control over cash disbursements.

3. The petty cashier, who should be a responsible employee, makes payments from the fund and obtains signed receipts for the payments. The Petty Cash account is debited when the fund is established or increased in size, and petty cash disbursements are recorded whenever the fund is replenished.

4. A bank reconciliation is performed to prove the accuracy of the depositor's and the bank's records. When the reconciliation is performed, the bank statement balance is adjusted for such items as outstanding cheques and deposits made after banking hours on the day of the bank statement. The records of the depositor are adjusted for such items as service charges, collections the bank has made for the depositor, and interest earned on the average chequing account balance.

5. When the net method of recording invoices is used, cash discounts lost are reported as an expense in the income statement. By comparison, when the gross method is used, discounts taken are reported as revenues. Therefore, the net method directs management's attention to instances where the company failed to take advantage of discounts.

Demonstration Problem

Complete the following table for a bank reconciliation as of September 30. Place an "x" in the appropriate columns to indicate whether the item should be added to or deducted from the book or bank balance, or whether it should not appear on the reconciliation. If the book balance is to be adjusted, place a "Dr." or "Cr." in the Must Adjust column to indicate whether the Cash balance should be debited or credited.

	Book Balance			Bank Balance		Not Shown on the Reconciliation
	Add	Deduct	Must Adjust	Add	Deduct	
1. Interest earned on the account.						
2. Deposit made on September 30 after the bank was closed.						
3. Cheques that were outstanding on August 31 and that cleared the bank in September.						
4. NSF cheque from customer returned on September 15 but not recorded by the company.						
5. Cheques written and mailed to payees on September 30.						
6. Deposit made on September 5 that was processed on September 8.						
7. Unrecorded withdrawal by owner using Automatic Teller Machine.						
8. Bank service charge.						

	Book Balance			Bank Balance		Not Shown on the Reconciliation
	Add	Deduct	Must Adjust	Add	Deduct	
9. Cheques written and mailed to payees on October 5.						
10. Cheque written by another depositor but charged against the company's account.						
11. Principal and interest collected by the bank but not recorded by the company.						
12. Special charge for collection of note in No. 11 on company's behalf.						
13. Cheque written against the account and cleared by the bank; erroneously omitted by the bookkeeper.						

Solution to Demonstration Problem

	Book Balance			Bank Balance		Not Shown on the Reconciliation
	Add	Deduct	Must Adjust	Add	Deduct	
1. Interest earned on the account.	x		Dr.			
2. Deposit made on September 30 after the bank was closed.				x		
3. Cheques that were outstanding on August 31 and that cleared the bank in September.						x
4. NSF cheque from customer returned on September 15 but not recorded by the company.		x	Cr.			
5. Cheques written and mailed to payees on September 30.					x	
6. Deposit made on September 5 that was processed on September 8.						x

	Book Balance			Bank Balance		Not Shown on the Reconcil- iation
	Add	Deduct	Must Adjust	Add	Deduct	
7. Unrecorded with- drawal by owner using Automatic Teller Machine.		x	Cr.			
8. Bank service charge.		x	Cr.			
9. Cheques written and mailed to payees on October 5.						x
10. Cheque written by another depositor but charged against the com- pany's account.				x		
11. Principal and in- terest collected by the bank but not recorded by the company.	x		Dr.			
12. Special charge for collection of note in No. 11 on com- pany's behalf.		x	Cr.			
13. Cheque written against the ac- count and cleared by the bank; er- roneously omitted by the bookkeeper.		x	Cr.			

Appendix F

RECORDING VOUCHERS, MANUAL SYSTEM

Explain the use of a Voucher Register and Cheque Register and prepare entries to record and pay liabilities when these registers are used in a manual accounting system.
(L. O. 7)

When a voucher system is in use, an account called Vouchers Payable replaces the Accounts Payable account described in previous chapters. And for every transaction that will result in a cash disbursement, a voucher is prepared and credited to this account. For example, when merchandise is purchased, the voucher covering the transaction is recorded with a debit to Purchases and a credit to Vouchers Payable. Likewise, when a plant asset is purchased or an expense is incurred, the voucher of the transaction is recorded with a debit to the proper plant asset or expense account and a credit to Vouchers Payable.

In a manual system, vouchers are recorded in a **Voucher Register** similar to Illustration F–1. Such a register has a Vouchers Payable Credit column and a number of debit columns. The exact debit columns vary from company to company, but merchandising concerns always provide a Purchases Debit col- umn. Also, as long as space is available, special debit columns are provided for transactions that occur frequently. In addition, an Other Accounts Debit col- umn is provided for transactions that do not occur often.

In recording vouchers in a register like that of Illustration F–1, all information about each voucher, other than information about its payment, is entered as soon as the voucher is approved for recording. The information as to payment date and the number of the paying cheque is entered later as each voucher is paid.

In posting a Voucher Register like that in Illustration F–1, the columns are first totaled and crossfooted to prove their equality. The Vouchers Payable column total is then credited to the Vouchers Payable account. The totals of the Purchases, Transportation-In, Sales Salaries Expense, Advertising Expense, Delivery Expense, and Office Salaries Expense columns are debited to these accounts. None of the individual amounts in these columns are posted. However, the individual amounts in the Other Accounts column are posted as individual amounts, and the column total is not posted.

The Unpaid Vouchers File

When a voucher system is in use, some vouchers are paid as soon as they are recorded. Others must be filed until payment is due. As an aid in taking cash discounts, vouchers for which payment is not due are generally filed in an unpaid vouchers file under the dates on which they are to be paid.

The file of unpaid vouchers takes the place of a subsidiary Accounts Payable Ledger. Actually, the file is a subsidiary ledger of amounts owed creditors. Likewise, the Vouchers Payable account is in effect a controlling account controlling the unpaid vouchers file. Therefore, after posting is completed at the end of a month, the balance of the Vouchers Payable account should equal the sum of the unpaid vouchers in the unpaid vouchers file. This is verified each month by preparing a schedule or an adding machine list of the unpaid vouchers in the file and comparing its total with the balance of the Vouchers Payable account. In addition, the unpaid vouchers in the file are compared with the unpaid vouchers shown in the Voucher Register's record of payments column. The number of each paying cheque and the payment date are entered in the Voucher Register's payments column as each voucher is paid. Therefore, the vouchers in the register without cheque numbers and payment dates should be the same as those in the unpaid vouchers file.

The Voucher System Cheque Register

In a voucher system, the Cash Disbursements Journal is replaced by a simpler *Cheque Register*. All cheques drawn in payment of vouchers are recorded in the Cheque Register. No obligation is paid until a voucher covering the payment is prepared and recorded in the Voucher Register. Likewise, no cheque is drawn except in payment of a specific voucher. Therefore, all cheques drawn result in debits to Vouchers Payable and credits to Cash, unless a discount must be recorded. Then, there are credits to both Purchases Discounts and to Cash. A Cheque Register is shown in Illustration F–2. Note that it has columns for debits to Vouchers Payable and credits to Purchases Discounts and to Cash. In posting, all amounts entered in these columns are posted in the column totals.

Illustration F–1
A Voucher Register

Page 32   Voucher

Date 19—		Voucher No.	Payee	When and How Paid		Vouchers Payable Credit	Purchases Debit	Transportation-In Debit	
				Date	Cheque No.				
Oct.	1	767	A. B. Seay Co.	10/6	733	800.00	800.00		1
	1	768	Daily Sentinel	10/9	744	53.00			2
	2	769	Seaboard Supply Co.	10/12	747	235.00	155.00	10.00	3
	6	770	George Smith	10/6	734	85.00			4
	6	771	Frank Jones	10/6	735	95.00			5
	6	772	George Roth	10/6	736	95.00			6
	30	998	First National Bank	10/30	972	505.00			33
									34
	30	999	Pacific Telephone Co.	10/30	972	18.00			35
	31	1000	Tarbell Wholesale Co.			235.00	235.00	36	
	31	1001	Office Equipment Co.	10/31	974	195.00			37
	31		Totals			5,079.00	2,435.00	156.00	38
						(213)	(511)	(514)	39
									40
									41

Illustration F–2
A Cheque Register

Cheque Register

Date 19—		Payee	Voucher No.	Ch. No.	Vouchers Payable Debit	Purchases Discounts Credit	Cash Credit
Oct.	1	C. B. & Y. RR Co.	765	728	14.00		14.00
	3	Frank Mills	766	729	73.00		73.00
	3	Ajax Wholesale Co.	753	730	250.00	5.00	245.00
	4	Normal Supply Co.	747	731	100.00	2.00	98.00
	5	Office Supply Co.	763	732	43.00		43.00
	6	A. B. Seay Co.	767	733	800.00	16.00	784.00
	6	George Smith	770	734	85.00		85.00
	6	Frank Jones	771	735	95.00		95.00
	30	First National Bank	998	972	505.00		505.00
	30	Pacific Telephone Co.	999	973	18.00		18.00
	31	Office Equipment Co.	1001	974	195.00		195.00
	31	Totals			6,468.00	28.00	6,440.00
					(213)	(512)	(111)

Register Page 32

	Sales Salaries Expense Debit	Adver-tising Expense Debit	Delivery Expense Debit	Office Salaries Expense Debit	Other Accounts Debit		
					Account Name	PR	Amount Debit
1							
2		53.00					
3					Store Supplies	117	70.00
4				85.00			
5	95.00						
6	95.00						
33					Notes Payable	211	500.00
34					Interest Expense	721	5.00
35					Telephone Expense	655	18.00
36							
37					Office Equipment	134	195.00
38	740.00	115.00	358.00	340.00			935.00
39	(611)	(612)	(615)	(615)			(√)
40							
41							

Purchases Returns

Occasionally, an item must be returned after the voucher recording its purchase has been prepared and entered in the Voucher Register. In such cases, the return is recorded with a general journal entry like the following:

Nov.	5	Vouchers Payable		15.00	
		Purchases Returns and Allowances			15.00
		Returned defective merchandise.			

In addition to the entry, the amount of the return is deducted on the voucher, and the credit memorandum and other documents verifying the return are attached to the voucher. Then, when the voucher is paid, a cheque is drawn for its corrected amount.

Summary of the Appendix in Terms of the Learning Objective

7. When a voucher system is used, all transactions that will require payments by cheque are recorded in a Voucher Register, which serves as a book of original entry. A Purchases Journal is not used. Then, cheques drawn in payment of vouchers are recorded in the Cheque Register, which replaces the Cash Disbursements Journal. The file of unpaid vouchers takes the place of a subsidiary Accounts Payable Ledger.

Glossary

Define or explain the words and phrases listed in the chapter Glossary. (L. O. 6)

Bank reconciliation an analysis that explains the difference between the balance of a chequing account as recorded in the depositor's records and the balance as shown on the bank statement. p. 348

Canceled cheques cheques that have been stamped or perforated by the bank to show they have been paid. p. 348

Cash Over and Short account an income statement account in which cash overages and cash shortages arising from making change are recorded. p. 346

Discounts lost an expense resulting from the failure to take advantage of cash discounts on purchases. p. 354

Gross method of recording purchases a method of recording purchases by which offered cash discounts are not deducted from the invoice price in determining the amount to be recorded. p. 354

Internal control system the procedures adopted by a business to encourage adherence to prescribed managerial policies, to protect its assets from waste, fraud, and theft, and to ensure accurate and reliable accounting data. p. 333

Invoice a document, prepared by a vendor, on which are listed the items sold, the sales prices, the customer's name, and the terms of sale. p. 340

Invoice approval form a document on which the accounting department notes that it has performed each step in the process of checking an invoice and approving it for recording and payment. p. 341

Liquid asset an asset, such as cash, that can be easily converted into other types of assets or used to buy services or satisfy obligations. p. 333

Liquidity a characteristic of an asset indicating how easily the asset can be converted into other types of assets or used to buy services or satisfy obligations. p. 333

Net method of recording purchases a method of recording purchases by which offered cash discounts are deducted from the invoice price in determining the amount to be recorded. p. 354

Outstanding cheques cheques that were drawn by the depositor, deducted on the depositor's records, and sent to the payees, but that have not yet reached the depositor's bank for payment and deduction. p. 350

Purchase order a business form that is sent to a vendor as a written order for the purchase of goods or services. p. 340

Purchase requisition a business form used within a business to ask the purchasing department of the business to buy needed items. p. 339

Receiving report a form used within a business to notify the proper persons of the receipt of goods ordered and of the quantities and condition of the goods. p. 340

Reconcile to explain or account for the difference between two amounts. p. 348

Vendee the purchaser of goods or services. p. 340

Vendor the seller of goods or services. p. 340

Voucher a business paper used in summarizing a transaction and approving it for recording and payment. p. 341

Voucher Register a book of original entry in which approved vouchers are entered. p. 358

Voucher system a set of procedures that are designed to control the incurrence of obligations and cash disbursements. p. 338

An asterisk (*) identifies the questions, exercises, and problems that are based on Appendix F at the end of the chapter.

Questions for Class Discussion

1. Name the broad principles of internal control.
2. Why should the person who keeps the record of an asset be a different person from the one responsible for custody of the asset?
3. Internal control procedures are important in every business, but at what stage in the development of a business do they become critical?
4. Why should responsibility for a sequence of related transactions be divided among different departments or individuals?
5. In a small business, it is sometimes impossible to separate the functions of record-keeping and asset custody, and it is sometimes impossible to divide responsibilities for related transactions. What should be substituted for these control procedures?
6. Are the principles of internal control for computerized accounting systems different from the principles of internal control for manual accounting systems?
7. What are some of the effects of computers on internal control?
8. What is meant by the phrase *all receipts should be deposited intact*? Why should all receipts be deposited intact on the day of receipt?
9. Why should a company's bookkeeper not be given responsibility for receiving cash for the company nor the responsibility for signing cheques or making cash disbursements in any other way?
10. In purchasing merchandise in a large store, why are the department managers not permitted to deal directly with the sources of supply?
11. What are the duties of the selling department managers in the purchasing procedures of a large store?
12. Tell (*a*) who prepares, (*b*) who receives, and (*c*) the purpose of each of the following business papers:
    Purchase requisition.   Receiving report.
    Purchase order.   Invoice approval form.
    Invoice.   Voucher.
13. Do all companies need a voucher system? At what approximate point in a company's growth would you recommend the installation of such a system?
14. When a disbursing officer issues a cheque in a large business, he or she usually cannot know from personal contact that the assets, goods, or services paid for by the cheque were received by the business or that

the purchase was properly authorized. However, if the company has an internal control system, the officer can depend on the system. Exactly what documents does the officer depend on to tell that the purchase was authorized and properly made and the goods were actually received?

15. Why are some cash payments made from a petty cash fund? Why are not all payments made by cheque?

16. What is a petty cash receipt? When a petty cash receipt is prepared, who signs it?

17. Explain how a petty cash fund operates.

18. Why should a petty cash fund be reimbursed at the end of each accounting period?

19. What are two results of reimbursing the petty cash fund?

20. What is a bank statement? What kind of information appears on a bank statement?

21. What is the meaning of the phrase *to reconcile a bank balance*?

22. Why should you reconcile the bank statement balance of cash and the depositor's book balance of cash?

23. Which of the following items, disclosed in the process of preparing a bank reconciliation, require entries on the books of the depositor?
    a. Outstanding cheques.
    b. Service charges.
    c. Deposits left in the night depository of the bank on the date the bank statement was prepared.
    d. Collection by the bank of the depositor's note receivable.

24. What valuable information becomes readily available to management when invoices are recorded at net amounts? Is this information readily available when invoices are recorded at gross amounts?

*25. What kind of transactions are entered in a Voucher Register?

*26. What kind of transactions are entered in a Cheque Register?

Multiple Choice

1. The broad principles of internal control require that:
   a. Responsibility for specific tasks be shared by more than one employee so that one serves as a check on the other.
   b. Employees who handle cash and negotiable assets should be bonded.
   c. An employee who has custody over an asset should also keep the accounting records for that asset to ensure that the records are kept current.
   d. Responsibility for a series of related transactions such as for placing orders for, receiving, and paying for merchandise should be lodged in one person so that responsibility is clearly assigned.
   e. All of the above are correct.

2. Regarding internal control procedures for cash receipts:

   a. At the end of each day, each salesclerk who receives cash should analyze and correct any errors in the cash register's record of receipts before the records are submitted to the accounting department.

   b. An accounting department employee should count the cash received from sales and promptly deposit the cash receipts in the bank.

   c. Mail containing cash receipts should be opened by an accounting department employee who is responsible for recording the amount of the receipts and for depositing the receipts in the bank.

   d. All cash disbursements, other than from petty cash, should be made by cheque.

   e. All of the above are correct.

3. When a petty cash fund is used:

   a. An entry should be prepared to record each payment from the petty cash fund.

   b. Payments from the petty cash fund should be recorded with entries that include a credit to the Cash account.

   c. Reimbursements of the petty cash fund should be credited to the Cash account.

   d. The petty cashier's summary of petty cash payments serves as a journal which is posted to the appropriate General Ledger accounts.

   e. The balance in the Petty Cash account should be reported in the balance sheet as a long-term investment since this amount is kept in the fund on a long-term basis.

4. Regarding the process of preparing a bank reconciliation at the end of an accounting period:

   a. All of the reconciling items shown on a bank reconciliation must be entered in the accounting records after the reconciliation is completed.

   b. Items that appear on the reconciliation as corrections to the bank statement balance should be entered in the accounting records.

   c. Items that appear on the reconciliation as corrections to the book balance of cash should be entered in the accounting records.

   d. Outstanding cheques should be subtracted from the book balance of cash.

   e. Outstanding cheques should be added to the bank balance of cash.

5. When invoices are recorded at net amounts:

   a. Purchase discounts taken are recorded in a Purchases Discounts account.

   b. The Purchases account is debited for the amount of any purchases discount offered plus the amount to be paid if the purchase discount is taken.

   c. The amount of purchases discounts lost is not recorded in a separate account.

   d. The amount of purchases discounts taken is not recorded in a separate account.

   e. The cash expenditures for purchases will always be less than if the invoices are recorded at gross amounts.

6. In a company that records invoices at net amounts, an invoice for goods purchased from Able Company was filed in error and the discount was lost. The entry to record the lost discount is:
   a. Debit Accounts Payable—Able Company and credit Cash.
   b. Debit Discounts Lost and credit Accounts Payable—Able Company.
   c. Debit Purchases Discounts and credit Accounts Payable—Able Company.
   d. Credit Discounts Lost and debit Cash.
   e. Some other entry.

Mini Discussion Cases

Case 7–1

To add to Innocente's problems (Mini Discussion Case 5–1), auditors hired by him (after the purchase was completed) discovered that the purchased accounts receivable were substantially overstated. Reconstruction of events prior to the purchase by Gerald Innocente revealed that all cash sales made during the period January 1 to August 15 (date of the purchase of business) were recorded as sales on account; the cash was "pocketed" and fictitious accounts receivable created. Cash sales during the period recorded as credit sales totaled $40,000.

Required

1. Discuss the effect on the financial statements of the manner in which cash sales were handled.
2. Discuss the safeguards or internal control that was lacking in the situation.

Case 7–2

Refer to Case 7–1.

Required

Discuss procedures that should have been followed prior to the purchase of the business to ensure the accuracy of accounts receivable.

Exercises

Exercise 7–1
Analyzing internal control
(L. O. 1, 2)

Roper Company is a young business that has grown rapidly. The company's bookkeeper, who was hired two years ago, left town suddenly after the owner discovered that money had been disappearing over the past 18 months. An audit disclosed that the bookkeeper had written and signed cheques made payable to the bookkeeper's cousin, and then recorded the cheques as salaries expense. The cousin, who cashed the cheques but had never worked for the company, left town with the bookkeeper. As a result, the company incurred a loss of $12,000. Evaluate Roper Company's internal system and indicate which principles of internal control appear to have been ignored in this situation.

Exercise 7–2
Recommending internal control procedures
(L. O. 1, 2)

What internal control procedures would you recommend in each of the following situations?

a. Fox Lunches has one employee that sells sandwiches at a stand next to a college campus. Each day, the employee is given enough sandwiches to last through the lunch period and enough cash to make change. The money is kept in a box at the lunch stand.

b. A used goods variety store has one employee that is given cash and sent to garage sales each weekend. The employee pays cash for merchandise to be resold at the variety store.

Exercise 7–3
Petty cash fund
(L. O. 3)

A company established a $125 petty cash fund on May 1. Two weeks later, on May 15, there was $9.95 in cash in the fund and receipts for these expenditures: postage, $26.40; transportation-in, $20.50; miscellaneous general expenses, $33; and office supplies, $35.15. (a) Give in general journal form the entry to establish the fund and (b) the entry to reimburse it on May 15. (c) Assume that since the fund was exhausted so quickly, it was not only reimbursed on May 15 but also increased in size to $175. Give the entry to reimburse and increase the fund to $175.

Exercise 7–4
Petty cash fund
(L. O. 3)

A company established a $100 petty cash fund on April 10. On April 30, there was $26.60 in cash in the fund and receipts for these expenditures: transportation-in, $12.25; miscellaneous general expenses, $22.70; and office supupplies, $35.45. The petty cashier could not account for the $3 shortage in the fund. Give in general journal form (a) the entry to establish the fund and (b) the April 30 entry to reimburse the fund and reduce it to $75.

Exercise 7–5
Internal control over cash receipts
(L. O. 1, 2)

Some of Usher Company's cash receipts from customers are sent to the company in the mail. Usher Company's bookkeeper opens the letters and deposits the cash received each day. What internal control problems are inherent in this arrangement? What changes would you recommend?

Exercise 7–6
Bank reconciliation
(L. O. 4)

French's Store deposits all receipts intact on the day received and makes all payments by cheque; and on October 31, after all posting was completed, its Cash account showed a $4,530 debit balance. However, its October 31 bank statement showed only $3,870 on deposit in the bank on that day. Prepare a bank reconciliation for the store, using the following information:

a. Outstanding cheques, $600.

b. Included with the October canceled cheques returned by the bank was a $12 debit memorandum for bank services.

c. Cheque No. 426, returned with the canceled cheques, was correctly drawn for $36 in payment of the telephone bill and was paid by the bank on October 9, but it had been recorded with a debit to Telephone Expense and a credit to Cash as though it were for $63.

d. The October 31 cash receipts, $1,275, were placed in the bank's night depository after banking hours on that date and were unrecorded by the bank at the time the October bank statement was prepared.

Exercise 7–7
Adjusting entries resulting from bank reconciliation
(L. O. 4)

Give in general journal form any entries that French's Store should make as a result of having prepared the bank reconciliation of the previous exercise.

Exercise 7–8
Recording invoices at gross or net amounts
(L. O. 5)

Cates Company incurred $42,000 of operating expenses in June, a month in which its sales were $150,000. The company began June with a $78,000 merchandise inventory and ended the month with an $84,000 inventory. During the month, it purchased merchandise having a $96,000 invoice price, all of which was subject to a 2% discount for prompt payment. The company took advantage of the discounts on $66,000 of the purchases; but through an error in filing, it did not earn and could not take the discount on a $30,000 invoice paid on June 30.

Required

1. Prepare a June income statement for the company under the assumption that it records invoices at gross amounts.

2. Prepare a second income statement for the company under the assumption that it records invoices at net amounts.

Exercise 7–9
Completion of bank reconciliation
(L. O. 4)

Complete the following bank reconciliation by filling in the missing amounts:

NELSON COMPANY
Bank Reconciliation
March 31, 1990

Book balance of cash	$?		Bank statement balance	.$4,400
Add: Collection of note	500		Add: Deposit of March 31	?
Interest earned	15		Bank error	30
	$4,715			$?
Deduct: Service charge	?		Deduct: Outstanding cheques	925
NSF cheque	300			
Reconciled balance	.$?		Reconciled balance	.$4,405

Problems

Problem 7–1
Establishing and reimbursing petty cash fund
(L. O. 3)

A concern completed the following petty cash transactions during June of the current year:

June   1   Drew a $150 cheque, cashed it, and gave the proceeds and the petty cashbox to Gus Troy, an office clerk who was to act as petty cashier.

5   Purchased computer paper with petty cash, $28.80.

7   Paid $8.55 COD delivery charges on merchandise purchased for resale.

10   Paid $7.50 parcel post charges on merchandise sold to a customer and delivered by mail.

12   Gave Mr. Hank Bronson, husband of the business owner, $20 from petty cash for cab fare and other personal expenses.

June 19 Paid $9.25 COD delivery charges on merchandise purchased for re-sale.

   23 Paid a service station attendant $7.50 for washing the personal car of Lil Bronson, the business owner.

   24 Paid Ready Delivery Service $15.50 from petty cash to deliver mer-chandise sold to a customer.

   26 Paid $45.50 for minor repairs to an office typewriter.

   29 Gus Troy sorted the petty cash receipts by accounts affected and exchanged them for a cheque to reimburse the fund for expenditures and, since there was only $5.50 in cash in the fund, for the shortage for which he could not account.

Required

1. Prepare a general journal entry to record the cheque establishing the petty cash fund.

2. Prepare a summary of petty cash payments that has these categories: Office supplies, Transportation-in, Delivery expense, Withdrawals, and Miscellaneous expenses. Sort the payments into the appropriate catego-ries, total the expenses in each category, and prepare the general journal entry to reimburse the fund.

Problem 7–2
Establishing, reimbursing, and increasing petty cash fund
(L. O. 3)

A business completed these transactions:

Aug. 10 Drew a $100 cheque to establish a petty cash fund, cashed it, and delivered the proceeds and the petty cashbox to Jack Tate, an office secretary who was to act as petty cashier.

   15 Paid Sid's Delivery Service $14 to deliver merchandise sold to a customer.

   21 Purchased office supplies with petty cash, $24.50.

   28 Paid $27 from petty cash to have the office windows washed.

   30 Joe Peach, the owner of the business, signed a petty cash receipt and took $12 from petty cash for lunch money.

Sept. 4 Paid $17.25 COD delivery charges on merchandise purchased for resale.

   5 Jack Tate noted that there was only $5.25 cash remaining in the fund. Thus, he sorted the paid petty cash receipts by accounts af-fected and exchanged them for a cheque to reimburse the fund. However, since the fund had been so rapidly exhausted, the cheque was made for an amount large enough to increase the size of the fund to $125.

   7 Paid Sid's Delivery Service $10.25 to deliver merchandise to a cus-tomer.

   12 Paid the Eastside Cleaner's delivery person $18.20 on the delivery to the office of clothes Mr. Peach had dropped off at the cleaners.

   14 Paid $20.50 COD delivery charges on merchandise purchased for resale.

   17 Gave Mrs. Peach, the wife of the business owner, $15 from petty cash for cab fare and other personal expenditures.

Sept. 21   Paid $35 for minor repairs to an office typewriter.
       26   Purchased office supplies with petty cash, $9.90.
       29   Paid $8.75 COD delivery charges on merchandise purchased for resale.
       30   Jack Tate sorted the petty cash receipts by accounts affected and exchanged them for a cheque to reimburse the fund for expenditures and, since there was only $5.40 in cash in the fund, for the shortage that he could not explain.

Required

1. Prepare a general journal entry to record the cheque establishing the petty cash fund.

2. Prepare a summary of petty cash payments prior to September 5 that has these categories: Office supplies, Transportation-in, Delivery expense, Withdrawals, and Miscellaneous expenses. Sort the payments into the appropriate categories and total each category. Prepare a similar summary of petty cash payments after September 5.

3. Prepare entries to reimburse the fund and increase its size on September 5 and to reimburse the fund on September 30.

Problem 7–3
Petty cash fund; reimbursement and analysis of errors
(L. O. 3)

The Hayden Company has only one journal in its accounting system and records all transactions in that General Journal. However, the company recently set up a petty cash fund to facilitate payments of small items. The following transactions involving the petty cash fund were noted by the petty cashier as occurring during April (the last month of the company's fiscal year):

Apr. 2   Received a company cheque for $75 to establish the petty cash fund.
      10   Received a company cheque to replenish the fund for the following expenditures made since April 1 and to increase the fund to $150.
           a.   Payment of $10.50 to Ed's Trucking for freight on merchandise delivered to Atkins Company.
           b.   Purchased postage stamps for $22.
           c.   Gave Janet Knox, owner of the business, $15 for personal use.
           d.   Paid $22.75 to Perry Company for repairs of office equipment.
           e.   Discovered that only $3.25 remained in the petty cash box.
      30   Having decided that the April 10 increase in the fund was too large, received a company cheque to replenish the fund for the following expenditures made since April 10 but allowing the fund to be reduced in size to $100:
           a.   Payment of $27.50 for emergency repairs to the company's office computer printer.
           b.   Payment of $25 for janitorial service.
           c.   Purchased office supplies for $36.75.
           d.   Payment of $53.20 to King Advertising for a space advertisement in a weekly newsletter.

Required

1. Prepare general journal entries to record the establishment of the fund on April 2 and its replenishments on April 10 and on April 30.
2. If Hayden Company had failed to replenish the petty cash fund on April 30, what would have been the effect on net income for the fiscal year ended April 30 and on total assets on April 30? Explain your answer.

Problem 7–4
Preparation of bank reconciliation and recording adjustments
(L. O. 4)

The following information was available to reconcile Prince Company's book balance of cash with its bank statement balance as of December 31:

a. The December 31 cash balance according to the accounting records was $12,510, and the bank statement balance for that date was $11,939.
b. Two cheques, No. 277 for $463 and No. 278 for $418, were outstanding on November 30 when the book and bank statement balances were last reconciled. Cheque No. 278 was returned with the December canceled cheques, but Cheque No. 277 was not.
c. Cheque No. 302 for $356 and Cheque No. 304 for $328, both written and entered in the accounting records in December, were not among the canceled cheques returned.
d. When the December cheques were compared with entries in the accounting records, it was found that Cheque No. 287 had been correctly drawn for $771 in payment for store supplies but was entered in the accounting records in error as though it were drawn for $717.
e. Two debit memoranda and a credit memorandum were included with the returned cheques and were unrecorded at the time of the reconciliation. The credit memorandum indicated that the bank had collected a $2,150 note receivable for the company, deducted a $15 collection fee, and credited the balance to the company's account. One of the debit memoranda was for $195 and had attached to it an NSF cheque in that amount that had been received from a customer, Bob Lasale, in payment of his account. The second debit memorandum was for a special printing of cheques and was for $54.
f. The December 31 cash receipts, $3,550, had been placed in the bank's night depository after banking hours on that date and did not appear on the bank statement.

Required

1. Prepare a December 31 bank reconciliation for the company.
2. Prepare the general journal entries necessary to bring the company's book balance of cash into conformity with the reconciled balance.

Problem 7–5
Preparation of bank reconciliation and recording adjustments
(L. O. 4)

Norris Company reconciled its book and bank statement balances of cash on February 28 and showed two cheques outstanding at that time, No. 371 for $1,000 and No. 374 for $512. The following information was available for the March 31 reconciliation:

From the March 31 bank statement:

```
BALANCE OF PREVIOUS STATEMENT ON 28/2/— . . . . . . . . . . . . . .        6,886.00
   5 DEPOSITS AND OTHER CREDITS TOTALING . . . . . . . . . . . . . .       10,231.00
   9 CHEQUES AND OTHER DEBITS TOTALING . . . . . . . . . . . . . . .        8,693.00
      SERVICE CHARGE AMOUNT . . . . . . . . . . . . . . . . . . . . .          11.00
CURRENT BALANCE AS OF THIS STATEMENT . . . . . . . . . . . . . . . .         8,413.00
```

CHEQUING ACCOUNT TRANSACTIONS °°°

DATE	AMOUNT	TRANSACTION DESCRIPTION
Mar. 2	1,122.00+	Deposit
Mar. 12	1,984.00+	Deposit
Mar. 19	1,843.00+	Deposit
Mar. 22	1,700.00+	Deposit
Mar. 28	185.00−	NSF cheque
Mar. 31	11.00−	Service charge
Mar. 31	3,582.00+	Credit memorandum

DATE	CHEQUE NO	AMOUNT	DATE	CHEQUE NO	AMOUNT
Mar. 1	371	1,000.00	Mar. 8	379	2,653.00
Mar. 2	376*	775.00	Mar. 13	380	475.00
Mar. 5	377	1,078.00	Mar. 18	382*	1,022.00
Mar. 11	378	270.00	Mar. 27	383	1,235.00

*Indicates a skip in cheque sequence.

From Norris Company's accounting records:

Cash Receipts Deposited

Date		Cash Debit
Mar.	2	1,122.00
	12	1,984.00
	19	1,843.00
	22	1,700.00
	31	890.00
		7,539.00

Cash Disbursements

Cheque No.		Cash Credit
376		775.00
377		1,087.00
378		270.00
379		2,653.00
380		475.00
381		490.00
382		1,022.00
383		1,235.00
384		172.00
		8,179.00

Cash

Date		Explanation	PR	Debit	Credit	Balance
Feb.	28	Balance				5,374.00
Mar.	31	Total receipts	R8	7,539.00		12,913.00
	31	Total disbursements	D9		8,179.00	4,734.00

Cheque No. 377 was correctly drawn for $1,078 in payment for office equipment; however, the bookkeeper misread the amount and entered it in the accounting records with a debit to Office Equipment and a credit to Cash as though it were for $1,087.

The NSF cheque was received from a customer, Pat Slade, in payment of his account. Its return is unrecorded. The credit memorandum resulted from a $3,600 note collected for Norris Company by the bank. The bank had deducted an $18 collection fee. Collection of the note has not been recorded.

Required

1. Prepare a March 31 bank reconciliation for the company.

2. Prepare in general journal form the entries needed to adjust the book balance of cash to the reconciled balance.

Problem 7–6
Recording invoices at gross or net amounts
(L. O. 5)

The July 31 credit balance in the Sales account of Horton Sales showed it had sold $117,000 of merchandise during the month. The concern began July with a $132,100 merchandise inventory and ended the month with a $108,300 inventory. It had incurred $39,000 of operating expenses during the month, and it had also recorded the following transactions:

July 2 Received merchandise purchased at a $12,000 invoice price, invoice dated June 26, terms 2/10, n/30.

4 Received a $1,200 credit memorandum (invoice price) for merchandise received on July 2 and returned for credit.

10 Received merchandise purchased at a $19,000 invoice price, invoice dated July 9, terms 2/10, n/30.

14 Received merchandise purchased at an $18,000 invoice price, invoice dated July 12, terms 2/10, n/30.

18 Paid for the merchandise received on July 10, less the discount.

21 Paid for the merchandise received on July 14, less the discount.

26 After the credit memorandum received on July 4 was attached to the invoice dated June 26, the invoice was mistakenly filed for payment today, which is the last day of its credit period. This caused the discount to be lost. Paid the invoice.

Required

1. Assume the concern records invoices at gross amounts. (*a*) Prepare general journal entries to record the transactions. (*b*) Prepare a July income statement for the concern.

2. Assume the concern records invoices at net amounts. (*a*) Prepare general journal entries to record the transactions. (*b*) Prepare a second income statement for the concern under this assumption.

*Problem 7–7
Using a voucher system
(L. O. 7)

Hitchcock Company completed these transactions involving vouchers payable:

Aug. 4 Recorded Voucher No. 524 payable to Evans Company for merchandise having a $3,420 invoice price, invoice dated July 31, terms FOB factory, 2/10, n/30. The vendor had prepaid the freight, $162, adding the amount to the invoice and bringing its total to $3,582.

6 Recorded Voucher No. 525 payable to *The Star* for advertising expense, $396. Issued Cheque No. 424 in payment of the voucher.

7 Received a credit memorandum for merchandise having a $540 invoice price. The merchandise had been received from Evans Company on August 4, recorded on Voucher No. 524, and later returned for credit.

Aug. 9   Recorded Voucher No. 526 payable to Western Realty for one month's rent on the space occupied by the store, $1,800. Issued Cheque No. 425 in payment of the voucher.

11   Recorded Voucher No. 527 payable to North Supply Company for store supplies, $234, terms n/10 EOM.

13   Recorded Voucher No. 528 payable to Rawlins Company for merchandise having a $4,500 invoice price, invoice dated August 11, terms FOB factory, 2/10, n/60. The vendor had prepaid the freight charges, $180, adding the amount to the invoice and bringing its total to $4,680.

14   Recorded Voucher No. 529 payable to Payroll for sales salaries, $1,800, and office salaries, $1,350. Issued Cheque No. 426 in payment of the voucher. Cashed the cheque and paid the employees.

18   Recorded Voucher No. 530 payable to Apex Company for merchandise having a $2,700 invoice price, invoice dated August 16, terms 2/10, n/60, FOB factory. The vendor had prepaid the freight charges, $126, adding the amount to the invoice and bringing its total to $2,826.

21   Issued Cheque No. 427 in payment of Voucher No. 528.

25   Recorded Voucher No. 531 payable to Rawlins Company for merchandise having a $5,400 invoice price, invoice dated August 23, terms FOB factory, 2/10, n/60. The vendor had prepaid the freight charges, $252, adding the amount to the invoice and bringing its total to $5,652.

27   Discovered that Voucher No. 524 had been filed in error for payment on the last day of its credit period rather than on the last day of its discount period, causing the discount to be lost. Issued Cheque No. 428 in payment of the voucher, less the return.

31   Recorded Voucher No. 532 payable to Payroll for sales salaries, $1,800, and office salaries, $1,350. Issued Cheque No. 429 in payment of the voucher. Cashed the cheque and paid the employees.

Required

1. Assume that Hitchcock Company records vouchers at gross amounts. Prepare a Voucher Register, a Cheque Register, and a General Journal, and record the transactions.

2. Prepare a Vouchers Payable account and post those portions of the journal and register entries that affect the account.

3. Test the accuracy of the Vouchers Payable account balance by preparing a schedule of vouchers payable.

Alternate Problems

Problem 7–1A
Establishing and reimbursing petty cash fund
(L. O. 3)

A concern completed the following petty cash transactions during October of the current year:

Oct. 2   Drew a $125 cheque, cashed it, and turned the proceeds and the petty cashbox over to Norm Bowers, an office clerk who was to act as petty cashier.

Oct. 5   Paid $9.15 parcel post charges on merchandise sold to a customer and delivered by mail.

8   Purchased office supplies with petty cash, $14.50.

9   Paid $28.35 from petty cash for repairs to an office copier.

12   Paid $10 COD delivery charges on merchandise purchased for resale.

15   Paid Mercury Delivery Service $11.25 to deliver merchandise sold to a customer.

21   Gave Dennis Moore, the owner of the business, $20 from petty cash for personal use.

23   Paid $12.55 COD delivery charges on merchandise purchased for resale.

27   Dennis Moore, owner of the business, signed a petty cash receipt and took $12 from petty cash for lunch money.

30   Norm Bowers exchanged his paid petty cash receipts for a cheque reimbursing the fund for expenditures and a shortage of cash in the fund that he could not account for. He reported a cash balance of $2.20 in the fund.

Required

1. Prepare a general journal entry to record the cheque establishing the petty cash fund.

2. Prepare a summary of petty cash payments that has these categories: Office supplies, Transportation-in, Delivery expense, Withdrawals, and Miscellaneous expenses. Sort the payments into the appropriate categories, total the expenses in each category, and prepare the general journal entry to reimburse the fund.

Problem 7–2A
Establishing, reimbursing, and increasing petty cash fund
(L. O. 3)

A business completed these petty cash transactions:

May 4   Drew a $75 cheque to establish a petty cash fund, cashed it, and turned the proceeds and the petty cashbox over to Gayle Bates, an office worker who was appointed petty cashier.

6   Paid $12.55 parcel post charges on merchandise sold to a customer and delivered by mail.

8   Paid $14 to have the office windows washed.

11   Purchased office supplies with petty cash, $25.25.

12   Susan Dixon, owner of the business, signed a petty cash receipt and took $8 from petty cash for coffee money.

14   Paid $13.20 COD delivery charges on merchandise purchased for resale.

15   Gayle Bates noted that only $2 remained in the petty cashbox. Thus, she sorted the petty cash receipts in terms of the accounts affected and exchanged the receipts for a cheque to reimburse the fund. However, since the fund had been exhausted so quickly, the cheque was made sufficiently large to increase the size of the fund to $150.

18   Paid $35 from petty cash for minor repairs to an office machine.

May 20 Paid $12.75 COD delivery charges on merchandise purchased for resale.

22 Paid A. M. Delivery Service $15.20 to deliver merchandise sold to a customer.

26 Purchased office supplies with petty cash, $18.

27 Susan Dixon, owner of the business, signed a petty cash receipt and took $15 from petty cash for lunch money.

June 1 Paid $16.50 COD delivery charges on merchandise purchased for resale.

5 Purchased paper clips and pencils with petty cash, $10.80.

10 Paid $18.75 COD delivery charges on merchandise purchased for resale.

12 Gayle Bates sorted the petty cash receipts and exchanged them for a cheque to replenish the fund for expenditures and, since there was only $1.50 in cash in the fund, for the unexplained shortage.

Required

1. Prepare a general journal entry to record the cheque establishing the petty cash fund.

2. Prepare a summary of petty cash payments prior to May 15 that has these categories: Delivery expense, Office supplies, Miscellaneous expenses, Withdrawals, and Transportation-in. Sort the payments into the appropriate categories and total each category. Prepare a similar summary of petty cash payments after May 15.

3. Prepare entries to reimburse the fund and increase its size on May 15 and to reimburse the fund on June 12.

Problem 7–3A
Petty cash fund;
reimbursement and
analysis of errors
(L. O. 3)

The accounting system used by the Franklin Company requires that all entries be journalized in a General Journal. To facilitate payments of small items, Franklin Company recently established a petty cash fund. The following transactions involving the petty cash fund occurred during August (the last month of the company's fiscal year):

Aug. 3 A company cheque for $200 was drawn and made payable to the petty cashier to establish the petty cash fund.

14 A company cheque was drawn to replenish the fund for the following expenditures made since August 1 and to increase the fund to $300:

a. Purchased postage stamps for $44.

b. Payment of $42.30 to Meeks Trucking for delivery of merchandise to customers.

c. Gave Beth Rogers, owner of the business, $50 for personal use.

d. Paid $60.50 to Appliance Company for repairs of office equipment.

e. Discovered that only $1.20 remained in the petty cashbox.

31 The petty cashier noted that $2.60 remained in the fund. Having decided that the August 14 increase in the fund was not large enough, a company cheque was drawn to replenish the fund for the

following expenditures made since August 14 and to increase it to $350:

a. Payment of $97.25 for office supplies to support the company's computer.

b. Payment of $52.15 for items classified as miscellaneous general expense.

c. Payment of $63 for janitorial service.

d. Payment of $85 to Southern Advertising Company for a space advertisement in a weekly newsletter.

Required

1. Prepare general journal entries to record the establishment of the fund on August 3 and its replenishments on August 14 and on August 31.

2. If Franklin Company had failed to replenish the petty cash fund on August 31, what would have been the effect on net income for the fiscal year ended August 31 and on total assets on August 31? Explain your answer. (Hint: The amount of Office Supplies to appear on a balance sheet is determined by a physical count of the supplies on hand.)

Problem 7–4A
Preparation of bank reconciliation and recording adjustments
(L. O. 4)

The following information was available to reconcile Golf Company's book balance of cash with its bank statement balance as of February 28:

a. After all posting was completed on February 28, the company's Cash account had a $7,180 debit balance, but its bank statement showed a $9,415 balance.

b. Cheques No. 217 for $365 and No. 222 for $709 were outstanding on the January 31 bank reconciliation. Cheque No. 222 was returned with the February canceled cheques, but Cheque No. 217 was not.

c. In comparing the canceled cheques returned with the bank statement with the entries in the accounting records, it was found that Cheque No. 297 for the purchase of office equipment was correctly drawn for $724 but was entered in the accounting records as though it were for $742. It was also found that Cheque No. 331 for $482 and Cheque No. 333 for $240, both drawn in February, were not among the canceled cheques returned with the statement.

d. A credit memorandum enclosed with the bank statement indicated that the bank had collected a $3,600 noninterest-bearing note for the concern, deducted a $36 collection fee, and had credited the remainder to the concern's account.

e. A debit memorandum for $464 listed a $452 NSF cheque plus a $12 NSF charge. The cheque had been received from a customer, Jan Bellors, and was among the canceled cheques returned.

f. Also among the canceled cheques was an $18 debit memorandum for bank services. None of the memoranda had been recorded.

g. The February 28 cash receipts, $1,952, were placed in the bank's night depository after banking hours on that date, and their amount did not appear on the bank statement.

Required

1. Prepare a bank reconciliation for the company.
2. Prepare entries in general journal form to bring the company's book balance of cash into conformity with the reconciled balance.

Problem 7–5A
Preparation of bank reconciliation and recording adjustments (L. O. 4)

Shepard Company reconciled its bank balance on November 30 and showed two cheques outstanding at that time, No. 404 for $628 and No. 409 for $124. The following information is available for the December 31 reconciliation:

From the December 31 bank statement:

BALANCE OF PREVIOUS STATEMENT ON 30/11/—	4,302.00
5 DEPOSITS AND OTHER CREDITS TOTALING.	7,344.00
8 CHEQUES AND OTHER DEBITS TOTALING.	5,683.00
SERVICE CHARGE AMOUNT	7.00
CURRENT BALANCE AS OF THIS STATEMENT	5,956.00

CHEQUING ACCOUNT TRANSACTIONS °°

DATE	AMOUNT	TRANSACTION DESCRIPTION
Dec. 2	535.00+	Deposit
Dec. 11	2,268.00+	Deposit
Dec. 21	1,560.00+	Deposit
Dec. 29	1,496.00+	Deposit
Dec. 30	576.00−	NSF cheque
Dec. 30	7.00−	Service charge
Dec. 30	1,485.00+	Credit memorandum

DATE	CHEQUE NO	AMOUNT	DATE	CHEQUE NO	AMOUNT
Nov. 25	404	628.00	Dec. 14	413	125.00
Dec. 4	410*	734.00	Dec. 16	414	280.00
Dec. 2	411	540.00	Dec. 28	415	770.00
Dec. 7	412	2,030.00			

*Indicates a skip in cheque sequence.

From Shepard Company's accounting records:

Cash Receipts Deposited

Date		Cash Debit
Dec.	2	535.00
	11	2,268.00
	21	1,560.00
	29	1,496.00
	30	765.00
		6,624.00

Cash Disbursements

Cheque No.		Cash Credit
410		734.00
411		540.00
412		2,030.00
413		125.00
414		280.00
415		707.00
416		310.00
417		391.00
		5,117.00

Cash

Date	Explanation	PR	Debit	Credit	Balance
Nov. 30	Balance				3,550.00
Dec. 31	Total receipts	R8	6,624.00		10,174.00
31	Total disbursements	D9		5,117.00	5,057.00

Cheque No. 415 was correctly drawn for $770 in payment for store equipment; however, the bookkeeper misread the amount and entered it in the accounting records with a debit to Store Equipment and a credit to Cash as though it were for $707. The bank paid and deducted the correct amount.

The NSF cheque was received from a customer, Fred Gantry, in payment of his account. Its return was unrecorded. The credit memorandum resulted from a $1,500 note which the bank had collected for the company. The bank had deducted a $15 collection fee and deposited the balance in the company's account. Collection of the note has not been recorded.

Required

1. Prepare a bank reconciliation for Shepard Company.
2. Prepare in general journal form the entries needed to bring the company's book balance of cash into agreement with the reconciled balance.

Problem 7–6A
Recording invoices at gross or net amounts
(L. O. 5)

The June 30 credit balance in the Sales account of Crewes Sales showed it had sold $325,000 of merchandise during the month. The concern began June with a $275,000 merchandise inventory and ended the month with a $217,000 inventory. It had incurred $105,000 of operating expenses during the month, and it had also recorded the following transactions:

June 2 Received merchandise purchased at a $36,000 invoice price, invoice dated May 30, terms 2/10, n/30.
  8 Received a $6,000 credit memorandum (invoice price) for merchandise received on June 2 and returned for credit.
  11 Received merchandise purchased at a $54,000 invoice price, invoice dated June 9, terms 2/10, n/30.
  15 Received merchandise purchased at a $63,750 invoice price, invoice dated June 13, terms 2/10, n/30.
  19 Paid for the merchandise received on June 11, less the discount.
  23 Paid for the merchandise received on June 15, less the discount.
  29 After the credit memorandum received on June 8 was attached to the invoice dated May 30, the invoice was mistakenly filed for payment today, which is the last day of its credit period. This caused the discount to be lost. Paid the invoice.

Required

1. Assume the concern records invoices at gross amounts. (*a*) Prepare general journal entries to record the transactions. (*b*) Prepare a June income statement for the concern.
2. Assume the concern records invoices at net amounts. (*a*) Prepare general journal entries to record the transactions. (*b*) Prepare a second income statement for the concern under this assumption.

*Problem 7–7A
Using a voucher system
(L. O. 7)

Judd Company completed these transactions involving vouchers payable:

May 1 Recorded Voucher No. 415 payable to Stewart Company for merchandise having a $1,800 invoice price, invoice dated April 28, terms FOB destination, 2/10, n/30.

May 4   Recorded Voucher No. 416 payable to Johnson Company for merchandise having a $2,800 invoice price, invoice dated May 2, terms FOB factory, 2/10, n/60. The vendor had prepaid the freight charges, $100, adding the amount to the invoice and bringing its total to $2,900.

7   Received a credit memorandum for merchandise having a $600 invoice price. The merchandise was received on May 1. Voucher No. 415, and returned for credit.

12   Issued Cheque No. 630 in payment of Voucher No. 416.

15   Recorded Voucher No. 417 payable to Payroll for sales salaries, $960, and office salaries, $640. Issued Cheque No. 631 in payment of the voucher. Cashed the cheque and paid the employees.

19   Recorded Voucher No. 418 payable to Decor Designers for the purchase of office equipment having a $720 invoice price, terms n/10 EOM.

21   Recorded Voucher No. 419 payable to *The SUN* for advertising expense, $300. Issued Cheque No. 632 in payment of the voucher.

26   Recorded Voucher No. 420 payable to Roxy Company for merchandise having a $2,020 invoice price, invoice dated May 23, terms FOB factory, 2/10, n/60. The vendor had prepaid the freight charges, $80, adding the amount to the invoice and bringing its total to $2,100.

29   Discovered that Voucher No. 415 had been filed in error for payment on the last day of its credit period rather than on the last day of its discount period, causing the discount to be lost. Issued Cheque No. 633 in payment of the voucher, less the return.

31   Recorded Voucher No. 421 payable to Payroll for sales salaries, $960, and office salaries, $640. Issued Cheque No. 634 in payment of the voucher. Cashed the cheque and paid the employees.

Required

1. Assume that Judd Company records vouchers at gross amounts. Prepare a Voucher Register, a Cheque Register, and a General Journal, and record the transactions.

2. Prepare a Vouchers Payable account and post those portions of the journal and register entries that affect the account.

3. Test the accuracy of the Vouchers Payable account balance by preparing a schedule of unpaid vouchers.

Provocative Problems

Provocative Problem 7–1
The Retiring Employee
(L. O. 1, 2)

The bookkeeper at Small Company will retire next week after more than 30 years with the store, having been hired by the father of the store's present owner. She has always been a very dependable employee, and as a result has been given more and more responsibilities over the years. Actually, for the past 15 years, she has "run" the store's office, keeping books, verifying invoices, and issuing cheques in their payment, which in the absence of the store's owner, Sally Ennis, she could sign. In addition, at the end of each day, the store's salesclerks turn over their daily cash receipts to the bookkeeper.

After counting the money and comparing the amounts with the cash register tapes, which she is responsible for removing from the cash registers, she makes the journal entry to record cash sales and then deposits the money in the bank. She also reconciles the bank balance with the book balance of cash each month.

Mrs. Ennis, the store's owner, realizes she cannot expect a new bookkeeper to accomplish as much as the old bookkeeper. And since the store is not large enough to warrant more than one office employee, she recognizes she must take over some of the old bookkeeper's duties when she retires. Mrs. Ennis already places all orders for merchandise and supplies and closely supervises all employees and does not want to add more to her duties than necessary.

Name the internal control principle violated here and tell which of the old bookkeeper's tasks should be taken over by Mrs. Ennis in order to improve the store's internal control over cash.

Provocative Problem 7–2
Sporting Goods Company
(L. O. 1, 2)

The Sporting Goods Company has enjoyed rapid growth since its beginning several years ago. Last year its sales were in excess of $15 million. However, its purchasing procedures may not have kept pace with its growth. When a plant supervisor or department head needs raw materials, plant assets, or supplies, he or she telephones a request to the purchasing department manager. The purchasing department manager prepares a purchase order in duplicate, sends one copy to the company selling the goods, and keeps the other copy in the files. When the seller's invoice is received, it is sent directly to the purchasing department. When the goods arrive, receiving department personnel count and inspect the items and prepare one copy of a receiving report which is sent to the purchasing department. The purchasing department manager attaches the receiving report and the retained copy of the purchase order to the invoice. If all is in order, the invoice is stamped "approved for payment" and signed by the purchasing department manager. The invoice and its supporting documents are then sent to the accounting department to be recorded and filed until due. On its due date, the invoice and its supporting documents are sent to the office of the company treasurer where a cheque is prepared and mailed. The number of the paying cheque is entered on the invoice and the invoice is sent to the accounting department for an entry to record its payment.

Do the procedures of Sporting Goods Company make it fairly easy for someone in the company to institute the payment of fictitious invoices by the company? If so, who is most likely to commit the fraud and what would that person have to do to receive payment of a fictitious invoice? What changes should be made in the company's purchasing procedures, and why should each change be made?

Analytical and Review Problems

A&R Problem 7–1

Your assistant prepared the following bank reconciliation statement. Obviously the statement is unacceptable and the task of preparing a proper reconciliation falls upon you.

HACKNEY COMPANY
Bank Reconciliation
October 31, 198A

Balance per books October 31, ...		$ 6,000
Add:		
Note collected	$1,000	
Interest on note	110	
Deposit in transit	2,900	4,010
		10,010
Deduct:		
Bank charges	10	
NSF cheque	100	
Outstanding cheques	1,500	
Error in Cheque No. 78 issued for $872 and . .		
recorded in the books as $827	45	1,655
Indicated bank balance		8,355
Balance per bank statement		5,555
Discrepancy		$ 2,800

Required

1. Prepare a proper bank reconciliation showing the true cash balance.
2. Prepare the necessary journal entries.

A&R Problem 7–2

The bank statement for October arrived in Friday's mail. You were especially anxious to receive the statement as one of your assignments was to prepare a bank reconciliation for the Saturday meeting. You got around to preparing the reconciliation rather late in the afternoon and found all the necessary data with the exception of the bank balance. The bottom portion of the bank statement was smudged, and several figures, including the balance, were obliterated. A telephone call to the bank was answered by a recording with the information that the bank was closed until 10 A.M. Monday. Since the reconciliation had to be prepared you decided to plug-in the bank balance.

In preparation you assembled the necessary material as follows:

a. Cash balance per books was $4,800.
b. From the canceled cheques returned by the bank you determined that six cheques remained outstanding. The total of these cheques was $2,100.
c. In checking the canceled cheques you noted that Cheque No. 274 was properly made for $481 but was recorded in the cash disbursement journal as $418. The cheque was in payment of an account.
d. Included with the bank statement were two memoranda; the credit memorandum was for collection of a note for $1,200 and $90 of interest thereon and the debit memorandum was for $12 of bank charges.
e. While you were sorting the canceled cheques, one of the cheques caught your attention. You were astounded by the similarity of name with that of your company and the similarity of the cheques. The cheque was for $340 and was obviously in error charged to your company's account.
f. From the deposit book you determined that a $2,200 deposit was made after hours on October 31.

Required

1. Prepare a bank reconciliation statement as of October 31 (plug in the indicated bank balance).
2. Prepare the necessary journal entries.

A&R Problem 7–3

The newly hired junior account of E. D. Smith Company prepared the November 30 bank reconciliation statement as follows:

E. D. SMITH COMPANY
Bank Reconciliation
November 30, 198A

Balance per books		$3,400
Add:		
Collection of note by bank	$1,500	
Interest thereon	120	
Error re E. D. Smythe Company		
cheque	300	
Error re Cheque No. 282	54	1,974
		5,374
Deduct:		
Bank charges		15
True cash balance		$5,359
Balance per bank		$4,700
Add:		
Deposit in transit	1,800	
NSF cheque	325	2,125
		6,825
Deduct:		
Outstanding cheques		1,466
True cash balance		$5,359

The controller took one glance at the reconciliation statement prepared by the junior accountant and screamed, "Where did we get him?" Therefore, the task of preparing a correct bank reconciliation fell upon you.

You determined the following:

a. All amounts in the reconciliation prepared by the junior accountant were correct.
b. The $300 E. D. Smythe Company cheque was erroneously credited by the bank to the E. D. Smith Company account.
c. E. D. Smith Company's Cheque No. 282 was properly drawn for $439 but was entered in the cash disbursement journal as $493. The cheque was in payment of an account.
d. The NSF cheque returned by the bank was from one of E. D. Smith Company's customers.

Required

1. Prepare a proper bank reconciliation statement indicating the true cash balance.
2. Prepare the required journal entries.

Carl Spinks acquired a sports equipment distribution business with a staff of six salespersons and two clerks. Because of the trust that Carl had in his employees—after all, they were all his friends and just like members of his family—he believed that an honour system with regard to the operation of the petty cash fund was adequate. Consequently, Carl placed $300 in a coffee jar, which, for convenience, was kept in a cupboard in the common room. All employees had access to the petty cash fund and withdrew amounts as required. No vouchers were required for withdrawals. As required, additional funds were placed in the coffee jar and the amount of the replenishment was charged to "miscellaneous selling expense."

Required

1. From the internal control point of view, discuss the weaknesses of the petty cash fund operation and suggest steps necessary for improvement.
2. Does the petty cash fund operation as described above violate any of the generally accepted accounting principles? If yes, which and how is/are the principle(s) violated?

8 Temporary Investments and Receivables

The focus of the last chapter was on accounting for cash, which is the most liquid of all assets. This chapter continues the discussion of liquid assets by focusing on temporary investments of cash, on accounts receivable, and on short-term notes receivable.

Learning Objectives

After studying Chapter 8, you should be able to:

1. Journalize entries to account for temporary investments; and calculate, record, and report the lower of cost or market of temporary investments in marketable equity securities.

2. Prepare entries to account for credit card sales.

3. Prepare entries to account for credit customers, including allowance method entries and direct write-off method entries to account for bad debts.

4. Calculate the interest on promissory notes and prepare entries to record the receipt of promissory notes and their payment or dishonour.

5. Calculate the discount and proceeds on discounted notes receivable and prepare entries to record the discounting of notes receivable and, if dishonoured, their dishonour.

6. Define or explain the words and phrases listed in the chapter Glossary.

Since cash is the typical means by which companies pay their obligations, good management generally requires that companies keep some surplus cash balances. Also, seasonal fluctuations in sales volume often result in surplus cash balances during some months of each year. Rather than leave these surplus cash balances in chequing accounts that pay, at best, low rates of interest, many concerns invest their surplus cash in the hope of earning higher returns.

Temporary Investments

Journalize entries to account for short-term investments; and calculate, record, and report the lower of cost or market of short-term investments in marketable equity securities. (L. O. 1)

Investments of surplus cash may be in a variety of government or corporate debt obligations or in stocks (equity securities). If the investments can be converted into cash quickly, and if management intends to hold the investments as a source of cash to satisfy the needs of current operations, the investments are called **temporary investments** or **short-term investments.** This means that they are classified on the balance sheet as current assets.

Some investments that are held as a source of cash qualify as current assets because they mature in a short period of time. These include short-term debt obligations of the government or other corporations that mature and will be repaid within one year or the current operating cycle of the business, whichever is longer. Investments in other securities that do not mature in a short period of time can be classified as current assets only if they are marketable. In other words, such securities must be salable without excessive delays. For example, stocks that are actively traded on a stock exchange qualify as marketable.

When temporary investments are purchased, you should record the investments at cost. For example, if Ford Motor Company's short-term notes payable are purchased for $40,000, you record the purchase as follows:

Aug.	16	Temporary Investments	40,000.00	
		Cash		40,000.00
		Bought $40,000 of Ford Motor Company notes due October 16.		

Assume that when these notes mature, the cash proceeds are $40,000 plus $800 interest. When the receipt is recorded, the interest is credited to a revenue account, as follows:

Oct.	16	Cash	40,800.00	
		Temporary Investments.		40,000.00
		Interest Earned		800.00
		Received cash proceeds from mature notes.		

When you determine the cost of an investment, you must include any commissions paid. For example, if 3,000 shares of Canadian Pacific (CP) common stock are purchased as a temporary investment, at 23⅜ ($23.375 per share)[1] plus a $625 broker's commission, the entry to record the transaction is:

Oct.	15	Temporary Investments	70,750.00	
		Cash		70,750.00
		Bought 3,000 shares of CP stock at $23⅜ plus $625 broker's commission.		

If cash dividends are received on stock held as a temporary investment, the dividends are credited to a revenue account, as follows:

Dec.	12	Cash	750.00	
		Dividends Earned		750.00
		Received dividend of 25 cents per share.		

When a temporary investment is sold, the difference between the cost of the investment and the cash proceeds from the sale is recorded as a gain or loss. For example, if 1,500 of the CP common shares are sold on December 20 for 22½ per share less a $350 commission, the sale is recorded as follows:

Dec.	20	Cash	33,400.00	
		Loss on Sale of Temporary Investments.	1,975.00	
		Temporary Investments.		35,375.00
		(1,500 × $22.50) − $350 = $33,400.		
		$70,750 ÷ 2 = $35,375.		

Temporary investments in marketable equity securities should be reported on the balance sheet at the **lower of cost or market (LCM).** In calculating the lower of cost or market (LCM), the total cost of all marketable securities held as temporary investments is compared with the total market value on the balance sheet date. For example, assume that on December 31, 1990, the company that purchased the CP stock has two other temporary investments in marketable equity securities. Lower of cost or market is determined by comparing the total cost and total market of the entire portfolio, as follows:

Temporary Investments	Cost	Market	LCM
Imasco common stock.	$ 42,600	$ 43,500	
Imperial Oil common stock	30,500	28,200	
Canadian Pacific common stock	35,375	34,000	
Total	$108,475	$105,700	$105,700

---

[1] Stocks are quoted on stock exchanges on the basis of dollars and ⅛ dollars per share. For example, a stock quoted at 23⅛ sold for $23.125 per share and one quoted at 36½ sold for $36.50 per share.

To record the reduction in the value of the temporary investment portfolio, the following entry is made:

Dec.	31	Loss on Market Decline of Temporary Investments.	2,775.00	
		Allowance to Reduce Temporary Investments		
		to Market		2,775.00
		$108,475 − $105,700 = $2,775.		

The Loss on Temporary Investments account is closed to Income Summary and reported on the income statement. The Allowance to Reduce Temporary Investments to Market account is a contra asset account. It is subtracted from the cost of the temporary investments so that they are reported in the current asset section of the balance sheet at the lower of cost or market, as follows:

Current assets:	
Cash.	xxx
Temporary investments, at lower of cost or	
market (cost is $108,475)	105,700

When the market value of temporary investments increases above cost, the increases are not recorded until the investments are sold. However, if temporary investments are written down to a market value below cost, subsequent increases in market value up to the original cost are recorded.

The use of lower of cost or market is often criticized because it is a departure from the *cost principle*. On the other hand, those who support the use of LCM argue that it provides a conservative balance sheet valuation.

In addition to cash and temporary investments, the liquid assets of a business include receivables that result from credit sales to customers. In the following sections of this chapter, we first discuss the procedures used to account for sales when customers use credit cards issued by banks or credit card companies. Then, we focus on accounting for credit sales when a business grants credit to its customers. This involves (1) maintaining a separate account receivable for each customer, (2) accounting for bad debts that result from credit sales, and (3) accounting for notes receivable.

Credit Card Sales

Prepare entries to account for credit card sales. (L. O. 2)

Many customers use credit cards such as VISA, MasterCard, or American Express to charge purchases from various businesses. This practice gives customers the ability to make purchases without carrying cash or writing checks. Also, customers usually can defer payment to the credit card company. Furthermore, once credit is established with the credit card company, the customer does not have to establish credit with each store. Finally, if customers use a credit card, they can avoid having to make several monthly payments to a variety of creditors.

There are good reasons why businesses allow customers to use credit cards. First, the business does not have to evaluate the credit standing of each customer or make decisions about who should get credit and how much. Second, the business avoids the risk of extending credit to customers who cannot pay. Third, the business often receives cash from the credit card company quicker than it would if customers were granted credit.

With some credit cards, usually those issued by banks, the business deposits a copy of each credit card receipt in its bank account just as it would deposit a customer's cheque. Thus, the business receives a cash credit immediately upon deposit. With other credit cards, the business sends the appropriate copy of each receipt to the credit card company and then is paid by the company. Until payment is received, the business has an account receivable from the credit card company. In return for the services provided to the business, credit card companies charge a fee ranging from 2% to 5% of credit card sales. This charge is deducted from the cash payment to the business.

Accounting for credit card sales depends on whether cash is received immediately upon deposit or is delayed until paid by the credit card company. If cash is received immediately, the entry to record credit card sales is:

Jan.	25	Cash	96.00	
		Credit Card Expense.	4.00	
		Sales.		100.00
		To record credit card sales less a 4% credit card expense.		

If the business must send the receipts to the credit card company and wait for payment, the entry to record credit card sales is:

Jan.	25	Accounts Receivable, Credit Card Company	100.00	
		Sales.		100.00
		To record credit card sales.		

When cash is received from the credit card company, the entry to record the receipt is:

Feb.	10	Cash	96.00	
		Credit Card Expense.	4.00	
		Accounts Receivable, Credit Card Company.		100.00
		To record cash receipt less 4% credit card expense.		

In the above entries, notice that the credit card expense was not recorded until cash was received from the credit card company. This is a matter of convenience. By following this procedure, the business avoids having to calculate the credit card expense each time a sale is recorded. Instead, the expense related to many sales can be calculated once and recorded when cash is received. However, the *matching principle* requires that you report credit card expense in the same period as the sale. Therefore, if the sale and the cash receipt occur in different periods, you must accrue and report the credit card expense in the period of sale.

Credit card expense is sometimes disclosed in the income statement as a type of discount that is deducted from sales to get net sales. Other companies classify it as a selling expense or even as an administrative expense. Arguments can be made for all three alternatives.

Maintaining a Separate Account for Each Customer

Prepare entries to account for credit customers, including allowance method entries and direct write-off method entries to account for bad debts. (L. O. 3)

In previous chapters, when we recorded credit sales, we debited a single account called Accounts Receivable. However, when a business has more than one credit customer, the accounts must be designed so that they show how much each customer has purchased, how much each customer has paid, and how much remains to be collected from each customer. To provide this information, businesses with credit customers must maintain a separate account receivable for each customer.

One possible way of keeping a separate account for each customer would be to keep all of these accounts in the same ledger that contains the financial statement accounts. However, this usually is not done. Instead, the ledger that contains the financial statement accounts, the **General Ledger,** continues to hold a single Accounts Receivable account. Then, a supplementary record is established in which a separate account is maintained for each customer. This supplementary record is called the **Accounts Receivable Ledger.**

Illustration 8–1 shows the relationship between the Accounts Receivable account in the General Ledger and the individual customer accounts in the Accounts Receivable Ledger. In Illustration 8–1, notice that the sum of the balances in the Accounts Receivable Ledger is equal to the balance of the Accounts Receivable account in the General Ledger. To maintain this relationship, each time credit sales are posted to the Accounts Receivable account, they are also posted to the appropriate customer accounts in the Accounts Receivable Ledger. Also, cash receipts from credit customers must be posted to both the Accounts Receivable account in the General Ledger and to the appropriate customer accounts.

You should understand that when debits (or credits) to Accounts Receivable are posted twice, this does not violate the requirement that debits equal credits. The equality of debits and credits is maintained *in the General Ledger.* The Accounts Receivable Ledger is simply a supplementary record that provides detailed information concerning each customer.

Because the balance in the Accounts Receivable account is always equal to the sum of the balances in the customers' accounts, the Accounts Receivable account is said to control the Accounts Receivable Ledger and is called a **controlling account.** And since the Accounts Receivable Ledger is a supplementary record that is controlled by an account in the General Ledger, it is called a **subsidiary ledger.**

The Accounts Receivable account and the Accounts Receivable Ledger are not the only examples of controlling accounts and subsidiary ledgers. Most companies buy on credit from several suppliers and must use a controlling account and subsidiary ledger for accounts payable. Another example might be an Office Equipment account, which would control a subsidiary ledger in which each item of equipment is recorded in a separate account.

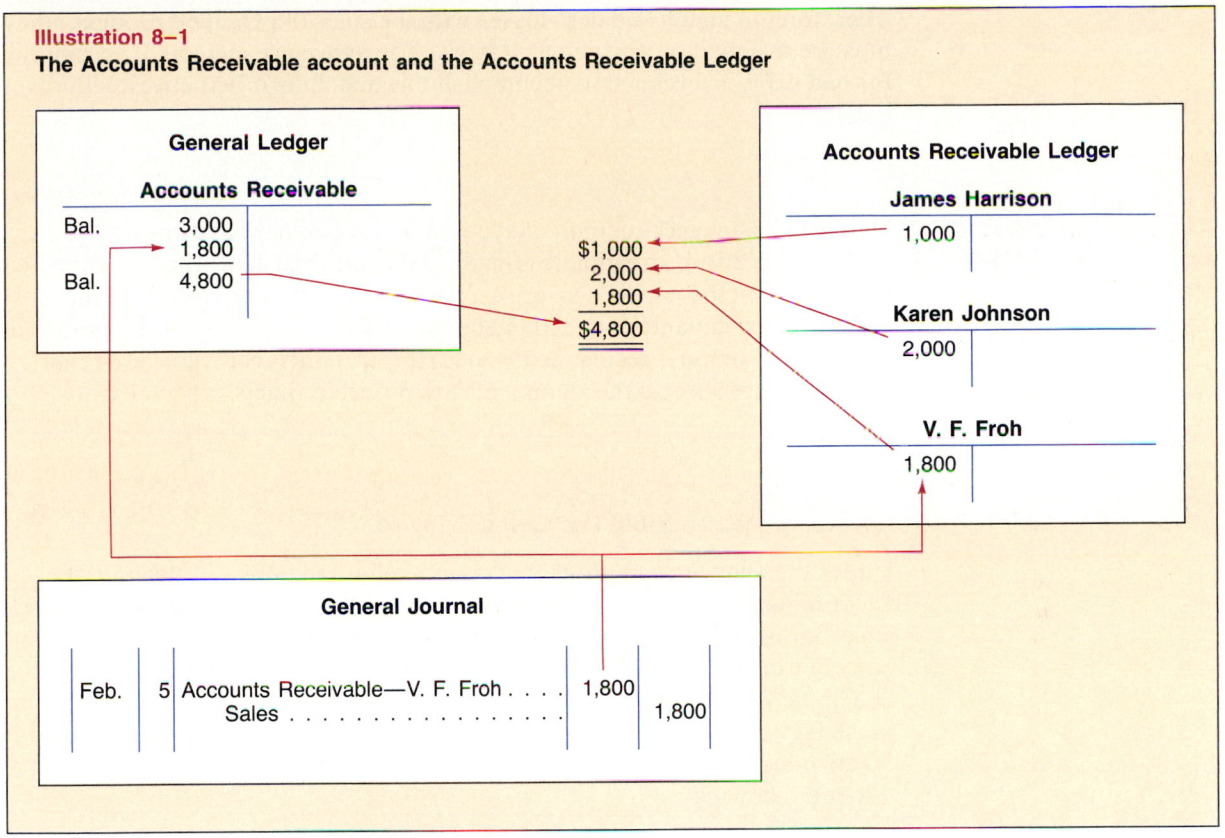

Illustration 8–1
The Accounts Receivable account and the Accounts Receivable Ledger

Bad Debts

When a company grants credit to its customers, there usually are a few customers who do not pay. The accounts of such customers are called **bad debts** and are an expense of selling on credit.

You might ask: Why do merchants sell on credit if bad debts result? The answer is that they sell on credit to increase sales and profits. They are willing to take a reasonable loss from bad debts to increase sales and profits. Therefore, bad debt losses are an expense of selling on credit, an expense incurred to increase sales.

The reporting of bad debts expenses on the income statement is governed by the *matching principle*. This means that bad debts expenses should be reported in the same accounting period as are the revenues they helped produce.

Matching Bad Debt Losses with Sales

When credit sales are made, management usually realizes that some portion of those sales will result in bad debts. However, the fact that a credit sale will not be collected often does not become apparent for some time. If a customer fails to pay, most businesses send out several repeat billings. Final acceptance that the customer is not going to pay should wait until every means of collection has been exhausted. Usually, this does not happen until one or more accounting periods after the period in which the sale was made. It may take a year or more.

Therefore, to match bad debt losses with the sales they helped produce, they must be matched on an estimated basis. The **allowance method of accounting for bad debts** is designed to accomplish this matching of expenses with revenues.

Allowance Method of Accounting for Bad Debts

Under the allowance method of accounting for bad debts, at the end of each accounting period, an estimate is made of the total bad debts that are expected to result from the period's sales. An allowance is then provided for the loss. This has two advantages: (1) the estimated loss is charged to the period in which the revenue is recognized; and (2) the accounts receivable are reported on the balance sheet at the amount of cash proceeds that is expected from their collection.

Recording the Estimated Bad Debts Expense

Under the allowance method of accounting for bad debts, at the end of each accounting period, the estimated bad debts expense is recorded with a work sheet adjustment and an adjusting entry. For example, assume that Fritz Company had charge sales of $300,000 during the first year of its operations. At the end of the year, $20,000 remains uncollected in accounts receivable. Based on these facts, Fritz Company estimates that $1,500 of accounts receivable will be uncollectible. This estimated expense is recorded with an adjusting entry like the following:

Dec.	31	Bad Debts Expense	1,500.00	
		Allowance for Doubtful Accounts		1,500.00
		To record the estimated bad debts.		

The debit of this entry causes the estimated bad debts expense to appear on the income statement of the year in which the sales were made. As a result, the estimated $1,500 expense of selling on credit is matched with the $300,000 of revenue it helped to produce.

Note that the credit of the entry is to the contra account, **Allowance for Doubtful Accounts.** A contra account must be used because at the time of the adjusting entry, it is not known for certain which customers will not pay. (The total loss from bad debts can be estimated from past experience. However, the exact customers who will not pay cannot be known until every means of collection is exhausted.) Therefore, since the bad accounts are not identifiable at the time of the adjusting entry, they cannot be removed from the subsidiary Accounts Receivable Ledger. As a result, the Allowance for Doubtful Accounts account must be credited instead of the controlling account. If the controlling account were credited, the controlling account balance would no longer equal the sum of the balances in the subsidiary ledger.

Bad Debts in the Accounts and in the Financial Statements

The process of evaluating customers and approving them for credit usually is not assigned to the selling departments of a business. Otherwise, given their primary objective of increasing sales, selling departments might not use good judgment in approving customers for credit. Because selling departments do not approve customers for credit, bad debts expense normally appears on the income statement as an administrative expense rather than as a selling expense. Since the sales department is not responsible for granting credit, it should not be held responsible for bad debts expense.

Recall that Fritz Company has $20,000 of outstanding accounts receivable at the end of its first year of operations. Thus, after the bad debts adjusting entry is posted, the company's Accounts Receivable and Allowance for Doubtful Accounts accounts show these balances:

Accounts Receivable		Allowance for Doubtful Accounts	
Dec. 31 20,000			Dec. 31 1,500

The Allowance for Doubtful Accounts credit balance of $1,500 has the effect of reducing accounts receivable (net of the allowance) to their estimated **realizable value.** This term *realizable value* means the expected proceeds from converting the assets into cash. Although $20,000 is legally owed to Fritz Company, only $18,500 is likely to be realized in cash.

When the balance sheet is prepared, the allowance for doubtful accounts is subtracted from the accounts receivable to show the amount that is expected to be realized from the accounts, as follows:

Current assets:		
Cash.		$11,300
Temporary investments at lower of cost or		
market (cost is $16,000).		14,500
Accounts receivable	$20,000	
Less allowance for doubtful accounts. . . .	(1,500)	18,500
Merchandise inventory.		52,700
Prepaid expenses		1,100
Total current assets.		$98,100

In the above example, compare the presentations of temporary investments and accounts receivable, and recall that contra accounts are subtracted in both cases. Even though the contra account to the Temporary Investments account is not shown on the statement, you can easily determine the $1,500 balance of the contra account by comparing the $16,000 cost with the $14,500 net amount. Sometimes, the contra account to Accounts Receivable is presented in a similar fashion, as follows:

Accounts receivable (net of $1,500 estimated	
uncollectible accounts)	18,500

Writing Off a Bad Debt

When an allowance for doubtful accounts is provided, accounts deemed un-collectible are written off against this allowance. For example, after spending a year trying to collect, Fritz Company finally decided the $100 account of Jack Vale was uncollectible and made the following entry to write it off:

Jan.	23	Allowance for Doubtful Accounts	100.00	
		Accounts Receivable—Jack Vale		100.00
		To write off an uncollectible account.		

Posting the credit of the entry to the Accounts Receivable account removes the amount of the bad debt from the controlling account. Posting it to the Jack Vale account removes the amount of the bad debt from the subsidiary ledger. After the entry is posted, the general ledger accounts appear as follows:

Accounts Receivable				Allowance for Doubtful Accounts			
Dec. 31	20,000	Jan. 23	100	Jan. 23	100	Dec. 31	1,500

Notice two aspects of the entry and the accounts. First, although bad debts are an expense of selling on credit, the allowance account rather than an ex-pense account is debited in the write-off. The allowance account is debited because the expense was recorded at the end of the period in which the sale occurred. At that time, the loss was estimated and the expense was recorded in the bad debts adjusting entry.

Second, although the write-off removed the amount of the account receiva-ble from the ledgers, it did not affect the estimated realizable amount of Fritz Company's accounts receivable, as the following tabulation shows:

Accounts receivable.	$20,000	$19,900
Less allowance for doubtful accounts . . .	1,500	1,400
Estimated realizable accounts receivable . .	$18,500	$18,500

Bad Debt Recoveries

Sometimes, after an account is written off as uncollectible, the customer vol-untarily pays all or part of the amount owed. When this happens, the payment should be recorded in the customer's account. This information should be retained in the customer's account for use in future credit evaluations of the customer. When a customer fails to pay and his or her account is written off, the customer's credit standing is impaired. Later, when the customer pays, the payment helps restore the credit standing.

When an account that was previously written off as a bad debt is collected, two entries are made. The first reinstates the customer's account and has the effect of reversing the original write-off. The second entry records the collec-tion of the reinstated account. For example, assume that on August 15 Jack Vale pays in full the account that Fritz Company had previously written off.

The entries to record the bad debt recovery are:

Aug.	15	Accounts Receivable—Jack Vale.	100.00	
		Allowance for Doubtful Accounts		100.00
		To reinstate the account of Jack Vale written off on		
		January 23.		
	15	Cash	100.00	
		Accounts Receivable—Jack Vale		100.00
		Received full payment of account.		

In this case, Jack Vale paid the entire amount previously written off. Sometimes after an account is written off, the customer will pay a portion of the amount owed. The question then arises, should the entire balance of the account be returned to accounts receivable or just the amount paid? The answer is a matter of judgment. If you believe the customer will pay in full, the entire amount owed should be returned. However, only the amount paid should be returned if you believe that no more will be collected.

Estimating the Amount of Bad Debts Expense

As you already learned, the allowance method of accounting for doubtful accounts requires an adjusting entry at the end of each accounting period to estimate the bad debts expense for the period. That entry takes the following form:

| Dec. | 31 | Bad Debts Expense . . . . | ???? | |
| | | Allowance for Doubtful Accounts . . . . | | ???? |

What is the process by which a company estimates the amount to record in this entry? There are two broad alternatives. One is to focus on the income statement relationship between bad debts expense and sales. The other is to focus on the balance sheet relationship between accounts receivable and allowance for doubtful accounts. Both alternatives require a careful analysis of past experience.

Estimating Bad Debts by Focusing on the Income Statement

The income statement approach to estimating bad debts is based on the idea that some particular percentage of a company's credit sales will become uncollectible. Hence, in the income statement, the amount of bad debts expense should be that same percentage of credit sales.

Suppose, for example, that Baker Company had credit sales of $400,000 in 1990. Based on past experience and the experience of similar companies, Baker Company estimates that 0.6% of credit sales are uncollectible. Using this estimate, Baker Company can expect $2,400 of bad debts expense to result from the year's sales ($400,000 × 0.006 = $2,400). The adjusting entry to record this expense is:

Dec.	31	Bad Debts Expense	2,400.00	
		Allowance for Doubtful Accounts		2,400.00

Importantly, this entry *does not* mean the December 31, 1990, balance in Allowance for Doubtful Accounts will be $2,400. For three reasons, it will probably be some other amount.

1. The bad debts percentage (0.6%) is only an estimate. The actual amount of accounts receivable that become uncollectible will likely be larger or smaller than this.
2. Some of the accounts that resulted from 1990 credit sales may have been written off prior to December 31, 1990. If so, the entries to write them off involved debits to Allowance for Doubtful Accounts. Thus, the account balance was increased by the $2,400 estimated expense but also decreased by the amounts previously written off.
3. There probably was a credit balance in the account at the beginning of the year. In each past year, bad debts were estimated at year-end, and accounts that became uncollectible were written off. The balance in Allowance for Doubtful Accounts reflects these events from past years as well as those in the current year.

Often, when the addition to the Allowance for Doubtful Accounts account is based on a percentage of sales, the passage of several accounting periods is required before it becomes apparent that the percentage is either too large or too small. In such cases, when it becomes apparent that the percentage is incorrect, a change in the percentage to be used in future periods should be made.

Estimating Bad Debts by Focusing on the Balance Sheet

The balance sheet approach to estimating bad debts is based on the idea that some portion of the receivables on the balance sheet date will become uncollectible. Hence, after the bad debts adjusting entry is posted, the Allowance for Doubtful Accounts balance should equal the portion of outstanding accounts receivable estimated to be uncollectible. To obtain this required balance in the Allowance for Doubtful Accounts account, you simply compare the balance before the adjustment with the required balance. The difference between the two is debited to Bad Debts Expense and credited to Allowance for Doubtful Accounts. The balance sheet approach may take two forms: (1) a simplified approach and (2) aging of accounts receivable.

A Simplified Balance Sheet Approach. Using the simplified balance sheet approach, a company estimates that a certain percentage of its outstanding receivables will become uncollectible. This estimated percentage is based on past experience and the experience of similar companies. Then, the dollar amount of outstanding receivables is multiplied by the estimated percentage to determine the estimated dollar amount of uncollectible accounts. This amount must appear in the balance sheet as the Allowance for Doubtful Accounts balance. To establish this balance in the account, an adjusting entry is made with a debit to Bad Debts Expense and a credit to Allowance for Doubtful Accounts. The amount of the adjustment is the amount necessary to provide the required balance in Allowance for Doubtful Accounts.

For example, assume that on December 31, 1990, Baker Company of the previous illustration has $50,000 of outstanding accounts receivable. Past experience indicates that 5% of outstanding receivables will become uncollectible. Thus, after the adjusting entry is posted, Allowance for Doubtful Accounts should have a $2,500 credit balance. Assume that before making the necessary adjustment, the account appears as follows:

Allowance for Doubtful Accounts

Feb. 6	800	Dec. 31	2,000
July 10	600	balance	
Nov. 20	400		

Understand that the $2,000 beginning balance appeared on the December 31, 1989, balance sheet. Then, during 1990, accounts of specific customers were written off on February 6, July 10, and November 20. As a result, the account has a $200 credit balance prior to the December 31, 1990, adjustment. The adjusting entry to give the account the required $2,500 balance is:

Dec.	31	Bad Debts Expense	2,300.00	
		Allowance for Doubtful Accounts		2,300.00

Aging of Accounts Receivable. Both the income statement approach and the simplified balance sheet approach use the knowledge gained from past experience to estimate bad debts expense. However, neither method of analysis is as refined as the balance sheet approach that involves **aging of accounts receivable.**

With the aging approach, each account is examined in the process of estimating the amount that is uncollectible. Sometimes, the sales and credit department managers have information about specific accounts that allows the managers to decide whether the accounts should be classified as uncollectible. More often, the outstanding receivables are classified in terms of how long they have been outstanding. Then, the estimate of uncollectible accounts is based on the idea that the longer an amount is outstanding, the more likely it will be uncollectible.

To age the accounts receivable outstanding at the end of the period, you must examine each account and classify the outstanding amounts in terms of how long they have been outstanding. After the outstanding amounts have been classified, past experience is used to estimate a percentage of each class that will become uncollectible. These percentages are applied to the amounts in the classes to determine the required allowance for doubtful accounts. This is done by setting up a schedule like the one for Baker Company shown in Illustration 8–2.

Illustration 8–2
Estimating bad debts by aging the accounts

BAKER COMPANY
Schedule of Accounts Receivable by Age

Customer's Name	Not Due	1 to 30 Days Past Due	31 to 60 Days Past Due	61 to 90 Days Past Due	Over 90 Days Past Due
Charles Abbot.	$ 450.00				
Frank Allen	710.00				
George Arden.		$ 200.00	$ 300.00		
Paul Baum					$ 640.00
Totals	$37,000.00	$6,500.00	$3,500.00	$1,900.00	$1,000.00
	×2%	×5%	×10%	×25%	×40%
Estimated uncollectible accounts	$ 740.00	$ 325.00	$ 350.00	$ 475.00	$ 400.00

The analysis of Illustration 8–2 indicates that the adjusted balance in Baker Company's Allowance for Doubtful Accounts should be $2,290 ($740 + $325 + $350 + $475 + $400 = $2,290). Since the account was previously assumed to have a preadjusted credit balance of $200, the aging of accounts receivable approach requires the following adjusting entry:

Dec.	31	Bad Debts Expense	2,090.00	
		Allowance for Doubtful Accounts		2,090.00

Recall from page 395 that when the income statement approach was used, bad debts expense was estimated to be $2,400. When the simplified balance sheet approach was used (page 396), the estimate was $2,300. And when aging of accounts receivable was used, the estimate was $2,090. It is not surprising that the amounts are different. After all, each approach is only an estimate. However, the aging of accounts receivable allows a more detailed examination of outstanding accounts and is usually most reliable.

Direct Write-Off Method of Accounting for Bad Debts

The allowance method of accounting for bad debts is designed to satisfy the requirements of the *matching principle*. Therefore, it is the method that should be used in most cases. However, under certain circumstances another method, called the **direct write-off method,** may be acceptable. Under this method, no attempt is made to estimate uncollectible accounts at the end of each period. No adjusting entry is made. Instead, when you decide that an account is uncollectible, it is written off directly to Bad Debts Expense with an entry like this:

Nov.	23	Bad Debts Expense	52.00	
		Accounts Receivable—Dale Hall		52.00
		To write off the uncollectible account.		

The debit of the entry charges the bad debt directly to the current year's Bad Debts Expense account. The credit removes the balance of the account from the subsidiary ledger and from the controlling account.

If an account previously written off directly to Bad Debts Expense is later collected in full, you record the recovery with the following entries:

Mar.	11	Accounts Receivable—Dale Hall	52.00	
		Bad Debts Expense.		52.00
		To reinstate the account of Dale Hall previously written off.		
	11	Cash	52.00	
		Accounts Receivable—Dale Hall		52.00
		In full payment of account.		

Sometimes a bad debt previously written off directly to the Bad Debts Expense account is recovered in the year following the write-off. If at that time the Bad Debts Expense account has no balance from other write-offs and no write-offs are expected, the credit of the entry recording the recovery can be to a revenue account called Bad Debt Recoveries.

Direct Write-Off Mismatches Revenues and Expenses

The direct write-off method usually mismatches revenues and expenses. The mismatch occurs because bad debt expenses often are not reported in the same period as the credit sales that become uncollectible. Nevertheless, some small businesses use the direct write-off method when past experience indicates that the amount of bad debts is very small in relation to other financial statement items. For example, the method may be used in a concern where bad debt losses are immaterial in relation to total sales and net income. In such cases, the use of direct write-off comes under the accounting *principle of materiality*.

The Materiality Principle

The basic idea of the **materiality principle** is that the requirements of any accounting principle may be ignored if the effect on the financial statements is unimportant to financial statement readers. In other words, failure to follow the requirements of an accounting principle is acceptable when the failure does not produce an error or misstatement large enough to influence a financial statement reader's judgment of a given situation.

Installment Accounts and Notes Receivable

Many companies allow their credit customers to make periodic payments over several months. When this is done, the selling company's asset may be in the form of an installment account receivable or a note receivable. The evidence of an **installment account receivable,** like any other account receivable, includes sales slips or invoices that describe each sales transaction. A note receivable, on the other hand, is a written document that promises payment and is signed by the customer. In either case, when payments will be made over several months or if the credit period is long, the customer usually is charged interest. Although the credit period of installment accounts and notes receivable often may be more than one year, they are normally classified as current assets if the company regularly offers customers such terms.

Generally, notes receivable are preferred over accounts receivable when the credit period is long and the receivable relates to a single sale of fairly large amount. Notes are also used to replace accounts receivable when customers ask for additional time to pay their past-due accounts. In these situations, creditors prefer notes to accounts receivable because the notes may be converted into cash before becoming due by discounting (selling) them to a bank. Also, notes are preferred for legal reasons. If a lawsuit is needed to collect, a note represents written acknowledgment by the debtor of both the debt and its amount.

Promissory Notes

Calculate the interest on promissory notes and prepare entries to record the receipt of promissory notes and their payment or dishonour.
(L. O. 4)

A promissory note is an unconditional promise in writing to pay on demand or at a fixed or determinable future date a definite sum of money. In the note shown in Illustration 8–3, Hugo Brown promises to pay Frank Black or his order a definite sum of money at a fixed future date. Hugo Brown is the **maker of the note.** Frank Black is the **payee.** To Hugo Brown, the illustrated note is a *note payable,* a liability. To Frank Black, the same note is a *note receivable,* an asset.

The Hugo Brown note bears interest at 12%. Interest is a charge for the use of money. To a borrower, interest is an expense. To a lender, it is a revenue. A note may be interest bearing or it may be noninterest bearing. If a note bears interest, the rate or the amount of interest must be stated on the note.

Calculating Interest

Unless otherwise stated, the rate of interest on a note is the rate charged for the use of the principal for one year or 365 days (366 in a leap year). The formula for calculating interest is:

$$\begin{array}{c} \text{Principal} \\ \text{of the} \\ \text{note} \end{array} \times \begin{array}{c} \text{Annual} \\ \text{rate of} \\ \text{interest} \end{array} \times \begin{array}{c} \text{Time of the} \\ \text{note expressed} \\ \text{in days plus} \\ \text{three days} \\ \text{of grace} \end{array} = \text{Interest}$$

For example, interest on a $1,000, 12%, six-month note, dated May 15, is calculated:

$$\$1,000 \times \frac{187}{365} \times .5 = \$61.48$$

Illustration 8–3
A promissory note

$1000.00	Windsor, Ontario	March 9, 1990

Thirty days after date _____I_____ promise to pay to

the order of _____Frank Black_____

One thousand and no / 100 -- dollars

for value received with interest at _____12%_____

payable at _____First National Bank Windsor, Ontario_____

Hugo Brown

The **maturity date of a note** (legal due date) is the day on which the note must be repaid. Most notes mature in less than a full year, and this period or time of the note often is expressed in days. When the time of a note is expressed in days, the maturity date is the specified number of days after the day the note is dated plus three days of grace. As a simple example, a one-day note dated June 15 matures and is due on June 19. Also, a 90-day note dated July 10 matures on October 11. This October 11 due date is calculated as follows:

Number of days in July	31
Minus the date of the note	10
Gives the number of days the note runs in July	21
Add the number of days in August	31
Add the number of days in September	30
Total through September 30	82
Days in October needed to equal the 90-day time of the note, also the maturity date of the note—October 8 . .	8
Add three days of grace—October 11	3
Total time the note runs in days	93

Occasionally, the time of a note is expressed in months. In such cases, the note matures and is payable in the month of its maturity on the same day of the month as its date plus the three days of grace. For example, a note dated July 10 and payable three months after that date is payable on October 13.

Recording the Receipt of a Note

Notes receivable are recorded in a single Notes Receivable account. Each note may be identified in the account by writing the name of the maker in the Explanation column on the line of the entry to record its receipt or payment. Only one account is needed because the individual notes are on hand. Therefore, the maker, rate of interest, due date, and other information may be learned by examining each note.

A note received at the time of a sale is recorded as follows:

Dec.	5	Notes Receivable	650.00	
		Sales.		650.00
		Sold merchandise, terms six-month, 9% note.		

When a business accepts a note as a way of granting a time extension on a past-due account receivable, the business often tries to collect part of the past-due account in cash. This reduces the customer's debt and requires the acceptance of a note for a smaller amount. For example, Symplex Company agrees to accept $232 in cash and a $500, 60-day, 14% note from Joseph Cook to settle his $732 past-due account. When Symplex receives the cash and note, the following entry is made:

Oct.	5	Cash	232.00	
		Notes Receivable	500.00	
		Accounts Receivable—Joseph Cook		732.00
		Received cash and a note in settlement of an account.		

When Cook pays the note, the receipt is recorded with this entry:

Dec.	7	Cash	512.08	
		Notes Receivable		500.00
		Interest Earned		12.08
		Collected the Joseph Cook note.		
		$500 × 14% × 63/365 = $12.08.		

Dishonoured Notes Receivable

Calculate the discount and proceeds on discounted notes receivable and prepare entries to record the discounting of notes receivable and, if dishonoured, their dishonour.
(L. O. 5)

Occasionally, the maker of a note either cannot or will not pay the note at maturity. When a note's maker refuses to pay at maturity, the note is said to be dishonoured. **Dishonouring a note** does not relieve the maker of the obligation to pay. Furthermore, every legal means should be used to collect. However, collection may require lengthy legal proceedings.

The balance of the Notes Receivable account should show only the amount of notes that have not matured. Therefore, when a note is dishonoured, you should remove the amount of the note from the Notes Receivable account and charge it back to the account of its maker. To illustrate, Symplex Company holds an $800, 14%, 60-day note of George Jones. At maturity, Jones dishonours the note. To remove the dishonoured note from the Notes Receivable account, the company makes the following entry:

Oct.	7	Accounts Receivable—George Jones	819.33	
		Interest Earned		19.33
		Notes Receivable.		800.00
		To charge the account of George Jones for his dishonoured note.		

Charging a dishonoured note back to the account of its maker serves two purposes. First, it removes the amount of the note from the Notes Receivable account, leaving in the account only notes that have not matured. It also records the dishonoured note in the maker's account. The second purpose is important. If in the future the maker of the dishonoured note again applies for credit, his or her account will show all past dealings, including the dishonoured note.

Note that Jones owes both the principal and the interest. Therefore, the entry records the full amount owed in Jones's account and credits the interest to Interest Earned. This procedure assures that the interest will be included in future efforts to collect from Jones.

Discounting Notes Receivable

As we previously stated, a note receivable often is preferred to an account receivable. One reason is that the owner of a note can convert the note into cash before it matures by **discounting the note receivable.** In essence, this involves selling the note to a bank or to some other buyer. When a note receivable is discounted, the owner endorses and delivers the note to the bank in exchange for cash. The bank holds the note to maturity and then collects its maturity value from the maker.

To illustrate, assume that on May 28, Symplex Company received a $1,200, 60-day, 12% note dated May 27 from John Owen. It held the note until June 2 and then discounted it at its bank at 14%. Since the maturity date of this note is July 29, the bank must wait 57 days after discounting the note to collect from Owen. These 57 days are called the **discount period** and are calculated as follows:

Time of the note in days		63
Less time held by Symplex Company:		
Number of days in May	31	
Less the date of the note	27	
Days held in May	4	
Days held in June	2	
Total days held.		6
Discount period in days		57

At the end of the discount period, the bank expects to collect the **maturity value** of this note from Owen. Therefore, as is customary, it bases its discount on the maturity value of the note, which is calculated as follows:

Principal of the note	$1,200.00
Interest on $1,200 for 63 days at 12% . .	24.85
Maturity value	$1,224.85

In this case, the bank's discount rate, or the rate of interest it charges for lending money, is 14%. Therefore, in discounting the note, it will deduct 54 days' interest at 14% from the note's maturity value and will give Symplex Company the remainder. The amount of interest deducted in advance is called the **bank discount**, and the remainder is called the **proceeds of the discounted note**. The bank discount and the proceeds are calculated as follows:

Maturity value of the note	$1,224.85
Less interest on $1,224.85 for 57 days at 14% . .	26.78
Proceeds.	$1,198.30

In this case, notice that the proceeds, $1,198.07, are $1.93 less than the $1,200 principal amount of the note. Therefore, Symplex will make this entry to record the discount transaction:

June	2	Cash	1,198.07	
		Interest Expense.	1.93	
		Notes Receivable.		1,200.00
		Discounted the John Owen note for 57 days at 14%.		

In this entry, notice that the $24.85 of interest Symplex would have earned by holding the note to maturity is offset against the $26.78 discount charged by the bank. The $1.93 difference is debited to Interest Expense.

In the situation just described, the principal of the discounted note exceeded the proceeds. However, in many cases, the proceeds exceed the principal. When this happens, the difference is credited to Interest Earned. For example, suppose that instead of discounting the John Owen note on June 2, Symplex held the note and discounted it on June 29. If the note is discounted on June 29 at 14%, the discount period is 30 days, the discount is $14.00, and the proceeds of the note are $1,210.76, calculated as follows:

Maturity value of the note	$1,224.85
Less interest on $1,224.85 at 14% for 30 days . .	14.09
Proceeds.	$1,210.76

Since the proceeds exceed the principal, the transaction is recorded as follows:

June	29	Cash	1,210.76	
		Interest Earned		10.76
		Notes Receivable.		1,200.00
		Discounted the John Owen note for 30 days at 14%.		

Contingent Liability

A person or company that discounts a note receivable is ordinarily required to endorse the note. This endorsement, unless it is qualified, makes the endorser contingently liable for payment of the note.[2] The **contingent liability** depends on the note's dishonour by its maker. If the maker pays, the endorser has no liability. However, if the maker defaults, the endorser's contingent liability becomes an actual liability, and the endorser must pay the note for the maker.

Since it can become an actual liability, a contingent liability may affect the credit standing of the person or concern contingently liable. Therefore, a discounted note should be noted in the Explanation column of the Notes Receivable account. Also, the existence of a contingent liability should be disclosed in the financial statements. For example, assume that Symplex Company holds $500 of notes receivable in addition to the John Owen note. After the entry to record the discounting of John Owen's note is posted, the Notes Receivable account appears as follows:

Notes Receivable

Date		Explanation	PR	Debit	Credit	Balance
May	28	John Owen note	G6	1,200.00		1,200.00
June	7	Earl Hill note	G6	500.00		1,700.00
	26	Discounted the John Owen note	G7		1,200.00	500.00

The contingent liability that results from discounting a note receivable is commonly disclosed in a footnote to the balance sheet. If Symplex Company follows this practice, the company's June 30 balance sheet will show the $500 of notes it has not discounted and the contingent liability that resulted from discounting the John Owen note as follows:

Current assets:
Cash . . . . $ 5,315
Accounts receivable 21,275
Notes receivable (Footnote 2). 500

Footnote 2: Symplex Company is contingently liable for $1,200 of notes receivable discounted.

---

[2] A qualified endorsement is one in which the endorser states in writing that he or she will not be liable for payment.

Full-Disclosure Principle

The balance sheet disclosure of contingent liabilities is required by the **full-disclosure principle.** The meaning of this principle is that a concern's financial statements including the footnotes should contain all relevant information about the operations and financial position of the entity. Any data that is important enough to affect a statement reader's evaluation of the concern's operations and financial position should be reported. This does not mean that the concern should report excessive amounts of detail. It simply means that nothing of a significant nature should be withheld and enough information should be provided to make the reports understandable. Examples of items that need to be reported to satisfy the full-disclosure principle include the following:

Contingent Liabilities. In addition to discounted notes, a company that is contingently liable due to possible additional tax assessments, pending lawsuits, or product guarantees should disclose these items in its statements.

Long-Term Commitments under a Contract. If a company has signed a long-term lease that requires a material annual payment, this should be disclosed even though the liability does not appear in the accounts. Also, if the company has pledged certain of its assets as security for a loan, this should be revealed.

Accounting Methods Used. Whenever there are several acceptable accounting methods that may be followed, a company should report in each case the method used, especially when a choice of methods can materially affect reported net income. For example, a company should report by means of financial statement footnotes such items as the inventory method or methods used, depreciation methods used, and the method of recognizing revenue under long-term construction contracts.[3]

Dishonour of a Discounted Note

A bank always tries to collect a discounted note directly from the maker. If it is able to do so, the one who discounted it will not hear from the bank and will need to do nothing more in regard to the note. However, if a discounted note is dishonoured, the bank must promptly notify each endorser of the note if it is to hold the endorsers liable on the note. The process of notifying endorsers that a note has been dishonoured is called protesting the note. To protest a note, the bank prepares and mails a **notice of protest** to each endorser. A notice of protest is a statement, usually witnessed by a notary public, that says the note was duly presented to the maker for payment and payment was refused. The cost of protesting a note is called a **protest fee,** and the bank will look to the one who discounted the note for payment of both the note's maturity value and the protest fee.

For example, suppose that instead of paying the $1,200 note previously illustrated, John Owen dishonoured it. In such a situation, the bank would immediately notify Symplex Company of the dishonour by mailing a notice of

---

[3] *CICA Handbook,* par. 1505.09.

protest and a letter asking payment for the note's maturity value plus the protest fee. If the protest fee is, say, $20, Symplex must pay the bank $1,244.85. To record the payment, Symplex will charge the $1,244.85 to the account of John Owen, as follows:

July	30	Accounts Receivable—John Owen.	1,244.85	
		Cash		1,244.85
		To charge the account of Owen for the maturity value of his dishonoured note plus the protest fee.		

Upon receipt of the $1,244.85, the bank will deliver the dishonoured note to Symplex Company. Symplex will then make every legal effort to collect from Owen, not only the maturity value of the note and protest fee but also interest on both from the date of dishonour until the date of final settlement. However, after exhausting every legal means to collect, it may have to write the account off as a bad debt. Normally, in such cases, no additional interest is taken onto the books before the write-off.

Although dishonoured notes often become bad debts, some are also eventually paid by their makers. For example, if 30 days after dishonour, John Owen pays the maturity value of his dishonoured note, the protest fee, and interest at 12% on both for 30 days beyond maturity, he will pay the following:

Maturity value	$1,224.85
Protest fee.	20.00
Interest on $1,244.85 at 12% for 30 days . .	12.28
Total	$1,257.13

Symplex will record receipt as follows:

Aug.	28	Cash	1,257.13	
		Interest Earned		12.28
		Accounts Receivable—John Owen		1,244.85
		Dishonoured note and protest fee collected with interest.		

End-of-Period Adjustments

If any notes receivable are outstanding at the end of an accounting period, their accrued interest should be calculated and recorded. For example, on December 16, Perry Company accepted a $3,000, 60-day, 12% note from a customer in granting an extension on a past-due account. When the company's accounting period ends on December 31, the $14.79 of interest that has accrued on this note is recorded with the following adjusting entry:

Dec.	31	Interest Receivable.	14.79	
		Interest Earned		14.79
		To record accrued interest.		

The adjusting entry causes the interest earned to appear on the income statement of the period in which it was earned. It also causes the interest receivable to appear on the balance sheet as a current asset.

Collecting Interest Previously Accrued

When the note is collected, Perry Company's entry to record the receipt is:

Feb.	17	Cash	3,062.14	
		Interest Earned		47.35
		Interest Receivable		14.79
		Notes Receivable		3,000.00
		Received payment of a note and its interest.		

The entry's credit to Interest Receivable records collection of the interest accrued at the end of the previous period.

Recording the Collection When Reversing Entries Are Used

In Appendix B at the end of Chapter 4, we explained how some companies make reversing entries on the first day of a new accounting period. These entries are not necessary but are often used as a bookkeeping convenience. In the above example, if Perry Company had used reversing entries, the December 31 accrual of interest would have been reversed on January 1, as follows:

Jan.	1	Interest Earned.	14.79	
		Interest Receivable		14.79
		To reverse accrual of interest.		

Since the Interest Earned account was closed to Income Summary on December 31, the above entry would give the Interest Earned account a debit balance of $14.79. Also, the Interest Receivable balance would be reduced from $14.79 debit to $0. Then, the cash receipt on February 17 would be recorded as follows:

Feb.	17	Cash	3,062.14	
		Interest Earned		62.14
		Notes Receivable		3,000.00
		Received payment of a note and its interest.		

Note that as a result of these two entries, the Interest Earned account balance is $62.14 − $14.79, or $47.35. This balance is exactly the same as when the receipt was recorded without the use of reversing entries (see the February 17 entry above).

Alternative Method of Interest Calculation

In calculating interest in the foregoing examples, the "exact," or proper, method was used. For classroom purposes, however, instructors may prefer to use a less accurate simplified method of interest calculation in order to focus on comprehension rather than on lengthy procedural calculation. To simplify interest calculations, the following assumptions are made:

1. Treat a year as having 360 days divided into 12 months of 30 days each.
2. Use the exact days of the note; that is, do not give consideration to the days of grace.

Thus, interest on a 90-day, 12%, $1,500 note is calculated as:

$$\$1,500 \times \frac{12}{100} \times \frac{90}{360} = \$45$$

To facilitate the use of the alternative method of interest calculation, certain exercises and problems may be designated for use of this method.

Summary of the Chapter in Terms of Learning Objectives

1. Temporary investments are recorded at cost; dividends, interest, and gains and losses on the investments are recorded in appropriate income statement accounts. The total cost of the entire portfolio of temporary investments in marketable securities is compared with its market value to determine the lower of cost or market. Write-downs to market are credited to a contra account.

2. When credit card receipts are deposited in a bank account, the credit card expense is recorded at the time of the deposit. When credit card receipts must be submitted to the credit card company for payment, Accounts Receivable is debited for the sales amount. Then, credit card expense is recorded at the time cash is received from the credit card company. However, credit card expense should be accrued at the end of each accounting period.

3. Under the allowance method, bad debts expense is recorded as an adjustment at the end of each accounting period. The amount of the entry is determined either by (a) focusing on the income statement relationship between bad debts expense and credit sales or (b) focusing on the balance sheet. The later approach may involve aging the accounts or using a percentage relationship between accounts receivable and allowance for doubtful accounts. Then, uncollectible accounts are written off against Allowance for Doubtful Accounts. The direct write-off method charges Bad Debts Expense only when accounts are written off as uncollectible.

4. Interest rates are typically stated in annual terms. When a note's time to maturity is more or less than one year, the time must be expressed as a percentage of one year and multiplied by the annual amount of interest to determine the interest on the note. Dishonoured notes are credited to Notes Receivable and debited to Accounts Receivable and to the account of the maker.

5. The bank's discount rate is applied to the maturity value of a note to determine the discount, which is subtracted from the maturity value to determine the proceeds. If a discounted note receivable is dishonoured, the original payee usually becomes liable to pay the note including any protest fee.

Demonstration Problem

The Garden Company had the following transactions during 1990:

May 8   Purchased 600 shares of Abitibi Price common stock as a temporary investment. The cost of $20 per share plus $975 in broker's commissions was paid in cash.

July 3   Received $800 in dividends from the Abitibi Price stock.

14   Wrote off a $750 account receivable from 1989. (Garden Company uses the allowance method.)

26   Bank credit card sales amounted to $15,000. Deposited the sales slips in the local bank, which deducts 5% as its fee.

30   Received $400 in partial settlement of a $2,000 account receivable. The remaining balance was converted to a $1,600, one-year, 12% note receivable.*

Aug. 4   Wrote off a $1,100 account receivable arising from a sale earlier in 1990.

15   Accepted a $2,000 down payment and a $10,000 note receivable from a customer in exchange for an inventory item that normally sells for $12,000. The note was dated August 15, bears 12% interest, and matures in six months.

Sept. 2   Sold 200 shares of Abitibi Price stock at $23.50 per share, and continued to hold the other 400 shares. The broker's commission on the sale was $225.

Nov.15   Discounted the $10,000 note (dated August 15) at the local bank at a rate of 16%.*

Dec. 2   Purchased 400 shares of McDonald's stock for $60 per share plus $1,600 in commissions. The stock is to be held as a temporary investment.

Required

1. Prepare journal entries to record the above transactions on the books of The Garden Company.

2. Prepare adjusting journal entries as of December 31, 1990, for the following items:

   a. The market prices of the equity securities held by The Garden Company are: $24 per share for the Abitibi Price stock, and $55 per share for the McDonald's stock.

   b. Bad debts expense is estimated by an aging of accounts receivable. The unadjusted balance of the Allowance for Doubtful Accounts account is a $1,000 debit, while the desired balance is estimated to be a $20,400 credit.

   c. Interest is accrued on the note dated July 30, 1990.

---
* Alternative method of calculation.

Solution to Demonstration Problem

1.

May	8	Temporary Investments.	12,975.00	
		Cash [(600 × $20) + $975]		12,975.00
		Purchased 600 shares of Abitibi Price.		
July	3	Cash.	800.00	
		Dividends Earned		800.00
		Received dividends on Abitibi Price stock.		
	14	Allowance for Doubtful Accounts	750.00	
		Accounts Receivable		750.00
		Wrote off an uncollectible account.		
	26	Cash.	14,250.00	
		Credit Card Expense	750.00	
		Sales		15,000.00
		$15,000 × .05 = $750.		
	30	Notes Receivable.	1,600.00	
		Cash.	400.00	
		Accounts Receivable		2,000.00
		Accepted a $1,600, one-year, 12% note receivable and $400 in cash in settlement of a customer's account.		
Aug.	4	Allowance for Doubtful Accounts	1,100.00	
		Accounts Receivable		1,100.00
		Wrote off an uncollectible account.		
	15	Cash.	2,000.00	
		Notes Receivable.	10,000.00	
		Sales		12,000.00
		Sold merchandise to customer for $2,000 cash and $10,000 note receivable.		
Sept.	2	Cash.	4,475.00	
		Gain on Sale of Investment.		150.00
		Temporary Investments		4,325.00
		Sold 200 shares of Abitibi Price for $23.50 per share less a $225 commission. $12,975 × 200/600 = $4,325.		
Nov.	15	Cash.	10,176.00	
		Interest Earned.		176.00
		Notes Receivable		10,000.00
		$10,000 + ($10,000 × 12% × 6/12) = $10,600. $10,600 × 16% × 3/12 = $424. $10,600 − $424 = $10,176.		
Dec.	2	Temporary Investments.	25,600.00	
		Cash		25,600.00
		Purchased 400 shares of McDonald's for $60 per share plus $1,600 in commissions.		

2.

1990				
Dec.	31	Loss on Market Decline of Temporary Investments . . .	2,650.00	
		Allowance to Reduce Temporary		
		Investments to Market		2,650.00
		To record the decline in market value of		
		temporary investments.		

Temporary Investments	Shares	Cost per Share	Total Cost	Value per Share	Total Market	Difference
Abitibi Price . .	400	$21.625	$ 8,650	$24.00	$ 9,600	
McDonald's . .	400	64.00	25,600	55.00	22,000	
Total			$34,250		$31,600	$2,650

	31	Bad Debts Expense.	21,400.00	
		Allowance for Doubtful Accounts		21,400.00
		To adjust the allowance account from		
		$1,000 debit balance to $20,400 credit balance.		
	31	Interest Receivable	80.00	
		Interest Earned.		80.00
		To accrue interest on July 30 note receivable		
		($1,600 × 12% × 5/12).		

Glossary

Define or explain the words and phrases listed in the chapter Glossary. (L. O. 6)

Accounts Receivable Ledger a subsidiary ledger having an account for each customer. p. 390

Aging of accounts receivable a process of classifying accounts receivable in terms of how long they have been outstanding for the purpose of estimating the amount of uncollectible accounts. p. 397

Allowance for doubtful accounts the estimated amount of accounts receivable that will be uncollectible. p. 392

Allowance method of accounting for bad debts an accounting procedure that (1) estimates the bad debts arising from credit sales and reports bad debt expense during the period of the sales; and (2) reports accounts receivable in the balance sheet net of estimated uncollectibles, which is their estimated realizable value. p. 392

Bad debt an uncollectible receivable. p. 391

Bank discount the amount of interest charged by a bank when the bank accepts a discounted note from a customer. Also, the interest a bank deducts in advance when making a loan. p. 404

Contingent liability a potential liability that will become an actual liability if and only if certain events occur. p. 405

Controlling account a general ledger account the balance of which is always equal to the sum of the balances in a related subsidiary ledger. p. 390

Direct write-off method of accounting for bad debts a procedure whereby uncollectible accounts are not estimated in advance and are not charged to expense until they prove to be uncollectible. p. 398

Discount period of a note the number of days following the date on which a note is discounted at the bank until the maturity date of the note. p. 403

Discounting a note receivable selling a note receivable to a bank or other concern, usually with the provision that the seller assumes a contingent liability to pay the note if it is dishonoured. p. 403

Dishonouring a note refusal of a promissory note's maker to pay the amount due upon maturity of the note. p. 402

Full-disclosure principle the accounting requirement that financial statements including the footnotes contain all relevant information about the operations and financial position of the entity and that the information be presented in an understandable manner. p. 406

General Ledger the collection of financial statement accounts of a business. p. 390

Installment accounts receivable accounts receivable that allow the customer to make periodic payments over several months and which typically earn interest. p. 400

Lower of cost or market (LCM) a method of reporting whereby the total cost of the entire portfolio of temporary investments in marketable equity securities is compared to the total market value on the date of the balance sheet and the lesser amount is reported in the balance sheet. p. 387

Maker of a note one who signs a note and promises to pay it at maturity. p. 400

Materiality principle the idea that the requirements of any accounting principle may be ignored if the effect on the financial statements is unimportant to financial statement readers. p. 399

Maturity date of a note the date on which a note and any interest are due and payable. p. 401

Maturity value of a note principal of the note plus any interest due on the note's maturity date. p. 403

Notice of protest a written statement, usually witnessed by a notary public, that says a note was duly presented to the maker for payment and payment was refused. p. 406

Payee of a note the one to whom a promissory note is made payable. p. 400

Proceeds of a discounted note the maturity value of a note minus any interest deducted because of its being discounted before maturity. p. 404

Protest fee the fee charged for preparing and issuing a notice of protest. p. 406

Realizable value the expected proceeds from converting an asset into cash. p. 393

Short-term investments another name for **temporary investments.** p. 386

Subsidiary ledger a collection of accounts other than general ledger accounts which shows the details underlying the balance of a controlling account in the General Ledger. p. 390

Temporary investments investments such as government or corporate debt obligations and marketable equity securities that can be converted into cash quickly and are held as a source of cash to satisfy the needs of current operations. p. 386

An asterisk (*) identifies questions, exercises, and problems that are to be done using the alternative method of interest calculation.

Questions for Class Discussion

1. Under what conditions should investments be classified as current assets?
2. In a balance sheet, what valuations should be reported for temporary investments in marketable equity securities?
3. What kind of account is credited when you record a loss on market decline of temporary investments?
4. Under what conditions are increases in the market value of temporary investments recorded in the accounts?
5. If 1,000 shares of Bander Corporation common stock are purchased as a temporary investment and the price paid was 67⅜ plus a $400 brokerage commission, what amount should be debited to the Temporary Investments account?
6. If a temporary investment that cost $6,780 was sold for $7,500, how should the difference between the two amounts be recorded?

7. Why do customers often prefer to charge their purchases to credit cards?

8. How do businesses benefit from allowing their customers to use credit cards?

9. Where is credit card expense disclosed on a classified income statement?

10. If a business allows its customers to use a credit card that requires the business to send the credit card receipts to the credit card company and wait to be paid, when is the credit card expense usually recorded?

11. What functions are served by the Accounts Receivable controlling account?

12. How is the equality of a controlling account and its subsidiary ledger maintained?

13. In meeting the requirements of the matching principle, why must bad debts expenses be matched with sales on an estimated basis?

14. What term describes the balance sheet valuation of accounts receivable less allowance for doubtful accounts?

15. What is a contra account? Why is estimated bad debts expense credited to a contra account rather than to the Accounts Receivable controlling account?

16. When bad debts are estimated by the income statement approach, what relationship is the focus of attention?

17. A company had $560,000 of charge sales in a year. How many dollars of bad debts expense may the company expect to experience from these sales if its past bad debts expense has averaged one fourth of 1% of charge sales?

18. Classify the following accounts: (*a*) Accounts Receivable, (*b*) Allowance for Doubtful Accounts, and (*c*) Bad Debts Expense.

19. Explain why writing off a bad debt against the allowance account does not reduce the estimated realizable value of a company's accounts receivable.

20. What are three reasons why Bad Debts Expense usually does not have the same adjusted balance as Allowance for Doubtful Accounts?

21. When bad debts are estimated by the simplified balance sheet approach, what relationship is the focus of attention?

22. Why does the direct write-off method of accounting for bad debts commonly fail in matching revenues and expenses?

23. What is the essence of the accounting principle of materiality?

24. Why might a business prefer a note receivable to an account receivable?

25. Define:
    a. Promissory note.
    b. Payee of a note.
    c. Maturity date.
    d. Dishonoured note.
    e. Notice of protest.
    f. Discount period of a note.
    g. Maker of a note.
    h. Principal of a note.
    i. Maturity value.
    j. Contingent liability.

26. What are the due dates of the following notes: (*a*) a 90-day note dated
    July 10, (*b*) a 60-day note dated April 14, and (*c*) a 90-day note dated
    November 12?

27. Distinguish between bank discount and cash discount.

28. What does the full-disclosure principle require in a company's account-
    ing statements?

Multiple Choice

1. In accounting for a portfolio of temporary investments in marketable
   equity securities:
   a. The lower of cost or market of each investment is calculated; then,
        the lower of cost or market amounts are summed to determine the
        lower of cost or market for the whole portfolio.
   b. The total cost of the investment portfolio is determined and com-
        pared to the total market value of the investment portfolio to deter-
        mine the lower of cost or market of the portfolio.
   c. A loss on the market decline of temporary investments is debited to
        Allowance to Reduce Temporary Investments to Market.
   d. Any cash received as dividends from temporary investments is deb-
        ited to Dividends Earned.
   e. Increases in the market value of the temporary portfolio are credited
        to Gain from Temporary Investments.

2. In accounting for credit card sales:
   a. The entry to record credit card sales always includes a debit to Ac-
        counts Receivable.
   b. When the bank credits the seller's chequing account immediately
        upon the seller's deposit of sales receipts, the seller records the
        credit card sales with a debit to Cash.
   c. Credit card expense that results from credit sales made in Period
        One should be reported as expense in Period Two if the cash from
        the sale is received in Period Two.
   d. When the bank credits the seller's chequing account immediately
        upon the seller's deposit of sales receipts, the seller does not incur
        any credit card expense as a result of making credit card sales.
   e. When the seller must submit accumulated sales receipts to the credit
        card company and then time passes before cash is received from the
        credit card company, the seller does not incur any credit card ex-
        pense as a result of making credit card sales.

3. Just before adjusting entries are made at year-end, Pickle Company's
   Accounts Receivable balance is $200,000 and Allowance for Doubtful
   Accounts has a debit balance of $2,000. Credit sales for the year were
   $1,500,000; the experience of past years suggests that 2% of credit sales
   prove to be uncollectible. However, an aging of accounts receivable results in a $45,000 estimate of uncollectibles. Using the aging of accounts
   receivable method, the Bad Debt Expense for the year is:

    a. $47,000.

    b. $45,000.

    c. $43,000.

    d. $30,000.

    e. None of the above is correct.

*4. Roth Company purchased $6,000 of merchandise from Kraft Company on December 16, 1990. Kraft accepted Roth's $6,000, 90-day, 10% note as payment. Assuming no reversing entries, what entry should Kraft make on March 16, 1991, when the note is paid?

a. Cash . . . . | 6,150.00 |
    Interest Earned . . . . | | 150.00
    Notes Receivable . . . . | | 6,000.00

b. Cash . . . . | 6,150.00 |
    Notes Receivable . . . . | | 6,150.00

c. Cash . . . . | 6,150.00 |
    Interest Earned . . . . | | 125.00
    Interest Receivable . . . . | | 25.00
    Notes Receivable . . . . | | 6,000.00

d. Cash . . . . | 6,125.00 |
    Interest Earned . . . . | | 125.00
    Notes Receivable . . . . | | 6,000.00

    e. None of the above.

*5. The proceeds from discounting a $3,000, 10%, 90-day note, if it is discounted 60 days before maturity at 12%, are:

    a. $3,075.00.

    b. $3,050.00.

    c. $3,061.50.

    d. $3,013.50.

    e. None of the above.

6. The accounting rule requiring that financial statements and their accompanying notes disclose all information of a material nature relating to the financial position and operating results of the company for which the statements are prepared is the:

    a. Realization principle.

    b. Full-disclosure principle.

    c. Cost principle.

    d. Materiality principle.

    e. Objectivity principle.

Mini Discussion Cases

Case 8–1

In addition to recording cash sales as indicated in Mini Discussion Case 7–1, there were also a number of fictitious sales recorded as receivables. Inventory represented by the fictitious sales was removed by the seller to another location. Interviews with employees in the stockroom also indicated that there was some substitution of inventory by the previous owner. That is, he removed the newest lines in inventory to his other place of business and brought in older and slow-moving items.

The auditor's report indicated $120,000 of fictitious sales and the corresponding cost of goods sold of $80,000.

The auditors were not able to fully document the amount of inventory substitution.

Required

1. Discuss the effect on the financial statements of the fictitious sales.
2. Discuss the safeguards or internal control that was lacking in the situation.

Case 8–2

John Crane could not understand the discounting procedure followed with regard to customers' notes receivable. Specifically, he could not understand why the discount was based on the maturity value of the note and not on the face value or the face value plus accrued interest to the discount date.

Required

Explain to John Crane why the maturity value of the note receivable is discounted.

Exercises

Exercise 8–1
Transactions that involve temporary investments
(L. O. 1)

Prepare general journal entries to record the following transactions involving Rather Company's temporary investments, all of which occurred during 1990.

a. On April 20, paid $50,000 to purchase $50,000 of Chrysler Corporation's short-term (90-day) notes payable, which are dated April 20, and pay interest at a 10% rate.
b. On May 15, bought 1,000 shares of General Electric common stock at 56½ plus a $640 brokerage fee.
c. On June 1, paid $30,000 to purchase West Corporation's 9% notes payable, $30,000 principal value, due June 15, 1997.
d. On July 19, received a cheque from Chrysler Corporation in payment of the principal and 90 days' interest on the notes purchased in (*a*).
e. On October 20, received a $1 per share cash dividend on the General Electric common stock purchased in transaction (*b*).
f. On November 5, sold 500 shares of General Electric common stock for $59 per share, less a $375 brokerage fee.
g. On December 1, received a cheque from West Corporation for six months' interest on the notes purchased in (*c*).

Exercise 8–2
Reducing temporary investments to lower of cost or market
(L. O. 1)

On December 31, 1990, DataFile Corporation owned the following temporary investments in marketable equity securities.

	Cost	Market Value
Firestone common stock	$12,400	$13,700
General Tire common stock.	16,800	16,100
Texas Instruments common stock	23,200	21,300
First Republic common stock	28,500	28,700

DataFile Corporation had no temporary investments prior to 1990. Calculate the lower of cost or market of DataFile Corporation's temporary investments and, if necessary, prepare a general journal entry to record the decline in market value of the investments.

Exercise 8–3
Adjusting the Allowance for Market Decline of Temporary Investments account
(L. O. 1)

Hays Company's annual accounting period ends on December 31. The cost and market values of the company's temporary investments in marketable equity securities were as follows on sequential balance sheet dates:

	Cost	Market Value
Temporary investments in marketable equity securities:		
On December 31, 1989	$15,000	$14,000
On December 31, 1990	17,000	15,500

Prepare a general journal entry on December 31, 1990, to adjust the balance in the contra account to Temporary Investments.

Exercise 8–4
Credit card transactions
(L. O. 2)

Compton Company allows customers to use two alternative credit cards in charging purchases. With the First Net Bank Card, Compton receives an immediate credit upon depositing sales receipts in its chequing account. First Net Bank makes a 3% service charge for credit card sales. The second credit card Compton accepts is Canadex Card. Compton sends the accumulated Canadex Card receipts to the Canadex Company on a weekly basis and is paid by Canadex Company approximately 10 days later. Canadex charges 3.5% of sales for using its card. Prepare entries in general journal form to record the following credit card transactions of Compton Company:

Oct. 1 Sold merchandise for $3,500 on this day, accepting the customers' First Net Bank Card. At the end of the day, the First Net Bank Card receipts were deposited in the company's account at the bank.

2 Sold merchandise for $225, accepting the customer's Canadex Card.

7 Mailed $6,000 of credit card receipts to Canadex Company, requesting payment.

19 Received Canadex Company's cheque for the October 7 billing, less the normal service charge.

Exercise 8–5
Subsidiary ledger accounts
(L. O. 3)

Bayfield Company recorded the following transactions during May 1990:

May	4	Accounts Receivable—Ed Morris.	900.00	
		Sales.		900.00
	8	Accounts Receivable—Alice Brown	750.00	
		Sales.		750.00
	19	Accounts Receivable—Carl Edison.	600.00	
		Sales.		600.00
	20	Sales Returns and Allowances	150.00	
		Accounts Receivable—Carl Edison		150.00
	26	Accounts Receivable—Ed Morris.	300.00	
		Sales.		300.00

Required

1. Open a General Ledger having T-accounts for Accounts Receivable, Sales, and Sales Returns and Allowances. Also, open a subsidiary Accounts Receivable Ledger having a T-account for each customer. Post the above entries to the customer accounts.

2. List the balances of the accounts in the subsidiary ledger, total the balances, and compare the total with the balance of the Accounts Receivable controlling account.

Exercise 8–6
Allowance for Doubtful Accounts
(L. O. 3)

On December 31, at the end of its annual accounting period, a company estimated it would lose as bad debts an amount equal to one half of 1% of its $540,000 of charge sales made during the year, and it made an addition to its Allowance for Doubtful Accounts equal to that amount. On the following March 9, it decided the $400 account of Bob Sweete was uncollectible and wrote it off as a bad debt. Two months later, on May 8, Mr. Sweete unexpectedly paid the amount previously written off. Give the required entries in general journal form to record these transactions.

Exercise 8–7
Bad debts expense
(L. O. 3)

At the end of each year, a company uses the simplified balance sheet approach to estimate bad debts. On December 31, 1990, it has outstanding accounts receivable of $57,000 and estimates that 3% will be uncollectible. (*a*) Give the entry to record bad debts expense for 1990 under the assumption that Allowance for Doubtful Accounts had a $350 credit balance before the adjustment. (*b*) Give the entry under the assumption that Allowance for Doubtful Accounts has a $400 debit balance before the adjustment.

Exercise 8–8
Dishonour of a note
(L. O. 3)

Prepare general journal entries to record these transactions:

Apr. 6   Accepted a $1,000, 60-day, 12% note dated this day from Mary Greene in granting a time extension on her past-due account.

June 8   Mary Greene dishonoured her note when presented for payment.

Dec. 31   After exhausting all legal means of collecting, wrote off the account of Mary Greene against the Allowance for Doubtful Accounts.

Exercise 8–9
Discounting a note
receivable
(L. O. 4, 5)

Prepare general journal entries to record these transactions:

May 11   Sold merchandise to Jack Voit, $2,500, terms 2/10, n/60.
July 11   Received $300 in cash and a $2,200, 90-day, 10% note dated July 11 in granting a time extension on the amount due from Jack Voit.
Aug. 3   Discounted the Jack Voit note at the bank at 12%.
Oct. 12   Since a notice protesting the Jack Voit note had not been received, assumed that it had been paid.

Exercise 8–10
Dishonour of a
discounted note
(L. O. 4, 5)

Prepare general journal entries to record these transactions:

Mar. 6   Accepted a $4,500, 60-day, 12% note dated March 4 from Ronald Becker granting a time extension on his past-due account.
       9   Discounted the Ronald Becker note at the bank at 14%.
May   8   Received notice protesting the Ronald Becker note. Paid the bank the maturity value of the note plus a $20 protest fee.
      23   Received payment from Ronald Becker of the maturity value of his dishonoured note, the protest fee, and interest at 12% on both for 15 days beyond maturity.

Exercise 8–11
Analysis of sales terms
and discounted note
(L. O. 4, 5)

On August 7, Barstow Sales sold Mark Gittes merchandise having a $6,250 catalogue list price, less a 20% trade discount, terms 2/10, n/60. (Trade discounts were explained on page 231.) Gittes was unable to pay and was granted a time extension on receipt of his 60-day, 15% note for the amount of the debt, dated October 6. Barstow Sales held the note until October 21, when it discounted the note at its bank at 16%. The note was not protested. Answer these questions:

a.   How many dollars of trade discount were granted on the sale?
b.   How many dollars of cash discount could Gittes have earned?
c.   What was the maturity date of the note?
d.   How many days were in the note's discount period?
e.   How much bank discount was deducted by the bank?
f.   What were the proceeds of the discounted note?

Problems

Problem 8–1
Accounting for temporary
investments
(L. O. 1)

Solomon Company had no temporary investments on December 31, 1989, but had the following transactions involving temporary investments during 1990:

Jan.   10   Paid $40,000 to buy six-month Certificate of Deposit, $40,000 principal amount, 8%, dated January 10.
Feb.   3   Purchased 600 shares of BCE common stock at 30½ plus a $300 brokerage fee.
       16   Purchased 400 shares of Alcan common stock at 43¼ plus a $200 brokerage fee.
Mar.   1   Paid $30,000 for Canada Savings Bonds, $30,000 principal amount, 9% dated March 1, 1990, due March 1, 1994.

Mar. 28   Purchased 1,000 shares of Syntex common stock at 45⅛ plus a $675 brokerage fee.

June   1   Received a $0.30 per share cash dividend on the BCE common shares.

       17   Sold 400 shares of BCE common stock at 32 less a $200 brokerage fee.

July   12   Received a cheque for the principal and accrued interest on the Certificate of Deposit that matured on July 10.

Aug.   14   Received a $0.35 per share cash dividend on the Alcan common shares.

Sept.   1   Received a cheque for six months' interest on the Canada Savings Bonds purchased on March 1.

        1   Received a $0.30 per share cash dividend on the remaining BCE common shares owned by Solomon Company.

Nov.   14   Received a $0.35 per share cash dividend on the Alcan common shares.

On December 31, 1990, the market prices of the equity securities held by Solomon Company were: BCE, 33½; Alcan, 42; and Syntex, 38⅞.

Required

1. Prepare general journal entries to record the above transactions.
2. Prepare a schedule to calculate the lower of cost or market of Solomon's temporary investments in marketable *equity* securities.
3. Prepare adjusting entries, if necessary, to record accrued interest on Solomon Company's investments in debt obligations and to reduce the marketable equity securities to the lower of cost or market.

Problem 8–2
Credit sales and credit card sales
(L. O. 2, 3)

Barrows Company allows a few customers to make sales on credit. Other customers may use either of two credit cards. The First City Bank makes a 4% service charge for sales on its credit card but immediately credits the chequing account of its commercial customers when credit card receipts are deposited. Barrows deposits the First City Bank credit card receipts at the close of each business day.

When customers use the Canadex Credit Card, Barrows Company accumulates the receipts for two or three days and then submits them to the Canadex Credit Company for payment. Canadex makes a 3% service charge and usually pays within one week of being billed.

Barrows Company completed the following transactions:

July   3   Sold merchandise on credit to Bob Jones for $1,170. (Terms of all credit sales are 2/15, n/60.)

       4   Sold merchandise for $2,160 to customers who used their First City Bank credit cards. Sold merchandise for $2,400 to customers who used their Canadex credit cards.

       5   Sold merchandise for $1,600 to customers who used their Canadex credit cards.

July 7 Wrote off the account of K. Perry against Allowance for Doubtful Accounts. The $250 balance in Perry's account stemmed from a credit sale in December of last year.

8 The Canadex credit card receipts accumulated since July 3 were submitted to the credit card company for payment.

18 Received Bob Jones's cheque paying for the purchase of July 3.

19 Received the amount due from Canadex Credit Company.

Required

Prepare general journal entries to record the above transactions.

Problem 8–3
Estimating bad debts expense
(L. O. 3)

On December 31, 1990, Wheaton Company's unadjusted trial balance included the following items:

	Debit	Credit
Cash sales.		150,300
Credit sales		308,500
Accounts receivable.	133,400	
Allowance for doubtful accounts	1,380	

Required

1. Prepare the adjusting entry on the books of Wheaton Company to estimate bad debts under each of the following independent assumptions:
   a. Bad debts are estimated to be 1.5% of total sales.
   b. Bad debts are estimated to be 3% of credit sales.
   c. An analysis suggests that 7% of outstanding accounts receivable on December 31, 1990, will become uncollectible.

2. Show how Accounts Receivable and Allowance for Doubtful Accounts would appear on the December 31, 1990, balance sheet given the facts in 1. *b* above.

3. Show how Accounts Receivable and Allowance for Doubtful Accounts would appear on the December 31, 1990, balance sheet given the facts in 1. *c* above.

Problem 8–4
Aging accounts receivable
(L. O. 3)

Miller Corporation had credit sales of $4.2 million in 1990. On December 31, 1990, the company's Allowance for Doubtful Accounts had a credit balance of $4,800. The accountant for Miller Corporation has prepared a schedule of the December 31, 1990, accounts receivable by age, and on the basis of past experience has estimated the percentage of the receivables in each age category that will become uncollectible. This information is summarized as follows:

December 31, 1990, Accounts Receivable	Age of Accounts Receivable	Uncollectible Percent Expected
$420,000	Not due (under 30 days)	1.75
216,000	1 to 30 days past due	3.25
66,000	31 to 60 days past due	18.00
42,000	61 to 90 days past due	45.00
24,000	over 90 days past due	75.00

Required

1. Calculate the amount that should appear in the December 31, 1990, balance sheet as allowance for doubtful accounts.
2. Prepare the general journal entry to record bad debts expense for 1990.
3. On April 2, 1991, Miller Corporation concluded that a customer's $7,800 accounts receivable was uncollectible and that the account should be written off. What effect will this action have on Miller Corporation's 1991 net income? Explain your answer.

Problem 8–5
Recording accounts receivable transactions and bad debt adjustments
(L. O. 3)

Salinas Company began operations on January 1, 1989. During the next two years, the company completed a number of transactions that involved credit sales, accounts receivable collections, and bad debts. These transactions are summarized as follows:

1989

a. Sold merchandise on credit for $174,200, terms n/60.
b. Wrote off uncollectible accounts receivable in the amount of $750.
c. Received cash of $132,400 in payment of outstanding accounts receivable.
d. In adjusting the accounts on December 31, concluded that 2% of the outstanding accounts receivable would become uncollectible.

1990

a. Sold merchandise on credit for $238,800, terms n/60.
b. Wrote off uncollectible accounts receivable in the amount of $980.
c. Received cash of $196,400 in payment of outstanding accounts receivable.
d. In adjusting the accounts on December 31, concluded that 2% of the outstanding accounts receivable would become uncollectible.

Required

Prepare general journal entries to record the 1989 and 1990 summarized transactions of Salinas Company and the adjusting entries to record bad debts expense at the end of each year.

Problem 8–6
Journalizing notes receivable and bad debts transactions
(L. O. 3, 4, 5)

Prepare entries in general journal form to record these transactions by Barley Company:

Jan. 5 Accepted a $4,590, 60-day, 10% note dated this day in granting a time extension on the past-due account of Grace Murrow.
Mar. 9 Grace Murrow paid the maturity value of her $4,590 note.
      11 Accepted an $1,800, 60-day, 11% note dated this day in granting a time extension on the past-due account of Paul Peters.
May 13 Paul Peters dishonoured his note when presented for payment.
      14 Accepted a $3,000, 90-day, 13% note dated May 12 in granting a time extension on the past-due account of Ralph Hunter.
      25 Discounted the Ralph Hunter note at the bank at 15%.

Aug. 17 Since notice protesting the Ralph Hunter note had not been received, assumed that it had been paid.

16 Accepted a $2,400, 60-day, 11% note dated August 15 in granting a time extension on the past-due account of Elmer Cooper.

Sept. 11 Discounted the Elmer Cooper note at the bank at 13%.

Oct. 18 Received notice protesting the Elmer Cooper note. Paid the bank the maturity value of the note plus a $20 protest fee.

19 Received a $3,600, 60-day, 12% note dated this day from Cathy Reese in granting a time extension on her past-due account.

Nov. 21 Discounted the Cathy Reese note at the bank at 15%.

Dec. 22 Received notice protesting the Cathy Reese note. Paid the bank the maturity value of the note plus a $20 protest fee.

30 Received payment from Cathy Reese of the maturity value of her dishonoured note, the protest fee, and interest on both for 9 days beyond maturity at 12%.

31 Wrote off the accounts of Paul Peters and Elmer Cooper against Allowance for Doubtful Accounts.

Problem 8–7
Analysis and journalizing of notes receivable transactions
(L. O. 4, 5)

Prepare general journal entries to record the following transactions of Crafter Company:

1989

Dec. 14 Accepted a $3,000, 60-day, 12% note dated this day in granting Ed Stafford a time extension on his past-due account.

31 Made an adjusting entry to record the accrued interest on the Ed Stafford note.

31 Closed the Interest Earned account.

1990

Jan. 13 Discounted the Ed Stafford note at the bank at 15%.

Feb. 15 Received notice protesting the Ed Stafford note. Paid the bank the maturity value of the note plus a $20 protest fee.

Mar. 3 Accepted a $2,100, 11%, 60-day note dated this day in granting a time extension on the past-due account of Roy Frix.

27 Discounted the Roy Frix note at the bank at 14%.

May 5 Since notice protesting the Roy Frix note had not been received, assumed that it had been paid.

June 9 Accepted a $2,400, 60-day, 10% note dated this day in granting a time extension on the past-due account of June Quigley.

Aug. 8 Received payment of the maturity value of the June Quigley note.

11 Accepted an $1,800, 60-day, 11% note dated this day in granting Rita Adair a time extension on her past-due account.

31 Discounted the Rita Adair note at the bank at 13%.

Oct. 13 Received notice protesting the Rita Adair note. Paid the bank the maturity value of the note plus a $20 protest fee.

Nov. 9 Received payment from Rita Adair of the maturity value of her dishonoured note, the protest fee, and interest on both for 26 days beyond maturity at 11%.

Dec. 27 Wrote off the Ed Stafford account against Allowance for Doubtful Accounts.

Alternate Problems

Griffen Company had no temporary investments on December 31, 1989, but had the following transactions involving temporary investments during 1990:

Jan. 9   Paid $60,000 to buy six-month Certificate of Deposit, $60,000 principal amount, 8%, dated January 9.

Feb. 2   Purchased 800 shares of Inco common stock at 35½ plus a $400 brokerage fee.

      15   Purchased 600 shares of Seagram common stock at 64¼ plus a $300 brokerage fee.

Mar. 2   Paid $45,000 for Canada Savings Bonds, $45,000 principal amount, 9%, dated March 2, 1990, due March 2, 1994.

      16   Purchased 1,200 shares of Nynex common stock at 55⅛ plus a $975 brokerage fee.

June 2   Received a $0.45 per share cash dividend on the Inco common shares.

      16   Sold 600 shares of Inco common stock at 37 less a $300 brokerage fee.

July 11   Received a cheque for the principal and accrued interest on the Certificate of Deposit that matured on July 9.

Aug. 13   Received a $0.55 per share cash dividend on the Seagram common shares.

Sept. 2   Received a cheque for six months' interest on the Canada Savings Bonds purchased on March 2.

      2   Received a $0.45 per share cash dividend on the remaining Inco common shares owned by Griffen Company.

Nov. 13   Received a $0.55 per share cash dividend on the Seagram common shares.

On December 31, 1990, the market prices of the equity securities held by Griffen Company were: Inco, 38½; Seagram, 63; and Nynex, 47⅞.

Required

1. Prepare general journal entries to record the above transactions.
2. Prepare a schedule to calculate the lower of cost or market of Griffen's temporary investments in marketable equity securities.
3. Prepare adjusting entries, if necessary, to record accrued interest on Griffen Company's investments in debt obligations and to reduce the marketable equity securities to the lower of cost or market.

Chilton Company allows a few customers to make sales on credit. Other customers may use either of two credit cards. The Canadex Bank makes a 3% service charge for sales on its credit card but immediately credits the chequing account of its commercial customers when credit card receipts are deposited. Chilton deposits the Canadex Bank credit card receipts at the close of each business day.

When customers use the Western Credit Card, Chilton Company accumulates the receipts for two or three days and then submits them to the Western

Credit Company for payment. Western makes a 4% service charge and usually pays within one week of being billed.

Chilton Company completed the following transactions:

Apr. 4   Sold merchandise on credit to Joe Blake for $1,750. (Terms of all credit sales are 2/15, n/60.)

5   Sold merchandise for $3,250 to customers who used their Canadex Bank credit cards. Sold merchandise for $3,600 to customers who used their Western credit cards.

6   Sold merchandise for $2,400 to customers who used their Western credit cards.

8   Wrote off the account of T. Kurth against Allowance for Doubtful Accounts. The $500 balance in Kurth's account stemmed from a credit sale in August of last year.

9   The Western credit card receipts accumulated since April 4 were submitted to the credit card company for payment.

19   Received Joe Blake's cheque paying for the purchase of April 4.

20   Received the amount due from Western Credit Company.

Required

Prepare general journal entries to record the above transactions.

Problem 8–3A
Estimating bad debts expense
(L. O. 3)

On December 31, 1990, Defore Corporation's unadjusted trial balance included the following items:

	Debit	Credit
Cash sales.		360,000
Credit sales		585,000
Accounts receivable.	210,000	
Allowance for doubtful accounts		200

Required

1. Prepare the adjusting entry on the books of Defore Corporation to estimate bad debts under each of the following independent assumptions:
    a. Bad debts are estimated to be 2% of total sales.
    b. Bad debts are estimated to be 3.5% of credit sales.
    c. An analysis suggests that 7.5% of outstanding accounts receivable on December 31, 1990, will become uncollectible.

2. Show how Accounts Receivable and Allowance for Doubtful Accounts would appear on the December 31, 1990, balance sheet given the facts in 1. *b* above.

3. Show how Accounts Receivable and Allowance for Doubtful Accounts would appear on the December 31, 1990, balance sheet given the facts in 1. *c* above.

Problem 8–4A
Aging accounts receivable
(L. O. 3)

Software Corporation had credit sales of $6.5 million in 1990. On December 31, 1990, the company's Allowance for Doubtful Accounts had a debit balance of $7,400. The accountant for Software Corporation has prepared a schedule of the December 31, 1990, accounts receivable by age, and on the basis of past experience has estimated the percentage of the receivables in each age category that will become uncollectible. This information is summarized as follows:

December 31, 1990, Accounts Receivable	Age of Accounts Receivable	Uncollectible Percent Expected
$600,000	Not due (under 30 days)	2
300,000	1 to 30 days past due	3
70,000	31 to 60 days past due	15
40,000	61 to 90 days past due	40
32,000	over 90 days past due	80

Required

1. Calculate the amount that should appear in the December 31, 1990, balance sheet as allowance for doubtful accounts.
2. Prepare the general journal entry to record bad debts expense for 1990.
3. On May 21, 1991, Software Corporation concluded that a customer's $9,600 accounts receivable was uncollectible and that the account should be written off. What effect will this action have on Software Corporation's 1991 net income? Explain your answer.

Problem 8–5A
Recording accounts receivable transactions and bad debt adjustments
(L. O. 3)

After beginning operations on January 1, 1989, Johanson Company completed a number of transactions during 1989 and 1990 that involved credit sales, accounts receivable collections, and bad debts. These transactions are summarized as follows:

1989
a. Sold merchandise on credit for $157,800, terms n/30.
b. Received cash of $128,900 in payment of outstanding accounts receivable.
c. Wrote off uncollectible accounts receivable in the amount of $300.
d. In adjusting the accounts on December 31, concluded that 1.5% of the outstanding accounts receivable would become uncollectible.

1990
a. Sold merchandise on credit for $198,800, terms n/30.
b. Received cash of $165,300 in payment of outstanding accounts receivable.
c. Wrote off uncollectible accounts receivable in the amount of $700.
d. In adjusting the accounts on December 31, concluded that 1.5% of the outstanding accounts receivable would become uncollectible.

Required
Prepare general journal entries to record the 1989 and 1990 summarized transactions of Johanson Company and the adjusting entries to record bad debts expense at the end of each year.

Problem 8–6A
Journalizing notes receivable and bad debts transactions
(L. O. 3, 4, 5)

Prepare entries in general journal form to record these transactions by Wheat Company:

Jan. 10 Accepted a $3,000, 60-day, 12% note dated this day in granting a time extension on the past-due account of David Huerta.

Mar. 14 David Huerta dishonoured his note when presented for payment.

19 Accepted a $2,100, 90-day, 10% note dated this day in granting a time extension on the past-due account of Rose Jones.

28 Discounted the Rose Jones note at the bank at 16%.

June 26 Since notice protesting the Rose Jones note had not been received, assumed the note had been paid.

27 Accepted $700 in cash and a $1,300, 60-day, 12% note dated this day in granting a time extension on the past-due account of Jake Thomas.

July 24 Discounted the Jake Thomas note at the bank at 14%.

Aug. 31 Received notice protesting the Jake Thomas note. Paid the bank the maturity value of the note plus a $20 protest fee.

Sept. 4 Accepted a $1,500, 60-day, 11% note dated this day in granting a time extension on the past-due account of Ginnie Bauer.

Oct. 13 Discounted the Ginnie Bauer note at the bank at 14%.

Nov. 9 Received notice protesting the Ginnie Bauer note. Paid the bank the maturity value of the note plus a $20 protest fee.

Dec. 6 Received payment from Ginnie Bauer of the maturity value of her dishonoured note, the protest fee, and interest at 11% on both for 30 days beyond maturity.

28 Decided the accounts of David Huerta and Jake Thomas were uncollectible and wrote them off against Allowance for Doubtful Accounts.

*Problem 8–7A
Analysis and journalizing of notes receivable transactions
(L. O. 4, 5)

Prepare general journal entries to record the following transactions of Raines Company:

1989

Dec. 9 Accepted a $3,300, 60-day, 12% note dated this day in granting a time extension on the past-due account of Tom Linden.

31 Made an adjusting entry to record the accrued interest on the Tom Linden note.

31 Closed the Interest Earned account.

1990

Jan. 8 Discounted the Tom Linden note at the bank at 14%.

Feb. 10 Since notice protesting the Tom Linden note had not been received, assumed that it had been paid.

Mar. 2 Accepted a $2,000, 90-day, 11% note dated this day in granting a time extension on the past-due account of Lois Goetz.

8 Discounted the Lois Goetz note at the bank at 14%.

June 3 Received notice protesting the Lois Goetz note. Paid the bank the maturity value of the note plus a $25 protest fee.

July 3 Received payment from Lois Goetz of the maturity value of her dishonoured note, the protest fee, and interest on both for 30 days beyond maturity at 11%.

July 3 Accepted a $1,500, 60-day, 10% note dated July 2 in granting a time extension on the past-due account of Janet Casey.

Sept. 3 Janet Casey dishonoured her note when presented for payment.

Sept. 4 Accepted $600 in cash and a $1,200, 60-day, 10% note dated this day in granting a time extension on the past-due account of Dick Beaumont.

Oct. 10 Discounted the Dick Beaumont note at the bank at 13%.

Nov. 6 Received notice protesting the Dick Beaumont note. Paid the bank its maturity value plus a $25 protest fee.

Dec. 28 Decided the Janet Casey and Dick Beaumont accounts were uncollectible and wrote them off against Allowance for Doubtful Accounts.

Provocative Problems

Provocative Problem 8–1
Personal Sales
(Review problem)

When his auditor arrived early in January to begin the annual audit, Sam Groves, the owner of Personal Sales, asked that careful attention be given to accounts receivable. Two things caused this request: (1) During the previous week, Mr. Groves had met Bob Peck, a former customer, and had asked him about his account which had recently been written off as uncollectible. Mr. Peck had indignantly replied that he had paid his $425 account in full, and he later produced canceled cheques endorsed by Personal Sales to prove it. (2) The income statement prepared for the quarter ended the previous December 31 showed an unusually large volume of sales returns. The bookkeeper who had prepared the statement was a new employee, having begun work on October 1, after being hired on the basis of out-of-town letters of reference. In addition to doing all the record-keeping, the bookkeeper also acts as cashier, receiving and depositing the cash from both cash sales and those received through the mail.

In the process of performing the audit, the auditor prepared from the company's records the following analysis of the accounts receivable for the period October 1 through December 31:

	Dodd	Reid	Mead	Farr	Soto	Lamb	Teas
Balance, October 1	$ 510	$300	$ 820	$600	$ 315	$1,210	$ 975
Sales.	1,680	315	1,275		1,580	1,000	1,450
Total	$2,190	$615	$2,095	$600	$1,895	$2,210	$2,425
Collections.	(1,225)		(950)		(985)	(1,175)	(1,475)
Returns	(205)	(100)	(95)		(195)	(150)	(60)
Bad debts written off		(515)		(600)			
Balance, December 31 . . .	$ 760	$–0–	$1,050	$–0–	$ 715	$ 885	$ 890

The auditor contacted all charge customers and learned that although their account balances as of December 31 agreed with the amounts shown in the company's records, the individual transactions did not. The customers reported credit purchases that totaled $8,150 during the three-month period and returns of $305 for which credit had been granted. Correspondence with Mr. Farr, the customer whose $600 account had been written off, revealed that he had become bankrupt and his creditor claims had been settled by his receiver in bankruptcy at $0.25 on the dollar. The cheques had been mailed by his receiver on October 30, and all had been paid and returned by the bank, properly endorsed by the recipients.

Under the assumption the bookkeeper has embezzled cash from the company, determine the total amount he has taken and attempted to conceal with false accounts receivable entries. Account for the deficiency by listing the concealment methods used and the amount he attempted to conceal with each method. Also outline an internal control system that will help protect the company's cash from future embezzlement. Assume the company will hire a new bookkeeper, but that it is small and can have only one office employee who must do all the bookkeeping.

Provocative Problem 8–2
Every-Sport Store
(L. O. 3)

Dennis Hoover has operated Every-Sport Store for five years. Three years ago, he liberalized the store's credit policy in an effort to increase credit sales. Credit sales have increased, but now Dennis is concerned with the effects of the more liberalized credit policy. Bad debts written off (the store uses the direct write-off method) have increased materially in the last three years, and now Dennis wonders if the increase justifies the substantial bad debt losses which he is certain have resulted from the more liberal credit policy.

An examination of the store's credit sales records, bad debt losses, and accounts receivable for the five years' operations reveal:

	1st Year	2nd Year	3rd Year	4th Year	5th Year
Credit sales	$180,000	$198,000	$270,000	$325,000	$360,000
Cost of goods sold	108,000	118,800	162,000	195,000	216,000
Gross profit from credit sales	$ 72,000	$ 79,200	$108,000	$130,000	$144,000
Expenses other than bad debts	54,000	59,220	81,360	96,840	108,000
Income before bad debts	$ 18,000	$ 19,980	$ 26,640	$ 33,160	$ 36,000
Bad debts written off	180	790	1,350	4,210	4,300
Income from credit sales	$ 17,820	$ 19,190	$ 25,290	$ 28,950	$ 31,700
Bad debts by year of sales	$ 720	$ 595	$ 3,510	3,850	$ 5,000

The last line in the tabulation results from reclassifying bad debt losses so that the losses appear in the same years as do the sales that resulted in the losses. Since some of the fifth-year sales had not been collected at year-end, the $5,000 of fifth-year losses includes $2,845 of estimated bad debts that are still in the accounts receivable.

Prepare a schedule showing in columns by years: income from credit sales before bad debt losses, bad debts incurred, and the resulting income from credit sales. Then, below the income figures show for each year bad debts written off as a percentage of sales followed on the next line by estimated bad debts expense incurred as a percentage of sales. Also prepare a report for Mr. Hoover in which you answer his concern about the new credit policy and recommend any changes you consider desirable in his accounting for bad debts.

Analytical and Review Problems

A&R Problem 8–1

West Company maintains a portfolio of investments in securities. The investments are classified as "temporary," and West uses the LCM method. The following data relate to the investment portfolio at year-end. There were no dispositions during 1991 and there was only one addition.

	Cost	Market
December 31, 1990	$38,200	$35,500
December 31, 1991	42,300	43,900

Required

Present the December 31, 1990 and 1991, adjusting entries with supporting explanations.

A&R Problem 8–2

The following pertains to the dealings of Burnaby Company and one of its customers, James Clarke.

Oct.   1 Received a 12%, 90-day note from James Clarke in full settlement of his account.

      31 Recorded the necessary adjusting entry pertaining to the Clarke note, this being the end of the company's fiscal year.

Nov. 5. Discounted at 10% the Clarke note at the bank.

Jan.   3 Received notification from the bank that the Clarke note was dishonoured, when due, and the bank charged the company's account with the maturity value of the note and the standard $25 protest fee.

Feb. 2 Received from James Clarke a certified cheque for the amount owing, including interest for the 30 days since the maturity of the note.

Required

1. Prepare the balance of the necessary entries without amounts in connection with the James Clarke note payable on the basis of the additional information provided above (the October 1 entry has already been prepared).

2. Indicate how the following are determined:
   a. Cash proceeds from the Clarke note on November 5.
   b. Interest on November 5.
   c. The amount of cash charged the Burnaby account by the bank when the Clarke note was dishonoured.
   d. Amount of cash received from Clarke on February 2.

3. Calculate the amounts referred to in (2) on the assumption that the Clarke note was for $1,000 (unless otherwise directed by your instructor).*

Oct.	1	Notes Receivable.	XXX	
		Accounts Receivable—James Clarke		XXX

A&R Problem 8–3

Hard Pressed Company required a loan of $4,800 and was offered two alternatives by the Security Bank. The alternatives are:

a. Hard Pressed would give the bank a one-year $4,800 note payable, dated December 1, 1990, with interest at 25%.*

b. Hard Pressed would give the bank a one-year $6,000 noninterest-bearing note payable dated December 1, 1990. The bank would precalculate and deduct interest at 20%.*

---

*Interest to be calculated on monthly basis and no days of grace.

Required

1. Prepare *all* the necessary entries (including repayment on November 30, 1991) with regard to alternative (*a*). Assume that Hard Pressed Company's fiscal year ends December 31.

2. Repeat the journal entries for alternative (*b*).

A&R Problem 8–4

The Tor-Mont Company has been in business three years and has applied for a significant bank loan. Prior to considering the applications, the bank asks you to conduct an audit for the last three years. Concerning accounts receivable, you find that the company has been charging off receivables as they finally proved uncollectible and treating them as expenses at the time of write-off.

Your investigation indicates that receivable losses have approximated (and can be expected to approximate) 2% of net sales. Until this first audit, the company's sales and direct receivable write-off experience was:

Year of Sales	Amount of Sales	Accounts written off in		
		19X1	19X2	19X3
19X1	$300,000	$1,500	$4,000	$ 800
19X2	400,000	—	2,000	4,800
19X3	500,000	—	—	5,000

Required

1. Indicate the amount by which net income was understated or overstated each year because the company used the direct write-off method rather than the generally acceptable allowance method.

2. Prepare all the entries for each of the three years that would have been made if Tor-Mont had used the allowance method from the start of the business.

3. Which of the entries in (2) are year-end adjusting entries?

A&R Problem 8–5

After three years in business, Handi Vacuum Company asks you to review its accounting procedures, particularly as they relate to accounts receivable. In your perusal of the company's records, your attention is drawn to the fact that the balance sheet carries no allowance for doubtful accounts. You are informed that the company expensed uncollectible accounts when written off with recoveries credited to income as collected.

In your examination of receivables you determine that the company sells vacuums on an installment plan; the installment contracts provided for uniform monthly collections over a time span of 18 months from date of sale. The amount of bad debt write-off was determined on December 31 of each year. The amount of the write-off was the total of contract balances on which at least four consecutive payments had lapsed.

Statistics for the past three years are as follows:

Year	Sales
199A	$180,000
199B	240,000
199C	220,000

Accounts written off to expense:

	199A	199B	199C
199A accounts	$1,800	$1,500	
199B accounts		2,700	$2,800
199C accounts			3,100

Estimated probable losses on the outstanding accounts as of December 31, 199C, for

199B accounts	$,600
199C accounts	1,000

Recoveries of accounts written off:

199A accounts	$240
199B accounts	400

Your recommendation to the company is to account for bad debts on the allowance basis. The allowance is to be based on a percentage of sales which is derived from the experience of the three-year period. Before implementing your recommendation, however, the president related the situation to an old classmate while attending a class reunion. His friend asked him, "Why do you want to bother with allowances and write-offs? Why not recognize revenue as cash is collected? And keep your receivables in two batches—those that are current and those that are delinquent. However, no matter how old they are, no revenue was recognized, and, therefore, there is no need for any write-off." Upon his return to the office the following Monday the president summons you and expresses much disappointment in your work and your recommendation. He proceeds to tell you of the alternative method that he got for free. He refuses to listen to you. However, he agrees to read your report evaluating the method currently being followed and the two alternative approaches proposed.

Required

1. Prepare the necessary report, especially focusing attention on: revenue recognition, matching of revenues and expenses, and reporting of accounts receivable.
2. Prepare all the entries for each of the years that would have been made if Handi had used the allowance method from the start of the business.
3. Are there approaches other than the percent of sales that may be used to determine bad debt expenses? If yes, discuss these.
4. Indicate the amount by which net income was understated or overstated each year because the company used the direct write-off method rather than the more acceptable allowance method.

A&R Problem 8–6

Michael Taylor, a merchant, kept only limited records. Major purchases, including merchandise, were paid by cheque, but most other disbursements were paid out of cash receipts. Cash in excess of $300 on hand at the end of the week was deposited in the bank. No record was kept of cash in bank nor was a record kept of sales. A record of accounts receivable was maintained by keeping a copy of the charge ticket; this copy was given to the customer when the account was paid.

Taylor had started in business the first week of January 1990, with $50,000 in cash. The first week's transactions included the rental of a suitable building at $500 per month with the first payments due on January 15, the date of the lease. On January 5, Taylor purchased equipment for $12,000 list price payable in 10 equal monthly installments of $1,200 each beginning February 5. Had Taylor paid cash, he would have received a 5% discount on the list price. Taylor estimated that the equipment would be useful for 10 years at which time it would be sold for salvage at $400. On January 6, merchandise costing $25,000 arrived.

An analysis of the bank statements for the year showed total deposits of $290,000. This amount included the initial investment and a $10,000 loan for which Taylor signed a 12%, one-year note dated June 30. The balance in the bank statement on December 31, 1990, was $9,400, but there were December-dated cheques amounting to $2,100 not paid by the bank until January. Cash on hand on December 31 was $300. An inventory of merchandise taken on December 31, 1990, showed $36,800 at cost. Tickets for accounts receivable totaled $8,400, but $380 of that amount is probably not collectible. Customers ordered special merchandise not carried in stock by depositing 50% of the selling price. Of such deposits by customers, $400 were outstanding on December 31. Unpaid suppliers' invoices for merchandise amounted to $8,200. Taylor paid himself in cash a salary of $200 per week (52 weeks). Expenses paid in cash were as follows:

Utilities	$1,400
Telephone.	320
Advertising	420
Sales personnel (part-time)	8,800

Analysis of the cheque stubs indicated that cheques were drawn for the following:

Monthly rental payments.

Monthly payments for equipment.

Merchandise purchases.

Business taxes for the year, $500.

Three-year insurance policy dated February 1, 1990, on equipment and contents; the premium for the three years was $1,800.

Delivery service, $1,100.

At year-end, Taylor estimated that unpaid utilities for December would amount to $150, and delivery service of $100 for December remained unpaid. Early in January 1991, the banker telephoned Taylor and requested a set of financial statements. Taylor felt that he did not have the time or knowledge to prepare the requested statements in good form and engages you to prepare these for him.

Required

Prepare the December 31, 1990, balance sheet and income statement for the year ended December 31, 1990. Support amounts used in the statements.

9 Inventories and Cost of Goods Sold

The operations of merchandising businesses involve the purchase and resale of tangible commodities. In Chapter 5, when we first introduced the topic of accounting for merchandising businesses, we left several important matters for later consideration. In this chapter, we return to the topic and examine the methods businesses use at the end of each period to assign dollar amounts to merchandise inventory and to cost of goods sold. The principles and procedures that are explained in this chapter are used in department stores, grocery stores, automobile dealerships, and any other businesses that purchase goods for resale.

Learning Objectives

After studying Chapter 9, you should be able to:

1. Calculate the cost of an inventory based on (*a*) specific invoice prices, (*b*) weighted-average cost, (*c*) FIFO, and (*d*) LIFO, and explain the financial statement effects of choosing one method over the others.

2. Calculate the lower-of-cost-or-market amount of an inventory.

3. Explain the effect of an inventory error on the income statements of the current and succeeding years.

4. Prepare entries to record merchandise transactions and maintain subsidiary inventory records under a perpetual inventory system.

5. Estimate an inventory by the retail method and by the gross profit method.

6. Define or explain the words and phrases listed in the chapter Glossary.

The assets that a business purchases and holds for resale are called *merchandise inventory*. As a rule, the items held as merchandise inventory are sold within one year or one operating cycle. Therefore, merchandise inventory is a current asset, usually the largest current asset on the balance sheet of a merchandiser.

Matching Merchandise Costs with Revenues

Accounting for inventories affects both the balance sheet and the income statement. However, "the method of determining cost should be one which results in the fairest matching of costs against revenues regardless of whether or not the method corresponds to the physical flow of goods."[1] The matching process is already a familiar topic. For inventories, it consists of determining how much of the cost of the goods that were available for sale during a period should be deducted from the period's revenue and how much should be carried forward as inventory to be matched against a future period's revenue.

In a periodic inventory system, when the cost of goods available for sale is allocated between cost of goods sold and ending inventory, the key problem is to assign a cost to the ending inventory. However, you should remember that when you assign a cost to the ending inventory, you are also determining cost of goods sold. This is true because the ending inventory is subtracted from the cost of goods available for sale to determine cost of goods sold.

Items to Include in Merchandise Inventory

The merchandise inventory of a business includes all goods owned by the business and held for sale, regardless of where the goods may be located at the time inventory is counted. In applying this rule, most items present no problem. All that is required is to see that all items are counted, that nothing is omitted, and that nothing is counted more than once. However, goods in transit, goods sold but not delivered, goods on consignment, and obsolete and damaged goods are items that require special attention.

Should merchandise be included in the inventory of a business if the goods are in transit from a supplier to a business on the date the business takes an inventory? The answer to this question depends on whether the rights and risks of ownership have passed from the supplier to the purchasing business. If ownership has passed to the purchaser, they should be included in the purchaser's inventory. Usually, if the buyer is responsible for paying the freight charges, ownership passes as soon as the goods are loaded aboard the means of transportation. (As mentioned in Chapter 5, the terms would be FOB the seller's factory or warehouse.) On the other hand, if the seller is to pay the freight charges, ownership passes when the goods arrive at their destination (FOB destination).

Goods on consignment are goods shipped by their owner (known as the **consignor**) to another person or firm (called the **consignee**) who is to sell the goods for the owner. Consigned goods belong to the consignor and should appear on the consignor's inventory.

Damaged goods and goods that have deteriorated or have become obsolete should not be counted in the inventory if they are not salable. If such goods are

---

[1] *CICA Handbook* (Toronto: The Canadian Institute of Chartered Accountants), par. 3030.09.

salable but at a reduced price, they should be included in the inventory at a conservative estimate of their **net realizable value** (sale price less the cost of making the sale). This causes the accounting period in which the goods deteriorated, were damaged, or became obsolete to suffer the resultant loss.

Elements of Inventory Cost

As applied to inventories, *cost* means the sum of the applicable expenditures and charges directly or indirectly incurred in bringing an article to its existing condition and location.[2] Therefore, the cost of an inventory item includes the invoice price, less the discount, plus any additional or incidental cost necessary to put the item into place and condition for sale. The additional costs may include import duties, transportation-in, storage, insurance, and any other applicable costs such as those incurred during an ageing process (for example, the ageing of wine).

If incurred, any of the foregoing enter into the cost of an inventory. However, in pricing an inventory, many concerns do not take into consideration the incidental costs of acquiring merchandise. They price the inventory on the basis of invoice prices only. As a result, the incidental costs are allocated to cost of goods sold during the period in which they are incurred.

In theory, a share of each incidental cost should be assigned to every unit purchased. This causes a portion of each to be carried forward in the inventory to be matched against the revenue of the period in which the inventory is sold. However, the expense of computing costs on such a precise basis may outweigh the benefit from the extra accuracy. Therefore, many businesses take advantage of the *principle of materiality* and charge such costs to cost of goods sold.

Taking an Ending Inventory

As you learned in Chapter 5, when a **periodic inventory system** is used, the dollar amount of the ending inventory is determined as follows: count the units of each product on hand, multiply the count for each product by its cost, and add the costs for all products. In making the count, items are less likely to be counted twice or omitted from the count if prenumbered **inventory tickets** like the one in Illustration 9–1 are used. Before beginning the inventory count, a sufficient number of the tickets, at least one for each product on hand, is issued to each department in the store. Next, a clerk counts the quantity of each product. From the count and the price tag attached to the merchandise, the clerk fills in the information on the inventory ticket and attaches it to the counted items. After the count is completed, each department is examined for uncounted items. At this stage, inventory tickets are attached to all counted items, and any products without tickets attached are uncounted. After all items are counted and tickets attached, the tickets are removed and sent to the accounting department for completion of the inventory. To ensure that no ticket is lost or left attached to merchandise, all the prenumbered tickets issued are accounted for when the tickets arrive in the accounting department.

---

[2] Ibid., see paragraphs 3030.02 to 3030.06.

Illustration 9–1
Inventory ticket used to tag item as it is counted

```
                    INVENTORY
                    TICKET no. ——— 786 ———

                    Item

                    _____

                    Quantity counted  [        ]

                    Sales price      $[        ]

                    Cost price       $[        ]

                    Purchase date     [        ]

                    Counted by ———————————————

                    Checked by ———————————————
```

In the accounting department, the unit and cost information on the tickets is aggregated by multiplying the number of units of each product by its unit cost. This gives the dollar amount of each product in the inventory, and the total for all the products is the dollar total of the inventory.

Assigning Costs to Inventory Items

Calculate the cost of an inventory based on (*a*) specific invoice prices, (*b*) weighted-average cost, (*c*) FIFO, and (*d*) LIFO, and explain the financial statement effects of choosing one method over the others. (L. O. 1)

In completing an inventory count, it is necessary to assign costs to the inventory items. When all units are purchased at the same unit cost, this process is easy. However, when identical items were purchased at different costs, a problem arises as to which costs apply to the ending inventory and which apply to the goods sold. There are four commonly used methods of assigning costs to goods in the ending inventory and to goods sold. They are (1) specific invoice prices; (2) weighted-average cost; (3) first-in, first-out; and (4) last-in, first-out. All four methods fall within generally accepted accounting principles.

To illustrate the four methods, assume that at the end of its annual accounting period, a company has on hand 12 units of Product X. Also, assume that the inventory at the beginning of the year and purchases during the year were as follows:

Jan. 1	Beginning inventory	10 units @ $100 =	$1,000
Mar. 13	Purchased	15 units @ $108 =	1,620
Aug. 17	Purchased	20 units @ $120 =	2,400
Nov. 10	Purchased	10 units @ $125 =	1,250
Total		55 units	$6,270

Specific Invoice Prices

When it is possible to identify each item in an inventory with a specific purchase and its invoice, **specific invoice inventory pricing** may be used to assign costs. For example, assume that 6 of the 12 unsold units of Product X were from the November purchase and 6 were from the August purchase. With this information, specific invoice prices can be used to assign cost to the ending inventory and to cost of goods sold as follows:

Total cost of 55 units available for sale		$6,270
Less ending inventory priced by means of specific invoices:		
6 units from the November purchase at $125 each . . .	$750	
6 units from the August purchase at $120 each	720	
12 units in the ending inventory.		1,470
Cost of goods sold.		$4,800

Weighted Average

When **weighted-average inventory pricing** is used, the unit prices of the beginning inventory and of each purchase are weighted by the number of units in the beginning inventory and each purchase. The total of these amounts is then divided by the total number of units available for sale to find the weighted-average cost per unit as follows:

10 units @ $100 =	$1,000
15 units @ $108 =	1,620
20 units @ $120 =	2,400
10 units @ $125 =	1,250
55	$6,270

$6,270 ÷ 55 = $114 weighted-average cost per unit

After the weighted-average cost per unit is determined, this average is used to assign costs to the inventory and the units sold as follows:

Total cost of 55 units available for sale	$6,270
Less ending inventory priced on a weighted-average cost basis: 12 units at $114 each.	1,368
Cost of goods sold	$4,902

First-In, First-Out

When **first-in, first-out inventory pricing (FIFO)** is used, the items in the beginning inventory are assumed to be sold first. Additional sales are assumed to come in the order in which they were purchased. Thus, the costs of the last items received are assigned to the ending inventory, and the remaining costs are assigned to goods sold. For example, when first-in, first-out is used, the costs of Product X are assigned to the inventory and goods sold as follows:

Total cost of 55 units available for sale.		$6,270
Less ending inventory priced on a basis of FIFO:		
10 units from the November purchase at $125 each . .	$1,250	
2 units from the August purchase at $120 each	240	
12 units in the ending inventory		1,490
Cost of goods sold.		$4,780

You need to understand that the use of FIFO is acceptable whether or not the physical flow of goods actually follows a first-in, first-out pattern. The physical flow of products depends on the nature of the product and the way the products are stored. If a product is perishable (for example, fresh tomatoes), the business will attempt to sell them in a first-in, first-out pattern. Other products, for example, bolts or screws that are kept in a large bin, may tend to be sold on a last-in, first-out basis. In either case, the FIFO method of allocating cost may be used.

Last-In, First-Out

Under the **last-in, first-out inventory pricing (LIFO)** method, the cost of the last goods received are charged to cost of goods sold and matched with revenue from sales. Again, this method is acceptable even though the physical flow of goods may not be on a last-in, first-out basis.

One argument for the use of LIFO is based on the idea that a going concern must replace the inventory items it sells. When goods are sold, replacements are purchased. Thus, it is a sale that causes the replacement of goods. If costs and revenues are then matched, replacement costs should be matched with the sales that induced the acquisitions. Although the costs of the most recent purchases are not quite the same as the costs of the replacements, the costs of the most recent purchases are the most current costs. Thus, the costs of recent purchases closely approximate replacement costs.

Under LIFO, costs are assigned to the 12 remaining units of Product X and to the goods sold as follows:

Total cost of 55 units available for sale		$6,270
Less ending inventory priced on a basis of LIFO:		
10 units in the beginning inventory at $100 each . .	$1,000	
2 units from the March purchase at $108 each. . .	216	
12 units in the ending inventory		1,216
Cost of goods sold.		$5,054

Notice that when LIFO is used to match costs and revenues, the ending inventory is priced at the cost of the oldest 12 units.

Comparison of Methods

In a stable market where prices remain unchanged, the choice of an inventory pricing method has little importance. When prices are unchanged over a period of time, all methods give the same cost figures. However, in a changing market where prices are rising or falling, each method may give a different result. These differences are shown in Illustration 9-2, where we assume that Product X sales were $6,000 and operating expenses were $500. In Illustration 9–2, note the differences that resulted from the choice of an inventory pricing method. Since purchase prices were rising throughout the period, FIFO resulted in the lowest cost of goods sold, the highest gross profit, and the highest net income. On the other hand, LIFO resulted in the highest cost of goods sold, the lowest gross profit, and the lowest net income. As you would expect, the results of using the weighted-average method fall between FIFO and LIFO. The results of using specific invoice prices depend entirely on which units were actually sold.

Each of the four pricing methods is generally accepted, and arguments can be made for using each. In one sense, one might argue that specific invoice prices exactly match costs and revenues. However, this method is of practical use only for relatively high-priced items of which only a few units are kept in stock and sold. Weighted-average costs tend to smooth out price fluctuations. FIFO provides an inventory valuation on the balance sheet that most closely approximates current replacement cost. LIFO causes the last costs incurred to be assigned to cost of goods sold. Therefore, it results in a better matching of current costs with revenues on the income statement.

Because the choice of an inventory pricing method often has material effects on the financial statements, the choice of a method should be disclosed in the footnotes to the statements. This information is important to an understanding of the statements and is required by the *full-disclosure principle*.[3]

The Consistency Principle

Since the choice of an inventory pricing method can have a material effect on the financial statements, some companies might be inclined to make a new choice each year. Their objective would be to select whichever method would result in the most favorable financial statements. However, if this were allowed, readers of financial statements would find it extremely difficult to compare the company's financial statements from one year to the next. If income increased, the reader would have difficulty deciding whether the increase resulted from more successful operations or from the change in the accounting method. The *consistency principle* is intended to avoid this problem.

The **consistency principle** requires that a company use the same accounting methods period after period, so that the financial statements of succeeding periods will be comparable.[4] The *consistency principle* is not limited just to inventory pricing methods. Whenever a company must choose between alter-

---

[3] Ibid., par. 3030.10.

[4] Ibid, par. 1000.20.

Illustration 9–2
The income statement effects of alternative inventory pricing methods

	Specific Invoice Prices	Weighted Average	FIFO	LIFO
Sales.	$6,000	$6,000	$6,000	$6,000
Cost of goods sold:				
Merchandise inventory, January 1	$1,000	$1,000	$1,000	$1,000
Purchases.	5,270	5,270	5,270	5,270
Cost of goods available for sale	$6,270	$6,270	$6,270	$6,270
Merchandise inventory, December 31 . .	1,470	1,368	1,490	1,216
Cost of goods sold.	$4,800	$4,902	$4,780	$5,054
Gross profit	$1,200	$1,098	$1,220	$ 946
Operating expenses	500	500	500	500
Income before taxes	$ 700	$ 598	$ 720	$ 446

native generally accepted accounting methods, consistency requires that the company continue to use the selected method period after period. As a result, a reader of a company's financial statements may assume that in keeping its records and in preparing its statements, the company used the same procedures employed in previous years. Only on the basis of this assumption can meaningful comparisons be made of the data in a company's statements year after year.

Changing Accounting Procedures

In achieving comparability, the *consistency principle* does not mean that a company can never change from one accounting method to another. Rather, if a company justifies a different acceptable method or procedure as an improvement in financial reporting, a change may be made. However, when such a change is made, the *full-disclosure principle* requires that the nature of the change, justification for the change, and the effect of the change on net income be disclosed in footnotes to the statements.[5]

Lower of Cost or Market

Calculate the lower-of-cost-or-market amount of an inventory.
(L. O. 2)

As we have discussed, the *cost* of the ending inventory is determined by using one of the four pricing methods (FIFO, LIFO, weighted average, or specific invoice prices). However, the cost of the inventory is not necessarily the amount that is reported on the balance sheet. Generally accepted accounting principles require that the inventory be reported at market value whenever market is lower than cost. Thus, merchandise inventory is shown on the balance sheet at the *lower of cost or market*.

---

[5] Ibid., par. 1506.15.

Market Normally Means Replacement Cost

Over the years the traditional rule for pricing inventory items has been the *lower of cost* or *market*. *Cost* is the price that was paid for an item when it was purchased. While *market* is normally interpreted as the price that would have to be paid to purchase or replace the item on the inventory date, its application has varied with differences in results. Consequently, the *CICA Handbook* has recommended that:

> In view of the lack of precision in meaning, it is desirable that the term "market" not be used in describing the basis of valuation. A term more descriptive of the method of determining market, such as "replacement cost," "net realizable value" or "net realizable value less normal profit margin" would be preferable.[6]

The argument advanced to support the use of cost or replacement was that if the replacement cost of an inventory item had declined, then its selling price would probably have to be reduced. Since this might result in a loss, the loss should be anticipated and taken in the period of the price decline. However, selling prices do not always follow cost prices exactly or quickly. As a result, the application of the rule has been modified, as shown in the next sections, to avoid misstatements of income in the year of the price decline and again in the succeeding year.

Lower of cost or market may be applied to merchandise inventory in either of two ways. First, it may be applied to the inventory as a whole. Alternatively, it may be applied separately to each product in the inventory. To illustrate, assume that a company's year-end inventory contains three products (X, Y, and Z) with the following costs and replacement costs:

Product	Units on Hand	Per Unit Cost	Per Unit Market	Total Cost	Total Market	Lower of Cost or Market (by product)
X	20	$8	$7	$160	$140	$140
Y	10	5	6	50	60	50
Z	5	9	7	45	35	35
				$255		$225

Replacement cost (market) of whole inventory . . . $235

Note that when the whole inventory is priced at market, the total is $235, which is $20 lower than the $255 cost. Alternatively, when the lower of cost or market is applied separately to each product, the sum is only $225. A company may use either approach to calculate lower of cost or market of merchandise inventory.

Recall from Chapter 8 that lower of cost or market also is used to value a company's temporary investments in marketable equity securities. However, in that case, only one approach is allowed. The total cost and total market value of the entire portfolio of investments is compared to determine the lower

---

[6] Ibid, par. 3030.11.

of cost or market. Thus, while the lower-of-cost-or-market calculation for merchandise inventory may be done two different ways, the calculation for temporary investments is restricted to one way.

Inventory Should Never Be Valued at More than Its Net Realizable Value

The idea that *market* is defined as *replacement cost* is subject to an important exception. This exception is that inventory should, according to some accountants, not be valued at more than its *net realizable value,* which is the expected sales price less additional costs to sell. Understand that merchandise is written down to market because the value of the merchandise to the company has declined. Sometimes, the net realizable value is even less than replacement cost. In that case, the merchandise is worth no more than net realizable value and should be written down to that amount.

For example, assume that merchandise was purchased for $100 and was originally priced to sell for $125. By year-end, a general decline in prices resulted in a replacement cost of $90. However, assume that the merchandise in question has been damaged. Management expects that the merchandise can be sold for $95 if it is first cleaned at a cost of $10. Therefore, net realizable value is $95 − $10, or $85. Since net realizable value ($85) is less than replacement cost ($90), the merchandise should be written down to net realizable value.

Inventory Should Never Be Valued at Less than Net Realizable Value minus a Normal Profit Margin

A second exception to the idea that *market* means *replacement cost* is that merchandise should, according to some accountants, not be written down to an amount that is less than net realizable value minus a normal profit margin. To illustrate, suppose that a company normally buys merchandise for $80 and sells it for $100. The gross profit of $20 is 20% of the selling price. Now suppose the selling price falls from $100 to $90. A normal gross profit margin would be $90 × 20% = $18. Therefore, the inventory should not be written down below $90 − $18 = $72, even if replacement cost is less than $72. If the inventory were written down below $72, the income statement of the current period would show an abnormally low gross profit margin. And when the merchandise is sold for $90 the next period, the income statement of that period would show an abnormally high gross profit margin.

Principle of Conservatism

Generally accepted accounting principles require that inventory be written down to market when market is less than cost. On the other hand, inventory generally cannot be written up to market when market exceeds cost. If writing inventory down to market is justified, why not also write inventory up to market? What is the reason for this apparent inconsistency?

The reason inventory is not written up above cost to a higher market value is that the "gain" from a market value increase is not realized until a sales transaction provides verifiable evidence of the amount of the gain. But why, then, are inventories written down when market is below cost?

Accountants often justify the lower-of-cost-or-market rule by citing the **conservatism principle.** This principle is sometimes expressed simplistically as "recognize all losses but anticipate no profits." More realistically, the principle of conservatism attempts to give the accountant guidance in uncertain situations where amounts must be estimated. "When uncertainty exists, estimates of a conservative nature attempt to ensure net assets or net income are not overstated."[7]

Explain the effect of an inventory error on the income statements of the current and succeeding years.
(L. O. 3)

Inventory Errors—Periodic System

When the *periodic inventory system* is used, you must be especially careful in taking the end-of-period inventory. If an error is made, it will cause misstatements in cost of goods sold, gross profit, net income, current assets, and owner's equity. Also, the ending inventory of one period is the beginning inventory of the next. Therefore, the error will carry forward and cause misstatements in the succeeding period's cost of goods sold, gross profit, and net income. Furthermore, since the amount involved in an inventory often is large, the misstatements can materially damage the usefulness of the financial statements.

To illustrate the effects of an inventory error, assume that in each of the years 1989, 1990, and 1991, a company had $100,000 in sales. If the company maintained a $20,000 inventory throughout the period and made $60,000 in purchases in each of the years, its cost of goods sold each year was $60,000 and its annual gross profit was $40,000. However, assume the company incorrectly calculated its December 31, 1989, inventory at $18,000 rather than $20,000. The error has the effects shown in Illustration 9–3.

Observe in Illustration 9–3 that the $2,000 understatement of the December 31, 1989, inventory caused a $2,000 overstatement in 1989 cost of goods sold and a $2,000 understatement in gross profit and net income. Also, since the ending inventory of 1989 became the beginning inventory of 1990, the error caused an understatement in the 1990 cost of goods sold and a $2,000 overstatement in gross profit and net income. However, by 1991 the error had no effect.

In Illustration 9–3, the December 31, 1989, inventory is understated. Had it been overstated, it would have caused opposite results—the 1989 net income would have been overstated and the 1990 income understated.

Since inventory errors correct themselves by causing offsetting errors in the next period, you might be inclined to think that they are not serious. Do not make this mistake. Management, creditors, and owners base many important decisions on fluctuations in reported net income. Therefore, inventory errors must be avoided.

Perpetual Inventory Systems

The previous discussion of inventories was focused on the periodic inventory system. Under the periodic system, the Merchandise Inventory account is updated only once each accounting period, at the end of the period. Then, the Merchandise Inventory account reflects the current balance of inventory only until the first purchase or sale in the following period. Thereafter, the Merchandise Inventory account no longer reflects the current balance.

---

[7]Ibid., par. 1000.18.

Illustration 9–3
Effects of inventory errors—periodic inventory system

	1989		1990		1991	
Sales.		$100,000		$100,000		$100,000
Cost of goods sold:						
Beginning inventory	$20,000		$18,000*		$20,000	
Purchases	60,000		60,000		60,000	
Goods for sale	$80,000		$78,000		$80,000	
Ending inventory	18,000*		20,000		20,000	
Cost of goods sold. . . .		62,000		58,000		60,000
Gross profit		$ 38,000		$ 42,000		$ 40,000
*Should have been $20,000.						

By contrast, the **perpetual inventory system** updates the Merchandise Inventory account after each purchase and each sale. As long as all entries have been posted, the account shows the current amount of inventory on hand. The system takes its name from the fact that the Merchandise Inventory account is ''perpetually'' up-to-date. When a perpetual inventory system is used, management is able to monitor the inventory on hand on a regular basis. This aids in planning future purchases.

Before computers were widely used in accounting, perpetual inventory systems were limited to companies that sold a limited number of products of relatively high value. The cost and effort of maintaining perpetual inventory records were simply too great for other types of companies. However, since computers have made the record-keeping chore much easier, an increasing number of companies are switching from periodic to perpetual.

Comparing Journal Entries under Periodic and Perpetual Inventory Systems

Prepare entries to record merchandise transactions and maintain subsidiary inventory records under a perpetual inventory system.
(L. O. 4)

Illustration 9–4 shows in parallel columns the typical journal entries made under periodic and perpetual inventory systems. In Illustration 9–4, observe the entries for the purchase of transaction 1. The perpetual system does not use a Purchases account. Instead, the cost of the items purchased is debited directly to Merchandise Inventory. Also, in transaction 2, the perpetual system credits the cost of purchase returns directly to the Merchandise Inventory account instead of using a Purchases Returns and Allowances account.

Transaction 3 involves the sale of merchandise. Note that the perpetual system requires two entries to record the sale, one to record the revenue and another to record cost of goods sold. Thus, a Cost of Goods Sold account is used in the perpetual system. In the periodic system the elements of cost of goods sold are not transferred to such an account. Instead, they are transferred to Income Summary in the process of recording the closing entries.

The closing entries under the two systems are shown as item 4 in Illustration 9–4. Under the periodic system, all of the cost elements related to inventories are transferred to Income Summary. By comparison, under the perpetual system, those cost elements were already recorded in a Cost of Goods Sold account. Thus, the closing entries simply transfer the balance in the Cost of

Illustration 9–4
A comparison of entries under periodic and perpetual inventory systems

X Company purchases merchandise for $15 per unit and sells it for $25. The company begins the current period with 5 units of product on hand, which cost a total of $75.

	Periodic			**Perpetual**	

1. Purchased on credit 10 units of merchandise for $15 per unit.

| Purchases | 150 | | Merchandise Inventory | 150 | |
| Accounts Payable | | 150 | Accounts Payable | | 150 |

2. Returned 3 units of merchandise originally purchased in (1) above.

| Accounts Payable | 45 | | Accounts Payable | 45 | |
| Purchases Returns and Allowances | | 45 | Merchandise Inventory | | 45 |

3. Sold 8 units for $200 cash.

Cash	200		Cash	200	
Sales		200	Sales		200
			Cost of Goods Sold	120	
			Merchandise Inventory		120

4. Closing entries:

Merchandise Inventory (Ending)	60		Income Summary	120	
Sales	200		Cost of Goods Sold		120
Purchases Returns and Allowances	45				
Income Summary		305	Sales	200	
			Income Summary		200
Income Summary	225				
Merchandise Inventory (Beginning)		75			
Purchases		150			

	Units	**Cost**
Beginning inventory	5	$ 75
Purchases	10	150
Purchases returns	(3)	(45)
Goods available	12	$180
Goods sold	(8)	(120)
Ending inventory	4	$ 60

Goods Sold account to Income Summary. Of course, Sales must be closed under both inventory systems.

In Illustration 9–4, both inventory systems result in the same amounts of sales, cost of goods sold, and end-of-period merchandise inventory.

Subsidiary Inventory Records—Perpetual System

When a company sells more than one product and uses the perpetual inventory system, the Merchandise Inventory account serves as a controlling account to a subsidiary Merchandise Inventory Ledger. This ledger contains a separate record for each product in stock. This ledger may be computerized or kept on a manual basis. In either case, the record for each product shows the number of

Illustration 9–5
First-in, first-out cost flow

Item _____ *Product Z* _____   Location in stockroom _____ *Bin 8* _____

Maximum _____ 25 _____   Minimum _____ 5 _____

Date	Received			Sold			Balance		
	Units	Cost	Total	Units	Cost	Total	Units	Cost	Total
Jan. 1							10	10.00	100.00
Jan. 5				5	10.00	50.00	5	10.00	50.00
Jan. 8	20	10.50	210.00				5	10.00	
							20	10.50	260.00
Jan. 10				3	10.00	30.00	2	10.00	
							20	10.50	230.00

units and cost of each purchase, the number of units and cost of each sale, and the resulting balance of product on hand.

Illustration 9–5 shows an example of a subsidiary merchandise inventory record. This particular record is for Product Z, which is stored in Bin 8 of the stockroom. In this case, the record also shows the company's policy of maintaining no more than 25 or no less than 5 units of Product Z on hand.

First-In, First-Out— Perpetual Inventory System

In Illustration 9–5, note that the beginning inventory consisted of 10 units that cost $10 each. The first transaction occurred on January 5 and was a sale of 5 units. Next, 20 units were purchased on January 8 at a cost of $10.50 per unit. And on January 10, 3 units were sold. Observe that these 3 units were "costed out" at $10 per unit. This indicates that a first-in, first-out basis is being assumed for this product. The entries to record the sale in the General Journal were the following:

Jan.	10	Cash (or Accounts Receivable).	xxx	
		Sales.		xxx
	10	Cost of Goods Sold	30.00	
		Merchandise Inventory		30.00
		3 × $10.00 = $30.00.		

The ending inventory of 22 units consists of 2 units at $10.00 plus 20 units at $10.50 for a total cost of $230.00.

Weighted Average— Perpetual Inventory System

Perpetual inventories also may be kept on a last-in, first-out basis. When this is done, each sale is recorded as being from the last units received. When these are exhausted, sales are from the next to last, and so on. For example, if LIFO was used for Product Z, the subsidiary merchandise inventory record would appear as in Illustration 9–6.

Compare Illustration 9–6 (weighted average) with Illustration 9–5 (FIFO). Observe that in both illustrations, the sale of 5 units on January 5 is recorded the same way. The cost of these units came from the 10 units in the beginning inventory. However, the sale of 3 units on January 10 is recorded differently under the two methods. Assuming weighted average, as in Illustration 9–6, the January 10 sale is "costed out" at the new average cost of $10.40 per unit. This results in an inventory cost of $228.50, for the 22 units remaining.

The general journal entries to record the January 10 sale, assuming weighted average, are as follows:

Jan.	10	Cash (or Accounts Receivable).	xxx	
		Sales.		xxx
	10	Cost of Goods Sold	31.20	
		Merchandise Inventory		31.20
		3 × $10.40 = $31.20.		

The Difference Between Weighted Average (Perpetual) and Weighted Average (Periodic)

Under the weighted average (periodic) system the cost amount is calculated as the average cost of all the units on hand or purchased during the period. Thus, the cost per unit used is the same for the sales on January 3 and January 10. Under the weighted average (perpetual) system, a purchase was made on January 8 which necessitated the calculation of a revised average cost. It is this revised cost which was used for the sale on January 10.

A comparison of weighted average—perpetual and periodic is summarized as follows:

	Wtd. Avg. (perpetual)	Wtd. Avg. (periodic)
Cost of goods sold:		
January 5 sale. . .	5 × $10.00 = $ 50.00	
January 10 sale . .	3 × $10.40 = 31.20	
Total	$ 81.20	8 × $10.33* = $ 82.67
Ending inventory:		
Total	22 × $10.40 = $228.80	22 × $10.33 = $227.33
Total goods available	$310.00	$310.00

*($100.00 + $210.00) ÷ (10 + 20) = $10.3333

In addition to FIFO and weighted average, perpetual inventory systems can be designed to accomodate a LIFO cost flow assumption. However, illustration of this alternative is deferred to a later course.

Illustration 9–6
Weighted average

Item	Product Z				Location in stockroom			Bin 8		
Maximum	25				Minimum			5		

	Received			Sold			Balance		
Date	Units	Cost	Total	Units	Cost	Total	Units	Cost	Total
Jan. 1							10	10.00	100.00
Jan. 5				5	10.00	50.00	5	10.00	50.00
Jan. 8	20	10.50	210.00				25	10.40	260.00
Jan. 10				3	10.40	31.20	22	10.40	228.80

The Retail Method of Estimating Inventories

Estimate an inventory by the retail method and by the gross profit method. (L. O. 5)

Good management requires that income statements be prepared more often than once each year, and inventory information is necessary each time an income statement is prepared. However, taking a physical inventory in a retail store is both time-consuming and expensive. Therefore, many retailers use the so-called **retail inventory method** to estimate inventories without stopping to take a physical count of inventory. Some companies use the retail inventory method to estimate monthly or quarterly statements. Then, they take a physical inventory at the end of each year. These monthly or quarterly statements are called **interim statements**, since they are prepared in between the regular year-end statements. Other companies also use the retail inventory method to prepare the year-end statements. However, all companies must take a physical inventory at least once each year to correct for any errors or shortages.

Estimating an Ending Inventory by the Retail Method

When the retail method is used to estimate an inventory, a store's records must show the amount of inventory it had at the beginning of the period both *at cost* and *at retail*. You already know what the cost of an inventory is. The retail amount of an inventory simply means the dollar amount of the inventory at the marked selling prices of the inventory items.

In addition to the beginning inventory, the accounting records must also show the amount of goods purchased during the period both at cost and at retail. Also, the records must show the amount of net sales at retail. This is the balance of the Sales account less returns and discounts. With this information, the ending inventory is estimated as follows:

Step 1: Compute the amount of goods that were for sale during the period both at cost and at retail.

Step 2:   Divide the goods available "at cost" by the goods available "at retail" to obtain a **retail method cost ratio.**

Step 3:   Deduct sales (at retail) from goods available for sale (at retail) to determine the ending inventory at retail.

Step 4:   Multiply the ending inventory at retail by the cost ratio to reduce the inventory to a cost basis.

Illustration 9–7 shows these calculations.

This is the essence of Illustration 9–7: (1) The store had $100,000 of goods (at marked selling prices) for sale during the period. (2) These goods cost 60% of the $100,000 total amount at which they were marked for sale. (3) The store's records (its Sales account) showed that $70,000 of these goods were sold, leaving $30,000 of merchandise unsold and presumably in the ending inventory. Therefore, (4) since cost in this store is 60% of retail, the estimated cost of this ending inventory is $18,000.

An ending inventory calculated as in Illustration 9–7 is an estimate arrived at by deducting sales (goods sold) from goods for sale. As we said before, this method may be used for interim statements or even for year-end statements. However, at least once each year a physical count of the inventory must be taken to correct for any errors or shortages.

Using the Retail Method to Reduce a Physical Inventory to Cost

In a store, items for sale normally have price tickets attached that show selling prices. So, when a store takes a physical inventory, it commonly takes the inventory at the marked selling prices of the inventoried items. It then reduces the dollar total of this inventory to a cost basis by applying its cost ratio. It does this because the selling prices are readily available and the application of the cost ratio eliminates the need to look up the invoice price of each inventoried item.

For example, assume that the store of Illustration 9–7, in addition to estimating its inventory by the retail method, also takes a physical inventory at the marked selling prices of the inventoried goods. Assume further that the total retail amount of this physical inventory is $29,600. Under these assumptions, the store may calculate the cost for this inventory, without having to look up the cost of each inventoried item, simply by applying its cost ratio to the $29,600 inventory total as follows:

$$\$29,600 \times 60\% = \$17,760$$

The $17,760 cost figure for this store's ending physical inventory is a satisfactory figure for year-end statement purposes. It is also acceptable for tax purposes.

Inventory Shortage

An inventory determined as in Illustration 9–7 is an estimate of the amount of goods on hand. However, since it is arrived at by deducting sales from goods for sale, it does not reveal any shortages due to breakage, loss, or theft. However, you can estimate the amount of such shortages by comparing the inven-

---

Illustration 9–7
Calculating the ending inventory cost by the retail method

		At Cost	At Retail
(Step 1)	Goods available for sale:		
	Beginning inventory.	$20,500	$ 34,500
	Net Purchases	39,500	65,500
	Goods available for sale	$60,000	$100,000
(Step 2)	Cost ratio: ($60,000/$100,000) × 100 = 60%		
(Step 3)	Deduct sales at retail		70,000
	Ending inventory at retail		$ 30,000
(Step 4)	Ending inventory at cost ($30,000 × 60%) . .	$18,000	

---

tory as calculated in Illustration 9–7 with the amount that results from taking a physical inventory.

For example, in Illustration 9–7, we estimated that the ending inventory at retail was $30,000. However, in the previous section, we assumed that this same store took a physical inventory and counted only $29,600 of merchandise on hand (at retail). Therefore, the store must have had an inventory shortage at retail of $30,000 − $29,600 = $400. Stated in terms of cost, the shortage is $400 × 60% = $240.

Markups and Markdowns

The calculation of a cost ratio often is not as simple as that shown in Illustration 9–6. It is not simple because after merchandise is purchased and marked at retail prices, a store may decide to change the retail prices by marking the goods up or down. When goods are first purchased and marked at selling price, the amount or percentage by which the marked selling prices exceed cost is called a **normal markup.** It is also called a **markon.** For example, if a store's normal markup is 50% on cost and it applies this markup to an item that cost $10, it will mark the item for sale at $15. Normal markups appear in the calculation of a store's cost ratio as the difference between net purchases at cost and at retail.

After goods are first priced to sell at the normal markup, if the prices are increased, the amount of the additional price increases are called **additional markups.** And if selling prices are decreased, the amounts of the decreases are called **markdowns.** Stores may add markups to the price of goods because the quality or style of the goods make them especially attractive to customers. Goods often are marked down for a clearance sale or whenever the goods are moving slowly.

When the retail inventory method is used, the store must keep a record of additional markups and markdowns. This information is used in the calculation of the ending inventory as shown in Illustration 9–8.

In Illustration 9–8, notice that the store's $80,000 of goods for sale at retail were reduced $54,000 by sales and $2,000 by markdowns, a total of $56,000. To understand the markdowns, visualize this effect of a markdown. The store had

Illustration 9–8
The effect of markups and markdowns on the retail method

	At Cost	At Retail
Goods available for sale:		
Beginning inventory.	$18,000	$27,800
Net purchases.	34,000	50,700
Additional markups		1,500
Goods available for sale	$52,000	$80,000
Cost ratio: ($52,000 ÷ $80,000) × 100 = 65%		
Sales at retail		$54,000
Markdowns.		2,000
Total sales and markdowns		$56,000
Ending inventory at retail ($80,000 less $56,000) . .		$24,000
Ending inventory at cost ($24,000 × 65%)	$15,600	

an item for sale during the period at $25. The item did not sell, so the manager marked its price down from $25 to $20. By this act the retail amount of goods for sale in the store was reduced by $5. The total of such markdowns during the year amounted to $2,000.

In the calculations of Illustration 9–8, note that the estimated ending inventory at retail is $24,000. Therefore, since "cost" is 65% of retail, the ending inventory at "cost" is $15,600.

Observe in Illustration 9–8 that markups enter into the calculation of the cost ratio but markdowns do not. Why are markdowns excluded from the cost ratio calculation? The reason for this is that a more conservative figure for the ending inventory results, a figure that approaches "the lower of cost or market." Further discussion of this phase of the retail inventory method is reserved for a more advanced accounting course.

Gross Profit Method of Estimating Inventories

Sometimes, when a business does not use a perpetual inventory method and does not use the retail method, it still may need to estimate the cost of its inventory. For example, if a fire destroys the inventory or a burglary results in the theft of the inventory, the business must estimate the inventory so that it can file a claim with its insurance company. In cases such as this, the cost of the inventory can be estimated by the **gross profit inventory method.** With this method, a business's historical relationship between cost of goods sold and sales is applied to sales of the current period as a way of estimating cost of goods sold during the current period. Then, cost of goods sold is subtracted from the cost of goods available for sale to get the estimated cost of the ending inventory.

To use the gross profit method, several items of accounting information must be available. This includes information about the normal gross profit margin or rate, the cost of the beginning inventory, the cost of net purchases, transportation-in, and the amount of sales and sales returns.

Illustration 9–9
The gross profit method of estimating inventory

Goods available for sale:		
Inventory, January 1, 1990.		$ 12,000
Net purchases.	$20,000	
Add transportation-in	500	20,500
Goods available for sale		$ 32,500
Less estimated cost of goods sold:		
Sales.	$31,500	
Less sales returns	(1,500)	
Net sales	$30,000	
Estimated cost of goods sold (70% × $30,000) . .		(21,000)
Estimated March 27 inventory and inventory loss . .		$ 11,500

For example, assume that the inventory of a company was totally destroyed by a fire that occurred on March 27, 1990. The company's average gross profit rate during the past five years has been 30% of net sales. On the date of the fire, the company's accounts showed the following balances:

Sales	$31,500
Sales returns.	1,500
Inventory, January 1, 1990	12,000
Net purchases	20,000
Transportation-in.	500

With this information, the gross profit method may be used to estimate the company's inventory loss. To apply the gross profit method, the first step is to recognize that whatever portion of each dollar of net sales was gross profit, the remaining portion was cost of goods sold. Thus, if the company's gross profit rate averages 30%, then 30% of each dollar of net sales was gross profit, and 70% was cost of goods sold. Illustration 9–9 shows how the 70% is used to estimate the inventory that was lost.

To understand Illustration 9–9, recall that in a normal situation an ending inventory is subtracted from goods available for sale to determine the cost of goods sold. Then observe in Illustration 9–9 that the opposite subtraction is made. Estimated cost of goods sold is subtracted from available goods for sale to determine the estimated ending inventory.

As we mentioned, the gross profit method often is used to estimate the amount of an insurance claim. Also, it sometimes is used by accountants to see if an inventory amount determined by management's physical count of the items on hand is a reasonable amount.

Summary of the Chapter in Terms of Learning Objectives

1. When specific invoice prices are used to price an inventory, each item in the inventory is identified and the cost of the item is determined by referring to the item's purchase invoice. With weighted-average cost, the total cost of the beginning inventory and of purchases is divided by the number of units available to determine the weighted-average cost per unit. This is multiplied by the number of units in the ending inventory to determine the cost of the inventory. FIFO prices the ending inventory based on the assumption that the first units purchased are the first units sold. LIFO is based on the assumption that the last units purchased are the first units sold. All of these methods are acceptable.

2. When lower of cost or market is applied to merchandise inventory, market usually means replacement cost. But market is never higher than net realizable value and never lower than net realizable value minus a normal profit. Lower of cost or market may be applied separately to each product or to the merchandise inventory as a whole.

3. When the periodic inventory system is used, an error in counting the ending inventory affects assets (inventory), net income (cost of goods sold), and owner's equity. Since the ending inventory is the beginning inventory of the next period, an error at the end of one period affects the cost of goods sold and the net income of the next period. These next period effects offset the financial statement effects in the previous period.

4. Under a perpetual inventory system, purchases and purchases returns are recorded in the Merchandise Inventory account. At the time sales are recorded, the cost of goods sold is credited to Merchandise Inventory. As a result, the Merchandise Inventory is kept up-to-date throughout the accounting period.

5. When the retail method is used, sales are subtracted from the retail amount of goods available to determine the ending inventory at retail. This is multiplied by the cost ratio to reduce the inventory amount to cost. To calculate the cost ratio, the cost of goods available is divided by the retail value of goods available (including markups but excluding markdowns).

With the gross profit method, you multiply sales by (1 − the gross profit rate) to estimate cost of goods sold. Then, you subtract the answer from the cost of goods available for sale to estimate the cost of the ending inventory.

Demonstration Problem

Following is Tale Company's beginning inventory and purchases during 1990:

		Item X		Item Y	
Date		Units	Cost per Unit	Units	Cost per Unit
Jan 1	Inventory	400	$14	200	$11
Mar 10	Purchase	200	15	300	12
May 9	Purchase	300	16		
Jun 17	Purchase			450	18
Sep 22	Purchase	250	20		
Nov 28	Purchase	100	21	110	17

At December 31, 1990, there were 550 units of X on hand and 320 units of Y.

Required

1. Using the above information, apply FIFO inventory pricing and calculate the cost of goods available for sale in 1990, the ending inventory, and the cost of goods sold for each item and for both items combined.

2. In preparing the financial statements for 1990, the bookkeeper misunderstood the instructions and computed the cost of goods sold according to LIFO. Ignore income taxes and determine the size of the misstatement of 1990's income from this error. Assuming that the December 31, 1991, inventory is correctly calculated using FIFO, determine the size of the misstatement of 1991's income. Assume no income taxes.

3. Assume the following additional facts, and use the retail method to estimate the lower of cost or market of the ending inventory:

Retail value of the beginning inventory . .	$13,051
Retail value of purchases	41,381
Additional markups (at retail).	3,600
Sales	33,600
Markdowns	4,432

Solution to Demonstration Problem

1. FIFO basis:

Item X:

Jan 1 inventory (400 @ $14)		$ 5,600
Purchases:		
Mar 10 purchase (200 @ $15)	$3,000	
May 9 purchase (300 @ $16).	4,800	
Sep 22 purchase (250 @ $20)	5,000	
Nov 28 purchase (100 @ $21)	2,100	14,900
Cost of goods available for sale.		$20,500
Ending inventory at FIFO cost:		
Nov 28 purchase (100 @ $21)	$2,100	
Sep 22 purchase (250 @ $20)	5,000	
May 9 purchase (200 @ $16).	3,200	
Ending inventory.		10,300
Cost of goods sold		$10,200

Item Y:

Jan 1 inventory (200 @ $11)		$ 2,200
Purchases:		
Mar 10 purchase (300 @ $12)	$3,600	
Jun 17 purchase (450 @ $18)	8,100	
Nov 28 purchase (110 @ $17)	1,870	13,570
Cost of goods available for sale.		$15,770
Ending inventory at FIFO cost:		
Nov 28 purchase (110 @ $17)	$1,870	
Jun 17 purchase (210 @ $18)	3,780	
Ending inventory.		5,650
Cost of goods sold		$10,120

Combined:

Cost of goods available ($20,500 + $15,770) . .	$36,270
Cost of ending inventory ($10,300 + $5,650) . .	15,950
Cost of goods sold ($10,200 + $10,120)	$20,320

2. LIFO basis:

Item X:

Cost of goods available for sale.		$20,500
Ending inventory at LIFO cost:		
Jan 1 inventory (400 @ $14)	$5,600	
Mar 10 purchase (150 @ $15)	2,250	
LIFO cost of ending inventory.		7,850
Cost of goods sold		$12,650

Item Y:

Cost of goods available for sale.		$15,770
Ending inventory at LIFO cost:		
Jan 1 inventory (200 @ $11)	$2,200	
Mar 10 purchase (120 @ $12)	1,440	
LIFO cost of ending inventory		3,640
Cost of goods sold		$12,130

Combined:

Cost of goods available ($20,500 + $15,770) . .	$36,270
Cost of ending inventory ($7,850 + $3,640) . . .	11,490
Cost of goods sold	$24,780

If LIFO is mistakenly used when FIFO should have been used, cost of goods sold in 1990 would be overstated by $4,460, which is the difference between the FIFO and LIFO amounts of ending inventory. Income would be understated in 1990 by $4,460. In 1991, income would be overstated by $4,460 because of the understatement of the beginning inventory.

3. Retail method of estimating inventory:

	At Cost	At Retail
Goods available for sale:		
Beginning inventory ($5,600 + $2,200 = $7,800) . .	$ 7,800	$13,051
Purchases ($14,900 + $13,570 = $28,470)	28,470	41,381
Markups.		3,600
Goods available for sale	$36,270	$58,032
Cost ratio: ($36,270 ÷ $58,032) × 100 = 62.5%		
Sales at retail		$33,600
Markdowns		4,432
Total sales and markdowns		$38,032
Ending inventory at retail ($58,032 − $38,032)		$20,000
Ending inventory at cost ($20,000 × 62.5%)	$12,500	

Glossary

Define or explain the words and phrases listed in the chapter Glossary. (L. O. 6)

Conservatism principle the accounting principle that guides accountants to ensure that net assets or net income are not overstated. p. 445

Consignee one who receives and holds goods owned by another party for the purpose of selling the goods for the owner. p. 437

Consignor an owner of goods who ships them to another party who will then sell the goods for the owner. p. 437

Consistency principle the accounting requirement that a company use the same accounting methods period after period so that the financial statements of succeeding periods will be comparable. p. 442

First-in, first-out inventory pricing (FIFO) the pricing of an inventory under the assumption that the first items received were the first items sold. p. 440

Gross profit inventory method a procedure for estimating an ending inventory in which the past gross profit rate is used to estimate cost of goods sold, which is then subtracted from the cost of goods available for sale to determine the estimated ending inventory. p. 454

Interim statements monthly or quarterly financial statements prepared in between the regular year-end statements. p. 451

Inventory ticket a form attached to the counted items in the process of taking a physical inventory. p. 438

Last-in, first-out inventory pricing (LIFO) the pricing of an inventory under the assumption that the last items received were the first items sold. p. 441

Markdown a reduction in the marked selling price of merchandise. p. 453

Markon the normal amount or percentage of cost that is added to the cost of merchandise to arrive at its selling price. p. 453

Markup (Additional Markup) an increase in the sales price of merchandise above the normal markon given to the goods. p. 453

Net realizable value the expected sales price of an item less any additional costs to sell. p. 445

Normal markup another name for markon. p. 453

Periodic inventory system an accounting system in which the Merchandise Inventory account is updated only once each accounting period, based on a physical count of the inventory. p. 438

Perpetual inventory system an inventory system in which cost of goods sold is recorded after each sale and the Merchandise Inventory account is updated after each purchase and each sale. p. 446

Retail inventory method a method for estimating an ending inventory based on the ratio of the amount of goods for sale at cost to the amount of goods for sale at marked selling prices. p. 451

Retail method cost ratio the ratio of goods available for sale at cost to goods available for sale at retail prices. p. 452

Specific invoice inventory pricing the pricing of an inventory where the purchase invoice of each item in the ending inventory is identified and used to determine the cost assigned to the inventory. p. 440

Weighted-average inventory pricing an inventory pricing system in which the unit prices of the beginning inventory and of each purchase are weighted by the number of units in the beginning inventory and each purchase. The total of these amounts is then divided by the total number of units available for sale to find the unit cost of the ending inventory and of the units that were sold. p. 440

Questions for Class Discussion

1. With respect to periodic inventory systems, it has been said that cost of goods sold and ending inventory are opposite sides of the same coin. What is meant by this?
2. Where is merchandise inventory disclosed in the financial statements?
3. If Barnes Company is the consignee and Smith Company is the consignor with respect to goods that are being offered for sale, the goods should show up on the inventory of which company?
4. If Craft sells goods to James, FOB Craft's factory, and the goods are still in transit from Craft to James, which company should include the goods in its physical count of inventory?
5. Of what does the cost of an inventory item consist?
6. Why are incidental costs often ignored in pricing an inventory? Under what accounting principle is this permitted?
7. Give the meanings of the following when applied to inventory: (*a*) FIFO, (*b*) LIFO, (*c*) cost, and (*d*) perpetual inventory.
8. If prices are rising, will the LIFO or the FIFO method of inventory valuation result in the higher gross profit?
9. If prices are falling, will the LIFO or the FIFO method of inventory valuation result in the higher ending inventory?
10. If prices are falling, will the LIFO or the FIFO method of inventory valuation result in the lower cost of goods sold?
11. May a company change its inventory pricing method each accounting period?
12. Does the accounting principle of consistency preclude any changes from one accounting method to another?
13. What effect does the full-disclosure principle have if a company changes from one acceptable accounting method to another?
14. What is meant when it is said that under a periodic inventory system, inventory errors "correct themselves"?
15. If inventory errors under a periodic inventory system "correct themselves," why be concerned when such errors are made?
16. What guidance for accountants is provided by the principle of conservatism?
17. What accounts are used in a periodic inventory system but are not used in a perpetual inventory system?
18. What account is used in a perpetual inventory system but is not used in a periodic inventory system.
19. Assuming a weighted average cost why do perpetual inventory systems

and periodic inventory systems result in different amounts of cost of goods sold and ending inventory?

20. What is the usual meaning of the word *market* as it is used in determining the lower of cost or market for merchandise inventory?

21. In what way is the use of lower of cost or market with merchandise inventory less restrictive than when it is used with temporary investments in marketable equity securities?

22. In deciding whether to reduce an item of merchandise to the lower of cost or market, what is the importance of the item's net realizable value?

23. Give the meanings of the following when applied in the retail method of estimating an inventory: (*a*) pricing inventory at retail, (*b*) cost ratio, (*c*) normal markup, (*d*) markon, (*e*) additional markup, and (*f*) markdown.

24. A company uses a periodic inventory system, records its merchandise purchases at cost, and assumes a FIFO cost flow. If a fire results in the loss of the company's inventory, what method might the company use to estimate the amount of inventory lost?

Multiple Choice

1. The following data relate to a single inventory item for Jones Company:

Date		Units	Cost per Unit
June 1	Beginning inventory	100	$4
3	Purchase	20	5
15	Sale	30	
18	Purchase	40	6
25	Sale	25	

Using a perpetual inventory system and costing inventory by FIFO, the ending inventory is:

a. $220.
b. $425.
c. $485.
d. $520.
e. $740.

2. Refer to the data about Jones Company in (1) above. Using a periodic inventory system and costing inventory by weighted average, the ending inventory is:

a. $220.
b. $425.
c. $485.
d. $520.
e. $740.

3. With a periodic inventory system, an undiscovered error that overstates the 1990 year-end inventory will cause:

a. An overstatement of 1990 net income and an understatement of 1991 net income.

b. An understatement of assets on the 1990 balance sheet.

c. An overstatement of 1990 cost of goods sold.

d. An overstatement of 1990 net income and no effect on 1991 net income.

e. None of the foregoing.

4. With a perpetual inventory system:

a. A sale of merchandise requires two entries, one to record the revenue and one to record the cost of goods sold.

b. A separate Cost of Goods Sold account is used.

c. The Merchandise Inventory account balance shows the amount of merchandise on hand.

d. Subsidiary inventory records are maintained for each type of product.

e. All of the above are correct.

5. The following data relates to Trenor Company's inventory during the year:

	Cost	Retail
Beginning inventory	$298,000	$490,000
Purchases	190,000	317,000
Purchases returns	3,200	5,000
Markups		6,000
Markdowns.		62,000
Sales		270,000

Using the retail method, the estimated cost of the ending inventory is:

a. $152,800.

b. $285,600.

c. $309,400.

d. $476,000.

e. $784,800.

6. The gross profit method:

a. Requires that detailed records be maintained concerning the cost, sales value, markups, and markdowns of inventory items.

b. Is used to estimate the cost of inventory lost in a fire when a perpetual inventory system was used to account for inventory.

c. Is used to estimate the cost of inventory lost in a fire when a periodic inventory system other than the retail method was used to account for inventory.

d. Is used to estimate the cost of inventory lost in a fire when the retail method was used to account for inventory.

e. None of the above is correct.

Mini Discussion Cases

Case 9–1

Your friend is the controller of Elora Manufacturing Company and has come to you for some advice about the valuation of the finished goods inventory. The inventory is currently listed on the books of the company at its cost of $87,500. The controller has recently learned that the goods could have been purchased from an overseas supplier for $73,900. The controller is unsure as to whether she should price the inventory on the year-end financial statements, which are to be prepared in two weeks, at the higher or lower value. She says that if she prices them at the lower value, she will violate both the cost and the consistency principles.

Required

Advise your friend and give the reasons behind your advice.

Case 9–2

In November of 1990 the accountant for the Vogler Cove Company discovered that the December 31, 1989, inventory had been misstated in the 1989 financial statements. The inventory should have been $57,000 but had been entered on the statements as $75,000. His assistant indicated that the company would have to correct and restate the 1989 statements when preparing the statements for the 1990 year-end. The accountant said that no corrections will be necessary since the error will have corrected itself by the end of 1990 and that the Retained Earnings figure will be correct as of December 31, 1990.

Required

Comment on the positions taken by the accountant and his assistant. What do you propose should be done in preparing the financial statements for 1990? Why?

Exercises

Exercise 9–1
Alternative cost flow assumptions, periodic inventory system
(L. O. 1)

Hoyt Company began a year and purchased merchandise as follows:

Jan. 1	Beginning inventory	20 units @ $10.00 =	$ 200
Feb. 9	Purchased	100 units @ $11.50 =	1,150
June 16	Purchased	40 units @ $12.50 =	500
Aug. 22	Purchased	80 units @ $14.00 =	1,120
Dec. 15	Purchased	60 units @ $15.00 =	900
	Total	300 units	$3,870

Required

The company uses a periodic inventory system, and the ending inventory consists of 75 units, 25 from each of the last three purchases. Determine the share of the $3,870 cost of the units for sale that should be assigned to the ending inventory and to goods sold under each of the following: (*a*) costs are assigned on the basis of specific invoice prices, (*b*) costs are assigned on a weighted-average cost basis, (*c*) costs are assigned on the basis of FIFO, and (*d*) costs are assigned on the basis of LIFO. Which method produces the highest/lowest net income?

Exercise 9–2
Alternative cost flow assumptions, periodic inventory system
(L. O. 1)

Higgins Company began a year and purchased merchandise as follows:

Jan. 1	Beginning inventory	20 units @ $15.00 =	$ 300
Feb. 9	Purchased	100 units @ $14.00 =	1,400
June 16	Purchased	40 units @ $12.50 =	500
Aug. 22	Purchased	80 units @ $11.50 =	920
Dec. 15	Purchased	60 units @ $10.00 =	600
	Total.	300 units	$3,720

Required

The company uses a periodic inventory system, and the ending inventory consists of 75 units, 25 from each of the last three purchases. Determine the share of the $3,720 cost of the units for sale that should be assigned to the ending inventory and to goods sold under each of the following: (*a*) costs are assigned on the basis of specific invoice prices, (*b*) costs are assigned on a weighted-average cost basis, (*c*) costs are assigned on the basis of FIFO, and (*d*) costs are assigned on the basis of LIFO. Which method will produce the highest/lowest net income?

Exercise 9–3
Lower of cost or market
(L. O. 2)

Starnes Company's ending inventory includes the following items:

Product	Units on Hand	Cost per Unit	Replacement Cost per Unit
W	15	$ 8	$12
X	20	15	12
Y	25	8	7
Z	18	5	5

After evaluating each product's selling price and normal profit margin, replacement cost is found to be the best measure of market. Calculate lower of cost or market for the inventory (*a*) as a whole and (*b*) applied separately to each product.

Exercise 9–4
Lower of cost or market
(L. O. 2)

Calculate the lower of cost or market for the inventory in each of the following independent cases:

1. Toy Company's inventory consists of 60 units of Product P, all of which have been damaged. The company bought the inventory for $12 per unit. Replacement cost is $11 per unit. Expected sales price is $15 per unit, but this can be realized only if $5 additional cost per unit is paid.
2. Doll Company's inventory consists of 110 units of Product Q which were purchased for $30 per unit. Replacement cost is $21 per unit. Expected sales price is $33 per unit, and a normal profit margin based on this price is $10.

Exercise 9–5
Analysis of inventory errors
(L. O. 3)

Matz Company had $95,000 of sales during each of three consecutive years, and it purchased merchandise costing $70,000 during each of the years. It also maintained a $20,000 inventory from the beginning to the end of the three-year period. However, in accounting under a periodic inventory system, it made an error at the end of year 1 that caused its ending year 1 inventory to appear on its statements at $25,000, rather than the correct $20,000.

Required

1. State the actual amount of the company's gross profit in each of the years.
2. Prepare a comparative income statement like the one illustrated in this chapter to show the effect of this error on the shop's cost of goods sold and gross profit in year 1, year 2, and year 3.

Exercise 9–6
Perpetual inventory system—FIFO cost flow
(L. O. 4)

In its beginning inventory on January 1, 1990, J Company had 30 units of merchandise which had cost $3 per unit. Prepare general journal entries for J Company to record the following transactions during 1990, assuming a perpetual inventory system and a first-in, first-out cost flow:

Mar. 12 Purchased on credit 120 units of merchandise at $5.25 per unit.
   15 Returned 20 defective units from the March 12 purchase to the supplier.
Sept. 22 Purchased for cash 70 units of merchandise at $3.50 per unit.
Oct. 15 Sold 85 units of merchandise for cash at a price of $5.50 per unit.
Dec. 31 Prepare entries to close the revenue and expense accounts to Income Summary.

Exercise 9–7
Perpetual inventory system—weighted average cost system
(L. O. 4)

In its January 1, 1990, inventory, X Company had 50 units of merchandise which had cost $4 per unit. Prepare general journal entries for X Company to record the following transactions during 1990, assuming a perpetual inventory system and a weighted average cost system:

Mar. 17 Purchased on credit 90 units of merchandise at $4.25 per unit.
June 25 Sold 60 units of merchandise for cash at $8.50 per unit.
Aug. 19 Purchased for cash 80 units of merchandise at $4.50 per unit.
Nov. 15 Sold 85 units of merchandise for cash at a price of $8.50 per unit.
Dec. 31 Prepare entries to close the revenue and expense accounts to Income Summary.

Exercise 9–8
Estimating ending inventory—retail inventory method
(L. O. 5)

During an accounting period, Fish Store sold $280,000 of merchandise at marked retail prices. At the period end, the following information was available from its records:

	At Cost	At Retail
Beginning inventory	$ 50,500	$ 75,000
Net purchases	194,500	267,000
Additional markups.		8,000
Markdowns.		7,200

Use the retail method to estimate the store's ending inventory at cost.

Exercise 9–9
Reducing physical inventory to cost—retail method
(L. O. 5)

Assume that in addition to estimating its ending inventory by the retail method, Fish Store of Exercise 9–8 also took a physical inventory at the marked selling prices of the inventory items. Assume further that the total of this physical inventory at marked selling prices was $60,200. Then (a) determine the amount of this inventory at cost and (b) determine the store's inventory shrinkage from breakage, theft, or other cause at retail and at cost.

Exercise 9–10
Estimating ending inventory—gross profit method
(L. O. 5)

On January 1, a store had a $51,000 inventory at cost. During the first quarter of the year, it purchased $195,000 of merchandise, returned $1,500, and paid freight charges on merchandise purchased totaling $10,500. During the past several years, the store's gross profit on sales has averaged 35%. Under the assumption the company had $288,000 of sales during the first quarter of the year, use the gross profit method to estimate its end of the first quarter inventory.

Problems

Problem 9–1
**Alternative cost flows—
periodic system**
(L. O. 1)

Crown Company began a year with 850 units of Product A in its inventory that cost $85 each, and it made successive purchases of the product as follows:

Apr.	1	1,500 units @ $85 each
June 10		1,750 units @ $90 each
Aug. 29		1,200 units @ $95 each
Nov. 15		1,500 units @ $90 each

The company uses a periodic inventory system. On December 31, a physical count disclosed that 2,000 units of Product A remained in inventory.

Required

1. Prepare a calculation showing the number and total cost of the units that were for sale during the year.
2. Prepare calculations showing the amounts that should be assigned to the ending inventory and to cost of goods sold assuming (*a*) a FIFO basis, (*b*) a LIFO basis, and (*c*) a weighted-average cost basis. Round your calculation of the weighted-average cost per unit to three decimal places.

Problem 9–2
**Income statement
comparisons and cost flow
assumptions**
(L. O. 1)

Breakward Company sold 8,500 units of its product at $25 per unit during 1990. It incurred operating expenses of $4 per unit in selling the units, and it began the year and made successive purchases of the product as follows:

January 1 beginning inventory	800 units costing $16.00 per unit
Purchases:	
January 30.	1,300 units costing $17.00 per unit
April 8	2,700 units costing $17.50 per unit
July 19.	4,200 units costing $18.25 per unit
November 20	700 units costing $20.00 per unit

Required

Prepare a comparative income statement for the company showing in adjacent columns the net incomes earned from the sale of the product assuming the company uses a periodic inventory system and prices its ending inventory on the basis of: (*a*) FIFO, (*b*) LIFO, and (*c*) weighted-average cost. Round your calculation of the weighted-average cost per unit to three decimal places.

Problem 9–3
Lower of cost or market
(L. O. 2)

Case 1: In this case, an evaluation of the expected selling price and normal profit margin for each product shows that replacement cost is the best measure of market. The inventory includes:

Product	Units on Hand	Cost	Replacement Cost
X	225	$ 7	$ 6
Y	450	12	10
Z	525	35	40

Case 2: In this case, the inventories of Products V and W have been damaged. If $4 additional cost per unit is paid to repackage the Product V units, they can

be sold for $45 per unit. The Product W units can be sold for $25 per unit after paying additional cleaning costs of $3 per unit. The inventory includes:

Product	Units on Hand	Cost	Replacement Cost
V	325	$45	$42
W	150	25	26

Case 3: In this case, Product U normally is sold for $70 per unit and has a profit margin of 25%. However, the expected selling price has fallen to $44 per unit. Product T normally is sold for $32 per unit and has a profit margin of 30%. However, the expected selling price of Product T has fallen to $30 per unit. The inventory includes:

Product	Units on Hand	Cost	Replacement Cost
U	200	$49	$35
T	110	24	20

Required

In each of the above independent cases, calculate the lower of cost or market (*a*) for the inventory as a whole and (*b*) for the inventory, applied separately to each product.

Problem 9–4
Analysis of inventory errors
(L. O. 3)

Smoots Company keeps its inventory records on a periodic basis. The following amounts were reported in the company's financial statements:

	Financial Statements for Year Ended December 31		
	1990	1991	1992
(a) Cost of goods sold	$ 48,000	$ 56,000	$ 50,000
(b) Net income	15,000	21,000	12,000
(c) Total current assets	90,000	96,000	82,000
(d) Owners' equity	102,000	110,000	100,000

In making the physical counts of inventory, the following errors were made:

Inventory on December 31, 1990 . . . . Overstated $5,000
Inventory on December 31, 1991 . . . . Understated 8,000

Required

1. For each of the financial statement items listed above as (*a*), (*b*), (*c*), and (*d*), prepare a schedule similar to the following and show the adjustments that would have been necessary to correct the reported amounts.

	1990	1991	1992
Cost of goods sold:			
Reported.			
Adjustments: Dec. 31, 1990 error			
Dec. 31, 1991 error			
Corrected			

2. What is the error in the aggregate net income for the three-year period that resulted from the inventory errors?

Alternate Problems

Problem 9–1A
Alternative cost flows—periodic system
(L. O. 1)

Edgar Company began a year with 1,000 units of Product Z in its inventory that cost $40 each, and it made successive purchases of the product as follows:

Mar. 2	1,500 units @ $45 each
June 19	1,550 units @ $50 each
Aug. 13	1,600 units @ $55 each
Nov. 6	1,600 units @ $52 each

The company uses a periodic inventory system. On December 31, a physical count disclosed that 2,000 units of Product Z remained in inventory.

Required

1. Prepare a calculation showing the number and total cost of the units that were for sale during the year.

2. Prepare calculations showing the amounts that should be assigned to the ending inventory and to cost of goods sold assuming (*a*) a FIFO basis, (*b*) a LIFO basis, and (*c*) a weighted-average cost basis. Round your calculation of the weighted-average cost per unit to three decimal places.

Problem 9–2A
Income statement comparisons and cost flow assumptions
(L. O. 1)

Lakewood Company sold 4,500 units of its product at $45 per unit during 1990. It incurred operating expenses of $10 per unit in selling the units, and it began the year and made successive purchases of the product as follows:

January 1 beginning inventory	600 units costing $15 per unit
Purchases:	
January 8	1,200 units costing $16 per unit
April 2	2,000 units costing $18 per unit
July 18	2,500 units costing $20 per unit
November 23	1,500 units costing $22 per unit

Required

Prepare a comparative income statement for the company showing in adjacent columns the net incomes earned from the sale of the product assuming the company uses a periodic inventory system and prices its ending inventory on the basis of: (*a*) FIFO, (*b*) LIFO, and (*c*) weighted-average cost. Round your calculation of the weighted-average cost per unit to three decimal places.

Problem 9–3A
Lower of cost or market
(L. O. 2)

Case 1: In this case, an evaluation of the expected selling price and normal profit margin for each product shows that replacement cost is the best measure of market. The inventory includes:

Product	Units on Hand	Cost	Replacement Cost
A	800	$20	$23
B	900	32	29
C	400	22	21

Case 2: In this case, the inventories of Products D and E have been damaged. If $15 additional cost per unit is paid to repackage the Product D units, they can

be sold for $50 per unit. The Product E units can be sold for $70 per unit after paying additional cleaning costs of $18 per unit. The inventory includes:

Product	Units on Hand	Cost	Replacement Cost
D	330	$44	$46
E	500	60	55

Case 3: In this case, Product F normally is sold for $60 per unit and has a profit margin of 30%. However, the expected selling price has fallen to $50 per unit. Product G normally is sold for $75 per unit and has a profit margin of 25%. However, the expected selling price of Product G has fallen to $65 per unit. The inventory includes:

Product	Units on Hand	Cost	Replacement Cost
F	330	$42	$30
G	190	65	56

Required

In each of the above independent cases, calculate the lower of cost or market (*a*) for the inventory as a whole and (*b*) for the inventory, applied separately to each product.

Problem 9–4A
Analysis of inventory errors
(L. O. 3)

Milicia Company keeps its inventory records on a periodic basis. The following amounts were reported in the company's financial statements:

	Financial Statements for Year Ended December 31		
	1990	1991	1992
(*a*) Cost of goods sold	$ 67,000	$ 75,000	$ 65,000
(*b*) Net income	24,000	39,000	21,000
(*c*) Total current assets	108,000	115,000	100,000
(*d*) Owners' equity	144,000	157,000	162,000

In making the physical counts of inventory, the following errors were made:

Inventory on December 31, 1990	Understated $ 9,000
Inventory on December 31, 1991	Overstated 14,000

Required

1. For each of the financial statement items listed above as (*a*), (*b*), (*c*), and (*d*), prepare a schedule similar to the following and show the adjustments that would have been necessary to correct the reported amounts.

	1990	1991	1992
Cost of goods sold:			
Reported	____	____	____
Adjustments: Dec. 31, 1990 error	____	____	____
Dec. 31, 1991 error	____	____	____
Corrected	====	====	====

2. What is the error in the aggregate net income for the three-year period that resulted from the inventory errors?

Problem 9–5A
Inventory records under FIFO and weighted average—perpetual system
(L. O. 4)

The Turner Company sells a product called TurnUp and uses a perpetual inventory system to account for its merchandise. The beginning balance of TurnUps and transactions during January of this year were as follows:

Jan. 1 Balance: 25 units costing $8 each.
      3 Purchased 50 units costing $9 each.
      7 Sold 20 units.
     19 Sold 15 units.
     21 Purchased 30 units costing $11 each.
     24 Sold 15 units.
     29 Sold 32 units.

Required

1. Under the assumption the concern keeps its records on a FIFO basis, enter the beginning balance and the transactions on a subsidiary inventory record like the one illustrated in this chapter.

2. Under the assumption the concern keeps its inventory records on a weighted average basis, enter the beginning inventory and the transactions on a second subsidiary inventory record.

3. Assume the 32 units sold on January 29 were sold on credit to Sally Rugby at $25 each and prepare general journal entries to record the sale on a FIFO basis.

Problem 9–6A
Retail inventory method
(L. O. 5)

Calico Stores takes a year-end physical inventory at marked selling prices and uses the retail method to reduce the inventory total to a cost basis for statement purposes. It also uses the retail method to estimate the amount of inventory it should have at the end of a year, and by comparison determines any inventory shortage due to shoplifting or other cause. At the end of last year, its physical inventory at marked selling prices totaled $145,200, and the following information was available from its records:

	At Cost	At Retail
Beginning inventory	$ 52,930	$ 80,200
Purchases	267,840	405,000
Purchases returns	5,520	8,400
Additional markups.		8,200
Markdowns		5,300
Sales		340,000
Sales returns		4,400

Required

1. Use the retail method to estimate the store's year-end inventory at cost.

2. Use the retail method to reduce the company's year-end physical inventory to a cost basis.

3. Prepare a schedule showing the inventory shortage at cost and at retail.

Problem 9–7A
Retail inventory method
(L. O. 5)

The records of Ware Products Company provided the following information for the year ended December 31:

	At Cost	At Retail
January 1 beginning inventory	$ 99,000	$146,100
Purchases	419,820	780,000
Purchases returns	8,970	17,100
Additional markups		18,000
Markdowns		9,900
Sales		850,500
Sales returns		13,050

Required

1. Prepare an estimate of the company's year-end inventory by the retail method.

2. Under the assumption the company took a year-end physical inventory at marked selling prices that totaled $77,100, prepare a schedule showing the store's loss from theft or other cause at cost and at retail.

Problem 9–8A
Gross profit method
(L. O. 5)

When the Accessory Store was opened for business on the morning of March 10, it was discovered that thieves had broken in and stolen the store's entire inventory. The following information for the period January 1 through March 10 was available to establish the amount of loss:

January 1 merchandise inventory at cost	$125,100
Purchases	370,000
Purchases returns	3,225
Transportation-in	15,750
Sales	720,400
Sales returns	13,200

Required

Under the assumption the store had earned an average 38% gross profit on sales during the past five years, prepare a statement showing the estimated loss.

Problem 9–9A
Gross profit method
(L. O. 5)

Hebert Florists wants to prepare interim financial statements for the first quarter of 1990. The company uses a periodic inventory system but would like to avoid making a physical count of inventory. During the last five years, the company's gross profit rate has averaged 30%; and the following information for the year's first quarter is available from its records:

January 1 beginning inventory	$ 70,560
Purchases	115,240
Purchases returns	3,900
Transportation-in	9,420
Sales	227,000
Sales returns	5,040

Required

Use the gross profit method to prepare an estimate of the company's March 31 inventory.

Provocative Problems

Provocative Problem 9–1
Fischer Boots
(L. O. 5)

The retail outlet of Fischer Boots suffered extensive smoke and water damage and a small amount of fire damage on September 10. The company carried adequate insurance, and the insurance company's claims adjuster appeared the same day to inspect the damage. After completing his survey, the adjuster agreed with Amy Harris, the store's owner, that the inventory could be sold to a company specializing in fire sales for about one fourth of its cost. The adjuster offered Ms. Harris $112,500 in full settlement for the damage to the inventory. He suggested that the offer be accepted and said he had authority to deliver at once a cheque for that amount. He also pointed out that a prompt settlement would provide funds to replace the inventory in time for the store to participate in the Christmas shopping season.

Ms. Harris felt the loss might exceed $112,500, but she recognized that a time-consuming count and inspection of each item in the inventory would be required to establish the loss more precisely. She was anxious to get back into business before the Christmas rush, the season making the largest contribution to annual net income, and was reluctant to take the time for the inventory count. Yet, she was also unwilling to take a substantial loss on the insurance settlement.

Ms. Harris asked for and received a one-day period in which to consider the insurance company offer, and immediately went to her records for the following information:

a.

	At Cost	At Retail
January 1 inventory	$ 159,975	$ 250,200
Purchases, January 1 through September 10 . .	1,049,625	1,638,450
Net sales, January 1 through September 10 . . .		1,627,650

b. On February 15, the remaining inventory of winter footwear was marked down from $72,000 to $54,000 and placed on sale in the annual end-of-the-winter-season sale. Three fourths of the boots were sold. The markdown on the remainder was canceled, and the boots were returned to their regular retail prices. (A markdown cancellation is subtracted from a markdown, and a markup cancellation is subtracted from a markup.)

c. In June, a special line of imported Italian boots proved popular, and 84 pairs were marked up from their normal $220.50 retail price to $243.00 per pair. Sixty pairs were sold at the higher price; and on July 20, the markup on the remaining 24 pairs was canceled and they were returned to their regular $220.50 price.

d. Between January 1 and September 10, markdowns totaling $8,100 were taken on several odd lots of shoes. Recommend whether or not you think Ms. Harris should accept the insurance company's offer. Back your recommendation with figures.

Provocative Problem 9–2
Value Furniture Store
(L. O. 5)

Value Furniture Store has been in operation for six years, during which it has earned a 34% average gross profit on sales. However, night before last, June 2, it suffered a disastrous fire that destroyed its entire inventory; and Fred Arne, the store's owner, has filed a $99,200 inventory loss claim with the store's insurance company. When asked on what he based his claim, he replied that during the day before the fire he had marked every item in the store down 20% in preparation for the annual summer clearance sale, and during the marking down process he had taken an inventory of the merchandise in the store. Furthermore, he said, "It's a big loss, but every cloud has a silver lining, because I am giving you fellows (the insurance company) the benefit of the 20% markdown in filing this claim."

When it was explained to Mr. Arne that he had to back his loss claim with more than his word as to the amount of the loss, he produced the following information from his pre-sale inventory and accounting records, which fortunately were in a fireproof vault and were not destroyed in the fire.

1. The store's accounts were closed on December 31 of last year.
2. After posting was completed, the accounts showed the following June 2 balances:

Merchandise inventory, January 1 balance . .	$ 86,500
Purchases.	232,800
Purchases returns.	2,450
Freight-in	5,880
Sales.	373,420
Sales returns	8,420

3. Mr. Arne's pre-fire inventory totaled $124,000 at pre-markdown prices.

From the information given, present figures to show the amount of loss suffered by Mr. Arne. Also, show how he arrived at the amount of his loss claim. Can his pre-sale inventory be used to substantiate the actual amount of his loss? If so, use the pre-sale inventory figure to substantiate the actual loss.

Analytical and Review Problems

A&R Problem 9–1

The LIFO versus FIFO controversy has spanned a number of decades. Proponents of each of the inventory procedures attribute certain merits to each.

Required

Identify the inventory procedure to which the following merits are attributed by writing either "LIFO" or "FIFO" opposite each of the letters (*a*) to (*n*).

Inventory procedure

a. _____Matches actual physical flow of goods.

b. _____Matches old costs with new prices.

c. _____Costs inventory at approximate replacement cost.

d. _____Matches new cost with new prices.

e. _____Emphasizes balance sheet.

f. _____Emphasizes income statement.

g. _____Opens door for "profit manipulation."

h. _____Understates the current ratio in a period of inflation.

i. _____Overstates inventory turnover in a period of inflation.

j. _____Gives higher profits in a period of inflation.

k. _____Matches current costs with current revenues.

l. _____More accurately reflects net income available to owners.

m. _____Gives lower profits in a period of deflation.

n. _____Results in a procession of costs in the same order as incurred.

A&R Problem 9–2

The following information is taken from the records of Fergus Company for four consecutive operating periods:

	Periods			
	1	**2**	**3**	**4**
Beginning inventory	$24,000	$36,000	$26,000	$32,000
Ending inventory	36,000	26,000	32,000	14,000
Net income	20,000	24,000	28,000	36,000

Assuming that the company made the errors below:

Period	Error in Ending Inventory	
1	Overstated	$6,000
2	Understated	4,000
3	Overstated	5,000

Required

1. Compute the revised net income for each of the four periods.

2. Assuming that the company's ending inventory for period 4 is correct, how would these errors affect the total net income for the four periods combined? Explain.

A&R Problem 9–3

The records of Weber Company as of December 31, 1991, show the following:

	Net Purchases	Net Income	Accounts Payable	Inventory
Balance per company's books	$197,000	$18,400	$24,300	$17,000
(a)				
(b)				
(c)				
(d)				
(e)				
Correct balances				

The accountant of Weber Company discovers in the first week of January 1992 that the following errors were made by his staff.

a. Goods costing $4,000 were in transit (FOB shipping point) and were not included in the ending inventory. The invoice had been received and the purchase recorded.

b. Damaged goods (cost $3,500) which were being held for return to the supplier were included in inventory. The goods had been recorded as a purchase and the entry for the return of these goods had also been made.

c. Inventory items costing $2,000 were incorrectly excluded from the final inventory. These goods had not been recorded as a purchase and had not been paid for by the company.

d. Goods which were shipped FOB destination had not yet arrived and were not included in inventory. However, the invoice had arrived on December 30, 1991, and the purchase for $1,800 was recorded.

e. Goods which cost $2,200 were segregated and not included in inventory because a customer expressed an intention to buy the goods. The sale of the goods for $3,800 had been recorded in December 1991.

Required

Using the format provided above, show the correct amount for net purchases, net income, accounts payable, and inventory for Weber Company as at December 31, 1991.

A&R Problem 9–4

The False Creek Company accounts for Product Y using LIFO and periodic procedures. Data relative to this product for the year ended December 31, 1991, are: Inventory January 1, 1991, 9,000 units at $9.

Purchases	Sales
1st quarter 18,000 units at $11	12,000 units at $17
2nd quarter 40,000 units at $12	32,000 units at $18
3rd quarter 32,000 units at $15	36,000 units at $20
4th quarter 16,000 units at $18	24,000 units at $23

Required

1. Compute the gross margin on sales of Product X for 1991.
2. Repeat part (1) assuming that 8,000 rather than 16,000 units were purchased in the 4th quarter.
3. Repeat part (1) assuming that 24,000 rather than 16,000 units were purchased in the 4th quarter.
4. Solve parts (1), (2), and (3) on the assumption that False Creek used the FIFO rather than LIFO inventory method.
5. Which method permits the manipulation of net income?
6. Which method emphasizes the balance sheet?
7. Which method emphasizes the income statement?
8. Which method matches current costs with current revenues?
9. Which method results in a processing of costs in the same order as incurred?
10. Which method costs inventory at approximately replacement cost?

A&R Problem 9–5

For each of the statements enter agree or disagree and state why you agree or disagree.

a. An improper valuation of inventory affects the income statement but does not affect the balance sheet.

b. Under the perpetual inventory system, an income statement may be prepared without taking a physical inventory.

    c. In general, the inventory policy should be to select an assumed flow of goods that matches the physical flow of the goods.

    d. The cost principle is the justification for the lower of cost or replacement rule.

    e. Under the periodic inventory method, cost of goods sold is computed as a residual.

    f. Under the perpetual inventory method, a physical inventory count is never taken.

    g. Damaged or obsolete inventory is valued at cost for balance sheet purposes until such time as sold.

    h. The LIFO inventory costing method lends itself most to manipulation of reported net incomes between periods.

    i. The specific inventory cost method of inventory flow is more likely to be employed by a jewelry store than a groceteria.

    j. The LIFO inventory costing method emphasizes the income statement rather than the balance sheet.

10 Plant and Equipment

In this chapter you will learn how to account for tangible assets that are used in the operations of a business. You will learn how to calculate depreciation on these assets and to account for the costs of repairing and improving them.

Learning Objectives

After studying Chapter 10, you should be able to:

1. Tell what is included in the cost of a plant asset and allocate the cost of lump-sum purchases to the separate assets being purchased.

2. Describe the reasons for depreciation accounting and calculate depreciation by the straight-line and units-of-production methods.

3. Describe how depreciation is disclosed in the financial statements and explain how the original cost of a plant asset is recovered through the sale of the asset's product or service.

4. Describe the use of accelerated depreciation for financial accounting and tax accounting purposes and calculate accelerated depreciation under (*a*) the double-declining-balance method and (*b*) the sum-of-the-years'-digits method.

5. Explain how subsidiary ledgers and related controlling accounts are used to maintain control over plant assets.

6. Define or explain the words and phrases listed in the chapter Glossary.

Tangible assets that are used in the production or sale of other assets or services and that have a useful life longer than one accounting period are called *plant and equipment* or *plant assets*. In past years, such assets were often described as **fixed assets.** However, the more descriptive terms *plant and equipment* or perhaps *property, plant, and equipment* are now used more often.

The characteristic that distinguishes plant assets from merchandise is that plant assets are held for use while merchandise is held for sale. For example, a typewriter is merchandise to an office equipment business that purchased the typewriter with the intention of selling it. But, if the business owns another typewriter that is used in business operations to prepare correspondence and so forth, this typewriter is classified as plant and equipment.

Plant assets also must be distinguished from long-term investments. Although both are held for more than one accounting period, investments are not used in the principal operations of the business. For example, land that is held for future expansion is classified as a long-term investment. On the other hand, land on which the factory of the business is located is a plant asset. It is classified as a plant asset because it is presently used in business operations. In addition, standby equipment that is held for use in case of a breakdown or during peak periods of production is a plant asset. However, when equipment is removed from service and held for sale, it ceases to be a plant asset.

The characteristic that distinguishes plant assets from tangible current assets such as supplies is that supplies are expected to be used up within one year or the current operating cycle of the business. By comparison, plant assets have longer useful lives that often extend over many accounting periods. Therefore, as the usefulness of plant assets expires over several accounting periods, the cost of plant assets must be allocated to these periods which benefit from their use.[1]

Cost of a Plant Asset

Tell what is included in the cost of a plant asset and allocate the cost of lump-sum purchases to the separate assets being purchased.
(L. O. 1)

Cost is the basis for recording the acquisition of a plant asset. The cost of a plant asset includes all normal and reasonable expenditures necessary to get the asset in place and ready to use. For example, the cost of a factory machine includes its invoice price, less any cash discount for early payment, plus freight, unpacking, and assembling costs. Cost also includes any expenditures to install the asset such as for a concrete base or foundation, electrical or power connections, and adjustments needed to place the machine in operation. In short, the cost of a plant asset includes all normal, necessary, and reasonable costs incurred in getting the asset in place and ready to produce.

A cost must be normal and reasonable as well as necessary if it is to be properly included in the cost of a plant asset. For example, if a machine is damaged by being dropped during unpacking, repairs should not be added to its cost. They should be charged to an expense account. Also, a fine paid for moving a heavy machine on city streets without proper permits is not part of the cost of the machine. However, if proper permits are obtained, the cost of the permits is included in the cost of the asset.

---

[1] *CICA Handbook* (Toronto: The Canadian Institute of Chartered Accountants), par. 1000.43.

Sometimes, when a plant asset is purchased, additional costs to repair or remodel the asset must be incurred before the asset meets the needs of the purchaser. In such cases, the repairing or remodeling expenditures should be charged to the asset. Furthermore, depreciation charges should not begin until the asset is put in use.

When a plant asset is constructed by a business for its own use, cost includes material and labor costs plus a reasonable amount of overhead or indirect expenses such as heat, lights, power, and depreciation on the machinery used in constructing the asset. Cost also includes architectural and design fees, building permits, and insurance during construction. However, insurance on the same asset after it has been placed in production is an expense.

When land is purchased for a building site, its cost includes the amount paid for the land plus any real estate commissions. It also includes escrow and legal fees, fees for examining and insuring the title, and any accrued property taxes paid by the purchaser, as well as expenditures for surveying, clearing, grading, draining, and landscaping. All are part of the cost of the land. Furthermore, any assessments incurred at the time of purchase or later for such things as the installation of streets, sewers, and sidewalks should be debited to the Land account since they add a more or less permanent value to the land.

Land purchased as a building site sometimes has an old building that must be removed. In such cases, the entire purchase price, including the amount paid for the building, should be charged to the Land account. Also, the cost of removing the old building, less any amounts recovered through the sale of salvaged materials, should be charged to this account.

Since land has an unlimited life, it is not subject to depreciation. However, **land improvements** such as parking lot surfaces, fences, and lighting systems have limited useful lives. Such costs improve the usefulness of land but must be charged to separate Land Improvement accounts and subjected to depreciation. Finally, a separate Building account must be charged for the cost of purchasing or constructing a building that will be used as a plant asset.

Purchases of land, land improvements, and buildings often are made in a single transaction at a single, lump-sum price. When this occurs, you must apportion the cost of the purchase among the assets, based on the relative market values of the purchased assets. Often, these values must be estimated by appraisal or by using the tax-assessed valuations of the assets.

For example, assume that land appraised at $30,000, land improvements appraised at $10,000, and a building appraised at $60,000 are purchased together for $90,000. The cost may be apportioned on the basis of appraised values as follows:

	Appraised Value	Percent of Total	Apportioned Cost
Land	$ 30,000	30	$27,000
Land improvements	10,000	10	9,000
Building.	60,000	60	54,000
Totals	$100,000	100	$90,000

Nature of Depreciation

Describe the reasons for depreciation accounting and calculate depreciation by the straight-line and units-of-production methods.
(L. O. 2)

Since plant assets are purchased for use, you may think of a plant asset as a quantity of usefulness that will contribute to the operations of the business throughout the service life of the asset. However, since the life of any plant asset (other than land) is limited, this quantity of usefulness expires as the asset is used. This expiration of a plant asset's quantity of usefulness is generally described as *depreciation;* and in accounting, the term is used to describe the process of allocating and charging the cost of this usefulness to the accounting periods that benefit from the asset's use.

For example, when a company purchases an automobile for use in the business, it purchases a quantity of usefulness, a quantity of transportation. The cost that will expire during the useful life of the car is the cost of the car less the proceeds that will be received when the car is sold or traded in at the end of its service life. This cost that will expire over the useful life of the car must be allocated to the accounting periods that benefit from the car's use; in other words, it must be depreciated. Note that the depreciation process does not measure the decline in the car's market value each period. Nor does it measure the physical deterioration of the car each period. Depreciation is a process of allocating cost.

The foregoing is in line with the pronouncements of the Canadian Institute of Chartered Accountants which described depreciation accounting as follows:

> An accounting procedure in which the cost or other recorded value of a fixed asset less estimated salvage (if any) is distributed over its estimated useful life in a systematic and rational manner. It is a process of allocation, not valuation.[2]

Service (Useful) Life of a Plant Asset

The **service life** of a plant asset is the length of time it will be used in the operations of the business. This may not be the same as the asset's potential life. For example, although typewriters have a potential life of six to eight years, a company may plan to trade in its old typewriters on new ones every three years. In this case, the typewriters have a three-year service life. Furthermore, in this company, the cost of the typewriters, less their expected trade-in value, should be charged to depreciation expense over this three-year period.

The service life of a plant asset often is difficult to predict because several factors may be involved. Wear and tear from use determine the useful life of some assets. However, two additional factors, **inadequacy** and **obsolescence**, often need to be considered. Usually, when a business acquires plant assets, it attempts to anticipate how much the business will grow and then acquires assets of a size and capacity to take care of its foreseeable needs. However, if a business grows more rapidly than anticipated, the capacity of the assets may become too small for the productive demands of the business. When this happens, the assets become inadequate.

Obsolescence, like inadequacy, is difficult to anticipate because the exact occurrence of new inventions and improvements normally cannot be predicted. Yet, new inventions and improvements often cause a plant asset to

---

[2] *Terminology for Accountants,* 3rd ed. (Toronto: The Canadian Institute of Chartered Accountants, 1983), p. 52.

AS A MATTER OF ETHICS

The economic situation surrounding a company has been quite dismal for a couple of years, and there are no signs of improvement for at least two more years. As a result, net income has been depressed, and the future seems bleak.

A significant item in the calculation of income is the depreciation of factory equipment. Because of frequent product changes, the equipment has been depreciated over only three years. However, in order to improve the income picture, management has in-structed Charles Roberts, the company's accountant, to begin using estimated useful lives of six years.

In trying to determine whether to follow management's instructions, Charles is torn between his loyalty to his employer and his responsibility to the public and the shareholders and others who use the company's financial statements. He is also trying to decide what the independent public accountant who audits the financial statements will think about the change.

become obsolete and make it wise to discard the obsolete asset long before it wears out.

Many times, a company is able to estimate the service life of a new asset based on its past experience with similar assets. In other cases, when it has no experience with a particular type of asset, a company must depend on the experience of others or on engineering studies and judgment.

Salvage Value

The total amount of depreciation that should be taken over an asset's service life is the asset's cost minus its estimated **salvage value.** The salvage value of a plant asset is the amount that will be recovered at the end of the asset's service life. Some assets such as typewriters, trucks, and automobiles are traded in on similar new assets at the end of their service lives. The salvage values of such assets are their trade-in values. Other assets may have no trade-in value and little or no salvage value. For example, at the end of its service life, some machinery can be sold only as scrap metal.

The disposal of some plant assets requires the outlay of costs such as the cost to wreck a building. In these cases, the expected salvage value of an asset is the *net* amount to be realized from the sale of the asset. The net amount to be realized is the expected amount to be received for the asset less its disposal cost. In the case of a machine, for example, the cost to remove the machine may equal the amount that can be realized from its sale. In such a case, the machine has no salvage value.

Allocating Depreciation

Many methods of allocating a plant asset's total depreciation to the several accounting periods in its service life have been suggested and used in past years. However, at the present time, most companies use the *straight-line method* of depreciation in their financial accounting records and on their financial statements. Also, some types of assets are depreciated according to the *units-of-production method*. Later in the chapter, after these two methods are explained, we will discuss some other depreciation methods, which are called *accelerated depreciation methods*.

Illustration 10–1
The financial statement effects of straight-line depreciation

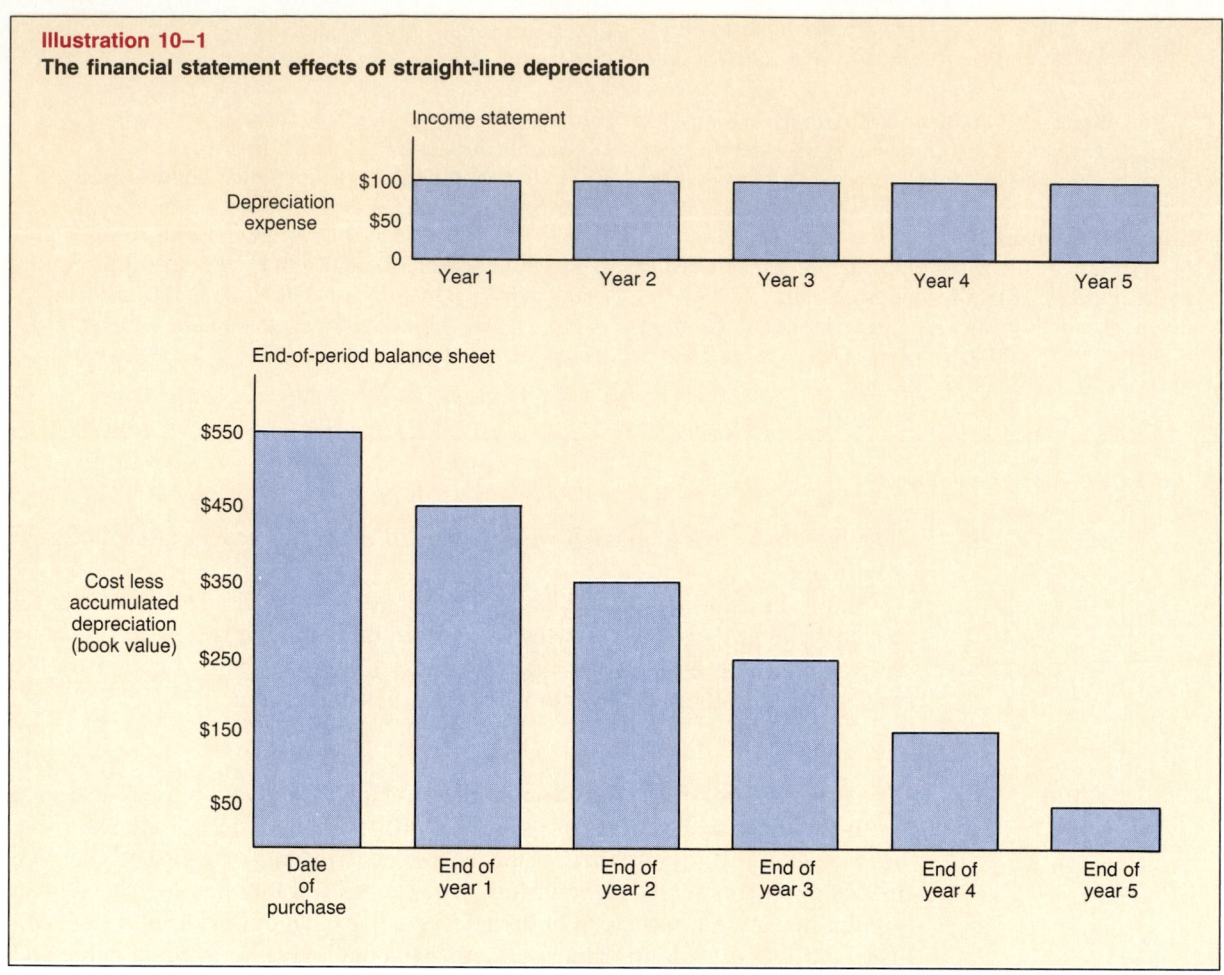

Straight-Line Method

When **straight-line depreciation** is used, the cost of the asset minus its estimated salvage value is divided by the estimated number of accounting periods
in the asset's service life. The result is the amount of depreciation to be taken
each period. For example, if a machine costs $550, has an estimated service
life of five years, and an estimated $50 salvage value, its depreciation per year
by the straight-line method is $100 and is calculated as follows:

$$\frac{\text{Cost} - \text{Salvage}}{\text{Service life in years}} = \frac{\$550 - \$50}{5} = \$100$$

Note that the straight-line method allocates an equal share of an asset's total
depreciation to each accounting period in its life. The financial statement effects of recording straight-line depreciation on the machine are shown in Illustration 10–1.

In Illustration 10–1, note that the cost minus accumulated depreciation, or
book value, decreases in a straight-line fashion over the five-year life of the

asset. (The book value of a plant asset is its cost less accumulated depreciation; it is the net amount shown for the asset on the books and in the balance sheet.) Also, note that the amount of depreciation expense reported in the income statement is the same each period ($100).

Units-of-Production Method

The purpose of recording depreciation is to charge each accounting period in which an asset is used with a fair share of its cost. The straight-line method charges an equal share to each period; and when plant assets are used about the same amount in each accounting period, this method rather fairly allocates total depreciation. However, in some lines of business, the use of certain plant assets varies greatly from accounting period to accounting period. For example, a contractor may use a particular piece of construction equipment for a month and then not use it again for many months. For such an asset, since its use fluctuates from period to period, **units-of-production depreciation** may provide a better matching of expenses with revenues than straight-line depreciation.

When the units-of-production method is used to depreciate an asset, the cost of an asset minus its estimated salvage value is divided by the estimated units it will produce during its entire service life. This calculation gives depreciation per unit of production. Then, the amount the asset is depreciated in any one accounting period is determined by multiplying the units produced in that period by the depreciation per unit. Units of production often is expressed as units of product. However, units of production also may be measured in terms of units used such as the distance driven or hours used.

For example, a truck that cost $24,000 is estimated to have a $4,000 salvage value. Also, the truck's service life in terms of kilometres is estimated to be 125,000 kms. Therefore, the depreciation per km., or the depreciation per unit of production, is $0.16 and is calculated as follows:

$$\frac{\text{Cost} - \text{Salvage value}}{\text{Estimated units of production}} = \text{Depreciation per unit of production}$$

or

$$\frac{\$24,000 - \$4,000}{125,000 \text{ kilometres}} = \$0.16 \text{ per kilometre}$$

If these estimates are used and the truck is driven 20,000 kms. during its first year, depreciation for the first year is $3,200. This is 20,000 kms. at $0.16 per km. If the truck is driven 15,000 kms. in the second year, depreciation for the second year is 15,000 times $0.16, or $2,400.

Depreciation for Partial Years

Plant assets may be purchased or disposed of any time during the year. When an asset is purchased (or disposed of) at some time other than the beginning (or end) of an accounting period, depreciation must be recorded for part of a year. Otherwise, the year of purchase or the year of disposal is not charged with its share of the asset's depreciation.

For example, assume that a machine was purchased and placed in service on October 8, 1991, and the annual accounting period ends on December 31. The machine costs $4,600, has an estimated service life of five years, and an estimated salvage value of $600. Since the machine was purchased and used nearly three months during 1991, the annual income statement should reflect depreciation expense on the machine for part of the year. The amount of depreciation to be reported often is based on the assumption that the machine was purchased on the first of the month nearest the actual date of purchase. Therefore, since the purchase was on October 8, three months' depreciation must be recorded on December 31. If the purchase had been on October 16 or later during October, depreciation would be calculated as if the purchase had been on November 1.

Three months are $\frac{3}{12}$ of one year. Therefore, if straight-line depreciation is used, the three months' depreciation is calculated as follows:

$$\frac{\$4,600 - \$600}{5} \times \frac{3}{12} = \$200$$

The entry to record depreciation for 1991 on the machine purchased on October 8, 1991, is:

Dec.	31	Depreciation Expense, Machinery	200.00	
		Accumulated Depreciation, Machinery.		200.00
		To record depreciation for three months.		

On December 31, 1992, and at the end of each of the following three years, a journal entry to record a full year's depreciation on this machine is required. The entry is:

Dec.	31	Depreciation Expense, Machinery	800.00	
		Accumulated Depreciation, Machinery.		800.00
		To record depreciation for one year.		

After the December 31, 1995, depreciation entry is recorded, the accounts showing the history of this machine appear as follows:

Machinery		Accumulated Depreciation Machinery	
Oct. 8, 1991 4,600		Dec. 31, 1991	200
		Dec. 31, 1992	800
		Dec. 31, 1993	800
		Dec. 31, 1994	800
		Dec. 31, 1995	800

If this machine is disposed of during 1996, two entries must be made to record the disposal. The first records 1996 depreciation to the date of disposal, and the second records the actual disposal. For example, assume that the machine is sold for $800 on June 24, 1996. To record the disposal, depreciation for six months (depreciation to the nearest full month) must first be recorded. The entry for this is:

June	24	Depreciation Expense, Machinery	400.00	
		Accumulated Depreciation, Machinery.		400.00
		To record depreciation for one-half year.		

After making the entry to record depreciation to the date of sale, a second entry to record the actual sale is made. This entry is:

June	24	Cash	800.00	
		Accumulated Depreciation, Machinery	3,800.00	
		Machinery		4,600.00
		To record sale of machine at book value.		

In this instance, the machine was sold for its book value. In the next chapter, you will learn how to account for the more typical situation in which plant assets are sold for more or less than book value.

Depreciation on the Balance Sheet

Describe how depreciation is disclosed in the financial statements and explain how the original cost of a plant asset is recovered through the sale of the asset's product or service. (L. O. 3)

In presenting information about the plant assets of a business, the *full-disclosure principle* requires that you give a general description of the depreciation method or methods used.[3] Usually, this is presented in a footnote. Also, the financial statements are more informative if you show both the cost and accumulated depreciation of plant assets by major classes. This may be accomplished in the statements or in related footnotes, and might appear as follows:

	Cost	Accumulated Depreciation	Book Value
Plant assets:			
Store equipment.	$ 12,400	$1,500	$10,900
Office equipment	3,600	450	3,150
Building	72,300	7,800	64,500
Land	15,000		15,000
Totals	$103,300	$9,750	$93,550

A presentation such as the above provides better information to financial statement readers than would be given if undepreciated costs were the only amounts reported. To illustrate, $50,000 of assets with $40,000 of accumulated depreciation may be quite different than $10,000 of new assets. Yet, the net undepreciated cost is the same in both cases.

---

[3] *CICA Handbook*, par. 3060.05.

Balance Sheet Plant Asset Values

From the discussion so far, you should recognize that the recording of depreciation is not primarily a valuation process. Rather, it is a process of allocating the cost of plant assets to the accounting periods that benefit from their use. Because depreciation is a process of cost allocation rather than valuation, plant assets are reported on balance sheets at their remaining (undepreciated) costs, not at market values.

The fact that balance sheets show undepreciated costs rather than market values may seem to be a failure of accounting. However, plant assets are held for use in the business; they are not held for sale. As a result, many accountants argue that the market values of plant assets are not particularly useful in evaluating the financial position and future prospects of the business. You should understand that a balance sheet is prepared under the assumption the company is a going concern. This means the company is expected to continue in business long enough to recover the original costs of its plant assets through the sale of its products.

The assumption that a company will continue in business long enough to recover its plant asset costs through the sale of its products is known in accounting as the *continuing-concern* or *going-concern concept*. This concept is used to justify carrying plant assets on the balance sheet at cost less accumulated depreciation—in other words, at the share of their cost applicable to future periods. The going-concern concept also explains why an item such as stationery imprinted with the company name is carried at cost even though the stationery is salable only as scrap paper. In all such instances, the intention is to use the assets in carrying on the business operations. They are not for sale, so their market or realizable values are not reported on the balance sheet.

Recovering the Costs of Plant Assets

An uninformed financial statement reader may make the mistake of thinking that the accumulated depreciation shown on a balance sheet represents funds accumulated to buy new assets when present assets must be replaced. However, an informed reader recognizes that accumulated depreciation represents the portion of an asset's cost that has been charged off to depreciation expense during its life. Accumulated depreciation accounts are contra accounts with credit balances that cannot be used to buy anything. If a business has cash with which to buy assets, it is shown on the balance sheet as a current asset *Cash,* not as accumulated depreciation.

A company that earns a profit or breaks even (neither earns a profit nor suffers a loss) eventually recovers the original cost of its plant assets through the sale of its products. This is best explained with a condensed income statement like that of Illustration 10–2 which shows that Even Steven Company broke even during the year of the illustrated income statement. However, in breaking even, the company also recovered $5,000 of the cost of its plant assets through the sale of its products. It recovered the $5,000 because $100,000 flowed into the company from sales and only $95,000 flowed out to pay for goods sold, rent, and salaries. No cash flowed out for depreciation expense. As a result, the company recovered this $5,000 portion of the cost of its plant assets through the sale of its products. Furthermore, if the company remains in business for the life of its plant assets, either breaking even or earning a profit, it will recover their entire cost in this manner.

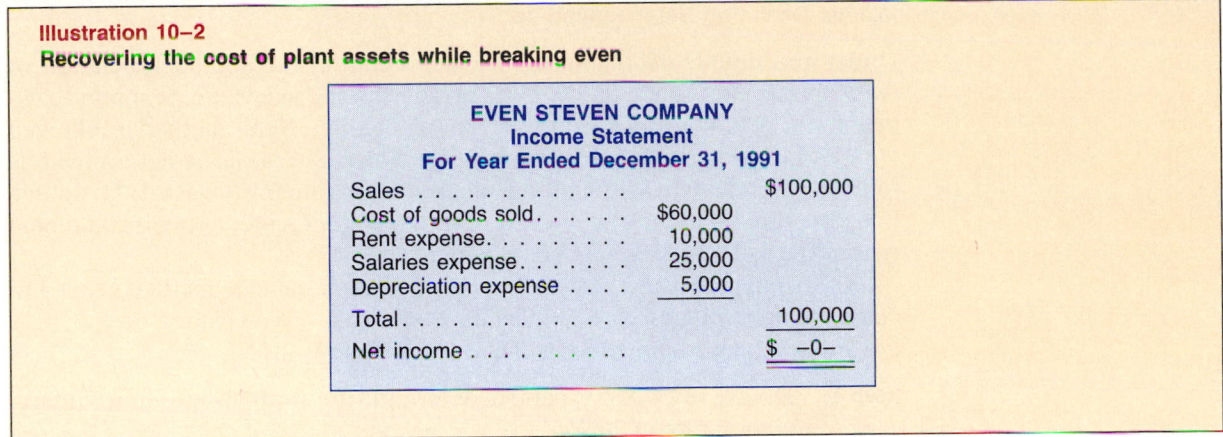

Illustration 10–2
Recovering the cost of plant assets while breaking even

EVEN STEVEN COMPANY
Income Statement
For Year Ended December 31, 1991

Sales		$100,000
Cost of goods sold	$60,000	
Rent expense	10,000	
Salaries expense	25,000	
Depreciation expense	5,000	
Total		100,000
Net income		$ –0–

At this point you might ask, "Where is the recovered $5,000?" The answer is that the company may have the $5,000 in the bank. However, the cash (funds) may also have been spent to increase merchandise inventory, to buy additional equipment, to pay off a debt, or they may have been withdrawn from the business by the owner. In short, the funds may still be in the bank or they may have been used for any purpose for which a business uses funds.

Accelerated Depreciation methods

Describe the use of accelerated depreciation for financial accounting and tax accounting purposes and calculate accelerated depreciation under (*a*) the double-declining-balance method, and (*b*) the sum-of-the-years'-digits method. (L. O. 4)

Some depreciation methods result in larger depreciation charges during the early years of an asset's life and smaller charges in the later years. These are called **accelerated depreciation** methods. Two of the more common methods are **double-declining-balance depreciation** and **sum-of-the-years'-digits depreciation.** Some accountants reason that accelerated depreciation methods provide better annual expenses associated with plant and equipment. Repair and maintenance costs are usually lower in the earlier years of an asset's life and greater in the later years. The higher depreciation expense is recorded in the early years with lower repair costs. The lower depreciation expense is recorded in the later years with the higher repair costs. Thus, the total annual costs (depreciation plus repairs) are approximately the same from year to year over the life of the asset. This argument, however, does not appear to have gained a great deal of support since most companies still use straight-line depreciation for accounting purposes.

The **Income Tax Act** requires that companies use double-declining-balance depreciation for tax purposes and specifies different depreciation rates for the various types of assets. For example, a rate of 20% would be used for general equipment and a rate of 5% for brick or masonary buildings. The Act stipulates that the depreciation (capital cost allowance) calculated is the maximum which may be claimed for tax purposes and that the rate is applied to the undepreciated capital cost (book value) to determine the allowed amount. Further discussion of the details of tax depreciation is deferred to a more advanced course.

Double-Declining-Balance Method

Under the double-declining-balance depreciation method, depreciation of twice the straight-line rate, without considering salvage value, is applied each year to the declining book value of a new plant asset. If this method is followed with twice the straight-line rate, depreciation on an asset is determined as follows: (1) calculate a straight-line depreciation rate for the asset; (2) double this rate; and (3) at the end of each year in the asset's life, apply this doubled rate to the asset's remaining book value.

For example, assume that the double-declining-balance method is used to calculate depreciation on a $10,000 new asset that has an estimated five-year life and a salvage value of $750. The steps to follow are:

Step 1: Divide 100% by 5 (years) to determine the straight-line annual depreciation rate of 20%.

Step 2: Double this 20% rate to get a declining-balance rate of 40%.

Step 3: Calculate the annual depreciation charges as shown in the following table:

Year	Annual Depreciation Calculation	Annual Depreciation Expense	End-of-Year Accumulated Depreciation	End-of-Year Book Value
1st year.	40% of $10,000	$4,000.00	$4,000.00	$6,000.00
2nd year	40% of 6,000	2,400.00	6,400.00	3,600.00
3rd year.	40% of 3,600	1,440.00	7,840.00	2,160.00
4th year.	40% of 2,160	864.00	8,704.00	1,296.00
5th year.	40% of 1,296	518.40	9,222.40	777.60

Under the double-declining-balance method, the book value of a plant asset never reaches zero. Therefore, when the asset is sold, exchanged, or scrapped, any remaining book value is used to determine the gain or loss on the disposal. However, if an asset has a salvage value, the asset may not be depreciated beyond its salvage value. For example, if instead of a $750 salvage value, the foregoing $10,000 asset has an estimated $1,000 salvage value, depreciation for its fifth year is limited to $296. This is the amount required to reduce the asset's book value to its $1,000 salvage value.

Sum-of-the-Years'-Digits Method

Under the sum-of-the-years'-digits method, the whole numbers from 1 to the number of years in an asset's service life are added. The sum of these numbers becomes the denominator of a series of fractions used to allocate total depreciation to the periods in the asset's service life. The numerators of the fractions are the same whole numbers that represent the years in the asset's life in their reverse order. For example, assume a machine is purchased that costs $7,000, has an estimated five-year life, and has an estimated $1,000 salvage value. The sum-of-the-years'-digits in the assest's life are:

$$1 + 2 + 3 + 4 + 5 = 15$$

and annual depreciation charges are calculated as follows:

Year	Annual Depreciation Calculation	Annual Depreciation Expense	End-of-Year Accumulated Depreciation	End-of-Year Book Value
1st year.	⁵/₁₅ of $6,000	$2,000	$2,000	$4,000
2nd year	⁴/₁₅ of 6,000	1,600	3,600	2,400
3rd year.	³/₁₅ of 6,000	1,200	4,800	1,200
4th year.	²/₁₅ of 6,000	800	5,600	400
5th year.	¹/₁₅ of 6,000	400	6,000	–0–
Total depreciation		$6,000		

The sum-of-the-years' digits in an asset's life may be calculated by using the formula: $SYD = n[(n + 1)/2]$. For example, sum-of-the-years' digits for a five-year life is:

$$5\left(\frac{5 + 1}{2}\right) = 15$$

Although this method is seldom used, it is relatively easy to calculate and provides a close approximation for the double-declining-balance method. Therefore, it is useful for rough calculations.

Apportioning Accelerated Depreciation

When accelerated depreciation is used and accounting periods do not coincide with the years in an asset's life, depreciation must be apportioned between accounting periods. For example, consider the above case where the sum-of-the-years'-digits method is used to calculate depreciation on a machine. Annual depreciation on the machine is $2,000 during its first year, $1,600 during its second year, and so on for its five-year life. Now assume this machine is placed in use on April 1 and the annual accounting period ends on December 31. As a result, the machine will be in use for three fourths of a year during the first accounting period in its life. Therefore, this period should be charged with $1,500 depreciation ($2,000 × ¾ = $1,500). Likewise, the second accounting period should be charged with $1,700 depreciation [(¼ × $2,000) + (¾ × $1,600) = $1,700]. Similar calculations should be used for the remaining periods in the asset's life.

Control of Plant Assets

Explain how subsidiary ledgers and related controlling accounts are used to maintain control over plant assets. (L. O. 5)

Good internal control requires that each plant asset be separately identified, usually with a serial number that is etched or affixed to the asset. Periodically, an inventory of plant assets should be taken in which the existence and continued use of each asset are verified. Formal records of plant assets on hand should be maintained.

In keeping plant asset records, concerns usually divide their plant assets into functional groups and provide in the General Ledger a separate asset account and accumulated depreciation account for each group. The asset account and related accumulated depreciation account for each group serve as controlling accounts that control detailed subsidiary records. For example, in a store, the Store Equipment account and the Accumulated Depreciation, Store Equipment account control the **Store Equipment Ledger.** This is a sub-

Plant Asset
No. _132-1_

SUBSIDIARY PLANT ASSET AND DEPRECIATION RECORD

Item _Office chair_   Account _Office Equipment_
Description _Padded, straight-back, wood_

Mfg. Serial No. _____   Purchased from _Office Equipment Co._
Where Located _Office_
Person Responsible for the Asset _Office Manager_
Estimated Life _6 years_   Estimated Salvage Value _$10.00_
Depreciation per Year _$30.00_   per Month _$2.50_

Date	Explanation	PR	Asset Record			Depreciation Record		
			Dr.	Cr.	Bal.	Dr.	Cr.	Bal.
July 2, 1989		G1	190.00		190.00			
Dec. 31, 1990		G23					15.00	15.00
Dec. 31, 1991		G42					30.00	45.00
Dec. 31, 1992		G65					30.00	75.00

Final Disposition of the Asset _____

Plant Asset
No. _132-2_

SUBSIDIARY PLANT ASSET AND DEPRECIATION RECORD

Item _Desk_   Account _Office Equipment_
Description _Wood, left hand return_

Mfg. Serial No. _____   Purchased from _Office Equipment Co._
Where Located _Office_
Person Responsible for the Asset _Office Manager_
Estimated Life _6 years_   Estimated Salvage Value _$30.00_
Depreciation per Year _$120.00_   per Month _$10.00_

Date	Explanation	PR	Asset Record			Depreciation Record		
			Dr.	Cr.	Bal.	Dr.	Cr.	Bal.
July 2, 1989		G1	750.00		750.00			
Dec. 31, 1990		G23					60.00	60.00
Dec. 31, 1991		G42					120.00	180.00
Dec. 31, 1992		G65					120.00	300.00

Final Disposition of the Asset _____

Illustration 10–3 *(concluded)*

Office Equipment   **Account No. 132**

Date		Explanation	PR	Debit		Credit		Balance	
1989									
July	*2*	*Desk and chair*	G1	940	00			940	00

Accumulated Depreciation,
Office Equipment   **Account No. 133**

Date		Explanation	PR	Debit		Credit		Balance	
1989									
Dec.	*31*		G23			75	00	75	00
1990									
Dec.	*31*		G42			150	00	225	00
1991									
Dec.	*31*		G65			150	00	375	00

sidiary ledger that has a separate record for each individual item of store equipment. The same is true for the Office Equipment account and the Accumulated Depreciation, Office Equipment account, which control the **Office Equipment Ledger.**

Whether plant asset records are computerized or handwritten, they provide the same basic information. To illustrate plant asset records, assume that a concern's office equipment consists of just one desk and a chair. The general ledger accounts for these assets are Office Equipment and Accumulated Depreciation, Office Equipment. Both are controlling accounts that control sections of the subsidiary record for the desk and chair. The general ledger and subsidiary ledger records of these assets are shown in Illustration 10–3.

At the top of each subsidiary record, observe the plant asset numbers assigned to these two items of office equipment. In each case, the assigned number consists of the number of the Office Equipment account, 132, followed by the asset's number. The remaining information on the subsidiary records is more or less self-evident. Note how the $940 balance of the general ledger account, Office Equipment, is equal to the sum of the $190 and $750 balances in the asset record section of the two subsidiary records. The general ledger account controls this section of the subsidiary ledger. Observe also how the Accumulated Depreciation, Office Equipment account controls the depreciation record section of the subsidiary records. The disposition section at the bottom of the subsidiary records is used to record the final disposal of the asset. When the asset is discarded, sold, or exchanged, a notation telling of the final disposition is entered here. The record is then removed from the subsidiary ledger and filed for future reference.

Plant Assets of Low Cost

Individual plant asset records are expensive to keep. Therefore, many companies establish a minimum, say, $50 or $100, and do not keep such records for assets costing less than the minimum. Rather, they charge the cost of such assets directly to an expense account at the time of purchase. As long as the amounts are small, this is acceptable under the *materiality principle*.

Summary of the Chapter in Terms of Learning Objectives

1. The cost of plant assets includes all normal and reasonable expenditures necessary to get the assets in place and ready to use. The cost of a lump-sum purchase should be allocated to the individual assets based on their relative market values.

2. Plant assets other than land have limited service lives. Therefore, the cost of the assets must be allocated to the accounting periods that benefit from their use. When the allocation is done according to the straight-line method, you divide the cost minus salvage value by the number of periods in the service life of the asset to determine the depreciation expense of each period. Under the units-of-production method, you divide the cost minus salvage value by the estimated number of units the asset will produce to determine the depreciation per unit.

3. Financial statements should include a description of the depreciation methods used. Also, financial statements are more informative if cost and accumulated depreciation are reported by major class of asset. When the revenues of a business are large enough to cover all expenses, the cost of depreciation is recovered through revenues.

4. Although double-declining-balance and sum-of-the-years'-digits depreciation are acceptable for financial accounting purposes, they are seldom used. Most companies prefer to use straight-line depreciation methods. Depreciation for tax purposes is tied into a system which is based upon double-declining-balance depreciation.

5. To maintain control over plant assets, detailed records should be kept. These records usually require the use of subsidiary ledgers that are controlled by asset and accumulated depreciation accounts.

Demonstration Problem

On July 14, 1990, a company paid $600,000 to acquire a fully equipped factory. The purchase included the following:

Asset	Appraised Value	Estimated Salvage Value	Estimated Service Life	Depreciation Method
Land.	$160,000			
Land improvements	80,000	$ –0–	10 years	Straight line
Building	320,000	100,000	10 years	Sum-of-the-years' digits
Machinery.	176,000	16,000	10,000 units	Units of production*
Computers	64,000	4,000	4 years	Double-declining balance (at twice the straight-line rate)
Total.	$800,000			

*The machinery was used to produce 700 units in 1990 and 1,800 units in 1991.

Required

1. Allocate the total $600,000 cost among the five separate assets.
2. Compute the depreciation expense that should be reported for 1990 (half-year) and for 1991.

Solution to Demonstration Problem

1.

Asset	Appraised Value	Percent of Total Value	Allocated Cost
Land	$160,000	20	$120,000
Land improvements	80,000	10	60,000
Building.	320,000	40	240,000
Machinery.	176,000	22	132,000
Computers	64,000	8	48,000
Total.	$800,000	100	$600,000

2. Depreciation for each asset:

Land improvements:

Cost	$60,000
Salvage value	–0–
Net cost	$60,000
Service life	10 years
Annual expense . . . . $60,000 ÷ 10 =	$6,000
1990 depreciation . . . . $6,000 × ($\frac{1}{2}$) =	$3,000
1991 depreciation	6,000

Building:

Cost.	$240,000
Salvage value	100,000
Net cost.	$140,000

Sum-of-the-years' digits = $(10 \times 11) \div 2 = 55$

1990 depreciation: $140,000 \times (^{10}/_{55}) \times (\frac{1}{2}) = $12,727

1991 depreciation: $140,000 \times (^{10}/_{55}) \times (\frac{1}{2}) = $12,727
                                    $140,000 \times (^{9}/_{55}) \times (\frac{1}{2}) = 11,455

Total	$24,182

Machinery:

Cost. $132,000
Salvage value   16,000
Net cost. $116,000

Total expected units   10,000
Expected cost per unit ($116,000 ÷ 10,000) $11.60

Year	Units × Unit Cost	Depreciation
1990	700 × $11.60	$ 8,120
1991	1,800 × $11.60	20,880

Computers:

Cost $48,000
Salvage value   4,000
Straight-line rate (100%/4 years) 25%
Twice the straight-line rate (25% × 2) . .   50%

Year	Rate	Beginning Book Value	Depreciation Expense	Accumulated Depreciation	Ending Book Value
1990	50%/2	$48,000	$12,000	$12,000	$36,000
1991	50%	36,000	18,000	30,000	18,000

Note: The percentage for 1990 is 50%/2 because the computers were in use for only one half of the year.

Glossary

Define or explain the words and phrases listed in the chapter Glossary. (L. O. 6)

Accelerated depreciation any depreciation method that results in greater amounts of depreciation expense in the early years of a plant asset's life and lesser amounts in later years. p. 489

Book value the carrying amount for an item in the accounting records. When applied to a plant asset, it is the cost of the asset minus its accumulated depreciation. p. 484

Double-declining-balance depreciation a depreciation method in which twice the straight-line rate of depreciation, without considering salvage value, is applied to the beginning-of-period book value of a plant asset to determine the asset's depreciation charge for the period. p. 490

Fixed asset another name for plant asset, no longer widely in use. p. 480

Inadequacy a situation in which a plant asset does not produce enough product to meet current needs. p. 482

Income Tax Act the codification of the Canadian federal tax laws. p. 489

Land improvements assets that improve or increase the usefulness of land but which have a limited useful life and are subject to depreciation. p. 481

Obsolescence a situation in which, because of new inventions and improvements, an old plant asset can no longer produce its product on a competitive basis. p. 482

Office Equipment Ledger a subsidiary ledger that contains a separate record for each item of office equipment owned. p. 493

Salvage value the portion of a plant asset's cost that will be recovered at the end of its service life through a sale or as a trade-in allowance on a new asset. p. 483

Service life the period of time a plant asset is used in the production and sale of other assets or services. p. 482

Store Equipment Ledger a subsidiary ledger that contains a separate record for each item of store equipment owned. p. 491

Straight-line depreciation a depreciation method that allocates an equal share of the total estimated amount a plant asset will be depreciated during its service life to each accounting period in that life. p. 484

Sum-of-the-years'-digits depreciation a depreciation method that allocates depreciation to each year in a plant asset's life on a fractional basis. The denominator of the fractions used is the sum-of-the-years' digits in the estimated service life of the asset, and the numerators are the years' digits in reverse order. p. 490

Units-of-production depreciation a depreciation method that allocates depreciation on a plant asset based on the relation of the units of product produced by the asset during a given period to the total units the asset is expected to produce during its entire life. p. 485

Questions for Class Discussion

1. What are the characteristics of an asset classified as plant and equipment?

2. What is the balance sheet classification of land held for future expansion? Why is such land not classified as a plant asset?

3. What is the difference between land and land improvements?

4. What in general is included in the cost of a plant asset?

5. Tack Company asked for bids from several machine manufacturers for the construction of a special machine. The lowest bid was $37,500. The company decided to build the machine itself and did so at a total cash outlay of $30,000. It then recorded the machine's construction with a debit to Machinery for $37,500, a credit to Cash for $30,000, and a credit to Gain on the Construction of Machinery for $7,500. Was this a proper entry? Discuss.

6. As used in accounting, what is the meaning of the term *depreciation?*

7. Is it possible to keep a plant asset in such an excellent state of repair that recording depreciation is unnecessary?

8. A machine that normally lasts 10 years is purchased even though management knows future growth of the company's operations will require that the machine be replaced in approximately 4 years. What factor in this situation tends to suggest that the machine should be depreciated over 4 years?

9. A company purchases a machine that normally has a service life of 12 years. However, the company's management believes that the development of a more efficient machine will make it necessary to replace the machine in 8 years. What period of useful life should be used in calculating depreciation on this machine?

10. A building estimated to have a useful life of 30 years was completed at a cost of $120,000. It was estimated that at the end of the building's life it would be wrecked at a cost of $13,000 and that materials salvaged from the wrecking operation would be sold for $25,000. How much straight-line depreciation should be charged on the building each year?

11. When straight-line depreciation is used, an equal share of the total amount a plant asset is to be depreciated during its life is assigned to each accounting period in that life. Describe a situation in which this may not be a fair basis of allocation. Name a depreciation method that might be fairer in the situation described.

12. Define the following terms as used in accounting for plant assets:
    a. Trade-in value.   *c*. Book value.   *e*. Inadequacy.
    b. Market value.   *d*. Salvage value.   *f*. Obsolescence.

13. What is the sum-of-the-years' digits in the life of a plant asset that will be used for 20 years?

14. Does the recording of depreciation cause a plant asset to appear on the balance sheet at market value? What is accomplished by recording depreciation?

15. Does the balance of the Accumulated Depreciation, Machinery account represent funds accumulated to replace the machinery as it wears out? Describe in your own words what the balance of such an account represents.

16. What method of depreciation is normally used for tax purposes?
17. What is the purpose of periodically taking an inventory of plant assets?
18. What possible justification is there for charging to expense a plant asset that cost $75?
19. What is the implication of the going-concern concept on the valuation of plant assets in the accounting records?
20. Explain how a business that breaks even recovers the cost of its plant assets through the sale of its products. Where are the funds thus recovered?

Multiple Choice

1. Cornwall Company recently purchased a new production machine which involved the following dollar amounts:

Gross purchase price.	$500,000
Sales tax	35,000
Freight to move machine to plant . .	2,500
Assembly costs.	2,200
Cost of foundation for machine . . .	1,800
Cost of spare parts to be used in	
maintenance of the machine . . .	3,000
Purchase discount taken.	15,000

The amount to be recorded as the cost of the machine is:
   a. $491,500.
   b. $524,300.
   c. $520,000.
   d. $526,500.
   e. $529,500.

2. Cummins, Inc., recently purchased a new machine for $120,000 on January 1, 1991. Its estimated useful life is five years or 80,000 units of product, and salvage value is $10,000. During 1991, 8,000 units of product were produced. Assuming (1) straight-line depreciation and (2) units-of-production depreciation, respectively, the book value of the machine on December 31, 1991, is:
   a. $96,000; $108,000.
   b. $96,000; $ 99,000.
   c. $88,000; $108,000.
   d. $98,000; $109,000.
   e. $22,000; $ 11,000.

3. When disclosing depreciation in the financial statements:
   a. Depreciation for the current period is subtracted from the asset account balance in the balance sheet.
   b. Total accumulated depreciation is subtracted as an expense in the income statement.
   c. Total accumulated depreciation is subtracted from the asset account balance in the balance sheet.
   d. Depreciation for the current period is subtracted as an expense in the income statement.
   e. Both (c) and (d) are correct.

4. Flexoral Industries recently purchased a new machine for $180,000 on January 1, 1990. Its estimated useful life is five years, and salvage value is $15,000. Depreciation expense for 1991 using (1) double-declining balance and (2) sum-of-the-years'-digits depreciation, respectively, is:
   a. $28,800; $48,000.
   b. $39,600; $48,000.
   c. $39,600; $44,000.
   d. $43,200; $48,000.
   e. $43,200; $44,000.

5. In keeping plant asset records:
   a. Detailed subsidiary records serve as controlling accounts for the related general ledger account.
   b. Computerized records always provide more information than handwritten records.
   c. The asset account and related accumulated depreciation account for each group of assets serve as controlling accounts that control detailed subsidiary records.
   d. To record a purchase of an office desk, separate general journal entries are made to Office Equipment and to the subsidiary account Office Desk.
   e. The Office Equipment Ledger controls the Office Equipment account and the Accumulated Depreciation, Office Equipment account.

Mini Discussion Cases

Case 10–1

The Halifax Company and the Dartmouth Company have each purchased similar properties consisting of land and a small commercial building. The two properties each cost approximately $850,000 and are used for rental purposes.

Management of the Halifax Company wishes to allocate a large portion of the purchase price to the building because of the company's excellent overall profitability. They argue that a large depreciation expense will reduce income taxes, alleviate shareholders' demands for dividends, and allow the company to retain cash for future investment. In contrast, the Dartmouth Company, which has been must less profitable, wishes to allocate a large portion of the purchase price to the land in order to show lower depreciation expense and thus enhance their profits.

Required
a. Evaluate the approaches taken by each of the companies.
b. Indicate, with reasons, how the allocation of the purchase price between the land and building should be conducted for each company.

Case 10–2

Your friend, who has had no experience with accounting, says that there are a couple of items on the balance sheet that he does not understand. For example, he knows that the building, shown at $75,000, could be sold for almost twice that amount. He also wonders where all the cash has gone; accumulated depreciation is $37,650 but the cash account only shows $9,825.

Required

Explain what is wrong with your friend's reasoning about accounting.

Exercises

Exercise 10–1
Cost of a plant asset
(L. O. 1)

Johnson Corporation purchased a machine for $19,000, terms 2/10, n/60, FOB shipping point. The seller prepaid the freight charges, $1,055, adding the amount to the invoice and bringing its total to $20,055. The machine required a special steel mounting and power connections costing $2,735, and another $2,590 was paid to assemble the machine and get it into operation. In moving the machine onto its steel mounting, it was dropped and damaged. The damages cost $675 to repair, and after being repaired, $280 of raw materials were consumed in adjusting the machine so it would produce a satisfactory product. The adjustments were normal for this type of machine and were not the result of its having been damaged. However, the product produced while the adjustments were being made was not salable. Prepare a calculation to show the cost of this machine for accounting purposes.

Exercise 10–2
Allocating cost between land, land improvements, and buildings
(L. O. 1)

Charter Company paid $520,000 for real estate plus $10,800 in closing costs. The real estate included land appraised at $160,000, land improvements appraised at $64,000, and a building appraised at $416,000. The plan is to use the building as a factory. Prepare a calculation showing the allocation of cost to the assets purchased and present the journal entry to record the purchase.

Exercise 10–3
Lump-sum purchase of plant assets
(L. O. 1)

Western Company bought two pickup trucks and a forklift from a financially distressed supplier and had them shipped to the company's plant. The purchase price was $25,000 plus $1,250 that was paid for the shipping charge. The forklift was only half as large as a truck and weighed half as much. Appraised values of the trucks and forklift and costs of initial repairs to get them ready for service were as follows:

	Truck 1	Truck 2	Forklift
Appraised values	$14,000	$12,250	$8,750
Repair costs	900	600	450

Determine the cost of each asset for accounting purposes.

Exercise 10–4
Recording the costs of real estate
(L. O. 1)

After planning to build a new manufacturing plant, Enslow Company purchased a large lot on which a small building was located. The negotiated purchase price of this real estate amounted to $375,000 for the lot plus $450,000 for the building. The company paid $60,000 to have the old building torn down and $75,000 for landscaping of the lot. Finally, it paid $2.7 million construction costs for a new building, which included $120,000 for lighting and paving of a parking lot next to the building. Present a single general journal entry to record the costs incurred by the company, all of which were paid in cash.

Exercise 10–5
Calculating depreciation;
four alternative methods
(L. O. 2, 3)

Barney Company installed a machine in its factory at a $114,000 cost. The machine's useful life was estimated at five years or 36,100 units of product with a $5,700 trade-in value. During its second year, the machine produced 8,600 units of product. Determine the machine's second-year depreciation with depreciation calculated in each of the following ways: (*a*) straight-line rate, (*b*) units-of-production basis, (*c*) double-declining-balance basis, and (*d*) sum-of-the-years'-digits basis.

Exercise 10–6
Calculating depreciation;
three alternative methods
(L. O. 2, 3)

On September 1, 1990, Fox Company purchased a machine for $675,000. The machine was expected to last six years and have a salvage value of $45,000. Calculate depreciation expense for 1991, assuming (*a*) straight-line depreciation, (*b*) sum-of-the-years'-digits depreciation, and (*c*) double-declining-balance depreciation.

Exercise 10–7
Partial year's depreciation
(L. O. 2, 5)

Daffy Company purchased and installed a machine on June 2, 1990, at a total cost of $54,000. Straight-line depreciation was taken on December 31 of each year for 1990 through 1993, based on the assumption of a six-year life and no salvage value. Then on August 31, 1994, the company decides to prepare financial statements for the period January through August. Present the entries to record the depreciation on December 31, 1990; December 31, 1991; and August 31, 1994.

Exercise 10–8
Straight-line and double-declining-balance depreciation
(L. O. 2, 3)

In January 1990, Thompson Company purchased computer equipment for $30,000. The equipment will be used in research and development activities for five years and then sold at an estimated salvage value of $2,000. Prepare a schedule showing each year's depreciation assuming (*a*) five-year straight-line depreciation and (*b*) double-declining-balance depreciation.

Exercise 10–9
Double-declining-balance depreciation
(L. O. 3)

Hatfield Company purchased and installed a plant asset that cost $24,000 and was estimated to have a four-year life and a $2,100 trade-in value. Use double-declining-balance depreciation to determine the amount of depreciation to be charged against the machine in each of the four years of its life.

Exercise 10–10
Income statement effects of alternative depreciation methods
(L. O. 2, 3)

Gafford Company recently paid $180,000 for equipment that will last four years and have a salvage value of $30,000. By using the machine in its operations for four years, the company expects to earn $60,000 annually, after deducting all expenses except depreciation. Present a schedule showing income before depreciation, depreciation expense, and net income for each year and the total amounts for the four-year period assuming (*a*) straight-line depreciation, (*b*) sum-of-the-years'-digits depreciation, and (*c*) double-declining-balance depreciation.

Problems

Problem 10–1
Alternative depreciation methods; retirement of plant assets
(L. O. 2, 3, 5)

Part 1. A machine that cost $75,000, has a five-year life, and has an estimated $10,500 salvage value was installed in Blake Company's factory. The factory management estimated the machine would produce 150,000 units of product during its life. It actually produced the following numbers of units: year 1, 21,000; year 2, 33,000; year 3, 30,000; year 4, 28,500; and year 5, 37,500.

Required
1. Prepare a calculation showing the number of dollars of this machine's cost that should be charged to depreciation over its five-year life.
2. Prepare a form with the following column headings:

Year	Straight Line	Units of Production	Declining Balance	Sum-of-the-Years' Digits

Then show the depreciation for each year and the total depreciation for the machine under each depreciation method. Use twice the straight-line rate for the declining-balance method.

Part 2. Craft Company purchased a used machine for $17,100 on January 3. The next day it was repaired at a cost of $2,025 and was installed on a new platform that cost $1,575. It was estimated the machine would be used for three years and would then have a $2,700 salvage value. Depreciation was to be charged on a straight-line basis. A full year's depreciation was charged on December 31, at the end of the first year of the machine's use; and on September 1, in its second year of use, the machine was retired from service.

Required
1. Prepare general journal entries to record the purchase of the machine, the cost of repairing it, and its installation. Assume cash was paid in each case.
2. Prepare entries to record depreciation on the machine on December 31 and on September 1.
3. Prepare entries to record the retirement of the machine under each of the following unrelated assumptions: (*a*) the machine was sold for $12,000; (*b*) it was sold for $6,900; and (*c*) it was destroyed in a fire, and the insurance company paid $6,525 in full settlement of the loss claim.

Problem 10–2
Plant asset records
(L. O. 2, 4)

Brady Salvage Company completed the following transactions involving plant assets:

1990
Jan. 5 Purchased on credit from Dexter Equipment an electronic scale priced at $3,975. The serial number of the scale was E-56273, its service life was estimated at five years with a trade-in value of $375, and it was assigned plant asset No. 545-1.
Apr. 3 Purchased on credit from Dexter Equipment a Moore mixer priced at $6,141. The serial number of the mixer was M-41652, its service

life was estimated at six years with a trade-in value of $525, and it was assigned plant asset No. 556-2.

Dec. 31 Recorded straight-line depreciation on the plant equipment for 1990.

1991

Nov. 4 Sold the Moore mixer to Sharpstowne Steel for $3,750 cash.

    4 Purchased a new Master mixer from Penford Equipment for $5,400. The serial number of the mixer was PM-87651, its service life was estimated at eight years with a trade-in value of $720, and it was assigned plant asset No. 556-3.

Dec. 31 Recorded straight-line depreciation on the plant equipment for 1991.

Required

1. Open general ledger accounts for Plant Equipment and for Accumulated Depreciation, Plant Equipment. Prepare a subsidiary plant asset record card for each item of equipment purchased.

2. Prepare general journal entries to record the transactions and post to the proper general ledger and subsidiary ledger accounts.

3. Prove the December 31, 1991, balances of the Plant Equipment and Accumulated Depreciation, Plant Equipment accounts by preparing a list showing the cost and accumulated depreciation on each item of plant equipment owned by Brady Salvage Company on that date.

Problem 10–3
Real estate costs and partial year's depreciation
(L. O. 1, 2, 3)

In early 1991, Angara Company paid $1,207,500 for real estate that included a tract of land on which two buildings were located. The plan was to demolish Building One and build a new store in its place. Building Two was to be used as a company office and was appraised to have a value of $341,250, with a useful life of 15 years and a $26,250 salvage value. A lighted parking lot near Building Two had improvements valued at $136,500 that were expected to last another 10 years and have no salvage value. In its existing condition, the tract of land was estimated to have a value of $887,250.

Angara Company incurred the following additional costs:

Cost to demolish Building One	$ 131,250
Cost to landscape new building site.	42,000
Cost to build new building (Building Three), having a useful life of 30 years and a $157,500 salvage value . . .	1,575,000
Cost of new land improvements near Building Three, which have a 15-year useful life and no salvage value . .	183,750

Required

1. Prepare a form having the following column headings: Land, Building Two, Building Three, Land Improvements Two, and Land Improvements Three. Allocate the costs incurred by Angara Company to the appropriate columns and total each column.

2. Prepare a single journal entry dated March 1 to record all of the costs incurred, assuming they were all paid in cash.

3. Prepare December 31 adjusting entries to record depreciation for the 10 months of 1991 during which the assets were in use. Use sum-of-the-

years'-digits depreciation for the newly constructed Building Three and Land Improvements Three and straight-line depreciation for Building Two and Land Improvements Two.

Problem 10–4
Plant asset costs and depreciation.
(L. O. 1, 2, 3)

Baku Company recently negotiated a lump-sum purchase of several assets from a bus dealer who was planning to change locations. The purchase was completed on October 31, 1990, at a total cash price of $624,000 and included a garage with land and certain land improvements and a new heavy, general-purpose truck. The estimated market values of the assets were: garage, $429,000; land, $132,000; land improvements, $66,000; and truck, $33,000.

Required

1. Prepare a schedule to allocate the lump-sum purchase price to the separate assets that were purchased. Also present the general journal entry to record the purchase.
2. Calculate the 1991 depreciation expense on the garage using the sum-of-the-years'-digits method and assuming a 12-year life and a $21,600 salvage value.
3. Calculate the 1990 depreciation expense on the land improvements assuming a 10-year life and double-declining-balance depreciation.
4. The truck is in a 10% class for tax purposes and is expected to last five years and have a salvage value of $2,400. Prepare a schedule showing each year's depreciation on the truck, assuming (*a*) five-year straight-line depreciation and (*b*) double-declining-balance depreciation.

Problem 10–5
Recording cost, depreciation, and sale of plant assets
(L. O. 1, 3, 5)

On October 27, 1988, a company made a lump-sum purchase of two machines from another company that was going out of business. The machines cost $109,350 and were placed in use on November 3, 1988. This additional information about the machines is available:

Machine No.	Appraised Value	Salvage Value	Estimated Life	Installation Cost	Depreciation Method
1	$54,000	$2,700	4 years	$1,350	Sum-of-the-years' digits
2	67,500	4,500	4 years	2,250	Double-declining balance

Depreciation was taken on the machines at the end of 1988, 1989, and 1990; and during the first week in January 1991, the company decided to sell and replace them. Consequently, on January 8, 1991, it sold Machine 1 for $10,500, and on January 9 it sold Machine 2 for $20,250.

Required
Prepare a form with the following columnar headings:

Machine No.	1988 Depreciation	1989 Depreciation	1990 Depreciation	1991 Depreciation	1992 Depreciation

Enter the machine numbers and the amounts of depreciation that would be taken each calendar year if the machines had been used throughout their four-year useful lives.

Alternate Problems

Problem 10–1A
Alternative depreciation methods; retirement of plant assets
(L. O. 2, 3, 5)

Part 1. FlatIrons Company purchased and installed a new machine that cost $195,000, had a five-year life, and an estimated $27,300 salvage value. Management estimated that the machine would produce 120,000 units of product during its life. Actual production of units of product was as follows: year 1, 16,800; year 2, 26,400; year 3, 24,000; year 4, 22,800; and year 5, 30,000.

Required

1. Prepare a calculation showing the number of dollars of this machine's cost that should be charged to depreciation over its five-year life.
2. Prepare a form with the following column headings:

Year	Straight Line	Units of Production	Declining Balance	Sum-of-the-Years' Digits

Then show the depreciation for each year and the total depreciation for the machine under each depreciation method. Use twice the straight-line rate for the declining-balance method.

Part 2. On January 9, Gilman Company purchased a used machine for $68,400. The next day it was repaired at a cost of $8,100 and was mounted on a new cradle that cost $6,300. It was estimated the machine would be used for three years and would then have a $10,800 salvage value. Depreciation was to be charged on a straight-line basis. A full year's depreciation was charged on December 31 of the first and the second years of the machine's use; and on March 29 of its third year of use, the machine was retired from service.

Required

1. Prepare general journal entries to record the purchase of the machine, the cost of repairing it, and its installation. Assume cash was paid in each case.
2. Prepare entries to record depreciation on the machine at the end of the first and second years and on March 29 of the third year.
3. Prepare entries to record the retirement of the machine under each of the following unrelated assumptions: (*a*) the machine was sold for $35,250; (*b*) it was sold for $24,150; and (*c*) it was destroyed in a fire, and the insurance company paid $22,050 in full settlement of the loss claim.

Problem 10–2A
Plant asset records
(L. O. 2, 4)

Parker Lewis Company completed the following transactions involving plant assets:

1990
Jan. 2 Purchased on credit from Southwest Equipment an electric packer priced at $19,875. The serial number of the packer was S-67422, its service life was estimated at five years with a trade-in value of $1,875, and it was assigned plant asset No. 420-1.

Apr. 4   Purchased on credit from Southwest Equipment a Donen vibrator priced at $30,705. The serial number of the vibrator was S-33246, its service life was estimated at six years with a trade-in value of $2,625, and it was assigned plant asset No. 430-2.

Dec. 31   Recorded straight-line depreciation on the plant equipment for 1990.

1991

Nov. 3   Sold the Donen vibrator to Cement Products for $18,750 cash.

7   Purchased a new Supermix vibrator from Stonework Equipment for $27,000. The serial number of the vibrator was CS-83215, its service life was estimated at eight years with a trade-in value of $3,600, and it was assigned plant asset No. 430-3.

Dec. 31   Recorded straight-line depreciation on the plant equipment for 1991.

Required

1. Open general ledger accounts for Plant Equipment and for Accumulated Depreciation, Plant Equipment. Prepare a subsidiary plant asset record card for each item of equipment purchased.

2. Prepare general journal entries to record the transactions and post to the proper general ledger and subsidiary ledger accounts.

3. Prove the December 31, 1991, balances of the Plant Equipment and Accumulated Depreciation, Plant Equipment accounts by preparing a list showing the cost and accumulated depreciation on each item of plant equipment owned by Parker Lewis Company on that date.

Problem 10–3A
Real estate costs and partial year's depreciation
(L. O. 1, 2, 3)

In early 1991, Nobles Company paid $975,000 for real estate that included a tract of land on which two buildings were located. The plan was to demolish Building A and build a new store in its place. Building B was to be used as a company office and was appraised to have a value of $315,000, with a useful life of 20 years and a $45,000 salvage value. A lighted parking lot near Building B had improvements valued at $105,000 that were expected to last another five years and have no salvage value. In its existing condition, the tract of land was estimated to have a value of $630,000.

Nobles Company incurred the following additional costs:

Cost to demolish Building A	$ 71,250
Cost to landscape new building site	81,000
Cost to build new building (Building C), having a useful life of 25 years and a $75,000 salvage value	1,125,000
Cost of new land improvements near Building C, which have an 8-year useful life and no salvage value	187,500

Required

1. Prepare a form having the following column headings: Land, Building B, Building C, Land Improvements B, and Land Improvements C. Allocate the costs incurred by Nobles Company to the appropriate columns and total each column.

2. Prepare a single journal entry dated June 1 to record all of the costs incurred, assuming they were all paid in cash.

3. Prepare December 31 adjusting entries to record depreciation for the seven months of 1991 during which the assets were in use. Use sum-of-

the-years'-digits depreciation for the newly constructed Building C and Land Improvements C and straight-line depreciation for Building B and Land Improvements B.

Problem 10–4A
Plant asset costs and depreciation
(L. O. 1, 2, 3)

Willo Company recently negotiated a lump-sum purchase of several assets from a road equipment dealer who was planning to change locations. The purchase was completed on September 30, 1990, at a total cash price of $870,000 and included a garage with land and certain land improvements and a new heavy, general-purpose truck. The estimated market values of the assets were: sales garage, $552,750; land, $331,650; land improvements, $100,500; and truck, $20,100.

Required

1. Prepare a schedule to allocate the lump-sum purchase price to the separate assets that were purchased. Also present the general journal entry to record the purchase.

2. Calculate the 1991 depreciation expense on the garage using the sum-of-the-years'-digits method and assuming a 15-year life and a $37,500 salvage value.

3. Calculate the 1990 depreciation expense on the land improvements assuming an eight-year life and double-declining-balance depreciation.

4. The truck is in a 10% class for tax purposes and is expected to last five years and have a salvage value of $2,250. Prepare a schedule showing each year's depreciation on the truck, assuming (*a*) five-year straight-line depreciation and (*b*) double-declining-balance depreciation.

Problem 10–5A
Recording cost, depreciation, and sale of plant assets
(L. O. 1, 3, 5)

On April 3, 1988, Locklin Company made a lump-sum purchase of two machines from another company that was going out of business. The machines cost $328,500 and were placed in use on April 6, 1988. This additional information about the machines is available:

Machine No.	Appraised Value	Salvage Value	Estimated Life	Installation Cost	Depreciation Method
1	$160,000	$ 8,000	4 years	$4,000	Sum-of-the-years' digits
2	200,000	12,000	4 years	6,500	Double-declining balance

Depreciation was taken on the machines at the end of 1988, 1989, and 1990; and during the first week in January 1991, the company decided to sell and replace them. Consequently, on January 5, 1991, it sold Machine 1 for $27,000, and on January 6 it sold Machine 2 for $60,750.

Required

Prepare a form with the following columnar headings:

Machine No.	1988 Depreciation	1989 Depreciation	1990 Depreciation	1991 Depreciation	1992 Depreciation

Enter the machine numbers and the amounts of depreciation that would be taken each year if the machines had been used throughout their four-year useful lives.

Provocative Problems

Provocative Problem 10–1
Fizicalle Company
(L. O. 1)

Fizicalle Company temporarily recorded the costs of a new plant in a summary account called Land and Buildings. Management has now asked you to examine this account and prepare any necessary entries to correct the account balances. In doing so, you find the following debits and credits to the account:

Debits

Jan.	4	Cost of land and buildings acquired for new plant site	$185,500
	12	Attorney's fee for title search	1,775
	25	Cost of wrecking old building on plant site.	17,000
Feb.	3	Six months' liability and fire insurance on new building	5,610
June	30	Payment to building contractor on completion of building.	705,000
July	3	Architect's fee for new building.	50,325
	7	City assessment for street improvements	12,150
	15	Cost of landscaping new plant site.	7,500
			$984,860

Credits

Jan.	27	Proceeds from sale of salvaged materials from old building	$ 3,750
July	3	Refund of one month's insurance premium	935
Dec.	31	Depreciation at 2 1/2% per year	21,000
	31	Balance	959,175
			$984,860

Your investigation suggests that 40 years is a reasonable life expectancy for a building of the type involved and that an assumption of zero salvage value is reasonable. To summarize your analysis, you decide to prepare a schedule with columns headed Date, Description, Total Amount, Land, Buildings, and Other Accounts and to enter the items found in the Land and Buildings account on the schedule, distributing the amounts to the proper columns. You should show credits on the schedule by enclosing the amounts in parentheses. Realizing that the accounts have not been closed, you should also draft any required correcting entry or entries. Assume that an account called Depreciation Expense, Land and Buildings was debited in recording the $21,000 of depreciation.

Provocative Problem 10–2
Rockwall and Stoneleigh Companies
(A Review Problem)

Rockwall Company and Stoneleigh Company are almost identical. Each began operations on January 1 of this year with $190,000 of equipment having an eight-year life and a $21,000 salvage value. Each purchased merchandise during the year as follows:

Jan.	1	315 units @ $400 per unit =	$126,000
Apr.	14	450 units @ $420 per unit =	189,000
June	24	675 units @ $435 per unit =	293,625
Nov.	6	350 units @ $500 per unit =	175,000
			$783,625

Now, on December 31 at the end of the first year, each has 440 units of merchandise in its ending inventory. However, Rockwall Company will use straight-line depreciation in arriving at its net income for the year, while Stoneleigh Company will use double-declining-balance depreciation. Also, Rockwall Company will use FIFO in costing its ending inventory, and Stoneleigh Company will use LIFO. The December 31 trial balances of the two concerns carried these amounts:

	Rockwall Company		Stoneleigh Company	
Cash	$ 18,375		$ 18,375	
Accounts receivable	42,000		42,000	
Equipment	190,000		190,000	
Accounts payable		$ 96,000		$ 96,000
H. Rockwall, capital		232,000		
M. Stoneleigh, capital				232,000
Sales		892,500		892,500
Purchases	783,625		783,625	
Salaries expense.	78,750		78,750	
Rent expense.	64,050		64,050	
Other cash expenses	43,700		43,700	
Totals	$1,220,500	$1,220,500	$1,220,500	$1,220,500

Required

Prepare an income statement for each company and a schedule accounting for the difference in their reported net incomes. Write a short answer to this question: Which, if either, of the companies is the more profitable and why?

Analytical and Review Problems

A&R Problem 10–1

At the last meeting of the executive committee of H. Fergus, Ltd., Pierre Lacroix, controller, was severely criticized by both President Fergus and George Taylor, vice president of production. The subject of criticism was in the recognition of periodic depreciation. President Fergus was unhappy with the fact that what he referred to as "a fictitious item" was deducted, resulting in depressed net income. In his words, "Depreciation is a fiction when the assets being depreciated are worth far more than we paid for them. What the controller is doing is unduly understating our net income. This in turn is detrimental to our shareholders because it results in the undervaluation of our shares on the market."

Vice President Taylor was equally adamant about the periodic depreciation charges; however, he came on from another side. He said, "Our maintenance people tell me that the level of maintenance is such that our plant and equipment will virtually last forever." He further stated that charging depreciation on top of maintenance expenses is double-counting—it seems reasonable to either charge maintenance or depreciation but not both.

The time taken by other pressing matters did not permit Lacroix to answer; instead, the controller was asked to prepare a report to the executive committee to deal with the issues raised by the president and vice president.

Required

The controller asks you, his assistant, to prepare the required report.

A&R Problem 10–2

The vice president of finance of Brant, Ltd., presented you with the following contentious accounting issue facing the company:

> Brant has not in the past recorded depreciation on its fixed assets. The president noted this fact in last year's report to the shareholders as follows: ''Our fixed assets are increasing, not decreasing in value. The recording of a fictitious expense (depreciation) will make our statements misleading.'' The Board of Directors share in the president's opinion; however, they agreed to have depreciation recorded this year in order to obtain an unqualified opinion.

Required

Evaluate the president's statement in the light of applicable GAAP.

A&R Problem 10–3

The following amounts would be charged in the second year of the asset's service life by three different methods:

		Method	
Year	a	b	c
1			
2	$45,000	$54,000	$60,000
3			
4			
5			

Required

1. Identify the three methods used and complete the table showing depreciation expense by each method for each year. Assume a five-year service life with no salvage value.

2. Assuming that income before depreciation is $25,000 for each of the five years, show the amount of income after depreciation for the period covered by the assets. Briefly explain the impact which the depreciation method may have on reported net income for a business.

A&R Problem 10–4

The Load Trucking Company purchased a large earth-mover four years ago at a cost of $161,000. At that time it was estimated that the economic life of the equipment would be 12 years and that its ultimate salvage value would be $5,000.

Assuming the company uses straight-line depreciation, state whether each of the following events requires a revision of the original depreciation rate, with reasons for your answer:

a. Due to the persistent inflation, the present replacement cost of the same type of equipment is $196,000.

b. Because of the higher replacement cost (as described in [a] above) the ultimate salvage value is now estimated at $10,000.

c. The company, in connection with having its line of credit increased, was required by the bank to have the assets appraised. The earth-mover was estimated to have a current value of $128,000.

d. At the time the appraisal was made in (*c*) above, it was determined that technological change was progressing more slowly than originally estimated and that the earth-mover would probably remain in service for 15 years with the ultimate salvage value as originally estimated at the end of 12 years.

A&R Problem 10–5

Two companies, RB Ltd., and JE Ltd., purchased identical assets costing $600,000 at the beginning of 1990. RB Ltd. depreciated its assets on a straight-line basis assuming a $20,000 salvage value and a useful life of 10 years. JE Ltd. decided to use the declining-balance method also assuming a useful life of 10 years.

Required

1. Which method (the one used by RB or by JE) is correct and should be used?
2. What will be the difference, if any, in the reported incomes of the two companies in each of years 1990, 1991, and 1992 assuming that their net incomes, before depreciation, are identical?
3. Prepare the balance sheet figures with respect to the assets purchased for RB Ltd. and JE Ltd. as at the end of 1992.

11 Plant and Equipment, Natural Resources, and Intangible Assets

In this chapter, we continue to examine the accounting issues related to property, plant, and equipment. In studying the chapter, you will learn how to account for disposals of plant assets, how to calculate depreciation when new information causes you to revise depreciation rates, and how to account for the costs of maintaining or improving plant assets. In addition, the chapter introduces you to the issues of accounting for natural resources and intangible assets.

Learning Objectives

After studying Chapter 11, you should be able to:

1. Prepare entries to record the sale or discarding of a plant asset.
2. Prepare entries to record the exchange of plant assets and the recognition of book gains and losses.
3. Make the calculations and prepare the entries to account for revisions in depreciation rates.
4. Make the calculations and prepare the entries to account for plant asset repairs and betterments.
5. Prepare entries to account for natural resources and for intangible assets, including entries to record depletion and amortization.
6. Define or explain the words and phrases listed in the chapter Glossary.

Plant Asset Disposals

Prepare entries to record
the sale or discarding of a
plant asset.
(L. O. 1)

Sooner or later, plant assets wear out, become obsolete, or become inadequate. When this occurs, the assets are discarded, sold, or traded in on new assets. The entry to record the disposal of a plant asset depends on which action is taken.

Discarding a Plant Asset

When an asset's accumulated depreciation is equal to its cost, the asset is said to be fully depreciated. If a fully depreciated asset is discarded, the entry to record the disposal is:

Jan.	7	Accumulated Depreciation, Machinery	1,500.00	
		Machinery		1,500.00
		Discarded a fully depreciated machine.		

Sometimes a fully depreciated asset is kept in use. In such situations, the asset's cost and accumulated depreciation should not be removed from the accounts; they should remain on the books until the asset is sold, traded, or discarded. Otherwise, the accounts do not show its continued existence. However, no additional depreciation should be recorded, since the reason for recording depreciation is to charge an asset's cost to depreciation expense. The total amount of depreciation expense related to an asset must not exceed the cost of the asset.

Sometimes an asset is discarded before being fully depreciated. For example, suppose an error was made in estimating the service life of a $1,000 machine, and it becomes worthless and is discarded after having only $800 of depreciation recorded against it. In such a situation, there is a loss, and the entry to record the disposal is:

Jan.	10	Loss on Disposal of Machinery	200.00	
		Accumulated Depreciation, Machinery	800.00	
		Machinery		1,000.00
		Discarded a worthless machine.		

Discarding a Damaged Plant Asset

Occasionally, before the end of its service life, a plant asset is wrecked or destroyed in an accident. For example, a machine that cost $900 and that had been depreciated $400 was totally destroyed in a fire. If the loss was partially covered by insurance and the insurance company paid $350 to settle the loss claim, the entry to record the machine's destruction is:

Jan.	12	Cash	350.00	
		Loss from Fire	150.00	
		Accumulated Depreciation, Machinery	400.00	
		Machinery		900.00
		To record the destruction of machinery and the receipt of insurance compensation.		

If the machine were uninsured, the entry to record its destruction would not have a debit to Cash, and the loss from fire would be $500.

Selling a Plant Asset

If a plant asset is sold and the selling price exceeds the asset's book value, there is a gain. And if the price is less than book value, there is a loss. For example, assume that a machine that cost $5,000 and had been depreciated $4,000 is sold for a price in excess of its book value, say, for $1,200. In this case, there is a gain, and the entry to record the sale is:

Jan.	4	Cash	1,200.00	
		Accumulated Depreciation, Machinery	4,000.00	
		Machinery		5,000.00
		Gain on the Sale of Plant Assets		200.00
		Sold a machine at a price in excess of book value.		

However, if the machine is sold for $750, there is a $250 loss. The entry to record the sale is:

Jan.	4	Cash	750.00	
		Loss on the Sale of Plant Assets.	250.00	
		Accumulated Depreciation, Machinery	4,000.00	
		Machinery		5,000.00
		Sold a machine at a price below book value.		

Exchanging Plant Assets

Prepare entries to record the exchange of plant assets and the recognition of book gains and losses. (L. O. 2)

Some plant assets are sold at the end of their useful lives. Others, such as machinery, automobiles, and office equipment, are commonly exchanged for new assets that are similar in purpose. In such exchanges, a trade-in allowance is normally received on the old asset, and the balance is paid in cash. When a plant asset is exchanged for a similar plant asset, a book loss is experienced when the trade-in allowance is less than the book value of the traded asset. A book gain results from a trade-in allowance that exceeds the book value of the traded asset.

Recognizing a Book Loss

To illustrate recognition of a book loss on an exchange of plant assets, assume that a machine that cost $18,000 and has been depreciated $15,000 is traded in on a new machine that has a $21,000 cash price. A $1,000 trade-in allowance is received, and the $20,000 balance is paid in cash. Under these assumptions, the book value of the old machine is $3,000, calculated as follows:

Cost of old machine.	$18,000
Less accumulated depreciation	15,000
Book value.	$ 3,000

Since the $1,000 trade-in allowance results in a $2,000 loss on the exchange, the transaction should be recorded as follows:

Jan.	5	Machinery.	21,000.00	
		Loss on Exchange of Machinery	2,000.00	
		Accumulated Depreciation, Machinery	15,000.00	
		Machinery		18,000.00
		Cash		20,000.00
		Exchanged old machine and cash for a		
		similar machine.		

The $21,000 debit to Machinery puts the new machine in the accounts at its cash price. The debit to Loss on Exchange of Machinery records the loss. The old machine is removed from the accounts with the $15,000 debit to Accumulated Depreciation and the $18,000 credit to Machinery.

Recognizing a Book Gain

To illustrate recognition of a book gain on an exchange of plant assets, assume that in acquiring the $21,000 machine of the previous section, a $4,500 trade-in allowance, rather than a $1,000 trade-in allowance, was received, and a $16,500 balance was paid in cash. The transaction is recorded as follows:

Jan.	5	Machinery.	21,000.00	
		Accumulated Depreciation, Machinery	15,000.00	
		Machinery		18,000.00
		Cash		16,500.00
		Gain on Exchange of Machinery.		1,500.00

Notice that the new machine is recorded in the books at its equivalent cash price. When assets are exchanged for newer or more efficient assets, the accountant may need to apply judgement in determining how much of the trade-in amount is, in fact, a discount on the new asset and how much is a reflection of the old asset's true value. The determination of the equivalent cash price of the asset acquired will provide guidance in calculating the proper gain or loss on the exchange.

Nonrecognition of a Book Loss or Gain

In the previous two sections, recognition of book loss and book gain was discussed and illustrated. Such accounting procedure is dictated by adherence to the cost principle; that is, recording the new plant asset at the cash equivalent amount, the price that would be paid without a trade-in. In the illustrations above, $21,000 was given as the new machine's cash price. There are times when the cash price of the new machine may not be readily available; however, the old machine may have a ready market at an easily determinable amount. In such cases the cash equivalent amount of the new machine would be the sum of cash paid and the fair value of the trade-in. Once the cash equivalent amount of the new machine is determined, the recording of the trade-in transaction is the same as illustrated in the previous sections.

Under Section 3830 of the *CICA Handbook,* a gain or loss on an exchange of similar assets would not be recognized. The new asset is recorded at an amount equal to the sum of the book value of the trade-in plus the cash paid. For example, an old typewriter that cost $500 was traded in at $50 on a new $600 typewriter, with the $550 difference being paid in cash. Depreciation on the old typewriter in the amount of $420 had been taken. In this case the old typewriter's book value is $80; and with the trade-in of $50, there was a $30 book loss on the exchange. In accordance with Section 3830 the following method may be used in recording the exchange.

Jan.	7	Office Equipment.	630.00	
		Accumulated Depreciation, Office Equipment	420.00	
		Office Equipment		500.00
		Cash		550.00
		Traded an old typewriter and cash for a new typewriter.		

The $630 at which the new typewriter is taken into the accounts is calculated as follows:

Book value of old typewriter ($500 less $420)	$ 80
Cash paid ($600 less the $50 trade-in allowance) . .	550
Cost basis of the new typewriter.	$630

In other cases, when there is an immaterial loss on an exchange, the violation of the cost principle is permissible under the *principle of materiality.* Under this principle an adherence to any accounting principle is not required when the cost to adhere is proportionally great and the lack of adherence does not materially affect reported periodic net income. In this case, failing to record the $30 loss on the exchange would not materially affect the average company's statements.

Revising Depreciation Rates

Make the calculations and prepare the entries to account for revisions in depreciation rates. (L. O. 3)

Since depreciation must be based on an asset's useful life, which is an estimate about the future, you should understand that depreciation is an estimate. Furthermore, you should be alert to the possibility that during the life of an asset, new information will show that the original estimate of useful life was wrong. The question that arises is: If your estimate of an asset's useful life changes, what should be done about it? The answer is that the new estimate of useful life should be used to calculate depreciation in the remaining periods of the asset's life. In other words, you correct the estimate by spreading the remaining cost to be depreciated over its remaining (revised) useful life.

For example, assume that seven years ago a machine was purchased at a cost of $10,500. At that time, the machine was estimated to have a 10-year life with a $500 salvage value. Therefore, it was depreciated at the rate of $1,000 per year [($10,500 − $500) ÷ 10 = $1,000]. At the beginning of the asset's eighth year, its book value is $3,500, calculated as follows:

Cost	$10,500
Less seven years' accumulated depreciation . .	7,000
Book value	$ 3,500

Assume that at the beginning of its eighth year, the estimated number of years remaining in this machine's useful life is changed from three to five years with no change in salvage value. Therefore, depreciation for each of the machine's remaining years should be calculated as follows:

$$\frac{\text{Book value} - \text{Salvage value}}{\text{Remaining useful life}} = \frac{\$3,500 - \$500}{5 \text{ years}} = \$600 \text{ per year}$$

And $600 of depreciation should be recorded on the machine at the end of the eighth and each succeeding year in its life.

Since this asset was depreciated at the rate of $1,000 per year for the first seven years, you might argue that depreciation expense was overstated during the first seven years. However, depreciation is understood to be an estimate based on the best information available at the time the depreciation is taken.

Changing the useful life of a plant asset is an example of a **change in an accounting estimate.** "Estimating . . . requires the exercise of judgement and reappraisal as new events occur, as more experience is acquired, or as additional information is obtained."[1] Therefore, generally accepted accounting principles require that changes in accounting estimates, such as this change in estimated useful life, be reflected only in future financial statements, not by attempts to correct past statements.

---

[1] *CICA Handbook* (Toronto: The Canadian Institute of Chartered Accountants) par. 1506.21.

Ordinary and Extraordinary Repairs

Make the calculations and prepare the entries to account for plant asset repairs and betterments. (L. O. 4)

Repairs made to keep an asset in its normal good operating condition are described as **ordinary repairs.** For example, to keep a wood-frame building in good condition, you must periodically have it repainted and have its roof repaired. Also, a machine must be cleaned, oiled, and adjusted, and any worn small parts must be replaced. Such repairs and maintenance are necessary, and their cost should appear on the current income statement as an expense.

Extraordinary repairs are major repairs made not to keep an asset in its normal good state of repair but to increase its overall service potential by making it significantly more efficient or by significantly increasing its service life. The current thought on these types of expenditures is that they should be debited to the asset's account and depreciated over the asset's remaining life. For example, a machine was purchased for $8,000 and depreciated under the assumption it would last eight years and have no salvage value. As a result, at the end of the machine's sixth year, its book value is $2,000 calculated as follows:

Cost of machine	$8,000
Less six years' accumulated depreciation . .	6,000
Book value	$2,000

Assume that, at the beginning of the machine's seventh year, it is given a major overhaul that extends its estimated useful life three years beyond the eight originally estimated. The $2,100 cost of the overhaul should be recorded as follows:

Jan.	12	Machinery.	2,100.00	
		Cash (or Accounts Payable).		2,100.00
		To record extraordinary repairs.		

In addition, depreciation for each of the five years remaining in the machine's life should be calculated as follows:

	Before Extraordinary Repairs	Effect of Extraordinary Repairs	After Extraordinary Repairs
Cost	$8,000	+$2,100	$10,100
Accumulated depreciation	6,000		6,000
Book value.	$2,000	+ 2,100	$ 4,100
Annual depreciation expense for remaining five years ($4,100/5)			$ 820

And, if the machine remains in use for five years after the major overhaul, the five annual depreciation charges of $820 each will exactly write off its new book value which includes the extraordinary repairs. As you will notice in the next section, the accounting treatment of the cost of extraordinary repairs and betterments is the same.

Betterments

A **betterment** involves modifying an existing plant asset to make it more efficient, usually by replacing part of the asset with an improved or superior part. The result of a betterment is a more efficient or more productive asset, but not necessarily one that has a longer life. For example, if the manual controls on a machine are replaced with automatic controls, the cost of labor may be reduced.

When a betterment is made, its cost should be debited to the improved asset's account, for example, the Machinery account, and depreciated over the remaining service life of the asset. Also, the cost and applicable depreciation of the replaced asset portion should be removed from the accounts.

Revenue and Capital Expenditures

The value or asset obtained by a **revenue expenditure** expires before the end of the current accounting period. As a result, a revenue expenditure appears on the current income statement as an expense that is deducted from the period's revenues. Expenditures for ordinary repairs, rent, and salaries are examples. Expenditures for betterments and for extraordinary repairs, on the other hand, are examples of what are called **capital expenditures** or **balance sheet expenditures.** They benefit future periods and should appear on the balance sheet as asset increases.

You must be careful to distinguish between capital and revenue expenditures when transactions are recorded because if errors are made, such errors often affect a number of accounting periods. For instance, an expenditure for a betterment initially recorded in error as an expense overstates expenses in the year of the error and understates net income. Also, since the cost of a betterment should be depreciated over the remaining useful life of the bettered asset, depreciation expense of future periods is understated.

Natural Resources

Prepare entries to account for natural resources and for intangible assets, including entries to record depletion and amortization.
(L. O. 5)

Natural resources such as standing timber, mineral deposits, and oil reserves are known as wasting assets. In their natural state, they represent inventories that will be converted into a product by cutting, mining, or pumping. However, until cut, mined, or pumped, they are noncurrent assets and commonly appear on a balance sheet under captions such as "Timberlands," "Mineral deposits," or "Oil reserves." Sometimes, this caption appears under the "Property, plant, and equipment" category of assets, and sometimes it is shown as a separate category.

Natural resources are accounted for at cost and appear on the balance sheet at cost less accumulated **depletion.** The amount such assets are depleted each year by cutting, mining, or pumping is commonly calculated on a units-of-production basis. For example, if a mineral deposit has an estimated 500,000 tons of available ore and is purchased for $500,000, the depletion charge per ton of ore mined is $1. Furthermore, if 85,000 tons are mined during the first year, the depletion charge for the year is $85,000 and is recorded as follows:

Dec.	31	Depletion of Mineral Deposit	85,000.00	
		Accumulated Depletion, Mineral Deposit		85,000.00
		To record depletion of the mineral deposit.		

On the balance sheet prepared at the end of the first year, the mineral deposit should appear at its $500,000 cost less accumulated depletion of $85,000. If the 85,000 tons of ore are sold by the end of the first year, the entire $85,000 depletion charge reaches the income statement as the depletion cost of the ore mined and sold. However, if a portion remains unsold at the year-end, the depletion cost of the unsold ore is carried forward on the balance sheet as part of the cost of the unsold ore inventory, a current asset.

Often, machinery must be installed or a building constructed in order to exploit a natural resource. The costs of such assets should be depreciated over the life of the natural resource with annual depreciation charges that are in proportion to the annual depletion charges. For example, if a machine is installed in a mine and one eighth of the mine's ore is removed during a year, one eighth of the amount the machine is to be depreciated should be recorded as a cost of the ore mined.

Intangible Assets

Assets that have no physical existence but that represent certain legal rights and economic relationships beneficial to the owner are called **intangible assets**. Patents, copyrights, leaseholds, goodwill, trademarks, and organization costs are examples. Notes and accounts receivable are also intangible in nature. However, these appear on the balance sheet as current assets rather than under the intangible assets classification.

When an intangible asset is purchased, it is recorded at cost. Thereafter, its cost must be systematically **amortized** or written off to expense over the asset's estimated useful life. Normally, the amortization period of an intangible asset should not exceed 40 years.

Amortization of intangible assets is similar to depreciation; both are processes of cost allocation. However, amortization of intangibles is limited to the straight-line method unless it can be demonstrated that another method is more appropriate. Also, while depreciation is recorded in a contra account (Accumulated Depreciation), amortization of intangible asset cost traditionally is credited directly to the asset account. As a result, intangible assets are reported in the balance sheet at that portion of cost not previously written off. Normally, intangible assets are shown in a separate balance section that follows immediately after the plant and equipment section.

Patents

The federal government grants **patents** to encourage the invention of new machines and mechanical devices. A patent gives its owner the exclusive right to manufacture and sell a patented machine or device for 17 years. When patent rights are purchased, all costs of acquiring the rights may be debited to an account called Patents. Also, the costs of a successful lawsuit in defense of a patent may be debited to this account.

A patent gives its owner exclusive rights to the patented device for 17 years. However, its cost should be amortized or written off over a shorter period if its useful life is estimated to be less than 17 years. For example, if a patent that cost $25,000 has an estimated useful life of 10 years, the following adjusting entry is made at the end of each year in the patent's life to write off $\frac{1}{10}$ of its cost:

Dec.	31	Amortization of Patents	2,500.00	
		Patents.		2,500.00
		To write off $\frac{1}{10}$ of patent costs.		

The entry's debit causes $2,500 of patent costs to appear on the annual income statement as one of the costs of the patented product manufactured. The credit directly reduces the balance of the Patents account. Note that the amount of amortization is written off directly to the Patents account.

Copyrights

A **copyright** is granted by the federal government and in most cases gives its owner the exclusive right to publish and sell a musical, literary, or artistic work for the life of the composer, author, or artist and for 50 years thereafter. Most copyrights actually have value for a much shorter time, and their costs should be amortized over the shorter period. Often, the only cost of a copyright is the fee paid to the Copyright Office. If this fee is not material, it may be charged directly to an expense account. Otherwise, the copyright costs should be capitalized, and the periodic amortization of a copyright should be charged to Amortization Expense, Copyrights.

Leaseholds

Property is rented under a contract called a **lease.** The person or company that owns the property and grants the lease is called the **lessor.** The person or company that secures the right to possess and use the property is called the **lessee.** The rights granted to the lessee under the lease are called **leasehold.**

Some leases require no advance payment from the lessee but do require monthly rent payments. Usually in such cases, a Leasehold account is not needed, and the monthly payments are debited to a Rent Expense account. Sometimes, a long-term lease is written so that the last year's rent must be paid in advance at the time the lease is signed. When this occurs, the last year's advance payment is debited to the Leasehold account. It remains there until the last year of the lease. At that time the Leasehold balance is transferred to Rent Expense.

Often, a long-term lease, one for 20 or 25 years, becomes valuable after a few years because its required rent payments are much less than current rentals for identical property. In such cases, the increase in value of the lease should not be entered on the books since no extra cost was incurred to acquire it. However, if the property is subleased and a cash payment is made for the rights under the old lease, the new tenant should debit the payment to a Leasehold account and write it off as additional rent expense over the remaining life of the lease.

Leasehold Improvements

Long-term leases often require the lessee to pay for any alterations or improvements to the leased property, such as new partitions and store fronts. Normally, the costs of **leasehold improvements** are debited to an account called Leasehold Improvements. Also, since the improvements become part of the property and revert to the lessor at the end of the lease, you must amortize the cost of the improvements over the life of the lease or the life of the improvements, whichever is shorter. The amortization entry commonly debits Rent Expense and credits Leasehold Improvements.

Goodwill

The term **goodwill** has a special meaning in accounting. Accountants say that *a business has goodwill when its rate of expected future earnings is greater than the rate of earnings normally realized in its industry*. Above-average earnings and the existence of goodwill may be demonstrated as follows with Companies A and B, both of which are in the same industry:

	Company A	Company B
Net assets (other than goodwill).	$100,000	$100,000
Normal rate of return in this industry . .	10%	10%
Normal return on net assets.	$ 10,000	$ 10,000
Expected net income	10,000	15,000
Expected earnings above average . . .	$ –0–	$ 5,000

Company B is expected to have an above-average earnings rate compared to its industry and is said to have goodwill. This goodwill may be the result of excellent customer relations, the location of the business, monopolistic privileges, superior management, or a combination of factors. Furthermore, a prospective investor would normally be willing to pay more for Company B than for Company A if the investor agreed the extra earnings rate should be expected. Thus, goodwill is an asset that has value.

Accountants agree that goodwill should not be recorded unless it is purchased. This normally occurs only when a business is acquired or sold in its entirety. Before a business is to be purchased, the buyer and seller may estimate the amount of goodwill in several different ways. Three examples follow:

1. The buyer and seller may place an arbitrary value on the goodwill of a business being sold. For instance, a seller may be willing to sell a business that has an above-average earnings rate for $115,000, and a buyer may be willing to pay that amount. If they both agree that the net assets of the business other than its goodwill have a $100,000 value, they are arbitrarily valuing the goodwill at $15,000.

2. Goodwill may be valued at some multiple of the portion of expected earnings that is above average. For example, if a company is expected to have $5,000 each year in above-average earnings, its good-

will may be valued at, say, four times the portion of its earnings which are above average, or at $20,000. In this case, you may also say that the goodwill is valued at four years' above-average earnings. However, regardless of how it is described, this too is placing an arbitrary value on the goodwill.

3. The portion of a company's earnings that is above average may be capitalized in order to place a value on its goodwill. For example, assume that a business is expected to have earnings each year that are $5,000 above average and the normal rate of return on invested capital in this company's industry is 10%. If the excess earnings are capitalized at 10%, goodwill is valued at $50,000 ($5,000 ÷ 10% = $50,000). Note that this method values the goodwill at the amount that must be invested at the normal rate of return in order to earn the extra $5,000 each year ($50,000 × 10% = $5,000). This is a satisfactory method if the extra earnings are expected to continue for all future periods. However, that may not happen. Therefore, extra earnings are sometimes capitalized at a rate that is higher than the normal rate of the industry. For example, in the present case, assume a capitalization rate that is twice the normal rate, or 20%. If the extra earnings are capitalized at 20%, the goodwill is valued at $25,000 ($5,000 ÷ 20% = $25,000).

There are other ways to think about the amount that should be assigned to goodwill. Nevertheless, in the final analysis, goodwill is always valued at the price a seller is willing to accept and a buyer is willing to pay.

Trademarks and Trade Names

Companies often design a unique symbol or select a unique name that they use in marketing their products. Sometimes, the ownership and exclusive right to use such a **trademark** or **trade name** can be established simply by demonstrating that the company has used the trademark or trade name before other businesses. However, ownership generally can be established more definitely by registering the trademark or trade name with the Patent Office. The cost of developing, maintaining, or enhancing the value of a trademark or trade name, perhaps through advertising, should be charged to expense in the period or periods incurred. However, if a trademark or trade name is purchased, the purchase cost should be debited to an asset account and amortized over its estimated useful life.

Amortization of Intangibles

Some intangibles, such as patents, copyrights, and leaseholds, have limited useful lives that are determined by law, contract, or the nature of the asset. Other intangibles, such as goodwill, trademarks, and trade names, have indeterminable lives. In general, the cost of intangible assets should be amortized over the periods expected to be benefited by their use, which in no case is longer than their legal existence. However, as we stated earlier, the amortization period of intangible assets normally should not be longer than 40 years. This limitation applies even if the life of the asset (for example, goodwill) may continue indefinitely.

Summary of the Chapter in Terms of Learning Objectives

1. When a plant asset is discarded or sold, the cost and accumulated depreciation are removed from the accounts. Any cash proceeds are recorded and compared to the book value at the date of sale or retirement to determine the gain or loss.

2. When a plant asset is exchanged for a new asset that is similar in purpose, the book value of the old asset is compared to its market value or trade-in allowance to determine whether the exchange results in a gain or loss. The new asset is recorded at its equivalent cash price, and the gain or loss on the exchange is recognized.

If the assets exchanged are similar and the gain or loss is not material in amount, then the new asset may be recorded at the book value of the asset given up plus or minus any cash paid or received, and no gain or loss is recognized.

3. When the estimated useful life of a plant asset is changed, the remaining cost to be depreciated is spread over the remaining (revised) useful life of the asset. The remaining cost to be depreciated is the original cost less the accumulated depreciation to date and less the estimated salvage value.

4. The cost of ordinary repairs is charged to expense of the current period in which the expense is incurred. Extraordinary repairs extend the useful life of a plant asset and are capitalized by debiting the asset account. Betterments make a plant asset more efficient and also are debited to the asset account.

5. The cost of a natural resource is recorded in an asset account. Then, depletion of the natural resource is recorded by allocating the cost to expense according to a units-of-production basis. The depletion is credited to an accumulated depletion account. Intangible assets are recorded at the cost incurred to purchase the assets. The allocation of intangible asset cost to expense is done on a straight-line basis and is called amortization. Normally, amortization is credited directly to the asset account.

Demonstration Problem

On January 13, 1989, the Maxwell Company purchased seven identical machines and paid $147,000 cash to the seller. The service life of each machine was predicted to be five years, and the salvage value of each was estimated at $1,000. All seven machines were placed into service at once. Depreciation is based on the assumption that machines are purchased and sold on the first of the month nearest the actual dates of purchase and sale. The straight-line method is used. Prepare entries to record each of the following transactions:

a. Machine No. 1 was used until July 7, 1994, when it was retired from service and sold for $1,000 cash. Record depreciation on Machine No. 1 for 1994 and record the sale of the machine.

b. Machine No. 2 was used until December 20, 1991, when it was stolen. On December 24, the insurance company paid Maxwell $4,800 cash, which equalled the estimate of the asset's fair value. Record depreciation on Machine No. 2 for 1991 and record the settlement with the insurance company.

c. Machine No. 3 was used until January 4, 1992, at which time it was sold for $13,000 cash. Record the sale of Machine No. 3.

d. Machine No. 4 was used until December 21, 1992, at which time it was traded in on Machine No. 8, with a cash payment of $20,000. Machine No. 8 had a cash price of $22,000. Record depreciation on Machine No. 4 for 1992 and record the exchange for Machine No. 8.

e. Machine No. 5 was used until December 23, 1992, when it was traded in on Machine No. 9, with a cash payment of $18,000. Machine No. 9 had a cash price of $25,500. Record depreciation on Machine No. 5 for 1992 and record the exchange for Machine No. 9.

f. Machine No. 6 was used until January 9, 1993, at which time it received a major overhaul which extended its useful life until the end of 1995 and left its expected salvage value at $1,000. The cost of the overhaul was $7,100, which was paid in cash. Record the overhaul, compute the machine's book value after the overhaul, and record depreciation for 1993.

g. Machine No. 7 was used only as a backup for the other six machines. Because the machines were more dependable than expected, Machine No. 7 did not deteriorate as quickly as the other machines. Therefore, during 1992, the company manager predicted that its useful life would probably extend until the end of 1996. The estimated salvage value was unchanged. Record depreciation expense on Machine No. 7 for 1992.

Solution to Demonstration Problem

For Machines Nos. 1–7, the initial cost of each is $147,000 ÷ 7 = $21,000. Annual depreciation for each machine is ($21,000 − $1,000) ÷ 5 = $4,000.

a.
	1994				
	July	7	Cash	1,000.00	
			Accumulated Depreciation, Machine No. 1	20,000.00	
			Machine No. 1		21,000.00
			($21,000 − $20,000 = $1,000).		

Machine No. 1 was fully depreciated before it was retired and was sold for its salvage value. Therefore, there was no gain or loss on the disposal.

b.
	1991				
	Dec.	20	Depreciation Expense.	4,000.00	
			Accumulated Depreciation, Machine No. 2 . .		4,000.00
		24	Cash	4,800.00	
			Accumulated Depreciation, Machine No. 2	12,000.00	
			Loss on Theft	4,200.00	
			Machine No. 2		21,000.00
			$21,000 − $12,000 = $9,000.		
			$9,000 − $4,800 = $4,200.		

c.

	1992				
	Jan.	4	Cash	13,000.00	
			Accumulated Depreciation, Machine No. 3	12,000.00	
			Gain on Disposal.		4,000.00
			Machine No. 3		21,000.00
			$21,000 - $12,000 = $9,000.$		
			$13,000 - $9,000 = $4,000.$		

d.

	1992				
	Dec.	21	Depreciation Expense.	4,000.00	
			Accumulated Depreciation, Machine No. 4 . .		4,000.00
		21	Machine No. 8.	22,000.00	
			Accumulated Depreciation, Machine No. 4	16,000.00	
			Loss on Trade.	3,000.00	
			Cash.		20,000.00
			Machine No. 4		21,000.00
			$4,000 \times 4 = $16,000$		

e.

	1992				
	Dec.	23	Depreciation Expense.	4,000.00	
			Accumulated Depreciation, Machine No. 5. . .		4,000.00
		23	Machine No. 9.	25,500.00	
			Accumulated Depreciation, Machine No. 5	16,000.00	
			Cash.		18,000.00
			Machine No. 5		21,000.00
			Gain on Trade		2,500.00

f.

	1993				
	Jan.	9	Machine No. 6.	7,100.00	
			Cash.		7,100.00

Book value before the overhaul: $21,000 - $16,000 = $5,000.$
Book value after the overhaul: $28,100 - $16,000 = $12,100.$

	Dec.	31	Depreciation Expense.	2,220.00	
			Accumulated Depreciation, Machine No. 6. . .		2,220.00
			$($12,100 - $1,000) \div 5 = $2,220.$		

g. Book value at Dec. 31, 1991: $21,000 - $12,000 = $9,000.$
Revised remaining useful life is from Jan. 1, 1992 to Dec. 31, 1996, or
five years, and the revised annual depreciation charge is: ($9,000 -
$1,000) \div 5 = $1,600.$

	1992				
	Dec.	31	Depreciation Expense.	1,600.00	
			Accumulated Depreciation, Machine No. 7. . .		1,600.00

Glossary

Define or explain the words and phrases listed in the chapter Glossary.
(L. O. 6)

Amortize to periodically write off as an expense a share of the cost of an asset, usually an intangible asset. p. 521

Balance sheet expenditure another name for *capital expenditure*. p. 520

Betterment a modification to an existing plant asset to make it more efficient, usually by replacing part of the asset with an improved or superior part. p. 520

Capital expenditure an expenditure that benefits future periods because the value or asset obtained by the expenditure does not fully expire by the end of the current period. Also called a *balance sheet expenditure*. p. 520

Change in an accounting estimate a change in a calculated amount to be reported in the financial statements that results from new information or subsequent developments and accordingly from better insight or improved judgement. p. 518

Copyright an exclusive right granted by the federal government to publish and sell a musical, literary, or artistic work for a period of years. p. 522

Depletion the amount a wasting asset is reduced through cutting, mining, or pumping. p. 520

Extraordinary repairs major repairs that extend the service life of a plant asset significantly beyond the number of years originally estimated. p. 519

Goodwill that portion of the value of a business that results from the business's expected ability to earn a rate of return greater than the average in its industry. p. 523

Intangible asset an asset that has no physical existence but has value due to the rights resulting from its ownership and possession. p. 521

Lease a contract that grants the right to possess and use property. p. 522

Leasehold the rights granted to a lessee under the terms of a lease contract. p. 522

Leasehold improvements improvements to leased property made by the lessee. p. 523

Lessee an individual or enterprise that has been given possession of property under the terms of a lease contract. p. 522

Lessor the individual or enterprise that has given up possession of property under the terms of a lease contract. p. 522

Ordinary repairs repairs made to keep a plant asset in its normal good operating condition. p. 519

Patent an exclusive right granted by the federal government to manufacture and sell a machine or mechanical device for a period of years. p. 521

Revenue expenditure an expenditure that benefits only the current period because the value or asset obtained by the expenditure will fully expire before the end of the current accounting period. p. 520

Trademark a unique symbol designed by a company for use in marketing its products or services. p. 524

Trade name a unique name selected by a company for use in marketing its products or services. p. 524

Questions for Class Discussion

1. If an asset that has been depreciated is sold for cash and the remaining book value of the asset is more than the cash proceeds from the sale, should the difference be debited to depreciation expense? How should the difference be recorded?

2. What is the essential meaning of the accounting principle of materiality?

3. Distinguish between ordinary repairs and extraordinary repairs.

4. How should ordinary repairs to a machine be recorded? How should extraordinary repairs be recorded?

5. What is a betterment? How should a betterment to a machine be recorded?

6. Distinguish between revenue expenditures and capital expenditures and state the difference in how they should be recorded.

7. What is the difference between balance sheet expenditures and capital expenditures?

8. When should a loss on the exchange of a plant asset be recorded? When is it permissible to absorb a loss into the cost basis of the new plant asset? Should a gain on a plant asset exchange be recorded as such?

9. What is the name for the process of allocating the cost of natural resources to expense as the natural resources are used?

10. What are the characteristics of an intangible asset?

11. Is the declining-balance method an acceptable means of calculating depletion of natural resources?

12. What are the general procedures to be followed in accounting for an intangible asset?

13. Define (a) lease, (b) lessor, (c) leasehold, and (d) leasehold improvement.

14. In accounting, when is a business said to have goodwill?

15. If at the end of five years it is discovered that a machine that was expected to have a six-year life will actually have an eight-year life, how is this new information reflected in the accounts?

16. X Company bought an established business and paid for goodwill. If X Company plans to incur substantial advertising and promotional costs each year to maintain the value of the goodwill, must the company also amortize the goodwill?

Multiple Choice

1. On January 1, 1991, Blair Company purchased a computer for $210,000. Estimated useful life is five years, and salvage value is $30,000. The company uses sum-of-the-years'-digits depreciation. If the computer is sold for $100,000 on March 31, 1992, the gain (loss) on the sale will be:
   a. $(38,000).
   b. $(26,000).
   c. $ (8,000).
   d. $ 20,000.
   e. $ 38,000.

2. Campbell Company traded an old truck for a new one. The original cost of the old truck was $100,000, and its accumulated depreciation is $78,000. The new truck has a cash price of $150,000. However, Campbell received a $10,000 trade-in allowance. Assume any book gain or loss is material. Campbell should record the new truck at:
   a. $162,000.
   b. $150,000.
   c. $140,000.
   d. $138,000.
   e. $ 22,000.

3. Comfax Company purchased a machine at a cost of $28,400. At that time, the machine was depreciated on a straight-line basis assuming a 9-year life with a $1,400 salvage value. At the beginning of the 7th year, the estimated useful life of the machine is changed from 9 to 10 years with no change in salvage value. Depreciation for each of the machine's remaining years is:
   a. $3,000.
   b. $2,700.
   c. $2,600.
   d. $2,250.
   e. $1,900.

4. At the beginning of the 5th year of a machine's estimated 7-year useful life, the machine was overhauled, and as a result its estimated useful life was extended to 10 years. The machine originally cost $110,000, and the overhaul cost was $15,000. The cost of the overhaul should be recorded as follows:

a.	Machinery	15,000.00	
	Accumulated Depreciation, Machinery		15,000.00
b.	Repairs Expense	15,000.00	
	Cash		15,000.00
c.	Machinery	15,000.00	
	Cash		15,000.00
d.	Accumulated Depreciation, Machinery	15,000.00	
	Machinery		15,000.00
e.	Depreciation Expense	15,000.00	
	Cash		15,000.00

5. Miller Mines, Inc., paid $500,000 for an ore deposit. The deposit had an estimated 250,000 tons of ore that would be fully mined during the next 10 years. During the current year, 70,000 tons were mined and sold. The amount of depletion expense this year is:
   a. $140,000.
   b. $120,000.
   c. $ 70,000.
   d. $ 50,000.
   e. $ –0–.

6. The Red Company exchanged its used copy machine for a newer model. The old machine had cost $1,350 and had been depreciated $1,050. The new copier had a cash price of $1,800, but Red Company was given a $525 trade-in allowance. What amount of gain or loss should Red Company show on the exchange?
   a. $0.
   b. $225 gain.
   c. $300 gain.
   d. $300 loss.
   e. $525 gain.

Mini Discussion Cases

Case 11–1

You have just been appointed auditor of the Conestoga Company. During your first examination of the records you discover that the company charges all of its repairs and maintenance costs to their respective asset accounts. Management indicates that regular maintenance increases the life of an asset; therefore, the maintenance costs, instead of being charged to expense as incurred, will be reflected in the increased depreciation charges as the asset is being used.

Required
Evaluate Conestoga's policy with respect to GAAP. Why is their policy (in)correct?

Case 11–2

Two of your classmates are having a discussion about accounting for intangible assets. Classmate 1 says that all intangible assets should be written off immediately since they have no physical substance. Classmate 2 argues that intangible assets should be written off over their lifetime as is provided by law.

Required
Mediate between your classmates explaining, with reasons, the proper accounting treatment for intangible assets.

Exercises

Exercise 11–1
Recording sales of plant assets
(L. O. 1)

A machine with an expected service life of six years and salvage value of $3,000 was purchased by Aster Company for $39,000. After taking straight-line depreciation for four years, the machine was sold. Present a general journal entry dated December 31 to record the sale assuming the cash proceeds from the sale were: (*a*) $15,000; (*b*) $18,450; and (*c*) $13,750.

Exercise 11–2
Asset disposal in midyear
(L. O. 1)

Daffy Company purchased and installed a machine on January 2, 1990, at a total cost of $54,000. Straight-line depreciation was taken each year for four years, based on the assumption of a six-year life and no salvage value. The machine was disposed of on August 31, during its fifth year. Present the entries to record the partial year's depreciation on August 31 and to record the disposal under each of the following unrelated assumptions: (a) the machine was sold for $20,000; (b) it was sold for $8,400; and (c) the machine was totally destroyed in a fire, and the insurance company settled the insurance claim for $11,000.

Exercise 11–3
Recording plant asset disposal or trade-in
(L. O. 1, 2)

On January 4, 1990, Taylor Company disposed of a machine that cost $29,000 and that had been depreciated $18,000. Present without explanations the entries to record the disposal under each of the following unrelated assumptions:

a. The machine was sold for $4,300 cash.
b. The machine was traded in on a new machine of like purpose having a $32,500 cash price. A $12,500 trade-in allowance was received, and the balance was paid in cash. Any gain or loss is recognized.
c. A $4,300 trade-in allowance was received for the machine on a new machine of like purpose having a $32,500 cash price. The balance was paid in cash, and the loss was considered material.
d. The loss in transaction (c) was considered immaterial.

Exercise 11–4
Exchanging plant assets
(L. O. 2)

Frantz Company traded in its old truck on a new truck, receiving a $16,650 trade-in allowance and paying the remaining $55,350 in cash. The old truck cost $49,500, and straight-line depreciation of $27,000 had been recorded under the assumption it would last five years and have a $4,500 salvage value. Answer the following questions: (a) What was the book value of the old truck? (b) What is the loss on the exchange? (c) Assuming the loss is deemed to be material, what amount should be debited to the New Truck account? (d) Assuming the loss is not material, what amount should be debited to the New Truck account?

Exercise 11–5
Revising depreciation rates
(L. O. 3)

Clayton Company depreciated a machine that cost $82,000 on a straight-line basis for five years under the assumption it would have an eight-year life and a $4,800 trade-in value. At that point, Clayton recognized that the machine had five years of remaining useful life, after which it would have an estimated $3,600 trade-in value. (a) Determine the machine's book value at the end of its fifth year. (b) Determine the amount of depreciation to be charged against the machine during each of the remaining years in its life.

Exercise 11–6
Ordinary repairs, extraordinary repairs, and betterments
(L. O. 4)

Darnell Company paid $67,500 for a machine that was expected to last six years and have a salvage value of $9,000. Present general journal entries dated December 31 to record the following costs related to the machine:

a. During the second year of the machine's life, $1,350 was paid for repairs necessary to keep the machine in good working order.

b. During the third year of the machine's life, $6,900 was paid for replacement parts that were expected to increase the machine's productivity by 15% each year.

c. During the fourth year of the machine's life, $9,300 was paid for repairs that were expected to increase the service life of the machine from six to eight years.

Exercise 11–7
Extraordinary repairs
(L. O. 4)

Mather Company owns a building that appeared on its balance sheet at the end of last year at its original $456,000 cost less $328,320 accumulated depreciation. The building has been depreciated on a straight-line basis under the assumption it would have a 25-year life and no salvage value. During the first week in January of the current year, major structural repairs were completed on the building at a $144,000 cost. The repairs did not improve the building's usefulness but they did extend its expected life for 13 years beyond the 25 years originally estimated. (*a*) Determine the building's age on last year's balance sheet date. (*b*) Give the entry to record the cost of the repairs. (*c*) Determine the book value of the building after its repairs were recorded. (*d*) Give the entry to record the current year's depreciation.

Exercise 11–8
Depletion of natural resources
(L. O. 5)

On January 1, 1990, Bayless Company paid $162,000 for an ore body containing 720,000 tons of ore. The company also installed machinery in the mine that cost $144,000, had an estimated 12-year life and no salvage value, and that was capable of removing the entire ore body in 6 years. The machine will be abandoned when the ore is completely mined. Bayless began mining operations on May 1, and it mined 58,000 tons of ore during the remaining nine months of the year. Give the entries to record the December 31, 1990, depletion of the ore body and the depreciation of the mining machinery.

Exercise 11–9
Amortization of intangible assets
(L. O. 5)

Marley Company purchased the copyright to a trade manual for $112,500 on January 1, 1990. The copyright legally protects its owner for 25 more years. However, management believes the trade manual can be successfully published and sold for only five more years. Prepare journal entries to record (*a*) the purchase of the copyright and (*b*) annual amortization of the copyright on December 31, 1990.

Exercise 11–10
Calculating goodwill
(L. O. 5)

J. Klaus has devoted years to building a profitable business that earns an attractive return. Now Klaus is considering the possibility of selling the business and is attempting to estimate the value of goodwill in the business. The recorded net assets of the business (excluding goodwill) amount to $225,000, and in a typical year, net income amounts to $40,500. Most businesses of this type are expected to earn a return of about 15% on net assets. Calculate goodwill assuming (*a*) the amount of goodwill is estimated to be six times the portion of earnings that are above average, and (*b*) the amount of goodwill is estimated by capitalizing above-average earnings at a rate of 12%.

Problems

Problem 11–1
Purchases, betterments, and sales of plant assets
(L. O. 2, 4)

The Whitestone Company completed these transactions involving the purchase and operation of delivery trucks:

1990

June 26 Paid cash for a new truck, $34,200 plus $1,710 provincial sales taxes. The truck was estimated to have a four-year life and a $9,000 salvage value.

July 5 Paid $1,890 for special racks and cleats installed in the truck. The racks and cleats did not increase the truck's estimated trade-in value.

Dec. 31 Recorded straight-line depreciation on the truck.

1991

June 25 Paid $2,460 to install an air-conditioning unit in the truck. The unit increased the truck's estimated trade-in value by $300.

Dec. 31 Recorded straight-line depreciation on the truck.

1992

Mar. 15 Paid $330 for repairs to the truck's fender damaged when the driver backed into a loading dock.

Dec. 31 Recorded straight-line depreciation on the truck.

1993

Aug. 31 Traded the old truck and $29,310 in cash for a new truck. The new truck was estimated to have a three-year life and a $9,600 trade-in value, and the invoice for the exchange showed these items:

Price of the truck	$37,200
Trade-in allowance granted	(9,000)
Balance.	$28,200
Provincial sales taxes	1,110
Balance paid in cash	$29,310

Sept. 4 Paid $3,690 for special cleats and racks installed in the truck.

Dec. 31 Recorded straight-line depreciation on the new truck.

Required

Prepare general journal entries to record the transactions.

Problem 11–2
Depreciating and exchanging plant assets
(L. O. 1, 2)

A company completed the following transactions involving machinery:

Machine No. 366-90 was purchased on May 1, 1986, at an installed cost of $48,600. Its useful life was estimated at four years with a $5,400 trade-in value. Straight-line depreciation was recorded on the machine at the end of 1986 and 1987, and on August 5, 1988, it was traded on Machine No. 366-91. A $27,000 trade-in allowance was received, and the balance was paid in cash.

Machine No. 366-91 was purchased on August 5, 1988, at an installed cash price of $63,000, less the trade-in allowance received on Machine No. 366-90. The new machine's life was estimated at five years with a $6,300 trade-in value. Sum-of-the-years'-digits depreciation was recorded on each December 31 of its life; and on January 5, 1993, it was sold for $9,000.

Machine No. 367-10 was purchased on January 6, 1988, at an installed cost of $45,000. Its useful life was estimated at five years, after which it would have a $4,500 trade-in value. Declining-balance depreciation at twice the straight-line rate was recorded on the machine at the end of 1988, 1989, and 1990; and on January 3, 1991, it was traded on Machine No. 367-11. An $8,100 trade-in allowance was received, the balance was paid in cash, and the loss was considered immaterial.

Machine No. 367-11 was purchased on January 3, 1991, at an installed cash price of $53,100, less the trade-in allowance received on Machine No. 367-10. It was estimated the new machine would produce 75,000 units of product during its useful life, after which it would have a $5,400 trade-in value. Units-of-production depreciation was recorded on the machine for 1991, a period in which it produced 7,500 units of product. Between January 1 and October 3, 1992, the machine produced 11,250 more units, and on the latter date it was sold for $36,000.

Required

Prepare general journal entries to record: (*a*) the purchase of each machine, (*b*) the depreciation recorded on the first December 31 of each machine's life, and (*c*) the disposal of each machine. Treat the entries for the first two machines as one series of transactions and those of the next two machines as an unrelated second series. Only one entry is needed to record the exchange of one machine for another.

Problem 11–3
Intangible assets and natural resources
(L. O. 5)

Part 1. Ten years ago, Domo Products Company leased space in a building for a period of 20 years. The lease contract calls for $67,500 annual rental payments on each January 1 throughout the life of the lease and also provides that the lessee must pay for all additions and improvements to the leased property. Recent construction nearby has made the location more valuable; and on December 28, Domo Products Company subleased the space to Techkon, Inc., for the remaining 10 years of the lease, beginning on the next January 1. Techkon, Inc., paid $150,000 for the privilege of subleasing the property and in addition agreed to assume and pay the building owner the $67,500 annual rental charges. After taking possession of the leased space, Techkon, Inc., paid for remodeling the office portion of the leased space at a cost of $210,000. The remodeled office portion is estimated to have a life equal to the remaining life of the building, 20 years, and was paid for on January 9.

Required

Prepare entries for Techkon, Inc., to record: (*a*) Techkon, Inc.'s payment to sublease the building space, (*b*) its payment of the annual rental charge to the building owner, and (*c*) payment for the new office portion. Also, prepare the adjusting entries required at the end of the first year of the sublease to amortize (*d*) a proper share of the $150,000 cost of the sublease and (*e*) a proper share of the office remodeling cost.

Part 2.   On May 7 of the current year, Vanex Company paid $1,224,000 for mineral land estimated to contain 7,500,000 tons of recoverable ore. It installed machinery costing $216,000, having an 18-year life and no salvage value, and capable of exhausting the mine in 15 years. The machinery was paid for on June 28, three days before mining operations began. During the first six months' operations the company mined 309,375 tons of ore.

Required

Prepare entries to record (*a*) the purchase of the mineral land, (*b*) the installation of the machinery, (*c*) the first six months' depletion under the assumption that the land will be valueless after the ore is mined, and (*d*) the first six months' depreciation on the machinery, which will be abandoned after the ore is fully mined.

Problem 11–4
Goodwill
(L. O. 5)

Excelsior Company's balance sheet on December 31, 1990, is as follows:

Cash	$ 94,500
Merchandise inventory	136,500
Buildings	420,000
Accumulated depreciation	(110,250)
Land	236,250
Total assets	$ 777,000
Accounts payable	$ 63,000
Long-term note payable	162,750
Common stock	393,750
Retained earnings	157,500
Total liabilities and owners' equity . .	$ 777,000

   In Excelsior Company's industry, earnings average 12% of common shareholders' equity. Excelsior Company, however, is expected to earn $110,250 annually. The owners of Excelsior Company believe that the balance sheet amounts are reasonable estimates of fair market values except for goodwill. In discussing a plan to sell the company, they argue that goodwill should be recognized by capitalizing the amount of earnings above average at a rate of 15%. On the other hand, the prospective purchaser argues that goodwill should be valued at five times the earnings above average.

Required

1. Calculate the amount of goodwill claimed by Excelsior Company's owners.
2. Calculate the amount of goodwill according to the purchaser.
3. Suppose the purchaser finally agrees to pay the full price requested by Excelsior Company's owners. If the expected earnings level is obtained and the goodwill is amortized over the longest permissible time period, what will be the net income for the first year after the company is purchased?
4. If the purchaser pays the full price requested by Excelsior Company's owners, what percentage of the purchaser's investment will be earned as net income the first year?

Problem 11–5
Depreciation, repairs, and exchanges of plant assets
(L. O. 1, 2, 3, 4)

Part 1. On January 8, 1984, a company purchased and placed in operation a machine estimated to have a 10-year life and no salvage value. The machine cost $135,000 and was depreciated on a straight-line basis. On January 3, 1988, a $5,400 device that increased its output by one fourth was added to the machine. The device did not change the machine's estimated life or its zero salvage value. During the first week of January 1991, the machine was completely overhauled at a $40,500 cost (paid for on January 9). The overhaul added three additional years to the machine's estimated life but did not change its zero salvage value. On June 30, 1992, the machine was destroyed in a fire and the insurance company settled the loss claim for $45,000.

Required

Prepare general journal entries to record: (*a*) the purchase of the machine, (*b*) the 1984 depreciation, (*c*) the addition of the new device, (*d*) the 1988 depreciation, (*e*) the machine's overhaul, (*f*) the 1991 depreciation, and (*g*) the insurance settlement.

Part 2. A company purchased Machine One at a $55,800 installed cost on January 1, 1986. It was depreciated on a straight-line basis at the end of 1986, 1987, 1988, and 1989 under the assumption it would have a 10-year life and a $10,800 salvage value. After more experience and before recording 1990 depreciation, the company revised its estimate of the machine's remaining years downward from six years to four and revised the estimate of its salvage value downward to $9,000. On April 1, 1992, after recording 1990, 1991, and part of a year's depreciation for 1992, the company traded in Machine One on Machine Two, receiving a $22,500 trade-in allowance. The cash paid for Machine Two was $73,350 less the trade-in allowance. On December 31, 1992, Machine Two was depreciated on a straight-line basis under the assumption it would have a six-year life and a $10,350 salvage value.

Required

Prepare entries to record: (*a*) the purchase of Machine One, (*b*) its 1986 depreciation, (*c*) its 1990 depreciation, (*d*) the exchange of the machines, and (*e*) the 1992 depreciation on Machine Two.

Alternate Problems

Problem 11–1A
Purchases, betterments, and sales of plant assets
(L. O. 2, 4)

The Franklin Company completed these transactions involving the purchase and operation of delivery vans:

1990
July 2 Paid cash for a new van, $27,360 plus $1,360 provincial sales taxes. The van was estimated to have a four-year life and a $7,200 salvage value.

July 6 Paid $1,512 for special racks and cleats installed in the van. The racks and cleats did not increase the van's estimated trade-in value.

Dec. 31 Recorded straight-line depreciation on the van.

1991
June 26 Paid $1,968 to install an air-conditioning unit in the van. The unit increased the van's estimated trade-in value by $240.

Dec. 31 Recorded straight-line depreciation on the van.

1992

May 15 Paid $285 for repairs to the van's fender damaged when the driver backed into a loading dock.

Dec. 31 Recorded straight-line depreciation on the van.

1993

Sept. 27 Traded the old van and $23,448 in cash for a truck. The truck was estimated to have a three-year life and a $7,680 trade-in value, and the invoice for the exchange showed these items:

Price of the truck	$29,760
Trade-in allowance granted	(7,200)
Balance	$22,560
Provincial sales taxes	888
Balance paid in cash	$23,448

Oct.   2 Paid $2,952 for special cleats and racks installed in the truck.

Dec. 31 Recorded straight-line depreciation on the truck.

Required

Prepare general journal entries to record the transactions.

Problem 11–2A
Depreciation and exchanges of plant assets
(L. O. 1, 2)

Keto Company completed the following transactions involving machinery:

Machine No. 267-90 was purchased on April 2, 1986, at an installed cost of $77,760. Its useful life was estimated at four years with an $8,640 trade-in value. Straight-line depreciation was recorded on the machine at the end of 1986 and 1987, and on July 3, 1988, it was traded on Machine No. 267-91. A $43,200 trade-in allowance was received, and the balance was paid in cash. Assume any gains or losses are recognized.

Machine No. 267-91 was purchased on July 3, 1988, at an installed cash price of $100,800, less the trade-in allowance received on Machine No. 267-90. The new machine's life was estimated at five years with a $10,080 trade-in value. Sum-of-the-years'-digits depreciation was recorded on each December 31 of its life; and on January 7, 1993, it was sold for $14,400.

Machine No. 267-95 was purchased on January 9, 1988, at an installed cost of $72,000. Its useful life was estimated at five years, after which it would have a $7,200 trade-in value. Declining-balance depreciation at twice the straight-line rate was recorded on the machine at the end of 1988, 1989, and 1990; and on January 2, 1991, it was traded on Machine No. 267-96. A $12,960 trade-in allowance was received, the balance was paid in cash, and the loss was considered immaterial.

Machine No. 267-96 was purchased on January 2, 1991, at an installed cash price of $84,960, less the trade-in allowance received on Machine No. 267-95. It was estimated the new machine would produce 60,000 units of product during its useful life, after which it would have an $8,640 trade-in value. Units-of-production depreciation was recorded on the machine for 1991, a period in which it produced 6,000 units of product. Between January 1 and October 2,

1992, the machine produced 9,000 more units, and on the latter date it was sold for $57,600.

Required
Prepare general journal entries to record: (*a*) the purchase of each machine, (*b*) the depreciation recorded on the first December 31 of each machine's life, and (*c*) the disposal of each machine. Treat the entries for the first two machines as one series of transactions and those of the next two machines as an unrelated second series. Only one entry is needed to record the exchange of one machine for another.

Problem 11–3A
Intangible assets and natural resources
(L. O. 5)

Part 1. Five years ago, D. C. Corporation leased space in a building for a period of 20 years. The lease contract calls for $81,000 annual rental payments on each January 1 throughout the life of the lease and also provides that the lessee must pay for all additions and improvements to the leased property. Recent construction nearby has made the location more valuable; and on December 30, D. C. Corporation subleased the space to T. P., Inc., for the remaining 15 years of the lease, beginning on the next January 1. T. P., Inc., paid $360,000 for the privilege of subleasing the property and in addition agreed to assume and pay the building owner the $81,000 annual rental charges. After taking possession of the leased space, T. P., Inc., paid for remodeling the office portion of the leased space at a cost of $270,000. The remodeled office portion is estimated to have a life equal to the remaining life of the building, 25 years, and was paid for on January 10.

Required
Prepare entries for T. P., Inc., to record: (*a*) T. P., Inc.'s payment to sublease the building space, (*b*) its payment of the annual rental charge to the building owner, and (*c*) payment for the new office portion. Also, prepare the adjusting entries required at the end of the first year of the sublease to amortize (*d*) a proper share of the $360,000 cost of the sublease and (*e*) a proper share of the office remodeling cost.

Part 2. On May 8 of the current year, Huber Company paid $1,080,000 for mineral land estimated to contain 9,000,000 tons of recoverable ore. It installed machinery costing $187,500, having an eight-year life and no salvage value, and capable of exhausting the mine in five years. The machinery was paid for on June 28, four days before mining operations began. During the first six months' operations the company mined 720,000 tons of ore.

Required
Prepare entries to record (*a*) the purchase of the mineral land, (*b*) the installation of the machinery, (*c*) the first six months' depletion under the assumption that the land will be valueless after the ore is mined, and (*d*) the first six months' depreciation on the machinery, which will be abandoned after the ore is fully mined.

Problem 11–4A
Goodwill
(L. O. 5)

Batts Company's balance sheet on December 31, 1990, is as follows:

Cash	$ 170,100
Merchandise inventory	245,700
Buildings.	756,000
Accumulated depreciation	(198,450)
Land	425,250
Total assets	$1,398,600
Accounts payable	$ 113,400
Long-term note payable.	295,200
Common stock	706,500
Retained earnings.	283,500
Total liabilities and owners' equity . .	$1,398,600

In Batts Company's industry, earnings average 11% of common shareholders' equity. Batts Company, however, is expected to earn $198,900 annually. The owners of Batts Company believe that the balance sheet amounts are reasonable estimates of fair market values except for goodwill. In discussing a plan to sell the company, they argue that goodwill should be recognized by capitalizing the amount of earnings above average at a rate of 20%. On the other hand, the prospective purchaser argues that goodwill should be valued at four times the earnings above average.

Required

1. Calculate the amount of goodwill claimed by Batts Company's owners.
2. Calculate the amount of goodwill according to the purchaser.
3. Suppose the purchaser finally agrees to pay the full price requested by Batts Company's owners. If the expected earnings level is obtained and the goodwill is amortized over the longest permissible time period, what will be the net income for the first year after the company is purchased?
4. If the purchaser pays the full price requested by Batts Company's owners, what percentage of the purchaser's investment will be earned as net income the first year?

Problem 11–5A
Depreciation, repairs, and exchanges of plant assets
(L. O. 1, 2, 3, 4)

Part 1.   On January 6, 1984, Knappe Company purchased a machine estimated to have a 10-year life and no salvage value. The machine cost $216,000 and was depreciated on a straight-line basis. On January 4, 1988, an $8,640 improvement was added to the machine which had the effect of increasing its output by one fourth. The improvement did not change the machine's estimated life or its zero salvage value. On January 8, 1991, the machine was completely overhauled at a $64,800 cost. The overhaul added three additional years to the machine's estimated life but did not change its zero salvage value. On June 30, 1992, the machine was destroyed in a fire and the insurance company settled the loss claim for $72,000.

Required

Prepare general journal entries to record: (*a*) the purchase of the machine, (*b*) the 1984 depreciation, (*c*) the addition of the new improvement, (*d*) the 1988 depreciation, (*e*) the machine's overhaul, (*f*) the 1991 depreciation, and (*g*) the insurance settlement.

Part 2. A company purchased Machine One at a $139,500 installed cost on January 11, 1986. It was depreciated on a straight-line basis at the end of 1986, 1987, 1988, and 1989 under the assumption it would have a 10-year life and a $27,000 salvage value. After more experience and before recording 1990 depreciation, the company revised its estimate of the machine's remaining years downward from six years to four and revised the estimate of its salvage value downward to $22,500. On April 11, 1992, after recording 1990, 1991, and part of a year's depreciation for 1992, the company traded in Machine One on Machine Two, receiving a $56,250 trade-in allowance. The cash paid for Machine Two was $183,375 less the trade-in allowance. Machine Two was depreciated on a straight-line basis on December 31, 1992, under the assumption it would have a six-year life and a $25,875 salvage value.

Required

Prepare entries to record: (*a*) the purchase of Machine One, (*b*) its 1986 depreciation, (*c*) its 1990 depreciation, (*d*) the exchange of the machines, and (*e*) the 1992 depreciation on Machine Two.

Provocative Problems

Provocative Problem 11–1
Troubled Company
(L. O. 1, 4)

While examining the accounting records of Troubled Company, you discover two entries during 1991 that appear questionable. The first entry recorded the cash proceeds from an insurance settlement as follows:

Nov.	14	Cash.	51,000.00	
		Loss from Fire	21,000.00	
		Accumulated Depreciation Machinery.	54,000.00	
		Machinery		126,000.00
		Received payment of fire loss claim.		

Your investigation shows that this entry was intended to record the receipt of an insurance company's $51,000 cheque to settle a claim resulting from the destruction of a machine in a small plant fire on November 4, 1991. The machine originally cost $108,000 and was put in operation on January 7, 1987. It was depreciated on a straight-line basis for four years under the assumption it would have an eight-year life and no salvage value. During the first week of January 1991, the machine had been overhauled at a cost of $18,000. The overhaul did not increase the machine's capacity or its salvage value. However, it was expected that the overhaul would lengthen the machine's service life two years beyond the eight originally expected.

The second entry that appears questionable was intended to record the receipt of a check from selling a portion of a tract of land. The tract was adjacent to the company's plant and had been purchased the year before. It cost $120,000, and $11,250 was paid for clearing and grading it. Both amounts had been debited to the Factory Land account. The land was to be used for storing finished product; but after the grading was completed, it was obvious the company did not need the entire tract. Troubled Company had received an offer from a purchaser who was willing to pay $67,500 for the east half or $90,000 for the west half. The company decided to sell the west half, and it recorded receipt of the purchaser's cheque with the following entry:

Dec.	10	Cash	90,000.00	
		Factory Land		90,000.00
		Sold unneeded factory land.		

Were any errors made in recording these transactions? If so, describe the errors and in each case give an entry or entries that will correct the account balances under the assumption the 1991 revenue and expense accounts have not been closed.

Provocative Problem 11–2
Sticks and Stones
Companies
(A Review Problem)

Sticks Company and Stones Company are similar businesses that sell competing products. Both companies began operations five years ago and are up for sale. Branch Company is considering both Sticks and Stones with the prospect of buying one of them.

In evaluating the two companies, the management of Branch has observed that Sticks Company has reported an average annual net income of $142,020. Stones Company, on the other hand, has reported an average of $171,000. However, the companies have not used the same accounting procedures, and Branch Company management is concerned that the numbers are not comparable. The current balance sheets of the two companies show these items:

	Sticks Company	Stones Company
Cash	$ 80,400	$ 98,400
Accounts receivable	619,200	702,000
Allowance for doubtful accounts.	(38,400)	–0–
Merchandise inventory..............	855,600	1,033,200
Store equipment	345,600	307,200
Accumulated depreciation, store equipment . .	(288,000)	(192,000)
Total assets..................	$1,574,400	$1,948,800
Current liabilities	$ 748,800	$ 826,800
Owners' equity	825,600	1,122,000
Total liabilities and owners' equity........	$1,574,400	$1,948,800

Sticks Company has used the allowance method in accounting for bad debts and has added to its allowance each year an amount equal to 1% of sales. However, this seems excessive since an examination shows that only $18,000 of its accounts are probably uncollectible. Stones Company has used the direct write-off method but has been slow to write off bad debts. An examination of its accounts shows $36,000 of accounts that are probably uncollectible.

During the past five years, Sticks Company has priced its inventories on a LIFO basis with the result that its current inventory appears on its balance sheet at an amount that is $144,000 below replacement cost. Stones Company has used FIFO, and its ending inventory appears at approximately its replacement cost.

Both companies have assumed eight-year lives and no salvage value in depreciating equipment; however, Sticks Company has used sum-of-the-years'-

digits depreciation, while Stones Company has used straight line. The management of Branch Company is of the opinion that straight-line depreciation has resulted in Stones Company's equipment appearing on its balance sheet at approximately its fair market value and that straight-line would have had the same result for Sticks Company.

Branch Company is willing to pay what its management considers fair market value for the assets of either business, not including cash, but including goodwill measured at four times average annual earnings in excess of 15% on the fair market value of the net tangible assets. Branch Company's management defines net tangible assets as all assets other than goodwill, including accounts receivable, minus liabilities. Branch Company will also assume the liabilities of the purchased business, paying its owner the difference between total assets purchased and the liabilities assumed.

Required

Prepare the following schedules: (*a*) a schedule showing the net tangible assets of each company at their fair market values according to Branch Company management, (*b*) a schedule showing the revised net incomes of the companies based on FIFO inventories and straight-line depreciation, (*c*) a schedule showing the calculation of each company's goodwill, and (*d*) a schedule showing the amount Branch Company would pay for each business.

Analytical and Review Problems

A&R Problem 11–1

Danny's Doorways traded in an old planing machine for a new heavy-duty automated model. The following data are available:

Old machine—cost	$5,250*
Accumulated depreciation	3,500
List price of new model	9,875
Amount paid with trade-in.	8,625
Expected life of 10 years with a $750 residual value. Danny's uses straight-line depreciation.	
*Market value at time of trade-in = $1,000	

Required

1. Prepare the journal entry to record the purchase of the new machine.
2. Using the data above, explain why it is important to current and future periods to determine the proper "cost" for assets subject to depreciation, particularly when trade-ins are involved.

A&R Problem 11–2

The Machinery and the Accumulated Depreciation accounts in the ledger of Algonquin Aluminum Company contain the following entries:

Machinery account:

Debits

Prior to December 31, 1990, Machines No. 1, 2, 3, and 4 at $24,000	$96,000
May 3, 1991, Machine No. 5	30,000
August 30, 1991, Machine No. 6 . .	36,000

Credits

August 31, Machine No. 2	3,600
September 30, Machine No. 4	9,200

Accumulated Depreciation-Machinery account:

Debits

No entries

Credits

Prior to December 31, 1990	$51,500
May 3, 1991	2,000
August 30, 1991	4,000
September 30, 1991	4,500

The following events took place during 1991:

a. Machine No. 5 replaced Machine No. 1 which became obsolete and was removed from the premises at no cost to the company. Accumulated depreciation on Machine No. 1 on December 31, 1990, amounted to $18,400. Machine No. 5 was purchased for $30,000 cash.

b. Machine No. 2 was traded in on Machine No. 6 costing $36,000. The fair market value of Machine No. 2 on August 30 was $3,600, and the accumulated depreciation on December 31, 1990, amounted to $14,400.

c. Machine No. 4 was totally destroyed by fire on September 30. Accumulated depreciation on this machine on December 31, 1990, amounted to $14,000. The machine was insured, and Seneca received $9,200 from the insurace company.

The company uses straight-line depreciation, four-year service life with no salvage value and computes depreciation to the nearest month.

Required

1. Give the probable entries that were made by Seneca's accountant.
2. Give the entries that you would make (assume that all gains and losses are material).

A&R Problem 11–3

The following data are taken from the financial statements of Huron Company, Limited:

	1990	1991	1992	1993
Total assets, December 31	$630,000	$660,000	$675,000	$825,000
Total liabilities, December 31	90,000	120,000	105,000	157,500
Net income	72,000	79,500	85,500	93,000

Additional information indicates that $150,000 was spent on a new plant completed in November of 1993 and currently undergoing preproduction testing.

You have been asked by a client to determine the value of the business. Your investigation indicates that the asset values reflected in the statements are sound values and that the normal rate of earnings for the industry is 12%.

Required

Determine the value of the business on the assumption that excess earnings are to be capitalized at 25%.

A&R Problem 11–4   **Part 1.** Taylor has been depreciating equipment over a 20-year life on a straight-line basis. The equipment cost $102,000 and has an estimated residual value of $12,000. On the basis of experience, since acquisition on January 2 five years ago, managment has decided that a total life of 14 years instead of 20 years is more appropriate, with no change in residual value. The change is to be effective January 1 of the fifth year.

Required

Prepare the December 31 adjusting entry to recognize depreciation expense for the fifth year. Show calculations.

Part 2. Taylor discovered during the year that the cost of an operational asset purchased on January 3, three years before January of the current year, was debited to operating expenses. The asset cost $40,000 and was estimated to have a five-year service life with no residual value. The company uses the diminishing-balance method of depreciation at twice the straight-line rate for assets of this nature.

Required

Compute the understatment/overstatement of net income for each of the three years as a result of the error.

A&R Problem 11–5   Interprovincial Oil Company drilled 10 oil wells at an average cost of $8 million each. Four of the oil wells were found to be "producers," with estimated total reserves of 10 million barrels, while the remaining six were "dry." Interprovincial's experience was representative of the industry. The same year 1 million barrels of crude were pumped.

Accountant A argues that the following entries are proper for the recording of the above:

Oil wells.	80,000,000	
Cash (or Payables)		80,000,000
Depletion expense	8,000,000	
Accumulated depletion—oil wells		8,000,000

Accountant B argues that the entries should be:

Oil wells.	32,000,000	
Loss on drilling of dry wells	48,000,000	
Cash (Payables).		80,000,000
Depletion expense	3,200,000	
Accumulated depletion—oil wells		3,200,000

Required

You have been asked to arbitrate the case. Present your supported views.

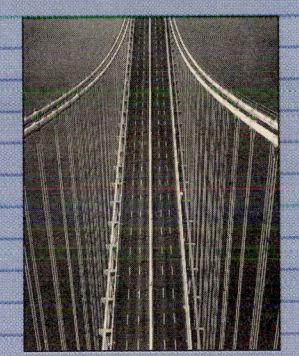

Liabilities, Partners' Equities, and the Evolving Development of Accounting Principles

Many different kinds of liabilities are incurred by businesses in the process of conducting business operations. These liabilities include short-term obligations such as accounts payable, wages payable, notes payable, unearned revenues, property taxes payable, product warranties, and payroll liabilities. They also include long-term liabilities such as capital leases, and long-term notes payable. You will learn the fundamental principles of accounting for liabilities such as these as you study the next two chapters. Then, in Chapter 14 you will learn about some special accounting issues that relate to partnerships.

Part four consists of the following:

12. Current and Long-Term Liabilities

13. Payroll Accounting

14. Partnership Accounting

12 Current and Long-Term Liabilities

You already know that liabilities are one of the three elements in the accounting equation. Some of the liabilities we've discussed in previous chapters include accounts payable, notes payable, wages payable, and unearned revenues. In this chapter, we examine liabilities such as property taxes payable, product warranties, single-payment notes payable, installment notes payable, and leases. We also introduce the important concept of present values and reconsider the topic of contingent liabilities. As you study this chapter, you will learn how to define, classify, and measure liabilities.

Learning Objectives

After studying Chapter 12, you should be able to:

1. Explain the difference between current and long-term liabilities.
2. Explain the meaning of definite and estimated liabilities.
3. Record transactions that involve liabilities such as property taxes payable, product warranties, and short-term notes payable.
4. Explain the difference between liabilities and contingent liabilities.
5. Calculate the present value of a sum of money that will be received a number of periods in the future or will be received periodically.
6. Prepare entries to account for long-term noninterest-bearing notes payable, for installment notes payable, and for capital and operating leases.
7. Define or explain the words and phrases listed in the chapter Glossary.

The Definition and Classification of Liabilities

Liabilities are obligations that require the future payment of assets or performance of services. Not every expected future payment is a liability. To qualify as a liability, the debtor must, as a result of past transactions, be presently obligated to make a future payment. Because liabilities result from past transactions, they normally are enforceable as legal claims against the enterprise.

Current and Long-Term Liabilities

Explain the difference between current and long-term liabilities.
(L. O. 1)

Current Liabilities. A business typically has several kinds of liabilities which are classified as either current or long-term liabilities. *Current liabilities* are debts or other obligations the liquidation of which is expected to require the use of existing current assets or the creation of other current liabilities. Current liabilities are due within one year of the balance sheet date or the operating cycle of the business, whichever is longer.[1] Examples of current liabilities are accounts payable, short-term notes payable, wages payable, dividends payable, product warranty liabilities, payroll and other taxes payable, and unearned revenues.

Long-Term Liabilities. Obligations that will not require the use of existing current assets because they do not mature within one year (or one operating cycle, whichever is longer) are classified as **long-term liabilities.** Examples of long-term liabilities include leases, long-term notes payable, product warranty liabilities, and bonds payable. However, you should understand that any given liability such as a note payable may be either current or long term. The critical difference is the question of whether or not payment will be made within one year or the current operating cycle of the business, whichever is longer.

Definite versus Estimated Liabilities

Explain the meaning of definite and estimated liabilities.
(L. O. 2)

Three important questions concerning liabilities are: Who will be paid? When is payment due? How much is to be paid? In many situations, the answers to these three questions are determined at the time the liability is incurred. For example, an account payable may be for precisely $100, payable to R. L. Tucker, and due on August 15, 1991. This type of liability is definite with respect to all three questions.

When the Identity of the Creditor Is Uncertain. Other types of liabilities may be indefinite with respect to one or more of the three questions. For example, in the case of dividends payable, the amount that will be paid and the due date are definite. The question of who will be paid, however, is not answerable until after the date of record. Even though the identity of the creditor may be uncertain, there is no doubt that the debtor is obligated to pay and a liability should be recognized.

---

[1] *CICA Handbook* (Toronto: The Canadian Institute of Chartered Accountants), par. 1510.03.

When the Due Date Is Uncertain. An example of a liability with an uncertain due date is unearned legal fees that a lawyer accepts in return for the obligation to provide services to a client upon call. In this case, the amount of the liability is known. And the client for whom services will be provided is also known. However, the question of when the services will be performed is not definite. Usually, such arrangements are short term and are classified as current liabilities.

When the Amount to Be Paid Is Uncertain. When an obligation definitely exists but the amount that will be paid is uncertain, the obligation is called an **estimated liability.** Two important examples of estimated liabilities are property taxes and product warranties.

Property Taxes Payable

Record transactions that involve liabilities such as property taxes payable, product warranties, and short-term notes payable. (L. O. 3)

Property taxes are levied on an annual basis usually by governmental authorities such as counties, municipalities, and school districts. However, the exact amount of tax to be paid may not become known until the tax year is partially over. For example, the 1991 tax that will be paid on each item of property may not be fixed in amount until September 1991. And the tax may not be due until October 1991. Thus, if financial statements are prepared monthly, the tax expense must be estimated when statements are prepared for January through August.

For example, throughout 1991, a company owns property that has been assessed by the city as having a valuation of $400,000 for property tax purposes. The tax on the property during the previous year (1990) was $11,400. In preparing monthly financial statements during 1991, before the actual tax is known, the company estimates a monthly tax expense of $11,400 ÷ 12 = $950. Until the 1991 tax becomes definite, the company will make monthly adjusting entries as follows:

1991 Jan.	31	Property Taxes Expense.	950.00	
		Estimated Property Taxes Payable		950.00
		To record estimated property taxes for the month of January.		

In September 1991, the city announces that the tax levy for 1991 will be $3 per $100 of assessed value. Now, the company calculates the actual 1991 tax as ($400,000 ÷ $100) × $3 = $12,000, which is $1,000 per month. For the first eight months (January through August), the estimated tax was less than the actual tax by $50 × 8 = $400. This may be recorded at the end of September along with the $1,000 monthly tax, as follows:

Sept.	30	Property Taxes Expense.	1,400.00	
		Estimated Property Taxes Payable		1,400.00
		To record property taxes for the month of September and to correct for $50 estimate error during first eight months.		

When the annual tax is paid at the end of October 1991, the entry to record the payment is:

Oct.	31	Property Taxes Expense (October).	1,000.00	
		Prepaid Property Taxes (November and December)	2,000.00	
		Estimated Property Taxes Payable.	9,000.00	
		Cash		12,000.00
		To pay property tax for 1991.		

Product Warranty Liabilities

Product warranty liability is another example of an estimated liability. Most companies provide warranties or guarantees for their products. A **product warranty** is a promise to the customer; the promise obligates the seller or manufacturer for a limited period of time to pay for items such as replacement parts or repair costs if the product breaks or fails to perform. For example, an automobile may be sold with a warranty that covers the mechanical parts for a period of one year or 12,000 kilometres, whichever comes first. The warranty may also include labor costs to install replacement parts.

When a product with a warranty is sold, the *matching principle* requires that you record all expenses to produce the sale in the same period as the sale. Therefore, the expense of the warranty must be recognized at the time of the sale. Since the exact amount of expense is not known at the time of the sale, the amount must be estimated based on past experience.

For example, a used auto is sold with a one-year or 12,000-km. warranty. The warranty covers mechanical parts, but the customer must pay any labor charges. Suppose the auto was sold on September 1, 1990, at a price of $16,000. Past experience shows that warranty expenses usually average about 2% of sales revenue. The entry to record the expense is:

Sept.	1	Warranty Expense	320.00	
		Estimated Warranty Liability		320.00
		$16,000 \times .02 = \$320$.		

Now suppose the customer has a problem with the car and returns it for warranty repairs on January 9, 1991. The auto dealer performs the warranty work by replacing parts that cost $90 and charges the customer $110 for labor. The entry to record the warranty work and the customer's payment is as follows:

Jan.	9	Cash	110.00	
		Estimated Warranty Liability.	90.00	
		Auto Parts Inventory		90.00
		Service Revenue		110.00
		To record warranty work and service revenue.		

What happens if the total warranty costs actually are different from the estimated $320 amount? On any sale, some difference is likely. Over the longer term, management must monitor warranty costs to be sure that 2% is the best estimate. When continued experience shows that warranty costs have changed, the percentage should be modified.

Contingent Liabilities

We first discussed contingent liabilities in Chapter 8. Discounted notes receivable were presented as an example of contingent liabilities. Contingent liabilities are not existing obligations and, therefore, are not recorded in the books as liabilities. However, the *full-disclosure principle* requires that you disclose contingent liabilities in the financial statements or in footnotes.

What Distinguishes Liabilities from Contingent Liabilities?

Explain the difference between liabilities and contingent liabilities. (L. O. 4)

Contingent liabilities become definite obligations only if some uncertain event takes place. For example, discounted notes receivable are contingent liabilities that become definite obligations only if the original signers of the notes fail to pay them.

Are product warranties a liability or contingent liability? A product warranty requires service or payment only if the product fails. That sounds like a contingent liability. However, the AcSC states that *if a contingency is likely and if the liability can be reasonably estimated, it should be recorded in the books as a liability.*[2] Product warranties usually are recorded as liabilities because the failure of some percentage of the products sold is likely and past experience allows a reasonable estimate of the amount of the liability.

What Are Other Examples of Contingent Liabilities?

Potential Legal Claims. In today's legal environment, many companies find themselves being sued for damages for a variety of reasons. The question is should the defendant report a liability or a contingent liability during the time a lawsuit is outstanding and not yet settled? The answer is that unless a payment for damages is likely and can be reasonably estimated, the potential claim of the plaintiff is a contingent liability of the defendant.

Debt Guaranties. Sometimes a company will guarantee the payment of a supplier, customer, or other company's debt, usually by cosigning the note payable of the other company. When this is done, the guarantor is contingently liable for the debt of the other company.

Short-Term Notes Payable

A current liability that requires further attention is short-term notes payable. When a business purchases merchandise on credit and then needs to gain an extension of the credit period, a short-term note payable may be substituted for the account payable. Also, short-term notes payable frequently arise in borrowing from a bank.

---

[2] Ibid., par. 3290.12.

Note Given to Secure a Time Extension on an Account

A note payable may be given to secure an extension of time in which to pay an account payable. For example, assume that Brock Company cannot pay its past-due $600 account with Ajax Company. As a result, Ajax Company agrees to accept Brock Company's 60-day, 12%, $600 note in granting an extension on the due date of the debt. Brock Company will record the issuance of the note as follows:

Aug.	23	Accounts Payable—Ajax Company.	600.00	
		Notes Payable.		600.00
		Gave a 60-day, 12% note to extend the due date on the amount owed.		

Observe that the note does not pay the debt. Rather, the form of the debt is changed from an account payable to a note payable. Ajax Company should prefer the note to the account because, in case of default and a lawsuit to collect, the note is written evidence of the debt and its amount.

When the note becomes due, Brock Company will give Ajax Company a cheque for $612 and record the payment of the note and its interest with this entry:

Oct.	22	Notes Payable	600.00	
		Interest Expense.	12.00	
		Cash		612.00
		Paid our note with interest.		

In Chapter 8 two methods for calculating interest, the "exact" method and the "alternative" method, were used. Even though the exact method is correct and calculators facilitate the arithmetic, we shall use the alternative method in this chapter so that both instructors and students may concentrate on the comprehension of the principles rather than on the lengthy procedural calculations. Therefore, assume a year of 360 days and months of 30 days and do not consider days of grace when doing the interest computations.

Borrowing from a Bank

In lending money, banks typically require that the borrower sign a promissory note. Oftentimes, the note is written for the amount of money loaned. The customer (debtor) promises to repay the amount of the note plus interest at a specified rate. In this case, the lending transaction is called a *loan*. In other cases, called *discounts,* the note is written for the sum of the amount borrowed plus interest. In other words, with a loan, the bank collects interest when the loan is repaid. With a discount, the bank deducts interest at the time the loan is made. To illustrate loans and discounts, assume that H. A. Green wishes to borrow approximately $2,000 for 60 days at the prevailing 15% rate of interest.

A Loan. In a loan transaction, the bank lends Green $2,000 in exchange for a signed promissory note. The note reads: "Sixty days after date I promise to pay $2,000 plus interest at 15%." Green records the transaction as follows:

Sept.	10	Cash	2,000.00	
		Notes Payable.		2,000.00
		Gave the bank a 60-day, 15% note.		

When the note and interest are paid, Green makes this entry:

Nov.	9	Notes Payable	2,000.00	
		Interest Expense	50.00	
		Cash		2,050.00
		Paid our 60-day, 15% note.		

Observe that in a loan transaction, the interest is paid at the time the loan is repaid.

A Discount. If Green's bank deducts interest at the time a loan is made, the bank will discount Green's $2,000 note. If it discounts the note at 15% for 60 days, it will deduct from the face amount of the note 60 days' interest at 15%, which is $50, and will give Green the difference, $1,950. The $50 deducted interest is called **bank discount.** The net amount received by Green, $1,950, is called the *proceeds* of the discounted note. Green records the transaction as follows:

Sept.	10	Cash	1,950.00	
		Discount on Notes Payable	50.00	
		Notes Payable.		2,000.00
		Discounted our $2,000 note payable at 15%.		

When the note matures, Green is required to pay the bank the face amount of the note, $2,000; Green records the payment like this:

Nov.	9	Notes Payable	2,000.00	
		Cash		2,000.00
		Paid our discounted note payable.		

Also, Green must record the interest expense, as follows:

Nov.	9	Interest Expense	50.00	
		Discount on Note Payable		50.00
		To record interest expense.		

In this example, note that this last entry could have been avoided if the $50 interest had been debited to Interest Expense in the entry of September 10, as follows:

Sept.	10	Cash	1,950.00	
		Interest Expense	50.00	
		Notes Payable.		2,000.00
		Discounted our $2,000 note payable at 15%.		

As a matter of convenience, when a note is signed and will be due within the same accounting period, many companies use this more efficient procedure.

In a discount transaction, since interest is deducted at the time the loan is made, the note states that only the principal amount is to be repaid at maturity. The note does not call for interest to be paid at maturity. Such a note may read: "Sixty days after date I promise to pay $2,000, with no interest." As a result, this type of note is commonly called a noninterest-bearing note. However, banks are not in business to lend money interest free. Interest is paid in a discount transaction. Since it is deducted at the time the loan is made, the note states that no additional interest will be collected at maturity. Nevertheless, interest is collected in a discount transaction and at a rate slightly higher than in a loan transaction at the same stated interest rate. For example, Green paid $50 for the use of $1,950 for 60 days, so the effective interest rate was a little in excess of 15% on the $1,950 received.

End-of-Period Adjustments

Discount on Notes Payable

When a note payable is discounted at a bank, and the note does not become due until the next accounting period, the interest deducted in advance should be debited to Discount on Note Payable. Then, at the end of the period, an adjusting entry is required. For example, on December 11, 1990, a company discounted at 15% its own $6,000, 60-day, noninterest-bearing note payable. It recorded the transaction as follows:

1990				
Dec.	11	Cash	5,850.00	
		Discount on Notes Payable	150.00	
		Notes Payable.		6,000.00
		Discounted our noninterest-bearing, 60-day note at 15%.		

If this company operates with accounting periods that end each December 31, 20 days' interest on this note, or $50 of the $150 discount, is an expense of the 1990 accounting period. Interest for the remaining 40 days, or $100, is an expense of 1991. Therefore, if revenues and expenses are matched, the company must make the following December 31, 1990, adjusting entry:

1990				
Dec.	31	Interest Expense.	50.00	
		Discount on Notes Payable		50.00
		To record 1990 interest expense.		

The adjusting entry removes from the Discount on Notes Payable account the $50 of interest that is applicable to 1990. It leaves in the account the $100 that is an expense of 1991. The $50 then appears on the 1990 income statement as an expense, and the $100 appears on the December 31, 1990, balance sheet. If this is the only note the company has outstanding, the $100 is deducted on the balance sheet as follows:

Current liabilities:
Notes payable $6,000
   Less discount on notes payable 100 $5,900

When the adjusted discount on notes payable is subtracted as a contra liability, the net liability on the balance sheet shows the amount received in discounting the note plus the accrued interest on the note to the balance sheet date. In this example, $5,850 was received in discounting the note, and accrued interest on the note is $50. Together they total $5,900, which is the net liability to the bank on December 31.

Accrued Interest Expense

Interest on an interest-bearing note accrues as time passes. Therefore, if any interest-bearing notes payable are outstanding at the end of an accounting period, the accrued interest should be recorded. For example, a company gave its bank a $4,000, 60-day, 12% note on December 16 to borrow that amount of money. If the company's accounting period ends on December 31, by then 15 days' or $20 interest has accrued on this note. You should record the interest with this adjusting entry:

Dec.	31	Interest Expense.	20.00	
		Interest Payable.		20.00
		To record accrued interest on a note payable.		

The adjusting entry causes the $20 accrued interest to appear on the income statement as an expense of the period that benefits from 15 days' use of the money. It also causes the interest payable to appear on the balance sheet as a current liability.

When the note matures in the next accounting period, its payment is recorded as follows:

Feb.	14	Notes Payable	4,000.00	
		Interest Payable	20.00	
		Interest Expense.	60.00	
		Cash		4,080.00
		Paid a $4,000 note and its interest.		

Interest on this note for 60 days is $80. In the illustrated entry, the $80 is divided between the interest accrued at the end of the previous period, $20, and interest applicable to the current period, $60.

The Concept of Present Value

Calculate the present value of a sum of money that will be received a number of periods in the future or will be received periodically.
(L. O. 5)

The concept of present value enters into many financing and investing decisions and any resulting liabilities. Therefore, an understanding of present value is important for all business students. The concept is based on the idea that the right to receive, say, $1 a year from today is worth less than $1 today. In other words, $1 to be received one year hence has a **present value** of less than $1. How much less depends on how much can be earned on invested funds. To state the concept in general terms, present value is the amount of money that could be currently invested at a given interest rate to accumulate a total value equal to a given amount to be received or paid at some future date. For example, if a 10% annual return can be earned, the expectation of receiving $1 one year from now has a present value of $0.9091. This can be verified as follows: $0.9091 invested today to earn 10% annually will earn $0.09091 in one year, and when the $0.09091 earned is added to the $0.9091 invested—

Investment	$0.9091
Earnings	0.09091
Total.	$1.00001

the investment plus the earnings equal $1.00001, which rounds to the $1 expected.

Likewise, the present value of $1 to be received two years hence is $0.8264 if a 10% compound annual return is expected. This also can be verified as follows: $0.8264 invested to earn 10% compounded annually will earn $0.08264 the first year it is invested, and when the $0.08264 earned is added to the $0.8264 invested—

Investment	$0.8264
First-year earnings	0.08264
End-of-year-1 amount	$0.90904

the investment plus the first year's earnings total $0.90904. During the second year, this $0.90904 will earn $0.090904, which when added to the end-of-year-1 amount—

End-of-year-1 amount	$0.90904
Second-year earnings	0.090904
End-of-year-2 amount	$0.999944

equals $0.999944, which rounds to the $1 expected at the end of the second year.

Present Value Tables

The *present value* of $1 to be received any number of years in the future can be calculated by using the formula, $1/(1 + i)^n$. The i is the interest rate, and n is the number of years to the expected receipt. However, you do not need to use the formula, since there are **present value tables** that show present values computed with the formula at various interest rates. An example is Table 12–1, which shows the present value amounts rounded to four decimal places. (Four decimal places would not be sufficiently accurate for some uses but will suffice here.)

Observe in Table 12–1 that the first amount in the 10% column is the 0.9091 used in the previous section to introduce the concept of present value. The 0.9091 in the 10% column means that the expectation of receiving $1 one period hence, when discounted at 10%, has a present value of $0.9091. Also note that the second amount in the 10% column is the 0.8264 previously used. This number means that the expectation of receiving $1 two periods hence, discounted at 10%, has a present value of $0.8264.

Using a Present Value Table

To demonstrate the use of a present value table such as Table 12–1, assume that a company has an opportunity to invest $55,000 in a project. The investment will return $20,000 at the end of the first year, $25,000 at the end of the second year, $30,000 at the end of the third year, and nothing thereafter. Also assume that the company believes the risks of the project justify a 12% return, compounded annually.

Will the project return the original investment plus the 12% demanded? The calculations of Illustration 12–1 indicate that it will. In Illustration 12–1, the expected returns in the second column are multiplied by the present value amounts in the third column to determine the present values in the last column. Since the total of the present values exceeds the required investment by $4,142, the project will return the $55,000 investment, plus a 12% return thereon, plus an additional $4,142.

In Illustration 12–1, the present value of each year's return was separately calculated. Then, the present values were totaled. When the periodic returns are unequal, as in this example, you must separately calculate the present value of each. However, in cases where the periodic returns are equal, there are shorter ways to calculate the sum of their present values.

For instance, suppose a $17,500 investment will return $5,000 at the end of each year in its five-year life and an investor wants to know the present value of these returns, discounted at 12%. In this case, the periodic returns are equal,

Table 12–1
Present Value of $1 at Compound Interest

Periods Hence	4½%	5%	6%	7%	8%	9%	10%	12%	14%	16%
1	0.9569	0.9524	0.9434	0.9346	0.9259	0.9174	0.9091	0.8929	0.8772	0.8621
2	0.9157	0.9070	0.8900	0.8734	0.8573	0.8417	0.8264	0.7972	0.7695	0.7432
3	0.8763	0.8638	0.8396	0.8163	0.7938	0.7722	0.7513	0.7118	0.6750	0.6407
4	0.8386	0.8227	0.7921	0.7629	0.7350	0.7084	0.6830	0.6355	0.5921	0.5532
5	0.8025	0.7835	0.7473	0.7130	0.6806	0.6499	0.6209	0.5674	0.5194	0.4761
6	0.7679	0.7462	0.7050	0.6663	0.6302	0.5963	0.5645	0.5066	0.4556	0.4104
7	0.7348	0.7107	0.6651	0.6228	0.5835	0.5470	0.5132	0.4523	0.3996	0.3538
8	0.7032	0.6768	0.6274	0.5820	0.5403	0.5019	0.4665	0.4039	0.3506	0.3050
9	0.6729	0.6446	0.5919	0.5439	0.5003	0.4604	0.4241	0.3606	0.3075	0.2630
10	0.6439	0.6139	0.5584	0.5084	0.4632	0.4224	0.3855	0.3220	0.2697	0.2267
11	0.6162	0.5847	0.5268	0.4751	0.4289	0.3875	0.3505	0.2875	0.2366	0.1954
12	0.5897	0.5568	0.4970	0.4440	0.3971	0.3555	0.3186	0.2567	0.2076	0.1685
13	0.5643	0.5303	0.4688	0.4150	0.3677	0.3262	0.2897	0.2292	0.1821	0.1452
14	0.5400	0.5051	0.4423	0.3878	0.3405	0.2993	0.2633	0.2046	0.1597	0.1252
15	0.5167	0.4810	0.4173	0.3625	0.3152	0.2745	0.2394	0.1827	0.1401	0.1079
16	0.4945	0.4581	0.3937	0.3387	0.2919	0.2519	0.2176	0.1631	0.1229	0.0930
17	0.4732	0.4363	0.3714	0.3166	0.2703	0.2311	0.1978	0.1456	0.1078	0.0802
18	0.4528	0.4155	0.3503	0.2959	0.2503	0.2120	0.1799	0.1300	0.0946	0.0691
19	0.4333	0.3957	0.3305	0.2765	0.2317	0.1945	0.1635	0.1161	0.0830	0.0596
20	0.4146	0.3769	0.3118	0.2584	0.2146	0.1784	0.1486	0.1037	0.0728	0.0514

Illustration 12–1
Present value of a series of unequal amounts

Years Hence	Expected Returns	Present Value of $1 at 12%	Present Value of Expected Returns
1	$20,000	0.8929	$17,858
2	25,000	0.7972	19,930
3	30,000	0.7118	21,354
Total present value of the returns			$59,142
Less investment required.			55,000
Excess over 12% demanded			$ 4,142

and a short way to determine their total present value at 12% is to add the present values of $1 at 12% for periods 1 through 5 (from Table 12–1) as follows—

```
0.8929
0.7972
0.7118
0.6355
0.5674
3.6048
```

and then to multiply $5,000 by the total. The $18,024 result ($5,000 × 3.6048 = $18,024) is the same as would be obtained if you calculate the present value of each year's return and then add the present values. Although the result is the same either way, the method demonstrated here requires four fewer multiplications.

Present Value of $1 Received Periodically for a Number of Periods

Table 12–2 is based on the idea demonstrated in the above paragraph. To summarize, the present value of a series of equal returns to be received at periodic intervals is nothing more than the sum of the present values of the individual returns. Note the amount on the table's fifth line in the 12% column. It is the same 3.6048 amount that was calculated in the previous paragraph by adding the first five present values of $1 at 12%. All the amounts shown in Table 12–2 could be determined by adding amounts found in Table 12–1. However, there would be some slight variations due to rounding.

A table such as Table 12–2 is used to determine the present value of a series of equal amounts to be received at periodic intervals. For example, what is the present value of a series of ten $1,000 amounts, with one $1,000 amount to be received at the end of each of 10 successive years, discounted at 8%? To determine the answer, look down the 8% column to the amount opposite 10 periods (years in this case). It is 6.7101, and $6.7101 is the present value of $1 to be received annually at the end of each of 10 years, discounted at 8%. Therefore, the present value of the ten $1,000 amounts is $1,000 × 6.7101, or $6,710.10.

Interest Periods Less than One Year in Length

In the examples so far, the interest rates were applied to time periods that were one year in length. However, interest often is applied to time periods that are shorter than one year. For instance, although interest rates on corporate bonds are usually quoted on an annual basis, the interest on such bonds is normally paid semiannually. As a result, the present value of the interest to be received on such bonds must be based on interest periods that are six months in length.

To illustrate a calculation based on six-month interest periods, assume an investor wants to know the present value of the interest that will be received over a period of five years on some corporation bonds. The bonds have a $10,000 par value, and interest is paid on them every six months at a 14% annual rate. Although the interest rate is stated as an annual rate of 14%, it is actually a rate of 7% per six-month interest period. Therefore, the investor will receive $10,000 × 7%, or $700 in interest on these bonds at the end of each six-month interest period. In five years, there are 10 such periods. Therefore, if these 10 receipts of $700 each are discounted at the interest rate of the bonds, to determine their present value, look down the 7% column of Table 12–2 to the amount opposite 10 periods. It is 7.0236, and the present value of the ten $700 semiannual receipts is 7.0236 × $700, or $4,916.52.

For a more complete discussion of discounting, you should turn to Appendix G at the end of the book. Appendix G expands the discussion of how present value tables are developed and explains the development of future value tables. Large present value and future value tables are included in the appendix, which also has numerous exercises related to discounting.

Table 12–2
Present Value of $1 Received Periodically for a Number of Periods

Periods Hence	4½%	5%	6%	7%	8%	9%	10%	12%	14%	16%
1	0.9569	0.9524	0.9434	0.9346	0.9259	0.9174	0.9091	0.8929	0.8772	0.8621
2	1.8727	1.8594	1.8334	1.8080	1.7833	1.7591	1.7355	1.6901	1.6467	1.6052
3	2.7490	2.7232	2.6730	2.6243	2.5771	2.5313	2.4869	2.4018	2.3216	2.2459
4	3.5875	3.5460	3.4651	3.3872	3.3121	3.2397	3.1699	3.0374	2.9137	2.7982
5	4.3900	4.3295	4.2124	4.1002	3.9927	3.8897	3.7908	3.6048	3.4331	3.2743
6	5.1579	5.0757	4.9173	4.7665	4.6229	4.4859	4.3553	4.1114	3.8887	3.6847
7	5.8927	5.7864	5.5824	5.3893	5.2064	5.0330	4.8684	4.5638	4.2883	4.0386
8	6.5959	6.4632	6.2098	5.9713	5.7466	5.5348	5.3349	4.9676	4.6389	4.3436
9	7.2688	7.1078	6.8017	6.5152	6.2469	5.9953	5.7590	5.3283	4.9464	4.6065
10	7.9127	7.7217	7.3601	7.0236	6.7101	6.4177	6.1446	5.6502	5.2161	4.8332
11	8.5289	8.3064	7.8869	7.4987	7.1390	6.8052	6.4951	5.9377	5.4527	5.0286
12	9.1186	8.8633	8.3838	7.9427	7.5361	7.1607	6.8137	6.1944	5.6603	5.1971
13	9.6829	9.3936	8.8527	8.3577	7.9038	7.4869	7.1034	6.4236	5.8424	5.3423
14	10.2228	9.8986	9.2950	8.7455	8.2442	7.7862	7.3667	6.6282	6.0021	5.4675
15	10.7395	10.3797	9.7123	9.1079	8.5595	8.0607	7.6061	6.8109	6.1422	5.5755
16	11.2340	10.8378	10.1059	9.4467	8.8514	8.3126	7.8237	6.9740	6.2651	5.6685
17	11.7072	11.2741	10.4773	9.7632	9.1216	8.5436	8.0216	7.1196	6.3729	5.7487
18	12.1600	11.6896	10.8276	10.0591	9.3719	8.7556	8.2014	7.2497	6.4674	5.8179
19	12.5933	12.0853	11.1581	10.3356	9.6036	8.9501	8.3649	7.3658	6.5504	5.8775
20	13.0079	12.4622	11.4699	10.5940	9.8182	9.1286	8.5136	7.4694	6.6231	5.9288

Exchanging a Note for a Plant Asset

Prepare entries to account for long-term noninterest-bearing notes payable, for installment notes payable, and for capital and operating leases. (L. O. 6)

When a high-cost asset is purchased, particularly if the credit period is long, a note is sometimes given in exchange for the purchased asset. If the amount of the note is approximately equal to the cash price for the asset and the stated interest rate on the note is approximately the prevailing market rate, the transaction is recorded as follows:

Feb.	12	Store Equipment	4,500.00	
		Notes Payable		4,500.00
		Exchanged a $4,500, three-year, 16% note payable for a refrigerated display case.		

A note given in exchange for a plant asset has two elements, which may or may not be stipulated in the note. They are (1) a dollar amount equivalent to the bargained cash price of the asset, and (2) an interest factor to compensate the supplier for the use of the funds that otherwise would have been received in a cash sale. Therefore, when a note is exchanged for a plant asset and the face amount of the note approximately equals the cash price of the asset and the note's interest rate approximates the prevailing market rate, the asset is recorded at the face amount of the note as in the previous illustration.

Notes that Have an Unreasonable or No Stated Interest Rate

Sometimes no interest rate is stated on a note, or the stated interest rate does not approximate a prevailing market rate. In such cases, the face amount of the note will not be equal to the cash price for the asset. Nevertheless, the asset must be recorded at its cash price or at the present value of the note, whichever is more clearly determinable.[3] To record the asset at the face amount of the note would misstate the asset, liability, and interest expense. Furthermore, these misstatements may be material, especially in case of a long-term note.

To illustrate a situation in which a note with no stated interest rate is exchanged for a plant asset, assume that on January 2, 1991, a noninterest-bearing, five-year, $10,000 note payable is exchanged for a factory machine. Also assume that the cash price of the asset is not readily determinable. If the prevailing market rate of interest on the day of the exchange is 14%, the present value of the note on that day is $5,194. This amount may be calculated by multiplying the face amount of the note by the fifth amount in the 14% column of Table 12–1 ($10,000 × 0.5194 = $5,194). The exchange should be recorded as follows:

1991 Jan.	2	Factory Machinery	5,194.00	
		Discount on Notes Payable	4,806.00	
		Long-Term Notes Payable		10,000.00
		Exchanged a five-year, noninterest-bearing note for a machine.		

The $5,194 debit amount in the entry is the present value of the note on the day of the exchange. It is also the cost of the machine and is the amount you must use to calculate depreciation. In the entry, the debit to Discount on Notes Payable and credit to Long-Term Notes Payable together measure the liability that resulted from the transaction. They should appear on a balance sheet prepared immediately after the exchange as follows:

Long-term liabilities:
   Long-term notes payable $10,000
   Less unamortized discount based on the 14% interest
      rate prevailing on the date of issue. 4,806 $5,194

Amortizing the Discount on a Note Payable

The $4,806 discount is a contra liability and is also the interest element of the transaction. Column 3 of Illustration 12–2 shows those parts of the $4,806 that should be amortized and charged to Interest Expense at the end of each of the five years in the life of the note.

---

[3] *APB Opinion No. 21*, par. 12.

Illustration 12–2
Amortization schedule for a five-year, $10,000 note payable, discounted at 14%

Year	(a) Face Amount of Note	(b) Unamortized Discount at Beginning of Year	(c) Beginning-of-Year Carrying Amount (a) − (b)	(d) Discount to Be Amortized Each Year (c) × 14%	(e) Unamortized Discount at the End of Year (b) − (d)	(f) End-of-Year Carrying Amount (a) − (e)
1991	$10,000	$4,806	$5,194	$ 727	$4,079	$ 5,921
1992	10,000	4,079	5,921	829	3,250	6,750
1993	10,000	3,250	6,750	945	2,305	7,695
1994	10,000	2,305	7,695	1,077	1,228	8,772
1995	10,000	1,228	8,772	1,228	–0–	10,000

The first year's amortization entry is:

1991					
Dec.	31	Interest Expense.		727.00	
		Discount on Notes Payable			727.00
		To amortize a portion of the discount on our long-term note.			

The $727 amortized is interest at 14% on the note's $5,194 value on the day it was exchanged for the machine. The $727 is rounded to the nearest whole dollar, as are all amounts in Illustration 12–2.

Posting the amortization entry causes the note to appear on the December 31, 1991, balance sheet as follows:

Long-term liabilities:		
Long-term notes payable.	$10,000	
Less unamortized discount on the 14% interest rate prevailing on the date of issue	4,079	$5,921

Compare the net amount at which the note is carried on the December 31, 1991, balance sheet with the net amount shown for the note on the balance sheet prepared on its date of issue. Observe that the **carrying amount of the note** increased $727 between the two dates. (The $727 is the amount of discount amortized and charged to Interest Expense at the end of 1991.)

At the end of 1992 and each succeeding year, the remaining amounts of discount shown in Column (d) of Illustration 12–2 should be amortized and charged to Interest Expense. This will cause the carrying amount of the note to increase each year by the amount of discount amortized that year and to reach $10,000, the note's maturity value, at the end of the fifth year. Payment of the note will be recorded as follows:

1996				
Jan.	2	Long-Term Notes Payable.	10,000.00	
		Cash		10,000.00
		Paid our long-term noninterest-bearing note.		

Look again at Illustration 12–2. Each end-of-year carrying amount in Column (f) is determined by subtracting the end-of-year unamortized discount in Column (e) from the $10,000 face amount of the note. For example, $10,000 − $4,079 = $5,921. Each beginning-of-year carrying amount is the same as the previous end-of-year amount. In Column (d), the amount of discount to be amortized each year is determined by multiplying the beginning-of-year carrying amount in Column (c) by the 14% interest rate prevailing at the time of the exchange. For example, $5,921 × 14% = $829 (rounded). Each end-of-year amount of unamortized discount in Column (e) is the discount remaining after subtracting the discount amortized that year. For example, $4,806 − $727 = $4,079.

In the balance sheet at the end of each year, the carrying amount of a note payable must be divided into two parts. The portion to be paid during the next year must be shown as a current liability, with the remaining portion shown as a long-term liability.

Installment Notes Payable

Although some promissory notes require a single lump-sum payment of the amount borrowed plus interest, most long-term notes require a series of payments. These notes are called **installment notes** because each payment includes not only interest but also part of the amount originally borrowed.

When an installment note is used to borrow money, the borrower records the note just like a single-payment note. For example, suppose a company borrows $60,000 by signing a 12% installment note that requires six annual payments. The borrower records the note as follows:

1990				
Dec.	31	Cash	60,000.00	
		Notes Payable.		60,000.00
		Borrowed by signing a 12% note.		

An installment note payable requires the borrower to pay back the debt in a series of periodic payments. Usually, each payment includes all of the interest accrued to the date of the payment plus some portion of the original amount borrowed (the principal amount). The terms of installment notes commonly call for one of two alternative payment patterns.

Installment Payments of Accrued Interest plus Equal Amounts of Principal

Some installment notes require payments that consist of accrued interest to date plus equal amounts of principal. Since each periodic payment reduces the amount borrowed, the next period's interest is reduced and the total amount of the payment is smaller than the previous payment. For example, suppose that the $60,000, 12% note recorded above requires that $10,000 of principal plus accrued interest be paid at the end of each year. The entries to record the first and the second annual payments are as follows:

1991				
Dec.	31	Notes Payable ($60,000 ÷ 6)	10,000.00	
		Interest Expense ($60,000 × 0.12)	7,200.00	
		Cash		17,200.00
		To record first installment payment.		
1992				
Dec.	31	Notes Payable ($60,000 ÷ 6)	10,000.00	
		Interest Expense ($50,000 × 0.12)	6,000.00	
		Cash		16,000.00
		To record second installment payment.		

Note that the balance of the debt at the beginning of each interest period is used to calculate the interest expense for the period. As a result, each payment is smaller than the previous payment.

Installment Payments that Are Equal in Total Amount

At this point, if you are not sure of your understanding of the concept of present value, you should turn back to page 557 and review this concept. Also, for additional study of discounting, Appendix G (at the end of the book) contains an expanded analysis of present and future values.

Many installment notes require a series of payments where the total amount of each payment is equal to each of the other payments. Since the payments are equal in amount, they consist of changing amounts of interest and principal. For example, assume that the $60,000, 12% note does not require six principal payments of $10,000 each plus accrued interest. Instead, assume that the note requires a series of six equal payments to be made at the end of each year. Each payment is to be $14,594.

Allocating Each Payment between Interest and Principal. Each payment of $14,594 includes both principal and interest. To determine the amounts of interest and principal that are included in each payment, understand that $60,000 is the present value of $14,594 to be paid annually for six years, discounted at 12%. (In this chapter, all dollar amounts are rounded to the nearest whole dollar.) The allocation of each payment between interest and principal is shown in Illustration 12-3. Because the illustration shows how the principal balance is reduced through the periodic payments, the presentation is sometimes called an installment note amortization schedule.

In Illustration 12–3, observe that interest expense is calculated each period as 12% multiplied by the beginning-of-period principal balance. Then, the interest expense is subtracted from the periodic payment to determine the portion of the payment that is a repayment of principal. Each number in the table is rounded to the nearest whole dollar.

Illustration 12–3
Installment note amortization schedule

Period Ending	(a) Beginning-of-Period Principal Balance	(b) Periodic Payment	(c) Interest Expense for the Period (a) × 12%	(d) Portion of Payment that Is Principal (b) − (c)	(e) End-of-Period Principal Balance (a) − (d)
Dec. 31, 1991	$60,000	$14,594	$7,200	$ 7,394	$52,606
Dec. 31, 1992	52,606	14,594	6,313	8,281	44,325
Dec. 31, 1993	44,325	14,594	5,319	9,275	35,050
Dec. 31, 1994	35,050	14,594	4,206	10,388	24,662
Dec. 31, 1995	24,662	14,594	2,959	11,635	13,027
Dec. 31, 1996	13,027	14,590*	1,563	13,027	–0–

*Note that the final payment is $4 smaller than the first five payments due to rounding. Although the note called for equal payments, a minor adjustment to the final payment is commonly necessary to repay the exact amount of debt.

The journal entry to record the first periodic payment is:

1991				
Dec.	31	Notes Payable	7,394.00	
		Interest Expense	7,200.00	
		Cash		14,594.00
		To record first installment payment.		

Similar entries are used to record each of the remaining payments.

How to Calculate the Periodic Payments. In the example, the $60,000, 12% loan required six annual payments of $14,594. Illustration 12–3 proves that these payments are precisely the amounts needed to repay the loan. But how do you calculate the $14,594?

The correct amount of the periodic payments may be calculated by using a table for the present value of $1 received (or paid) periodically for a number of periods. (See Table 12–2.) In Table 12–2, the present value of $1 paid at the end of each year for six years, discounted at 12%, is $4.1114. This relationship between the periodic payments of $1 and the present value of $4.1114 may be expressed as a ratio, as follows:

$$\frac{\text{Periodic payment}}{\text{Present value}} = \frac{1}{4.1114}$$

This ratio of periodic payments to present value is the same for all situations in which six payments ($n = 6$) are discounted at an interest rate of 12% ($i = 12\%$). In other words, when the present value is $60,000, the periodic payments can be calculated as follows:

$$\frac{\text{Periodic payment}}{\$60,000} = \frac{1}{4.1114}$$

$$\text{Periodic payment} = \frac{\$60,000 \times 1}{4.1114} = \$14,593.57, \text{ or } \$14,594$$

Liabilities from Leasing

How to Classify Leases

In recent years, many businesses have chosen to lease plant assets rather than purchase them. By leasing instead of purchasing, a business avoids the immediate cash outflow to pay for the asset. Instead, a lease typically requires a series of payments to be made over the life of the lease.

Although leases require a series of future payments, some leases, which are called **operating leases**, are not recorded as liabilities. In general, the terms of operating leases are such that the lessee does not acquire an ownership interest in the leased property. Because some leases are not recorded as liabilities and therefore do not appear on the balance sheet, leasing is sometimes said to be a form of off-balance sheet financing.

While operating leases generally do not give the lessee the benefits of ownership, other leases have essentially the same economic consequences as if the lessee secured a loan and purchased the leased asset. Such leases are called **capital leases** or **financing leases.** When an asset is leased under a capital lease, the lessee records the asset as if it has been purchased and also records a liability equal to the present value of the future lease payments.

According to the *CICA Handbook*, a lease that meets any one of the following criteria is a capital lease.[4]

1. Ownership of the leased asset is transferred to the lessee at the end of the lease period, or the lease gives the lessee the option of purchasing the leased asset at less than fair value at some point during or at the end of the lease period.
2. The period of the lease is 75% or more of the estimated service life of the leased asset.
3. The present value of the minimum lease payments is 90% or more of the fair value of the leased asset.

A lease that does not meet at least one of the three criteria is classified as an operating lease.

To illustrate accounting for leases, assume that Alpha Company plans to produce a product that requires the use of a new machine that costs approximately $35,000 and has an estimated 10-year life with no salvage value. Alpha Company does not have $35,000 in available cash and plans to lease the machine as of December 31, 1990. It will lease the machine under one of the following contracts, each of which requires Alpha Company to pay maintenance, taxes, and insurance on the machine: (1) Lease the machine for five years, with annual payments of $7,500 payable at the end of each of the five

---

[4] Ibid., par. 3065.06.

years. The machine will be returned to the lessor at the end of the lease period. (2) Lease the machine for five years, with annual payments of $10,000 payable at the end of each of the five years. The machine will become the property of Alpha Company at the end of the lease period.

Accounting for an Operating Lease

The first lease contract does not meet any of the first two criteria of a capital lease. Also, assuming the interest rate available to Alpha Company is 16%, the present value of the lease payments is $7,500 × 3.2743 = $24,557.25, which is less than 90% of $35,000. Therefore, the lease does not meet the third criterion of a capital lease. Since the lease does not meet any of the criteria, it must be classified as an operating lease.

If Alpha Company chooses this contract, it should make no entry to record the lease contract. However, each annual rental payment should be recorded as follows:

1991				
Dec.	31	Machinery Rentals Expense.	7,500.00	
		Cash		7,500.00
		Paid the annual rent on a leased machine.		

Alpha Company should also charge to expense all payments for taxes, insurance, and any repairs to the machine. But, since the leased machine is not recorded as an asset, depreciation expense is not recorded. In addition, Alpha should add a footnote to its income statement that gives a general description of the leasing arrangements.

Accounting for a Capital Lease

The second lease contract meets the first and third criteria in the *CICA Handbook* and is a capital lease. In effect, it is a purchase transaction with the lessor company financing the purchase of the machine for Alpha Company. Therefore, the AcSC ruled that the asset and the lease liability should be recorded on the lease date at the present value of the lease payments.

Recording the Lease Liability. If Alpha Company chooses the second lease contract and the interest rate available to Alpha on such contracts is 16% annually, it should (based on the fifth amount in the 16% column of Table 12–2) multiply $10,000 by 3.2743 to get a $32,743 present value for the five lease payments. Alpha should then make this entry:

1990				
Dec.	31	Machinery.	32,743.00	
		Discount on Lease Financing	17,257.00	
		Long-Term Lease Liability		50,000.00
		Purchased a machine through a long-term lease contract.		

The $32,743 is the cost of the machine. As with any plant asset, it should be charged off to depreciation expense over the machine's expected service life. Note, however, that the expected service life of a leased asset may be limited to the term of the lease. If the lessee does not have the right to ownership at the end of the lease and the lease period is less than the asset's expected life, the lease period becomes the useful life of the asset.

Reporting a Long-Term Lease Liability on the Balance Sheet. The $17,257 discount is the interest factor in the transaction. The long-term lease liability less the amount of the discount measures the net liability that results from the purchase. The two items should appear on a balance sheet prepared immediately after the transaction as follows:

Long-term liabilities:
  Long-term lease liability[5] $50,000
  Less unamortized discount based on the 16% interest
     rate available on the date of the contract 17,257 $32,743

Entries to Record Depreciation, Lease Payments, and Interest. If Alpha Company plans to depreciate the machine on a straight-line basis over its 10-year life, it should make the following entries at the end of the first year in the life of the lease:

1991				
Dec.	31	Depreciation Expense, Machinery	3,274.30	
		Accumulated Depreciation, Machinery.		3,274.30
		To record depreciation on the machine.		
	31	Long-Term Lease Liability.	10,000.00	
		Cash		10,000.00
		Made the annual payment on the lease.		
	31	Interest Expense.	5,239.00	
		Discount on Lease Financing		5,239.00
		Amortized a portion of the discount on the lease financing.		

The first two entries need no comment. The $5,239 amortized in the third entry is interest at 16% for one year on the $32,743 beginning-of-year carrying amount of the lease liability ($32,743 × 16% = $5,239). The $5,239 is rounded to the nearest whole dollar, as are all amounts in Illustration 12–4.

Posting the entries that record the $10,000 payment and the amortization of the discount causes the **carrying amount of the lease** to appear on the December 31, 1991, balance sheet as follows:

[5]To simplify the illustration, the fact that the first installment on the lease should be classified as a current liability is ignored here and should be ignored in the problems at the end of the chapter.

Illustration 12–4
Amortization schedule for a lease liability

Year	Beginning-of-Year Lease Liability	Beginning-of-Year Unamortized Discount	Beginning-of-Year Carrying Amount	Discount to Be Amortized (16%)	Unamortized Discount at End of Year	End-of-Year Lease Liability	End-of-Year Carrying Amount
1991	$50,000	$17,257	$32,743	$5,239	$12,018	$40,000	$27,982
1992	40,000	12,018	27,982	4,477	7,541	30,000	22,459
1993	30,000	7,541	22,459	3,593	3,948	20,000	16,052
1994	20,000	3,948	16,052	2,568	1,380	10,000	8,620
1995	10,000	1,380	8,620	1,380*	–0–	–0–	–0–

* Adjusted for rounding.

Long-term liabilities:
Long-term lease liability $40,000
Less unamortized discount based on the 16% interest
rate prevailing on the date of the contract 12,018 $27,982

At the end of 1992 and each succeeding year, the remaining amounts in Column 5 of Illustration 12–4 should be amortized. This, together with $10,000 annual payments, will reduce the carrying amount of the lease liability to zero by the end of the fifth year.

Return again to Illustration 12–4. To determine the amount of discount to be amortized each year, the beginning-of-year carrying amount of the lease liability was multiplied by 16%. For example, the 1992 amount to be amortized is $4,477 ($27,982 × 16% = $4,477 rounded). Each end-of-year carrying amount was determined by subtracting the end-of-year unamortized discount from the remaining end-of-year lease liability. For example, the December 31, 1992, carrying amount is $30,000 − $7,541 = $22,459.

Summary of Chapter in Terms of Learning Objectives

1. Current liabilities are due within one year of the balance sheet date or within one operating cycle, whichever is longer. The liquidation of current liabilities requires the use of existing assets or the creation of other current liabilities. Long-term liabilities are those that do not have to be paid within one year or one operating cycle.

2. A liability is definite when you know the answer to all three of these questions: (a) Who will be paid? (b) When is payment due? (c) How much will be paid? When the amount to be paid is not precisely known, the obligation is called an estimated liability.

3. Expenses for property taxes and product warranties often must be recorded before the amounts to be paid are known. Therefore, you must estimate the amounts of the liabilities based on the information currently available. After more information becomes available, the liabilities are corrected with corresponding adjustments to expense. Short-term notes payable are recorded at their face amounts when the stated interest rates of the notes are reasonable approximations of current market rates of interest. When the notes are not interest bearing or the stated rates of interest do not reflect the current market rate, the notes are recorded at their present values.

4. An obligation that qualifies as a liability generally does not depend on a future, uncertain event. In contrast, when an economic entity is obligated to make a future payment only if some future event takes place, the potential obligation is called a contingent liability. However, if the future event is probable and the amount of the payment can be reasonably estimated, the obligation qualifies as a liability.

5. The present value of an amount to be received or paid in the future is the amount that could be currently invested at the given rate of interest and would accumulate a total value equal to the amount to be received or paid. The present value of a series of equal payments is the sum of the present values of each payment.

6. A long-term, noninterest-bearing note must be recorded at its present value. Each period during the life of the note, interest expense is calculated by multiplying the carrying value of the note by the interest rate that was used to discount the note.

Installment notes typically require either of two alternative methods of payment: (1) payments that include accrued interest plus a principal amount equal to the total principal divided by the number of payments; or (2) payments that are equal in amount and that consist of a declining amount of interest and an increasing amount of principal. If the second payment pattern is used, the payments are determined by expressing the amount borrowed as the present value of the payments, discounted at the rate of interest specified in the note.

When accounting for a capital lease you must record the leased asset and the lease liability at the present value of the lease payments. On the other hand, you debit the periodic payments of an operating lease to Rent Expense as they are incurred.

Demonstration Problem

Prepare journal entries for the 1990 transactions of Kearns Company listed below.

a. Kearns accrued estimated property taxes during the first eight months of 1990 at the rate of $20,000 per month. On September 10, Kearns learned that the 1990 tax bill would be $217,200. The due date for these taxes is December 31. Show the property tax entries on September 30 and October 31.

b. During September, Kearns sold $140,000 of merchandise under a 180-day warranty. Prior experience shows that the costs of fulfilling the warranty will equal 5% of the selling price. Record the month's warranty expense and liability as a September 30 adjusting entry. Also record an October 8 expenditure of $300 to service an item sold in September.

c. On October 10, Kearns arranged with a supplier to pay 25% of Kearns' overdue $10,000 account payable to the supplier. The remaining balance was converted to a $7,500, 90-day note bearing 12% interest.

d. On October 15, Kearns borrowed $98,333 by discounting its $100,000, 60-day note to the bank. The discount rate charged by the bank was 10%.

e. On December 1, Kearns acquired a machine by giving a $60,000, noninterest-bearing note due in one year. The rate of interest available to Kearns for this type of debt was 12%.

f. On December 14, Kearns paid the note described in (d).

g. On January 1, 1990, Kearns signed a $500,000, 10%, installment note that calls for five annual installment payments that are equal in amount. The payments will be made on December 31, 1990–1994.

h. On December 31, Kearns accrued the interest on the notes described in (c) and (e). Show separate adjusting entries, assuming a 360-day year.

i. For the installment note in (g), (i) calculate the amount of each installment payment, (ii) prepare an amortization schedule, and (iii) present the entry for the first installment payment on December 31, 1990.

In addition to the above transactions, Kearns entered into a three-year lease of machinery on January 1, 1990, and agreed to make three payments on December 31, 1990, 1991, and 1992. Each payment will be $30,158, which will include 10% interest. Title to the machinery will pass to Kearns at the end of the lease, and the lease should be recorded as a capital lease.

j. Show the entry to record the lease.

k. Prepare a table that shows the interest expense in each year of the lease.

l. Show the entries to record the first payment on December 31, 1990, the interest expense for 1990, and the depreciation expense for 1990. The machine's useful life is predicted to be five years, with no salvage value, and straight-line depreciation is used.

m. Show how the leased asset and lease liability would appear on the balance sheet as of December 31, 1990.

Solution to Demonstration Problem

a.	Sept.	30	Property Tax Expense	2,900.00	
			Estimated Property Taxes Payable		2,900.00

Liability on September 30 ($217,200 × 9/12)	$162,900
Recorded liability as of August 31 ($20,000 × 8) . .	160,000
Additional liability to record on September 30	$ 2,900

	Oct.	31	Property Tax Expense	18,100.00	
			Estimated Property Taxes Payable		18,100.00
			$217,200 ÷ 12 = $18,100.		
b.	Sept.	30	Warranty Expense.	7,000.00	
			Estimated Warranty Liability.		7,000.00
			$140,000 × 5% = $7,000.		
	Oct.	8	Estimated Warranty Liability	300.00	
			Cash.		300.00
c.		10	Accounts Payable.	10,000.00	
			Cash.		2,500.00
			Notes Payable		7,500.00
d.		15	Cash	98,333.00	
			Interest Expense	1,667.00	
			Notes Payable		100,000.00
e.	Dec.	1	Machine	53,574.00	
			Discount on Notes Payable.	6,426.00	
			Notes Payable		60,000.00
			$60,000 × .8929 = $53,574.		
f.		14	Notes Payable.	100,000.00	
			Cash.		100,000.00
h.			For the Note in (c)		
		31	Interest Expense	205.00	
			Interest Payable		205.00
			$7,500 × 12% × $^{82}/_{360}$ = $205.		
			For the Note in (e)		
		31	Interest Expense	535.74	
			Discount on Notes Payable		535.74
			$53,574 × 12% × $^{30}/_{360}$ = $535.74.		

i.   (i)   Calculating the dollar amount of the five equal payments for the installment note.

From Table 12–2, the present value of $1 to be paid annually for 5 years, discounted at 10%, is $3.7908

Periodic payment = $500,000/3.7908 = $131,898

   (ii)   The amortization schedule for the installment note.

Period Ending	Beginning-of-Period Principal Balance	Periodic Payment	Interest Expense for the Period	Portion of Payment that is Principal	End-of-Period Principal Balance
Dec. 31, 90	$500,000	$131,898	$50,000	$ 81,898	$418,102
Dec. 31, 91	418,102	131,898	41,810	90,088	328,014
Dec. 31, 92	328,014	131,898	32,801	99,097	228,917
Dec. 31, 93	228,917	131,898	22,892	109,006	119,911
Dec. 31, 94	119,911	131,902*	11,991	119,911	–0–

*Payment increased by $4 because of rounding.

(iii)   The entry for the first payment on this note on December 31, 1990.

1990					
Dec.	31	Interest Expense	50,000.00	
		Notes Payable	81,898.00	
		Cash		131,898.00
		Made first payment on installment note.		

j.

	31	Machinery	75,000.00	
		Discount on Lease Financing	15,474.00	
		Long-Term Lease Liability		90,474.00
		Present value is:		
		$30,158 \times 2.4869 = \$75,000$ (rounded).		
		$30,158 \times 3 = \$90,474$.		

k.

Year	Beginning-of-Year Lease Liability	Beginning-of-Year Unamortized Discount	Beginning-of-Year Carrying Amount	Discount to Be Amortized	Unamortized Discount at End of Year	End-of-Year Lease Liability	End-of-Year Carrying Amount
1990	$90,474	$15,474	$75,000	$7,500	$7,974	$60,316	$52,342
1991	60,316	7,974	52,342	5,234	2,740	30,158	27,418
1992	30,158	2,740	27,418	2,740*	–0–	–0–	–0–

*Adjusted for rounding.

l.

Dec.	31	Long-Term Lease Liability	30,158.00	
		Cash.		30,158.00
	31	Interest Expense	7,500.00	
		Discount on Lease Financing		7,500.00
	31	Depreciation Expense.	15,000.00	
		Accumulated Depreciation.		15,000.00
		$75,000 \div 5 = \$15,000$.		

m.

Long-term liabilities:
Long-term lease liability $60,316
Less unamortized discount based on the 10%
interest rate available on the date of the
contract.   7,974 $52,342

Glossary

Define or explain the words and phrases listed in the chapter Glossary. (L. O. 7)

Bank discount interest charged and deducted by a bank at the time a loan is made. p. 554

Capital lease a lease that meets any of three criteria established by the *CICA Handbook*, the implication of which is that the lease has essentially the same economic consequences as if the lessee had secured a loan and purchased the leased asset. p. 567

Carrying amount of a lease the remaining lease liability minus the unamortized discount on the lease financing. p. 569

Carrying amount of a note the face amount of a note minus the unamortized discount on the note. p. 563

Estimated liability an obligation that definitely exists but for which the amount to be paid is uncertain. p. 550

Financing lease another name for a capital lease. p. 567

Installment notes promissory notes that require a series of payments which consist of interest plus a portion of the original amount borrowed. p. 564.

Long-term liabilities obligations that will not require the use of existing current assets in their liquidation because they do not mature within one year or one operating cycle, whichever is longer. p. 549

Operating lease a lease that does not meet any of the criteria of the *CICA Handbook* that would make it a capital lease. p. 567

Present value the amount of money that could be currently invested at a given interest rate to accumulate a total value equal to a given amount to be received or paid at some future date(s). p. 557

Present value table a table that shows the present values of one amount to be received at various future dates when discounted at various interest rates, or that shows the present values of a series of equal payments to be received for a varying number of periods when discounted at various interest rates. p. 558

Product warranty a promise to a customer that obligates the seller or manufacturer for a limited period of time to pay for items such as replacement parts or repair costs if the product breaks or fails to perform. p. 551

Questions for Class Discussion

1. What is a liability?
2. Are all expected future payments liabilities?
3. Define (*a*) a current liability and (*b*) a long-term liability.
4. If a liability is payable in 15 months, should it be classified as a current liability or as a long-term liability?
5. There are three important questions about which a liability may or may not be definite. What are those questions?
6. What is the nature of an estimated liability?
7. If a company has a definite obligation to pay a given amount of money to an outside party but the date the obligation must be paid is indefi-

nite, should the obligation be reported as a liability on the balance sheet or disclosed as a contingent liability?

8. If a property tax liability is estimated at the end of year 1 and the actual payment of the liability in year 2 turns out to be more than the amount that was estimated, how is the excess accounted for in year 2?

9. What is the difference between a liability and a contingent liability?

10. Under what conditions should a contingency be reported on the balance sheet as a liability?

11. Why are product warranties often recorded as liabilities instead of being disclosed as contingent liabilities?

12. The legal position of a company may be improved by its acceptance of a promissory note in exchange for granting a time extension on the due date of a customer's debt. Why?

13. What is the difference between a loan and a discount as those terms relate to borrowing money from a bank?

14. Which is to the advantage of a bank: (*a*) making a loan to a customer in exchange for the customer's $1,000, 60-day, 9% note or (*b*) making a loan to the customer by discounting the customer's $1,000 noninterest-bearing note for 60 days at 9%? Why?

15. Distinguish between bank discount and cash discount.

16. What determines the present value of $1,000 to be received at some future date?

17. Is $1,000 to be received in one year always worth less than a series of two $500 payments to be received semiannually for the next year?

18. If a $5,000 noninterest-bearing, five-year note is exchanged for a machine, the face amount of the note equals the sum of two different economic costs. What are these two costs?

19. If the Machinery account is debited for $5,000 and Notes Payable is credited for $5,000 in recording the machine of Question 18, what effects will this have on the financial statements?

20. What are two commonly used payment patterns on installment notes?

21. How is the interest portion of an installment note payment calculated?

22. What is the advantage of leasing a plant asset instead of purchasing it?

23. Distinguish between a capital lease and an operating lease. Which causes an asset and a liability to appear on the balance sheet?

24. When a capital lease is to be recorded, how do you determine the amount to be debited to the asset account?

Multiple Choice

1. Which of the following items normally would be classified as a current liability of a company that has a 15-month current operating cycle?
   a. Accounts payable due in 13 months.
   b. A note payable due in 11 months.
   c. Salaries payable.

    d. The portion of a long-term lease liability that is due within 15 months.

    e. All of the above.

2. Estimated liabilities include:

    a. Obligations to pay a specific amount on a specific date when the party to be paid is not known.

    b. Obligations to pay a specific amount to a specific person when the due date is not known.

    c. Obligations to pay a specific person on a specific date when the amount to be paid is uncertain but can be reasonably estimated.

    d. Obligations to pay an amount to an outside party if some uncertain future event occurs.

    e. All of the above.

3. A future payment should be reported on the balance sheet as a liability if:

    a. The payment is contingent on a future event that is likely and the amount of the payment is certain.

    b. The payment is contingent on a future event that is not likely but the amount of the payment can be reasonably estimated.

    c. The payment is contingent on a future event that is likely but the amount of the payment cannot be reasonably estimated.

    d. The payment is contingent on a future event that is likely and the amount of the payment can be reasonably estimated.

    e. Both (*a*) and (*d*) are correct.

4. When an installment note requires a series of payments that are equal in amount:

    a. The payments consist of changing amounts of interest, but the principal amount remains constant.

    b. The payments consist of changing amounts of the principal portion of the payment, but the interest portion of the payment remains constant.

    c. The interest expense for a given period is calculated by multiplying the face amount of the note by the interest rate.

    d. The portion of the payment that is a repayment of principal is determined by multiplying the beginning-of-period principal balance by the interest rate and deducting that amount of interest expense from the periodic payment.

    e. The payments consist of an increasing amount of interest and a decreasing amount of principal.

5. A company enters into an agreement whereby the company will make three semiannual payments of $500 each, the first to be made in 6 months, plus an additional $10,000 payment to be made 18 months from now. If the annual rate of interest is 12%, the present value of these payments is:

    a. $ 8,318.90.

    b. $ 9,732.50.

    c. $11,500.00.

    d. $12,097.49.

    e. $14,257.07.

6. On December 31, 1990, Jacks Company leased for 18 years a building
    with a fair value of $1,000,000 and an estimated useful life of 25 years.
    Annual lease payments of $125,522.44 begin on December 31, 1991, and
    the prevailing interest rate available to Jacks Company was 12%. Which
    of the following expenses will be recognized on this lease during 1991?
    a. Rental expense, $125,522.44.
    b. Interest expense, $109,200.00.
    c. Interest expense, $120,000.00.
    d. Rental expense, $55,555.56.
    e. Interest expense, $5,000.00.

Mini Discussion Cases

Case 12–1

Your friend has indicated that according to GAAP all possible liabilities should
be recorded in the financial statements. Therefore, he continues, even those
items called contingent liabilities must be accrued in accordance with the conservatism principle. Otherwise, the financial statements would be misleading.

Required

Is your friend correct? Why (not)?

Case 12–2

Jamie Keyes, ace lefthander with the York Bluebirds, is negotiating for re-
newal of his contract. Prior to making an offer to Keyes, George Megabucks—
owner of the team—asks you to check out three alternatives he intends to
present to the pitcher. George is only willing to offer a three-year contract but
is offering three different payment schemes as follows:

a. $200,000 payable at the end of each year for 10 years.
b. $500,000 payable at the end of each year for 3 years.
c. $1,200,000 payable on signing the three-year contract.

Required

1. Identify the accounting issues raised in the case.
2. Discuss how the issues should be resolved in light of GAAP.

Exercises

Exercise 12–1
Property tax expense
(L. O. 3)

Throughout 1991, K Company owned property that was subject to county
property taxes and had an assessed valuation for tax purposes of $900,000.
The 1990 tax levy was $0.60 per $100 of assessed valuation, and the company
expected the 1990 rate to remain unchanged. In early June, the county announced that the 1991 tax levy would be $0.66 per $100 and that taxes would be
due July 31, 1991. Prepare entries to record property tax expense for the
months of May, June, and July (including the payment of the annual tax on
July 31).

Exercise 12–2
Product warranty expense
(L. O. 3)

Fawn Company manufactures one product for $12 per unit and sells it for $20 per unit. In October, the company sold 150,000 units subject to a one-year warranty. According to the warranty, customers must pay a $2.25 service charge to return a broken unit and have it replaced by a new unit. When a unit under warranty fails, the company simply discards the broken unit and replaces it with a new one. Past experience suggests a 2% failure rate of new products sold, and customers actually returned 1,800 broken units during the month of October. Prepare summary entries for the month of October to record product warranty expense and to record the replacement of 1,800 broken units.

Exercise 12–3
Short-term notes payable
(L. O. 3)

On December 1, 1990, Blatz Company borrowed $150,000 by giving a 90-day, 12% note payable. The company has an annual, calendar-year accounting period and does not make reversing entries. Prepare general journal entries to record: (*a*) the issuance of the note, (*b*) the required year-end adjusting entry, and (*c*) the entry to pay the note.

Exercise 12–4
Discounted notes payable
(L. O. 3)

On December 1, 1990, Nozzle Company discounted its own $150,000, 90-day note payable at the bank. The discount rate was 12%. Prepare general journal entries to record: (*a*) the issuance of the note; (*b*) the required December 31, 1990, adjusting entry; (*c*) the payment of the note; and (*d*) the interest expense on the note during 1991.

Exercise 12–5
Present value calculations
(L. O. 5)

Present calculations to show the following: (*a*) the present value of $30,000 to be received nine years hence, discounted at 16%; (*b*) the total present value of three payments consisting of $35,000 to be received one year hence, $45,000 to be received two years hence, and $60,000 to be received three years hence, all discounted at 14%; and (*c*) the present value of seven payments of $9,000 each, with a payment to be received at the end of each of the next seven years, discounted at 12%.

Exercise 12–6
Present value of investment
(L. O. 5)

Smith Company is offered a contract whereby it will be paid $12,000 every 6 months for the next 10 years. The first payment would be received six months from today. What will the company be willing to pay for this contract if it expects a 14% annual return on the investment? What if it expects an annual return of only 10%?

Exercise 12–7
Present value of investment
(L. O. 5)

Titsch Company is offered a contract whereby it will be paid $24,000 annually for the next 10 years. The first payment would be received one year from today. What will the company be willing to pay for this contract if it expects a 14% return on the investment? What if it expects an annual return of only 10%?

Exercise 12–8
Choosing between payment patterns based on present values
(L. O. 5)

An individual has offered to sell a machine for $13,500. A potential buyer has agreed to purchase the machine for the stated price but, as an alternative, has given the seller the option of receiving 10 annual payments of $2,250 each, the first payment to be one year from now. Assuming the seller expects an annual return of at least 9%, which of the two alternatives should the seller accept?

Exercise 12–9
Exchanging a noninterest-bearing note for a plant asset
(L. O. 6)

Catter Company purchased equipment on January 1 of the current year. The terms of purchase included $21,000 cash plus a $35,000, noninterest-bearing, five-year note. The available interest rate on this date was 12%. (*a*) Prepare the entry to record the purchase of the machine. (*b*) Show how the liability will appear on a balance sheet prepared on the day of the purchase. (*c*) Prepare the entry to amortize a portion of the discount on the note at the end of its first year.

Exercise 12–10
Installment note with payments of accrued interest plus equal amounts of principal
(L. O. 6)

On December 31, 1990, Cutter Company borrowed $95,000 by signing a 5-year, 12% installment note. The note requires annual payments on December 31 of accrued interest plus equal amounts of principal. Prepare journal entries to record the first payment on December 31, 1991, and the last payment on December 31, 1995.

Exercise 12–11
Installment note with equal payments
(L. O. 6)

On December 31, 1990, Butter Company borrowed $95,000 by signing a 5-year, 12% installment note. The note requires annual payments of $26,354 to be made on December 31. Prepare journal entries to record the first payment on December 31, 1991, and the second payment on December 31, 1992.

Exercise 12–12
Calculating installment note payments
(L. O. 6)

Flag Company borrowed $100,000 by signing a 6-year, 14% installment note. The terms of the note require six annual payments of an equal amount, the first of which is due one year after the date of the note. Calculate the amount of the installment payments, based on the present values contained in Table 12–2.

Exercise 12–13
Liabilities from leasing
(L. O. 6)

On December 31, 1990, a day when the available interest rate was 12%, Davis Company leased a machine for five years under a contract calling for a $45,000 annual lease payment at the end of each of the next five years, with the machine becoming the property of the lessee at the end of that period. The company decided to lease the machine. Prepare entries to record: (*a*) the leasing of the machine; (*b*) the amortization of the discount on the lease financing at December 31, 1991; and (*c*) the December 31, 1991, payment under the lease.

Problems

Problem 12–1
Product warranty expense and property tax expense
(L. O. 2, 3)

Part 1.   Collie Company sells a single product subject to a six-month warranty that covers replacement parts but not labour. The company uses a periodic inventory system to account for merchandise. Prepare journal entries to record the following transactions completed by the company during the month of April:

Apr. 2 Purchased 1,200 units of merchandise for $30 per unit, paying cash.

3 Purchased $3,900 of spare parts for making repairs to merchandise that is expected to be returned for warranty work.

8 Sold 500 units of merchandise for $60 per unit, receiving cash.

11 Repaired 30 units of merchandise that customers returned under the warranty. Replacement parts cost $750, and the customers paid $570 for labour.

18 Sold 600 units of merchandise for $65 per unit.

21 Repaired 22 units of merchandise under the product warranty. Replacement parts cost $506, and the customers paid $396 for labour.

29 Recorded warranty expense for April. Past experience shows that 4% of the units sold require warranty work, and the average cost of replacement parts is $24 per unit returned. Average labour charges are $18.50.

Part 2. Terrapin Company expects to accrue 1991 property taxes at the end of each month using the experience of 1990 as a means of estimating the tax. In January 1990, Terrapin's property was appraised at $900,000. The 1990 tax levy was $2.40 per $100. In January 1991, Terrapin's property was reappraised at $990,000. (The reappraisal was not expected to affect the tax levy of $2.40 per $100.) Early in June 1991, the annual tax levy was set at $2.80 per $100. On November 30, 1991, Terrapin paid the 1991 tax. Complete financial statements are prepared by the company on a monthly basis, and the company does not use reversing entries.

Required
Prepare entries at the end of January, June, November, and December 1991 to record property tax expense for each of those months and to record the annual tax payment.

Problem 12–2
Journalizing notes payable transactions
(L. O. 3)

Prepare general journal entries to record these transactions of Davies Company:

1990
Jan. 8 Purchased merchandise on credit from Grant Company, invoice dated January 7, terms 2/10, n/60, $15,600.

Feb. 5 Borrowed money at First Provincial Bank by discounting our own $25,000 note payable for 60 days at 12%. Since the note matures before the end of the year, the discount should be charged to Interest Expense.

Mar. 10 Gave Grant Company $2,100 cash and a $13,500, 60-day, 12% note to secure an extension on our account that was due.

Apr. 5 Paid the note discounted at First Provincial Bank on February 5.

May 10 Paid the note given Grant Company on March 10.

Nov. 1 Borrowed money at First Provincial Bank by discounting our own $30,000 note payable for 90 days at 14%.

Dec. 16 Borrowed money at InterCity Bank by giving a $25,000, 60-day, 15% note payable.

Dec. 31   Made an adjusting entry to record interest on the November 1 note to First Provincial Bank.

31   Made an adjusting entry to record the accrued interest on the December 16 note to InterCity Bank.

1991

Jan. 30   Paid the November 1 note to First Provincial Bank. Also recorded interest expense related to the note.

Feb. 14   Paid the note given InterCity Bank on December 16.

Problem 12–3
Present values of alternative payment patterns
(L. O. 5)

Tropical Adventures is negotiating with a naval architect and shipyard in planning the construction of a 90-foot trimaran that Tropical Adventures expects to acquire and place in charter service. The yacht will be completed and ready for service four years hence. If Tropical Adventures pays for the yacht on completion (Payment Plan A), it will cost $500,500. However, two alternative payment plans are available. Plan B would require an immediate payment of $365,650. Plan C would require four annual payments of $105,850, the first of which would be made one year hence. In evaluating the three alternatives, the management of Tropical Adventures has decided to assume an interest rate of 10%.

Required

Calculate the present value of each payment and indicate which plan Tropical Adventures should follow.

Problem 12–4
Exchanging a noninterest-bearing note for a plant asset
(L. O. 6)

On January 2, 1990, a company gave its own $150,000 noninterest-bearing, five-year note payable in exchange for a machine the cash price of which was not readily determinable. The market rate for interest on such notes on the day of the exchange was 8% annually.

Required
(Round all amounts in your answers to the nearest whole dollar.)

1. Prepare a form with the following column headings and calculate and fill in the required amounts for the five years the note is outstanding.

Year	Face Amount of Note	Unamortized Discount at Beginning of Year	Beginning-of-Year Carrying Amount	Discount to Be Amortized Each Year	Unamortized Discount at the End of Year	End-of-Year Carrying Amount

2. Prepare general journal entries to record: (*a*) the acquisition of the machine, (*b*) the discount amortized at the end of each year, and (*c*) the payment of the note on January 2, 1995.

3. Show how the note should appear on the December 31, 1992, balance sheet.

Problem 12–5
Installment notes
(L. O. 6)

On June 30, 1990, Potter Company borrowed $450,000 at the bank by signing a five-year, 12% installment note. The terms of the note require equal semi-annual payments beginning December 31, 1990.

Required
(Round all amounts in your answers to the nearest whole dollar.)

1. Calculate the amount of the installment payments. (Use Table 12–2 on page 561.)
2. Prepare a table with column headings like the table in Illustration 12–3. Complete the table for the Potter Company note.
3. Prepare general journal entries to record the first and the last payments on the note.
4. Assume that the note does not require equal payments. Instead, assume the note requires payments of accrued interest plus equal amounts of principal. Prepare general journal entries to record the first and the last payments on the note.

Problem 12–6
Capital leases and exchanges of plant assets
(L. O. 6)

Isden Production Company leased a machine on January 1, 1990, under a contract calling for annual payments of $48,000 on December 31 at the end of each of five years, with the machine becoming the property of the lessee company after the fifth $48,000 payment. The machine was estimated to have an eight-year life and no salvage value, and the interest rate available to Isden for equipment loans on the day the lease was signed was 14%. The machine was delivered on January 5, 1990, and was immediately placed in operation. At the beginning of the eighth year in the machine's life, it was overhauled at a $3,060 total cost. The overhaul was paid for on January 10, and it did not increase the machine's efficiency but it did add an additional year to its expected service life. On March 31, during the ninth year in the machine's life, it was traded in on a new machine of like purpose having a $144,000 cash price. A $12,000 trade-in allowance was received, and the balance was paid in cash.

Required
(Round all amounts in your answers to the nearest whole dollar.)

1. Prepare a schedule with the column headings of Illustration 12–4. Enter the years 1990 through 1994 in the first column and complete the schedule by filling in the proper amounts.
2. Prepare the entry to record the leasing of the machine.
3. Prepare December 31, 1991, entries to record annual depreciation on a straight-line basis, to record the lease payment, and to amortize the discount in the life of the lease. Also show how the machine and the lease liability should appear on the December 31, 1991, balance sheet.
4. Prepare the entries to record the machine's overhaul and the depreciation on the machine at the end of its eighth year.
5. Prepare the March 31, 1998, entries to record the exchange of the machines.

Problem 12–7
Accounting for capital and operating leases
(L. O. 6)

The Colossal Freight Company needs two new trucks, each of which has an estimated service life of nine years. The trucks could be purchased for $149,200 each, but Colossal does not have enough cash to pay for them. Instead, Colossal agrees to lease Truck 1 for six years, after which the truck remains the property of the lessor. In addition, Colossal agrees to lease Truck 2 for eight years, after which the truck remains the property of the lessor. According to the lease contracts, Colossal must pay $30,000 annually for each truck ($60,000 for two trucks), with the payments to be made at the end of each lease year. Both leases were signed on December 31, 1989, at which time the prevailing interest rate available to Colossal for equipment loans was 12%.

Required

(Round all amounts in your answers to the nearest whole dollar.)

1. Prepare any required entries to record the lease of (*a*) Truck 1 and (*b*) Truck 2.
2. Prepare the required entries as of the end of the first year in (*a*) the life of Truck 1 and (*b*) the life of Truck 2. Use straight-line depreciation. (Hint: If the length of a capital lease is less than the asset's estimated service life and the asset remains the property of the lessor, depreciation must be taken over the length of the lease.)
3. Truck 1 was returned to the lessor on December 31, 1995, the end of the sixth year. Prepare the required entries as of the end of the sixth year in (*a*) the life of Truck 1 and (*b*) the life of Truck 2.
4. Show how Truck 2 and the lease liability for the truck should appear on the balance sheet as of the end of the sixth year in the life of the lease (after the year-end lease payment).

Alternate Problems

Problem 12–1A
Product warranty expense and property tax expense
(L. O. 2, 3)

Part 1. Saxon Company sells a single product subject to a one-year warranty that covers replacement parts but not labour. The company uses a periodic inventory system to account for merchandise. Prepare journal entries to record the following transactions completed by the company during the month of September:

Sept. 1 Purchased 4,500 units of merchandise for $85 per unit, paying cash.
      2 Purchased $45,600 of spare parts for making repairs to merchandise that is expected to be returned for warranty work.
      5 Sold 2,500 units of merchandise for $200 per unit, receiving cash.
    10 Repaired 90 units of merchandise that customers returned under the warranty. Replacement parts cost $5,670, and the customers paid $5,940 for labour.
    17 Sold 2,000 units of merchandise for $250 per unit.
    22 Repaired 55 units of merchandise under the product warranty. Replacement parts cost $3,355, and the customers paid $3,520 for labour.

Sept. 30 Recorded warranty expense for September. Past experience shows that 4% of the units sold require warranty work, and the average cost of replacement parts is $62 per unit returned. Average labour charges are $65.

Part 2. Tidwell Company accrues property taxes at the end of each month and uses recent experience as a means of estimating the tax. In early 1990, Tidwell's property was appraised at $700,000. The 1990 tax levy was $1.30 per $100. In January 1991, Tidwell's property was reappraised at $780,000. (The reappraisal was not expected to affect the tax levy of $1.30 per $100.) Early in July 1991, the annual tax levy was set at $1.50 per $100. On October 31, 1991, Tidwell paid the 1990 tax. Complete financial statements are prepared by the company on a monthly basis, and the company does not use reversing entries.

Required

Prepare entries at the end of January, July, October, and November 1991 to record property tax expense for each of those months and to record the annual tax payment.

Problem 12–2A
Journalizing notes payable transactions
(L. O. 3)

Prepare general journal entries to record these transactions:

1990
Jan. 27 Purchased merchandise on credit from Haller Company, invoice dated January 7, terms 2/10, n/60, $56,160.
Feb. 18 Borrowed money at National Bank by discounting our own $75,000 note payable for 60 days at 12%. Since the note matures before the end of the year, the discount should be charged to Interest Expense.
Apr. 4 Gave Haller Company $5,160 cash and a $51,000, 60-day, 14% note to secure an extension on our past-due account.
   19 Paid the note discounted at National Bank on February 18.
June 3 Paid the note given Haller Company on April 4.
Nov. 16 Borrowed money at National Bank by discounting our own $90,000 note payable for 90 days at 13%.
Dec. 1 Borrowed money at First Provincial Bank by giving a $60,000, 60-day, 12% note payable.
   31 Made an adjusting entry to record interest on the November 16 note to National Bank.
   31 Made an adjusting entry to record the accrued interest on the December 1 note to First Provincial Bank.

1991
Jan. 30 Paid the December 1 note to First Provincial Bank.
Feb. 14 Paid the November 16 note to National Bank.

Problem 12–3A
Present values of alternative payment patterns
(L. O. 5)

Skylane Airways is negotiating with an airframe outfitter in planning the interior finishings of an eight-passenger turboprop that Skylane Airways expects to acquire and place in charter service. The airplane will be completed and ready for service four years hence. If Skylane pays for the airplane upon completion (Payment Plan A), it will cost $1,895,000. However, two alternative payment plans are available. Plan B would require an immediate payment of $1,422,750. Plan C would require four annual payments of $400,250, the first of which would be made one year hence. In evaluating the three alternatives, the management of Skylane has decided to assume an interest rate of 9%.

Required

Calculate the present value of each payment and indicate which plan Skylane should follow.

Problem 12–4A
Exchanging a noninterest-bearing note for a plant asset
(L. O. 6)

On January 1, 1990, Technic Company gave its own $500,000 noninterest-bearing, six-year note payable in exchange for a machine, the cash price of which was not readily determinable. The market rate for interest on such notes on the day of the exchange was 9% annually.

Required

(Round all amounts in your answers to the nearest whole dollar.)

1. Prepare a form with the following column headings and calculate and fill in the required amounts for the six years the note is outstanding.

Year	Face Amount of Note	Unamortized Discount at Beginning of Year	Beginning-of-Year Carrying Amount	Discount to Be Amortized Each Year	Unamortized Discount at the End of Year	End-of-Year Carrying Amount

2. Prepare general journal entries to record: (*a*) the acquisition of the machine, (*b*) the discount amortized at the end of each of the first three years, and (*c*) the payment of the note on January 1, 1996.
3. Show how the note should appear on the December 31, 1992, balance sheet.

Problem 12–5A
Installment notes
(L. O. 6)

Schaefer Company financed a major expansion of its production capacity by borrowing money and signing an installment note at the bank. The four-year, 14%, $200,000 note is dated June 30, 1990, and requires equal semiannual payments beginning December 31, 1990.

Required

(Round all amounts in your answers to the nearest whole dollar.)

1. Calculate the amount of the installment payments. (Use Table 12–2 on page 561.)
2. Prepare a table with column headings like the table in Illustration 12–3. Complete the table for the Schaefer Company note.
3. Prepare general journal entries to record the first and the last payments on the note.
4. Assume that the note does not require equal payments. Instead, assume the note requires payments of accrued interest plus equal amounts of principal. Prepare general journal entries to record the first and the last payments on the note.

Problem 12–6A
**Capital leases and
exchanges of plant assets**
(L. O. 6)

Edenroc Production Company leased a machine on January 2, 1990, under a contract calling for annual payments of $65,000 on December 31 at the end of each of five years, with the machine becoming the property of the lessee company after the fifth $65,000 payment. The machine was estimated to have a six-year life and no salvage value, and the interest rate available to Edenroc for equipment loans on the day the lease was signed was 14%. The machine was delivered on January 4, 1990, and was immediately placed in operation. At the beginning of the sixth year in the machine's life, it was overhauled at an $8,500 total cost. The overhaul was paid for on January 8, and it did not increase the machine's efficiency but it did add an additional two years to its expected service life. On April 30, during the eighth year in the machine's life, it was traded in on a new machine of like purpose having a $275,000 cash price. A $15,000 trade-in allowance was received, and the balance was paid in cash.

Required

(Round all amounts in your answers to the nearest whole dollar.)

1. Prepare a schedule with the column headings of Illustration 12–4. Enter the years 1990 through 1994 in the first column and complete the schedule by filling in the proper amounts.
2. Prepare the entry to record the leasing of the machine.
3. Prepare December 31, 1991, entries to record annual depreciation on a straight-line basis, to record the lease payment, and to amortize the discount on lease financing. Also show how the machine and the lease liability should appear on the December 31, 1991, balance sheet.
4. Prepare the entries to record the machine's overhaul and the depreciation on the machine at the end of its sixth year.
5. Prepare the April 30, 1997, entries to record the exchange of the machines.

Problem 12–7A
**Accounting for capital and
operating leases**
(L. O. 6)

The Southwest News Company leased two new printing presses. Each of the presses has an estimated service life of seven years. Press 1 was leased for five years. Press 2 was leased for six years. Each lease agreement calls for $40,000 annual lease payments at the end of the year ($80,000 for both presses). When the period of each lease expires, each press will be returned to the lessor. Both leases were signed on December 31, 1989, at which time the prevailing interest rate available to Southwest News for equipment loans was 9%. Each of the presses could have been purchased for $180,000 cash.

Required

(Round all amounts in your answers to the nearest whole dollar.)

1. Prepare any required entries to record the lease of (*a*) Press 1 and (*b*) Press 2.
2. Prepare the required entries as of the end of the first year in (*a*) the life of Press 1 and (*b*) the life of Press 2. Use straight-line depreciation.
   (Hint: If the length of a capital lease is less than the asset's estimated service life and the asset remains the property of the lessor, depreciation must be taken over the length of the lease.)

3. Press 1 was returned to the lessor on December 31, 1994, the end of the fifth year. Prepare the required entries as of the end of the fifth year in (*a*) the life of Press 1 and (*b*) the life of Press 2.

4. Show how Press 2 and the lease liability for the press should appear on the balance sheet as of the end of the fifth year in the life of the lease (after the year-end lease payment).

Provocative Problems

Provocative Problem 12–1
Canadian Sea Company
(L. O. 3)

Canadian Sea Company is a worldwide provider of processed food products and services. In the company's 1987 annual report, the footnotes to the financial statements included the following item:

> 8. Legal Matters
> Ocean Foods Ltd., a wholly-owned subsidiary of the company, is a defendant in a suit brought by owners of 10 tuna fishing vessels which was filed in February, 1985, in a Nova Scotia court. The complaint alleges that the defendant has engaged in price fixing and other violations of federal antitrust laws in connection with the purchase of raw tuna from the plaintiffs. Plaintiffs have also asserted, in the same litigation, contract, tort and punitive damage claims. Ocean Foods has vigorously defended against this action and in November, 1985, filed its own antitrust counterclaims against the plaintiffs. Most of the plaintiffs have settled with the defendants, and settlement negotiations are in progress with the remaining plaintiffs. Management is of the opinion, based on facts presently available, that this action will finally be settled for an amount approximating the amount which has been accrued in the company's 1987 consolidated financial statements. This amount was not material to 1987 results.

Comment on the reasons why the management of Canadian Sea Company decided to include the above statements among the footnotes to the company's financial statements. Since the legal action against the company had not been resolved when the financial statements were issued, what reasons would have led the company to accrue an expense in the 1987 income statement? Under what circumstances might the company have included a footnote such as the above but avoided reporting an expense on the 1987 income statement?

Provocative Problem 12–2
Lettwinn Corporation
(L. O. 6)

Lettwinn Corporation is planning to acquire some new equipment from Clifton Company and has asked you to assist in analyzing the situation. The equipment may be purchased for $415,000 and then will be leased by Lettwinn under a 10-year lease contract to a customer for $75,000 payable at the end of each year. After the lease expires, Lettwinn expects to sell the equipment for $115,000.

1. Suppose Lettwinn has $415,000 cash available to buy the equipment and requires a 14% rate of return on its investments. Should the company buy the equipment and lease it to the customer?

2. As an alternative to paying cash, Lettwinn can invest the $415,000 in other operations for five years and earn 14% annually on its investment. If this is done, the equipment may be purchased by signing a $750,000,

five-year, noninterest-bearing note payable to Clifton Company. Should Lettwinn pay $415,000 now or sign the $750,000 note?

3. Now suppose Lettwinn does not have the option of signing a $750,000, five-year, noninterest-bearing note. Instead, the company may either pay $415,000 cash or lease the equipment from Clifton Company for eight years, after which the equipment would become the property of Lettwinn. The lease contract would require $93,750 payments at the end of each year. If Lettwinn leases the equipment, it will invest the $415,000 available cash in other operations and earn 14% on the investment. Should Lettwinn pay cash or lease the equipment from Clifton?

Analytical and Review Problems

A&R Problem 12-1

Refer to Mini Discussion Case 12–2 and prepare journal entries for each of the alternatives as of the date of signing the contract and at the end of the first year. Also indicate balance sheet presentation as of the end of the first year. Assume:

1. The going rate of interest is 12%.
2. The company amortizes and/or depreciates assets on a straight-line basis.
3. Use interest method to recognize interest expense.

A&R Problem 12-2

On September 1, 1990, Wong Company acquired a machine by paying $10,000 cash and signing a two-year note that carried a face amount of $60,000 due at the end of the two-year period; the note did not specify interest. Assume the going rate of interest for this company for this type of loan is 12%. The accounting period ends December 31.

Required

Give the entry to record the purchase of the machine and complete a tabulation as follows (round amounts to nearest dollar):

	Straight-line Method	Interest Method
1. Cash to be paid at maturity	$_____	$_____
2. Total interest expense	$_____	$_____
3. Interest expense on income statement for 1990 . .	$_____	$_____
4. Amount of the liability reported on balance sheet at end of 1990	$_____	$_____
5. Depreciation expense for 1990 (assume straight-line, partial year, no residual value, and useful life of five years).	$_____	$_____

A&R Problem 12-3

For the purpose of stimulating sales, Aroma Coffee Company places a coupon in each can of coffee sold; the coupons are redeemable in dishes. Each premium cost the company $1.00 (the cost of printing is negligible). Ten coupons must be presented by the customers to receive one premium. The following data are available:

Year	Cans of Coffee Sold	Premiums Purchased	Coupons Redeemed
1990	1,000,000	65,000	600,000
1991	1,200,000	100,000	950,000
1992	900,000	70,000	750,000

It is estimated that only 80% of the coupons will be presented for redemption.

Required

a. Compute the amount of the premium inventory, liability for premiums outstanding, and the expenses applicable to each yer.

b. Give all the necessary entries for each year.

COMPREHENSIVE PROBLEM

Campbell Stoop Company
(Review of Chapters 1–12)

Presented below is the December 31, 1990, unadjusted trial balance for the Campbell Stoop Company, which retails doors and related items. Some of these items are manufactured by other companies under patents created by Bill Campbell, the owner of the company. The company is the legal owner of the patents.

CAMPBELL STOOP COMPANY
Unadjusted Trial Balance
December 31, 1990

Cash	$ 6,360	
Accounts receivable	12,000	
Allowance for doubtful accounts		$ 860
Merchandise inventory	15,000	
Equipment	36,000	
Accumulated depreciation, equipment		14,200
Building.	75,000	
Accumulated depreciation, building.		27,000
Patents	17,500	
Accounts payable		9,600
Estimated warranty liability		3,900
Interest payable		–0–
Notes payable		40,000
Bill Campbell, capital (December 31, 1989, balance) . .		49,623
Bill Campbell, withdrawals.	4,000	
Sales		137,500
Interest earned.		400
Purchases	70,000	
Depreciation expense, equipment	–0–	
Depreciation expense, building	–0–	
Wages expense	22,000	
Bad debts expense	–0–	
Patent amortization expense	–0–	
Legal expense	23,000	
Warranty expense	–0–	
Interest expense	2,023	
Miscellaneous expenses	200	
Totals	$283,083	$283,083

The following additional information is available:

a. The process of reconciling the bank statement of December 31, 1990, showed these items:

Balance per bank	$5,700
Balance per books	6,360
Outstanding cheques.	725
Deposit in transit	1,000
Interest earned	40
Service charges (miscellaneous expense) . .	25
Included with the bank statement was a canceled cheque the company had failed to record. The amount of the cheque, which was a payment of an account payable, can be determined from the above information	?

b. An examination of customers' accounts shows that accounts totaling $420 should be written off as uncollectible. In addition, the ending balance of the allowance account should be $990.

c. Two items of equipment (No. 3 and No. 5) were purchased two years ago and are being depreciated by the straight-line method. These facts are known about these assets:

	No. 3	No. 5
Original cost	$20,000	$16,000
Expected salvage value	3,600	1,000
Useful life	4 years	5 years

d. The building was acquired at the beginning of 1986 and is being depreciated under the sum-of-the-years'-digits method. These facts are also known:

Original cost	$75,000
Expected salvage value	20,000
Useful life	10 years

e. Early in 1990, $20,000 of legal costs were incurred defending the patents against infringement. The bookkeeper had recorded these costs as legal expenses. As of January 1, 1990, the remaining useful life of the patents is expected to be five years.

f. The expected cost of servicing items sold this year under warranty is estimated to be 2% of sales. No warranty expense has been recorded for 1990.

g. There are two notes payable. The first note is dated January 1, 1990, is not due for several more years, has a principal amount of $15,000, and bears interest at 12% per year. Its terms require Campbell to pay the interest annually on January 1. No interest has yet been recognized for this note in 1990. The second note is paid with installments of $2,821 on March 31 and September 30 of each year. The annual interest rate is 10% (5% semiannual). The $25,000 balance on the books was correctly determined on September 30, 1990, and the $2,023 of interest expense represents the proper total for the first nine months of the year. (In preparing the balance sheet, classify the entire principal of both notes as long-term liabilities; include the interest payable among the current liabilities.)

h. In drafting the income statement and preparing the closing entries, a measure of the ending inventory is needed. It is measured with the retail method, and this information is known for 1990:

	Cost	Retail
Beginning inventory	$15,000	$ 27,000
Purchases	70,000	133,000
Additional markups		6,666
Markdowns		9,068
Sales		137,500

Required

1. Prepare a work sheet for the company using the information below.
2. Journalize entries resulting from the bank reconciliation and journalize the adjusting entries. Also present all calculations that support the entries.
3. Journalize closing entries for the company.
4. Prepare a single step income statement with a supporting calculation of cost of goods sold, a statement of changes in owner's equity, and a balance sheet.

13 Payroll Accounting

Wages or salaries generally amount to one of the largest expenses incurred by a business. Accounting for these items involves much more than simply recording liabilities and cash payments to employees. It also includes accounting for: (1) amounts withheld from employees' wages, (2) payroll costs levied on the employer, and (3) employee (fringe) benefits paid by the employer. As you study this chapter, you will learn the general processes all businesses follow to account for these items.

Learning Objectives

After studying Chapter 13, you should be able to:

1. List the taxes and other items frequently withheld from employees' wages, make the calculations necessary to prepare a Payroll Register, and prepare the entry to record an accrued payroll.
2. Prepare journal entries to pay employees and explain the operation of a payroll bank account.
3. Calculate the payroll costs levied on employers and prepare the entries to record the accrual and payment of these amounts.
4. Calculate and record employee fringe benefit costs and show the effect of these items on the total cost of employing labour.
5. Define or explain the words and phrases listed in the chapter Glossary.

An understanding of payroll accounting and the design and use of payroll records require some knowledge of the laws and programs that affect payrolls. Consequently, the more pertinent of these are discussed in the first portion of this chapter before the subject of payroll records is introduced.

Unemployment Insurance

To alleviate hardships caused by interruptions in earnings through unemployment, the federal government, with the concurrence of all provincial governments, implemented an employee-employer financed unemployment insurance plan in 1940. The 1940 Unemployment Insurance Act created a federal agency, the Unemployment Commission, which was charged with the administration of the act. Under the act, all employment in Canada was subjected to compulsory insurance unless specifically exempt by the legislation. Exempted classifications included employment as (1) a member of the Canadian Forces; (2) a private-duty nurse; (3) a teacher; (4) a farmer; (5) a hunter or trapper; (6) a domestic; (7) a permanent civil servant; (8) employee of husband, wife, and so forth; (9) a commission salesperson of insurance, real estate, and securities; and (10) employment where annual remuneration was in excess of $7,800. In 1971 the then existing legislation was rescinded, and the Unemployment Insurance Act, 1971, was passed. Under this act, compulsory **unemployment insurance** coverage was extended to all Canadian workers who are not self-employed. As of January 1, 1990, over 13.5 million employees, including teachers, hospital workers, and top-level executives, were covered by the insurance plan.

The purpose of an unemployment insurance program is usually two-fold:

1. To pay unemployment compensation for limited periods to unemployed individuals eligible for benefits.
2. To establish and operate employment facilities that assist unemployed individuals in finding suitable employment and assist employers in finding employees.

Such was the purpose of the original Unemployment Insurance Act from its passage to April 1, 1966. On that date the employment function was transferred to the Department of Manpower and Immigration. The Unemployment Commission continued the compensation function with responsibility for (1) revenue collection and control and (2) administration of claims and benefits. On July 1, 1971, the collection function was assumed by Revenue Canada, Taxation Division.

The unemployment insurance fund from which benefits are paid is jointly financed by employees and their employers. Under the original act, equal contributions were made by each group. Under the current act, in 1990 an employer is required to deduct from his/her employees' wages 2.25% of insured earnings, to add his/her contribution of 1.4 times the amount deducted from employees' wages, and to remit both amounts to the Receiver General of Canada. Insured earnings refer to average weekly *gross pay* in the range of $140 to $700. Employees paid in whole or in part on a time-worked or fixed-salary basis must be employed at least 15 hours in a weekly pay period or earn 20% of the maximum weekly insurable earnings ($640 in 1990) in order to be insurable.

The maximum amount deductible per year is $748.80 (in 1990). This amount is adjusted for weekly or monthly pay periods by dividing by the appropriate number; that is, 52, 12, and so on.

The Unemployment Insurance Act, in addition to setting rates, requires that an employer:

1. Withhold from the wages of each employee each payday an amount of unemployment insurance tax calculated at the current rate.
2. Pay an unemployment insurance tax equal to 1.4 times the amount withheld from the wages of all employees.
3. Periodically remit both the amounts withheld from employees' wages and the employer's tax to the Receiver General of Canada. (Remittance is discussed later in this chapter.)
4. Complete a "Record of Employment" form for employees who experience an "interruption of earnings" because of termination of employment, illness, injury, or pregnancy.
5. Keep a record for each employee that shows among other things wages subject to unemployment insurance and taxes withheld. (The law does not specify the exact form of the record, but most employers keep individual employee earnings records similar to the one shown later in this chapter.)

Weekly Unemployment Benefits

The amount of weekly benefits received by an unemployed individual who qualifies is based on his/her average insurable weekly earnings. The federal government has varied the benefit period from region to region on the basis of percentage and duration of unemployment in the region.

Withholding Employees' Income Tax

With few exceptions, employers are required to calculate, collect, and remit to the Receiver General of Canada the income taxes of their employees. Historically, although the first federal income tax law became effective in 1917, it applied to only a few individuals having high earnings, and it was not until World War II that income taxes were levied on substantially all wage earners. At that time Parliament recognized that many individual wage earners could not be expected to save sufficient money with which to pay their income taxes once each year. Consequently, Parliament instituted a system of pay-as-you-go withholding of taxes each payday at their source. This pay-as-you-go withholding of employee income taxes requires an employer to act as a tax collecting agent of the federal government.

The amount of income taxes to be withheld from an employee's wages is determined by his/her wages and the amount of the **personal tax credits.** Each individual is entitled, in 1990, to the following personal tax credits (as applicable):

1. Basic personal amount $6,169
2. Married or equivalent   5,655
3. Dependants under 19 years old:
   First and second dependant (each) . . .   399   with maximum earnings stipulated
   Third and each additional (each).   798

The personal tax credit total for each taxpayer determines the level of income tax deductions from the individual's gross pay. For example, an individual with a gross weekly salary of $500 and personal tax credits of $6,169 (1990 net claim code 1 on the TD1 form) would have $97.55 of income taxes withheld. Another individual with the same gross salary but with personal tax credits of $12,210 (claim code 5) would have $70.20 withheld.

Employers are responsible for determining and withholding each payday the required amount from each of their employees' pay for income taxes. However, to do so an employer must know the exemptions claimed by each employee. Consequently, every employee is required to file with the employer an Employee's Tax Deduction Return, Form TD1, on which he/she claims the credit entitled. The taxpayer must file a revised Form TD1 each time the exemptions change during a year.

In determining the amounts of income taxes to be withheld from the wages of employees, employers normally use tax withholding tables provided by Revenue Canada, Taxation. The tables indicate the tax to be withheld from any amount of wages and with any number of credits. The to-be-withheld amounts include both federal and provincial income taxes except for the province of Quebec. The province of Quebec levies and collects its own income tax and its own pension plan contributions. Employers in that province remit separately, to the respective authority, federal and provincial tax deductions.

In addition to determining and withholding income taxes from each employee's wages every payday, employers are required to:

1. Remit the withheld taxes to the Receiver General of Canada.
2. On or before the last day of February following each year give each employee a T-4 statement which tells the employee:
   a. Total wages for the preceding year.
   b. Taxable benefits received from the employer.
   c. Income taxes withheld.
   d. Deductions for registered pension plan.
   e. Canada Pension Plan contributions.
   f. Unemployment insurance deductions.
3. On or before the last day of February following each year forward to the district Taxation office copies of the employees' T-4 statements plus a T-4 form on which is summarized the information contained on the employees' T-4 statements.

The Canada Pension Plan

The **Canada Pension Plan** applies, with few exceptions, to everyone who is working. Every employee and the self-employed between the ages of 18 and 70 must make contributions in required amounts to the Canada Pension Plan. Self-employed individuals are required to remit periodically appropriate amounts to the Receiver General of Canada. Employee contributions are deducted by the employer from salary, wages, or other remuneration paid to the employee. Furthermore, each employer is required to contribute an amount equal to that deducted from his employees' earnings.

Contributions are based on earnings with the first $2,800 of each employee's annual being exempt. On earnings above that amount and up to the 1990 ceiling of $28,900 a year, the employee contributes at a rate of 2.2%. The total contribution from both employee and employer is 4.4% on the $26,100 of annual earnings between $2,800 and $28,900. Thus, the maximum contribution to the Canada Pension Plan is $574.20 each from the employee and the employer. The $2,800 exemption is adjusted for weekly or monthly pay periods by dividing by the appropriate number; that is, 52, 12, and so on.

Employers are responsible for making the proper deductions from their employees' earnings. The employer remits these deductions each month, together with his own contributions, to the Receiver General of Canada.

Self-employed individuals pay the combined rate for employees and employers, or 4.4% on annual earnings between $2,800 and the tax-exempt ceiling of $28,900.

Most employers use **wage bracket withholding tables** similar to the one for 1989 shown in Illustration 13–1 in determining Canada Pension Plan and unemployment insurance to be withheld from employee's gross earnings. The illustrated table is for a weekly pay period; different tables are provided for different pay periods. Somewhat similar tables are available for determining income tax withholdings.

Determining the amount of withholdings from an employee's gross wages is quite easy when withholding tables are used. First, the employee's wage bracket is located in the first two columns. Then the amounts to be withheld for Canada Pension Plan and unemployment insurance are found on the line of the wage bracket in the appropriate columns.

Workers' Compensation

Legislation is in effect in all provinces for payments to employees for an injury or disability arising out of or in the course of their employment. Under the provincial workers' compensation acts, employers are in effect required to "insure" their employees against injury or disability that may arise as a result of employment. Premiums are normally based on: (1) accident experience of the industrial classification to which each business is assigned and (2) the total payroll.

Procedures for payment are as follows:

1. At the beginning of each year every covered employer is required to submit to the Workers' Compensation Board an estimate of his/her expected payroll for the ensuing year.
2. Provisional premiums are then established by the board by relating estimated requirements for disability payments to estimated payroll. Provisional premium notices are then sent to all employers.
3. Provisional premiums are normally payable in from three to six installments during the year.
4. At the end of each year actual payrolls are submitted to the board, and final assessments are made based on actual payrolls and actual payments. Premiums are normally between 1% and 3% of gross payroll and are borne by the employer.

Illustration 13–1
Wage bracket withholding tables

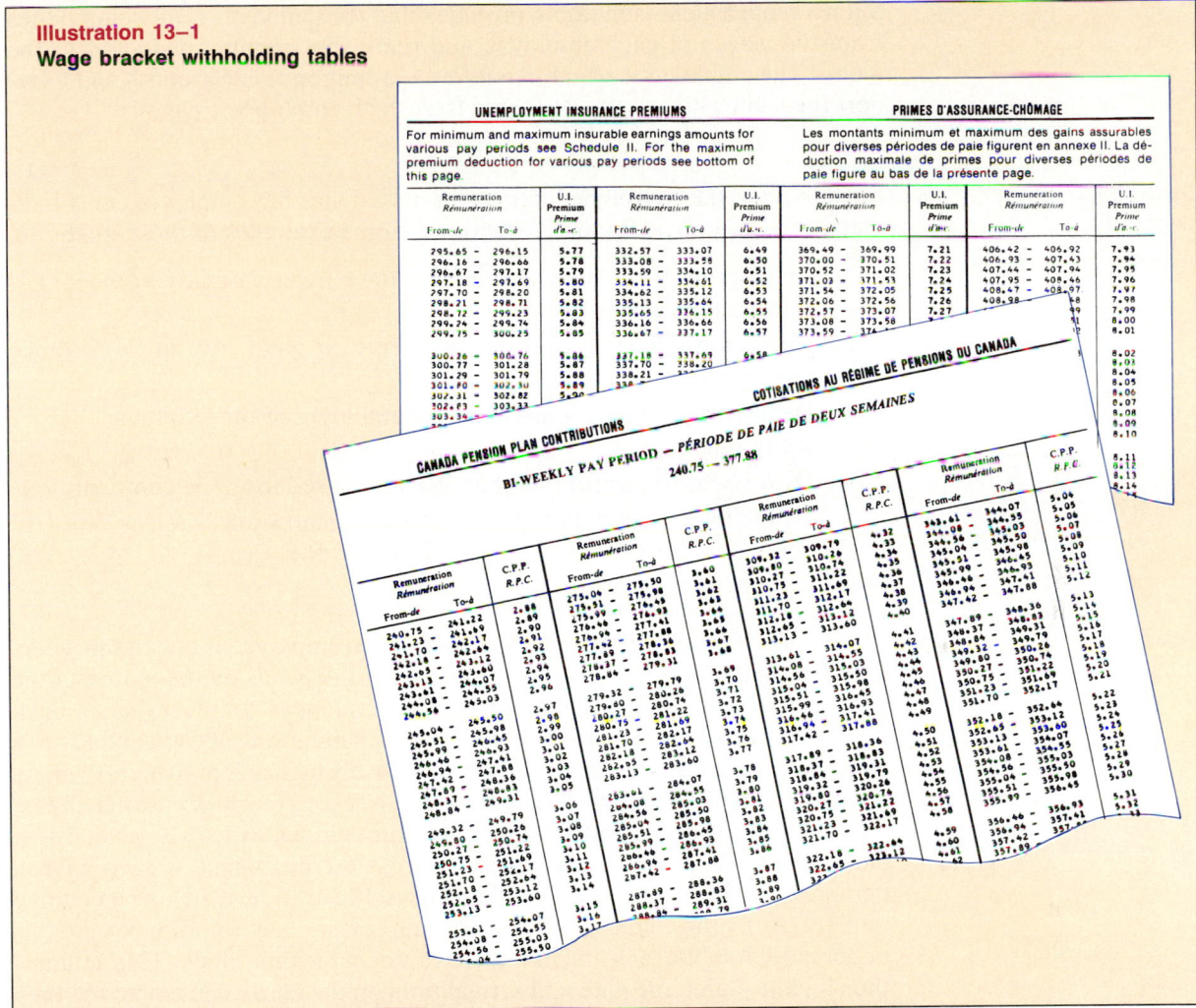

Wages, Hours, and Union Contracts

All provinces have laws establishing maximum hours of work and minimum pay rates; and while the details vary with each province, generally, employers are required to pay an employee for hours worked in excess of 40 in any one week at the employee's regular pay rate plus an overtime premium of at least one half of his or her regular rate. This gives an employee an overtime rate of at least 1½ times his or her regular hourly rate for hours in excess of 40 in any one week. In addition, employers commonly operate under contracts with their employees' union that provide even better terms. For example, union contracts often provide for time and a half for work on Saturdays, and double time for Sundays and holidays. When an employer is under such a union contract, since the contract terms are better than those provided for by law, the contract terms take precedence over the law.

In addition to specifying working hours and wage rates, union contracts often provide for the collection of employees' union dues by the employer.

Such a requirement commonly provides that the employer shall deduct dues from the wages of each employee and remit the amounts deducted to the union. The employer is usually required to remit once each month and to report the name and amount deducted from each employee's pay.

Other Payroll Deductions

In addition to the payroll deductions discussed thus far, employees may individually authorize additional deductions. Some examples of these might be:

1. Deductions to accumulate funds for the purchase of Government of Canada bonds.
2. Deductions to pay health, accident, hospital, or life insurance premiums.
3. Deductions to repay loans from the employer or the employees' credit union.
4. Deductions to pay for merchandise purchased from the company.
5. Deductions for donations to charitable organizations such as Boy Scouts, Girl Scouts, United Way Fund, or Red Cross.

Timekeeping

Compiling a record of the time worked by each employee is called **timekeeping.** The method used to compile such a record depends on the nature of the company's business and the number of its employees. In a very small business, timekeeping may consist of no more than notations of each employee's working time made in a memorandum book by the manager or owner. In many companies, however, time clocks are used to record on **clock cards** each employee's time of arrival and departure. The time clocks are usually placed near entrances to the office, store, or factory. At the beginning of each payroll period, a clock card for each employee (see Illustration 13–2) is placed in a rack for use by the employee. Upon arriving at work, each employee takes his or her card from the rack and places it in a slot in the time clock. This actuates the clock to stamp the date and arrival time on the card. The employee then returns the card to the rack. Upon leaving the plant, store, or office for lunch or at the end of the day, the procedure is repeated. The employee takes the card from the rack, places it in the clock, and the time of departure is automatically stamped. As a result, at the end of each pay period, the card shows the hours the employee was at work.

The Payroll Register

List the taxes and other items frequently withheld from employees' wages, make the calculations necessary to prepare a Payroll Register, and prepare the entry to record an accrued payroll. (L. O. 1)

Each pay period the total hours worked as compiled on clock cards or otherwise is summarized in a Payroll Register, an example of which is shown in Illustration 13–3. The illustrated register is for a weekly pay period and shows the payroll data for each employee on a separate line.

In Illustration 13–3, the columns under the heading Daily Time show the hours worked each day by each employee. The total of each employee's hours is entered in the column headed Total Hours. If hours worked include overtime hours, these are entered in the column headed O.T. Hours.

The Regular Pay Rate column shows the hourly pay rate of each employee. Total hours worked multiplied by the regular pay rate equals regular pay.

Illustration 13–2
An employee's clock card

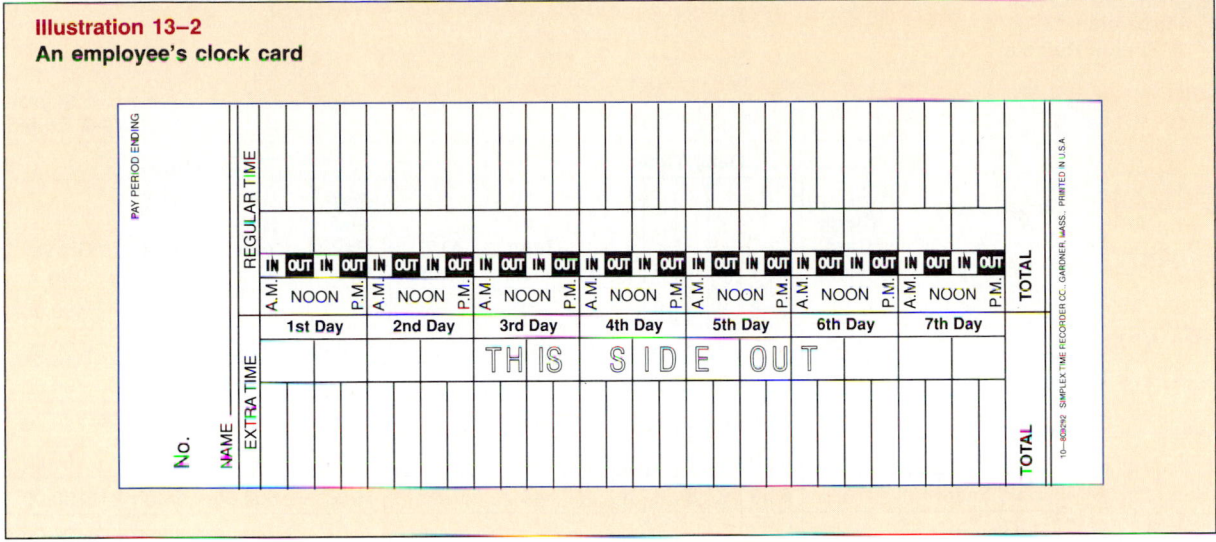

Courtesy Simplex Time Recorder Co.

Overtime hours multiplied by the overtime premium rate (50% in this case) equals overtime premium pay. And, regular pay plus overtime premium pay is the **employee's gross pay.**

The amounts withheld from each employee's gross pay are recorded in the Deductions columns of the payroll register. For example, you determine the income tax deductions by matching the gross pay of each employee to the tax deduction tables and then enter the results in the tax deduction column. In this and the remaining illustrations of this chapter, we assume that the deduction rate is 20% on the first $50,000 earned by each employee.

As previously stated, the income tax withheld depends on each employee's gross pay and personal tax credits. You can determine these amounts by referring to the appropriate wage bracket withholding tables. You then enter them in the column headed Income Taxes.

The column headed Hosp. Ins. shows the amounts withheld to pay for hospital insurance for the employees and their families. The total withheld from all employees is a current liability of the employer until paid to the insurance company. Likewise, the total withheld for employees' union dues is a current liability until paid to the union.

Additional columns may be added to the Payroll Register for any other deductions that occur sufficiently often to warrant special columns. For example, a company that regularly deducts amounts from its employees' pay for Canada savings bonds may add a special column for this deduction.

An employee's gross pay less total deductions is the **employee's net pay** and is entered in the Net Pay column. The total of this column is the amount the employees are to be paid. The numbers of the cheques used to pay the employees are entered in the column headed Cheque No.

Illustration 13–3
A Payroll Register

Payroll
Week Ended

| Employees | Clock Card No. | Daily Time | | | | | | | Total Hours | O.T. Hours | Earnings | | | |
		M	T	W	T	F	S	S			Regular Pay Rate	Regular Pay	O.T. Premium Pay	Gross Pay
Robert Austin	114	8	8	8	8	8			40		10.00	400.00		400.00
Judy Cross	102	8	8	8	8	8			40		15.00	600.00		600.00
John Cruz	108	0	8	8	8	8	8		40		14.00	560.00		560.00
Kay Keife	109	8	8	8	8	8	8		48	8	14.00	672.00	56.00	728.00
Lee Miller	112	8	8	8	8	0			32		14.00	448.00		448.00
Dale Sears	103	8	8	8	8	8	4		44	4	15.00	660.00	30.00	690.00
Totals												3,340.00	86.00	3,426.00

The Distribution columns are used to classify the various salaries in terms of different kinds of expense. Here you enter each employee's gross salary in the proper column according to the type of work performed. The column totals then indicate the amounts to be debited to the salary expense accounts.

Recording the Payroll

Generally, a Payroll Register such as the one shown is a supplementary memorandum record. As such, you do not post its information directly to the accounts. Instead, you must first record the payroll with a general journal entry, which is then posted to the accounts. The entry to record the payroll shown in Illustration 13–3 is:

Mar.	23	Sales Salaries Expense.	2,336.00	
		Office Salaries Expense.	1,090.00	
		UIC Payable.		73.98
		Employees' Income Taxes Payable		685.20
		Employees' Hospital Insurance Payable		90.00
		CPP Payable		68.28
		Accrued Payroll Payable		2,508.54
		To record the March 23 payroll.		

The debits of the entry were taken from the Payroll Register's distribution column totals. They charge the employees' gross earnings to the proper salary expense accounts. The credits to UIC Payable, Employees' Income Taxes Payable, Employees' Hospital Insurance Payable, and CPP Payable record these amounts as current liabilities. The credit to Accrued Payroll Payable records as a liability the net amount to be paid to the employees.

**Register
March 23, 19—**

	Deductions				Payment		Distribution	
U.I. Premium	Income Taxes	Hosp. Ins.	C.P.P.	Total Deductions	Net Pay	Cheque No.	Sales Salaries	Office Salaries
9.00	80.00	10.00	7.62	106.62	293.38	893		400.00
13.50	120.00	16.00	12.02	161.52	438.48	894	600.00	
12.60	112.00	16.00	11.14	151.74	408.26	895	560.00	
14.40	145.60	16.00	14.83	190.83	537.17	896	728.00	
10.08	89.60	16.00	8.67	124.35	323.65	897	448.00	
14.40	138.00	16.00	14.00	182.40	507.60	898		690.00
73.98	685.20	90.00	68.28	917.46	2,508.54		2,336.00	1,090.00

Illustration 13–4

Cash Disbursements Journal

Date	Cheque No.	Payee	Account Debited	PR	Other Accts. Debit	Accts. Pay. Debit	Accr. Payroll Pay. Debit	Pur. Dis. Credit	Cash Credit
Mar. 23	893	Robert Austin	Accrued Payroll				293.38		293.38
23	894	Judy Cross	"				438.48		438.48
23	895	John Cruz	"				408.26		408.26
23	896	Kay Keife	"				537.17		537.17
23	897	Lee Miller	"				323.65		323.65
23	898	Dale Sears	"				507.60		507.60

Paying the Employees

Prepare journal entries to pay employees and explain the operation of a payroll bank account.
(L. O. 2)

Almost every business pays its employees with cheques. In a company that has few employees, these cheques often are drawn on the regular bank account and entered in a Cash Disbursements Journal (or Cheque Register) like the one described in Chapter 6. Since each cheque is debited to the Accrued Payroll Payable account, posting labour can be saved by adding an Accrued Payroll Payable column in the journal. If such a column is added, entries to pay the employees of the Illustration 13–3 payroll will appear as in Illustration 13–4.

Although not required by law, most employers furnish each employee an earnings statement each payday. The statement gives the employee a record of hours worked, gross pay, deductions, and net pay. The statement often takes

Illustration 13–5
A payroll cheque

Robert Austin	40		10.00	400.00		400.00	9.00	80.00	7.62	10.00	106.62	293.38
Employee	Total Hours	O.T. Hours	Reg. Pay Rate	Regular Pay	O.T. Prem. Pay	Gross Pay	F.I.C.A. Taxes	Income Taxes	Union Dues	Hosp. Ins.	Total Deduc- tions	Net Pay

STATEMENT OF EARNINGS AND DEDUCTIONS FOR EMPLOYEE'S RECORDS—DETACH BEFORE CASHING CHECK

- -

VALLEY SALES COMPANY
2590 Chula Vista Street • Eugene, Oregon

No. 893

PAY TO THE
ORDER OF _____ *Robert Austin* _____   Date *March 23, 19--* $ *293.38*

Two hundred ninety-three dollars and thirty-eight cents ----------------------------

Merchants National Bank
Eugene, Oregon

VALLEY SALES COMPANY

James R. Morris

the form of a detachable paycheque portion that is removed before the cheque is cashed. A paycheque with a detachable earnings statement is reproduced in Illustration 13–5.

Payroll Bank Account

A business with many employees normally uses a special **payroll bank account** to pay its employees. When such an account is used, one cheque for the total payroll is drawn on the regular bank account and deposited in the special payroll bank account. Then, individual payroll cheques are drawn on this special account. Because only one cheque for the payroll total is drawn on the regular bank account each payday, use of a special payroll bank account simplifies internal control, especially the reconciliation of the regular bank account. It may be reconciled without considering the payroll cheques outstanding, and there may be many of these.

When a company uses a special payroll bank account, you must complete the following steps to pay the employees:

1. First, record the information shown on the Payroll Register in the usual manner with a general journal entry similar to the one previously illustrated. This entry causes the sum of the employees' net pay to be credited to the liability account (Accrued Payroll Payable).

2. Next, have a single cheque written that is payable to Payroll Bank Account for the total amount of the payroll and enter the payment in the Cheque Register. This requires a debit to Accrued Payroll Payable and a credit to Cash.

3. Next, have the cheque deposited in the payroll bank account. This transfers an amount of money equal to the payroll total from the regular bank account to the special payroll bank account.
4. Last, have individual payroll cheques drawn on the special payroll bank account and delivered to the employees. As soon as all employees cash their cheques, the funds in the special account will be exhausted.

A special Payroll Cheque Register may be used in connection with a payroll bank account. However, most companies do not use such a register. Instead, the payroll cheque numbers are entered in the Payroll Register so that it serves as a Cheque Register.

Employee's Individual Earnings Record

An **Employee's Individual Earnings Record**, as shown in Illustration 13–6, provides for each employee in one record a full year's summary of the employee's working time, gross earnings, deductions, and net pay. In addition, it accumulates information that—

1. Serves as a basis for the employer's payroll tax returns.
2. Indicates when an employee's earnings have reached the maxima for CPP and UIC deductions.
3. Supplies data for the T4 slip, which must be given to the employee at the end of the year.

The payroll information on an Employee's Individual Earnings Record is taken from the Payroll Register. The information as to earnings, deductions, and net pay is first recorded on a single line in the Payroll Register. Then, each pay period, the information is posted from the Payroll Register to the earnings record. Note the last column of the record. It shows an employee's cumulative earnings and is used to determine when the earnings reach the maximum amounts taxed and are no longer subject to the various payroll taxes.

Payroll Deductions Required by the Employer

Calculate the payroll costs levied on employers and prepare the entries to record the accrual and payment of these amounts. (L. O. 3)

Under the previous discussion of the Canada Pension Plan, it was pointed out that pension deductions are required in like amounts on both employed workers and their employers. A covered employer is required by law to deduct from the employees' pay the amounts of their Canada Pension Plan, but in addition, the employer must pay an amount equal to the sum of the employees' Canada pension. Commonly, the amount deducted by the employer is recorded at the same time the payroll to which it relates is recorded. Also, since both the employees' and employer's shares are reported on the same form and are paid in one amount, the liability for both is normally recorded in the same liability account, the Canada Pension Plan Payable account.

In addition to the Canada Pension Plan, an employer is required to pay unemployment insurance that is 1.4 times the sum of the employees' unemployment insurance deductions. Most employers record both of these payroll deductions with a general journal entry that is made at the time the payroll to

Illustration 13–6
Employee's Individual Earnings Record

Employee's Name _____ Robert Austin _____ SIN. No. _____ 123-456-789 _____ Employee No. _____ 114 _____

Home Address _____ 111 South Greenwood _____ Notify in Case of Emergency _____ Margaret Austin _____ Phone No. _____ 964-9834 _____

Employed _____ June 7, 1980 _____ Date of Termination _____ Reason _____

Date of Birth _____ June 6, 1962 _____ Date Becomes 65 _____ June 6, 2027 _____ Male (X) Female ( ) Married (X) Single ( ) Number of Exemptions _____ 1 _____ Pay Rate _____ $10.00

Occupation _____ Clerk _____ Place _____ Office _____

Date		Time Lost		Time Worked			O.T.		U.I.				Total			Cumu-
Per. Ends	Paid	Hrs.	Rea-son	Total	O.T. Hours	Reg. Pay	Prem. Pay	Gross Pay	U.I. Prem.	Income Taxes	Hosp. Ins.	CPP	Deduc-tions	Net Pay	Cheque No.	lative Pay
1/5	1/5			40		400.00		400.00	9.00	80.00	10.00	7.62	106.62	293.38	173	400.00
1/12	1/12			40		400.00		400.00	9.00	80.00	10.00	7.62	106.62	293.38	201	800.00
1/19	1/19			40		400.00		400.00	9.00	80.00	10.00	7.62	106.62	293.38	243	1,200.00
1/26	1/26	4	Sick	36		360.00		360.00	8.10	72.00	10.00	6.74	96.84	263.16	295	1,560.00
2/2	2/2			40		400.00		400.00	9.00	80.00	10.00	7.62	106.62	293.38	339	1,960.00
2/9	2/9			40		400.00		400.00	9.00	80.00	10.00	7.62	106.62	293.38	354	2,360.00
2/16	2/16			40		400.00		400.00	9.00	80.00	10.00	7.62	106.62	293.38	397	2,760.00
2/23	2/23			40		400.00		400.00	9.00	80.00	10.00	7.62	106.62	293.38	446	3,160.00
3/23	3/23			40		400.00		400.00	9.00	80.00	10.00	7.62	106.62	293.38	893	4,760.00

which they relate is recorded. For example, the entry to record the employer's amounts on the payroll of Illustration 13–3 is:

Mar.	23	Payroll Expense	171.85	
		Unemployment Insurance Payable		103.57
		Canada Pension Plan Payable.		68.28
		To record the employer's payroll taxes.		

The debit of the entry records as an expense the payroll taxes levied on the employer, and the credits record the liabilities for the taxes. The $103.57 credit to Unemployment Insurance Payable is 1.4 times the sum of the amounts deducted from the pay of the employees whose wages are recorded in the Payroll Register of Illustration 13–3, and the credit to Canada Pension Plan Payable is equal to the total of the employees' pension plan deductions.

Paying the Payroll Deductions

Income tax, unemployment insurance, and Canada Pension Plan amounts withheld each payday from the employees' pay plus the employer's portion of unemployment insurance and Canada Pension Plan are current liabilities until paid to the Receiver General of Canada. The normal method of payment is to pay the amounts due at any chartered bank or remit directly to the Receiver General of Canada. Payment of these amounts must be made before the 15th of the month following the month that deductions were made from the earnings of the employees. Payment of these liabilities is recorded in the same manner as payment of any other liabilities.

Accruing Taxes on Wages

Mandatory payroll deductions are levied on wages actually paid. In other words, accrued wages are not subject to payroll deductions until they are paid. Nevertheless, if the requirements of the *matching principle* are to be met, both accrued wages and the accrued deductions on the wages should be recorded at the end of an accounting period. However, since the amounts of such deductions vary little from one accounting period to the next and often are small in amount, many employers apply the *materiality principle* and do not accrue payroll deductions.

Employee (Fringe) Benefit Costs

Calculate and record employee fringe benefit costs and show the effect of these items on the total cost of employing labour. (L. O. 4)

In addition to the wages earned by employees and the related payroll amounts paid by the employer, many companies provide their employees a variety of benefits. Since the costs of these benefits are paid by the employer and the benefits are in addition to the amount of wages earned, they are often called **employee fringe benefits.** For example, an employer may pay for part (or all) of the employees' medical insurance, life insurance, and disability insurance. Another typical employee benefit involves employer contributions to a retirement income plan. Perhaps the most typical employee benefit is vacation pay.

Employer Contributions to Employee Insurance and Retirement Plans

The entries to record employee benefit costs depend on the nature of the benefit. Some employee retirement plans are quite complicated and involve accounting procedures that are too complex for discussion in this introductory course. In other cases, however, the employer simply makes periodic cash contributions to a retirement fund for each employee and records the amounts contributed as expense. Other employee benefits that require periodic cash payments by the employer include employer payments of insurance premiums for employees.

In the case of employee benefits that simply require the employer to make periodic cash payments, the entries to record the employer's obligations are similar to those used for payroll deductions.[1] For example, assume an employer with five employees has agreed to pay medical insurance premiums of

---

[1] Some payments of employee benefits must be added to the gross salary of the employee for the purpose of calculating income tax, CPP, and UIC payroll deductions. However, in this chapter and in the problems at the end of the chapter, the possible effect of employee benefit costs on payroll taxes is ignored to avoid undue complexity in the introductory course.

$40 per month for each employee. The employer also will contribute 10% of each employee's salary to a retirement program. If each employee earns $1,500 per month, the entry to record these employee benefits for the month of March is:

Mar.	31	Employees' Benefits Expense.	950.00	
		Employees' Medical Insurance Payable.		200.00
		Employees' Retirement Program Payable		750.00
		($1,500 × 5) × 10% = $750.		

Vacation Pay

Nearly all employers promise their employees paid vacation time as a benefit of employment. For example, many employees receive 2 weeks' vacation in return for working 50 weeks each year. The effect of a 2-week vacation is to increase the employer's payroll expenses by 4% (2/50 = .04). However, new employees often do not begin to accrue vacation time until after they've worked for a period of time, perhaps as much as a year. The employment contract may say that no vacation is granted until the employee works one year; but if the first year is completed, the employee receives the full 2 weeks. In this type of situation, the expense associated with vacation pay depends on the employee turnover rate. If the turnover experience of the employer suggests that only 90% of employees actually will be granted vacation time, the additional expense of a 2-week vacation benefit would be 90% of 4%, or 3.6%.

To account for vacation pay, an employer should estimate and record the additional expense during the weeks the employees are working and earning the vacation time. For example, assume that a company with a weekly payroll of $20,000 grants two weeks' vacation after one year's employment. Based on past turnover rates, the employer estimates that 90% of employees actually will be granted vacation time. The entry to record the estimated vacation pay is:

Date	Employees' Benefits Expense.	720.00	
	Estimated Vacation Pay Liability		720.00
	$20,000 × .04 × .9 = $720.		

As employees take their vacations and receive their vacation pay, the entries to record the vacation payroll take the following general form:

Date	Estimated Vacation Pay Liability	xxx	
	UIC and CPP Taxes Payable		xxx
	Employees' Income Taxes Payable		xxx
	Other withholding liability accounts such as Employees'		
	Hospital Insurance Payable		xxx
	Accrued Payroll Payable		xxx

Mandatory payroll deductions and employee benefits costs are often a major category of expense incurred by a company. They may amount to well over 25% of the salaries earned by employees.

Computerized Payroll Systems

Manually prepared records like the ones described in this chapter are used in many small companies. However, an increasing number of companies use computers to process their payroll. The computer programs are designed to take advantage of the fact that the same calculations are performed each pay period. Also, much of the same information must be entered for each employee in the Payroll Register, on the employee's earnings record, and on the employee's paycheque. The computers simultaneously store or print the information in all three places.

Summary of the Chapter in Terms of Learning Objectives

1. Amounts withheld from employees' wages include federal income taxes, unemployment insurance, and Canada Pension Plan. Payroll costs levied on employers include unemployment insurance, Canada Pension, and workers' compensation.

An employee's gross pay may be the employee's specified wage rate multiplied by the total hours worked plus an overtime premium rate multiplied by the number of overtime hours worked. Alternatively, it may be the given periodic salary of the employee. Taxes withheld and other deductions for items such as union dues, insurance premiums, and charitable contributions are subtracted from gross pay to determine the net pay.

A Payroll Register is used to summarize all employees' hours worked, regular and overtime pay, payroll deductions, net pay, and distribution of gross pay to expense accounts during each pay period. It provides the necessary information for journal entries to record the accrued payroll and to pay the employees.

2. A payroll bank account is a separate account that is used solely for the purpose of paying employees. Each pay period, an amount equal to the total net pay of all employees is transferred from the regular bank account to the payroll bank account. Then, cheques are drawn against the payroll bank account for the net pay of the employees.

3. When a payroll is accrued at the end of each pay period, payroll deductions and levies also should be accrued with a debit to Payroll Expense and credits to appropriate liability accounts.

4. Fringe benefit costs that involve simple cash payments by the employee should be accrued with an entry similar to the one used to accrue payroll levies. To account for the expense associated with vacation pay, you should estimate the expense on an annual basis and allocate the estimated amount to the pay periods during the year. These allocations are recorded with a debit to Employees' Benefits Expense and a credit to Estimated Vacation Pay Liability. Then, payments to employees on vacation are charged to the estimated liability.

Demonstration Problem

Presented below are various items of information about three employees of the Jasmine Company for the week ending October 20, 1990.

	Babcock	Dawson	Sanders
Wage rate (per hour)	$10	$30	$16
Overtime premium	50%	50%	50%
Annual vacation	2 weeks	4 weeks	2 weeks
Cumulative wages as of October 13, 1990 . .	$17,500	$49,200	$5,200
For the week (pay period) ended October 20, 1990:			
Hours worked	46	40	50
Medical insurance:			
Jasmine's contribution	$25	$ 25	$ 25
Withheld from employee	15	15	15
Union dues withheld	40	60	40
Income tax withheld	98	480	176
Unemployment insurance withheld	11	14	14
Canada pension withheld	10	—	18

Payroll deduction rates:

Income taxes	assume 20% of gross wages
Unemployment insurance	2.25% to a maximum of $14 per week
Canada Pension Plan	2.2% less annual exemption of $2,800; maximum per year is $574.

Required

In solving the following requirements, round all amounts to the nearest whole dollar. Prepare schedules that determine, for each employee and for all employees combined, the following information:

1. Wages earned for the regular 40-hour week, total overtime pay, and gross wages.
2. Vacation pay accrued for the week.
3. Deductions withheld from the employees' wages.
4. Costs imposed on the employer.
5. Employees' net pay for the week.
6. Employer's total payroll-related cost (wages, mandatory deductions, and fringe benefits).

Present journal entries to record the following:

7. Payroll expense.
8. Payroll deductions and employees' benefits expense.

Solution to Demonstration Problem

1. The gross wages (including overtime) for the week.

	Babcock	Dawson	Sanders	Total
Regular wage rate	$ 10	$ 30	$ 16	
Regular 40-hour workweek	×40	×40	×40	
Regular pay	$400	$1,200	$640	$2,240
Overtime rate	$ 15	$ 45	$ 24	
Overtime hours	×6	×–0–	×10	
Total overtime pay	$ 90	$ –0–	$240	330
Gross wages	$490	$1,200	$880	$2,570

2. The vacation pay accrued for the week.

	Babcock	Dawson	Sanders	Total
Annual vacation	2 weeks	4 weeks	2 weeks	
Weeks worked in year	50 weeks	48 weeks	50 weeks	
Vacation pay as a percentage of regular pay	4.00%	8.33%	4.00%	
Regular pay this week	×$ 400	×$1,200	×$ 640	
Vacation pay this week	$ 16	$ 100	$ 26	$142

The information in the following table is needed for parts 3 and 4:

Employees	Earnings through October 13	Earnings This Week	Earnings Subject to	
			CPP	Unemployment Ins.
Babcock	$17,500	$ 490	$ 436	$ 490
Dawson	49,200	1,200	—	640
Sanders	5,200	880	826	640
Totals		$2,570	$1,262	$1,770

3. Amounts withheld from the employees.

	Babcock	Dawson	Sanders	Total
Income tax withheld	$ 98	$480	$176	$754
CPP withheld	10	—	18	28
UIC withheld	11	14	14	39
Totals	$119	$494	$208	$821

4. The costs imposed on the employer.

	Babcock	Dawson	Sanders	Total
CPP (1.0)	$10	—	$18	$28
Unemployment insurance (1.4) . .	15	$20	20	55
Totals	$25	$20	$38	$83

5. The net amount paid to the employees.

	Babcock	Dawson	Sanders	Total
Regular pay	$400	$1,200	$640	$2,240
Overtime pay	90	−0−	240	330
Gross pay	$490	$1,200	$880	$2,570
Withholdings:				
Income tax withholding	$ 98	$480	$176	$ 754
CPP withholding	10	—	18	28
UIC withholding	11	14	14	39
Medical insurance	15	15	15	45
Union dues	40	60	40	140
Total withholdings	$174	$569	$263	$1,006
Net pay to employees	$316	$631	$617	$1,564

6. The total payroll-related cost to the employer.

	Babcock	Dawson	Sanders	Total
Regular pay.	$400	$1,200	$ 640	$2,240
Overtime pay	90	–0–	240	330
Gross pay.	$490	$1,200	$ 880	$2,570
Deductions and fringe benefits:				
CPP.	$ 10	$ —	$ 18	$ 28
UIC	15	20	20	55
Vacation pay	16	100	26	142
Medical insurance	25	25	25	75
Total deductions and				
fringe benefits	$ 66	$ 145	$ 89	$ 300
Total payroll related cost	$556	$1,345	$969	$2,870

7. Journal entry for payroll expense.

1990					
Oct.	20	Payroll Expense		2,570.00	
		Employees' Income Taxes Payable			754.00
		Employees' CPP Payable			28.00
		Employees' UIC Payable.			39.00
		Employees' Medical Insurance Payable.			45.00
		Employees' Union Dues Payable			140.00
		Accrued Payroll Payable			1,564.00
		To record payroll expense.			

8. Journal entries to record payroll tax and fringe benefit expense

1990					
Oct.	20	Payroll Expense		83.00	
		CPP Payable			28.00
		UIC Payable.			55.00
		To record payroll expense.			
	20	Employees' Benefits Expense		217.00	
		Accrued Vacation Pay			142.00
		Medical Insurance Payable			75.00
		To record fringe benefits expense.			

Glossary

Define or explain the words and phrases listed in the chapter Glossary. (L. O. 5)

Canada Pension Plan A national contributory retirement pension scheme. p. 597

Clock card a card issued to each employee that the employee inserts in a time clock to record the time of arrival and departure to and from work. p. 600

Employee fringe benefits payments by an employer, in addition to wages and salaries, that are made to acquire employee benefits such as insurance coverage and retirement income. p. 607

Employee's gross pay the amount an employee earns before any deductions for taxes withheld or other items such as union dues or insurance premiums. p. 601

Employee's Individual Earnings Record a record of an employee's hours worked, gross pay, deductions, net pay, and certain personal information about the employee. p. 605

Employee's net pay the amount an employee is paid, determined by subtracting from gross pay all deductions for taxes and other items that are withheld from the employee's earnings. p. 601

Payroll bank account a special bank account a company uses solely for the purpose of paying employees by depositing in the account each pay period an amount equal to the total employees' net pay and drawing the employees' payroll cheques on that account. p. 604

Payroll deduction an amount deducted usually based on the amount of an employee's gross pay. p. 605

Personal tax credits amounts which may be deducted from an individual's income taxes and which determine the amount of income taxes to be withheld. p. 596

Timekeeping the process of recording the time each employee is on the job. p. 600

Unemployment insurance an employee-employer financed unemployment insurance plan. p. 595

Wage bracket withholding table a table showing the amounts to be withheld from employees' wages at various levels of earnings. p. 598

Questions for Class Discussion

1. Who pays under the Canada Pension Plan?
2. Who pays premiums under the workers' compensation laws?
3. What benefits are paid to unemployed workers for funds raised by the Federal Unemployment Insurance Act?
4. Who pays federal unemployment insurance? What is the rate?
5. What are the objectives of unemployment insurance laws?
6. To whom and when are payroll deductions remitted?
7. What determines the amount that must be deducted from an employee's wages for income taxes?
8. What is a tax withholding table?

9. What is the Canada Pension Plan deduction rate for self-employed individuals?

10. How is a clock card used in recording the time an employee is on the job?

11. How is a special payroll bank account used in paying the wages of employees?

12. At the end of an accounting period a firm's special payroll bank account has a $562.35 balance because the payroll cheques of two employees have not cleared the bank. Should this $562.35 appear on the firm's balance sheet? If so, where?

13. What information is accumulated on an employee's individual earnings record? Why must this information be accumulated? For what purposes is the information used?

14. What payroll charges are levied on the employer? What amounts are deducted from the wages of an employee?

15. What are employee fringe benefits? Name some examples.

Multiple Choice

1. Net pay is:
   a. The amount of an employee's pay due in income tax.
   b. Gross pay minus deductions.
   c. The amount of an employee's pay before any deductions.
   d. Gross pay plus employer's tax.
   e. None of the above.

2. The weekly payroll register shows:
   a. The number of hours worked by each employee each day during the week.
   b. The regular pay rate of each employee.
   c. The earnings of each employee.
   d. The deductions for each employee to determine the net pay.
   e. All of the above.

3. Which of the following steps must be completed when a company uses a special payroll bank account?
   a. Record the information shown on the Payroll Register with a general journal entry.
   b. Write a single cheque that is payable to Payroll Bank Account for the total amount of the payroll and enter the payment in the Cheque Register.
   c. Deposit a cheque for the total amount of the payroll in the payroll bank account.
   d. Write individual payroll cheques to be drawn on the payroll bank account.
   e. All of the above.

4. Making a record of the time each employee is at his or her place of work is:

a. Auditing.
b. Budgeting.
c. Timekeeping.
d. Bookkeeping.
e. Spying.

5. If the payroll bank account has a $210 balance because an employee's payroll cheque has not cleared, the $210 should appear:
   a. On the balance sheet as a current asset.
   b. On the balance sheet as a current liability.
   c. On the income statement as an expense.
   d. On the balance sheet as a current asset and on the income statement as an expense.
   e. On none of the foregoing.

6. Datacom employes two people at $1,800 per month and two people at $4,000 per month. Every employee receives one month's vacation each year. Although no employees took vacation during May, all are expected to take their vacation later this year. In addition, Datacom pays medical insurance premiums of $145 per month per employee and contributes 6% of total salaries to a retirement program. The entry to record these benefits for Datacom employees for the month of May is as follows:

a.	Employees' Benefits Expense.	2,330.55	
	Estimated Vacation Pay Liability.		1,054.55
	Employees' Medical Insurance Payable.		580.00
	Employees' Retirement Program Payable		696.00
b.	Salaries Expense	11,600.00	
	Estimated Vacation Pay Liability.		1,054.55
	Employees' Medical Insurance Payable.		580.00
	Employees' Retirement Program Payable		696.00
	Accrued Payroll Payable		9,269.45
c.	Estimated Vacation Pay Expense.	1,054.55	
	Employees' Medical Insurance Expense.	580.00	
	Employees' Retirement Program Expense.	696.00	
	Salaries Expense	11,600.00	
	Accrued Payroll Payable		13,930.55
d.	Employees' Benefits Expense.	2,330.55	
	Cash		2,330.55
e.	No entry is required.		

Mini Discussion Case

Case 13-1

You are the accountant for a high-tech company most of whose employees have an annual salary in excess of $30,000 per year. In discussing the cost of salary increases for the coming year, senior management has asked you to outline what additional costs are involved. After all, they reason, there are caps on the amounts deducted for both unemployment insurance and Canada

Pension Plan. Therefore, these would not add to the company's cost since the employees are already over the maximum amounts.

Required

Respond to senior management.

Exercises

Exercise 13–1
Calculating gross and net pay
(L. O. 1)

Terry Rosten, an employee of the Hine Company Limited, worked 46 hours during the week ended January 5. Her pay rate is $16 per hour, and her wages are subject to no deductions other than income taxes, unemployment insurance, and Canada Pension. The overtime premium is 50% and is applicable to any time greater than 40 hours per week. Calculate her regular pay, overtime premium pay, gross pay, UIC, CPP, income tax deductions (assume a tax deduction rate of 20%), total deductions, and net pay.

Exercise 13–2
Journalizing payroll information
(L. O. 2)

On January 5, at the end of its first weekly pay period in the year, Clive Company's payroll record showed that its sales employees had earned $3,420 and its office employees had earned $1,800. The employees were to have $101 of UIC and $110 of CPP withheld plus $738 of income taxes, $120 of union dues, and $540 of hospital insurance premiums. Calculate the amount of taxes to be withheld and give the general journal entry to record the payroll.

Exercise 13–3
Calculating payroll deductions and recording the payroll
(L. O. 1)

The following information as to earnings and deductions for the pay period ended May 12 was taken from a company's payroll records:

Employees' Names	Weekly Gross Pay	Earnings to End of Previous Week	Income Taxes	Health Insurance Deductions
Beth Johnson	$ 620	$ 6,785	$106.00	$ 82.00
Dan Tremont	590	6,320	81.00	82.00
Art Nathan	500	5,500	52.00	56.50
Sally Becker	1,500	18,200	456.00	42.50
	$3,210		$695.00	$263.00

Calculate the employees' UIC and CPP withholdings, the amounts paid to each employee, and prepare a general journal entry to record the payroll. Assume all employees work in the office.

Exercise 13–4
Calculating and recording payroll taxes
(L. O. 3)

Use the information provided in Exercise 13–3 to complete the following requirements:

1. Prepare a general journal entry to record the employer's payroll costs resulting from the payroll.
2. Prepare a general journal entry to record the following employee benefits incurred by the company: (1) health insurance costs equal to the

amounts contributed by each employee and (2) contributions equal to 10% of gross pay for each employee's retirement income program.

Exercise 13–5
Analyzing total labor costs
(L. O. 4)

Carelli Company's employees earn a gross pay of $20 per hour and work 40 hours each week. Carelli Company contributes 10% of gross pay to a retirement program for employees and pays medical insurance premiums of $40 per week per employee. What is Carelli Company's total cost of employing a person for one hour? (Assume that individual wages are less than the $28,900 Canada Pension Plan limit.)

Exercise 13–6
Calculating fringe benefit costs
(L. O. 4)

Luddite Corporation grants those employees who have worked for the company one complete year vacation time of two weeks. After 10 years of service, employees receive four weeks of vacation. Luddite estimates that 96% of its employees with less than 10 years' service will be granted two weeks' of vacation this year, and 99% of those who will have completed 10 or more years of service during the year will be granted four weeks vacation (1% are expected to resign during their 10th year). The monthly payroll for January includes $160,000 to persons who will not complete 10 years of service this year and $72,000 to persons who, if they do not resign, will have completed 10 years of service by year-end. On January 31, record the January expense arising from the vacation policy of the company.

Exercise 13–7
Analyzing the cost of payroll taxes and fringe benefits
(L. O. 3, 4)

Ridder Company's payroll costs and fringe benefit expenses include the normal CPP and UIC contributions, retirement fund contributions of 10% of total earnings, and health insurance premiums of $180 per employee per month. Given the following list of employee annual salaries, payroll costs and fringe benefits constitute what percentage of salaries?

Belton	$31,000
Dirk.	59,700
Hopkins	57,500
Jiles	38,600
Kress.	44,200

Exercise 13–8
Other payroll deductions
(L. O. 1)

Curtis Worthington is single and earns a weekly salary of $825. In response to a citywide effort to obtain charitable contributions to the local United Way programs, Worthington has requested that his employer withhold 1% of his salary (net of CPP, UIC, and income taxes—assume a tax deduction rate of 20%). Under this program, what will be Worthington's annual contribution to the United Way?

Problems

Problem 13–1
The Payroll Register and the payroll bank account
(L. O. 1, 2)

On January 6, at the end of the first weekly pay period of the year, a company's Payroll Register showed that its employees had earned $16,850 of sales salaries and $4,150 of office salaries. Withholdings from the employees' salaries were to include $410 of UIC, $440 of CPP, $2,965 of income taxes, $840 of hospital insurance, and $275 of union dues.

Required

1. Prepare the general journal entry to record the January 6 payroll.
2. Prepare a general journal entry to record the employer's payroll deductions resulting from the January 6 payroll.
3. Under the assumption the company uses a payroll bank account and special payroll cheques in paying its employees, give the cheque register entry (Cheque No. 542) to transfer funds equal to the payroll from the regular bank account to the payroll bank account.
4. Answer this question: After the cheque register entry is made and posted, are additional debit and credit entries required to record the payroll cheques and pay the employees?

Problem 13–2
The Payroll Register, the payroll bank account, and payroll deductions
(L. O. 1, 2, 3)

The payroll records of Boutade Corporation provided the following information for the weekly pay period ended December 21:

Employees	Clock Card No.	Daily Time M	T	W	T	F	S	S	Pay Rate	Income Taxes	Hospital Insurance	Union Dues	Earnings to End of Previous Week
Paul Lapin	11	8	8	7	7	8	1	0	$22.00	$180.00	$ 50.00	$15.50	$40,000
Ruth Moule	12	8	7	8	8	8	4	0	18.00	150.00	50.00		48,000
Carl Simms	13	8	8	8	8	8	0	0	20.00	120.00	50.00	15.50	5,300
Nick Paxton	14	8	8	8	8	8	2	0	24.00	117.00	45.00	15.50	35,600
Diana Wood	15	8	7	8	8	7	3	0	28.00	200.00	50.00	15.50	52,800
										$767.00	$245.00	$62.00	

Required

1. Enter the relevant information in the proper columns of a Payroll Register and complete the register for CPP and UIC deductions. Charge the wages of Diana Wood to Office Salaries Expense and the wages of the remaining employees to Service Wages Expense.
2. Prepare a general journal entry to record the payroll register information.
3. Make the cheque register entry (Cheque No. 399) to transfer funds equal to the payroll from the regular bank account to the payroll bank account under the assumption the company uses special payroll cheques and a payroll bank account in paying its employees. Assume the first payroll cheque is numbered 530 and enter the payroll cheque numbers in the Payroll Register.
4. Prepare a general journal entry to record the employer's payroll costs resulting from the payroll.

Problem 13–3
The Payroll Register, payroll taxes, and employee fringe benefits
(L. O. 1, 3, 4)

A company accumulated the following payroll information for the weekly pay period ended December 22:

Employees	Clock Card No.	Daily Time							Pay Rate	Income Tax Deductions	Medical Insurance	Union Dues	Earnings to End of Previous Week
		M	T	W	T	F	S	S					
Mike Jens	31	7	8	8	8	8	3	0	$13.00	$112.00	$30.00	$15.00	$20,000
Seth Wain	32	8	6	8	8	8	4	0	15.50	133.00	35.00	15.00	6,200
Bob Mack	33	8	8	8	8	8	0	0	14.50	116.00	45.00	15.00	32,200
Kris Roan	34	8	9	8	8	9	1	0	16.00	143.00	45.00		5,400

Required

1. Enter the relevant information in the proper columns of a Payroll Register and complete the register with CPP and UIC deductions. Assume the first employee is a salesperson, the second two work in the shop, and the last one works in the office.

2. Prepare a general journal entry to record the payroll register information.

3. Make the cheque register entry to transfer funds equal to the payroll from the regular bank account to the payroll bank account (Cheque No. 522) under the assumption the company uses special payroll cheques and a payroll bank account in paying its employees. Assume the first payroll cheque is numbered 230 and enter the payroll cheque numbers in the Payroll Register.

4. Prepare a general journal entry to record the employer's payroll deductions resulting from the payroll.

5. Prepare general journal entries to accrue employee fringe benefit costs for the week. Assume the company matches the employees' payments for medical insurance and contributes an amount equal to 10% of each employees' gross pay to a retirement program. Also, each employee accrues vacation pay at the rate of 5% of the wages and salaries earned. The company estimates that all employees eventually will be paid their vacation pay.

Problem 13–4
General journal entries for payroll transactions
(L. O. 2)

A company has three employees, each of whom has been employed since January 1, earns $2,000 per month, and is paid on the last day of each month. On March 1, the following accounts and balances appeared in its ledger:

a. Employees Income Taxes Payable, $1,020 (liability for February only).
b. Unemployment Insurance Payable, $324 (liability for February).
c. Canada Pension Plan Payable, $264 (liability for February).
d. Employees' Medical Insurance Payable, $1,080 (liability for January and February).

During March and April, the company completed the following transactions related to payroll:

Mar. 11   Issued Cheque No. 320 payable to Receiver General of Canada. The $1,511 cheque was in payment of the February employee income taxes, UIC, and CPP amounts due.

31   Prepared a general journal entry to record the March Payroll Record which had the following column totals:

Income Taxes	UIC	CPP	Medical Insurance	Total Deductions	Net Pay	Office Salaries	Shop Wages
$1,020	$135	$132	$270	$1,557	$4,443	$2,500	$3,500

31   Recorded the employer's $270 liability for its 50% contribution to the medical insurance plan of employees.

31   Issued Cheque No. 351 payable to Payroll Bank Account in payment of the March payroll. Endorsed the cheque, deposited it in the payroll bank account, and issued payroll cheques to the employees.

31   Prepared a general journal entry to record the employer's payroll costs resulting from the March payroll.

Apr. 15   Issued Cheque No. 375 payable to the Receiver General in payment of the March mandatory deductions.

15   Issued Cheque No. 376 payable to All Canadian Insurance Company in payment of the employee medical insurance premiums for the first quarter.

Required

Prepare the necessary cheque register and general journal entries to record the transactions.

Alternate Problems

Problem 13–1A
The Payroll Register and the payroll bank account
(L. O. 1, 2)

Gogol Company's first weekly pay period of the year ended on January 8. On that date the column totals of the company's Payroll Register indicated its sales employees had earned $19,875, its office employees had earned $9,375, and its delivery employees had earned $2,250. Withholdings from the employees' salaries included $620 of UIC, $605 of CPP, $3,150 federal income taxes, $1,425 medical insurance deductions, and $340 of union dues.

Required

1. Prepare the general journal entry to record the January 8 payroll.
2. Prepare a general journal entry to record the employer's payroll deductions resulting from the January 8 payroll.

3. Under the assumption the company uses special payroll cheques and a payroll bank account in paying its employees, give the cheque register entry (Cheque No. 378) to transfer funds equal to the payroll from the regular bank account to the payroll bank account.

4. Answer this question: After the cheque register entry is made and posted, are additional debit and credit entries required to record the payroll cheques and pay the employees?

Problem 13–2A
The Payroll Register, the payroll bank account, and payroll deductions
(L. O. 1, 2, 3)

The following information was taken from the payroll records of Specialty Software Company for the weekly pay period ending December 24:

Employees	Clock Card No.	Daily Time M	T	W	T	F	S	S	Pay Rate	Income Taxes	Medical Insurance	Union Dues	Earnings to End of Previous Week
Lila Tomas	41	8	9	8	8	8	4	0	$20.00	$190.00	$ 35.00		$42,500
Mike Lowe	42	7	7	6	8	8	0	0	18.00	130.00	23.00	$20.00	55,800
Rick Corey	43	8	8	8	8	8	2	0	22.00	189.00	46.00	20.00	6,075
Maria Inez	44	6	7	8	8	7	2	0	19.00	145.00	56.00	20.00	35,600
James Sun	45	8	8	8	9	8	0	0	21.00	174.00	30.00		49,000
										$828.00	$190.00	$60.00	

Required

1. Enter the relevant information in the proper columns of a Payroll Register and complete the register with CPP and UIC deductions. The company pays time and one half for hours in excess of 40 each week. Also, work on Saturdays is paid at time and one half whether the total for the week is over 40 or not. Charge the wages of Lila Tomas to Office Salaries Expense and the wages of the remaining employees to Plant Salaries Expense.

2. Prepare a general journal entry to record the payroll register information.

3. Assume the company uses special payroll cheques drawn on a payroll bank account in paying its employees and make the cheque register entry (Cheque No. 484) to transfer funds equal to the payroll from the regular bank account to the payroll bank account. Also, assume the first payroll cheque is No. 632 and enter the payroll cheque numbers in the Payroll Register.

4. Prepare a general journal entry to record the employer's payroll deductions resulting from the payroll.

Problem 13–3A
**The Payroll Register,
payroll taxes, and
employee fringe benefits**
(L. O. 1, 2, 4)

The following information for the weekly pay period ended December 10 was taken from the records of a company:

| Employees | Clock Card No. | Daily Time | | | | | | | Pay Rate | Income Tax Deductions | Medical Insurance | Union Dues | Earnings to End of Previous Week |
		M	T	W	T	F	S	S					
Tom Darby	34	7	8	8	7	8	5	0	$15.00	$134.00	$25.50		$25,600
Ed Ward	35	8	8	7	8	8	3	0	13.00	112.00	18.00	$15.00	6,100
Jill White	36	8	8	8	8	7	1	0	14.50	116.00	30.50		29,200
Pam Taylor	37	8	7	9	9	7	4	0	12.00	110.00	22.00	15.00	6,700

Required

1. Enter the relevant information in the proper columns of a Payroll Register and complete the register with CPP and UIC deductions. Assume that the first employee works in the office, the second is a salesperson, and the last two work in the shop.

2. Prepare a general journal entry to record the payroll register information.

3. Make the cheque register entry (Cheque No. 389) to transfer funds equal to the payroll from the regular bank account to the payroll bank account. Assume the first payroll cheque is numbered 632 and enter the payroll cheque numbers in the Payroll Register.

4. Prepare a general journal entry to record the employer's payroll deductions resulting from the payroll.

5. Prepare a general journal entry to accrue employee fringe benefit costs for the week. Assume the company matches the employees' payments for medical insurance and contributes an amount equal to 10% of each employees' gross pay to a retirement program. Also, Darby and White accrue vacation pay at the rate of 7% of the wages and salaries earned. Ward and Taylor accrue vacation pay at the rate of 5%. The company estimates that all employees eventually will be paid their vacation pay.

Problem 13–4A
**General journal entries for
payroll transactions**
(L. O. 2)

A company has five employees, each of whom has been employed since January 1, earns $1,200 per month, and is paid on the last day of each month. On June 1 the following accounts and balances appeared on its ledger:

a. Employees' Income Taxes Payable, $1,250. (The balance of this account represents the liability for the May 31 payroll only.)

b. Unemployment Insurance Payable, $324 (liability for May only).

c. Canada Pension Payable, $264 (liability for May).

d. Employees' Medical Insurance Payable, $1,296 (liability for April and May).

During June and July, the company completed the following payroll-related transactions:

June 10 Issued Cheque No. 726 payable to the Receiver General for Canada. The $1,736 cheque was in payment of the May employee income taxes, CPP, and UIC amounts due.

   30 Prepared a general journal entry to record the June Payroll Record which had the following column totals:

Federal Income Taxes	CPP	UIC	Medical Insurance	Total Deductions	Net Pay	Office Salaries	Shop Wages
$1,195	$132	$135	$344	$1,806	$4,194	$2,500	$3,500

   30 Recorded the employer's $344 liability for its 50% contribution to the medical insurance plan of employees.

   30 Issued Cheque No. 766 payable to Payroll Bank Account in payment of the June payroll. Endorsed the check, deposited it in the payroll bank account, and issued payroll cheques to the employees.

   30 Prepared a general journal entry to record the employer's payroll costs resulting from the June payroll.

July 15 Issued Cheque No. 790 payable to Receiver General in payment of the June mandatory deductions.

   15 Issued Cheque No. 791 payable to Blacke Insurance Company. The cheque was in payment of the April, May, and June employee health insurance premiums.

Required

Prepare the necessary cheque register and general journal entries to record the transactions.

Provocative Problems

Provocative Problem 13–1
Archery Unlimited Company
(L. O. 1, 3)

Archery Unlimited Company has 80 regular employees, has recently received an order for a line of archery equipment from a chain of department stores. The order should be very profitable and will probably be repeated each year. In filling the order, Archery Unlimited can manufacture the various bows and other supplies with present machines and employees. However, it will have to add 20 persons to its work force for 40 hours per week for 10 weeks to finish the crossbows and pack them for shipment.

The company can hire these workers and add them to its own payroll, or it can secure the services of 20 people through Personnel, Inc. Archery Unlimited will pay Personnel, Inc., $10.50 per hour for each hour worked by each person supplied. The people will be employees of Personnel, Inc., and it will pay their wages and all taxes on the wages. On the other hand, if Archery Unlimited employs the workers and places them on its payroll, it will pay them $10 per hour and will also pay the following payroll costs on their wages: Canada Pension Plan and unemployment insurance. The company will also have to pay medical insurance costs of $10 per employee per week.

Should Archery Unlimited place the temporary help on its own payroll, or should it secure their services through Personnel, Inc.? Justify your answer.

Provocative Problem 13–2
Astrolabs Company
(L. O. 3, 4)

Astrolabs Company employs a scientific specialist at an annual salary of $66,000. The company pays the usual portion of mandatory unemployment insurance and Canada Pension. The company also pays $85 per month for the employee's medical insurance. Effective June 1, the company agreed to contribute 15% of the specialist's gross pay to a retirement program.

What was the total monthly cost of employing the specialist in January, March, July, and December? Assuming the employee works 180 hours each month, what is the cost per hour in January? If the annual gross salary is increased by $4,000, what will be the increase in the total annual costs of employing the specialist?

Analytical and Review Problems

A&R Problem 13–1

Using current year's withholding tables for Canada Pension Plan, unemployment insurance, and income tax, update the Payroll Register of Illustration 13–3. In computing income tax withholdings, state *your* assumption as to each employee's personal deductions. Assume that hospital insurance deductions continue at the same amounts as in Illustration 13–3.

A&R Problem 13–2

The following data were taken from the Payroll Register of Muskoka Company:

Gross salary.	XXX
Employees' income tax deductions	XXX
UI deductions	XXX
CPP deductions.	XXX
Hospital insurance deductions	XXX
Union dues deductions	XXX

Muskoka contributes an equal amount to the hospital insurance plan, in addition to the statutory payroll taxes, and 6% of gross salaries to a pension program.

Required

Record in general journal form the payroll, payment of the employees, and remittance to the appropriate authority amounts owing in connection with the payroll. (Note: All amounts are to be indicated as XXX.)

14 Partnership Accounting

The three common types of business organization, single proprietorships, partnerships, and corporations, were introduced in the early chapters of this book. In this chapter, we look more closely at the partnership form of business organization. The partnership form is widely used, especially in businesses where the owners know each other well. Many professional businesses, including public accounting firms, are organized as partnerships.

Learning Objectives

After studying Chapter 14, you should be able to:

1. List the characteristics of a partnership and explain the importance of mutual agency and unlimited liability to a person about to become a partner.

2. Allocate partnership earnings to partners (*a*) on a stated fractional basis, (*b*) in the partners' capital ratio, and (*c*) through the use of salary and interest allowances.

3. Prepare entries for (*a*) the sale of a partnership interest, (*b*) the admission of a new partner by investment, and (*c*) the retirement of a partner by the withdrawal of partnership assets.

4. Prepare entries required in the liquidation of a partnership.

5. Define or explain the words and phrases listed in the chapter Glossary.

Characteristics of a Partnership

List the characteristics of a partnership and explain the importance of mutual agency and unlimited liability to a person about to become a partner. (L. O. 1)

The provincial Partnership Acts and the Civil Code, with minor variations, define a **partnership** as: ''The relation which subsists between persons carrying on a business in common with a view of profit.'' Another definition of a partnership is ''an association of two or more competent persons under a contract to combine some or all of their property, labour, and skills in the operation of a business.'' Both of these definitions say something about the legal nature of a partnership. However, the nature of the partnership form of business becomes clearer when you understand some of the specific features that characterize partnerships.

A Voluntary Association

A partnership is a voluntary association between the partners. This voluntary nature of a partnership is important because a person assumes some risk by entering a partnership. For example, each partner is responsible for the business acts of his or her partners when the acts are within the scope of the partnership. Also, a partner is personally liable for all of the debts of his or her partnership. As a result, you never have to join a partnership without agreeing who will be the partners. Normally, you should select only financially responsible people who have good judgment.

Based on a Contract

One advantage of a partnership as a form of business organization is that it is easy to organize. All that is necessary is for two or more legally competent people to agree to become partners. Their agreement becomes a **partnership contract**. This contract should be carefully written so that all anticipated points of future disagreement are covered. However, even if the partners make their agreement orally and fail to put it in writing, the partnership contract is binding.

Limited Life

The life of a partnership is always limited. Death, bankruptcy, or anything that takes away the ability of one of the partners to contract automatically ends a partnership. In addition, since a partnership is based on a contract, the contract may state a period of time after which the partnership ends. If the contract does not specify a time period, the partnership ends when the business for which it was created is completed. Or, if no time is stated because the business is expected to go on indefinitely, the partnership may be terminated at will by any one of the partners.

Mutual Agency

In most partnerships, the partners are understood to be mutual agents of the partnership. **Mutual agency** means that every partner can act as an agent of the partnership by committing it to any contract within the apparent scope of its business. For example, a partner in a merchandising business can sign contracts that bind the partnership to buy merchandise, lease a store building, borrow money for the business, or hire employees. These are all within the scope of a merchandising firm. On the other hand, a partner in a law firm, acting alone, cannot contract on behalf of his or her partners to buy merchandise for resale or to rent a store building. These are not within the normal scope of a law firm's business.

Partners may agree to limit the agency powers of any one or more of the partners to negotiate certain contracts for the partnership. Such an agreement is binding on the partners and on outsiders who know of the agreement. However, it is not binding on outsiders who do not know that it exists. Outsiders who are not aware of the agreement have a right to assume that each partner has the normal agency rights of a partner.

Because mutual agency exposes all partners to the actions of any one partner, you should carefully evaluate potential partners before agreeing to join a partnership. The importance of this advice becomes clear when you consider the fact that most partnerships are also characterized by unlimited liability. Mutual agency plus unlimited liability are the reasons most partnerships have only a few partners.

Unlimited Liability

Normally, when a partnership cannot pay its debts, the creditors may satisfy their claims from the personal assets of the partners. Also, if the property of a partner is insufficient to meet his or her share of the partnership's debts, the creditors may turn to the assets of the remaining partners who are able to pay. Thus, one partner may be called on to pay all the debts of the partnership. This **unlimited liability of partners** is a very important characteristic of partnerships.

Unlimited liability may be illustrated as follows. Ned Albert and Carol Bates each invested $5,000 in a store to be operated as a partnership. They also agreed to share net incomes and losses equally. Albert has no property other than his $5,000 investment. Bates has sizable savings in addition to her investment. After renting a store, the partners bought merchandise for $30,000, paying $10,000 in cash and promising to pay the balance at a later date. However, before the business opened, the store burned and the merchandise was totally destroyed. There was no insurance, and all the partnership assets were lost. Albert has no other assets. Because of unlimited liability, the partnership creditors can collect the full $20,000 of their claims from Bates. However, Bates may look to Albert for payment of half at a later date, if Albert ever is able to pay.

Limited Partnerships

So far, we have said that all partners normally have unlimited liability. Sometimes, however, a group of individuals want to invest in a partnership but are unwilling to accept the risk of unlimited liability. This can be accomplished by using a unique form of business called a **limited partnership**. A limited partnership has two classes of partners, general partners and limited partners. At least one of the partners, the **general partner(s)**, must assume unlimited liability for the debts of the partnership. However, the remaining **limited partners** have no personal liability beyond the amounts they invest in the business. Usually, a limited partnership is managed by the general partner(s). The limited partners have no active role except for certain major decisions as specified in the partnership agreement. To distinguish limited partnerships from those in which all of the partners have unlimited liability, the latter are often called **general partnerships**

Advantages and Disadvantages of a Partnership

Limited life, mutual agency, and unlimited liability are disadvantages of a partnership. Yet, there are other reasons why a partnership may be a preferred form of business organization. A partnership has the advantage of being able to bring together more money and skills than a single proprietorship. A partnership is easier to organize than a corporation. Also, a partnership may escape some of the federal and provincial regulations and taxes that are imposed on corporations. Finally, partners may act without having to hold shareholders' or directors' meetings, which are required of a corporation.

Partnership Accounting

Accounting for a partnership is no different than accounting for a single proprietorship except for transactions that directly affect the partners' equities. Because ownership rights in a partnership are divided between two or more partners, there must be:

1. A capital account for each partner.
2. A withdrawals account for each partner.
3. A careful measurement and division of earnings.

When partners invest in a partnership, the capital account of each partner is credited for the amount of that partner's investment. Thereafter, each partner's withdrawals are debited to his or her withdrawals account. And, in the end-of-period closing procedure, a net income is allocated to the partners by crediting each partner's capital account for his or her share. Obviously, these closing procedures are like those you would use for a single proprietorship. The only difference is that separate capital and withdrawals accounts are maintained for each partner. Thus, the closing procedures for a partnership require no further consideration. However, we should examine more carefully the matter of allocating earnings among partners.

Nature of Partnership Earnings

Partners cannot enter into an employer-employee contractual relationship with themselves. They cannot legally hire themselves and pay themselves a salary. If partners devote their time and services to the affairs of their partnership, they are understood to do so for profit, not for salary. Therefore, when the net income or loss of a partnership is calculated, salary allowances to partners are not deducted as expenses. However, when the net income or loss of the partnership is allocated among the partners, the partners may agree to base part of the allocation on the relative amounts of service provided by the partners.

Just as salary allowances to partners are not expenses of the partnership, neither is interest on the partners' investments. Partners are understood to invest in a partnership for profit, not for interest. Nevertheless, partners may agree that the division of partnership earnings should include a return on invested capital. For example, if one partner contributes five times as much capital as another, fairness would require that this fact be taken into consideration when earnings are allocated among the partners. Likewise, if the services of one partner are more valuable than those of another, some provision should be made for the unequal service contributions.

Division of Earnings

Allocate partnership earnings to partners (*a*) on a stated fractional basis, (*b*) in the partners' capital ratio, and (*c*) through the use of salary and interest allowances. (L. O. 2)

In the absence of a contrary agreement, the law states that the income or loss of a partnership is shared equally by the partners. However, partners may agree to any method of sharing. If they agree on a method of sharing incomes but say nothing of losses, then losses are shared in the same way as incomes.

Several methods of allocating partnership earnings among the partners are commonly used. Three frequently used methods are to allocate earnings based on: (1) stated fractions assigned to each partner, (2) the ratio of capital investments, or (3) salary and interest allowances and the remainder in a fixed ratio.

Earnings Allocated on a Stated Fractional Basis

The easiest way to divide partnership earnings is to give each partner a stated fraction of the total. A division on a fractional basis may provide for an equal sharing if service and capital contributions are equal. An equal sharing may also be provided when the greater capital contribution of one partner is offset by a greater service contribution of another. Or, if the service and capital contributions are unequal, a fixed ratio may provide for an unequal sharing. All that is necessary in any case is for the partners to agree as to the fractional share each will receive.

For example, assume that the partnership agreement of Morse and North states that Morse will receive two thirds and North will receive one third of the partnership earnings and the partnership's net income for a year is $30,000. Therefore, after all revenue and expense accounts are closed at the end of the year, the Income Summary account has a $30,000 credit balance. The entry to close the Income Summary account and to allocate the partnership's earnings to the partners is as follows:

Dec.	31	Income Summary	30,000.00	
		A. P. Morse, Capital		20,000.00
		R. G. North, Capital		10,000.00
		To close the Income Summary account and allocate the earnings.		

Division of Earnings Based on the Ratio of Capital Investments

If the nature of a partnership's business is such that earnings are closely related to money invested, a division of earnings based on the ratio of partners' investments offers a fair sharing method. To illustrate this method, assume that Chase, Davis, and Fall have agreed to share earnings in the ratio of their investments. These are Chase, $50,000, Davis, $30,000, and Fall, $40,000. If net income for the year is $48,000, the respective shares of the partners are calculated as follows:

Step 1: Chase, capital . . . . $ 50,000
Davis, capital   30,000
Fall, capital   40,000
Total invested $120,000

Step 2: Share of earnings to Chase: $\dfrac{\$50,000}{\$120,000} \times \$48,000 = \$20,000$

Share of earnings to Davis: $\dfrac{\$30,000}{\$120,000} \times \$48,000 = \$12,000$

Share of earnings to Fall: $\dfrac{\$40,000}{\$120,000} \times \$48,000 = \$16,000$

The entry to allocate the earnings to the partners is then:

Dec.	31	Income Summary	48,000.00	
		T. S. Chase, Capital		20,000.00
		S. A. Davis, Capital		12,000.00
		R. R. Fall, Capital		16,000.00
		To close the Income Summary account and allocate the earnings.		

Salaries and Interest Allowances

Sometimes partners' service contributions are not equal. Also, the capital contributions of the partners may not be equal. Even in partnerships in which all partners work full time, the services of one partner may be more valuable than the services of another. If the service contributions are not equal, the partners may use salary allowances to compensate for the differences. Or, when capital contributions are not equal, they may allocate part of the earnings in the form of interest to compensate for the unequal investments. When service and investment contributions are both unequal, they may use a combination of salary and interest allowances in an effort to share earnings fairly.

For example, in Hill and Dale's net partnership, Hill is to provide annual services that they agree are worth an annual salary of $36,000. Dale is less experienced in the business, so his service contribution to the business is worth only $24,000. Also, Hill will invest $30,000 in the business, and Dale will invest $10,000. To compensate the partners fairly, given the differences in their service and capital contributions, Hill and Dale agree that they will share incomes or losses as follows:

1. Partners are to be granted annual salary allowances of $36,000 to Hill and $24,000 to Dale.
2. Partners are to be granted an interest allowance equal to 10% of each partner's beginning-of-year capital balance.
3. The remaining balance of income or loss is to be shared equally.

Illustration 14–1
Sharing income when income exceeds interest and salary allowances

	Share to Hill	Share to Dale	Totals
Total net income			$ 69,000
Allocated as salary allowances:			
Hill.	$36,000		
Dale		$24,000	
Total allocated as salary allowances			(60,000)
Balance of income after salary allowances. . .			$ 9,000
Allocated as interest:			
Hill (10% on $30,000)	3,000		
Dale (10% on $10,000)		1,000	
Total allocated as interest			(4,000)
Balance of income after salary and interest allowances			$ 5,000
Balance allocated equally:			
Hill.	2,500		
Dale		2,500	
Total allocated equally			(5,000)
Balance of income			$ –0–
Shares of the partners	$41,500	$27,500	

Note that the provisions for salaries and interest in this partnership agreement are called *allowances*. They are called allowances because, in a legal sense, partners do not work for salaries and they do not invest in a partnership to earn interest. They invest and work for earnings. Therefore, when a partnership agreement provides for salaries and interest, these allowances are not reported as salaries and interest expense. They are only a means of sharing income or losses.

Under the Hill and Dale agreement, a first year net income of $69,000 would be shared as in Illustration 14–1.

After the shares in the net income are determined, the following entry is used to close the Income Summary account. Note that the credit amounts in the entry are taken from the first two column totals of the computation shown in Illustration 14–1.

Dec.	31	Income Summary	69,000.00	
		Hill, Capital		41,500.00
		Dale, Capital		27,500.00
		To close the Income Summary account and allocate the earnings.		

In Illustration 14–1, the $69,000 net income exceeded the salary and interest allowances of the partners. However, the partners would use the same method to share a loss or to share a net income that was smaller than their salary and interest allowances. For example, assume that Hill and Dale earned

Illustration 14–2

Sharing income when interest and salary allowances exceed income

	Share to Hill	Share to Dale	Totals
Total net income			$ 45,000
Allocated as salary allowances:			
Hill.	$36,000		
Dale		$24,000	
Total allocated as salary allowances			(60,000)
Balance of income after salary allowances. . .			$(15,000)
Allocated as interest:			
Hill (10% on $30,000)	3,000		
Dale (10% on $10,000)		1,000	
Total allocated as interest			(4,000)
Balance of income after salary and interest allowances			$(19,000)
Balance allocated equally:			
Hill.	(9,500)		
Dale		(9,500)	
Total allocated equally.			19,000
Balance of income			$ –0–
Shares of the partners	$29,500	$15,500	

Illustration 14–3

A statement of changes in partners' equity

HILL AND DALE
Statement of Changes in Partners' Equity
For Year Ended December 31, 19—

	Hill		Dale		Total
Beginning capital balances		$ –0–		$ –0–	$ –0–
Plus:					
Investments by owners		30,000		10,000	40,000
Net income:					
Salary allowances.	$36,000		$24,000		
Interest allowances	3,000		1,000		
Balance	(9,500)		(9,500)		
Total net income		29,500		15,500	45,000
Total.		$ 59,500		$ 25,500	$ 85,000
Less partners' withdrawals		(20,000)		(12,000)	(32,000)
Ending capital balances		$ 39,500		$ 13,500	$ 53,000

only $45,000 during the first year of operations. A $45,000 net income would be shared by the partners as in Illustration 14–2.

    The same procedures used to allocate a net income between Hill and Dale would also be used to allocate a net loss. The only difference is that the income-and-loss-sharing procedure would begin with a negative amount of income (a net loss). The amount allocated equally would then be a larger negative amount.

Partnership Financial Statements

In most respects, partnership financial statements are like those of a single proprietorship. On the balance sheet of a partnership, the owner's equity section often shows the separate capital account balance of each partner. The **statement of changes in partners' equity** shows the total capital balances at the beginning of the period, any additional investments made by the partners, the net income or loss of the partnership, withdrawals by the partners, and the ending capital balances. Usually, this statement shows these changes for each partner's capital account and includes the allocation of income among the partners. For example, recall that Hill and Dale began their partnership by making investments of $30,000 and $10,000, respectively. During the first year of operations, in which the partnership earned $45,000, assume that Hill withdrew $20,000 and Dale withdrew $12,000. The statement of changes in partners' equity appears in Illustration 14–3.

Withdrawal or Addition of a Partner

Prepare entries for (a) the sale of a partnership interest, (b) the admission of a new partner by investment, and (c) the retirement of a partner by the withdrawal of partnership assets.
(L. O. 3)

A partnership is based on a contract between specific individuals. Therefore, when a partner withdraws from a partnership, the old partnership ceases to exist. Nevertheless, the business may continue to operate as a new partnership among the remaining partners.

The withdrawal of a partner from a partnership may take place two different ways. First, the withdrawing partner may sell his or her interest to another person who pays for the interest by transferring cash or other assets to the withdrawing partner. Second, cash or other assets of the partnership may be distributed to the withdrawing partner in settlement of his or her interest in the partnership.

When a new partner is admitted to a partnership, the old partnership technically ends and is replaced by a new partnership. Similar to the withdrawal of a partner, there are two ways a new partner may be admitted to an existing partnership. First, the new partner may purchase an interest directly from one or more of its partners. In other words, the new partner may pay cash to one or more of the existing partners in exchange for an interest in the partnership. Second, a new partner may join an existing partnership by investing cash or other assets in the business.

Sale of a Partnership Interest

Assume that Abbott, Burns, and Camp are partners in a partnership that owes no liabilities and has the following assets and owners' equity:

Assets		Owners' Equity	
Cash	$ 3,000	Abbott, capital	$ 5,000
Other assets.	12,000	Burns, capital	5,000
		Camp, capital	5,000
Total assets	$15,000	Total owners' equity	$15,000

Camp's equity in this partnership is $5,000. If Camp sells this equity to Davis for $7,000, Camp is selling a $5,000 recorded interest in the partnership assets. The entry on the partnership books to transfer the equity is:

Feb.	4	Camp, Capital	5,000.00	
		Davis, Capital		5,000.00
		To transfer Camp's equity in the partnership to Davis.		

After this entry is posted, the assets and owners' equity of the new partnership are:

Assets		Owners' Equity	
Cash	$ 3,000	Abbott, capital	$ 5,000
Other assets.	12,000	Burns, capital	5,000
		Davis, capital	5,000
Total assets	$15,000	Total owners' equity.	$15,000

Two aspects of this transaction are especially important. First, the $7,000 Davis paid to Camp is not recorded in the partnership books. Camp sold and transferred a $5,000 recorded equity in the partnership assets to Davis. The entry that records the transfer is a debit to Camp, Capital and a credit to Davis, Capital for $5,000. Furthermore, the entry is the same whether Davis pays Camp $7,000, or $70,000. The amount is paid directly to Camp. Since the partnership is not a party to the transaction, the assets and the total equity of the partnership are not affected by the transaction.

The second important aspect of this transaction is the question of whether Davis's purchase of Camp's interest qualifies Davis as a new partner. In fact, Abbott and Burns must agree to the sale and transfer if Davis is to become a partner. Abbott and Burns cannot prevent Camp from selling the interest to Davis. But Abbott and Burns do not have to accept Davis as a partner. If Abbott and Burns agree to accept Davis, a new partnership is formed and a new contract with a new income-and-loss-sharing ratio must be drawn.

What if either Abbott or Burns refuses to accept Davis as a partner? Under the Provincial Partnership Act, Davis gets Camp's share of partnership income and losses. And if the partnership is liquidated, Davis gets Camp's share of partnership assets. However, Davis gets no voice in the management of the firm until admitted as a partner.

Investing Assets in an Existing Partnership

Instead of purchasing the equity of an existing partner, an individual may gain an equity by investing assets in the business. Then, the invested assets become the property of the partnership. For example, assume that the partnership of Evans and Gage has assets and owners' equity as follows:

Assets		Owners' Equity	
Cash.	$ 3,000	Evans, capital	$20,000
Other assets.	37,000	Gage, capital	20,000
Total assets	$40,000	Total owners' equity.	$40,000

Also, assume that Evans and Gage have agreed to accept Hart as a partner with a one-half interest in the business upon his investment of $40,000. The entry to record Hart's investment is:

Mar.	2	Cash	40,000.00	
		Hart, Capital		40,000.00
		To record the investment of Hart.		

After the entry is posted, the assets and owners' equity of the new partnership appear as follows:

Assets		Owners' Equity	
Cash.	$43,000	Evans, capital	$20,000
Other assets.	37,000	Gage, capital	20,000
		Hart, capital	40,000
Total assets	$80,000	Total owners' equity.	$80,000

In this case, Hart has a 50% equity in the assets of the business. However, he does not necessarily have a right to one half of its net income. The sharing of incomes and losses is a separate matter on which the partners must agree. As you learned earlier in the chapter, the sharing of profits and losses may be in the ratio of the partners' relative capital contributions. However, the method of sharing also may depend on other factors.

A Bonus to the Old Partners

Sometimes, when the current value of a partnership is greater than the amounts of equity recorded in the accounting records, the partners may require an incoming partner to give a bonus for the privilege of joining the firm. For example, Judd and Kirk operate a partnership business, sharing its earnings equally. The partnership's accounting records show that Judd's recorded equity in the business is $38,000 and Kirk's recorded equity is $32,000. Judd and Kirk agree to accept Lee's $50,000 investment in the business in return for a one-third share of the partnership's earnings and a one-third equity in net assets. Lee's equity is determined with a calculation as follows:

Equities of the existing partners ($38,000 + $32,000) . .	$ 70,000
Investment of the new partner	50,000
Total partnership equity.	$120,000
Equity of Lee (⅓ of total)	$ 40,000

Notice that although Lee invested $50,000 in the partnership, his equity in the recorded net assets of the partnership is only $40,000. The $10,000 difference usually is described as a bonus that is allocated to the existing partners (Judd and Kirk). Therefore, the entry to record Lee's investment is:

May.	15	Cash	50,000.00	
		Lee, Capital		40,000.00
		Judd, Capital		5,000.00
		Kirk, Capital		5,000.00
		To record the investment of Lee.		

Notice that the $10,000 difference between the $50,000 invested by Lee and the $40,000 credited to his capital account is shared by Judd and Kirk according to their income-and-loss-sharing ratio. Such a bonus is always shared by the old partners in their income-and-loss-sharing ratio. This ratio is used because the bonus compensates the old partners for increases in the worth of the partnership that have not yet been recorded as income.

Recording Goodwill

As discussed above, when a new partner's investment exceeds his or her equity in the partnership's net assets, the entry to record the new partner's admission normally allocates a bonus to the existing partners. Occasionally, however, an alternative method is used to record the admission of a new partner. The alternative method involves recording goodwill on the books of the partnership. The debit to Goodwill is matched with credits that increase the equities of the existing partners.

The goodwill method of recording a new partner's admission would be used only if the evidence indicates that future earnings of the partnership are large enough to justify the increased partnership equity. Evidence of such future earnings might be provided by a historical record of earnings that are consistently in excess of the average for the industry.

In practice, goodwill is seldom recognized upon the admission of a new partner. Instead, the bonus method usually is used.

Bonus to the New Partner

Sometimes, the members of an existing partnership may be very eager to bring a new partner into their firm. The business may need additional cash or the new partner may have exceptional abilities or business contacts that will increase profits. In such a situation, the old partners may be willing to give the new partner a larger equity in the business than the amount of his or her investment. In this case, the old partners give a bonus to the new partner.

For example, Jay Moss and Mike Owen are partners with capital account balances of $30,000 and $18,000, respectively. They share income and losses in a 2:1 ratio. The partners are anxious to have Kay Pitt join their partnership and will grant her a one-fourth equity in the firm if she will invest $12,000. If Pitt accepts, her equity in the new firm is calculated as follows:

Equities of the existing partners ($30,000 + $18,000) . .	$48,000
Investment of the new partner	12,000
Total equities in the new partnership.	$60,000
Equity of Pitt (¼ of total)	$15,000

And the entry to record Pitt's investment is:

June	1	Cash	12,000.00	
		Moss, Capital ($3,000 × ⅔).	2,000.00	
		Owen, Capital ($3,000 × ⅓)	1,000.00	
		Pitt, Capital		15,000.00
		To record the investment of Pitt.		

Note that Pitt's bonus is contributed by the old partners in their income-and-loss-sharing ratio. Also remember that Pitt's one-fourth equity does not necessarily entitle her to one fourth of the earnings of the business. The sharing of income and losses is a separate matter for agreement by the partners.

Withdrawal of a Partner

When a new partnership is formed, the partnership contract should state the procedures to be followed when a partner retires from the partnership. These procedures often state that a withdrawing partner shall withdraw assets equal to the current value of the partner's equity. To accomplish this, the procedures may require an audit of the accounting records and a revaluation of the partnership assets. The revaluation places the assets on the books at current values. It also causes the partners' capital accounts to reflect the current value of their equity.

For example, assume that Blue is retiring from the partnership of Smith, Blue, and Short. The partners have always shared incomes and losses in the ratio of one half to Smith, one fourth to Blue, and one fourth to Short. Their partnership agreement provides for an audit and asset revaluation upon the retirement of a partner. Just prior to the audit and revaluation, their balance sheet shows the following assets and owners' equity:

Assets			Owners' Equity	
Cash		$11,000	Smith, capital	$22,000
Merchandise inventory . .		16,000	Blue, capital	10,000
Equipment	$20,000		Short, capital	10,000
Less accum. depr.. . . .	5,000	15,000		
Total assets.		$42,000	Total owners' equity	$42,000

The audit and appraisal indicate that the merchandise inventory is overvalued by $4,000. Also, due to market changes, the partnership's equipment should be valued at $25,000, less accumulated depreciation of $8,000. The entries to record these revaluations are:

Oct.	31	Smith, Capital	2,000.00	
		Blue, Capital	1,000.00	
		Short, Capital	1,000.00	
		Merchandise Inventory		4,000.00
		To revalue the inventory.		
	31	Equipment	5,000.00	
		Accumulated Depreciation, Equipment		3,000.00
		Smith, Capital		1,000.00
		Blue, Capital		500.00
		Short, Capital		500.00
		To revalue the equipment.		

Note in the illustrated entries that the partners share the amount of the revaluations in their income-and-loss-sharing ratio. This is fair because revaluations of assets are actually gains and losses. If the partnership were not terminated, these gains and losses would sooner or later show up on the income statement as increases and decreases in net income. The revaluation simply records the effect of the gains and losses earlier than would have occurred.

After the entries revaluing the partnership assets are recorded, the balance sheet for the Smith, Blue, and Short partnership is as follows:

Assets			**Owners' Equity**	
Cash		$11,000	Smith, capital	$21,000
Merchandise inventory ..		12,000	Blue, capital	9,500
Equipment	$25,000		Short, capital	9,500
Less accum. depr.. ...	8,000	17,000		
Total assets		$40,000	Total owners' equity	$40,000

After the revaluation, if Blue retires and takes cash equal to his revalued equity, the entry to record the withdrawal is:

Oct.	31	Blue, Capital	9,500.00	
		Cash		9,500.00
		To record the withdrawal of Blue.		

In withdrawing, Blue does not have to take cash in settlement of his equity. He may take any combination of assets to which the partners agree, or he may take the new partnership's promissory note. Also, the withdrawal of Blue generally creates a new partnership between the remaining partners. Therefore, a new partnership contract and a new income-and-loss-sharing agreement may be required.

Withdrawing Partner Takes Fewer Assets than Recorded Equity

Sometimes, when a partner retires, the remaining partners may not wish to revalue the assets on the books of the partnership. Nevertheless, the current values of the partnership assets must be determined so that the amount of assets to be taken by the retiring partner can be established. For example, the partners may agree that the assets are overvalued. As a result, the retiring partner should be given assets of less value than the book value of his or her equity. Also, even if the assets are not overvalued, a retiring partner may be willing to take less than the current value of his or her equity just to get out of the partnership.

When a partner retires and takes assets of less value than the partner's recorded equity, the partner in effect leaves a portion of the equity in the business. In such cases, the remaining partners share the unwithdrawn equity portion in their income-and-loss-sharing ratio. For example, assume that Black, Brown, and Green are partners who share incomes and losses in a 2:2:1 ratio. Their assets and equities are as follows:

Assets		Owners' Equity	
Cash	$ 5,000	Black, capital	$ 6,000
Merchandise inventory	9,000	Brown, capital	6,000
Store equipment.	4,000	Green, capital	6,000
Total assets	$18,000	Total owners' equity.	$18,000

Brown is anxious to withdraw from the partnership and offers to take $4,500 in cash in settlement for his equity. Black and Green agree to the $4,500 withdrawal, and Brown retires. The entry to record the retirement is:

Mar.	4	Brown, Capital	6,000.00	
		Cash		4,500.00
		Black, Capital		1,000.00
		Green, Capital.		500.00
		To record the withdrawal of Brown.		

In retiring, Brown withdrew $1,500 less than his recorded equity. This is divided between Black and Green in their income-and-loss-sharing ratio. The income-and-loss-sharing ratio of the original partnership was Black, 2; Brown, 2; and Green, 1. Therefore, the ratio for sharing between Black and Green was 2:1, and the unwithdrawn book equity of Brown is shared by Black and Green in this ratio.

Withdrawing Partner Takes More Assets than Recorded Equity

There are two common reasons why a retiring partner might withdraw more assets than his or her recorded equity. First, the partnership assets may be undervalued on the books. Also, the continuing partners may want to encourage the retiring partner to withdraw by giving up assets of greater value than the retiring partner's recorded equity.

When assets are undervalued, the partners may not wish to change the recorded values. If a retiring partner is allowed to withdraw assets of greater value than that partner's recorded equity, the retiring partner is, in effect, withdrawing his or her own equity plus a portion of the continuing partners' equities.

For example, assume that Jones, Thomas, and Finch are partners that share incomes and losses in a 3:2:1 ratio. The assets and owners' equity of the partnership are as follows:

Assets		Owners' Equity	
Cash.	$ 5,000	Jones, capital	$ 9,000
Merchandise inventory	10,000	Thomas, capital	6,000
Equipment.	3,000	Finch, capital	3,000
Total assets	$18,000	Total owners' equity.	$18,000

Finch wishes to withdraw from the partnership. Jones and Thomas plan to continue the business. The partners agree that some of the partnership's assets are undervalued, but they do not wish to increase the recorded values. They further agree that if current values were recorded, the asset total would be increased by $6,000 and the equity of Finch would be increased by $1,000. Therefore, the partners agree that $4,000 is the proper value for Finch's equity and that amount of cash may be withdrawn. The entry to record the withdrawal is:

May	7	Finch, Capital	3,000.00	
		Jones, Capital	600.00	
		Thomas, Capital	400.00	
		Cash.		4,000.00
		To record the withdrawal of Finch.		

Death of a Partner

A partner's death automatically dissolves a partnership. As a result, the deceased partner's estate is entitled to receive the amount of his or her equity. The partnership contract should contain provisions for settlement in case a partner dies. Included should be provisions for (a) an immediate closing of the books to determine earnings since the end of the previous accounting period and (b) a method for determining and recording current values for the assets and liabilities. After these steps are taken, the remaining partners and the deceased partner's estate must agree to a disposition of the deceased partner's equity. This may involve selling the equity to the remaining partners or to an outsider, or it may involve the withdrawal of assets in settlement. We explained the appropriate entries for both cases in the previous paragraphs.

Liquidations

Prepare entries required in the liquidation of a partnership.
(L. O. 4)

When a partnership is liquidated, its business is ended. The assets are converted into cash, and the creditors are paid. The remaining cash is then distributed to the partners, and the partnership is dissolved. **Partnership liquidations** may follow a variety of different steps. However, we will limit the following discussion to three typical situations.

All Assets Realized before a Distribution; Assets Are Sold at a Profit

One case involving a partnership liquidation is the situation in which all of the partnership assets are converted into cash at a profit, before any cash is distributed to the partners. The following example shows the necessary accounting entries to be made under these conditions.

Ottis, Skinner, and Parr have operated a partnership for a number of years, sharing incomes and losses in a 3:2:1 ratio. Due to several unsatisfactory conditions, the partners decide to liquidate as of December 31. On that date, the books are closed, and the income from operations is transferred to the partners' capital accounts. Thereafter, the partnership's balance sheet appears as follows:

Assets		Liabilities and Owners' Equity	
Cash	$10,000	Accounts payable	$ 5,000
Merchandise inventory	15,000	Ottis, capital	15,000
Other assets	25,000	Skinner, capital	15,000
		Parr, capital	15,000
		Total liabilities and	
Total assets	$50,000	owners' equity	$50,000

In a liquidation, some gains or losses normally result from the sale of noncash assets. These losses and gains are called "losses and gains from realization." Just like any other net incomes or losses, the losses and gains from realization are shared by the partners in their income-and-loss-sharing ratio. For example, if Ottis, Skinner, and Parr sell their inventory for $12,000 and their other assets for $34,000, the sales and the net gain allocation are recorded as follows:

Jan.	12	Cash	12,000.00	
		Loss or Gain from Realization	3,000.00	
		Merchandise Inventory		15,000.00
		Sold the inventory at a loss.		
	15	Cash	34,000.00	
		Other Assets		25,000.00
		Loss or Gain from Realization		9,000.00
		Sold the other assets at a profit.		
	15	Loss or Gain from Realization	6,000.00	
		Ottis, Capital		3,000.00
		Skinner, Capital		2,000.00
		Parr, Capital		1,000.00
		To allocate the net gain from realization to the partners in their 3:2:1 income-and-loss-sharing ratio.		

Notice in the last entry that the losses and gains from realization were shared in the partners' income-and-loss-sharing ratio. In solving liquidation problems, do not make the mistake of allocating the losses and gains in the ratio of the partners' capital balances.

After the merchandise and other assets of Ottis, Skinner, and Parr are sold and the net gain is allocated, a new balance sheet shows the following:

Assets		**Liabilities and Owners' Equity**	
Cash	$56,000	Accounts payable	$ 5,000
		Ottis, capital	18,000
		Skinner, capital	17,000
		Parr, capital	16,000
		Total liabilities and	
Total assets	$56,000	owners' equity	$56,000

Observe that the one asset, cash, $56,000, exactly equals the sum of the liabilities and the equities of the partners.

After partnership assets are realized and the gain or loss shared, the realized cash is distributed to the proper parties. Since creditors have first claim, they are paid first. After the creditors are paid, the remaining cash is divided among the partners. Each partner has the right to cash equal to his or her equity or, in other words, cash equal to the balance of his or her capital account. The entries to record the final cash payments and distribution to Ottis, Skinner, and Parr are:

Jan.	15	Accounts Payable	5,000.00	
		Cash		5,000.00
		To pay the claims of the creditors.		
	15	Ottis, Capital	18,000.00	
		Skinner, Capital	17,000.00	
		Parr, Capital	16,000.00	
		Cash		51,000.00
		To distribute the remaining cash to the partners according to their capital account balances.		

Notice that after gains and losses are shared and the creditors are paid, each partner receives cash equal to the balance remaining in his capital account. The partners receive these amounts because a partner's capital account balance represents the partner's equity in the remaining partnership asset, cash. In making the entry to distribute cash to the partners, be sure that you do not make the mistake of distributing it in the partners' income-and-loss-sharing ratio. Gains and losses from realization are allocated according to the income-and-loss-sharing ratio; but cash must be distributed to the partners in relation to their capital account balances.

All Assets Realized before a Distribution; Assets Sold at a Loss; Each Partner's Capital Account Is Sufficient to Absorb His or Her Share of the Loss

In a partnership liquidation, the assets are sometimes sold at a net loss. For example, assume that the Ottis, Skinner, and Parr partnership does not sell its assets at a profit. Instead, assume that the inventory is sold for $10,000 and the other assets for $12,000. The entries to record the sales and loss allocation are:

Jan.	12	Cash	10,000.00	
		Loss or Gain from Realization	5,000.00	
		Merchandise Inventory		15,000.00
		Sold the inventory at a loss.		
	15	Cash	12,000.00	
		Loss or Gain from Realization	13,000.00	
		Other Assets		25,000.00
		Sold the other assets at a loss.		
	15	Ottis, Capital	9,000.00	
		Skinner, Capital	6,000.00	
		Parr, Capital	3,000.00	
		Loss or Gain from Realization		18,000.00
		To allocate the loss from realization to the partners in their income-and-loss-sharing ratio.		

After the entries are posted, a balance sheet shows that the partnership cash exactly equals the liabilities and the equities of the partners, as follows:

Assets		Liabilities and Owners' Equity	
Cash	$32,000	Accounts payable	$ 5,000
		Ottis, capital	6,000
		Skinner, capital	9,000
		Parr, capital	12,000
		Total liabilities and	
Total assets	$32,000	owners' equity	$32,000

The following entries are required to distribute the cash to the proper parties:

Jan.	15	Accounts Payable	5,000.00	
		Cash		5,000.00
		To pay the partnership creditors.		
	15	Ottis, Capital	6,000.00	
		Skinner, Capital	9,000.00	
		Parr, Capital	12,000.00	
		Cash		27,000.00
		To distribute the remaining cash to the partners according to the balances of their capital accounts.		

Notice again that after losses are shared and creditors are paid, the remaining cash is distributed to the partners in the ratio of their capital account balances.

All Assets Realized before a Distribution; Assets Sold at a Loss; a Partner's Capital Account Is Not Sufficient to Cover His or Her Share of the Loss

Sometimes, the liquidation losses allocated to a partner will exceed that partner's capital account balance. In such cases, the partner must, if possible, cover the deficit by paying cash into the partnership. For example, contrary to the previous illustrations, assume that the Ottis, Skinner, and Parr partnership sells its merchandise for $3,000 and sells its other assets for $4,000. The entries to record the sales and the loss allocation are:

Jan.	12	Cash	3,000.00	
		Loss or Gain from Realization	12,000.00	
		Merchandise Inventory		15,000.00
		Sold the inventory at a loss.		
	15	Cash	4,000.00	
		Loss or Gain from Realization	21,000.00	
		Other Assets		25,000.00
		Sold the other assets at a loss.		
	15	Ottis, Capital	16,500.00	
		Skinner, Capital	11,000.00	
		Parr, Capital	5,500.00	
		Loss or Gain from Realization		33,000.00
		To allocate the loss from realization to the partners in their income-and-loss-sharing ratio.		

After you post the entry to allocate the realization loss, the capital account of Ottis has a $1,500 debit balance and appears as follows:

Ottis, Capital

Date	Explanation	Debit	Credit	Balance
Dec. 31	Balance			15,000.00
Jan. 15	Share of loss from realization	16,500.00		(1,500.00)

The partnership agreement states that one half of all losses or gains should be allocated to Ottis. Therefore, since Ottis's capital account balance is not large enough to absorb his share of the loss, he is obligated to pay $1,500 into the partnership to cover the **deficit**. If Ottis is able to pay, the following entry is made:

Jan.	15	Cash	1,500.00	
		Ottis, Capital		1,500.00
		To record the additional investment of Ottis to cover his share of realization losses.		

After the $1,500 is received, the partnership has $18,500 in cash. The following entries are then made to distribute the case to the proper parties:

Jan.	15	Accounts Payable	5,000.00	
		Cash		5,000.00
		To pay the partnership creditors.		
	15	Skinner, Capital	4,000.00	
		Parr, Capital	9,500.00	
		Cash		13,500.00
		To distribute the remaining cash to the partners according to the balances of their capital accounts.		

When a partnership's liquidation losses create a debit balance in one partner's capital account balance, that partner may be unable to make up the deficit. In such cases, since each partner has unlimited liability, the deficit must be borne by the remaining partner or partners. For example, assume that Ottis is unable to pay the $1,500 necessary to cover the deficit in his capital account. If Ottis is unable to pay, his deficit must be shared by Skinner and Parr in their income-and-loss-sharing ratio. The partners share income and losses in the ratio of Ottis, 3; Skinner, 2; and Parr, 1. Therefore, Skinner and Parr share in a 2:1 ratio. This means that Skinner and Parr must share the $1,500 by which Ottis's share of the losses exceeded his capital account balance in a 2:1 ratio. Normally, the defaulting partner's deficit is transferred to the capital accounts of the remaining partners. This is accomplished for Ottis, Skinner, and Parr with the following entry:

Jan.	15	Skinner, Capital	1,000.00	
		Parr, Capital	500.00	
		Ottis, Capital		1,500.00
		To transfer the deficit of Ottis to the capital accounts of Skinner and Parr.		

After the deficit is transferred, the capital accounts of the partners appear as in Illustration 14–4. The entries to record the final payments to creditors and distribution to the partners are as follows:

Jan.	15	Accounts Payable	5,000.00	
		Cash.		5,000.00
		To pay the partnership creditors.		
	15	Skinner, Capital	3,000.00	
		Parr, Capital	9,000.00	
		Cash.		12,000.00
		To distribute the remaining cash to the partners		
		according to their capital account balances.		

You should understand that the inability of Ottis to meet his loss share at this time does not relieve him of liability. If he becomes able to pay at some future time, Skinner and Parr may collect the full $1,500 from him. Skinner may collect $1,000, and Parr, $500.

The sharing of an insolvent partner's deficit by the remaining partners in their original income-and-loss-sharing is generally regarded as equitable. In England, however, in the case of *Garner* v. *Murray*, Judge Joyce ruled that the debit balance of the insolvent partner's Capital account is a personal debt due to the other partners and to be borne by them in the ratio of their Capital account balances immediately prior to liquidation.

While the *Garner* v. *Murray* still appears to be good law, it is considered by most to be inequitable. The decision applies only when the partnership agreement does not cover this situation and, although rendered in 1904, has not been applied in Canada. It is common practice to provide in the partnership agreement for the sharing of a partner's debit balance by the remaining partners in their income-and-loss-sharing ratio.

Summary of the Chapter in Terms of Learning Objectives

1. A partnership is a voluntary association between the partners that is based on a contract. The life of a partnership is limited by agreement or by the death or incapacity of a partner. Normally, each partner can act as an agent of the other partners and commit the partnership to any contract within the apparent scope of its business. All partners in a general partnership are personally liable for all the debts of the partnership. Limited partnerships include one or more general partners plus one or more (limited) partners whose liabilities are limited to the amount of their investments in the partnership. The risk of becoming a partner results in part from the fact that partnership characteristics include mutual agency and unlimited liability.

2. A partnership's net incomes or losses are allocated to the partners according to the partnership agreement. The agreement may specify that each partner will receive a given fraction, or that the allocation of incomes and losses will reflect salary allowances and/or interest allowances. When salary and/or interest allowances are granted, the residual net income or loss usually is allocated equally or on a stated fractional basis.

3. When a new partner buys a partnership interest directly from one or more of the existing partners, the amount of cash paid from one partner to

Illustration 14–4
Allocating liquidation losses and partner's deficit to capital accounts

Ottis, Capital

Date	Explanation	Debit	Credit	Balance
Dec. 31	Balance			15,000.00
Jan. 15	Share of loss from realization	16,500.00		1,500.00
15	Deficit to Skinner and Parr		1,500.00	–0–

Skinner, Capital

Date	Explanation	Debit	Credit	Balance
Dec. 31	Balance			15,000.00
Jan. 15	Share of loss from realization	11,000.00		4,000.00
15	Deficit to Skinner and Parr	1,000.00		3,000.00

Parr, Capital

Date	Explanation	Debit	Credit	Balance
Dec. 31	Balance			15,000.00
Jan. 15	Share of loss from realization	5,500.00		9,500.00
15	Deficit to Skinner and Parr	500.00		9,000.00

another does not affect the total recorded equity of the partnership. The recorded equity of the selling partner(s) is simply transferred to the capital account of the new partner. Alternatively, a new partner may purchase an equity by investing additional assets in the partnership. When this occurs, part of the new partner's investment may be credited as a bonus to the capital accounts of the existing partners. Also, to gain the participation of the new partner, the existing partners may give the new partner a bonus whereby portions of the existing partners' capital balances are transferred to the new partner's capital account. Occasionally, goodwill is recorded when a new partner invests in a partnership.

4. When a partnership is liquidated, losses and gains from selling the partnership assets are allocated to the partners according to their income-and-loss-sharing ratio. If a partner's capital account has a deficit balance that the partner cannot pay, the other partners must share the deficit in their relative income-and-loss-sharing ratio.

Demonstration Problem

The following events affect the partner's capital accounts in several successive partnerships. On a work sheet with six money columns, one for each of five partners and a totals column, show the effects of the following events on the partners' capital accounts:

13/4/88   Kelly and Emerson create K&E Co. Each invests $10,000, and they agree to share profits equally.

31/12/88   K&E Co. earns $15,000 in the year. Kelly withdraws $4,000 from the partnership, and Emerson withdraws $7,000.

1/1/89   Reed is made a partner in KE&R Co. after contributing $12,000 cash. The partners agree that each will get a 10% interest allowance on their beginning capital balances. In addition, Emerson and Reed are to receive $5,000 salary allowances. The remainder of the income is to be divided evenly.

31/12/89   The partnership's income for the year is $40,000, and these withdrawals occur: Kelly, $5,000; Emerson, $12,500; and Reed, $11,000.

1/1/90   For $20,000, Kelly sells her interest to Merritt, who is accepted by Emerson and Reed as a partner in the new ER&M Co. The profits are to be shared equally after Emerson and Reed each receive $25,000 salaries.

31/12/90   The partnership's income for the year is $35,000, and these withdrawals occur: Emerson, $2,500; and Reed, $2,000.

1/1/91   Davis is admitted as a partner after investing $60,000 cash in the new Davis & Associates partnership. Davis is given a 50% interest in capital after the other partners transfer $3,000 to his account from each of theirs. A 20% interest allowance (on the beginning-of-year capital balances) will be used in sharing profits, but there will be no salaries. Davis will get 40% of the remainder, and the other three partners will each get 20%.

31/12/91   Davis & Associates earns $127,600 for the year, and these withdrawals occur: Emerson, $25,000; Reed, $27,000; Merritt, $15,000; and Davis, $40,000.

1/1/92   Davis buys out Emerson and Reed for the balances of their capital accounts, after a revaluation of the partnership assets. The revaluation gain is $50,000, which is divided in the previous 1:1:1:2 ratio. Davis pays the others from personal funds. Merritt and Davis will share profits on a 1:9 ratio.

29/2/92   The partnership had $10,000 of income since the beginning of the year. Merritt retires and receives partnership cash equal to her capital balance. Davis takes possession of the partnership assets in his own name, and the company is dissolved.

Solution to Demonstration Problem

Event	Kelly	Emerson	Reed	Merritt	Davis	Total
13/4/88						
Initial investment	$ 10,000	$ 10,000				$ 20,000
31/12/88						
Income (equal)	7,500	7,500				15,000
Withdrawals	(4,000)	(7,000)				(11,000)
Ending balance	$ 13,500	$ 10,500				$ 24,000
1/1/89						
New investment			$ 12,000			12,000
31/12/89						
10% interest	1,350	1,050	1,200			3,600
Salaries		5,000	5,000			10,000
Remainder (equal)	8,800	8,800	8,800			26,400
Withdrawals	(5,000)	(12,500)	(11,000)			(28,500)
Ending balance	$ 18,650	$ 12,850	$ 16,000			$ 47,500
1/1/90						
Transfer interest	(18,650)			$ 18,650		–0–
31/12/90						
Salaries		25,000	25,000			50,000
Remainder (equal)		(5,000)	(5,000)	(5,000)		(15,000)
Withdrawals		(2,500)	(2,000)			(4,500)
Ending balance	$ –0–	$ 30,350	$ 34,000	$ 13,650		$ 78,000
1/1/91						
New investment					$ 60,000	60,000
Bonuses to Davis		(3,000)	(3,000)	(3,000)	9,000	–0–
Adjusted balance		$ 27,350	$ 31,000	$ 10,650	$ 69,000	$ 138,000
31/12/91						
20% interest		5,470	6,200	2,130	13,800	27,600
Remainder (1:1:1:2)		20,000	20,000	20,000	40,000	100,000
Withdrawals		(25,000)	(27,000)	(15,000)	(40,000)	(107,000)
Ending balance		$ 27,820	$ 30,200	$ 17,780	$ 82,800	$ 158,600
Gain (1:1:1:2)		10,000	10,000	10,000	20,000	50,000
Adjusted balance		$ 37,820	$ 40,200	$ 27,780	$ 102,800	$ 208,600
Transfer interests		(37,820)	(40,200)		78,020	–0–
Adjusted balance		$ –0–	$ –0–	$ 27,780	$ 180,820	$ 208,600
29/2/92						
Income (1:9)				1,000	9,000	10,000
Adjusted balance				$ 28,780	$ 189,820	$ 218,600
Settlements				(28,780)	(189,820)	(218,600)
Final balance				$ –0–	$ –0–	$ –0–

Glossary

Define or explain the words and phrases listed in the chapter Glossary. (L. O. 5)

Deficit a negative balance in an account. p. 645

General partner(s) a partner who assumes unlimited liability for the debts of the partnership. p. 627

General partnership a partnership in which all partners have unlimited liability for partnership debts. p. 628

Limited partners partners who have no personal liability for debts of the limited partnership beyond the amounts they have invested in the partnership. p. 627

Limited partnership a partnership that has two classes of partners, limited partners and one or more general partners. p. 627

Mutual agency a characteristic of the relationship between the partners in a partnership whereby each partner is able to bind the partnership to contracts within the apparent scope of the partnership business. p. 626

Partnership an association by contract of two or more persons to carry on a business as co-owners for profit. p. 626

Partnership contract the agreement between partners that sets forth the terms under which the affairs of a partnership will be conducted. p. 626

Partnership liquidations the winding up of a partnership business by converting its assets to cash and distributing the cash to the proper parties. p. 640

Statement of Changes in Partners' Equity a financial statement that shows the total capital balances at the beginning of the period, any additional investments by the partners, the net income or loss of the period, the partners' withdrawals during the period, and the ending capital balances. p. 633

Unlimited liability of partners the legal characteristic of a partnership that makes each general partner responsible for paying all the debts of the partnership if the other partners are unable to pay their shares. p. 627

Questions for Class Discussion

1. Groan and Moan are partners. Groan dies, and his son claims the right to take his father's place in the partnership. Does he have this right? Why?

2. If Sue Wiles cannot legally enter into a contract, can she become a partner?

3. If a partnership contract does not state the period of time the partnership is to exist, when does the partnership end?

4. What does the term *mutual agency* mean as applied to a partnership?

5. Kurt and Ellen are partners in the operation of a store. Without consulting Kurt, Ellen enters into a contract for the purchase of merchandise for resale by the store. Kurt contends that he did not authorize the order and refuses to take delivery. The vendor sues the partners for the contract price of the merchandise. Will the partnership have to pay? Why?

6. Would your answer to Question 5 differ if Kurt and Ellen were partners in a public accounting firm?

7. May partners limit the right of a member of their firm to bind their partnership to contracts? Is such an agreement binding (*a*) on the partners and (*b*) on outsiders?

8. What does the term *unlimited liability* mean when it is applied to members of a general partnership?

9. South organized a limited partnership and is the only general partner. North invested $20,000 in the partnership and was admitted as a limited partner with the understanding that he would receive 10% of the profits. After two unprofitable years, the partnership ceased doing business. At that point, partnership liabilities were $85,000 larger than partnership assets. How much money can the creditors of the partnership obtain from North in satisfaction of the unpaid partnership debts?

10. How does a general partnership differ from a limited partnership?

11. George, Burton, and Dillman have been partners for three years. The partnership is dissolving. George is leaving the firm while Burton and Dillman plan to carry on the business. In the final settlement, George places a $75,000 salary claim against the partnership. His contention is that since he devoted all of his time for three years to the affairs of the partnership, he has a claim for a salary of $25,000 for each year. Is his claim valid? Why?

12. The partnership agreement of Barnes and Ardmore provides for a two-thirds, one-third sharing of income but says nothing about losses. The first year of partnership operations resulted in a loss, and Barnes argues that the loss should be shared equally since the partnership agreement said nothing about sharing losses. Do you agree?

13. A and B are partners who agree that A will receive a $50,000 salary allowance after which remaining incomes or losses will be shared equally. If B's capital account is credited $1,000 as his share of the net income in a given period, how much net income did the partnership earn?

14. W, X, and Y are partners with capital account balances of $7,000 each. Z pays W $8,000 for his one-third interest and is admitted to the partnership. The bookkeeper debits W, Capital and credits Z, Capital for $7,000. Z objects; he wants his capital account to show an $8,000 balance, the amount he paid for his interest. Explain why Z's capital account is credited for $7,000.

15. If the partners in Blatt Partnership want the financial statements to show the procedures used to allocate the partnership income among the partners, on what financial statement should the allocation appear?

16. After all partnership assets are converted to cash and all liabilities have been paid, the remaining cash should equal the sum of the balances of the partners' capital accounts. Why?

17. Fern, Vern, and Hern are partners. In a liquidation, Fern's share of partnership losses exceeds her capital account balance. She is unable

to meet the deficit from her personal assets, and the excess losses are shared by her partners. Does this relieve Fern of liability?

18. A partner withdraws from a partnership and receives assets of greater value than the book value of his equity. Should the remaining partners share the resulting reduction in their equities in the ratio of their relative capital balances or in their income-and-loss-sharing ratio?

Multiple Choice

1. Which of the following is a characteristic of a partnership?
   a. A partnership is a voluntary association between two or more persons.
   b. A partnership is organized by means of a partnership contract.
   c. The life of a partnership is always limited.
   d. Unless the partnership contract specifies otherwise, each partner can act on behalf of the other partners and commit the partnership to any contract within the scope of its business.
   e. All of the above are characteristics of a partnership.

2. Jekyll and Hyde form a partnership with initial investments of $50,000 and $25,000, respectively. The partners agree to annual salary allowances of $30,000 to Jekyll and $20,000 to Hyde. Also, they agree to an interest allowance equal to 10% of each partner's beginning-of-year capital balance. The remaining balance of income or loss is to be shared equally. How would a first year net income of $15,000 be shared between Jekyll and Hyde?
   a. Jekyll, $ 8,750; Hyde, $6,250.
   b. Jekyll, $ 7,500; Hyde, $7,500.
   c. Jekyll, $ 9,500; Hyde, $5,500.
   d. Jekyll, $13,750; Hyde, $1,250.
   e. Jekyll, $ 9,000; Hyde, $6,000.

3. Crosby and Stills operate a partnership and share earnings equally. Crosby's recorded equity is $80,000, and Still's recorded equity is $70,000. Crosby and Stills agree to accept Nash's $60,000 investment in the business in return for a one-quarter share of the partnership's earnings and a one-quarter equity in net assets. The entry to record Nash's investment in the partnership would include:
   a. A credit to Crosby, Capital for $13,750.
   b. A credit to Stills, Capital for $7,500.
   c. A credit to Nash, Capital for $60,000.
   d. A debit to Stills, Capital for $11,250.
   e. Both (a) and (c) are correct.

4. The balance sheet for the partnership of Miller, Perry, and Thornton before liquidation is as follows:

Assets			Liabilities and Owners' Equity		
Cash.	$ 6,000		Accounts payable.		$15,000
Merchandise inventory	42,000		Miller, capital		30,000
Other assets	27,000		Perry, capital		10,000
			Thornton, capital		20,000
			Total liabilities and		
Total assets	$75,000		owners' equity		$75,000

The merchandise inventory and other assets are sold for a total of $60,000. If incomes and losses are shared on a 3:2:1 ratio, what amount of cash should Perry receive upon distribution of the remaining cash?

   a. $20,000.

   b. $10,000.

   c. $ 7,000.

   d. $17,000.

   e. $ 8,500.

5. If a partnership contract provides for interest at 10% annually on each partner's investment, the interest:

   a. Is ignored when earnings are not sufficient to pay interest.

   b. Provides for the sharing of a portion of the partnership earnings in the capital ratio.

   c. Is an expense of the business.

   d. Must be paid because the partnership contract provides for it.

   e. Is interest in the legal sense of the term.

6. If Rayfield and Simms are partners sharing profits and losses equally and possessing capital balances of $60,000 and $40,000, respectively, and Jones pays $50,000 for a one-third interest in profits, losses, and capital, the entry of Jones should be recorded:

   a. In a manner that recognizes goodwill and allocates the goodwill to the old partners.

   b. In a manner that provides a bonus to Jones.

   c. In a manner that provides a bonus to the old partners.

   d. In a manner that does not involve a bonus and does not involve goodwill.

   e. With a credit of $33,000 to the capital account of Jones.

Mini Discussion Cases

Case 14–1

Two students were overhead discussing the virtues and pitfalls of the partnership form of business organization. Their conclusion was that the disadvantages far outweighed the advantages. The partnership form had many pitfalls and should be entered into as a last resort. Entry should be made with extreme caution and with as many protective features as can be negotiated.

Required

The above conclusion seems to be extreme. You are asked to critically evaluate the conclusion of the two students.

Case 14–2

There are certain types of businesses that cannot incorporate and must be operated as sole proprietorships or partnerships.

Required

1. List types of businesses that cannot be incorporated.
2. Discuss why the businesses you listed must be organized as sole proprietorships or partnerships but not as corporations.

Exercises

Exercise 14–1
Journalizing partnership entries
(L. O. 2)

On February 1, 1990, Young and Olde formed a partnership in which Young contributed $70,000 and Olde contributed land valued at $80,000 and a building valued at $90,000. The partnership also is to assume responsibility for Olde's $30,000 long-term note payable. The partners agreed to share profits as follows: Young is to receive an annual salary allowance of $35,000, each partner is to receive 10% of his or her original capital investment, and any remaining profit or loss is to be shared equally. On November 20, 1990, Young withdrew cash of $40,000 and Olde withdrew $30,000. Present general journal entries to record the initial capital investments of the partners, the cash withdrawals of the partners, and the December 31 closing of the withdrawals accounts and the Income Summary account, which had a credit balance of $68,000.

Exercise 14–2
Income allocation in a partnership
(L. O. 2)

Newberg and Scampi began a partnership by investing $52,000 and $78,000, respectively. During its first year, the partnership earned $180,000. Prepare calculations that show how the income should be allocated to the partners under each of the following plans for sharing net incomes and losses:

a. The partners failed to agree on a method of sharing income.
b. The partners agreed to share incomes and losses in their investment ratio.
c. The partners agreed to share income by allowing an $85,000 per year salary allowance to Newberg, a $65,000 per year salary allowance to Scampi, 10% interest on beginning capital balances, and the remainder equally.

Exercise 14–3
Income allocation in a partnership
(L. O. 2)

Assume the partners in Exercise 14–2 agreed to share net incomes and losses by allowing yearly salary allowances of $85,000 to Newberg and $65,000 to Scampi, 10% interest allowances on their investments, and the balance equally. (*a*) Determine the shares of Newberg and Scampi in a first-year net income of $145,300. (*b*) Determine the partners' shares in a first-year net loss of $30,200.

Exercise 14–4
Sale of a partnership interest
(L. O. 3)

The partners in the Duprix Partnership have agreed that partner Dupont may sell his $70,000 equity in the partnership to Queen, for which Queen will pay Dupont $55,000. Present the partnership's journal entry to record the sale on April 30.

Exercise 14–5
Admission of a new partner
(L. O. 3)

The Hagen-Baden Partnership has total partners' equity of $380,000, which is made up of Hagen, Capital, $300,000, and Baden, Capital, $80,000. The partners share net incomes and losses in a ratio of 75% to Hagen and 25% to Baden. On July 1, Megan is admitted to the partnership and given a 20% interest in equity and in gains and losses. Prepare the journal entry to record the entry of Megan under each of the following unrelated assumptions: Megan invests cash of (a) $95,000; (b) $115,000; and (c) $55,000.

Exercise 14–6
Retirement of a partner
(L. O. 3)

Hollis, Evans, and Bowen have been partners sharing net incomes and losses in a 3:5:2 ratio. On October 31, the date Bowen retires from the partnership, the equities of the partners are Hollis, $130,000; Evans, $200,000; and Bowen, $50,000. Present general journal entries to record Bowen's retirement under each of the following unrelated assumptions:

a. Bowen is paid $50,000 in partnership cash for his equity.
b. Bowen is paid $60,000 in partnership cash for his equity.
c. Bowen is paid $45,000 in partnership cash for his equity.

Exercise 14–7
Liquidation of a partnership
(L. O. 4)

The Whiz-Bam-Boom partnership was begun with investments by the partners as follows: Whiz, $115,600; Bam, $88,600; and Boom, $95,800. The first year of operations did not go well, and the partners finally decided to liquidate the partnership, sharing all losses equally. On December 31, after all assets were converted to cash and all creditors were paid, only $30,000 in partnership cash remained.

Required

1. Calculate the capital account balances of the partners after the liquidation of assets and payment of creditors.
2. Assume that any partner with a deficit pays cash to the partnership to cover the deficit. Then, present the general journal entries on December 31 to record the cash receipt from the deficient partner(s) and the final disbursement of cash to the partners.
3. Now make the contrary assumption that any partner with a deficit is not able to reimburse the partnership. Present journal entries (a) to transfer the deficit of any deficient partners to the other partners and (b) to record the final disbursement of cash to the partners.

Exercise 14–8
Liquidation of a partnership
(L. O. 4)

Prince, Count, and Earl are partners who share incomes and losses in a 1:3:4 ratio. After lengthy disagreements among the partners and several unprofitable periods, the partners decided to liquidate the partnership. Before the liquidation, the partnership balance sheet showed total assets, $238,000; liabilities, $200,000; Prince, Capital, $8,000; Count, Capital, $10,000; and Earl, Capital, $20,000. The cash proceeds from selling the assets were sufficient to repay all but $45,000 to the creditors. Calculate the loss from selling the assets, allocate the loss to the partners, and determine how much of the remaining liability should be paid by each partner.

Exercise 14–9
Liquidation of a limited partnership
(L. O. 4)

Assume that the Prince, Count, and Earl partnership of Exercise 14–8 is a limited partnership. Prince and Count are general partners, and Earl is a limited partner. How much of the remaining $45,000 liability should be paid by each partner?

Problems

Problem 14–1
Methods of allocating partnership income
(L. O. 2)

Dell Willis, Lara Hart, and Susan Butler invested $66,400, $58,100, and $41,500, respectively, in a partnership. During its first year, the firm earned $175,500.

Required

Prepare entries to close the firm's Income Summary account as of December 31 and to allocate the net income to the partners under each of the assumptions below. (Round your answers to the nearest whole dollar.)

a. The partners could not agree as to the method of sharing incomes.
b. The partners agreed to share net incomes and losses in the ratio of their beginning investments.
c. The partners agreed to share income by allowing annual salary allowances of $52,000 to Willis, $58,000 to Hart, and $45,000 to Butler; allowing 10% interest on the partners' investments; and sharing the remainder equally.

Problem 14–2
Allocating partnership incomes and losses; sequential years
(L. O. 2)

Linda Meade and Richard Munez are in the process of forming a partnership to which Meade will devote one-third time and Munez will devote full time. They have discussed the following plans for sharing net incomes and losses:

a. In the ratio of their investments which they have agreed to maintain at $33,000 for Meade and $49,500 for Munez.
b. In proportion to the time devoted to the business.
c. A salary allowance of $3,500 per month to Munez and the balance in their investment ratio.
d. A $3,500 per month salary allowance to Munez, 10% interest on their investments, and the balance equally.

The partners expect the business to generate income as follows: year 1, $20,000 net loss; year 2, $60,000 net income; and year 3, $95,000 net income.

Required

1. Prepare three schedules with the following columnar headings:

Income/ Loss Sharing Plan	Year		
	Calculations	Meade	Munez

2. Complete a schedule for each of the first three years by showing how the partnership net income or loss for each year should be allocated to the partners under each of the four plans being considered. Round your answers to the nearest whole dollar.

Problem 14–3
Partnership income allocation, statement of changes in partners' equity, and closing entries
(L. O. 2)

Lou Cass, Red Sanders, and Barbara Archer formed the CSA Partnership by making capital contributions of $116,640, $129,600, and $142,560, respectively. They anticipate annual net incomes of $195,000 and are considering the following alternative plans of sharing net incomes and losses: (a) equally; (b) in the ratio of their initial investments; or (c) salary allowances of $35,000 to Cass, $20,000 to Sanders, and $45,000 to Archer, interest allowances of 10% on initial investments, with any remaining balance shared equally.

Required
1. Prepare a schedule with the following column headings:

Income/Loss Sharing Plan	Calculations	Share to Cass	Share to Sanders	Share to Archer	Totals

Use the schedule to show how a net income of $195,000 would be distributed under each of the alternative plans being considered. Round your answers to the nearest whole dollar.

2. Prepare a statement of changes in partners' equity showing the allocation of income to the partners, assuming they agree to use alternative (c) and the net income earned is $85,000. During the year, Cass, Sanders, and Archer withdrew $15,000, $20,000, and $23,000, respectively.

3. Prepare the December 31 journal entry to close Income Summary assuming they agree to use alternative (c) and the net income is $85,000. Also close the withdrawals accounts.

Problem 14–4
Withdrawal of a partner
(L. O. 3)

Part 1. Pushkin, Tolstoy, and Chekhov are partners with capital balances as follows: Pushkin, $183,750; Tolstoy, $131,250; and Chekhov, $315,000. The partners share incomes and losses in a 1:2:3 ratio. Prepare general journal entries to record the August 1 withdrawal of Tolstoy from the partnership under each of the following unrelated assumptions:

a. Tolstoy sells his interest to Gogol for $168,000 after Pushkin and Chekhov approve the entry of Gogol as a partner.
b. Tolstoy gives his interest to a son-in-law, Lermontov. Pushkin and Chekhov accept Lermontov as a partner.
c. Tolstoy is paid $131,250 in partnership cash for his equity.
d. Tolstoy is paid $194,250 in partnership cash for his equity.
e. Tolstoy is paid $27,250 in partnership cash plus delivery equipment recorded on the partnership books at $115,000 less accumulated depreciation of $63,000.

Part 2.   Assume that Tolstoy does not retire from the partnership described in Part 1. Instead, Nabokov is admitted to the partnership on August 1 with a 25% equity. Prepare general journal entries to record the entry of Nabokov into the partnership under each of the following unrelated assumptions:

a. Nabokov invests $210,000.
b. Nabokov invests $157,500.
c. Nabokov invests $262,500.

Problem 14–5
Liquidation of a partnership
(L. O. 4)

Maxwell, Adams, and Nelson plan to liquidate their partnership. They have always shared losses and gains in a 1:4:5 ratio, and on the day of the liquidation their balance sheet appeared as follows:

MAXWELL, ADAMS AND NELSON
Balance Sheet
June 30, 19—

Assets		Liabilities and Owners' Equity	
Cash	$ 27,500	Accounts payable	$ 52,150
Other assets	180,500	Pam Maxwell, capital	30,500
		Greg Adams, capital.	80,350
		Linda Nelson, capital	45,000
		Total liabilities and	
Total assets	$208,000	owners' equity.	$208,000

Required

Prepare general journal entries to record the sale of the other assets and the distribution of the cash to the proper parties under each of the following unrelated assumptions:

a. The other assets are sold for $195,250.
b. The other assets are sold for $150,000.
c. The other assets are sold for $85,000, and any partners with resulting deficits can and do pay in the amount of their deficits.
d. The other assets are sold for $75,000, and the partners have no assets other than those invested in the business.

Problem 14–6
Withdrawal of a partner
(L. O. 3)

Until May 28, 1990, Block, Sun, and Steen were partners that shared incomes and losses in the ratio of their beginning-of-year capital account balances. On May 28, Sun suffered a heart attack and died. Block and Steen immediately ended the business operations and prepared the following adjusted trial balance:

BLOCK, SUN, AND STEEN
Adjusted Trial Balance
May 28, 1990

Cash	$ 23,625	
Accounts receivable	55,125	
Allowance for doubtful accounts.		$ 2,625
Supplies inventory	111,750	
Equipment	70,875	
Accumulated depreciation, equipment		18,375
Land	23,625	
Building.	262,500	
Accumulated depreciation, building		49,875
Accounts payable		15,750
Note payable (secured by mortgage)		52,500
Bob Block, capital		157,500
Joan Sun, capital.		157,500
Tim Steen, capital		78,750
Bob Block, withdrawals	8,250	
Joan Sun, withdrawals.	8,250	
Tim Steen, withdrawals	8,250	
Revenues.		204,750
Expenses.	165,375	
Totals	$737,625	$737,625

Required

1. Prepare May 28 entries to close the revenue, expense, income summary, and withdrawals accounts of the partnership.

2. Assume the estate of Sun agreed to accept the land and building and to assume the mortgage note thereon in settlement of its claim against the partnership assets, and that Block and Steen planned to continue the business and rent the building from the estate. Give the partnership's June 15 entry to transfer the land, building, and mortgage note in settlement with the estate.

3. Assume that in place of the foregoing, the estate of Sun demanded a cash settlement, and the business had to be sold to a competitor who gave $355,000 for the noncash assets and assumed the mortgage note but not the accounts payable. Give the June 15 entry to transfer the noncash assets and mortgage note to the competitor, and give the entries to allocate the loss to the partners and to distribute the partnership cash to the proper parties.

Alternate Problems

Problem 14–1A
Methods of allocating partnership income
(L. O. 2)

Rhonda Zeller, Brian Jackson, and Debby Rogers invested $92,400, $74,800, and $52,800, respectively, in a partnership. During its first year, the firm earned $198,000.

Required

Prepare entries to close the firm's Income Summary account as of December 31 and to allocate the net income to the partners under each of the assumptions below. (Round your answers to the nearest whole dollar.)

a. The partners could not agree as to the method of sharing incomes.

b. The partners had agreed to share net incomes and losses in the ratio of their beginning investments.

c. The partners had agreed to share income by allowing annual salary allowances of $75,000 to Zeller, $40,500 to Jackson, and $45,500 to Rogers; allowing a share of the income equal to 10% interest on the partners' investments; and sharing the remainder equally.

Problem 14–2A
Allocating partnership incomes and losses; sequential years
(L. O. 2)

Harriet Monroe and Ozzie Young are in the process of forming a partnership to which Monroe will devote one-fourth time and Young will devote full time. They have discussed the following plans for sharing net incomes and losses:

a. In the ratio of their investments which they have agreed to maintain at $49,800 for Monroe and $74,700 for Young.

b. In proportion to the time devoted to the business.

c. A salary allowance of $5,250 per month to Young and the balance in their investment ratio.

d. A $5,250 per month salary allowance to Young, 10% interest on their investments, and the balance equally.

The partners expect the business to generate income as follows: year 1, $30,500 net loss; year 2, $82,500 net income; and year 3, $215,000 net income.

Required

1. Prepare three schedules with the following columnar headings:

Income/ Loss Sharing Plan	Year			
	Calculations		Monroe	Young

2. Complete a schedule for each of the first three years by showing how the partnership income for each year would be allocated to the partners under each of the four plans being considered. Round your answers to the nearest whole dollar.

Problem 14–3A
Partnership income allocation, statement of changes in partners' equity, and closing entries
(L. O. 2)

Betty Iris, Jim Dolan, and Bob Carrow formed the IDC Partnership by making capital contributions of $245,000, $280,000, and $175,000, respectively. They anticipate annual net incomes of $390,000 and are considering the following alternative plans of sharing net incomes and losses: (a) equally; (b) in the ratio of their initial investments; or (c) interest allowances of 12% on initial investments, salary allowances of $95,000 to Iris, $46,000 to Dolan, and $60,000 to Carrow, with any remaining balance shared equally.

Required

1. Prepare a schedule with the following column headings:

Income/Loss Sharing Plan	Calculations	Share to Iris	Share to Dolan	Share to Carrow	Totals

   Use the schedule to show how a net income of $390,000 would be distributed under each of the alternative plans being considered. Round your answers to the nearest whole dollar.

2. Prepare a statement of changes in partners' equity showing the allocation of income to the partners, assuming they agree to use alternative (*c*) and the net income actually earned is $135,000. During the year, Iris, Dolan, and Carrow withdrew $40,000, $30,000, and $20,000, respectively.

3. Prepare the December 31 journal entry to close Income Summary assuming they agree to use alternative (*c*) and the net income is $135,000. Also close the withdrawals accounts.

Problem 14–4A
Withdrawal of a partner
(L. O. 3)

Part 1. Gagin, Fagin, and Onegin are partners with capital balances as follows: Gagin, $153,000; Fagin, $51,000; and Onegin, $102,000. The partners share incomes and losses in a 2:4:2 ratio. Prepare general journal entries to record the November 30 withdrawal of Onegin from the partnership under each of the following unrelated assumptions:

a. Onegin sells his interest to Sagin for $42,800 after Gagin and Fagin approve the entry of Sagin as a partner.

b. Onegin gives his interest to a son-in-law, Narwood. Gagin and Fagin accept Narwood as a partner.

c. Onegin is paid $102,000 in partnership cash for his equity.

d. Onegin is paid $75,000 in partnership cash for his equity.

e. Onegin is paid $36,000 in partnership cash plus delivery equipment recorded on the partnership books at $78,000 less accumulated depreciation of $45,000.

Part 2. Assume that Onegin does not retire from the partnership described in Part 1. Instead, Smitz is admitted to the partnership on November 30 with a 20% equity. Prepare general journal entries to record the entry of Smitz under each of the following unrelated assumptions:

a. Smitz invests $76,500.

b. Smitz invests $54,000.

c. Smitz invests $123,000.

Problem 14–5A
Liquidation of a partnership
(L. O. 4)

Poppy, Sweetbean, and Olive, who have always shared incomes and losses in a 3:1:1 ratio, plan to liquidate their partnership. Just prior to the liquidation their balance sheet appeared as follows:

POPPY, SWEETBEAN, AND OLIVE
Balance Sheet
October 15, 19—

Assets		Liabilities and Owners' Equity	
Cash	$ 13,500	Accounts payable	$ 56,700
Other assets	237,600	E. Poppy, capital.	91,200
		L. Sweetbean, capital	60,000
		N. Olive, capital	43,200
		Total liabilities and	
Total assets	$251,100	owners' equity.	$251,100

Required

Under the assumption the other assets are sold and the cash is distributed to the proper parties on October 15, give the entries for the sales, the loss or gain allocations, and the distributions if—

a. The other assets are sold for $270,000.

b. The other assets are sold for $170,100.

c. The other assets are sold for $72,600, and any partners with resulting deficits can and do pay in the amount of their deficits.

d. The other assets are sold for $55,200, and the partners have no assets other than those invested in the business.

Problem 14–6A
Withdrawal of a partner
(L. O. 3)

Rayburn, Myers, and Newton are partners. Rayburn devotes full time to partnership affairs; Myers and Newton devote very little time; and as a result, they share incomes and losses in a 4:1:1 ratio. Of late, the business has not been too profitable, and the partners have decided to liquidate. Just prior to the first realization sale, a partnership balance sheet appeared as follows:

RAYBURN, MYERS, AND NEWTON
Balance Sheet
July 10, 1990

Assets			Liabilities and Owners' Equity	
Cash		$ 4,500	Accounts payable.	$12,600
Accounts receivable. .		17,100	Rayburn, capital.	10,800
Merchandise inventory		28,800	Myers, capital	21,600
Equipment	$21,600		Newton, capital	21,600
Less accum. depr. .	5,400	16,200		
			Total liabilities and	
Total assets		$66,600	owners' equity	$66,600

The assets were sold, the creditors were paid, and the remaining cash was distributed to the partners on the following dates:

July 11   The accounts receivable were sold for $11,300.

12   The merchandise inventory was sold for $19,800.

14   The equipment was sold for $8,800.

15   The creditors were paid.

17   The remaining cash was distributed to the partners.

Required

1. Prepare general journal entries to record the asset sales, the allocation of the realization loss, and the payment of the creditors.

2. Under the assumption that any partners with capital deficits can and do pay in the amount of their deficits on July 17, give the entry to record the receipt of the cash and the distribution of partnership cash to the remaining partners.

3. Under the assumption that any partners with capital deficits cannot pay, give the entry to allocate the deficits to the remaining partners. Then give the entry to distribute the partnership cash to the remaining partners.

Provocative Problems

Provocative Problem 14–1
White and Black
Partnership
(L. O. 2)

Karen White and Joe Black agreed to share the annual net incomes or losses of their partnership as follows. If the partnership earns a net income, the first $50,000 is allocated 25% to White and 75% to Black so as to reflect the time devoted to the business by each partner. Income in excess of $50,000 is shared equally. However, if business operations result in a loss for the year, the partners have agreed to share the loss equally.

Required

1. Prepare a schedule showing how the 1990 net income of $59,000 should be allocated to the partners.

2. Immediately after the closing entries for 1990 were posted on December 31, 1990, the partners discover $70,000 of unrecorded accounts payable. These accounts payable relate to expenses incurred by the business. Black suggests that the $70,000 should be allocated equally between the partners as a loss. White disagrees and argues that an entry should be made to record the accounts payable and correct the capital accounts to reflect an $11,000 net loss for 1990. (*a*) Present the January 1, 1991, journal entry to record the accounts payable and allocate the loss to the partners according to Black's suggestion. (*b*) Now give the January 1, 1991, journal entry to record the accounts payable and correct the capital accounts according to White's argument. Show how you calculated the amounts in the entry.

3. Which partner do you think is right? Why?

Provocative Problem 14–2
The Fitness Place
(L. O. 3)

Maddie Hall and Amanda Miller are partners that own and operate The Fitness Place, an exercise and casual wear shop. Hall has a $75,000 equity in the business, and Miller has a $60,000 equity. They share incomes and losses by allowing annual salary allowances of $33,750 to Hall and $27,000 to Miller, with any remaining balance being shared 60% to Hall and 40% to Miller.

Susie Hall, Maddie Hall's daughter, has been working in the store on a salary basis. In addition to working in the store, Susie is a popular aerobics teacher and is well known among other aerobics teachers and a number of students. As a result, Susie attracts a great deal of business to the store. The partners believe that at least one third of the past three years' sales can be traced directly to Susie's association with the store, and it is reasonable to assume she was instrumental in attracting even more.

Susie is paid $1,800 per month, but feels this is not sufficient to induce her to remain with the firm as an employee. However, she likes her work and would like to remain in the fitness-wear business. What she really wants is to become a partner in the business.

Her mother is anxious for her to remain in the business and proposes the following:

a. That Susie be admitted to the partnership with a 20% equity in the partnership assets.

b. That she, Maddie Hall, transfer from her capital account to that of Susie's one half the 20% interest; that Susie contribute to the firm's assets a noninterest-bearing note for the other half; and that she, Maddie Hall, will guarantee payment of the note.

c. That incomes and losses be shared by continuing the $33,750 and $27,000 salary allowances of the original partners and that Susie be given a $21,600 annual salary allowance, after which any remaining income or loss would be shared 40% to Maddie Hall, 40% to Amanda Miller, and 20% to Susie Hall.

Prepare a report to Ms. Miller on the advisability of accepting Maddie Hall's proposal. Under the assumption that net incomes for the past three years have been $65,400, $68,500, and $70,500, respectively, prepare schedules showing (a) how net income was allocated during the past three years and (b) how it would have been allocated had the proposed new agreement been in effect. Also, (c) prepare a schedule showing the partners' capital interests as they would be immediately after the admission of Susie.

Provocative Problem 14–3
Venerable Partnership
(L. O. 3)

The balance sheet of the Venerable Partnership on December 31, 1990, is as follows:

Assets		Liabilities and Owners' Equity	
Cash	$ 45,250	Hamilton, capital	$ 22,750
Other assets	56,250	Adams, capital	33,750
Land	33,750	Hay, capital.	78,750
		Total liabilities and	
Total assets	$135,250	owners' equity	$135,250

The income-and-loss-sharing percentages are: Hamilton, 20%; Adams, 30%; and Hay, 50%. Hamilton wishes to withdraw from the partnership, and the partners finally agree that the land owned by the partnership should be transferred to Hamilton in full payment for his equity. In reaching this decision, they recognize that the land has appreciated since it was purchased and is now worth $60,000. If Hamilton retires on January 1, 1991, what journal entries should be made on that date?

Analytical and Review Problems

A&R Problem 14-1

Jay and Mar entered into a partnership to carry on a business under the firm name of Jay-Mar Sportsland. Prior to the final signing of the agreement Jay asks you to evaluate the "income/loss distribution clause" contained in the agreement.

Your examination revealed that the agreement called for the following: Equal sharing of net income and losses after an initial allocation of $40,000 to Jay and $10,000 to Mar in order to reflect the difference in time and expertise devoted to the business by each partner. The initial allocation would be made regardless of the level of net income/loss.

Required

Prepare a report to Jay on the particular clause of the agreement. Your report should show the consequence on each partner of operating results as follows: (*a*) net income of $80,000; (*b*) net income of $20,000; (*c*) operation at break-even, that is, no net income or loss; (*d*) loss of $20,000; (*e*) loss of $80,000.

A&R Problem 14-2

The summarized balance sheet of Bell, Trunk, and Field showed:

Assets		Equities	
Cash	$ 20,000	Liabilities	$ 60,000
Other assets	280,000	Bell, capital.	80,000
		Trunk, capital.	120,000
		Field, capital	40,000
Total assets	$300,000	Total equities.	$300,000

The partnership has operated successfully for nearly 25 years, and Field, because of his age and health, is pushing for sale of the business. In fact, he has found Arn, a buyer who is willing to pay $320,000 cash and take over the liabilities. Both Bell and Trunk are not anxious to sell what they refer to as "our little gold mine."

Field is adamant about getting out and has proposed the following:

1. Either sell to Arn, or Bell and Trunk (a new partnership) should buy out Field at an amount Field would receive if the business was sold to Arn.

2. Admit Arn to partnership upon the purchase of Field's share for an amount Field and Arn will negotiate.

The present partnership agreement calls for a distribution of net income/loss on a 3:5:2 basis. If Arn is admitted to partnership the ratio would not change; he would be entitled to Field's 20% share of net income/loss. If Bell and Trunk buy out for an amount based on the Arn offer, Bell and Trunk would continue to share net income/loss on the same relative basis. They would (the new partnership of Bell and Trunk) have to borrow sufficient funds from the bank to retain a minimum cash balance of $10,000.

Required

1. Prepare the general journal entry for admission of Arn to the partnership upon his purchase of Field's interest for an undisclosed amount.

2. Prepare the necessary entries to record Field's withdrawal from the partnership. The amount paid to Field is equal to the amount he would have received if the partnership was sold to Arn.

A&R Problem 14–3

Yee, Fee, and Dee were partners sharing income and losses equally. The business was considered very successful until the last two or three years. Changes in technology and additional competition from abroad led the partners to conclude that they should sell. As Yee stated, "We had many good years with each of us withdrawing various amounts, nearly $5 million in total. Why wait for rigor mortis to set in? Let's get out while we still can." These sentiments were shared by both Fee and Dee.

Both Yee and Dee were taking their wives on a round-the-world cruise to celebrate their 40th and 50th anniversaries. Consequently, Fee was authorized to negotiate the sale of the business.

Upon Yee's and Dee's return, Fee informed them that he had disposed of the business for a price that both Yee and Dee agreed was excellent. Consequently, Dee demanded an accounting when informed that he owed Yee and Fee $5,000 each.

The partnership balance sheet at the time of the sale of the business to Nu-Technology, Inc., was as follows:

YEE, FEE, AND DEE
Balance Sheet
June 15, 1985

Assets

Cash	$ 2,000	
Accounts receivable (net of $800 allowance)	80,000	
Inventory.	120,000	
Prepayments	8,000	
Total current assets		$210,000
Goodwill, patents, and other intangibles		60,000
Plant and equipment (net of $420,000 accumulated depreciation . .		80,000
Total assets		$350,000

Liabilities

Accounts payable.	120,000	
Notes payable.	80,000	
Total liabilities		$200,000

Partners' Equity

Yee, capital	60,000	
Fee, capital	60,000	
Dee, capital	30,000	
Total partners' equity		150,000
Liabilities and partners' equity		$350,000

Required

1. What value was placed on the assets? (The book value of liabilities was agreed upon.)
2. Show the computations Fee made to arrive at the amount owed by Dee to Yee and Fee.

3. How much did Yee and Fee receive prior to settlement with Dee?
4. Present the general journal entries to record the sale of the partnership and the closing of the partnership books.

A&R Problem 14–4

Repeat the requirements of A&R Problem 14–3 on the assumption that Fee gave Dee a cheque for $40,000 as his share of the cash available to the partners upon the sale of the business.

A&R Problem 14–5

Refer to A&R Problem 14–3. What factors, other than those given, would influence Nu-Technology, Inc., to place the value they did on the partnership business?

Accounting for Corporations and Bonds

Most students of business will at some time work for a corporation. Perhaps all students will own (either directly or indirectly through a retirement fund) some debt or stock securities issued by corporations. For these reasons, you should have a basic understanding of corporations and the methods used to account for corporations and for stocks and bonds. These topics are discussed in Part Five, which consists of the following chapters:

15. Organization and Operation of Corporations

16. Additional Corporate Transactions; Reporting Income and Retained Earnings; Earnings per Share

17. Bonds as Liabilities and Investments

15 Organization and Operation of Corporations

Of the three common types of business organizations (proprietorships, partnerships and corporations), corporations are fewest in number. However, they transact substantially more business than do the other two combined. Thus, from an overall economic point of view, corporations are clearly the most important form of business organization. As you study this chapter, you will learn how corporations are organized and operated and some of the procedures used to account for corporations.

Learning Objectives

After studying Chapter 15, you should be able to:

1. Explain the advantages, disadvantages, and organization of corporations and the differences in accounting for partnerships and corporations.
2. Record the issuance of no-par value stock and the issuance of par stock.
3. Record transactions involving stock subscriptions and explain the effects of subscribed stock on corporation assets and shareholders' equity.
4. Explain the differences between common and preferred stocks and allocate dividends between common and preferred stocks.
5. Describe convertible preferred stock and explain the meaning of par, redemption, book, and market values of stock.
6. Define or explain the words and phrases listed in the chapter Glossary.

Advantages of the Corporate Form

Explain the advantages, disadvantages, and organization of corporations, and the differences in accounting for partnerships and corporations. (L. O. 1)

Corporations have become the dominant type of business in our country because of the advantages offered by this form of business organization. Among the advantages are the following:

Corporations Are Separate Legal Entities

Unlike a proprietorship or partnership, a corporation is a separate legal entity; it is separate and distinct from its owners. Because it is a separate legal entity, a corporation, through its agents, may conduct its affairs with the same rights, duties, and responsibilities as a person.

Shareholders Are Not Liable for a Corporation's Debts

As a separate legal entity a corporation is responsible for its own acts and its own debts. Its shareholders are not liable for either. From the viewpoint of an investor, this lack of shareholders' liability is perhaps the most important advantage of the corporate form of business.

Ownership Rights of Corporations Are Easily Transferred

The ownership of a corporation is represented by shares of stock that generally can be transferred and disposed of any time the owners wish. Also, the transfer of shares from one shareholder to another has no effect on the corporation or its operations.

Corporations Have Continuity of Life

A corporation's life may continue for the time stated in its articles of incorporation or charter. This may be of any length permitted by the laws of the jurisdiction of its incorporation. Also, if the stated time expires, the corporation's articles of incorporation or charter may be renewed and the period extended. Thus, a corporation that continues to be successful may have a perpetual life.

Shareholders Do Not Have a Mutual Agency Relationship

The shareholders of a corporation do not have the mutual agency relationship that is typical of partnerships. Therefore, a shareholder, acting as a shareholder, does not have the power to bind the corporation to contracts. The participation of shareholders in the affairs of the corporation is limited to the right to vote in the shareholders' meetings. As a result, if you become a shareholder in a corporation, you do not have to worry about the character of the other shareholders to the same extent that you would if the business were a partnership.

Ease of Capital Assembly

Buying stock in a corporation often is more attractive to investors than is investing in a partnership. This is because: (1) shareholders are not liable for the corporation's actions and debts, (2) shareholders do not have a relationship of mutual agency regarding the corporation, and (3) stock often is easily transferred or sold. These advantages make it possible for some corporations to assemble large amounts of capital from the combined investments of many shareholders. Actually, a corporation's ability to raise capital is limited only by its ability to convince investors that it can use their funds profitably. This is very different from most partnerships where mutual agency and unlimited liability limit the number of investors who are willing to become partners.

Disadvantages of the Corporate Form

Governmental Regulation

Corporations are created by fulfilling the requirements of federal or provincial corporation laws. These laws subject a corporation to considerable regulation and control. Single proprietorships and partnerships escape this regulation as well as the filing of many governmental reports required of corporations.

Taxation

As business units, corporations are subject to the same taxes as single proprietorships and partnerships. In addition, corporations are subject to taxes that are not levied on either of the other two. The most burdensome of these taxes are income taxes, which may amount to as much as 50% of a corporation's pretax income. However, for the shareholders of a corporation, the tax burden does not end there. The income of a corporation is taxed twice, first as income of the corporation and again as personal income when it is distributed to the shareholders as dividends. This differs from single proprietorships and partnerships, which as business units are not subject to income taxes. Normally, their income is taxed only as the personal income of their owners.

The tax characteristics of a corporation are generally viewed as a disadvantage. In some cases, however, they work to the advantage of shareholders. Corporation and individual tax rates are progressive. In other words, high levels of income are taxed at higher rates and lower levels of income are taxed at lower rates. Therefore, taxes may be saved or at least delayed if a large amount of income is divided between two or more tax-paying entities. So, if an individual has a large personal income and pays taxes at a high rate, the individual may benefit if some of the income is earned by a corporation owned by the individual. Then, if the corporation avoids paying dividends, the income of the corporation is, at least temporarily, taxed only once at the lower corporate rate. Additionally, the dividend tax credit gives some relief from the effects of double taxation.

Organizing a Corporation

A corporation is created by securing a certificate of incorporation or a charter from the federal or provincial government. Under the Canada Business Corporations Act, 1975, incorporation is a matter of right. One person, over 18, of sound mind, and not bankrupt may incorporate by submitting completed articles of incorporation and other required documentation to the Director, Corporations Branch, Department of Consumer and Corporate Affairs. Once the documentation is in order, the Director issues a certificate of incorporation and a corporation comes into existence. The subscribers then purchase the corporation's stock, after which the shareholders meet and elect a board of directors who are responsible for directing the corporation's affairs.

Organization Costs

The costs of organizing a corporation, such as legal fees, promoters' fees, and amounts paid the provincial or federal government to secure approval of articles of incorporation, are called **organization costs** and are debited on incurrence to the account, Organization Costs. Theoretically, the sum of these costs represent an intangible asset from which the corporation will benefit throughout its life. However, the life of a corporation is always indeterminable; consequently, the period over which it will benefit from being organized is indeterminable. Nevertheless, a corporation should make a reasonable estimate of the benefit period, which, in line with the CICA recommendations, should not exceed 40 years, and write off its organization costs over this period. Although not necessarily related to the benefit period, income tax rules permit a corporation to write off 50% of the post-1972 organization costs as a tax-deductible expense at an annual 10% rate on a diminishing balance basis. Consequently, some corporations adopt the tax period over which to write off such costs. There is no theoretical justification for this, but it is generally accepted in practice. Also, organization costs often are not material in amount, in which case a write-off over five years is justified under the *materiality principle*.

Management of a Corporation

The organizational structure by which shareholders govern the activities of a corporation is not the same in all corporations. However, Illustration 15–1 shows two alternative structures that are widely used. Notice that ultimate control of a corporation rests with its shareholders. However, this control is exercised indirectly through the election of the board of directors. The individual shareholders' right to participate in management begins and ends with a vote in the shareholders' meeting, where each shareholder usually has one vote for each share of stock owned.

Normally, a corporation's shareholders meet once each year to elect directors and vote on any other business matters which, according to the corporation's bylaws, must be approved by the shareholders. If a group of shareholders own or control the votes of 50% plus one share of a corporation's stock, they can elect the board and control the corporation. However, in many companies, a large number of shareholders do not attend the annual meeting or get involved in the voting process. As a result, a much smaller percentage is frequently able to dominate the election of board members.

Shareholders who do not attend shareholders' meetings usually can delegate their voting rights to an agent. This is done by signing a legal document called a **proxy**, which gives the agent the right to vote the stock.

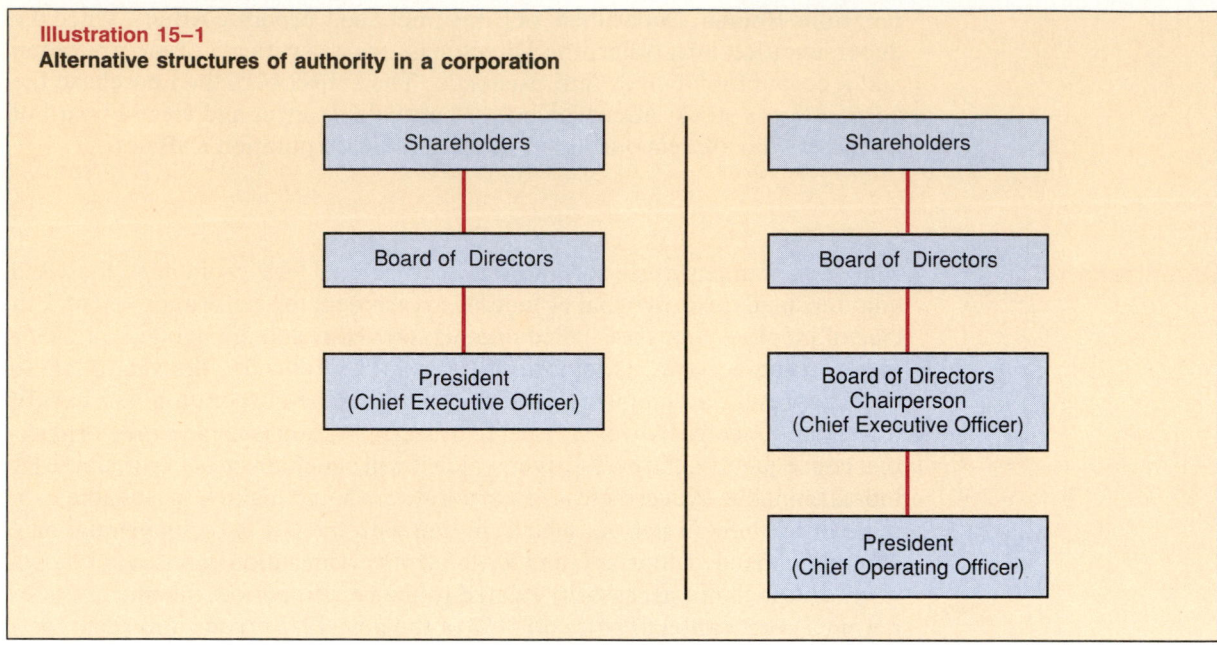

Illustration 15–1
Alternative structures of authority in a corporation

A corporation's board of directors is responsible and has final authority for the direction of corporate affairs. However, it may act only as a collective body. An individual director, as a director, has no power to transact corporate business. Although the board has final authority, it usually limits its actions to establishing policy. Day-by-day direction of corporate business is delegated to executive officers who are appointed by the board to manage the business.

Traditionally, the chief executive officer (CEO) of the corporation is the president. Under the president, there may be several vice presidents who are assigned specific areas of management responsibility such as finance, production, and marketing. In addition, the corporation secretary keeps the minutes of the meetings of the shareholders and directors. In a small corporation, the secretary also may be responsible for keeping a record of the shareholders and the transfer of shares between shareholders.

In recent years, many corporations have a slightly different structure in which the board of directors chairperson assumes the position of chief executive officer. When this is done, the president usually is designated the chief operating officer (COO).

Stock Certificates and the Transfer of Stock

When a person invests in a corporation by buying its stock, the person receives a stock certificate as proof of the shares purchased. Usually, in a small corporation, only one certificate is issued for each block of stock purchased. This certificate may be for any number of shares. For example, the certificate of Illustration 15–2 is for 50 shares. Large corporations commonly use preprinted

AS A MATTER OF ETHICS

The board of directors and the officers of Skyline Corporation are meeting to discuss and plan the agenda for the corporation's 1991 annual shareholders' meeting. The first item considered by the directors and officers was whether to report a large government contract that Skyline has just obtained. Although this contract will significantly increase income and cash flows in 1991 and beyond, the management felt that there is no need to reveal the news at the shareholders' meeting. After all, the meeting is intended to be the forum for describing the past year's activities, not the plans for the next year.

After concluding that the contract will not be mentioned, the group moved on to the next topic for the shareholders' meeting. This topic is a motion for the shareholders to approve a compensation plan that will award the managers the rights to acquire large quantities of shares over the next several years. According to the plan, the managers will have a three-year option to buy shares at a fixed price that equals the market value of the stock as measured 30 days after the upcoming shareholders' meeting. In other words, the managers will be able to buy stock in 1992, 1993, or 1994 by paying the 1991 market value. Obviously, if the stock increases in value over the next several years, the managers will realize large profits without having to invest any cash. The financial vice president asks the group whether they should reconsider the decision about the government contract in light of its possible relevance to the vote on the stock option plan.

certificates, each of which represents 100 shares, plus blank certificates that may be made out for any number of shares.

When a shareholder sells shares of a corporation, the seller completes and signs the transfer endorsement on the back of the certificate and sends it to the corporation's secretary (or transfer agent). The old certificate is canceled and retained, and a new certificate is issued to the new shareholder. If the old certificate represents more shares than were sold, the corporation issues two certificates. One goes to the new shareholder for the shares sold, and another certificate is issued to the original shareholder for the remaining shares that were not sold.

Transfer Agent and Registrar

If a corporation's stock is traded on a major stock exchange, the corporation must have a registrar and a transfer agent. The registrar keeps the shareholder records and prepares official lists of shareholders for shareholders' meetings and for payment of dividends. Usually, registrars and transfer agents are large banks or trust companies.

When a shareholder wants to sell some shares of stock, the owner usually requests a stockbroker to act on the owner's behalf and sell the shares. Then, the owner completes the transfer endorsement on the back of the stock certificate and gives the certificate to the stockbroker who sends it to the corporation's transfer agent. The transfer agent cancels the old certificate and issues one or more new certificates and sends them to the registrar. The registrar enters the transfer in the shareholder records and sends the new certificate or certificates to the proper owners.

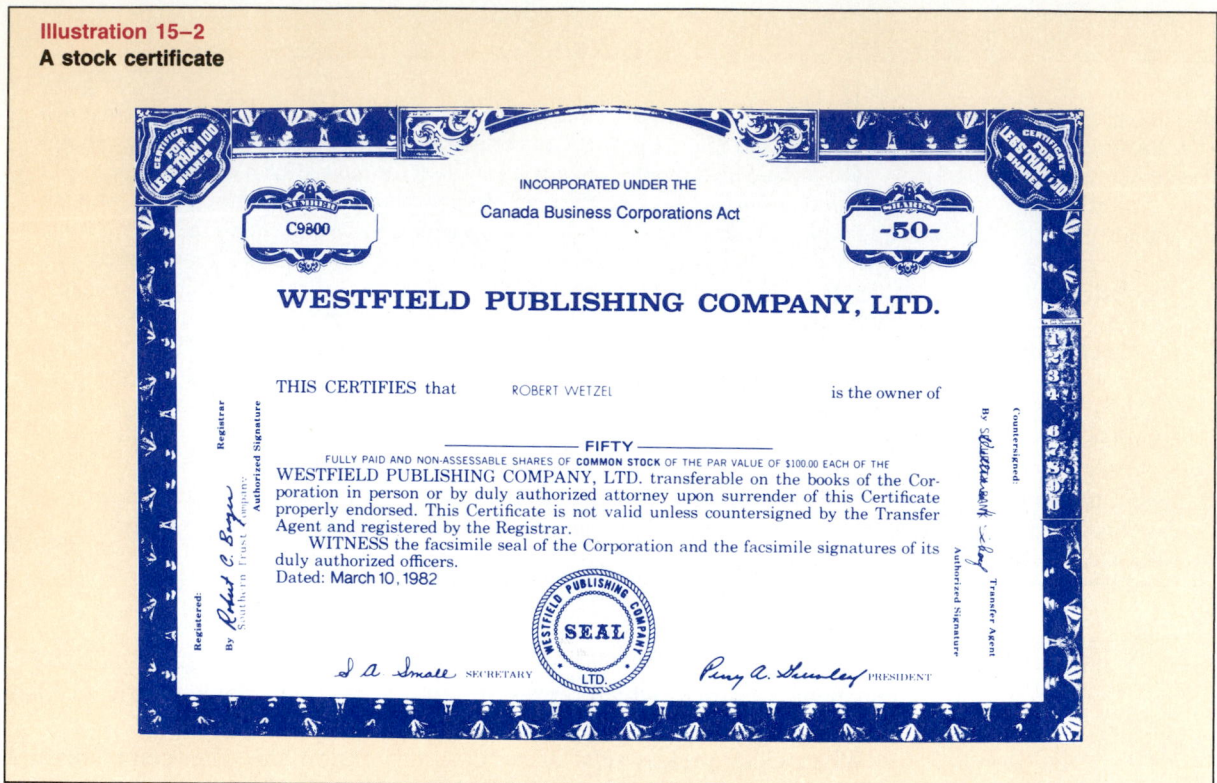

Illustration 15–2
A stock certificate

Corporation Accounting

Corporation accounting was initially discussed in Chapter 4. In that discussion, we explained the entries to record several basic transactions of corporations. The entries included recording an issue of common stock for cash and closing a net income or a net loss from Income Summary to Retained Earnings. Also, the declaration and later payment of cash dividends were recorded. *At this point, you should review the Chapter 4 discussion of these entries, which was presented on pages 172 through 175.* After completing that review, keep in mind that the shareholders' equity accounts of a corporation are divided into (1) contributed capital accounts and (2) retained earnings accounts. Also, remember that when a corporation's board of directors declares a cash dividend on the *date of declaration*, a legal liability of the corporation is incurred. The board of directors declares that on a specific future date, the *date of record*, the shareholders according to the corporation's records will be designated as those to receive the dividend. Finally, on the *date of payment*, the liability for the declared cash dividend is paid by the corporation.

The financial statements of a corporation were first illustrated in Chapter 5. The income statement was shown in Illustration 5–1 on page 221; the retained earnings statement was shown in Illustration 5–3 on page 226; and the balance sheet was shown in Illustration 5–4 on page 226. When you review these illustrations, you should note that income taxes were deducted on the income statement as an expense. Recall that a business organized as a corporation must pay income taxes, while a proprietorship or partnership does not pay income taxes. Also, cash dividends to shareholders are not an expense of the corporation; they are not deducted on the income statement. Instead, dividends are a *distribution of* net income and are subtracted on the retained earnings statement. Finally, notice that the shareholders' equity in Illustration 5–4 is divided into common stock and retained earnings.

Shareholders' Equity Accounts Compared to Partnership Accounts

To demonstrate the use of separate accounts for contributed capital and retained earnings as found in corporation accounting and to contrast their use with the accounts used in partnership accounting, assume the following. On January 5, 1990, a partnership involving two partners and a corporation having five shareholders were formed. Also assume that $25,000 was invested in each. In the partnership, J. Olm invested $10,000 and A. Baker invested $15,000. In the corporation, each of the five shareholders bought 500 shares of its common stock at $10 per share. Without dates and explanations, general journal entries to record the investments are:

Partnership			Corporation		
Cash	10,000		Cash	25,000	
J. Olm, Capital		10,000	Common Stock		25,000
Cash	15,000				
A. Baker, Capital		15,000			

After the entries are posted, the owners' equity accounts of the two companies appear as follows:

Partnership
J. Olm, Capital

Date	Dr.	Cr.	Bal.
Jan. 5, 1990		10,000	10,000

Corporation
Common Stock

Date	Dr.	Cr.	Bal.
Jan. 5, 1990		25,000	25,000

A. Baker, Capital

Date	Dr.	Cr.	Bal.
Jan. 5, 1990		15,000	15,000

To continue the illustration, assume that during 1990, each company earned a net income of $8,000 and also distributed $5,000 to its owners. According to the partnership agreement, incomes are allocated 40% to Olm and 60% to

Baker. The cash distribution to the partners was divided equally. The corporation declared the dividends on December 20, 1990, and both companies made the cash payments to owners on December 25, 1990. The entries to record the distribution of cash to partners and the declaration and payments of dividends to shareholders are as follows:

Partnership		Corporation	
Partnership		**Corporation**	
J. Olm, Withdrawals	2,500	Dividends Declared	5,000
A. Baker, Withdrawals	2,500	Dividends Payable	5,000
Cash	5,000		
		Dividends Payable	5,000
		Cash	5,000

At the end of the year, the entries to close the Income Summary accounts are as follows:

Partnership		Corporation	
Partnership		**Corporation**	
Income Summary	8,000	Income Summary	8,000
J. Olm, Capital	3,200	Retained Earnings	8,000
A. Baker, Capital	4,800		

Finally, the entries to close the withdrawals accounts and the Dividends Declared account are:

Partnership		Corporation	
Partnership		**Corporation**	
J. Olm, Capital	2,500	Retained Earnings	5,000
A. Baker, Capital	2,500	Dividends Declared . . .	5,000
J. Olm, Withdrawals . . .	2,500		
A. Baker, Withdrawals . .	2,500		

After posting the above entries, the owners' equity accounts of the two companies are as follows:

Partnership
J. Olm, Capital

Date	Dr.	Cr.	Bal.
Jan. 5, 1990		10,000	10,000
Dec. 31, 1990		3,200	13,200
Dec. 31, 1990	2,500		10,700

Corporation
Common Stock

Date	Dr.	Cr.	Bal.
Jan. 5, 1990		25,000	25,000

A. Baker, Capital

Date	Dr.	Cr.	Bal.
Jan. 5, 1990		15,000	15,000
Dec. 31, 1990		4,800	19,800
Dec. 31, 1990	2,500		17,300

Retained Earnings

Date	Dr.	Cr.	Bal.
Dec. 20, 1990	5,000		5,000
Dec. 31, 1990		8,000	3,000

J. Olm, Withdrawals

Date	Dr.	Cr.	Bal.
Dec. 25, 1990	2,500		2,500
Dec. 31, 1990		2,500	–0–

Dividends Declared

Date	Dr.	Cr.	Bal.
Dec. 20, 1990	5,000		5,000
Dec. 31, 1990		5,000	–0–

A. Baker, Withdrawals

Date	Dr.	Cr.	Bal.
Dec. 25, 1990	2,500		2,500
Dec. 31, 1990		2,500	–0–

Observe that in the partnership, after all entries have been posted, the $28,000 equity of the owners appears in the capital accounts of the partners:

J. Olm, Capital	$10,700
A. Baker, capital	17,300
Total owners' equity	$28,000

By comparison, the shareholders' equity of the corporation is divided between contributed capital and the Retained Earnings account, as follows:

Common stock	$25,000
Retained earnings	3,000
Total shareholders' equity	$28,000

Authorization and Issuance of Stock

When a corporation is organized, it is normally authorized to issue an unlimited number of shares. If all of the authorized shares have the same rights and characteristics, the stock is called **common stock**. However, a corporation may be authorized to issue both common and preferred stock. (Preferred stock is discussed later in this chapter.) If a corporation chooses to place a limitation on the number of shares it may issue, such limitation must be stated in the articles, not in the by-laws. When a balance sheet is prepared, both the amount of stock authorized and the amount issued are commonly disclosed as shown on page 682.

Sale of Stock for Cash

When stock is sold for cash and immediately issued, an entry in general journal form like the following may be used to record the sale and issuance:

June	5	Cash	300,000.00	
		Common Stock		300,000.00
		Sold and issued 30,000 shares of common stock, at $10 per share.		

Exchanging Stock for Noncash Assets

A corporation may accept assets other than cash in exchange for its stock. In the process, the corporation also may assume some liabilities. Transactions such as these are recorded as follows:

Apr.	3	Machinery	10,000.00	
		Buildings	65,000.00	
		Land	15,000.00	
		Long-Term Notes Payable		50,000.00
		Common Stock		40,000.00
		Exchanged 4,000 shares of common stock for machinery, buildings, land, and assumption of note payable.		

A corporation also may issue shares of its stock to its promoters in exchange for their services in organizing the corporation. In this case, the corporation receives the intangible asset of being organized in exchange for its stock. The transaction is recorded as follows:

Apr.	5	Organization Costs	5,000.00	
		Common Stock		5,000.00
		Gave promoters 500 shares of common stock in exchange for services in organizing the corporation.		

Sale of Stock through Subscriptions

Record transactions involving stock subscriptions and explain the effects of subscribed stock on corporation assets and shareholders' equity.
(L. O. 3)

Usually, stock is sold for cash and immediately issued. However, corporations sometimes sell stock by means of **stock subscriptions**. For example, when a new corporation is formed, the organizers may realize that the new business has limited immediate needs for cash but will need additional capital in the future. To get the corporation started on a sound footing, the organizers may sell stock to investors who agree to contribute some cash now and also agree to make additional contributions in the future.

When stock is sold through subscriptions, the investor signs a subscription blank or a subscription list and agrees to buy a certain number of the shares at a specified price. The agreement also states when payments are to be made. When the subscription is accepted by the corporation, it becomes a contract and the corporation acquires an asset. The asset is the right to receive payment from the subscriber. At the same time, the subscriber obtains an equity in the corporation.

To illustrate the sale of stock through subscriptions, assume that on May 6, Northgate Corporation accepted subscriptions to 5,000 shares of common stock at $12 per share. The subscription contracts called for a 10% down payment to accompany the subscriptions and the balance in two equal installments due in three months and six months. You record the subscriptions as follows:

May	6	Subscriptions Receivable, Common Stock	60,000.00	
		Common Stock Subscribed		60,000.00
		Accepted subscriptions to 5,000 shares of common stock at $12 per share.		

Notice that at the time the subscriptions are accepted, the subscriptions receivable account is debited for the total amount of the subscription. This is the amount the subscribers agree to pay. Also notice that the **Common Stock Subscribed** account is credited for the same amount. Later, the subscriptions receivable will be converted into cash when the subscribers pay for their stock. And when payment is completed, the subscribed stock will be issued and will become outstanding stock.

Receipt of the down payments and the two installment payments are recorded with these entries.

May	6	Cash	6,000.00	
		Subscriptions Receivable, Common Stock		6,000.00
		Collected 10% down payments on the common stock subscribed.		
Aug.	6	Cash	27,000.00	
		Subscriptions Receivable, Common Stock		27,000.00
		Collected the first installment payments on the common stock subscribed.		
Nov.	6	Cash	27,000.00	
		Subscriptions Receivable, Common Stock		27,000.00
		Collected the second installment payments on the common stock subscribed.		

In this case, the down payments accompanied the subscriptions. Therefore, the May 6 entries to record the receipt of the subscriptions and to record the down payments could have been combined.

When stock is sold through subscriptions, the stock usually is not issued until the subscriptions are paid in full. Also, if dividends are declared before subscribed stock has been issued, the dividends go only to outstanding shares, not to the subscribed shares. However, as soon as the subscriptions are paid, the stock is issued. The entry to record the issuance of the Northgate common stock appears as follows:

Aug.	5	Common Stock Subscribed	60,000.00	
		Common Stock		60,000.00
		Issued 5,000 shares of common stock sold through subscriptions.		

Most subscriptions are collected in full, but not always. Sometimes a subscriber fails to pay. If this happens, the subscription contract must be canceled. In such a case, if the subscriber has made a partial payment on the contract, the amount paid may be returned. Or, an amount of stock equal to the partial payment may be issued. Or, in some jurisdictions, the subscriber's partial payment may be kept by the corporation to compensate for any damages suffered.

Subscriptions Receivable and Stock Subscribed on the Balance Sheet

Subscriptions receivable are reported on the balance sheet as a current asset or as a long-term asset, depending on when collection is expected. If a corporation prepares a balance sheet after accepting subscriptions to its stock but before the stock is issued, both the issued stock and the subscribed stock should be reported on the balance sheet, as follows:

Common stock, unlimited number of shares authorized, 20,000 shares issued	$200,000
Common stock subscribed, 5,000 shares	60,000
Total common stock issued and subscribed	$260,000

Par and No-Par Value

Record the issuance of par value stock and the issuance of no-par stock. (L. O. 2)

The Canada Business Corporations Act, 1975, as well as the more recently passed provincial counterparts, require that all shares be of **no-par** or nominal value. These acts also require the total consideration received by the corporation for each share issued must be added to the stated capital account maintained for the shares of that class or series. Some provinces still permit the issuance of par value shares. **Par value** is an arbitrary value a corporation places on a share of its stock.

When a corporation issues par value stock, the par is printed on each certificate and is used in accounting for the stock. If the stock is issued at par, the entry to record the issue is the same as if the stock was no-par value. If, however, the stock is issued at a price above the stock's par value, the stock is said to be issued at a **premium.** For example, if a corporation sells and issues its $10 par value common stock at $12 per share, the stock is sold at a $2 per share premium. Although a premium is an amount in excess of par paid by purchasers of newly issued stock, it is not considered a profit to the issuing corporation. Rather, a premium is part of the investment of shareholders who pay more than the par for the stock.

In accounting for stock sold at a premium, the premium is recorded separately from the par value of the stock to which it applies. For example, if a corporation sells and issues 10,000 shares of its $10 par value common stock for cash at $12 per share, the sale is recorded as follows:

Dec.	1	Cash.	120,000.00	
		Common Stock.		100,000.00
		Premium on Common Stock		20,000.00
		Sold and issued 10,000 shares of $10 par value common stock at $12 per share.		

When a balance sheet is prepared, stock premium is disclosed under ''Other contributed capital.''

Rights of Common Shareholders

When investors buy a corporation's common stock, they acquire all the *specific* rights granted by the corporation's articles of incorporation or charter to its common shareholders. They also acquire the *general* rights granted shareholders by the laws of the jurisdiction in which the company is incorporated. The laws vary, but common shareholders generally have the following rights:

1. The right to vote in the shareholders' meetings.
2. The right to sell or otherwise dispose of their stock.
3. The right to share pro rata with other common shareholders in any dividends declared.
4. The right to share in any assets remaining after creditors are paid if the corporation is liquidated.

In addition, if desired, the articles of incorporation may provide additional rights. For example, the articles may specifically provide for the **preemptive right.** This right holds that no shares of a class shall be issued unless the shares have first been offered to the shareholders holding shares of that class, and that those shareholders have a first opportunity to acquire the offered shares in proportion to their holdings of the shares of that class, at such a price and on such terms as those shares are to be offered to others.

Classes of Shares

The Canada Business Corporations Act allows corporations to issue registered no-par-value shares by class and by series of the class so long as there exists one ''residual'' class of shares that may vote at all meetings of shareholders (except for meetings of specified classes of shareholders) and that may receive the remaining assets of a corporation upon dissolution. The act does not use the adjectives *common* and *preferred* but simply refers to shares in general. Classes of shares may continue to be called common, preferred, Class A, Class B, and so on; however, the act does require the articles to set out the rights, privileges, restrictions, and conditions attaching to each class and series of shares. Because of their widespread usage the terms *common* and *preferred* are used throughout this book.

Preferred Stock

Explain the differences between common and preferred stocks and allocate dividends between common and preferred stocks.
(L. O. 4)

A corporation may issue more than one kind or class of stock. If two classes are issued, one is usually called **preferred stock** and the other is common stock.

The name *preferred* comes from the fact that preferred shares have a higher priority or senior status relative to common shares in one or more ways. These commonly include a preference as to payment of dividends and may include a preference in the distribution of assets if the corporation is liquidated.

In addition to the preferences it receives, preferred stock carries all the rights of common stock, unless such rights are specifically denied in the corporation's articles of incorporation or charter. Preferred stock often is denied the right to vote in the shareholders' meetings.

Preferred Dividends

A preference as to dividends gives the preferred shareholders the right to receive their preferred dividends before the common shareholders receive a dividend. In other words, dividends cannot be paid to common shareholders unless preferred shareholders also receive a dividend. The amount of dividends that the preferred shareholders must receive usually is expressed as a dollar amount per share or as a percentage that is applied to the par value. For example, 9%, $100 par value, preferred stock must be paid $9 per share before the common shares can receive any dividend. However, a preference as to dividends does not grant an absolute right to dividends. If the board of directors does not declare a dividend, then neither the preferred nor the common shareholders receive a dividend.

Cumulative and Noncumulative Preferred Stock

Preferred stock is either **cumulative** or **noncumulative**. If it is cumulative, any undeclared dividends accumulate each year until paid. If it is noncumulative, the right to receive dividends is forfeited in any year that dividends are not declared.

If preferred stock is cumulative and the corporation fails to declare a dividend to the preferred shareholders as called for in the corporate charter, the unpaid dividend is called a **dividend in arrears**. The accumulation of dividends in arrears on cumulative preferred stocks does not guarantee payment. However, with cumulative preferred stock, the preferred shareholders must be paid both the current dividend and any dividends in arrears before any dividend is paid to common shareholders.

To show the difference between cumulative and noncumulative preferred stock, assume that a corporation has outstanding 1,000 shares of $9 preferred stock issued at $100 per share and 4,000 shares of common stock issued at $50 per share. During the first two years of the corporation's operations, the board of directors declared cash dividends of: year 1, $5,000; and year 2, $42,000. The allocations are:

	To Preferred	To Common
Assuming noncumulative preferred:		
Year 1.	$ 5,000	$ –0–
Year 2:		
First: Current preferred dividend	$ 9,000	
Remainder to common		$33,000
Assuming cumulative preferred:		
Year 1.	$ 5,000	$ –0–
Year 2:		
First: Dividends in arrears	$ 4,000	
Next: Current preferred dividend	9,000	
Remainder to common		$29,000
Totals.	$13,000	$29,000

Notice that the year 2 allocation of dividends depends on whether the preferred stock is noncumulative or cumulative. With noncumulative preferred stock, the preferred shareholders never receive the $4,000 that was unpaid in year 1. However, when the preferred stock is cumulative, the $4,000 must be paid before the common shareholders receive a dividend.

Disclosure of Dividends in Arrears in the Financial Statements

Unlike interest expense, which is incurred as time passes and therefore must be accrued, dividends do not accrue. A liability for a dividend does not come into existence until the dividend is declared by the board of directors. Therefore, if a preferred dividend date passes and the corporation's board fails to declare the dividend on its cumulative preferred stock, the dividend in arrears is not a liability. It does not appear on the balance sheet as a liability. However, when you prepare the financial statements, the *full-disclosure principle* requires that you report the amount that preferred dividends are in arrears on the balance sheet date. Normally, this information is given in a footnote to the financial statements. If there is no such disclosure, readers of the financial statements have the right to assume that preferred dividends are not in arrears.

Participating and Nonparticipating Preferred Stock

Dividends to preferred stock are generally limited each year to the stated amount or to an amount that is determined by applying the preferred percentage to the par value. When preferred stock is so limited, it is called *nonparticipating preferred stock*. Most preferred stock is nonparticipating. However, some preferred stock may be paid additional dividends in excess of the stated percentage or amount that is preferred. Such preferred stock is called **participating preferred stock.**

Large corporations with publicly traded stock rarely issue participating preferred stock. However, this kind of stock sometimes is issued by smaller corporations that need to raise more capital than the organizers can provide. If the organizers are not willing to share control but are willing to share profits with other investors, the corporation may issue participating preferred stock that has limited voting rights.

To illustrate participating preferred stock, assume that the 1,000 shares of $9 preferred stock in the above example are participating, and participation is based on equal percentage of average stated (average issue price) value of each class of shares. Also, assume that cash dividends of $48,000 are declared in year 3. The allocation between preferred and common shares is as follows:

	To Preferred	To Common
First, to preferred [9% × (1,000 × $100)]	$ 9,000	
Next, to common [9% × (4,000 × $50)]		$18,000
Remainder maintains equal percentage to preferred and common: ($49,000 − $9,000 − $18,000 = $21,000)		
$21,000 × ($100,000 ÷ $300,000)	7,000	
$21,000 × ($200,000 ÷ $300,000)		14,000
Totals	$16,000	$32,000

Observe that the first step satisfies the preferred stock's right to $9 (9% of stated value) before any dividends are paid to common. Next, the common shares receive 9% of stated value. Finally, any additional dividends are allocated on the basis of the relative stated par value amounts outstanding. As a result, both preferred and common shares are paid the same percentage (16% of stated value in this case). This is confirmed by the following calculation:

	Total Stated Value	Total Dividend	Percent of stated value
Preferred (1,000 × $100)	$100,000	$16,000	16
Common (4,000 × $50)	200,000	32,000	16
Totals	$300,000	$48,000	16

In this example, no matter how much larger the dividend declaration might be, the preferred stock has the right to participate with common on an equal percentage basis. Thus, the preferred stock in this example is called *fully participating preferred stock*. In other cases, the right to receive additional dividends beyond the basic preferred amount is limited to a stated amount or percentage. For example, a $9 preferred stock might have the right to participate in dividend declarations, up to an additional $2 per share or 2% of stated value. This type of stock is called *partially participating preferred stock*.

Why Preferred Stock Is Issued

Two common reasons why preferred stock is issued are best shown with an example. Suppose that the organizers of a business have $100,000 to invest but wish to organize a corporation that requires $200,000 capital. If they sell and issue $200,000 of common stock, they will have to share control with other shareholders. However, if they issue $100,000 of common stock to themselves and can sell to outsiders, at $100 per share, 1,000 shares of $8 cumulative preferred stock that has no voting rights, they will retain control of the corporation.

Also, suppose the organizers expect their new corporation to earn an annual after-tax return of $24,000. If they sell and issue $200,000 of common stock, this will mean a 12% return. However, if they sell and issue $100,000 of each kind of stock, retaining the common for themselves, they can increase their own return to 16%, as follows:

Net after-tax income	$24,000
Less preferred dividends (1,000 × $8)	(8,000)
Balance to common shareholders (equal to 16% on their $100,000 investment)	$16,000

In this case, the common shareholders earn 16% because the dividends on the preferred stock are less than the amount that can be earned on the preferred shareholders' investment. This issuance of preferred stock is an example of **financial leverage**. Whenever the dividend rate on preferred stock is less than the rate the corporation earns on its operations, the effect is to increase or *lever* the rate earned by common shareholders. Financial leverage also occurs if money is borrowed and the creditors are paid an interest rate less than the rate earned from using the borrowed money.

There are other reasons why corporations issue preferred stock. For example, a corporation's preferred stock may appeal to some investors who believe that its common stock is too risky. Also, if a corporation's management wants to issue common stock but believes the current market price for the common stock is too low, the corporation may issue preferred stock that is convertible into common stock. Later, if the price of the common stock recovers, the preferred shareholders may be asked to convert their shares into common shares.

Convertible Preferred Stock

Describe convertible preferred stock and explain the meaning of par, redemption, book, and market values of stock.
(L. O. 5)

To make an issue of preferred stock more attractive, investors may be given the right to exchange their preferred shares for a fixed number of shares of the issuing company's common stock. **Convertible preferred stocks** offer investors more security than would common stock. Also, if the issuing company prospers and its common stock increases in price, the investors have the opportunity to share in the prosperity by converting their preferred stock into the more valuable common stock. Conversion is always at the option of the investors and therefore does not occur unless it is to their advantage.

To see how the conversion of preferred stock is recorded, assume that a corporation has outstanding 1,000 shares of $10 convertible preferred stock. The stock was originally issued for $103 per share. Each preferred share is convertible into four shares of common stock. If all of the preferred shares are converted on May 1, the entry to record the conversion is:

May	1	Preferred Stock	103,000.00	
		Common Stock		103,000.00
		To record the conversion of preferred stock.		

Note that when the preferred stock is converted into common stock, the balance in the preferred stock account is removed and added to the stated value of the common stock account. No gain or loss is recorded.

Stock Values

In addition to a par value and average stated value, stocks may have a redemption value, a market value, and a book value.

Redemption Value of Callable Preferred Stock

Some issues of preferred stock are callable. This means that the issuing corporation has the right to retire the **callable preferred stock** by paying a specified amount to the preferred shareholders. The amount that must be paid to call and retire a callable preferred share is its **redemption value** or **call price**. This amount is set at the time the stock is issued. To retire a callable preferred stock, the issuing corporation must pay any dividends in arrears in addition to the redemption value of the stock.

Market Value

The market value of a share of stock is the price at which a share can be bought or sold. Market values are influenced by earnings, dividends, future prospects, and general market conditions.

Book Value

The **book value of a share of stock** is one share's equity in the corporation's net assets as recorded in the corporation's accounts. To determine the book value per share when the only outstanding stock is common stock, you divide total shareholders' equity by the number of shares outstanding. For example, if total shareholders' equity is $285,000 and there are 10,000 shares outstanding, the book value per share is $28.50 ($285,000 ÷ 10,000 = $28.50).

To compute book values when both common and preferred stock are outstanding, you must allocate the total shareholders' equity between the preferred and common shares. The preferred stock's portion is its redemption value (or stated value if there is no redemption value) plus any cumulative dividends in arrears. The remaining shareholders' equity is then assigned to the common shares outstanding. To determine the book value of each class, you divide the portion of shareholders' equity assigned to a class by the number of shares of that class outstanding. For instance, assume a corporation has the shareholders' equity as shown in Illustration 15–3.

If the preferred stock is redeemable at $103 per share and two years of cumulative preferred dividends are in arrears, the book values of the corporation's shares are calculated as follows:

Total shareholders' equity.			$ 447,000
Less equity applicable to preferred shares:			
Redemption value	$103,000		
Cumulative dividends in arrears	14,000	(117,000)	
Equity applicable to common shares			$330,000
Book value of preferred shares ($117,000 ÷ 1,000)		$117	
Book value of common shares ($330,000 ÷ 10,000)		33	

Illustration 15–3
Shareholders' equity with preferred and common stock

Shareholders' Equity

Preferred stock, $7 cumulative and nonparticipating, 2,000 shares authorized, 1,000 shares issued and outstanding	$105,000
Common stock, no-par value, unlimited number of shares authorized, 10,000 shares issued and outstanding.	$260,000
Total contributed capital	$365,000
Retained earnings	82,000
Total shareholders' equity	$447,000

In their annual reports to shareholders, corporations sometimes report the increase in the book value of the corporation's shares that has occurred during a year. Also, book value may have significance in a contract. For example, a shareholder may enter into a contract to sell shares at their book value on some future date. However, book value should not be confused with *liquidation value*. If a corporation is liquidated, its assets will probably sell at prices quite different from the amounts at which they are carried on the books. Also, book value generally has little bearing on the market value of stock. Dividends, earning capacity, and future prospects are usually of much more importance.

Summary of the Chapter in Terms of Learning Objectives

1. Advantages of the corporate form of business include the following: (*a*) corporations are separate legal entities, (*b*) shareholders are not liable for the corporate debts, (*c*) corporations have continuity of life, and (*d*) shareholders are not agents of the corporation. A disadvantage is that corporations are closely regulated by government. Also, corporations must pay various taxes, especially income taxes, which is often a disadvantage.

A corporation is governed by its board of directors, which is elected by its shareholders. Officers that manage the corporation include a president, perhaps one or more vice presidents, and a secretary. The chief executive officer may be the president or the board of directors chairperson.

2. When par value stock is issued, the par value is credited to the stock account, and any excess is credited to a separate contributed capital account. If the stock has no par, the entire proceeds are credited to the stock account.

3. If a corporation sells stock through subscriptions, the right to receive payment is an asset of the corporation, and the subscriber's equity is recorded in a contributed capital account. The Common Stock Subscribed account is transferred to Common Stock when the shares are issued, which normally occurs after all payments are received.

4. Preferred stock has a priority or senior status relative to common stock in one or more ways. Usually, this means that common shareholders cannot be paid dividends unless a specified amount of dividends is also paid to preferred shares. Also, preferred stock may have a priority status if the corporation is liquidated. The dividend preference for many preferred stocks is cumulative, and a few preferred stocks also participate in dividends beyond the preferred amount.

5. Upon the conversion of convertible preferred stock into common stock, the carrying value of the preferred stock or bonds is transferred to a contributed capital account that relates to common stock. No gain or loss is recorded.

Par value is an arbitrary amount assigned to a share of stock when the class of stock is authorized. If preferred stock is callable, the amount that must be paid to retire the stock is its redemption value plus any dividends in arrears. The book value of preferred stock is any dividend arrearage plus the stock's stated value or, if it is callable, its redemption value. The remaining shareholders' equity is divided by the number of outstanding common shares to determine the book value per share of the common stock. Market value is the price a stock commands if bought or sold.

Demonstration Problem

Barton Corporation was created on January 1, 1990. Listed below are the transactions relating to shareholders' equity, which occurred during the first two years of the company's operations. Prepare the journal entries to record these transactions. Also prepare the balance sheet presentation of the organization costs, liabilities, and shareholders' equity as of December 31, 1990, and December 31, 1991. Include appropriate footnotes.

1990
Jan. 1 Authorized the issuance of unlimited number of shares of no-par-value common stock and 100,000 shares of no-par-value preferred stock. The preferred stock pays a $10 annual dividend and is cumulative.

1 Issued 200,000 shares of common stock at $12 per share.

1 Issued 100,000 shares of common stock in exchange for a building valued at $820,000 and merchandise inventory valued at $380,000.

1 Accepted subscriptions for 150,000 shares of common stock at $12 per share. The subscribers made no down payments, and the full purchase price was due on April 1, 1990.

1 Reimbursed the company's founders for $100,000 of organization costs which are to be amortized over 10 years.

1 Issued 12,000 shares of preferred stock for $110 per share.

Apr. 1 Collected the full subscription price for the January 1 common stock and issued the stock.

Dec. 31 The Income Summary account for 1990 had a $125,000 credit balance before being closed to Retained Earnings; no dividends were declared on either the common or preferred stocks.

1991
June 4 Issued 100,000 shares of common stock for $15 per share.

Dec. 10 Declared dividends payable on January 10, 1992, as follows:

To preferred shareholders for 1990 . .	$120,000
To preferred shareholders for 1991 . .	120,000
To common shareholders for 1991. . .	300,000

31 The Income Summary account for 1991 had a $1,000,000 credit balance before being closed to Retained Earnings.

Solution to Demonstration Problem

1990					
Jan	1	Cash.	2,400,000.00	
		Common Stock		2,400,000.00
		Issued 200,000 shares of common stock.		
	1	Building	820,000.00	
		Merchandise Inventory.	380,000.00	
		Common Stock		1,200,000.00
		Issued 100,000 shares of common stock.		
	1	Subscriptions Receivable	1,800,000.00	
		Common Stock Subscribed.		1,800,000.00
		Accepted subscriptions for 150,000 shares of common stock.		
	1	Organization Costs.	100,000.00	
		Cash		100,000.00
		Reimbursed the founders for organization costs.		
	1	Cash.	1,320,000.00	
		Preferred Stock		1,320,000.00
		Issued 12,000 shares of preferred stock.		
Apr.	1	Cash.	1,800,000.00	
		Subscriptions Receivable.		1,800,000.00
		Collected balance due on subscribed common stock.		
	1	Common Stock Subscribed	1,800,000.00	
		Common Stock		1,800,000.00
		Issued 150,000 shares of subscribed common stock.		
Dec.	31	Income Summary.	125,000.00	
		Retained Earnings.		125,000.00
		To close the Income Summary account and update Retained Earnings.		
1991				
June	4	Cash.	1,500,000.00	
		Common Stock		1,500,000.00
		Issued 100,000 shares of common stock.		

Dec.	10	Retained Earnings	540,000.00	
		Dividends Payable, Common Stock		300,000.00
		Dividends Payable, Preferred Stock		240,000.00
		Declared current dividends and dividends in arrears to common and preferred shareholders, payable on January 10, 1992.		
	31	Income Summary	1,000,000.00	
		Retained Earnings		1,000,000.00
		To close the Income Summary account and update Retained Earnings.		

Balance Sheet Presentations

	As of 31/12/90	As of 31/12/91
Assets:		
Organization costs	$ 90,000	$ 80,000
Liabilities:		
Dividends payable, common stock		$ 300,000
Dividends payable, preferred stock		240,000
Total liabilities		$ 540,000
Shareholders' equity:		
Contributed capital:		
Preferred stock, no par value, $10, cumulative dividend, 100,000 shares authorized, 12,000 shares issued	$1,320,000	$1,320,000
Common stock, no par value, unlimited number of shares authorized, 450,000 shares issued in 1990, and 550,000 shares in 1991	$5,400,000	$6,900,000
Total contributed capital	$6,720,000	$8,220,000
Retained earnings (see Note 1)	125,000	585,000
Total shareholders' equity	$6,845,000	$8,805,000

Note 1: As of December 31, 1990, there were $120,000 of dividends in arrears on the cumulative preferred stock.

Glossary

Define or explain the words and phrases listed in the chapter Glossary. (L. O. 6)

Book value of a share of stock the equity of one share of outstanding stock in the issuing corporation's net assets as recorded in the corporation's accounts. p. 688

Callable preferred stock preferred stock that the issuing corporation, at its option, may retire by paying to the shareholders the redemption value of the stock plus any dividends in arrears. p. 688

Call price of preferred stock another name for *redemption value*. p. 688

Common stock stock of a corporation that has only one class of stock, or if there is more than one class, the class that has no preferences relative to the corporation's other classes of stock. p. 679

Common Stock Subscribed a shareholders' equity account in which a corporation records the subscription value of unissued common stock that investors have contracted to purchase. p. 681

Convertible preferred stock preferred stock that, at the option of the shareholder, may be exchanged for a fixed number of the issuing corporation's common shares. p. 687

Cumulative preferred stock preferred stock that has the right to receive all preferred dividends including undeclared dividends from past years before outstanding common shares can receive any dividend. p. 684

Dividend in arrears a dividend to cumulative preferred stock which remains unpaid after the date for payment called for in the corporate charter. p. 684

Financial leverage increasing the return to common stock as a result of paying preferred shareholders or creditors a given dividend or interest rate that is less than the rate earned from using the assets received by the corporation from the preferred shareholders or creditors. p. 687

Noncumulative preferred stock a preferred stock for which the right to receive dividends is forfeited in any year in which dividends are not declared. p. 684

No-par stock a class of stock that does not have an arbitrary (par) value placed on the stock at the time the stock is first authorized. p. 682

Organization costs costs of bringing a corporation into existence, such as legal fees, promoters' fees, and amounts paid to incorporate the business. p. 673

Participating preferred stock preferred stock that has the right to share in dividends above the fixed amount or percentage that is preferred. p. 685

Par value an arbitrary value placed on a share of stock at the time the stock is authorized. p. 682

Preemptive right the right of common shareholders to protect their proportionate interests in a corporation by having the first opportunity to purchase additional shares of common stock issued by the corporation. p. 683

Preferred stock stock the owners of which are granted a priority status over common shareholders in one or more ways such as in the payment of dividends or in the distribution of assets upon liquidation. p. 684

Premium on stock the difference between the par value of stock and the amount contributed by shareholders when the amount contributed is more than par value. p. 682

Proxy a legal document that gives an agent of a shareholder the right to vote the shareholder's shares. p. 674

Redemption value of preferred stock the amount a corporation must pay in addition to dividends in arrears if and when it exercises its right to retire a share of callable preferred stock. p. 688

Stated value of no-par stock the amount that is credited to the no-par stock account at the time the stock is issued. p. 682

Stock subscription a contractual commitment by an investor to purchase unissued shares of stock and become a shareholder. p. 680

Questions for Class Discussion

1. What are the advantages and disadvantages of the corporate form of business organization?
2. Why is the income of a corporation said to be taxed twice?
3. Who is responsible for directing the affairs of a corporation?
4. Who serves as the chief executive officer of a corporation?
5. What is a proxy?
6. What are organization costs? List several.
7. How are organization costs classified on the balance sheet?
8. What are the duties and responsibilities of a corporation's registrar and transfer agent?
9. List the general rights of common shareholders.
10. What is the preemptive right of common shareholders?
11. Laws place no limit on the amounts partners may withdraw from a partnership. On the other hand, laws regulating corporations place definite limits on the amount of dividends shareholders may withdraw from a corporation. Why is there a difference?
12. What is a stock premium?
13. In what account would you record a premium on common stock?
14. Does a corporation earn a profit by selling its stock at a premium?
15. What is stated value of no-par-value stock?
16. What is the main advantage of no-par stock?
17. What distinguishes preferred stock from common stock?
18. What is the difference between cumulative and noncumulative preferred stock?
19. What is the difference between participating and nonparticipating preferred stock?
20. What are the balance sheet classifications of the accounts: (*a*) Subscriptions Receivable, Common Stock and (*b*) Common Stock Subscribed?

21. What is the difference between the par value and redemption value of callable preferred stock?
22. What is the difference between the market value and book value of a stock?

Multiple Choice

1. An advantage of the corporate form of organization is:
   a. The ease of organization.
   b. That shareholders have a mutual agency relationship with the corporation.
   c. The ease of capital assembly.
   d. The lack of governmental regulation compared to single proprietorships and partnerships.
   e. The method of taxation.

2. A contractual commitment to purchase unissued shares of stock and become a shareholder is a:
   a. Proxy.
   b. Preemptive right.
   c. Stock subscription.
   d. Preferred stock.
   e. Promissory note.

3. Iota Corporation accepted subscriptions to 5,000 shares of $10 par value common stock at $84 per share. A 10% down payment was made at the time of the subscription contract, and the balance was to be paid in full six months later. The entries to record receipt of the final balance and the issuance of the stock would include:
   a. A debit to Subscriptions Receivable, Common Stock for $378,000.
   b. A credit to Subscriptions Receivable, Common Stock for $420,000.
   c. A debit to Common Stock Subscribed for $420,000.
   d. A credit to Contributed Capital in Excess of Par Value, Common Stock for $333,000.
   e. A credit to Common Stock for $50,000.

4. Jinn Corporation has shareholders' equity as follows:

Preferred stock, $5, cumulative and nonparticipating, 10,000 shares authorized, 5,000 shares issued and outstanding	$750,000
Common stock, unlimited number of shares authorized, 15,000 shares issued and outstanding . .	$700,000
Total contributed capital	$1,450,000
Retained earnings	700,000
Total shareholders equity	$2,150,000

Dividends have not been declared for the past two years, but in the third year, Jinn Corporation declared $160,000 of dividends distributable to both preferred and common shareholders. Determine the amount of dividends to be paid the common shareholders.

a. $ 50,000.
b. $160,000.
c. $ 75,000.
d. $ 85,000.
e. $135,000.

5. Raysome, Inc.'s callable preferred stock has a redemption value of $90 plus any dividends in arrears. The shareholders' equity of the company is as follows:

Preferred stock, $75 par value, 10%, cumulative and nonparticipating, 5,000 shares authorized, 1,000 issued and outstanding (dividends are in arrears for two years)	$ 75,000	
Contributed capital in excess of par value, preferred stock	5,000	
Total capital contributed by preferred shareholders . . .		$ 80,000
Common stock, $20 par value, 50,000 shares authorized, 12,000 shares issued and outstanding . .	$240,000	
Contributed capital in excess of par value, common stock	60,000	
Total capital contributed by common shareholders . . .		300,000
Total contributed capital		$380,000
Retained earnings		145,000
Total shareholders' equity		$525,000

The book values per share of the preferred and common shares are:

a. Preferred shares, $105.00; common shares, $35.00.
b. Preferred shares, $ 75.00; common shares, $37.50.
c. Preferred shares, $ 90.00; common shares, $36.25.
d. Preferred shares, $ 80.00; common shares, $27.08.
e. Preferred shares, $ 95.00; common shares, $25.83.

6. X Corporation has outstanding 1,000 shares of $10, preferred stock issued at $100 per share and 6,000 shares of common stock issued at $20 per share. X Corporation paid out dividends for the last four years as follows: 198A, $9,000; 198B, $10,000; 198C, $17,000; 198D, $33,000. If the preferred stock is cumulative and fully participating based on percentage of stated capital, the allocation of 198B dividends between preferred and common stock is:

a. $0 preferred, $10,000 common.
b. $1,429 preferred, $7,571 common.
c. $4,545 preferred, $4,455 common.
d. $10,000 preferred, $0 common.
e. None of the above.

7. Mark Company's shareholders' equity section of its year-end balance sheet is as follows:

Preferred stock, $9, cumulative and nonparticipating, 2000 shares outstanding . .	$212,000
Common stock, 50,000 shares outstanding . . .	$530,000
Total contributed capital	$742,000
Retained earnings	$200,000
Total shareholders' equity	$942,000

The preferred stock has one year of dividends in arrears and a redemption value of $107. The book value per common share is:

a. $14.32.

b. $14.60.

c. $14.20.

d. $10.60.

e. Some other amount.

Mini Discussion Case

Case 15–1

James Service operated the Dawson Inn Motel and Restaurant as a sole proprietorship for five years. The business was successful, and he had two modest expansions since starting.

Service had reached a level of operation that required a major decision of sell or expand. After much deliberation and consultation with a close friend, Service decided to undertake a major expansion. Prior to proceeding with the expansion, he incorporated the business.

Carrying the plans for the expansion under his arm, he set out to keep an appointment with his banker. Service was somewhat annoyed with the banker's apparent lack of interest in the plans. It appeared to Service that the banker was more interested in obtaining Service's and his wife's personal guarantees for the required loan than in his plans. On returning home he remarked to his wife that he couldn't understand the banker's attitude—in prior borrowings the banker had never asked for any sort of guarantees.

Required:

Discuss the banker's attitude.

Exercises

Exercise 15–1
Recording issuances of stock
(L. O. 2)

Prepare general journal entries on November 12 to record the following issuances of stock by various corporations:

1. One hundred shares of no-par-value common stock are issued for $30,000 cash.

2. One thousand shares of no-par common stock are issued to promoters in exchange for their efforts in organizing the corporation. The promoters' efforts are estimated to be worth $11,500.

3. Assume the same facts as in (2) above, except that the stock has a $10 par value.

Exercise 15–2
Comparative entries for partnership and corporation
(L. O. 1, 2)

Jack Hunt and Dana Blake begin a new business on January 7 by investing $85,000 each in the company. Assume that on December 24, it is decided that $22,000 of the company's cash will be distributed equally between the owners. Cheques for $11,000 are prepared and given to the owners on December 29. On December 31, the company reports a $30,000 net income. Prepare journal entries to record the investments by the owners, the distribution of cash to the owners, and the closing of the Income Summary account assuming: (a) the business is a partnership between equal partners; and (*b*) the business is a corporation that issued 1,500 shares of no-par-value common stock to each owner.

Exercise 15–3
Accounting for par and no-par stock
(L. O. 2)

On June 8, Daily Corporation sold and issued 10,000 shares of its common stock for $315,000. Give the entry to record the sale under each of the following independent assumptions: (*a*) the stock is no-par stock; (*b*) the stock has a $20 par value; and (*c*) the stock has a $30 par value.

Exercise 15–4
Stock subscriptions
(L. O. 3)

On May 13, Keefert Corporation accepted subscriptions to 30,000 shares of its no-par-value common stock at $15 per share. The subscription contracts called for one fourth of the subscription price to accompany each contract as a down payment and the balance to be paid on July 15. Give the entries to record: (*a*) the subscriptions, (*b*) the down payments, (*c*) receipt of the remaining amounts due on the subscriptions, and (*d*) issuance of the stock.

Exercise 15–5
Allocating dividends between common and cumulative preferred stock
(L. O. 4)

Farley Corporation has outstanding 15,000 shares of $4.50, cumulative and nonparticipating preferred stock and 35,000 shares of no-par-value common stock. During the first four years in its life, the corporation declared and paid the following amounts in dividends: first year, $–0–; second year, $85,000; third year, $150,000; and fourth year, $75,000. Determine the total dividends paid to each class of shareholders each year.

Exercise 15–6
Allocating dividends between common and non-cumulative preferred stock
(L. O. 4)

Refer to the facts presented in Exercise 15–5 and determine the total dividends paid to each class of shareholders assuming the preferred stock is noncumulative.

Exercise 15–7
Allocating dividends between common and participating preferred stock
(L. O. 4)

Ewing Corporation has outstanding 15,000 shares of $4, cumulative and fully participating (as a percentage of stated value) preferred stock issued at $50 per share and 50,000 shares of common stock issued at $10 per share. It has regularly paid all dividends on the preferred stock. This year the board of directors declared and paid a total of $150,000 in dividends to the two classes of shareholders. Determine the percentage of stated value each class of shareholders received this year and the dividend per share paid to each class.

Exercise 15–8
Effect of preferred stock on rates of return
(L. O. 4)

Four individuals have agreed to begin a new business that will require a total investment of $2 million. Each of the four will contribute $300,000, and the remaining $800,000 will be raised from other investors. Two alternative plans for raising the money are being considered: (1) issue at $100 per share common stock to all investors, or (2) issue at $100 per share common stock to the four founders and at $100 per share, $9, preferred stock to the remaining investors. In either case, all of the shares will be issued at $100. If the business is expected to earn an after-tax net income of $250,000, which of the two plans will provide the highest return to the four founders? What rate of return will the founders earn under each alternative?

Exercise 15–9
Effect of preferred stock on rates of return
(L. O. 4)

What would be your answer to Exercise 15–8 if the business is expected to earn an annual, after-tax net income of only $150,000?

Exercise 15–10
Book value per share of stock
(L. O. 5)

The shareholders' equity section from Tingle Corporation's balance sheet is as follows:

Shareholders' Equity

Preferred stock, $10, cumulative and nonparticipating, $105 redemption value, 5,000 shares issued and outstanding	$ 500,000
Common stock, no-par value, 90,000 shares issued and outstanding	900,000
Retained earnings.	400,000
Total shareholders' equity.	$1,800,000

Required

1. Determine the book value per share of the preferred stock and of the common stock under the assumption there are no dividends in arrears on the preferred stock.
2. Determine the book value per share for each kind of stock under the assumption that two years' dividends are in arrears on the preferred stock.

Problems

Problem 15–1
Stock subscriptions
(L. O. 2, 3)

Leotine Corporation is authorized to issue 20,000 shares of $10 cumulative and nonparticipating preferred stock and an unlimited number of shares of no-par-value common stock. Leotine Corporation then completed these transactions:

Aug. 6   Accepted subscriptions to 150,000 shares of common stock at $20 per share. Down payments equal to 20% of the subscription price accompanied each subscription.

15   Gave the corporation's promoters 4,000 shares of common stock for their services in getting the corporation organized. The board valued the services at $75,000.

Sept. 4   Accepted subscriptions to 10,000 shares of preferred stock at $130 per share. The subscriptions were accompanied by 40% down payments.

10   Collected the balance due on the August 6 common stock subscriptions and issued the stock.

30   Accepted subscriptions to 5,000 shares of preferred stock at $120 per share. The subscriptions were accompanied by 40% down payments.

Oct. 9   Collected the balance due on the September 4 preferred stock subscriptions and issued the stock.

Required

1. Prepare general journal entries to record the transactions.
2. Prepare the contributed capital section of the corporation's balance sheet as of the close of business on October 9.

Settliff Company is authorized by its charter to issue an unlimited number of shares of no-par-value common stock and 35,000 shares of $11, cumulative and nonparticipating preferred stock. The company completed the following transactions:

1989

June   6   Issued 35,000 shares of common stock at $10 per share for cash.
       29   Gave the corporation's promoters 4,500 shares of common stock for their services in getting the corporation organized. The directors valued the services at $50,000.
July   2   Exchanged 90,000 shares of common stock for the following assets at fair market values: land, $200,000; buildings, $420,000; and machinery, $300,000.
Dec. 31   Closed the Income Summary account. A $50,000 loss was incurred.

1990

Jan. 24   Issued 2,500 shares of preferred stock at $100 per share.
Feb. 20   Accepted subscriptions to 7,000 shares of common stock at $15.20 per share. Down payments of 30% accompanied the subscription contracts.
Dec. 31   Closed the Income Summary account. A $175,000 net income was earned.

1991

Jan.   3   The board of directors declared an $11 per share dividend to preferred shares and $0.70 per share to outstanding common shares, payable on February 3 to the January 24 shareholders of record.
Feb.   3   Paid the previously declared dividends.
May 20   Settliff Company's $100,000 note payable (plus interest of $7,500) was due and payable on this date. The interest had already been credited to Interest Payable. The lender accepted 10,500 shares of Setliff's common stock in payment of this note and accrued interest.
Dec. 31   Closed the Dividends Declared and Income Summary accounts. A $275,000 net income was earned.

Required

1. Prepare general journal entries to record the transactions.
2. Prepare the shareholders' equity section of a balance sheet as of the close of business on December 31, 1991.

Part 1.   The balance sheet of Romero Services Corporation includes the following information:

Shareholders' Equity

Preferred stock, $10, cumulative and nonparticipating, 2,000 shares authorized and issued	$200,000
Common stock, no-par value, unlimited number of shares authorized and 50,000 shares issued	500,000
Retained earnings	150,000
Total shareholders' equity	$850,000

Required

Assume that the preferred stock has a redemption value of $106 plus any dividends in arrears. Calculate the book value per share of the preferred and common stocks under each of the following assumptions:

a. There are no dividends in arrears on the preferred stock.

b. One year's dividends are in arrears on the preferred stock.

c. Three years' dividends are in arrears on the preferred stock.

Part 2.   Since its organization, Transom Corporation has had outstanding 5,000 shares of $12, preferred stock issued at $100 per share and 75,000 shares of common stock issued at $10 per share. No dividends have been paid this year, and none were paid during either of the past two years. However, the company has recently prospered, and the board of directors wants to know how much cash will be required for dividends if a $2.30 per share dividend is paid on the common stock.

Required

Prepare a schedule that shows the amounts of cash required for dividends to each class of shareholders under each of the following assumptions:

a. The preferred stock is noncumulative and nonparticipating.

b. The preferred stock is cumulative and nonparticipating.

c. The preferred stock is cumulative and fully participating as a percentage of stated value.

d. The preferred stock is cumulative and participating to 14% of stated value.

Problem 15–4
Allocating dividends in sequential years between preferred and common stock
(L. O. 4)

Cummings Credit Company has outstanding 3,000 shares of $11, preferred stock issued at $100 per share and 70,000 shares of common stock issued at $10 per share. During a seven-year period, the company paid out the following amounts in dividends: 1987, $–0–; 1988, $50,000; 1989, $–0–; 1990, $55,000; 1991, $67,000; 1992, $70,000; and 1993, $150,000.

Required

1. Prepare three schedules with columnar headings as follows:

Year	Calculations	Preferred Dividend per Share	Common Dividend per Share

2. Complete a schedule under each of the following assumptions. There
    were no dividends in arrears for the years prior to 1987. (Round your
    answers to the nearest penny.)
    a. The preferred stock is noncumulative and nonparticipating.
    b. The preferred stock is cumulative and nonparticipating.
    c. The preferred stock is cumulative and fully participating (based on
        percentage of stated value).

Problem 15–5
Calculation of book values
(L. O. 5)

Fredrick Corporation's common stock is selling on a stock exchange today at
$28.75 per share, and a just-published balance sheet shows the shareholders'
equity of the corporation as follows:

Shareholders' Equity

Preferred stock, $8.50, cumulative and nonparticipating,	
4,000 shares authorized and outstanding	$ 400,000
Common stock, unlimited number of shares authorized, 10,000 . .	
shares outstanding	1,000,000
Retained earnings	476,000
Total shareholders' equity	$1,876,000

Required

Answer these questions: (1) What is the market value of the corporation's
common stock? (2) What are the par values of its (a) preferred stock and
(b) common stock? (3) If there are no dividends in arrears, what are the book
values of the (a) preferred stock and (b) common stock? (4) If two years' dividends are in arrears on the preferred stock, what are the book values of the
(a) preferred stock and (b) common stock? (Assume the preferred stock is not
callable.)

Alternate Problems

Problem 15–1A
Stock subscriptions
(L. O. 2, 3)

Zanobia Corporation is authorized to issue 15,000 shares of $10, cumulative
and nonparticipating preferred stock and an unlimited number of shares of
no-par-value common stock. Zanobia Corporation then completed these
transactions:

May   6   Accepted subscriptions to 95,000 shares of common stock at $15 per
          share. Down payments equal to 30% of the subscription price ac-
          companied each subscription.

     10   Gave the corporation's promoters 2,500 shares of common stock for
          their services in getting the corporation organized. The board val-
          ued the services at $45,000.

June 5   Accepted subscriptions to 6,000 shares of preferred stock at $110
          per share. The subscriptions were accompanied by 50% down pay-
          ments.

      8   Collected the balance due on the May 6 common stock subscrip-
          tions and issued the stock.

     29   Accepted subscriptions to 3,000 shares of preferred stock at $105
          per share. The subscriptions were accompanied by 50% down pay-
          ments.

July 12   Collected the balance due on the June 5 preferred stock subscriptions and issued the stock.

Required

1. Prepare general journal entries to record the transactions.
2. Prepare the contributed capital section of the corporation's balance
    sheet as of the close of business on July 12.

Problem 15–2A
Shareholders' equity
transactions
(L. O. 2, 3, 4)

Hernandez Company is authorized to issue an unlimited number of shares
of no-par-value common stock and 45,000 shares of $12, cumulative and nonparticipating preferred stock. The company completed the following
transactions:

1989
Apr. 5   Issued 125,000 shares of common stock at $1 per share for cash.
     28   Gave the corporation's promoters 80,000 shares of common stock
          for their services in getting the corporation organized. The directors
          valued the services at $175,000.
May   7   Exchanged 200,000 shares of common stock for the following assets
          at fair market values: land, $85,000; buildings, $200,000; and machinery, $325,000.
Dec. 31   Closed the Income Summary account. A $90,000 loss was incurred.

1990
Jan. 15   Issued 4,000 shares of preferred stock at $100 per share.
Mar. 20   Accepted subscriptions to 40,000 shares of common stock at $1.90
          per share. Down payments of 25% accompanied the subscription
          contracts.
Dec. 31   Closed the Income Summary account. A $250,000 net income was
          earned.

1991
Jan. 9   The board of directors declared a $12 per share dividend to preferred shares and $0.20 per share to outstanding common shares,
          payable on January 22 to the January 15 shareholders of record.
     22   Paid the previously declared dividends.
Mar. 13   Hernandez Company's $40,000 note payable (plus interest of
          $2,500) was due and payable on this date. The interest had already
          been credited to Interest Payable. The lender accepted 25,000
          shares of Hernandez's common stock in payment of this note and
          accrued interest.
Dec. 31   Closed the Dividends Declared and Income Summary accounts. A
          $250,000 net income was earned.

Required

1. Prepare general journal entries to record the transactions.
2. Prepare the shareholders' equity section of a balance sheet as of the
    close of business on December 31, 1991.

Problem 15–3A
Calculating book values; allocating dividends between preferred and common stock
(L. O. 4, 5)

Part 1. The balance sheet of World Boat Charters Corporation includes the following information:

Shareholders' Equity

Preferred stock, $9, cumulative and nonparticipating, 3,500 shares authorized and issued	$ 350,000
Common stock, unlimited number of shares authorized, 70,000 . . . shares issued	700,000
Retained earnings	80,000
Total shareholders' equity	$1,130,000

Required

Assume that the preferred stock has a redemption value of $105 plus any dividends in arrears. Calculate the book value per share of the preferred and common stocks under each of the following assumptions:

a. There are no dividends in arrears on the preferred stock.
b. One year's dividends are in arrears on the preferred stock.
c. Three years' dividends are in arrears on the preferred stock.

Part 2. Since its organization, Medley Corporation has had outstanding 4,800 shares of $11, preferred stock issued at $100 per share and 72,000 shares of common stock issued at $10 per share. No dividends have been paid this year, and none were paid during either of the past two years. However, the company has recently prospered and the board of directors wants to know how much cash will be required for dividends if a $1.85 per share dividend is paid on the common stock.

Required

Prepare a schedule showing the amounts of cash required for dividends to each class of shareholders under each of the following assumptions:

a. The preferred stock is noncumulative and nonparticipating.
b. The preferred stock is cumulative and nonparticipating.
c. The preferred stock is cumulative and fully participating (based on percentage of stated value).
d. The preferred stock is cumulative and participating to 14% of stated value.

Problem 15–4A
Allocating dividends in sequential years between preferred and common stock
(L. O. 4)

Kato Ranch Company has outstanding 1,500 shares of $10, preferred stock issued at $100 per share and 30,000 shares of common stock issued at $10 per share. During a seven-year period, the company paid out the following amounts in dividends: 1987, $–0–; 1988, $40,000; 1989, $–0–; 1990, $25,000; 1991, $30,000; 1992, $42,000; and 1993, $85,000.

Required

1. Prepare three schedules with columnar headings as follows:

Year	Calculations	Preferred Dividend per Share	Common Dividend per Share

2. Complete a schedule under each of the following assumptions. There were no dividends in arrears for the years prior to 1987. (Round your calculations of dividends per share to the nearest penny.)
   a. The preferred stock is noncumulative and nonparticipating.
   b. The preferred stock is cumulative and nonparticipating.
   c. The preferred stock is cumulative and fully participating (based on percentage of stated value).

Problem 15–5A
Calculation of book values
(L. O. 5)

Lanno Corporation's common stock is selling on a stock exchange today at $20.25 per share, and a just-published balance sheet shows the shareholders' equity in the corporation as follows:

Shareholders' Equity

Preferred stock, $9.80, cumulative and nonparticipating, 3,200 shares authorized and outstanding	$ 320,000
Common stock, unlimited number of shares authorized and 85,000 shares outstanding	850,000
Retained earnings	275,000
Total shareholders' equity	$1,445,000

Required

Answer these questions: (1) What is the market value of the corporation's common stock? (2) What are the average stated values of its (*a*) preferred stock and (*b*) common stock? (3) If there are no dividends in arrears, what are the book values of the (*a*) preferred stock and (*b*) common stock? (4) If two years' dividends are in arrears on the preferred stock, what are the book values of the (*a*) preferred stock and (*b*) common stock? (Assume the preferred stock is not callable.)

Provocative Problems

Provocative Problem 15–1
X-L Sports, Inc.
(L. O. 1, 2)

Jae Xu and Bob Lyle have operated a sports equipment company, X-L Sports, for a number of years as partners sharing net incomes and gains in a 3 to 2 ratio. Because the business is growing, the two partners entered into an agreement with Tom Celic to reorganize their firm into a corporation. The new corporation, X-L Sports, Inc., is authorized to issue 75,000 shares of no-par-value common stock. On the date of the reorganization, August 15, 1990, a trial balance of the partnership ledger appears as follows:

X-L SPORTS
Trial Balance
August 15, 1990

Cash	$ 38,255	
Accounts receivable	69,750	
Allowance for doubtful accounts		$ 2,625
Merchandise inventory.	316,875	
Store equipment	73,500	
Accumulated depreciation, store equipment . .		15,750
Buildings	375,000	
Accumulated depreciation, buildings		75,000
Land	93,750	
Accounts payable		41,625
Notes payable		262,500
Jae Xu, capital		339,380
Bob Lyle, capital		230,250
Totals	$967,130	$967,130

The agreement between the partners and Celic carries these provisions:

1. The partnership assets are to be revalued as follows:
    a. The $2,250 account receivable of Blue Tigers is known to be uncollectible and is to be written off as a bad debt.
    b. After writing off the Blue Tigers account, the allowance for doubtful accounts is to be increased to 4% of the remaining accounts receivable.
    c. The merchandise inventory is to be written down to $285,000 to allow for damaged and shopworn goods.
    d. Insufficient depreciation has been taken on the store equipment. Therefore, its book value is to be decreased to $48,750 by increasing the balance of the accumulated depreciation account.
    e. The building is to be written up to its replacement cost, $487,500, and the balance of the accumulated depreciation account is to be increased to show the building to be one fifth depreciated.
2. After the partnership assets are revalued, the assets and liabilities are to be transferred to the corporation in exchange for its stock, with each partner accepting stock at $10 per share for his equity in the partnership.
3. Tom Celic is to buy any remaining authorized stock for cash at $10 per share.

After reaching the agreement outlined, the three principals hired you as accountant for the new corporation. Your first task is to determine the amount of stock each person should receive, and to prepare entries on the corporation's books to record the issuance of stock in exchange for the partnership's assets and liabilities and the issuance of stock to Celic for cash. In addition, prepare a balance sheet for the corporation as it should appear after all its stock is issued.

Provocative Problem 15–2
Andrews Corporation
(L. O. 4)

The management of Andrews Corporation is considering the expansion of its business operations to a new and exciting line of business in which newly invested assets can be expected to earn 20% per year. At present, Andrews Corporation has only 18,000 shares of no-par-value common stock outstanding, which was issued at $50 per share, no other contributed capital accounts, and retained earnings of $270,000. Existing operations consistently earn approximately $175,000 each year. To finance the new expansion, management is considering three alternatives: (*a*) Issue 5,000 shares of $13, cumulative, nonparticipating, nonvoting, preferred stock. The investment advisors of the company conclude that these shares could be issued at $100 per share. (*b*) Issue 2,000 shares of $100 par, 13%, cumulative, fully participating, nonvoting, preferred stock. The investment advisors conclude that these shares could be sold for $250 per share. (*c*) Issue 6,250 shares of common stock at $80 per share.

In evaluating these three alternatives, Andrews Company management asked you to calculate the dividends that would be distributed to each class of shareholder based on the assumption that each year the board of directors will declare dividends equal to the total net income earned by the corporation. Your calculations should show the distribution of dividends to preferred and common shareholders under each of the three alternative financing plans. You should also calculate dividends per share of preferred and dividends per share of common.

As a second part of your analysis, assume that you own 1,000 of the common shares outstanding prior to the expansion and that you will not acquire or purchase any of the newly issued shares. Based on your whole analysis, would you prefer that the proposed expansion in operations be rejected? If not, comment on the relative merits of each alternative from your point of view as a common shareholder.

Provocative Problem 15–3
Reinhold Corporation and Rollins Company
(L. O. 4, 5)

Having recently inherited $75,000, Brian Parker is thinking about investing the money in one of two securities. They are: Reinhold Corporation common stock or the preferred stock issued by Rollins Company. The companies manufacture and sell competing products, and both have been in business about the same length of time—four years in the case of Reinhold Corporation and five years for Rollins Company. Also, the two companies have about the same amounts of shareholders' equity, as the following equity sections from their latest balance sheets show:

REINHOLD CORPORATION

Common stock, no-par value, unlimited number of shares authorized, 5,000,000 shares issued	$5,000,000
Retained earnings	2,000,000
Total shareholders' equity	$7,000,000

ROLLINS COMPANY

Preferred stock, $100 par value, 8%, cumulative and nonparticipating, unlimited number of shares authorized, 20,000 shares issued	$2,000,000*
Common stock, no-par value, unlimited number of shares authorized, 400,000 shares issued	4,000,000
Retained earnings	200,000
Total shareholders' equity	$6,200,000

*The current and one prior year's dividends are in arrears on the preferred stock.

Reinhold Corporation did not pay a dividend on its common stock during its first year's operations; however, since then, for the past three years, it has paid a $0.20 per share annual dividend on the stock. The stock is currently selling for $1.50 per share. The preferred stock of Rollins Company, on the other hand, is selling for $95 per share. Mr. Parker favours this stock as an investment. He feels the stock is a real bargain since it is not only selling below its par value but also $21 below book value, and as he says, "Since it is a preferred stock, the dividends are guaranteed." Too, he feels the common stock of Reinhold Corporation, selling at 7% above book value and 50% above its average stated value, while paying only a $0.20 per share dividend, is overpriced.

Required

a. Is the preferred stock of Rollins Company selling at a price $21 below its book value, and is the common stock of Reinhold Corporation selling at a price 7% above book value and 50% above its average stated value?

b. From an analysis of the shareholders' equity sections, express your opinion of the two stocks as investments and describe some of the factors Mr. Parker should consider in choosing between the two securities.

Analytical and Review Problems

A&R Problem 15–1

Until March 2 of the current year, Knox, Lacy, and Mann were partners sharing losses and gains in a 5:3:2 ratio. On that date they received their certificate of incorporation of KLM Company, Limited. All the assets and liabilities of the partnership were taken over by the new corporation.

The trial balance of the partnership just before the transfer and the opening trial balance of the corporation appear below:

KNOX, LACY AND MANN
Post Closing Trial Balance
March 2, 19—

Cash.	$ 4,500	
Accounts receivable	20,500	
Allowance for doubtful accounts		$ 500
Merchandise inventory	33,000	
Store equipment	13,500	
Accumulated depreciation, store eqiupment.		3,500
Land	8,500	
Building	65,000	
Accumulated depreciation, building		9,500
Accounts payable		15,500
Mortgage payable		12,000
John Knox, capital		45,000
Robert Lacy, capital		40,000
George Mann, capital		19,000
	$145,000	$145,000

KLM COMPANY, LIMITED
Trial Balance
March 2, 19—

Cash	$ 4,500	
Accounts receivable	20,500	
Allowance for doubtful accounts		$ 1,500
Merchandise inventory	25,000	
Store equipment	8,000	
Land	22,000	
Building	52,000	
Accounts payable		15,500
Mortgage payable		12,000
Share capital, common, no par value 20,600 shares . .		103,000
	$132,000	$132,000

Required

1. Journal entries to close the books of the partnership and to open the books of the corporation.

2. What is the value of shares received by each of three shareholders?

3. How many shares did each shareholder receive?

A&R Problem 15–2

During the first year after incorporation, the following transactions affecting shareholders' equity were completed:

a. Immediately after incorporation sold 50,000 shares at $40 per share for cash.

b. Near mid-year received a subscription for 1,000 shares at $30 per share, collected 50% in cash, balance due in two equal installments within one year.

c. Two months later issued 500 shares for a used machine that would be used in operations. The machine had cost $20,000 new and was carried by the seller at a book value of $13,000. It was appraised at $16,000 six months previously by a reputable independent appraiser.

d. Collected half of the unpaid subscriptions in (b).

Required
Give entries for each of the above transactions.

A&R Problem 15–3

Section 39 of the Canada Business Corporations Act states in part:

> The directors acting in good faith and with a view to the best interests of a corporation may authorize the corporation to pay a commission to any person in consideration of his purchasing or agreeing to purchase shares of the corporation from the corporation.

Required
Draft a letter to the minister in charge of administering the Act, criticizing the provision with respect to accounting implications.

After 10 years in the Navy, Gerald Labonte decided not to reenlist. He located in Windsor, Ontario, and began looking for opportunities. By accident he discovered that an unfilled demand by farmers existed for a prepackaged variety of standard-sized nuts and bolts. After an initial market testing in various parts of Essex and Kent Counties, Mr. Labonte was convinced he had found his niche. He incorporated Continental Bolt Company, Limited, and recruited a cadre of commission salesmen throughout the country. The business proved to be in instant success.

However, the more the sales increased and, of course, profit, the more was Mr. Labonte's need for cash. It got to the point of Mr. Labonte remarking, "I am going broke while making a profit." He was so desperate for cash that he sold to Mr. Balzeg a 10% interest for the equivalent of 1/10 of the then annual net income. One year later he could not stand Mr. Balzeg's questioning of his policies. Consequently, he offered and Mr. Balzeg accepted a sum five times what Mr. Balzeg originally paid for his shares. The company was an instant success, at least on paper. Mr Labonte hocked everything he could lay his hands on and then some. He even pledged his house for a bank loan to the company.

A year after Mr. Labonte started the Canadian Company, he incorporated one in the United States. Sales were growing at a 25% annual rate, and the relationship of net income to sales continued at 10%. These rates of growth and profitability were expected to continue over the next few years. All earnings were reinvested in the business.

In the midst of this success, bankers and suppliers were growing more and more uneasy. It was taking Mr. Labonte longer and longer to pay supplier accounts, and interest on outstanding bank loans was being paid out of proceeds of new loans. Mr. Labonte realized that he was nearing the end of his juggling act and that he had to get long-term financing. The condensed financial statements are presented below:

CONTINENTAL BOLT COMPANY, LIMITED
Condensed Balance Sheet
December 31, 199A

Cash	$ 200
Accounts receivable (net)	105,000
Inventory	105,000
Other assets	25,300
	$235,500
Accounts payable	$ 26,250
Bank loans (demand) payable	116,000
Share capital	7,000
Retained earnings	86,250
	$235,500

CONTINENTAL BOLT COMPANY, LIMITED
Condensed Income Statement
For the Year Ended December 31, 199A

Sales	$420,000
Cost of sales	210,000
	210,000
Expenses, including income taxes	168,000
Net income	$ 42,000

Required

Focus on Mr. Labonte's remark: "I am going broke while making a profit." Using the financial statements given in the case, discuss the basis for support or prove Mr. Labonte's remark to be erroneous. Your answer should be supported by projected balance sheets and income statements through at least December 31, 199D. In preparing the projected statements assume that (*a*) sales will increase at 25% per annum and net income will remain constant as a percentage of sales (10%); (*b*) receivables, inventory, and payables will grow at the same rate as sales (25% per annum); (*c*) the amount of other assets are expected to increase at a 50% annual rate; (*d*) no dividends will be declared; (*e*) the bank will not permit the loan to exceed $120,000; and (*f*) the amount of cash (could be negative) is the variable necessary to balance; if negative, additional borrowing required to have at least a zero balance in the cash account.

A&R Problem 15–5

This problem continues the case of Continental Bolt Company, Limited. As best as Mr. Labonte could figure out, in the next two years he needed to raise $200,000 to substantially eliminate the bank loan and provide an adequate cash balance. To provide for growth for the following five-year period (total of seven years from now) and the anticipated more rapid growth of the U.S. market, Mr. Labonte decided to aim at raising $500,000. The amount would replace the bank loan and provide for the necessary working capital.

What appears to be excess cash in the earlier years would in fact be required to partially finance the expanded operations and accommodate purchasing arrangements with new suppliers. It was intended that large lots of product would be purchased principally from Japanese suppliers at a substantial saving. The "catch" was that payment had to be made at the time shipment was made, and shipping time was three to five months. Consequently, inventory turnover would be reduced from the current twice a year to once a year.

Once he had this plan formulated, he approached Michael Brown, professor of business administration, at the University of Southwestern Ontario, with an invitation to serve on the board of directors. Dr. Brown accepted, and the two started to set out alternatives to raise the necessary capital. At first they thought of approaching Eric Denham, a wealthy manufacturer, who was just "itching" to get back into the swing of things. He was forced to retire at age 55 as chairman of the board of DKS, Limited, an auto parts manufacturer, in which he held a 38% interest. Two alternatives that would be presented to him were as follows:

1. A straight loan of $500,000 for 10 years at 15% (the same rate the bank charged on the current loan).
2. A loan of $200,000 for 10 years at 15% and $300,000 for 40% interest in Continental Bolt common stock (class B).

The price for the common shares in the second alternative had been determined using what Dr. Brown and Mr. Labonte considered to be a conservative price/earnings multiple based on the projected income for the first year after the financing.

Another proposal was to approach underwriters to arrange for an issue of $200,000 of 12% nonvoting preferred stock (class A) and $300,000 of common stock (class B). The common stock issue would represent 40% of the total common stock outstanding after the issue. In making calculations of the implications of these proposals, Brown prepared the following pro forma partial income statement:

CONTINENTAL BOLT COMPANY, LIMITED
Pro Forma Income Statement
For the First Year after Financing

Sales	$800,000
Cost of sales	360,000
	440,000
Expenses, excluding interest charges and income taxes*	220,000
	$220,000

*Income tax rate is expected to average 40%.

Assume that Retained Earnings at the beginning of the year covered by the pro forma income statement were estimated at $200,000 and the bank loan was fully repaid out of the proceeds of new financing.

Required

1. For each of the proposals, calculate the return on the ending common (class B) shareholders' equity and indicate, giving your reasons, which proposal you would recommend to Mr. Labonte.

2. Which of the two alternatives is Eric Denham likely to prefer, if either? Explain your thinking.

3. Discuss some of the problems that you think might be encountered in attempting to locate a willing underwriter for the latter proposal given the size and nature of the issue.

16 Additional Corporate Transactions; Reporting Income and Retained Earnings; Earnings per Share

This chapter begins with a discussion of dividends and other transactions between a corporation and its shareholders. In this section of the chapter, you will learn about stock dividends, stock splits, and repurchases of stock by the issuing corporation. The second section of the chapter explains how income and retained earnings information is classified and reported. The third section explains how accountants report the earnings per share of a corporation. Your understanding of these topics will help you be able to interpret and evaluate corporate financial statements.

Learning Objectives

After studying Chapter 16, you should be able to:

1. Record cash dividends, stock dividends, and stock splits and explain their effects on the assets and shareholders' equity of a corporation.

2. Record purchases and sales of treasury stock and retirements of stock and describe their effects on shareholders' equity.

3. Describe restrictions and appropriations of retained earnings and the disclosure of such items in the financial statements.

4. Explain how the income effects of discontinued operations, extraordinary items, changes in accounting principles, and prior period adjustments are reported.

5. Calculate earnings per share for companies with simple capital structures and explain the difference between primary and fully diluted earnings per share.

6. Define or explain the words and phrases listed in the chapter Glossary.

CORPORATE DIVIDENDS AND OTHER STOCK TRANSACTIONS

In Chapter 3, we first described a corporation's retained earnings as the total amount of its net incomes less its net losses and dividends declared since it began operations. Years ago, retained earnings were commonly called **earned surplus.** However, the term is rarely used anymore.

Retained Earnings and Dividends

Record cash dividends, stock dividends, and stock splits and explain their effects on the assets and shareholders' equity of a corporation.
(L. O. 1)

Most jurisdictions require that a corporation cannot pay cash dividends unless retained earnings are available. However, the payment of a cash dividend reduces both cash and shareholders' equity. Therefore, a corporation cannot pay a cash dividend simply because it has a credit balance in Retained Earnings; it also must have enough cash on hand to pay the dividend. If cash or assets that will shortly become cash are not available, a board of directors may choose to avoid a dividend declaration even though the Retained Earnings balance is adequate. Even if a corporation has a large Retained Earnings balance, the board of directors may refuse to declare a dividend because the available cash is needed in the operations of the business.

In deciding whether to declare dividends, a board of directors must recognize that operating activities are a source of cash. Perhaps some cash from operating activities should be paid out in dividends and some should be retained for emergencies. In addition, some cash may be retained to pay dividends in years when current operating activities do not generate enough cash to pay normal dividends. Furthermore, management may want to retain some cash from operating activities to finance expanded operations.

As was noted in Chapter 15, shareholders enjoy limited liability. Consequently, corporation laws provide for the protection of creditors and others dependent on the continuity of the corporation. To this end, the more recently passed corporations acts include a solvency test. For example, the Canada Business Corporation Act 1975 provides in section 40 that:

> A corporation shall not declare or pay a dividend if there are responsible grounds for believing that
> (*a*) the corporation is, or would after the payment be, unable to pay its liabilities as they become due; or
> (*b*) the realizable value of the corporation's assets would thereby be less than the aggregate of its liabilities and stated capital of all classes.

Entries for the declaration and distribution of a cash dividend were presented on page 678 and need not be repeated here. It should be noted that asset distributions in excess of a credit balance in Retained Earnings are liquidating dividends—a return of original investment.

Stock Dividends

Sometimes, a corporation will distribute additional shares of its own stock to its shareholders without receiving any consideration from the shareholders. This type of distribution is called a **stock dividend.** You should understand that a stock dividend and a cash dividend are very different. A cash dividend transfers assets from the corporation to the shareholders. As a result, a cash dividend reduces the corporation's assets and its shareholders' equity. On the other hand, a stock dividend does not transfer assets from the corporation to the shareholders; it has no effect on assets and no effect on *total* shareholders' equity.

However, a stock dividend does have an effect on the *components* of shareholders' equity. To record a stock dividend, you must transfer some of the Retained Earnings balance to contributed capital accounts. For example, assume that Northwest Corporation's shareholders' equity is as follows:

Shareholder's Equity

Common stock, no-par value, unlimited number of shares authorized, 10,000 shares issued and outstanding . .	$108,000
Retained earnings.	35,000
Total shareholders' equity.	$143,000

On December 31, the directors of Northwest Corporation declared a 10% or 1,000-share stock dividend distributable on January 20 to the shareholders of record on January 15.

If the market value of Northwest Corporation's stock on December 31 is $15 per share, the dividend declaration is recorded as follows:

Dec.	31	Stock Dividends Declared.	15,000.00	
		Common Stock Dividend Distributable		15,000.00
		To record the declaration of a 1,000-share common stock dividend.		

Note that the debit is to Stock Dividends Declared. In previous chapters, when we discussed cash dividends, they were debited to Dividends Declared. However, since a corporation may declare stock dividends as well as cash dividends, a convenient system of accounts would include separate Cash Dividends Declared and Stock Dividends Declared accounts.

In the year-end closing process, the Stock Dividends Declared account is closed to Retained Earnings, as follows:

Dec.	31	Retained Earnings	15,000.00	
		Stock Dividends Declared		15,000.00

The distribution of the stock on January 20 is recorded as follows:

Jan.	20	Common Stock Dividend Distributable	15,000.00	
		Common Stock		15,000.00
		To record the distribution of a 1,000-share common stock dividend.		

Note that these entries shift $15,000 of the shareholders' equity from retained earnings to contributed capital or, in other words, $15,000 of retained earnings is *capitalized*. Note also that the amount of retained earnings capitalized is equal to the market value of the 1,000 shares issued ($15 × 1,000 shares = $15,000).[1]

As you already learned, a stock dividend does not distribute assets to the shareholders; it has no effect on the corporation's assets. Also, it has no effect on total shareholders' equity and no effect on the percentage of the company owned by each individual shareholder. To illustrate these last points, assume that Johnson owned 100 shares of Northwest Corporation's stock prior to the stock dividend. Then, the 10% stock dividend gave each shareholder 1 new share for each 10 shares previously held. Therefore, Johnson received 10 new shares.

Illustration 16–1 shows Northwest Corporation's total contributed and retained capital and the book value of Johnson's 100 shares before the dividend and after the dividend.

Illustration 16–1 shows that before the stock dividend, Johnson owned 100/10,000 or 1/100 of the Northwest Corporation stock, and his holdings had a $1,430 book value. After the dividend, he owns 110/11,000 or 1/100 of the corporation, and his holdings still have a $1,430 book value. In other words, there was no effect on Johnson's investment except that it was repackaged from 100 units into 110. Also, the only effect on the corporation's capital was a transfer of $15,000 from retained earnings to contributed capital. To summarize, there was no change in the corporation's total assets, no change in its total capital or equity, and no change in percentage of that equity owned by Johnson.

Why Stock Dividends Are Distributed

If stock dividends have no effect on corporation assets and shareholders' equities other than to repackage the equities into more units, why are such dividends declared and distributed? The primary reason for stock dividends is related to the market price of a corporation's common stock. For example, if a profitable corporation grows by retaining earnings, the price of its common stock also tends to grow. Eventually, the price of a share may become high enough to discourage some investors from buying the stock. Thus, the corporation may declare stock dividends to keep the price of its shares from increasing too much. For this reason, some corporations declare small stock dividends each year.

Some shareholders may like stock dividends for another reason. Often, corporations that declare stock dividends continue to pay the same cash dividend per share after a stock dividend as before. The result is that shareholders receive more cash each time dividends are declared.

---

[1] The Canada Business Corporations Act requires that the value of a stock dividend be added to the stated capital account. In other jurisdictions, for example, Ontario, the amount to be capitalized is left to the board of directors.

Illustration 16–1
The effect of Northwest Corporation's stock dividend on shareholders

Before the 10% stock dividend:

Common stock (10,000 shares).	$108,000
Retained earnings	35,000
Total contributed and retained capital	$143,000

$143,000 ÷ 10,000 shares outstanding = $14.30 per share book value.
$14.30 × 100 = $1,430, the book value of Johnson's 100 shares.

After the 10% stock dividend is distributed:

Common stock (11,000 shares).	$123,000
Retained earnings	20,000
Total contributed and retained capital	$143,000

$143,000 ÷ 11,000 shares outstanding = $13 per share book value.
$13 × 110 = $1,430, the book value of Johnson's 110 shares.

Amount of Retained Earnings Capitalized

If a corporation declares a **stock dividend,** the Canada Business Act requires that the corporation capitalize an amount of retained earnings that equals the market value of the shares to be distributed. A requirement to capitalize a specified amount of retained earnings is without justification. If the board of directors can decide the amount of cash dividends, then the power to decide the amount of retained earnings should also be left to their discretion. The authors therefore believe that the provision of the Ontario Corporations Act is correct. That is, the board of directors decides the amount of retained earnings to be capitalized.

Stock Dividends on the Balance Sheet

Since a stock dividend is "payable" in stock rather than in assets, it is not a liability of its issuing corporation. Therefore, if a balance sheet is prepared between the declaration and distribution dates of a stock dividend, the amount of the dividend distributable should appear on the balance sheet in the shareholders' equity section, as follows:

Common stock, no par value, unlimited number of shares authorized, 10,000 shares issued and outstanding	$108,000
Common stock dividend distributable, 1,000 shares	**15,000**
Total common stock issued and to be issued	$123,000
Retained earnings	20,000
Total shareholders' equity	$143,000

Stock Splits

Sometimes, when a corporation's stock is selling at a high price, the corporation will call it in and issue two, three, or more new shares in the place of each previously outstanding share. For example, a corporation that has outstanding stock selling for $375 a share may call in the old shares and issue to the shareholders 4 shares, or 10 shares, or any number of shares of stock in exchange for each share formerly held. In the case of par value stock, the par value of the new shares is proportionally reduced. This is known as a **stock split**. The usual purpose of a stock split is to reduce the market price of the stock and thereby facilitate trading in the stock. Less frequently than a stock split, a corporation may have a **reverse stock split**. In that case a corporation calls in the old shares and issues 1 new share for each 2 shares, 3 shares, 10 shares, or any number of shares previously held. The usual purpose of a reverse stock split is to reduce the number of shares outstanding and to cause an increase in the per share market value.

A stock split (or reverse stock split) has no effect on total shareholders' equity, the equities of the individual shareholders, or on the balances of any of the contributed or retained capital accounts. Consequently, all that is required in recording a stock split or a reverse stock split is a memorandum entry in the stock account reciting the facts of the split. For example, such a memorandum might read, ''Issued 10 new shares common stock for each old share previously outstanding.'' There would also be a change in the number of shares outstanding on the balance sheet.

Reacquisition of Shares

Under the Canada Business Corporations Act, a corporation may purchase for cancellation shares of its own outstanding stock. However, in some jurisdictions a corporation may reacquire shares of its own outstanding stock and reissue these shares at a future date. Such reacquired shares are known as **treasury stock**.

Treasury Stock

Record purchases and sales of treasury stock and retirements of stock and describe their effects on shareholders' equity. (L. O. 2)

Corporations often reacquire shares of their own stock. This is done for a variety of reasons. Some shares may be given to employees as a bonus. Others may be used to pay for the acquisition of another corporation. Sometimes, shares are repurchased to avoid a ''hostile takeover'' by an investor who seeks control of the company. Occasionally, shares are bought in order to maintain a favourable market for the stock. For example, in the 1986 annual report of W. R. Grace & Co., the chief executive officer described the reason for the company's repurchases of its stock as follows:

> The year began with the unexpected need to repurchase 13.6 million Grace common shares plus some preferred shares for nearly $600 million. This was an unplanned action made necessary when Grace's largest shareholder divested its entire holdings. And, it was done to avoid a potentially dangerous downturn in the market value of your Grace shares.

Whatever the reason, if a corporation reacquires shares of its own stock, the reacquired shares are called *treasury stock*. Treasury stock is a corporation's stock that was issued and then reacquired by the issuing corporation. Notice that the acquired stock must be the issuing corporation's own stock. The acquisition of another corporation's stock does not create treasury stock. Also, treasury stock must have been issued and then reacquired. This distinguishes treasury stock from unissued stock.

Illustration 16–2
Curry Corporation's balance sheet prior to the purchase of treasury stock

CURRY CORPORATION
Balance Sheet
May 1, 1990

Assets		Shareholders' Equity	
Cash	$ 30,000	Common stock, no-par value,	
Other assets	95,000	authorized and issued	
		10,000 shares	$100,00
		Retained earnings	25,000
Total assets.	$125,000	Total shareholders' equity.	$125,000

Although treasury stock differs from unissued stock in that it was previously issued, in other respects it has the same status as unissued stock. Neither is an asset. Both are subtracted from authorized stock to determine outstanding stock when such things as book values are calculated. Neither receives cash dividends nor has a vote in the shareholders' meetings.

Purchase of Treasury Stock[2]

When a corporation purchases its own stock, it reduces in equal amounts both its assets and its shareholders' equity. To illustrate, assume that on May 1 of the current year, the condensed balance sheet of Curry Corporation appears as in Illustration 16–2.

On May 1, Curry Corporation purchases 1,000 shares of its outstanding stock at $11.50 per share, and the transaction is recorded as follows:

May	1	Treasury Stock, Common	11,500.00	
		Cash		11,500.00
		Purchased 1,000 shares of treasury stock at $11.50 per share.		

The debit of the entry records a reduction in the equity of the shareholders. The credit records a reduction in assets. Both are equal to the cost of the treasury stock. After the entry is posted, a new balance sheet shows the reductions as in Illustration 16–3.

In Illustration 16–3, notice that the cost of the treasury stock appears in the shareholders' equity section as a deduction from common stock and retained

---

[2] There are alternate ways of accounting for treasury stock transactions. This text will discuss the so-called cost basis or single transaction method. This method is recommended by the CICA.

Illustration 16–3
Curry Corporation's balance sheet immediately after the purchase of treasury stock

CURRY CORPORATION
Balance Sheet
May 1, 1990

Assets		Shareholders' Equity	
Cash	$ 18,500	Common stock, no par value,	
Other assets	95,000	authorized and issued 10,000	
		shares of which 1,000 are in	
		the treasury	$100,000
		Retained earnings of which	
		$11,500 is restricted by the	
		purchase of treasury stock	25,000
		Total.	$125,000
		Less cost of treasury stock.	11,500
Total assets.	$113,500	Total shareholders' equity	$113,500

earnings. In comparing the two balance sheets (Illustrations 16–2 and 16–3), you can see that the treasury stock purchase reduced both assets and shareholders' equity by the $11,500 cost of the stock. Also, the amount of *issued stock* is not changed by the purchase of treasury stock. The dollar amount of issued stock remains at $100,000 and is unchanged from the first balance sheet. However, the purchase does reduce the amount of *outstanding stock*. Curry Corporation's outstanding stock was reduced from 10,000 to 9,000 shares.

There is a distinction between issued stock and outstanding stock. Issued stock may or may not be outstanding. Outstanding stock was issued and remains currently in the hands of shareholders. Only outstanding stock receives cash dividends and has a vote in the meetings of shareholders.

Restricting Retained Earnings by the Purchase of Treasury Stock

Describe restrictions and appropriations of retained earnings and the disclosure of such items in the financial statements. (L. O. 3)

The purchase of treasury stock by a corporation has the same effect on its assets and shareholders' equity as the payment of a cash dividend. Both transfer corporate assets to shareholders and thereby reduce assets and shareholders' equity. Therefore, in jurisdictions which permit treasury stock, a corporation may purchase treasury stock or it may pay cash dividends, but the sum of both cannot exceed the amount of its retained earnings available for dividends. Tests of solvency also apply.

Unlike the payment of a cash dividend, the purchase of treasury stock does not reduce the balance of the Retained Earnings account. Instead, the purchase places a restriction on the amount of retained earnings available for dividends. Note how **restricted retained earnings** are shown in Illustration 16–3. Usually, the restriction also is described in a footnote to the financial statements.

The restriction of retained earnings because of treasury stock purchases is a matter of law. Other types of legal restrictions on retained earnings may be imposed by law or by contract.

Reissuing Treasury Stock

Treasury stock may be reissued at cost, above cost, or below cost. If reissued at cost, the entry to record the transaction is the reverse of the entry used to record the purchase.

If treasury stock is sold at a price that is above cost, the amount received in excess of cost is credited to a contributed capital account called Contributed Capital, Treasury Stock Transactions. For example, if Curry Corporation sells for $12 per share 500 of the treasury shares purchased at $11.50 per share, the entry to record the transaction is as follows:

June	3	Cash	6,000.00	
		Treasury Stock, Common.		5,750.00
		Contributed Capital, Treasury Stock Transactions . . .		250.00
		Sold at $12 per share 500 treasury shares that cost $11.50 per share.		

When treasury stock is reissued at a price below cost, the entry to record the sale depends on whether there is a preexisting credit balance in the Contributed Capital, Treasury Stock Transactions account. If none exists, the amount by which sales price is less than cost is debited to Retained Earnings. However, if the contributed capital account has a credit balance, the difference between sales price and cost is charged to the contributed capital account to the extent possible. After the credit balance in the contributed capital account is eliminated, any remaining difference between sales price and cost is debited to Retained Earnings. For example, if Curry Corporation sells its remaining 500 shares of treasury stock at $10 per share, the entry to record the sale is:

July	10	Cash	5,000.00	
		Contributed Capital, Treasury Stock Transactions.	250.00	
		Retained Earnings	500.00	
		Treasury Stock, Common.		5,760.00
		Sold at $10 per share 500 treasury shares that cost $11.50 per share.		

Retirement of Stock

Under the Canada Business Corporations Act, as well as under the more recently passed provincial acts, for example, Ontario, a corporation may purchase and retire shares of its own outstanding stock if it can satisfy a solvency test as follows:

1. The corporation would after the payment be able to pay its liabilities as they become due.
2. The realizable value of the corporation's assets would, after the payment, be greater than the aggregate of its liabilities and stated capital of all classes.

When stock is purchased for retirement, the debit to the stated capital account is the product of the number of shares acquired multiplied by the weighted average per share invested by the shareholders. If the shares are purchased for less than the weighted average per share invested by the shareholders, the differentce is credited to an account such as Contributed Capital from Retiremment of Stock. On the other hand, if the shares are purchased for more than the weighted average per share invested by the shareholders, the difference is debited to contributed capital from previous stock retirement transactions to the extent of its balance with any remainder debited to Retained Earnings.

For example, assume a corporation originally issued its no-par-value common stock at $12 per share. If the corporation later purchased and retired 1,000 shares of this stock at the price for which it was issued, the entry to record the retirement is:

Apr.	12	Common Stock.	12,000.00	
		Cash		12,000.00
		Purchased and retired 1,000 shares of common stock at $12 per share.		

If on the other hand the corporation paid $11 per share instead of $12, the entry for the retirement is:

Apr.	12	Common Stock.	12,000.00	
		Cash		11,000.00
		Contributed Capital from the Retirement of Common Stock		1,000.00
		Purchased and retired 1,000 shares of common stock at $11 per share.		

Or, if the corporation paid $15 per share, the entry for the purchase and retirement is:

Apr.	12	Common Stock.	12,000.00	
		Retained Earnings	3,000.00	
		Cash		15,000.00
		Purchased and retired 1,000 shares of common stock at $15 per share.		

In jurisdictions which have par values when such shares are reacquired for cancellation, all capital items related to the shares being retired are removed from the accounts, and the difference between the purchase price and the weighted average per share invested by the shareholders is treated in a like manner to that illustrated above for no-par value shares.

Appropriations of Retained Earnings

A corporation may voluntarily **appropriate retained earnings** for some special purpose as a means of explaining to shareholders why the retained earnings are not being declared as dividends. In contrast to retained earnings restrictions, which are binding by law or by contract, appropriations of retained earnings are voluntarily made by the board of directors. In earlier years, such appropriations were recorded by transferring portions of retained earnings from the Retained Earnings account to another shareholders' equity account such as Retained Earnings Appropriated for Contingencies or Retained Earnings Appropriated for Plant Expansion. When the contingency or other reason for an appropriation was passed, the appropriation account was eliminated by returning its balance to the Retained Earnings account.

Today, appropriations of retained earnings are seldom seen on balance sheets. Instead, management's reasons for not declaring dividends usually are conveyed in a letter to the shareholders that is published with the financial statements.

REPORTING INCOME AND RETAINED EARNINGS INFORMATION

Income Statement Items Not Related to Continuing Operations

When the revenue and expense transactions of a company consist of routine, continuing operations, the company's single-step income statement will show revenues followed by a list of operating expenses and finally by net income. Often, however, the activities of a business include items that are not closely related to its continuing operations. In these cases, the income effects of such items should be separated from the revenues and expenses of continuing operations. Otherwise, the income statement will fail to provide readers with clear information about the results of business activities.

To see how various income statement items should be classified, look at Illustration 16–4. Observe that the income statement is separated into four sections labeled 1 through 4. The first portion of the income statement (the portion labeled as 1) shows the revenues, expenses, and income generated by the company's continuing operations. This portion looks just like the single-step income statement we first discussed in Chapter 5. The next income statement section, labeled 2, relates to discontinued operations.

Discontinued Operations

Explain how the income effects of discontinued operations, extraordinary items, changes in accounting principles, and prior period adjustments are reported. (L. O. 4)

Large companies often have several different lines of business operations or have several different classes of customers. A company's operations that involve a particular line of business or class of customers may qualify as a **segment of the business.** To qualify as a segment of a business, the assets, activities, and financial results of operations involving a particular line of business or class of customers must be distinguished from other parts of the business.

Separating Discontinued Operations on the Income Statement

Normally, the revenues and expenses of all business segments are added together and reported as the continuing operations of the business (as in section 1 of Illustration 16–4). However, when a business sells or disposes of a business segment, the results of that segment's operations should be separated and

Illustration 16–4
Income statement for a corporation

CONNELLY CORPORATION
Income Statement
For Year Ended December 31, 1990

	Net sales.		$ 8,443,000
	Gain on sale of old equipment.		30,000
	Total		$ 8,473,000
	Costs and expenses:		
	Cost of goods sold	$5,950,000	
1	Depreciation expense.	35,000	
	Other selling, general, and administrative expenses.	515,000	
	Interest expense	20,000	
	Income taxes	792,000	(7,312,000)
	Unusual loss on sale of surplus land		(45,000)
	Infrequent gain on relocation of a plant		72,000
	Income from continuing operations.		$ 1,188,000
	Discontinued operations:		
	Income from operation of discontinued Division A		
2	(net of $166,000 income taxes).	$ 400,000	
	Loss on disposal of Division A (net of $60,000 tax benefit)	(150,000)	250,000
	Income before extraordinary items and cumulative		
	effect of a change in accounting principle		$ 1,438,000
	Extraordinary items:		
	Gain on sale of unused land expropriated for a highway		
3	interchange (net of $35,000 income taxes).	$ 142,500	
	Loss from earthquake damage (net of $310,000 income taxes) . .	(670,000)	500,500
	Net income.		$ 937,500
	Earnings per common share (250,000 shares outstanding):		
	Income from continuing operations		$ 4.75
4	Discontinued operations		1.00
	Extraordinary items		(2.11)
	Net income		$ 3.64

reported as you see in section 2 of Illustration 16–4. In the illustration, the results of the discontinued operations are completely separated from the results of other activities. This separation makes it easier for financial statement readers to evaluate the continuing operations of the business.

Separating the Results of Operating a Segment That Is Being Discontinued from the Gain or Loss on Disposal

Within section 2 of Illustration 16–4, note that the income from *operating* Division A (the operation that is being discontinued) during the period is reported separately from the loss on the final *disposal* of Division A. Also, the income tax effects of the discontinued operations are separated from the income tax expense shown in section 1 of Illustration 16–4. Thus, the results of the discontinued operations are reported net of tax. Also, the amount of tax related to each item is disclosed. Similarly, unusual items, items that do not qualify as extraordinary, should be reported separately. For example, an actual statement is presented in Illustration 16–5 which discloses separately an unusual item—write-down of oil and gas properties.

The above discussion summarizes the method of *reporting* the results of discontinued operations and unusual items on the income statement. The detailed requirements for *measuring* the income or losses of discontinued operations are discussed in a more advanced accounting course.

Extraordinary Items

Section 3 of the income statement in Illustration 16–4 discloses gains and losses that are extraordinary. The *CICA Handbook*[3] identifies extraordinary items as items which result from transactions or events that have all of the following characteristics: (*a*) they are not expected to occur frequently over several years, (*b*) they do not typify the normal business activities of the entity, and (*c*) they do not depend primarily on decisions or determinations by management or owners. Thus, the essential characteristics of extraordinary items are frequency of occurrences, atypical activity and result primarily from nonmanagement decisions. Examples are government expropriations of property or natural disasters. Gains or losses resulting from the risks inherent in an entity's normal business activities such as losses on accounts receivable or inventories, and gains and losses on disposals of long-term assets would not be considered extraordinary.

Each extraordinary item should be disclosed separately and adequately described to allow users of the financial statements to understand the nature of the transactions or events and the extent to which income has been affected.

Prior Period Adjustments

Prior period adjustments are accounted for and reported as direct charges (or credits, including disclosure of the applicable income tax) to Retained Earnings; they cause the opening balance of retained earnings to be restated. To qualify as prior period adjustments, items must be rare in occurrence and must meet the specific criteria set out in paragrahs 3600.02–.03 of the *CICA Handbook*. Settlement of lawsuits arising in prior periods and one-time income tax settlement are normally the only items that qualify as prior period adjustments.

Accounting Changes

Accounting changes (Section 1506 of the *CICA Handbook*) include (*a*) accounting errors, (*b*) changes in accounting policy, and (*c*) changes in estimates. The first two types of items—accounting errors arising in prior periods and changes in accounting policy necessitated by a change in circumstances or the development of new accounting principles—receive parallel treatment to that described for prior period adjustments. That is, they are applied retroactively with a restatement of the opening retained earnings. The latter, change in estimate, is accorded prospective treatment. As a company gains more experience in such areas as estimating bad debts, warranty costs, and useful lives of depreciable assets, there is often a sound basis for revising previous estimates.

---

[3] *CICA Handbook*, section 3480.

Illustration 16–5

CANADA NORTHWEST ENERGY LIMITED
Consolidated Statement of Earnings and Retained Earnings
For the year ended September 30, 1988
(With Comparative Figures for the Year Ended September 30, 1987)
(In thousands of dollars except per share amounts)

	1988	1987
Revenue:		
Gross oil and gas sales	$ 107,736	$ 86,217
Less: Royalties–Crown and other	10,267	9,367
Net oil and gas sales	97,469	76,850
Other income (Note 6)	14,780	13,208
	112,249	90,058
Expenses:		
Operating	27,220	16,794
General and administrative (Note 2)	11,361	10,112
Interest on long term debt (Note 2)	14,759	1,603
Depletion and depreciation	49,768	29,468
	103,108	57,977
Earnings before the following:	9,141	32,081
Income and other taxes:		
Current	6,387	7,061
Deferred	(199)	6,944
Provincial government royalty tax credits	(3,000)	(2,072)
	3,188	11,933
Earnings before unusual item	5,953	20,148
Unusual item (Note 10)	(118,000)	
Net earnings (loss)	(112,047)	20,148
Preferred share dividends	11,031	10,366
Net earnings (loss) attributable to common shares	(123,078)	9,782
Retained earnings, beginning of year	162,099	19,317
Reduction of stated capital (Note 5)		133,000
Retained earnings, end of year	$ 39,021	$ 162,099
Information per common share:		
Average number of common shares outstanding	19,445,976	19,244,792
Earnings (loss) before unusual item	$ (0.26)	$ 0.51
Net earnings (loss) after unusual item	$ (6.32)	$ 0.51

Notes to Consolidated Financial Statements

10 Unusual Items

Write down of oil and gas properties net of deferred income taxes of $8,800	$118,000

Future net revenues have been calculated based on average prices for the two months ended September 30, 1988, without escalation or discounting. If prices in effect at the Company's year end had been used, the write down of oil and gas properties, net of deferred income taxes of $8,800, would have been $186,000. If the average price for the year had been used the write down net of deferred income taxes of $2,000 would have been $22,000.

Illustration 16–6

CONNELLY CORPORATION
Statement of Retained Earnings
For the Year Ended December 31, 1990

Retained earnings, December 31, 1989	$4,745,000
Prior period adjustment for accounting error:	
Cost of the land that was incorrectly charged to expense	
(net of $60,000 income taxes)	130,000
Retained earnings, December 31, 1989, as restated	$4,875,000
Plus net income	937,500
Less cash dividends declared.	(240,000)
Retained earnings, December 31, 1990	$5,572,500

Such changes affect only the present and future statements. A detailed discussion and comparative statement presentation of the above items are left to a more advanced textbook; however, a simple illustration is to be found in Illustration 16–6.

EARNINGS PER SHARE

Among the most commonly quoted statistics on the financial pages of daily newspapers is **earnings per share** of common stock. Investors use earnings per share data when they evaluate the past performance of a corporation, project its future earnings, and weigh investment opportunities.

Companies with Simple Capital Structures

Calculate earnings per share for companies with simple capital structures and explain the difference between primary and fully diluted earnings per share. (L. O. 5)

Earnings per share calculations may be simple or complex. The calculations are not as difficult for companies that have simple capital structures. A company has a **simple capital structure** if it has only common stock and perhaps nonconvertible preferred stock outstanding. In other words, to have a simple capital structure, the company cannot have outstanding any options or rights to purchase common stock at a specified price or any securities that are convertible into common stock.

Calculating Earnings per Share When the Number of Common Shares Outstanding Does Not Change

Consider a company that has only common stock and nonconvertible preferred stock outstanding. If the number of common shares outstanding does not change during the period, earnings per share is calculated as follows:

$$\text{Earnings per share} = \frac{\text{Net income} - \text{Preferred dividends}}{\text{Common shares outstanding}}$$

For example, assume that in 1989, Blackwell Company earned a $40,000 net income and paid its preferred dividends of $7,500. On January 1, 1989, the company had 5,000 common shares outstanding and this number did not change during the year. Earnings per share for 1989 is:

$$\text{Earnings per share} = \frac{\$40,000 - \$7,500}{5,500} = \$6.50$$

However, the calculation becomes more complex if the number of common shares outstanding changes during the period. The number of common shares outstanding may change (1) because the company sells additional shares or buys treasury shares or (2) because of stock dividends and stock splits.

Adjusting the Denominator for Sales or Purchases of Common Shares

If additional shares are sold or shares are reacquired during the year, earnings per share is based on the weighted-average number of shares outstanding during the year. For example, suppose that in 1990, Blackwell Company again earned $40,000 and preferred dividends were $7,500. However, on July 1, 1990, Blackwell sold 4,000 additional common shares. Also, on November 1, 1990, Blackwell purchased 3,000 treasury shares. In other words, 5,000 shares were outstanding for six months; then 9,000 shares were outstanding for four months; then 6,000 shares were outstanding for two months. If these changes occurred, you calculate the weighted-average number of shares outstanding during 1990 as follows:

Time Period	Shares Outstanding	Weighted by Portion of Year Outstanding
January–June	5,000	$(6/12) = 2,500$
July–October	(5,000 + 4,000)	$(4/12) = 3,000$
November–December	(9,000 − 3,000)	$(2/12) = 1,000$
Weighted-average common shares outstanding		6,500

The calculation of earnings per share for 1990 is:

$$\text{Earnings per share} = \frac{\$40,000 - \$7,500}{6,500} = \$5$$

Adjusting the Denominator for Stock Splits and Stock Dividends

A stock split or stock dividend is different from a stock sale. When stock is sold, the company receives new assets that it uses to generate additional earnings. On the other hand, stock splits and stock dividends do not provide additional assets for the company. Instead, a stock split or stock dividend simply means that the company's earnings must be allocated to a larger number of outstanding shares.

Because of the nature of stock splits and stock dividends, you must treat them differently from stock sales when you calculate the weighted-average number of shares outstanding. When a stock split or stock dividend occurs, the number of shares outstanding during previous portions of the year must be retroactively restated to reflect the stock split or dividend. For example, consider the above example of Blackwell Company. However, assume that the stock transactions in 1990 included a stock split, as follows:

Jan. 1:	5,000 common shares were outstanding.
July 1:	Blackwell sold 4,000 additional shares of common stock.
Nov. 1:	Blackwell purchased 3,000 common shares as treasury stock.
Dec. 1:	**Outstanding common shares were split 2 for 1.**

Given these changes in the number of shares outstanding during 1990, you calculate the weighted-average number of shares outstanding as follows:

Time Period	Shares Outstanding	Restated for Stock Split	Weighted by Portion of Year Outstanding
January–June	5,000	2	$(6/12) =$ 5,000
July–October	(5,000 + 4,000)	2	$(4/12) =$ 6,000
November	(9,000 − 3,000)	2	$(1/12) =$ 1,000
December	12,000	—	$(1/12) =$ 1,000
Weighted-average common shares outstanding			13,000

Note that every time stock was sold or purchased, the resulting number of outstanding shares was restated for the subsequent stock split. The same type of restatement is required for stock dividends. If, for example, the 2 for 1 stock split on December 1 had been a 10% stock dividend, the previous amounts of outstanding shares would have been adjusted by a multiplier of 1.10 instead of 2.

The calculation of Blackwell Company's earnings per share for 1990 is:

$$\text{Earnings per share} = \frac{\$40,000 - \$7,500}{13,000} = \$2.50$$

Companies with Complex Capital Structures

Companies with **complex capital structures** have outstanding securities such as bonds or preferred stock that are convertible into common stock. Earnings per share calculations for companies with complex capital structures are more complicated. Often, such companies must present two types of earnings per share calculations. One is called **basic earnings per share**, and the other is called **fully diluted earnings per share.**

Suppose that a corporation has convertible preferred stock outstanding throughout the current year. However, consider what the effects would have been if the preferred shares had been converted at the beginning of the year. The result of this assumed conversion would have been to increase the number of common shares outstanding and to reduce preferred dividends. The net result may have been to reduce earnings per share, or to increase earnings per share. When the assumed conversion of a security reduces earnings per share, the security is said to be **dilutive**; those that increase earnings per share are **antidilutive.** Fully diluted earnings per share is calculated as if *all* dilutive secu-

Illustration 16–7
Reporting primary and fully diluted earnings per share

BCE INC.
Earnings per Share

	1988	1987	1986
Earnings per common share (notes 8, 20 and 23)	$3.09	$3.91	$3.83
Assuming full dilution	3.09	3.85	3.77

NOVA CORPORATION OF ALBERTA
Net Income per Common Share

	1988	1987	1986
Before extraordinary item:			
Basic	$1.76	$0.70	$0.18
Fully diluted	1.66	0.67	0.17
After extraordinary item:			
Basic	1.76	0.70	0.12
Fully diluted	1.66	0.67	0.12

TRIDEL ENTERPRISES INC.

	1988	1987
Earnings per share before extraordinary gain (note 17)	$3.56	$1.78
Adjusted earnings per share before extraordinary gain (note 18)	3.23	
Fully diluted earnings per share before extraordinary gain (note 17) . .	2.85	1.59
Earnings per share (note 17)	7.90	1.78
Adjusted earnings per share (note 18)	6.96	
Fully diluted earnings per share (note 17)	6.03	1.59

rities (antidilutive securities are excluded from the calculation) had already been converted. The complexities of fully diluted earnings per share are left for more advanced accounting courses.

Presentations of Earnings per Share on the Income Statement

Because of the importance attached to earnings per share data, generally accepted accounting principles require that you show this information on the face of published income statements or in the notes to the financial statements cross-referenced to the income statement. Separate earnings per share calculations are normally presented for (1) income before extraordinary items, (2) extraordinary items, and (3) net income. Some corporations provide additional calculations such as unusual items in Illustrations 16–4 and 16–5. Examples from published statements are presented in Illustration 16–7.

Summary of Chapter in Terms of Learning Objectives

1. Whereas cash dividends transfer corporate assets to the shareholders, stock dividends do not. Stock dividends and stock splits have no effect on assets, no effect on total shareholders' equity, and no effect on the equity of each shareholder. Depending on the jurisdiciton, stock dividends are recorded by capitalizing retained earnings equal to the market value of the distributed shares or capitalizing an amount set by the board of directors.

2. When outstanding shares are repurchased by the issuing corporation and held as treasury stock, the cost of the shares is debited to Treasury Stock, which is subtracted in the shareholders' equity section of the balance sheet. If treasury stock is reissued, proceeds in excess of cost are credited to Contributed Capital, Treasury Stock Transactions. If the proceeds are less than cost, the difference is debited to Contributed Capital, Treasury Stock Transactions to the extent a credit balance exists in that account. Any remaining amount is debited to Retained Earnings. If the shares are reacquired and retired, the stated capital account is debited for the weighted average per share invested by the shareholders. If the purchase price is more or less than the weighted average per share, the difference is treated as in the sale of treasury stock.

3. In most jurisdictions, retained earnings are legally restricted by an amount equal to the cost of reacquired shares. Retained earnings also may be restricted by contract. Corporations may voluntarily appropriate retained earnings to inform shareholders why dividends are not larger in amount. More often, however, this information is expressed in a letter to the shareholders.

4. If management implemented a plan to discontinue a business segment, the net income or loss from operating the segment and the gain or loss on disposal should be separately reported on the income statement below income from continuing operations. Next, extraordinary gains or losses are listed.

Prior period adjustments, which include the income effects of accounting errors made in prior periods, are reported on the statement of retained earnings.

Changes in accounting estimates are made because new information shows the old estimates to be invalid. When an accounting estimate is changed, the new estimate is used to calculate revenue or expense in the current and future periods.

5. Companies with simple capital structures do not have outstanding securities that are convertible into common stock. For such companies, earnings per share is calculated by dividing net income less dividends to preferred stock by the weighted-average number of outstanding common shares. In calculating the weighted-average number of shares outstanding, the number of shares outstanding prior to a stock dividend or stock split must be restated to reflect the effect of the stock dividend or stock split.

Companies with complex capital structures have outstanding securities that are convertible into common stock. These companies may have to report both basic earnings per share and fully diluted earnings per share. In calculating basic earnings per share, the denominator is the weighted-average number of common shares outstanding. Fully diluted earnings per share assumes the conversion of all dilutive securities.

Demonstration Problem

Part A

Crown Corporation's books on January 1 showed the following balances (summarized):

Cash	$ 35,000
Other current assets	25,000
Operational assets (net)	235,000
Other assets	55,000
	$350,000
Current liabilities	$ 30,000
Long-term liabilities.	60,000
Capital stock, 2,000 shares . .	210,000
Retained earnings	50,000
	$350,000

The board of directors is considering a cash dividend, and you have been requested to provide certain assistance as the independent accountant. The following matters have been referred to you:

1. What is the maximum amount of cash dividends that can be paid at January 1? Explain.
2. What entries would be made assuming a $26,000 cash dividend is declared with the following dates specified: (*a*) declaration date, (*b*) date of record, and (*c*) date of payment.
3. Assuming a balance sheet is prepared between declaration date and payment date, how would the dividend declaration be reported?

Part B

The records of North Corporation showed the following balances on November 1, 19A:

Capital stock (27,500 shares)	$385,000
Retained earnings	195,000

On November 5, 19A, the board of directors declared a stock dividend of one additional share for each five shares outstanding; issue date, January 10, 19B. The market value of the stock immediately after the declaration was $18 per share.

Required

Give entries in parallel columns for the stock dividend assuming, for problem purposes, (*a*) market value is capitalized, (*b*) $55,000 is capitalized (amount decided by the board), and (*c*) average paid in is capitalized. Assume the company records the dividend on declaration and credits an account titled, Stock Dividends Distributable (not a liability).

Part C

Complete the following matrix:

		Method of Reflecting the Effect	
		Prospective	**Retroactive**
a.	Change in estimate	_____	_____
b.	Change in principle or method	_____	_____
c.	Correction of error	_____	_____

Part D

Western Corporation had outstanding 10,000 shares of no-par common stock sold initially for $20 per share. The Retained Earnings balance is $31,600. The corporation purchased 200 shares at $22 per share and 300 shares of its common at $25 per share. Subsequently, the 500 shares of the common treasury stock were retired.

Required

Give entries to record the treasury stock transactions.

Part E

A company split its common stock 2 for 1 on June 30 of its fiscal year ended December 31. Before the split, there were 4,000 shares of common stock outstanding. How many shares of common stock should be used in computing EPS? How many shares of common stock should be used in computing a comparative EPS amount for the preceding year?

Solution to Demonstration Problem

Part A

Requirement 1

The maximum cash dividend that can be paid at January 1 depends in part on the statutory provisions, i.e., solvency test; however, the *cash* available is limiting in this situation. Possible alternatives are:

1. Limit to cash, $35,000.
2. Limit to retained earnings, $50,000. This would require property dividends, liability dividends, or generating additonal cash through borrowing or other means.

Requirement 2

a.	Date of declaration:		
	Retained Earnings	26,000	
	Dividends Payable.		26,000
b.	Record date. No entry; prepare list of shareholders.		
c.	Date of payment:		
	Dividends Payable	26,000	
	Cash		26,000

Requirement 3

Between declaration and payment dates, dividends payable for whatever amount is declared ($26,000) would be reported as a current liability. Retained earnings would be reported as $50,000 − $26,000 = $24,000.

Part B

	Amount Capitalized		
	(a) Market Value	**(b)** Decision of the Board	**(c)** Average Paid in
November 5, 19A:			
To record declaration:[a]			
Retained Earnings	99,000[b]	55,000[c]	77,000[d]
Stock Dividends Distributable (5,500 shares × $10) . .	99,000	55,000	77,000
January 10, 19B:			
To record stock issued:			
Stock Dividend Distributable . .	55,000	55,000	55,000
Capital Stock (5,500 shares)	55,000	55,000	55,000

Note: Alternative accounting: An equally acceptable alternative manner of accounting and reporting the stock dividend would be to disclose the November 5, 19A, stock dividend declaration in the *notes* to the 19A financial statements. Then the entry to record the January 10, 19B, issuance of the dividend shares would be the same as the declaration entry given above, except that Capital Stock would be credited instead of Stock Dividends Distributable.

[a] 27,500 shares outstanding; 27,500 ÷ 5 = 5,500 shares issued for stock dividend.
[b] Capitalize market value: 5,500 shares × $18 = $99,000.
[c] Capitalize amount decided by the board = $55,000.
[d] Capitalize average paid in: $385,000 ÷ 27,500 = $14 per share, average.
5,500 shares × $14 = $77,000.

Part C

	Method of Reflecting the Effect	
	Prospective	Retroactive
a. Change in estimate	✓	
b. Change in principle or method		✓
c. Correction of error		✓

Part D

Treasury Stock (200 shares @ $22).	4,400	
Cash.		4,400
Treasury Stock (300 shares @ $25).	7,500	
Cash.		7,500
Capital Stock (500 shares @ $20).	10,000	
Retained Earnings.	1,900	
Treasury Stock		11,900

Note: Restriction of Retained Earnings (required by law) for $4,400 and $7,500 (the cost of treasury stock) may be recorded by journal entry or disclosed by footnote.

Part E

In computing EPS for the year, 8,000 shares of common stock should be used. The *CICA Handbook* prescribes retroactive treatment for stock dividends and stock splits for all periods presented. Therefore, 8,000 shares would also be used to compute EPS (restated) for the preceding year as well. The two EPS amounts are therefore (a) comparable and (b) both related to the current capital structure.

Glossary

Define or explain the words and phrases in the chapter Glossary.
(L. O. 6)

Antidilutive securities convertible securities the assumed conversion of which would have the effect of increasing earnings per share. p. 729

Appropriated retained earnings retained earnings voluntarily earmarked for a special use as a way of informing shareholders that assets from earnings equal to the appropriations are not available for dividends. p. 723

Basic earnings per share earnings per share statistics that are calculated for corporations with a simple capital structure and for corporations with complex capital structures before giving effect to the dilutive securities. p. 729

Changes in accounting estimates adjustments to previously made assumptions about the future such as salvage values and the length of useful lives of buildings and equipment. p. 725

Complex capital structure a capital structure that includes outstanding rights or options to purchase common stock or securities that are convertible into common stock. p. 729

Dilutive securities convertible securities the assumed conversion of which would have the effect of decreasing earnings per share. p. 729

Earned surplus a synonym for retained earnings; no longer in general use. p. 714

Earnings per share the amount of net income (or components of income) that accrues to common shares divided by the weighted-average number of common shares outstanding. p. 727

Extraordinary gain or loss a gain or loss which by its nature is not typical of the normal activities of the business. p. 725

Fully diluted earnings per share earnings per share statistics that are calculated as if all dilutive securities had already been converted. p. 729

Infrequent gain or loss a gain or loss that is not expected to occur again, given the operating environment of the business. p. 725

Liquidating dividends distributions of corporate assets to shareholders, which are charged to contributed capital accounts and which therefore represent amounts that had been originally contributed by the shareholders. p. 714

Prior period adjustment items that are reported in the current statement of retained earnings as restatements of the beginning retained earnings balance, limited primarily to corrections of errors that were made in past years; settlement of lawsuits arising in prior years and one-time income tax settlements. p. 725

Restricted retained earnings retained earnings that are not available for dividends because of law or binding contract. p. 720

Segment of a business operations of a company that involve a particular line of business or class of customer, providing the assets, activities, and financial results of the operations can be distinguished from other parts of the business. p. 723

Simple capital structure a capital structure that does not include any rights or options to purchase common shares or any securities that are convertible into common stock. p. 727

Stock dividend a distribution by a corporation of shares of its own stock to its shareholders without any consideration being received in return. p. 714

Stock split the act of a corporation to call in its stock and issue more than one new share in the place of each share previously outstanding. p. 718

Treasury stock issued stock that was reacquired and is currently held by the issuing corporation. p. 718

Unusual gain or loss a gain or loss (that doesn't qualify as extraordinary) that is abnormal and unrelated or only incidentally related to the ordinary activities and environment of the business. p. 725

Questions for Class Discussion

1. What effect does the declaration of a cash dividend have on the assets, liabilities, and shareholders' equity of the corporation that declares the dividend? What is the effect of the subsequent payment of the cash dividend?

2. Why are cash dividends charged against contributed capital accounts called liquidating dividends?

3. What effect does the declaration of a stock dividend have on the assets, liabilities, and total shareholders' equity of the corporation that declares the dividend? What is the effect of the subsequent distribution of the stock dividend?

4. What amount of retained earnings should be capitalized in accounting for a stock dividend?

5. What is the difference between a stock dividend and a stock split?

6. If a balance sheet is prepared between the date of declaration and the date of payment or distribution of a dividend, how should the dividend be shown if it is (a) a cash dividend, or (b) a stock dividend?

7. What is treasury stock?

8. Southern Products Corporation bought 15,000 shares of Regional Steel Corporation stock and turned it over to the treasurer of Southern Products for safekeeping. Is this treasury stock? Why or why not?

9. What effect does the reacquisition of the corporation's own stock have on assets and total shareholders' equity?

10. Distinguish between issued stock and outstanding stock.

11. Why do laws place limitations on the reacquisition of a corporation's stock?

12. In the annual income statement of a corporation, what other sections of the statement might appear below ''Income from continuing operations?''

13. If a company operates one of its business segments at a loss during much of 1990 and then finds a buyer and disposes of that segment during November of that year, what two items concerning that segment should appear on the company's 1990 income statement?

14. Where on the income statement should a company disclose a gain that by its nature is not typical of the ordinary activities of the business and that is expected to recur no more often than once every few years?

15. Which of the following items would qualify as an extraordinary gain or loss: (*a*) operating losses resulting from a strike against a major supplier, (*b*) a gain from the sale of surplus equipment, or (*c*) a loss from damage to a building caused by a tornado (a type of storm that rarely occurs in the geographical region of the company's operations).

16. In past years, Daley Company paid its sales personnel annual salaries without additional incentive payments. This year, a new policy is being instituted whereby they will receive sales commissions rather than annual salaries. Does this new policy require a prior period adjustment? Explain why or why not.

17. After taking five years' straight-line depreciation on an asset that was expected to have an eight-year life, a company concluded that the asset would last another six years. Does this decision involve a change in accounting principles? If not, how would you describe this change?

18. How are earnings per share calculated for a corporation with a simple capital structure?

19. In calculating the weighted-average number of common shares outstanding, how are stock splits and stock dividends treated?

20. Why are not all convertible securities considered in the calculation of earnings per share?

21. What is the difference between basic earnings per share and fully diluted earnings per share?

22. What is the difference between simple capital structures and complex capital structures?

Multiple Choice

1. Which one of the following items is likely to be affected by a stock split?
   a. Total assets.
   b. Market value per share of stock.
   c. Total shareholders' equity.
   d. Total book value of the shares held by an individual shareholder.
   e. All of the above.

2. Failure to record the declaration and distribution of a dividend in stock would:
   a. Cause the balance sheet to be out of balance.
   b. Cause the outstanding stock to exceed the shareholders' equity.
   c. Cause an understatement of shareholders' equity.
   d. Cause an overstatement of shareholders' equity.
   e. Have no effect on total shareholders' equity.

3. Which of the following statements is true with regard to stock dividends and stock splits?
   a. The distribution of stock dividends reduces both cash and shareholders' equity while a stock split reduces neither one.
   b. Stock dividends and stock splits have the same effect on total assets and total retained earnings of the issuing corporation.

    c. A stock dividend does not transfer assets from a corporation to the shareholders but requires that an amount of retained earnings be capitalized.

    d. In a stock split, Retained Earnings is debited and the stock account is credited for the average stated value of the shares issued.

    e. All of the above.

4. The purchase of treasury stock by a corporation:

    a. Requires a debit to Retained Earnings.

    b. Reduces in equal amounts both its total assets and its total shareholders' equity.

    c. Is recorded with an increase to assets and a decrease to assets.

    d. Decreases the amount of issued stock.

    e. Does not change the amount of outstanding stock.

5. Which of the following qualifies as an extraordinary gain or loss?

    a. A manufacturer of three-wheeled recreational vehicles incurred a loss as a result of a customer's lawsuit over injuries the customer suffered from using the product.

    b. A loss due to compensating a worker for injuries the worker suffered while working at the companys plant.

    c. A gain from the exchange of British pounds for dollars which resulted from credit sales of goods to British customers.

    d. A loss of plant and equipment damaged as a result of a meteorite shower.

    e. None of the above are extraordinary items.

6. Tupelo Corporation earned $120,000 in 1990 and preferred dividends were $30,000. On January 1, 1990, the company had 12,000 common shares outstanding. However, on May 1, 1990, Tupelo Corporation reacquired 3,000 of its shares. Earnings per share for 1990 is:

    a. $13.33.

    b. $12.00.

    c. $10.00.

    d. $9.00.

    e. $7.50.

Mini Discussion Case

Case 16–1

The acquisition of previously issued shares, whether for retirement or for subsequent reissue, continues to be a controversial matter. There are people who argue that there is something unsavory about a corporation "trafficking" in its own shares. On the other hand, there are people who hold that a corporation should have a wide latitude in adjusting its capital structure.

Required

Discuss the pros and cons of a corporation's right to reacquire its own shares for:

a. Retirement.

b. Reissue at a future date.

Exercises

Exercise 16–1
Stock dividends
(L. O. 1)

Brazos Corporation's shareholders' equity appeared as follows on March 15:

Common stock, no-par value, unlimited number of shares authorized, 25,000 shares issued	$250,000
Retained earnings	48,750
Total shareholders' equity	$298,750

On March 15, when the stock was selling at $13.50 per share, the corporation's directors voted a 5% stock dividend distributable on April 11 to the March 25 shareholders of record. The stock was selling at $13 per share at the close of business on April 12. (Assume Brazos was incorporated under the Canada Business Corporations Act.)

Required

1. Prepare general journal entries to record the declaration and distribution of the dividend.
2. Under the assumption that Rebecca Brady owned 800 of the shares on March 15 and received her dividend shares on April 11, prepare a schedule showing the number of shares she held on March 25 and on April 12, with their total book values and total market values. Assume no change in total shareholders' equity from March 15 to April 12.

Exercise 16–2
Stock dividends and stock splits
(L. O. 1)

On July 31, 1990, Fairey Corporation's common stock was selling for $50 per share, and the shareholders' equity section of the corporation's balance sheet appeared as follows:

Common stock, no-par value, unlimited number of shares authorized, 10,000 shares issued	$100,000
Retained earnings	220,000
Total shareholders' equity	$320,000

Required

1. Assume the corporation declares and immediately issues a 100% stock dividend and capitalizes $10 per share of retained earnings. Answer the following questions about the shareholders' equity of the corporation after the new shares are issued:
   a. What is the retained earnings balance?
   b. What is the total amount of shareholders' equity?
   c. How many shares are outstanding?
2. Assume that instead of declaring a 100% stock dividend, the corporation effects a 2 for 1 stock split. Answer the following questions about the shareholders' equity of the corporation after the stock split takes place:
   a. What is the retained earnings balance?
   b. What is the total amount of shareholders' equity?
   c. How many shares are outstanding?

Exercise 16–3
Treasury stock purchases
(L. O. 2, 3)

On May 31, Narco, Inc.'s shareholders' equity section appeared as follows:

Shareholders' Equity

Common stock, 15,000 shares issued . .	$750,000
Retained earnings	150,250
Total shareholders' equity	$900,250

On May 31, the corporation purchased 500 shares of treasury stock at $75 per share. Give the entry to record the purchase and prepare a shareholders' equity section as it would appear immediately after the purchase.

Exercise 16–4
Sales of treasury stock
(L. O. 2)

On June 30, Narco, Inc., of Exercise 16–3 sold at $80 per share 300 of the treasury shares purchased on May 31, and on September 15, it sold the remaining treasury shares at $65 per share. Prepare general journal entries to record the sales.

Exercise 16–5
Retirement of stock
(L. O. 2)

The shareholders' equity section of Hackbart Company's December 31, 1990, balance sheet is as follows:

Common stock, no-par value, unlimited number of shares authorized, 80,000 shares issued	$560,000
Retained earnings.	250,000
Total shareholders' equity.	$810,000

On the date of the balance sheet, the company purchased and retired 1,000 shares of its common stock. Prepare general journal entries to record the purchase and retirement under each of the following independent assumptions: (a) the stock was purchased for $5 per share, (b) the stock was purchased for $7 per share, and (c) the stock was purchased for $14 per share.

Exercise 16–6
Income statement categories
(L. O. 4)

The following list of items was extracted from the December 31, 1990, trial balance of Yellow Company. Using the information contained in this listing, prepare Yellow Company's income statement for 1990. You need not complete the earnings per share calculations.

	Debit	Credit
Salaries expense	$21,000	
Income tax expense (continuing operations).	22,500	
Loss from operating segment G (net of $27,000 tax)	63,000	
Sales		$140,250
Cumulative effect on prior years' income of change from double-declining-balance to straight-line depreciation (net of $4,500 tax).		10,800
Extraordinary gain on condemnation of land owned by Yellow Company (net of $15,000 tax). .		39,000
Depreciation expense	19,800	
Gain on sale of segment G (net of $12,000 tax) . . .		30,000
Cost of goods sold.	43,500	

Exercise 16–7
Change in accounting principles
(L. O. 4)

Davis Company has one depreciable asset that cost $480,000 and has decided to switch from straight-line depreciation to double-declining-balance depreciation. In prior years, the company depreciated the asset for two years based on straight-line depreciation, no salvage value, and an eight-year life. Calculate the amount of depreciation expense to be reported in the current year and the cumulative effect of the change on prior years' incomes. Indicate whether the cumulative effect of the change on prior years' incomes should be added, subtracted, or disregarded when calculating the current year's net income.

Exercise 16–8
Classifying income items not related to continuing operations
(L. O. 4)

In preparing the annual financial statements for Terry Corporation, the correct manner of reporting the following items was not clear to the company's employees. Explain where each of the following items should appear in the financial statements:

a. The company keeps its delivery equipment for several years before disposing of the old equipment and buying new equipment. This year, for the first time in eight years, the company sold old equipment for a gain of $7,500 and then purchased new equipment.

b. After amortizing a trademark for five years based on an expected life of seven years, the company decided this year that the value of the trademark would last four more years. As a result, the amortization for the current year is $5,000 instead of $10,000.

c. This year the accounting department of the company discovered that two years ago, a cost had been charged to maintenance expense when it should have been charged to land. The after-tax effect of the charge to maintenance expense was $35,000.

Exercise 16–9
Weighted-average shares outstanding and earnings per share
(L. O. 5)

Janes Corporation reported $249,500 net income in 1990 and declared preferred dividends of $22,000. The following changes in common shares outstanding occurred during the year:

Jan. 1:   30,000 common shares were outstanding.
Mar. 1:   Sold 20,000 common shares for cash.
July 1:   Declared and issued a 50% common stock dividend, or
          (50,000 × 50%) = 25,000 additional shares.

Calculate the weighted-average number of common shares outstanding during the year and earnings per share.

Exercise 16–10
Weighted-average shares outstanding and earnings per share
(L. O. 5)

Stahl Incorporated reported $605,625 net income in 1990 and declared preferred dividends of $37,500. The following changes in common shares outstanding occurred during the year:

Jan. 1:   45,000 common shares were outstanding.
Apr. 1:   Sold 55,000 common shares for $10 per share.
Aug. 1:   Purchased 5,000 shares to be held as treasury stock.
Nov. 1:   Declared and issued a 3 for 1 stock split.

Calculate the weighted-average number of common shares outstanding during the year and earnings per share.

Exercise 16–11
Reporting earnings per share
(L. O. 5)

Rachet Corporation's 1990 income statement, excluding the earnings per share portion of the statement, was as follows:

Sales		$225,000
Costs and expenses:		
Depreciation	$ 12,000	
Income taxes	18,000	
Other expenses	132,000	162,000
Income from continuing operations		$ 63,000
Loss from operating discontinued business segment		
(net of $11,400 taxes)	$ 30,000	
Loss on sale of business segment (net of $13,500 tax) . .	39,000	(69,000)
Loss before extraordinary items		$ (6,000)
Extraordinary gain (net of $24,000 taxes)		130,500
Net income		$124,500

Assume that the weighted-average number of common shares outstanding during the year was 90,000. Assume that the weighted-average number of common shares outstanding during the year was 112,000.

Required

Present the earnings per share portion of the 1990 income statement.

Problems

Problem 16–1
Treasury stock transactions and stock dividends
(L. O. 1, 2, 3)

Davenport (federal incorporation) Corporation's shareholders' equity on December 31, 1989, consisted of the following:

Common stock, no-par value, unlimited number of shares	
authorized, 205,000 shares issued	$257,300
Retained earnings	145,200
Total shareholders' equity	$402,500

During 1990, the company completed these transactions:

Feb. 10   Purchased 15,000 shares of treasury stock at $1.25 per share.

Mar. 25   The directors voted a $0.05 per share cash dividend payable on April 20 to the April 10 shareholders of record.

Apr. 20   Paid the dividend declared on March 25.

June 8   Sold 5,000 of the treasury shares at $1.30 per share.

Nov. 9   Sold 10,000 of the treasury shares at $0.80 per share.

Dec. 21   The directors voted a $0.10 per share cash dividend payable on January 20 to the January 5 shareholders of record, and they voted a 3% stock dividend distributable on February 2 to the January 21 shareholders of record. The market value of the stock was $1.15 per share.

      31   Closed the Income Summary account and carried the company's $50,500 net income to Retained Earnings.

      31   Closed the Cash Dividends Declared and Stock Dividends Declared accounts.

Required

1. Prepare general journal entries to record the transactions.
2. Prepare a retained earnings statement for the year and the shareholders' equity section of the company's year-end balance sheet.

Problem 16–2
Cash dividend, stock dividend, and stock split
(L. O. 1)

Last May 31, Rubinett Corporation (federal incorporation) had a $2.1 million credit balance in its Retained Earnings account. On that date, the corporation's contributed capital consisted of 105,000 no-par-value common shares which had been issued at $15 and were outstanding. It then completed the following transactions:

June 1 The board of directors declared a $5 per share dividend on the common stock, payable on July 5 to the June 15 shareholders of record.
July 5 Paid the dividend declared on June 1.
     12 The board declared a 25% stock dividend, distributable on August 10 to the July 28 shareholders of record. The stock was selling at $50 per share.
Aug. 10 Distributed the stock dividend declared on July 12.
     31 Since August 31 is the end of the company's fiscal year, closed the Income Summary account, which had a credit balance of $656,250. Also closed the Cash Dividends Declared and Stock Dividends Declared accounts.
Sept. 8 The board of directors voted to split the corporation's stock 5 for 1. The split was completed on October 5.

Required

1. Prepare general journal entries to record these transactions.
2. Under the assumption Jill Owens owned 1,500 of the shares on May 31 and neither bought nor sold any shares during the period of the transactions, prepare a schedule with columns for the date, supporting calculations, book value per share, and book value of Owens' shares. Then complete the schedule by calculating the book value per share of the corporation's stock and the book value of Owens' shares at the close of business on May 31, June 1, July 5, August 10, August 31, and September 8. Assume that the only income earned by the company during these periods was the $656,250 earned and closed on August 31.
3. Prepare three shareholders' equity sections for the corporation, the first showing the shareholders' equity on May 31, the second on August 31, and the third on September 8.

Problem 16–3
Calculating net income from balance sheet comparison
(L. O. 1, 2, 3)

The equity sections from the 1989 and 1990 balance sheets of Teller Industries, Inc., appeared as follows:

Shareholders' Equity
(As of December 31, 1989)

Common stock, no-par value, unlimited number of shares authorized, 80,000 shares issued	$ 980,000
Retained earnings	750,250
Total shareholders' equity	$1,730,250

Shareholders' Equity
(As of December 31, 1990)

Common stock, no-par value, unlimited number of shares authorized, 87,920 shares issued of which 800 are in the treasury.	$1,178,000
Retained earnings, of which $17,600 is restricted	675,120
Total.	$1,853,120
Less cost of treasury stock	17,600
Total shareholders' equity	$1,835,520

On April 8, July 5, September 20, and again on December 15, 1990, the board of directors declared $0.40 per share dividends on the outstanding stock. The treasury stock was purchased on July 25. On September 20 (while the stock was selling for $25 per share) the corporation declared a 10% stock dividend on the outstanding shares. The new shares were issued on October 19.

Required

Under the assumption that there were no transactions affecting retained earnings other than the ones given, determine the 1990 net income of Teller Industries, Inc. Show your calculations.

Problem 16–4
Classifying income items in a published income statement
(L. O. 4)

Fremont Corporation had several unusual transactions during 1990 and has prepared the following list of trial balance items from which the appropriate items should be selected and used in constructing the 1990 income statement for the company.

	Debit	Credit
Loss on sale of antique automobile displayed in company showroom (an unusual transaction for the company that occurs about once every four years when a new customer attraction is obtained)	$ 27,900	
Cost of goods sold	170,400	
Gain on settlement with supplier to compensate for negative customer reaction to receipt of products with faulty materials Fremont had purchased from the supplier. (In this industry, attempts to obtain such settlements with suppliers are not unusual but occur very infrequently.)		$ 46,800
Income tax expense.	71,250	
Revenue received in advance late last year and incorrectly credited to a revenue account instead of a liability account (net of $9,750 income taxes).	23,500	
Depreciation expense.	28,350	
Gain on sale of investment in stock (Fremont regularly maintains a large portfolio of stock investments as part of its business activities, expecting to enhance the earnings of the company through purchases and sales of such securities.)		85,350
Accumulated depreciation, buildings.		76,500
Effect on prior years' income of switching from straight-line depreciation to declining-balance depreciation, justified in this case as an improvement in financial reporting	91,650	
Other operating expenses	140,850	
Loss on write-down of assets (net of $17,100 income taxes)	40,950	
Interest earned		10,800
Gain on condemnation of land by city. (This is probably the only time in the company's past or future that it will have land condemned by a government. The event is highly unusual.) (net of $39,000 income taxes)		136,500
Sales.		569,400
Accrued liabilities		48,000

Required

Prepare Fremont Corporation's income statement for 1990, excluding the earnings per share statistics.

Problem 16–5
Changes in accounting principles
(L. O. 4)

On January 1, 1985, Russell Corporation purchased a large item of machinery for use in its manufacturing operations. The machine cost $1,000,000 and was expected to have a salvage value of $65,000. Depreciation was taken through 1989 on a double-declining-balance method assuming a 10-year life. Early in 1990, the company concluded that given the economic conditions in the industry, a straight-line method would result in more meaningful financial statements. They argue that straight-line depreciation would allow better comparisons with the financial results of other firms in the industry.

Required

1. Is Russell Corporation allowed to change depreciation methods in 1990?

2. Prepare a table that shows the depreciation expense to be reported each year of the asset's life under both depreciation methods and the cumulative effect of the change on prior years' incomes. (Round your answers to the nearest whole dollar.)

3. State the amount of depreciation expense to be reported in 1990. How should the cumulative effect be reported? Does the cumulative effect increase or decrease net income?

4. Now assume that Russell Corporation had used straight-line depreciation through 1989 and justified a change to double-declining-balance depreciation in 1990. What amount of depreciation expense should be reported in 1990? Does the reporting of the cumulative effect of the change differ from your answer to Requirement 3?

Problem 16–6
Earnings per share calculations and presentation
(L. O. 5)

Except for the earnings per share statistics, the 1990, 1989, and 1988 income statements of Glowworm Corporation were originally presented as follows:

	1990	1989	1988
Sales	$918,000	$692,400	$774,000
Costs and expenses	796,800	537,600	562,800
Income from continuing operations	$121,200	$154,800	$211,200
Loss on write-down of assets	—	(99,600)	(66,000)
Income (loss) before extraordinary items . .	$121,200	$ 55,200	$145,200
Extraordinary gains (losses)	35,400	(81,600)	(45,600)
Net income (loss)	$156,600	$(26,400)	$ 99,600

Information on common stock:	
Shares outstanding on January 1, 1988	28,800
Sale of shares on June 1, 1988.	+3,600
Purchase of treasury shares on October 1, 1988 . .	−1,800
Shares outstanding on December 31, 1988	30,600
Sale of shares on March 1, 1989	+6,120
Sale of shares on April 1, 1989	+9,720
Stock split of 2 for 1 on September 1, 1989	+46,440
Shares outstanding on December 31, 1989	+92,880
Purchase of treasury shares on March 1, 1990 . . .	−3,600
Sale of shares on June 1, 1990.	+16,920
Stock dividend of 20% on November 1, 1990	+21,240
Shares outstanding on December 31, 1990	127,440

Required

1. Calculate the weighted-average number of common shares outstanding during (*a*) 1988, (*b*) 1989, and (*c*) 1990.

2. Present the earnings per share portions of: (*a*) the 1988 income statement, (*b*) the 1989 income statement, and (*c*) the 1990 income statement.

Alternate Problems

Problem 16–1A
Treasury stock transactions and stock dividends
(L. O. 1, 2, 3)

Brevet Corporation's shareholders' equity on December 31, 1989, consisted of the following:

Common stock, no-par value, unlimited number of shares authorized, 10,500 shares issued	$304,500
Retained earnings.	95,000
Total shareholders' equity.	$399,500

During 1990, the company completed these transactions:

Apr. 8   Purchased 900 shares of treasury stock at $40 per share.

27   The directors voted a $0.45 per share cash dividend payable on May 26 to the May 15 shareholders of record.

May 26   Paid the dividend declared on April 27.

July 19   Sold 500 of the treasury shares at $45 per share.

Oct. 10   Sold 400 of the treasury shares at $35 per share.

Dec. 22   The directors voted a $0.45 per share cash dividend payable on January 25 to the January 10 shareholders of record, and they voted a 2% stock dividend distributable on February 15 to the February 1 stockholders of record. The market value of the stock was $42 per share, and the directors used this amount to capitalize retained earnings.

31   Closed the Income Summary account and carried the company's $25,000 net income to Retained Earnings.

31   Closed the Cash Dividends Declared and Stock Dividends Declared accounts.

Required

1. Prepare general journal entries to record the transactions.

2. Prepare a retained earnings statement for the year and the shareholders' equity section of the company's year-end balance sheet.

Problem 16–2A
Cash dividend, stock dividend, and stock split
(L. O. 1)

Last August 31, Redondo Corporation had a $650,000 credit balance in its Retained Earnings account. On that date, the corporation's contributed capital consisted of 5,000 shares of no-par-value common stock which had been issued at $115 and were outstanding. It then completed the following transactions:

Sept. 1   The board of directors declared a $7 per share dividend on the common stock, payable on October 4 to the September 15 shareholders of record.

Oct. 4   Paid the dividend declared on September 1.

Nov. 11   The board declared a 10% stock dividend, distributable on December 8 to the November 20 shareholders of record. The stock was selling at $125 per share, and the directors decided to capitalize this amount.

Dec. 8   Distributed the stock dividend declared on November 11.

   31   Since December 31 is the end of the accounting year, closed the Income Summary account, which had a credit balance of $192,500. Also closed the Cash Dividends Declared and Stock Dividends Declared accounts.

Jan. 10   The board of directors voted to split the corporation's stock 5 for 1. The shareholders voted approval of the split, and the split was completed on February 5.

Required

1. Prepare general journal entries to record these transactions and to close the Income Summary account at year-end. (No entry is required for the split; however, a memorandum reciting the facts would be entered in the Common Stock account.)

2. Under the assumption Chris Reed owned 500 of the shares on August 31 and neither bought nor sold any shares during the period of the transactions, prepare a schedule with columns for the date, supporting calculations, book value per share, and book value of Reed's shares. Then complete the schedule by calculating the book value per share of the corporation's stock and the book value of Reed's shares at the close of business on August 31, September 1, October 4, December 8, December 31, and February 5. Assume that the only income earned by the company during these periods was the $192,500, which was earned and closed on December 31.

3. Prepare three shareholders' equity sections for the corporation, the first showing the shareholders' equity on August 31, the second on December 31, and the third on February 5.

Problem 16–3A
Calculating net income from balance sheet comparison
(L. O. 1, 2, 3)

The equity sections from the 1989 and 1990 balance sheets of St. James Corporation appeared as follows:

Shareholders' Equity
(As of December 31, 1989)

Common stock, no-par value, unlimited number of shares authorized, 60,000 shares issued	$ 730,000
Retained earnings.	595,250
Total shareholders' equity.	$1,325,250

Shareholders' Equity
(As of December 31, 1990)

Common stock, no-par value, unlimited number of shares authorized, 62,965 shares issued of which 700 are in the treasury	$ 866,650
Retained earnings of which $14,500 is restricted	475,250
Total	$1,341,900
Less cost of treasury stock	14,500
Total shareholders' equity.	$1,327,400

On April 2, June 8, September 25, and again on December 18, 1990, the board of directors declared $0.20 per share dividends on the outstanding stock. The treasury stock was purchased on June 25. On October 25, while the stock was selling for $30 per share, the corporation declared a 5% stock dividend on the outstanding shares. The new shares were issued on October 21.

Required

Under the assumption that there were no transactions affecting retained earnings other than the ones given, determine the 1990 net income of St. James Corporation. Show your calculations.

Problem 16–4A
Classifying income items in a published income statement
(L. O. 4)

Milano Company had several unusual transactions during 1990 and has prepared the following list of trial balance items from which the appropriate items should be selected and used in constructing the 1990 income statement for the company.

	Debit	Credit
Depreciation expense	$ 21,900	
Sales		438,000
Cost of goods sold	131,100	
Gain on sale of artwork in company offices (an unusual transaction for the company that occurs only when major redecorations are required and expensive new artwork is purchased, which happens about every five to seven years)		48,750
Loss on a patent infringement suit initiated four years ago. (This patent is essential to the operations of the business and it is not unusual for companies in this industry to be involved in patent infringement suits. However, the lawsuit appears to have settled the matter in this case and the problem is not expected to arise in the foreseeable future.)	210,000	
Income tax expense	54,900	
Gain on payment from supplier to compensate for loss of customers who had been sold products containing inferior materials purchased from the supplier. (In this industry, such settlements with suppliers occur quite frequently.)		36,000
Maintenance expense costs (net of $7,500 income taxes) incurred in late December of last year and incorrectly charged to building.	18,150	
Gain on sale of investment in stock (The stock was originally donated to Milano by an elderly shareholder and was held out of courtesy until that shareholder's death. Milano has never held stock investments before and has no intention of doing so in the future.) (net of $10,500 income taxes)		65,700
Accumulated depreciation, buildings		54,000
Loss on write-down of assets (net of $13,200 income taxes)	31,500	
Interest earned		5,250
Other operating expenses	108,450	
Effect on prior years' income of switching from accelerated depreciation to straight-line depreciation		70,500
Estimated product warranty liability		34,500

Required

Prepare Milano Company's income statement for 1990, excluding the earnings per share statistics.

Problem 16–5A
Changes in accounting principles
(L. O. 4)

On January 1, 1986, the Jett Company purchased a major item of machinery for use in its operations. The machine cost $650,000 and was expected to have a salvage value of $50,000. Depreciation was taken through 1990 on a declining-balance method at twice the straight-line rate assuming an eight-year life. Early in 1990, the company concluded that given the economic conditions in the industry, a straight-line method would result in more meaningful financial statements. They argue that straight-line depreciation would allow better comparisons with the financial results of other firms in the industry.

Required

1. Is Jett Company allowed to change depreciation methods in 1990?
2. Prepare a table that shows the depreciation expense to be reported each year of the asset's life under both depreciation methods and the cumulative effect of the change on prior years' incomes (round your answers to the nearest whole dollar).
3. State the amount of depreciation expense to be reported in 1990. How should the cumulative effect be reported? Does the cumulative effect increase or decrease net income?
4. Now assume that Jett Company had used straight-line depreciation through 1989 and justified a change to double-declining-balance depreciation in 1990. What amount of depreciation expense should be reported in 1990? Does the reporting of the cumulative effect of the change differ from your answer to Requirement 3?

Problem 16–6A
Earnings per share calculations and presentation
(L. O. 5)

Except for the earnings per share statistics, the 1990, 1989, and 1988 income statements of Berber Company were originally presented as follows:

	1990	1989	1988
Sales	$720,000	$ 652,500	$597,000
Costs and expenses	622,500	585,000	480,000
Income from continuing operations	$ 97,500	$ 67,500	$117,000
Loss on write-down of assets	—	(180,000)	—
Income (loss) before extraordinary items	$ 97,500	$(112,500)	$117,000
Extraordinary gains (net of tax)	168,000	—	9,000
Net income (loss)	$265,500	$(112,500)	$126,000

Information on common stock:

Shares outstanding on January 1, 1988	30,000
Sale of shares on April 1, 1988	+12,000
Purchase of treasury shares on May 1, 1988	−6,000
Stock dividend of 10% on September 1, 1988	+3,600
Shares outstanding on December 31, 1988	39,600
Sale of shares on April 1, 1989	+9,000
Sale of shares on July 1, 1989	+13,500
Shares outstanding on December 31, 1989	62,100
Purchase of treasury shares on April 1, 1990	−4,500
Sale of shares on June 1, 1990	+22,500
Stock split of 2 for 1 on November 1, 1990	+80,100
Shares outstanding on December 31, 1990	160,200

Required

1. Calculate the weighted-average number of common shares outstanding during (*a*) 1988, (*b*) 1989, and (*c*) 1990.
2. Present the earnings per share portions of (*a*) the 1988 income statement, (*b*) the 1989 income statement, and (*c*) the 1990 income statement.

Provocative Problems

Provocative Problem 16–1
Cornfield Corporation
(L. O. 1, 2, 3)

On January 1, 1988, Hal Peeks purchased 800 shares of Cornfield Corporation stock at $45.50 per share. On that date, the corporation had the following shareholders' equity:

Common stock, no-par value, unlimited number of shares authorized, 250,000 shares issued and outstanding	$7,000,000
Retained earnings.	2,500,000
Total shareholders' equity.	$9,500,000

Since purchasing the 800 shares, Mr. Peeks has neither purchased nor sold any additional shares of the company's stock. On December 31 of each year, he has received dividends on the shares held as follows: 1988, $1,408; 1989, $1,672; and 1990, $2,200.

On June 15, 1988, at a time when its stock was selling for $51.25 per share (amount capitalized), Cornfield Corporation declared a 10% stock dividend that was distributed one month later. On October 25, 1989, the corporation split its stock 2 for 1. On May 10, 1990, it purchased 10,000 shares of treasury stock at $35.50 per share. The shares were still in its treasury at year-end.

Required

Assume that Cornfield Corporation's outstanding stock had a book value of $35.75 per share on December 31, 1988, a book value of $20 per share on December 31, 1989, and a book value of $22.25 on December 31, 1990. Do the following:

1. Prepare statements that show the nature of the shareholders' equity in the corporation at the end of 1988, 1989, and 1990.
2. Prepare a schedule that shows the amount of the corporation's net income each year for 1988, 1989, and 1990. Assume that the changes in the company's retained earnings during the three-year period resulted from earnings and dividends.

Provocative Problem 16–2
BiState Company
(L. O. 1)

BiState (federal incorporation) Company's shareholders' equity on September 15 consisted of the following amounts:

Common stock, no-par value, unlimited number of shares authorized, 50,000 shares issued and outstanding	$2,875,000
Retained earnings	1,286,000
Total shareholders' equity	$4,161,000

On September 15, when the stock was selling at $100 per share, the corporation's directors voted a 20% stock dividend, distributable on October 5 to the

September 25 shareholders of record. The directors also voted a $3.45 per share annual cash dividend, payable on November 23 to the November 15 shareholders of record. The amount of the latter dividend was a disappointment to some shareholders, since the company had for a number of years paid a $4 per share annual cash dividend.

Nancy Cooper owned 1,000 shares of BiState Company stock on September 25, received her stock dividend shares, and continued to hold all of her shares until after the November 23 cash dividend. She also observed that her stock had a $100 per share market value on September 15, a market value it held until the close of business on September 25, when the market value declined to $90.50 per share.

Required

Give the entries to record the declaration and distribution or payment of the dividends involved here, and answer these questions:

a. What was the book value of Cooper's total shares on September 15 (after taking into consideration the cash dividend declared on that day)? What was the book value on October 5, after she received the dividend shares?

b. What fraction of the corporation did Cooper own on September 15? What fraction did she own on October 5?

c. What was the market value of Cooper's total shares on September 15? What was the market value at the close of business on September 25?

d. What did Cooper gain from the stock dividend?

Provocative Problem 16–3
Rutland Corporation
(L. O. 4)

Rutland Corporation had several rather special transactions and events in 1990 which are described below:

a. Rutland Corporation's continuing operations involve a high technology production process. Technical developments in this area occur regularly, and the production machinery becomes obsolete surprisingly often. Because such developments occurred recently, Rutland decided that it was forced to sell certain items of machinery at a loss and replace those items with a different type of machinery. The problem is how to report the loss.

b. Early last year, Rutland purchased a new type of equipment for use in its production process. Although much of the production equipment is depreciated over 5 years, a careful analysis of the situation led the company to decide that the new equipment should be depreciated over 10 years. Nevertheless, in the rush of year-end activities, the new equipment was included with the older equipment and depreciated on a five-year basis. In preparing adjustments at the end of 1990, the accountant discovered that $90,000 depreciation was taken on the new equipment last year, when only $45,000 should have been taken.

c. Rutland has a mining operation in several foreign countries, one of which has been subject to political unrest. After a sudden change in governments, the new ruling body resolved that the amount of foreign investment in the country was excessive. As a result, Rutland was forced to transfer ownership in its mines in that country to the new government. Rutland was able to continue its mining operation in a neighboring country and was allowed to transfer much of its mining equipment to the neighbouring country. Nevertheless, the price paid to Rutland for its mines resulted in a significant loss.

d. Two years earlier, Rutland Corporation purchased some highly specialized equipment that was to be used in the operations of a new division that Rutland intended to acquire. The new division was in a separate line of business and would have been a separate segment of the business. After lengthy negotiations, the acquisition of the division was not accomplished and the company abandoned any hope of entering that line of business. Although the equipment had never been used, it was sold in 1990 at a loss. Rutland Corporation does not have a history of expanding into new lines of business and has no plans of doing so in the future.

Required

Examine Rutland Corporation's special transactions and events and describe how each one should be reported on the income statement or statement of retained earnings. Also state the specific characteristics of the item that support your decision.

Analytical and Review Problems

A&R Problem 16–1

Part 1. The more recent business corporations acts restrict the directors by the "solvency" test in the matter of declaration and payment of dividends in money or property. A similar restriction is not, however, imposed in the case of a stock dividend.

Required

Discuss why a restriction is deemed necessary in the former but not in the latter situation.

Part 2. In the case of stock dividends the Canada Business Corporations Act prescribes that the amount of retained earnings to be capitalized is the product of the number of shares issued as a stock dividend multiplied by the market value of each share. The revised Ontario Business Corporations Act does not stipulate the amount to be capitalized, simply stating that the amount to be added to the stated capital account is the amount declared by the directors.

Required

Can a case be made for either of the positions? Support your answer.

A&R Problem 16–2

In Canada, the concept of treasury stock has been one of controversy. There is a strong feeling that corporations should not be permitted to "traffic" in their own shares, that is, reacquire their own shares for reissue at a future date. Some also feel that reacquisition of own shares for retirement should be prohibited, and any adjustment of shareholders' equity should be made through the corporation's dividend policy in order to give equal treatment to all shareholders.

Required

Comment on the above by making a case for and against: (*a*) treasury shares and (*b*) reacquisition of shares for retirement.

A&R Problem 16–3

Included with the most recent dividend cheque was the following statement.

> On behalf of the board of directors I regret to inform you that they (the board) found it necessary to reduce your latest quarterly dividend from 50 to 25 cents per share. The board hopes that future economic conditions will permit the maintenance of the quarterly dividends at the new amount and the eventual restoration to the previously established levels.

Within a few days of payment of the dividend, the president was confronted by the following letter from an irate shareholder:

> Dear Mr. President:
>
> I was extremely disappointed with the reduced dividend and with no guarantee from you that even the reduced dividend will be maintained. Have you no compassion? I am a widow dependent on the meagre pension and dividends on the few shares I hold. Is it not enough that my income has been eroded by inflation? Why must you add to my misery by reducing, by half, the dividend I was certain of receiving?
>
> Before my husband died he instructed me to keep your company's shares because they were as solid as the rock of Gibralter and I could depend not only on dividends but increasing dividends as well as increasing market value of the shares. I believed my husband, and now you go and cut the dividend; furthermore, the shares have declined by 30% from their high of a couple of years ago.
>
> I think there is something funny going on; my granddaughter informs me that the company has nearly $400 million of retained earnings, and reduction of the dividend was just another example of corporate irresponsibility. I have always believed in fair play and await your reply before agreeing or disagreeing with my granddaughter's conclusion.
>
> Sincerely yours,
>
> J.P.
> Concerned shareholder

Required

The president has asked you to draft a reply letter and to be certain to address all the issues J. P. raised.

A&R Problem 16–4

The following information was taken from a published annual report of a Canadian brewer:

Year Ended March 31	(000)
Earnings before unusual item	$68,895
Provision for loss on returnable bottles . .	17,600
Loss from discontinued operations	—
Earnings before extraordinary item	51,295
Extraordinary item	—
Net earnings	$51,295
Earnings per share:	
Before unusual item:	
Basic	$2.41
Fully diluted	$2.23
Before extraordinary item:	
Basic	$1.80
Fully diluted	$1.69
Net earnings:	
Basic	$1.80
Full diluted	$1.69

Required

Determine (*a*) the weighted average number of shares outstanding and (*b*) the number of shares that would result from the conversion of convertible securities and/or exercise of stock purchase warrants.

A&R Problem 16–5

Morton Corporation's fiscal year is the calendar year. During the most recent year, its common shares outstanding changed as follows:

Shares outstanding, Jan. 1	150,000
2-for-1 stock split July 1	150,000
Shares sold Oct. 1	60,000
Shares outstanding Dec. 31	360,000

Required

For purposes of calculating EPS at the end of the year, determine the number of shares outstanding.

17 Bonds as Liabilities and Investments

In Chapter 12, you learned to account for notes payable that require a single payment on the date the note matures and notes that require a series of payments consisting of interest plus a part of the amount borrowed. This chapter discusses bonds, which are liabilities issued by corporations as well as a variety of governmental bodies. The chapter concludes with a brief introduction to bond investments.

Learning Objectives

After studying Chapter 17, you should be able to:

1. Describe the various characteristics of differing bond issues and prepare entries to record bonds that are issued between interest dates.

2. Calculate the price of a bond issue that sells at a discount and prepare entries to account for bonds issued at a discount.

3. Prepare entries to account for bonds issued at a premium.

4. Explain the purpose and operation of a bond sinking fund and prepare entries for sinking fund operations, for the retirement of bonds, and for the conversion of bonds into stock.

5. Describe the procedures used to account for investments in bonds.

6. Define or explain the words and phrases listed in the chapter Glossary.

Borrowing by Issuing Bonds

Corporations often borrow money by issuing **bonds**.[1] Like notes payable, bonds involve a written promise to pay interest and principal or **par value**. The par value, also called the **face amount**, is printed on the bond. The interest rate stated on the bond is applied to the par value to determine the annual interest to be paid. Also, the par value is the amount that is repaid when the bond matures. Most bonds require that the borrower pay interest semiannually and repay the par value at a fixed future date (the maturity date).

Difference between Notes Payable and Bonds

When a business (or an individual) borrows money by signing a note payable, the money is generally borrowed from a single creditor such as a bank. In contrast to a note payable, a bond issue typically includes a large number of bonds, usually in denominations of $1,000, that are sold to many different lenders. After they are originally issued, bonds are frequently bought and sold by investors and may be owned by a number of people before they mature.

Difference between Stocks and Bonds

The phrase *stocks and bonds* commonly appears on the financial pages of newspapers and is often a topic of conversation. However, the difference between stocks and bonds should be clearly understood. A share of stock represents an equity or ownership right in a corporation. For example, if a person owns 1,000 of the 10,000 shares a corporation has outstanding, the person has an equity in the corporation measured at 1/10 of the corporation's total shareholders' equity. Also, the person has an equity in 1/10 of the corporation's earnings. On the other hand, if a person owns a $1,000, 11%, 20-year bond issued by a corporation, the bond represents a debt or a liability of the corporation. The owner of the bond has two rights: (1) the right to receive 11% or $110 interest each year the bond is outstanding and (2) the right to be paid $1,000 when the bond matures 20 years after its date of issue.

Why Issue Bonds Instead of Stock

A corporation that needs long-term funds may consider issuing additional shares of stock or issuing bonds. Each has its advantages and disadvantages. Present shareholders may see the issuance of additional shares as a disadvantage if the shares are issued to new shareholders. Since the new shareholders are owners, the additional stock spreads ownership, control of management, and earnings over more shares. Bondholders, on the other hand, are creditors and do not share in either management or earnings. However, a disadvantage of issuing bonds is that the interest on the bonds must be paid whether or not there are any earnings.

---

[1] The federal government and other governmental units, such as cities, provinces, and crown corporations, also issue bonds. Although the examples in this chapter are of bonds issued by business corporations, the methods used to account for bonds are the same for all organizations.

Illustration 17–1
Financing with stock or with bonds

	Plan A	Plan B
Earnings before bond interest and income taxes . .	$ 900,000	$ 900,000
Deduct interest expense.		(100,000)
Income before corporation income taxes.	$ 900,000	$ 800,000
Deduct income taxes (assumed 40% rate)	(360,000)	(320,000)
Net income	$ 540,000	$ 480,000
Plan A income per share (300,000 shares)	$1.80	
Plan B income per share (200,000 shares)		$2.40

A potential advantage of issuing bonds instead of stock is that if bonds are issued, the result may be increased earnings for the common shareholders. For example, assume a corporation that has 200,000 shares of common stock outstanding needs $1 million to expand its operations. Management estimates that after the expansion, the company can earn $900,000 annually before bond interest, if any, and before corporation income taxes. Two plans for securing the needed funds are proposed. Plan A calls for issuing 100,000 additional shares of the corporation's common stock at $10 per share. This will increase the total outstanding shares to 300,000. Plan B calls for the sale at par of $1 million of 10% bonds. Illustration 17–1 shows how the plans will affect the corporation's earnings.

Corporations must pay federal and provincial income taxes. These federal and provincial taxes may amount to as much as 40% or more of the corporation's before-tax income. However, interest expense is a deductible expense in arriving at income subject to taxes. Therefore, when the combined provincial and federal tax rate is 40%, as in Illustration 17–1, the tax reduction from issuing bonds equals 40% of the annual interest on the bonds. In other words, the tax saving in effect pays 40% of the interest cost.

Characteristics of Bonds

Describe the various characteristics of differing bond issues and prepare entries to record bonds that are issued between interest dates.
(L. O. 1)

Over the years, corporation lawyers and financiers have created a wide variety of bonds, each with different combinations of characteristics. We describe some of the more common characteristics of different bond issues in the following paragraphs.

Serial Bonds

Some bond issues include bonds that mature at different points in time so that the entire bond issue is repaid gradually over a period of years. Bonds of this type are called **serial bonds**. For example, a $1 million issue of serial bonds may include $100,000 of bonds that mature each year from year 6 through year 15.

Sinking Fund Bonds

In contrast to serial bonds, sinking fund bonds all mature on the same date. However, sinking fund bonds require that a separate pool of assets (a sinking fund) be established specifically for the purpose of providing the cash necessary to retire the bonds at maturity. We will discuss bond sinking funds later in this chapter.

Coupon Bonds

Interest payments on registered bonds are usually made by cheques mailed to the registered owners. If interest is not paid in this manner, the bonds are called coupon bonds. Coupon bonds obtain their name from the interest coupons attached to each bond. Each coupon calls for payment on the interest payment date of the interest due on the bond. The coupons are detached as they become due and are deposited with a bank for collection.

Registered Bonds and Bearer Bonds

Most bonds are registered, which means that the name and address of the owner of a registered bond are recorded with the issuing corporation. This offers some protection from loss or theft. If bonds are not registered, they are made payable to bearer and are called bearer bonds. Whoever holds bearer bonds is presumed to be the rightful owner of the bonds. Generally, bearer bonds are also coupon bonds so that the holder of the bonds receives interest payments by clipping the coupons and depositing them with a bank for collection. At maturity, the holder or bearer usually follows the same process and deposits the bond certificates with a bank for collection.

Secured Bonds and Debentures

When bonds are secured, specific assets of the issuing corporation are pledged or mortgaged to be sold, if necessary, to repay the bonds. Mortgages are discussed later in this chapter. Unsecured bonds that depend on the general credit standing of the issuing corporation for security are called debentures. A company generally must be financially strong if it is to successfully issue unsecured bonds.

The Process of Issuing Bonds

When a corporation issues bonds, it normally sells the bonds to an investment firm called the *underwriter*. The underwriter in turn resells the bonds to the public. The legal document that states the rights and obligations of the company and the bondholders is called the bond indenture. In other words, the bond indenture is the written, legal contract between the issuing company and the bondholders. Each bondholder receives a *bond certificate* which is evidence of the corporation's debt to the bondholder.

When bonds are going to be issued to a large number of bondholders, they are represented by a *trustee*. The trustee monitors the corporation's actions so that the corporation fulfills its obligations as stated in the bond indenture. In most cases, the trustee is a large bank or trust company that is selected by the issuing company.

Accounting for the Issuance of Bonds

When a corporation issues bonds, the bond certificates are printed and the indenture is drawn and deposited with the trustee of the bondholders. At that point, a memorandum describing the bond issue is commonly entered in the Bonds Payable account. Such a memorandum might read, "Authorized to issue $8 million of 9%, 20-year bonds dated January 1, 19—, and with interest payable semiannually on each July 1 and January 1." Note that the bonds in this example are typical of most bonds in that interest is payable semiannually.

After the bond indenture is deposited with the trustee of the bondholders, all or a portion of the bonds may be sold. If all are sold at their par value, an entry like the following is made to record the sale:

Jan.	1	Cash	8,000,000.00	
		Bonds Payable		8,000,000.00
		Sold 9%, 20-year bonds at par on their interest date.		

When the semiannual interest is paid on these bonds, the transaction is recorded as follows:

July	1	Interest Expense	360,000.00	
		Cash		360,000.00
		Paid the semiannual interest on the bonds.		

And when the bonds are paid at maturity, an entry like the following is made:

Jan.	1	Bonds Payable	8,000,000.00	
		Cash		8,000,000.00
		Paid bonds at maturity.		

Bonds Sold between Interest Dates

Sometimes bonds are sold on their date of issue, which is also their interest date, as in the previous illustration. More often they are sold after their date of issue and between interest dates. In such cases, it is customary to charge and collect from the purchasers the interest that has accrued on the bonds since the last interest payment date and to return this accrued interest to the purchasers on the next interest date. For example, assume that on March 1, a corporation sold at par $100,000 of 9% bonds on which interest is payable semiannually on each January 1 and July 1. The entry to record the sale between interest dates is:

Mar.	1	Cash	101,500.00	
		Interest Payable		1,500.00
		Bonds Payable		100,000.00
		Sold $100,000 of 9%, 20-year bonds on which two months' interest has accrued		

At the end of four months, on the July 1 semiannual interest date, the purchasers of these bonds are paid a full six months' interest. This payment includes four months' interest earned by the bondholders after March 1 and the two months' accrued interest collected from them at the time the bonds were sold. The entry to record the payment is:

July	1	Interest Payable	1,500.00	
		Interest Expense	3,000.00	
		Cash		4,500.00
		Paid the semiannual interest on the bonds.		

It may seem strange to charge bond purchasers for accrued interest and then to return this accrued interest in the next interest payment. However, bond transactions are made on a "plus accrued interest" basis because it is easier for the bond issuer. For instance, if a corporation sold bonds on a variety of dates during an interest period and did not collect accrued interest, it would have to keep records of the purchasers and the dates on which they bought their bonds. Otherwise, it could not pay the correct amount of interest to each bondholder. However, if each buyer is charged for accrued interest at the time of purchase, the corporation does not have to keep records of the purchasers and their purchase dates. It can pay a full period's interest to all purchasers for the period in which they bought their bonds; each receives the interest earned and gets back the accrued interest paid at the time of the purchase.

Bond Interest Rates

A corporation issuing bonds specifies in the bond indenture and on each bond certificate the interest rate to be paid. This rate is called the **contract rate.** Even though bond interest normally is paid semiannually, the contract rate usually is stated on an annual basis. The contract rate of interest is applied to the par value of the bonds to determine the amount of interest to be paid each year. For example, if a corportaion issues a $1,000, 8% bond on which interest is paid semiannually, $80 will be paid each year in two semiannual installments of $40 each.

Although the contract rate establishes the interest a corporation will pay, it is not necessarily the interest the corporation will incur in issuing bonds. The interest it will incur depends on what lenders consider their risks will be in lending to the corporation and on the current **market rate for bond interest** available to the corporation. The market rate for bond interest is the rate borrowers are willing to pay and lenders are willing to take for the use of money at the level of risk involved. It fluctuates daily as the supply and demand for loanable funds fluctuate. It goes up when the demand for bond money increases and the supply decreases, and it goes down when the supply increases and the demand decreases.

Also, note that on any single day, the market rate for bond interest is not the same for all corporations. The rate for a specific corporation's bonds depends on the level of risk investors attach to those bonds. As the level of risk increases, the rate increases.

In many cases, the corporation issuing bonds offers a contract rate of interest equal to what it estimates the market will demand on the day the bonds are to be issued. If its estimate is correct and the contract rate and market rate coincide on the day the bonds are issued, the bonds will sell at par, their face amount. However, when bonds are sold, their contract rate may not coincide with the market rate. As a result, bonds often sell at a discount or at a premium. Sometimes, the issuing corporation offers a contract rate that results in very large discounts.

At this point, if you are not sure of your understanding of the concept of present value, you should turn back to Chapter 12 and review this concept. Also, for additional study of discounting, Appendix G (at the end of the book) contains an expanded analysis of present and future values.

Bonds Sold at a Discount

Calculate the price of a bond issue that sells at a discount and prepare entries to account for bonds issued at a discount. (L. O. 2)

A **discount on bonds payable** results when a corporation issues and sells bonds that have a contract rate below the prevailing market rate. Given the level of risk, investors can get the market rate of interest elsewhere for the use of their money. So they will buy the bonds only at a price that will yield the prevailing market rate on the investment. In other words, to determine the price of the bonds, you discount the cash flows from the bond investment at the current market rate for bond interest. The price of the bonds is the *present value* of the expected cash flows.

To illustrate how bond prices are determined, assume that on a day when the market rate for bond interest is 9%, a corporation offers to sell and issue bonds that have a $100,000 par value, a 10-year life, and on which interest will be paid semiannually at an 8% annual rate.[2] In exchange for current dollars, the buyers of these bonds obtain the right to receive two different future cash inflows. They are:

1. The right to receive $100,000 at the end of the bond issue's 10-year life.
2. The right to receive $4,000 in interest at the end of each 6-month interest period throughout the 10-year life of the bonds.

To determine the price of the bonds, you must calculate the present value of the future cash flows by discounting the amounts to be received at the market

---

[2]The spread between the contract rate and the market rate of interest on a new bond issue is seldom more than a fraction of a percent. However, a spread of a full percent is used here to simplify the illustrations.

rate of interest. If the market rate is 9% annually, it is 4½% semiannually; and in 10 years, there are 20 semiannual periods. Therefore, you use the last number in the 4½% column of Table 12–1, page 559, to discount the $100,000 receipt; and you use the last number in the 4½% column of Table 12–2, page 561, to discount the series of $4,000 amounts. The present value of these cash flows and the price informed buyers will offer for the bonds is:

Present value of $100,000 to be received 20 periods hence, discounted at 4½% per period ($100,000 × 0.4146) . . .	$41,460
Present value of $4,000 to be received periodically for 20 periods, discounted at 4½% ($4,000 × 13.0079)	52,032
Present value of the bonds	$93,492

If the corporation accepts the $93,492 offered for its bonds and sells them on their date of issue, the sale will be recorded with an entry like this:

Jan.	1	Cash	93,492.00	
		Discount on Bonds Payable	6,508.00	
		Bonds Payable.		100,000.00
		Sold 8%, 10-year bonds at a discount on their date of issue.		

If the corporation prepares financial statements on the day the bonds are sold, the bonds will appear in the long-term liability section of the balance sheet as follows:

Long-term liabilities:		
First-mortgage, 8% bonds payable, due		
January 1, 2001	$100,000	
Less unamortized discount based on the 9% market rate		
for bond interest prevailing on the date of issue	6,508	$93,492

On a balance sheet, any unamortized discount on bonds payable is deducted from the par value of the bonds to show the **carrying amount of the bonds payable,** which is the amount at which the bonds are recorded in the books.

Amortizing the Discount

In the discussion above, the corporation recieved $93,492 for its bonds, but in 10 years it must pay the bondholders $100,000. The difference, the $6,508 discount, is a cost of using the $93,492. This cost is incurred because the contract rate of interest on the bonds was below the prevailing market rate. It is a cost that must be paid when the bonds mature. However, each semiannual interest period in the life of the bond issue benefits from the use of the $93,492. Therefore, each period should bear a fair share of this cost.

Straight-Line Method. The process of allocating a discount among the periods in the life of the bond issue is called *amortizing* the discount. A simple amortization method is the **straight-line method of amortizing bond discount or premium**. This method allocates an equal portion of the discount to each interest period. To apply the straight-line method in the present example, you divide the $6,508 discount by 20, the number of interest periods in the life of the bond issue. The $325 answer ($6,508 ÷ 20 = $325.40, or $325)[3] is the amount of discount to be amortized at the end of each interest period. The periodic amortization of discount is recorded with the semiannual cash payment of interest, as follows:

July	1	Interest Expense	4,325.00	
		Discount on Bonds Payable.		325.00
		Cash		4,000.00
		To record payment of six months' interest and amortization of the discount.		

Illustration 17–2 shows the interest expense to be recorded, the discount to be amortized, and so forth, when the straight-line method is applied to the present example. In Illustration 17–2, notice the following points:

1. The bonds were sold at a $6,508 discount, which when subtracted from their face amount gives a beginning-of-period-1 carrying amount of $93,492.

2. The semiannual $4,325 interest expense amounts equal $4,000 paid to bondholders plus $325 amortization of discount.

3. Interest paid to bondholders each period is determined by multiplying the par value of the bonds by the contract rate of interest ($100,000 × 4% = $4,000).

4. The discount amortized each period is $6,508 ÷ 20 = $325.40, or $325.

5. The unamortized discount at the end of each period is determined by subtracting the discount amortized that period from the unamortized discount at the beginning of the period.

6. The end-of-period carrying amount of the bonds is determined by subtracting the end-of-period amount of unamortized discount from the face amount of the bonds. For example, at the end of period 1: $100,000 − $6,183 = $93,817.

Straight-line amortization once was generally accepted. However, generally accepted accounting principles now allow the straight-line method only when the results do not materially differ from those obtained through use of the **interest method of amortizing bond discount or premium**.[4]

---

[3] In this chapter and in the problems at the end of the chapter, all calculations involving bonds have been rounded to the nearest whole dollar.

[4] *APB Opinion No. 21*, par. 15.

Illustration 17-2
Calculation of interest expense and bond discount amortization: straight-line method

Period	Beginning-of-Period Carrying Amount	Interest Expense to Be Recorded	Interest to Be Paid the Bondholders	Discount to Be Amortized	Unamortized Discount at End of Period	End-of-Period Carrying Amount
1	$93,492	$4,325	$4,000	$325	$6,183	$ 93,817
2	93,817	4,325	4,000	325	5,858	94,142
3	94,142	4,325	4,000	325	5,533	94,467
4	94,467	4,325	4,000	325	5,208	94,792
5	94,792	4,325	4,000	325	4,883	95,117
6	95,117	4,325	4,000	325	4,558	95,442
7	95,442	4,325	4,000	325	4,233	95,767
8	95,767	4,325	4,000	325	3,908	96,092
9	96,092	4,325	4,000	325	3,583	96,417
10	96,417	4,325	4,000	325	3,258	96,742
11	96,742	4,325	4,000	325	2,933	97,067
12	97,067	4,325	4,000	325	2,608	97,392
13	97,392	4,325	4,000	325	2,283	97,717
14	97,717	4,325	4,000	325	1,958	98,042
15	98,042	4,325	4,000	325	1,633	98,367
16	98,367	4,325	4,000	325	1,308	98,692
17	98,692	4,325	4,000	325	983	99,017
18	99,017	4,325	4,000	325	658	99,342
19	99,342	4,325	4,000	325	333	99,667
20	99,667	4,333*	4,000	333*	-0-	100,000

*Adjusted to compensate for accumulated rounding of amounts.

Interest Method. When the interest method is used, the amount of recorded interest expense changes each period. To calculate the amount of interest expense each period, you must multiply the beginning-of-period carrying amount of the bonds by a constant rate of interest. The constant interest rate is the market rate for the bonds at the time the bonds were issued.

After interest expense for a period is calculated, you can determine the amount of discount to be amortized. This is calculated by subtracting the cash payment of interest from the interest expense. Illustration 17-3 shows the interest expense to be recorded, the cash payment of interest, the discount to be amortized, and the remaining balance sheet amounts when the interest method is applied to the bonds in this discussion.

Compare Illustration 17-3 with 17-2 and note these unique aspects of the interest method as shown in Illustration 17-3.

1. The interest expense amounts result from multiplying each beginning-of-period carrying amount by the 4½% semiannual market rate that prevailed when the bonds were issued. For example, $93,492 × 4½% = $4,207 and $93,699 × 4½% = $4,216.

2. The discount to be amortized each period is determined by subtracting the amount of interest to be paid the bondholders from the amount of interest expense.

Illustration 17–3
Calculation of interest expense and bond discount amortization: interest method

Period	Beginning-of-Period Carrying Amount	Interest Expense to Be Recorded	Interest to Be Paid the Bondholders	Discount to Be Amortized	Unamortized Discount at End of Period	End-of-Period Carrying Amount
1	$93,492	$4,207	$4,000	$207	$6,301	$ 93,699
2	93,699	4,216	4,000	216	6,085	93,915
3	93,915	4,226	4,000	226	5,859	94,141
4	94,141	4,236	4,000	236	5,623	94,377
5	94,377	4,247	4,000	247	5,376	94,624
6	94,624	4,258	4,000	258	5,118	94,882
7	94,882	4,270	4,000	270	4,848	95,152
8	95,152	4,282	4,000	282	4,566	95,434
9	95,434	4,295	4,000	295	4,271	95,729
10	95,729	4,308	4,000	308	3,963	96,037
11	96,037	4,322	4,000	322	3,641	96,359
12	96,359	4,336	4,000	336	3,305	96,695
13	96,695	4,351	4,000	351	2,954	97,046
14	97,046	4,367	4,000	367	2,587	97,413
15	97,413	4,384	4,000	384	2,203	97,797
16	97,797	4,401	4,000	401	1,802	98,198
17	98,198	4,419	4,000	419	1,383	98,617
18	98,617	4,438	4,000	438	945	99,055
19	99,055	4,457	4,000	457	488	99,512
20	99,512	4,488*	4,000	488	–0–	100,000

*Adjusted to compensate for accumulated rounding of amounts.

When the interest method is used to amortize a discount, the periodic amortizing entries are like the entries used with the straight-line method; only the dollar amounts are different. For example, the entry to pay the bondholders and amortize a portion of the discount at the end of the first semiannual interest period of the bond issue in Illustration 17–3 is:

July	1	Interest Expense	4,207.00	
		Discount on Bonds Payable.		207.00
		Cash		4,000.00
		To record payment to the bondholders and amortization of a portion of the discount.		

Similar entries, differing only in the amount of interest expense recorded and discount amortized, are made at the end of each semiannual interest period in the life of the bond issue.

Consider the differences between the interest method of amortizing a discount and the straight-line method (previously discussed). The following table shows these financial statement differences:

	Interest-Method Amortization			Straight-Line Amortization		
Period	Beginning-of-Period Carrying Amount	Interest Expense to Be Recorded	Interest Expense as a Percentage of Carrying Amount	Beginning-of-Period Carrying Amount	Interest Expense to Be Recorded	Interest Expense as a Percentage of Carrying Amount
1 ..	$93,492	$4,207	4.5	$93,492	$4,325	4.63
11 ..	96,037	4,322	4.5	96,742	4,325	4.47
19 ..	99,055	4,457	4.5	99,342	4,325	4.35

The table shows the beginning-of-period carrying amount of the bond liability and the interest expense for each of three six-month periods during the life of the bonds. The first three columns of the table show that in every six-month period, the interest method provides an interest expense amount that is 4.5% of the beginning-of-period carrying amount. The last three columns show the amounts that you get if you use the straight-line method. Observe that when the straight-line method is used, the percentage changes each period. Recall that the bonds were issued at a price that reflected a discounting of cash flows at 4.5% per six-month period. The interest method is most consistent with this fact; and it is the preferred method.

Because the above example involves a bond discount, the straight-line method causes a declining percentage. When a premium is amortized, the straight-line method results in an increasing percentage. In either case, however, the straight-line method can be used only where the results do not differ materially from those obtained through use of the interest method.

Bonds Sold at a Premium

Prepare entries to account for bonds issued at a premium.
(L. O. 3)

When a corporation offers to sell bonds that carry a contract rate of interest above the prevailing market rate for the risks involved, the bonds will sell at a **premium.** Buyers will bid up the price of the bonds, going as high, but no higher, than a price that will return the current market rate of interest on the investment. What price will they pay? They will pay the present value of the expected cash flows from the investment, determined by discounting these cash flows at the market rate of interest for the bonds. For example, assume that on a given day a corporation offers to sell bonds that have a $100,000 par value and a 10-year life. The interest is to be paid semiannually at an 11% annual rate. On the day of issue, the market rate of interest for the corporation's bonds is 10%. Buyers of these bonds will discount the expected receipt of $100,000, 20 six-month periods hence, and the expected receipt of $5,500 semiannually for 20 periods at the current market rate of 5% per six-month period, as follows:

Present value of $100,000 to be received 20 periods hence, discounted at 5% per period ($100,000 × 0.3769).	$ 37,690
Present value of $5,500 to be received periodically for 20 periods, discounted at 5% ($5,500 × 12.4622).	68,542
Present value of the bonds	$106,232

Investors will offer the corporation a total of $106,232 for its bonds. If the corporation accepts and sells the bonds on their date of issue, say, May 1, 1990, it will record the sale as follows:

1990				
May	1	Cash	106,232.00	
		Premium on Bonds Payable		6,232.00
		Bonds Payable		100,000.00
		Sold bonds at a premium on their date of issue.		

It may then show the bonds on a balance sheet prepared on the day of the sale as follows:

Long-term liabilities:
First-mortgage, 11% bonds payable, due May 1, 2000 . . $100,000
Add unamortized premium based on the 10% market
   rate for bond interest prevailing on the date of issue . .   6,323 $106,232

On a balance sheet, any unamortized premium on bonds payable is added to the par value of the bonds to show the carrying amount of the bonds, as illustrated.

Amortizing the Premium

In the present example, the corporation received $106,232 for its bonds. However, when the bonds mature, the corporation will have to repay only $100,000. The difference, the $6,232 premium, represents a reduction in the cost of using the $106,232. It should be amortized over the life of the bond issue and have the effect of reducing the recorded interest expense. Illustration 17–4 shows the interest expense and the premium amortization each period when the $6,232 is amortized by the interest method.

Observe in Illustration 17–4 that the premium to be amortized each period is determined by subtracting the interest to be recorded from the interest to be paid the bondholders.

Based on Illustration 17–4, the entry to record the first semiannual interest payment and premium amortization is:

1990				
Nov.	1	Interest Expense	5,312.00	
		Premium on Bonds Payable	188.00	
		Cash		5,500.00
		To record payment of the bondholders and		
		amortization of a portion of the premium.		

Note that the amortization of the premium has the effect of reducing interest expense. Similar entries, with decreasing amounts of interest expense and increasing amounts of premium amortized, are made at the end of the remaining periods in the life of the bond issue.

Illustration 17–4
Calculation of interest expense and bond premium amortization: interest method

Period	Beginning-of-Period Carrying Amount	Interest Expense to Be Recorded	Interest to Be Paid the Bondholders	Premium to Be Amortized	Unamortized Premium at End of Period	End-of-Period Carrying Amount
1	$106,232	$5,312	$5,500	$188	$6,044	$106,044
2	106,044	5,302	5,500	198	5,846	105,846
3	105,846	5,292	5,500	208	5,638	105,638
4	105,638	5,282	5,500	218	5,420	105,420
5	105,420	5,271	5,500	229	5,191	105,191
6	105,191	5,260	5,500	240	4,951	104,951
7	104,951	5,248	5,500	252	4,699	104,699
8	104,699	5,235	5,500	265	4,434	104,434
9	104,434	5,222	5,500	278	4,156	104,156
10	104,156	5,208	5,500	292	3,864	103,864
11	103,864	5,193	5,500	307	3,557	103,557
12	103,557	5,178	5,500	322	3,235	103,235
13	103,235	5,162	5,500	338	2,897	102,897
14	102,897	5,145	5,500	355	2,542	102,542
15	102,542	5,127	5,500	373	2,169	102,169
16	102,169	5,108	5,500	392	1,777	101,777
17	101,777	5,089	5,500	411	1,366	101,366
18	101,366	5,068	5,500	432	934	100,934
19	100,934	5,047	5,500	453	481	100,481
20	100,481	5,019*	5,500	481	–0–	100,000

*Adjusted to compensate for accumulated rounding of amounts.

Accrued Interest Expense

When bonds are sold, the bond interest periods often do not coincide with the issuing company's accounting periods. In these cases, you must make an adjustment for accrued interest at the end of each accounting period. For example, we previously assumed that the bonds of Illustration 17–4 were issued on May 1, 1990, and interest was first recorded and paid on November 1 of that year. By December 31, 1990, two months' interest has accrued on these bonds. If the accounting period ends on that date, the following adjusting entry is required:

1990				
Dec.	31	Interest Expense ($5,302 × ⅔)	1,767.00	
		Premium on Bonds Payable ($198 × ⅔)	66.00	
		Interest Payable ($5,500 × ⅔)		1,833.00
		To record two months' accrued interest and amortize one third of the premium applicable to the interest period.		

Two months are one third of a semiannual interest period. Therefore, the amounts in the entry are one third of the amounts applicable to the second interest period in the life of the bond issue. Similar entries will be made on each December 31 throughout the life of the issue. However, the amounts will differ, since in each case they will apply to a different interest period.

On May 1, 1991, the entry to record the semiannual payment of interest is:

1991				
May	1	Interest Payable.	1,833.00	
		Interest Expense ($5,302 × 4/6)	3,535.00	
		Premium on Bonds Payable ($198 × 4/6)	132.00	
		Cash		5,500.00
		Paid the interest on the bonds, a portion of which was previously accrued, and amortized four months' premium.		

Redemption of Bonds

Bond indentures commonly include a provision that give the issuing corporation the option of redeeming the bonds prior to their maturity date. Often, the provision states that if the corporation calls and redeems the bonds before they mature, the corporation must pay the par value plus a redemption premium. Bonds that can be redeemed at the option of the issuing corporation are known as **callable bonds.** One reason corporations insert redemption clauses in the bond indenture is that if interest rates decline sharply, the corporations can redeem and replace the outstanding bonds with new bonds that pay a lower interest rate.

Not all bonds are callable. However, even though the right is not provided, the issuing corporation often can retire its bonds by purchasing them on the open market. When bonds are redeemed or purchased in the open market by the issuing corporation, the price paid usually is not equal to the carrying value of the bonds. Since the market rate of interest changes as economic conditions change, the present value of a bond's remaining cash flows to the bondholder also changes. Therefore, the price paid to purchase and retire bonds may result in a gain or loss. For example, assume that a company has outstanding $1 million of bonds. After interest is recorded on a given interest date, there remains a $12,000 unamortized premium. The bonds are selling at 98½ (98½% of par value). If the company buys and retires 1/10 of the issue, the entry to record the purchase and retirement is:

Apr.	1	Bonds Payable	100,000.00	
		Premium on Bonds Payable	1,200.00	
		Gain on the Retirement of Bonds.		2,700.00
		Cash		98,500.00
		To record the retirement of bonds.		

In this case, the retirement resulted in a $2,700 gain because the bonds were purchased at a price $2,700 below their carrying value.

In the last paragraph, we stated that the bonds were selling at 98½. Bond quotations are commonly made in this manner. For example, a bond may be quoted for sale at 101¼. This means the bond is for sale at 101¼% of its par value, plus accrued interest, if applicable.

Bond Sinking Fund

Explain the purpose and operation of a bond sinking fund and prepare entries for sinking fund operations, for the retirement of bonds, and for the conversion of bonds into stock.
(L. O. 4)

One reason investors may buy bonds instead of stocks is that bonds usually provide greater security than stocks. Often, a corporation will give additional security to the bondholders by agreeing in the bond indenture to create a **bond sinking fund.** This fund consists of assets that are committed to be used to repay the bondholders at maturity.

When a bond indenture specifies that a bond sinking fund is to be created, the issuing corporation normally is required to make periodic cash deposits with a sinking fund trustee. The trustee's duties are to safeguard the cash, to invest it in securities of reasonably low risk, and to add the interest or dividends earned to the sinking fund. Generally, when the bonds become due, it is also the duty of the sinking fund trustee to sell the sinking fund securities and use the proceeds to pay the bondholders.

When a sinking fund is created, the amount that must be deposited periodically to provide enough money to retire a bond issue at maturity will depend on the net rate of interest that can be earned on the invested funds. It is a net rate because the fee for the trustee's services commonly is deducted from the earnings.

To illustrate the operation of a sinking fund, assume a corporation issues $1 million par value, 10-year bonds. The bond indenture requires that the corporation make annual deposits with a sinking fund trustee at the end of each year in the bond issue's life. Based on the assumption that the trustee will be able to earn an annual return of 8% on the invested assets, net of expenses, the corporation must deposit $69,029 each year.[5] Illustration 17–5 shows that these deposits will generate an amount that is sufficient to retire the bonds at maturity.

When a sinking fund is created by periodic deposits, the entry to record the amount deposited each year appears as follows:

Dec.	31	Bond Sinking Fund	69,029.00	
		Cash		69,029.00
		To record the annual sinking fund deposit.		

The sinking fund trustee invests the amount deposited, and each year the trustee sends to the issuing corporation a report of the earnings on the investments. The corporation then records the sinking fund earnings in its accounts and reports them on its income statement. For example, if $69,029 is deposited at the end of the first year in the sinking fund and 8% is earned, the corporation that issued the bonds records the second year's sinking fund earnings as follows:

Year	2			
Dec.	31	Bond Sinking Fund	5,522.00	
		Sinking Fund Earnings.		5,522.00
		To record the sinking fund earnings.		

---

[5] To understand how the periodic deposits to a sinking fund are calculated, you should study Appendix G at the end of the book. Using the "future value of an annuity of 1 per period" table in Appendix G, the payment of $69,029 is calculated as $1,000,000 ÷ 14.486 = $69,029.

Illustration 17–5
Expected asset accumulation of a bond sinking fund that earns 8%

End of Year	Beginning-of-Period Sinking Fund Balance	8% Interest Earned on Fund Balance	Amount Deposited	Total Increase in Sinking Fund	End-of-Period Sinking Fund Balance
1	$ –0–	$ –0–	$69,029	$ 69,029	$ 69,029
2	69,029	5,522	69,029	74,551	143,580
3	143,580	11,486	69,029	80,515	224,095
4	224,095	17,928	69,029	86,957	311,052
5	311,052	24,884	69,029	93,913	404,965
6	404,965	32,397	69,029	101,426	506,391
7	506,391	40,511	69,029	109,540	615,931
8	615,931	49,274	69,029	118,303	734,234
9	734,234	58,739	69,029	127,768	862,002
10	862,002	68,969*	69,029	137,998	1,000,000

*Adjusted to compensate for accumulated rounding of amounts.

A sinking fund is the property of the company that created the fund and should appear on its balance sheet in the long-term investments section.

When bonds mature, it is usually the duty of the sinking fund trustee to convert the fund's investments into cash and pay the bondholders. Normally, the sinking fund securities, when sold, produce either a little more or a little less cash than is needed to pay the bondholders. If more cash than needed is produced, the extra cash is returned to the corporation; and if less cash is produced than needed, the corporation must make up the deficiency. For example, if the securities in the sinking fund of a $1 million bond issue produce $1,001,325 when converted to cash, the trustee will use $1 million to pay the bondholders and will return the extra $1,325 to the corporation. The corporation will then record the payment of its bonds and the return of the extra cash with an entry like the following:

Jan.	3	Cash	1,325.00	
		Bonds Payable	1,000,000.00	
		Bond Sinking Fund.		1,001,325.00
		To record payment of our bonds and the return		
		of extra cash from the sinking fund.		

Restriction on Dividends Due to Outstanding Bonds

To protect a corporation's financial position and the interests of its bondholders, a bond indenture may restrict the dividends the corporation may pay while its bonds are outstanding. Commonly, the restriction provides that the corporation may pay dividends in any year only to the extent that the year's earnings exceed sinking fund requirements.

Converting Bonds to Stock

To make a bond issue more attractive, bondholders may be given the right to exchange their bonds for a fixed number of shares of the issuing company's common stock. Such **convertible bonds** offer investors initial investment security, and if the issuing company prospers and its shares increase in price, an opportunity to share in the prosperity by converting their bonds to the more valuable shares. Conversion is always at the bondholders' option and therefore does not take place unless it is to their advantage.

When bonds are converted into stock, the conversion changes a liability into owners' equity. The generally accepted rule for measuring the contribution for the issued shares is that the carrying amount of the converted bonds becomes the book value of the capital contributed for the new shares. For example, assume the following: (1) A company has outstanding $1 million of bonds on which there is $8,000 unamortized discount. (2) The bonds are convertible at the rate of a $1,000 bond for 90 shares of the company's no-par-value common stock. And (3) $100,000 in bonds have been presented on their interest date for conversion. The entry to record the conversion is:

May	1	Bonds Payable	100,000.00	
		Discount on Bonds Payable.		800.00
		Common Stock.		99,200.00
		To record the conversion of bonds.		

Note in this entry that the bonds' $99,200 carrying amount sets the accounting value for the capital contributed. Usually, when bonds have a conversion privilege, it is not exercised until the stock's market value and normal dividend payments are sufficiently high to make the conversion profitable to the bondholders.

Investments in Bonds

Describe the procedures used to account for investments in bonds. (L. O. 5)

So far, the discussion of bonds has focused on the issuing corporation. We now shift our attention to the purchasers of bonds. When bonds are purchased as an investment, they are recorded at cost, including any brokerage fees. If interest has accrued at the date of purchase, the purchaser also pays for the accrued interest and records it with a debit to Interest Receivable. The entry to record a bond purchase is as follows:

May	1	Investment in X Corporation Bonds	46,400.00	
		Interest Receivable	1,500.00	
		Cash		47,900.00
		Purchased 50 $1,000, 9%, 10-year bonds dated December 31, 1990, at a price of 92 plus a $400 brokerage fee and accrued interest.		

Note that the $46,400 cost of the bonds was 92% × $50,000 par value plus the $400 brokerage fee, which leaves a discount of $3,600. Most companies do not record the discount (or premium) in a separate account. The investment account is simply debited for the net cost. The accrued interest on May 1 was $\frac{4}{12} \times 9\% \times \$50,000$, or $1,500.

Short-Term Investments in Bonds

Assuming interest is paid semiannually on June 30 and December 31, the entry to record the receipt of interest on June 30 is as follows:

June	30	Cash	2,250.00	
		Interest Receivable.		1,500.00
		Interest Earned.		750.00
		To record the first semiannual receipt of interest.		

This entry correctly reflects the fact that the purchaser owned the bonds for two months during which time interest amounted to $\frac{2}{12} \times 9\% \times \$50,000$, or $750. However, recall that the bonds were purchased at a discount and observe that the June 30 entry does not include any amortization of the discount. This is acceptable only if the bonds are held as a short-term, temporary investment. Under these conditions, the bond investment is reported at cost in the current asset section of the balance sheet. The market value of the bonds on the date of the balance sheet should also be disclosed, as follows:

Current assets:
    Investment in X Corporation bonds (market value is $xx,xxx) . . $46,400

When the bonds are sold, the gain or loss on the sale is calculated as the difference between the sale proceeds and cost.

Long-Term Investments in Bonds

What if the bonds are held as a long-term investment? In this case, you should expect the market value of the bonds to move generally toward par value as the maturity date approaches. In a similar fashion, any discount (or premium) should be amortized so that each interest period includes some amortization in the calculation of interest earned. The procedures for amortizing discount or premium on bond investments parallel those that were discussed and applied previously to bonds payable. The only difference is that the amount of discount (or premium) to be amortized is debited (or credited) directly to the investment account. As a consequence, on the maturity date, the investment account balance will equal the par value on the bonds.

Sale of Bonds by Investors

An investor who buys a bond may not hold it to maturity but may sell it after a period of months or years. When this occurs, the price at which the bond is sold is determined by the market rate for bond interest on the day of the sale. The market rate for bond interest on the day of the sale determines the price because the new investor could get this current rate elsewhere. Therefore, the new investor will discount the right to receive the bond's face amount at maturity and the right to receive its interest for the remaining periods of life at the current market rate to determine the price to pay for the bond. As a result, since bond interest rates vary over time, a bond that originally sold at a premium may later sell at a discount, and vice versa.

Mortgages as Security for Notes Payable and Bonds

Earlier in this chapter, we said that some bonds are secured and some are unsecured. This is also true of notes payable. When bonds or notes are unsecured, the obligation to pay interest and par or principal is equal in standing with other unsecured liabilities of the issuing company. If the company becomes financially troubled and is unable to pay, none of the unsecured creditors has preference over any other.

The ability of a company to borrow money by signing an unsecured note or issuing unsecured bonds depends on the company's general credit standing. In many cases, a company cannot obtain debt financing without providing security to the creditors. In other cases, the rate of interest that creditors would charge to provide unsecured debt is very high. As a result, many notes payable and bond issues are secured by a mortgage.

A **mortgage** is a legal agreement that helps protect a lender if a borrower fails to make the payments required by a note payable or bond indenture. A mortgage gives the lender the right to be paid from the cash proceeds from the sale of the borrower's mortgaged assets.

The terms of a mortgage are written in a separate legal document, the **mortgage contract.** The mortgage contract is given to the trustee of the bond issue or to the lender along with the note payable. A mortgage contract commonly requires the borrower to pay all property taxes on the mortgaged property, to keep the mortgaged property repaired, and to keep it adequately insured. In addition, it normally grants the mortgage holder (the lender) the right to foreclose if the borrower fails to pay. In a foreclosure, a court either sells the property or grants possession of the mortgaged property to the lender who sells it. When the property is sold, the proceeds go first to pay court costs and the claims of the mortgage holder. Any money remaining is then paid to the former owner of the property.

Summary of the Chapter in Terms of Learning Objectives

1. A bond issue usually is divided into bonds that have a par value of $1,000 each so that many investors can participate in the issue. A share of stock represents an equity interest in a corporation while bonds are liabilities. A bond issue may be of serial bonds, which mature at different points in time, or of bonds that all mature on the same date. Some of the latter are sinking fund bonds, for which a fund of assets is established to retire the bonds. If bonds are registered, the name and address of each bondholder is recorded with the issuing corporation. In contrast, bearer bonds are payable to whomever holds or "bears" the bonds. Interest on coupon bonds is paid when the coupons are detached and presented for payment. Mortgages are used to secure some bonds, and other bonds, called debentures, are unsecured.

When bonds are sold between interest dates, the accrued interest is charged to the purchaser, who then is repaid that interest on the next interest payment date.

2. The contract rate of interest is applied to the par value of bonds to determine the annual cash payment of interest, which usually is paid in two installments. The present value of a bond is determined by discounting the series of interest payments, discounting the repayment of the par value, and adding the two present values.

When issued at a discount, the Bonds Payable account is credited for the par value of the bonds and the difference between the cash proceeds and the par value is debited to Discount on Bonds Payable. Each time interest is paid, the discount is amortized, the effect being to increase interest expense. The interest method of amortization is required by generally accepted accounting principles, but the straight-line method may be used if the results are not materially different from the interest method.

3. When the market rate for a corporation's bonds is less than the contract rate, the bonds will sell at a premium. The premium is recorded by the issuer in a separate account and is amortized over the life of the bonds in a manner that is similar to the amortization of bond discount.

4. A corporation that issues sinking fund bonds makes periodic deposits of cash with a sinking fund trustee. The trustee invests the assets, reports the earnings to the issuing corporation, and uses the accumulated sinking fund assets to repay the bondholders on the maturity date of the bonds.

When convertible bonds are converted into common stock, the carrying value of the bonds is transferred to contributed capital accounts that relate to common stock. No gain or loss is recorded.

5. The cost of a bond investment (including brokerage fees) usually is debited to an Investment in Bonds account without separately identifying any premium or discount on the investment. If held as a short-term investment, cash receipts of interest are recorded as interest earned, and no attempt is made to amortize the premium or discount on bond investment. However, if bonds are held as a long-term investment, the difference between the cost and par value of the investment must be amortized. The methods used to amortize premium or discount on bond investments parallel the amortization of premium or discount on bonds payable.

Demonstration Problem

The Janni Company patented and successfully test-marketed a new product. However, to expand its ability to produce and market the product, the company needed $1.5 million of additional financing. On January 1, 1990, the company borrowed the money by issuing three separate groups of five-year bonds, each of which has a face amount of $500,000. On January 1, 1990, the market interest rate for all three groups of bonds was 10% per year.

    a. Group A will pay 10% annual interest on June 30 and December 31, 1990–94.

    b. Group B will pay 12% annual interest on June 30 and December 31, 1990–94.

    c. Group C will pay 8% annual interest on June 30 and December 31, 1990–94.

Required

1. For the 10% (Group A) bonds, present (*a*) the January 1, 1990, entry to record the issuance of the bonds; and (*b*) the June 30, 1990, entry to record the first payment of interest.

2. For the 12% (Group B) bonds, (*a*) calculate the issuance price of the bonds; (*b*) present the January 1, 1990, entry to record the issuance of the bonds; (*c*) prepare a schedule that shows periodic interest expense and premium amortization, using the interest method; (*d*) present the June 30, 1990, entry to record the first payment of interest; and (*e*) present a January 1, 1992, entry to record the retirement of the bonds at the contractual call price of $505,000.

3. For the 8% (Group C) bonds, (*a*) calculate the issuance price of the bonds; (*b*) present the January 1, 1990, entry to record the issuance of the bonds; (*c*) prepare a schedule that shows periodic interest expense and discount amortization, using the interest method; and (*d*) present the June 30, 1990, entry to record the first payment of interest.

Solution to Demonstration Problem

1. *a.* The entry for issuance of the 10% bonds on January 1, 1990:

1990				
Jan.	1	Cash.	500,000.00	
		Bonds Payable, Group A		500,000.00
		Issued 10% bonds at face value.		

b. The entry for the first payment of interest on the bonds on June 30, 1990:

1990				
June	30	Interest Expense	25,000.00	
		Cash		25,000.00
		Paid interest on 10% bonds.		

2. *a.* Calculating the issue price of the 12% bonds:

Present value of $500,000 to be paid 10 periods hence, discounted at 5% ($500,000 × 0.6139).	$306,950
Present value of $30,000 to be paid periodically for 10 periods, discounted at 5% ($30,000 × 7.7217) . .	231,651
Present value of the bonds	$538,601

b. The entry for issuance of the 12% bonds on January 1, 1990:

1990				
Jan.	1	Cash.	538,601.00	
		Bonds Payable, Group B		500,000.00
		Premium on Bonds Payable, Group B.		38,601.00
		Issued 12% bonds at a premium.		

c. The premium amortization table for the 12% bonds (interest method):

Period Ending	Beginning-of-Period Carrying Balance	Interest Expense to Be Recorded	Interest to Be Paid the Bondholders	Premium to Be Amortized	Unamortized Premium at End of Period	End-of-Period Carrying Amount
30/6/90 . .	$538,601	$26,930	$30,000	$3,070	$35,531	$535,531
31/12/90 . .	535,531	26,777	30,000	3,223	32,308	532,308
30/6/91 . .	532,308	26,615	30,000	3,385	28,923	528,923
31/12/91 . .	528,923	26,446	30,000	3,554	25,369	525,369
30/6/92 . .	525,369	26,268	30,000	3,732	21,637	521,637
31/12/92 . .	521,637	26,082	30,000	3,918	17,719	517,719
30/6/93 . .	517,719	25,886	30,000	4,114	13,605	513,605
31/12/93 . .	513,605	25,680	30,000	4,320	9,285	509,285
30/6/94 . .	509,285	25,464	30,000	4,536	4,749	504,749
31/12/94 . .	504,749	25,251*	30,000	4,749	–0–	500,000

*Adjusted to compensate for accumulated rounding of amounts.

d. The entry for the first payment of interest on bonds on June 30, 1990:

1990					
June	30	Interest Expense	26,930.00	
		Premium on Bonds Payable, Group B	3,070.00	
		Cash		30,000.00
		Paid interest on 12% bonds.		

e. The entry that would be made on January 1, 1992, for the retirement of the 12% bonds at the contractual call price of $505,000:

1992					
Jan.	1	Bonds Payable, Group B.	500,000.00	
		Premium on Bonds Payable, Group B	25,369.00	
		Gain on the Retirement of Bonds.		20,369.00
		Cash		505,000.00
		Retired 12% bonds at contractual call price of $505,000.		

3. *a.* Calculating the issue price of the 8% bonds:

Present value of $500,000 to be paid 10 periods hence, discounted at 5% ($500,000 × 0.6139).	$306,950
Present value of $20,000 to be paid periodically for 10 periods, discounted at 5% ($20,000 × 7.7217) . .	154,434
Present value of the bonds.	$461,384

b. The entry for issuance of the 8% bonds on January 1, 1990:

1990					
Jan.	1	Cash	461,384.00	
		Discount on Bonds Payable, Group C	38,616.00	
		Bonds Payable, Group C		500,000.00
		Issued 8% bonds at a discount.		

c. The discount amortization table for the 8% bonds (interest method):

Period Ending	Beginning-of-Period Carrying Balance	Interest Expense to Be Recorded	Interest to Be Paid the Bondholders	Discount to Be Amortized	Unamortized Discount at End of Period	End-of-Period Carrying Amount
30/6/90 . .	$461,384	$23,069	$20,000	$3,069	$35,547	$464,453
31/12/90 . .	464,453	23,223	20,000	3,223	32,324	467,676
30/6/91 . .	467,676	23,384	20,000	3,384	28,940	471,060
31/12/91 . .	471,060	23,553	20,000	3,553	25,387	474,613
30/6/92 . .	474,613	23,731	20,000	3,731	21,656	478,344
31/12/92 . .	478,344	23,917	20,000	3,917	17,739	482,261
30/6/93 . .	482,261	24,113	20,000	4,113	13,626	486,374
31/12/93 . .	486,374	24,319	20,000	4,319	9,307	490,693
30/6/94 . .	490,693	24,535	20,000	4,535	4,772	495,228
31/12/94 . .	495,228	24,772*	20,000	4,772	–0–	500,000

* Adjusted to compensate for accumulated rounding of amounts.

d. The entry for the first payment of interest on the bonds on June 30, 1990:

1990					
June	30	Interest Expense	23,069.00	
		Discount on Bonds Payable, Group C		3,069.00
		Cash		20,000.00
		Paid interest on 8% bonds.		

Glossary

Define or explain the words or phrases listed in the chapter Glossary. (L. O. 6)

Bearer bond a bond that is not registered and is made payable to whoever holds the bond (the bearer). p. 758

Bond a long-term liability of a corporation or governmental unit, usually issued in denominations of $1,000, that requires periodic payments of interest and final payment of par value when it matures. p. 756

Bond indenture the contract between the issuing corporation and the bondholders that states the rights and obligations of both parties. p. 758

Bond sinking fund a separate pool of assets that is established by deposits from the issuing corporation of a bond issue and from earnings on investments of the assets, and which is established for the purpose of providing the cash to repay the bondholders when the bonds mature. p. 770

Callable bond a bond that may be redeemed or repaid before its maturity date at the option of the issuing corporation. p. 769

Carrying amount of bonds payable the par value of bonds payable less any unamortized discount or plus any unamortized premium. p. 762

Contract rate of bond interest a rate of interest specified in the bond indenture as the rate that is applied to the par value of the bonds to determine the annual amount of cash payments to the bondholders. p. 760

Convertible bond a bond that may be exchanged for shares of its issuing corporation's stock at the option of the bondholder. p. 772

Coupon bond a bond that is issued with interest coupons attached to the bond certificate so that as each interest payment date approaches, the bondholder detaches a coupon and submits it to the issuing corporation as a demand for payment. p. 758

Debenture an unsecured bond. p. 758

Discount on bonds payable the difference between the par value of a bond and the price at which it is issued when the issue price is below par. p. 761

Face amount of a bond the bond's par value. p. 756

Interest method of amortizing bond discount or premium a method that calculates interest expense by multiplying the beginning-of-period carrying value of the bonds by the market rate of interest at the date of issuance and then subtracts the cash payment of interest from interest expense to determine the periodic amortization of discount or premium. p. 763

Market rate for bond interest the interest rate that a corporation is willing to pay and investors are willing to take for the use of their money to buy that corporation's bonds. p. 760

Mortgage a legal agreement that helps protect a lender by giving the lender the right to be paid from the cash proceeds from the sale of specified assets that belong to the borrower. p. 774

Mortgage contract a legal document that states the rights of the lender and the obligations of the borrower with respect to assets that are pledged as security for a bond or note payable. p. 774

Par value of a bond the face amount of the bond, which is the amount the borrower agrees to repay at maturity and the amount on which interest payments are based. p. 756

Premium on bonds payable the difference between the par value of a bond and the price at which it is issued when issued at a price above par. p. 766

Registered bond a bond for which the name and address of the owner are recorded with the issuing corporation. p. 758

Serial bonds an issue of bonds that mature at different points in time so that the entire bond issue is repaid gradually over a period of years. p. 757

Sinking fund bonds bonds that require the issuing corporation to make deposits to a separate fund of assets during the life of the bonds for the purpose of repaying the bondholders at maturity. p. 758

Straight-line method of amortizing bond discount or premium a method that allocates to each accounting period an equal amount of discount or premium. p. 763

Questions for Class Discussion

1. What is the difference between a note payable and a bond issue?
2. What is the primary difference between a share of stock and a bond?
3. Why may bonds be preferred to stock as a means of long-term financing?
4. What is a bond indenture? What are some of the provisions commonly contained in an indenture?
5. What role is played by the underwriter when bonds are issued?
6. What is the function of the trustee on a bond issue?
7. Define or describe: (*a*) registered bonds, (*b*) coupon bonds, (*c*) serial bonds, (*d*) sinking fund bonds, (*e*) callable bonds, (*f*) convertible bonds, and (*g*) debenture bonds.
8. Why does a corporation that issues bonds between interest dates collect accrued interest from the purchasers of the bonds?
9. As it relates to a bond issue, what is the meaning of ''contract rate of interest''? What is the meaning of ''market rate for bond interest''?
10. What determines bond interest rates?
11. When the straight-line method is used to amortize bond discount, how is the interest expense for each period calculated?
12. When the interest method is used to amortize bond discount or premium, how is the interest expense for each period calculated?
13. If a $1,000 bond is sold at 98¼, at what price is it sold? If a $1,000 bond is sold at 101½, at what price is it sold?
14. If the quoted price for a bond is 97¾, does this include accrued interest?
15. What purpose is served by creating a bond sinking fund?
16. How are bond sinking funds classified for balance sheet purposes?
17. If when a bond issue matures the sinking fund has insufficient assets to repay the bondholders, who pays the bondholders the deficiency? If the sinking fund has more than enough cash to repay the bondholders, what happens to the extra cash?

18. Why might a corporation issue convertible preferred stock or convertible bonds?

19. What two legal documents are involved when a company signs a note payable that is secured by a mortgage? What is the purpose of each?

Multiple Choice

1. On May 1, a corporation sold $200,000 of 9% bonds on which interest is payable semiannually on each January 1 and July 1. If the bonds were sold at par value plus accrued interest, the entry to record the first semiannual interest payment on July 1 would include:
    a. A debit to Bonds Payable for $9,000.
    b. A credit to Cash for $18,000.
    c. A debit to Interest Payable for $3,000.
    d. A credit to Interest Payable for $6,000 and a debit to Interest Expense for $9,000.
    e. A debit to Interest Payable for $6,000.

2. What would be the selling price of 10% bonds that have a $100,000 par value and an eight-year life if interest is to be paid semiannually? Assume the market rate of interest is 12% and the bonds were sold six months before the first interest payment.
    a. $115,644.
    b. $110,836.
    c. $100,000.
    d. $ 89,900.
    e. $ 86,050.

3. On December 31, 1990, Cetto Corporation received $109,444 from the sale of 16% bonds payable, $100,000 par value, interest payable June 30 and December 31. The bonds were sold to yield a 14% market rate of interest, which resulted in $109,444 cash proceeds from the sale. The entry to record the second payment of interest on December 31, 1991, would include a debit to Premium on Bonds Payable in the amount of:
    a. $ 339.
    b. $ 363.
    c. $ 678.
    d. $7,637.
    e. $7,661.

4. When the bond indenture requires the issuing corporation to establish a bond sinking fund:
    a. The issuing corporation usually is required to make periodic cash deposits with a sinking fund trustee.
    b. Interest and dividends earned from investing the assets in the sinking fund are credited to Sinking Fund Earnings and reported on the income statement of the issuing corporation.
    c. The issuing corporation reports the accumulated amount of assets in the fund on its balance sheet as a long-term investment.
    d. The final entry to retire the bonds with sinking fund assets may in-

clude a debit or credit to Cash if the total amount of sinking fund assets differs from the par value of the bonds.

   e. All of the above.

5. A corporation has $50,000 of convertible bonds outstanding. The unamortized discount on these bonds is $600, and the market value of the bonds is $45,000. If the bonds are converted, the sum of the credits to contributyed capital accounts in the entry to record the conversion will be:

   a. $50,000.

   b. $600.

   c. $50,600.

   d. $49,400.

   e. $45,000.

6. When an investor purchases corporate bonds:

   a. And the bonds are held as a long-term investment, any premium or discount on the investment must be amortized in the process of recording interest income

   b. And the bonds are held as a short-term investment, any premium or discount on the investment must be amortized in the process of recording interest income.

   c. The investment should be recorded at cost, excluding any brokerage fees.

   d. Accrued interest on the date of purchase should be included in the amount of interest earned that is recognized when the first cash interest payment is received.

   e. And the purchase price includes a premium, the amount of interest earned recorded in later periods will exceed the amount of cash received each period.

Mini Discussion Case

Case 17–1

The June 1986 issue of *Investment Research Overview* published by Richardson Greenshields of Canada Limited states:

   Strip bonds (or "zero-coupon" bonds, as they are called in the United States) began to sell in Canada in 1982. In the four years since that time an estimated $5 billion bonds have been "stripped" and sold by investment dealers in Canada. Harold B. Ehrlich, chairman, Berstein Macaulay Money Management Ltd., is quoted as saying, "When the history books are written, I am convinced zero-coupon bonds will be one of the great financial inventions of the 1970s and 1980s."

Required

Differentiate coupon and zero-coupon bonds and critically evaluate the claim made by Harold B. Ehrlich.

Exercises

In solving the exercises at the end of this chapter, round all dollar amounts to the nearest whole dollar.

Exercise 17–1
Bonds sold between interest dates
(L. O. 1)

On March 31 of the current year, Ester Corporation sold at par plus accrued interest $2 million of its 9.8% bonds. The bonds were dated January 1 of the current year, with interest payable on each July 1 and January 1. (*a*) Give the entry to record the sale. (*b*) Give the entry to record the first interest payment. Answer these questions: (*c*) How many months' interest were accrued on these bonds when they were sold? (*d*) How many months' interest were paid on July 1? (*e*) How many months' interest did the bondholders earn during the first interest period?

Exercise 17–2
Straight-line amortization of bond discount
(L. O. 2)

On May 1 of the current year, Beasley Corporation sold $1 million of its 10.2%, 20-year bonds. The bonds were dated May 1 of the current year, with interest payable on each November 1 and May 1. Give the entries to record the sale at 95½ and the first semiannual interest payment under the assumption that the straight-line method is used to amortize the discount.

Exercise 17–3
Calculating sales price of bonds sold at discount
(L. O. 2)

On November 1 of the current year, Henrett Corporation sold $3 million of its 10.8%, 10-year bonds at a price that reflected a 14% market rate for bond interest. Interest is payable each May 1 and November 1. Calculate the sales price of the bonds and prepare a general journal entry to record the sale of the bonds. (Use the present value tables, Tables 12–1 and 12–2, pages 559 and 561.)

Exercise 17–4
Interest method of amortizing bond discount
(L. O. 2)

Henrett Corporation of Exercise 17–3 uses the interest method of amortizing bond discount or premium. Under the assumption the Henrett Corporation sold its bonds for $2,491,428, prepare a schedule with the columnar headings of Illustration 17–3 and present the amounts in the schedule for the first two interest periods. Also, prepare general journal entries to record the first and second payments of interest to bondholders.

Exercise 17–5
Calculating sales price of bonds sold at premium
(L. O. 3)

Frissel Corporation sold $900,000 of its own 13%, 9-year bonds on November 1, 1990, at a price that reflected a 12% market rate of bond interest. The bonds pay interest each May 1 and November 1. (*a*) Calculate the price at which the bonds sold, and (*b*) prepare a general journal entry to record the sale. (Use the present value tables, Tables 12–1 and 12–2, pages 559 and 561.)

Exercise 17–6
Interest method of amortizing bond premium
(L. O. 3)

Assume the bonds of Exercise 17–5 sold for $948,685 and that Frissel Corporation uses the interest method to amortize bond discount or premium. Prepare general journal entries to accrue interest on December 31, 1990, and to record the first payment of interest on May 1, 1991.

Exercise 17–7
Retirement of bonds
(L. O. 4)

Golfer Corporation sold $800,000 of its 10.2%, 20-year bonds at 98¾ on their date of issue, January 1, 1990. Five years later, on January 1, after the bond interest for the period had been paid and 25% of the total discount on the issue had been amortized, the corporation purchased $200,000 par value of the bonds on the open market at 102¼ and retired them. Give the entry to record the retirement.

Exercise 17–8
Bond sinking fund
(L. O. 4)

On January 1, 1989, Daisy Corporation sold $2.5 million of 10-year sinking fund bonds. The corporation expects to earn 10% on assets deposited with the sinking fund trustee and is required to deposit $156,864 with the trustee at the end of each year in the life of the bonds. (a) Prepare a general journal entry to record the first deposit of $156,864 with the trustee on January 1, 1990. (b) Prepare a general journal entry on December 31, 1990, to record the $15,686 earnings for 1990 reported to the corporation by the trustee. (c) After the final payment to the trustee, the sinking fund had an accumulated balance of $2,503,765. Prepare the general journal entry to record the payment to the bondholders on January 1, 1999.

Exercise 17–9
Convertible preferred stock and convertible bonds
(L. O. 4)

Naft Corporation has outstanding 4,000 shares of 7%, $100 par value, preferred stock that is convertible into the corporation's no-par common stock at the rate of one share of preferred for six shares of common. The preferred stock was issued at a premium of $10 per share. All shares are presented for conversion.

Piper Corporation has outstanding $20,000,000 of 9%, 20-year bonds on which there is $350,000 of unamortized bond premium. The bonds are convertible into the corporation's no-par-value common stock at the rate of one $1,000 bond for 200 shares of the stock, and $1 million of the bonds are presented for conversion.

Present entries dated June 10 to record the conversions on the books of the two corporations.

Exercise 17–10
Bonds as temporary investments
(L. O. 5)

On November 1, 1990, Rennco Company purchased 50 $1,000 par value, 11%, 10-year Quatrain Corporation bonds dated December 31, 1989. The bonds pay interest semiannually on June 30 and December 31. Rennco Company bought the bonds at 98 plus accrued interest and an $800 brokerage fee. Rennco intends to hold the bonds as a temporary investment. Prepare journal entries for Rennco Company to record the purchase and to record the receipt of interest on December 31, 1990.

Problems

In solving the problems at the end of this chapter, round all dollar amounts to the nearest whole dollar.

Problem 17–1
Straight-line method of amortizing bond discount
(L. O. 2)

Baxter Corporation sold $750,000 of its own 8.5%, 10-year bonds on their date of issue, December 31, 1989. Interest was payable on the bonds on each June 30 and December 31, and they were sold at a price to yield the buyers a 9% annual return. The corporation uses the straight-line method of amortizing discount or premium.

Required

1. Prepare a calculation to show the price at which the bonds were sold. (Use the present value tables, Tables 12–1 and 12–2, pages 559 and 561.)

2. Prepare a form with the columnar headings of Illustration 17–2 and fill in the amounts for the first two interest periods of the bond issue. Round all amounts to the nearest whole dollar.

3. Prepare entries in general journal form to record the sale of the bonds and the first two payments of interest.

Problem 17–2
Interest method of amortizing bond premium
(L. O. 3)

Redman Corporation sold $1 million of its own 11%, 10-year bonds on December 31, 1989. The bonds were dated December 31, 1989, with interest payable on each June 30 and December 31, and were sold to yield the buyers a 10% annual return. The corporation uses the interest method of amortizing premium or discount.

Required

1. Prepare a calculation to show the price at which the bonds were sold. (Use the present value tables, Tables 12–1 and 12–2, pages 559 and 561.)

2. Prepare a form with the columnar headings of Illustration 17–4 and fill in the amounts for the first two interest periods of the bond issue. Round all amounts to the nearest whole dollar.

3. Prepare entries in general journal form to record the sale of the bonds and the first two payments of interest.

Problem 17–3
Interest method of amortizing bond discount; bond sinking fund
(L. O. 2, 4)

Prepare general journal entries to record the following transactions of Warren Corporation. Use the present value tables, Tables 12–1 and 12–2, pages 559 and 561, as necessary, to calculate the amounts in your entries. Remember to round all amounts to the nearest whole dollar.

1989

Dec. 31   Sold $1.2 million of its own 11.2%, 10-year bonds dated December 31, 1989, with interest payable on each June 30 and December 31. The bonds sold for a price that reflected a 14% market rate of bond interest.

1990

June 30   Paid the semiannual interest on the bonds and amortized a portion of the discount calculated by the interest method.

Dec. 31   Paid the semiannual interest on the bonds and amortized a portion of the discount calculated by the interest method.

   31   Deposited $68,381 with the sinking fund trustee to establish the sinking fund to repay the bonds.

1991

Dec. 30   Received the report of the sinking fund trustee that the sinking fund had earned $8,260.

1999

Dec. 31   Received a report from the sinking fund trustee which noted that the bondholders had been paid $1.2 million on that day. Included was a $3,420 check for the extra cash accumulated in the sinking fund.

Problem 17–4
Straight-line method of amortizing bond premium; retirement of bonds
(L. O. 3, 4)

Prepare general journal entries to record the following bond transactions of Cradle Corporation:

1989

Nov.   1   Sold $2.5 million par value of its own 9.5%, 10-year bonds at a price to yield the buyers a 9% annual return. The bonds were dated November 1, 1989, with interest payable on each May 1 and November 1.

Dec. 31   Made an adjusting entry to record the accrued interest on the bonds and to amortize the premium applicable to 1989. The straight-line method was used to calculate the premium amortized.

1990

May   1   Paid the semiannual interest on the bonds and amortized the remainder of the premium applicable to the first interest period.

Nov.   1   Paid the semiannual interest on the bonds and amortized the premium applicable to the second interest period of the issue.

1991

Nov.   1   After recording the entry paying the semiannual interest on the bonds on this date and amortizing a portion of the premium, Cradle Corporation purchased $\frac{1}{10}$ of the bonds at 100¾ and retired them. Present only the entry to record the purchase and retirement of the bonds.

Problem 17–5
Comparison of straight-line and interest methods
(L. O. 2, 3)

On December 31, 1989, Nelsbore Corporation sold $3 million of 10-year, 9.5% bonds payable at a price that reflected a 10% market rate of bond interest. The bonds pay interest on June 30 and December 31. Use the present value tables, Tables 12–1 and 12–2, pages 559 and 561, as necessary, in calculating the amounts in your answers.

Required

1. Present a general journal entry to record the sale of the bonds.
2. Present general journal entries to record the first and second payments of interest on June 30, 1990, and on December 31, 1990, assuming straight-line amortization of premium or discount.
3. Present general journal entries to record the first and second payments of interest on June 30, 1990, and on December 31, 1990, assuming the use of the interest method to amortize premium or discount.
4. Prepare a schedule like the one on page 766 that has columns for the beginning-of-period carrying amount, interest expense to be recorded, and interest expense as a percentage of carrying amount, assuming use of the (1) interest method and (2) straight-line method. In completing the schedule, present the amounts for period 1 and period 2.

Alternate Problems

In solving the following alternate and provocative problems, round all dollar amounts to the nearest whole dollar.

Problem 17–1A
Interest method of amortizing bond discount
(L. O. 2)

Nunley Corporation sold $1.5 million of its own 9.2%, 10-year bonds on their date of issue, December 31, 1989. Interest was payable on the bonds on each June 30 and December 31, and they were sold at a price to yield the buyers a 10% annual return. The corporation uses the interest method of amortizing discount or premium.

Required

1. Prepare a calculation to show the price at which the bonds were sold. (Use the present value tables, Tables 12–1 and 12–2, pages 559 and 561.)
2. Prepare a form with the columnar headings of Illustration 17–2 and fill in the amounts for the first two interest periods of the bond issue. Round all amounts to the nearest whole dollar.
3. Prepare entries in general journal form to record the sale of the bonds and the first two payments of interest.

Problem 17–2A
Straight-line method of amortizing bond premium
(L. O. 3)

On December 31, 1989, Molly Corporation sold $2.4 million of its own 13.5%, 10-year bonds. The bonds were dated December 31, 1989, with interest payable on each June 30 and December 31, and were sold to yield the buyers a 12% annual return. The corporation uses the straight-line method of amortizing premium or discount.

Required

1. Prepare a calculation to show the price at which the bonds were sold. (Use the present value tables, Tables 12–1 and 12–2, pages 559 and 561.)
2. Prepare a form with the columnar headings of Illustration 17–4 and fill in the amounts for the first two interest periods of the bond issue. Round all amounts to the nearest whole dollar.
3. Prepare entries in general journal form to record the sale of the bonds and the first two payments of interest.

Problem 17–3A
Straight-line method of amortizing bond discount; bond sinking fund
(L. O. 2, 4)

Prepare general journal entries to record the following transactions of Transcon Corporation. Use the present value tables, Tables 12–1 and 12–2, pages 559 and 561, as necessary, to calculate the amounts in your entries. Remember to round all amounts to the nearest whole dollar.

1989
Dec. 31   Sold $900,000 of its own 13.3%, 10-year bonds dated December 31, 1989, with interest payable on each June 30 and December 31. The bonds sold for a price that reflected a 14% market rate of bond interest.

1990

June 30   Paid the semiannual interest on the bonds and amortized a portion of the discount calculated by the straight-line method.

Dec. 31   Paid the semiannual interest on the bonds and amortized a portion of the discount calculated by the straight-line method.

      31   Deposited $46,542 with the sinking fund trustee to establish the sinking fund to repay the bonds.

1991

Dec. 30   Received the report of the sinking fund trustee that the sinking fund had earned $6,516.

1999

Dec. 31   Received a report from the sinking fund trustee which noted that the bondholders had been paid $900,000 on that day. Included was a $2,840 check for the extra cash accumulated in the sinking fund.

Problem 17–4A
Interest method of amortizing bond premium; retirement of bonds
(L. O. 3, 4)

Prepare general journal entries to record the following bond transactions of Bennett Corporation:

1989

Oct. 1   Sold $3.5 million par value of its own 9.7%, 10-year bonds at a price to yield the buyers a 9% annual return. The bonds were dated October 1, 1989, with interest payable on each April 1 and October 1.

Dec. 31   Made an adjusting entry to record the accrued interest on the bonds and to amortize the premium applicable to 1989. The interest method was used in calculating the premium amortized.

1990

Apr. 1   Paid the semiannual interest on the bonds and amortized the remainder of the premium applicable to the first interest period.

Oct. 1   Paid the semiannual interest on the bonds and amortized the premium applicable to the second interest period of the issue.

1991

Oct. 1   After recording the entry paying the semiannual interest on the bonds on this date and amortizing a portion of the premium, Bennett Corporation purchased ¹/₁₀ of the bonds at 101¼ and retired them. Present only the entry to record the purchase and retirement of the bonds.

Problem 17–5A
Comparison of straight-line and interest methods
(L. O. 2, 3)

On December 31, 1989, Frankens Corporation sold $5 million of 10-year, 11.5% bonds payable at a price that reflected a 10% market rate of bond interest. The bonds pay interest on June 30 and December 31, Use the present value tables, Tables 12–1 and 12–2, pages 559 and 561, as necessary, to calculate the amounts in your answers.

Required

1. Present a general journal entry to record the sale of the bonds.
2. Present general journal entries to record the first and second payments of interest on June 30, 1990, and on December 31, 1990, assuming straight-line amortization of premium or discount.

3. Present general journal entries to record the first and second payments of interest on June 30, 1990, and on December 31, 1990, assuming the use of the interest method to amortize premium or discount.

4. Prepare a schedule like the one on page 766 that has columns for the beginning-of-period carrying amount, interest expense to be recorded, and interest expense as a percentage of carrying amount, assuming use of the (1) interest method and (2) straight-line method. In completing the schedule, present the amounts for period 1 and period 2.

Provocative Problems

Provocative Problem 17–1
Transfer Sales Company
(L. O. 1)

Transfer Sales Company is planning a major expansion of its operations and needs $2.5 million to finance the expansion. The company has been presented with three alternative financing proposals. Each involves issuing bonds that pay interest semiannually. The alternatives are:

Plan A: Issue at par $2.5 million of 10-year, 12% bonds.

Plan B: Issue $2,830,000 of 10-year, 10% bonds.

Plan C: Issue $2,250,000 of 10-year, 14% bonds.

Regardless of which plan is followed, the market rate of interest for the bonds is expected to be 12%.

For each bond issue, calculate the cash proceeds of the issue, the interest expense for the first six-month period, and the expected cash outflow each six-month period for interest. Use the interest method to amortize bond premium or discount. Which plan has the smallest cash demands on the company prior to the final payment at maturity? Which requires the largest payment upon maturity?

Provocative Problem 17–2
Hardin Corporation
(L. O. 1)

The shareholders' equity of Hardin Corporation consists of 250,000 shares of outstanding common stock on which the corporation has earned an average of $0.50 per share during each of the last three years. In an effort to increase earnings, management is planning an expansion that will require the investment of an additional $1.5 million in the business. The $1.5 million is to be acquired either by selling an additional 150,000 shares of the company's common stock at $10 per share or selling at par $1.5 million of 8%, 20-year bonds. Management estimates that the expansion will double the company's before-tax earnings the first year after it is completed and will increase before-tax earnings an additional 25% over that level in the years that follow.

Hardin Corporation's management wants to finance the expansion in the manner that will serve the best interests of present shareholders and has asked you to evaluate the two alternatives from this perspective. In your report, express an opinion as to the relative merits and disadvantages of each of the proposed ways of securing the funds needed for the expansion. Attach to your report a schedule that shows expected earnings per share of the common shareholders under each method of financing. In preparing your schedule, assume the company presently pays out in income taxes 50% of its before-tax earnings and that it will continue to pay out the same share after the expansion.

Analytical and Review Problems

A&R Problem 17–1

The accounts of Clues Corporation showed the following balances as of December 31, 1990:

Bonds Payable	$1,500,000
Bond Discount.	30,900

The 9% 10-year bonds dated August 1, 1989, were issued on December 1, 1989, and the cash proceeds were $1,510,200. Interest is payable semiannually.

Required

Reconstruct the entries pertaining to the bond issue that were made on the company's books. Assume that the company's fiscal year coincides with the calendar year.

A&R Problem 17–2

On June 30, 1990, Guida Corporaton issued $500,000 par value 10%, 10-year bonds convertible at the rate of a $1,000 bond for 50 common shares. The bonds were dated June 30, 1990, and were sold at a price to yield investors 12%. Interest was payable annually.

Required

a. Prepare entries on the following dates (Guida uses straight-line to amortize discounts or premiums): June 30, 1990; December 31, 1990 (year-end); June 30, 1991; and June 30, 1992, to record conversion of 40 of the bonds.

b. On the assumption that Guida used the interest method for amortization of discounts and premiums prepare entries on the following dates:

December 31, 1990.
June 30, 1991.
June 30, 1992.

A&R Problem 17–3

On May 1, 1990, Tony Temple purchased as a long-term investment 20, $1,000 par value, 12% bonds, due 5½ years from date of purchase. Interest on the bonds is due and payable annually on November 1. Temple does not use discount or premium accounts related to investments of this nature and uses straight-line amortization.

Required

a. On the assumption that Temple's *total* cash outlay for the bonds was $17,040, prepare entries on the following 1990 dates:

May 1, 1990.
November 1, 1990.
December 31, 1990 (year-end).

b. On the assumption that Temple's total cash outlay for the bonds was $22,520 prepare the entries on the following dates:

> May 1, 1990.
> November 1, 1990.
> December 31, 1990 (year-end).

A&R Problem 17–4

Vacon Co., Limited, had excellent prospects; however, it currently was experiencing a severe cash flow problem which was expected to persist for the next three or four years. Vacon was able to arrange a sale of "low" coupon bonds which would: (a) relieve the immediate cash flow problem and (b) not require large interest cost outflow during the life of the bonds. The bond issue was for $1 million par value, 3% annual, five-year bonds. The bonds were dated and issued April 1, 1990, to yield 12%. Vacon's fiscal year ends December 31.

Required (round calculations to the nearest dollar)
1. Journalize the bond issue.
2. Prepare the December 31, 1990, adjusting journal entry assuming interest method amortization.
3. Prepare the necessary April 1, 1991, journal entry (assume amortizaton of discount is also recorded at the time of interest payment).

A&R Problem 17–5

Assume that C. Ashley Inc. purchased, as long-term investment, $100,000 of the Vacon Co., Limited, bonds (A&R Problem 17–4) on the date of issue. Ashley's fiscal period ends December 31.

Required (round calculations to nearest dollar)
1. Prepare the journal entry to record the investment in Vacon Co. bonds.
2. Prepare the December 31, 1990, adjusting entry.
3. Prepare the April 1, 1991, entry.
4. Prepare the October 1, 1991, entry or entries to record the sale of one half of the Vacon Co. bonds at a gain of $5,000.
5. Prepare the December 31, 1991, adjusting entry.

A&R Problem 17–6

Little Corporation issued $1 million par value, 12% annual, 10-year bonds. The bonds were dated April 1, 1990; however, because of market conditions they were not sold until August 1, 1990. All of the bonds were sold on August 1 at *total* proceeds of $1,051,600.

Little's fiscal period ends December 31, and the company intends to use straight-line amortization of premium.

Required

Prepare the necessary journal entries as of: (a) August 1, 1990; (b) December 31, 1990; (c) April 1, 1991; and (d) December 31, 1991.

Financial Statements: Interpretation and Modifications

Your study of Part Six will contribute a great deal to your ability to understand and use financial statements. You will learn about the statement of changes in financial position and how businesses account for and report their investments in other companies and their operations in foreign countries. Finally, you will learn some important techniques to use in analyzing financial statements.

Part Six consists of the following chapters:

18 Statement of Changes in Financial Position (SCFP)

Cash is the lifeblood of a business enterprise. It is the fuel that keeps a business alive. Without cash, employees and suppliers are not paid, loans are not repaid, and owners do not receive dividends. In other words, a business must have an adequate amount of cash to operate. For these reasons, decision makers pay close attention to a company's cash position and the events and transactions that cause that position to change. Information about the events and transactions that affect the cash position of a company is reported in a financial statement called the **statement of changes in financial position (SCFP).** By studying this chapter, you will learn how to prepare and interpret an SCFP.

Learning Objectives

After studying Chapter 18, you should be able to:

1. Explain the differences between operating, investing, and financing activities and assign a company's cash inflows and outflows to these categories.
2. Calculate cash inflows and outflows by inspecting the noncash account balances of a company and related information about its transactions.
3. Identify and report on the SCFP any simultaneous investing and financing transactions.
4. Prepare a working paper for a statement of changes in financial position.
5. Define or explain the words or phrases listed in the chapter Glossary.

Why Cash Information Is Important

Information about cash flows can influence decision makers in many ways. For example, if a company's regular operations bring in more cash than it uses, investors will value the company more highly than if property and equipment must be sold to finance operations. Information about cash flows can help creditors decide whether a company will have enough cash to pay its debts as they mature. Management and investors use cash flow information to evaluate a company's ability to meet unexpected obligations. Cash flow information is also used to evaluate a company's ability to take advantage of new business opportunities that may arise. These are just a few of the many ways that different people use cash flow information.

The importance of cash flow information to decision makers has directly influenced the thinking of accounting authorities. For example, the CICA's stated objectives of financial reporting clearly reflect the importance of cash flow information. The CICA stated that financial statements should include information:

About how a business obtains and spends cash,

About its borrowing and repayment activities,

About the sale and repurchase of its ownership securities,

About dividend payments and other distributions to its owners, and

About other factors that affect a company's liquidity or solvency.[1]

To accomplish these objectives, a financial statement is needed to summarize, classify, and report the periodic cash inflows and outflows of a business. This information is contained in a statement of changes in financial position (SCFP).

Statement of Changes in Financial Position (SCFP)

Explain the differences between operating, investing, and financing activities and assign a company's cash inflows and outflows to these categories. (L. O. 1)

In September 1985, the CICA's Accounting Standards Committee revised Section 1540 of the *Handbook*. This recommendation now requires businesses to include a statement of changes in financial position (SCFP) which is to present information about a company's cash receipts and disbursements during the reporting period.

Illustration 18–1 shows the content of the SCFP. In the Illustration, note that cash flows are grouped in three categories: cash flows from operating activities, cash flows from investing activities, and cash flows from financing activities. Within each category, there may be both inflows and outflows. Because all cash inflows and outflows are reported, the statement reconciles the beginning-of-period and end-of-period balances of cash plus cash equivalents.

Presenting Cash Flows from Operating Activities

When you prepare a SCFP, the net cash provided (or used) by operating activities is determined first. This item is important because it represents the cash which the company generates on an ongoing basis from its normal operations.

When you calculate cash from operations, first list net income. It is then adjusted for items that are necessary to reconcile net income to the net cash

---

[1] *CICA Handbook* (Toronto: The Canadian Institute of Chartered Accountants), par. 1540.01.

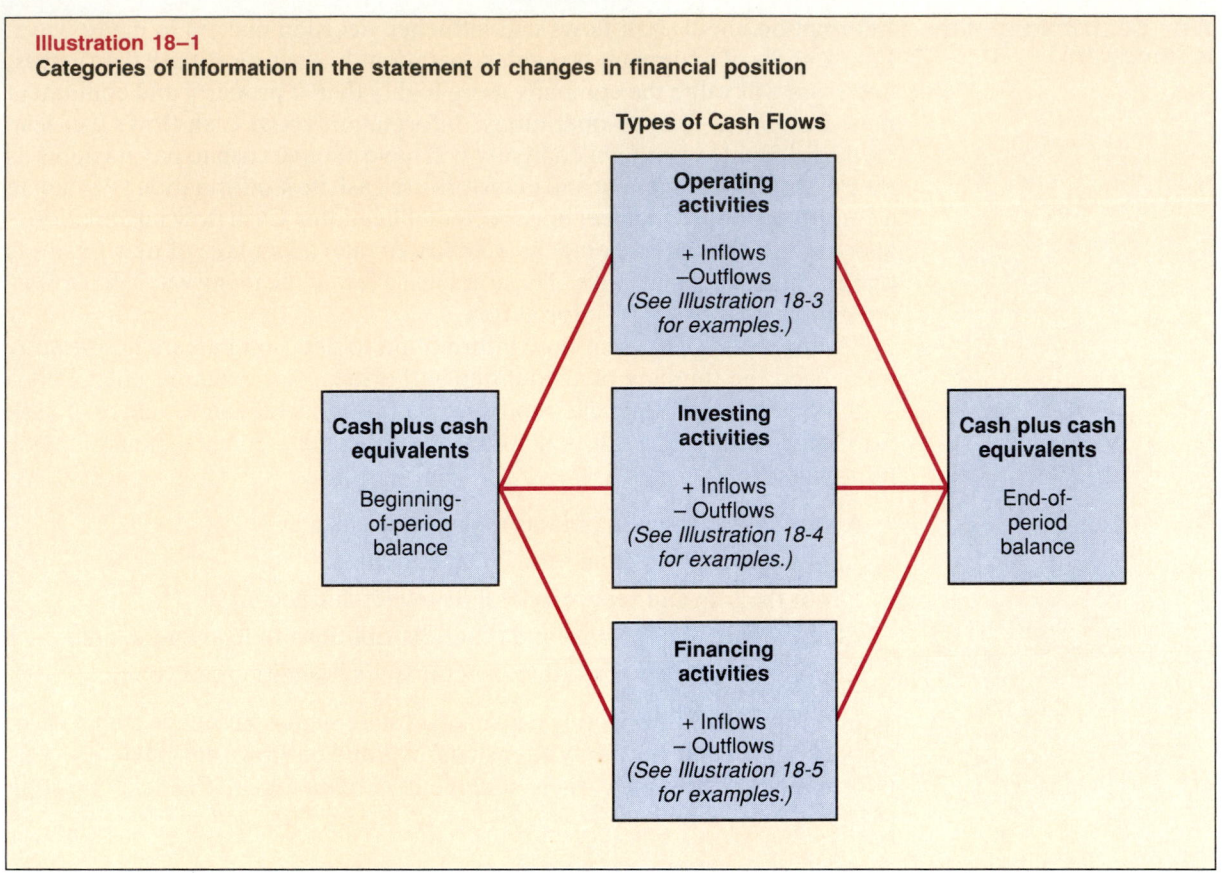

Illustration 18–1
Categories of information in the statement of changes in financial position

Types of Cash Flows

Operating activities

+ Inflows
−Outflows
(See Illustration 18-3 for examples.)

Cash plus cash equivalents

Beginning-of-period balance

Investing activities

+ Inflows
− Outflows
(See Illustration 18-4 for examples.)

Cash plus cash equivalents

End-of-period balance

Financing activities

+ Inflows
− Outflows
(See Illustration 18-5 for examples.)

provided (or used) by operating activities. That is, net income is adjusted to exclude amounts that were included in the determination of net income but that did not provide operating cash inflows or outflows during the period. For example, you know that depreciation expense is subtracted in the calculation of net income. But depreciation expense does not involve a current cash payment. Therefore, depreciation expense is added back to net income in the process of reconciling net income to the net cash provided (or used) by operating activities.

Designing the Statement of Changes in Financial Position (SCFP)

Illustration 18–2 contains the SCFP for Grover Company. Notice that in the operating activities section of the statement, there are three types of adjustments indicated. These will be explained below. In each of the other two categories, the cash outflows are subtracted from the cash inflows to determine the cash provided (or used) by those categories of transactions.

Compare Illustration 18–2 with Illustration 18–1. Notice that in Illustration 18–1, the beginning and ending balances are called *cash plus cash equivalents*. However, in Illustration 18–2, the beginning and ending balances refer only to cash. The balances in Illustration 18–2 are called *cash* because Grover Com-

Illustration 18–2

GROVER COMPANY
Statement of Changes in Financial Position
For Year Ended December 31, 1990

Cash flows from operating activities:			
Net income		$ 38,000	
Adjustments to reconcile net income to net			
cash provided by operating activities:			
Increase in accounts receivable	$(20,000)		
Increase in merchandise inventory	(14,000)		
Increase in prepaid expenses. . . .	(2,000)		
1 Decrease in accounts payable	(5,000)		
Decrease in interest payable	(1,000)		
Increase in income taxes payable	10,000		
2 Depreciation expense	24,000		
3 Loss on sale of plant assets	6,000		
Gain on retirement of bonds	(16,000)		
Total adjustments		(18,000)	
Net cash provided by operating activities . .			$ 20,000
Cash flows from investing activities:			
Cash paid for purchase of plant assets.		(70,000)	
Cash received from sale of plant assets		12,000	
Net cash provided by investing activities			(58,000)
Cash flows from financing activities:			
Cash received from issuance of stock		15,000	
Cash received from issuance of bonds		60,000	
Cash paid to retire bonds		(18,000)	
Cash paid for dividends		(14,000)	
Net cash used in financing activities			43,000
Net increase in cash.			5,000
Cash balance at beginning of 1990			12,000
Cash balance at end of 1990.			$ 17,000)

pany does not own any **cash equivalents.** However, this difference between the two illustrations raises the question: What are cash equivalents?

Cash and Cash Equivalents

In Section 1540 of the *CICA Handbook,* the Accounting Standards Committee concluded that a statement of cash flows should explain the differences between the beginning and ending balances of cash and cash equivalents. "Cash and cash equivalents would normally include cash, net of short-term borrowings, and temporary investments and may, in some cases, include certain other elements of working capital when they are equivalent to cash."[2]

The idea of classifying short-term, highly liquid investments as cash equivalents is based on the assumption that companies make these investments to earn a return on idle cash balances. However, some companies have other reasons for investing in items that meet the criteria of cash equivalents. For

[2] Ibid., par. 1540.03.

Illustration 18–3
Reconciliation of net income to cash flows from operating activities

Net Income or Net Loss

Plus	Minus
Decreases in noncash current assets.	Increases in noncash current assets.
Increases in current liabilities.	Decreases in current liabilities.
Expenses which do not require a cash outflow during the period.	Income which did not result in a cash inflow during the period.
Losses from investing and financing activities.	Gains from investing and financing activities.

example, an investment company that specializes in the purchase and sale of securities may buy such items as part of its investing activities.

Sometimes, items that meet the criteria of cash equivalents are not held as temporary investments of idle cash balances. Companies that have such investments are allowed to exclude them from the cash equivalents classification. However, the companies must develop a clear policy for determining which items are included and which are excluded. These policies must be disclosed in the footnotes to the financial statements and must be followed consistently from period to period.

Classifying Cash Transactions

Calculate cash inflows and outflows by inspecting the noncash account balances of a company and related information about its transactions.
(L. O. 2)

A SCFP describes the change in cash plus cash equivalents. Therefore, cash payments to purchase cash equivalents and cash receipts from selling cash equivalents are not reported on the statement. All other cash receipts and payments are classified as operating, investing, or financing activities. Within each category, individual cash receipts and payments are summarized and described in a manner that clearly presents the general nature of the company's cash transactions. Then, the summarized cash receipts and payments within each category are netted against each other. A category provides a net cash inflow if the receipts in the category exceed the payments. And if the payments in a category exceed the receipts, the category is a net user of cash during the period.

Operating Activities

In Illustration 18–2, look at the types of adjustments that are made to revise net income into cash flows resulting from **operating activities.** You should recognize that operating activities generally include only transactions that relate to the calculation of net income. However, some income statement items are not related to operating activities. These items will be discussed later.

As disclosed in a SCFP, operating activities involve the production or purchase of merchandise and the sale of goods and services to customers. Operating activities also include the expenditures related to administering the business. In fact, cash flows from operating activities include all cash flows from transactions that are not defined as investing or financing activities. Illustration 18–3 shows typical cash inflows and outflows from operating activities.

Three types of adjustments to net income are shown in Illustration 18–2. The adjustments grouped under (1) are for changes in noncash current assets and current liabilities that relate to operating activities. The adjustment identified as (2) is for an item that relates to operating activities but which did not provide cash inflows or cash outflows during the period. The adjustments grouped under (3) eliminate gains and losses that do not relate to operating activities. These gains and losses resulted from investing and financing activities.

Adjustments for Changes in Current Assets and Current Liabilities

To help you understand why adjustments for changes in noncash current assets and current liabilities are necessary, we will use the transactions of a very simple company as an example. Assume that Simple Company's income statement shows only two items, as follows:

Sales	$20,000
Operating expenses	12,000
Net income	$ 8,000

For a moment assume that all of Simple Company's sales and operating expenses are for cash. The company has no current assets other than cash and has no current liabilities. Given these assumptions, the net cash provided by operating activities during the period is $8,000, which is the cash received from customers less the cash paid for operating expenses. The net cash provided by operating activities also equals net income.

Adjustments for Changes in Noncash Current Assets

Now assume that Simple Company's sales are on account. Also assume that its Accounts Receivable balance was $2,000 at the beginning of the year and $2,500 at the end of the year. Under these assumptions, cash receipts from customers equal sales of $20,000 minus the $500 increase in Accounts Receivable, or $19,500. Therefore, the net cash provided by operating activities is $19,500 − $12,000 = $7,500.

When the net cash flow is calculated, net income of $8,000 is adjusted for the $500 increase in accounts receivable to get a net cash provided by operating activities of $7,500. The calculations are as follows:

Receipts from customers ($20,000 − $500)	$19,500
Payments for operating expenses	−12,000
Cash provided (or used) by operating activities . .	$ 7,500
Net income.	$ 8,000
Less the increase in Accounts Receivable	−500
Cash provided (or used) by operating activities . .	$ 7,500

Notice that the increase in Accounts Receivable is *subtracted* from net income.

As another example, assume that the Accounts Receivable balance decreased from $2,000 to $1,200. Under this assumption, cash receipts from customers equal sales of $20,000 plus the $800 decrease in Accounts Receivable, or $20,800. The net cash provided by operating activities is $20,800 − $12,000 = $8,800. Or the $800 decrease in Accounts Receivable is *added* to the $8,000 net income to get $8,800 net cash provided by operating activities.

Adjustments like these for Accounts Receivable are required for all noncash current assets related to operating activities. When a noncash current asset increases, part of the assets derived from operating activities are allocated to the increase. This leaves a smaller amount as a net cash inflow. Therefore, when you calculate the net cash inflow, the noncash current asset increase must be *subtracted* from net income. But when a noncash current asset decreases, the opposite adjustment is necessary. These adjustments for changes in current assets related to operating activities are as follows:

Net income
Add: Decreases in noncash current assets
Subtract: Increases in noncash current assets

Net cash provided (or used) by operating activities

Adjustments for Changes in Current Liabilities

To illustrate the adjustments for changes in current liabilities, return to the original assumptions about Simple Company. Sales of $20,000 are for cash, and operating expenses are $12,000. However, assume now that Simple Company has one current liability, Interest Payable, that relates to operating expenses. Also assume that the beginning-of-year balance in Interest Payable was $500 and the end-of-year balance was $900. This increase means that the operating expenses of $12,000 include $400 of interest that was not paid in cash during the period. Therefore, the cash payments for operating expenses were $11,600, or ($12,000 − $400). Under these assumptions, the calculation of net cash provided by operating activities is $8,400, or $20,000 in receipts from customers less $11,600 payments for expenses. Or, the cash inflow from operations is $8,400, determined by the net income of $8,000 plus the $400 increase in Interest Payable.

Alternatively, if the Interest Payable balance decreased, say by $600, the cash outflow for operating expenses would have been the $12,000 expense plus the $600 liability decrease, or $12,600. Then the calculation of net cash flow is $20,000 − $12,600 = $7,400. That is, $8,000 − $600 = $7,400. In other words, a *decrease* in Interest Payable is *subtracted* from net income.

Adjustments like these for Interest Payable are required for all current liabilities related to operating activities. When a current liability decreases, part of the assets derived from operating activities are allocated to pay for the decrease. Therefore, the decrease is subtracted from net income to determine the remaining net cash inflow. And when a current liability increases, the opposite adjustment is necessary. These adjustments for changes in current liabilities related to operating activities are:

```
Net income
Add: Increase in current liabilities
Subtract: Decrease in current liabilities
Net cash provided (or used) by operating activities
```

Adjustments for Other Operating Items that Do Not Provide or Use Cash

Some operating items that appear on an income statement do not provide or use cash during the current period. One example is depreciation. Other examples are amortization of intangible assets, depletion of natural resources, and bad debts expense.

These expenses are recorded with debits to expense accounts and credits to noncash accounts. They reduce net income but do not require cash outflows during the period. Therefore, when adjustments to net income are made, these noncash expenses must be added back to net income.

In addition to noncash expenses such as depreciation, net income may include some revenues that do not provide cash inflows during the current period. An example is equity method earnings from a stock investment in another entity. If net income includes revenues that do not provide cash inflows, the revenues must be subtracted from net income in the process of reconciling net income to the net cash provided by operating activities.

The adjustments for expenses and revenues that do not provide or use cash during the current period are:

```
Net income
Add: Expenses that do not use cash
Subtract: Revenues that do not provide cash
Net cash provided (or used) by operating activities
```

Adjustments for Nonoperating Items

Some income statement items are not related to the operating activities of the company. These are gains and losses that result from investing and financing activities. Examples are gains or losses on the sale of plant assets and gains or losses on the retirement of bonds payable.

Remember that you must reconcile net income to the net cash provided (or used) by *operating* activities. Therefore, net income must be adjusted to exclude gains and losses from investing and financing activities. In making these adjustments, gains from financing and investing activities are subtracted from net income, and losses are added back to net income.

```
Net income
Add: Losses from investing or financing activities
Subtract: Gains from investing or financing activities
Net cash provided (or used) by operating activities
```

In order to determine the net cash flows provided (or used) by operating activities, you need balance sheets at the beginning and end of the period, the current period's income statement, and other information about selected transactions. Illustration 18–9 shows the income statement and balance sheet information for Grover Company. Based upon this information, Illustration 18–2 presents the reconciliation of net income to net cash provided by operating activities.

Investing Activities

Transactions that involve making and collecting loans or that involve purchasing and selling plant assets, other productive assets, and investments (other than cash equivalents) are called **investing activities.** Usually, investing activities involve the purchase or sale of assets that are classified on the balance sheet as plant and equipment, intangible assets, or long-term investments. However, the purchase and sale of short-term investments other than cash equivalents are also investing activities. Illustration 18–4 shows examples of cash flows from investing activities.

The second type of receipt listed in Illustration 18–4 involves proceeds from collecting the principal amount of loans. Regarding this item, you must examine carefully any cash receipts that relate to notes receivable. If the notes resulted from sales to customers, the cash receipts are classified as operating activities. This is true even if the notes are long-term notes. But, if a company loans money to other parties, the cash receipts from collecting the loans are classified as investing activities. Nevertheless, the CICA concluded that collections of *interest* are not investing activities; they are reported as operating activities.

Financing Activities

A company's transactions with its owners and long-term creditors are typically called **financing activities.** Also, financing activities include borrowing cash on a short-term basis. However, cash payments to settle credit purchases of merchandise, whether on account or by note, are operating activities. Payments of interest expense are also operating activities. Examples of cash flows from financing activities are shown in Illustration 18–5.

Noncash Investing and Financing Activities

Identify and report on the SCFP any simultaneous investing and financing transactions. (L. O. 3)

Some important investing and financing activities do not involve cash receipts or payments during the current period. In the *CICA Handbook* the Accounting Standards Committee recognized that **noncash investing and financing activities** are important events that should be disclosed. For example, a company might purchase land and buildings and finance 100% of the purchase by giving a long-term note payable. Because this transaction clearly involves both investing and financing activities, it must be reported in both sections of the current period's SCFP even though no cash was received or paid. That is, the transaction is treated as if two cash transactions occurred simultaneously.

Other investing and financing activities may involve some cash receipt or payment but also involve giving or receiving other types of consideration. An example is if you purchase machinery valued at $12,000 by paying cash of

---

Illustration 18–4
Cash flows from investing activities

Cash Inflows	Cash Outflows
Proceeds from selling productive assets (e.g., land, buildings, equipment, natural resources, and intangible assets).	Payments to purchase property, plant, and equipment or other productive assets (excluding merchandise inventory).
Proceeds from collecting the principal amount of loans.	Payments to acquire equity securities of other companies.
Proceeds from selling investments in the equity securities of other companies.	Payments to acquire debt securities of other entities, except cash equivalents.
Proceeds from selling investments in the debt securities of other entities, except cash equivalents.	Payments in the form of loans made to other parties.
Proceeds from the sale (discounting) of loans made by the enterprise.	

Illustration 18–5
Cash flows from financing activities

Cash Inflows	Cash Outflows
Proceeds from the issuance of equity securities (e.g., common and preferred stock).	Payments of dividends and other distributions to owners.*
Proceeds from the issuance of bonds and notes payable.	Payments to purchase treasury stock.
Proceeds from other short- or long-term borrowing transactions.	Repayments of cash loans.
	Payments of the principal amounts involved in long-term credit arrangements.

*Some companies treat dividends as an operating activity outflow while others disclose them in a separate category. Section 1540 of the *Handbook* requires that dividends be disclosed but does not offer any guidance as to their category in the SCFP.

$5,000 and trading in old machinery that has a market value of $7,000. In this case, the SCFP reports a cash inflow of $7,000 from the sale of the old machine and a cash outflow of $12,000 on the purchase of the new machine.

Illustration 18–6 shows an example of how a company might disclose its noncash investing and financing activities. In Illustration 18–6, notice the last item which describes an exchange of machinery. Following the requirements of the CICA, the statement describes *both* the cash and noncash aspects of this transaction. The $5,000 cash payment is reported in Decco Company's SCFP as a net investing activity. Nevertheless, the statement includes both the cash and noncash aspects of the transaction.

Examples of transactions that must be disclosed as noncash investing and financing activities include the following:

The conversion of debt securities to equity securities.

The conversion of preferred stock into common stock.

The leasing of assets in a transaction that qualifies as a capital lease.

Illustration 18–6
Decco Company—disclosure of noncash investing and financing activities

The company issued 1,000 shares of common stock for the purchase of land and buildings with fair values of $5,000 and $15,000, respectively.

> Investing activity (outflow): Purchase of property for $20,000.
> Financing activity (inflow): Issue of common stock for $20,000.

The company entered into a capital lease obligation of $12,000 for new computer equipment.

> Investing activity (outflow): Acquisition of capital lease assets for $12,000.
> Financing activity (inflow): Capital lease obligation assumed for $12,000.

The company exchanged old machinery with a fair value of $7,000 and a book value of $8,000 for new machinery valued at $12,000. The balance of $5,000 was paid in cash.

> Net investing activity (outflow): Trade-in acquisition of new machinery for a net
> outflow of $5,000.

The purchase of long-term assets financed by a note payable to the seller.

The exchange of a noncash asset for other noncash assets.

The purchase of noncash assets in exchange for equity or debt securities.

Preparing a Statement of Changes in Financial Position

The information you need to prepare a statement of changes in financial position (SCFP) comes from a variety of sources. These include comparative balance sheets at the beginning and the end of the accounting period, an income statement for the period, and a careful analysis of each noncash balance sheet account. However, since our goal is to report cash inflows and cash outflows, we might begin our investigation by looking at the transactions recorded in the Cash account.

Analyzing the Cash Account

All of a company's cash receipts and cash payments are recorded in the Cash account in the general ledger. Therefore, the Cash account would seem to be the logical place to look for information about cash flows from operating, investing, and financing activities. To demonstrate, review the summarized Cash account of Grover Company presented below.

Summarized Cash Account, Grover Company

Balance, 31/12/89	12,000		
Receipts from customers	570,000	Payments for merchandise	319,000
Proceeds from sale of plant		Payments for wages and other	
assets	12,000	operating expenses	218,000
Proceeds from stock issuance	15,000	Interest payments	8,000
		Income tax payments	5,000
		Payments for purchase of plant	
		assets	10,000
		Payments to retire bonds	18,000
		Dividend payments	14,000
Balance, 31/12/90	17,000		

In this account, the individual cash transactions are already summarized in terms of major types of receipts and payments. For example, individual receipts from customers were totaled and are listed in the account as a single debit. All that remains is to determine whether each type of cash inflow or outflow is an operating, investing, or financing activity and to place it in its proper category on the SCFP.

While an analysis of the Cash account may appear to be an easy way to prepare a SCFP, it has two serious drawbacks. First, most companies have so many individual cash receipts and disbursements it is not practical to review them all. Imagine what a problem this would be for Stelco, INCO, Loblaws, or Molsons, or even for a relatively small business. Second, the Cash account usually does not contain a description of each cash transaction. Therefore, even though the Cash account shows the amount of each debit and credit, you generally cannot determine the type of transaction by looking at the Cash account. Thus, the Cash account does not provide the information that you need to prepare a SCFP. To obtain the necessary information, you must analyze the changes in the noncash accounts.

Analyzing Noncash Accounts to Determine Cash Flows

When a company records cash inflows and outflows with debits and credits to the Cash account, it also records credits and debits in other accounts. Some of these accounts are balance sheet accounts. Others are revenue and expense accounts that are closed to Retained Earnings, a balance sheet account. As a result, all cash transactions eventually affect the noncash balance sheet accounts. Therefore, the nature of the cash inflows and outflows can be determined by examining the changes in the noncash balance sheet accounts. Illustration 18–7 shows this important relationship between the Cash account and the noncash balance sheet accounts.

In Illustration 18–7, notice that the balance sheet equation labeled (1) is expanded in (2) so that cash is separated from the other assets. Then the equation is rearranged in (3) so that cash is set equal to the sum of the liability and equity accounts less the noncash asset accounts. The illustration then points out in (4) that changes in one side of the equation (cash) must be equal to the changes in the other side (noncash accounts). Part (4) shows that if you discover the changes in liabilities, owners' equity, and noncash assets, it is possible to fully explain the changes in cash. This information is all that you need to prepare a statement of cash flows.

This overall process has one added advantage. The examination of each noncash account also identifies any noncash investing and financing activities that occurred during the period. As you learned earlier, these noncash items must also be disclosed.

When you begin to analyze the changes in the noncash balance sheet accounts, recall that Retained Earnings is affected by revenues, expenses, and dividend declarations. Therefore, you need to look at the income statement accounts to help explain the change in Retained Earnings. In fact, the income statement accounts provide important information that relates to the changes in several balance sheet accounts.

Illustration 18–7
Why an analysis of the noncash accounts explains the change in cash

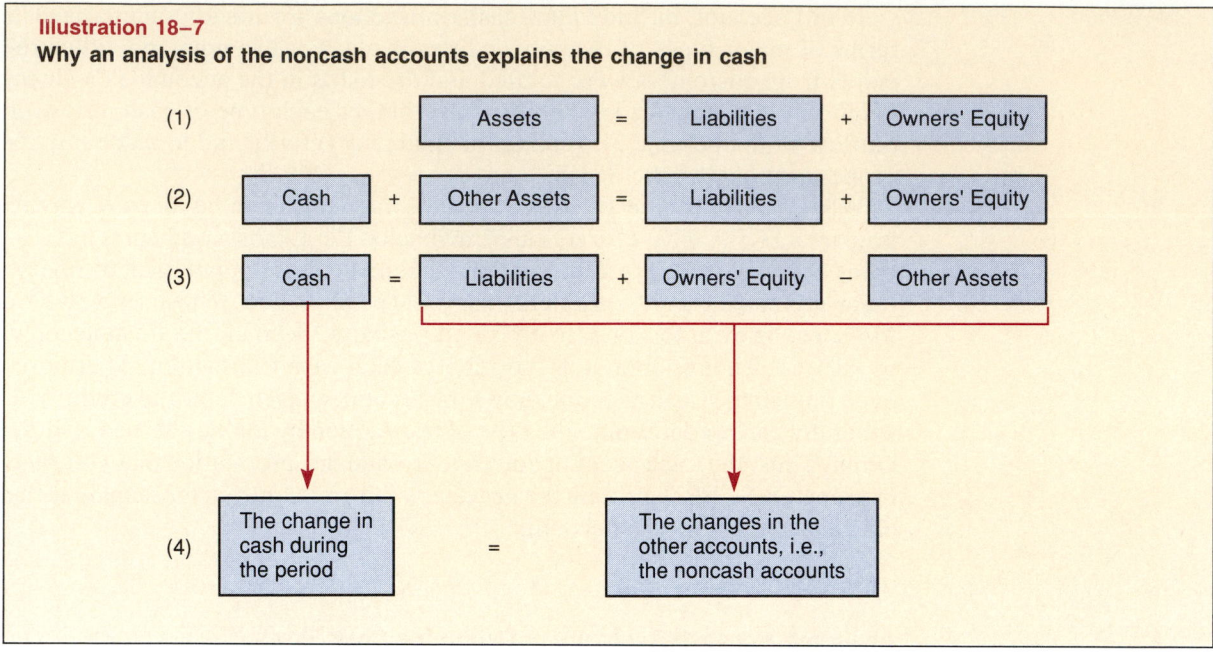

Some of these relationships between income statement accounts, balance sheet accounts, and possible cash flows are summarized in Illustration 18–8. For example, to determine the cash receipts from customers during a period, you must adjust the amount of sales revenue (i.e., net income) for the increase or decrease in Accounts Receivable.[3] If the Accounts Receivable balance did not change, you may infer that the cash collected from customers is equal to sales revenue. On the other hand, if the Accounts Receivable balance decreased, cash collections must have been equal to sales revenue plus the reduction in Accounts Receivable. And if the Accounts Receivable balance increased, the cash collected from customers must have been equal to Sales less the increase in Accounts Receivable.

If you analyze all of the noncash balance sheet accounts and the related income statement accounts in this fashion, you will obtain the information you need for a statement of cash flows. So that you will clearly understand this process, we will illustrate this process by examining the accounts of Grover Company.

---

[3] This introductory explanation assumes that there is no bad debts expense. However, if bad debts occur and are written off directly to Accounts Receivable, the change in the Accounts Receivable balance will be due in part to the write-off. The remaining change results from credit sales and from cash receipts. This chapter does not discuss the allowance method of accounting for bad debts since it would make the analysis unnecessarily complex at this time.

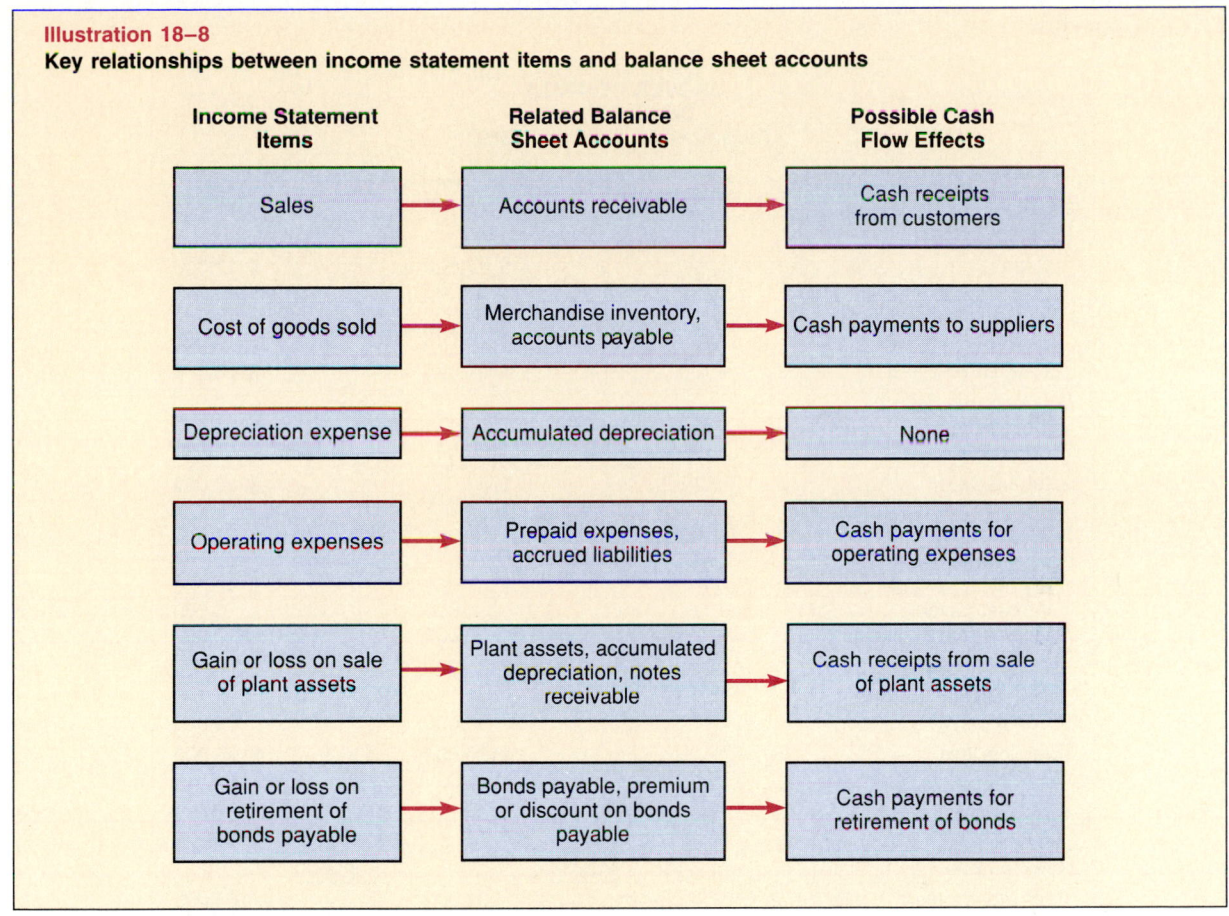

Illustration 18–8
Key relationships between income statement items and balance sheet accounts

Grover Company— A Comprehensive Example

Grover Company's December 31, 1989 and 1990, balance sheets and its 1990 income statement are presented in Illustration 18–9. The objective is to prepare a SCFP that explains the $5,000 increase in Cash, based on these financial statements and the additional information about 1990 transactions that follows. The letter that identifies each item of information is also used in the working paper to cross reference related debits and credits.

(a) Net income was $38,000.
(b) Accounts receivable increased by $20,000.
(c) Merchandise inventory increased by $14,000.
(d) Prepaid expenses increased by $2,000.
(e) Accounts payable decreased by $5,000.
(f) Interest payable decreased by $1,000.
(g) Income taxes payable increased by $10,000.
(h) Depreciation expenses was $24,000.

Illustration 18–9

GROVER COMPANY
Balance Sheet
December 31, 1990 and 1989

	1990		1989	
Assets				
Current assets:				
Cash		$ 17,000		$ 12,000
Accounts receivable		60,000		40,000
Merchandise inventory		84,000		70,000
Prepaid expenses		6,000		4,000
Total current assets		$167,000		$126,000
Long-term assets:				
Plant assets	$250,000		$ 210,000	
Less accumulated depreciation	60,000	190,000	48,000	162,000
Total assets.		$357,000		$288,000
Liabilities				
Current liabilities:				
Accounts payable		$ 35,000		$ 40,000
Interest payable		3,000		4,000
Income taxes payable		22,000		12,000
Total current liabilities		$ 60,000		$ 56,000
Long-term liabilities:				
Bonds payable		90,000		64,000
Total liabilities		$150,000		$120,000
Shareholders' Equity				
Contributed capital:				
Common stock, no-par value	$ 95,000		$ 80,000	
Retained earnings	112,000		88,000	
Total shareholders' equity		207,000		168,000
Total liabilities and shareholders' equity . .		$357,000		$288,000

Income Statement
For Year Ended December 31, 1990

Sales		$ 590,000
Cost of goods sold.	$300,000	
Wages and other operating expenses	216,000	
Interest expense	7,000	
Income taxes expense.	15,000	
Depreciation expense	24,000	(562,000)
Loss on sale of plant assets		(6,000)
Gain on retirement of debt		16,000
Net income		$ 38,000

(i) Loss on sale of plant assets was $6,000; assets that cost $30,000 with accumulated depreciation of $12,000 were sold for $12,000 cash.

(j) Gain on retirement of bonds was $16,000; bonds with a book value of $34,000 were retired with a cash payment of $18,000.

(k) Plant assets that cost $70,000 were purchased; the payment consisted of $10,000 cash and the issuance of a $60,000 note payable.

(l) Sold 3,000 shares of common stock for $15,000.

(m) Paid cash dividends of $14,000.

Preparation of the SCFP

Direct Approach

The direct approach uses (a) comparative balance sheets (in which beginning-period and ending-period balances are compared), (b) the current income statement, and (c) supplementary data to clarify certain transactions. To illustrate the direct approach, consider data given in Illustration 18–9 and above. The related SCFP is shown in Illustration 18–2. The comparative balance sheets show that cash increased by $5,000 during 1990. Therefore, $5,000 must be the amount on the bottom line of the SCFP (Illustration 18–2). This change is explained by examining and identifying the causes of the cash inflows and outflows.

Analysis of Cash Flows

In Illustration 18–2 the $20,000 cash from operations consists of the following four elements: (a) reported net income (from the income statement), (b) increases and decreases in current assets and current liabilities (#1, from comparative balance sheets), (c) expenses not requiring cash outlay in the current period (#2, from income statement), and (d) gains and losses arising from investing and financing activities (#3, from income statement).

The $58,000 cash outflow from investing activities consists of two items. First, the $70,000 purchase of plant assets which was partially financed by a $60,000 bond issue (the bond issue is reported under financing activities) and the sale of plant assets for $60,000 cash. The details of the assets sold, which had an original cost of $30,000, can be found in the additional information. The purchase of assets costing $70,000 and the sale of assets costing $30,000 explains the $40,000 net increase in the Plant Assets account.

The $43,000 cash inflow from financing activities consists of four items. First, there was a $15,000 stock issue which is given in the additional information and can be determined from the comparative balance sheets. Second, there was an issue of bonds for $60,000. Third, bonds with a book value of $34,000 were redeemed for a payment of $18,000. These two items together account for the net increase of $26,000 in the Bond account ($60,000 − $34,000). Fourth, dividends of $14,000 were paid during the period. Net income less the dividends account for the increase in retained earnings of $24,000 ($38,000 − $14,000).

Although the direct method technique may be adequate when doing relatively simple SCFPs, in many cases a more formal method is desirable. This is the working paper approach which is illustrated and discussed below.

Preparing the SCFP Working Paper

Prepare a working paper for a statement of changes in financial position. (L. O. 4)

Illustration 18–10 shows the working paper for Grover Company. Notice that the beginning and ending balance sheets are recorded on the working paper and, following the balance sheets, information is entered in the Analysis of Changes columns about cash flows from operating, investing, and financing activities and about noncash investing and financing activities. Note that the working paper does not include a reconstruction of the income statement. Instead, net income is entered as the first source of cash flows from operating activities.

Entering the Analysis of Changes on the Working Paper

After the balance sheets are entered, we recommend that you use the following sequence of procedures to complete the working paper.

Operating Activities

1. Enter net income as an operating cash inflow (a debit) and as a credit to Retained Earnings, entry (*a1*); enter the difference in the cash balance, entry (*a2*).
2. In the statement of cash flows section, adjustments to net income are entered as debits if they increase cash inflows and as credits if they decrease cash inflows. Following this rule, adjust net income for the change in each noncash current asset and current liability related to operating activities. For each adjustment to net income, the offsetting debit or credit should reconcile the beginning and ending balances of a current asset or current liability (see entries (*b*) to (*g*)). For example, an increase in Accounts Receivable would be entered as a debit on the asset line and a credit in the operating activity section. (See entry (*b*) in Illustration 18–10.)
3. Enter the adjustments to net income for income statement items, such as depreciation, that did not provide or use cash during the period (entry (*h*)). For each adjustment, the offsetting debit or credit should help reconcile a noncash balance sheet account.
4. Adjust net income to eliminate any gains or losses from investing and financing actvities. Since the cash inflow of a gain is excluded from operating activities, it is entered as a credit (entry (*j*)). On the other hand, losses are entered with debits (entry (*i*)). For each of these adjustments, the related debit and/or credits help reconcile balance sheet accounts and also involve entries to show the cash flow from investing or financing activities.

Investing Activities

Investing activities usually refer to transactions that affect long-term assets. Recall from the information that was provided about Grover Company's transactions that the company purchased plant assets and also sold plant assets. Both of these transactions are investing activities.

Purchase of Plant Assets. Grover Company purchased plant assets that cost $70,000 by issuing $60,000 of bonds payble to the seller and paying the $10,000 balance in cash. The effect of these transactions is similar to a cash inflow followed immediately by a cash outflow. Therefore, this transaction

Illustration 18–10

GROVER COMPANY
Working Paper for Statement of Changes in Financial Position
For Year Ended December 31, 1990

	December 31, 1989	Analysis of Changes		December 31, 1990
		Debit	Credit	
Balance sheet—debits:				
Cash	12,000	(a2) 5,000		17,000
Accounts receivable	40,000	(b) 20,000		60,000
Merchandise inventory	70,000	(c) 14,000		84,000
Prepaid expenses	4,000	(d) 2,000		6,000
Plant assets	210,000	(k1) 70,000	(i) 30,000	250,000
	336,000			417,000
Balance sheet—credits:				
Accumulated depreciation	48,000	(i) 12,000	(h) 24,000	60,000
Accounts payable	40,000	(e) 5,000		35,000
Interest payable	4,000	(f) 1,000		3,000
Income taxes payable	12,000		(g) 10,000	22,000
Bonds payable	64,000	(j) 34,000	(k2) 60,000	90,000
Common stock, no par value	80,000		(l) 15,000	95,000
Retained earnings	88,000	(m) 14,000	(a1) 38,000	112,000
	336,000			417,000
Statement of changes in financial position:				
Operating activities:				
Net income		(a1) 38,000		
Increase in accounts receivable			(b) 20,000	
Increase in merchandise inventory			(c) 14,000	
Increase in prepaid expenses			(d) 2,000	
Decrease in accounts payable			(e) 5,000	
Decrease in interest payable			(f) 1,000	20,000
Increase in income taxes payable		(g) 10,000		
Depreciation expense		(h) 24,000		
Loss on sale of plant assets		(i) 6,000		
Gain on retirement of bonds			(j) 16,000	
Investing activities:				
Receipts from sale of plant assets		(i) 12,000		(58,000)
Purchase of plant assets			(k1) 70,000	
Financing activities:				
Payments to retire bonds			(j) 18,000	
Receipts from issuance of stock		(l) 15,000		43,000
Payments of dividends			(m) 14,000	
Receipts from issuance of bonds		(k2) 60,000		
Increase in cash balance			(a2) 5,000	5,000
		342,000	342,000	

is reported as both a financing and an investing activity. That is, a financing cash inflow of $60,000 (entry (k2)) and an investing cash outflow of $70,000 (entry (k1)).

Sale of Plant Assets. Grover Company sold plant assets that cost $30,000 and had accumulated depreciation of $12,000. The result of the sale was a loss of

$6,000 and a cash receipt of $12,000 (entry (*i*)). This cash receipt is reported in the statement of cash flows as a cash inflow from investing activities (see Illustration 18–2).

Recall from Grover Company's income statement that depreciation expense was $24,000. Depreciation does not use or provide cash. However, we should notice the effects of depreciation expense, the plant asset purchase, and the plant asset sale on the Plant Assets and Accumulated Depreciation accounts. These accounts are reconstructed, as follows:

Plant Assets					Accumulated Depreciation	
31/12/89 Bal.	210,000				31/12/89 Bal.	48,000
Purchase	70,000	Sale	30,000	Sale 12,000	Depreciation expense	24,000
31/12/90 Bal.	250,000				31/12/90 Bal.	60,000

The beginning and ending balances of these accounts were taken from Grover Company's balance sheets (Illustration 18–9). Reconstructing the accounts shows that the beginning and ending balances of both accounts are completely reconciled by the purchase, the sale, and the depreciation expense. As a result, you can conclude that you did not omit any of the investing activities that relate to plant assets.

Financing Activities

Financing activities usually relate to a company's long-term debt and shareholders' equity accounts. In the information about Grover Company, there were four transactions that involved financing activities. One of these, the $60,000 issuance of bonds payable (entry (*k2*)) to purchase plant assets, was discussed above as a simultaneous investing and financing activity. The remaining three transactions were the retirement of bonds, the issuance of common stock, and the payment of cash dividends.

Payment to Retire Bonds Payable. Grover Company's December 31, 1989, balance sheet showed bonds payable of $64,000, of which $34,000 were retired for $18,000 cash in 1990 (entry (*j*)). The income statement reports the $16,000 difference as a gain (entry (*j*)). The SCFP shows the $18,000 payment as a cash outflow from financing activities (see Illustration 18–2).

Notice that the beginning and ending balances of Bonds Payable are reconciled by the $60,000 issuance of new bonds and the retirement of $34,000 of old bonds. This is shown in the reconstructed Bonds Payable account that follows:

Bonds Payable			
		31/12/89 Bal.	64,000
Retired bonds	34,000	Issued bonds	60,000
		31/12/90 Bal.	90,000

Receipt from Common Stock Issuance. During 1990, Grover Company issued 3,000 shares of common stock for $5 per share. This $15,000 cash receipt is reported on the statement of cash flows as a financing activity (entry (*l*)). Look at the December 31, 1989 and 1990, balance sheets in Illustration 18–9. Notice that the Common Stock account balance increased from $80,000 at the beginning of 1990 to $95,000 at the end of 1990. Thus, the $15,000 stock issue reconciles the change in the Common Stock account.

Payment of Cash Dividends. According to the facts provided about Grover Company's transactions, cash dividends of $14,000 were paid during 1990. This payment is reported as a cash outflow from financing activities (entry (*m*)). Also note that the effects of this $14,000 payment and the reported net income of $38,000 fully reconcile the beginning and ending balances of Retained Earnings. This is shown in the reconstructed Retained Earnings account that follows:

Retained Earnings

		31/12/89 Bal.	88,000
Cash dividend	14,000	Net income	38,000
		31/12/90 Bal.	112,000

All of Grover Company's cash inflows and outflows were described in the previous paragraphs. We also described one simultaneous investing and financing transaction. In the process of making these analyses, we reconciled the changes in all of the noncash balance sheet accounts. The change in the Cash account is reconciled by the statement of changes in financial position, as shown in Illustration 18–2.

Summary of Chapter in Terms of Learning Objectives

1. Operating activities include transactions that relate to production or purchase of merchandise, sale of goods and service to customers, and administrative functions. Investing activities include purchases and sales of noncurrent assets and short-term investments that are not cash equivalents. Transactions with long-term creditors, owners, and that involve short-term sources of cash and cash equivalents are financing activities.

2. Cash receipts and payments are recorded in the Cash account and in offsetting balance sheet accounts or temporary accounts such as revenues and expenses. The temporary accounts are closed to Retained Earnings. Therefore, you can analyze the changes in the noncash balance sheet accounts brought about by income statement transactions and other events to determine cash receipts and cash payments. For example, cash collected from customers is calculated by adjusting sales revenues for the change in accounts receivable. Also, cash paid for interest is calculated by adjusting interest expense for the change in interest payable.

3. To calculate the net cash provided (or used) by operating activities, you first list the net income and then adjust it for three types of events. They are: (*a*) changes in noncash current assets and current liabilities related to operating activities, (*b*) revenues and expenses that did not provide or use cash, and (*c*) gains and losses from investing and financing activities.

4. To prepare a SCFP working paper, you first enter the beginning and ending balances of the balance sheet accounts in columns one and four. Then, the three sections of the SCFP are established. Net income is entered as the first item in the operating activities section. Then you adjust the net income for events (*a*)–(*c*) identified in paragraph 3, above. This reconciles the changes in the noncash current assets and current liabilities related to operations. Any remaining balance sheet account changes are reconciled, and their cash effects are reported in the appropriate sections, being careful to enter properly any simultaneous investing and financing activities which may have occurred.

Demonstration Problem

Given the following condensed income statement and a partial list of account balances, calculate the cash provided by operating activities:

BUTTERFIELD COMPANY
Income Statement
For the Year Ended December 31, 1991

Sales		$225,000
Cost of goods sold		130,000
Gross profit from sales.		$ 95,000
Operating expenses:		
Salaries and wages	$31,250	
Depreciation expense	3,750	
Rent expense	9,000	
Amortization of patents	750	
Office expense.	1,000	
Bond interest expense.	3,375	49,125
Net income		$ 45,875

Butterfield Company's partial list of comparative account balances as of December 31, 1991 and 1990:

	1991	1990
Cash	$ 2,600	$ 2,200
Accounts receivable (net)	23,200	21,800
Inventory	17,900	19,300
Prepaid expenses	1,200	1,400
Accounts payable	11,400	12,100
Salaries and wages payable	250	650
Interest payable	1,500	750
Unamortized bond discount.	500	875

Solution to Demonstration Problem

BUTTERFIELD COMPANY
Cash Provided by Operating Activities
For the Year Ended December 31, 1991

Cash provided by operating activities:		
Net income		$45,875
Adjustments to reconcile net income to		
cash provided by operations:		
Increase in accounts receivable	$(1,400)	
Decrease in inventory	1,400	
Decrease in prepaid expenses	200	
Decrease in accounts payable	(700)	
Decrease in salaries and wages payable	(400)	
Increase in interest payable.	750	
Depreciation expense	3,750	
Amortization of patents	750	
Amortization of bond discount	375	4,725
Cash provided by operating activities.		$50,600

Glossary

Define or explain the words or phrases listed in the chapter Glossary. (L. O. 5)

Cash equivalent an investment that is readily convertible to a known amount of cash. p. 797

Financing activities transactions with the owners or long-term creditors of the business or that involve borrowing cash on a short-term basis. p. 802

Investing activities transactions that involve making and collecting loans or that involve purchasing and selling plant assets, other productive assets, or investments (other than cash equivalents). p. 802

Noncash investing and financing transactions those transactions where a company will exchange long-term assets for other long-term assets or for long-term debt and/or shares. The transaction is reported as if two simultaneous cash transactions took place. p. 802

Operating activities activities that involve the production or purchase of merchandise and the sale of goods and services to customers, including expenditures to administer the business. p. 798

Statement of changes in financial position (SCFP) a financial statement that reports the cash inflows and outflows for an accounting period, and that classifies those cash flows as operating activities, investing activities, and financing activities. p. 794

Questions for Class Discussion

1. What information is shown on a statement of changes in financial position (SCFP)?

2. What are the three categories of cash flows shown on a SCFP?

3. What are some examples of items that are reported on a SCFP as investing activities?

4. What are some examples of items that are reported on a SCFP as financing activities?

5. If a company reports a net income for the year, is it possible for the company to show a net cash outflow from operating activities? Explain your answer.

6. A machine that was held as a long-term asset for use in business operations is sold for cash. Where should this cash flow appear on the SCFP?

7. A business purchases merchandise inventory for cash. Where should this cash flow appear on the SCFP?

8. If a corporation pays cash dividends, where on the corporation's SCFP should the payment be reported?

9. A company purchases land for $200,000 and finances 100% of the purchase with a long-term note payable. Should this transaction be reported on a SCFP? If so, where on the statement should it be reported?

10. A company purchases land for $100,000, paying $20,000 cash and borrowing the remainder on a long-term note payable. How should this transaction be reported on a SCFP?

11. Why are expenses such as depreciation and amortization of goodwill added to net income when cash flow from operations is calculated?

12. A company had $70,000 of merchandise inventory at the beginning of a period and $40,000 of merchandise inventory at the end of the same period. How should this decrease in inventory be treated in the calculation of the SCFP?

13. A company reports a net income of $15,000 that includes a $3,000 gain on sale of plant assets. Why is this gain subtracted from net income in the process of reconciling net income to the net cash provided or used by operating activities?

14. Is depreciation a source of cash?

15. On June 3, a company borrowed $50,000 by giving its bank a 60-day, interest-bearing note. On the SCFP where should this item be reported?

16. A company borrowed $50,000 by giving its bank a 60-day, 12% interest-bearing note. When the note was repaid, the company also paid interest of $1,000. On the SCFP where should the $1,000 interest payment be reported?

17. When a working paper for the preparation of a SCFP is prepared, all changes in noncash balance sheet accounts are accounted for on the working paper. Why?

18. A company retired a long-term note payable by issuing, at par, shares of common stock. How is this event analyzed on the SCFP working paper?

Multiple Choice

1. On December 31, 1990, the balance in the Salary Expense account was $16,400. The Salaries Payable account had a January 1 balance of $1,300 and a December 31 balance of $2,400. How much cash was paid for salaries in 1990?
   a. $14,000.
   b. $15,300.
   c. $16,400.
   d. $17,700.
   e. $18,800.

2. Repayment of a cash loan is an example of a:
   a. Cash flow from operating activities.
   b. Cash flow from investing activities.
   c. Cash flow from financing activities.
   d. Noncash investing and financing activity.
   e. Cash payment to purchase a cash equivalent.

3. Banghart Company's Merchandise Inventory account balance decreased during a period from a beginning balance of $40,000 to an ending balance of $35,000. Cost of goods sold for that same period was

$210,000. If the Accounts Payable balance increased $3,000 during the period, what was the amount of cash paid for merchandise?
a. $202,000.
b. $208,000.
c. $210,000.
d. $212,000.
e. $218,000.

4. The following information concerns the Omega Corporation for 1990:

Cash balance, January 1, 1990.	$56,000
Cash generated by operations	43,000
Cash dividends paid by Omega	29,000
Depreciation expense for 1990.	12,000
Sale of warehouse	42,000
Purchase of marketable equity securities . .	40,000

What is Omega's December 31, 1990, cash balance?
a. $60,000.
b. $72,000.
c. $84,000.
d. $96,000.
e. $136,000.

5. A company's operations included the following activities:

Net income	$22,400
Depreciation expense, buildings	2,300
Depletion expense, oil wells	5,000
Amortization of bond discount	500
Payment of dividends declared last year . .	3,200
Cost of treasury stock purchased	5,000
Proceeds from sale of equipment	2,200
Increase in current assets (except cash) . .	800
Increase in current liabilities	600

Given the above information, what is the amount of cash from operations?
a. $34,800.
b. $31,400.
c. $31,900.
d. $32,400.
e. $30,000.

6. Proper accounting for the acquisition of a building in exchange for a mortgage requires:
a. Disclosure in the statement of changes in financial position of only the mortgage issuance and not the building acquisition.
b. Disclosure in the statement of changes in financial position of both the building acquisition and mortgage issuance.
c. No disclosure in the statement of changes in financial position.
d. Disclosure in the statement of changes in financial position of only the building acquisition and not the mortgage issuance.
e. None of the above.

Mini Discussion Cases

Case 18–1

George Nature, sole owner and chief executive of Nature Decoy Company, operated from the basement of his home. He made carved decoys at a cost of $350 each and sold them for $500. The cost of selling the decoys was $50 each. He had no other expenses, and therefore, Nature Decoy Company's income was $100 each.

All production costs were paid in cash, as the custom in this so-called cottage industry was not to provide credit to customers. Nature kept his inventory at the end of each month equal to the number of decoys sold during that month. All sales were made on 30-day credit, and the terms were strictly enforced. The operation was steady with sales of 50 decoys per month since the business was started two years ago. The balance sheet on May 31, 1990, was as follows:

Cash	$15,000	Liabilities.	-0-
Accounts receivable	25,000		
Inventory	17,500	George Nature, capital	$57,500
	$57,500		$57,500

During Rotary's Art in the Park display, at which Nature had a showing of his decoys, sales took off. In June he sold 250 decoys, and in July, 500. By the middly of July it appeared that sales would continue to increase at 50 decoys a month.

The established policy of the company was to maintain an end-of-month inventory equal to the sales of the month. For example, at the end of May, inventory was 50 decoys, and at the end of June, 250 decoys.

The sales picture was so good that George decided to go on vaction the third week of July. Three days after he left, he received a telephone call from home to return immediately. The bank was "bouncing" his cheques and his suppliers were irate. He asked about the company's production, sales, and collections and was told they were all on schedule. He was heard to remark, "How can I be going broke while making such a good profit?"

Puzzled by the situaton, George Nature turns to you to solve the apparent mystery.

Case 18–2

During the Gulf Canada Corp. takeover of Hiram Walker Resources, in the spring of 1986, much was written by financial analysts on the reasons for the takeover. The most common reason was that Gulf was primarily interested in the cash-generating portions of Walker Resources. Gulf Canada was a cash "user" company and needed a cash-generating unit.

Required

Discuss the characteristics of a company that (*a*) makes it a cash-generating company and (*b*) one that is a cash user company.

Exercises

Exercise 18–1
Classifying transactions on SCFP
(L. O. 1)

Examine each of the following items to determine where on the SCFP the item should be included. Prepare a table for your answers and record your answers by placing check marks in the appropriate columns.

	Operating Activities	Investing Activities	Financing Activities
a. A six-month note receivable was accepted in exchange for a building that had been used in operations.	_____	_____	_____
b. A cash dividend that was declared in a previous period was paid in the current period.	_____	_____	_____
c. Surplus merchandise inventory was sold for cash.	_____	_____	_____
d. Paid cash to purchase a trademark.	_____	_____	_____
e. Long-term bonds payable were retired by issuing common stock.	_____	_____	_____
f. Borrowed cash from the bank by signing a six-month note payable.	_____	_____	_____

Exercise 18–2
Calculating cash flows
(L. O. 3)

In each of the following cases, use the information provided about the 1990 operations of Barney Company to calculate the adjustment to net income needed to determine cash provided by operations:

Case A:	Rent expense	$19,000
	Prepaid rent, January 1.	4,500
	Rent paid	17,500
Case B:	Salaries expense	$14,000
	Salaries paid	11,000
	Salaries payable, December 31	8,000
Case C:	Sales revenue.	$60,000
	Accounts receivable, January 1	12,000
	Accounts receivable, December 31	9,000

Exercise 18–3
Calculating cash flows
(L. O. 3)

In each of the following cases, use the information provided about the 1990 operations of Lehman Company to calculate the adjustment to net income needed to determine cash provided by operations:

Case A:	Interest revenue	$34,000
	Interest receivable, January 1.	2,500
	Interest receivable, December 31.	1,800
Case B:	Utilities expense	$16,800
	Utilities payable, January 1	7,500
	Utilities payable, December 31	4,700
Case C:	Cost of goods sold.	$59,000
	Merchandise inventory, January 1	18,600
	Accounts payable, January 1	14,300
	Merchandise inventory, December 31	19,200
	Accounts Payable, December 31	11,700

Exercise 18–4
Cash flows from operating activities
(L. O. 2, 4)

Use the following income statement and information about changes in non-cash current assets and current liabilities to present the cash flows from operating activities:

ECOSYSTEMS COMPANY
Income Statement
For Year Ended December 31, 1990

Sales.		$225,000
Cost of goods sold		130,000
Gross profit from sales		$ 95,000
Operating expenses:		
Salaries and wages.	$31,250	
Depreciation expense	3,750	
Rent expense.	9,000	
Amortization of goodwill	1,750	
Interest expense	2,375	48,125
Total		$ 46,875
Gain on sale of machinery		1,000
Net income		$ 47,875

Changes in current asset and current liability accounts during the year, all of which related to operating activities, were as follows:

Accounts receivable.	$4,000 decrease
Merchandise inventory	5,000 increase
Accounts payable	7,000 increase
Salaries and wages payable	3,000 decrease

Exercise 18–5
Cash flows from operating activities
(L. O. 3)

Megan Corporation's 1990 income statement showed the following: net income, $42,000; depreciation expense, $7,000; amortization expense, $3,500; and loss on sale of plant assets, $4,000. An examination of the company's current assets and current liabilities showed that the following changes occurred because of operating activities: accounts receivable increased $5,600; merchandise inventory decreased $7,000; prepaid expenses increased $2,800; accounts payable decreased $4,200; other payables increased $1,900. Calculate the cash flow from operating activities.

Exercise 18–6
Noncash investing and financing activities
(L. O. 4)

Explain how each of the transactions below should be reported on the SCFP.

a. The income statement shows a $5,000 loss on exchange of machinery. The loss relates to an old machine that had a book value of $25,000 when it was exchanged for a new machine that had a cash price of $20,000.

b. Outstanding bonds payable carried on the books at $100,000 were retired by issuing 800 shares of common stock.

c. Land valued at $250,000 was purchased by paying cash of $50,000 and signing a long-term note payable for the balance.

d. The income statement shows a $30,000 gain on the sale of a building. The building had a book value of $90,000 and was sold for $120,000. The company received $50,000 cash and accepted a long-term promissory note for the balance of the sales price.

Exercise 18–7
SCFP
(L. O. 2, 4)

Gail Company's 1990 and 1989 balance sheets showed the following items:

	December 31	
	1990	1989
Debits		
Cash	$ 15,000	$ 12,000
Accounts receivable	24,000	27,000
Merchandise inventory.	63,000	54,000
Equipment	53,000	45,000
Totals	$155,000	$138,000
Credits		
Accumulated depreciation, equipment	$ 14,000	$ 9,000
Common stock, no par value	75,000	75,000
Retained earnings	66,000	54,000
Totals	$155,000	$138,000

An examination of the company's activities during 1990, including the income statement, reveals the following:

a.	Sales (all on credit)		$190,000
b.	The only decreases in Accounts Receivable were receipts from customers.		
c.	Cost of goods sold	$103,000	
d.	All merchandise purchases were for cash.		
e.	Depreciation expense	5,000	
f.	Other operating expenses	60,000	168,000
	Net income		$ 22,000

g. Equipment was purchased for $8,000 cash.
h. The company declared and paid $10,000 of cash dividends during the year.

Required

Prepare a SCFP. Do not prepare a working paper but show any supporting calculations.

Problems

Problem 18–1
SCFP (direct method)
(L. O. 1, 2, 3)

Mason Corporation's 1990 and 1989 balance sheets carried the following items:

	December 31	
	1990	1989
Debits		
Cash	$ 63,000	$ 24,000
Accounts receivable	48,000	54,000
Merchandise inventory.	126,000	108,000
Equipment	111,000	90,000
Totals	$348,000	$276,000
Credits		
Accumulated depreciation, equipment	$ 27,000	$ 18,000
Accounts payable	51,000	30,000
Income taxes payable	6,000	12,000
Common stock	198,000	180,000
Retained earnings	66,000	36,000
Totals	$348,000	$276,000

Additional information about the company's activities during 1990 follows:

a. Net income was $60,000.

b. Accunts receivable decreased.

c. Merchandise inventory increased.

d. Accounts payable increased.

e. Income taxes payable decreased.

f. Depreciation expense was $9,000.

g. Equipment was purchased for $21,000 cash.

h. Fifteen hundred shares of stock were issued for cash at $12 per share.

i. The company declared and paid $30,000 of cash dividends during the year.

Required

Prepare a SCFP using the direct method. Do not prepare a working paper. Instead, prepare the statement directly from your examination of the balance sheets and the additional information provided about the income statement and other transactions of the company.

Problem 18–2
SCFP working paper
(L. O. 1, 4)

Refer to the facts about Mason Corporation presented in Problem 18–1 and prepare a statement of cash flows working paper. Identify the debits and credits in the Analysis of Changes columns with letters that correspond to the list of information about the company presented in Problem 18–1.

Problem 18–3
Reconciling net income to cash flows from operating activities
(L. O. 1, 2, 3)

Skipper Corporation's 1990 and 1989 balance sheets included the following items:

	December 31	
	1990	**1989**
Debits		
Cash	$ 97,800	$ 25,800
Accounts receivable	48,000	60,000
Merchandise inventory.	189,000	192,000
Prepaid expenses	6,000	7,200
Equipment	220,600	154,000
Totals.	$561,400	$439,000
Credits		
Accumulated depreciation, equipment	$ 36,600	$ 32,800
Accounts payable	129,000	107,400
Short-term notes payable	15,000	9,000
Long-term notes payable	76,000	60,000
Common stock.	195,000	150,000
Retained earnings	109,800	79,800
Totals.	$561,400	$439,000

Additional information about the 1990 activities of the company is as follows:

a. Net income was $48,000.

b. Accounts receivable decreased.

c. Merchandise inventory decreased.

d. Prepaid expenses decreased.

e. Accounts payable increased.

f. Depreciation expense was $12,600.

g. Equipment that cost $14,800 and was depreciated $8,800 was sold for $4,200 cash, which caused a loss of $1,800.

h. Equipment that cost $81,400 was purchased by paying cash of $41,400 and (i) by signing a long-term note payable for the balance.

j. Borrowed $6,000 by signing a short-term note payable.

k. Paid $24,000 to reduce a long-term note payable.

l. Issued 500 shares of common stock for cash at $90 per share.

m. Declared and paid cash dividends of $18,000.

Required

Prepare a schedule that reconciles net income to the net cash provided or used by operating activities.

Problem 18–4
SCFP (direct method)
(L. O. 1, 2, 3)

Refer to the information about Skipper Corporation presented in Problem 18–3.

Required:

Prepare a SCFP using the direct method. Do not prepare a working paper. Instead, prepare the statement directly from your examination of the balance sheets and the additional information provided about the income statement and other transactions of the company. Show your supporting calculations.

Problem 18–5
SCFP working paper
(L. O. 4)

Refer to the facts about Skipper Corporation presented in Problem 18–3. Prepare a SCFP working paper which identifies the debits and credits in the Analysis of Changes columns with letters that correspond to the list of information about the company presented in Problem 18–3.

Alternate Problems

Problem 18–1A
SCFP (direct method)
(L. O. 1, 2, 3)

Cemco Corporation's 1990 and 1989 balance sheets carried the following items:

	December 31	
	1990	**1989**
Debits		
Cash	$ 50,400	$ 19,200
Accounts receivable	38,400	43,200
Merchandise inventory.	100,800	86,400
Equipment	88,800	72,000
Totals	$278,400	$220,800
Credits		
Accumulated depreciation, equipment	$ 21,600	$ 14,400
Accounts payable	40,800	24,000
Income taxes payable	4,800	9,600
Common stock	158,400	144,000
Retained earnings	52,800	28,800
Totals	$278,400	$220,800

Additional information about the company's activities during 1990 follows:

a. Net income was $48,000.

b. Accounts receivable decreased.

c. Merchandise inventory increased.

d. Accounts payable increased.

e. Income taxes payable decreased.

f. Depreciation expense was $7,200.

g. Equipment was purchased for $16,800 cash.

h. Twelve hundred shares of stock were issued for cash at $12 per share.

i. The company declared and paid $24,000 of cash dividends during the year.

Required

Prepare a SCFP using the direct method. Do not prepare a working paper. Instead, prepare the statement directly from your examination of the balance sheets and the additional information provided about the income statement and other transactions of the company.

Problem 18–2A
SCFP working paper
(L. O. 1)

Refer to the facts about Cemco Corporation presented in Problem 18–1A and prepare a working paper. Identify the debits and credits in the Analysis of Changes columns with letters that correspond to the above list of information about the company.

Problem 18–3A
Reconciling net income to cash flows from operating activities
(L. O. 1, 2, 3)

Columbus Corporation's 1990 and 1989 balance sheets included the following items:

	December 31	
	1990	**1989**
Debits		
Cash	$146,700	$ 38,700
Accounts receivable	72,000	90,000
Merchandise inventory.	283,500	288,000
Prepaid expenses	9,000	10,800
Equipment	330,900	231,000
Totals	$842,100	$658,500
Credits		
Accumulated depreciation, equipment	$ 54,900	$ 49,200
Accounts payable	193,500	161,100
Short-term notes payable	22,500	13,500
Long-term notes payable	114,000	90,000
Common stock	292,500	225,000
Retained earnings	164,700	119,700
Totals	$842,100	$658,500

Additional information about the 1990 activities of the company is as follows:

a. Net income was $72,000.
b. Accounts receivable decreased.
c. Merchandise inventory decreased.
d. Prepaid expenses decreased.
e. Accounts payable increased.
f. Depreciation expense was $18,900.
g. Equipment that cost $22,200 and was depreciated $13,200 was sold for $6,300 cash, which caused a loss of $2,700.
h. Equipment that cost $122,100 was purchased by paying cash of $62,100 and by signing a long-term note payable for the balance.
i. Borrowed $9,000 by signing a short-term note payable.
j. Paid $36,000 to reduce a long-term note payable.
k. Issued 500 shares of common stock for cash at $135 per share.
l. Declared and paid cash dividends of $27,000.

Required
Prepare a schedule that reconciles net income to the net cash provided or used by operating activities.

Problem 18–4A
SCFP (direct method)
(L. O. 1, 2, 3)

Refer to the information about Columbus Corporation presented in Problem 18–3A.

Required
Prepare a SCFP using the direct method. Do not prepare a working paper. Instead, prepare the statement directly from your examination of the balance sheets and the additional information provided about the income statement and other transactions of the company. Show your supporting calculations.

Problem 18–5A
SCFP working paper
(L. O. 1, 7)

Refer to the facts about Columbus Corporation presented in Problem 18–3A. Prepare a SCFP working paper which identifies the debits and credits in the Analysis of Changes columns with letters that correspond to the list of information about the company in Problem 18–3A.

Provocative Problems

Provocative Problem 18–1
Yaupon, Inc.
(L. O. 2)

Yaupon, Inc.'s 1990 statement of changes in financial position appeared as follows:

Cash flows from operating activities:		
Net income		$111,100
Accounts receivable increase	$(14,700)	
Inventory decrease.	47,600	
Prepaid expense increase	(4,600)	
Accounts payable decrease	(16,300)	
Income tax payable increase	4,400	
Depreciation expense	12,000	
Loss on disposal of equipment	13,400	
Gain on bond retirement	(7,700)	34,100
Net cash provided by operating activities . .		$145,200
Cash flows from investing activities:		
Receipt from sale of office equipment	$ 5,100	
Purchase of store equipment.	(33,000)	
Net cash used by investing activities		(27,900)
Cash flows from financing activities:		
Payment to retire bonds payable.	$(42,300)	
Payment of dividends.	(30,000)	
Net cash used by financing activities		(72,300)
Net increase in cash		$ 45,000
Cash balance at beginning of year		45,400
Cash balance at end of year		$ 90,400

Yaupon, Inc.'s beginning and ending balance sheets were as follows:

	December 31	
	1990	**1989**
Debits		
Cash	$ 90,400	$ 45,400
Accounts receivable	114,900	100,200
Merchandise inventory.	212,700	260,300
Prepaid expenses	9,000	4,400
Equipment	99,100	108,600
Totals	$526,100	$518,900
Credits		
Accumulated depreciation, equipment	$ 18,200	$ 30,200
Accounts payable	58,500	74,800
Income taxes payable	10,900	6,500
Dividends payable	–0–	7,500
Bonds payable	–0–	50,000
Common stock	300,000	300,000
Retained earnings	138,500	49,900
Totals	$526,100	$518,900

An examination of the company's statements and accounts showed:

a. All sales were made on credit.
b. All merchandise purchases were on credit.
c. Accounts Payable balances resulted from merchandise purchases.
d. Prepaid expenses relate to other operating expenses.
e. Equipment that cost $42,500 and was depreciated $24,000 was sold for cash.
f. Equipment was purchased for cash.
g. The change in the balance of Accumulated Depreciation resulted from depreciation expense and from the sale of equipment.
h. The change in the balance of Retained Earnings resulted from dividend declarations and net income.
i. Cash receipts from customers were $772,800.
j. Cash payments for merchandise inventory amounted to $425,400.
k. Cash payments for other operating expenses were $169,800.
l. Income taxes paid were $32,400.

Required

Present Yaupon, Inc.'s income statement for 1990. Show your supporting calculations.

Provocative Problem 18–2
James Company
(L. O. 1, 3)

The following items include the 1990 and 1989 balance sheets and the 1990 income statement of the James Company. Additional information about the company's 1990 transactions is presented after the financial statements.

JAMES COMPANY
Balance Sheet
December 31, 1990 and 1989

	1990		1989	
Assets				
Current assets:				
Cash and cash equivalents	$ 1,000		$ 800	
Accounts receivable.	4,500		3,100	
Merchandise inventory	19,000		16,000	
Prepaid expenses	700		600	
Total current assets		$25,200		$20,500
Long-term investments:				
Icahn Corporation common stock.		10,000		12,000
Plant assets:				
Land		9,000		4,000
Buildings	$60,000		$60,000	
Less accumulated depreciation	38,000	22,000	36,000	24,000
Equipment	$21,000		$16,000	
Less accumulated depreciation	6,000	15,000	4,000	12,000
Total assets		$81,200		$72,500

Liabilities

Current liabilities:		
Notes payable	$ 5,000	$ 3,500
Accounts payable	9,000	10,000
Other accrued liabilities	5,300	4,200
Interest payable	400	300
Taxes payable	300	500
Total current liabilities	$20,000	$18,500
Long-term liabilities:		
Bonds payable, due in 1999	25,000	22,000
Total liabilities	$45,000	$40,500

Shareholders' Equity

Contributed capital:		
Common stock	$16,000	$14,000
Retained earnings	22,000	18,000
Total	$38,000	$32,000
Less cost of treasury stock	1,800	–0–
Total shareholders' equity	36,200	32,000
Total liabilities and shareholders' equity	$81,200	$72,500

JAMES COMPANY
Income Statement
For Year Ended December 31, 1990

Revenues:		
Sales	$120,000	
Gain on sale of stock investment	3,000	
Dividend income	500	
Interest income	400	$123,900
Expenses and losses:		
Cost of goods sold	$ 50,000	
Other expenses	54,800	
Interest expense	2,000	
Income tax expense	2,500	
Depreciation expense, buildings	2,000	
Depreciation expense, equipment	4,000	
Loss on sale of equipment	600	
Total expenses and losses		115,900
Net income		$ 8,000

Additional Information:

1. Received $5,000 from the sale of Icahn Corporation common stock that originally cost $2,000.

2. Received a cash dividend of $500 from the Icahn Corporation.

3. Received $400 cash from the First National Bank on December 31, 1990, as interest income.

4. Sold old equipment for $1,400. The old equipment originally cost $4,000 and had accumulated depreciation of $2,000.

5. Purchased land costing $5,000 on December 31, 1990, in exchange for a note payable. Both principal and interest are due on June 30, 1991.

6. Purchased new equipment for $9,000 cash.

7. Purchased treasury stock for $1,800.

8. Paid $3,500 of notes payable.

9. Sold additional bonds payable at par of $3,000 on January 1, 1990.

10. Issued 1,000 shares of common stock for cash at $2 per share.

11. Declared and paid a $4,000 cash dividend on October 1, 1990.

(The working papers that accompany the text include forms for this problem.)

Required

a. Prepare a working paper for James Company's 1990 SCFP.

b. Prepare the SCFP for 1990.

Analytical and Review Problems

A&R Problem 18–1

Adjustments to Derive Cash Flow from Operations

	Adjust by	
Income element	**Adding**	**Subtracting**
1. Changes in current assets:		
a. Increases	_____	_____
b. Decreases.	_____	_____
2. Changes in current liabilities:		
a. Increases	_____	_____
b. Decreases.	_____	_____
3. Depreciation of plant assets	_____	_____
4. Amortization of intangible assets. .	_____	_____
5. Interest expense:		
a. Premium amortized.	_____	_____
b. Discount amortized	_____	_____
6. Sale of noncurrent asset:		
a. Gain	_____	_____
b. Loss	_____	_____

Required

Indicate by an x in the appropriate column whether an item is added or subtracted to derive cash flow from operations.

A&R Problem 18–2

Baker Corporation earned $84,000 net income during 1991. Machinery was sold for $116,000, and a $24,000 loss on the sale was recorded. Machinery purchases totaled $330,000 including a July purchase for which an $80,000 promissory note was issued. Bonds were retired at their face value, and the issuance of new common shares produced an infusion of cash.

Baker's comparative balance sheets were as follows (in thousands):

	December 31	
	1991	**1990**
Cash	$ 104	$ 84
Receivables	196	222
Inventory	324	310
Machinery	1,350	1,260
Accumulated depreciation.	(190)	(210)
Total assets	$1,784	$1,666
Accounts payable	$ 238	$ 286
Notes payable	272	210
Dividends payable.	32	20
Bonds payable.	228	320
Common stock.	700	560
Retained earnings	314	270
Total liabilities and shareholders' equity . .	$1,784	$1,666

a. What was Baker's depreciation expense in 1991?

b. What was the amount of cash flow from operations?

c. What was the amount of cash flow from investing activities?

d. What was the amount of the cash dividend declared? Paid?

e. By what amount would you expect the total sources of cash to differ from the total uses of cash?

f. What was the amount of cash flow from financing activities?

A&R Problem 18–3

The data below refers to the activities of Brennan Corporation.

Required

For each item, identify both the dollar amount and its classification—that is, whether it would appear as a positive or a negative adjustment to net income in the measurement of cash flow from operations or as some other source or use of cash.

1. Declared a $15,000 cash dividend; paid $12,000 during the year.

2. Sold for $90,000 cash land that had cost $75,000 two years earlier.

3. Sold for cash 2,000 shares for $6 a share.

4. Bought machinery for $24,000 in exchange for a note due in eight months.

5. Bought a computer which had fair value of $35,000 by giving in exchange real estate that had cost $15,000 in an earlier period.

6. Equipment depreciation, $18,000.

7. Issued for cash on December 31, 1990, 10-year 10% $250,000 par-value bonds at $18,000 discount.

8. Bought its own shares for $7,500 and immediately canceled it.

9. Paid a lawyer $6,200 for services performed, billed, and recorded correctly in 1990.

10. Reported net income of $63,000 for the year ended December 31, 1991.

19 Equity Investments, Consolidations, and International Operations

Most large corporations invest in the shares of other corporations, and many have operations in foreign countries. The financial statement effects of such investments and foreign operations often are very important. As a result, your study of these topics in this chapter will enrich your ability to understand and interpret the financial reports of most large businesses.

Learning Objectives

After studying Chapter 19, you should be able to:

1. State the criteria for classifying equity investments as current assets or as long-term investments.
2. Describe the circumstances under which the cost method, the equity method, and consolidated financial statements are used to account for long-term stock investments.
3. Prepare entries to account for long-term equity investments according to the cost method and the equity method and to reflect lower of cost or market.
4. Prepare consolidated balance sheets and explain how to report any excess of investment cost over book value or minority interests.
5. Describe the primary problems of accounting for international operations and prepare entries to account for sales to foreign customers.
6. Define or explain the words and phrases listed in the chapter Glossary.

Stocks as Investments

In Chapters 15 and 16, we discussed stock transactions in which the issuing corporation sold or repurchased its own shares. The focus of our discussion was the shareholders' equity accounts of the issuing corporation. However, such transactions represent only a small portion of the share transactions that take place each day. Most share transactions are between shareholders and do not involve the issuing corporation. These purchase/sales transactions between investors usually are arranged through brokers who charge a commission for their services.

Brokers who act as agents for their customers buy and sell shares and bonds on exchanges such as the Toronto Stock Exchange. Some securities are not listed or traded on an organized stock exchange. Instead, they are bought and sold in the "over-the-counter" market. Each security in this market is handled by one or more brokers who receive from other brokers offers to buy or sell the security at specific "bid" or "asked" prices.

Recall that stock prices are quoted on the basis of dollars and ⅛ dollars per share; that is, a stock quoted at 29¼ means $29.25 per share, and a stock quoted at 28⅞ means $28.875 per share. For example, the purchases and sales of Bell Canada Enterprise's common stock and International Nickel Company's common stock on Friday, March 31, 1989, were reported in many newspapers as follows:

Stock	High	Low	Close	Net Change
BCE	37⅛	36⅞	37⅛	+¼
Inco	34⅞	34½	34⅞	+⅜

These reported prices are the highest and lowest prices at which the shares traded during the day and the price of the last transaction that occurred before the stock exchange closed at the end of the day. The net change is the difference between the closing price that day and the closing price for the previous day.

Classifying Investments

State the criteria for classifying equity investments as current assets or as long-term investments.
(L. O. 1)

Equity securities include common and preferred stocks. **Temporary investments** are identified by the *CICA Handbook* as those that are "capable of reasonably prompt liquidation."[1]

If an investment in marketable equity securities is held as "an investment of cash available for current operations," it is classified as a current asset.[2] You already learned how to account for short-term investments in marketable equity securities when you studied Chapter 8.

Investments that are not held as a ready source of cash are called **long-term investments.** They include funds earmarked for a special purpose, such as bond sinking funds, as well as land or other assets that are owned but not used

---

[1] *CICA Handbook* (Toronto: The Canadian Institute of Chartered Accountants), par. 3010.02.

[2] Ibid., par. 3010.01.

in the regular operations of the business. Long-term investments also include investments in bonds and stocks that are not marketable or that, although marketable, are not intended to serve as a ready source of cash. These assets are reported on the balance sheet in a separate category titled *Long-term investments*.

Accounting for Long-Term Investments in Shares

Describe the circumstances under which the cost method, the equity method, and consolidated financial statements are used to account for long-term stock investments. (L. O. 2)

The method used to account for a long-term stock investment depends on the relationship between the investor and the investee. In deciding what type of relationship exists between the investor and the investee, three alternatives are considered:

1. The investor is not able to significantly influence the operations of the investee.
2. The investor has a significant influence but does not control the investee.
3. The investor controls the investee.

When a company invests in another company's stock, the shares owned by the investor often represent a small percentage of the total amount of shares outstanding. As a result, the investor does not have the ability to influence the operations of the investee corporation. According to generally accepted accounting principles, if an investor owns less than 20% of a corporation's voting stock, you usually should presume that the investor does not have a significant influence over the investee.[3]

Sometimes, an investor buys a large block of a corporation's voting stock and is able to exercise a significant influence over the investee corporation. An investor that owns 20% or more of a corporation's voting stock normally is presumed to have a significant influence over the investee. There may be cases, however, where the accountant concludes that the 20% test of significant influence should be overruled by other, more persuasive, evidence.[4]

If an investor owns more than 50% of a corporation's voting stock, the investor can dominate all of the other shareholders in electing the corporation's board of directors. Thus, the investor has control over the investee corporation's management.

As we stated earlier, the method of accounting for a stock investment depends on the relationship between the investor and the investee. Illustration 19–1 shows each type of investor/investee relationship and the corresponding accounting methods used. In Illustration 19–1, note that if the investor does not have a significant influence, the accounting method used is the **cost method.** However, when the cost method is used, lower of cost or market also might be applied. If the investor has a significant influence, the accounting method used is the **equity method.** Finally, if the investor controls the investee, the investor reports **consolidated financial statements** to the public. Each of these accounting methods is explained in the following sections.

---

[3] Ibid., par. 3050.21.

[4] Ibid.

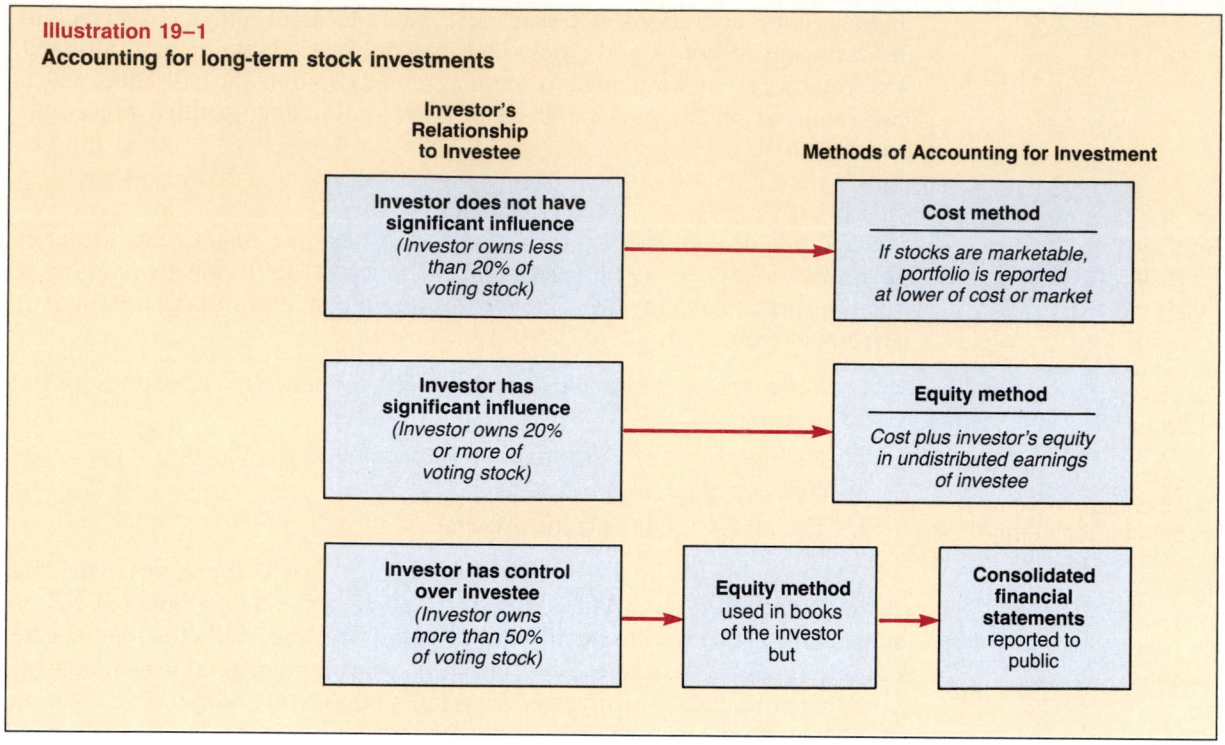

Illustration 19–1
Accounting for long-term stock investments

The Cost Method of Accounting for Equity Investments

Prepare entries to account for long-term equity investments according to the cost method and the equity method and to reflect lower of cost or market.
(L. O. 3)

When shares are purchased, the purchase is recorded at total cost, which includes any commission paid to the broker. For example, 1,000 (10%) of Dot Corporation's 10,000 outstanding common shares were purchased as an investment at 23¼ plus a $300 broker's commission. The entry to record the transaction is:

Sept.	10	Investment in Dot Corporation Stock	23,550.00	
		Cash		23,550.00
		Purchased 1,000 shares of stock for $23,250 plus a $300 broker's commission.		

When the cost method is used and a cash dividend is received on the stock, the dividend is recorded as follows:

Oct.	5	Cash	1,000.00	
		Dividends Earned		1,000.00
		Received a $1 per share dividend on the stock.		

Dividends do not accrue as time passes; therefore, you never make an end-of-period entry to record accrued dividends. However, if a balance sheet is prepared after a cash dividend is declared but before it is paid, you should record the declaration with a debit to Dividends Receivable and a credit to Dividends Earned.

When a stock dividend is declared, the shares distributed to the shareholders are not revenue or income. Therefore, an investor does not make a journal entry to record a stock dividend. However, a memorandum entry or a notation about the additional shares should be made in the investment account. Also, receipt of a stock dividend does affect the per share cost of the old shares. For example, if a 20-share dividend is received on 100 shares originally purchased for $15 per share ($100 \times \$15 = \$1,500$), the cost of all 120 shares is $1,500, and the cost per share is $12.50 ($1,500 \div 120$ shares = $12.50 per share).

Under the cost method, when an investment in stock is sold and the proceeds net of any sales commission differ from cost, a gain or loss must be recorded. For example, consider the 1,000 shares of Dot Corporation common stock that were purchased at a cost of $23,550. If these shares are sold at 25¾ less a sales commission of $315, there is a $1,885 gain, and the transaction is recorded as follows:

Jan.	7	Cash	25,435.00	
		Investment in Dot Corporation Stock		23,550.00
		Gain on Sale of Investments		1,885.00
		Sold 1,000 shares of stock for $25,750 less a $315 commission.		

If the net amount received for these shares had been less than their $23,550 cost, there would have been a loss on the transaction.

Lower of Cost or Market

If the cost method is used to account for a stock investment that is not marketable, the asset is reported on the balance sheet at cost. However, as you learned in Chapter 8, investments in marketable equity securities are divided into two portfolios: (1) those that are current assets (temporary investments) and (2) those that are long-term investments. For temporary investments, the total current market value of the portfolio is calculated and compared to the total cost of the portfolio. The portfolio is then reported at the lower of cost or market.[5]

In the case of long-term investments, they are shown at cost with market value disclosed even if cost is below market value so long as the decline in value is temporary. However, when there has been a loss in value other than a temporary decline, the investment should be written down to recognize the loss. The write-down (loss) would be included in determining net income. When the investment has been written down to recognize a loss, the new carrying value is deemed to be the new cost basis for subsequent accounting purposes. A subsequent increase in value would be recognized only when realized. For purposes of calculating a gain or loss on the sale of the invest-

---

[5] Ibid., par. 3010.06.

ments, the cost of the investments sold should be calculated on the basis of the average carrying value.[6]

The Equity Method of Accounting for Common Stock Investments

If a common stock investor has significant influence over the investee, the equity method of accounting for the investment must be used. When the stock is acquired, the purchase is recorded at cost just as it is under the cost method. For example, on January 1, 1990, James, Inc., purchased 3,000 shares (30%) of RMS, Inc., common stock for a total cost of $70,650. The entry to record the purchase on the books of James, Inc., is as follows:

Jan.	1	Investment in RMS, Inc..	70,650.00	
		Cash		70,650.00
		Purchased 3,000 shares of common stock.		

Under the equity method, the earnings of the investee corporation not only increase the net assets of the investee corporation but also increase the investor's equity in the assets. Therefore, when the investee closes its books and reports the amount of its earnings, the investor takes up its share of those earnings in its investment account. For example, RMS, Inc., reported net income of $20,000. James, Inc.'s entry to record its share of these earnings is:

Dec.	31	Investment in RMS, Inc..	6,000.00	
		Earnings from Investment in RMS, Inc..		6,000.00
		To record 30% equity in investee's earnings of $20,000.		

The debit records the increase in James, Inc.'s equity in RMS, Inc. The credit causes 30% of RMS, Inc.'s net income to appear on James, Inc.'s income statement as earnings from the investment. Then, James, Inc., closes the earnings to its Income Summary account and on to its Retained Earnings account just as it would close earnings from any investment.

If, instead of a net income, the investee corporation incurs a net loss, the investor debits the loss to an account called Loss from Investment and credits (reduces) its Investment in Stock account. It then transfers the loss to its Income Summary account and on to its Retained Earnings account.

Dividends paid by an investee corporation decrease the investee's assets and retained earnings, and also decrease the investor's equity in the investee. Since, under the equity method, the investor records its equity in the full amount of earnings reported by an investee, the receipt of cash dividends is not income. Instead, dividend receipts from the investee represent a change in the form of the investor's assets; part of the investment is converted into cash. For example, RMS, Inc., declared and paid $10,000 in dividends on its common stock. The entry to record James, Inc.'s share of these dividends, which it received on January 9, 1991, is:

---

[6]Ibid., par. 3050.27–.35.

Jan.	9	Cash	3,000.00	
		Investment in RMS, Inc.		3,000.00
		To record receipt of 30% of the $10,000 dividend		
		paid by RMS, Inc.		

Notice that when the equity method is used, the carrying value of a common stock investment equals the cost of the investment plus the investor's equity in the undistributed earnings of the investee. For example, after the above transactions are recorded on the books of James, Inc., the investment account appears as follows:

Investment in RMS, Inc.

Date		Explanation	Debit	Credit	Balance
1990					
Jan.	1	Investment	70,650		70,650
Dec.	31	Share of earnings	6,000		76,650
1991					
Jan.	9	Share of dividend		3,000	73,650

When an equity method stock investment is sold, the gain or loss on the sale is determined by comparing the proceeds from the sale with the carrying value of the stock on the date of sale. For example, on January 10, 1991, James, Inc., sold its RMS, Inc., shares for $80,000. The entry to record the sale is as follows:

Jan.	10	Cash	80,000.00	
		Investment in RMS, Inc.		73,650.00
		Gain on Sale of Investments		6,350.00
		Sold 3,000 shares for $80,000.		

Parent and Subsidiary Corporations

Corporations commonly own shares in and may even control other corporations. For example, if Par Company owns more than 50% of the voting stock of Sub Company, Par company can elect Sub Company's board of directors and thus control its activities and resources. In this case, the controlling corporation, Par Company, is known as the **parent company**, and Sub Company is called a **subsidiary.**

When a corporation owns all the outstanding shares of a subsidiary, it can take over the subsidiary's assets, cancel its stock, and merge the subsidiary into the parent company. However, instead of operating the business as a single corporation, there often are financial, legal, and tax advantages if a large business is operated as a parent corporation that controls one or more subsidiary corporations. Actually, most large companies are parent corporations that own one or more subsidiaries.

When a business is operated as a parent company with subsidiaries, separate accounting records are kept for each corporation. Also, from a legal viewpoint, the parent and each subsidiary are separate entities with all the rights, duties, and responsibilities of a separate corporation. However, investors in the parent company depend on the parent to present consolidated financial statements. Consolidated statements show the financial position and results of all operations under the parent's control, including those of any subsidiaries. These statements are prepared as if the business is organized as a single company. In other words, the assets and liabilities of all affiliated companies are combined on a single balance sheet. Also, their revenues and expenses are combined on a single income statement and their cash flows are combined on a single statement of cash flows. The relationship between the consolidated entity and the separate parent and subsidiary corporations is shown in the top portion of Illustration 19–2.

Consolidated Balance Sheets

Prepare consolidated balance sheets and explain how to report any excess of investment cost over book value or minority interests.
(L. O. 4)

The bottom portion of Illustration 19–2 shows the process of preparing a consolidated balance sheet from the separate balance sheets of the parent and the subsidiary. When parent and subsidiary balance sheets are consolidated, duplications in items are eliminated so that the combined figures do not show more assets and equities than actually exist. For example, a parent's investment in a subsidiary is evidenced by shares of stock that are carried as an asset in the parent company's records. However, these shares actually represent an equity in the subsidiary's assets. Therefore, if the parent's investment in a subsidiary and the subsidiary's assets were both shown on the consolidated balance sheet, the same resources would be counted twice. To prevent this, the parent's investment and the subsidiary's capital accounts are offset and eliminated in preparing a consolidated balance sheet.

Likewise, a single enterprise cannot owe a debt to itself. This would be like a student who "borrows" $20 for a date from funds saved for next semester's expenses and who then prepares a balance sheet that shows the $20 as both a receivable from himself and a payable to himself. To prevent such double counting, intercompany debts and receivables are also eliminated in preparing a consolidated balance sheet.

Balance Sheets Consolidated at Time of Acquisition

When a parent's and a subsidiary's assets are combined in the preparation of a consolidated balance sheet, a work sheet normally is used to organize the data. For example, Illustration 19–3 shows a work sheet to consolidate the accounts of Par Company and its subsidiary called Sub Company. In the work sheet, the account balances are on December 31, 1989, which was the day Par Company acquired Sub Company. On that day, Par Company paid cash to purchase all of Sub Company's outstanding common stock. The shares had a book value of $115,000, or $11.50 per share, on the books of Sub Company. In this first illustration, we assume that Par Company paid $115,000, or book value, for the outstanding shares.

In Illustration 19–3, notice that the eliminations columns include two sets of debits and credits. One set is identified by the letter (a), and the other set is identified by the letter (b).

Illustration 19–2

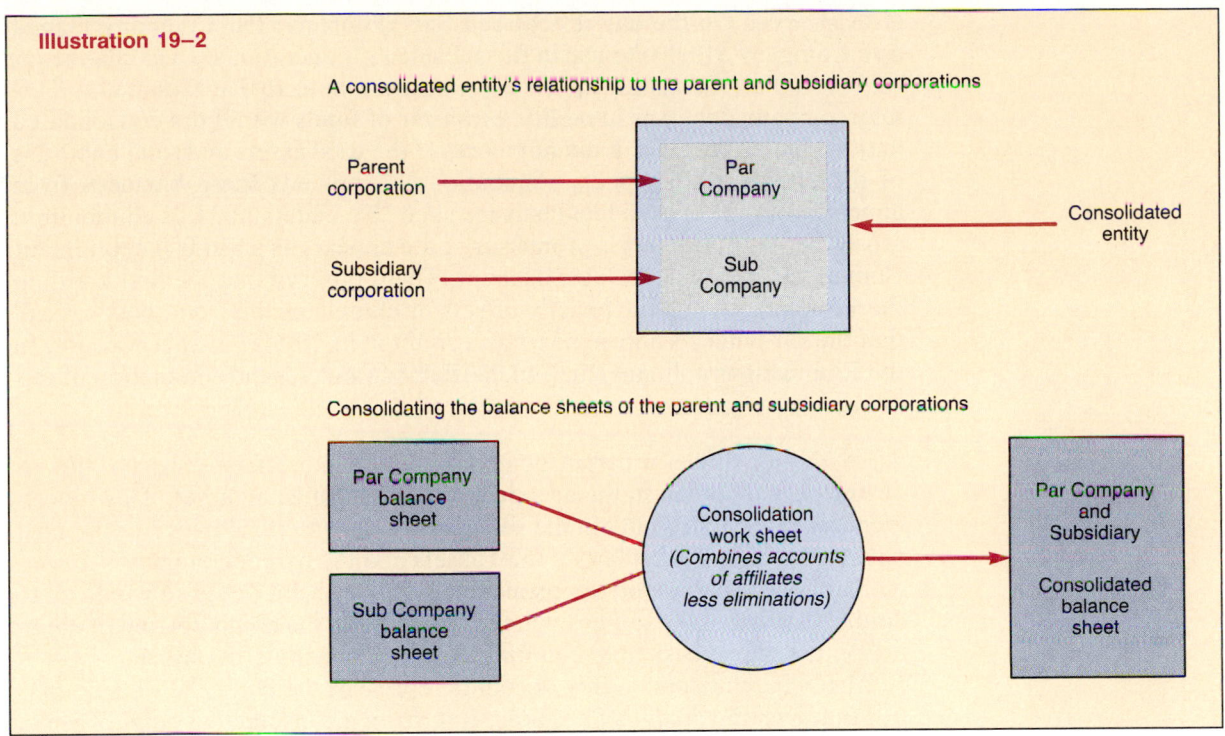

A consolidated entity's relationship to the parent and subsidiary corporations

Consolidating the balance sheets of the parent and subsidiary corporations

Illustration 19–3
Consolidated work sheet for 100% owned subsidiary; shares purchased at book value

PAR COMPANY AND SUB COMPANY
Work Sheet for a Consolidated Balance Sheet
December 31, 1989

	Par Company	Sub Company	Eliminations Debit	Eliminations Credit	Consolidated Amounts
Assets					
Cash	5,000	15,000			20,000
Notes receivable	10,000			(a) 10,000	
Investment in Sub Company	115,000			(b) 115,000	
Other assets	190,000	117,000			307,000
	320,000	132,000			327,000
Liabilities and Equities					
Accounts payable	15,000	7,000			22,000
Notes payable.		10,000	(a) 10,000		
Common stock	250,000	100,000	(b) 100,000		250,000
Retained earnings	55,000	15,000	(b) 15,000		55,000
	320,000	132,000	125,000	125,000	327,000

Elimination (a). On the day it acquired Sub Company, Par Company loaned Sub Company $10,000 to use in the subsidiary's operations. In exchange for the cash, Sub Company signed a promissory note to Par Company. This intercompany debt was in reality a transfer of funds within the consolidated entity. Therefore, since it did not increase the total assets and total liabilities of the affiliated companies, elimination (a) prevents these balances from appearing on the consolidated balance sheet. To understand this elimination, recall that the subsidiary's promissory note appears as a $10,000 debit in Par Company's Notes Receivable account. Then, observe that the first credit in the Eliminations column exactly offsets or eliminates this item. Next, recall that the subsidiary's note appears as a credit in its Notes Payable account. In the Eliminations columns, the $10,000 debit completes the elimination of this intercompany debt.

Elimination (b). When a parent company buys a subsidiary's shares, the investment is recorded in the accounts of the parent as an asset. This investment represents an equity in the subsidiary's net assets. However, you must not show both the subsidiary's (net) assets and the parent company's investment in the subsidiary on a consolidated balance sheet. To do so would be to double count those resources. On the work sheet, the credit portion of elimination (b) prevents double counting of Sub company's net assets.

Also, shareholders' equity accounts represent the equity of outside parties that own the company's shares. But, from a consolidated point of view, there are no outside parties that own the subsidiary's shares. Therefore, the shareholders' equity account balances of Sub Company should not appear on a consolidated balance sheet. On the work sheet, the debits of elimination (b) prevent Sub Company's shareholders' equity balances from appearing on the consolidated balance sheet.

After the intercompany items are eliminated on a work sheet as in Illustration 19–3, the assets of the parent and the subsidiary and the remaining equities in these assets are combined and carried into the work sheet's last column. The combined amounts are then used to prepare a consolidated balance sheet that shows all the assets and equities of the parent and its subsidiary.

Parent Company Does Not Buy All of Subsidiary's Shares and Pays More than Book Value

In the above example, Par Company purchased all of its subsidiary's shares and paid book value for it. However, a parent company often purchases less than 100% of a subsidiary's shares and commonly pays a price that is either more or less than book value. To illustrate, assume Par Company purchased only 80% of Sub Company's outstanding shares. Also assume that Par company paid $13 per share, a price that was $1.50 more than the stock's book value.

These new assumptions result in a more complicated work sheet entry to eliminate the parent's investment and the subsidiary's shareholders' equity accounts. The entry is complicated by (1) the minority interest in the subsidiary and (2) the excess over book value paid by the parent company for the subsidiary's shares.

Illustration 19–4
Consolidated work sheet; 80% of subsidiary shares purchased at more than book value

PAR COMPANY AND SUB COMPANY
Work Sheet for a Consolidated Balance Sheet
December 31, 1989

	Par Company	Sub Company	Eliminations Debit	Eliminations Credit	Consolidated Amounts
Assets					
Cash	16,000	15,000			31,000
Notes receivable	10,000			*(a)* 10,000	
Investment in Sub Company	104,000			*(b)* 104,000	
Other assets	190,000	117,000			307,000
Excess of cost over book value			*(b)* 12,000		12,000
	320,000	132,000			350,000
Liabilities and Equities					
Accounts payable	15,000	7,000			22,000
Notes payable	10,000	10,000	*(a)* 10,000		
Common stock	250,000	100,000	*(b)* 100,000		250,000
Retained earnings	55,000	15,000	*(b)* 15,000		55,000
Minority interest				*(b)* 23,000	23,000
	320,000	132,000	137,000	137,000	350,000

Minority Interest. When a parent buys a controlling interest in a subsidiary, the parent company is the subsidiary's majority shareholder. However, when the parent owns less than 100% of the subsidiary's shares, the subsidiary has other shareholders who own a **minority interest** in its assets and share its earnings.

When you prepare a consolidated work sheet for a parent and a subsidiary that has a minority interest, the equity of the minority interest must be recognized. This is done in the process of eliminating the shareholders' equity balances of the subsidiary, as shown in Illustration 19–4. In this case, the minority shareholders have a 20% interest in the subsidiary. Therefore, on the work sheet, 20% of the subsidiary's shareholders' equity amounts [($100,000 + $15,000) × 20% = $23,000] is reclassified as the minority interest.

Excess of Investment Cost over Book Value. In Illustration 19–4, we assume that Par Company paid $13 per share for its 8,000 shares of Sub Company's stock. Therefore, the cost of these shares exceeded their book value by $12,000, calculated as follows:

Cost of stock (8,000 shares at $13 per share) . .	$104,000
Book value (8,000 shares at $11.50 per share) . .	92,000
Excess of cost over book value	$ 12,000

Now observe how in the process of eliminating the parent's investment in the subsidiary, this excess of cost over book value is set out on the work sheet. Then, it is carried into the Consolidated Amounts column as an asset.

After the work sheet of Illustration 19–4 was completed, the consolidated amounts in the last column were used to prepare the consolidated balance sheet of Illustration 19–5. Note the treatment of the minority interest in the balance sheet. The minority shareholders have a $23,000 equity in the consolidated assets of the affiliated companies. Some accountants argue that this item should be disclosed in the shareholders' equity section. Others believe it should be shown in the long-term liabilities section. However, the minority interest usually is shown as a separate item between the liabilities and shareholders' equity sections, as you see in Illustration 19–5.

Next, observe that the $12,000 excess over book value that Par Company paid for Sub Company's shares appears on the consolidated balance sheet as an asset called "Goodwill from consolidation." There are several reasons why a parent might pay more than book value for its equity in a subsidiary. (1) One reason may be that certain of the subsidiary's assets are carried on the subsidiary's books at less than fair value. (2) Another reason may be that certain of the subsidiary's liabilities are carried at book values that are greater than fair values. (3) Also, the subsidiary's earnings prospects may be good enough to justify paying more than the net fair (market) value of its assets and liabilities. In this illustration, we assume that the book values of Sub Company's assets and liabilities are equal to their fair values. However, Sub Company's expected earnings justified paying $104,000 for an 80% equity in the subsidiary's net assets (assets less liabilities).

When a company pays more than book value because the subsidiary's assets are undervalued or its liabilities are overvalued, the cost in excess of book value must be allocated to those assets and liabilities so that they are restated at fair values. After the subsidiary's assets and liabilities have been restated to reflect fair values, any remaining cost in excess of book value is reported on the consolidated balance sheet as "Goodwill from consolidation."[7]

Occasionally, a parent company pays less than book value for its interest in a subsidiary. The probable reason for a price below book value is that some of the subsidiary's assets are carried on its books at amounts in excess of fair value. Therefore, the CICA ruled that the excess of book value over cost should be allocated to reduce the balance sheet valuations of the overvalued assets.[8]

Earnings and Dividends of a Subsidiary

As you already learned, a parent uses the equity method in its books to account for its investment in a subsidiary. As a result, the parent's recorded net income and Retained Earnings account include the parent's equity in the net income earned by the subsidiary since the date of acquisition. Also, the balance of the parent's Investment in Subsidiary account increases (or decreases) each year by an amount equal to the parent's equity in the subsidiary's earnings (or loss) less the parent's share of any dividends paid by the subsidiary.

---

[7] Ibid., par. 1580.44.

[8] Ibid.

Illustration 19–5

PAR COMPANY AND SUBSIDIARY
Consolidated Balance Sheet
December 31, 1989
Assets

Cash	$ 31,000
Other assets	307,000
Goodwill from consolidation	12,000
Total assets	$350,000

Liabilities and Shareholders' Equity

Liabilities:		
Accounts payable		$ 22,000
Minority interest		23,000
Shareholders' equity:		
Common stock	$250,000	
Retained earnings	55,000	
Total shareholders' equity		305,000
Total liabilities and shareholders' equity . .		$350,000

For example, assume that Sub Company earned $12,500 during 1990, its first year as a subsidiary, and at year-end paid out $7,500 in dividends. Par Company records its 80% equity in these earnings and dividends as follows:

Dec.	31	Investment in Sub Company	10,000.00	
		Earnings from Investment in Subsidiary		10,000.00
		To record 80% of the net income reported by Sub Company.		
	31	Cash	6,000.00	
		Investment in Sub Company		6,000.00
		To record the receipt of 80% of the $7,500 dividend paid by Sub Company.		

Consolidated Balance Sheets at a Date after Acquisition

Illustration 19–6 shows the December 31, 1990, work sheet to consolidate the balance sheets of Par Company and Sub Company. To simplify the illustration, it is assumed that Par Company had no transactions during the year other than to record its equity in Sub Company's earnings and dividends. Also, the other assets and liabilities of Sub Company did not change, and the subsidiary has not paid its note to Par Company.

Compare Illustration 19–6 with 19–4 to see the changes in Par Company's balance sheet (the first column). Par Company's cash increased from $16,000 to $22,000 because of the dividends received from Sub Company. The Investment in Sub Company account increased from $104,000 to $108,000 as a result of the equity method entries during the year. Finally, Par Company's Retained

Illustration 19–6

Work sheet for a consolidated balance sheet, one year after acquisition

PAR COMPANY AND SUB COMPANY
Work Sheet for a Consolidated Balance Sheet
December 31, 1990

	Par Company	Sub Company	Eliminations Debit	Eliminations Credit	Consolidated Amounts
Assets					
Cash	22,000	20,000			42,000
Notes receivable	10,000			(a) 10,000	
Investment in Sub Company	108,000			(b) 108,000	
Other assets	190,000	117,000			307,000
Excess of cost over book value			(b) 12,000		12,000
	330,000	137,000			361,000
Liabilities and Equities					
Accounts payable	15,000	7,000			22,000
Notes payable		10,000	(a) 10,000		
Common stock	250,000	100,000	(b) 100,000		250,000
Retained earnings	65,000	20,000	(b) 20,000		65,000
Minority interest				(b) 24,000	24,000
	330,000	137,000	142,000	142,000	361,000

Earnings increased by $10,000, which was the parent's equity in the subsidiary's earnings.

In the second column of Illustration 19–6, note only two changes: (1) Sub Company's cash balance increased by $5,000, which is the difference between its $12,500 net income and $7,500 payment of dividends; and (2) retained earnings also increased from $15,000 to $20,000, which is explained by the $12,500 net income less $7,500 dividends. Note that the $20,000 balance is eliminated on the work sheet.

Two additional items need explanation. First, the minority interest set out on the December 31, 1990, work sheet (Illustration 19–6), is greater than on the December 31, 1989, work sheet (Illustration 19–4). The minority shareholders have a 20% equity in Sub Company. So, the $24,000 shown on the December 31, 1990, work sheet is 20% of Sub Company's Common Stock and Retained Earnings balances on December 31, 1990. This $24,000 is $1,000 greater than the beginning-of-year minority interest because the subsidiary's retained earnings increased $5,000 during the year; the minority shareholder's share of this increase is 20%, or $1,000.

Second, the $12,000 excess cost over book value shown in Illustration 19–6 is unchanged from a year earlier. However, generally accepted accounting principles require that this cost be amortized.[9] The procedures of amortizing this cost are explained in a more advanced course.

---

[9] Ibid., par. 1580.58.

Other Consolidated Statements

In addition to the balance sheet, the consolidated financial statements include a consolidated income statement, consolidated retained earnings statement, and consolidated statement of cash flows. However, you can have a general understanding of these statements without further discussion of the procedures to prepare them. At this point, you need only recognize that all duplications in items are eliminated. Also, when one affiliate records profit on sales to the other affiliate, the profit is eliminated in the consolidated statements. Finally, the amounts of net income and retained earnings that are reported in consolidated statements are equal to the amounts recorded by the parent under the equity method.

The Corporation Balance Sheet

A number of balance sheet sections have been illustrated in this and previous chapters. To bring together the information from all these sections, the balance sheet of Betco Corporation is shown in Illustration 19–7. Three items of information in this balance sheet tell you that it is a consolidated balance sheet. They are the title and the two items "Goodwill from consolidation" and "Minority interest."

In Illustration 19–7, notice the asset called "Investment in Galt Corporation common stock." You should understand that Galt Corporation is not the subsidiary. When the balance sheet was prepared, Betco Corporation's investment in its subsidiary was eliminated. Therefore, the Galt Corporation stock is an investment in an unconsolidated company.

Accounting for International Operations

Describe the primary problems of accounting for international operations and prepare entries to account for sales to foreign customers.
(L. O. 5)

Many companies have business activities in more than one country. In fact, the operations of some large corporations involve so many different countries that they are called **multinational businesses.** The problems of managing and accounting for a company that has international operations can be very complex; and detailed study of these issues should be reserved for advanced courses in business.

However, you should know about two accounting problems that relate to international operations. Both of these problems occur because businesses with transactions in more than one country have to deal with more than one currency. To make the analysis clearer, we will discuss these problems from the perspective of companies that have a base of operations in Canada. Therefore, we will assume that the companies in our examples prepare their financial statements in terms of the Canadian dollar. Hence, the **reporting currency** of such firms is the Canadian dollar.

Exchange Rates between Currencies

You should understand that there is an active market for the purchase and sale of foreign currencies. Canadian dollars may be exchanged for U.S. dollars, British pounds, French francs, or other currencies. The price of one currency is stated in terms of another currency and is called a **foreign exchange rate.** For example, on March 31, 1989, the current exchange rate for British pounds and Canadian dollars was $2.0111, which means that one pound could have been exchanged for $2.0111. On the same day, the exchange rate between West German marks and Canadian dollars was $0.6292. These foreign exchange rates fluctuate daily based on the changing supply and demand for each currency.

Illustration 19–7

BETCO CORPORATION
Consolidated Balance Sheet
December 31, 1990
Assets

Current assets:		
Cash		$ 15,000
Marketable securities		5,000
Accounts receivable	$ 50,000	
Less allowance for doubtful accounts	1,000	49,000
Merchandise inventory		115,000
Subscriptions receivable, common stock		15,000
Prepaid expenses		1,000
Total current assets		$200,000
Long-term investments:		
Bond sinking fund		$ 15,000
Galt Corporation common stock (cost approximates market)		5,000
Total long-term investments		20,000
Plant assets:		
Land		$ 50,000
Buildings	$285,000	
Less accumulated depreciation	30,000	255,000
Store equipment	$ 85,000	
Less accumulated depreciation	20,000	65,000
Total plant assets		370,000
Intangible assets:		
Goodwill from consolidation		10,000
Total assets		$600,000

Liabilities

Current liabilities:		
Notes payable	$ 10,000	
Accounts payable	14,000	
Income taxes payable	16,000	
Total current liabilities		$ 40,000
Long-term liabilities:		
Bonds payable, 8%, secured by mortgage, due in 1997	$100,000	
Less unamortized discount based on the 8¼% market rate for bond interest prevailing on the date of issue	2,000	98,000
Total liabilities		$138,000
Minority interest		15,000

Shareholders' Equity

Contributed capital:		
Common stock, no par value, authorized 50,000 shares, issued 30,000 shares of which 1,000 are in the treasury	$333,000	
Unissued common stock subscribed, 2,500 shares	25,000	
Total contributed capital	$358,000	
Retained earnings (Note 1)	105,000	
Total contributed and retained capital	$463,000	
Less cost of treasury stock	16,000	
Total shareholders' equity		447,000
Total liabilities and shareholders' equity		$600,000

Note 1: Retained earnings in the amount of $31,000 is restricted under an agreement with the corporation's bondholders and because of the purchase of treasury stock, leaving $74,000 of retained earnings not so restricted.

Sales (or Purchases) Denominated in a Foreign Currency

When a Canadian company makes a sale to a foreign customer, a special problem may arise in accounting for the sale and account receivable. If the sales terms require the foreign customer's payment to be in Canadian dollars, no special problem arises. But if the terms of the sale state that payment is to be in a foreign currency, the Canadian company must go through special steps to account for the sale and account receivable.

For example, suppose a Canadian company, the Guelph Company, makes a credit sale to London Outfitters, a British company. The sale occurs on December 12, 1990, and the price is 10,000 pounds due February 10, 1991. Guelph Company keeps its accounting records in terms of Canadian dollars. Therefore, to record the sale, Guelph Company must translate the sales price from pounds to dollars. This is done using the current exchange rate available on the date of the sale. Assuming the current exchange rate on December 12 is $1.80, the sale is recorded as follows:

Dec.	12	Accounts Receivable—London Outfitters	18,000.00	
		Sales.		18,000.00
		10,000 × $1.80 = $18,000.		

Now assume that Guelph Company prepares annual financial statements on December 31. On that date, the current exchange rate is $1.84. Therefore, the current dollar value of Guelph Company's receivable is $18,400, or 10,000 × $1.84. This is $400 higher than the amount originally recorded on December 12. According to generally accepted accounting principles, the receivable must be reported in the balance sheet at its current dollar value. Hence, Guelph Company must make the following entry to record the increase in the dollar value of the receivable:

Dec.	31	Accounts Receivable—London Outfitters	400.00	
		Exchange Gain or Loss		400.00
		10,000 × $1.84 = $18,400		
		10,000 × $1.80 = 18,000		
		$ 400		

The Exchange Gain or Loss is closed to Income Summary and included on the income statement.[10] Assume that on February 10, Guelph Company receives London Outfitters' payment of 10,000 pounds and immediately exchanges the pounds for Canadian dollars. On this date, the foreign exchange rate is $1.78. Therefore, Guelph Company receives $17,800, or 10,000 × $1.78. The receipt and the loss associated with the decline in the exchange rate are recorded as follows:

---

[10] Ibid., par. 1650.20.

Feb.	10	Cash (10,000 × $1.78)	17,800.00	
		Exchange Gain or Loss	600.00	
		Accounts Receivable—London Outfitters		18,400.00
		Received foreign currency payment of account and converted into dollars.		

Accounting for credit purchases from a foreign supplier are similar to the above example of a credit sale to a foreign customer. If the Canadian company is required to make payment in a foreign currency, the account payable must be translated into dollars before it can be recorded by the Canadian company. Then, if the exchange rate changes before payment is made, an exchange gain or loss must be recognized by the Canadian company.

Consolidated Statements with Foreign Subsidiaries

A second problem of accounting for international operations involves the preparation of consolidated financial statements when the parent company has a foreign subsidiary. For example, suppose a Canadian company owns a controlling interest in a French subsidiary. The reporting currency of the Canadian parent is the dollar. However, the French subsidiary maintains its financial records in francs. Before a consolidated working paper can be prepared, the financial statements of the French company must be translated into Canadian dollars. After the translation is completed, the preparation of consolidated statements is not any different than for any other subsidiary.

The procedures for translating a foreign subsidiary's account balances depend on the nature of the subsidiary's operations. However, the general process is one of selecting appropriate foreign exchange rates and applying those rates to the account balances of the foreign subsidiary. Business students do not need any more detailed discussion of these procedures. For those who will major in accounting, a thorough analysis of these procedures is included in a senior level course in advanced accounting.

Summary of the Chapter in Terms of Learning Objectives

1. Equity investments are classified as current assets if they are marketable and are held as a source of cash to be used in current operations. All other equity investments are classified as long-term investments.

2. The cost method is used if the investor does not have a significant influence over the investee corporation. Usually, this means the investor owns less than 20% of the investee's voting stock. Also, when the cost or equity method is used, lower of cost or market is applied to the equity investments. The equity method is used if the investor has a significant influence over the investee which usually means the investor owns 20% or more of the investee's voting stock.

Consolidated financial statements are used by an investor if the investor controls another corporation. If an investor corporation controls another corporation because the investor owns more than 50% of the investee's voting stock, the investor's financial reports are prepared on a consolidated basis.

3. With the cost method, the investment account is maintained at cost and dividends received are credited to a revenue account. With the equity method, the investor records its share of the investee's earnings with a debit to the investment account and a credit to a revenue account. Then, dividend receipts change the form of the investor's assets from investment to cash.

4. To prepare a consolidated balance sheet, all items that are duplicated on the books of the subsidiary and the parent are eliminated. These eliminations always include offsetting the parent's investment account against the shareholders' equity accounts of the subsidiary. If subsidiary shares are held by outside parties, that portion of the subsidiary's shareholders' equity is reclassified as minority interest. Also, if the cost of the parent's investment differs from the book value of the investment, the difference is recognized. The remaining account balances of the affiliates are added to get the consolidated amounts.

5. If a Canadian company makes a credit sale to a foreign customer and the sales terms call for payment in a foreign currency, the company must translate the foreign currency into dollars in order to record the receivable. Then, if the current exchange rate changes before payment is received, an exchange gain or loss must be recognized. The same problem arises if a Canadian company makes a credit purchase from a foreign supplier and is required to make payment in a foreign currency. Also, if a Canadian company has a foreign subsidiary that maintains its accounts in a foreign currency, the account balances must be translated into dollars before they can be consolidated with the parent's accounts.

Demonstration Problem

Presented below are a series of events and facts related to Brown Company's investment activities during 1990 and 1991. Show the appropriate journal entries and the portions of each year's balance sheet and income statement that result from these events and facts:

1990

Sept. 9   Purchased as a long-term investment 1,000 shares of Packard, Inc., common stock for $80,000 cash. These shares represent less than 3% of the outstanding shares and are not readily marketable.

Oct.   2   Purchased as a long-term investment 2,000 shares of BCE common stock for $60,000 cash. The stock is actively traded on the Toronto Stock Exchange.

       17   Purchased as a long-term investment 1,000 shares of Apple Computers common stock for $40,000 cash. The stock is actively traded in the over-the-counter market.

Nov.   1   Received $5,000 cash dividends from Packard.

       30   Received $3,000 cash dividends from BCE.

Dec. 15   Received $1,400 cash dividends from Apple Computers.

       31   Market values for the investments in marketable equity securities are: BCE, $48,000; Apple Computers, $45,000; Packard, $80,000.

Dec. 31   After closing the accounts, selected account balances are:

Common stock	$3,000,000
Retained earnings	750,000

1991
Jan.   5   Purchased 120,000 shares (a 30% interest) of Hanson Company common stock, a corporation that was just created by two former employees. Brown paid $600,000 cash, will have influence over the management of the company, and plans to hold the shares as a long-term investment.

Feb. 15   Packard, Inc., was taken over by other investors, and Brown sold its shares for $125,000 cash.

May 30   Received $3,100 cash dividends from BCE.

June 15   Received $1,600 cash dividends from Apple Computers.

Aug. 17   Sold the BCE stock for $52,000 cash.

    19   Bought as a long-term investment 2,000 shares of Loblaws common stock for $50,000. The stock is actively traded on the Toronto Stock Exchange.

Dec. 15   Received $1,800 cash dividends from Apple Computers.

    19   Received $13,000 cash dividends from Hanson Company.

    31   Total profits for Hanson Company for 1991 are determined to be $140,000.

    31   Market values of the investments in marketable equity securities are: Apple Computers, $39,000; Loblaws, $48,000.

    31   After closing the accounts, selected account balances are:

Common stock	$3,400,000
Retained earnings	970,000

Solution to Demonstration Problem

Journal entries during 1990:

Sept.	9	Investment in Packard, Inc., Common Stock	80,000.00	
		Cash		80,000.00
		Acquired 1,000 shares as long-term investment.		
Oct.	2	Investment in BCE Common Stock	60,000.00	
		Cash		60,000.00
		Acquired 2,000 shares as long-term investment.		
	17	Investment in Apple Computers Common Stock	40,000.00	
		Cash		40,000.00
		Acquired 1,000 shares as long-term investment.		
Nov.	1	Cash	5,000.00	
		Dividends Earned		5,000.00
		Received dividend from Packard, Inc.		
	30	Cash	3,000.00	
		Dividends Earned		3,000.00
		Received dividend from BCE.		

Dec.	15	Cash	1,400.00	
		Dividends Earned....................		1,400.00
		Received dividend from Apple Computers.		

December 31, 1990, balance sheet items:

Long-term investments in equity securities,
at cost (market value, $173,000) $180,000

Since the shares are held as a long-term investment, it is not unreasonable to assume that the small decline in market value is temporary.

Income statement items for the year ended December 31, 1990:

Dividends earned. . . . . $ 9,400

Journal entries during 1991:

Jan.	5	Investment in Hanson Company Common Stock	600,000.00	
		Cash		600,000.00
		Acquired 120,000 shares as long-term investment. Equity method to be used.		
Feb.	15	Cash	125,000.00	
		Investment in Packard, Inc., Common Stock		80,000.00
		Gain on Sale of Investments.		45,000.00
		Sold 1,000 shares for cash.		
May	30	Cash	3,100.00	
		Dividends Earned		3,100.00
		Received dividend from BCE.		
June	15	Cash	1,600.00	
		Dividends Earned		1,600.00
		Received dividend from Apple Computers.		
Aug.	17	Cash	52,000.00	
		Loss on Sale of Investments	8,000.00	
		Investment in BCE Common Stock		60,000.00
		Sold 2,000 shares for cash.		
	19	Investment in Loblaws Common Stock	50,000.00	
		Cash		50,000.00
		Acquired 2,000 shares as long-term investment.		
Dec.	15	Cash	1,800.00	
		Dividends Earned		1,800.00
		Received dividend from Apple Computers.		
	19	Cash	13,000.00	
		Investment in Hanson Company Common Stock		13,000.00
		Received dividend from Hanson Company, deducted from investment account under the equity method.		
	31	Investment in Hanson Company Common Stock	42,000.00	
		Earnings from Investment in Hanson Company . .		42,000.00
		$140,000 \times 30\% = \$42,000$.		

December 31, 1991, balance sheet items:
Long-term investments in equity securities:

At cost (market value, $87,000)	$ 90,000
At equity.	$629,000
	$719,000

Since the shares are held as a long-term investment, it is not unreasonable to assume that the small decline in market value is temporary.

Income statement items for the year ended December 31, 1991:

Dividends earned	$ 6,500
Earnings from equity method investment . .	42,000
Gain on sale of investments	45,000
Loss on sale of investments	(8,000)
Total	$85,500

Glossary

Define or explain the words and phrases listed in the chapter Glossary. (L. O. 6)

Consolidated financial statements financial statements that show the results of all operations under the parent's control, including those of any subsidiaries. Assets and liabilities of all affiliated companies are combined on a single balance sheet, revenues and expenses are combined on a single income statement, and cash flows are combined on a single statement of changes in financial position as though the business were in fact a single company. p. 833

Cost method of accounting for equity investments an accounting method whereby the investment is recorded at total cost and maintained at that amount; subsequent invested earnings and dividends do not affect the investment account. p. 834

Equity method of accounting for equity investments an accounting method whereby the investment is recorded at total cost, and the investment account balance is subsequently increased to reflect the investor's equity in earnings of the investee, and decreased to reflect the investor's equity in dividends of the investee. p. 836

Foreign exchange rate the price of one currency stated in terms of another currency. p. 845

Long-term investments investments not intended as a ready source of cash in case of need, such as bond sinking funds, land, bonds, and shares that are not held as a temporary investment of cash available for current operations. p. 832

Minority interest the portion of a subsidiary company's shareholders' equity that is not owned by the parent corporation. p. 841

Multinational business a company that operates in a large number of different countries. p. 845

Parent company a corporation that owns a controlling interest (more than 50% of the voting shares is required) in another corporation. p. 837

Reporting currency the currency in which a company presents its financial statements. p. 845

Subsidiary a corporation that is controlled by another (parent) corporation because the parent owns more than 50% of the subsidiary's voting shares p. 837

Temporary investments common and preferred shares that are actively traded so that sales prices or bid and ask prices are currently available on a national securities exchange or in the over-the-counter market. p. 832

Questions for Class Discussion

1. What is meant by the term *marketable securities*?
2. Under what conditions should an equity investment be classified on the balance sheet as a long-term investment?
3. What types of assets are classified as long-term investments?
4. In accounting for common stock investments, when should the cost method be used? When should the equity method be used?

5. Under what circumstances would a company prepare consolidated financial statements?

6. When the cost method is used to account for a long-term equity investment, what events cause the investor to record revenue from the investment?

7. If a company prepares consolidated financial statements, what method would the company normally use on its books to account for its investment in the subsidiary?

8. When a parent corporation uses the equity method to account for its investment in a subsidiary, what recognition is given by the parent corporation to the income or loss reported by the subsidiary? What recognition is given to dividends declared by the subsidiary?

9. Under what circumstances is lower of cost or market applied to long-term investments in shares?

10. When a long-term investment in equity securities is written down to a market value that is less than cost, how is the loss reported on the financial statements?

11. What are consolidated financial statements?

12. What account balances must be eliminated in preparing a consolidated balance sheet?

13. Why are the shareholders' equity accounts of a subsidiary eliminated in the process of preparing a consolidated balance sheet?

14. What is meant by *minority interest*? Where is this item disclosed on a consolidated balance sheet?

15. Why would a parent corporation pay more than book value for the shares of a subsidiary?

16. When a parent pays more than book value for the shares of a subsidiary, how should this additional cost be reported on the consolidated balance sheet?

17. What are two basic problems of accounting for international operations?

18. If a Canadian company makes a credit sale to a foreign customer and the customer is required to make payment in Canadian dollars, might the Canadian company have an exchange gain or loss as a result of the sale?

19. A Canadian company makes a credit sale to a foreign customer, and the customer is required to make payment in a foreign currency. The foreign exchange rate was $1.40 on the date of the sale and is $1.30 on the date the customer pays the receivable. Will the Canadian company record an exchange gain or an exchange loss?

20. On December 31, 1990, a Canadian company has an account receivable from a British customer which requires the customer to pay 6,000 pounds to the Canadian company. How do you determine the amount to be reported on the Canadian company's December 31 balance sheet?

21. In preparing its December 31, 1990, financial statements, a Canadian company had to report an account receivable that was denominated in a foreign currency. The receivable stemmed from a sale made on November 14, 1989. In translating the receivable into dollars, should the accountant use the foreign exchange rate on November 14 or on December 31?

Multiple Choice

1. Which of the following criteria must be satisfied in order for an equity investment to be classified as long term?
   a. The shares must be marketable securities.
   b. The shares must not be marketable securities that are held as a ready source of cash.
   c. The shares must not be marketable securities.
   d. The shares must not be held longer than one year.
   e. The shares must be common shares.

2. Under which of the following circumstances would a company account for its investment in another company's stock according to the equity method?
   a. The investor company owns 18% of the investee company's common shares and exercises a significant influence over the operations of the investee company.
   b. The investment represents 40% of the investee's outstanding preferred (nonvoting) stock.
   c. The investor owns 21% of the investee company's voting stock, but other facts disclose that the investor does not have a significant influence over the investee.
   d. The investment represents 30% of the investee's outstanding bonds payable.
   e. The investment represents 2% of the investee's outstanding common shares.

3. On January 1, 1990, Abbott Labs purchased 4,000 shares (40%) of Costello Company's common stock at a total cost of $103,000. Costello Company's net income over the next two years totaled $35,000, and the company declared and paid $25,000 in dividends on its outstanding common shares. Abbott Labs sold its Costello Company shares on January 14, 1993, for $27.75 per share. The entry to record the sale is as follows:

a.	Cash	111,000.00	
	Investment in Costello Company.		107,000.00
	Gain on Sale of Investments		4,000.00
b.	Cash	111,000.00	
	Investment in Costello Company.		103,000.00
	Gain on Sale of Investments		8,000.00

c.	Cash	111,000.00	
	Loss on Sale of Investments	2,000.00	
	Investment in Costello Company.		113,000.00
d.	Cash	111,000.00	
	Loss on Sale of Investments	6,000.00	
	Investment in Costello Company.		117,000.00
e.	Cash	111,000.00	
	Investment in Costello Company.		111,000.00

4. Lewis Company purchased 90% of Martin Company's shares at a total cost of $135,000, which amounted to $15 per share. The book value of the stock was $12.50 per share. Calculate the following amounts to report in Lewis Company's consolidated balance sheet on the date of acquisition: (1) investment in Martin Company, (2) excess of cost over book value, and (3) minority interest.
    a. (1) $135,000; (2) $ –0– ; (3) $15,000.
    b. (1) $135,000; (2) $25,000; (3) $15,000.
    c. (1) $112,500; (2) $22,500; (3) $12,500.
    d. (1) $ –0– ; (2) $22,500; (3) $12,500.
    e. Cannot be determined from information given.

5. In regard to consolidated statements, which one of the following is true:
    a. Minority interest is a current liability on the consolidated balance sheet.
    b. Goodwill from consolidation arises when the cost of the parent's investment in the subsidiary is more than the fair value of the subsidiary's net assets (assets less liabilities).
    c. If the parent clearly has a significant financial influence over the subsidiary, consolidated financial statements should be prepared even though the parent may own less than 50% of the subsidiary's outstanding stock.
    d. Consolidated financial statements are the primary source of information used by minority interests in evaluating the activities of a subsidiary.
    e. None of the above is true.

6. If a Canadian company makes a credit sale of merchandise to a British customer and the sales terms require the customer's payment to be in British pounds:
    a. The Canadian company may be required to record an exchange gain or loss on the date of the sale.
    b. The British company may eventually have to record an exchange gain or loss.
    c. The Canadian company will incur an exchange loss if the foreign exchange rate between pounds and dollars increases from $1.70 at the date of sale to $1.80 at the date the account is settled.
    d. The British company will incur an exchange loss if the foreign exchange rate between pounds and dollars decreases from $1.70 at the date of sale to $1.623 at the date the account is settled.
    e. None of the above is correct.

Mini Discussion Cases

Case 19-1

Paula Company has 10,000 shares (a 5% interest) of Sarah Company which were purchased as a temporary investment in 1987 at a cost of $100,000. Paula Company has total current assets of $400,000 and total current liabilities of $250,000 as of December 31, 1990.

Paula Company also has debentures outstanding which require Paula to maintain a current asset to current liability ratio of 1.5:1. The market value of Sarah Company's shares as at December 31, 1990, is $12 per share.

Required

Should the Sarah Company shares be classified as a temporary investment or as an investment in equity securities on the balance sheet of Paula Company? Discuss the consequences of the classification of Sarah Company's shares on Paula's balance sheet.

Case 19-2

When a company purchases more than 50% of another company's shares and pays more than book value, any amount not allocated to specific assets is reported in an account called Goodwill on Consolidation. However, when a price which is less than book value is paid, the entire excess of book value over cost must be allocated to reduce the balance sheet valuations of the assets.

Required

Discuss the apparent inconsistency in the treatment of the two amounts described above. Explain why you do (not) believe these treatments are appropriate.

Exercises

Exercise 19-1
Classifying equity investments; lower of cost or market
(L. O. 1, 3)

During 1990, Kest Corporation made five investments in equity securities. These securities, with their December 31, 1990, market values, are as follows:

a. Manor Corporation common stock: 3,000 shares, $36,000 cost, $32,000 market value. Purpose of investment is to develop a supplier relationship with Manor Corporation.

b. Blalock Company preferred stock: 1,000 shares, $22,000 cost, $23,500 market value. Purpose of investment is to earn dividends while holding as a source of cash for operations.

c. Cedar Company common stock: 1,500 shares, $37,000 cost, $39,000 market value. Purpose of investment is to hold for expected increase in value over the next few years.

d. Dipprey Corp. common stock: 1,200 shares, $44,000 cost, $41,000 market value. Purpose of investment is expected gains from increases in market value during next two years.

e. Neeley Company preferred stock: 800 shares, $25,000 cost, $26,000 market value. Purpose of the investment is to earn a return on surplus cash balances.

Determine the lower-of-cost-or-market amount of the long-term equity investments as of December 31, 1990. If necessary, prepare a journal entry dated December 31, 1990, to record any decline in market value. If a loss is recorded, explain how it should be reported by Kest Corporation.

Exercise 19–2
Equity investment transactions
(L. O. 2, 3)

Prepare general journal entries to record the following events on the books of K-Stop Company:

1990
Jan.   5   Purchased 10,000 shares of Mert Company common stock for $125,000 plus broker's fee of $2,150. Mert Company has 200,000 shares of common stock outstanding, and K-Stop Company does not have a significant influence on Mert Company policies.
May 12   Mert Company declared and paid a cash dividend of $0.90 per share.
Dec. 31   Mert Company announced that net income for the year amounted to $86,000.

1991
May 25   Mert Company declared and paid a cash dividend of $0.45 per share.
Aug. 20   Mert Company declared and issued a stock dividend of one additional share for each 10 shares already outstanding.
Dec. 30   K-Stop Company sold 5,500 shares of Mert Company for $73,200.
        31   Mert Company announced that net income for the year amounted to $80,000.

Exercise 19–3
Equity investment transactions
(L. O. 2, 3)

Prepare general journal entries to record the following events on the books of Akvar Company:

1990
Jan.   3   Purchased 10,000 shares of Betel Company for $133,000 plus broker's fee of $1,890. Betel Company has 50,000 shares of common stock outstanding and has acknowledged the fact that its policies will be significantly influenced by Akvar Company.
Oct. 15   Betel Company declared and paid a cash dividend of $0.70 per share.
Dec. 31   Betel Company announced that net income for the year amounted to $77,600.

1991
May 29   Betel Company declared and paid a cash dividend of $1.80 per share.
Aug. 24   Betel Company declared and issued a stock dividend of one additional share for each 10 shares already outstanding.
Dec. 31   Betel Company announced that net income for the year amounted to $65,000.
        31   Akvar Company sold 5,500 shares of Betel Company for $63,000.

Exercise 19–4
Comparison of cost and equity methods
(L. O. 2, 3)

On December 31, 1989, Able Company and Baker Company each purchased 6,000 shares of Charlie Company stock at a cost of $30 per share. On that date, the shareholders' equity of Charlie Company appeared as follows:

Common stock (30,000 shares)	$600,000
Retained earnings	300,000
Total	$900,000

Because of certain legal agreements, Baker Company does not have a significant influence over Charlie Company. However, Able Company is presumed to have a significant influence over Charlie Company.

During 1990 and 1991, Charlie Company earned an annual net income of $90,000 and paid cash dividends of $30,000 each year. On December 31, 1991, calculate the carrying value of (a) Able Company's investment in Charlie Company and (b) Baker Company's investment in Charlie Company.

Exercise 19–5
Consolidated statement elimination entry at acquisition
(L. O. 4)

On December 31, Small Company had the following shareholders' equity:

Common stock, 9,500 shares issued and outstanding . .	$ 95,000
Retained earnings.	65,000
Total shareholders' equity	$160,000

On the same day (December 31), Puff Company purchased 6,650 of Small Company's outstanding shares, paying $20 per share, and a work sheet to consolidate the balance sheets of the two companies was prepared. In general journal form, give the entry made on this work sheet to eliminate Puff Company's investment and the related shareholders' equity accounts of Small Company.

Exercise 19–6
Consolidated statement elimination entry after acquisition
(L. O. 4)

During the year following its acquisition by Puff Company (see Exercise 19–5), Small Company earned $25,000, paid out $12,000 in dividends, and retained the balance for use in its operations. In general journal form, give the entry under these assumptions to eliminate Puff Company's investment and Small Company's shareholders' equity account balances as of the end of the year.

Exercise 19–7
Consolidated balance sheet
(L. O. 4)

On December 31, 1990, Holter Company purchased 70% of Cats Corporation's 10,000 outstanding common shares. The balance sheets of the two companies on that date were as follows:

	Holter Company	Cats Corporation
Assets		
Investment in Cats Corporation.	$ 98,000	
Other assets	402,000	$160,000
Total assets	$500,000	$160,000
Liabilities and Shareholders' Equity		
Liabilities.	$100,000	$ 20,000
Common stock	250,000	100,000
Retained earnings.	150,000	40,000
Total liabilities and shareholders' equity . .	$500,000	$160,000

Present the consolidated balance sheet for Holter Company and its subsidiary on December 31, 1990. (Do not prepare a consolidated work sheet.)

Exercise 19–8
Calculating consolidated net income
(L. O. 3, 4)

On January 1, 1990, Rayer Corporation purchased 80% of Safte Corporation's outstanding shares. During the year ended December 31, 1990, Rayer earned a net income (excluding its equity in the earnings of Safte Corporation) of $75,000. Safte Corporation earned a net income of $40,000 and paid cash dividends of $15,000 during 1990. Calculate the net income to be reported on Rayer Corporation's consolidated income statement for 1990.

Exercise 19–9
Receivables denominated in a foreign currency
(L. O. 5)

On June 15, 1990, Wilder Company made a credit sale to a Swedish company. The terms of the sale required the Swedish company to pay 46,000 kronor (Swedish) on January 15, 1991. Wilder prepares quarterly financial statements on March 31, June 30, September 30, and December 31. The current foreign exchange rates for kronor during the time the receivable was outstanding were:

June 15, 1990.	$0.1680
June 30, 1990.	0.1825
September 30, 1990	0.1960
December 31, 1990.	0.1800
January 15, 1991	0.1700

Calculate the exchange gain or loss that Wilder Company should report on each of its quarterly income statements during the last three quarters of 1990 and the first quarter of 1991. Also calculate the amount that should be reported on Wilder Company's balance sheets at the end of each of those quarters.

Exercise 19–10
Foreign currency transactions
(L. O. 5)

Rhonder Company of Brandon, Manitoba, sells its products to customers in Canada and in Norway. On October 15, 1990, Rhonder Company sold merchandise on credit to the Norway Products Company at a price of 40,000 kroner. The exchange rate on that day was 1 krone equals $0.1572. On December 31, 1990, when Rhonder Company prepared its financial statements, the exchange rate was 1 krone for $0.1690. Norway Products paid its bill in full on January 12, 1991, at which time the exchange rate was 1 krone for $0.1625. Rhonder Company immediately exchanged the 40,000 kroner for Canadian dollars. Prepare journal entries on October 15, December 31, and January 12, to account for the sale and account receivable on the books of Rhonder Company.

Problems

Problem 19–1
Equity investments—cost and equity methods
(L. O. 2, 3)

Ranger Company was organized on January 2, 1990, for the purpose of investing in the shares of other companies. Ranger Company immediately issued 50,000 shares of common stock for which it received $250,000 cash. On January 9, 1990, Ranger Company purchased 10,000 shares (20%) of Trumpe Company's outstanding stock at a cost of $250,000. The following transactions and events subsequently occurred:

1990
Apr. 30   Trumpe Company declared and paid a cash dividend of $1 per share.
Dec. 31   Trumpe Company announced that its net income for the year was $125,000.

1991

June 12   Trumpe Company declared and issued a stock dividend of one share for each two shares already outstanding.

Aug. 10   Trumpe Company declared and paid a cash dividend of $0.80 per share.

Dec. 31   Trumpe Company announced that its net income for the year was $95,000.

1992

Jan.   4   Ranger Company sold all of its investment in Trumpe Company for $275,000 cash.

Part 1.   Because Ranger Company owns 20% of Trumpe Company's outstanding shares, Ranger Company is presumed to have a significant influence over Trumpe Company.

Required

1.   Give the entries on the books of Ranger Company to record the above events regarding its investment in Trumpe Company.

2.   Calculate the cost per share of Ranger Company's investment as reflected in the investment account on January 1, 1992.

3.   Calculate Ranger Company's retained earnings balance on January 5, 1992, after a closing of the books.

Part 2.   Although Ranger Company owns 20% of Trumpe Company's outstanding shares, a thorough investigation of the surrounding circumstances indicates that Ranger Company does not have a significant influence over Trumpe Company, and the cost method is the appropriate method of accounting for the investment.

Required

1.   Give the entries on the books of Ranger Company to record the above events regarding its investment in Trumpe Company.

2.   Calculate the cost per share of Ranger Company's investment as reflected in the investment account on January 1, 1992.

3.   Calculate Ranger Company's retained earnings balance on January 5, 1992, after a closing of the books.

Problem 19–2
Consolidated statements, at acquisition and one year later
(L. O. 4)

On January 1, 1990, Northwood Company purchased 80% of Souther Company's outstanding stock at $48 per share. On that date, Northwood Company had retained earnings of $517,500. Souther Company had retained earnings of $135,000 and had outstanding 15,000 shares of common stock.

Part 1.

Required

1.   Give the elimination entry to be used on a work sheet for a consolidated balance sheet dated January 1, 1990.

2.   Determine the amount of consolidated retained earnings that should be shown on a consolidated balance sheet dated January 1, 1990.

Part 2.   During the year ended December 31, 1990, Northwood Company paid cash dividends of $67,500 and earned net income of $127,500 excluding earnings from its investment in Souther Company. Souther Company earned net income of $63,000 and paid dividends of $30,000. Except for Northwood Company's Retained Earnings account and the Investment in Souther Company account, the balance sheet accounts for the two companies on December 31, 1990, are as follows:

	Northwood Company	Souther Company
Assets		
Cash	$157,800	$124,200
Notes receivable.	54,000	
Merchandise.	367,200	178,200
Building, net	348,000	216,000
Land	210,000	189,000
Investment in Souther Company	?	
Total assets	$?	$707,400
Liabilities and Shareholders' Equity		
Accounts payable	$439,500	$260,400
Note payable.		54,000
Common stock.	672,000	225,000
Retained earnings	?	168,000
Total liabilities and shareholders' equity . .	$?	$707,400

Northwood Company loaned $54,000 to Souther Company during 1990, for which Souther Company signed a note. On December 31, 1990, the note had not been repaid.

Required

1. Calculate the December 31, 1990, balances in Northwood Company's Investment in Souther Company account and Retained Earnings account.

2. Complete a work sheet to consolidate the balance sheets of the two companies.

Problem 19–3
Consolidated work sheet and balance sheet
(L. O. 4)

The following items appeared in the first two columns of a work sheet prepared to consolidate the balance sheets of Upper Company and Lower Company on the day Upper Company gained control of Lower Company by purchasing 6,375 shares of its common stock at $65 per share. Lower Company has a total of 7,500 shares outstanding.

	Upper Company	Lower Company
Assets		
Cash	$ 28,125	$ 41,250
Note receivable, Lower Company	37,500	
Accounts receivable, net	105,000	90,000
Inventories	157,500	131,250
Investment in Lower Company	414,375	
Equipment, net	300,000	262,500
Buildings, net	318,750	
Land	75,000	
Total assets	$1,436,250	$525,000

	Upper Company	Lower Company
Liabilities and Shareholders' Equity		
Accounts payable	$ 78,750	$ 37,500
Note payable, Upper Company		37,500
Common stock	937,500	375,000
Retained earnings	420,000	75,000
Total liabilities and shareholders' equity . .	$1,436,250	$525,000

At the time Upper Company acquired control of Lower Company, it took Lower Company's note in exchange for $37,500 in cash, and it sold and delivered $7,500 of equipment at cost to Lower Company on open account (account receivable). Both transactions are reflected in the foregoing accounts.

Required

1. Prepare a work sheet to consolidate the balance sheets of the two companies and prepare a consolidated balance sheet.
2. Under the assumption that Lower Company earned $37,500 during the first year after it was acquired by Upper Company, paid out $22,500 in dividends, and retained the balance of its earnings in its operations, give the entry to eliminate Upper Company's investment in the subsidiary and Lower Company's shareholders' equity accounts at the year's end.

Problem 19–4
Foreign currency transactions
(L. O. 5)

Paramount Sales Corporation, a Canadian company that has customers in several foreign countries, had the following transactions in 1990 and 1991:

1990

June 6 Sold merchandise for 125,000 francs to Poirot Co. of Brussels, payment in full to be received in 60 days. On this day, the foreign exchange rate for francs into dollars was $0.02822.

July 17 Sold merchandise to Nordhoff Distributors of West Germany for $8,880 cash. The exchange rate for marks into dollars was $0.5920.

Aug. 1 Received Poirot Company's payment for its purchase of June 6 and exchanged the francs for dollars. The current foreign exchange rate for francs into dollars was $0.02840.

Oct. 25 Sold merchandise on credit to British Imports, Ltd., a company located in London, England. The price of 3,000 pounds was to be paid 90 days from the date of sale. On October 25, the exchange rate for pounds into dollars was $1.7730.

Nov. 30 Sold merchandise for 350,000 yen to Yamoto Company of Japan; payment in full to be in 60 days. The exchange rate for yen into dollars was $0.007710.

Dec. 31 Prepared adjusting entries to recognize exchange gains or losses on the annual financial statements. Rates for exchanging foreign currencies into dollars on this day included the following:

Francs (Belgium)	$0.02833
Marks (W. German)	0.5944
Pounds (England)	1.7125
Yen (Japan)	0.007897

1991

Jan. 23   Received British Imports, Ltd.'s full payment for the sale of October 25 and immediately exchanged the pounds for dollars. The exchange rate for pounds into dollars was $1.7628.

29   Received full payment from Yamoto Company for the sale of November 30 and immediately exchanged the yen for dollars. The exchange rate for yen into dollars was $0.007779.

Required

1. Prepare general journal entries to account for these transactions of Paramount Sales Corporation.

2. Calculate the exchange gain or loss to be reported on Paramount Sales Corporation's 1990 income statement.

Alternate Problems

Problem 19–1A
Stock investments—cost and equity methods
(L. O. 2)

Universal Company was organized on January 1, 1990, for the purpose of investing in the shares of other companies. Universal Company immediately issued 46,000 shares of $5 par, common stock for which it received $230,000 cash. On January 7, 1990, Universal Company purchased 20,000 shares (20%) of Suburban Company's outstanding stock at a cost of $230,000. The following transactions and events subsequently occurred:

1990

May 20   Suburban Company declared and paid a cash dividend of $0.90 per share.

Dec. 31   Suburban Company announced that its net income for the year was $150,000.

1991

July   8   Suburban Company declared and issued a stock dividend of one share for each four shares already outstanding.

Nov. 15   Suburban Company declared and paid a cash dividend of $0.70 per share.

Dec. 31   Suburban Company announced that its net income for the year was $160,000.

1992

Jan.   4   Universal Company sold all of its investment in Suburban Company for $240,000 cash.

Part 1.   Because Universal Company owns 20% of Suburban Company's outstanding stock, Universal Company is presumed to have a significant influence over Suburban Company.

Required

1. Give the entries on the books of Universal Company to record the above events regarding its investment in Suburban Company.

2. Calculate the cost per share of Universal Company's investment as reflected in the investment account on January 3, 1992.

3. Calculate Universal Company's retained earnings balance on January 5, 1992, after a closing of the books.

Part 2. Although Universal Company owns 20% of Suburban Company's outstanding stock, a thorough investigation of the surrounding circumstances indicates that Universal Company does not have a significant influence over Suburban Company, and the cost method is the appropriate method of accounting for the investment.

Required

1. Give the entries on the books of Universal Company to record the above events regarding its investment in Suburban Company.
2. Calculate the cost per share of Universal Company's investment as reflected in the investment account on January 3, 1992.
3. Calculate Universal Company's retained earnings balance on January 5, 1992, after a closing of the books.

Problem 19–2A
Consolidated statements, at acquisition and one year later
(L. O. 4)

On January 1, 1990, Larger Company purchased 90% of Smaller Company's outstanding shares at $24 per share. On that date, Larger Company had retained earnings of $350,500. Smaller Company had retained earnings of $225,000 and had outstanding 20,000 shares of common stock.

Part 1.

Required

1. Give the elimination entry to be used on a work sheet for a consolidated balance sheet dated January 1, 1990.
2. Determine the amount of consolidated retained earnings that should be shown on a consolidated balance sheet dated January 1, 1990.

Part 2. During the year ended December 31, 1990, Larger Company paid cash dividends of $45,000 and earned net income of $90,000 excluding earnings from its investment in Smaller Company. Smaller Company earned net income of $45,000 and paid dividends of $25,000. Except for Larger Company's Retained Earnings account and the Investment in Smaller Company account, the balance sheet accounts for the two companies on December 31, 1990, are as follows:

	Larger Company	Smaller Company
Assets		
Cash	$140,200	$106,800
Notes receivable.	45,000	
Merchandise.	220,800	175,300
Building, net	284,250	240,000
Land	186,000	183,500
Investment in Smaller Company	?	
Total assets	$?	$705,600
Liabilities and Shareholders' Equity		
Accounts payable	$215,250	$215,600
Note payable		45,000
Common stock	675,000	200,000
Retained earnings	?	245,000
Total liabilities and shareholders' equity . .	$?	$705,600

Larger Company loaned $45,000 to Smaller Company during 1990, for which Smaller Company signed a note. On December 31, 1990, the note had not been repaid.

Required

1. Calculate the December 31, 1990, balances in Larger Company's Investment in Smaller Company account and Retained Earnings account.
2. Complete a work sheet to consolidate the balance sheets of the two companies.

Problem 19–3A
Consolidated work sheet and balance sheet
(L. O. 4)

The following items appeared in the first two columns of a work sheet prepared to consolidate the balance sheets of Parent Company and Subsidiary Company on the day Parent Company gained control of Subsidiary Company by purchasing 29,750 shares of its common stock at $13 per share. Subsidiary Company has a total of 35,000 common shares outstanding.

	Parent Company	Subsidiary Company
Assets		
Cash	$ 37,250	$ 72,500
Note receivable, Subsidiary Company . . .	54,000	
Accounts receivable, net	110,000	80,000
Inventories	215,000	162,500
Investment in Subsidiary Company	386,750	
Equipment, net	461,250	257,500
Buildings, net	337,500	
Land	150,000	
Total assets	$1,751,750	$572,500
Liabilities and Shareholders' Equity		
Accounts payable	$ 257,500	$ 98,500
Note payable, Parent Company		54,000
Common stock	875,000	350,000
Retained earnings	619,250	70,000
Total liabilities and shareholders' equity . .	$1,751,750	$572,500

At the time Parent Company acquired control of Subsidiary Company, it took Subsidiary Company's note in exchange for $54,000 in cash, and it sold and delivered $3,000 of equipment at cost to Subsidiary Company on open account (account receivable). Both transactions are reflected in the foregoing accounts.

Required

1. Prepare a work sheet to consolidate the balance sheets of the two companies and prepare a consolidated balance sheet.
2. Under the assumption that Subsidiary Company earned $50,000 during the first year after it was acquired by Parent Company, paid out $32,500 in dividends, and retained the balance of its earnings in its operations, give the entry to eliminate Parent Company's investment in the subsidiary and Subsidiary Company's shareholders' equity accounts at the year's end.

Problem 19–4A
Foreign currency transactions
(L. O. 5)

Global Sales Company, a Canadian company that has customers in several foreign countries, had the following transactions in 1990 and 1991:

1990

July 16   Sold merchandise for 950,000 yen to Shisedu Company of Japan, payment in full to be received in 60 days. On this day, the current foreign exchange rate for yen into dollars was $0.007897.

Aug. 21   Sold merchandise to Klaus Retailers of West Germany for $9,500 cash. The foreign exchange rate for marks into dollars was $0.6027.

Sept. 14   Received Shisedu Company's payment for its purchase of July 16 and exchanged the yen for dollars. The exchange rate for yen into dollars was $0.007779.

Oct.   6   Sold merchandise on credit to Trafalgar Distributors, Inc., a company located in London. The price of 5,000 pounds was to be paid 90 days from the date of sale. On October 6, the foreign exchange rate for pounds into dollars was $1.7644.

Nov. 18   Sold merchandise for 30,000 francs to Belgique Suppliers of Brussels, payment in full to be in 60 days. The exchange rate for Belgian francs into dollars was $0.2818.

Dec. 31   Prepared adjusting entries to recognize exchange gains or losses on the annual financial statements. Rates of exchanging foreign currencies into dollars on this day included the following:

Francs (Belgium).	$0.2850
Marks (West Germany)	0.5903
Pounds (England)	1.7420
Yen (Japan)	0.007791

1991

Jan.   4   Received Trafalgar Distributors, Inc.'s full payment for the sale of October 6 and immediately exchanged the pounds for dollars. The exchange rate for pounds into dollars was $1.7695.

Jan. 17   Received full payment from Belgique Suppliers for the sale of November 18 and exchanged the francs for dollars. The exchange rate for francs into dollars was $0.2822.

Required

1. Prepare general journal entries to account for these transactions of Global Sales Company.

2. Calculate the exchange gain or loss to be reported on Global Sales Company's 1990 income statement.

Provocative Problems

Provocative Problem 19–1
Tamerack, Ltd.
(L. O. 2, 3)

When corporations have their annual meetings with shareholders, the managements often have to deal with difficult questions from shareholders. For example, at a recent shareholders' meeting of Tamerack, Ltd., one of the shareholders made the following statements. ''I have owned shares of Tamerack for several years but am now questioning whether management is telling the truth in the annual financial statements. At the end of 1990, you announced that Tamerack had just acquired a 30% interest in the outstanding shares of Franklin Company, Ltd. You also stated that the 105,000 shares had cost Tamerack about $10.5 million. In the financial statements for 1991, you told us that the investments of Tamerack were proving to be very profitable and reported that earnings from all investments had amounted to more than $5.25 million. In the financial statements for 1992, you explained that Tamerack had sold the Franklin shares during the first week of the year, receiving $11,750,000 cash proceeds from the sale. Nevertheless, the income statement for 1992 reports only a $260,000 gain on the sale (before taxes). I realize that Franklin did not pay any dividends during 1991, but it was very profitable. As I recall, it reported net income of $3.3 million for 1991. Personally, I do not think you should have sold the shares. But, much more importantly, you reported to us that our company gained only $260,000 from the sale. How can that be true if the shares were purchased for $10,500,000 and were sold for $11,750,000?''

Explain to this shareholder why the $260,000 gain is correctly reported.

Provocative Problem 19–2
Canadian Motor Inns, Limited
(L. O. 4)

Canadian Motor Inns (CMI) is engaged in the business of operating hotels and restaurants. A recent annual report of CMI included the following footnote to its financial statements:

> (7) MINORITY INTEREST IN SUBSIDIARY
> In December, . . . the Company's previously wholly owned subsidiary, Universal Communication Systems, Ltd., sold 750,000 shares of its common stock to the public resulting in net proceeds of $8,725,000. This reduced the Company's holding in that subsidiary to approximately 84% of the outstanding common stock.

Given this information, would you expect the future consolidated financial statements of Canadian Motor Inns to report its investment in Universal Communication Systems according to the equity method? Why or why not? Also, assume that Canadian Motor Inns prepared a consolidated balance sheet immediately after the subsidiary's sale of shares to the public. Did the sale of shares have any effects on that balance sheet? If so, explain the effects.

Analytical and Review Problems

A&R Problem 19–1

On January 1, 1990, Tony Company purchases 40% of Danny Company's outstanding voting shares. On December 31, 1991, Tony Company's account Investment in Danny Company showed a balance of $400,000. Danny Company reported the following information for the years of 1990 and 1991:

	Net Income	Dividends Paid
1990	$150,000	$50,000
1991	200,000	50,000

Required
Calculate the purchase price paid by Tony Company for the Danny Company shares.

A&R Problem 19–2

On January 1, 1990, Peter Ltd. purchases a 40% interest (i.e., 7,500 shares) in Stanley Company's outstanding voting shares for $236,250. During 1990 and 1991 Peter recorded the following entries:

Dec.	1	1990	Cash.	10,500	
			Dividend revenue		10,500
			To record receipt of dividend.		
Dec.	31	1990	Investment in Stanley Co.	26,250	
			Investment revenue		26,250
			To record increase in market value of Stanley Co. shares.		
Dec.	1	1991	Cash.	10,500	
			Dividend revenue		10,500
			To record receipt of dividend.		
Dec.	15	1991	Investment in Stanley Co.	30,000	
			Investment revenue		30,000
			To record receipt of 750 shares of Stanley Co. as a stock dividend.		
Dec.	31	1991	Investment in Stanley Co.	45,750	
			Investment revenue		45,750
			To record increase in market value of Stanley Co. shares.		

Stanley Company's results for 1990 and 1991 were as follows:

	1990	1991
Net income	$70,500	$52,500
Cash dividends paid	26,250	26,250

Required

a. Identify any errors you feel that Peter Ltd. may have made with respect to the entries shown above.

b. Prepare any necessary correcting entries as of December 31, 1991, assuming the books have not yet been closed.

A&R Problem 19–3

The consolidated Statements of Retained Earnings and accompanying note are reproduced from the Northern Communication Limited Annual Report for 1990.

Consolidated Statement of Retained Earnings
Year Ended December 31
(in thousands)

	1990	1989
Balance at beginning of year	$ 933.0	$ 677.4
Net earnings	411.4	333.9
	1,344.4	1,001.3
Dividends—preferred shares	(36.4)	(22.3)
—common shares	(58.0)	(46.0)
Balance at end of year	$1,250.0	$ 933.0

Note: At December 31, 1990, Well Wisher Enterprises Inc. (WWE) owned 52.0 percent of the outstanding common shares.

Required

1. Prepare the necessary journal entry on the books of Well Wisher Enterprises to record (*a*) its share of Northern Communication's net income for 1990 and (*b*) its share of the dividends paid by Northern Communication.

2. Would WWE's consolidated statements include Northern Communication?

A&R Problem 19–4

The following is an excerpt from the notes to the financial statements of ABC Sciences Ltd.:

> ABC Sciences holds a 35.4% interest in Halifax-based Eastern Laboratories which develops, manufactures, and distributes chemicals solely in the Canadian market. ABC Sciences accounts for its investment in Eastern Chemicals by the equity method. During 1990, Eastern had a strong year, with revenues increasing 79.6% while net income more than doubled to $7.6 million. ABC Sciences's share of this net income was . . .

Required

1. Is ABC Sciences using the cost or equity method to account for its investment in Eastern Chemicals? Support your answer.

2. Prepare the journal entry to record ABC Sciences's share of Eastern's net income.

3. If Eastern paid out 50% of its 1990 net income as cash dividends, what entry would ABC Sciences make to record the receipt of cash?

20 Analyzing Financial Statements

As a result of studying the previous chapters, you have learned the fundamental methods and principles that are used to generate financial statements. The focus of this chapter is on the analysis of financial statements. In studying this chapter, you will expand your understanding of how the information in financial statements can be used to evaluate the activities and financial status of a business.

Learning Objectives

After studying Chapter 20, you should be able to:

1. List the three broad objectives of financial reporting by business enterprises.
2. Describe, prepare, and interpret comparative financial statements and common-size comparative statements.
3. Calculate and explain the interpretation of the ratios, turnovers, and rates of return used to evaluate (*a*) short-term liquidity, (*b*) long-term risk and capital structure, and (*c*) operating efficiency and profitability.
4. State the limitations associated with using financial statement ratios and the sources from which standards for comparison may be obtained.
5. Define or explain the words and phrases listed in the chapter Glossary.

Financial Reporting

Many different people receive and analyze financial information about business firms. These people range from managers, employees, directors, customers, suppliers, owners, lenders, and potential investors to brokers, regulatory authorities, lawyers, economists, labour unions, financial advisors, and the financial press. Some of these groups, such as managers and some regulatory agencies, are able to require a company to prepare specialized financial reports that meet their specific interests. Many other groups must rely on the **general purpose financial statements** that companies publish periodically. General purpose financial statements usually include (1) an income statement, (2) a balance sheet, (3) a statement of retained earnings or statement of changes in shareholders' equity, and (4) a statement of changes in financial position. A variety of additional financial information such as the financial statement footnotes typically is published with the statements. See, for example, the financial statements and related information from the annual report of Abitibi-Price in Appendix I. Also, news announcements by company managers often are a timely source of financial information.

Financial reporting is the process of preparing and issuing financial information about a company. While financial reporting includes more than general purpose financial statements, the same broad objectives apply to both.

Objectives of Financial Reporting

List the three broad objectives of financial reporting by business enterprises.
(L. O. 1)

The great variety of persons who use financial information about a business have differing reasons for analyzing that information. However, most users are "generally interested in [the business's] ability to generate favourable cash flows because their decisions relate to amounts, timing, and uncertainties of expected cash flows." Based on this general assumption about the interests of financial information users, the *CICA Handbook,* par. 1000.12, states:

> The objective of financial statements is to communicate information that is useful to investors, creditors and other users in making resource allocation decisions and/or assessing management stewardship. Consequently, financial statements provide information about:
> (a) an entity's economic resources, obligations and equity;
> (b) changes in an entity's economic resources, obligations and equity; and
> (c) the economic performance of the entity.

The financial information must have certain attributes to be useful to investors, creditors, and other users. The *CICA Handbook,* par. 1000.15–19, identifies these as the qualitative characteristics of understandability, relevance, reliability, and comparability and expands on these as follows:

Understandability

> For the information provided in financial statements to be useful, it must be capable of being understood by investors, creditors and other users. Investors, creditors and other users are assumed to have a reasonable understanding of business and economic activities and accounting, together with a willingness to study the information with reasonable diligence.

Relevance

For the information provided in financial statements to be useful, it must be relevant to the decisions made by investors, creditors and other users. Information is relevant by its nature when it can influence the decisions of investors, creditors and other users by helping them evaluate the financial impact of past, present or future transactions and events or confirm, or correct, previous evaluations. Relevance is achieved through information that has predictive value or feedback value and by its timeliness.

Reliability

For the information provided in financial statements to be useful, it must be reliable. Information is reliable when it is in agreement with the actual underlying transactions and events, the agreement is capable of independent verification and the information is reasonably free from error and bias. Reliability is achieved through representational faithfulness, verifiability and neutrality. Neutrality is affected by the use of conservatism in making judgments under conditions of uncertainty.

Comparability

Comparability is a characteristic of the relationship between two pieces of information rather than of a particular piece of information by itself. It enables investors, creditors and other users to identify similarities in and differences between the information provided by two sets of financial statements. Comparability is important when comparing the financial statements of two different entities and when comparing the financial statements of the same entity over two periods or at two different points in time.

The concepts of financial statements are intended to help accountants decide how accounting problems should be solved. In addition, they provide important background information for the person who is learning how to understand and analyze financial statements.

The primary idea of analysis of financial statements is that financial reporting should help readers predict the amounts, timing, and uncertainty of future net cash inflows to the business. The methods of analysis and techniques explained in this chapter contribute to this process.

When the financial statements of a business are analyzed, individual statement items usually are not too significant. However, relationships between items and groups of items plus changes that occurred are significant. As a result, financial statement analysis involves describing relationships between items and groups of items and changes in items.

Comparative Statements

Describe, prepare, and interpret comparative financial statements and common-size comparative statements.
(L. O. 2)

You can see changes in financial statement items most clearly when item amounts for two or more successive accounting periods are placed side by side in columns on a single statement. Statements prepared in this manner are called **comparative statements.** Each financial statement can be presented in the form of a comparative statement.

In its most simple form, a comparative balance sheet consists of the item amounts from two or more successive balance sheets arranged side by side so that you can see the changes in the amounts. However, the statement can be improved by also showing the changes in dollar amounts and in percentages. When this is done, as in Illustration 20–1, large dollar and large percentage changes are readily apparent.

A comparative income statement is prepared in the same way as a comparative balance sheet. Income statement amounts for two or more successive periods are placed side by side, with dollar and percentage changes in additional columns. Illustration 20–2 shows such a statement.

Analyzing and Interpreting Comparative Statements

In analyzing and interpreting comparative data, you should select for study any items that show significant dollar or percentage changes. Then, you try to determine the reasons for each change and if possible whether they are favourable or unfavourable. For example, in Illustration 20–1, the first item, "Cash," shows a decrease of $5,500. The next item, "Temporary investments," shows an extremely large decrease. Also, the "Long-term investments" were completely eliminated during the year. At first glance these changes appear unfavourable. However, these decreases must be evaluated in light of other changes that occurred. The increases in "Store equipment," "Buildings," and "Land," show that the company materially increased its plant assets between the two balance sheet dates. Further study suggests that the company has apparently constructed a new building on land that was held as an investment until needed in this expansion. Also, the company apparently paid for the new plant assets by reducing cash, selling the Apex Company common stock, and issuing a $50,000 note payable.

To help control operations, a comparative income statement is usually more valuable than a comparative balance sheet. For example, in Illustration 20–2, "Gross sales" increased 14.1% and "Net sales" increased 13.9%. At the same time, "Sales returns" increased 32.4%, or at a rate more than twice that of gross sales. Usually, returned sales represent wasted sales effort and dissatisfied customers. Therefore, the increased rate of "Sales returns" should be investigated, and the reason for the increase determined if possible.

In addition to the large increase in the "Sales returns," it is significant that the rate of increase in "Cost of goods sold" is greater than that of "Net sales." This unfavourable trend should be corrected if possible.

In attempting to find reasons for Ranger Wholesale Company's increase in sales, the increases in advertising and in plant assets must be considered. You might expect an increase in advertising to increase sales. Also, the increase in plant assets may have been necessary to support a larger sales volume.

Illustration 20–1

RANGER WHOLESALE COMPANY
Comparative Balance Sheet
December 31, 1990, and December 31, 1989

	Years Ended December 31		Amount of Increase or (Decrease) during 1990	Percent of Increase or (Decrease) during 1990
	1990	1989		
Assets				
Current assets:				
Cash	$ 15,000	$ 20,500	$ (5,500)	(26.8)
Temporary investments	3,000	70,000	(67,000)	(95.7)
Accounts receivable, net	68,000	64,000	4,000	6.3
Merchandise inventory	90,000	84,000	6,000	7.1
Prepaid expenses	5,800	6,000	(200)	(3.3)
Total current assets	$181,800	$244,500	$ (62,700)	(25.6)
Long-term investments:				
Real estate	$ –0–	$ 30,000	$ (30,000)	(100.0)
Apex Company common stock.	–0–	50,000	(50,000)	(100.0)
Total long-term investments	$ –0–	$ 80,000	$ (80,000)	(100.0)
Plant and equipment				
Office equipment, net	$ 3,500	$ 3,700	$ (200)	(5.4)
Store equipment, net	17,900	6,800	11,100	163.2
Buildings, net	176,800	28,000	148,800	531.4
Land	50,000	20,000	30,000	150.0
Total plant and equipment	$248,200	$ 58,500	$189,700	324.3
Total assets	$430,000	$383,000	$ 47,000	12.3
Liabilities				
Current liabilities:				
Notes payable	$ 5,000	$ –0–	$ 5,000	
Accounts payable	43,600	55,000	(11,400)	(20.7)
Taxes payable	4,800	5,000	(200)	(4.0)
Wages payable	800	1,200	(400)	(33.3)
Total current liabilities	$ 54,200	$ 61,200	$ (7,000)	(11.4)
Long-term liabilities:				
Notes payable (secured by mortgage).	$ 60,000	$ 10,000	$ 50,000	500.0
Total liabilities	$114,200	$ 71,200	$ 43,000	(60.4)
Shareholders' Equity				
Common stock, 25,000 shares	$250,000	$250,000	–0–	–0–
Retained earnings	65,800	61,800	4,000	6.5
Total shareholder's equity	$315,800	$311,800	$ 4,000	1.3
Total liabilities and equity	$430,000	$383,000	$ 47,000	12.3

Illustration 20–2

RANGER WHOLESALE COMPANY
Comparative Income Statement
For Years Ended December 31, 1990, and 1989

	Years Ended December 31		Amount of Increase or (Decrease) during 1990	Percent of Increase or (Decrease) during 1990
	1990	1989		
Gross sales	$973,500	$853,000	$120,500	14.1
Sales returns and allowances	13,500	10,200	3,300	32.4
Net sales.	$960,000	$842,800	$117,200	13.9
Cost of goods sold	715,000	622,500	92,500	14.9
Gross profit from sales	$245,000	$220,300	$ 24,700	11.2
Operating expenses:				
Selling expenses:				
Advertising expense	$ 7,500	$ 5,000	$ 2,500	50.0
Sales salaries expense	109,500	97,500	12,000	12.3
Store supplies expense	3,200	2,800	400	14.3
Depreciation expense, store equipment	2,400	1,700	700	41.2
Delivery expense.	14,800	14,000	800	5.7
Total selling expenses	$137,400	$121,000	$ 16,400	13.6
General and administrative expenses:				
Office salaries expenses.	$ 41,000	$ 40,050	$ 950	2.4
Office supplies expenses	1,300	1,250	50	4.0
Insurance expense.	1,600	1,200	400	33.3
Depreciation expense, office equipment	300	300	–0–	–0–
Depreciation expense, buildings	2,850	1,500	1,350	90.0
Bad debts expense.	2,250	2,200	50	2.3
Total general and admin. expenses.	$ 49,300	$ 46,500	$ 2,800	6.0
Total operating expenses	$186,700	$167,500	$ 19,200	11.5
Operating income	$ 58,300	$ 52,800	$ 5,500	10.4
Less interest expense	6,300	1,500	4,800	320.0
Income before taxes	$ 52,000	$ 51,300	$ 700	1.4
Income taxes.	19,000	18,700	300	1.6
Net income.	$ 33,000	$ 32,600	$ 400	1.2
Earnings per share	$1.32	$1.30	$0.02	1.5

Calculating Percentage Increases and Decreases

To calculate the percentage increases and decreases shown on comparative statements, you divide the dollar increase or decrease in an item by the amount shown for the item in the base year. If no amount is shown in the base year, or if the base year amount is negative (such as a net loss), a percentage increase or decrease cannot be calculated. For example, in Illustration 20–1, there were no notes payable at the end of 1989, and a percentage change for this item cannot be calculated.

In this text, percentages and ratios typically are rounded to one or two decimal places. However, there is no uniform agreement on this matter. In general, percentages should be carried out far enough to assure that meaningful information is conveyed. However, they should not be carried so far that the significance of relationships tends to become "lost" in the length of the numbers.

Trend Percentages

Trend percentages or index numbers emphasize changes that have occurred from period to period and are used to compare data that covers a number of years. You calculate trend percentages as follows:

1. Select a base year and assign each item amount on the base year statement a weight of 100%.
2. Then, express each item from the statements for the years after the base year as a percentage of its base year amount. To determine these percentages, divide the item amounts in the years after the base year by the amount of the item in the base year.

For example, if 1985 is selected as the base year for the following data, you divide the "Sales" amount in each year by $210,000 to get the trend percentages for sales. To get the trend percentages for cost of goods sold, you divide the "Cost of goods sold" amount in each year by $145,000. And the gross profit trend percentages equal the "Gross profit" amount in each year divided by $65,000.

	1990	1989	1988	1987	1986	1985
Sales	$324,000	$310,000	$284,000	$292,000	$204,000	$210,000
Cost of goods sold . .	229,000	218,000	198,000	204,000	139,000	145,000
Gross profit	$ 95,000	$ 92,000	$ 86,000	$ 88,000	$ 65,000	$ 65,000

When these divisions are made, the trends for these three items appear as follows:

	1990	1989	1988	1987	1986	1985
Sales	154%	148%	135%	139%	97%	100%
Cost of goods sold . .	158	150	137	141	96	100
Gross profit	146	142	132	135	100	100

Note that the sales trend is upward after the second year. However, cost of goods sold increases at a slightly more rapid rate. This indicates a contracting gross profit rate and should receive attention.

You should understand that the trend for a single balance sheet or income statement item is seldom very informative. However, you may learn a great deal from comparing the trends of related items. For example, a downward sales trend with an upward trend for merchandise inventory, accounts receivable, and bad debts expense indicates an unfavourable situation. On the other hand, an upward sales trend with a downward trend or a slower upward trend for accounts receivable, merchandise inventory, and selling expenses suggests an increase in operating efficiency.

Illustration 20–3

RANGER WHOLESALE COMPANY
Common-Size Comparative Balance Sheet
December 31, 1990, and December 31, 1989

	Years Ended December 31		Common-Size Percentages	
	1990	**1989**	**1990**	**1989**
Assets				
Current assets:				
Cash.	$ 15,000	$ 20,500	3.49	5.35
Temporary investments	3,000	70,000	0.70	18.28
Accounts receivable, net.	68,000	64,000	15.81	16.71
Merchandise inventory	90,000	84,000	20.93	21.93
Prepaid expenses	5,800	6,000	1.35	1.57
Total current assets	$181,800	$244,500	42.28	63.84
Long-term investments:				
Real estate	–0–	$ 30,000		7.83
Apex Company common stock	–0–	50,000		13.05
Total long-term investments	–0–	$ 80,000		20.88
Plant and equipment:				
Office equipment, net	$ 3,500	$ 3,700	0.81	0.97
Store equipment, net.	17,900	6,800	4.16	1.78
Buildings, net	176,800	28,000	41.12	7.31
Land.	50,000	20,000	11.63	5.22
Total plant and equipment	$248,200	$ 58,500	57.72	15.28
Total assets	$430,000	$383,000	100.00	100.00
Liabilities				
Current liabilities:				
Notes payable	$ 5,000	–0–	1.16	
Accounts payable.	43,600	$ 55,000	10.14	14.36
Taxes payable	4,800	5,000	1.12	1.31
Wages payable	800	1,200	0.19	0.31
Total current liabilities	$ 54,200	$ 61,200	12.61	15.98
Long-term liabilities:				
Notes payable (secured by mortgage)	$ 60,000	$ 10,000	13.95	2.61
Total liabilities	$114,200	$ 71,200	26.56	18.59
Shareholders' Equity				
Common stock, 25,000 shares.	$250,000	$250,000	58.14	65.27
Retained earnings.	65,800	61,800	15.30	16.14
Total shareholders' equity	$315,800	$311,800	73.44	81.41
Total liabilities and equity.	$430,000	$383,000	100.00	100.00

Common-Size Comparative Statements

Although the comparative statements illustrated so far show how each item
has changed over time, they do not emphasize the relative importance of each
item. Changes in the relative importance of each financial statement item are
shown more clearly by **common-size comparative statements**.

In common-size statements, each item is expressed as a percentage of a base amount; that is, the items are shown in common-size figures—figures that are fractions of 100%. For example, on a common-size balance sheet (1) the amount of total assets is assigned a value of 100%. (2) This means that the total amount of liabilities plus owners' equity also equals 100%. Then (3), each asset, liability, and owners' equity item is shown as a percentage of total assets (or total liabilities plus owners' equity). If you show a company's successive balance sheets in this way (see Illustration 20–3), proportional changes are emphasized.

On a common-size income statement, the amount of net sales is assigned a value of 100%. Then, each statement item appears as a percentage of net sales. Such a statement is an informative and useful tool. If you think of the 100% sales amount as representing one sales dollar, then the remaining items show how each sales dollar was distributed to costs, expenses, and profit. For example, on the comparative income statement in Illustration 20–4, the 1989 cost of goods sold consumed 73.86 cents of each sales dollar. In 1990, cost of goods sold consumed 74.48 cents of each sales dollar. While this increase is small, if the cost of goods sold percentage in 1990 had remained at the 1989 level, almost $6,000 of additional gross profit would have been earned.

Common-size percentages point out efficiencies and inefficiencies that are otherwise difficult to see. For this reason, they are a valuable management tool. To illustrate, sales salaries of Ranger Wholesale Company took a higher percentage of each sales dollar in 1990 than in 1989. On the other hand, office salaries took a smaller percentage. Although the amount of bad debts expense in 1990 was more than in 1989, bad debts expense took a smaller portion of each sales dollar in 1990 than in 1989.

Analysis of Short-Term Liquidity

Calculate and explain the interpretation of the ratios, turnovers, and rates of return used to evaluate (*a*) short-term liquidity, (*b*) long-term risk and capital structure, and (*c*) operating efficiency and profitability. (L. O. 3)

The amount of a business's current assets less its current liabilities is called the **working capital** or **net working capital** of the business. A business must maintain an adequate amount of working capital to meet current debts, carry sufficient inventories, and take advantage of cash discounts. Indeed, a business that runs out of working capital cannot continue its operations. Because current assets and current liabilities are so necessary to current operations, an important part of evaluating the financial position of a business involves the analysis of working capital.

When you evaluate the working capital of a business, you must look beyond the dollar amount by which current assets exceed current liabilities. To see why this is true, consider the following example of Ace Company and Box Company:

	Ace Company	Box Company
Current assets	$100,000	$20,000
Current liabilities . . .	90,000	10,000
Working capital	$ 10,000	$ 10,000

Illustration 20–4

RANGER WHOLESALE COMPANY
Common-Size Comparative Income Statement
For Year Ended December 31, 1990 and 1989

	Years Ended December 31		Common-Size Percentages	
	1990	**1989**	**1990**	**1989**
Gross sales	$973,500	$853,000	101.41	101.21
Sales returns and allowances	13,500	10,200	1.41	1.21
Net sales	$960,000	$842,800	100.00	100.00
Cost of goods sold	715,000	622,500	74.48	73.86
Gross profit from sales	$245,000	$220,300	25.52	26.14
Operating expenses:				
Selling expenses:				
Advertising expense	$ 7,500	$ 5,000	0.78	0.59
Sales salaries expense	109,500	97,500	11.41	11.57
Store supplies expense	3,200	2,800	0.33	0.33
Depreciation expense, store equipment	2,400	1,700	0.25	0.20
Delivery expense	14,800	14,000	1.54	1.66
Total selling expenses	$137,400	$121,000	14.31	14.36
General and administrative expenses:				
Office salaries expense	$ 41,000	$ 40,050	4.27	4.75
Office supplies expense	1,300	1,250	0.14	0.15
Insurance expense	1,600	1,200	0.17	0.14
Depreciation expense, office equipment	300	300	0.03	0.04
Depreciation expense, buildings	2,850	1,500	0.30	0.18
Bad debts expense	2,250	2,200	0.23	0.26
Total general and administrative expenses . . .	$ 49,300	$ 46,500	5.14	5.52
Total operating expenses	$186,700	$167,500	19.45	19.87
Operating income	$ 58,300	$ 52,800	6.07	6.26
Less interest expense	6,300	1,500	0.66	0.18
Income before taxes	$ 52,000	$ 51,300	5.42	6.09
Income taxes	19,000	18,700	1.98	2.22
Net income	$ 33,000	$ 32,600	3.44	3.87
Earnings per share	$1.32	$1.30	—	—

Ace Company and Box Company have the same amount of working capital. However, Ace Company's current liabilities are nine times greater than its working capital, while Box Company's current liabilities and working capital are equal. As a result, to pay its liabilities on time, Ace Company must experience much less shrinkage and delay in converting its current assets to cash than Box Company. Thus, the dollar amount of a company's working capital does not adequately measure its working capital position. The ratio of its current assets to its current liabilities is a much better measure.

Current Ratio

The relation of a company's current assets to its current liabilities is called the **current ratio.** To calculate the current ratio, you simply divide total current assets by total current liabilities. For example, the current ratio of Box Company is:

$$\frac{\text{Current assets, \$20,000}}{\text{Current liabilities, \$10,000}} = 2.0$$

In other words, Box Company's current assets are two times its current liabilities, or the current ratio is 2 to 1.

The current ratio expresses the relation of current assets and current liabilities mathematically. A high current ratio indicates a strong current position; that is, a higher ratio generally means the company is more capable of meeting its current obligations.

On the other hand, a company might have a current ratio that is too high. This would mean that the company has overinvested in current assets relative to its needs. Normally, surplus current assets do not generate very much additional revenue. Therefore, if a company invests too much of its capital in current assets, the investment is not used efficiently.

Years ago, bankers and other creditors often used a current ratio of 2 to 1 as a rule of thumb in evaluating the debt-paying ability of a credit-seeking company. A company with a 2 to 1 current ratio was generally thought to be a good credit risk in the short run. However, most credit grantors realize that the 2 to 1 rule of thumb is not an adequate test of debt-paying ability. They realize that whether or not a company's current ratio is good or bad depends upon at least three factors:

1. The nature of the company's business.
2. The composition of its current assets.
3. The turnover of certain of its current assets.

Whether or not a company's current ratio is adequate depends on the nature of its business. A public utility that has no inventories other than supplies and grants little or no credit can operate on a current ratio of less than 1 to 1. On the other hand, a company that sells high fashion clothing may occasionally misjudge future styles. If this happens, the company's inventory may be of little sales value. Such a company may need a current ratio of much more than 2 to 1.

Therefore, when the adequacy of working capital is studied, consideration must be given to the type of business under review. Before you decide whether a company's current ratio is too low (or too high), you should compare the company's current ratio with those of other companies in the same industry. Another important source of insight is to observe how the ratio compares to past periods.

The composition of a company's current assets also should be considered when you evaluate the company's working capital. Cash and temporary investments are more liquid than are accounts and notes receivable. And short-term receivables normally are more liquid than is merchandise inventory. Cash can be used to pay current debts at once. But accounts receivable and merchandise must be converted into cash before payments can be made.

Acid-Test Ratio

An easily calculated check on current asset composition is the **acid-test ratio,**
also called the **quick ratio** because it is the ratio of "quick assets" to current
liabilities. Quick assets are cash, temporary investments, accounts receivable, and notes receivable. They are the current assets that can quickly be
turned into cash. The traditional rule of thumb for an acceptable acid-test ratio
is 1 to 1. However, as is true for all financial ratios, you should be skeptical
about rules of thumb. The acid-test ratio of Ranger Wholesale Company as of
the end of 1990 is calculated as follows:

Quick assets:		Current liabilities:	
Cash.	$15,000	Notes payable.	$ 5,000
Temporary investments	3,000	Accounts payable.	43,600
Accounts receivable	68,000	Taxes payable.	4,800
Total.	$86,000	Wages payable	800
		Total.	$54,200

$$\frac{\text{Quick assets, \$86,000}}{\text{Current liabilities, \$54,200}} = 1.59, \text{ or } 1.6 \text{ to } 1$$

The working capital requirements of a company are affected by how fast the
company converts and replaces some of its current assets. For example, assume that Dot Company and Fox Company sell the same amounts of merchandise on credit each month. However, Dot Company grants 30-day terms to its
customers, while Fox Company grants 60 days. Both collect their accounts at
the end of these credit periods. As a result of the difference in terms, Dot
Company turns over or collects its accounts twice as fast as Fox Company.
Also, as a result of the more rapid turnover, Dot Company requires only one
half the investment in accounts receivable that is required of Fox Company
and can operate with a smaller current ratio.

Accounts Receivable Turnover

One way to measure how fast a company converts its accounts receivable into
cash is to calculate the **accounts receivable turnover.** To calculate the accounts
receivable turnover, you divide credit sales (or net sales) for a year by the
average accounts receivable balance during the year. If the company has
short-term notes receivable, those balances should be included with the accounts receivable. The average balance usually is estimated by averaging the
beginning and ending balances. For example, Ranger Wholesale Company's
accounts receivable turnover for 1990 is calculated as follows:

a.	December 31, 1989, accounts receivable . .	$ 64,000
b.	December 31, 1990, accounts receivable . .	68,000
c.	Average balance $(a + b) \div 2$	66,000
d.	Net sales for year	960,000

$$\frac{\text{Net sales, \$960,000}}{\text{Average accounts receivable, \$66,000}} = 14.5$$

If accounts receivable are collected quickly, the accounts receivable turnover will be high. In general, this is favourable because it means that the company does not have to invest large amounts of capital in accounts receivable. However, an accounts receivable turnover may be too high, if it means that credit terms are so limited that they have a negative effect on sales volume.

Sometimes the ending accounts receivable balance is used as a substitute for the average balance in calculating accounts receivable turnover. This is acceptable if the effect is not material. If possible, credit sales should be used rather than the sum of cash and credit sales. Also, accounts receivable before subtracting the allowance for doubtful accounts should be used. However, information as to credit sales is seldom available in published financial statements. Likewise, many published balance sheets report accounts receivable at their net amount. Therefore, you may be forced to use total sales and net accounts receivable.

Days' Sales Uncollected

Accounts receivable turnover is one way to measure how fast a company collects its accounts. Another way is to calculate the **days' sales uncollected.** To illustrate the calculation of days' sales uncollected, assume a company had charge sales of $250,000 during a year and $25,000 of accounts and short-term notes receivable at the year's end. That means $\frac{1}{10}$ of its charge sales are uncollected. In other words, the charge sales made during $\frac{1}{10}$ of a year, or the charge sales of 36.5 days ($\frac{1}{10} \times 365$ days in a year = 36.5 days) are uncollected. This calculation of days' sales uncollected in equation form is as follows:

$$\frac{\text{Accounts receivable, \$25,000}}{\text{Charge sales, \$250,000}} \times 365 = 36.5 \text{ days' sales uncollected}$$

Days' sales uncollected has more meaning if you know the credit terms. According to a rule of thumb, a company's days' sales uncollected should not exceed one and one third times the days in its credit period when it does not offer discounts and one and one third times the days in its discount period when it does. If the company, whose days' sales uncollected is calculated in the illustration just given, offers 30-day terms, then 36.5 days is within the rule-of-thumb amount. However, if its terms are 2/10, n/30, its days' sales uncollected seem excessive.

Turnover of Merchandise Inventory

Working capital requirements also are affected by how long a company holds merchandise inventory before selling it. This can be measured by calculating the **merchandise turnover,** which is the number of times the average inventory is sold during an accounting period. A high turnover generally indicates good merchandising. Also, from a working capital point of view, a company with a high turnover requires a smaller investment in inventory than one producing the same sales with a low turnover. On the other hand, the merchandise turnover may be too high if a company keeps such a small inventory that sales volume is restricted.

To calculate merchandise turnover, you divide cost of goods sold by average inventory. Cost of goods sold is the amount of merchandise at cost that was sold during an accounting period. Average inventory is the average amount of merchandise at cost on hand during the period. The 1990 merchandise turnover of Ranger Wholesale Company is calculated as follows:

$$\frac{\text{Cost of goods sold, \$715,000}}{\text{Average merchandise inventory, \$87,000}} = \frac{\text{Merchandise turnover}}{\text{of 8.2 times}}$$

In the above calculation, the cost of goods sold is taken from the company's 1990 income statement. The average inventory is estimated by averaging the beginning inventory ($84,000) and the ending inventory ($90,000), or ($84,000 + $90,000) ÷ 2 = $87,000. In cases where the beginning and ending inventories do not represent the inventory normally on hand, a more accurate turnover may be secured by using the average of all the 12 month-end inventories.

Standards of Comparison

State the limitations associated with using financial statement ratios and the sources from which standards for comparison may be obtained.
(L. O. 4)

After you compute ratios and turnovers in the process of analyzing financial statements, you then have to decide whether the calculated amounts suggest good, bad, or just average performance by the company. To make these judgments, you must have some basis for comparison. The following are possibilities:

1. An experienced analyst may compare the ratios and turnovers of the company under review with mental standards acquired from past experiences.
2. For purposes of comparison, an analyst may calculate the ratios and turnovers of a selected group of competitive companies in the same industry as the one whose statements are under review.
3. Ratios and turnovers such as those published by Dun & Bradstreet may be used for comparison.
4. Some local and national trade associations gather data from their members and publish standard or average ratios for their trade or industry. When available, these give the analyst a very good basis of comparison.
5. Rule-of-thumb standards may be used as a basis for comparison.

Of these five standards, the ratios and turnovers of a selected group of competitive companies normally are the best bases for comparison. Rule-of-thumb standards should be applied with great care and then only if they seem reasonable in light of past experience.

Analysis of Long-Term Risk and Capital Structure

The analysis of working capital generally is intended to evaluate the short-term liquidity of the company. However, analysts are also interested in the long-run ability of the company to meet its obligations and provide security to its creditors. Indicators of this ability include debt and equity ratios, the relation of pledged plant assets to secured liabilities, and the company's capacity to earn enough to pay fixed interest charges.

Debt and Equity Ratios

Financial statement analysts are always interested in the portion of a company's assets contributed by its owners and the portion contributed by creditors. These are measured by ratios that express total liabilities as a percentage of total assets and total shareholders' equity as a percentage of total assets. The debt and equity ratios of Ranger Wholesale Company are calculated as follows:

		1990	1989
a.	Total liabilities.	$114,200	$ 71,200
b.	Total owners' equity.	315,800	311,800
c.	Total liabilities and owners' equity	$430,000	$383,000
	Percentages provided by creditors ($a \div c$) × 100.	26.6%	18.6%
	Percentages provided by shareholders ($b \div c$) × 100	73.4	81.4

Creditors like to see a high proportion of owners' equity because owners' equity acts as a cushion that absorbs losses. The greater the equity of the owners in relation to liabilities, the greater are the losses that can be absorbed by the owners before the creditors begin to lose.

From the creditors' standpoint, a high percentage of owners' equity is desirable. However, if a business can earn a return on borrowed capital that is higher than the cost of borrowing, the return to shareholders is increased.

Pledged Plant Assets to Secured Liabilities

Companies commonly borrow by issuing a note or bonds secured by a mortgage on certain of their plant assets. The ratio of pledged plant assets to secured liabilities is often calculated to measure the protection provided to the secured creditors by the pledge of assets. To calculate this ratio, you divide the pledged assets' book value by the liabilities for which the assets are pledged. It is calculated for Ranger Wholesale Company as of the end of 1990 and 1989 as follows:

		1990	1989
	Buildings, net.	$176,800	$28,000
	Land	50,000	20,000
a.	Book value of pledged plant assets	$226,800	$48,000
b.	Notes payable (secured by mortgage) . .	$ 60,000	$10,000
	Ratio of pledged assets to secured liabilities ($a \div b$).	3.8 to 1	4.8 to 1

The usual rule-of-thumb minimum for this ratio is 2 to 1. However, the ratio needs careful interpretation because it is based on the *book value* of the pledged assets. Book values often bear little relation to the amount that would be received for the assets in a foreclosure or a liquidation. As a result, estimated liquidation values or foreclosure values are a better measure of the protection provided by pledged assets. Also, the long-term earning ability of the company with pledged assets is equally important to secured creditors as is the pledged assets' book value.

Times Fixed Interest Charges Earned

The number of **times fixed interest charges were earned** often is calculated to measure the security of the return offered to creditors. The amount of income before the deduction of fixed interest charges and income taxes is the amount available to pay the fixed interest charges. Therefore, to calculate the number of times fixed interest charges were earned, you divide income before fixed interest charges and income taxes by fixed interest charges. The result is the number of times fixed interest charges were earned. Often, fixed interest charges are considered reasonably safe if the company earns its fixed interest charges two or more times each year.

The number of times fixed interest charges were earned by Ranger Wholesale Company are calculated as follows:

		1990	1989
a.	Income before interest and taxes	$58,300	$52,800
b.	Interest expense	6,300	1,500
	Times fixed interest charges earned (a ÷ b) . .	9.3	35.2

Analysis of Operating Efficiency and Profitability

Financial statement analysts are especially interested in the ability of a company to use its assets efficiently to produce profits for its owners. Several ratios are available to help you evaluate operating efficiency and profitability.

Profit Margin

The operating efficiency of a company can be expressed in terms of two components. The first is the company's **profit margin,** which is the ability to earn a net income from sales. This is measured by expressing net income as a percentage of sales. For example, the profit margin of Ranger Wholesale Company in 1990 is calculated as follows:

$$\frac{\$33,000, \text{ net income}}{\$960,000, \text{ net sales}} \times 100 = 3.4\%$$

To evaluate the profit margin of a company, you must consider the nature of the industry in which the company operates. For example, a publishing company might be expected to have a profit margin between 10 and 15%, while a retail supermarket might have a normal profit margin of 1 or 2%.

Total Asset Turnover

The second component of operating efficiency is **total asset turnover,** which is the ability of the company to use its assets to generate sales. To calculate this statistic, you divide net sales by the average total assets employed in the business. For Ranger Wholesale Company, the total asset turnover is:

$$\frac{\$960{,}000,\ \text{net sales}}{(\$430{,}000 + \$383{,}000) \div 2} = 2.4$$

Note that average total assets is estimated by averaging the total assets at the beginning and end of the period.

In general, the higher the total asset turnover, the more efficient the company is in using its assets. However, as in the case of profit margin, your evaluation of total asset turnover depends on the nature of the industry in which the company operates.

Profit margin and total asset turnover measure the two basic components of operating efficiency. However, they also are used to evaluate management performance since the management of a company is responsible for its operating efficiency.

Return on Total Assets Employed

Although operating efficiency has two basic components that are measured by profit margin and total asset turnover, analysts also calculate a summary measure of these components. The summary measure is **return on total assets employed.** To calculate this measure you divide net income by the average total assets employed during the year and multiply the answer by 100. For example, the return on the total assets employed by Ranger Wholesale Company during 1990 is as follows:

		1990
a.	Net income.	$ 33,000
b.	Average total assets employed ($430,000 + $383,000) ÷ 2 . .	406,500
	Return on total assets employed (a ÷ b) × 100	8.1%

Note that the beginning and ending amounts of total assets are divided by 2 to estimate the average total assets employed during the year.

The above calculation shows that Ranger Wholesale Company earned 8.1% return on its average total assets employed in the business during 1990. However, you cannot tell whether this return is good or bad without some basis of comparison. An important basis of comparison is the returns earned by similar-size companies engaged in the same kind of business. Also, you should evaluate the trend in the return earned by the company in recent years.

Earlier, we said that the return on total assets employed summarizes the two components of operating efficiency—profit margin and total asset turnover. Illustration 20–5 shows the relationship between these three measures. Notice that both profit margin and total asset turnover contribute to overall operating efficiency, as measured by return on total assets employed.

Illustration 20–5
Profit margin, total asset turnover, and return on total assets employed

Profit margin	$\times$	**Total asset turnover**	=	**Return on total assets employed**
$\dfrac{\text{Net income}}{\text{Net sales}}$	$\times$	$\dfrac{\text{Net sales}}{\text{Average total assets}}$	=	$\dfrac{\text{Net income}}{\text{Average total assets}}$

For Ranger Wholesale Company:

3.4%	$\times$	2.4	=	8.1%

Return on Common Shareholders' Equity

A primary reason for the operation of a business is to earn a net income for its owners. The **return on the common shareholders' equity** measures the success achieved in this area. Usually an average of the beginning-of-year and end-of-year equities is used in calculating the return. For Ranger Wholesale Company, the 1990 calculation is as follows:

		1990
a.	Net income after taxes.	$ 33,000
b.	Average shareholders' equity	313,800
	Rate of return on shareholders' equity (a ÷ b) × 100 . .	10.5%

When there is preferred stock outstanding, the preferred dividend requirements must be subtracted from net income to arrive at the common shareholders' share of income to be used in this calculation.

Compare Ranger Wholesale Company's return on shareholders' equity (10.5%) with its return on total assets employed (8.1%) and note that the return on the shareholders' equity is greater. This occurred because Ranger Wholesale Company successfully employs **financial leverage** in its capital structure. This means that the company borrows assets from creditors and employs those assets to earn a return that is higher than the rate of interest the company has to pay the creditors.

Price-Earnings Ratio

A commonly used statistic in comparing investment opportunities is **price earnings ratio.** To calculate a price earnings ratio, you divide market price per share by earnings per share. For example, if Ranger Wholesale Company's common stock sold at $15 per share at the end of 1990, the stock's end-of-year price earnings ratio is calculated as:

$$\frac{\text{Market price per share, \$15}}{\text{Earnings per share, \$1.32}} = 11.4$$

In comparing price earnings ratio, you must remember that such ratios vary from industry to industry. For example, in the steel industry, a price earnings ratio of 8 to 10 is normal, while in a growth industry, such as high-technology electronics, a price earnings ratio of 20 might be expected.

Dividend Yield

When investors evaluate whether to buy a stock at a given price per share, they often consider how much return they expect to receive in the form of cash dividends. A statistic that is used to compare the dividend-paying performance of different investment alternatives is **dividend yield.** To calculate the dividend yield of a stock you divide the annual amount of dividends paid by the market price per share and multiply the answer by 100. For example, Ranger Wholesale Company paid cash dividends in 1990 of $29,000, which amounted to $1.16 per share. If the market price per share is $15, the dividend yield is:

$$\frac{\$1.16}{\$15} \times 100 = 7.7\%$$

Review of Financial Statement Ratios and Statistics for Analysis

To evaluate short-term liquidity:

$$\text{Current ratio} = \frac{\text{Current assets}}{\text{Current liabilities}}$$

$$\text{Acid-test ratio} = \frac{\text{Cash} + \text{Temporary investments} + \text{Current receivables}}{\text{Current liabilities}}$$

$$\text{Accounts receivable turnover} = \frac{\text{Credit sales}}{\text{Average accounts receivable}}$$

$$\text{Merchandise turnover} = \frac{\text{Cost of goods sold}}{\text{Average merchandise inventory}}$$

To evaluate long-term risk and capital structure:

$$\text{Debt ratio} = \frac{\text{Total liabilities}}{\text{Total assets}} \times 100$$

$$\text{Equity ratio} = \frac{\text{Total shareholders' equity}}{\text{Total assets}} \times 100$$

$$\frac{\text{Pledged plant asset}}{\text{to secured liabilities}} = \frac{\text{Book value of pledged plant assets}}{\text{Total secured liabilities}}$$

$$\text{Times fixed interest charged earned} = \frac{\text{Income before interest and taxes}}{\text{Interest expense}}$$

To evaluate operating efficiency and profitability:

$$\text{Profit margin} = \frac{\text{Net income}}{\text{Net sales}} \times 100$$

$$\text{Total asset turnover} = \frac{\text{Net sales}}{\text{Average total assets}}$$

$$\text{Return on total assets employed} = \frac{\text{Net income}}{\text{Average total assets}} \times 100$$

$$\frac{\text{Return on common}}{\text{shareholders' equity}} = \frac{\text{Net income} - \text{Preferred dividends}}{\text{Average common shareholders' equity}}$$

$$\text{Price earnings ratio} = \frac{\text{Market price per common share}}{\text{Earnings per share}}$$

$$\text{Dividend yield} = \frac{\text{Annual dividends declared}}{\text{Market price per share}}$$

Summary of the Chapter in Terms of Learning Objectives

1. Financial reporting is intended to provide information that is useful to investors, creditors, and others in making investment, credit, and similar decisions. The information should help the users assess the amounts, timing, and uncertainty of prospective cash flows. Information should be provided about an enterprise's economic resources, claims against those resources, and the events that change its resources and the claims to those resources.

2. Comparative financial statements show amounts for two or more successive periods, sometimes with the changes in the items disclosed in absolute and of a base amount such as total assets or net sales.

3. In evaluating the short-term liquidity of a company, you might calculate a current ratio, an acid-test ratio, the accounts receivable turnover, the days' sales uncollected, and the merchandise turnover.

In evaluating the long-term risk and capital structure of a company, you might calculate debt and equity ratios, pledged plant assets to secured liabilities, and the number of times fixed interest charges were earned.

In evaluating operating efficiency and profitability, you might calculate profit margin, total asset turnover, return on total assets employed, and return on common shareholders' equity. Other statistics used to evaluate the profitability of alternative investments include price-earnings ratios, and dividend yield.

4. To decide whether financial statement ratios are desirable, too high, or too low, you must have some bases for comparison. These may come from past experience and personal judgment, from ratios of similar companies, or from ratios published by trade associations or other public sources. Traditional rules-of-thumb should be applied with great care and only if they seem reasonable in light of past experience.

Demonstration Problem

Use the financial statements of Precision Company, Inc., to satisfy the following requirements:

1. Prepare a comparative income statement showing the percentage increase or decrease for 1991 over 1990.
2. Prepare common-size, comparative balance sheets for 1991 and 1990.

3. Compute the following ratios for the year ended December 31, 1991:
   a. Current ratio.
   b. Acid-test ratio.
   c. Accounts receivable turnover.
   d. Days' sales uncollected.
   e. Turnover of merchandise inventory.
   f. Total liabilities as a percentage of total assets.
   g. Pledged plant assets to secured liabilities.
   h. Times fixed interest charges earned.
   i. Profit margin.
   j. Total asset turnover.
   k. Return of total assets employed.
   l. Return on common shareholders' equity.

PRECISION COMPANY, INC.
Comparative Balance Sheet
December 31, 1991, and December 31, 1990

Assets	1991	1990
Current assets:		
Cash.	$ 79,000	$ 42,000
Temporary investments.	65,000	96,000
Accounts receivable, net	120,000	100,000
Merchandise inventory	250,000	265,000
Total current assets.	$ 514,000	$ 503,000
Plant and equipment:		
Store equipment, net	$ 400,000	$ 350,000
Office equipment, net	45,000	50,000
Buildings, net	625,000	675,000
Land	100,000	100,000
Total plant and equipment	$1,170,000	$1,175,000
Total assets	$1,684,000	$1,678,000
Liabilities		
Current liabilities:		
Accounts payable	$ 164,000	$ 190,000
Short-term notes payable.	75,000	90,000
Taxes payable.	26,000	12,000
Total current liabilities.	$ 265,000	$ 292,000
Long-term liabilities:		
Notes payable (secured by		
mortgage on building and land) . .	$ 400,000	$ 420,000
Total liabilities	$ 665,000	$ 712,000
Shareholders' Equity		
Common stock, 95,000 shares	$ 475,000	$ 475,000
Retained earnings.	544,000	491,000
Total shareholders' equity.	$1,019,000	$ 966,000
Total liabilities and equity	$1,684,000	$1,678,000

PRECISION COMPANY, INC.
Comparative Income Statement
For Years Ended December 31, 1991, and December 31, 1990

	1991	1990
Sales	$2,486,000	$2,075,000
Cost of goods sold	1,523,000	1,222,000
Gross profit from sales	$ 963,000	$ 853,000
Operating expenses:		
Advertising expense	$ 145,000	$ 100,000
Sales salaries expense	240,000	280,000
Office salaries expense	165,000	200,000
Insurance expense	100,000	45,000
Supplies expense	26,000	35,000
Depreciation expense	85,000	75,000
Miscellaneous expense	17,000	15,000
Total operating expenses	$ 778,000	$ 750,000
Operating income	$ 185,000	$ 103,000
Less interest expense	44,000	46,000
Income before taxes	$ 141,000	$ 57,000
Income taxes	47,000	19,000
Net income	$ 94,000	$ 38,000
Earnings per share	$0.99	$0.40

Solution to Demonstration Problem

1.

PRECISION COMPANY, INC.
Comparative Income Statement
For Years Ended December 31, 1991, and December 31, 1990

	1991	1990	Increase (Decrease) in 1991 Amount	Percent
Sales	$2,486,000	$2,075,000	$411,000	19.8
Cost of goods sold	1,523,000	1,222,000	301,000	24.6
Gross profit from sales	$ 963,000	$ 853,000	$110,000	12.9
Operating expenses:				
Advertising expense	$ 145,000	$ 100,000	$ 45,000	45.0
Sales salaries expense	240,000	280,000	(40,000)	(14.3)
Office salaries expense	165,000	200,000	(35,000)	(17.5)
Insurance expense	100,000	45,000	55,000	122.2
Supplies expense	26,000	35,000	(9,000)	(25.7)
Depreciation expense	85,000	75,000	10,000	13.3
Miscellaneous expense	17,000	15,000	2,000	13.3
Total operating expenses	$ 778,000	$ 750,000	$ 28,000	3.7
Operating income	$ 185,000	$ 103,000	$ 82,000	79.6
Less interest expense	44,000	46,000	(2,000)	(4.3)
Income before taxes	$ 141,000	$ 57,000	$ 84,000	147.4
Income taxes	47,000	19,000	28,000	147.4
Net income	$ 94,000	$ 38,000	$ 56,000	147.4
Earnings per share	$0.99	$0.40	$0.59	147.5

2.

PRECISION COMPANY, INC.
Common-Size, Comparative Balance Sheet
December 31, 1991, and December 31, 1990

	Years Ended December 31		Common-Size Percentages	
	1991	1990	1991	1990
Assets				
Current assets:				
Cash	$ 79,000	$ 42,000	4.69	2.50
Temporary investments	65,000	96,000	3.86	5.72
Accounts receivable, net	120,000	100,000	7.13	5.96
Merchandise inventory	250,000	265,000	14.85	15.79
Total current assets	$ 514,000	$ 503,000	30.52	29.98
Plant and equipment:				
Store equipment, net	$ 400,000	$ 350,000	23.75	20.86
Office equipment, net	45,000	50,000	2.67	2.98
Buildings, net	625,000	675,000	37.11	40.23
Land	100,000	100,000	5.94	5.96
Total plant and equipment	$1,170,000	$1,175,000	69.48	70.02
Total assets	$1,684,000	$1,678,000	100.00	100.00
Liabilities				
Current liabilities:				
Accounts payable	$ 164,000	$ 190,000	9.74	11.32
Short-term notes payable	75,000	90,000	4.45	5.36
Taxes payable	26,000	12,000	1.54	0.72
Total current liabilities	$ 265,000	$ 292,000	15.74	17.40
Long-term liabilities:				
Notes payable (secured by mortgage on building and land) . .	$ 400,000	$ 420,000	23.75	25.03
Total liabilities	$ 665,000	$ 712,000	39.49	42.43
Shareholders' Equity				
Common stock, 95,000 shares	$ 475,000	$ 475,000	28.21	28.31
Retained earnings	544,000	491,000	32.30	29.26
Total shareholders' equity	$1,019,000	$ 966,000	60.51	57.57
Total liabilities and equity	$1,684,000	$1,678,000	100.00	100.00

3. Ratios for 1991:
   a. Current ratio: $514,000 ÷ $265,000 = 1.9.
   b. Acid-test ratio: $79,000 + $65,000 + $120,000 = $264,000
      $264,000 ÷ $265,000 = 1.0.
   c. Accounts receivable turnover:
      $$($120,000 + $100,000) ÷ 2 = $110,000$$
      $$$2,486,000 ÷ $110,000 = 22.6.$$
   d. Days' sales uncollected: ($120,000/$2,486,000) × 365 = 17.6 days.
   e. Turnover of merchandise inventory:
      $$($250,000 + $265,000) ÷ 2 = $257,500$$
      $$$1,523,000 ÷ $257,500 = 5.9 times.$$
   f. Total liabilities as a percentage of total assets:
      $$($665,000/$1,684,000) × 100 = 39.5\%.$$

g. Pledged assets to secured liabilities:
$$(\$625,000 + \$100,000) \div \$400,000 = 1.8.$$

h. Times fixed interest charges earned:
$$\$185,000 \div \$44,000 = 4.2 \text{ times.}$$

i. Profit margin: $(\$94,000/\$2,486,000) \times 100 = 3.8\%.$

j. Total asset turnover: $(\$1,684,000 + \$1,678,000) \div 2 = \$1,681,000$
$$\$2,486,000 \div \$1,681,000 = 1.48.$$

k. Return on total assets employed: $\$94,000 \div \$1,681,000 = 5.6\%$
$$\text{or } 3.8\% \times 1.48 = 5.6\%.$$

l. Return on common shareholders' equity:
$$(\$1,019,000 + \$966,000) \div 2 = \$992,500$$
$$(\$94,000/\$992,500) \times 100 = 9.5\%.$$

Glossary

Define or explain the
words and phrases listed in
the chapter Glossary.
(L. O. 5)

Accounts receivable turnover an indication of how long it takes a company to collect its accounts; calculated by dividing credit sales (or net sales) by the average accounts receivable balance. p. 882

Acid-test ratio the relation of quick assets, such as cash, temporary investments, accounts receivable, and notes receivable, to current liabilities; calculated as quick assets divided by current liabilities. p. 882

Common-size comparative statements comparative financial statements in which each amount is expressed as a percentage of a base amount. In the balance sheet, the amount of total assets is usually selected as the base amount and is expressed as 100%. In the income statement, net sales is usually selected as the base amount. p. 878

Comparative statement a financial statement with data for two or more successive accounting periods placed in columns side by side, sometimes with changes shown in dollar amounts and percentages. p. 874

Current ratio the relation of a company's current assets to its current liabilities; that is, current assets divided by current liabilities. p. 881

Days' sales uncollected the number of days of average credit sales volume that, if totaled, would equal the accounts receivable balance; calculated as the product of 365 times the accounts receivable balance divided by charge sales. p. 883

Dividend yield the annual amount of cash dividends paid per share of stock expressed as a percentage of the market price per share; used to compare the dividend paying performance of different investment alternatives. p. 889

Financial leverage the use of debt as a source of assets in the hope of earning a return on those assets that is higher than the rate of interest paid to creditors, thereby increasing the return to shareholders. p. 888

Financial reporting the process of preparing and issuing financial information about a company. p. 872

General purpose financial statements statements that are published periodically for use by a wide variety of interested parties and that include the income statement, balance sheet, statement of retained earnings or statement of changes in shareholders' equity, and statement of changes in financial position. p. 872

Merchandise turnover the number of times a company's average inventory is sold during an accounting period; calculated by dividing cost of goods sold by the average merchandise inventory balance. p. 883

Net working capital a synonym for working capital. p. 879

Price-earnings ratio a measure used to evaluate the profitability of alternative common stock investments; calculated as market price per share of common stock divided by earnings per share. p. 888

Profit margin a component of operating efficiency and profitability; calculated by expressing net income as a percentage of net sales. p. 886

Quick ratio a synonym for acid-test ratio. p. 882

Return on common shareholders' equity a measure of profitability in the use of assets provided by common shareholders; measured by expressing net income less preferred dividends as a percentage of average common share-holders' equity. p. 888

Return on total assets employed a summary measure of operating efficiency and management performance; calculated by expressing net income as a percentage of average total assets. p. 887

Times fixed interest charges earned a measure of a company's ability to sat-isfy fixed interest charges; calculated as income before interest and income taxes divided by fixed interest charges. p. 886

Total asset turnover a component of operating efficiency and profitability; calculated by dividing net sales by average total assets. p. 887

Working capital current assets minus current liabilities. p. 879

Questions for Class Discussion

1. Who are the intended readers of general purpose financial statements?
2. What statements are usually included in the general purpose financial statements published by corporations?
3. Explain the difference between financial reporting and financial state-ments.
4. General purpose financial statements should help readers make what kind of predictions?
5. What are the broad objectives of financial reporting?
6. Why are some comparative balance sheets prepared with columns that show increases and decreases in both dollar amounts and percentages?
7. Under what circumstances is it impossible to calculate a percentage increase or decrease in a comparative financial statement item?
8. When trends are calculated and compared, it is often informative to compare the trend of sales with the trends of several other financial statement items. What are some of the items that should be compared to sales in this fashion?
9. What is meant by *common-size* financial statements?
10. What items usually are assigned a value of 100% (*a*) on a common-size balance sheet and (*b*) on a common-size income statement?
11. Why is working capital given special attention in the process of analyz-ing balance sheets?
12. Which ratio provides the best indication of a company's ability to meet its debt obligations in the very near future, current ratio or acid-test ratio?
13. Indicate which of the following transactions increase working capital, which decrease working capital, and which have no effect on working capital:
    a. Collected accounts receivable.
    b. Borrowed money by giving a 90-day, interest-bearing note.
    c. Declared a cash dividend.
    d. Paid a cash dividend previously declared.

    e. Sold plant assets at their book value.

    f. Sold merchandise at a profit.

14. List several factors that have an effect on working capital requirements.

15. What are several reasons why a 2 to 1 current ratio may not be adequate for a particular company?

16. Why does turnover of accounts receivable provide information about a company's short-term liquidity?

17. What is the significance of the number of days' sales uncollected?

18. Why does turnover of merchandise inventory provide information about a company's short-term liquidity?

19. Why do creditors like to see a high proportion of total assets being financed by owners' equity?

20. Why is the capital structure of a company, as measured by debt and equity ratios, of importance to financial statement analysts?

21. Why must the ratio of pledged plant assets to secured liabilities be interpreted with care?

22. What is the relationship between profit margin, total asset turnover, and return on total assets employed?

23. Why might a company's return on total assets employed be different from its return on common shareholders' equity?

24. What ratios might you calculate for the purpose of evaluating management performance?

25. How might you use the information provided by price-earnings ratio and dividend yield?

Multiple Choice

1. Which of the following is not one of the broad objectives of financial reporting by business enterprises?

    a. Financial reporting should provide information that is useful to present and potential investors and creditors and other users in making rational investment, credit, and similar decisions.

    b. Financial reporting should provide information to help present and potential investors and creditors and other users in assessing the amounts, timing, and uncertainty of prospective cash receipts from dividends or interest and the proceeds from the sale, redemption, or maturity of securities or loans.

    c. Financial reporting should provide comparative data for two or more successive accounting periods so that users may analyze items that show significant changes as favorable or unfavorable.

    d. Financial reporting should provide information about the economic resources of an enterprise, the claims to those resources, and the effects of transactions, events, and circumstances that change its resources and claims to those resources.

    e. All of the above are identified by section 1000 of the *CICA Handbook* as objectives of financial reporting.

2. The XYZ Company had earnings per share of $2.44, net income of $29,280, and 12,000 common shares outstanding throughout the year for 198A. On December 31, 198A, the stock of XYZ Company sold for $32. What is XYZ's price-earnings ratio?
   a. 2.44.
   b. 13.11.
   c. 375.00.
   d. 915.00.
   e. None of the above.

3. The one transaction (below) which will reduce a company's current ratio is:
   a. Sale of merchandise at a profit.
   b. Payment of a cash dividend previously declared.
   c. Sale of office equipment at a price below book value.
   d. Declaration of a cash dividend.
   e. Sale of bonds at a discount.

4. The I. M. Slick Company had the following comparative income statements for 198A and 198B:

	198B	198A
Net sales.	$288,000	$240,000
Cost of goods sold	252,000	216,000
Gross profit from sales	36,000	24,000
Operating expenses.	18,000	12,000
Net income	$ 18,000	$ 12,000

The net income in common-size percentages for 198B and 198A respectively is:
   a. 87.5% and 90.0%.
   b. 12.5% and 10.0%.
   c.   6.25% and   5.0%.
   d. 150.0% and 100.0%.
   e. 50.0% and 50.0%.

5. A synonym for acid-test ratio is:
   a. Cash ratio.
   b. Quick ratio.
   c. Marketable ratio.
   d. Current ratio.
   e. Price-earnings ratio.

6. The number of times a company's average inventory is sold during an accounting period, calculated by dividing cost of goods sold by average merchandise inventory, is the:
   a. Accounts receivable turnover.
   b. Merchandise turnover.
   c. Average receivables turnover.
   d. Cost of goods sold turnover.
   e. Average sales turnover.

Mini Discussion Cases

Case 20-1

Analysts have often used working capital ratios to test for companies' financial health. Some years ago, however, there were several cases of companies with healthy working capital ratios which, shortly thereafter, were forced into bankruptcy apparently because they were not able to pay their debts as they became due.

Required

Discuss the shortcomings of working capital analysis. What other kinds of analyses might be used which would overcome these deficiencies? Why?

Case 20-2

A friend comes to you excitedly urging you to take advantage of an investment opportunity. As support for her recommendation the friend shows you the company's annual report and says, "This company has earnings per share of $6.73." She says that she has just purchased 500 of the company's shares at $45.50 and urges you to do the same before the price goes up any further.

Required

It is now 5:00 P.M. and the markets have closed for the day. Your friend has allowed you to borrow her copy of the annual report until tomorrow morning. What analyses are you going to use to evaluate this investment? What further information do you think you might require? Why?

Exercises

Exercise 20-1
Calculating trend percentages
(L. O. 2)

Calculate trend percentages for the following items using 1987 as the base year. Then state whether the situation shown by the trends appears to be favourable or unfavourable:

	1991	1990	1989	1988	1987
Sales	$595,000	$561,000	$527,000	$497,250	$425,000
Cost of goods sold	374,170	350,455	329,375	313,565	263,500
Accounts receivable	59,640	56,700	54,600	52,500	42,000

Exercise 20-2
Reporting percentage changes
(L. O. 2)

Where possible, calculate percentages of increase and decrease for the following unrelated items. The parentheses indicate deficit items.

	1991	1990
Equipment, net	$114,750	$85,000
Notes receivable	–0–	15,000
Notes payable	30,000	–0–
Retained earnings	(2,000)	20,000
Cash.	7,500	(500)

Exercise 20–3
Calculating common-size percentages
(L. O. 2)

Express the following income statement information in common-size percentages and evaluate the situation shown as favourable or unfavourable:

PADREN CORPORATION
Comparative Income Statement
For Years Ended December 31, 1990, and 1989

	1990	1989
Sales.	$250,000	$235,000
Cost of goods sold	165,000	151,575
Gross profit from sales	$ 85,000	$ 83,425
Operating expenses.	63,500	42,770
Net income.	$ 21,500	$ 40,655

Exercise 20–4
Evaluating short-term liquidity
(L. O. 3)

Rawhide Company's December 31 balance sheets included the following data:

	1990	1989	1988
Assets			
Cash	$ 8,800	$ 16,700	$ 25,900
Accounts receivable, net	63,000	51,000	47,500
Merchandise inventory	85,000	44,000	20,000
Prepaid expenses	10,800	7,500	3,500
Plant assets, net.	195,000	201,000	180,000
Total assets	$362,600	$320,200	$276,900
Liabilities and Shareholders' Equity			
Accounts payable	$ 82,600	$ 53,000	$ 39,400
Long-term notes payable secured by mortgage on plant assets.	105,000	105,000	80,000
Common stock, 10,000 shares	100,000	100,000	100,000
Retained earnings	75,000	62,200	57,500
Total liabilities and shareholders' equity . .	$362,600	$320,200	$276,900

Required

Compare the short-term liquidity positions of the company at the end of 1990, 1989, and 1988 by calculating the following ratios: (*a*) current ratio and (*b*) acid-test ratio. Comment on any changes that occurred.

Exercise 20–5
Evaluating short-term liquidity
(L. O. 3)

Refer to the information in Exercise 20–4 about Rawhide Company. The company's income statement for years ended December 31, 1990, and 1989, included the following data:

	1990	1989
Sales.	$530,000	$475,000
Cost of goods sold	$314,000	$290,000
Other operating expenses	173,000	152,000
Interest expense	12,000	11,500
Income taxes	8,200	6,800
Total costs and expenses.	$507,200	$460,300
Net income	$ 22,800	$ 14,700
Earnings per share	$2.28	$1.47

Required

For the years ended December 31, 1990, and 1989, calculate the following: (*a*) days' sales uncollected, (*b*) accounts receivable turnover, and (*c*) merchandise turnover. Comment on any changes that occurred from 1989 to 1990.

Exercise 20–6
Evaluating long-term risk and capital structure
(L. O. 3)

Refer to the information in Exercises 20–4 and 20–5 about Rawhide Company. Compare the long-term risk and capital structure positions of the company at the end of 1990 and 1989 by calculating the following ratios: (*a*) debt and equity ratios, (*b*) pledged plant assets to secured liabilities, and (*c*) times fixed interest charges earned. (Assume all sales were on credit.) Comment on any changes that occurred.

Exercise 20–7
Evaluating operating efficiency and profitability
(L. O. 3)

Refer to the financial statements of Rawhide Company presented in Exercises 20–4 and 20–5. To evaluate the operating efficiency and profitability of the company, calculate the following: (*a*) profit margin, (*b*) total asset turnover, and (*c*) return on total assets employed.

Exercise 20–8
Evaluating profitability
(L. O. 3)

Refer to the financial statements of Rawhide Company presented in Exercises 20–4 and 20–5. Additional information about the company is as follows:

Common stock market price, December 31, 1990 . . .	$32.00
Common stock market price, December 31, 1989 . . .	15.00
Annual cash dividends per share in 1990 and 1989 . .	1.00

Required

To evaluate the profitability of the company, calculate the following for 1990 and 1989: (*a*) return on common shareholders' equity, (*b*) price-earnings ratio on December 31, and (*c*) dividend yield.

Exercise 20–9
Determining income effects from common-size and trend percentages
(L. O. 3)

Common-size and trend percentages for a company's sales, cost of goods sold, and expenses follow:

Common-Size Percentages	1991	1990	1989	Trend Percentages	1991	1990	1989
Sales	100.0	100.0	100.0	Sales	95.3	97.4	100.0
Cost of goods sold . .	56.2	60.4	60.8	Cost of goods sold . .	87.3	95.2	100.0
Expenses	28.8	27.1	28.2	Expenses	95.2	97.0	100.0

Required

Present statistics to show whether the company's net income increased, decreased, or remained unchanged during the three-year period represented above.

Problems

The condensed statements of Falcon Hill Company, Ltd., follow:

FALCON HILL COMPANY, LTD.
Comparative Income Statement
For Years Ended December 31, 1991, 1990, and 1989
($000)

	1991	1990	1989
Sales.	$62,000	$57,000	$47,000
Cost of goods sold	43,883	39,330	31,654
Gross profit from sales . .	$18,117	$17,670	$15,346
Selling expenses	$ 8,915	$ 8,392	$ 7,280
Administrative expenses .	6,510	6,247	5,310
Total expenses	$15,425	$14,639	$12,590
Income before taxes . . .	$ 2,692	$ 3,031	$ 2,756
Income taxes	700	788	715
Net income	$ 1,992	$ 2,243	$ 2,041

FALCON HILL COMPANY, LTD.
Comparative Balance Sheet
December 31, 1991, 1990, and 1989
($000)

	1991	1990	1989
Assets			
Current assets.	$10,340	$ 9,660	$11,440
Long-term investments . .	–0–	75	700
Plant and equipment . . .	17,760	18,540	15,060
Total assets	$28,100	$28,275	$27,200
Liabilities and Capital			
Current liabilities	$ 4,700	$ 4,600	$ 4,400
Common stock	12,000	12,000	11,900
Other contributed capital .	1,300	1,325	1,050
Retained earnings	10,100	10,350	9,850
Total liabilities and capital	$28,100	$28,275	$27,200

Required

1. Calculate each year's current ratio.
2. Express the income statement data in common-size percentages.
3. Express the balance sheet data in trend percentages with 1989 as the base year.
4. Comment on any significant relationships revealed by the ratios and percentages.

The condensed comparative statements of Rydmore Range Corporation follow:

RYDMORE RANGE CORPORATION
Comparative Income Statement
For Years Ended December 31, 1992–1986
($000)

	1992	1991	1990	1989	1988	1987	1986
Sales	$792	$740	$660	$592	$540	$480	$400
Cost of goods sold	437	399	342	304	257	235	190
Gross profit from sales	$355	$341	$318	$288	$283	$245	$210
Operating expenses	297	264	218	167	165	138	110
Income before taxes	$ 58	$ 77	$100	$121	$118	$107	$100

RYDMORE RANGE CORPORATION
Comparative Balance Sheet
December 31, 1992–1986
($000)

	1992	1991	1990	1989	1988	1987	1986
Assets							
Cash	$ 8	$ 12	$ 14	$ 17	$ 18	$ 15	$ 20
Accounts receivable, net	92	90	88	66	57	54	44
Merchandise inventory	232	225	212	176	156	130	112
Other current assets	5	7	4	8	7	7	4
Long-term investments	–0–	–0–	–0–	39	39	39	39
Plant and equipment, net	372	382	358	180	182	176	178
Total assets	$709	$716	$676	$486	$459	$421	$397
Liabilities and Capital							
Current liabilities	$135	$140	$125	$100	$ 85	$ 70	$ 60
Long-term liabilities	165	189	201	84	87	90	85
Common stock	230	230	230	185	185	175	175
Retained earnings	179	157	120	117	102	86	77
Total liabilities and capital	$709	$716	$676	$486	$459	$421	$397

Required

1. Calculate trend percentages for the items of the statements using 1986 as the base year.

2. Analyze and comment on the situation shown in the statements.

Problem 20–3
Calculation of financial statement relations
(L. O. 3)

The year-end statements of Riverbank Corporation follow:

RIVERBANK CORPORATION
Income Statement
For Year Ended December 31, 1991

Sales		$676,500
Cost of goods sold:		
Merchandise inventory, December 31, 1990	$ 49,800	
Purchases	385,900	
Goods available for sale	$435,700	
Merchandise inventory, December 31, 1991	33,600	
Cost of goods sold		402,100
Gross profit from sales		$274,400
Operating expenses		195,900
Operating income		$ 78,500
Interest expense		10,800
Income before taxes		$ 67,700
Income taxes		23,700
Net income		$ 44,000

RIVERBANK CORPORATION
Balance Sheet
December 31, 1991

Assets		Liabilities and Shareholders' Equity	
Cash	$ 25,700	Accounts payable	$ 48,700
Temporary investments	27,600	Accrued wages payable	5,800
Accounts receivable, net.	45,200	Income taxes payable	6,900
Notes receivable.	5,300	Long-term note payable,	
Merchandise inventory.	53,600	secured by mortgage on	
Prepaid expenses	2,100	plant assets	105,000
Plant assets, net	352,700	Common stock, 45,000 shares .	225,000
		Retained earnings	120,800
		Total liabilities and	
Total assets	$512,200	shareholders' equity.	$512,200

Assume all sales were on credit. On the December 31, 1990, balance sheet, the assets totaled $350,300, common stock was $225,000, and retained earnings was $100,200.

Required

Calculate the following: (*a*) current ratio, (*b*) acid-test ratio, (*c*) days' sales uncollected, (*d*) merchandise turnover, (*e*) ratio of pledged plant assets to secured liabilities, (*f*) times fixed interest charges earned, (*g*) profit margin, (*h*) total asset turnover, (*i*) return on total assets employed, and (*j*) return on common shareholders' equity.

Problem 20–4
Comparative analysis of financial statement ratios
(L. O. 3)

Two companies that operate in the same industry as competitors are being evaluated by a bank that may lend money to each one. Summary information from the financial statements of the two companies is provided below:

Data from the Current Year-End Balance Sheets

	Quaser Company	Pulser Company
Assets		
Cash.	$ 20,200	$ 27,600
Accounts receivable	54,900	87,100
Notes receivable	9,000	7,700
Merchandise inventory.	67,200	102,000
Prepaid expenses	7,500	9,700
Plant and equipment, net.	300,700	308,600
Total assets.	$459,500	$542,700
Liabilities and Capital		
Current liabilities	$ 80,800	$110,100
Long-term notes payable.	88,000	102,000
Common stock	160,000*	190,000†
Retained earnings	130,700	140,600
Total liabilities and capital	$459,500	$542,700

Data from the Current Year's Income Statements

Sales	$745,000	$969,000
Cost of goods sold	550,000	718,000
Interest expense	8,600	14,900
Income tax expense	11,200	15,300
Net income	35,300	44,200

Beginning-of-Year Data

Accounts receivable, net.	$ 38,200	$ 70,000
Notes receivable	–0–	–0–
Merchandise inventory.	55,200	88,400
Total assets.	392,000	468,500
Common stock	160,000*	190,000†
Retained earnings	108,200	111,600

* 16,000 shares.
† 19,000 shares.

Required

1. Calculate current ratios, acid-test ratios, accounts (and notes) receivable turnovers, merchandise turnovers, and days' sales uncollected for the two companies. Then state which company you think is the better short-term credit risk and why.

2. Calculate profit margins, total asset turnovers, returns on total assets employed, and returns on common shareholders' equity. Assuming that each company paid cash dividends of $0.80 per share and each company's stock can be purchased at $18 per share, calculate price earnings ratio and dividend yield. Also state which company's stock you would recommend as the better investment and why.

Problem 20–5
Analysis of working capital
(L. O. 3)

City Sales Corporation began the month of August with $420,000 of current assets, a current ratio of 2.5 to 1, and an acid-test ratio of 1.5 to 1. During the month, it completed the following transactions:

Aug. 3 Bought $60,000 of merchandise on account. (The company uses a perpetual inventory system.)
  6 Sold for $70,000 merchandise that cost $38,000.
  9 Collected a $20,000 account receivable.
  12 Paid a $25,000 account payable.
  17 Wrote off an $8,500 bad debt against the Allowance for Doubtful Accounts account.
  21 Declared a $1 per share cash dividend on the 20,000 shares of outstanding common stock.
  25 Paid the dividend declared on August 21.
  27 Borrowed $80,000 by giving the bank a 60-day, 12% note.
  29 Borrowed $90,000 by signing a long-term secured note.
  31 Used the $170,000 proceeds of the notes to buy additional machinery.

Required

Prepare a schedule showing the company's current ratio, acid-test ratio, and working capital after each of the foregoing transactions. Round to two decimal places.

Alternate Problems

Problem 20–1A
Calculating ratios and percentages
(L. O. 2, 3)

The condensed statements of Tradent Corporation follow:

TRADENT CORPORATION
Comparative Income Statement
For Years Ended December 31, 1991, 1990, and 1989
($000)

	1991	1990	1989
Sales.	$98,000	$82,400	$71,000
Cost of goods sold	54,500	43,300	33,800
Gross profit from sales	$43,500	$39,100	$37,200
Selling expenses	$13,100	$10,350	$10,900
Administrative expenses	9,800	10,450	9,500
Total expenses	$22,900	$20,800	$20,400
Income before taxes	$20,600	$18,300	$16,800
Income taxes	7,210	6,405	5,880
Net income	$13,390	$11,895	$10,920

TRADENT CORPORATION
Comparative Balance Sheet
December 31, 1991, 1990, and 1989
($000)

	1991	1990	1989
Assets			
Current assets.	$22,600	$12,500	$14,900
Long-term investments	–0–	700	5,700
Plant and equipment	51,000	53,000	39,200
Total assets	$73,600	$66,200	$59,800
Liabilities and Capital			
Current liabilities	$11,000	$ 9,200	$ 7,700
Common stock	19,600	19,600	16,000
Retained earnings	43,000	37,400	36,100
Total liabilities and capital	$73,600	$66,200	$59,800

Required

1. Calculate each year's current ratio.
2. Express the income statement data in common-size percentages.
3. Express the balance sheet data in trend percentages with 1989 as the base year.
4. Comment on any significant relationships revealed by the ratios and percentages.

Problem 20–2A
Calculation and analysis of trend percentages
(L. O. 2)

The condensed comparative statements of Clear River Company, Ltd., follow:

CLEAR RIVER COMPANY, LTD.
Comparative Income Statement
For Years Ended December 31, 1992–1986
($000)

	1992	1991	1990	1989	1988	1987	1986
Sales	$450	$470	$460	$490	$530	$520	$560
Cost of goods sold	190	197	194	208	219	212	214
Gross profit from sales	$260	$273	$266	$282	$311	$308	$346
Operating expenses	200	207	205	224	231	235	255
Income before taxes	$ 60	$ 66	$ 61	$ 58	$ 80	$ 73	$ 91

CLEAR RIVER COMPANY, LTD.
Comparative Balance Sheet
December 31, 1992–1986
($000)

	1992	1991	1990	1989	1988	1987	1986
Assets							
Cash	$ 30	$ 33	$ 32	$ 36	$ 45	$ 42	$ 46
Accounts receivable, net	92	103	99	101	112	110	118
Merchandise inventory	143	149	147	156	159	169	162
Other current assets	20	21	22	24	23	26	28
Long-term investments.	80	60	40	87	87	87	90
Plant and equipment, net	362	368	372	287	292	297	302
Total assets.	$727	$734	$712	$691	$718	$731	$746
Liabilities and Capital							
Current liabilities	$162	$169	$152	$121	$143	$171	$216
Long-term liabilities	130	145	160	175	190	205	220
Common stock	205	205	205	205	205	205	205
Retained earnings	230	215	195	190	180	150	105
Total liabilities and capital	$727	$734	$712	$691	$718	$731	$746

Required

1. Calculate trend percentages for the items of the statements using 1986 as the base year.
2. Analyze and comment on the situation shown in the statements.

Problem 20–3A
Financial statement ratios
(L. O. 3)

The year-end statements of Tooner Corporation follow:

TOONER CORPORATION
Income Statement
For Year Ended December 31, 1991

Sales		$805,000
Cost of goods sold:		
Merchandise inventory, December 31, 1990 . .	$ 62,800	
Purchases	500,700	
Goods available for sale	$563,500	
Merchandise inventory, December 31, 1991 . .	48,200	
Cost of goods sold		515,300
Gross profit from sales		$289,700
Operating expenses		227,800
Operating income.		$ 61,900
Interest expense		9,500
Income before taxes		$ 52,400
Income taxes		15,720
Net income		$ 36,680

TOONER CORPORATION
Balance Sheet
December 31, 1991

Assets		Liabilities and Shareholders' Equity	
Cash	$ 18,500	Accounts payable	$ 40,700
Temporary investments	20,400	Accrued wages payable	5,200
Accounts receivable, net	43,400	Income taxes payable	5,800
Notes receivable	8,800	Long-term note payable,	
Merchandise inventory	49,200	secured by mortgage	
Prepaid expenses	4,800	on plant assets	95,000
Plant assets, net	272,100	Common stock, 160,000 shares	160,000
		Retained earnings	110,500
		Total liabilities and	
Total assets	$417,200	shareholders' equity	$417,200

Assume all sales were on credit. On the December 31, 1990, balance sheet, the assets totaled $360,600, common stock was $160,000, and retained earnings was $89,700.

Required

Calculate the following: (*a*) current ratio, (*b*) acid-test ratio, (*c*) days' sales uncollected, (*d*) merchandise turnover, (*e*) ratio of pledged plant assets to secured liabilities, (*f*) times fixed interest charges earned, (*g*) profit margin, (*h*) total asset turnover, (*i*) return on total assets employed, and (*j*) return on common shareholders' equity.

Problem 20–4A
Comparative analysis of financial statement ratios
(L. O. 3)

Two companies that operate in the same industry as competitors are being evaluated by a bank that may lend money to each one. Summary information from the financial statements of the two companies is provided below:

Data from the Current Year-End Balance Sheets

	Zesta Corporation	Festa Corporation
Assets		
Cash	$ 30,200	$ 57,100
Accounts receivable	105,500	118,500
Notes receivable	18,000	16,500
Merchandise inventory	98,700	133,300
Prepaid expenses	15,700	17,900
Plant and equipment, net	332,900	340,100
Total assets	$601,000	$683,400
Liabilities and Capital		
Current liabilities	$113,400	$141,800
Long-term notes payable	120,000	135,000
Common stock*	182,000	212,000
Retained earnings	185,600	194,600
Total liabilities and capital	$601,000	$683,400

Data from the Current Year's Income Statements

Sales	$703,500	$992,100
Cost of goods sold	518,000	708,200
Interest expense	14,100	17,800
Income tax expense	22,500	42,700
Net income	54,200	74,700

Beginning-of-Year Data

Accounts receivable, net.	$ 98,000	$100,500
Notes receivable	–0–	–0–
Merchandise inventory.	118,200	93,900
Total assets.	514,300	600,000
Common stock*.	182,000	212,000
Retained earnings	158,700	151,700

*All shares were issued at $20 per share.

Required

1. Calculate current ratios, acid-test ratios, accounts (and notes) receivable turnovers, merchandise turnovers, and days' sales uncollected for the two companies. Then state which company you think is the better short-term credit risk and why.

2. Calculate profit margins, total asset turnovers, returns on total assets employed, and returns on common shareholders' equity. Assuming that each company paid cash dividends of $3 per share and each company's stock can be purchased at $45 per share, calculate price earnings ratio and dividend yield. Also state which company's stock you would recommend as the better investment and why.

Problem 20–5A
Analysis of working capital
(L. O. 3)

Ft. Mason Corporation began the month of March with $286,000 of current assets, a current ratio of 2.2 to 1, and an acid-test ratio of 0.9 to 1. During the month, it completed the following transactions:

Mar. 3 Sold for $55,000 merchandise that cost $36,000.
5 Collected a $35,000 account receivable.
10 Bought $56,000 of merchandise on account. (The company uses a perpetual inventory system.)
12 Borrowed $60,000 by giving the bank a 60-day, 12% note.
15 Borrowed $90,000 by signing a long-term secured note.
22 Used the $150,000 proceeds of the notes to buy additional machinery.
24 Declared a $1.75 per share cash dividend on the 40,000 shares of outstanding common stock.
26 Wrote off a $14,000 bad debt against Allowance for Doubtful Accounts.
28 Paid a $45,000 account payable.
30 Paid the dividend declared on March 24.

Required

Prepare a schedule showing the company's current ratio, acid-test ratio, and working capital after each of the foregoing transactions. Round to two decimal places.

Provocative Problems

Provocative Problem 20–1
The Clorox Company
(L. O. 2, 3)

The Clorox Company is a diversified firm that develops, manufactures, and markets premium quality household products, architectural coatings, and food service products. In addition to the liquid bleach product from which it takes its name, the company markets the leading line of dry salad mixes. Founded in 1913, the Clorox Company has become an international company with sales in excess of $1 billion. Their 1986 annual report included a 10-year financial summary, from which the following information has been extracted:

(In thousands, except per-share data)	1986	1985	1984	1983
Operations				
Net sales	$1,089,070	$1,054,847	$974,566	$913,807
Percent change	+3.2	+8.2	+6.6	+5.4
Net earnings	95,610	86,124	79,709	65,507
Percent change	+11.0	+8.0	+21.7	+45.2
Common Stock				
Per share:				
Earnings from continuing operations	$3.60	$3.27	$3.09	$2.72
Earnings from discontinued operations	—	—	—	—
Net earnings				
Assuming no dilution	$3.60	$3.27	$3.09	$2.72
Assuming full dilution	$3.50	$3.17	$3.01	$2.64
Dividends	$1.40	$1.24	$1.08	$ .95
Shareholders' equity at end of year	20.61	18.37	16.40	13.48
Other Data				
Working capital	$240,180	$203,011	$144,424	$117,333
Total assets	849,225	778,062	701,396	603,875
Long-term debt	38,151	38,945	43,174	72,597
Shareholders' equity	549,793	485,856	431,313	325,998
Current ratio	2.4	2.0	1.8	1.7
Percent return on net sales—continuing operations	8.8	8.2	8.2	7.2
Percent return on average shareholders' equity	18.5	18.8	20.2	21.6

Courtesy of the Clorox Company

Discuss the format of the Clorox Company's presentation relative to the illustrations in the chapter. Then evaluate the company's performance over the four-year period as it is disclosed by the above data.

Provocative Problem 20–2
Tropical Trade Company
(L. O. 2, 3)

In your position as controller of Tropical Trade Company, you have the responsibility of keeping the board of directors informed about the financial activities and status of the company. In preparation for the next meeting of the board, you have calculated the following ratios, turnovers, and percentages to enable you to answer questions:

	1991	1990	1989
Current ratio	2.5 to 1	2.4 to 1	1.9 to 1
Acid-test ratio	0.9 to 1	1.2 to 1	1.3 to 1
Merchandise turnover	8.3 times	9.5 times	10.4 times
Accounts receivable turnover	7.5 times	8.1 times	8.9 times
Return on shareholders' equity	10.50%	12.25%	12.75%
Profit margin	3.4%	3.6%	3.8%
Total asset turnover	2.9 times	3.0 times	3.1 times
Return on total assets	9.9%	10.8%	11.8%
Sales to plant assets	4.1 to 1	3.8 to 1	3.5 to 1
Sales trend	136.00	124.00	100.00
Selling expenses to net sales	10.2%	15.4%	16.8%

Required

Using the statistics given, answer each of the following questions and explain how you arrived at your answer.

1. Is it becoming easier for the company to meet its current debts on time and to take advantage of cash discounts?
2. Is the company collecting its accounts receivable more rapidly?
3. Is the company's investment in accounts receivable decreasing?
4. Are dollars invested in inventory increasing?
5. Is the company's investment in plant assets increasing?
6. Is the shareholders' investment becoming more profitable?
7. Is the company using its assets efficiently?
8. Did the dollar amount of selling expenses decrease during the three-year period?

Provocative Problem 20–3
Lodestar and Cosmos
(L. O. 3)

Lodestar, Inc., and Cosmos, Inc., are competing companies with similar backgrounds. The stock of both companies is traded locally, and each stock can be purchased at its book value. Mary Link has an opportunity to invest in either company but is undecided as to which is the better managed company and which is the better investment. Prepare a report to Ms. Link stating which company you think is the better managed and which company's stock you think may be the better investment. Back your report with any ratios, turnovers, and other analyses you think pertinent.

Balance Sheets
December 31, 1990

	Lodestar, Inc.	Cosmos, Inc.
Assets		
Cash.	$ 40,200	$ 41,100
Accounts receivable, net .	101,600	108,300
Merchandise inventory . .	140,700	148,500
Prepaid expenses.	4,200	5,300
Plant and equipment, net.	462,200	443,100
Total assets	$ 748,900	$ 746,300
Liabilities and Capital		
Current liabilities	$ 130,200	$ 146,400
Long-term notes payable.	150,800	137,600
Common stock*	272,500	239,500
Retained earnings	195,400	222,800
Total liabilities and capital	$ 748,900	$ 746,300

Income Statements
For Year Ended December 31, 1990

	Lodestar, Inc.	Cosmos, Inc.
Sales.	$1,950,000	$2,056,000
Cost of goods sold	1,350,400	1,453,400
Gross profit on sales . . .	$ 599,600	$ 602,600
Operating expenses . . .	516,600	552,400
Operating income.	$ 83,000	50,200
Interest expense	12,300	11,900
Income before taxes . . .	$ 70,700	$ 38,300
Income taxes	24,200	13,100
Net income	$ 46,500	$ 25,200

December 31, 1989, Data

Accounts receivable . . .	$ 125,400	$ 170,400
Merchandise inventory . .	119,000	137,200
Total assets	700,600	662,400
Common stock*	272,000	239,000
Retained earnings	177,300	190,600

*Issued at $10 per share.

Provocative Problem 20–4
Abitibi-Price Inc.
(L. O. 2, 3)

Use the financial statements and related footnotes of Abitibi-Price Inc. shown in Appendix I to complete the following requirements:

Required

1. Calculate the following ratios and turnovers for 1989 and 1988: (*a*) current ratio; (*b*) acid-test ratio; (*c*) days' sales uncollected; (*d*) profit margin; (*e*) total asset turnover; (*f*) return on total assets employed; and (*g*) return on common shareholder's equity.

2. Prepare common-size statements for the portions of the 1989 and 1988 income statements that relate to continuing operations. [Net sales, income, and earnings per share are from continuing operations and before extraordinary items unless otherwise noted.]

3. After reviewing your answers to Requirements 1 and 2 and reviewing the financial statements and related disclosures of Abitibi-Price Inc., write a brief summary and evaluation of the results of 1989 compared to 1988.

Analytical and Review Problems

A&R Problem 20–1

DATA COMPANY, LTD.
Balance Sheet
As at December 31, 1990

Assets		Liabilities and Capital	
Cash	$_____	Current liabilities	$_____
Accounts receivable	_____	12% bonds payable	_____
Inventory	_____	Capital stock	2,500
Plant and equipment	_____	Retained earnings	_____
		Total liabilities and	
Total assets	$_____	capital	$_____

Required

Using the format shown above complete the balance sheet for Data Company Ltd., from the following ratios:

Net income	$ 1,200
Sales	$15,000
Current ratio	2 to 1
Liabilities to total assets	1 to 2
Inventory turnover	10 times
Average (collection period, based on 360 days) . .	60 days
Plant and equipment turnover	3 times
Total asset turnover	1.5 times
Expenses (including income tax at 40%)	$ 3,800
Dividends paid during the year	600

A&R Problem 20–2

On the basis of the information given, complete the balance sheet.

VIDIO COMPANY LIMITED
December 31, 1990

Assets		Liabilities and Capital	
Cash . . . . $_____		Current liabilities . . . . . . $_____	
Accounts receivable . . . . . . _____		8% bonds payable . . . . . _____	
Inventory . . . . _____		Capital stock 15,000	
Plant and equipment. . . . . . _____		Retained earnings . . . . . _____	
		Total liabilities and	
Total assets . . . . $_____		capital. . . . . $_____	

Sales (all credit)	$40,000
Cost of goods sold	24,000
Expenses.	13,000
Income taxes	1,000
Net income	2,000
Net income/shareholder's equity	10%
Bonds payable/shareholder's equity	1 to 4
Inventory turnover	4 times
Accounts receivable collection period (360-day year) . .	45 days
Current ratio	2 to 1
Total asset turnover	1.25 times

A&R Problem 20–3

A company began the month of May with $200,000 of current assets, a 2-to-1 current ratio, and a 1-to-1 acid-test (quick) ratio. During the month it completed the following transactions:

		Current Ratio			Acid-Test Ratio		
		Inc.	Dcr.	No. Change	Inc.	Dcr.	No. Change
a.	Bought $20,000 of merchandise on account (the company uses a perpetual inventory system)						
b.	Sold for $25,000 merchandise that cost $15,000						
c.	Collected an $8,500 account receivable						
d.	Paid a $12,000 account payable						
e.	Wrote off a $1,000 bad debt against the allowance for doubtful accounts						
f.	Declared a $1 per share cash dividend on the 10,000 shares of outstanding common stock						
g.	Paid the dividend declared in (f)						
h.	Borrowed $12,000 by giving the bank a 60-day, 10% note						
i.	Borrowed $30,000 by placing a 10-year mortgage on the plant						
j.	Used $20,000 of proceeds of the mortgage to buy additional machinery						

Required

1. Indicate the affect on (*a*) current ratio and (*b*) working capital of each transaction. Set up a chart in your answer similar to that shown above and use check marks to indicate your answers. (Working capital is defined as ''current assets minus current liabilities.'')
2. For the end of May, calculate the:
   a. Current ratio.
   b. Acid-test ratio.
   c. Working capital.

Part Seven

Managerial Accounting for Costs

In this part of *Financial Accounting Principles*, we focus on the development of information about the costs of manufacturing operations. This information is used by the managers of a business and also is used to prepare financial statements for outside parties. Since manufacturing companies face unique problems in accounting for their production activities, your study of this part will include Chapter 21, which explains the manufacturing accounting systems used by many companies. These systems are based on periodic inventories.

21. Accounting for Manufacturing Companies

21 Accounting for Manufacturing Companies

Manufacturing and merchandising companies are alike because both depend on the sale of one or more commodities or products for revenue. However, they differ in one important way. A merchandising company sells goods in essentially the same condition as they were in when they were purchased. A manufacturing company, on the other hand, buys raw materials that it manufactures into the finished products it sells. For example, a shoe store buys shoes and sells them in the same form they were in when they were purchased; but a manufacturer of shoes buys leather, cloth, glue, nails, and dye and turns these items into salable shoes.

Most of the topics you learned about in previous chapters apply equally well to service companies, merchandising companies, and manufacturing companies. However, whenever inventories and cost of goods sold were discussed, the examples and illustrations were limited to merchandising companies. In this chapter (and in Chapter 22), you will learn about the unique problems of accounting for manufacturing companies.

Learning Objectives
After studying Chapter 21, you should be able to:

1. Describe the basic differences in the financial statements of manufacturing companies and merchandising companies and the procedures used in a general accounting system for a manufacturing company.
2. Describe the unique accounts that manufacturing companies use, prepare a manufacturing statement, and explain its purpose and relationship to the primary financial statements.
3. Prepare a work sheet and the financial statements for a manufacturing company.
4. Prepare the adjusting and closing entries for a manufacturing company.
5. Explain the procedures for assigning costs to the different manufacturing inventories.
6. Define or explain the words and phrases listed in the chapter Glossary.

Alternative Systems of Accounting for Manufacturing Companies

Some manufacturing companies use accounting systems that are based on periodic inventories. In keeping records on raw materials to be used in production, goods that are in the production process, and finished goods that are ready for sale, each type of inventory is periodically counted to determine the ending inventory and the amount used or sold during the period. When a manufacturing company uses periodic inventories to determine the total cost of all goods manufactured during each accounting period, the accounting system is called a **general accounting system**

General accounting systems are explained in the rest of this chapter. However, many manufacturing companies use accounting systems that are based on perpetual inventories. Systems of accounting for manufacturing operations that incorporate perpetual inventories are called **cost accounting systems**. These systems provide information about the unit cost of manufacturing a product and are more effective in assisting management's efforts to control costs. Cost accounting systems are explained in Chapter 22.

What Is the Basic Difference between Accounting for Merchandisers and Manufacturers?

Describe the basic differences in the financial statements of manufacturing companies and merchandising companies and the procedures used in a general accounting system for a manufacturing company. (L. O. 1)

The basic difference in accounting for manufacturing and merchandising companies stems from the fact that a merchandising company buys the goods it sells in their ready-for-sale state. As a result, the merchandising company can easily determine the cost of the goods it has bought for sale by examining the debit balance of its Purchases account. In contrast, a manufacturer uses the raw materials it buys to create the products it sells. Therefore, the manufacturer must combine the balances of a number of material, labour, and overhead accounts to determine the cost of the goods it manufactured for sale.

To emphasize this difference, the cost of goods sold section from a merchandising company's income statement is condensed and presented below next to the cost of goods sold section of a manufacturing company.

Merchandising Company		Manufacturing Company	
Cost of goods sold:		Cost of goods sold:	
Beginning merchandise inventory	$14,200	Beginning finished goods inventory	$ 11,200
Cost of goods purchased	34,150	Cost of goods manufactured (see manufacturing statement)	170,500
Goods available for sale	$48,350	Goods available for sale	$181,700
Ending merchandise inventory	12,100	Ending finished goods inventory	10,300
Cost of goods sold	$36,250	Cost of goods sold	$171,400

In the manufacturing company's cost of goods sold section, notice that the inventory of goods for sale is called *finished goods inventory* rather than merchandise inventory. Also note that the *Cost of goods purchased* element of the merchandising company becomes *Cost of goods manufactured (see manufacturing statement)* on the manufacturer's income statement. These differences exist because the merchandising company buys its goods ready for sale, while the manufacturer creates its salable products from raw materials.

The words *see manufacturing statement* refer the income statement reader to a separate schedule. A **manufacturing statement** (see page 925) shows the costs of manufacturing the products produced by a manufacturing company. The records and techniques used in accounting for these costs are the distinguishing characteristics of manufacturing accounting.

Elements of Manufacturing Costs

In the process of manufacturing its products, a manufacturing company usually incurs a large variety of costs. There are, however, only three different types or classes of manufacturing costs. They are: direct materials, direct labour, and factory overhead.

Direct Materials

The physical items that enter into and become a part of a finished product are called **direct materials.** For example, the direct materials of a shoe manufacturer might include leather, dye, cloth, nails, and glue. Since direct materials physically become part of the finished product, the cost of direct materials is easily traced to units of product or batches of production. As a result, the direct materials cost of production can be charged directly to units of product or batches of production without using arbitrary or highly judgmental cost allocation procedures.

Direct materials must be distinguished from **indirect materials,** which include factory supplies such as grease and oil for machinery, cleaning fluids, and so on. Indirect materials are used in the manufacturing process but do not enter into or become a part of the finished product. As a result, the cost of indirect materials is not easily traced to specific units or batches of production. Therefore, in accounting for production costs, the cost of indirect materials is treated as factory overhead.

The commodities that a company buys for use in the manufacturing process are called **raw materials.** Usually, raw materials are used in the production process as *direct* materials. When they are purchased, they are debited to an account called Raw Material Purchases. In contrast, when materials are intended for use as *indirect* materials, they are debited to a Factory Supplies account. Occasionally, however, some raw material purchases may be used as factory supplies (indirect materials). When this is done, a special adjusting entry is required to transfer the cost of those materials from Raw Material Purchases to an account called Factory Supplies Used.

Direct Labour

The labour of those people who work specifically on the materials being converted into finished products is called **direct labour.** The cost of direct labour can be easily associated with and charged to the units or batches of production to which the labour was applied.

In accounting for manufacturing operations, direct labour must be distinguished from indirect labour. **Indirect labour** is used in the manufacturing process but is not applied specifically to the finished product. Therefore, indirect labour is not easily associated with or charged to units or batches of produc-

Illustration 21–1
Examples of factory overhead

Indirect labour	Factory utilities:
Indirect materials:	Electricity
Cleaning supplies	Natural gas
Machinery oil	Depreciation of plant and equipment
Repairs to factory buildings and	Amortization of patents
equipment	Small tools written off
Insurance on factory equipment	Factory worker's compensation
Taxes on factory equipment	insurance
Taxes on raw materials and work in	Other payroll costs associated with
process	the wages of factory workers

tion. Examples of indirect labour include the labour of supervisors, engineers, and janitors. These people do not work specifically on the manufactured products but do aid in production. The labour provided by these workers makes production possible but is not applied specifically to the finished product. Indirect labour is accounted for as a factory overhead cost.

In a general accounting system, an account called Direct Labour is debited for the wages of those workers who work directly on the product. Likewise, the wages of indirect workers are debited to one or more indirect labour accounts. Also, at the end of each period, the amounts of accrued direct and indirect labour are recorded in the direct and indirect labour accounts by means of adjusting entries. You can see that a manufacturing company's payroll accounting is similar to that of a merchandising company. No new techniques are required. Only the new direct and indirect labour accounts distinguish the payroll accounting of a manufacturer from that of a merchant.

Factory Overhead

All manufacturing costs other than direct materials and direct labour costs are called **factory overhead.** Factory overhead is also called **manufacturing overhead** or **factory burden.** Examples of factory overhead are shown in Illustration 21–1.

Factory overhead does not include selling and administrative expenses. Selling and administrative expenses are not factory overhead because they are not incurred in the manufacturing process. These costs might be called selling and administrative overhead, but not factory overhead.

All factory overhead costs are accumulated in overhead cost accounts that vary in number and description from company to company. The exact accounts used in each case depend on the nature of the company and the information each company wants. For example, one account called Expired Insurance on Plant Equipment may be maintained, or separate expired insurance accounts may be used for buildings and the different kinds of equipment. Factory overhead costs, such as factory utilities and indirect labour, are recorded and posted to the accounts as they are paid. In addition, items such as depreciation of machinery and expired insurance are recorded in the process of making adjusting entries.

AS A MATTER OF ETHICS

Three former university classmates got together to have dinner at an expensive restaurant to talk over the past and to share recent news about what they and their companies were doing. The evening was a long one but was entertaining and even fruitful with respect to business ideas.

When the check arrived, it was grabbed by one of the three. Because he was a self-employed entrepreneur, he said, "Here, let me pay it—I'll deduct it as a business expense on my tax return, and it won't cost me as much."

One of the others was the vice president of a me-

dium-size corporation. She snatched the check out of his hand and said, "I'll put this on a company credit card, and it won't cost us anything."

The third, who was a factory manager for a company that sold products to the government, smiled and folded his hands. When his silence got the attention of the other two, he said, "Neither of you understand the system yet. I'll put this on my credit card and call it overhead on a cost-plus contract my company is doing for the government. That way, my company will not only pay for our dinner but we'll make a profit on it."

Product Costs and Period Costs

A manufacturing company incurs both **period costs** and **product costs**. Product costs are incurred for the purpose of acquiring merchandise or manufacturing finished goods. Since product costs result in the acquisition of assets, they make up the cost of the assets. As Illustration 21–2 shows, product costs are not recorded in expense accounts. Instead, product costs are assigned to units of product and are reported in the balance sheet as inventories. They do not show up in the income statement until the units of product are sold; then product costs appear as cost of goods sold. Product costs include all manufacturing costs—direct materials, direct labour, and factory overhead.

Period costs are closely related to the periods of time in which they are incurred; they are not closely related to the manufacture of products. Thus, period costs are charged to expense in the period they are incurred. Period costs include all selling expenses and general administrative expenses.

Comparing the Flow of Product Costs for Merchandising and Manufacturing Companies

Illustration 21–3 shows the flow of product costs for a manufacturing company that uses a periodic inventory (general accounting) system. Notice that the costs of raw materials, direct labour, and overhead are recorded as they are incurred throughout the period. Also, some manufacturing costs such as depreciation and accrued wages are recorded with adjusting entries at the end of the period. Then, in the end-of-period closing process, the inventory accounts are brought up-to-date, and the cost of goods sold is established in the Income Summary account. In the rest of this chapter, you will learn more about the accounts shown in Illustration 21–3 and the procedures that are necessary to account for and report these cost flows.

Illustration 21–2
Product costs and period expenses in the financial statements

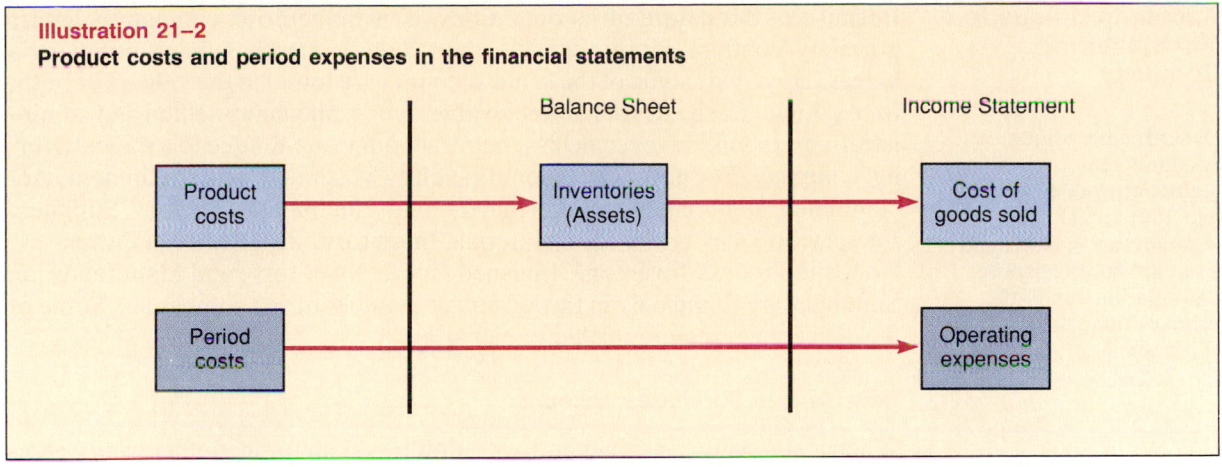

Illustration 21–3
Flow of product costs for a manufacturer that uses a periodic inventory system (assumes no beginning inventories)

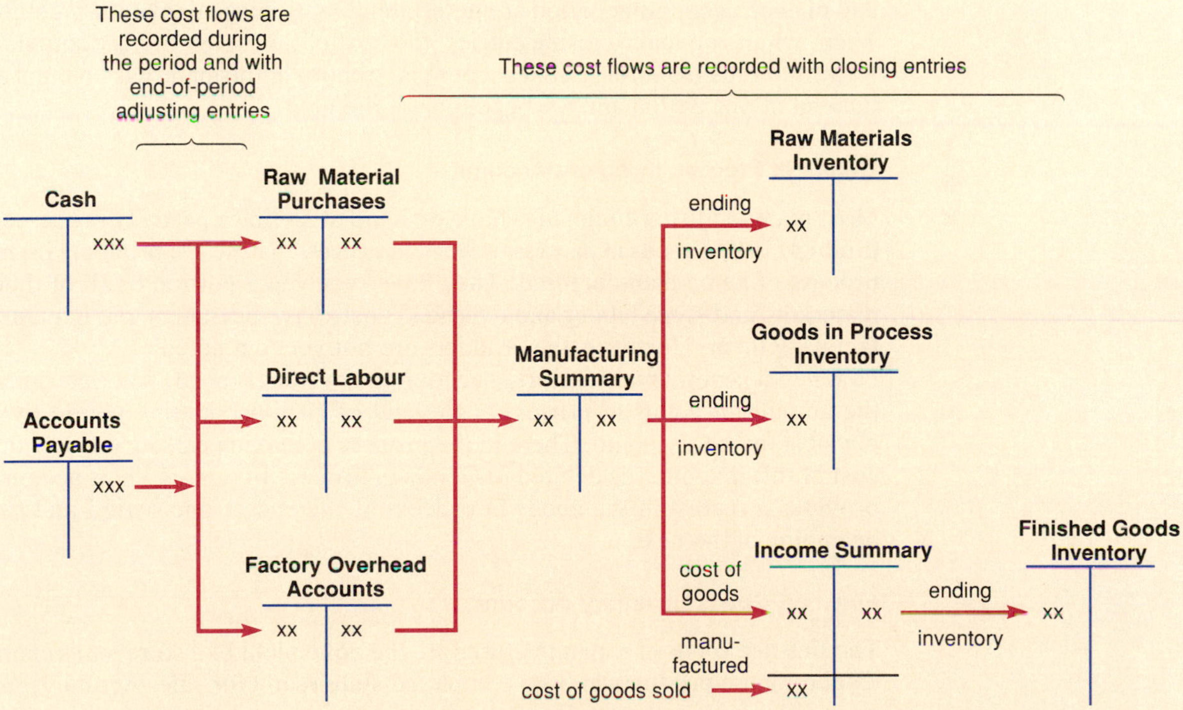

Accounts Unique to a Manufacturing Company

Describe the unique accounts that manufacturing companies use, prepare a manufacturing statement, and explain its purpose and relationship to the primary financial statements. (L. O. 2)

Because of the nature of its operations, a manufacturing company's ledger normally contains more accounts than does a merchandising company's ledger. However, some of the same accounts are found in the ledgers of both; for example, Cash, Accounts Receivable, Sales, and many selling and administrative expenses. Nevertheless, many accounts are unique to a manufacturing company. For instance, accounts such as Machinery and Equipment, Accumulated Depreciation of Machinery and Equipment, Factory Supplies, Factory Supplies Used, Raw Materials Inventory, Raw Material Purchases, Goods in Process Inventory, Finished Goods Inventory, and Manufacturing Summary are found only in the ledgers of manufacturing companies. Some of these accounts require further explanation.

Raw Material Purchases Account

When a company uses a general accounting system for manufacturing operations (a periodic inventory system), the cost of all direct materials is debited to a Raw Material Purchases account. Often a special column is provided in the Voucher Register or other special journal for the debits of the individual purchases. Thus, you are able to periodically post these debits as one amount, the column total.

Raw Materials Inventory Account

When a general accounting system is used, the raw materials on hand at the end of each accounting period are determined by a physical inventory count. Then, when you make closing entries, the cost of this inventory is debited to Raw Materials Inventory. That account is a record of the materials on hand at the end of one period and the beginning of the next.

Goods in Process Inventory Account

Most manufacturing companies have on hand at all times partially processed products called **goods in process** or **work in process.** These are products in the process of being manufactured. They have received a portion or all of their materials, and some labour and overhead costs have been incurred in manufacturing them. However, the products are not yet completed.

When a general manufacturing accounting system is used, you determine the amount of goods in process at the end of each accounting period by a physical inventory count. Then, in the process of making closing entries, the cost of this inventory is debited to Goods in Process Inventory. This account provides a record of the goods in process at the end of one period and the beginning of the next.

Finished Goods Inventory Account

The **finished goods** of a manufacturer are the equivalent of a store's merchandise; they are products in their completed state ready for sale. Actually, the only difference is that a manufacturing company creates its finished goods from raw materials, while a store buys its merchandise in a finished, ready-for-sale state.

A physical count of the ending finished goods inventory provides the neces-

Illustration 21–4

EXCEL MANUFACTURING COMPANY
Income Statement
For Year Ended December 31, 1990

Revenue:			
Sales			$310,000
Cost of goods sold:			
Finished goods inventory, December 31, 1989		$ 11,200	
Cost of goods manufactured (see manufacturing statement)		170,500	
Goods available for sale		$181,700	
Finished goods inventory, December 31, 1990		10,300	
Cost of goods sold			171,400
Gross profit			$138,600
Operating expenses:			
Selling expenses:			
Sales salaries expense	$18,000		
Advertising expense	5,500		
Delivery wages expense	12,000		
Shipping supplies expense	250		
Delivery equipment insurance expense	300		
Depreciation expense, delivery equipment	2,100		
Total selling expenses		$ 38,150	
General and administrative expenses:			
Office salaries expense	$15,700		
Miscellaneous general expense	200		
Bad debts expense	1,550		
Office supplies expense	100		
Depreciation expense, office equipment	200		
Interest expense	4,000		
Total general and administrative expenses		21,750	
Total operating expenses			59,900
Income before income taxes			$ 78,700
Less income taxes			32,600
Net income			$ 46,100
Net income per common share (20,000 shares outstanding)			$2.31

sary information to record the end-of-period balance in the Finished Goods Inventory account. This is done in the closing entry process. Like the other inventory accounts, Finished Goods Inventory provides a record of the finished goods at the end of one period and the beginning of the next.

The three inventories—raw materials, goods in process, and finished goods—are classified as current assets on the balance sheet. Factory supplies is also a current asset.

Income Statement of a Manufacturing Company

The income statement of a manufacturing company is similar to that of a merchandising company. To see this, compare the income statement of Kona Sales Incorporated, Illustration 5–1 on page 221, with that of Excel Manufacturing Company, Illustration 21–4. Notice that both types of businesses show

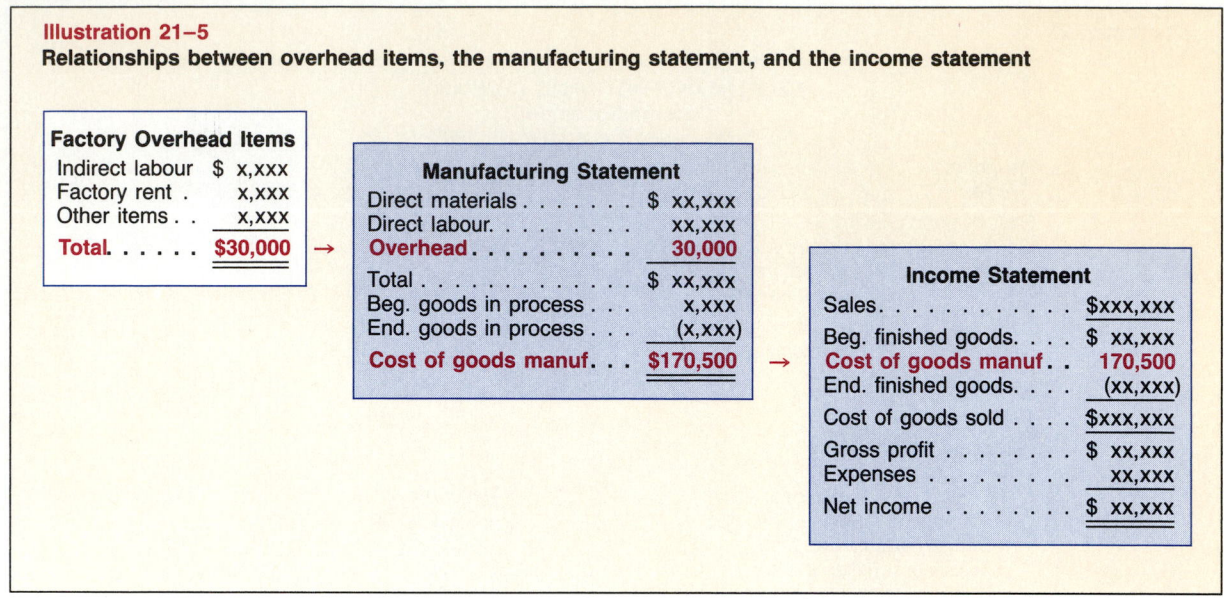

Illustration 21–5
Relationships between overhead items, the manufacturing statement, and the income statement

Factory Overhead Items

Indirect labour	$ x,xxx
Factory rent .	x,xxx
Other items . .	x,xxx
Total.	**$30,000**

Manufacturing Statement

Direct materials	$ xx,xxx
Direct labour.	xx,xxx
Overhead.	**30,000**
Total	$ xx,xxx
Beg. goods in process . . .	x,xxx
End. goods in process . . .	(x,xxx)
Cost of goods manuf. . .	**$170,500**

Income Statement

Sales.	$xxx,xxx
Beg. finished goods. . . .	$ xx,xxx
Cost of goods manuf . .	**170,500**
End. finished goods. . . .	(xx,xxx)
Cost of goods sold	$xxx,xxx
Gross profit	$ xx,xxx
Expenses	xx,xxx
Net income	$ xx,xxx

similar revenue, selling, and general and administrative expense sections. However, you can see that the cost of goods sold sections are slightly different. In this section, the "Cost of goods manufactured" item replaces "Purchases," and finished goods inventories replace merchandise inventories.

Observe the cost of goods sold section of Excel Manufacturing Company's income statement. Only the *total* cost of goods manufactured is shown. You could expand this section to show the detailed costs of the materials, direct labour, and factory overhead entering into the cost of goods manufactured. However, this would make the income statement long and unwieldy. Therefore, the common practice is to show only the total cost of goods manufactured on the income statement and to show the details in a supporting schedule. This schedule is called a **schedule of the cost of goods manufactured** or a **manufacturing statement.** To show how manufacturing costs enter the financial statements, Illustration 21–5 shows the relationship between overhead cost items, the manufacturing statement, and the income statement.

Manufacturing Statement

The cost elements of manufacturing are direct materials, direct labour, and factory overhead; and a manufacturing statement is normally designed to emphasize these elements. In Illustration 21–6, notice that section 1 of the statement shows the cost of direct materials used. Also observe that the format of the presentation in section 1 is the same as is used on the income statement of a merchandising company to show cost of goods purchased and sold.

Section 2 shows the cost of direct labour used in production, and section 3 shows factory overhead costs. If there are not too many overhead accounts, the balance of each may be listed in this third section, as in Illustration 21–6.

Illustration 21-6

EXCEL MANUFACTURING COMPANY
Manufacturing Statement
For Year Ended December 31, 1990

1	Direct materials:		
	Raw materials inventory, December 31, 1989		$ 8,000	
	Raw material purchases	$85,000		
	Freight on raw materials purchased	1,500		
	Delivered cost of raw materials purchased		86,500	
	Raw materials available for use		$94,500	
	Raw materials inventory, December 31, 1990		9,000	
	Direct materials used			$ 85,500
2	Direct labour			60,000
3	Factory overhead costs:		
	Indirect labour		$ 9,000	
	Supervision		6,000	
	Factory utilities		2,600	
	Repairs and maintenance of machinery		2,500	
	Factory taxes		1,900	
	Factory supplies used		600	
	Factory insurance expired		1,100	
	Small tools written off		200	
	Depreciation of machinery and equipment		3,500	
	Depreciation of factory building		1,800	
	Amortization of patents		800	
	Total factory overhead costs			30,000
4	Total manufacturing costs			$175,500
	Add goods in process inventory, December 31, 1989 . .			2,500
	Total goods in process during the year			$178,000
	Deduct goods in process inventory,			
	December 31, 1990			7,500
	Cost of goods manufactured			$170,500

However, if overhead accounts are numerous, only the total amount of overhead may be shown. In such cases, the total is supported by a separate schedule of overhead costs.

In section 4, the calculation of costs of goods manufactured is completed. Here the cost of the beginning goods in process inventory is added to the sum of the manufacturing costs to show the total cost of all goods in process during the period. From this total, you subtract the cost of the goods still in process at the end of the period to determine the cost of goods manufactured.

The manufacturing statement is prepared from the Manufacturing Statement columns of a work sheet. The items that appear on the statement are summarized in these columns, and all that is required in setting up the statement is to rearrange the items in the proper statement order. Illustration 21–7 shows the manufacturing work sheet.

Illustration 21–7

EXCEL MANUFACTURING COMPANY
Manufacturing Work Sheet for Year Ended December 31, 1990

Account Titles	Unadjusted Trial Balance		Adjustments		Manufacturing Statement		Income Statement		Statement of Retained Earnings or Balance Sheet	
	Dr.	Cr.	Dr.	Cr.	Dr.	Cr.	Dr.	Cr.	Dr.	Cr.
Cash	11,000								11,000	
Accounts receivable	32,000								32,000	
Allowance for doubtful accounts		300		(a) 1,550						1,850
Raw materials inventory	8,000				8,000	9,000			9,000	
Goods in process inventory	2,500				2,500	7,500			7,500	
Finished goods inventory	11,200						11,200	10,300	10,300	
Office supplies	150			(b) 100					50	
Shipping supplies	300			(c) 250					50	
Factory supplies	750			(d) 500					250	
Prepaid insurance	1,700			(e) 1,400					300	
Small tools	1,300			(f) 200					1,100	
Delivery equipment	9,000								9,000	
Accumulated depreciation of delivery equipment		1,900		(g) 2,100						4,000
Office equipment	1,700								1,700	
Accumulated depreciation of office equipment		200		(h) 200						400
Machinery	72,000								72,000	
Accumulated depreciation of machinery		3,000		(i) 3,500						6,500
Factory building	90,000								90,000	
Accumulated depreciation of factory building		1,500		(j) 1,800						3,300
Land	9,500								9,500	
Patents	12,000			(k) 800					11,200	
Accounts payable		14,000								14,000
Long-term notes payable		50,000								50,000
Common stock, 20,000 shares		100,000								100,000
Retained earnings		3,660								3,660
Sales		310,000						310,000		
Raw material purchases	85,100			(d) 100	85,000					
Freight on raw materials	1,500				1,500					
Direct labour	59,600		(l) 400		60,000					
Indirect labour	8,940		(l) 60		9,000					

Account	Trial Balance Dr	Trial Balance Cr	Adjustments Dr	Adjustments Cr	Cost of Goods Manufactured Dr	Cost of Goods Manufactured Cr	Income Statement Dr	Income Statement Cr	Balance Sheet Dr	Balance Sheet Cr
Supervision	6,000				6,000					
Factory utilities	2,600				2,600					
Repairs and maintenance of machinery	2,500				2,500					
Factory taxes	1,900				1,900					
Sales salaries expense	18,000						18,000			
Advertising expense	5,500						5,500			
Delivery wages expense	11,920		(l) 80				12,000			
Office salaries expense	15,700						15,700			
Miscellaneous general expense	200						200			
Interest expense	2,000		(m) 2,000				4,000			
	484,560	484,560								
Bad debts expense			(a) 1,550				1,550			
Office supplies expense			(b) 100				100			
Shipping supplies expense			(c) 250				250			
Factory supplies used			(d) 600		600					
Factory insurance expired			(e) 1,100		1,100					
Delivery equipment insurance expense			(e) 300				300			
Small tools written off			(f) 200		200					
Depreciation expense, delivery equipment			(g) 2,100				2,100			
Depreciation expense, office equipment			(h) 200				200			
Depreciation of machinery			(i) 3,500		3,500					
Depreciation of factory building			(j) 1,800		1,800					
Amortization of patents			(k) 800		800					
Accrued wages payable				(l) 540						540
Interest payable				(m) 2,000						2,000
Income tax expense			(n) 32,600				32,600			
Income taxes payable				(n) 32,600						32,600
			47,640	47,640	187,000	16,500				
Cost of goods manufactured to Income Statement columns						170,500	170,500			
					187,000	187,000	274,200	320,300	264,950	218,850
Net income							46,100			46,100
							320,300	320,300	264,950	264,950

Work Sheet for a Manufacturing Company

Prepare a work sheet and the financial statements for a manufacturing company.
(L. O. 3)

Examine Illustration 21–7 and note that there are no Adjusted Trial Balance columns. As we explained in Chapter 5, these columns may be omitted to save time and effort. To understand the work sheet in Illustration 21–7, recall that a work sheet is a tool the accountant uses to—

1. Achieve the effect of adjusting the accounts before entering the adjustments in a journal and posting them to the accounts.
2. Sort the adjusted account balances into columns according to the financial statement on which they appear.
3. Calculate and confirm the mathematical accuracy of the net income.

Comparing the Work Sheets of Manufacturing and Merchandising Companies

A primary difference between the work sheet of a manufacturing company and that of a merchandising company is an additional set of columns. The adjustments are made in the same way on both kinds of work sheets. Also, the mathematical accuracy of the net income is confirmed in the same way. However, remember that a manufacturing company prepares an additional schedule or statement (the manufacturing statement). Therefore, a manufacturing company's work sheet has two additional columns into which you must sort the items that appear on the manufacturing statement.

Preparing a Manufacturing Company's Work Sheet

To prepare a work sheet for a manufacturing company, you first enter the unadjusted account balances in the Trial Balance columns. Next, you enter the appropriate adjustments in the Adjustments columns.

Adjustments Information for Excel Manufacturing Company. The adjustments information for the work sheet shown in Illustration 21–7 is as follows:

a. Bad debts expense is estimated to be 0.5% of sales, or $1,550.
b. Office supplies used was $100.
c. Shipping supplies used was $250.
d. Factory supplies used was $500. In addition, raw materials that cost $100 were used as factory supplies.
e. Expired insurance on factory was $1,100; and expired insurance on the delivery equipment was $300.
f. The small tools inventory shows $1,100 of usable small tools on hand. As is often done, Excel Company accounts for small hand tools in the same manner as supplies.
g. Depreciation of delivery equipment was $2,100.
h. Depreciation of office equipment was $200.
i. Depreciation of factory machinery was $3,500.
j. Depreciation of factory building was $1,800.

    k. Yearly amortization of ¹⁄₁₇ of the cost of patents was $800.

    l. At year-end, accrued wages were: direct labour, $400; indirect labour, $60; and delivery wages, $80. All other employees are paid monthly on the last day of each month.

    m. Interest expense results from the long-term note payable and $2,000, which is one-half year's interest, has accrued on the notes.

    n. Income tax expense amounted to $32,600.

Sorting Adjusted Amounts to the Proper Financial Statement Columns. After the adjustments are completed, you must combine the amounts in the Unadjusted Trial Balance columns with the amounts in the Adjustments columns and sort the resulting amounts to the proper statement columns. Items that go in the Manufacturing Statement columns include raw materials, goods in process, direct labour, and all factory overhead items. Items that go in the Income Statement columns include the beginning finished goods inventory plus the revenue, selling, general and administrative, and financial expense items. Remember that items which appear in either the statement of retained earnings or the balance sheet go in the final two columns.

Entering the Ending Inventory Amounts. After the trial balance items with their adjustments are sorted to the proper statement columns, the ending inventory amounts are entered on the work sheet. Since the ending raw materials and goods in process inventories are subtracted on the manufacturing statement, they are entered in the Manufacturing Statement Credit column. And since these ending inventory balances are assets, they also must be entered in the final Debit column as balance sheet items.

    Note in Illustration 21–7 that the ending raw materials inventory is assumed to be $9,000, and the ending work in process inventory is assumed to be $7,500. These amounts were determined on the basis of a physical inventory taken at the end of the year.

    The ending finished goods inventory is also determined on the basis of a physical inventory taken at the end of the year. In Illustration 21–7, Excel Manufacturing Company's ending finished goods inventory of $10,300 is entered in the Income Statement Credit column and in the final Debit column as an asset to be reported on the balance sheet. You will note that this treatment of the finished goods inventory on the work sheet is exactly the same as is done for the ending merchandise inventory of a merchandising company.

    After the ending inventories are entered on the work sheet, you total and balance the Manufacturing Statement columns. The amount necessary to balance these columns is the cost of the goods manufactured; it must be entered in the Manufacturing Statement Credit column to make the two columns equal. Also, it is entered in the Income Statement Debit column, the same column in which the balance of the Purchases account of a merchant is entered. After this, you complete the work sheet in the usual manner.

Preparing the Financial Statements

After it is completed, the manufacturing work sheet is used to prepare the statements and to make adjusting and closing entries. The manufacturing statement is prepared from the information in the work sheet's Manufacturing Statement columns, the income statement from the information in the Income Statement columns, and the statement of retained earnings and balance sheet from information in the final two columns. After this, the adjusting and closing entries are entered in the journal and posted.

Adjusting Entries

Prepare the adjusting and closing entries for a manufacturing company. (L. O. 4)

The adjusting entries of a manufacturing company are prepared in the same way as those of a merchandising company. For each adjustment that appears in the work sheet Adjustments columns, you must record an adjusting entry in the General Journal.

In the case of Excel Manufacturing Company, the only adjustment that may require further attention is adjustment (d) as described on page 918 (see also Illustration 21–7). At the time they were purchased, most of the factory supplies were debited to a Factory Supplies account. The information for adjustment (d) states that $500 of these supplies were used. However, the factory also used $100 of its raw materials as factory supplies. Therefore, the adjusting entry to record all of the factory supplies used is:

Dec.	31	Factory Supplies Used.	600.00	
		Factory Supplies		500.00
		Raw Material Purchases		100.00
		To record factory supplies used.		

After Raw Material Purchases is credited for $100, the remaining $85,000 is correctly shown on the manufacturing statement as part of the direct materials cost calculation. (See Illustration 21–6.)

Closing Entries

The account balances that are used to calculate cost of goods manufactured reflect the manufacturing costs for the accounting period and must be closed at the end of the period. Normally, they are closed to a Manufacturing Summary account, which is in turn closed to the Income Summary account.

The entries to close the manufacturing accounts of Excel Manufacturing Company are as follows:

Dec.	31	Manufacturing Summary.	187,000.00	
		Raw Materials Inventory		8,000.00
		Goods in Process Inventory		2,500.00
		Raw Material Purchases		85,000.00
		Freight on Raw Materials.		1,500.00
		Direct Labour		60,000.00
		Indirect Labour.		9,000.00
		Supervision		6,000.00
		Factory Utilities		2,600.00
		Repairs and Maintenance of Machinery.		2,500.00
		Factory Taxes		1,900.00

		Factory Supplies Used			600.00
		Factory Insurance Expired			1,100.00
		Small Tools Written Off			200.00
		Depreciation of Machinery			3,500.00
		Depreciation of Building.			1,800.00
		Amortization of Patents			800.00
		To close those manufacturing accounts having debit balances.			
	31	Raw Materials Inventory	9,000.00		
		Goods in Process Inventory.	7,500.00		
		Manufacturing Summary			16,500.00
		To record the ending raw materials and goods in process inventories and to remove their balances from the Manufacturing Summary account.			

The above entries are taken from the information in the Manufacturing Statement columns of the Illustration 21–7 work sheet. Compare the first entry with the information shown in the Manufacturing Statement Debit column. Note how the debit to the Manufacturing Summary account is taken from the column total, and how each account with a balance in the column is credited to close it. Also observe that the second entry has the effect of subtracting the ending raw materials and goods in process inventories from the manufacturing costs shown in the work sheet's Debit column.

The effect of the two entries is to cause the Manufacturing Summary account to have a debit balance equal to the $170,500 cost of goods manufactured.

The $170,500 balance in Manufacturing Summary is closed to Income Summary along with the other cost and expense accounts that have balances in the Income Statement Debit column. This closing entry for Excel Manufacturing Company is shown below. Especially note the last account credited in the entry.

Dec.	31	Income Summary.	274,200.00	
		Finished Goods Inventory		11,200.00
		Sales Salaries Expense.		18,000.00
		Advertising Expense		5,500.00
		Delivery Wages Expense.		12,000.00
		Office Salaries Expense		15,700.00
		Miscellaneous General Expense.		200.00
		Interest Expense		4,000.00
		Bad Debts Expense.		1,550.00
		Office Supplies Expense		100.00
		Shipping Supplies Expense.		250.00
		Delivery Equipment Insurance Expense.		300.00
		Depreciation Expense, Delivery Equipment.		2,100.00
		Depreciation Expense, Office Equipment		200.00
		Income Tax Expense		32,600.00
		Manufacturing Summary		170,500.00
		To close the income statement accounts having debit balances.		

After the foregoing entry, the remainder of the income statement accounts of Illustration 21–7 are closed as follows:

Dec.	31	Finished Goods Inventory	10,300.00	
		Sales	310,000.00	
		Income Summary		320,300.00
		To close the Sales account and to record the ending finished goods inventory.		
	31	Income Summary.	46,100.00	
		Retained Earnings.		46,100.00
		To close the Income Summary account.		

Inventory Valuation Problems of a Manufacturer

Explain the procedures for assigning costs to the different manufacturing inventories.
(L. O. 5)

With a general accounting system for manufacturing operations, the physical count of inventories must result in separate valuations for the end-of-period amounts of raw materials, goods in process, and finished goods. There are no particular problems in obtaining a valuation for raw materials because these items are in the same form they were in when they were purchased. However, placing valuations on goods in process and finished goods is not as easy. These goods consist of direct materials to which certain amounts of labour and overhead have been added. They are not in the same form in which they were purchased. Therefore, the inventory values of these items are not simply the amounts that were paid to a supplier. Instead, their inventory values must be calculated by adding together estimates of the direct materials, direct labour, and factory overhead costs that were applied to each item.

Estimating Direct Material Costs in the Ending Inventories

Estimating the cost of direct materials that were applied to a goods in process or finished goods item is usually not too difficult. After the partially finished units of product in the work in process inventory are counted, a responsible plant official normally can estimate how much direct materials have been used in each unit and then calculate the cost of direct materials in the inventory. The same process is used to calculate the cost of direct materials in the finished goods inventory.

Estimating Direct Labour Costs in the Ending Inventories

The process of estimating the direct labour costs in the ending goods in process and finished goods inventories is essentially the same as for direct materials. A responsible plant official must estimate the percentage of completion of the units in the goods in process inventory and then calculate the direct labour cost that was applied to those units. A similar estimate must be made of the direct labour cost that was applied to the units in the finished goods inventory.

Estimating Factory Overhead Costs in the Ending Inventories

Factory overhead consists of many items, none of which is directly associated with specific units or batches of production. As a result, estimating factory overhead costs in the ending inventories presents a difficult problem. This problem is often solved by assuming that factory overhead costs are closely related to direct labour costs. Usually, this is a reasonable approach. There is often a close relation between direct labour costs and such indirect costs as supervision, factory utilities, repairs, and so forth. When this relation is used to apply overhead costs, you assume that the relation of overhead costs to the direct labour costs in each unit of goods in process and finished goods is the same as the relation between total factory overhead costs and total direct labour costs for the accounting period.

Estimating the Ending Inventory Costs of Excel Manufacturing Company

For example, examine the manufacturing statement in Illustration 21–6 and you will see that Excel Manufacturing Company's total direct labour costs were $60,000 and its overhead costs were $30,000. In other words, during the year the company incurred in the production of all its products $2 of direct labour for each $1 of factory overhead costs; overhead costs were 50% of direct labour cost.

$$\frac{\text{Overhead costs, } \$30,000}{\text{Direct labour, } \$60,000} \times 100 = 50\%$$

Therefore, in estimating the overhead applicable to a goods in process or finished goods item, Excel Manufacturing Company may assume that this 50% overhead rate applies. Since total overhead costs were 50% of total labour costs, it would appear reasonable to assume that this relationship applies to each goods in process and finished goods item.

Recall from Illustration 21–7 that the ending goods in process inventory was $7,500, and the ending finished goods inventory was $10,300. To see how these amounts might have been determined, assume that a physical count of the ending inventories showed that there were 1,000 partially finished units in the goods in process inventory and 800 units in the finished goods inventory. The costs of the ending inventories were determined as follows:

	Goods in Process			Finished Goods		
	Cost per Unit	Units of Product	Total Cost	Cost per Unit	Units of Product	Total Cost
Direct materials	$3.75	1,000	$3,750	$5.00	800	$ 4,000
Direct labour.	2.50	1,000	2,500	5.25	800	4,200
Factory overhead—						
50% of direct labour	1.25	1,000	1,250	2.625	800	2,100
			$7,500			$10,300

To summarize, the per unit costs for direct materials and direct labour were estimated by appropriate plant officials. The factory overhead cost per unit was calculated as 50% of the direct labour cost. And the number of units of product in each inventory was determined by physically counting the units on hand.

Summary of the Chapter in Terms of Learning Objectives

1. The only difference in the financial statements of manufacturers and merchandisers is in the descriptions of inventories and cost of goods sold. The manufacturer shows cost of goods manufactured instead of the cost of goods purchased and may describe its inventory as finished goods instead of as merchandise. A general accounting system for manufacturing operations is a periodic inventory system. Physical counts of the ending raw materials, goods in process, and finished goods are required. The costs of direct materials, direct labour, and factory overhead are combined to determine the financial statement valuations of goods in process, finished goods, and cost of goods sold.

2. Unique accounts of manufacturers include Raw Materials Purchases, Raw Materials Inventory, Goods in Process Inventory, Finished Goods Inventory, Manufacturing Summary, and several different accounts in which are recorded the costs of factory overhead. The manufacturing statement is a supporting schedule that shows the costs of direct materials, direct labour, and factory overhead that were incurred during the period. On the statement, these costs are adjusted for changes in the inventories to determine the cost of goods manufactured during the period.

3. The work sheet for a manufacturer includes two additional columns into which you sort the items that appear on the manufacturing statement. The cost of goods manufactured is determined in these columns and is extended to the Income Statement Debit column. Then, the financial statement information in the remaining columns is generated in the same manner as you would complete a merchandising company's work sheet.

4. Adjusting entries for a manufacturer include adjustments related to manufacturing costs as well as the typical revenue and expense adjustments for prepaid and accrued items. In the closing entry process, all items related to manufacturing costs are closed to a Manufacturing Summary account. This account is then closed with the expense accounts to Income Summary.

5. When a manufacturer determines the costs of its ending inventories, the raw materials and direct labour costs allocated to goods in process and finished goods are estimated by a responsible plant official. To determine the overhead cost allocated to goods in process and finished goods, the total overhead cost is first expressed as a percentage of total direct labour cost. Then, the overhead cost in each inventory is determined by multiplying this percentage by the direct labour cost allocated to each inventory.

Demonstration Problem

The following information for the year ended December 31, 1990, was taken from the accounting records of Froh Corporation. Use the information to prepare a schedule of factory overhead costs, a manufacturing statement (in which overhead is shown in total), and an income statement.

Advertising expense.	$ 85,000
Amortization of patents	16,000
Bad debts expense	28,000
Depreciation of production machinery	78,000
Depreciation of factory building	133,000
Depreciation of office equipment	37,000
Direct labour	250,000
Factory insurance	62,000
Factory utilities.	115,000
Repairs and maintenance of machinery	31,000
Factory supervision	74,000
Factory supplies used	21,000
Taxes on production machinery.	14,000
Finished goods inventory, December 31, 1990.	12,500
Finished goods inventory, December 31, 1989.	15,000
Goods in process inventory, December 31, 1990	9,000
Goods in process inventory, December 31, 1989	8,000
Income tax expense	53,400
Indirect labour	26,000
Insurance expense	55,000
Interest expense.	25,000
Raw materials inventory, December 31, 1990	78,000
Raw materials inventory, December 31, 1989	60,000
Raw materials purchases	313,000
Salaries expense	150,000
Sales	1,630,000

Solution to Demonstration Problem

FROH CORPORATION
Schedule of Factory Overhead Costs
For Year Ended December 31, 1990

Amortization of patents	$ 16,000
Depreciation of production machinery . . .	78,000
Depreciation of factory building	133,000
Factory insurance	62,000
Factory utilities.	115,000
Repairs and maintenance of machinery . .	31,000
Factory supervision	74,000
Factory supplies used	21,000
Taxes on production machinery.	14,000
Indirect labour	26,000
Total factory overhead.	$570,000

FROH CORPORATION
Manufacturing Statement
For Year Ended December 31, 1990

Direct materials:		
Raw materials inventory, December 31, 1989 . . .	$ 60,000	
Raw materials purchases	313,000	
Raw materials available for use.	$ 373,000	
Raw materials inventory, December 31, 1990 . . .	78,000	
Direct materials used.		$ 295,000
Direct labour.		250,000
Factory overhead costs.		570,000
Total manufacturing costs		$1,115,000
Goods in process inventory, December 31, 1989 . .		8,000
Total goods in process		$1,123,000
Goods in process inventory, December 31, 1990 . .		9,000
Cost of goods manufactured.		$1,114,000

FROH CORPORATION
Income Statement
For Year Ended December 31, 1990

Sales.		$1,630,000
Cost of goods sold:		
Finished goods inventory, December 31, 1989 . .	$ 15,000	
Cost of goods manufactured.	1,114,000	
Goods available for sale.	$1,129,000	
Finished goods inventory, December 31, 1990 . .	12,500	
Cost of goods sold		1,116,500
Gross profit		$ 513,500
Operating expenses:		
Advertising expense	$ 85,000	
Bad debts expense.	28,000	
Depreciation of office equipment	37,000	
Insurance expense	55,000	
Interest expense	25,000	
Salaries expense	150,000	
Total operating expenses		380,000
Income before income taxes.		$ 133,500
Income tax expense		53,400
Net income		$ 80,100

Glossary

Cost accounting system an accounting system that uses perpetual inventories in accounting for manufacturing operations and that is designed to assist management's efforts to control costs. p. 917

Direct labour labour the cost of which can be easily associated with and charged to units or batches of production because the labour is of those employees who work specifically on the conversion of raw materials into finished products. p. 918

Direct materials physical items the cost of which is easily traced to units of product or batches of production because the items enter into and become a part of a finished product. p. 918

Factory burden a synonym for *factory overhead* or *manufacturing overhead*. p. 919

Factory overhead all manufacturing costs other than for direct materials and direct labour. p. 919

Finished goods products that a company manufactures for sale and which have completed the manufacturing process and are ready for sale. p. 922

General accounting system for manufacturers an accounting system that uses periodic inventories to determine the total cost of all goods manufactured during each accounting period. p. 917

Goods in process products in the process of being manufactured that have received a portion or all of their materials and have had some labour and overhead applied but that are not completed. p. 922

Indirect labour labour the cost of which cannot be easily associated with specific units of product because the labour is by employees who, although contributing to production, do not work specifically on the manufactured products. p. 918

Indirect materials commodities used in production and accounted for as factory overhead because they do not enter into or become a part of the finished product and, therefore, are not easily traced to specific units or batches of production. p. 918

Manufacturing overhead a synonym for *factory overhead* or *factory burden*. p. 919

Manufacturing statement a schedule that shows the costs incurred to manufacture a product or products during a period. p. 924

Period costs costs such as selling and general administrative expenses that are charged to expense in the period incurred because they are not related to the purchase of merchandise or the manufacture of finished goods. p. 920

Product costs costs incurred to acquire merchandise or manufacture finished goods and that, therefore, are charged to inventory accounts until the goods are sold, at which time they are reported as cost of goods sold. p. 920

Raw materials commodities that are purchased for use in the manufacturing process as direct materials but that are sometimes used as indirect materials. p. 918

Schedule of the cost of goods manufactured a synonym for *manufacturing statement*. p. 924

Work in process a synonym for *goods in process*. p. 922

Questions for Class Discussion

1. What is the difference between a general accounting system for manufacturers and a cost accounting system?

2. What is the basic difference between a manufacturing company and a merchandising company?

3. Manufacturing costs consist of three elements. What are they?

4. How does the income statement of a manufacturing company differ from the income statement of a merchandising company?

5. What is the difference between direct materials and indirect materials?

6. What is the difference between raw materials and direct materials?

7. What is the difference between direct labour and indirect labour?

8. How is the cost of indirect labour charged to production?

9. Factory overhead costs include a variety of items. List several examples of factory overhead costs.

10. What is the difference between factory overhead and selling or administrative expenses?

11. If a general accounting system is used, when in the accounting cycle are the costs of raw material purchases, direct labour, and factory overhead allocated to cost of goods sold and to the ending raw materials, goods in process, and finished goods inventories?

12. Name several accounts that are often found in the ledgers of both manufacturing and merchandising companies. Name several accounts that are found only in the ledgers of manufacturing companies.

13. What are three inventory accounts that appear in the ledger of a manufacturing company?

14. How are the beginning and ending inventories of raw materials, goods in process, and finished goods extended to or entered in the financial statement columns of a work sheet?

15. Which inventories of a manufacturing company receive the same work sheet treatment as the merchandise inventories of a merchandising company?

16. Which inventories of a manufacturing company appear on its manufacturing statement? Which appear on the income statement?

17. What accounts are summarized in the Manufacturing Summary account? What accounts are summarized in the Income Summary account?

18. What are the three manufacturing cost elements emphasized on the manufacturing statement?

19. What account balances are carried into the Manufacturing Statement columns of the manufacturing work sheet? What account balances are

carried into the Income Statement columns? What account balances are carried into the Statement of Retained Earnings or Balance Sheet columns?

20. Why is the cost of goods manufactured entered in the Manufacturing Statement Credit column of a work sheet and again in the Income Statement Debit column?

21. May prices paid to a supplier for items of raw materials be used to determine the balance sheet valuation of the items in the raw materials inventory? Why? Do such prices also determine the balance sheet valuations of the goods in process and finished goods inventories? Why?

22. Republic Company used an overhead rate of 60% of direct labour cost to apply overhead to the items of its goods in process inventory. If the manufacturing statement of the company showed total overhead costs of $156,000, how much direct labour did it show?

Multiple Choice

1. Which of the following statements is true with regard to the procedures used in a general accounting system for a manufacturing company?
   a. Perpetual inventory records are maintained for raw materials and goods in process but not for finished goods.
   b. Labour that contributes to production but that is not easily identified with units of product is accounted for as factory overhead.
   c. Examples of direct labour include the labour of supervisors and engineers.
   d. All manufacturing costs other than direct materials are called factory overhead.
   e. Product costs are recorded in expense accounts.

2. A manufacturing statement:
   a. Shows the elements of manufacturing costs incurred during the period and calculates the cost of goods sold during the period.
   b. Shows the changes that occurred during the period in raw materials inventory, goods in process inventory, and finished goods inventory.
   c. Shows the elements of manufacturing costs incurred during the period and calculates the cost of goods manufactured during the period.
   d. Shows all of the cost items that make up the operating expenses incurred during the period.
   e. None of the above is correct.

3. On a work sheet for a manufacturing company:
   a. Raw material purchases appear in the Income Statement Debit column.
   b. The cost of goods manufactured appears in the Manufacturing Statement Credit column and the Income Statement Debit column.
   c. All of the factory overhead costs appear in the Manufacturing Statement Credit column.
   d. Ending finished goods inventory appears in the Manufacturing Statement Credit column.

    e. Raw material purchases appear in the Statement of Retained Earnings or Balance Sheet Debit column.

4. A Manufacturing Company has a beginning finished goods inventory of $16,600; a cost of goods manufactured of $29,400; and an ending finished goods inventory of $15,400. The cost of goods sold for this company is:

    a. $19,000.

    b. $30,600.

    c. $37,800.

    d. $46,000.

    e. Answer cannot be determined from the information given.

5. Given the following information, what is the cost of goods manufactured?

Beginning raw materials.	$ 5,500
Ending raw materials	4,000
Direct labour	12,250
Raw material purchases.	7,400
Depreciation on factory equipment	6,500
Factory repairs and maintenance.	3,300
Beginning finished goods inventory.	10,200
Ending finished goods inventory	8,900
Beginning goods in process inventory	5,700
Ending goods in process inventory	6,300

    a. $30,650.

    b. $30,350.

    c. $31,650.

    d. $36,650.

    e. $30,950.

6. During the annual accounting period, total manufacturing overhead was $70,000 and total direct labour was $175,000. If the ending balance of Finished Goods Inventory was $38,000, which included $10,000 of direct materials, the amount of direct labour included in the ending finished goods inventory was:

    a. $8,000.

    b. $10,000.

    c. $20,000.

    d. $28,000.

    e. Cannot be determined from information given.

Mini Dicussion Cases

Case 21–1

A friend has been operating a manufacturing business for the last few months and has come to you for assistance. He says that he understands the idea of direct versus indirect labour but has problems in applying the ideas in his operations.

His machine operators work on as many as 10 different products or jobs during each day, sometimes looking after more than one machine at the same time. Therefore, it is very difficult to assign the labour costs amongst these jobs. Your friend asks you, "Just what is direct labour?"

Required

Reply to your friend in the context of his problem. Should he treat his machine operators as indirect labour? Why or why not?

Case 21–2

The Sticky Cog Manufacturing Company has a policy whereby it always assumes that its work in process inventories are 50% complete. The accountant says that this makes the preparation of the year-end financial statements much easier because no one has to estimate the actual degree of completion. All that is required is to take a count of the uncompleted units.

Required

Evaluate the company's policy. Do you agree or disagree with this policy? Why?

Exercises

Exercise 21–1
Raw materials used as indirect materials
(L. O. 1)

This year Horizon Corporation began manufacturing operations and purchased on account $35,000 of raw materials. These materials included paint that is applied to the units being produced as they are finished. During the year, $205 of the paint was used to repaint some of the tools used in the factory. Prepare general journal entries to record the purchase of raw materials and the use of paint to repaint tools.

Exercise 21–2
Classifying product costs and period costs
(L. O. 1)

The following costs were incurred by a manufacturing company. Indicate which of these costs should be classified as product costs and which should be classified as period costs.

Advertising   Insurance on factory workers
Amortization of patents   Interest on long-term debt
Bad debts expense   Office salaries
Depreciation of factory building   Repairs to machinery
Direct materials used   Sales salaries
Income taxes   Small tools written off

Exercise 21–3
Preparing a manufacturing statement
(L. O. 2)

After Florian Corporation posted its adjusting entries on December 31, 1990, the general ledger included the following account balances. (Some accounts in the general ledger have not been listed.)

Sales	$950,000
Raw materials inventory, January 1, 1990	52,000
Goods in process inventory, January 1, 1990 . .	60,700
Finished goods inventory, January 1, 1990. . . .	76,500
Raw material purchases.	153,100
Direct labour	182,200
Factory supplies used	18,400
Indirect labour	44,800
Machinery repairs	8,000
Rent on factory building	66,000
Selling expenses, controlling	115,200
Administrative expenses, controlling	134,600

On December 31, 1990, the inventories of Florian Corporation were determined to be:

Raw materials inventory.	$47,500
Goods in process inventory.	42,200
Finished goods inventory	71,300

Given the above information, prepare a manufacturing statement for Florian Corporation.

Exercise 21–4
Preparing a manufacturing company's income statement
(L. O. 3)

Use the information provided in Exercise 21–3 and prepare an income statement for Florian Corporation.

Exercise 21–5
Closing entries for a manufacturing company
(L. O. 4)

Use the information provided in Exercise 21–3 and prepare closing entries for Florian Corporation.

Exercise 21–6
Calculating the cost of goods manufactured
(L. O. 2)

The following information was taken from the accounting records of Dunlop Company and Elmore Company:

	Dunlop Company	Elmore Company
Ending finished goods inventory	$ 360	$1,140
Direct labour	1,800	2,890
Factory electricity	240	480
Ending raw materials inventory	420	540
Machinery repairs	240	480
Raw material purchases.	2,040	2,640
Beginning goods in process inventory . .	600	1,020
Sales salaries	720	1,080
Beginning finished goods inventory. . . .	600	840
Indirect labour	480	960
Depreciation of factory.	540	900
Beginning raw materials inventory	780	600
General and administrative expenses . .	2,100	2,280
Factory supplies used.	180	240
Ending goods in process inventory	660	780

Calculate the cost of goods manufactured and the cost of goods sold for each company.

Exercise 21–7
Allocating costs to ending inventories
(L. O. 5)

Hopper Company's ending goods in process inventory included 800 units of product; its finished goods inventory included 1,600 units of product. Factory officials determined that goods in process included direct materials cost of $6.30 per unit and direct labour cost of $8.60. Finished goods units were estimated to have $6.45 of direct materials and $10.60 of direct labour. During the period, the company incurred $94,100 of direct labour and $70,600 of factory overhead. Factory overhead is assumed to be closely related to direct labour. Calculate the total cost of each ending inventory. Also calculate how much direct labour and how much factory overhead will be included in cost of goods sold.

Exercise 21–8
Closing entries for a manufacturing company
(L. O. 4)

Guzman Corporation's accounting system uses highly summarized controlling accounts. The following account balances and ending inventories on December 31, 1990, were taken from the company's accounting records:

Sales	$176,000
Raw material purchases	28,000
Direct labour	41,300
Factory overhead.	34,000
Selling expenses, controlling	19,100
General and administrative expenses, controlling . .	17,400
Income taxes	19,800
Raw materials inventory	5,200
Goods in process inventory	7,100
Finished goods inventory	4,300
Ending inventories:	
Raw materials	8,100
Goods in process	10,500
Finished goods.	6,600

Prepare closing entries for the company.

Exercise 21–9
Overhead rate calculation and analysis
(L. O. 5)

Ehler Company uses the relation between factory overhead and direct labour costs to apply factory overhead to its goods in process and finished goods inventories. The company incurred the following costs during a year: direct materials, $348,600; direct labour, $300,000; and factory overhead costs, $600,000. (*a*) Determine the company's overhead rate. (*b*) Under the assumption the company's $42,360 goods in process inventory had $8,600 of direct labour costs, determine the inventory's direct material costs. (*c*) Under the assumption the company's $53,600 finished goods inventory had $14,600 of direct material costs, determine the inventory's direct labour cost and factory overhead costs.

Exercise 21–10
Work sheet for a manufacturing firm
(L. O. 3)

The December 31 trial balance of Deitz Diesel Company follows:

DEITZ DIESEL COMPANY
Unadjusted Trial Balance
December 31, 1990

Cash	$ 1,350	
Accounts receivable	1,530	
Allowance for doubtful accounts.		$ 480
Raw materials inventory	570	
Goods in process inventory	1,230	
Finished goods inventory	750	
Factory supplies	990	
Prepaid factory insurance	1,050	
Factory machinery	6,480	
Accumulated depreciation, factory machinery . .		1,200
Common stock.		4,500
Retained earnings		1,800
Sales		24,300
Raw material purchases.	5,100	
Freight on raw materials	300	
Direct labour	3,300	
Indirect labour	1,020	
Factory utilities	1,740	
Machinery repairs	450	
Factory rent.	1,800	
Selling expenses, controlling	2,610	
Administrative expenses, controlling	2,010	
Totals	$32,280	$32,280

Additional information to be used in preparing a work sheet for 1990 financial statements is as follows:

a. Ending inventories:
      Raw materials, $960.
      Goods in process, $1,590.
      Finished goods, $540.
      Factory supplies, $210.
b. Allowance for doubtful accounts should be increased by $660.
c. Expired factory insurance for the year is $750.
d. Depreciation of factory machinery amounted to $840.
e. Accrued payroll on December 31:
      Direct labour, $1,320.
      Indirect labour, $480.
      Office salaries, $330. (Debit Administrative Expenses, controlling account.)

Required
Prepare a work sheet for the year ended December 31, 1990.

Problems

Problem 21–1
Allocating costs to work in process; preparing the manufacturing statement
(L. O. 2, 4, 5)

Doppler Company's December 31, 1990, work sheet had the following items in its manufacturing statement columns:

	Manufacturing Statement	
	Debit	**Credit**
Raw materials inventory.	47,000	50,600
Goods in process inventory	55,200	?
Raw material purchases.	173,000	
Direct labour	280,000	
Indirect labour	107,900	
Factory utilities.	60,800	
Machinery repairs	16,700	
Factory rent	47,000	
Property taxes, machinery	10,700	
Expired factory insurance	8,900	
Factory supplies used.	19,400	
Depreciation of machinery	46,000	
Amortization of patents	7,400	
	880,000	?
Cost of goods manufactured		?
	880,000	880,000

Doppler Company's work sheet does not show the amount of the ending goods in process inventory or the cost of goods manufactured. However, the company makes a single product, and on December 31, 1990, there were 2,600 units of goods in process. Each unit contained an estimated $7.40 of direct materials and had an estimated $10.00 of direct labour applied.

Required

1. Calculate the relation between direct labour and factory overhead costs and use this relation to place an accounting value on the ending goods in process inventory.
2. Prepare a 1990 manufacturing statement for the company.
3. Prepare entries to close the manufacturing accounts to Manufacturing Summary and to close the Manufacturing Summary account.

Problem 21–2
Preparing manufacturing and income statements; closing entries
(L. O. 2, 3, 4)

The following items appeared in the Manufacturing Statement and Income Statement columns of a work sheet prepared for Goodman Corporation on December 31, 1990:

	Manufacturing Statement		Income Statement	
	Debit	**Credit**	**Debit**	**Credit**
Raw materials inventory.	34,020	32,670		
Goods in process inventory	39,960	34,830		
Finished goods inventory			43,470	50,760
Sales.				976,050
Raw material purchases.	159,300			
Discounts on raw material purchases		2,160		
Direct labour	243,000			
Indirect labour	37,260			
Factory supervision	32,400			
Factory utilities.	49,680			
Machinery repairs	12,150			
Factory rent	19,440			
Property taxes, machinery	4,590			
Selling expenses, controlling			83,160	
Administrative expenses, controlling .			78,030	
Expired factory insurance	6,480			
Factory supplies used.	16,470			
Depreciation of machinery	28,350			
Small tools written off	1,080			
Amortization of patents	6,750			
Income tax expense . .			79,650	
	690,930	69,660		
Cost of goods manufactured		621,270	621,270	
	690,930	690,930	905,580	1,026,810
Net income.			121,230	
			1,026,810	1,026,810

Required

1. Prepare a manufacturing statement and an income statement for the company.
2. Journalize closing entries for the company.

Problem 21–3
Calculating cost components and preparing the manufacturing statement
(L. O. 3, 5)

Calderon Company began this year with the following inventories: raw materials, $41,400; goods in process, $46,350; and finished goods, $56,250. The company uses the relation between its factory overhead and direct labour costs to apply overhead to its inventories of goods in process and finished goods; and at the end of this year its inventories were assigned these costs:

	Raw Materials	Goods in Process	Finished Goods
Material costs	$38,700	$12,600	$20,250
Direct labour costs	–0–	16,200	25,200
Overhead costs	–0–	?	31,500
Totals	$38,700	?	$76,950

And this additional information was available from the company's records:

Total factory overhead costs incurred during the year . .	$371,200
Cost of all goods manufactured during the year	892,800

Required

On the basis of the information given plus data you derive from it, prepare a manufacturing statement for Calderon Company.

Problem 21–4
Preparing the work sheet, manufacturing statement, and income statement
(L. O. 2, 3, 4, 5)

The December 31, 1990, unadjusted trial balance of Norwich Manufacturing Company is as follows:

NORWICH MANUFACTURING COMPANY
Unadjusted Trial Balance
December 31, 1990

Cash	$ 24,225	
Accounts receivable	27,150	
Allowance for doubtful accounts.		$ 150
Raw materials inventory	27,825	
Goods in process inventory	25,800	
Finished goods inventory	36,525	
Prepaid factory insurance	3,075	
Factory supplies	9,825	
Machinery	170,625	
Accumulated depreciation, machinery . . .		58,800
Accounts payable		18,975
Common stock		75,000
Retained earnings		71,175
Sales		519,375
Raw material purchases	138,825	
Direct labour	119,625	
Indirect labour	27,450	
Factory utilities	10,200	
Machinery repairs	7,050	
Selling expenses, controlling	60,900	
Administrative expenses, controlling	54,375	
Totals	$743,475	$743,475

The following adjustments and inventory information were available at year-end:

a. Allowance for doubtful accounts should be increased to $1,275. (Debit Administrative Expenses, controlling account.)

b. An examination of policies shows $2,325 of factory insurance expired.

c. An inventory of factory supplies shows $7,275 of factory supplies used.

d. Depreciation of factory machinery was $23,475.

e. Accrued direct labour is $375; and accrued indirect labour is $225.

f. Accrued income taxes payable amount to $28,125.

g. Year-end inventories:
   (1) Raw materials, $27,525.
   (2) Goods in process consists of 1,200 units of product. Each unit is estimated to contain $8.40 of direct materials and $9.00 of direct labour.
   (3) Finished goods inventory consists of 1,120 units of product. Each unit is estimated to contain $16 of direct materials and $13 of direct labour.

Required

1. Enter the unadjusted trial balance on a work sheet form and make the adjustments from the information given. Then sort the items to the proper financial statement columns.

2. After the Direct Labour and factory overhead accounts have been adjusted and extended to the Manufacturing Statement columns, determine the relation between direct labour and overhead costs and use this relation to determine the overhead applicable to each unit of goods in process and finished goods. Next, calculate the balance sheet values for these inventories, enter the inventory amounts on the work sheet, and complete the work sheet.

3. From the work sheet prepare a manufacturing statement and an income statement.

4. Journalize the closing entires.

Problem 21–5
Preparing the work sheet and financial statements for a manufacturing firm
(L. O. 2, 3, 4, 5)

Enoch Company's unadjusted trial balance on December 31, 1990, the end of an annual accounting period, appears as follows:

ENOCH COMPANY
Unadjusted Trial Balance
December 31, 1990

Cash	$ 11,100	
Raw materials inventory	10,275	
Goods in process inventory	9,375	
Finished goods inventory	11,325	
Prepaid factory insurance	2,700	
Factory supplies	5,100	
Factory machinery	126,150	
Accumulated depreciation, factory machinery		$ 23,475
Small tools	3,075	
Patents	5,025	
Common stock		75,000
Retained earnings		12,525
Sales		277,500
Raw material purchases	46,500	
Discounts on raw material purchases		900
Direct labour	73,800	
Indirect labour	9,075	
Factory supervision	8,775	
Factory utilities	13,425	
Machinery repairs	3,150	
Factory rent	4,500	
Property taxes, machinery	1,275	
Selling expenses, controlling	23,550	
Administrative expenses, controlling	21,225	
Totals	$389,400	$389,400

Additional Information

a. Expired factory insurance, $1,800.

b. Factory supplies used, $4,425.

c. Depreciation of factory machinery, $7,650.

d. Small tools written off, $375.

e. Amortization of patents, $1,050.

f. Accrued wages payable:
    (1) Direct labour, $1,200.
    (2) Indirect labour, $525.
    (3) Factory supervision, $225.

g. Estimated income taxes payable, $22,500.

h. Ending inventories:
    (1) Raw materials, $9,900.
    (2) Goods in process consists of 750 units of product. Each unit is estimated to contain $4.50 of direct materials and $6.00 of direct labour.
    (3) Finished goods consists of 600 units of product. Each unit is estimated to contain $8.75 of direct materials and $12.00 of direct labour.

Required

1. Enter the unadjusted trial balance on a work sheet form. Make the adjustments from the information given and sort the items to the proper financial statement columns.

2. Determine the relation between factory overhead costs and direct labour cost and use the relation to calculate the overhead that should be charged to the ending goods in process and finished goods inventories. Then, complete the work sheet.

3. From the work sheet prepare a manufacturing statement and an income statement.

4. Journalize the closing entries.

Alternate Problems

Problem 21–1A
Allocating costs to work in process; preparing the manufacturing statement
(L. O. 2, 4, 5)

In Ingram Corporation's December 31, 1990, work sheet, the Manufacturing Statement columns appeared as shown below. The illustrated columns show the items as they appeared after all adjustments were completed but before the ending work in process inventory was calculated and entered and before the cost of goods manufactured was calculated.

Ingram Corporation makes a single product called Cifones. On December 31, 1990, the goods in process inventory consisted of 1,500 units of Cifones. Each unit was estimated to contain $13.80 of direct materials and $34.40 of direct labour.

	Manufacturing Statement	
	Debit	**Credit**
Raw materials inventory.	91,580	83,370
Goods in process inventory.	76,890	?
Raw material purchases.	351,640	
Direct labour.	432,000	
Indirect labour	70,000	
Factory supervision	52,840	
Factory utilities.	38,150	
Machinery repairs	27,220	
Factory rent	32,100	
Property taxes, machinery	8,200	
Factory insurance expired.	14,250	
Factory supplies used.	31,960	
Depreciation of machinery	73,000	
Small tools written off	2,200	
	1,302,030	?
Cost of goods manufactured		?
	1,302,030	1,302,030

Required

1. Calculate the relation between direct labour and factory overhead costs and determine an accounting valuation of the ending goods in process inventory.

2. After placing a value on the ending goods in process inventory, prepare a manufacturing statement for Ingram Corporation.

3. Prepare entries to close the manufacturing accounts to Manufacturing Summary and to close the Manufacturing Summary account.

Problem 21–2A
Preparing manufacturing and income statements; closing entries
(L. O. 2, 3, 4)

The following alphabetically arranged items were taken from the Manufacturing Statement and Income Statement columns of Juvenal Manufacturing Company's year-end work sheet:

Advertising.	$ 8,100	Goods in process,		
Depreciation of machinery	14,175	December 31.	$	50,625
Depreciation of office equipment .	3,375	Finished goods, January 1 . .		70,875
Depreciation of selling		Finished goods,		
equipment.	4,050	December 31.		56,700
Direct labour.	261,900	Miscellaneous production costs.		3,375
Factory supplies used.	7,425	Office salaries		28,350
Factory utilities	13,500	Raw material purchases		347,625
Freight on raw materials	10,125	Rent on factory building.		32,400
Income tax expense.	54,675	Rent expense, office space. . .		9,450
Indirect labour.	23,625	Rent expense, selling space . .		10,800
Inventories:		Repairs to machinery		12,150
Raw materials, January 1 . . .	66,150	Sales.		1,215,675
Raw materials, December 31 .	68,175	Sales discounts		22,950
Goods in process, January 1. .	55,350	Sales salaries		118,125
		Factory supervision		48,600

Required

Prepare a manufacturing statement and an income statement for the company.

Problem 21–3A
Calculating cost components and preparing the manufacturing statement
(L. O. 3, 5)

Mega Products Company incurred a total of $781,920 of direct material, direct labour, and factory overhead costs in manufacturing its product last year. Of this amount, $336,960 represented factory overhead costs. The company began last year with the following inventories: raw materials, $30,240; goods in process, $52,200; and finished goods, $63,000. It applies overhead to its goods in process and finished goods inventories on the basis of the relation of overhead to direct labour costs; and at the end of last year, it assigned the following costs to its inventories:

	Raw Materials	Goods in Process	Finished Goods
Material costs	$33,120	$16,920	$20,700
Direct labour costs	–0–	17,280	20,880
Overhead costs	–0–	?	31,320
Totals	$33,120	$?	$72,900

Required

Prepare a manufacturing statement for Mega Products Company using the above information and any other necessary data that can be derived from it.

Problem 21–4A
Preparing the work sheet, manufacturing statement, and income statement
(L. O. 2, 3, 4, 5)

Jakel Corporation's December 31, 1990, unadjusted trial balance included the following items:

JAKEL CORPORATION
Trial Balance
December 31, 1990

Cash	$ 45,900	
Accounts receivable	56,850	
Allowance for doubtful accounts		$ 1,350
Raw materials inventory	71,250	
Goods in process inventory	31,800	
Finished goods inventory	38,100	
Prepaid factory insurance	11,400	
Factory supplies	17,400	
Machinery	333,000	
Accumulated depreciation, machinery		133,500
Accounts payable		62,250
Common stock		90,000
Retained earnings		102,300
Sales		1,018,050
Raw material purchases	262,500	
Direct labour	177,900	
Indirect labour	40,500	
Factory utilities	34,650	
Machinery repairs	10,950	
Selling expenses, controlling	131,100	
Administrative expenses, controlling	144,150	
Totals	$1,407,450	$1,407,450

The following adjustments and inventory information was available at year-end:

a. Allowance for doubtful accounts should be increased to $2,700. (Debit Administrative Expenses, controlling account.)

b. An examination of policies showed $7,500 of factory insurance expired.

    c. An inventory of factory supplies showed $11,100 of factory supplies used.

    d. Estimated depreciation of factory machinery was $47,400.

    e. Accrued direct labour is $2,100; and accrued indirect labour is $900.

    f. Accrued income taxes payable amount to $59,100.

    g. Year-end inventories:

      (1) Raw materials, $55,050.

      (2) Goods in process consists of 1,700 units of product. Each unit is estimated to contain $12 of direct materials and $10 of direct labour.

      (3) Finished goods inventory consists of 2,200 units of product. Each unit is estimated to contain $18 of materials and $15 of direct labour.

Required

1. Enter the unadjusted trial balance on a work sheet form and make the adjustments from the information given. Then sort the items to the proper financial statement columns.

2. After the Direct Labour and factory overhead accounts have been adjusted and carried into the Manufacturing Statement columns, determine the relation between direct labour and overhead costs and use this relation to determine the overhead applicable to each unit of goods in process and finished goods. Next, calculate the balance sheet values for these inventories (rounded to the nearest whole dollar), enter the inventory amounts on the work sheet, and complete the work sheet.

3. From the work sheet prepare a manufacturing statement and an income statement.

4. Prepare closing journal entries.

Problem 21–5A
Preparing the work sheet and financial statements for a manufacturing company
(L. O. 2, 3, 4, 5)

Overton Manufacturing Company's unadjusted trial balance on December 31, 1990, the end of its annual accounting period, appears as follows:

OVERTON MANUFACTURING COMPANY
Unadjusted Trial Balance
December 31, 1990

Cash	$ 31,500	
Raw materials inventory	23,940	
Goods in process inventory	27,540	
Finished goods inventory	29,880	
Prepaid factory insurance	7,560	
Factory supplies	11,520	
Factory machinery	315,900	
Accumulated depreciation, factory machinery . .		$ 51,840
Small tools	6,660	
Patents	8,100	
Common stock		180,000
Retained earnings		61,920
Sales		647,460
Raw material purchases	111,240	
Discounts on raw material purchases		1,800
Direct labour	160,380	
Indirect labour	23,940	
Factory supervision	21,240	
Factory utilities	32,220	
Machinery repairs	7,920	
Factory rent.	12,960	
Property taxes, machinery.	1,440	
Selling expenses, controlling	56,520	
Administrative expenses, controlling	52,560	
Totals	$943,020	$943,020

Additional Information

a. Expired factory insurance, $3,960.

b. Factory supplies used, $11,340.

c. Depreciation of machinery, $17,820.

d. Small tools written off, $1,260.

e. Amortization of patents, $2,340.

f. Accrued wages payable:
   (1) Direct labour, $1,620.
   (2) Indirect labour, $900.
   (3) Factory supervision, $360.

g. Estimated income tax expense, $51,200.

h. Ending inventories:
   (1) Raw materials, $23,040.
   (2) Goods in process consists of 2,200 units of product. Each unit is estimated to contain $5 of direct materials and $3 of direct labour.
   (3) Finished goods consists of 1,700 units of product. Each unit is estimated to contain $7 of direct materials and $8 of direct labour.

Required

1. Enter the trial balance on a work sheet form. Make the adjustments from the information given and sort the items to the proper financial statement columns.

2. Determine the relation between direct labour and factory overhead costs and use this relation to calculate the overhead that should be charged to the ending goods in process and finished goods inventories. Then, complete the work sheet.

3. From the work sheet prepare a manufacturing statement and an income statement.

4. Journalize closing entries.

Provocative Problems

Provocative Problem 21–1
Universal Mechanism Company
(L. O. 1, 3, 5)

Universal Mechanism Company has been in operation for three years, manufacturing and selling a single product. Although sales have increased materially, profits have increased only slightly. The company president, Clark Kentz, has asked you to analyze the situation and tell him why. Mr. Kentz is primarily a production man and knows little about accounting. The company bookkeeper knows a debit from a credit and is an excellent clerk, but has limited knowledge of accounting.

The company's condensed income statements for the past three years show:

	1989	1990	1991
Sales	$270,000	$378,000	$432,000
Cost of goods sold:			
Finished goods inventory, beginning	$ –0–	$ 19,800	$ 59,400
Cost of goods manufactured.	178,200	276,480	302,940
Goods available for sale	$178,200	$296,280	$362,340
Finished goods inventory, ending	19,800	59,400	79,200
Cost of goods sold	$158,400	$236,880	$283,140
Gross profit from sales	$111,600	$141,120	$148,860
Selling and administrative expenses.	81,000	105,840	116,640
Net income	$ 30,600	$ 35,280	$ 32,220

Further investigation yields the following additional information:

a. The company sold 3,000 units of its product during the first year in business, 4,200 during the second year, and 4,800 during the third. All sales were priced at $110 per unit, and no discounts were granted.

b. There were 300 units in the finished goods inventory at the end of the first year, 900 at the end of the second, and 1,200 at the end of the third.

c. The units in the finished goods inventory were valued each year at 60% of their selling price, or at $66 per unit.

Required

Prepare a report for Mr. Kentz that shows (*a*) the number of units of product manufactured each year, (*b*) the cost each year to manufacture a unit of product, and (*c*) the selling and administrative expenses per unit of product sold each year. Also, (*d*) prepare an income statement that shows the correct net income each year, using a FIFO basis for pricing the finished goods inventory. And finally, (*e*) express an opinion as to why net income has not kept pace with the rising sales volume.

Provocative Problem 21–2
Pacific Salmon Boats
(L. O. 5)

Several years ago Laura Unger took over the operation of her family's salmon boat manufacturing company. The company previously specialized in manufacturing standard boats. However, it recently has turned more and more to building boats to the specifications of its customers. The seasonality of this business means that shop activity is rather slow during October, November, and December.

Laura has tried to increase business during the slow months. However, most prospective customers who come to the business during these months are shoppers; when Laura quotes a price for a boat, they commonly decide the price is too high and walk out. Laura thinks the trouble arises from her application of a rule established by her father when he ran the business. The rule is that in pricing a job to a customer, ''always set the price so as to make a 10% profit over and above all costs, and be sure that all costs are included.''

Laura says that in pricing a job, the direct material and direct labour costs are easy to figure but that overhead is another thing. Her overhead consists of depreciation of the factory building and machinery, manufacturing utilities, taxes, and so on. In total, these amount to $11,250 per month whether she builds any boats or not. Also, when she follows her father's rule, she has to charge more for a boat built during the slow months because the overhead is spread over fewer jobs. She readily admits that this seems to drive away business during the months she needs business most. Nevertheless, she finds it difficult to break her father's rule, for as she says, ''Dad did all right in this business for many years.''

Required

Explain why Laura charges more for a boat made in December than for one built in May, a very busy month. Use assumed figures to illustrate your point. Suggest how Laura might solve this pricing problem and still follow her father's rule.

Provocative Problem 21–3
Geronimo Production Company
(L. O. 3)

On January 1, 1990, Geronimo Production Company had outstanding 81,000 shares of common stock. The stock was issued at $10 per share. The assets and liabilities of the company on that date were as follows:

Cash	$180,000
Accounts receivable	90,000
Raw materials inventory	112,500
Goods in process inventory	135,000
Finished goods inventory.	157,500
Plant and equipment, net.	382,500
Accounts payable.	90,000

During 1990, the company paid no dividends, although it earned a 1990 net income (ignore income taxes) of $84,375. At year-end, the amounts of the company's accounts receivable, accounts payable, and common stock outstanding were the same as at the beginning of the year. However, its cash decreased by $16,875, its raw materials inventory increased by 40%, its goods in process inventory increased by 25%, and its finished goods inventory increased by one half during the year. The net amount of its plant and equipment decreased by $56,250 due to depreciation, chargeable four fifths to factory overhead costs and one fifth to general and administrative expenses. The year's direct labour costs were $225,000, and factory overhead costs excluding depreciation were 60% of that amount. Cost of goods sold was $562,500, and all sales were made at prices 50% above cost. Selling expenses were 14%, and general and administrative expenses excluding depreciation were 8% of sales.

Required

Based on the information given and on amounts you can derive therefrom, prepare a manufacturing work sheet for the company.

Analytical and Review Problems

A&R Problem 21–1

Depreciation of plant and equipment is normally considered as a cost attributable to a specific period of time. For example, the cost of a factory is allocated over the service life of that factory with specific amounts charged to each period. In accounting for manufacturing companies, depreciation calculated in a particular period may be carried forward to future period(s). Alternately, more than the calculated depreciation for the current period may be included in the current period's income statement.

Required

Do you agree with the above statements? Using a numerical example, prove or disprove the above statements.

A&R Problem 21–2

In manufacturing accounting, the inclusion of depreciation of plant and equipment as part of the overhead is, in fact, converting a fixed (long-term) asset into a current asset.

Required

Does conversion of fixed assets into current assets, via the process of depreciation, take place in nonmanufacturing companies, for example, merchandising companies? Discuss and support your answer.

Appendixes

To supplement the topical coverage of *Financial Accounting Principles*, we have included ten appendixes. Appendixes A through F are presented at the end of the chapters to which they relate. The remaining four appendixes make up the contents of Part Eight.

The appendixes to *Financial Accounting Principles* are:

A. Recording Prepaid and Unearned Items in Income Statement Accounts (Appendix to Chapter 3)

B. Reversing Entries (Appendix to Chapter 4)

C. The Adjusting Entry Approach to Accounting for Merchandise Inventories (Appendix to Chapter 5)

D. Accounting Principles and Financial Statement Concepts (Appendix to Chapter 5)

E. Application Programs for Business (Appendix to Chapter 6)

F. Recording Vouchers, Manual System (Appendix to Chapter 7)

G. Present and Future Values: An Expansion

H. The Accounting Problem of Changing Prices

I. Accounting for Corporate Income Taxes

J. Abitibi-Price Inc. Financial Statements (1989 Annual Reports)

G Present and Future Values: An Expansion

The concept of present values was introduced in Chapter 12 and was applied to accounting problems in Chapters 12 and 17. This appendix is designed to supplement the treatment of present values with additional discussion, more complete tables, and additional homework exercises. In studying this appendix, you also will learn about the concept of future values.

Learning Objectives

After studying Appendix G, you should be able to:

1. Explain what is meant by the present value of a single amount and the present value of an annuity, and be able to use tables to solve problems that involve present values.
2. Explain what is meant by the future value of a single amount and the future value of an annuity, and be able to use tables to solve problems that involve future values.

Present Value of a Single Amount

Explain what is meant by the present value of a single amount and the present value of an annuity, and be able to use tables to solve problems that involve present values.
(L. O. 1)

The present value of a single amount to be received or paid at some future date may be expressed as:

$$p = \frac{f}{(1 + i)^n} \tag{1}$$

where

p = present value
f = future value
i = rate of interest per period
n = number of periods

For example, assume $2.20 is to be received one period from now. This amount will be received because a smaller amount ($2.00) is invested now, for one period, at an interest rate of 10%. Using the formula:

$$p = \frac{f}{(1 + i)^n} = \frac{\$2.20}{(1 + .10)^1} = \$2.00$$

Alternatively, assume the present investment of $2.00 is to remain invested for two periods at 10% and the future amount to be received is $2.42. Using the formula:

$$p = \frac{f}{(1 + i)^n} = \frac{\$2.42}{(1 + .10)^2} = \$2.00$$

Note that n (the number of periods) does not have to be expressed in years. Any period of time such as a day, a month, a quarter, or a year may be used. However, whatever period is used, i (the interest rate) must be per the same period. Thus, if a problem requires that you express n in months, then an i of 1% means 1% per month. This means that each month, 1% of the invested amount at the beginning of the month is earned and added to the investment. Another way of expressing this is to say that interest is compounded monthly.

A present value table is designed to show present values for a variety of i's (interest rates) and a variety of n's (number of periods). Throughout the table, each present value is based on the assumption that f (the future value) is 1.00. Since the future value is assumed to be 1 (in other words, $f = 1$), the formula to construct a table of present values of a single future amount is as follows:

Since $f = 1$,

$$p = \frac{f}{(1 + i)^n} = \frac{1}{(1 + i)^n}$$

A table of present values of a single future amount often is called a *present value of 1* table. Table G–1 on page 1247 is such a table.

Future Value of a Single Amount

The formula for the present value of a single amount may be manipulated to solve for the future value of a single amount. Thus, the formula presented above as (1) may be manipulated as follows:

$$p = \frac{f}{(1 + i)^n} \tag{1}$$

Explain what is meant by
the future value of a single
amount and the future
value of an annuity, and be
able to use tables to solve
problems that involve
future values.
(L. O. 2)

multiply both sides of the equation by $(1 + i)^n$,

$$(1 + i)^n \times p = (1 + i)^n \times \frac{f}{(1 + i)^n}$$

cancel the common terms in the numerator and denominator,

$$(1 + i)^n \times p = \cancel{(1 + i)^n} \times \frac{f}{\cancel{(1 + i)^n}}$$

and the result is,

$$(1 + i)^n \times p = f$$

or

$$f = p \times (1 + i)^n \qquad\qquad (2)$$

For example, assume that $2.00 is invested for one period at an interest rate of 10%. The $2.00 amount will increase to a future value of $2.20. Using the formula:

$$f = p \times (1 + i)^n = \$2.00 \times (1 + .10)^1 = \$2.20$$

Alternatively, assume the present investment of $2.00 will remain invested for three periods at 10%. The amount that will be received three periods hence is $2.662, and is calculated with the formula as follows:

$$f = p \times (1 + i)^n = \$2.00 \times (1 + .10)^3 = \$2.662$$

A future value table is designed to show future values for a variety of i's (interest rates) and a variety of n's (number of periods). Throughout the table, each future value is based on the assumption that p (the present value) is 1.00. Since the present value is assumed to be 1 (in other words, $p = 1$), the formula to construct a table of future values of a single amount is as follows:

Since $p = 1$,

$$f = p(1 + i)^n = (1 + i)^n$$

A table of future values of a single amount is often called a *future value of 1* table. Table G–2 on page 1248 is such a table.

In Table G–2, look at the row where $n = 0$ and observe that regardless of the interest rate, the future value is 1. When $n = 0$, the period of time over which interest is earned is zero. Hence, no interest is earned. The future value is calculated as of the date of the investment. Since the table assumes that the investment is 1, the "future value" on that date is also 1.

You should also observe that a table showing the present values of 1 and a table showing the future values of 1 contain exactly the same information. Both tables are based on the same equation. That is,

$$p = \frac{f}{(1 + i)^n}$$

is nothing more than a reformulation of

$$f = p(1 + i)^n$$

Both tables reflect the same four variables, p, f, i, and n. Therefore, any problem that can be solved using one of the two tables can also be solved using the other table.

For example, suppose a person invests $100 for five years and expects to earn 12% per year. How much should the person receive five years hence?

To solve the problem using Table G–2, look in the table to find the future value of 1, five periods hence, compounded at 12%. In the table, $f = 1.7623$. Thus,

$$\$100 \times 1.7623 = \$176.23$$

To solve the problem using Table G–1, look in the table to find the present value of 1, five periods hence, discounted at 12%. In the table, where $n = 5$, and $i = 12\%$, $p = 0.5674$. Recall that $f = 1$ in the table. This relationship between present value and future value may be expressed as:

$$\frac{p}{f} = \frac{0.5674}{1}$$

This relationship between p and f is the same as in the problem where $100 is invested for five years. Thus,

$$\frac{0.5674}{1}$$

is the same as

$$\frac{\$100}{f}$$

$$\frac{0.5674}{1} = \frac{\$100}{f}$$

$$0.5674 \times f = \$100 \times 1$$

$$f = \frac{\$100}{0.5674} = \$176.24$$

The $0.01 difference between the two answers ($176.23 and $176.24) occurs only because the numbers in the tables were rounded.

Present Value of an Annuity

A series of equal payments is called an annuity. For example, if a person offers to make three annual payments of $100 each, the person is offering an annuity. The present value of an annuity is defined as the value of the payments one period prior to the first payment. Graphically, this may be presented as follows:

$$\$100 \quad \$100 \quad \$100$$

$$p \underline{\hspace{4cm}} f$$

To calculate the present value of this annuity, one might calculate the present value of each payment and add them together. For example, assuming an interest rate of 18%, the calculation is:

$$p = \frac{\$100}{(1 + .18)^1} + \frac{\$100}{(1 + .18)^2} + \frac{\$100}{(1 + .18)^3} = \$217.43$$

Another way to calculate the present value of the annuity is to use Table G–1. The calculation is as follows:

First payment: $p = \$100 \times 0.8475 = \$\ 84.75$
Second payment: $p = \$100 \times 0.7182 = \ \ \ 71.82$
Third payment: $p = \$100 \times 0.6086 = \ \ \ 60.86$

Total: $p = \$217.43$

Another way of using Table G–1 to solve the problem is to add the present values of three payments of 1 and multiply the answer times $100. Thus,

From Table G–1: $i = 18\%, n = 1, p = \ \ 0.8475$
                       $i = 18\%, n = 2, p = \ \ 0.7182$
                       $i = 18\%, n = 3, p = \ \ 0.6086$

                                              2.1743

$2.1743 \times \$100 = \$217.43$

The easiest way to solve the problem is to use a table that shows the present values of a series of payments. That type of table often is called a *present value of an annuity of 1* table. Table G–3 on page 1249 is such a table. Look in Table G–3 on the row where $n = 3$ and $i = 18\%$ and observe that the present value is 2.1743. Stated in other words, an annuity of 1 for three periods, discounted at 18%, is 2.1743.

Although a formula is used to construct a table showing the present values of an annuity,[1] you should understand that the table can be constructed simply by adding together the amounts in a present value of 1 table (such as Table G–1). To check your understanding of this, examine Table G–1 and Table G–3 to confirm that the following numbers were drawn from those tables.

From Table G–1		From Table G–3	
$i = 8\%, n = 1$	0.9259	$i = 8\%, n = 1$	0.9259
$i = 8\%, n = 2$	0.8573		
$i = 8\%, n = 3$	0.7938		
$i = 8\%, n = 4$	0.7350		
Total.	3.3120	$i = 8\%, n = 4$	3.3121

The minor difference in the results (3.3120 and 3.3121) occurs only because the numbers in the tables have been rounded.

---

[1] The formula for a table showing the present values of an annuity of 1 is:

$$p = \frac{1 - \frac{1}{(1 + i)^n}}{i}$$

Future Value of an Annuity

Earlier, we defined an annuity as any series of equal payments. Just as you can calculate the present value of an annuity, you can also calculate the future value of an annuity. The future value of an annuity is defined as the value of the annuity on the date of the final payment. Consider the earlier example of a person who offers to make three annual payments of $100 each. Graphically, the points in time at which the present value and the future value are calculated may be shown as follows:

To calculate the future value of this annuity, you might calculate the future value of each payment and add them together. Assuming an interest rate of 18%, the calculation is:

$$f = \$100(1 + .18)^2 + \$100(1 + .18)^1 + \$100(1 + .18)^0 = \$357.24$$

Another way to calculate the future value of the annuity is to use Table G–2. The calculation is as follows:

First payment: $f = \$100 \times 1.3924 = \$139.24$
Second payment: $f = \$100 \times 1.1800 = \quad 118.00$
Third payment: $f = \$100 \times 1.0000 = \quad \underline{100.00}$

Total: $f = \$357.24$

In the calculations and the graph above, note that the first payment is made two periods prior to the point at which future value is determined. Therefore, for the first payment, $n = 2$. For the second payment, $n = 1$. since the third payment occurs on the future value date, $n = 0$.

Instead of adding the future value of each payment, another approach is to add the future values of three payments of 1 and multiply the answer by $100. This approach appears as follows:

From Table G–2: $i = 18\%, n = 2, f = \quad 1.3924$
$i = 18\%, n = 1, f = \quad 1.1800$
$i = 18\%, n = 0, f = \quad \underline{1.0000}$

3.5724

$3.5724 \times \$100 = \underline{\underline{\$357.24}}$

The easiest way to solve the problem is to use a table that shows the future values of a series of payments. That type of table often is called a *future value of an annuity of 1* table. Table G–4 on page 1250 is such a table. Note in Table G–4 that when $n = 1$, the future values are equal to 1 ($f = 1$) for all rates of interest. When $n = 1$, the "annuity" consists of only one payment and the future value is determined on the date of the payment. Hence, the future value equals the payment.

Although a formula[2] is used to construct a table showing the future values of

---

[2] The formula for a table showing the future values of an annuity of 1 is:

$$f = \frac{(1 + i)^n - 1}{i}$$

an annuity of 1, you should understand that the table can be constructed simply by adding together the amount in a future value of 1 table (such as Table G–2). To check your understanding of this, examine Table G–2 and Table G–4 to confirm that the following numbers were drawn from those tables.

From Table G–2		From Table G–4	
$i = 8\%, n = 0$	1.0000	$i = 8\%, n = 1$	1.0000
$i = 8\%, n = 1$	1.0800		
$i = 8\%, n = 2$	1.1664		
$i = 8\%, n = 3$	1.2597		
Total.	4.5061	$i = 8\%, n = 4$	4.5061

Minor differences in the results may sometimes occur but only because the numbers in the tables have been rounded.

Observe that in Table G–2, the future value is 1.0000 when $n = 0$. However, in Table G–4, the future value is 1.0000 when $n = 1$. Why is this true?

When $n = 0$ in Table G–2, the future value is determined on the same date as the single payment of 1 is made. The investment period over which interest is earned is zero ($n = 0$). However, Table G–4 is designed so that one payment is made each period. When $n = 2$, two payments are assumed, or when $n = 1$, one payment is assumed. And since future value is calculated as of the date of the last payment, future value = 1 when $n = 1$.

Table G–1
Present value of 1 due in *n* periods

Periods	1.0%	1.5%	3.0%	4.0%	8.0%	10.0%	12.0%	14.0%	16.0%	18.0%	20.0%
1	0.9901	0.9852	0.9709	0.9615	0.9259	0.9091	0.8929	0.8772	0.8621	0.8475	0.8333
2	0.9803	0.9707	0.9426	0.9246	0.8573	0.8264	0.7972	0.7695	0.7432	0.7182	0.6944
3	0.9706	0.9563	0.9151	0.8890	0.7938	0.7513	0.7118	0.6750	0.6407	0.6086	0.5787
4	0.9610	0.9422	0.8885	0.8548	0.7350	0.6830	0.6355	0.5921	0.5523	0.5158	0.4823
5	0.9515	0.9283	0.8626	0.8219	0.6806	0.6209	0.5674	0.5194	0.4761	0.4371	0.4019
6	0.9420	0.9145	0.8375	0.7903	0.6302	0.5645	0.5066	0.4556	0.4104	0.3704	0.3349
7	0.9327	0.9010	0.8131	0.7599	0.5835	0.5132	0.4523	0.3996	0.3538	0.3139	0.2791
8	0.9235	0.8877	0.7894	0.7307	0.5403	0.4665	0.4039	0.3506	0.3050	0.2660	0.2326
9	0.9143	0.8746	0.7664	0.7026	0.5002	0.4241	0.3606	0.3075	0.2630	0.2255	0.1938
10	0.9053	0.8617	0.7441	0.6756	0.4632	0.3855	0.3220	0.2697	0.2267	0.1911	0.1615
11	0.8963	0.8489	0.7224	0.6496	0.4289	0.3505	0.2875	0.2366	0.1954	0.1619	0.1346
12	0.8874	0.8364	0.7014	0.6246	0.3971	0.3186	0.2567	0.2076	0.1685	0.1372	0.1122
13	0.8787	0.8240	0.6810	0.6006	0.3677	0.2897	0.2292	0.1821	0.1452	0.1163	0.0935
14	0.8700	0.8118	0.6611	0.5775	0.3405	0.2633	0.2046	0.1597	0.1252	0.0985	0.0779
15	0.8613	0.7999	0.6419	0.5553	0.3152	0.2394	0.1827	0.1401	0.1079	0.0835	0.0649
16	0.8528	0.7880	0.6232	0.5339	0.2919	0.2176	0.1631	0.1229	0.0930	0.0708	0.0541
17	0.8444	0.7764	0.6050	0.5134	0.2703	0.1978	0.1456	0.1078	0.0802	0.0600	0.0451
18	0.8360	0.7649	0.5874	0.4936	0.2502	0.1799	0.1300	0.0946	0.0691	0.0508	0.0376
19	0.8277	0.7536	0.5703	0.4746	0.2317	0.1635	0.1161	0.0829	0.0596	0.0431	0.0313
20	0.8195	0.7425	0.5537	0.4564	0.2145	0.1486	0.1037	0.0728	0.0514	0.0365	0.0261
21	0.8114	0.7315	0.5375	0.4388	0.1987	0.1351	0.0926	0.0638	0.0443	0.0309	0.0217
22	0.8034	0.7207	0.5219	0.4220	0.1839	0.1228	0.0826	0.0560	0.0382	0.0262	0.0181
23	0.7954	0.7100	0.5067	0.4057	0.1703	0.1117	0.0738	0.0491	0.0329	0.0222	0.0151
24	0.7876	0.6995	0.4919	0.3901	0.1577	0.1015	0.0659	0.0431	0.0284	0.0188	0.0126
25	0.7798	0.6892	0.4776	0.3751	0.1460	0.0923	0.0588	0.0378	0.0245	0.0160	0.0105
26	0.7720	0.6790	0.4637	0.3607	0.1352	0.0839	0.0525	0.0331	0.0211	0.0135	0.0087
27	0.7644	0.6690	0.4502	0.3468	0.1252	0.0763	0.0469	0.0291	0.0182	0.0115	0.0073
28	0.7568	0.6591	0.4371	0.3335	0.1159	0.0693	0.0419	0.0255	0.0157	0.0097	0.0061
29	0.7493	0.6494	0.4243	0.3207	0.1073	0.0630	0.0374	0.0224	0.0135	0.0082	0.0051
30	0.7419	0.6398	0.4120	0.3083	0.0994	0.0573	0.0334	0.0196	0.0116	0.0070	0.0042
31	0.7346	0.6303	0.4000	0.2965	0.0920	0.0521	0.0298	0.0172	0.0100	0.0059	0.0035
32	0.7273	0.6210	0.3883	0.2851	0.0852	0.0474	0.0266	0.0151	0.0087	0.0050	0.0029
33	0.7201	0.6118	0.3770	0.2741	0.0789	0.0431	0.0238	0.0132	0.0075	0.0042	0.0024
34	0.7130	0.6028	0.3660	0.2636	0.0730	0.0391	0.0212	0.0116	0.0064	0.0036	0.0020
35	0.7059	0.5939	0.3554	0.2534	0.0676	0.0356	0.0189	0.0102	0.0055	0.0030	0.0017
36	0.6989	0.5851	0.3450	0.2437	0.0626	0.0323	0.0169	0.0089	0.0048	0.0026	0.0014
37	0.6920	0.5764	0.3350	0.2343	0.0580	0.0294	0.0151	0.0078	0.0041	0.0022	0.0012
38	0.6852	0.5679	0.3252	0.2253	0.0537	0.0267	0.0135	0.0069	0.0036	0.0019	0.0010
39	0.6784	0.5595	0.3158	0.2166	0.0497	0.0243	0.0120	0.0060	0.0031	0.0016	0.0008
40	0.6717	0.5513	0.3066	0.2083	0.0460	0.0221	0.0107	0.0053	0.0026	0.0013	0.0007
41	0.6650	0.5431	0.2976	0.2003	0.0426	0.0201	0.0096	0.0046	0.0023	0.0011	0.0006
42	0.6584	0.5351	0.2890	0.1926	0.0395	0.0183	0.0086	0.0041	0.0020	0.0010	0.0005
43	0.6519	0.5272	0.2805	0.1852	0.0365	0.0166	0.0076	0.0036	0.0017	0.0008	0.0004
44	0.6454	0.5194	0.2724	0.1780	0.0338	0.0151	0.0068	0.0031	0.0015	0.0007	0.0003
45	0.6391	0.5117	0.2644	0.1712	0.0313	0.0137	0.0061	0.0027	0.0013	0.0006	0.0003
46	0.6327	0.5042	0.2567	0.1646	0.0290	0.0125	0.0054	0.0024	0.0011	0.0005	0.0002
47	0.6265	0.4967	0.2493	0.1583	0.0269	0.0113	0.0049	0.0021	0.0009	0.0004	0.0002
48	0.6203	0.4894	0.2420	0.1522	0.0249	0.0103	0.0043	0.0019	0.0008	0.0004	0.0002
49	0.6141	0.4821	0.2350	0.1463	0.0230	0.0094	0.0039	0.0016	0.0007	0.0003	0.0001
50	0.6080	0.4750	0.2281	0.1407	0.0213	0.0085	0.0035	0.0014	0.0006	0.0003	0.0001

Table G–2
Future value of 1 due in *n* periods

Periods	1.0%	1.5%	3.0%	4.0%	8.0%	10.0%	12.0%	14.0%	16.0%	18.0%	20.0%
0	1.0000	1.0000	1.0000	1.0000	1.0000	1.0000	1.0000	1.0000	1.0000	1.0000	1.0000
1	1.0100	1.0150	1.0300	1.0400	1.0800	1.1000	1.1200	1.1400	1.1600	1.1800	1.2000
2	1.0201	1.0302	1.0609	1.0816	1.1664	1.2100	1.2544	1.2996	1.3456	1.3924	1.4400
3	1.0303	1.0457	1.0927	1.1249	1.2597	1.3310	1.4049	1.4815	1.5609	1.6430	1.7280
4	1.0406	1.0614	1.1255	1.1699	1.3605	1.4641	1.5735	1.6890	1.8106	1.9388	2.0736
5	1.0510	1.0773	1.1593	1.2167	1.4693	1.6105	1.7623	1.9254	2.1003	2.2878	2.4883
6	1.0615	1.0934	1.1941	1.2653	1.5869	1.7716	1.9738	2.1950	2.4364	2.6996	2.9860
7	1.0721	1.1098	1.2299	1.3159	1.7138	1.9487	2.2107	2.5023	2.8262	3.1855	3.5832
8	1.0829	1.1265	1.2668	1.3686	1.8509	2.1436	2.4760	2.8526	3.2784	3.7589	4.2998
9	1.0937	1.1434	1.3048	1.4233	1.9990	2.3579	2.7731	3.2519	3.8030	4.4355	5.1598
10	1.1046	1.1605	1.3439	1.4802	2.1589	2.5937	3.1058	3.7072	4.4114	5.2338	6.1917
11	1.1157	1.1779	1.3842	1.5395	2.3316	2.8531	3.4785	4.2262	5.1173	6.1759	7.4301
12	1.1264	1.1956	1.4258	1.6010	2.5182	3.1384	3.8960	4.8179	5.9360	7.2876	8.9161
13	1.1381	1.2136	1.4685	1.6651	2.7196	3.4523	4.3635	5.4924	6.8858	8.5994	10.6993
14	1.1495	1.2318	1.5126	1.7317	2.9372	3.7975	4.8871	6.2613	7.9875	10.1472	12.8392
15	1.1610	1.2502	1.5580	1.8009	3.1722	4.1772	5.4736	7.1379	9.2655	11.9737	15.4070
16	1.1726	1.2690	1.6047	1.8730	3.4259	4.5950	6.1304	8.1372	10.7480	14.1290	18.4884
17	1.1843	1.2880	1.6528	1.9479	3.7000	5.0545	6.8660	9.2765	12.4677	16.6722	22.1861
18	1.1961	1.3073	1.7024	2.0258	3.9960	5.5599	7.6900	10.5752	14.4625	19.6733	26.6233
19	1.2081	1.3270	1.7535	2.1068	4.3157	6.1159	8.6128	12.0557	16.7765	23.2144	31.9480
20	1.2202	1.3469	1.8061	2.1911	4.6610	6.7275	9.6463	13.7435	19.4608	27.3930	38.3376
21	1.2324	1.3671	1.8603	2.2788	5.0338	7.4002	10.8038	15.6676	22.5745	32.3238	46.0051
22	1.2447	1.3876	1.9161	2.3699	5.4365	8.1403	12.1003	17.8610	26.1864	38.1421	55.2061
23	1.2572	1.4084	1.9736	2.4647	5.8715	8.9543	13.5523	20.3616	30.3762	45.0076	66.2474
24	1.2697	1.4295	2.0328	2.5633	6.3412	9.8497	15.1786	23.2122	35.2364	53.1090	79.4968
25	1.2824	1.4509	2.0938	2.6658	6.8485	10.8347	17.0001	26.4619	40.8742	62.6686	95.3962
26	1.2953	1.4727	2.1566	2.7725	7.3964	11.9182	19.0401	30.1666	47.4141	73.9490	114.4755
27	1.3082	1.4948	2.2213	2.8834	7.9881	13.1100	21.3249	34.3899	55.0004	87.2598	137.3706
28	1.3213	1.5172	2.2879	2.9987	8.6271	14.4210	23.8839	39.2045	63.8004	102.9666	164.8447
29	1.3345	1.5400	2.3566	3.1187	9.3173	15.8631	26.7499	44.6931	74.0085	121.5005	197.8136
30	1.3478	1.5631	2.4273	3.2434	10.0627	17.4494	29.9599	50.9502	85.8499	143.3706	237.3763
31	1.3613	1.5865	2.5001	3.3731	10.8677	19.1943	33.5551	58.0832	99.5859	169.1774	284.8516
32	1.3749	1.6103	2.5751	3.5081	11.7371	21.1138	37.5817	66.2148	115.5196	199.6293	341.8219
33	1.3887	1.6345	2.6523	3.6484	12.6760	23.2252	42.0915	75.4849	134.0027	235.5625	410.1863
34	1.4026	1.6590	2.7319	3.7943	13.6901	25.5477	47.1425	86.0528	155.4432	277.9638	492.2235
35	1.4166	1.6839	2.8139	3.9461	14.7853	28.1024	52.7996	98.1002	180.3141	327.9973	590.6682
36	1.4308	1.7091	2.8983	4.1039	15.9682	30.9127	59.1356	111.8342	209.1643	387.0368	708.8019
37	1.4451	1.7348	2.9852	4.2681	17.2456	34.0039	66.2318	127.4910	242.6306	456.7034	850.5622
38	1.4595	1.7608	3.0748	4.4388	18.6253	37.4043	74.1797	145.3397	281.4515	528.9100	1020.6747
39	1.4741	1.7872	3.1670	4.6164	20.1153	41.1448	83.0812	165.6873	326.4838	635.9139	1224.8096
40	1.4889	1.8140	3.2620	4.8010	21.7245	45.2593	93.0510	188.8835	378.7212	750.3783	1469.7716
41	1.5083	1.8412	3.3599	4.9931	23.4625	49.7852	104.2171	215.3272	439.3165	885.4464	1763.7259
42	1.5188	1.8688	3.4607	5.1928	25.3395	54.7637	116.7231	245.4730	509.6072	1044.8268	2116.4711
43	1.5340	1.8969	3.5645	5.4005	27.3666	60.2401	130.7299	279.8392	591.1443	1232.8956	2539.7653
44	1.5493	1.9253	3.6715	5.6165	29.5560	66.2641	146.4175	319.0167	685.7274	1454.8168	3047.7183
45	1.5648	1.9542	3.7816	5.8412	31.9204	72.8905	163.9876	363.6791	795.4438	1716.6839	3657.2620
46	1.5805	1.9835	3.8950	6.0748	34.4741	80.1795	183.6661	414.5941	922.7148	2025.6870	4388.7144
47	1.5963	2.0133	4.0119	6.3178	37.2320	88.1975	205.7061	472.6373	1070.3492	2390.3106	5266.4573
48	1.6122	2.0435	4.1323	6.5705	40.2106	97.0172	230.3908	538.8065	1241.6051	2820.5665	6319.7487
49	1.6283	2.0741	4.2562	6.8333	43.4274	106.7190	258.0377	614.2395	1440.2619	3328.2685	7583.6985
50	1.6446	2.1052	4.3839	7.1067	46.9016	117.3909	289.0022	700.2330	1670.7038	3927.3569	9100.4382

Table G–3
Present value of an annuity of 1 per period

Periods	1.0%	1.5%	3.0%	4.0%	8.0%	10.0%	12.0%	14.0%	16.0%	18.0%	20.0%
1	0.9901	0.9852	0.9709	0.9615	0.9259	0.9091	0.8929	0.8772	0.8621	0.8475	0.8333
2	1.9704	1.9559	1.9135	1.8861	1.7833	1.7355	1.6901	1.6467	1.6052	1.5656	1.5278
3	2.9410	2.9122	2.8286	2.7751	2.5771	2.4869	2.4018	2.3216	2.2459	2.1743	2.1065
4	3.9020	3.8544	3.7171	3.6299	3.3121	3.1699	3.0373	2.9137	2.7982	2.6901	2.5887
5	4.8534	4.7826	4.5797	4.4518	3.9927	3.7908	3.6048	3.4331	3.2743	3.1272	2.9906
6	5.7955	5.6972	5.4172	5.2421	4.6229	4.3553	4.1114	3.8887	3.6847	3.4976	3.3255
7	6.7282	6.5982	6.2303	6.0021	5.2064	4.8684	4.5638	4.2883	4.0386	3.8115	3.6046
8	7.6517	7.4859	7.0197	6.7327	5.7466	5.3349	4.9676	4.6389	4.3436	4.0776	3.8372
9	8.5660	8.3605	7.7861	7.4353	6.2469	5.7590	5.3282	4.9464	4.6065	4.3030	4.0310
10	9.4713	9.2222	8.5302	8.1109	6.7101	6.1446	5.6502	5.2161	4.8332	4.4941	4.1925
11	10.3676	10.0711	9.2526	8.7605	7.1390	6.4951	5.9377	5.4527	5.0286	4.6560	4.3271
12	11.2551	10.9075	9.9540	9.3851	7.5361	6.8137	6.1944	5.6603	5.1971	4.7932	4.4392
13	12.1337	11.7315	10.6350	9.9856	7.9038	7.1034	6.4235	5.8424	5.3423	4.9095	4.5327
14	13.0037	12.5434	11.2961	10.5631	8.2442	7.3667	6.6282	6.0021	5.4675	5.0081	4.6106
15	13.8651	13.3432	11.9379	11.1184	8.5595	7.6061	6.8109	6.1422	5.5755	5.0916	4.6755
16	14.7179	14.1313	12.5611	11.6523	8.8514	7.8237	6.9740	6.2651	5.6685	5.1624	4.7296
17	15.5623	14.9076	13.1661	12.1657	9.1216	8.0216	7.1196	6.3729	5.7487	5.2223	4.7746
18	16.3983	15.6726	13.7535	12.6593	9.3719	8.2014	7.2497	6.4674	5.8178	5.2732	4.8122
19	17.2260	16.4262	14.3238	13.1339	9.6036	8.3649	7.3658	6.5504	5.8775	5.3162	4.8435
20	18.0456	17.1686	14.8775	13.5903	9.8181	8.5136	7.4694	6.6231	5.9288	5.3527	4.8696
21	18.8570	17.9001	15.4150	14.0292	10.0168	8.6487	7.5620	6.6870	5.9731	5.3837	4.8913
22	19.6604	18.6208	15.9369	14.4511	10.2007	8.7715	7.6446	6.7429	6.0113	5.4099	4.9094
23	20.4558	19.3309	16.4436	14.8568	10.3711	8.8832	7.7184	6.7921	6.0442	5.4321	4.9245
24	21.2434	20.0304	16.9355	15.2470	10.5288	8.9847	7.7843	6.8351	6.0726	5.4509	4.9371
25	22.0232	20.7196	17.4131	15.6221	10.6748	9.0770	7.8431	6.8729	6.0971	5.4669	4.9476
26	22.7952	21.3986	17.8768	15.9828	10.8100	9.1609	7.8957	6.9061	6.1182	5.4804	4.9563
27	23.5596	22.0676	18.3270	16.3296	10.9352	9.2372	7.9426	6.9352	6.1364	5.4919	4.9636
28	24.3164	22.7267	18.7641	16.6631	11.0511	9.3066	7.9844	6.9607	6.1520	5.5016	4.9697
29	25.0658	23.3761	19.1885	16.9837	11.1584	9.3696	8.0218	6.9830	6.1656	5.5098	4.9747
30	25.8077	24.0158	19.6004	17.2920	11.2578	9.4269	8.0552	7.0027	6.1772	5.5168	4.9789
31	26.5423	24.6461	20.0004	17.5885	11.3498	9.4790	8.0850	7.0199	6.1872	5.5227	4.9824
32	27.2696	25.2671	20.3888	17.8736	11.4350	9.5264	8.1116	7.0350	6.1959	5.5277	4.9854
33	27.9897	25.8790	20.7658	18.1476	11.5139	9.5694	8.1354	7.0482	6.2034	5.5320	4.9878
34	28.7027	26.4817	21.1318	18.4112	11.5869	9.6086	8.1566	7.0599	6.2098	5.5356	4.9898
35	29.4086	27.0756	21.4872	18.6646	11.6546	9.6442	8.1755	7.0700	6.2153	5.5386	4.9915
36	30.1075	27.6607	21.8323	18.9083	11.7172	9.6765	8.1924	7.0790	6.2201	5.5412	4.9929
37	30.7995	28.2371	22.1672	19.1426	11.7752	9.7059	8.2075	7.0868	6.2242	5.5434	4.9941
38	31.4847	28.8051	22.4925	19.3679	11.8289	9.7327	8.2210	7.0937	6.2278	5.5452	4.9951
39	32.1630	29.3646	22.8082	19.5845	11.8786	9.7570	8.2330	7.0997	6.2309	5.5468	4.9959
40	32.8347	29.9158	23.1148	19.7928	11.9246	9.7791	8.2438	7.1050	6.2335	5.5482	4.9966
41	33.4997	30.4590	23.4124	19.9931	11.9672	9.7991	8.2534	7.1097	6.2358	5.5493	4.9972
42	34.1581	30.9941	23.7014	20.1856	12.0067	9.8174	8.2619	7.1138	6.2377	5.5502	4.9976
43	34.8100	31.5212	23.9819	20.3708	12.0432	9.8340	8.2696	7.1173	6.2394	5.5510	4.9980
44	35.4555	32.0406	24.2543	20.5488	12.0771	9.8491	8.2764	7.1205	6.2409	5.5517	4.9984
45	36.0945	32.5523	24.5187	20.7200	12.1084	9.8628	8.2825	7.1232	6.2421	5.5523	4.9986
46	36.7272	33.0565	24.7754	20.8847	12.1374	9.8753	8.2880	7.1256	6.2432	5.5528	4.9989
47	37.3537	33.5532	25.0247	21.0429	12.1643	9.8866	8.2928	7.1277	6.2442	5.5532	4.9991
48	37.9740	34.0426	25.2667	21.1951	12.1891	9.8969	8.2972	7.1296	6.2450	5.5536	4.9992
49	38.5881	34.5247	25.5017	21.3415	12.2122	9.9063	8.3010	7.1312	6.2457	5.5539	4.9993
50	39.1961	34.9997	25.7298	21.4822	12.2335	9.9148	8.3045	7.1327	6.2463	5.5541	4.9995

Table G–4
Future value of an annuity of 1 per period

Periods	1.0%	1.5%	3.0%	4.0%	8.0%	10.0%	12.0%	14.0%	16.0%	18.0%	20.0%
1	1.0000	1.0000	1.0000	1.0000	1.0000	1.0000	1.0000	1.0000	1.0000	1.0000	1.0000
2	2.0100	2.0150	2.0300	2.0400	2.0800	2.1000	2.1200	2.1400	2.1600	2.1800	2.2000
3	3.0301	3.0452	3.0909	3.1216	3.2464	3.3100	3.3744	3.4396	3.5056	3.5724	3.6400
4	4.0604	4.0909	4.1836	4.2465	4.5061	4.6410	4.7793	4.9211	5.0665	5.2154	5.3680
5	5.1010	5.1523	5.3091	5.4163	5.8666	6.1051	6.3528	6.6101	6.8771	7.1542	7.4416
6	6.1520	6.2296	6.4684	6.6330	7.3359	7.7156	8.1152	8.5355	8.9775	9.4420	9.9299
7	7.2135	7.3230	7.6625	7.8983	8.9228	9.4872	10.0890	10.7305	11.4139	12.1415	12.9159
8	8.2857	8.4328	8.8923	9.2142	10.6366	11.4359	12.2997	13.2328	14.2401	15.3270	16.4991
9	9.3685	9.5593	10.1591	10.5828	12.4876	13.5795	14.7757	16.0853	17.5185	19.0859	20.7989
10	10.4622	10.7027	11.4639	12.0061	14.4866	15.9374	17.5487	19.3373	21.3215	23.5213	25.9587
11	11.5668	11.8633	12.8078	13.4864	16.6455	18.5312	20.6546	23.0445	25.7329	28.7551	32.1504
12	12.6825	13.0412	14.1920	15.0258	18.9771	21.3843	24.1331	27.2707	30.8502	34.9311	39.5805
13	13.8093	14.2368	15.6178	16.6268	21.4953	24.5227	28.0291	32.0887	36.7862	42.2187	48.4966
14	14.9474	15.4504	17.0863	18.2919	24.2149	27.9750	32.3926	37.5811	43.6720	50.8180	59.1959
15	16.0969	16.6821	18.5989	20.0236	27.1521	31.7725	37.2797	43.8424	51.6595	60.9653	72.0351
16	17.2579	17.9324	20.1569	21.8245	30.3243	35.9497	42.7533	50.9804	60.9250	72.9390	87.4421
17	18.4304	19.2014	21.7616	23.6975	33.7502	40.5447	48.8837	59.1176	71.6730	87.0680	105.9306
18	19.6147	20.4894	23.4144	25.6454	37.4502	45.5992	55.7497	68.3941	84.1407	103.7403	128.1167
19	20.8109	21.7967	25.1169	27.6712	41.4463	51.1591	63.4397	78.9692	98.6032	123.4135	154.7400
20	22.0190	23.1237	26.8704	29.7781	45.7620	57.2750	72.0524	91.0249	115.3797	146.6280	186.6880
21	23.2392	24.4705	28.6765	31.9692	50.4229	64.0025	81.6987	104.7684	134.8405	174.0210	225.0256
22	24.4716	25.8376	30.5368	34.2480	55.4568	71.4027	92.5026	120.4360	157.4150	206.3448	271.0307
23	25.7163	27.2251	32.4529	36.6179	60.8933	79.5430	104.6029	138.2970	183.6014	244.4868	326.2369
24	26.9735	28.6335	34.4265	39.0826	66.7648	88.4973	118.1552	158.6586	213.9776	289.4945	392.4842
25	28.2432	30.0630	36.4593	41.6459	73.1059	98.3471	133.3339	181.8708	249.2140	342.6035	471.9811
26	29.5256	31.5140	38.5530	44.3117	79.9544	109.1818	150.3339	208.3327	290.0883	405.2721	567.3773
27	30.8209	32.9867	40.7096	47.0842	87.3508	121.0999	169.3740	238.4993	337.5024	479.2211	681.8528
28	32.1291	34.4815	42.9309	49.9676	95.3388	134.2099	190.6989	272.8892	392.5028	566.4809	819.2233
29	33.4504	35.9987	45.2189	52.9663	103.9659	148.6309	214.5828	312.0937	456.3032	669.4475	984.0680
30	34.7849	37.5387	47.5754	56.0849	113.2832	164.4940	241.3327	356.7868	530.3117	790.9480	1181.8816
31	36.1327	39.1018	50.0027	59.3283	123.3459	181.9434	271.2926	407.7370	616.1616	934.3186	1419.2579
32	37.4941	40.6883	52.5028	62.7015	134.2135	201.1378	304.8477	465.8202	715.7475	1103.4960	1704.1095
33	38.8690	42.2986	55.0778	66.2095	145.9506	222.2515	342.4294	532.0350	831.2671	1303.1253	2045.9314
34	40.2577	43.9331	57.7302	69.8579	158.6267	245.4767	384.5210	607.5199	965.2698	1538.6878	2456.1176
35	41.6603	45.5921	60.4621	73.6522	172.3168	271.0244	431.6635	693.5727	1120.7130	1816.6516	2948.3411
36	43.0769	47.2760	63.2759	77.5983	187.1021	299.1268	484.4631	791.6729	1301.0270	2144.6489	3539.0094
37	44.5076	48.9851	66.1742	81.7022	203.0703	330.0395	543.5987	903.5071	1510.1914	2531.6857	4247.8112
38	45.9527	50.7199	69.1594	85.9703	220.3159	364.0434	609.8305	1030.9981	1752.8220	2988.3891	5098.3735
39	47.4123	52.4807	72.2342	90.4091	238.9412	401.4478	684.0102	1176.3378	2034.2735	3527.2992	6119.0482
40	48.8864	54.2679	75.4013	95.0255	259.0565	442.5926	767.0914	1342.0251	2360.7572	4163.2130	7343.8578
41	50.3752	56.0819	78.6633	99.8265	280.7810	487.8518	860.1424	1530.9086	2739.4784	4913.5914	8813.6294
42	51.8790	57.9231	82.0232	104.8196	304.2435	537.6370	964.3595	1746.2358	3178.7949	5799.0378	10577.3553
43	53.3978	59.7920	85.4839	110.0124	329.5830	592.4007	1081.0826	1991.7088	3688.4021	6843.8646	12693.8263
44	54.9318	61.6889	89.0484	115.4129	356.9496	652.6408	1211.8125	2271.5481	4279.5465	8076.7603	15233.5916
45	56.4811	63.6142	92.7199	121.0294	386.5056	718.9048	1358.2300	2590.5648	4965.2739	9531.5771	18281.3099
46	58.0459	65.5684	96.5015	126.8706	418.4261	791.7953	1522.2176	2954.2439	5760.71.77	11248.2610	21938.5719
47	59.6263	67.5519	100.3965	132.9454	452.9002	871.9749	1705.8838	3368.8380	6683.4326	13273.9480	26327.2863
48	61.2226	69.5652	104.4084	139.2632	490.1322	960.1723	1911.5898	3841.4753	7753.7818	15664.2586	31593.7436
49	62.8348	71.6087	108.5406	145.8337	530.3427	1057.1896	2141.9806	4380.2819	8995.3869	18484.8251	37913.4923
50	64.4632	73.6828	112.7969	152.6671	573.7702	1163.9085	2400.0182	4994.5213	10435.6488	21813.0937	45497.1908

Exercises

Exercise G–1
Present value of an amount
(L. O. 1)

Ferrara Company is considering an investment which if paid for immediately is expected to return $750,000 six years hence. If Ferrara Company demands an 18% return, how much will Ferrara Company be willing to pay for this investment?

Exercise G–2
Future value of an amount
(L. O. 2)

Sandala Company invested $77,500 in a project that is expected to earn a 12% rate of return. The earnings will be reinvested in the project each year until the entire investment is liquidated 20 years hence. What will be the cash proceeds when the project is liquidated?

Exercise G–3
Present value of an annuity
(L. O. 1)

Zavala Company is considering a contract that will return $8,000 annually at the end of each year for 22 years. If Zavala Company demands an annual return of 18% and pays for the investment immediately, how much should it be willing to pay?

Exercise G–4
Future value of an annuity
(L. O. 2)

Carol Thornton is planning to begin an individual retirement program in which she will invest $1,200 annually at the end of each year. Ms. Thornton plans to retire after making 35 annual investments in a program that earns a return of 8%. What will be the value of the program on the date of the last investment?

Exercise G–5
Interest rate on an investment
(L. O. 1)

Mr. Lee has been offered the possibility of investing $0.0160 for 25 years, after which he will be paid $1. What annual rate of interest will Mr. Lee earn? (Use Table G–1 to find the answer.)

Exercise G–6
Number of periods of an investment
(L. O. 1)

Ms. Collins has been offered the possibility of investing $0.0779. The investment will earn 20% per year and will at the end of the investment return Ms. Collins $1. How many years must Ms. Collins wait to receive the $1? (Use Table G–1 to find the answer.)

Exercise G–7
Number of periods of an investment
(L. O. 2)

Mr. Farabee expects to invest $1 at 16% and at the end of the investment receive $55.0004. How many years will elapse before Mr. Farabee receives the payment? (Use Table G–2 to find the answer.)

Exercise G–8
Interest rate on an investment
(L. O. 2)

Ms. O'Connell expects to invest $1 for 12 years, after which she will receive $3.8960. What rate of interest will Ms. O'Connell earn? (Use Table G–2 to find the answer.)

Exercise G–9
Interest rate on an investment
(L. O. 1)

Mr. Wainwright expects an immediate investment of $18.7641 to return $1 annually for 28 years, the first payment to be received in 1 year. What rate of interest will Mr. Wainwright earn? (Use Table G–3 to find the answer.)

Exercise G–10
Number of periods of an investment
(L. O. 1)

Ms. Kubacek expects an investment of $6.0726 to return $1 annually for several years. If Ms. Kubacek is to earn a return of 16%, how many annual payments must she receive? (Use Table G–3 to find the answer.)

Exercise G–11
Interest rate on an investment
(L. O. 2)

Mr. Gibbs expects to invest $1 annually for 40 years and have an accumulated value of $1342.0251 on the date of the last investment. If this occurs, what rate of interest will Mr. Gibbs earn? (Use Table G–4 to find the answer.)

Exercise G–12
Number of periods of an investment
(L. O. 2)

Ms. Evans expects to invest $1 annually in a fund that will earn 10%. How many annual investments must Ms. Evans make to accumulate $201.1378 on the date of the last investment? (Use Table G–4 to find the answer.)

Exercise G–13
Present value of an annuity
(L. O. 1)

Jan Michaels financed a new automobile by paying $1,000 cash and agreeing to make 48 monthly payments of $350 each, the first payment to be made one month after the purchase. The loan was said to bear interest at an annual rate of 12%. What was the cost of the automobile?

Exercise G–14
Future value of an amount
(L. O. 2)

Edward Locker deposited $12,000 in a savings account that earns interest at an annual rate of 12%, compounded quarterly. The $12,000 plus earned interest must remain in the account three years before it can be withdrawn. How much money will be in the account at the end of three years?

Exercise G–15
Future value of an annuity
(L. O. 2)

Liz Storey plans to have $250 withdrawn from her monthly paycheque and deposited in a savings account that earns 12% annually, compounded monthly. If Liz continues with her plan for four years, how much will be accumulated in the account on the date of the last deposit?

Exercise G–16
Present value of bonds
(L. O. 1)

Cameron Company plans to issue 10%, 20-year, $750,000 par value, bonds payable that pay interest semiannually on June 30 and December 31. The bonds are dated December 31, 1990, and are to be issued on that date. If the market rate of interest for the bonds is 8% on the date of issue, what will be the cash proceeds from the bond issue?

Exercise G–17
Future value of an amount
plus an annuity
(L. O. 2)

Pecan Street Company has decided to establish a fund that will be used seven years hence to replace an aging productive facility. The company makes an initial contribution of $120,000 to the fund and plans to make quarterly contributions of $30,000 beginning in three months. The fund is expected to earn 12%, compounded quarterly. What will be the value of the fund seven years hence?

Exercise G–18
Present value of an amount
(L. O. 1)

Jetson Company expects to earn 16% on an investment that will return $450,000, 10 years hence. Use Table G–2 to calculate the present value of the investment.

Exercise G–19
Future value of an amount
(L. O. 2)

J. B. Pharries Company invests $50,000 at 18% for five years. Use Table G–1 to calculate the future value of the investment, five years hence.

H The Accounting Problem of Changing Prices

For many years, accountants have discussed the problem of how to account for changing prices. Sometimes, when prices are changing rapidly, the discussion is heated and attempts are made to improve accounting practices. Other times, when prices are changing at a slower rate, the problem of accounting for price changes gets less attention. In any case, the fact that the prices paid for economic goods and services change over time presents a major problem in accounting. In studying this appendix, you will learn why price changes are a problem in accounting. You will also gain an introductory understanding of proposed ways of dealing with this problem.

Learning Objectives

After studying Appendix H, you should be able to:

1. Explain why conventional financial statements fail to adequately account for price changes.
2. Explain how price changes should be measured and how to construct a price index.
3. Restate historical cost/nominal dollar costs into constant purchasing power amounts and calculate purchasing power gains and losses.
4. Explain the difference between current costs and historical costs stated in constant purchasing power amounts.
5. Define or explain the words and phrases listed in the appendix Glossary.

**Conventional
Financial Statements
Fail to Account for
Price Changes**

Explain why conventional
financial statements fail to
adequately account for
price changes.
(L. O. 1)

All accountants agree that conventional financial statements provide useful information for making economic decisions. However, many accountants also agree that conventional financial statements fail to adequately account for the impact of changing prices. Sometimes, this failure of conventional financial statements makes the statements misleading. That is, the statements may imply certain facts that are inconsistent with the real state of affairs. As a result, the information in the statements may lead decision makers to make decisions that are inconsistent with their objectives.

Failure to Account for Price Changes on the Balance Sheet

In what ways do conventional financial statements fail to account for changing prices? The general problem is that transactions are recorded in terms of the historical number of dollars paid. These amounts are not adjusted even though subsequent price changes may dramatically change the value of the purchased items. For example, Old Company purchased 10 acres of land for $25,000. Then, at the end of each accounting period, Old Company presented a balance sheet showing "Land, $25,000." Six years later, after price increases of 97%, New Company purchased 10 acres of land that was next to and nearly identical to Old Company's land. New Company paid $49,250 for the land. In comparing the conventional balance sheets of the two companies, you would see the following balances:

	Balance Sheets	
	Old Company	New Company
Land	$25,000	$49,250

Without knowing the details that led to these balances, a statement reader is likely to conclude that New Company either has more land than does Old Company or that New Company's land is more valuable. But, both companies own 10 acres that are of equal value. The entire difference between the prices paid by the two companies is explained by the 97% price increase between the two purchase dates. That is, $25,000 \times 1.97 = $49,250$.

Failure to Account for Price Changes on the Income Statement

The failure of conventional financial statements to adequately account for changing prices also shows up in the income statement. For example, assume that in the above example, machines were purchased instead of land. Also, assume that the machines of Old Company and New Company are identical except for age; both are being depreciated on a straight-line basis over a 10-year period with no salvage value. As a result, the annual income statements of the two companies show the following:

	Income Statements	
	Old Company	New Company
Depreciation expense, machinery	$2,500	$4,925

Although assets of equal value are being depreciated, the income statements show depreciation expense for New Company that is 97% higher than Old Company's. This is inconsistent with the fact that both companies own the same machines that are affected by the same depreciation factors. Furthermore, although Old Company will appear more profitable, it must pay more income taxes due to the apparent extra profits. Also, Old Company may not recover the full replacement cost of its machinery through the sale of its product.

Understanding Price-Level Changes

Explain how price changes should be measured and how to contruct a price index.
(L. O. 2)

In one way or another, all of us have experienced the effects of **inflation,** which is a general increase in the prices paid for goods and services. A general decrease in prices is called **deflation.** Of course, the prices of specific items do not all change at the same rate. Even when most prices are rising, the prices of some goods or services may be falling. For example, consider the following prices of four different items:

Item	Price/Unit in 1990	Price/Unit in 1989	Percentage Change
A.	$1.30	$1.00	+30
B.	2.20	2.00	+10
C.	1.80	1.50	+20
D.	2.70	3.00	−10
Totals	$8.00	$7.50	

The Problem of Describing Price Changes. How should you describe these price changes? One possibility is to state the percentage change in the price per unit of each item (see above). This information is useful for some purposes. But, it does not show the average effect or impact of the price changes.

The Average Change in Unit Prices. A better indication of the average effect would be to determine the average increase in the per unit prices of the four items. Thus: ($8.00 − $7.50) ÷ $7.50 = 6.7% average increase in per unit prices.[1] However, even this average probably fails to show the impact of the price changes on most individuals or businesses. It is a good indicator only if the typical buyer purchased an equal number of units of each item.

The Weighted-Average Change in Prices. What if the four items usually are purchased in unequal amounts? For example, assume that for each unit of A purchased, 2 units of B, 5 units of C, and 1 unit of D are purchased. When the items are purchased in unequal amounts, the impact of changing prices depends on the typical quantity of each item purchased. Hence, the average

---

[1] Throughout this appendix, only final answers are rounded. Percentages or index numbers are rounded to the nearest 1/10% and dollar amounts to the nearest whole dollar.

change in the price of the A, B, C, D "market basket" is calculated as follows:

Item	Units Purchased	1989 Prices		Units Purchased	1990 Prices	
A.	1 unit	$1.00	= $ 1.00	1 unit	$1.30	= $ 1.30
B.	2 units	$2.00	= 4.00	2 units	$2.20	= 4.40
C.	5 units	$1.50	= 7.50	5 units	$1.80	= 9.00
D.	1 unit	$3.00	= 3.00	1 unit	$2.70	= 2.70
Totals			$15.50			$17.40

Weighted-average price change = ($17.40 − $15.50) ÷ $15.50 = 12.3%

Based on this calculation, you can say that the annual rate of inflation in the prices of these four items was 12.3%. However, not every individual and business will purchase these four items in exactly the same proportion of 1 unit of A, 2 units of B, 5 units of C, and 1 unit of D. As a result, the stated inflation rate only approximates the impact of price changes on each buyer. But if these proportions represent the typical buying pattern, the stated 12.3% inflation rate fairly reflects the inflationary impact on the average buyer.

Construction of a Price Index

When the cost of purchasing a given market basket is determined for each of several periods, you can express the results as a **price index.** In constructing a price index, one year is arbitrarily selected as the "base" year. The cost of purchasing the market basket in that year is then assigned a value of 100. For example, suppose the cost of purchasing the A, B, C, D market basket in each year is:

1984	$ 9.00
1985	11.00
1986	10.25
1987	12.00
1988	13.00
1989	15.50
1990	17.40

If you select 1987 as the base year, the $12 cost for 1987 is assigned a value of 100. Then, an index number for each of the other years is calculated and expressed as a percent of the base year's cost. For example, the index number for 1986 is 85.4 or ($10.25 ÷ $12.00 × 100 = 85.4). The index numbers for the remaining years are calculated in the same way. Illustration H–1 presents the entire price index for the years 1984 through 1990.

With this price index for the A, B, C, D market basket, you can make comparative statements about the cost of purchasing these items in various years. For example, you can say that the price level in 1990 was 45.0% (145 ÷ 100) higher than it was in 1987; the price level in 1990 was 33.9% (145 ÷ 108.3) higher than it was in 1988; and 12.2% (145 ÷ 129.2) higher than it was in 1989. Stated another way, $1 in 1990 would purchase the same amount of A, B, C, D as would $0.52 in 1984 (75 ÷ 145 = 0.51724).

Illustration H–1
Constructing a price index

Year	Calculation of Price Level		Price Index
1984 . .	($ 9.00 ÷ $12.00) × 100	=	75.0
1985 . .	($11.00 ÷ $12.00) × 100	=	91.7
1986 . .	($10.25 ÷ $12.00) × 100	=	85.4
1987 . .	($12.00 ÷ $12.00) × 100	=	100.0
1988 . .	($13.00 ÷ $12.00) × 100	=	108.3
1989 . .	($15.50 ÷ $12.00) × 100	=	129.2
1990 . .	($17.40 ÷ $12.00) × 100	=	145.0

Specific versus General Price-Level Indexes

Price changes and price-level indexes can be calculated for narrow groups of commodities or services, such as housing construction material costs; or for broader groups of items, such as all construction costs; or for very broad groups of items, such as all items produced in the economy. A **specific price-level index**, such as for housing construction materials, indicates the changing purchasing power of a dollar spent for items in that specific category; that is, to pay for housing construction materials. A **general price-level index**, such as the Consumer Price Index, indicates the changing purchasing power of a dollar spent for a very broad range of items.

Using Price Index Numbers in Accounting

In accounting, one way general price indexes are used is to restate dollar amounts of cost that were paid in earlier years into the current price level. In other words, a specific dollar amount of cost in a previous year can be restated in terms of the comparable number of dollars that would have been incurred if the cost had been paid with dollars that have the current amount of purchasing power.

For example, suppose that in 1986, $1,000 was paid to purchase items A, B, C, D. Stated in terms of 1990 prices, that 1986 cost is $1,000 × (145 ÷ 85.4) = $1,698. Also, if $1,500 were paid for A, B, C, D in 1987, that 1987 cost restated in terms of 1990 prices, is $1,500 × (145 ÷ 100) = $2,175.

Note that the 1987 cost of $1,500 correctly states the number of monetary units (dollars) expended for items A, B, C, D in 1987. Also, the 1986 cost of $1,000 correctly states the units of money expended in 1986. However, in a very important way, the 1986 monetary units do not mean the same thing as the 1987 monetary units. A dollar (one monetary unit) in 1986 represented a different amount of purchasing power than a dollar in 1987. Both of these dollars represent different amounts of purchasing power than a dollar in 1990.

To communicate the amount of purchasing power expended or incurred, the historical number of monetary units must be restated in terms of dollars with the same amount of purchasing power. For example, the total amount of cost incurred during 1986 and 1987 could be stated in terms of the purchasing power of 1987 dollars, or stated in terms of the purchasing power of 1990 dollars. These calculations are presented in Illustration H–2.

Illustration H–2
Expressing costs in constant dollars

Year Cost Was Incurred	Monetary Units Expended (a)	Price Index Factor for Adjustment to 1987 Dollars (b)	Historical Cost Stated in 1987 Dollars (a × b = c)	Price Index Factor for Adjustment to 1990 Dollars (d)	Historical Cost Stated in 1990 Dollars (c × d)
1986	$1,000	100 ÷ 85.4 = 1.17096	$1,171	145 ÷ 100 = 1.45000	$1,698*
1987	1,500	—	1,500	145 ÷ 100 = 1.45000	2,175
Total cost . . .	$2,500		$2,671		$3,873

*An alternative calculation is $1,000 × (145 ÷ 85.4) = $1,698.

Accounting Systems that Make Adjustments for Price Changes

There are at least two important accounting systems that use price indexes to develop comprehensive financial statements. Both are alternatives to the conventional accounting system used in Canada. One alternative, called **current cost accounting**, is discussed later in the appendix. Current cost accounting uses specific price-level indexes (along with appraisals and other means) to develop statements that report assets and expenses in terms of the current costs to acquire those assets or services. The other alternative is called **historical cost/constant purchasing power accounting**

Historical Cost/ Constant Purchasing Power Accounting

Restate historical cost/ nominal dollar costs into constant purchasing power amounts and calculate purchasing power gains and losses.
(L. O. 3)

Conventional financial statements disclose revenues, expenses, assets, liabilities, and owners' equity in terms of the historical monetary units exchanged when the transactions occurred. As such, they are sometimes called **historical cost/nominal dollar financial statements.** This emphasizes the difference between conventional statements and historical cost/constant purchasing power statements. Historical cost/constant purchasing power accounting uses a general price index to restate the conventional financial statements into dollar amounts that represent current, general purchasing power.

You should understand that the same principles for determining depreciation expense, cost of goods sold, accruals of revenue, and so forth, apply to both historical cost/nominal dollar statements and historical cost/constant purchasing power statements. The same generally accepted accounting principles apply to both. The only difference between the two is that constant purchasing power statements reflect adjustments for general price-level changes; nominal dollar statements do not.

The Impact of General Price Changes on Assets

Monetary Assets. The effect of general price-level changes on investments in assets depends on the nature of the assets. Some assets, called **monetary assets,** represent money or claims to receive a fixed amount of money. The number of dollars owned or to be received does not change even though the purchasing power of the dollar may change. Examples of monetary assets are cash, accounts receivable, notes receivable, and investments in bonds.

Because the amount of money that will be received from a monetary asset is fixed, a monetary asset is not adjusted for general price-level changes on a historical cost/constant purchasing power balance sheet. For example, assume that $800 in cash was owned at the end of 1990. Regardless of how the price level has changed since the cash was acquired, the amount to be reported on the December 31, 1990, historical cost/constant purchasing power balance sheet is $800.

Purchasing Power Gains or Losses Result from Owning Monetary Assets. Because the amount of money that will be received from monetary assets does not change with price-level changes, there is a special risk associated with owning these assets. An investment in monetary assets held during a period of inflation results in a loss of purchasing power. During a period of deflation, an investment in monetary assets results in a gain of purchasing power.

For example, assume that the $800 cash balance on December 31, 1990, resulted from the following:

Cash balance, December 31, 1989	$ 200
Cash receipts, assumed to have been received uniformly throughout the year	1,500
Cash disbursements, assumed to have been made uniformly throughout the year	(900)
Cash balance, December 31, 1990	$ 800

Also assume that the general price index was 150.0 at the end of 1989; that it averaged 160.0 throughout 1990; and was 168.0 at the end of that year. In this example, the beginning cash balance of $200 and the net receipts less disbursements of $600 lost purchasing power as the price level rose during 1990. This reduction in purchasing power is a loss. To calculate the loss during the year, the beginning cash balance and each receipt or disbursement is adjusted for price changes to the end of the year. Then, the adjusted balance is compared with the actual balance to determine the loss.

The amount of the loss is calculated as follows:

	Nominal Dollar Amounts	Price Index Factor for Restatement to December 31, 1990	Restated to December 31, 1990	Gain or (Loss)
Beginning balance	$ 200	168.0 ÷ 150.0 = 1.12000	$ 224	
Receipts.	1,500	168.0 ÷ 160.0 = 1.05000	1,575	
Disbursements	(900)	168.0 ÷ 160.0 = 1.05000	(945)	
Ending balance, adjusted .			$ 854	
Ending balance, actual .	$ 800		(800)	
Purchasing power loss . .				$(54)

In the above calculation, note that the receipts and disbursements are adjusted from the *average* price level during the year (*160.0*) to the ending price level (168.0). Because the receipts and disbursements were assumed to have occurred uniformly throughout the year, the average price level is used to approximate the price level at the time each receipt and disbursement took place. If receipts and disbursements do not occur uniformly, then each receipt and each disbursement must be adjusted separately from the price index at the time of the receipt or disbursement to the price index at year-end.

Nonmonetary Assets. Assets that have fluctuating prices are called **nonmonetary assets.** In other words, nonmonetary assets include all assets other than monetary assets. The prices at which nonmonetary assets may be bought and sold tend to increase or decrease over time as the general price level increases or decreases. Therefore, as the general price level changes, investments in nonmonetary assets tend to retain the amounts of purchasing power originally invested. As a result, on historical cost/constant purchasing power balance sheets, nonmonetary assets are adjusted to reflect changes in the price level that occurred since the nonmonetary assets were acquired.

For example, assume that $500 was invested in land (a nonmonetary asset) at the end of 1982 and the investment was held throughout 1990. During this time, the general price index increased from 96.0 to 168.0. The historical cost/constant purchasing power balance sheets would disclose the following amounts:

Asset	December 31, 1982 Historical Cost/Constant Purchasing Power Balance Sheet (a)	Price Index Factor for Adjustment to December 31, 1990 (b)	December 31, 1990 Historical Cost/Constant Purchasing Power Balance Sheet (a × b)
Land	$500	168.0 ÷ 96.0 = 1.75000	$875

The $875 shown as the investment in land at the end of 1990 has the same amount of general purchasing power as did $500 at the end of 1982. Thus, no change in general purchasing power is recognized from holding the land.

The Impact of General Price Changes on Liabilities and Shareholders' Equity

The effect of general price-level changes on liabilities depends on the nature of the liability. Most liabilities are monetary items, but shareholders' equity and a few liabilities are nonmonetary items.[2]

Monetary Liabilities. Obligations that are fixed in terms of the amount owed are called **monetary liabilities.** The number of dollars to be paid does not change regardless of changes in the general price level. Since the amount of mone-

_____

[2] Depending on its nature, preferred stock may be treated as a monetary item. If so, it is an exception to the general rule that shareholders' equity items are nonmonetary items.

tary liabilities owed does not change when price levels change, monetary liabilities are not adjusted for price-level changes.

Purchasing Power Gains and Losses Result from Owing Monetary Liabilities. A company with monetary liabilities outstanding during a period of general price-level change experiences a **purchasing power gain or loss.** Assume, for example, that a note payable for $300 was outstanding on December 31, 1989, when the price index was 150.0. On April 5, 1990, when the price index was 157.0, a $700 increase in the note resulted in a $1,000 balance that remained outstanding throughout the rest of 1990. On December 31, 1990, the price index was 168.0. On the historical cost/constant purchasing power balance sheet for December 31, 1990, the note payable is reported at $1,000. The purchasing power gain or loss during 1990 is calculated as follows:

	Nominal Dollar Amounts	Price Index Factor for Restatement to December 31, 1990	Restated to December 31, 1990	Gain or (Loss)
Beginning balance	$ 300	168.0 ÷ 150.0 = 1.12000	$ 336	
April 5 increase.	700	168.0 ÷ 157.0 = 1.07006	749	
Ending balance, adjusted . .			$ 1,085	
Ending balance, actual. . . .	$1,000		(1,000)	
Purchasing power gain. . . .				$85

Stated in terms of general purchasing power at year-end, the amount borrowed was $1,085. Since the company can pay the note with $1,000, the $85 difference is a gain in general purchasing power earned by the firm. On the other hand, if the general price index had decreased during 1990, the monetary liability would have resulted in a general purchasing power loss.

To determine a company's total purchasing power gain or loss during a year, the accountant must analyze each monetary asset and each monetary liability. The final gain or loss is then described as *the purchasing power gain (or loss) on net monetary items owned or owed.*

Nonmonetary Liabilities and Shareholders' Equity. Obligations that are not fixed in amount are called **nonmonetary liabilities.** The amount needed to satisfy a nonmonetary liability tends to change with changes in the general price level. For example, product warranties may require that a manufacturer pay for repairs and replacements for a specified period of time after the product is sold. The amount of money required to make the repairs or replacements tends to change with changes in the general price level. As a result, there is no purchasing power gain or loss associated with such warranties. Further, the historical cost/constant purchasing power balance sheet amount of such a nonmonetary liability must be adjusted to reflect changes in the general price index that occur after the liability comes into existence. Shareholders' equity items, with the possible exception of preferred stock, are also nonmonetary items. Hence, they also must be adjusted for changes in the general price index.

Illustration H–3
The effect of price changes on monetary and nonmonetary items

Financial Statement Item	When the General Price Level Rises (inflation)		When the General Price Level Falls (deflation)	
	Balance Sheet Adjustment Required	Income Statement Gain or Loss	Balance Sheet Adjustment Required	Income Statement Gain or Loss
Monetary assets	No	Loss	No	Gain
Nonmonetary assets	Yes	None	Yes	None
Monetary liabilities	No	Gain	No	Loss
Nonmonetary equities and liabilities	Yes	None	Yes	None

Illustration H–3 summarizes the impact of general price-level changes on monetary and nonmonetary items. The illustration shows the adjustments made to prepare a historical cost/constant purchasing power balance sheet. It also shows what purchasing power gains and losses are recognized on a constant purchasing power income statement.

Historical Cost/ Constant Purchasing Power Accounting Fails to Report Current Values

As we said before, prices do not all change at the same rate. In fact, when the general price level is rising, some specific prices may be falling. If this were not so, if prices all changed at the same rate, then historical cost/constant purchasing power accounting would report current values on the financial statements.

For example, suppose that a company purchased land for $50,000 on January 1, 1989, when the general price index was 130.0. Then the price level increased until December 1990, when the price index was 168.0. A historical cost/constant purchasing power balance sheet for this company on December 31, 1990, would report the land at $50,000 × $64,615. If all prices increased at the same rate during that period, the price of the land would have increased from $50,000 to $64,615, and the company's historical cost/constant purchasing power balance sheet would coincidentally disclose the land at its current value.

However, since all prices do not change at the same rate, the current value of the land may differ substantially from the historical cost/constant dollar amount of $64,615. For example, assume that the company had the land appraised and determined that its current value on December 31, 1990, was $80,000. The difference between the original purchase price of $50,000 and the current value of $80,000 is explained as follows:

Unrealized holding gain	$80,000 − $64,615 =	$15,385
Adjustment for general price-level increase . .	$64,615 − $50,000 =	14,615
		$30,000

In that case, the historical cost/constant purchasing power balance sheet would report land at $64,615, which is $15,385 ($80,000 − $64,615) less than its current value. This illustrates an important fact about historical cost/constant purchasing power accounting; it does not attempt to report current value. Rather, historical cost/constant purchasing power accounting restates original transaction prices into equivalent amounts of current, *general* purchasing power. Only if current, *specific* purchasing power were the basis of valuation would the balance sheet display current values.

Current Cost Accounting

Explain the difference between current costs and historical costs stated in constant purchasing power amounts.
(L. O. 4)

Current Costs on the Income Statement

When the **current cost** approach to accounting is used, the reported amount of each expense is the number of dollars that would be required, at the time the expense was incurred, to acquire the resources consumed. For example, assume that the annual sales of a company included an item that was sold in May for $1,500. The item had been acquired on January 1 for $500. Also, suppose that in May, at the time of the sale, the cost to replace this item was $700. Then, the annual current cost income statement would show sales of $1,500 less cost of goods sold of $700. In other words, when an asset is acquired and then held for a time before it expires, the historical cost of the asset usually is different from its current cost at the time it expires. *Current cost accounting* measures the reported amount of expense at the time the asset expires.

The result of measuring expenses in terms of current costs is that revenue is matched with the current (at the time of the sale) cost of the resources that were used to earn the revenue. Thus, operating profit is not greater than zero unless revenues are large enough to replace all of the resources that were consumed in the process of producing those revenues. Therefore, the operating profit figure is an important (and improved) basis for evaluating the effectiveness of operating activities.

Current Costs on the Balance Sheet

On the balance sheet, current cost accounting reports assets at the amounts that would have to be paid to purchase them as of the balance sheet date. Liabilities are reported at the amounts that would have to be paid to satisfy the liabilities as of the balance sheet date. Note that this valuation basis is similar to historical cost/constant purchasing power accounting in that a distinction exists between monetary and nonmonetary assets and liabilities. Monetary assets and liabilities are fixed in amount regardless of price changes. Therefore, monetary assets are not adjusted for price changes. But all of the nonmonetary items must be evaluated at each balance sheet date to determine the best estimate of current cost.

For a moment, think about the large variety of assets reported on balance sheets. Given that there are so many different kinds of assets, you should not be surprised that accountants have difficulty obtaining reliable estimates of current costs. In some cases, specific price indexes provide the most reliable source of current cost information. In other cases, where an asset is not new and has been partially depreciated, its current cost may be estimated by determining the cost to acquire a similar but new asset. Depreciation on the old asset is then based on the current cost of the new asset. Clearly, the accountant's professional judgment is an important factor in developing current cost data.

Disclosing the Effects of Changing Prices

At the present time, the CICA encourages but does not require companies to disclose information about the effects of changing prices. Some of the items recommended for disclosure include:

a. Income from continuing operations on a current cost basis.

b. Purchasing power gain or loss on net monetary items.

c. The current cost or lower recoverable amount of inventory and property, plant, and equipment, net of inflation.

d. Cost of goods sold, depreciation, depletion, and amortization expense on the basis of current cost or lower recoverable amounts of the assets involved.

e. Explanations of the information disclosed.[3]

Summary of the Appendix in Terms of Learning Objectives

1. Conventional financial statements report transactions in terms of the historical number of dollars received or paid. Therefore, the statements are not adjusted to reflect general price-level changes or changes in the specific prices of the items reported.

2. To measure the effect of price changes for a group of items, you should estimate the relative quantities sold of the items in the market basket. Then, you calculate the total price of the entire market basket in each period. A price index expresses the market basket's price each period as a percentage of the price in a base period.

3. To restate a historical cost/nominal dollar cost in constant purchasing power terms, you multiply the nominal dollar cost by a factor that represents the change in the general price level since the cost was incurred. On the balance sheet, monetary assets and liabilities should not be adjusted for changes in prices. However, purchasing power gains or losses result from holding monetary assets and owing monetary liabilities during a period of general price changes.

4. Historical costs stated in constant purchasing power amounts are adjusted for changes in the general price level since the costs were incurred. By comparison, current costs on the balance sheet are the dollar amounts that would be required to purchase the assets at the balance sheet date. On the income statement, current costs are the dollar amounts that would be necessary to acquire the consumed assets on the date they were consumed.

---

[3] *CICA Handbook,* Section 4510.

Glossary

Define or explain the words and phrases listed in the appendix Glossary. (L. O. 5)

Current cost in general, the cost that would be required to acquire (or replace) an asset or service at the present time. On the income statement, the numbers of dollars that would be required, at the time the expense is incurred, to acquire the resources consumed. On the balance sheet, the amounts that would have to be paid to replace the assets or satisfy the liabilities as of the balance sheet date. p. 1264

Current cost accounting an accounting system that uses specific price-level indexes (and other means) to develop financial statements that report items such as assets and expenses in terms of the costs to acquire or replace those assets or services at the present time. p. 1259

Deflation a general decrease in the prices paid for goods and services. p. 1256

General price-level index a measure of the changing purchasing power of a dollar, spent for a very broad range of items; for example, the Consumer Price Index. p. 1258

Historical cost/constant purchasing power accounting an accounting system that adjusts historical cost/nominal dollar financial statements for changes in the general purchasing power of the dollar. p. 1259

Historical cost/nominal dollar financial statements conventional financial statements that disclose revenues, expenses, assets, liabilities, and owners' equity in terms of the historical monetary units exchanged at the time the transactions occurred. p. 1259

Inflation a general increase in the prices paid for goods and services. p. 1256

Monetary assets money or claims to receive a fixed amount of money; the number of dollars to be received does not change regardless of changes in the purchasing power of the dollar. p. 1259

Monetary liabilities fixed amounts that are owed; the number of dollars to be paid does not change regardless of changes in the general price level. p. 1261

Nonmonetary assets assets that are not claims to a fixed number of monetary units, the prices of which therefore tend to fluctuate with changes in the general price level. p. 1261

Nonmonetary liabilities obligations that are not fixed in terms of the number of monetary units needed to satisfy them, and that therefore tend to fluctuate in amount with changes in the general price level. p. 1262

Price index a measure of the changes in prices of a particular market basket of goods and/or services. p. 1257

Purchasing power gain or loss the gain or loss that results from holding monetary assets and/or owing monetary liabilities during a period in which the general price level changes. p. 1262

Specific price-level index an indicator of the changing purchasing power of a dollar spent for items in a category of items that includes a much narrower range of goods and services than does a general price index. p. 1258

Questions for Class Discussion

1. Some people argue that conventional financial statements fail to adequately account for inflation. What is the general problem with conventional financial statements that generates this argument?

2. During a period of inflation, is it possible for the prices of specific items to fall? Why or why not?

3. Explain the difference between an *average* change in per unit prices and a *weighted-average* change in per unit prices.

4. What is the significance of the base year in constructing a price index? How is the base year chosen?

5. What is the difference between a specific price index and a general price index?

6. What is the fundamental difference in the price-level adjustments made under current cost accounting and under historical cost/constant purchasing power accounting?

7. What are historical cost/nominal dollar financial statements?

8. What is the difference between monetary assets and nonmonetary assets?

9. What is the difference between monetary liabilities and nonmonetary liabilities? Give examples of both.

10. If the monetary assets held by a firm exceed its monetary liabilities throughout a period in which prices are rising, which results: a purchasing power gain or loss? What if monetary liabilities exceed monetary assets during a period in which prices are falling?

11. If accountants preferred to display current values in the financial statements, would they use historical cost/constant purchasing power accounting or current cost accounting?

12. Describe the meaning of *operating profit* under a current cost accounting system.

13. "The distinction between monetary assets and nonmonetary assets is just as important for current cost accounting as it is for historical cost/constant purchasing power accounting." Is this statement true? Why?

14. What are some of the items the CICA recommends for disclosure concerning the effects of price changes?

Exercises

Exercise H–1
Calculating inflation rates
(L. O. 2)

Market basket No. 1 consists of 2 units of A, 5 units of B, and 1 unit of D. Market basket No. 2 consists of 3 units of B, 4 units of C, and 2 units of D. The per unit prices of each item during 1990 and during 1991 were as follows:

Item	1990 Price per Unit	1991 Price per Unit
A ..	$3.00	$2.60
B ..	5.00	5.40
C ..	6.00	7.00
D ..	2.00	1.80

Required

Compute the annual rate of inflation for market basket No. 1 and for market basket No. 2. (Round your answers to the nearest 1/10%.)

Exercise H–2
Constructing a price index
(L. O. 2)

The following total prices of a specified market basket were calculated for each of the years 1987 through 1991:

Year	Total Price
1987 . .	$20,300
1988 . .	30,400
1989 . .	35,800
1990 . .	40,500
1991 . .	50,100

Required

1. Using 1989 as the base year, prepare a price index for the five-year period. (Round your answers to the nearest 1/10%.)
2. Convert the index from a 1989 base year to a 1991 base year.

Exercise H–3
Adjusting costs for historical cost/constant purchasing power statements
(L. O. 3)

A company's plant and equipment consisted of land purchased in late 1985 for $350,000, a building purchased in late 1987 for $470,000, and equipment purchased in late 1989 for $85,000. The general price index for December of the years 1985 through 1991 is as follows:

1985	100.0
1986	110.0
1987	120.0
1988	122.0
1989	125.0
1990	150.0
1991	160.5

Required

1. Assuming the above price index adequately represents end-of-year price levels, calculate the amount of each cost that would be shown on a historical cost/constant purchasing power balance sheet for (a) December 31, 1990, and (b) December 31, 1991. Ignore any accumulated depreciation.
2. Would the historical cost/constant purchasing power income statement for 1991 disclose any purchasing power gain or loss as a consequence of holding the above assets? If so, how much?

Exercise H–4
Classifying monetary and nonmonetary items
(L. O. 3)

Determine whether the following items are monetary or nonmonetary items.

1. Common stock.
2. Retained earnings.
3. Merchandise.
4. Prepaid rent.
5. Prepaid insurance.
6. Salaries payable.
7. Goodwill.

8. Furniture and fixtures.
9. Accounts payable.
10. Product warranties liability.
11. Trademarks.
12. Savings accounts.
13. Notes receivable.

Exercise H–5
Calculating amounts for current cost statements
(L. O. 4)

A company made the following purchases of land: in 1988 at a cost of $60,000, and in 1989 at a cost of $35,000. What is the current cost of the land purchases in (*a*) 1990 and (*b*) 1991, given the following specific price index for land costs? (Round your answers to the nearest whole dollar.)

1988	80.0
1989	100.0
1990	95.0
1991	110.0

Exercise H–6
Calculating general purchasing power gain or loss
(L. O. 3)

Calculate the general purchasing power gain or loss in 1991 given the following information:

Time Period	Price Index
December 1990	125.0
Average during 1991	135.0
December 1991	162.0

a. The cash balance on December 31, 1990, was $2,500. During 1991, cash sales occurred uniformly throughout the year and amounted to $20,500. Payments of expenses also occurred evenly throughout the year and amounted to $15,500. Accounts payable of $5,200 were paid in December.

b. Accounts payable amounted to $3,000 on December 31, 1990. Additional accounts payable amounting to $4,600 were recorded evenly throughout 1991. The only payment of accounts during the year was $5,200 in late December.

Problems

Problem H–1
Constructing and using a price index
(L. O. 2)

The costs of purchasing a common "market basket" in each of several years are as follows:

Year	Cost of Market Basket
1984 . .	$ 75,000
1985 . .	82,500
1986 . .	87,700
1987 . .	96,400
1988 . .	108,400
1989 . .	105,700
1990 . .	113,300
1991 . .	127,100

Required

1. Construct a price index using 1987 as the base year. (Round each index number to 1/10%.)

2. Using the index constructed in Requirement 1, what was the percent increase in prices from 1984 to 1990?

3. Using the index constructed in Requirement 1, how many dollars in 1991 does it take to have the same purchasing power as $1 in 1986?

4. Using the index constructed in Requirement 1, if $90,000 were invested in land during 1985 and $60,000 were invested in land during 1987, what would be reported as the total land investment on a constant purchasing power balance sheet prepared in 1991? What would your answer be if the investments were in Canada savings bonds rather than in land?

Problem H–2
Adjusting costs to historical cost/constant purchasing power amounts
(L. O. 3)

Maxima Company purchased machinery for $675,000 on December 30, 1987. The equipment was expected to last eight years and have no salvage value; straight-line depreciation was to be used. The equipment was sold on December 31, 1991, for $525,000. End-of-year general price index numbers during this period of time were as follows:

1987	195.0
1988	252.8
1989	272.4
1990	310.5
1991	330.2

Required
(Round all answers to the nearest whole dollar.)

1. What should be presented for the equipment and accumulated depreciation on a historical cost/constant purchasing power balance sheet dated December 31, 1989? Hint: Depreciation is the total amount of cost that has been allocated to expense. Therefore, the price index numbers that are used to adjust the nominal dollar cost of the asset should also be used to adjust the nominal dollar amount of depreciation.

2. How much depreciation expense should be shown on the historical cost/constant purchasing power income statement for 1990?

3. How much depreciation expense should be shown on the historical cost/constant purchasing power income statement for 1991?

4. How much gain on the sale of equipment would be reported on the historical cost/nominal dollar income statement for 1991?

5. After adjusting the equipment's cost and accumulated depreciation to the end-of-1991 price level, how much gain in (loss of) purchasing power was realized by the sale of the equipment?

Problem H–3
Calculating purchasing power gain or loss
(L. O. 3)

Brookes Express had three monetary items during 1991: cash, accounts receivable, and accounts payable. The changes in these accounts during the year were as follows:

Cash:
Beginning balance	$ 10,000
Cash proceeds from sale of surplus equipment (in mid-January 1991) . .	15,700
Cash receipts from customers (spread evenly throughout the year) . . .	95,300
Payments of accounts payable (spread evenly throughout the year) . . .	(51,200)
Payments of other cash expenses during March 1991	(20,400)
Dividends declared and paid in mid-September 1991	(18,000)
Ending balance	$ 31,400

Accounts receivable:
Beginning balance	$ 16,500
Sales to customers (spread evenly throughout the year)	105,200
Cash receipts from customers (spread evenly throughout the year) . . .	(95,300)
Ending balance	$ 26,400

Accounts payable:
Beginning balance	$ 18,800
Merchandise purchases (spread evenly throughout the year)	42,500
Special purchase near end of December 1991	14,000
Payments of accounts payable (spread evenly throughout the year) . . .	(51,200)
Ending balance	$ 24,100

General price index numbers at the end of 1990 and during 1991 are as follows:

December 1990	185.0
January 1991	188.0
March 1991	192.7
September 1991	195.7
December 1991	197.0
Average for 1991	193.0

Required

Calculate the general purchasing power gain or loss experienced by Brookes Express in 1991. (Round all amounts to the nearest whole dollar.)

Problem H–4
Historical cost/nominal dollars, historical cost/ constant purchasing power, and current costs
(L. O. 1, 4)

Krenidon, Incorporated purchased a tract of land for $150,000 in 1984 when the general price index was 85.5. At the same time, a price index for land values in the area of Krenidon's tract was 81.5. In 1985, when the general price index was 90.2 and the specific price index for land was 95.2, Krenidon bought another tract of land for $210,000. In late 1991, the general price index is 175.3, and the price index for land values is 162.5.

Required

1. In preparing a balance sheet at the end of 1991, what amount should be shown for land on:
   a. A historical cost/nominal dollar balance sheet.
   b. A historical cost/constant purchasing power balance sheet.
   c. A current cost balance sheet.
   (Round all amounts to the nearest whole dollar.)
2. In Krenidon, Incorporated's December 1991 meeting of the board of directors, one director insists that Krenidon has earned a gain in purchasing power as a result of owning the land. A second director argues that there could not have been a purchasing power gain or loss since land is a nonmonetary asset. Which director do you think is correct? Explain your answer.

Alternate Problems

Problem H–1A
Constructing and using a price index
(L. O. 2)

The costs of purchasing a common "market basket" in each of several years are as follows:

Year	Cost of Market Basket
1984 . .	$ 85,000
1985 . .	89,850
1986 . .	95,300
1987 . .	94,750
1988 . .	110,000
1989 . .	115,400
1990 . .	112,760
1991 . .	125,300

Required

1. Construct a price index using 1985 as the base year. (Round each index number to 1/10%.)
2. Using the index constructed in Requirement 1, what was the percent increase in prices from 1987 to 1991?
3. Using the index constructed in Requirement 1, how many dollars in 1991 does it take to have the same purchasing power as $1 in 1984?
4. Using the index constructed in Requirement 1, if $85,000 were invested in land during 1986 and $95,000 were invested in land during 1989, what would be reported as the total land investment on a constant purchasing power balance sheet prepared in 1990? What would your answer be if the investments were in Canada savings bonds rather than in land?

Problem H–2A
Adjusting costs to historical cost/constant purchasing power amounts
(L. O. 3)

Bowldt Corporation purchased machinery for $585,000 on December 30, 1987. The equipment was expected to last nine years and have no salvage value; straight-line depreciation was to be used. The equipment was sold on December 31, 1991, for $435,000. End-of-year general price index numbers during this period of time were as follows:

Year	Index
1987	98.2
1988	125.5
1989	135.4
1990	155.6
1991	168.3

Required

(Round all answers to the nearest whole dollar.)

1. What should be presented for the equipment and accumulated depreciation on a historical cost/constant purchasing power balance sheet dated December 31, 1989? Hint: Depreciation is the total amount of cost that has been allocated to expense. Therefore, the price index numbers that are used to adjust the nominal dollar cost of the asset should also be used to adjust the nominal dollar amount of depreciation.
2. How much depreciation expense should be shown on the historical cost/constant purchasing power income statement for 1990?

3. How much depreciation expense should be shown on the historical cost/constant purchasing power income statement for 1991?

4. How much gain on the sale of equipment would be reported on the historical cost/nominal dollar income statement for 1991?

5. After adjusting the equipment's cost and accumulated depreciation to the end-of-1991 price level, how much gain in (loss of) general purchasing power was realized by the sale of the equipment?

Problem H–3A
Calculating purchasing power gain or loss
(L. O. 3)

Eastbend Drafters had three monetary items during 1991: cash, accounts receivable, and accounts payable. The changes in these accounts during the year were as follows:

Cash:

Beginning balance	$ 20,300
Cash proceeds from sale of land (in mid-January 1991)	32,450
Cash receipts from customers (spread evenly throughout the year) . .	215,620
Payments of accounts payable (spread evenly throughout the year) . .	(120,050)
Dividends declared and paid during March 1991	(50,090)
Payments of other cash expenses in mid-September 1991	(41,000)
Ending balance	$ 57,230

Accounts receivable:

Beginning balance	$ 36,400
Sales to customers (spread evenly throughout the year)	240,020
Cash receipts from customers (spread evenly throughout the year) . .	(215,620)
Ending balance	$ 60,800

Accounts payable:

Beginning balance	$ 42,750
Merchandise purchases (spread evenly throughout the year)	95,300
Special purchase near end of December 1991	28,200
Payments of accounts payable (spread evenly throughout the year) . .	(120,050)
Ending balance	$ 46,200

General price index numbers at the end of 1990 and during 1991 are as follows:

December 1990	106.5
January 1991	107.8
March 1991	110.2
September 1991.	115.3
December 1991	118.0
Average for 1991	112.8

Required

Calculate the general purchasing power gain or loss experienced by Eastbend Drafters in 1991. (Round all amounts to the nearest whole dollar.)

Problem H–4A
Historical cost/nominal dollars, historical cost/ constant purchasing power, and current costs
(L. O. 1, 4)

Olmos Company purchased a tract of land for $180,000 in 1983 when the general price index was 84.2. At the same time, a price index for land values in the area of Olmos's tract was 90.5. In 1984, when the general price index was 88.6 and the specific price index for land was 102.3, Olmos bought another tract of land for $240,000. In late 1991, the general price index is 160.2, and the price index for land values is 245.6.

Required

1. In preparing a balance sheet at the end of 1991, what amount should be shown for land on:
   a. A historical cost/nominal dollar balance sheet.
   b. A historical cost/constant purchasing power balance sheet.
   c. A current cost balance sheet.
   (Round all amounts to the nearest whole dollar.)

2. In Olmos Company's December 1991 meeting of the board of directors, one director insists that Olmos had incurred a loss of purchasing power as a result of owning the land. A second director argues that there could not have been a purchasing power gain or loss since land is a nonmonetary asset. Which director do you think is correct? Explain your answer.

Provocative Problems

**Provocative Problem H–1
Laguna Corporation
historical cost/constant
dollar statements
(L. O. 3)**

Although Laguna Corporation is not required to present financial information adjusted for price changes, the company has often been willing to consider new, innovative ways of reporting to its shareholders. For example, it has presented supplemental historical cost/constant dollar financial statements in its annual reports. The constant dollar balance sheets of Laguna Corporation for December 31, 1990, and 1991, were as follows:

LAGUNA CORPORATION
Historical Cost/Constant Dollar Balance Sheets

	As Presented on December 31, 1991	As Presented on December 31, 1990
Assets		
Cash	$ 45,000	$ 20,000
Accounts receivable.	103,000	60,000
Note receivable	30,000	—
Inventory.	35,672	22,690
Equipment	208,454	181,922
Accumulated depreciation.	(66,275)	(34,450)
Land	166,930	108,280
Total assets	$522,781	$358,442
Liabilities and Shareholders' Equity		
Accounts payable	$ 72,000	$ 21,000
Notes payable	55,000	24,000
Common stock.	295,450	253,730
Retained earnings.	100,331	59,712
Total liabilities and shareholders' equity . . .	$522,781	$358,442

A new member of Laguna Corporation's board of directors has expressed interest in the relationship between historical cost/constant dollar statements and historical cost/nominal dollar statements. The board member understands that constant dollar statements are derived from nominal dollar statements, but wonders if the process can be reversed. Specifically, you are asked to show how the historical cost/constant dollar balance sheets for December 31, 1990, and 1991, could be restated back into nominal dollar statements.

Additional Information

1. The outstanding stock was issued in January 1990, and the company's equipment was purchased at that time. The equipment has no salvage value and is being depreciated over seven years.

2. The note receivable was acquired on June 30, 1991.

3. Notes payable consists of two notes, one for $24,000 which was issued on January 1, 1990, and the other for $31,000 which was issued on January 1, 1991.

4. The Land account includes two parcels, one of which was acquired for $100,000 on January 1, 1990. The remaining parcel was acquired in June 1991.

5. Selected numbers from a general price-level index are:

January 1990.	175.0
June 1990 (also average for 1990)	195.0
December 1990	205.3
June 1991 (also average for 1991)	220.0
December 1991	235.0

6. The inventory at the end of each year was acquired evenly throughout that year.

7. Hint: If all other accounts are properly adjusted from constant dollars back to nominal dollars, the correct retained earnings balance can be determined simply by "plugging" the amount necessary to make the balance sheet balance.

I Accounting for Corporate Income Taxes

The rules surrounding the accounting treatment for corporate income taxes have been under reexamination for the last seven years. Until very recently it appeared that significant changes were about to take place. However, the Accounting Standards Committee has decided to suspend the project and to proceed with the existing Standard. This Appendix is therefore based on the existing Section 3470 of the *CICA Handbook*.

Learning Objectives

After studying Appendix I, you should be able to:

1. Explain why income taxes for accounting purposes may be different from income taxes for tax purposes.
2. Prepare an income tax schedule and journal entries for a company where timing differences exist between accounting and taxable income.

You have already learned how to determine net income under GAAP for a profit oriented entity. However, the determination of taxable income for a corporation, while starting with the accounting net income, is done using the Canadian Income Tax Act. Almost always, this results in taxable income being different from the GAAP accounting income.

Explain why income taxes for accounting purposes may be different from income taxes for tax purposes.
(L. O. 1)

A major difference between accounting income and taxable income results from what are known as timing differences. These arise because some items are included as revenue or expense in one period under GAAP while they are included in a different period under the income tax rules. For example:

1. The application of accounting principles for installment sales requires that gross profit on these sales is recognized in accounting income before it is recognized in taxable income under the income tax rules.

2. Accounting principles require an estimate of future costs, such as costs of making good on guarantees; they also require a deduction of such costs from revenue in the year the guaranteed goods are sold. However, tax rules do not permit the deduction of such costs until they are actually incurred.

3. Reported net income also differs from taxable income because the taxpayer uses a method or procedure for accounting purposes that he/she feels fairly reflects periodic net income but is required to use a different method of procedure for tax purposes. For example, the last-in, first-out inventory method of cost allocation may be used for accounting purposes but is not permitted for tax purposes. Likewise, many companies use straight-line depreciation for accounting purposes but are required to use a different procedure, called capital cost allowances, for tax purposes.

Capital Cost Allowances

Depreciation accounting has been greatly influenced by income tax laws. The 1948 Income Tax Act replaced the complex body of rules that had developed for the purpose of limiting the amount of depreciation allowed for tax purposes. The act defined and set a limit on amounts which could be deducted, for tax purposes, in respect to the cost of depreciable assets. These amounts are known as **capital cost allowances** (CCA).

The capital cost allowances are identical in nature and purpose with the accountants' concept of depreciation and are based on the declining-balance method, discussed in Chapter 10. For tax purposes, the taxpayer may claim the maximum allowed or any part thereof in any year regardless of the depreciation method and the amounts he/she uses in the accounting records.

Although capital cost allowances are based on the declining-balance method, certain procedures have been set out by the Regulations of the Act. The more important of these are as follows:

1. All depreciable assets are grouped into a comparatively small number of classes and a maximum rate allowed is prescribed for each group. The assets most commonly in use are set out below according to the class to which they belong, with the maximum rate of allowance for each such class (as at the time of writing).

Class 3 (5%): Brick, cement, and stone buildings.

Class 6 (10%): Frame, log, stucco, and corrugated iron buildings.

Class 7 (15%): Ships, scows, canoes, and rowboats.

Class 10 (30%): Automobiles, trucks, and tractors.

Class 8 (20%): Machinery, equipment, and furniture.

2. The assets of a designated class are considered to form a separate pool of costs. The costs of asset additions are added to their respective pools of undepreciated capital cost. When assets are disposed of, the proceeds (up to the original cost) received from disposal are deducted from the proper pool. The balance of each pool of costs is also diminished by the accumulated capital cost allowance claimed. A capital cost allowance is claimed on the balance, referred to as the undepreciated capital cost (UCC), in the pool at the end of the fiscal year. However, when there are net additions to the pool, only one half of the amount added is used in the calculation of CCA. The effect is that the assets are assumed to have been acquired halfway through the fiscal year.

3. "Losses" and "gains" on disposal of individual assets disappear into the pool of undepreciated capital costs except when an asset is sold for more than its capital cost. In this case, proceeds of disposal in excess of the capital cost of the asset are normally treated as a capital gain. Where the proceeds of disposal (excluding the capital gain, if any) exceed the undepreciated capital cost of the class immediately before the sale, the amount of the excess is treated as a "recapture" of capital cost allowances previously made. Such a recapture is considered as ordinary income. When all of the assets in a class are disposed of and the proceeds are less than the undepreciated capital cost of the class immediately before the sale, the proceeds less the undepreciated capital cost may be deducted in determining the year's taxable income.

Companies must, with few exceptions, use capital cost allowances for tax purposes, but commonly use straight-line depreciation in their accounting records. A problem arising from this practice is discussed in the next section.

Taxes and the Distortion of Net Income

Prepare an income tax schedule and journal entries when timing differences exist. (L. O. 2)

When one accounting procedure is required for tax purposes and a different procedure is used in the accounting records, a problem arises as to how much income tax expense should be deducted each year on the income statement. If the tax actually incurred in such situations is deducted, reported net income often varies from year to year due to the postponement and later payment of taxes. Consequently, in such cases, since shareholders may be misled by these variations, many accountants are of the opinion that income taxes should be allocated in such a way that any distortion resulting from postponing taxes is removed from the income statement.

To appreciate the problem involved here, assume that a corporation has installed a $100,000 machine, the product of which will produce a half-million dollars of revenue in each of the succeeding four years and $80,000 of income before depreciation and taxes. Assume further that the company must pay income taxes at a 40% rate (round number assumed for easy calculation) and that it plans to use straight-line depreciation in its records but the capital cost allowance for tax purposes. If the machine has a four-year life and a $10,000 salvage value and if the maximum permitted capital cost allowance rate on this particular machine is 50%, annual depreciation calculated by each method will be as follows:

Year	Straight Line	Declining Balance
1990	$22,500	$25,000
1991	22,500	37,500
1992	22,500	18,750
1993	22,500	8,750*
Totals	$90,000	$90,000

*Use $8,750 in order to match salvage value. CCA allowed is $9,375.

In the year of acquisition, only one half of the CCA otherwise allowed may be claimed. In subsequent years, CCA may be claimed up to the maximum amounts allowed.

Since the company has elected capital cost allowance for tax purposes, it will be liable for $22,000 of income tax on the first year's income, $17,000 on the second, $24,500 on the third, and $28,500 on the fourth. The calculation of these taxes is shown in Illustration I–1.

Furthermore, if the company were to deduct its actual tax payable each year in arriving at income to be reported to its shareholders, it would report the amounts shown in Illustration I–2.

Observe in Illustrations I–1 and I–2 that total depreciation, $90,000, is the same whether calculated by the straight-line or the declining-balance method. Also note that the total tax paid over the four years, $92,000, is the same in each case. Then note the distortion of the final income figures in Illustration I–2 due to the postponement of taxes.

If this company should report successive annual income figures of $35,500, $40,500, $33,000, and then $29,000, some of its shareholders might be misled as to the company's earnings trend. Consequently, in cases such as this many accountants think income taxes should be allocated so that the distortion caused by the postponement of taxes is removed from the income statement. These accountants advocate that—

> When one accounting procedure is used in the accounting records and a different procedure is used for tax purposes, the tax expense deducted on the income statement should not be the actual tax liability but the amount that would be payable if the procedure used in the records were also used in calculating the tax.

If the foregoing is applied in this case, the corporation will report to its shareholders in each of the four years the amounts of income shown in Illustration I–3.

In examining Illustration I–2, recall that the company's taxes payable are actually $22,000 in the first year, $17,000 in the second, $24,500 in the third,

Illustration I–1
Calculation of income taxes

Annual income taxes	1991	1992	1993	1994	Total
Income before depreciation and income taxes	$80,000	$80,000	$80,000	$80,000	$320,000
Depreciation for tax purposes (declining balance)	25,000	37,500	18,750	8,750	90,000
Taxable income	$55,000	$42,500	$61,250	$71,250	$230,000
Annual income taxes (40% of taxable income)	$22,000	$17,000	$24,500	$28,500	$ 92,000

Illustration I–2
Calculation of remaining income

Income after deducting actual tax liabilities	1991	1992	1993	1994	Total
Income before depreciation and income taxes	$80,000	$80,000	$80,000	$80,000	$320,000
Depreciation per books (straight line)	22,500	22,500	22,500	22,500	90,000
Income before taxes	57,500	57,500	57,500	57,500	230,000
Income taxes (actual liability of each year)	22,000	17,000	24,500	28,500	92,000
Remaining income	$35,500	$40,500	$33,000	$29,000	$138,000

and $28,500 in the fourth, a total of $92,000. Then observe that when this $92,000 liability is allocated evenly over the four years, the distortion of the annual net incomes due to the postponement of taxes is removed from the published income statements.

Entries for the Allocation of Taxes

When income taxes are allocated as in Illustration I–3, the tax payable for each year and the deferred income tax are recorded with an adjusting entry. The adjusting entries for the four years of Illustration I–2 and the entries in general journal form for the payment of the taxes (without explanations) are as follows:

1991	Income Tax Expense	23,000	
	Income Taxes Payable		22,000
	Deferred Income Tax		1,000
	Income Taxes Payable	22,000	
	Cash		22,000
1992	Income Tax Expense	23,000	
	Income Taxes Payable		17,000
	Deferred Income Tax		6,000
	Income Taxes Payable	17,000	
	Cash		17,000

Illustration I–3
Tax expense based on accounting income

Net income that should be reported to shareholders	1991	1992	1993	1994	Total
Income before depreciation and income taxes	$80,000	$80,000	$80,000	$80,000	$320,000
Depreciation per books (straight line) . .	22,500	22,500	22,500	22,500	90,000
Income before taxes.	57,500	57,500	57,500	57,500	230,000
Income taxes (amounts based on straight-line depreciation).	23,000	23,000	23,000	23,000	92,000
Net income.	$34,500	$34,500	$34,500	$34,500	$138,000

1993	Income Tax Expense.	23,000		
	Deferred Income Tax	1,500		
	Income Taxes Payable			24,500
	Income Taxes Payable.	24,500		
	Cash			24,500
1994	Income Tax Expense.	23,000		
	Deferred Income Tax	5,500		
	Income Taxes Payable			28,500
	Income Taxes Payable.	28,500		
	Cash			28,500

Note: To simplify the illustration, it is assumed here that the entire year's tax liability is paid at one time. However, corporations are usually required to pay estimated taxes on a monthly basis.

In the entries the $23,000 debited to Income Tax Expense each year is the amount that is deducted on the income statement in reporting annual net income. Also, the amount credited to Income Taxes Payable each year is the actual tax liability of that year.

Observe in the entries that since the actual tax payable in each of the first two years is less than the amount debited to Income Tax Expense, the difference is credited to **Deferred Income Tax.** Then note that in the last two years, since the actual liability each year is greater than the debit to Income Tax Expense, the difference is debited to Deferred Income Tax. Now observe in the following illustration of the company's Deferred Income Tax account that the debits and credits exactly balance each other out over the four-year period:

Deferred Income Tax

Year	Explanation	Debit	Credit	Balance
1990			1,000	1,000
1991			6,000	7,000
1992		1,500		5,500
1993		5,500		–0–

In passing, it should be observed that many accountants believe the interests of government, business, and the public would be better served if there were more uniformity between taxable income and reported net income. However, since the federal income tax is designed to serve other purposes than raising revenue, it is apt to be some time before this is achieved.

Before concluding this appendix on income taxes, we should mention some additional features of the rules that govern accounting for income taxes.

1. In the example above, we assumed an income tax rate of 40% in each year. However, if the income tax rate changes, we use the rate in effect for that year. When the timing difference reverses, the average rate over the accumulation period should be used to avoid throwing the deferred tax amount into a debit balance (this point is covered more thoroughly in later courses).

2. In the example, 1991 income before taxes was *more than* taxable income because of a timing difference that was expected to reverse in 1993 or 1994. As a result, we recognized a deferred tax balance on the December 31, 1991, balance sheet. In other situations, just the opposite kind of timing difference may occur. In other words, a timing difference that will reverse in the future may cause income before taxes to be *less than* taxable income. These latter situations may, under certain conditions, result in the recognition of a deferred tax debit.

3. The Deferred Income Tax account balance may be reported as a long-term liability or as a current liability, depending on how far in the future the amount will reverse.

4. Federal tax laws generally require corporations to estimate their current year's tax liability and make advance payments of the estimated amount before the final tax return is filed. As a result, the end-of-year entries to record income taxes, such as those shown above, often have to be altered to take into consideration any previously recorded prepayments.

Exercises

Exercise I–1
Timing differences
(L.O. 1)

Indicate which of the following items might cause timing differences for a corporation:

a. Sales on account
b. Capital cost allowances
c. Wages paid to employees
d. Property taxes
e. Installment sales
f. Cost of goods sold
g. Warranty expenses
h. Rents received in advance
i. Cash sales

Exercise I–2
Taxable vs. accounting income
(L.O. 1)

a. Explain why accounting income is usually different from taxable income.
b. What reasons can you give for the two sets of rules?

Exercise I–3
Recording corporate income tax expense
(L.O. 2)

Granger Inc., began operations on January 1, 1990. During 1990, Granger's operations resulted in a current tax payable $350,000. In addition, Granger sold land for $110,000 that had cost $20,000. The sale qualified as an installment sale for tax purposes so the gain was subject to tax as cash was received. The purchaser agreed to pay for the land on June 1, 1991. Present the December 31, 1990, entry to record Granger's Inc.'s income taxes. Assume a tax rate of 45% and that the profit on the land is fully taxable.

Exericse I–4
Recording corporate income tax expense
(L.O. 2)

Banister Corporation would have had identical accounting and taxable income for the three years 1991–1993 were it not for the fact that for tax purposes an operational asset that cost $18,000 was depreciated by the sum-of-the-years'-digits (SYD) method (assumed for problem purposes to be acceptable) whereas for accounting purposes, the straight-line method was used. The asset has a three-year operational life and no residual value. Income before depreciation and income taxes for the years concerned follow:

	1991	1992	1993
Pretax accounting income (before depreciation)	$30,000	$35,000	$40,000

Assume an income tax rate of 40% for each year.

Required:

a. Calculate the accounting and taxable income for each year.
b. Prepare journal entries to record the income tax expense for each year.

Exercise I–5
Analyze timing differences; entries
(L.O. 2)

Collinge Corporation reports the following information for the year ended December 31, 1991:

Revenue	$325,000
Expenses	278,000
Net income before tax	$ 47,000

Additional information:

a. Revenues (above) do not include $10,000 of rent which is taxable in 1991 but was unearned at the end of 1991.

b. Capital cost allowances for 1991 are $18,000 greater than the depreciation expense included above.

c. Expenses (above) include $7,000 of estimated warranty expenses which are not deductible for tax purposes in 1991.

d. Assume an income tax rate of 40%.

Prepare a journal entry to record income taxes for Collinge Corp. on December 31, 1991.

Exercise I–6
Timing differences; entries
(L. O. 2)

Income tax returns of Vachon Corporation reflected the following:

	Year Ended Dec. 31		
	1991	**1992**	**1993**
Royalty income	$ 60,000		
Investment income	30,000	$20,000	$40,000
Rent income	10,000	10,000	10,000
	$100,000	$30,000	$50,000
Deductible expenses	30,000	20,000	20,000
Taxable income	$ 70,000	$10,000	$30,000

Assume the average income tax rate for each year was 40%.

The only differences between taxable income on the tax returns and the pretax accounting income relate to royalty income. For accounting purposes, royalty income was recognized ratably (equally) over the three-year period.

Required

Give journal entries such as would appear at the end of each year to reflect income tax and allocation.

(CGA adapted)

J Abitibi-Price Inc.
Financial Statements
(1989 Annual Report)

1989 ANNUAL REPORT

"

In a capital intensive company like Abitibi-Price, *changes feel like lightning.* **To manage them we first had to learn how to change ourselves. Change how we think. All of us. Top to bottom.**

"

BERND K. KOKEN, CHAIRMAN AND CHIEF EXECUTIVE OFFICER

Operations   Sales of $3.3 billion for the year 1989 were approximately the same as 1988 and compare with $3.0 billion in 1987. However, net earnings of $54.2 million or 70 cents per common share reflected a major drop from $191.1 million or $2.64 per share in 1988 and $125.7 million or $1.70 per share in 1987. Earnings for 1989 include a restructuring charge of $31.2 million which is referred to below. Without this charge, after-tax earnings for the year would have been $75.2 million or $1.00 per common share. Net earnings for 1988 included an extraordinary gain of $2.9 million resulting from the sale of land in South Carolina, U.S.A. There were no extraordinary items in 1989 or 1987.

The restructuring charge consisted of the write-off of an old newsprint machine at Grand Falls, Newfoundland which is to be permanently withdrawn from production in early 1990, a provision for employee termination costs relating to that closure, plus the write-off of the assets of a discontinued self-insulating hardboard siding operation at the Company's building products plant in Alpena, Michigan.

Apart from the restructuring charge, principal causes of the drop in 1989 earnings were significant declines in operating profits from newsprint, groundwood papers and coated papers. Common to the first two business segments in particular was the effect of the ongoing decline in the Canadian value of the U.S. dollar which, despite the degree of protection provided by the Company's hedging program, has continued to have a negative impact on earnings. In 1989, the U.S. dollar averaged Cdn. $1.184, down 4% from $1.231 in 1988 and down 11% from $1.326 in 1987.

Newsprint sales in 1989 totalled $1.1 billion, compared with $1.3 billion in 1988 and $1.2 billion in 1987. Operating profit showed a major decline to $78.9 million in 1989 from $250.1 million and $194.9 million in 1988 and 1987, respectively. In addition to the effect of the lower value of the U.S. dollar, the drop in 1989 sales and operating profit from 1988 reflected the reduction in sales volume and price discounting which have resulted from new capacity coming on the market while demand has remained flat. From 1987 to 1988, newsprint sales and operating profit improved because of higher shipments, price increases in most markets and the benefits realized from capital invested in the modernization of production facilities.

It is expected that the unfavourable supply/demand situation, with the attendant pricing pressures, will continue and the Company is not expecting any improvement in sales in 1990. However, in the manufacturing area, which is within the Company's control, steps were taken during 1989 to introduce a wide range of improvements which will lead to increases in productivity, product quality and cost effectiveness. These include the reduced use of chemicals and costly kraft pulp, an increase in the yield of the pulping operations, and capital expenditures to modernize machinery and processes.

The Alabama River Newsprint joint venture, which is referred to in Note 2 to the financial statements, is on budget and construction is expected to be completed in 1990 as scheduled.

In recognition of growing environmental concerns and the thrust towards the use of recycled products, the Company has announced definite steps in the area of recycled newsprint. It has already announced the installation of a deinking facility at its joint venture newsprint mill in Augusta, Georgia, which should be in operation by the end of 1990; it is studying the use of recycled wood fibre at a mill in Ontario; and it is studying the feasibility of a partnership to produce newsprint from recycled paper at a mill to be built in Scotland.

Sales of groundwood papers increased to $363 million in 1989 from $343 million in 1988 and $279 million in 1987, while operating profit of $23.3 million for the year compared with $44.0 million and $11.7 million in 1988 and 1987, respectively. The increase in 1989 groundwood papers sales was essentially due to an increase in capacity which became available at the beginning of the year with the conversion of a newsprint machine to the production of directory paper at the Alma, Quebec, mill. However, operating profit showed a significant drop in 1989 for the same reasons as newsprint – over-supply with pricing pressures, plus the decline in the Canadian value of the U.S. dollar. In addition, the Company suffered production problems and low efficiency levels at its Jonquière, Quebec, mill. The improvement in groundwood papers sales and operating profit from 1987 to 1988 was primarily the result of favourable market conditions which permitted near-capacity operations and improved prices. In addition, 1988 represented the first full year's sales of the Company's new clay-filled supercalendered paper. These positive factors more than offset the negative effect of the decline in the value of the U.S. dollar from 1987 to 1988.

The outlook for groundwood papers in 1990 is mixed. A continued softening of demand for the lower value grades is expected because of the oversupply of newsprint. However, demand should remain strong for high quality directory papers, forms papers and supercalendered grades, and the Company is expected to benefit from repositioning itself to place the emphasis on these grades as well as from actions taken during 1989 to improve production efficiencies.

At $145 million, sales of coated papers in 1989 compared with $151 million in 1988 and $131 million in 1987. At the same time, however, 1989 showed an operating loss of $7.6 million, as against operating profits of $13.4 million and $6.7 million in 1988 and 1987, respectively. The drop in sales and the operating loss in 1989 were due to a weakening of Canadian demand, increased competition

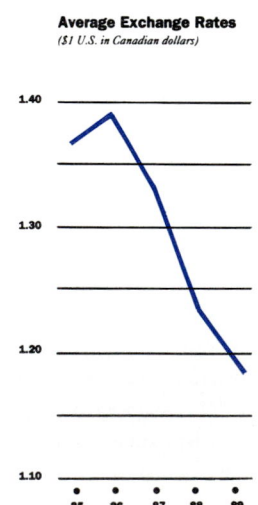

Average Exchange Rates
($1 U.S. in Canadian dollars)

from outside Canada, and the loss of production during the rebuild of a paper machine and an off-machine coater at the mill in Thunder Bay, Ontario. The improvement in coated papers' 1988 results over 1987 was attributable to increased demand for the Company's grades of paper, which resulted in record production levels and higher prices.

Although it is not anticipated that prices for present grades of coated papers will improve during 1990, it is expected that the increased production from the rebuild of the Thunder Bay paper machine plus the introduction of new grades will return the operation to profitability.

Sales of the distribution, office products and converted products segment of the Company's operations climbed to $1.4 billion in 1989 from $1.3 billion in 1988 and $1.1 billion in 1987, while 1989 operating profit of $49.3 million compared with $51.9 million in 1988 and $43.3 million in 1987. The increase in sales in 1989 reflected the full year's inclusion of the results of six businesses that were acquired in the last half of 1988. However, operating profit declined because of competitive pressures which forced a reduction in prices and profit margins in the distribution sector. The improvement in sales and operating profit from 1987 to 1988 reflected the acquisitions of the new businesses referred to above and the installation of new high-speed equipment to improve productivity and reduce costs in the converted products sector.

The outlook for the operation of the Company's distribution, office products and converted products segment in 1990 is one of increased profitability flowing from programs involving reorganization and rationalization, as well as from new equipment installations.

During 1989, the Company announced its intention to seek a buyer for its U.S. building products division, but subsequently announced that it would keep the operation as offers from potential buyers did not meet certain conditions and did not reflect the true value of the business. Sales of $193 million in 1989 compared with $198 million in 1988 and $222 million in 1987, while operating profit was $14.4 million, versus $11.4 million and $16.3 million in 1988 and 1987, respectively. Although housing starts in the U.S. market declined through the period from 1987 to 1989 and accounted for a major part of the fall-off in operating profit in 1988, in the period from 1988 to 1989 operating profit rose because the effect of reduced housing starts was more than offset by the results of a successful program to contain costs and reduce overheads. It is expected that the effects of this program will lead to improved operating performance in 1990.

Net Sales By Market
(percent)

United States
52%

Canada
41%

Offshore
7%

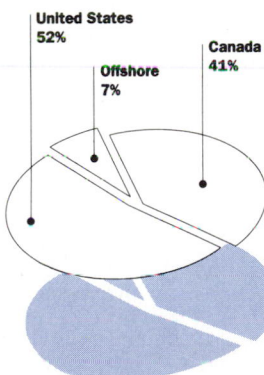

Interest expense charged to earnings in 1989 was $44.1 million, compared with $51.4 million in 1988 and $41.9 million in 1987. Interest through the period benefitted from the favourable effect of the declining U.S. exchange rate on that part of interest which was payable in U.S. funds. This, plus an increase in the amount of interest which was capitalized, explains the drop in the amount of interest charged to earnings from 1988 to 1989. However, from 1987 to 1988, the favourable effect of the lower U.S. exchange rate was more than offset by a reduction in the amount of interest which was capitalized and by higher interest charges associated with an increase in the average amount of long-term debt outstanding. Capitalized interest in 1989 was $9.6 million, compared with $6.1 million in 1988 and $9.0 million in 1987.

Other income, net of expense, amounted to $15.8 million in 1989, compared with $16.4 million in 1988 and $11.3 million in 1987. The decrease from 1988 to 1989 was attributable to lower interest earned on short-term investments as the amount of surplus funds temporarily placed in such investments was reduced to zero during the year. The effect of this was partially offset by interest received in the settlement of an insurance claim relating to the flooding of a powerhouse and dam serving the newsprint mill at Grand Falls, Newfoundland, and by a reduction in foreign exchange losses as a result of the Company's hedging program. The increase in other income from 1987 to 1988 was principally due to interest earned on a larger amount of surplus funds temporarily placed in short-term investments.

The effective tax rate in 1989 was 45% compared with 41% in 1988 and 44% in 1987. The increase in the 1989 rate was primarily due to the effect of the lower U.S. tax rate on loss operations in that country, while the reduction from 1987 to 1988 was mainly attributable to lower tax rates introduced with tax reform.

Financial position and liquidity   Over the three-year period from 1987 to 1989, the Company's cash position declined by $43.0 million, from $11.8 million at the beginning of 1987 to a deficit of $31.2 million at December 31, 1989, as cash derived from operations, new financings and other sources was exceeded by expenditures on capital projects, long-term debt repayments, the retirement of the Series A and C preferred shares, investments in new businesses and shareholder dividends.

In 1987, the Company borrowed U.S. $150 million in the form of a syndicated seven-year floating rate term loan, realizing Cdn. $197.2 million which was used to reduce short-term indebtedness and augment working capital. In that same year, a 51%-owned subsidiary, Gaspesia Pulp and Paper Company Ltd., borrowed U.S. $25 million in the form of a floating rate revolving loan, realizing Cdn. $32.6 million, which was used to finance its capital program.

In 1988, the Company redeemed its U.S. $50 million Series I Debentures at a cost of Cdn. $60.2 million; and in 1989, Gaspesia repaid its 1987 loan at a Canadian funds cost of $29.6 million and borrowed U.S. $24.5 million from another source under more favourable conditions, realizing Cdn. $28.9 million.

In the latter part of 1988, the Company negotiated amendments to its Trust Indenture in order to update it to current practices. In exchange for the elimination of incremental debt issuance tests, the floating charge on assets and certain other covenants, the Company agreed to increase interest rates on the Series F, G and H Sinking Fund Debentures by $1/2$ of 1%, with effect from December 19, 1988.

The Company's capital expenditures are primarily directed toward improvements in productivity and quality and the manufacture of higher-value products. In 1989, capital expenditures totalled $260.1 million, compared with $203.8 million in 1988 and $256.6 million in 1987. Capital expenditures in 1990 are expected to approximate $150 million, which will be financed by cash flow from operations and additional borrowing. The Company's capital expenditures program is designed with a degree of flexibility so that it can be tailored to fit the funds available.

Four quarterly common share dividends were paid in each of the three years, totalling $1 per share in 1989 and 1988 and 60 cents per share in 1987. Dividends declared during the period totalled 87.5 cents in 1989, $1 in 1988 and 70 cents in 1987. Differences between dividends paid and dividends declared for the years 1989 and 1987 are due to the fact that the dividend declared in the fourth quarter of a year is paid in the first quarter of the year following. At the time of the fourth quarter dividend declaration in December 1989, the quarterly dividend rate was reduced from 25 cents to 12.5 cents, effective with the payment made in January 1990; and when the fourth quarter dividend was declared in December 1987, for payment in January 1988, the quarterly rate was raised from 15 cents to 25 cents.

While the Company's cash requirements have been met mainly by funds generated from operations and, when necessary, from new long-term financings, for liquidity purposes the company has a policy of maintaining sufficient bank lines of credit to cover temporary extra demands for cash. Out of a total of $255 million of such lines of credit with several banks, $242.7 million remained unused at the end of 1989. Under a commercial paper program which the Company had arranged during the last half of 1989, it can issue short-term promissory notes up to a principal value of $200 million. At December 31, 1989, the amount of such notes outstanding totalled $124.1 million.

United States GAAP Reconciliation The Company's financial statements have been prepared in accordance with generally accepted accounting principles in Canada and conform in all material respects with those in the United States, except as noted in Note 18 to the financial statements.

CONSOLIDATED EARNINGS

Year ended December 31 *(millions of Canadian dollars)*	1989	1988	1987	ABITIBI·PRICE
Net sales	$ 3,257.7	$ 3,304.5	$ 2,988.0	
Cost of sales	2,706.5	2,566.2	2,385.1	
Selling and administrative expenses	275.0	257.8	234.1	
Depreciation and depletion	118.1	110.4	97.4	
	3,099.6	2,934.4	2,716.6	
Operating profit	158.1	370.1	271.4	
Interest expense – long-term (note 14)	(37.4)	(50.5)	(39.3)	
– short-term	(6.7)	(0.9)	(2.6)	
Restructuring costs (note 4)	(31.2)	–	–	
Other income and expense – net (note 5)	15.8	16.4	11.3	
	98.6	335.1	240.8	
Income taxes (note 6)	44.7	137.9	106.7	
	53.9	197.2	134.1	
Minority interest	0.3	(9.0)	(8.4)	
Earnings before extraordinary item	54.2	188.2	125.7	
Extraordinary item (note 8)	–	2.9	–	
Net earnings	54.2	191.1	125.7	
Provision for dividends on preferred shares	5.7	7.8	8.1	
Net earnings available to common shareholders	$ 48.5	$ 183.3	$ 117.6	
Per Common Share:				
Earnings before extraordinary item	$ 0.70	$ ·2.60	$ 1.70	
Net earnings	0.70	2.64	1.70	
Dividends declared	0.875	1.00	0.70	
Weighted average number of common shares outstanding *(millions)*	69.3	69.3	69.2	

CONSOLIDATED RETAINED EARNINGS

Year ended December 31 *(millions of Canadian dollars)*	1989	1988	1987
Retained earnings at beginning of year	$ 950.2	$ 836.2	$ 768.9
Net earnings	54.2	191.1	125.7
	1,004.4	1,027.3	894.6
Amalgamation adjustment	–	–	(1.8)
Dividends declared –			
Preferred shares	(5.7)	(7.8)	(8.1)
Common shares	(60.6)	(69.3)	(48.5)
Retained earnings at end of year	$ 938.1	$ 950.2	$ 836.2

CONSOLIDATED BALANCE SHEET

December 31 *(millions of Canadian dollars)*	1989	1988
ASSETS		
Current assets		
Cash and short-term investments	$ –	$ 44.6
Accounts receivable (note 10)	383.2	424.2
Inventories (note 11)	433.1	415.4
Prepaid expenses	27.6	26.3
	843.9	910.5
Fixed assets		
Property, plant and equipment	2,424.6	2,236.4
Logging equipment and development	102.4	99.4
Timber limits and water power rights	25.7	25.7
	2,552.7	2,361.5
Less – accumulated depreciation and depletion	1,017.0	932.9
	1,535.7	1,428.6
Other assets		
Interests in newsprint joint ventures (note 2)	100.6	96.1
Deferred pension cost	63.7	45.7
Goodwill	58.7	63.4
Long-term receivables, investments and other assets	58.5	86.3
	281.5	291.5
	$ 2,661.1	$ 2,630.6

The financial statements have been approved by the Board:

Director

Director

December 31	1989	1988	ABITIBI·PRICE
(millions of Canadian dollars)			

LIABILITIES

Current liabilities

	1989	1988
Bank indebtedness	$ 31.2	$ 7.1
Notes payable (note 12)	124.1	–
Accounts payable and accrued liabilities (note 13)	307.5	284.7
Income taxes payable	10.9	15.6
Dividends payable	9.3	18.6
Long-term debt due within one year (note 14)	33.3	30.5
	516.3	356.5
Long-term debt (note 14)	435.4	488.8
Unrealized gain on translation of long-term debt payable in U.S. funds	2.2	2.6
Deferred income taxes	434.0	412.8
Minority interest	41.8	42.1

SHAREHOLDERS' EQUITY

Stated capital (note 15)

Preferred Shares –

		1989	1988
Series A	– nil shares		
(1988	– 126,760 shares)	–	6.3
Series C	– nil shares		
(1988	– 1,500,000 shares)	–	75.0
Series F	– 2,706,450 shares		
(1988	– 2,964,419 shares)	31.1	34.1
Common Shares	– 69,266,738 shares		
(1988	– 69,265,550 shares)	262.2	262.2
Retained earnings		938.1	950.2
		1.231.4	1,327.8
		$ 2,661.1	$ 2,630.6

CHANGES IN CONSOLIDATED CASH POSITION

Year ended December 31 *(millions of Canadian dollars)*	1989		1988		1987
Operating Activities					
Earnings before extraordinary item	$ 54.2	$	188.2	$	125.7
Depreciation and depletion	118.1		110.4		97.4
Restructuring costs (note 4)	23.2		–		–
Deferred pension cost	(10.5)		(6.8)		(12.3)
Goodwill	3.5		2.0		1.8
Deferred income taxes	26.8		105.6		46.3
Minority interest	(0.3)		9.0		8.4
Other	(0.1)		(14.7)		(4.5)
	214.9		393.7		262.8
Change in operating working capital (note 9)	40.1		(30.8)		(16.4)
	255.0		362.9		246.4
Financing Activities					
Issue of notes payable – net	124.1		–		–
Issue of long-term debt	29.3		–		229.8
Repayment of long-term debt	(66.1)		(95.6)		(28.6)
Retirement of preferred shares	(84.4)		(5.6)		(1.8)
Other	0.4		1.0		0.2
	3.3		(100.2)		199.6
Investment Activities					
Acquisitions	–		(82.9)		–
Bank indebtedness of acquired businesses	–		(1.2)		–
Consideration represented by loans payable	–		14.9		–
	–		(69.2)		–
Investment in newsprint joint ventures	(3.3)		(12.2)		–
Investment in equity interest	–		(35.8)		–
Additions to fixed assets	(260.1)		(203.8)		(256.6)
Government capital grants and investment tax credits	1.1		8.5		24.3
Decrease in long-term receivables	13.2		3.0		4.4
Other	(2.2)		(11.3)		4.5
	(251.3)		(320.8)		(223.4)
Dividends Paid					
Preferred shareholders	(6.4)		(7.7)		(8.0)
Common shareholders	(69.3)		(69.3)		(41.6)
Minority shareholder of a subsidiary company	–		(12.2)		–
	(75.7)		(89.2)		(49.6)
Cash – **(Decrease) increase**	(68.7)		(147.3)		173.0
– **Beginning of year**	37.5		184.8		11.8
– **End of year**	$ (31.2)	$	37.5	$	184.8

Cash comprises cash and short-term investments, less bank indebtedness.

CONSOLIDATED SEGMENTED INFORMATION

ABITIBI-PRICE

Year ended December 31 (millions of Canadian dollars)	Sales To Customers	Inter-Segment Sales	Segment Sales	Depreciation And Depletion	Operating Profit	Additions To Fixed Assets	Total Assets
1989 BUSINESS SEGMENTS							
Newsprint	$ 1,058.9	$ 1.1	$ 1,060.0	$ 62.8	$ 78.9	$ 130.3	$ 1,201.8
Groundwood papers	362.9	0.9	363.8	28.1	23.3	52.8	570.8
Coated papers	144.6	26.1	170.7	6.7	(7.6)	35.1	165.5
Distribution, Office products and Converted products	1,404.1	0.9	1,405.0	10.1	49.3	31.7	488.1
Building products	192.8	–	192.8	8.2	14.4	6.3	144.6
Other	94.4	–	94.4	2.2	(0.2)	0.6	21.9
Eliminations		(29.0)	(29.0)				
	$ 3,257.7	$ –	$ 3,257.7	$ 118.1	$ 158.1	256.8	2,592.7
Corporate						3.3	68.4
						$ 260.1	$ 2,661.1
GEOGRAPHIC SEGMENTS							
Canada			$ 2,456.5		$ 147.7		$ 2,157.9
U.S.A.			801.2		10.4		434.8
			$ 3,257.7		$ 158.1		2,592.7
Corporate							68.4
							$ 2,661.1
1988 BUSINESS SEGMENTS							
Newsprint	$ 1,257.6	$ 2.0	$ 1,259.6	$ 61.3	$ 250.1	$ 110.6	$ 1,172.2
Groundwood papers	343.1	0.3	343.4	24.5	44.0	42.9	509.1
Coated papers	150.6	35.8	186.4	5.3	13.4	20.2	122.1
Distribution, Office products and Converted products	1,282.8	0.7	1,283.5	8.2	51.9	20.4	497.5
Building products	198.3	–	198.3	9.0	11.4	5.4	164.6
Other	72.1	–	72.1	2.1	(0.7)	0.9	21.6
Eliminations		(38.8)	(38.8)				
	$ 3,304.5	$ –	$ 3,304.5	$ 110.4	$ 370.1	200.4	2,487.1
Corporate						3.4	143.5
						$ 203.8	$ 2,630.6
GEOGRAPHIC SEGMENTS							
Canada			$ 2,550.1		$ 347.1		$ 2,099.8
U.S.A.			754.4		23.0		387.3
			$ 3,304.5		$ 370.1		2,487.1
Corporate							143.5
							$ 2,630.6
1987 BUSINESS SEGMENTS							
Newsprint	$ 1,174.4	$ 1.3	$ 1,175.7	$ 54.0	$ 194.9	$ 153.1	$ 1,142.3
Groundwood papers	278.8	0.2	279.0	19.8	11.7	72.9	465.4
Coated papers	131.3	37.6	168.9	5.1	6.7	5.6	101.3
Distribution, Office products and Converted products	1,078.9	0.8	1,079.7	7.2	43.3	14.4	336.5
Building products	221.6	–	221.6	9.2	16.3	6.1	180.9
Other	103.0	–	103.0	2.1	(1.5)	0.6	19.1
Eliminations		(39.9)	(39.9)				
	$ 2,988.0	$ –	$ 2,988.0	$ 97.4	$ 271.4	252.7	2,245.5
Corporate						3.9	286.8
						$ 256.6	$ 2,532.3
GEOGRAPHIC SEGMENTS							
Canada			$ 2,297.9		$ 248.0		$ 1,945.2
U.S.A.			690.1		23.4		300.3
			$ 2,988.0		$ 271.4		2,245.5
Corporate							286.8
							$ 2,532.3

Notes: (1) Geographic segments reflect the location of the source of the product sold.

(2) Canadian operations include sales to the U.S. market of $889.9 million (1988 – $957.8 million, 1987 – $890.0 million) and other export sales of $230.1 million (1988 – $270.6 million, 1987 – $243.1 million).

NOTES TO CONSOLIDATED FINANCIAL STATEMENTS

1 **Summary of significant accounting policies**

The consolidated financial statements are expressed in Canadian dollars and are prepared in accordance with accounting principles generally accepted in Canada.

(a) Principles of consolidation The financial statements consolidate the accounts of Abitibi-Price Inc. and all companies in which it holds more than a 50% interest. Investments in joint ventures and in companies in which Abitibi-Price does not have more than a 50% interest but in which it can exercise significant influence are included in the financial statements in accordance with the equity method of accounting.

Goodwill, which represents the excess of the cost of acquired businesses over the values attributed to the underlying net assets, is amortized over periods not exceeding 40 years.

(b) Translation of foreign currencies The assets and liabilities of self-sustaining foreign subsidiaries and affiliates are translated into Canadian funds at year-end exchange rates and the resulting unrealized exchange gains or losses are included in shareholders' equity. The earnings statements of such operations are translated at exchange rates prevailing during the year.

Monetary assets and liabilities of domestic companies and integrated foreign subsidiaries which are denominated in foreign funds are translated into Canadian funds at year-end exchange rates, non-monetary assets are translated at historical rates, and transactions included in earnings are translated at rates prevailing during the year, with the exception of depreciation which is translated at historical rates. Exchange gains or losses on translation are included in earnings, with the exception of gains or losses arising on the translation of long-term debt payable in U.S. funds. Such gains or losses which relate to debt that hedges the net investment in self-sustaining U.S. subsidiaries are included in shareholders' equity, while the balance, which relates to debt that is hedged by a future income stream denominated in U.S. funds, is deferred and included in earnings in the same years as the income stream.

(c) Inventories Inventories of finished products, work in process and materials and operating supplies are valued at the lower of average cost and net realizable value. Inventories of pulpwood and sawlogs are valued at average cost.

(d) Fixed assets and depreciation Fixed assets are recorded at cost, which includes capitalized interest and preproduction and start-up costs. Investment tax credits and grants received under government programs relating to capital expenditures are credited to fixed assets.

Depreciation is provided at rates considered adequate to amortize the cost over the productive lives of the assets. The principal asset category is primary production equipment which is depreciated over 20 years on a straight-line basis.

(e) Pension costs Earnings are charged with the cost of benefits earned by employees as services are rendered. The cost reflects management's best estimates of the pension plans' expected investment yields, wage and salary escalation, mortality of members, terminations and the ages at which members will retire. Adjustments arising from pension plan amendments, experience gains and losses and changes in assumptions are amortized to earnings over the estimated average remaining service lives of the members.

The difference between amounts included in earnings and Company contributions to the pension plans appears on the balance sheet as deferred pension cost.

(f) Income taxes Earnings are charged with income taxes relating to reported profits. Differences between such taxes and taxes currently payable, which result from timing differences between the recognition of income and expenses for accounting and for tax purposes, are reflected as deferred income taxes on the balance sheet.

Augusta Newsprint Company The Company's 50% share of the earnings and net assets of the joint venture newsprint operation at Augusta, Georgia, is as follows:

($ millions)	1989	1988	1987
Revenue	$ 107.1	$ 118.3	$ 112.1
Expenses	103.0	102.8	106.0
Earnings	$ 4.1	$ 15.5	$ 6.1
Assets	$ 175.8	$ 179.1	$ 199.3
Liabilities	107.5	112.8	143.4
Net assets	$ 68.3	$ 66.3	$ 55.9

The Company's share of the joint venture's earnings is included in "Cost of sales".

Liabilities above include $90.5 million (1988 – $101.4 million; 1987 – $133.1 million) of long-term borrowings which are without recourse to the Company or its co-venturer.

Under a marketing agreement, the joint venture's newsprint production is sold through a wholly-owned sales subsidiary of Abitibi-Price Inc.

Alabama River Newsprint Company   During 1988, the Company formed a joint venture partnership, Alabama River Newsprint Company, with Parsons & Whittemore, Incorporated of New York, as equal partners, to build and operate a newsprint mill at Claiborne, Alabama with an annual capacity of 220,000 tonnes. Financing for the project, without recourse to the partners, has been arranged in the form of a U.S. $337 million loan, of which U.S. $159 million was outstanding at December 31, 1989. The total investment in the project is estimated at U.S. $409 million, including construction expenditures of U.S. $342 million. Construction commenced in 1988 and is expected to be completed in 1990. Under a marketing agreement, the partnership's newsprint production will be sold through a wholly-owned sales subsidiary of Abitibi-Price Inc. Abitibi-Price's investment in the joint venture at December 31, 1989 was $30.7 million (1988 – $29.8 million), of which $15.6 million (1988 – $17.9 million) was represented by a note payable.

Pulpa y Papel Orinoco, S. A.   In 1988, a Venezuelan corporation, Pulpa y Papel Orinoco, S. A., was formed to construct a newsprint mill in that country under a joint venture arrangement that includes Abitibi-Price and Bowater Incorporated of Darien, Connecticut, each with a 24.5% interest, the Venezuelan Government with 36%, and a group of Venezuelan newspaper publishers with 15%. Work has not commenced on the Venezuelan project and it is too soon after recent events in that country to estimate a completion date. Abitibi-Price's investment in the joint venture at December 31, 1989 was $1.6 million.

3 **Acquisitions**

In 1988, Abitibi-Price acquired all of the outstanding shares of Datarex Systems Inc. of Orchard Park, New York, a distributor of information processing products, for a cash consideration of $51.1 million. The acquisition has been accounted for by the purchase method and has been included in the consolidated financial statements from September 1, 1988.

Also, during 1988, the Company purchased the assets of five businesses involved in the distribution of office and paper products for a total cost of $31.8 million, comprising cash of $16.9 million and loans payable of $14.9 million.

These 1988 acquisitions are summarized as follows:

($ millions)	Datarex	Other Businesses	Total
Net assets acquired at fair value:			
Bank indebtedness	$ (1.2)	$ –	$ (1.2)
Other working capital	21.8	19.9	41.7
Fixed assets	3.7	1.7	5.4
Goodwill	35.4	10.2	45.6
Long-term debt	(9.1)	–	(9.1)
Deferred income taxes	0.5	–	0.5
Total cost	$ 51.1	$ 31.8	$ 82.9

Goodwill, which represents the excess of the cost of the Company's investment over the values attributed to the underlying net assets acquired, is being amortized on a straight-line basis over 20 years.

In October 1988, Abitibi-Price acquired a 19.9% equity interest in Spicers Paper Limited, one of Australia's leading paper distributors and converters, which also has operations in New Zealand, Singapore and the U.S. West Coast. The total cost of the investment, which is being accounted for by the equity method, was $35.8 million, and the amount by which this exceeded the $26.8 million book value of the acquired shares is being amortized on a straight-line basis over 20 years. The investment in Spicers is included in "Long-term receivables, investments and other assets" on the balance sheet and the Company's share of Spicers' earnings is included in "Other income and expense".

4 **Restructuring costs**

Restructuring costs of $31.2 million in 1989 consist of:

($ millions)	
Write-off of a newsprint machine at Grand Falls, Newfoundland, which is to be permanently withdrawn from production in early 1990	$ 14.1
Provision for related employee termination costs at that time	8.0
	22.1
Write-off of the assets of the self-insulating hardboard siding operation at the Alpena, Michigan building products plant	9.1
	$ 31.2

5 Other income and expense

($ millions)	1989	1988	1987
Interest	$ 6.2	$ 17.3	$ 11.2
Interest on insurance claim	6.8	–	–
Spicers Paper Limited – equity income	1.9	0.5	–
Foreign exchange gain (loss)	0.5	(2.7)	(2.3)
Other	0.4	1.3	2.4
	$ 15.8	$ 16.4	$ 11.3

6 Income taxes

The Company's effective income tax rate is as follows:

($ millions)	1989	1988	1987
Earnings before income taxes, minority interest and extraordinary item	$ 98.6	$ 335.1	$ 240.8
Income taxes	44.7	137.9	106.7
Effective income tax rate	45.3%	41.2%	44.3%
Made up of:			
Combined basic Canadian federal/provincial income tax rates	40.7%	43.9%	48.1%
Increase (decrease) resulting from –			
Manufacturing and processing allowances	(1.7)	(3.3)	(4.2)
Foreign taxes	3.8	0.4	0.4
Other	2.5	0.2	–
Effective income tax rate	45.3%	41.2%	44.3%

7 Consolidated earnings information

($ millions)	1989	1988	1987
Maintenance and repairs	$ 159.5	$ 152.5	$ 147.3
Taxes other than payroll and income taxes	46.7	37.3	36.8
Pension expense – Company and government plans	9.0	12.5	7.6
Operating lease rentals	47.4	43.3	39.5

8 **Extraordinary item**

The extraordinary gain of $2.9 million reported for the year 1988 resulted from a sale of land in South Carolina, U.S.A. after income taxes of $2.0 million.

9 **Change in operating working capital**

($ millions)	1989	1988	1987
Cash used for changes in operating working capital components:			
Decrease (increase) in current assets:			
Accounts receivable	$ 41.0	$ 5.0	$ (30.7)
Inventories	(17.7)	(42.7)	(15.2)
Prepaid expenses	(1.3)	(10.7)	(1.3)
Increase (decrease) in current liabilities:			
Accounts payable and accrued liabilities, excluding dividend payable to a minority shareholder of a subsidiary company	22.8	(27.6)	23.7
Income taxes payable	(4.7)	3.5	7.1
	40.1	(72.5)	(16.4)
Operating working capital acquired with the purchase of a subsidiary company and other businesses		41.7	–
Change in operating working capital	$ 40.1	$ (30.8)	$ (16.4)

10 **Accounts receivable**

At December 31, 1989, the allowance for doubtful accounts receivable was $14.4 million (1988 – $12.9 million).

11 **Inventories**

($ millions)	1989	1988
Finished products and work in process	$ 237.8	$ 233.1
Pulpwood, sawlogs and expenditures on current logging operations	110.5	105.5
Materials and operating supplies	84.8	76.8
	$ 433.1	$ 415.4

12 **Notes payable and bank lines of credit**   **ABITIBI·PRICE**

Under a commercial paper program arranged in 1989, the Company can issue short-term promissory notes in U.S. currency up to a principal value of equivalent Cdn. $200 million. At December 31, 1989, the values of such notes outstanding was Cdn. $124.1 million. Interest on these notes, which is on a floating rate basis, was 8.65% on the notes outstanding of U.S. $107.1 million at the year-end.

At December 31, 1989 the company had $242.7 million in unused bank lines of credit. Any borrowings under these lines of credit would bear interest at the prevailing market rates.

13 **Accounts payable and accrued liabilities**

($ millions)	1989	1988
Trade accounts payable	$ 176.4	$ 161.7
Accrued vacation pay	43.8	42.7
Accrued salaries, wages and benefits	31.0	35.5
Accrued restructuring costs	8.0	–
Other	48.3	44.8
	$ 307.5	$ 284.7

14 **Long-term debt**

($ millions)	1989	1988
Abitibi-Price Inc.:		
Sinking Fund Debentures –		
11¹/₂% Series F, maturing 1995	$ 7.4	$ 8.3
11⁷/₈% Series G, maturing 1992 (U.S. $12 million)	13.9	23.9
10.65% Series H, maturing 2000 (U.S. $93.5 million)	108.3	121.8
Floating Rate Term Loan, maturing 1994		
(U.S. $150 million) (a)	173.8	178.9
Abitibi-Price Refinance Inc.:		
Floating Rate Cumulative/Term Loan,		
maturing 1993 (U.S. $96.4 million) (b)	111.7	115.0
Gaspesia Pulp and Paper Company Ltd.:		
Floating Rate Revolving Loan, maturing 1996		
(U.S. $24.5 million) (c)	28.4	–
Floating Rate Revolving Loan, maturing 1992		29.8
Other indebtedness	25.2	41.6
	468.7	519.3
Less: Amount due within one year	33.3	30.5
	$ 435.4	$ 488.8

(a)   Interest is at a rate approximating LIBOR. The loan is secured by an Abitibi-Price Inc. Series L Debenture. The Company has entered into interest rate exchange agreements, covering the period to 1994, for a principal amount of U.S. $100 million at an average fixed interest rate of 8.88%.

(b)　Interest is at rates approximating U.S. base rate or LIBOR for U.S. funds borrowings and at rates approximating EuroCanadian rate or Canadian bank prime for Canadian funds borrowings. The loan is secured by an Abitibi-Price Inc. Series K Debenture.

(c)　Gaspesia Pulp and Paper Company Ltd. may borrow on a revolving basis up to U.S. $29.4 million to December 31, 1996, with the balance of the loan becoming due on that date. Interest is at rates approximating LIBOR or U.S. base rate.

During 1988, the Company negotiated amendments to its Trust Indenture, eliminating the incremental debt issuance tests, the floating charge on the Company's assets and certain other covenants in order to update it to current practice. As part of the negotiations, the Company agreed to increase the coupon rates on the Series F, G and H Sinking Fund Debentures by $1/2$ of 1%, with effect from December 19, 1988.

Sinking fund and other long-term debt repayment obligations for the years 1991 to 1994 are estimated to be $16.9 million, $16.8 million, $123.6 million and $185.2 million, respectively.

All outstanding sinking fund debentures are currently redeemable at the option of the Company.

During the year ended December 31, 1989, interest of $9.6 million was capitalized on major capital additions (1988 – $6.1 million; 1987 – $9.0 million).

15　Stated capital

The Company is governed by the Canada Business Corporations Act and is authorized to issue an unlimited number of preferred shares and common shares.

Common Shares	Number of common shares	$ millions
Outstanding at January 1, 1987	69,211,114	$　259.8
Issued under terms of the Key Executive and Management Personnel Stock Option Plan		
1987	35,497	0.3
1988	18,939	0.3
1989	1,188	–
Amalgamation adjustment – 1987	–	1.8
Outstanding at December 31, 1989	69,266,738	$　262.2

At December 31, 1989, $2^1/2$ million common share purchase warrants were outstanding. Each warrant entitles the holder to purchase, on or prior to June 15, 1990, one common share for $30. No warrants have been exercised.

$7^1/2$% Cumulative Redeemable Preferred Shares Series A –　The balance of the Series A shares, which were issued at $50 per share, were retired in 1989 at a cost of $6.4 million (1988 – 3,600 shares with a book value of $0.2 million were purchased at a cost of $0.2 million; 1987 – 4,840 shares with a book value of $0.3 million at a cost of $0.2 million).

Floating Rate Preferred Shares Series C –   The Series C shares, which were issued at $50 per share, were redeemed by the Company at $50 per share in 1989. Dividends were payable at a floating rate of one-half the average prime rate of the five largest Canadian chartered banks plus 1%, with a maximum dividend rate of 9% per annum.

$0.94 Cumulative Redeemable Retractable Preferred Shares Series F –   The Series F shares, which were issued at $11.50 per share, are redeemable by the Company at $11.50 per share and are retractable at $11.50 per share at the option of the holder on January 1 in each year. In 1989, 257,969 shares were retracted (1988 – 468,814 shares; 1987 – 132,611 shares).

16   **Lease commitments**

The Company and its subsidiaries have entered into operating leases to charter ships and to lease property and equipment for various periods up to the year 2007 at rentals aggregating approximately $140.6 million. Minimum payments under these leases are as follows:

(\$ millions)	
1990	$ 33.6
1991	27.4
1992	17.8
1993	11.6
1994	10.2
Remaining years	40.0
	$ 140.6

17   **Pension plans**

The Company's pension plans, covering most employees, are primarily contributory, defined benefit plans that provide pension benefits based on length of service and final average earnings. The Company has an obligation to ensure that there are sufficient funds in these plans to pay the benefits earned and, although the Company's contributions vary from year to year, they are made in accordance with the annual contribution requirements of regulatory authorities. Pension contributions are generally invested in balanced funds with outside managers and at December 31, 1989 approximately 52% of the assets were held in equity securities, with the remainder in fixed income securities.

The following table reconciles the funded status of the pension plans with the amounts recognized on the Company's balance sheet:

($ millions)	1989	1988
Market value of assets	$ 850.5	$ 771.1
Actuarial present value of accumulated plan benefits based on current service and compensation levels		
Vested	588.6	523.4
Non-vested	3.0	5.2
	591.6	528.6
Adjustment for projected service and compensation levels	78.3	127.8
	669.9	656.4
Excess of market value of assets over projected benefit obligations	$ 180.6	$ 114.7
Consisting of:		
Unrecognized gain	$ 61.4	$ 7.5
Prior service cost not yet recognized in periodic pension expense	(53.1)	(58.4)
Balance of unrecognized net assets existing at January 1, 1986	108.6	119.9
Deferred pension cost recognized on the balance sheet	63.7	45.7
	$ 180.6	$ 114.7

Net pension cost (credit) of the Company plans included the following components:

($ millions)	1989	1988	1987
Service cost – benefits earned during the year for both defined benefit and defined contribution plans	$ 15.0	$ 16.4	$ 18.7
Interest cost on projected benefit obligations	59.1	55.9	50.6
Actual return on plan assets	(117.1)	(73.9)	(63.9)
Net total of other components	38.9	1.8	(9.0)
Net pension cost (credit)	$ (4.1)	$ 0.2	$ (3.6)

Pension benefit obligations were based on an assumed discount rate of 9.5% (1988 – 9.0%) and an assumed compensation rate increase of 6.0% (1988 – 6.0%). The assumed long-term rate of return on pension plan assets was 9.5% (1988 – 9.0%).

The financial statements have been prepared in accordance with generally accepted accounting principles ("GAAP") in Canada which, in the case of the Company, conform in all material respects with those in the United States, with the following exceptions:

(a) Earnings adjustments –

(i)   Unrealized exchange gains or losses arising on the translation of long-term debt payable in U.S. funds that is hedged by a future income stream denominated in U.S. funds are deferred and included in earnings in the same years as the income stream. If such gains or losses had been included in earnings as they occured, as required under U.S. GAAP, the effect would have been:

($ millions)	1989	1988	1987
Net earnings, as reported under Canadian GAAP	$ 54.2	$ 191.1	$ 125.7
Unrealized gain on translation of long-term debt payable in U.S. funds, net of income taxes	0.6	21.2	11.7
Net earnings, as adjusted to U.S. GAAP	$ 54.8	$ 212.3	$ 137.4

Per Common Share:

	1989	1988	1987
Net earnings, as reported	$ 0.70	$ 2.64	$ 1.70
Adjustment	0.01	0.31	0.17
Net earnings, as adjusted	$ 0.71	$ 2.95	$ 1.87

(ii) Under U.S. GAAP, the extraordinary item referred to on the earnings statement and in note 8 to the financial statements would be included in earnings before the extraordinary item.

(iii) The impact on net earnings adjusted to U.S. GAAP of Financial Accounting Standard 96 relating to income taxes, which is required to be implemented for fiscal years commencing after December 15, 1991, has not been determined.

(b) Preferred shares –   Under Securities and Exchange Commission reporting requirements, preferred shares which are retractable at the option of the holders would not be reported under Shareholders' Equity, but would be reported under a separate caption entitled "Retractable Preferred Shares". The Company's Series F shares are retractable at the option of the holders and at December 31, 1989, $31.1 million of these shares were outstanding (1988 – $34.1 million for Series F and $75.0 million for Series C).

19 Comparative figures

Certain comparative figures have been reclassified to conform to the current year's financial statements presentation.

MANAGEMENT'S REPORT The consolidated financial statements and all other information in the Annual Report are the responsibility of management and have been approved by the Board of Directors.

The financial statements have been prepared by management in accordance with accounting principles generally accepted in Canada and include some amounts which are based on best estimates and judgements. Financial information provided elsewhere in the Annual Report is consistent with that shown in the financial statements.

The integrity of the financial statements is supported by an extensive and comprehensive system of internal accounting controls and internal audits, the latter being coordinated with reviews and examinations performed by the shareholders' auditors in the course of satisfying themselves as to the reliability and objectivity of the financial statements.

The shareholders' and internal auditors have free and independent access to the Audit Committee which is comprised of six non-management members of the Board of Directors. The Audit Committee, which meets regularly through the year with members of financial management and the shareholders' and internal auditors, reviews the consolidated financial statements and recommends their approval to the Board of Directors.

The accompanying consolidated financial statements have been examined by the shareholders' auditors, Price Waterhouse, whose report follows.

AUDITORS' REPORT TO THE SHAREHOLDERS OF ABITIBI-PRICE INC. We have examined the consolidated balance sheets of Abitibi-Price Inc. as at December 31, 1989 and December 31, 1988 and the consolidated statements of earnings, retained earnings and changes in cash position for each of the three years in the period ended December 31, 1989. Our examinations were made in accordance with generally accepted auditing standards, and accordingly included such tests and other procedures as we considered necessary in the circumstances.

In our opinion, these consolidated financial statements present fairly the financial position of Abitibi-Price Inc. as at December 31, 1989 and December 31, 1988 and the results of its operations and the changes in its cash position for each of the three years in the period ended December 31, 1989 in accordance with generally accepted accounting principles applied on a consistent basis.

Price Waterhouse

Chartered Accountants
February 16, 1990
Toronto, Ontario

QUARTERLY FINANCIAL INFORMATION

(unaudited) (millions of dollars, except per share amounts)	1st Quarter	2nd Quarter	3rd Quarter	4th Quarter	TOTAL
1989 Net Sales	$ 810.1	$ 830.3	$ 816.4	$ 800.9	$ 3,257.7
Operating profit	48.5	57.8	32.8	19.0	158.1
Restructuring costs	–	–	–	(31.2)	(31.2)
Net earnings	26.3	28.8	13.6	(14.5)	54.2
Per common share:					
Net earnings	$ 0.35	$ 0.39	$ 0.18	$ (0.22)	$ 0.70
Dividends declared	0.25	0.25	0.25	0.125	0.875
Dividends paid	0.25	0.25	0.25	0.25	1.00
Price range per common share					
Toronto Stock Exchange					
High	$ 21.50	$ 20.38	$ 18.63	$ 17.13	
Low	19.13	18.38	16.25	13.13	
* New York Stock Exchange (U. S. dollars)					
High	18.25	17.25	15.50	14.63	
Low	15.88	15.38	13.75	11.38	
1988 Net Sales	$ 800.0	$ 835.5	$ 813.4	$ 855.6	$ 3,304.5
Operating profit	89.4	103.8	87.6	89.3	370.1
Earnings before extraordinary item	44.1	54.4	44.5	45.2	188.2
Net earnings	44.1	54.4	44.5	48.1	191.1
Per common share:					
Earnings before extraordinary item	$ 0.61	$ 0.76	$ 0.61	$ 0.62	$ 2.60
Net earnings	0.61	0.76	0.61	0.66	2.64
Dividends declared	0.25	0.25	0.25	0.25	1.00
Dividends paid	0.25	0.25	0.25	0.25	1.00
Price range per common share					
Toronto Stock Exchange					
High	$ 28.00	$ 23.13	$ 22.88	$ 20.88	
Low	22.38	19.13	19.75	18.50	
* New York Stock Exchange (U. S. dollars)					
High	21.75	19.00	19.00	17.13	
Low	18.25	15.38	16.13	15.38	
1987 Net Sales	$ 695.7	$ 756.4	$ 749.8	$ 786.1	$ 2,988.0
Operating profit	58.4	66.8	70.8	75.4	271.4
Net earnings	21.9	36.2	33.0	34.6	125.7
Per common share:					
Net earnings	$ 0.29	$ 0.49	$ 0.45	$ 0.47	$ 1.70
Dividends declared	0.15	0.15	0.15	0.25	0.70
Dividends paid	0.15	0.15	0.15	0.15	0.60
Price range per common share					
Toronto Stock Exchange					
High	$ 43.00	$ 40.50	$ 37.25	$ 35.75	
Low	28.00	33.50	31.00	19.50	
* New York Stock Exchange (U. S. dollars)					
High	–	–	28.00	27.25	
Low	–	–	23.25	15.38	

* Abitibi-Price's common shares were listed on the New York Stock Exchange on July 1, 1987.

ELEVEN-YEAR FINANCIAL REVIEW

	1989	1988	1987	1986
Sales and earnings *($ millions)*				
Net sales	$ 3,257.7	$ 3,304.5	$ 2,988.0	$ 2,763.5
Cost of sales	2,706.5	2,566.2	2,385.1	2,226.0
Selling and administrative expenses	275.0	257.8	234.1	203.1
Depreciation and depletion	118.1	110.4	97.4	88.7
Operating profit	158.1	370.1	271.4	245.7
Interest expense – long-term	37.4	50.5	39.3	35.1
– short-term	6.7	0.9	2.6	2.0
Restructuring costs	31.2	–	–	–
Other income and expense	15.8	16.4	11.3	4.0
Income taxes	44.7	137.9	106.7	91.9
Minority interest	0.3	9.0	8.4	10.6
Earnings before extraordinary items	54.2	188.2	125.7	110.1
Extraordinary items	–	2.9	–	(2.8)
Net earnings	54.2	191.1	125.7	107.3
Dividends declared *($ millions)*				
Preferred shares	$ 5.7	$ 7.8	$ 8.1	$ 8.7
Common shares *(2)*	60.6	69.3	48.5	41.5
Capital expenditures *($ millions)*	$ 260.1	$ 203.8	$ 256.6	$ 263.0
Financial position *($ millions)*				
Working capital	$ 327.6	$ 554.0	$ 622.3	$ 459.0
Fixed assets, net	1,535.7	1,428.6	1,358.1	1,232.6
Long-term debt	435.4	488.8	597.2	428.9
Deferred income taxes	434.0	412.8	318.1	273.5
Minority interest	41.8	42.1	33.1	36.9
Preferred shares	31.1	115.4	121.0	122.8
Common shareholders' equity	1,200.3	1,212.4	1,098.1	1,028.6
Per common share *(1)*				
Earnings before extraordinary items	$ 0.70	$ 2.60	$ 1.70	$ 1.50
Net earnings	0.70	2.64	1.70	1.46
Dividends declared *(2)*	0.875	1.00	0.70	0.60
Dividends paid *(2)*	1.00	1.00	0.60	0.60
Common shareholders' equity	17.32	17.50	15.86	14.86
Return on average common shareholders' equity	4.0%	15.6%	11.1%	10.9%
Long-term debt/long-term debt plus shareholders' equity	26.1%	26.9%	32.9%	27.1%
Number of employees (year end)	15,600	16,200	16,000	16,200

Notes

(1) Figures for the years 1979 to 1984 have been restated to reflect the 3-for-1 split of common shares which became effective May 1, 1985.

(2) Four quarterly dividends were paid in each of the years 1979 to 1988, but because of changes in dividend declaration dates, three dividends were declared in 1983 and five in 1985.

	1985	1984	1983	1982	1981	1980	1979
	$ 2,549.8	$ 2,137.2	$ 1,660.2	$ 1,634.3	$ 1,763.4	$ 1,364.7	$ 1,470.9
	2,075.3	1,794.0	1,439.7	1,352.4	1,356.3	1,076.5	1,134.3
	188.4	132.9	114.8	121.8	117.8	98.8	93.4
	82.1	76.8	68.6	70.1	61.7	53.3	49.5
	204.0	133.5	37.1	90.0	227.6	136.1	193.7
	43.6	40.4	18.9	25.2	28.2	25.7	20.0
	3.0	1.2	0.8	1.4	–	0.3	0.8
	–	–	–	–	–	–	–
	20.0	19.0	25.0	29.0	19.0	40.9	32.1
	69.4	30.2	0.7	22.4	87.2	51.9	80.5
	7.8	8.4	3.7	6.1	7.8	4.8	5.7
	100.2	72.3	38.0	63.9	123.4	94.3	118.8
	–	(2.2)	–	(2.6)	12.3	18.0	33.6
	100.2	70.1	38.0	61.3	135.7	112.3	152.4
	$ 9.3	$ 8.0	$ 7.4	$ 10.8	$ 10.0	$ 9.8	$ 9.1
	47.0	25.0	12.4	31.1	33.1	30.1	28.0
	$ 202.4	$ 126.3	$ 165.3	$ 187.9	$ 207.0	$ 231.0	$ 153.5
	$ 373.0	$ 409.5	$ 384.2	$ 437.3	$ 461.4	$ 414.3	$ 339.1
	1,132.0	1,010.3	993.6	917.9	837.1	730.0	594.1
	455.7	419.9	395.1	385.8	388.9	360.7	237.7
	236.9	209.3	191.8	187.6	174.7	127.9	105.4
	26.3	25.1	19.5	19.5	16.6	18.1	24.5
	124.1	104.2	113.8	122.7	130.8	139.9	143.0
	837.4	792.5	739.4	721.1	701.5	560.4	487.0
	$ 1.42	$ 1.02	$ 0.48	$ 0.87	$ 1.85	$ 1.50	$ 1.96
	1.42	0.99	0.48	0.82	2.05	1.82	2.56
	0.73	0.40	0.20	0.50	0.53	0.53	0.50
	0.58	0.40	0.30	0.50	0.53	0.53	0.50
	13.04	12.40	11.89	11.60	11.29	9.93	8.68
	11.2%	8.4%	4.2%	7.5%	18.0%	16.1%	25.5%
	32.2%	31.9%	31.7%	31.4%	31.8%	34.0%	27.4%
	15,500	14,800	15,100	14,600	17,800	17,300	18,300

(figures in thousands) **PRIMARY PRODUCTION**

	Newsprint* (tonnes)	Groundwood Papers (tonnes)	Kraft Products (tonnes)	Lumber (mfbm)	Coated Papers (tonnes)	Hardboard (msf-equivalent)
Production						
1984	1,721	374	115	181	121	1,111
1985	1,699	349	105	103	126	1,155
1986	1,798	350	87	83	132	1,058
1987	1,833	363	–	55	142	1,147
1988	1,900	407	–	52	144	1,032
1989	1,791	416	–	52	140	1,054
Capacity – 1990	1,953	443	–	83	174	1,267

*Newsprint figures include the total production of the 50%-owned joint ventures at Augusta, Georgia, and Claiborne, Alabama.

Index

A Complete Learning Solution

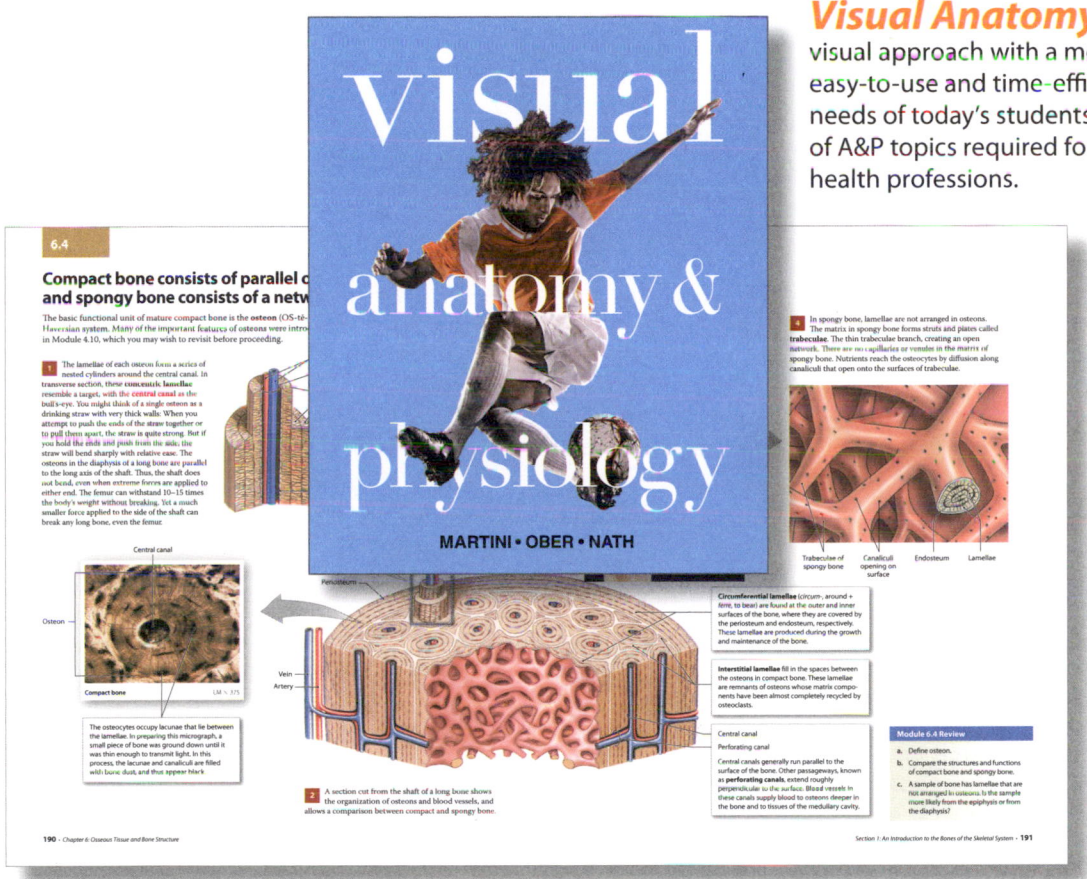

Visual Anatomy & Physiology combines a visual approach with a modular organization to deliver an easy-to-use and time-efficient book that uniquely meets the needs of today's students—without sacrificing the coverage of A&P topics required for careers in nursing and other allied health professions.

MasteringA&P is an online learning and assessment system proven to help students learn and designed to help instructors teach more efficiently.

- Lets instructors easily assign media that is automatically graded
- Provides students with personalized coaching through answer-specific feedback and hints
- Motivates students to come to class prepared
- Easily captures data to demonstrate assessment outcomes

To learn more about how ***Visual Anatomy & Physiology*** and **MasteringA&P** work together to provide a complete learning solution, please turn to pages vi–xvii.